Economics: New Classical versus Neoclassical Frameworks

Faifax

# ECONOMICS
## NEW CLASSICAL VERSUS NEOCLASSICAL
## FRAMEWORKS

## Xiaokai Yang

*Monash University and Harvard University*

First published 2001

2 4 6 8 10 9 7 5 3 1

Blackwell Publishers Inc.
350 Main Street
Malden, Massachusetts 02148
USA

Blackwell Publishers Ltd
108 Cowley Road
Oxford OX4 1JF
UK

*Library of Congress Cataloging-in-Publication Data*

Yang, Xiaokai.
    Economics : new classical versus neoclassical frameworks / Xiaokai Yang.
        p.      cm.
    Includes bibliographical references and index.
    ISBN 0-631-22001-1 (alk. paper) — ISBN 0-631-22002-X (pbk. : alk. paper)
    1. Neoclassical school of economics.   2. Classical school of economics.   3. Economics.
  I. Title.

  HB98.2.Y36 2001
  330.1—dc21

                                                                    00-033713

*British Library Cataloguing in Publication Data*
A CIP catalogue record for this book is available from the British Library.

Typeset in 10 on 11½ pt Ehrhardt
by Ace Filmsetting Ltd, Frome, Somerset
Printed in Great Britain by T. J. International, Padstow, Cornwall

This book is printed on acid-free paper.

*To Xiaojuan, Xiaoxi, James, and Edward*

# CONTENTS

# Tables

# PREFACE

This book belongs to a new species of economics textbook. It differs from Marshall's first-generation textbook which separates the analysis of demand and supply from the analysis of individuals' decisions in choosing their levels of specialization. It differs from his marginal analysis of demand and supply based on a neoclassical dichotomy between pure consumers and firms. I begin here from an analysis of individual consumer-producers' decisions in choosing levels of specialization, and then apply inframarginal analysis (total benefit–cost analysis across corner solutions in addition to marginal analysis of each corner solution) to investigate how the network size of division of labor in society is determined in the marketplace. According to this inframarginal analysis, demand and supply are two sides of the division of labor (Allyn Young, 1928). Hence demand and supply are determined not only by resource allocation for a given network pattern of division of labor, but also by the network pattern itself.

This book also differs from Samuelson's prototype of the second-generation economics textbook. It does not have a dichotomy between microeconomics and macroeconomics. Since a particular level of division of labor is associated with a certain size of market network, the extent of the market and aggregate demand are determined by individuals' decisions in choosing levels of specialization that yield the network size of division of labor for society as a whole. Hence many macroeconomic phenomena, such as unemployment and business cycles, are special features of the complicated network of division of labor.

In this text nonlinear programming, dynamic programming, and other forms of nonclassical mathematical programming are employed to resurrect the spirit of classical mainstream economics within a modern body of formalism. Since the spirit of the book is older than, while its body is younger than, neoclassical economics, I have chosen to name the new species *New Classical Economics*.

Despite the innovation in this text, it maintains continuity with mainstream economics through a synthesis of the latter's existing and emerging branches. Neoclassical microeconomics, based on the dichotomy between pure consumers and exogenously given firms, is covered in the text (part II). But possible corner solutions and inframarginal comparative statics of general equilibrium (discontinuous jumps of endogenous variables across corner and interior solutions in response to changes in parameters) in the neoclassical framework are emphasized. Neoclassical trade theory is synthesized into the text by highlighting its features of inframarginal comparative statics which generate jumps of equilibrium trade pattern across corner and interior solutions (chapter 12). New trade theory developed by Dixit and Stiglitz (1977), Krugman (1979, 1980, 1981), Ethier (1982), and others is covered in chapter 11. New equilibrium game models, such as the models of sequential equilibrium of Milgrom–Roberts and Kreps–Wilson and the commitment game model of Dewatripont–Maskin, are covered and applied to analyze the relationship between endogenous transaction costs and network size of division of labor in chapters 4, 9, and 12.

New models that formalize the notion of endogenous transaction costs caused by moral hazard and information asymmetry, the theory on structure of residual rights and incomplete contract, and the new theory of the firm are covered in chapters 9 and 12. These models are extended in this text to explore the relationship between endogenous transaction costs, evolution of division of labor, structure of property rights, and emergence of the institution of the firm. New endogenous growth models (AK models, R&D-based models, and models with endogenous evolution of division of labor) are covered in chapters 21, 22, 23, and 24. The different endogenous growth models are compared in the light of recent empirical work that tests them against observations.

Several new classical general equilibrium models are used to develop an overarching framework for explaining all micro and macro phenomena. I show that when the network size of division of labor is endogenized in a general equilibrium analysis, marginal comparative statics for a given pattern of the network can address conventional microeconomic resource allocation problems, while inframarginal comparative statics explain discontinuous jumps of the equilibrium size of network of division of labor and related aggregate variables across different structures. The inframarginal comparative statics (or dynamics) can then explain emergence of money, business cycles, and unemployment from division of labor. Hence, for our grand synthesis, macroeconomic analysis and microeconomic analysis are just at two different levels within an integrated framework.

Many insights of Buchanan, Cheung, Coase, and North into transaction costs, property rights, institution of the firm, and contract are formalized in the text. Challenges posed by nonlinear evolutionary economics (see Nelson, 1995, Conlisk, 1996, and references there) and by the Austrian School (see Kirzner, 1997, and references there) to the mainstream are acknowledged and absorbed into the text. For instance, the concept of Walrasian sequential equilibrium is developed in chapter 24 to predict concurrent evolution of economic organisms and evolution of information acquired by society through social experiment with various organisms using price mechanism. The recursive paradox (which means that a decision problem based on bounded rationality cannot be well defined) raised by nonlinear evolutionary economists is solved in a well-closed dynamic general equilibrium model based on adaptive behaviors and bounded rationality. The dynamic equilibrium model substantiates the proposition in nonlinear evolutionary economics that concurrent evolution of organisms and information about organisms acquired by society involves uncertainty about the direction of the evolution as well as certain of its tendencies (Nelson, 1995).

This text can be used at two different levels. Since each chapter includes some descriptive intuition with regard to larger formal models and mechanisms at work, with the aid of illustrations, the text could be used for third- or fourth-year (micro or macro) economics courses and third- or fourth-year courses in development economics, trade theory, industrial organization, economics of transaction costs and property rights, economics of contract and institution. The focus of undergraduate courses is on training in economic thinking. If the text is used for that purpose, questions for assignments and examinations could be chosen from those at the end of each chapter and difficult algebra and exercises could then be skipped.

The text can be used for a microeconomics course at graduate level. It can be used, equally, as a reference in graduate courses on macroeconomics, development economics, growth theory, economics of transaction costs and organization, economics of contract and institution, industrial organization, and trade theory. The focus of graduate courses is on formal basic training as well as on innovative, creative, and critical economic thinking. For the purposes of basic training, students are asked to pay more attention to duplication of major models in the text and to work out main exercises at the end of each chapter. One hour spent on duplicating the models is as effective as eight hours spent on listening and reading. The formal training is characterized by strong accumulation effects. If each model covered in the text is duplicated and well understood, the study will become increasingly easier. But if one of the major models cannot be duplicated or a lecture is missed out, study may become increasingly difficult later on.

For the purposes of creative and critical thinking, students are asked to pay more attention to the trial–error process in designing models and in choosing one from many possible frameworks. Not only must all original ideas stand the test of rigorous deduction, of logical consistency, and of empirical evidence, but also insights are encouraged that might be too sophisticated to be formalized by any available mathematical instruments. Questions and exercises at the end of each chapter include many good thesis topics for masters and Ph.D. programs. Free assistance can be obtained for such programs from the author upon request (xiaokai.yang@buseco.monash.edu.au).

The text could also be used for a one-year course. In that case, the teacher might pay more attention to basic training in the first semester and which might cover parts I–V. Then more attention could be paid to encouraging creative, independent, and critical economic thinking in the second semester. If it were used for a semester course, the teacher might choose major chapters in parts I–V, then quickly outline the main results in other chapters with the aid of illustrations.

This book is a response to increasing demand for a text on and survey of the technical substance of new classical economics and inframarginal analysis. It covers many of the new research results of new classical economics and inframarginal analysis and compares the new classical and neoclassical frameworks. Some of the new research results are here published for the first time. I hope that the reader will experience an intellectual adventure and find inframarginal analysis of network of division of labor as a bridge between the mainstream economics and this era of networking.

Since new classical economics can be applied to many fields of economics, my colleagues and I are developing a franchise network to promote teaching, research, and publication of new classical economics and inframarginal analysis. One of many franchise units is *Development Economics*, by Jeff Sachs and Xiaokai Yang, which applies new classical economics to development economics, synthesizing it with other new research in this field. This book will be published by Blackwell as well. Other possible franchise units under consideration include *Economics of Property Rights and Transaction Costs*, *Economics of e-Commerce and Networking Decisions*, and *New Classical Trade Theory*. Also, undergraduate editions of this text and *Development Economics* without much mathematics are other possible franchise units. If you are interested in involvement in this franchise network, please contact me at xiaokai_yang@ksg.harvard.edu or xiaokai.yang@buseco.monash.edu.au. We will provide training support and all necessary technical information for working out a book applying the new classical approach to a field of economics. Website www.inframarginal.com provides updated information on this franchise network. You can find research reviews, recent papers, dissertations, conference information, texts, and a list of economists contributing to this literature.

Many individuals and institutions have contributed to this project. I am very grateful to my teachers at Princeton University, Hugo Sonneschein who taught me the theory of general equilibrium, Edwin Mills who taught me development economics and urban economics, Gene Grossman and Avinish Dixit who taught me trade theory and new general equilibrium models with increasing returns, Gregory Chow, Whitney Newey, Anguish Deaton, and Richard Quandt who taught me econometrics, Joseph Stiglitz, Barry Nalebuff, and Sanddy Grossman who taught me information economics and game theory, Alan Blinder and John Taylor who taught me macroeconomics, and William Baumol, Michael Katz, and Robert Willig who taught me industrial organization.

I am also greatly indebted to my co-authors of the various research papers which are covered in this text: Jeff Borland, Been-Lon Chen, Wen-Li Cheng, Ben Heijdra, Geoff Hogbin, Chien-fu Lin, Monchi Lio, Mong-Chun Liu, Pak-Wai Liu, Siang Ng, Yew-Kwang Ng, Babu Nahata, Bob Rice, Jeff Sachs, He-Ling Shi, Guangzhen Sun, Ian Wills, Jianguo Wang, Kar-yiu Wong, Shuntian Yao, Dingsheng Zhang, Yiming Zhao, Lin Zhou. I have benefited immensely from comments and criticisms on research papers and books that relate to this text from Ken Arrow, Gary Becker, Avner Ben-Ner, Fischer Black, James Buchanan, Steven Cheung, Cyrus Chu, Eric van Damme, Herbert Dawid, Jürgen Eichberger, Karl Farmer, John Gallup, Robert Gilles, Oliver Hart, Heinz Kurz, Lachie McGregor, Douglas North, Lloyd Reynolds, Peter Ruys, Andrei Shleifer, Hugo Sonnenschein, Sherwin Rosen, Donald Smythe, Willy Spanjers, Guoqiang Tian, Andrew Warner, Chenggang Xu, Gang Yi, Weiying Zhang, and participants in numerous seminars and conference sessions. Many students at Harvard University, Monash University, Peking University, the Chinese University of Hong Kong, the University of Hong Kong, the National University of Taiwan, and the University of Louisville provided useful feedback to the teaching of the materials covered in this text. Special thanks go to Jeff Borland, Sherwin Rosen, Monchi Lio, Mei Wen, and Julan Du for drawing several references cited in the text to my attention. Mei Wen and Yiming Zhao have done an excellent job of drawing many graphs in this text. My gratitude also goes to six anonymous referees who commented on a draft of this book.

The financial support for this project and related research from the Center for International Development at Harvard University, Australian Research Council, Chinese University of Hong Kong, National Taiwan University, Institute of Economics of Academia Sinica, National Sciences Council of the Republic of China, China Economic Center and Guanghua School of Management of Peking University, and Centre for Economic Research at Tilburg University is gratefully acknowledged.

Last but not least, without the love, patience, and strong support of my family, this book would never have come into existence. I wish to express my deepest love and thanks to my wife, Xiaojuan Wu, and kids, Xiaoxi, James, and Edward.

Of course, any remaining errors are solely my own responsibility.

Xiaokai Yang
at Harvard University
September, 1999

# part I
# THE ECONOMIC ENVIRONMENT

# INTRODUCTION

## ◆ 0.1 What is Economics?

What is economics? A typical textbook answer to this question goes like this: economics is the discipline that studies the allocation of scarce resources between alternative uses to meet individuals' needs. However, this is a characteristically neoclassical conception of the subject, which implies a focus substantially different from that of classical mainstream economic thinking. Neoclassical economics is distinguished precisely by its preoccupation with the problem of resource allocation. Its analysis therefore centers on the process by which, for any given degree of scarcity of resources, relative prices and quantities of commodities produced and consumed are determined in the marketplace. By contrast, classical economists, building on the foundations laid down by Adam Smith (1776), were concerned rather with the question: what makes one country more wealthy than another? Smith in particular was preoccupied with the process by which the division of labor could *reduce* scarcity of resources and accordingly make a society more affluent.

In order to encompass both the neoclassical problem of resource allocation for a given degree of scarcity, and the classical problem of division of labor, a more general conception of the discipline is required. We therefore propose the following definition: *Economics is the study of trade-offs in economic activities*. There are several trade-offs in neoclassical economics in relation to problems of resource allocation. For a consumer seeking to raise utility through consumption, there is the trade-off between the feasible quantities of alternative consumption goods. For a given income, the quantity of good x that is consumed must be traded off against the quantity of good y that is consumed: it is not feasible to increase both at the same time. This trade off can be described in terms of the marginal opportunity cost of good x in terms of good y, which relates to the marginal rate of substitution between them (defined as the quantity of good y that must be given up to keep utility unchanged for each unit of good x that is increased at margin).

Important trade-offs occur also in production. For a firm producing a single good by means of the two factors K (capital) and L (labor), there is the trade-off between quantities of K and L used to create any given level of output. This trade-off relates to the marginal rate of substitution between the two factors (the amount of a factor that must be increased to compensate for a marginal unit decrease of the other factor in order to keep output unchanged). For a firm producing two goods x and y using a given amount of resources, there is the trade-off between the respective quantities of x and y that can be produced. This trade-off relates to the marginal rate of transformation between the two goods (defined as the amount of one good that must be given up to compensate for a marginal unit increase of the other). Each of the trade-offs between counteracting forces is sorted out by an individual decision-maker. The efficient trade-off is usually a compromise between the counteracting forces, which determines the individual's self-interested behavior.[1]

Moreover, the self-interested decisions of different individuals are often in conflict with each other in the marketplace. For instance, the sellers of a good would like to obtain a price as high as possible, while the buyers would like to pay a price as low as possible. Thus, the interactions between conflicting self-interested decisions in the marketplace involve trade-offs as well. In a competitive market those interactions cannot be manipulated unilaterally by a single person, so that each individual may not be completely happy with the outcome because of nonsatiated desires. Nonetheless, she or he must take that outcome as it is. Then the interactions will trade off the interests of sellers against the interests of buyers and coordinate and reconcile conflicting self-interested decisions to achieve a compromise, which is called equilibrium by economists. The coordination process generates an outcome that is not purposely pursued by any single decision-maker, and that may not be completely satisfactory to anyone. Nevertheless, everyone will not attempt unilaterally to deviate from it. Economists have therefore followed the lead of Adam Smith in describing the interactions that generate the outcome as an *invisible hand*. In a competitive market, the interactions between self-interested decisions take place indirectly through market prices. By contrast, in a game model, with more general game rules, they take place directly.

The trade-offs that occur in the marketplace are much more complicated than those that arise in the decision-making of individuals. A popular joke illustrates the common misunderstanding of the distinction between the two types of trade-off. In the joke, a light bulb is broken. An engineer, a manager, and an economist are consulted about what can be done with the situation. The engineer suggests checking if the bulb can be fixed or buying a high-quality bulb that can be used for a longer period than the broken one. The manager suggests buying a good-quality bulb at a reasonable price. The economist suggests doing nothing since the invisible hand will take care of everything.

However, what the economist in this story is really likely to suggest is that a compromise payment arrangement should be negotiated among those affected by the light bulb. That arrangement should take into account the conflicting preferences of the parties (perhaps one does not want to pay too much for the bulb while another wants a high-quality bulb with little concern for its price; or perhaps one likes very strong light while the other likes very soft light; and so on). Hence, the engineer focuses her attention on technical problems, which are part of the natural environment specified in an economic model; the manager focuses on the self-interested behavior of individuals (the optimization problem); while the economist focuses on the interactions between the conflicting self-interested behaviors and their outcome. The most important feature of the outcome is that it cannot be completely manipulated by a single decision-maker and that therefore it must be something of a compromise between the individuals' self-interested behaviors. Hence, while nobody is completely happy with the outcome, everybody has to accept it as it is. But this does not mean that nothing needs to be done. Instead, this process involves many individual decision-makers' self-interested actions and interactions between them.

*Economics* is the discipline that studies all trade-offs of the kind just discussed. It analyzes not only the trade-offs in decision-making of individuals, but also studies how the interactions of the self-interested decisions under various institutional arrangements trade off conflicting interests to generate outcomes that individual decision-makers have to accept. Hence, economics differs from management science and other business subjects which focus on the trade-offs in decision-making.

All of the trade-offs so far discussed relate to neoclassical problems of resource allocation for a given degree of scarcity of resources. However the degree of resource scarcity can itself be traded off against other forces. That kind of trade-off was the major concern of Smith and other classical mainstream economists. In this text, the focus is on the trade-off between the positive network effects of division of labor on aggregate productivity and various transaction costs at the level of decision-making as well as at the level of interactions between self-interested decisions. The efficient trade-off between economies of division of labor and transaction costs can explain how the degree of scarcity of resources (or its reciprocal, the wealth of the nations) is endogenously determined by individuals' self-interested decisions and the interactions between them. The central idea of classical economists that division of labor can reduce scarcity and raise the wealth of the nations will be formalized in this text. It will be shown that the outcome of interactions between the self-interested decisions of individuals in choosing their levels of specialization will determine the network size of division of labor for society as a whole in the marketplace. The pattern and size of the network of division of labor in turn determine demand and supply. In the next two sections, we will investigate further the relationship between the two types of trade-off, discussed here, relating respectively to the neoclassical problems of resource allocation and the classical problems of division of labor.

## ◆ 0.2 The Analytical Framework of Economics

An economic system is among the most complex systems known. Hence, we must somehow organize our economic analysis so as to divide the economic system into more manageable subsystems. A structure of economic analysis that organizes concepts and subsystems is referred to as a *framework*. There are many analytical frameworks in economics. For instance, in an Austrian framework, the notion of equilibrium as the outcome of interactions between self-interested decisions is rejected. In a framework of nonlinear evolutionary economics, the notion of optimization in decision-making is rejected. The choice of framework has profound implications for the meanings of concepts that are used and for the explanatory power of theories that might be developed.

Most modern mainstream economists adopt a hierarchical framework involving four levels of analysis. At the bottom level of the hierarchy, the mathematical concepts of functions and sets are used to describe the economic environment. For instance, utility functions are used to describe individuals' preferences, and production functions and production sets are used to describe production conditions. The notions of budget constraint and related ownership structure and pricing rules, or more general game rules in game models, are used to describe the institutional environment.

At the second level of the hierarchy, mathematical programming is used to describe individuals' self-interested behaviors. The results of the analysis at this level are referred to as the comparative statics of the decision in a static model, or the dynamics and comparative dynamics of the decision in a dynamic model. Such results explain individuals' self-interested behaviors by prices and the economic environment, which encompasses preferences, production conditions, and institutional arrangements.

At the third level of the hierarchy, more sophisticated mathematical tools, such as the fixed-point theorem in topology, are used to describe the outcome of interactions between self-interested decisions. The results of the analysis at this level are called the comparative statics of general equilibrium in a static model and the dynamics and comparative dynamics of general equilibrium in a dynamic model. Such results explain how the outcomes of interactions between self-interested decisions change in response to changes in the economic environment.

All analysis at the three levels just described is referred to as *positive analysis*. When economists conduct positive analysis they do not ask what is good or bad, or what should be done to change matters, for they are not then concerned with value judgments. What they are trying to do is to use *thought experiments* to figure out what is going to happen under certain conditions.[2] The following process is typical of such thought experiments. Begin with some assumptions about the intangible preferences and behaviors, and then use rigorous mathematics to establish connections between the intangible and tangible phenomena. One such tangible phenomenon is called the demand function, which is the relationship between the quantity purchased and the price of a good. We can thus infer intangible relationships from the tangible. If the observed phenomena are consistent with their predictions based on the established connection, then our assumptions about the intangible are accepted as working hypotheses, which can be used to explain economic phenomena. If the thought experiment generates predictions concerning tangible phenomena that are incompatible with observations, the hypothesis underlying the thought experiment is then rejected.

Some conjectures cannot be falsified or verified. For example, consider the statement: "The use value of a commodity is determined by the degree to which the desire of its user is satisfied." If the notions of use value and desire are not well defined in terms of mathematics, then we cannot establish a rigorous connection between the intangible and observable variables using mathematics, and so there is no way to verify or falsify the statement.

On the other hand the following statement can be verified or falsified. "If an individual's utility function is strictly concave (implying diminishing marginal utility, see chapter 1), then her utility maximizing decision in a competitive market based on private ownership will satisfy the law of demand (a negative relationship between the quantity of a good purchased and its price)." Data on quantities of goods purchased and prices can be collected. If the price goes up but the quantity purchased does not fall, then the statement is falsified. The testing of hypotheses based on thought experiments is referred to as *empirical research*, which is one of the fields of econometrics. Indeed, some such empirical research has falsified the foregoing statement.

Falsification of a hypothesis does not invalidate the chain of mathematical logic linking the assumption and the prediction in the hypothesis, provided of course that the process of deduction is mathematically correct. Hence, rejection of the above hypothesis may be attributable to the unrealism of the assumptions (namely, that utility functions are strictly concave, implying diminishing marginal utility, and that behavior is motivated by utility maximization); or it may be attributable to a problem with the analytical framework itself. Thus by safeguarding against incorrect logic in a thought experiment that generates a hypothesis, mathematics can help us to narrow down the list of possible explanations for the empirical rejection of that hypothesis. This enables us to focus our attention on the assumptions and the analytical framework.

At the fourth level of the hierarchical structure of economic analysis, economists raise questions that involve value judgments, such as "Is the outcome of interactions between self-interested decisions (equilibrium) in a competitive market based on the private owner-ship system good for society as a whole?" The analysis at this level is referred to as *welfare* or *normative analysis.*

Recently, economics has encountered several challenges. However, all of them do not constitute a serious challenge to the hierarchical structure of economic analysis. For in-stance, some writers who have contributed to the development of information economics, have proposed the formal incorporation of uncertainty into economics. Some game theo-rists have suggested the generalization of game rules in economic models. Such sugges-tions can be well absorbed into the established hierarchical structure of the discipline. They merely imply that the specification of the economic environment at the first level of the hierarchy should be refined. Some economists go even further and suggest that game rules should be endogenized as the outcomes of direct interactions among self-interested decisions. This suggestion implies that game rules should not be specified at the first level of the hierarchy of economic analysis, but rather should emerge from the analysis at the third level. Again, what is called for is some possible reform of the hierarchical structure of analysis rather than its abandonment.

Developments in nonlinear evolutionary economics (see Nelson, 1995 and Conlisk, 1996) challenge the notions of equilibrium and optimization in the hierarchical structure of economic analysis by emphasizing bounded rationality and calculation costs. But as we shall show in chapter 24, this challenge too can be well absorbed within the hierarchical structure of economic analysis. It implies simply that more sophisticated constraints, relat-ing to shortage of information and to calculation costs, should be specified at the first level of the hierarchy. If all of the constraints are considered, a variety of decision rules, such as routines, heuristic decision rules, imitation (herd behavior), may emerge from the interac-tions between self-interested behaviors. The challenge posed by the Austrian School and nonlinear evolutionary economists (see Kirzner, 1997, and references there) against the notion of equilibrium is absorbed, to some degree, by the recent development of sequential equilibrium and dynamic game models that generate equilibrium shortages of some goods (such that demand is not equal to supply), as the outcome of interactions between self-interested behaviors (see Qian, 1994a and b). Furthermore we are quite sure that the challenge posed by the Austrian School's notion of entrepreneurial discovery can be ab-sorbed by the new classical framework developed in this text on the basis of the four-level analytical hierarchy. We will show that dynamic general equilibrium models based on bounded rationality and limited information may generate spontaneous evolution of many interesting economic phenomena, including the evolution of information about social or-ganisms acquired by society through spontaneous social experiments.

The hierarchical structure of economic analysis is organized using mathematics. There are two main reasons for the extensive application of mathematics in economics. First, the rigorous language of mathematics significantly raises efficiency in debates about economic problems by enabling the two sides of a debate to know precisely what are the differences between them. Prior to the extensive use of mathematics, debates in economics were often difficult to settle because the two sides often had different definitions of the same concept. Karl Marx claimed that he was not a Marxist, because many Marxist interpretations of his notions were in conflict with each other and with his own original interpretation. It is, of course, Marx himself who should be held responsible for this since he did not well define his notions in terms of rigorous mathematics. Where the concepts used by economists are well defined in terms of mathematics, this kind of problem can be largely avoided.

The debate in astronomy between heliocentric theory and geocentric theory offers a further example of the benefits of mathematical rigor. Until approximately five centuries ago, the Ptolemaic system was generally used to explain the movements of the planets within an internally consistent mathematical framework. However, its fundamental assumption that the earth is the planetary center yielded increasing inconsistency between the predictions of the theory and new observations. In due course it was therefore supplanted by the Copernicus–Kepler system, which was similarly developed within a mathematical framework but which takes the sun instead of earth as the center of the universe. Since both theories are based on rigorous mathematics, the Ptolemy system can be rigorously falsified despite the fact that mathematics cannot guarantee that the Ptolemy system based on it is right. Also, Copernicus' assumption of a circular trajectory of the earth around sun can be falsified by Kepler and the original Copernican system can be refined by assuming oval trajectory of the earth. Hence, the application of mathematics can significantly improve debating efficiency and speed up the accumulation of knowledge.

The second justification for extensive and intensive use of mathematics in economics relates to the notion of mainstream economics. *Mainstream economics* may be right or wrong, or good or bad. Nonetheless, from a positive view, it is defined as that which has been taught in most economics courses from generation to generation. There is no such mainstream in many disciplines, such as sociology. What is taught in courses of sociology differs from lecturer to lecturer, and from generation to generation, with little clearly defined common ground. But by contrast microeconomics is nearly the same in most courses in which it is taught throughout the world. Its common ground includes much of the discourse and many of the notions that Alfred Marshall used a hundred years ago. The common mainstream shared by different fields of economics and by successive generations of teachers and students creates a unified dictionary among them. This significantly improves communication efficiency, thereby promoting division of labor not only between specialized fields of the discipline, but also between different generations of economists.

Marshall (1890) tried to formalize classical economic thinking within a mathematical framework. Much of the textbook which sets out his principles falls into two main parts. One (comprising chapters 8–12 of Book IV) is full of classical insights into the economic implications of specialization and division of labor without mathematical formalization. The other comprises the marginal analysis of demand and supply within an internally consistent mathematical framework. Thus in this second part Marshall successfully formalized the relatively unimportant elements of classical economic thinking on the *problem of resource allocation*. As we have noted, the essence of that problem is to find the efficient quantities of different goods, and the efficient quantities of factors allocated to producing those goods, for a given degree of scarcity (or a given transformation function) and a given pattern and level of division of labor. The *problem of economic organization*, by contrast, is to find the efficient level and pattern of division of labor in order to reduce scarcity by trading off the productivity gains against transaction costs. As Yang and Y.-K. Ng (1993) show, the failure of Marshall and other neoclassical economists to formalize these problems of economic organization can be explained by the fact that this would have involved corner solutions and related inframarginal analysis, for which the mathematical techniques were not available until the 1950s. A *corner solution* to an optimization problem is a solution that involves upper and/or lower bound values of some decision variables. *Inframarginal analysis* is total benefit–cost analysis across corner solutions in addition to the marginal analysis of each corner solution.[3]

The success of the second part of Marshall's principles textbook is based on an unrealistic dichotomy between pure consumers and pure producers (firms) which is essential for the avoidance of corner solutions. This dichotomy makes Marshall's marginal analysis incapable of explaining many interesting and important economic phenomena. These include, for example, the emergence of firms, cities, money, middlemen, business cycles, the hierarchical structure of transactions from division of labor; the evolution of the extent of the market, productivity, comparative advantages, and trade dependency.

However, Marshall's formalization of the resource allocation problem established a well-organized structure for mainstream economics. Within this structure, not only can different generations of economists and students share a common dictionary, but also teachers can set questions and exercises in classrooms and in examinations to which uniquely correct answers are expected. What teachers teach on the blackboard can be exactly duplicated by their students. Unfortunately, however, as we have observed, this mainstream does not carry the core of classical economic thinking on problems of specialization and the division of labor. As Buchanan (1994, p. 6) observes, "with one part of his mind always in classical teachings, Marshall recognized that this genuinely marvellous neoclassical construction requires that the Smithian proposition on labor specialization be abandoned." As an unexpected consequence of Marshall's success in formalizing problems of resource allocation, the core of classical economics concerning specialization and division of labor has been mostly forgotten.[4]

This example illustrates the influence of mathematical formalism in shaping the mainstream of economics. Insightful economic thinking may be forgotten if it is not formalized in terms of mathematics, while quite superficial economic thinking may have a chance to be part of the mainstream if it is so formalized.

It is clear then that whatever may be the potential benefits of mathematical formalism, it does not follow that all economic thinking decorated by sophisticated mathematics is necessarily insightful. Indeed many available economic models based on sophisticated mathematics are notably short of insights. Often this is because even the most advanced mathematical techniques known are still incapable of capturing the rich essence of extremely complex economic phenomena. It follows that many existing economic models based on apparently high-powered mathematics are too simple to be relevant, and therefore to be applicable to real-world policy or business problems. At the same time there are many important economic insights that are too complicated to be formalized in terms of mathematics. But the advantage of mathematical formalism in speeding up knowledge accumulation is such that the evolution of mainstream economics will undoubtedly be characterized by the progressive application of increasingly sophisticated mathematics, and by the eventual formalization of such insights. One extreme is to worship mathematical formalism and ignore nonmathematical insights into economics. The other is to totally ignore the implications of mathematical formalism. Both extremes are inappropriate.

The Austrian idea of spontaneous order (Hayek, 1944) is a good example of a potentially valuable economic insight. According to this idea, if nobody can manipulate the formation of institutions, then the emergence of any particular institution is an unintended outcome of the interactions that occur among many self-interested individuals, so that that institution incorporates all of the information that is dispersed among many individuals. But if one individual, or some group of individuals, were to design the institutional arrangements for society, then the resulting institutions would be necessarily inefficient because they could not incorporate all information dispersed in society. Formalization of this idea may need an evolutionary game model that can endogenize the spontaneous coevolution of game rules (institutions), and the institution information acquired by society. But so far, economists can only barely manage the simplest game model with concurrent evolution of strategies and information (the sequential equilibrium model). No game models can explain the concurrent evolution of game rules and the information acquired by society about those game rules. But the efforts of game theorists may eventually enable the formalization of Hayek's idea.

## ◆ 0.3 Neoclassical Economics vs. New Classical Economics

We have observed that the focus of the classical mainstream of economics was on the implications of specialization and division of labor for the wealth of the nations. According to classical economic thinking, the most important decisions of individuals involve their choice of occupation and level of specialization. The aggregate outcome of these decisions determines the community's level of division of labor (or, in modern language, the network size of division of labor). Demand and supply are two sides of division of labor. The most important function of the invisible hand is to coordinate individuals' decisions in choosing levels and patterns of specialization to enable utilization of the positive network effects of division of labor.

Since Leon Walras (1874), Carl Menger (1871), and Marshall (1890), the focus of economic analysis has been shifted from the function of the price system in coordinating specialization and division of labor to the function of the price system in allocating resources.

Marshall's neoclassical framework is characterized by the dichotomy between pure consumers and firms, the replacement of the concept of economies of specialization with the concept of economies of scale, and the marginal analysis of demand and supply.[5] Marshall's neoclassical framework cannot be used to analyze individuals' decisions in choosing levels and patterns of specialization, so that structure of division between pure consumers and firms is exogenously given. His marginal analysis of demand and supply, which would become the basis of neoclassical microeconomics in the mainstream, has nothing to do with individuals' decisions in choosing their levels of specialization. In this text we will use nonlinear programming and the notion of general equilibrium based on corner solutions to formalize Marshall's intuitive insights into the implications of "economic organisms" and division of labor in chapters 8–12 of his Book IV. This will enable us to resurrect the classical analysis of specialization and division of labor as the core of mainstream economics.

Samuelson's principles textbook (1947) was another dividing line. This text comprised microeconomics, that is, Marshall's marginal analysis of demand and supply, and macroeconomics incorporating Keynesian economics which tries to explain phenomena that cannot be predicted by Marshall's marginal analysis. Since the 1950s, when Samuelson's textbook became a prototype for principles textbooks in economics, there has not been a place for problems of specialization and division of labor in textbooks. Most textbooks pay only brief symbolic respect to classical economic thinking on these issues. Accordingly, since Samuelson, the analysis of individuals' decisions in choosing their levels and patterns of specialization, and of the function of the market in coordinating division of labor, has lost its core position in mainstream economics. George Stigler (1976) vividly described the consequence of this feature of mainstream economics since Samuelson: "Almost no one used or now uses the theory of division of labor, for the excellent reason that there is scarcely such a theory. . . . there is no standard, operable theory to describe what Smith argued to be the mainspring of economic progress. Smith gave the division of labor an immensely convincing presentation – it seems to me as persuasive a case for the power of specialization today as it appeared to Smith. Yet there is no evidence, so far as I know, of any serious advance in the theory of the subject since his time, and specialization is not an integral part of the modern theory of production, which may well be an explanation for the fact that the modern theory of economies of scale is little more than a set of alternative possibilities."

After the Second World War, many economists pointed out that neoclassical microeconomics cannot explain such phenomena as economic development, trade, and economic growth. This accounts for the emergence of development economics, trade theory, and growth theory, as separate branches of the discipline which are quite independent of neoclassical microeconomics. Since the 1960s, economists have realized that neoclassical microeconomics cannot explain the emergence of the institution of the firm, or the implications of transaction costs and property rights. Specialist branches dealing with these areas and new theories of the firm have been developed to fill these gaps.

A tale from the history of science may serve nicely as a parallel to this development process. After the incompatibility between the Ptolemaic system and new observations became apparent, new theories were developed to try to accommodate the new phenomena that had been observed. While the new theories could perhaps accommodate some of the new phenomena, they revealed inconsistencies with the core of the Ptolemaic system and among themselves. Copernicus recognized the unacceptability of adding more and more internally inconsistent theories to reconcile the conflict between the Ptolemaic system and the observations. He argued that the best way forward was to adopt his own, Copernican, system, which assumes the sun instead of the earth as the center of the planetary system. As soon as this had been done, the internal inconsistencies of the modified Ptolemaic system became irrelevant, and the unifying theory of Copernicus and Kepler stood ready to explain all phenomena that could not be predicted by its predecessor.

The situation of economics today is in important respects analogous to what happened in astronomy five centuries ago. The emergence of macroeconomics, trade theory, development economics, comparative economics, the economics of property rights and transaction costs, growth theory, and the new theory of the firm may all be viewed as responses to inconsistencies between the core of neoclassical economics and observed economic phenomena. What we shall attempt to do in this text is roughly analogous to what Copernicus and Kepler did. By restoring the problems of specialization and division of labor to their proper place at the core of mainstream economics, we will be able, within a single overarching framework, to explain and predict such interesting phenomena as the emergence of the firm, business cycles, unemployment, money, cities, and economic growth.

Since the 1980s, many economists have applied nonlinear, linear, and dynamic programming to the inframarginal analysis of individuals' decisions in choosing their levels of specialization, and to analysis of the function of the market in coordinating the network of division of labor (see the survey of the emerging literature by Yang and S. Ng, 1998). The new waves of economic thinking resurrect the classical spirit of economics in the modern body of new mathematical models. The new literature shows that, when inframarginal analysis of corner solutions is applied, demand and supply can be explained as two aspects of division of labor. The network size of division of labor is determined by interactions between self-interested decisions in choosing levels and patterns of specialization. It can be shown that many macroeconomic phenomena (such as unemployment, business cycles, and the emergence of money from division of labor), many institutional phenomena (such as the emergence of the institution of the firm, or of the hierarchical structure of transactions from division of labor), and many development and growth phenomena are simply different aspects of the evolution of division of labor, or different features of the network of division of labor.

In order to get more intuition about the distinction between Marshall's neoclassical framework and the framework used in the new literature of endogenous specialization, let us look at figure 0.1. figure 0.1(a) illustrates Marshall's neoclassical framework. The two circles with numbers represent two consumers who do not make production decisions. The two circles with x and y represent two firms producing respectively goods x and y. The solid lines represent flows of goods sold by firms and the broken lines denote flows of labor and other factors from consumers to firms.

In the *neoclassical framework* all goods consumed by consumers are bought from the firms, consumers cannot choose their levels of self-sufficiency. Therefore, the existence of the market and the institution of the firm is exogenously given. Productivity of the firm relates only to its operation scale and has nothing to do with the levels of specialization of workers and managers within the firm. Suppose for simplicity that each consumer sells one unit of labor, which is the sole production factor, to the firms. There are at least two patterns of specialization. In one pattern, consumer 1 sells all her labor to the firm producing x and consumer 2 sells all her labor to the firm producing y. Hence, the scale of labor employed by each firm is one unit and each individual is completely specialized. In another pattern of specialization, each consumer sells 0.5 units of her labor to each of the two firms, so that individuals are not specialized, but the size of labor employed by each firm is still one unit. According to the neoclassical notion of economies of scale, productivity in the pattern of complete specialization and in the pattern with no specialization is the same. But according to the classical notion of economies of specialization, the pattern with specialization should generate a higher productivity.

In a neoclassical model, with or without economies of scale, the two patterns of specialization are associated with the same general equilibrium. In other words, individuals' patterns and levels of specialization are not well defined and make no difference. According to classical economic thinking, on the other hand, the productivity implications of the level of division of labor of society which is determined by individuals' levels of specialization are the focus of the economic analysis. The pattern of division of labor is related to

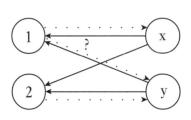

(a) Neoclassical framework

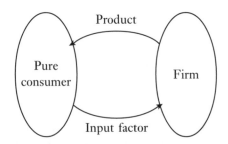

(b) Flow chart in neoclassical economics

◆ **Figure 0.1:** The neoclassical analytical framework

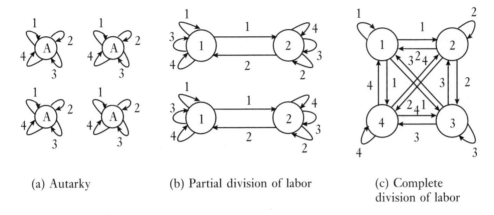

(a) Autarky                     (b) Partial division of labor              (c) Complete
                                                                          division of labor

◆ **Figure 0.2:** The new classical analytical framework

the number of transactions, which is referred to mathematically as one of the topological properties of the graph of an organism. Thus we may say that the focus of classical economics is on the implications of the topological properties of economic organisms. Quantities of goods consumed and produced can be denoted by the thickness of lines representing flows of goods and factors. Mathematically this characteristic is referred to as a nontopological property of the graph of an organism. Thus, because of its preoccupation with relative prices and quantities, we may say that neoclassical economics focuses on the implications of the nontopological properties of economic organisms. Since topological properties are not the focus of neoclassical economics, the chart in figure 0.1(b), which ignores these, becomes a common representation of the neoclassical economy in standard textbooks.

Now consider figure 0.2. In panel (a) a circle with A denotes a consumer-producer self-providing all goods that she needs. In other panels a circle with number i (=1, 2, 3, 4) denotes an individual selling good i, while an arrowed line with number i denotes a flow of good i. This figure illustrates the features of the *new classical framework* in the modern literature of endogenous specialization. In each panel there is an economy with four consumer-producers, each of whom consumes four goods and can choose to produce either one, two, three, or four goods. In panel (a), each consumer-producer is self-sufficient in all goods; thus there is no market, and the economy is divided into four separate components. Clearly the degree of commercialization (or marketization) and the degree of integration in this economy is low. Accordingly, the degree of concentration of production is low (there are four producers of each good), as is each person's level of specialization. If it is true that specialization can speed up the process of learning by doing, or can reduce total fixed learning costs by avoiding duplicated learning and training and by increasing the utilization rate of those costs in the society, then it follows that each person's pro-ductivity is low in the autarchic structure of panel (a). But on the other hand this structure does not have transaction costs. Since each person has the same configuration of pro-duction, the degree of diversification in autarky is also low.

In the organizational structure depicted in panel (b), the number of goods produced by each person has been reduced from four to three, so that relative to panel (a) each individual's level of specialization and productivity has increased. Markets for two goods have emerged from the division of labor, and the number of transactions and related transaction costs have increased. The economy now comprises two, rather than four, separate local business communities, so that the degree of market integration has increased. The number of producers of the (now traded) good 1 or 2 has decreased from four to two, so that the degree of production concentration is higher than in autarky. Since two different professions have emerged from the division of labor, the degree of diversity of the economic structure has increased as has each individual's level of specialization. The degree of interpersonal dependence, the degree of interaction between individuals, the degree of each person's trade dependence, the degree of commercialization for society, and the number of markets have all increased compared with autarky.

In panel (c), each individual is completely specialized in producing one good. Accordingly, the degree of market integration, the number of markets, the diversity of the economic structure, the number of transactions, the concentration of production, the degree of commercialization, productivity, and transaction costs are all higher than in panel (b).

We will show in part III and afterward that, because of the trade-off between the positive network effects of division of labor and transaction costs, as a transaction cost coefficient for a unit of goods traded falls in a static model, transaction costs caused by division of labor will be more likely to be outweighed by positive network effects of division of labor. Hence, the economy will evolve from autarky structure in (a) to that in (b), followed by that in (c). In a dynamic equilibrium model such evolution of division of labor may occur spontaneously in the absence of exogenous improvements in trading efficiency. The above concurrent phenomena will take place as different aspects of the evolution of division of labor. In this process, the emergence of the market is endogenously determined by individuals' self-interested decisions in choosing their levels and patterns of specialization and by the interactions of the self-interested decisions in the marketplace. Demand and supply are two aspects of the division of labor. As shown in chapters 8, 10, and 23, if producer goods are introduced, then the institution of the firm will endogenously emerge from the evolution in division of labor as well. Since the spirit of this text is older than neoclassical economics, while its body is younger than neoclassical economics, we would like to address our new species as *New Classical Economics*.

A comparison of figure 0.1 and figure 0.2 indicates that new classical economics is distinguished from neoclassical economics by the following features.

1   In new classical economics, the notions of economies of specialization and network effects of division of labor are used to describe production conditions, while in neoclassical economics, the notion of economies of scale is used to describe production conditions.

2   There is no *ex ante* dichotomy between pure consumers and firms in new classical economics, while this dichotomy is the basis of neoclassical economics.

3   Transaction costs have important implications for the equilibrium topological properties of economic organisms in new classical economics, while they may not have such implications in neoclassical economics.

4   In chapter 5, we shall show that in new classical economics individuals' optimum decisions are always corner solutions and that therefore interior solutions can never be optimal. In neoclassical economics, by contrast, the interior optimum is the rule and the corner solution is the exception.

In new classical economics, there are two kinds of decisions that each individual has to make. The first involves the choice of one's occupation and the level of specialization in that chosen occupation, which relates to how many (professional and self-sufficient) activities one engages in. This kind of decision is inherently associated with corner solutions (cases in which zero values attach to some activity levels). Marginal analysis for interior solutions does not work for this kind of decision-making. The second type of decision involves how one allocates one's limited resources among all the activities that one has decided to undertake. This kind of decision features marginal analysis of a corner or interior solution. Inframarginal analysis is a combination of these two types of decision-making.

Comparison of the two figures indicates that trade theory, development economics, and changes in aggregate demand (macroeconomic phenomena) based on a change in the network size of division of labor, are all related aspects of new classical economics. Neo-classical economics cannot simultaneously and naturally explain so many phenomena. Part IX will show that the emergence of money, cyclical unemployment, and long-run regular business cycles can also be explained by reference to the developed network of division of labor.

## ◆ 0.4 Structure of the Text and Suggestions for its Use

This text is divided into 10 parts, organized on the basis of the four-level hierarchical structure of economic analysis discussed in section 0.2. Part I analyzes the characteristics of the economic environment. Chapter 1, which deals with consumer preferences, focuses on the human aspect of that environment. This chapter has its counterpart in any standard microeconomics text. Chapter 2 focuses on the production environment, and illustrates different methods of specifying production environment in the neoclassical and new classical frameworks. A difference between the two methods relates to the distinction between the notion of economies of scale (nonconvex production sets) used in neoclassical economics and economies of division of labor (network effects) used in new classical economics. It is shown that one of the distinguishing features of the new classical framework is that consumer-producers are the only *ex ante* players, while firms emerge as *ex post* players from interactions among individuals' decisions in choosing the structure of transactions and residual rights.

Part II, on the Neoclassical Framework, covers standard neoclassical microeconomics, including applications of game theory within this framework. Possible corner solutions and inframarginal analysis (nonlinear programming) are emphasized in this part. Part III, on the New Classical Framework, develops simple new classical models with only two final goods to illustrate the basic concepts of new classical economics and to introduce the techniques required to manage the inframarginal analysis of new classical models. Part IV, the Institution of the Firm and Pricing through Bargaining and Contracting, introduces producer goods into the analysis to explain why and how the institution of the firm emerges from the evolution of division of labor. Various game models and models of moral hazard are then used to explore the effects of endogenous transaction costs on the equilibrium network size of division of labor, and on the equilibrium structure of residual rights and ownership. Particular attention is paid to the connection between strategic interactions and network effects of division of labor. Also, the implications of sequential equilibrium models for investigating economies of information asymmetry and endogenous transaction costs are explored. Chapter 10 covers principal–agent models and Grossman–Hart–Moore models of two-sided moral hazard and optimum ownership structure. The new classical framework is used to explore the implications of endogenous transaction costs caused by moral hazard for simultaneous endogenization of specialization, principal–agent relationships, and structure of residual rights.

Part V, Trade Theory and More General New Classical Models, applies the new classical framework to develop endogenous trade theory and the notion of endogenous comparative advantage. The results provide interesting support for Smith's view that differences in productivity between different specialists are the consequence rather than the cause of the division of labor. Then conventional exogenous comparative advantages in productivity and endowment are introduced to investigate the implications of the coexistence of endogenous and exogenous comparative advantage for economic analysis. Also, implications of inframarginal comparative statics of general equilibrium for discontinuous jumps of trade pattern between corner solutions are explored in connection with neoclassical trade models (the Ricardo model and the Heckscher–Ohlin model). Chapter 12 shows that since each country is both a consumer and a producer in the trade models, inframarginal analysis becomes essential and results based on marginal analysis may be misleading. Then a general new classical model with no explicit specification of functional forms is used to investigate the existence of a general equilibrium network of division of labor in chapter 13. The notions of topology and a weighted digraph of economic organisms are used to clearly define the general equilibrium network of division of labor and pattern of resource allocation. It will be shown that the equilibrium organism which comprises the equilibrium network of division of labor and equilibrium resource allocation are Pareto optimal. Hence, the most important function of "the invisible hand" is to coordinate individuals' decisions in choosing their levels and patterns of specialization and to utilize network effects of division of labor.

Part VI, Urbanization, Population, and the Trade-off between Working and Leisure, explores the implications of the network effect of division of labor for emergence of cities and for the equilibrium differential of land prices between urban and rural areas. We show how the trade-off between working and leisure in the new classical framework can explain concurrent increases in both leisure and working time for the market as a consequence of an evolution of division of labor that reduces the working time for self-sufficient production. The professional infrastructure sector and primary resources are then introduced into the new classical framework in order to endogenize transaction efficiency, and to explore the effects of population size and shortage of primary resources on the evolution of division of labor.

Part VII, on the Trade-off Between Economies of Division of Labor and Coordination Reliability of the Network of Division of Labor, examines the economics of property rights and the theory of insurance, in the light of transaction costs caused by the coordination failure risk of a large network of division of labor. A new classical theory of endogenous externality is developed as part of a new classical economics of property rights and transaction costs. Part VIII, the Hierarchical Structure of Division of Labor, develops the analysis to endogenize simultaneously the number of links and the level of division of labor in the roundabout production chain. Also, the number of layers of the hierarchical structure of transactions and cities based on a high level of division of labor is endogenized, and the intrinsic relationship between the hierarchical structure of organization, industrialization, and the evolution of division of labor is investigated.

Part IX, Economic Development and Economic Growth, uses various new classical dynamic general equilibrium models to explain many development phenomena as different aspects of the evolution of division of labor. In particular, a new classical sequential equilibrium model is used to explore the implications of spontaneous social experiments, through the price system, with various structures of the network of division of labor. This model features bounded rationality, adaptive behavior, uncertainty of the direction of the evolution of economic organisms, and spontaneous evolution of the information acquired by society through social experiments. Chapter 21 is exclusively devoted to the endogenous growth models based on the neoclassical framework. In chapter 22 these are then compared with new classical endogenous growth models based on spontaneous evolution of division of labor. The two types of endogenous growth models are also tested against empirical observations.

Part X, Macroeconomic Phenomena and the Endogenous Size of Networks of Division of Labor, develops a new classical model explaining the emergence of money from the evolution of division of labor. We also develop a new classical model of capital, which formalizes classical ideas about the intimate relationship between capital and the evolution of division of labor in roundabout production. A new classical model of endogenous business cycles and unemployment is then used to explore the implications of efficient long-run business cycles and long-run regularly cyclical unemployment for long-run endogenous growth. Also, the implications of all kinds of new classical models for explaining macroeconomic phenomena, such as an endogenous and efficient risk for mass unemployment caused by the trade-off between the positive network effects of division of labor on aggregate productivity and coordination reliability of a larger network of division of labor, are explored.

Despite an innovative structure, this text systematically teaches orthodox neoclassical microeconomics as well as new classical economics. Most chapters devote appropriate space to both new classical and neoclassical economics. We use a pedagogical approach of "reduction prior to deduction." This implies that specific examples of models or cases are first used to teach the basic concepts and technical substance before general theories and abstract deduction are introduced. In other words, we usually use specific models to explicitly solve for the optimum decisions and equilibrium, and their comparative statics. After this inquiry into applied theories, we may consider some pure theoretical problems, such as the existence theorem for a very general class of models. This pedagogical approach generates jumps between simple examples and general theories as you read one chapter after another. But it avoids the introduction of very abstract concepts and deduction before students get an intuitive understanding of them from specific examples. Most texts on theories present theorems and their proof before examples are presented, or specialize either in pure theories or in applied theories. Our pedagogical approach differs from these. Please give us some feedback on its relative performance.

Since new classical economics is relatively new to the reader, the entirety of part III is devoted to using the simplest specific new classical models to illustrate basic concepts and procedure for inframarginal analysis in new classical economics. Pure theories of new classical economics, such as the existence theorem of general equilibrium and the first welfare theorem for a general class of new classical models, will be covered in part V. For neoclassical economics, fairly complex examples are introduced from the outset and some pure theories, such as the existence theorems of utility function and equilibrium, are considered after the presentation of a few examples, since we suppose that the reader is quite familiar with the materials.

There are many different ways to use the text. First, it can be used at different levels of mathematical formalism. A teacher fond of exciting ideas in the economics of property rights and transaction costs, but who does not like mathematical models, might use the text in the following way. Chapters 13, 23, and others involving too much mathematics, could be skipped, as could the mathematical models in all chapters. Lectures could focus on the trade-offs that generate stories and the economic mechanism at work in each chapter. The text provides descriptive illustrations for each formal model developed. The text also features many graphs that highlight properties of demand and supply as two aspects of the network of division of labor. These are much more intuitive than conventional demand and supply curves. The teacher accustomed to explaining neoclassical microeconomics using such curves, but no formal mathematics, will certainly be more able to teach new classical economics using the graphs of network of division of labor in the absence of mathematical substance. If the teacher chooses to use this text in this way, then she can choose assignments and examination questions for students mainly from the questions at the end of each chapter, ignoring those exercises that involve mathematical models. Emphasis can then be put on the training and inspiring of creative and critical economic thinking with the aid of graphs.

If the teacher chooses to teach students the technical substance of the main models in the text, she can still choose between two levels. One is to cover proofs of the theorems with sophisticated mathematics, such as the existence theorem of the utility function (chapter 1), the existence theorem of neoclassical general equilibrium (chapter 4), the existence theorem of new classical general equilibrium (chapter 13), and the difficult dynamic models in part IX. The alternative is to cover only simple formal models at the level of applied theory and skip the proofs of the main theorems and more complicated models. For the complicated models and theorems, the teacher can still use a graphical approach to illustrate the central ideas, the trade-offs that generate the stories behind the mathematics, and the economic mechanisms at work.

Second, this text can be used for different fields of economics because of its nature as a general theoretical synthesis. Through revision and generalization of the core of mainstream economics, it is able to encompass, within one overarching framework, many areas of the discipline that have customarily been treated as separate branches. These include, for example: microeconomics, macroeconomics, development economics, international economics, urban economics, growth theory, industrial organization, applications of game theory in economics, economics of property rights, economics of transaction costs, economics of institutions and contracts, economics of organization, managerial economics, theory of hierarchy, new theory of the firm, theory of money, theory of insurance, theory of network and reliability, and so on. Hence, this book can be used not only as the main text for a general course, but also as a text for any of the above fields. For instance, to use the book as a text for a one-semester course on "economic development and trade," the teacher might choose chapter 2, parts III, IV, V, VI, IX, and X. A one-semester course on the "economics of property rights and transaction costs" might focus on chapter 2, parts III, IV, V, VII, VIII, and chapters 22 and 26. For a one-semester course on the "economics of organization and contracts," appropriate selections would be chapter 2, the game theory part of chapter 4, parts III, IV, V, VII, VIII, and chapters 22 and 25. Certainly there are many other ways to package appropriate chapters and parts of the text to suit particular subjects. And of course it would be particularly suitable for a subject specifically aimed at covering the new theories of trade, growth, institutions, and transaction costs.

If the text is chosen for a core course of economics, such as a graduate-level or upper undergraduate-level course in microeconomics or macroeconomics, then it can be adapted to suit a one-year course, a one-semester course, or a two-quarter course. For a one-year course, I suggest covering parts I–V in the first semester, with the emphasis on basic training. The teacher may press students to spend substantial time in this semester duplicating the major models covered. They might also be asked to do at least three exercises from each chapter covered. I suggest that, with respect to understanding the technical content of this course, one hour spent duplicating the major models in the text is as effective as perhaps eight hours spent reading and listening. But students should be reminded that the purpose of duplication is not simply to memorize results mechanically, but rather to help them acquire the capacity to design models that can formalize our insights into economic problems. The second semester could cover the rest of the text, with the emphasis on stimulating creative and critical thinking. For this kind of core course, appropriate prerequisites would be first-year microeconomics if the text is used for a third- or fourth-year undergraduate course, or intermediate microeconomics if the text is used for a graduate course.

## Key Terms and Review

What is economics about and what is mainstream economics?
What is the essence of classical mainstream economics?
What are the differences between neoclassical economics and new classical economics?
What are the implications of mathematical formalism for economic research and development of mainstream economics?
Positive, normative, and empirical analysis; the scientific approach to economics.
Marginal vs. inframarginal analysis.
Problems of resource allocation vs. problems of economic organization.

## Further Reading

*New classical economics and inframarginal analysis*: Marshall (1890, chs. 8–12 of Book IV), Young (1928), Stigler (1951, 1976), Houthakker (1956), Rosen (1978, 1983), Becker (1981), Becker and Murphy (1992), Yang (1994, 1996), Yang and S. Ng (1998) and references there, Yang and Y.-K. Ng (1993, chs. 0, 1), Borland and Yang (1992), Ben-Ner (1995), Smith (1776); *neoclassical microeconomics*: Mas-Collell, Whinston, and Green (1995), Varian (1984), Henderson and Quandt (1980), Kreps (1990), Stiglitz (1993), Marshall (1890), Samuelson (1955), Debreu (1991); *Evidence for evolution in division of labor*: Braudel (1984), Chandler (1990), Yang, Wang, and Wills (1992), Chen, Lin, and Yang (1999; see ch. 22 in this text); *classical mathematical programming, nonlinear and linear programming, and other mathematics used in economics*: Chiang (1984), Dixit (1990), Mas-Collell, Whinston, and Green (1995, mathematical appendix), Himmelblan (1972); *dynamic programming and dynamic models*: Beckmann (1968), Denardo (1975), Chow (1975), Kamien and Schwartz (1981), Seierstad and Sydsater (1987).

# QUESTIONS

1   Some economists argue that new classical economics and inframarginal analysis is relevant only to the evolution of division of labor that occurred before the Industrial Revolution. They claim that in a modern economy, each individual is completely specialized and buys everything from the market, so that the assumption of an exogenous level of specialization of individuals is acceptable. Comment on this view in connection with the following cases.

   a) The emergence of the CNN network is certainly very much a modern phenomenon. Also, according to an article in *The Economist* ("Newspapers and the Internet", July 17, 1999, pp. 17–19), as the internet develops, many specialized information sites become more competitive than nonspecialized conventional newspapers which cover a broad range of information, but not deeply in each field. New classical economics can explain this phenomenon better than neoclassical economics. According to new classical theory, an improvement in transaction efficiency (which might be caused by new telecommunication facilities), or a spontaneous evolution of division of labor, will make a higher level of division of labor between specialized media and information providers commercially viable. The corner equilibrium that involves the finer division of labor between CNN (which specializes in reporting news through TV networks) and other media will be the general equilibrium. Whether or not the demand for and supply of CNN's professional services are "effective" depends on the general equilibrium level of division of labor, since demand and supply are two sides of the division of labor. But this in turn is determined by the efficient balance point between the economies of specialization and transaction costs.

   b) Recently the *Wall Street Journal* reported that each wave of mergers of modern corporations is associated with more specialization and division of labor. In particular, the latest wave of rationalization in the corporate sector has the characteristic that many companies have moved to separate some of their functions from their core business. Services that were once self-provided are now bought from more specialized suppliers. Now salesmen frequently use the claim "we are professional" to attract clients. Managers talk about downsizing, out-sourcing, disintegration, and focusing on core competence. This is the modern phenomenon of economies of specialization and division of labor, and should be distinguished from economies of scale.

   c) The recent boom in franchising in the US is further evidence that new classical economics is very relevant to the modern economy. The institution of the franchise provides a way to trade intangible intellectual property between a franchiser and franchisees. A franchise contract usually gives the franchiser great discretionary power, and has the effect of increasing the specificity of the assets of franchisees. This is used to check and balance infringements upon the intangible intellectual property of the franchiser. Through this institutional arrangement, transaction efficiency in enforcing rights to intangible intellectual property is improved. Hence the boom in franchise networks enables a deeper division of labor between specialized producers of entrepreneurial ideas and specialized producers of tangible services or goods. Now many businessmen make a lot of money from specialized production of ideas through the franchise system. It turns out to be increasingly difficult to survive in the business arena in the US if an entrepreneur tries to produce both ideas and tangible services. Our new classical economics, then, can not only explain why the boom of the institution of the firm was a driving force for increasing the level of division of labor in the production of goods and services in the first industrial revolution; it is also powerful in explaining the current industrial revolution in the US, in which the franchising system is bringing about an increasing division of labor between the production of intangible intellectual property and the production of other goods.

   d) The development of the market for automatic toothbrushes is a modern phenomenon which converts the self-sufficient production and consumption of tooth brushing to specialized production of an automatic toothbrush and commercialized consumption of it. You may analyze the commercialization of robots: say the production cost of robots has been significantly reduced, so that each family can afford to use a robot for house-keeping. Then you may find that the income share of commercialized house-keeping is higher than the income share of food or automobiles. This postmodern phenomenon can certainly be better explained by new classical theory of endogenous specialization than by neoclassical theory of exogenous specialization.

2   Classical economists never used the concept of economies of scale. They tended rather to think in terms of the benefits of division of labor, and of the transportation and seasonal adjustment costs caused by division of labor. In the last quarter of the nineteenth century, economists started to use the concept of economies of scale to describe benefit of division of labor on the basis of the neoclassical dichotomy between pure consumers and firms. Marshall was acutely aware of the inadequacy of the concept of economies of scale for describing phenomena of economies of division of labor. He suggested the notion of external economies of scale to differentiate the economies of division of labor from the economies of scale of a firm. He also used this notion to try to salvage the classical concept of the invisible hand. However, Allyn Young's student, Frank Knight (1925), pointed out that the notion of external economies of scale involves a logical inconsistency, since economies of scale that are external to all firms are an empty box. Young (1928) indicated that the notion of external as well as internal economies of scale is simply a misrepresentation of the economies of division of labor. He argued (1928, p. 531) that "the view of the nature of the processes of industrial progress which is implied in the distinction between internal and external economies is necessarily a partial view. Certain aspects of those processes are illuminated, while, for that very reason, certain other aspects, important in relation to other problems, are obscured." According to Young, the notion of economies of scale misses qualitative aspects of economies of division of labor, though it may capture the quantitative aspect. Young evidently had in mind what today we call the network effect. He spelled this out as follows (1928, p. 539): "The mechanism of increasing returns is not to be discerned adequately by observing the effects of variations in the size of an individual firm or of a particular industry, for the progressive division of labor and specialization of industries is an essential part of the process by which increasing returns are realized. What is required is that industrial operations be seen as an interrelated whole." Suppose there are three *ex ante* identical individuals who prefer diverse consumption and specialized production of each of three goods x, y, and z. If an individual chooses to specialize completely in producing x, then she will demand y and z. If she chooses to self-provide x and y and not to produce z, then she has no demand for x and y from the market and will demand z. But if two individuals choose self-sufficiency of all goods, then the other cannot choose specialization. This implies that each person's decision as to her level of specialization not only determines her productivity, but also determines the extent of the market for the produce of others, thereby imposing a constraint on their decisions on their levels of specialization and productivity. The Young theorem (1928, pp. 534, 539) explores a typical feature of the network effects of the division of labor and the related market. The theorem states that "the securing of increasing returns depends on the progressive division of labor. . . . not only the division of labor depends upon the extent of the market, but the extent of the market also depends upon the division of labor. . . . demand and supply are two sides of the division of labor." Young also believed that Marshall's marginal analysis of demand and supply cannot be used to explain network size of division of labor. Discuss why Young's insights into the limitations of the concept of economies of scale were not formalized and taught in mainstream textbooks until recently.

3   Some economists take the study of specialization and division of labor as a subfield of economics. Comment on this view in connection with Houthakker's assertion (1956, p. 182) that "there is hardly any part of economics that would not be advanced by a further analysis of specialization." Use some examples to discuss his points.

## Notes

1 Note that self-interested behavior does not necessarily imply selfish behavior. If others' consumption positively contributes to an individual's objective function, then her self-interested behavior includes pursuit of charity, which is certainly different from selfishness.

2 We will discuss the difficulty in completely isolating positive analysis from value judgments in chapter 4.

3 Coase (1946, p. 173) noted "a consumer does not only have to decide whether to consume additional units of a product; he has also to decide whether it is worth his while to consume the product at all rather than spend his money in some other direction." He applies this inframarginal analysis to criticize marginal cost pricing rule (1946) and Pigou's (1940) marginal analysis of externality (Coase, 1960). Buchanan and Stubblebine (1962) coined the term inframarginal analysis. Formally, inframarginal analysis is based on linear, nonlinear, and dynamic programming and other nonclassical mathematical programming, while marginal analysis is based on classical mathematical programming. The application of inframarginal analysis to a decision problem can be found in Becker (1981), and Rosen (1983). Its application to the theory of incomplete contract can be found in Grossman and Hart (1986) and Hart (1995). The application of inframarginal analysis to general equilibrium models can be found in Yang and Wills (1990), Yang and Borland (1991), Dixit (1987, 1989), Yang and Shi (1992), Yang and Ng (1993), and in chapters in this text.

4 As a result, economists' research on specialization and division of labor since Marshall has been more limited than sociologists' research on the topic, represented by Emile Durkheim (1933).

5 The modern Arrow–Debreu model of general equilibrium, which features the first two properties of Marshall's framework, has generalized and consolidated that framework. Arrow and Debreu use the concept of a nonconvex production set to generalize the concept of economies of scale.

# chapter 1

# PREFERENCE AND THE UTILITY FUNCTION

## ◆ 1.1 The Scientific Approach to the Study of Human Behavior

This text starts with an inquiry into an individual's preferences, since each individual's economic activities are motivated by the pursuit of his or her happiness and satisfaction. This distinguishes economics from the natural sciences, and also poses some particularly difficult tasks for economics. The study of interactions among individuals who try to meet their desires has three important features. First, each individual's behavior is driven by his or her purpose in the economic arena. Hence, we need an objective function to describe the purpose of a player, who is not merely a passive object as in physics or chemistry. But the objective function of an individual may be in conflict with those of others. The study of such conflicts, and their reconciliation, distinguish economics from physics, chemistry, and other natural sciences. The mathematical approach to optimizing an objective function subject to some constraints is used to describe self-interested behavior. The notion of optimization is beyond physical- or chemical-state equations.

Second, while an individual's desires play a central role in economic analysis, these are not directly observable. Satisfaction of an individual's desires is not only intangible, but also involves that individual's subjective judgment of value. This implies that it is difficult, if not impossible, to measure degrees of satisfaction, and to conduct absolutely objective experiments. Most economists follow the approach of the thought experiment to investigate an individual's behavior. That is, they make some assumptions about what the individual's desires are, about the constraints facing her, and about her behavior in achieving her objectives subject to those constraints. Then, through rigorous mathematical deduction, they establish the connection between the intangible desires, the behavior, and the resulting tangible phenomena (such as quantities and prices of goods purchased). The relationship between the tangible quantities and prices has a certain correspondence to the assumed properties of the intangible desire and the individual's behavior. Economists can thus infer the intangible things from the tangible relationship. If observable phenomena are compatible with the relationships generated by mathematical deduction on the basis of the assumptions about intangible things, then economists take the assumptions about desires and behavior to be acceptable as working hypotheses. Otherwise, the theories are falsified by observations. This procedure is referred to as the scientific approach to positive analysis in economics. In positive analysis, economists do not claim that their assumptions are always right. What they try to do is to establish the hypotheses (theories) that can be tested against observations. The working hypotheses can then be either falsified or verified.

Finally, interactions between active players in the economy may generate something that is much more than the simple sum of individuals' behaviors. An analogy may illustrate the point. The human body comprises a heap of molecules, but it contains something that never exists in a single molecule. We call this thing "life" or "spirit". The spirit of an economic system comprising many individuals is, for instance, "price," "money," or "equilibrium", which never exists in a single individual's activity in the absence of others' interactions with her. Superadditivity and network effects (see chapters 2, 5, 6, 11, and 13) are other examples of analogues to life and spirit in molecular biology. The emergence of some phenomena from interactions among individual elements that are much more than the simple sum of those individual elements is a feature of the theory of complexity. This is an exciting feature of economics as well. This, together with the first feature that we have discussed, makes economics more complex than biology, physics, and chemistry. In chapters 4 and 6, we shall investigate how the spirit of an economy, equilibrium prices, emerges from interactions between individuals' behaviors.

In section 1.2, we make some assumptions about an individual's preferences that ensure the existence of a utility function, which allows for the application of mathematical programming to the study of individual behavior. Further assumptions, relating to individuals' desires for diverse consumption and to the second-order condition for a neoclassical consumer's decision problem, are made in section 1.3. The economic meaning of the assumptions is then discussed.

---

### Questions to Ask Yourself when Reading this Chapter

♦ Why do we need the notion of a utility function to do a thought experiment?

♦ Under what conditions can an individual's preferences be represented by a utility function?

♦ What assumptions about utility functions and preferences do economists make when they use utility functions to represent preferences? Why do they need these assumptions?

♦ What are the relationships between the important assumptions?

---

## ♦ 1.2 Preference and the Utility Function

Assume that $x_i$ is the amount of good i that is consumed and $x$ is an $m$ dimension column vector representing a bundle of $m$ goods that is consumed. Then a *consumption set* is defined by

$$X \subset R_+^m = \{x \in R^m : x_i \geq 0, \text{ for } i = 1, 2, \ldots, m\}, \tag{1.1}$$

where $R_+^m$ denotes a set of $m$ dimension vectors whose elements are nonnegative real numbers. We read $X \subset R_+^m$ as "set $X$ is contained in set $R_+^m$" which implies that each element of set $X$ is an element of set $R_+^m$. $X$ may or may not equal set $R_+^m$. If the amount of a consumption good must be an integer, or if the maximum amount of a consumption good is limited (for instance, leisure time for each day cannot be greater than 24 hours), then the consumption set $X$ is a subset of $R_+^m$ and $X \neq R_+^m$. In the rest of this volume, we assume that $X = R_+^m$, unless indicated otherwise.

The objectives of the decision-maker are summarized in a *preference relation*, which we denote by $\gtrsim$. $\gtrsim$ is a binary relation on the consumption set $X$, allowing the comparison of pairs of alternative consumption bundles $x, y \in X$. We read $x \gtrsim y$ as "$x$ is at least as good as $y$." From $\gtrsim$, we can derive two other important relations on $X$: $>$ and $\sim$.

The *strict preference relation*, $>$, is defined by $x > y$ iff (if and only if) $x \gtrsim y$ but not $y \gtrsim x$. $x > y$ is read "$x$ is preferred to $y$." The *indifference relation*, $\sim$, is defined by $x \sim y$ iff $x \gtrsim y$ and $y \gtrsim x$. $x \sim y$ is read "$x$ is indifferent to $y$."

In order to obtain some intuitive understanding of the concept of preference, which may seem to have no connection to our daily experience, you may conduct an experiment with your mom. Before the experiment, first prepare a piece of paper with two dimension coordinates as shown in figure 1.1. A point $x_1$ on the horizontal axis represents the amount of apples consumed and a point $x_2$ on the vertical axis represents the amount of bread consumed. Let a vector $x = (x_1, x_2)$ represent a bundle of consumption of the two goods. Suppose that $x(1) = (8, 2)$ denotes a bundle of consumption with $x_1 = 8$ (8 units of apples) and $x_2 = 2$ (2 units of bread). You may draw a vertical line that cuts point $x_1 = 8$ and a horizontal line that cuts point $x_2 = 2$. The intersection point of the two lines is $x(1) = (8, 2)$. All points that are in the first quadrant, including the horizontal and vertical axes, constitute the consumption set. Following the same method, you can plot points $x(2) = (2, 8)$, $x(3) = (3, 9)$, $x(4) = (9, 3)$, $x(5) = (4, 4)$, and other points that represent different bundles of consumption of the two goods, as shown in figure 1.1(a). Now, the experiment is ready.

You can then ask your mom to compare each pair of consumption bundles i and j, and in each case to choose one and only one of the three answers:

$$x(i) > x(j), \qquad x(j) > x(i), \qquad x(i) \sim x(j).$$

Suppose that her answers are:

$$x(3) \sim x(4) > x(1) \sim x(2) \sim x(5).$$

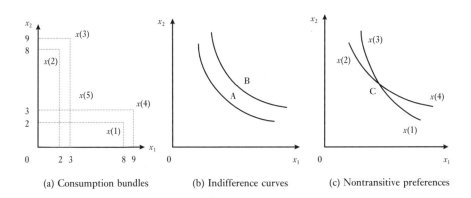

(a) Consumption bundles          (b) Indifference curves          (c) Nontransitive preferences

◆ **Figure 1.1:** Mom's preferences and indifference curves

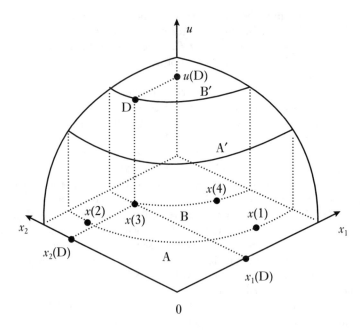

♦ **Figure 1.2:** A utility function

If you connect all equivalent points with smooth curves, you will obtain the two *indiffer-ence curves* shown in figure 1.1(b). All points on the same indifference curve generate the same degree of satisfaction. Hence, when your mom answered your questions, she indi-rectly told you her preferences and her degree of satisfaction for each consumption bundle. The degree is what economists call *utility*.

Now if we consider the degree of satisfaction in addition to consumption bundles themselves, there are three dimensions: $x_1$, $x_2$, and utility $u$. In order to view the third dimension, we draw the graph in figure 1.2. Note that the origin of the $x_1$ and $x_2$ coordinates in figure 1.1. is now moved to the bottom of the graph. The new vertical axis represents the degree of satisfaction, or utility. The two indifference curves in Fig. 1.1(b) are now copied in the $x_1$–$x_2$ plane in figure 1.2 as the broken curves A and B. We now move indifference curve A (representing a lower degree of satisfaction) straight up to the position of curve A' and move indifference curve B (representing a higher degree of satisfaction) up to the position of curve B'. If we do this also for other indifference curves, then we can obtain many similarly moved indifference curves in the three dimension space, where the indifference curves with higher degrees of satisfaction lie above those with lower degrees of satisfaction. All of the resulting indifference curves would consti-tute the surface of a hill, as shown in figure 1.2. This surface is the geometric represen-tation of a utility function that indicates the relationship between the degree of satisfaction and the amounts of the two goods consumed. For any point on the surface, for instance point D, we can find corresponding amounts of apples and bread, $x_1(D)$ and $x_2(D)$ respectively, and the corresponding degree of satisfaction $u(D)$. That is, we have a utility function such that

$$u = f(x_1, x_2).$$ (1.2)

However, the degree of satisfaction is an ordinal rather than a cardinal concept. That is, it is independent of the unit of measurement of utility. The same set of preferences may be represented by multiple utility functions, indicated by more or less closely spaced indifference curves, as long as the order between any pair of indifference curves is preserved. In other words, a steeper or a flatter hill surface may represent the same preferences that are associated with a set of the indifference curves on the $x_1$–$x_2$ plane.

Following our intuitive illustration of the notion of utility function, let us now define the concept rigorously.

A function $u: X \rightarrow R$ is a *utility function* representing preference relations $\succcurlyeq$ if, for all $x_1, x_2 \in X$,

$$x_1 \succcurlyeq x_2 \text{ iff } u(x_1) \geq u(x_2).$$

For instance, the previous experiment with your mom indicates that her preference can be represented by the utility function

$$u = f(x_1\ x_2) = x_1 x_2.$$

Since a utility function maps multidimensional variables into a one-dimensional real number, it will remarkably facilitate the analysis of self-interested behavior by applying mathematical programming which optimizes an objective function subject to constraints. Then we need not repeat the time-consuming experiment that you did with your mom. But it is conceivable that some irrational preferences may not be representable by a utility function. Hence, we are interested in the question: what kinds of preferences can be represented by a utility function? The answer to the question is given by the existence theorem of the utility function, proved by Debreu (1959).

We first prove that only rational preferences can be represented by a utility function. Then we examine other properties of preferences that are essential for the existence of a utility function.

The preference relation $\succcurlyeq$ on $X$ is *rational* if it possesses the following two properties:

i)   *Completeness.* For any $x, y \in X$, we have $x \succcurlyeq y$, or $y \succcurlyeq x$, or $x \sim y$.
ii)  *Transitivity.* For any $x, y, z \in X$, if $x \succcurlyeq y$ and $y \succcurlyeq z$, then $x \succcurlyeq z$.

If preferences are not complete, the individual cannot make judgments about what she wants for at least some pair of consumption bundles. In that case we cannot use a utility function to represent her preferences. If an individual's preferences are not transitive, they must involve inconsistency. For instance, the two indifference curves in figure 1.1(c) are associated with a preference relation that violates transitivity. The intersection of the two curves implies $x(1) \sim C \sim x(4)$, while the fact that point $x(4)$ is higher than point $x(1)$ implies $x(4) > x(1)$, which contradicts $x(1) \sim x(4)$. Similarly, $x(3) \sim C \sim x(2)$ contradicts $x(3) > x(2)$. A person with such preferences is said to be irrational. She is inconsistent in judging what she wants. Of course such preferences cannot be represented by a utility function. To verify the claim, we shall prove the following proposition.

**Proposition 1.1:** A preference relation can be represented by a utility function only if it is rational.

*Proof:* (Mas-Collell, et al., 1995). To prove this proposition, we show that if there is a utility function that represents preferences $\succcurlyeq$, then $\succcurlyeq$ must be complete and transitive.

   *Completeness.* Because $u(.)$ is a real-valued function defined on $X$, it must be that $\forall$ (for any) $x$, $y \in X$, either $u(x) \geq u(y)$ or $u(y) \geq u(x)$. But because $u(.)$ is a utility function representing $\succcurlyeq$, this implies that either $x \succcurlyeq y$ or $y \succcurlyeq x$ (recall the definition of a utility function). Hence, $\succcurlyeq$ must be complete.

   *Transitivity.* Suppose that $x \succcurlyeq y$ and $y \succcurlyeq z$. Because $u(.)$ represents $\succcurlyeq$, we must have $u(x) \geq u(y)$ and $u(y) \geq u(z)$. Therefore, $u(x) \geq u(z)$. Because $u(.)$ represents $\succcurlyeq$, this implies $x \succcurlyeq z$. Thus, we have shown that $x \succcurlyeq y$ and $y \succcurlyeq z$ imply $x \succcurlyeq z$, and so transitivity is established. *Q.E.D.*

   Now we consider an example which shows that rational preferences need not be representable by a utility function. With that motivation, we then consider further assumptions about preferences that are essential for the existence of a utility function.

   Consider the case of *the lexicographic preference relation.* For simplicity, assume that $X = R_+^2$. Define $x \succcurlyeq y$ if either "$x_1 > y_1$" or "$x_1 = y_1$ and $x_2 \geq y_2$." This is known as the lexicographic preference relation. The name derives from the way a dictionary is organized; that is, good 1 has the highest priority in determining the preference ordering, just as the first letter of a word does in the ordering of a dictionary. When the amount of good 1 in two consumption bundles is the same, the amount of good 2 in the two consumption bundles determines the consumer's preferences. It is not difficult to verify that the lexicographic preference is complete and transitive (see exercise 4, below). Nevertheless, it can be shown that no utility function exists that represents this preference ordering. This is intuitive. With this preference ordering, no two distinct bundles are indifferent. Therefore, we need two-dimensional real numbers to represent the preference orderings. Hence, a utility number from the one-dimensional real line is not enough to represent the preference ordering. A somewhat subtle argument required to establish this claim rigorously can be found in Mas-Collell et al. (1995, p. 46).

   The assumption that is needed to ensure the existence of a utility function is that the preference relation be continuous. The preference relation $\succcurlyeq$ on $X$ is *continuous* if it is preserved under limits. That is, for any sequence of pairs $\{(x^n, y^n)\}_{n=1}^{\infty}$ with $x^n \succcurlyeq y^n$ for all $n$, $x = \lim_{n \to \infty} x^n$ and $y = \lim_{n \to \infty} y^n$, we have $x \succcurlyeq y$. Continuity says that the consumer's preferences cannot exhibit "jumps," with, for instance, the consumer preferring each element in sequence $\{x^n\}$ to the corresponding element in sequence $\{y^n\}$, but suddenly reversing her preference at the limiting points of these sequences $x$ and $y$.

   An equivalent way of stating this notion of continuity is to say that for all $x$, the upper contour set $\{y \in X : y \succcurlyeq x\}$ and the lower contour set $\{y \in X : x \succcurlyeq y\}$ are both *closed*; that is, they include their boundaries.

   We can show that lexicographic preferences are not continuous. To see this, consider the sequence of bundles $x^n = (1/n, 0)$ and $y^n = (0, 1)$. For every $n$, we have $x^n > y^n$. But $\lim_{n \to \infty} y^n = (0, 1) > (0, 0) = \lim_{n \to \infty} x^n$. In words, as long as the first component of $x$ is larger than that of $y$, $x$ is preferred to $y$ even if $y_2$ is much larger than $x_2$. But as soon as the first components become equal, only the second components are relevant, and so the preference ranking is reversed at the limit points of the sequence. Lexicographic preferences relate to a hierarchical structure of desires. For instance, a hungry man may not be interested in feelings of accomplishment or prestige. But after his basic need for food and clothing is met, he might desire those feelings. From our daily experience we can perceive that our preferences are indeed hierarchical. Hence, the assumption of continuous preferences that exclude hierarchical preferences from consideration is unrealistic.

However, we have to confess that we economists are incapable of handling hierarchical preferences in terms of mathematics. Therefore, we confine our attention within a particular layer of the hierarchical structure of desires, so that the following theory of utility is applicable.

Though rationality and continuity of the preference relation are together sufficient for the existence of a utility function, there is a further assumption that makes the proof of the existence theorem easier and ensures some important properties of the demand function, such as Walras' law. This is the assumption of non-satiation. (A weaker assumption of local nonsatiation is made in Mas-Collell et al., 1995, p. 42, and Varian, 1992, p. 96.)

The preference relation $\geqslant$ on $X$ is *nonsatiated* if $x, y \in X$ and $y_i > x_i$ $\forall i$ implies $y > x$, where $\forall$ reads "for any." It is *strongly nonsatiated* if $y \geq x$ and $y \neq x$ implies $y > x$.

The assumption of nonsatiation is easier to accept if $x$ is interpreted as amounts of goods that a consumer possesses rather than the amounts of the goods that she consumes. This interpretation of $x$ and the assumption of strong nonsatiation, together with the assumption of free disposal, implies that more is better.

We are now ready to prove the existence theorem of the utility function.

**Proposition 1.2:** Suppose that the rational preference relations $\geqslant$ on $X$ is continuous and nonsatiated. Then there is a continuous utility function $u(x)$ that represents $\geqslant$.

*Proof:* For the case of $X = R_+{}^m$, we can prove the proposition with the aid of figure 1.3. Denote the diagonal ray in $R_+{}^m$ (the locus of vectors with all $m$ components equal) by $Z$. It will be convenient to let $e$ designate the $m$-vector whose elements are all equal to 1. Then $\alpha e \in Z \, \forall \, \alpha \geq 0$.

Note that $\forall \, x \in R_+{}^m$, nonsatiation implies that $x \geqslant 0$. Also note that for any $\bar{\alpha}$ such that $\bar{\alpha} e_i > x_i$ for $i = 1, 2, \ldots, m$ (as shown in figure 1.3), we have $\bar{\alpha} e \geqslant x$. Nonsatiation and continuity can then be shown to imply that there is a unique value $\alpha(x) \in [0, \bar{\alpha}]$ such that $\alpha(x)e \sim x$.

We now take $\alpha(x)$ as our utility function, that is, we assign a utility value $u(x) = \alpha(x)$ to every $x$. This utility level is also depicted in figure 1.3. We need to check two properties of this function. The first is that it represents the preference $\geqslant$, that is, $\alpha(x) \geq \alpha(y)$ iff $x \geqslant y$.

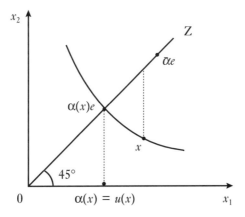

♦ **Figure 1.3:** Construction of a utility function

This follows from the construction of the utility function. Suppose first that $\alpha(x) \geq \alpha(y)$. By nonsatiation, this implies that $\alpha(x)e \succcurlyeq \alpha(y)e$. Since $\alpha(x)e \sim x$ and $\alpha(y)e \sim y$, we have $x \succcurlyeq y$. Suppose, on the other hand, that $x \succcurlyeq y$. Then $\alpha(x)e \sim x \succcurlyeq \alpha(y)e \sim y$; and so by nonsatiation, we must have $\alpha(x) \geq \alpha(y)$. Hence, $\alpha(x) \geq \alpha(y)$ iff $x \succcurlyeq y$. The second property is that the constructed utility function is a continuous function. Mas-Collell et al. (1995, p. 48) provide a proof of this.

## ◆ 1.3 The Convex Preference Relation, Quasi-concave Utility Functions, Diminishing Marginal Rates of Substitution, and Desire for Diverse Consumption

In addition to the conditions required for the existence of the utility function, we are also interested in some particular properties of preferences, and the correspondence between these properties and the features of the utility functions. The most important of the properties is convexity of the preference relation. It is important because it relates to the second-order condition for the consumer's decision problem and to an individual's desire for diverse consumption. In this section, we examine the relationships between convex preference ordering (convex upper contour set), quasi-concave utility functions, diminishing marginal rates of substitution, and a consumer's desire for diverse consumption, which is essential for the interior solution in neoclassical economics and for the trade-off between economies of specialization and transaction costs in new classical economics.

The preference relation $\succcurlyeq$ on $X$ is *convex* if $\forall\, x \in X$, the upper contour set $\{y \in X\colon y \succcurlyeq x\}$ is convex; that is if $y \succcurlyeq x$ and $z \succcurlyeq x$, then $\alpha y + (1-\alpha)z \succcurlyeq x\ \forall\, \alpha \in [0,1]$. Figure 1.4(a) gives an illustration of the definition. All points on and above the indifference curve that generates the utility level $u(x)$ constitute an upper contour set. For any points in the set, such as $y$ and $z$, their weighted average, which is a point on the segment between the two points, is an element of the set. A nonconvex preference relation and nonconvex upper contour set are illustrated in figure 1.4(b), where a weighted average of point $y$ and $z$ is out

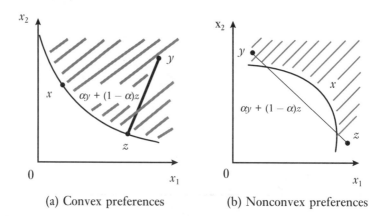

(a) Convex preferences          (b) Nonconvex preferences

◆ **Figure 1.4:** Convex vs. nonconvex preferences

of the upper contour set. It is straightforward that a convex upper contour set is associated with an indifference curve that is convex to the origin.

From the definition of a convex preference relation, we can see that the upper contour set is convex iff the following statement is true.

$$\forall y, z \in X \text{ and } \forall \alpha \in [0,1],$$
$$u(\alpha y + (1 - \alpha)z) \geq \text{Min } \{u(y), u(z)\} \tag{1.3}$$

A utility function having this property is said to be *quasi-concave*. Hence, convexity of the preference relation or of the upper contour set is equivalent to quasi-concavity of the utility function representing the preference relation. If the close interval of $\alpha$, $[0,1]$, is replaced with the open interval $(0,1)$, and semi-inequality $\geq$ is replaced with $>$ in (1.3), then a utility function that satisfies the condition is said to be *strictly quasi-concave*.

Now we assume that the utility function $u(.)$ on $X$ is twice continuously differentiable. The properties of continuity and differentiability make it easier to establish the connection between strict quasi-concavity of the utility function and diminishing marginal rate of substitution. But actually the utility function may not be continuous or differentiable at any point $x \in X$. Any strictly increasing transformation of a continuous function representing a preference relation $\succeq$ also represents $\succeq$. If the transformation is not continuous, then the new utility function representing the continuous preference relation $\succeq$ is discontinuous.

Figure 1.5 shows the graph of the Leontief preference orderings. The corresponding utility function is $u(x) = \text{Min } \{x_1/a, x_2/b\}$. It is not difficult to see that the Leontief preference relation is convex and continuous; but it is not differentiable at the kink point.

Assume that the continuous and differentiable utility function is $u(x)$, where $x = (x_1, x_2)$. The equation that represents an indifference curve for a fixed utility level $u_1$ is:

$$u(x) = u_1 \text{ or } f(x) \equiv u(x) - u_1 = 0. \tag{1.4}$$

Since a convex preference relation is associated with a convex upper contour set and the latter is associated with a set of convex indifference curves, we can establish the connection

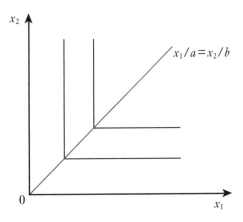

♦ **Figure 1.5:** Leontief preferences

between the first- and second-order derivatives of the indifference curves and the convexity of the preference ordering. According to your high-school mathematics, a downward sloping and convex curve can be represented by function $x_2 = g(x_1)$ that has a negative first-order derivative and a positive second-order derivative. Function $x_2 = g(x_1)$ is implicitly given by (1.4). Its first derivative can be derived from the implicit function theorem.

$$\frac{dx_2}{dx_1} = -\frac{\partial u / \partial x_1}{\partial u / \partial x_2} < 0, \text{ or } -\frac{dx_2}{dx_1} = \frac{\partial u / \partial x_1}{\partial u / \partial x_2} > 0 \tag{1.5}$$

where $-dx_2/dx_1$ is called the *marginal rate of substitution*, which is the amount of good 2 that must be given away to keep utility unchanged when the amount of good 1 is increased by a marginal unit. A strictly convex preference relation implies strictly convex indifference curves. Hence, the second-order derivative of $x_2 = g(x_1)$ should be positive. Having differentiated (1.5), the second-order derivative can be worked out as follows.

$$\frac{d^2 x_2}{dx_1^2} \equiv \frac{d\frac{dx_2}{dx_1}}{dx_1} = -\frac{\left(u_{11} + u_{12}\frac{dx_2}{dx_1}\right)u_2 - \left(u_{12} + u_{22}\frac{dx_2}{dx_1}\right)u_1}{u_2^2} \tag{1.6}$$

where, $u_i \equiv \frac{\partial u}{\partial x_i}$, $u_{ij} \equiv \frac{\partial^2 u}{\partial x_i \partial x_j}$, and $\frac{dx_2}{dx_1}$ is given by (1.5).

Inserting (1.5) into (1.6), it can be shown that the second-order derivative in (1.6) is positive iff

$$-\left(u_1^2 u_{22} - 2u_1 u_2 u_{12} + u_2^2 u_{11}\right) > 0 \tag{1.7}$$

Condition (1.7) is equivalent to the following condition for the sign of the *bordered Hessian determinant*.

$$\begin{vmatrix} u_{11} & u_{12} & u_1 \\ u_{12} & u_{22} & u_2 \\ u_1 & u_2 & 0 \end{vmatrix} > 0. \tag{1.8}$$

The utility function $u(x)$ that satisfies condition (1.8) is said to have a *negative definite bordered Hessian matrix*

$$\begin{pmatrix} u_{11} & u_{12} & u_1 \\ u_{12} & u_{22} & u_2 \\ u_1 & u_2 & 0 \end{pmatrix}.$$

This establishes the equivalence between a strictly convex preference relation and a negative definite bordered Hessian matrix of the utility function representing the preference relation. This deduction can be extended to utility functions with more than 2 consumption goods. For those cases, a negative definite bordered Hessian matrix requires alternatively changing signs of all principal minors of the bordered Hessian determinant, with a negative first-order principal minor. See Chiang (1984) for more details.

Since

$$\frac{d^2 x_2}{dx_1^2} \equiv \frac{d\,\dfrac{dx_2}{dx_1}}{dx_1} > 0 \text{ iff } -\frac{d^2 x_2}{dx_1^2} \equiv \frac{d\left[-\dfrac{dx_2}{dx_1}\right]}{dx_1} < 0, \tag{1.9}$$

where $-\dfrac{dx_2}{dx_1}$ is the marginal rate of substitution,

equation (1.7) is equivalent to a diminishing marginal rate of substitution. This establishes the equivalence between a twice continuously differentiable and strictly quasi-concave utility function and the *law of diminishing marginal rate of substitution*. This law implies that as the consumption of good 1 increases, progressively smaller amounts of good 2 must be given up in order to maintain an unchanged utility level. Graphically, the law implies that the tangent lines of the indifference curve become flatter as consumption of good 1 increases.

Finally, we examine the connection between convexity of the preference relation and the desire for diverse consumption. From figure 1.4(a), we can see that for a strictly convex preference relation, a weighted average (a mixture) of the two equally valued consumption bundles is preferred to either bundle alone. We call this feature of the preference relation *desire for diverse consumption*. Hence, strict convexity of the preference relation is equivalent to the desire for diverse consumption.

If the signs of the expressions in (1.7), (1.8), and (1.9) are reversed, the utility function $u(x)$ is *strictly quasi-convex*. A quasi-convex utility function represents nonconvex preferences for specialized consumption. The linear utility function $u = x_1 + bx_2$ is both quasi-concave and quasi-convex. It is neither strictly quasi-concave nor strictly quasi-convex. It represents razor-edge preferences between desire for specialized consumption and desire for diverse consumption.

So far, all the assumptions we have made about the preference relation and the utility function relate to *ex ante* properties of what an individual wants. It is an *ex post* matter if a consumption bundle that is actually chosen by an individual is diverse. This is because the individual's consumption decision depends not only on her preferences, but also on prices, which are themselves the consequence of interactions between self-interested behaviors, and endowments. In the text we take *ex ante* to mean "before individuals have made

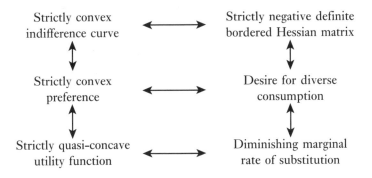

♦ **Figure 1.6:** Relationships between several important concepts

decisions," and *ex post* to mean "after individuals have made decisions and the economy has settled down in an equilibrium which is the consequence of interactions between all individuals' self-interested decisions." In the next chapter, we will see that even if individuals prefer diverse consumption in the sense discussed above, they may nevertheless be induced by relative prices to choose a specialized consumption pattern when their strictly convex preferences are represented by a quasi-linear utility function.

The relationships between convexity of the preference relation, convexity of the upper contour set, quasi-concavity of the utility function, a negative definite bordered Hessian matrix, a diminishing marginal rate of substitution, and the desire for diverse consumption are summarized in figure 1.6. Note that these relationships are based on the existence of a twice continuously differentiable utility function.

## ◆ 1.4 Ordinal vs. Cardinal Theory of Utility, and Diminishing Marginal Rate of Substitution vs. Diminishing Marginal Utility

Since an increasing transformation of a utility function preserves the preference orderings, it represents the same preference relation as does the original utility function (see exercise 2). For a twice continuously differentiable utility function, its continuous and increasing transformation preserves not only preference orderings, but also marginal rates of substitution. For instance, the utility function $u = x_1 x_2$ can be transformed to $v = u^{1/2} = x_1^{1/2} x_2^{1/2}$. It can be shown that the transformation changes neither the marginal rates of substitution nor the quasi-concavity of the utility function, since

$$-\frac{dx_2}{dx_1} = \frac{\partial v / \partial x_1}{\partial v / \partial x_2} = \frac{(dv/du)(\partial u / \partial x_1)}{(dv/du)(\partial u / \partial x_2)} = \frac{\partial u / \partial x_1}{\partial u / \partial x_2}.$$

In the next chapter, we will show that the demand function also will not be changed by the increasing transformation of the utility function as long as the marginal rate of substitution is not changed by the transformation.

However, we can show that $u(.)$ is not strictly concave, while $v(.)$ is strictly concave. A function $v(x)$ is *strictly concave* if $\forall \, y, z \in X$ we have

$$v(\alpha y + (1 - \alpha)z) > \alpha v(y) + (1 - \alpha)v(z), \tag{1.10}$$

where $\alpha \in [0, 1]$. It can be shown that for twice continuously differentiable $v$ (1.10) holds iff

$$v_{11} < 0, \; v_{22} < 0, \; v_{11}v_{22} - v_{12}^2 > 0, \tag{1.11}$$

where $v_{ij} \equiv \partial^2 v / \partial x_i \partial x_j$. (1.11) holds iff the Hessian matrix of $v(.)$,

$$\begin{pmatrix} v_{11} v_{12} \\ v_{12} v_{22} \end{pmatrix},$$

is negative definite. See Chiang (1984) for proof of these two propositions. $\partial v / \partial x_i$ is called *marginal utility* of good i. $\partial^2 v / \partial x_i^2 \equiv \partial(\partial v / \partial x_i) / \partial x_i < 0$ implies that marginal utility decreases as consumption of a good increases. This is referred to as *diminishing marginal utility*. It is easy to show that the utility function $v = x_1^{1/2} x_2^{1/2}$ satisfies (1.11). Hence this utility function is strictly concave, or it displays diminishing marginal utility. But, it can be shown that

$$u_{11}u_{22} - u_{12}^2 = -1 < 0, \ u_{11} = 0.$$

Thus the utility function $u = x_1 x_2$ is not concave and it does not have diminishing marginal utility. A property of a utility function that cannot (or can) be preserved by an increasing transformation of that function is called a *cardinal* (or *ordinal*) *property*. Hence, diminishing marginal utility is a cardinal property of a utility function, while diminishing marginal rate of substitution and related quasi-concavity are ordinal properties. Diminishing marginal utility is not necessary for convexity of indifference curves, which is associated with a quasi-concave utility function; nor is it essential for diminishing marginal rate of substitution, which relates to the second-order condition for the interior optimum consumption decision, as shown in the next chapter. It is not difficult to show that a concave function is quasi-concave, but a quasi-concave function is not necessarily concave.

An increasing transformation of a utility function changes the measurement unit of utility, preserving preference orderings as well as marginal rates of substitution. Let $u = x_1 x_2 = 100$ and $v = u^{1/2} = x_1^{1/2} x_2^{1/2} = 10$. Then the two equations generate the same indifference curve represented by $x_2 = 100/x_1$. Hence, if we call one unit of utility in terms of $v$ 10 units of utility in terms of $u$, then the increasing transformation from $u$ to $v$ does not change anything of substance in the analysis, just as the transformation of 1 kilogram to 2.2 pounds would not change real weight.

The view that a measurement unit of utility is essential is referred to as *cardinal theory of utility*, while the view that a measurement unit is not essential is referred to as *ordinal theory of utility*. We shall show in the next chapter that the ordinal theory of utility is enough for a positive analysis of demand and supply. But the cardinal theory may be needed when some social welfare function is used for welfare analysis, though welfare analysis may be conducted without the use of such a function.

## Key Terms and Review

Preferences and indifference curves.
Rational preferences, complete preferences, transitive preferences.
Nonsatiation, strong nonsatiation, and continuity of preferences.
Utility functions and conditions for the existence of utility functions.
Convex upper contour set, convex indifference curves, and convex preference relations.
Quasi-concave utility functions.
Marginal rates of substitution.
The law of diminishing marginal rate of substitution.
Marginal utility.
Diminishing marginal utility and strictly concave utility function.
Relationships between convex preferences, the quasi-concave utility function, concave utility function, diminishing marginal rate of substitution, negative definite bordered Hessian matrix, and desire for diverse consumption.
Cardinal vs. ordinal theories of utility.

## Further Reading

Mas-Collell et al. (1995, chs. 1–3), Varian (1992, ch. 7), Deaton and Muellbauer (1980), Debreu (1959), Samuelson (1947).

# QUESTIONS

**1** What is meant by the scientific approach to studying an individual's degree of satisfaction?

**2** Some economists, such as Hayek, hold that economics cannot be a science because society as a whole always knows much more than each individual member of it. This view implies that what is known by even the greatest economist is only a very small part of what society knows. Hence, it is an impossibility to make economics a science that is supposed to cover all economic knowledge in society. Comment on the view.

**3** Some economists challenge the mainstream approach to studying preferences and utility functions by pointing out that preferences should be endogenously determined by interactions between self-interested behaviors rather than exogenously given. For instance, pursuit of relative position and peer pressure may affect the evolution of individuals' preference. Other economists, such as Becker, argue that good economic theories can explain many economic phenomena as the unintended consequence of interactions between self-interested behaviors in the absence of changes of preferences. Comment on these alternative views, and discuss the merits and shortcomings of the mainstream approach to studying preferences as adopted in this text.

**4** Why do we need a utility function to represent an individual's preferences?

**5** What kind of preferences can be represented by a utility function?

**6** What is the restriction that the assumption of continuous preference imposes on economic analysis?

**7** Why do economists assume that individuals prefer diverse consumption?

**8** What is the connection between convex indifference curves, the quasi-concave utility function, diminishing marginal rate of substitution, and desire for diverse consumption?

**9** What is the relationship between diminishing marginal rate of substitution and diminishing marginal utility?

**10** What are ordinal and cardinal theories of utility?

# EXERCISES

**1** Prove the following proposition. If $\succcurlyeq$ is rational, then (i) $\succ$ is both irreflexive ($x \succ x$ never holds) and transitive. (ii) $\sim$ is reflexive ($x \sim x$ for all $x$) and transitive.

**2** Show that if $f: R \to R$ is a strictly increasing function and $u: X \to R$ is a utility function representing the preference relation $\succcurlyeq$, then the function $v: X \to R$ defined by $v(x) = f(u(x))$ is also a utility function representing the preference relation $\succcurlyeq$.

**3** Prove that if $\succcurlyeq$ is strongly nonsatiated, then it is nonsatiated.

4   Verify that the lexicographic ordering is complete, transitive, strongly nonsatiated, and strictly convex.

5   Identify the conditions under which the quasi-linear utility function $u = x_1 + x_2^\alpha$ is strictly quasi-concave. Draw indifference curves represented by the utility function in the $x_1$–$x_2$ plane.

6   Show an example of a preference relation that is not continuous but is representable by a utility function.

7   Suppose that in a two-good world, the consumer's utility function takes the form $u = [\alpha x_1^\rho + (1 - \alpha) x_2^\rho]^{1/\rho}$. This utility function is known as the constant elasticity of substitution (or CES) utility function. (a) Show that when $\rho = 1$, indifference curves become linear. (b) Show that as $\rho \to 0$, this utility function comes to represent the same preferences as the Cobb–Douglas utility function $u = x_1^\alpha x_2^{1-\alpha}$. (c) Show that as $\rho \to -\infty$, this utility function comes to represent the same preferences as the Leontief utility function $u = \text{Min}\{x_1, x_2\}$.

8   Assume that $x$ is the amount of goods consumed, $y$ is the amount of leisure time, $L = 24 - y$ is the amount of working time. The utility function is $u = x^\alpha y^{1-\alpha}$. Draw indifference curves on the x–L plane. Then draw indifference curves on the x–y plane.

9   Suppose the Leontief utility function is

$$u = \text{Min}\left(\frac{x}{a}, \frac{y}{b}\right).$$

Draw indifference curves on the x–y plane. Will utility increase if $x$ is increased and $y$ is unchanged? Under what condition will utility be raised by changes of $x$ and $y$?

10  Consider the following utility functions, and in each case determine: whether they are strictly quasi-concave and strictly concave; whether their marginal rates of substitution diminish; work out their Hessian matrix and bordered Hessian matrix; whether they are negative definite. (a) $u = ax + \ln y$, $a > 0$; (b) $u = xy / (x + y)$; (c) $u = x(y - a)$, $a > 0$; (d) $u = \ln x + b \ln y$, $b > 0$.

11  Identify from among the following those utility functions that represent the same preference relation. (a) $u = x^\alpha y^\beta$; (b) $u = x^\alpha + y^\beta$; (c) $u = \alpha \ln x + \beta \ln y$; (d) $u = \alpha x + \beta y$.

12  Which of the following utility functions represent preferences for diverse consumption? (a) $u = x^a + y^b$, $a, b > 0$; (b) $u = ax + y^2$, $a > 0$; (c) $u = bx + y$; (d) $u = \text{Min}\{x, y\}$.

# chapter 2

# PRODUCTION CONDITIONS

## ♦ 2.1 The Neoclassical Framework vs. the New Classical Framework

In most economics textbooks, the chapter following the one dealing with preferences and utility functions would be devoted to the derivation of demand functions from a constrained utility maximization problem. We will not follow that sequence here for the following reasons. Whereas the framework of most textbooks is neoclassical, the approach of the present book is more general. This will enable us to compare the neoclassical framework with the new classical framework and to explore the implications of the differences between the two. Within the new classical framework, the analysis of consumers' and producers' decisions cannot be separated. Hence, we start this chapter with an outline of the relationship between the neoclassical and new classical frameworks, and then proceed to an analysis of production conditions in the two frameworks.

Three features in particular distinguish the neoclassical framework.

(i) The dichotomy between pure consumers and firms is exogenously given, so that pure consumers cannot survive in the absence of firms and a market system to link them with firms. This implies that the existence of the institution of the firm and the market is in turn exogenously given. A pure consumer cannot choose the self-provision of any of the goods that she demands. Nor can she choose her level of specialization in producing goods.

(ii) The productivity of a firm is determined by its size, rather than by the levels of specialization of individuals within that firm, or by the level of division of labor of the firm or of society.

(iii) Analysis of demand and supply focuses on the determinants of relative quantities of goods consumed and produced, for a given pattern of organization between pure consumers and firms. This differs from Allyn Young's theory of demand and supply, in which these are seen as two related aspects of the division of labor. Young's idea implies that the focus of analysis should be on the endogenization of individuals' levels of specialization. All individuals' decisions on their levels and patterns of specialization determine the level and structure of division of labor for society as a whole, which in turn determine demand and supply. In many cases, the neoclassical analysis of demand and supply is associated with marginal analysis of interior solutions.

As discussed in the introductory chapter, the neoclassical framework was adopted to avoid corner solutions. But now many nonclassical mathematical programming methods are available for handling corner solutions, so that the neoclassical framework is no longer essential for mathematical formalism. We can use a mathematical framework to formalize classical economic thinking on specialization and division of labor and reorientate economics from problems of resource allocation to those of economic organization. Accordingly our economic analysis can start by examining the decision process by which individuals choose their levels and patterns of specialization. In other chapters of this text, we will show that there are two important differences between the neoclassical and new classical theories of production. In neoclassical economics, the Walrasian equilibrium and Pareto optimum production schedule are always associated with the production possibility frontier (PPF). Also, marginal cost pricing is efficient. But in new classical economics, the equilibrium and Pareto optimum production schedule may not be associated with the PPF. In a new classical Walrasian equilibrium, marginal cost pricing does not work.

In the rest of this chapter, we study the concepts of production function, production set, and endowment constraint, and examine their different meanings in the neoclassical and new classical frameworks. Section 2.2 studies the neoclassical production environment, and section 2.3 is devoted to the new classical production environment.

---

### Questions to Ask Yourself when Reading this Chapter

♦ What are the main differences between the production environment in the neoclassical framework and that in the new classical framework?

♦ What are the differences between economies of scale, economies of specialization, economies of scope, and economies of division of labor?

♦ What is the distinction between exogenous and endogenous comparative advantage?

♦ Why can fixed learning or training cost generate economies of division of labor?

---

## ♦ 2.2 The Neoclassical Production Environment

This section examines production conditions for firms, as defined by the neoclassical framework. In neoclassical production theory, the concepts of production function and production set are used to describe the relationship between inputs and outputs for a firm. The most important feature of this relationship is the connection between the scale of a firm's production operations and its productivity. Here, the *operation scale* of the firm is defined by either the output size or the input size of the firm, which may be independent of individuals' levels of specialization and the level of division of labor in the firm. In other words, the only variables involved in the neoclassical concepts of production function and production set are output levels of goods and input levels of factors. No part is played by variables that relate to the degree of interpersonal dependence, individuals' levels of specialization, the level of division of labor in the firm or in society, and the related size of the market network. In contrast, the new classical theory of production emphasizes the implications of individuals' levels of specialization and the level of division of labor in society for productivity.

The neoclassical dichotomy between pure consumers and firms presupposes that the existence of firms and of the market are given exogenously. Firms buy inputs from and sell outputs to the market. A neoclassical firm is defined by a production set. A production vector (or an input–output vector, or production plan) is a vector $y = (y_1, y_2, \ldots y_m) \in R^m$ that describes the outputs of the $m$ commodities from a production process. Here, positive numbers denote outputs and negative numbers denote inputs. Some elements of a production vector may be zero; this just means that the process has no net output of that commodity.

The set of all production vectors that constitute feasible plans for the firm is the *production set* for the firm, and is denoted by $Y \subset R^m$. Any $y \in Y$ is possible; any $y \notin Y$ is not. The production set $Y$ can be described using the *transformation function F(.)*, which has the property that $Y = \{y \in R^m : F(y) \leq 0\}$ and $F(y) = 0$ iff $y$ is an element of the boundary of $Y$. The set of boundary points of $Y$, $\{y \in R^m : F(y) = 0\}$, is known as the *production possibility frontier*, which can be called a *transformation curve* if $m = 2$. (See figure 2.1.)

If $F(.)$ is differentiable, and if the production vector $\bar{y}$ satisfies $F(\bar{y}) = 0$, then for any commodities $i$ and $j$, the ratio

$$-\frac{dy_i}{dy_j} = \frac{\partial F(\bar{y})/\partial y_j}{\partial F(\bar{y})/\partial y_i}$$

is called the *marginal rate of transformation (MRT) of good i for good j at $\bar{y}$*. The marginal rate of transformation is a measure of how much the output of good $j$ can be increased if the firm decreases the output of good $i$ by one marginal unit. It describes the trade-off between quantities of different outputs for given inputs.

In neoclassical economics, if there are global economies of scale, a firm will always completely specialize in producing one good. If production conditions display constant returns to scale, then a firm's level of specialization does not matter for productivity. Hence, in many neoclassical economic models each firm is assumed to produce a single good. For this case, it is convenient to describe the production condition for a firm using the concept of *production function*. Let a variable $z \geq 0$ denote the amount of the firm's output and $x = \{x_1, x_2, \ldots, x_n\} \geq 0$ denote the amounts of the firm's $n$ inputs. The *production function* $z = f(x)$ gives rise to the production set

$$Y = \{(z, x_1, x_2, \ldots, x_n) \in R_+^{n+1} : z \leq f(x_1, x_2, \ldots, x_n)\}.$$

Hence, the production function $z = f(x)$ is a relationship between dependent variable (output) $z$ and independent variables (inputs) $x$. Holding the level of output fixed, we can define the *marginal rate of substitution (MRS) of input i for input j at $\bar{x}$*

$$-\frac{dx_i}{dx_j} = \frac{\partial f(\bar{x})/\partial x_j}{\partial f(\bar{x})/\partial x_i}$$

The MRS measures the additional amount of input $j$ that must be used to keep output at level $\bar{z} = f(\bar{x})$ when the amount of input $i$ is decreased marginally. Hence, the MRS describes the trade off between quantities of different inputs in generating a certain level of output.

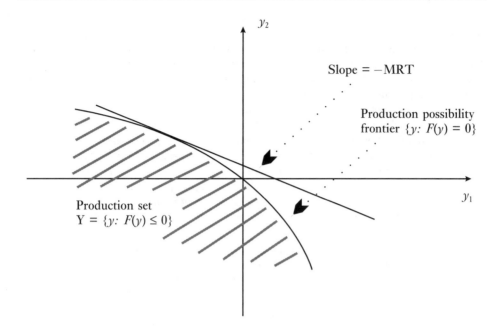

**Figure 2.1:** Production set and production possibility frontier

## Example 2.1: a Cobb–Douglas production function

We consider a firm that produces a single good, employing two inputs. Suppose that its production conditions are described by the following *Cobb–Douglas production function*

$$z = f(x, y) = Ax^\alpha y^\beta \tag{2.1}$$

where $z$ is the quantity of the good that is produced, and $x$ and $y$ are respective quantities of the two inputs, say capital and labor, that are employed in the production process. $\partial f/\partial x$ and $\partial f/\partial y$ are the respective *marginal productivities* of the two inputs. The exponentially weighted average of the two inputs $F \equiv x^{\alpha/(\alpha+\beta)} y^{\beta/(\alpha+\beta)}$ is called *the total factor* employed in production, and $f/F$ is called the *total factor productivity (TFP)* of $z$. The percentage change in output over the percentage change of capital input $(\partial f/f)/(\partial x/x) = (\partial f/\partial x)(x/f) = \alpha$ is called *elasticity of output with respect to capital* (or *capital elasticity of output*). Similarly, $(\partial f/f)/(\partial y/y) = (\partial f/\partial y)(y/f) = \beta$ is *labor elasticity of output*.

The most important properties of the production function and production set relate to the concepts of economies (or diseconomies) of scale and elasticity of substitution. Let us examine the first of these, which distinguishes neoclassical economics from new classical economics.

The production set $Y$ exhibits non-increasing returns to scale if for any $y \in Y$, we have $ty \in Y$ for all scalars $t \in [0, 1]$. A production function with a single output, $z = f(x)$, displays *decreasing returns to scale* if $tz > f(tx)$ for all scalars $t > 1$. That is, there exist diseconomies of scale if output increases less than proportionally as all inputs increase proportionally.

The production set $Y$ exhibits nondecreasing returns to scale if for any $y \in Y$, we have $ty \in Y$ for all scalars $t \geq 1$. A production function with a single output, $z = f(x)$ displays *increasing returns to scale* if $tz < f(tx)$ for all scalars $t > 1$. That is, there exist economies of scale if output increases more than proportionally as all inputs increase proportionally.

The production set $Y$ exhibits constant returns to scale if for any $y \in Y$, we have $ty \in Y$ for all scalars $t \geq 0$. That is, $Y$ displays nondecreasing as well as non-increasing returns to scale. A production function with a single output, $z = f(x)$, displays *constant returns to scale* if $tz = f(tx)$ for all scalars $t \geq 0$. That is, there exist constant returns to scale if output increases proportionally as all inputs increase.

The production set $Y$ is convex, if $y, y' \in Y$ and $\alpha \in [0, 1]$, then $\alpha y + (1 - \alpha)y' \in Y$. It can be verified that increasing returns to scale or economies of scale implies that the production set is not convex. If inaction is possible $(0 \in Y)$, convexity implies that $Y$ displays non-increasing returns to scale.

Consider the function $z(t) = f(tx, ty)$. The *elasticity of scale* is given by $e(x) = [dz(t)/z(t)]/(dt/t)$, evaluated at $t = 1$. We say that the technology exhibits *locally increasing*, *constant*, or *decreasing returns to scale* as $e(x)$ is greater, equal, or less than 1, respectively. It is easy to see that $e = \alpha + \beta$ for the Cobb–Douglas production function in (2.1), which displays economies of scale if $\alpha + \beta > 1$, diseconomies of scale if $\alpha + \beta < 1$, and constant returns to scale if $\alpha + \beta = 1$. The Cobb–Douglas production function belongs to a class of functions with constant $e$, which are called *homogeneous functions*.

The marginal rate of substitution for the homogeneous Cobb–Douglas production function is $-dy/dx = (\partial f/\partial x)/(\partial f/\partial y) = \alpha y/\beta x$. The capital elasticity of output is $\alpha$ and the labor elasticity of output is $\beta$.

### Example 2.2: a nonhomogeneous production function

The following production function is *nonhomogeneous*.

$$z = f(x, y) = A(x - a)^\alpha (y - b)^\beta$$

It displays variable economies of scale. It is not difficult to verify that $e > 1$ if $x$ tends to and is larger than $a$ or if $y$ tends to and is larger than $b$, and that $e < 1$ if $x$ and $y$ are sufficiently large and $\alpha + \beta < 1$.

The percentage change in the relative input level over the percentage change in relative marginal productivities of factors is called *elasticity of substitution* between the two factors. It will be shown in chapters 3 and 5 that under the conditions for the interior optimum the relative marginal productivities of factors equals their relative prices. Thus the elasticity of substitution describes the sensitivity of changes in the optimum relative quantities of factors in response to changes in their relative prices. Let the elasticity of substitution be $E$; then for the production function $z = f(x, y)$,

$$E = \frac{d(x/y)/(x/y)}{d\left(\frac{\partial f/\partial y}{\partial f/\partial x}\right)\bigg/\left(\frac{\partial f/\partial y}{\partial f/\partial x}\right)} = \frac{d \ln(x/y)}{d \ln\left(\frac{\partial f/\partial y}{\partial f/\partial x}\right)}.$$

In exercise 5, you are asked to show that the elasticity of substitution is 1 for the Cobb–Douglas production function and is a constant for any CES production function. It can be shown also that the nonhomogeneous production function in example 2.2 has variable elasticity of substitution.

Classical economists, such as Smith, never used the concept of economies of scale or increasing returns to scale.[1] They focused instead on the benefits of specialization and division of labor. The concept of a nonconvex production set generalizes the concept of economies of scale or increasing returns to scale. Young (1928, p. 533) argued that "the use of the notion of large-scale production misses the phenomenon of economies of division of labor" and that (1928, p. 539) "the mechanism of increasing returns is not to be discerned adequately by observing the effects of variations in the size of an individual firm or of a particular industry, for the progressive division of labor and specialization of industries is an essential part of the process by which increasing returns are realized."

Marshall (1890) tried to keep the connection between the concepts of economies of scale and economies of division of labor by distinguishing between internal and external economies of scale. *Internal economies of scale* correspond to the ordinary definition of economies of scale; that is, a firm's productivity goes up as its operation scale expands. *External economies of scale* imply that a firm's productivity goes up as the operation size of the sector or the size of the whole economy expands. Young argued (1928, p. 531) that "the view of the nature of the processes of industrial progress which is implied in the distinction between internal and external economies is necessarily a partial view. Certain aspects of those processes are illuminated, while, for that very reason, certain other aspects, important in relation to other problems, are obscured." Hence, it seemed to Young that the concept of external economies of scale is a misrepresentation of the classical concept of economies of specialization and division of labor.

In the next section, we shall define economies of specialization and division of labor and examine the distinction between economies of division of labor and nonconvexity of the production set.

## ◆ 2.3 The New Classical Production Environment

The focus of classical economics was on the effects of specialization and division of labor on economic growth and welfare. Plato (380 BC, pp. 102–6) considered the welfare implication of the division of labor and specialization and the connection between the division of labor, the market, and money. Xenophon also examined the connection between cities and the division of labor (see Gordon, 1975, p. 41). William Petty (1671, I, pp. 260–1) noted that specialization contributes to skillful clothmaking and pointed out that the Dutch could convey goods cheaply because they specialized each ship for a specific function. In another place, Petty gave a more striking example of the division of labor in the manufacture of a watch. He indicated (1683, pp. 471–2) that cities can promote the division of labor by reducing transaction costs. Joseph Harris (1757) and Josiah Tucker (1755, 1774) referred directly to the productivity implications of the division of labor, the possibility of the subdivision of labor, and the intimate relationship between a greater variety of goods, production roundaboutness, and a higher level of division of labor.

A number of works before Smith recognized the advantages of division of labor in improving the skill (or human capital, in modern terms) of individual workers, in reducing the time and effort involved in having to switch from one production operation to another, and in facilitating the invention of machinery. They also recognized the role of the market and population size in permitting specialization. These works include Denis Diderot (1713), Anonymous (1701, p. 591), Henry Maxwell (1721, p. 33), and Josiah Tucker (1755, 1774). Also, Turgot (1751, pp. 242–3) linked the development of division of labor with the concurrent increases in inequality of income distribution and in living standards for even the humblest member of society. He associated the division of labor with the introduction of money, the extension of commerce, and the accumulation of capital (1766, pp. 44–6, 64, 70).

Smith (1776) called public attention to the central role of specialization and division of labor in economic analysis by systematically investigating their implications for economic growth and prosperity. Among other contributions, he conjectured that the division of labor is limited by the extent of the market (1776, ch. 3 of bk. I), and that the extent of the market is determined by transportation efficiency (1776, pp. 31–2). He also proposed what is now referred to as the concept of endogenous comparative advantage, which implies that economies of specialization and division of labor may exist even if all individuals are *ex ante* identical, and that the differences in productivities between various specialists are consequences rather than causes of the division of labor (p. 28). Subsections 2.3.1 and 2.3.2 of this chapter formalize Smith's concepts of economies of specialization and division of labor.

David Ricardo (1817) pursued an alternative line of study of specialization and division of labor. He emphasized the significance of exogenous comparative advantage and what is referred to by Rosen (1978) as superadditivity, which implies a type of interpersonal or social complementarity of production that generates a higher aggregate productivity for division of labor than for nonspecialized production. Heckscher (1919) and Ohlin (1933) distinguished between exogenous technical comparative advantage and exogenous endowment comparative advantage, and showed that the latter can generate economies of division of labor in the absence of technical comparative advantage. Subsection 2.3.3 formalizes Ricardo's and Heckscher–Ohlin's concept of economies of division of labor based on exogenous comparative advantage.

According to Rae (1834, pp. 164–5, 352–7), an increase in the utilization rate of tools and materials is a far more significant advantage of the division of labor than time saved. Charles Babbage (1832, pp. 170–4) suggested that the division of labor can save on fixed learning cost by avoiding duplicated learning and training. Hegel (1821, p. 129), Babbage (1832, pp. 173–4), and Ure (1835, p. 21) argued that by simplifying the work of each specialist the division of labor enables the worker to be replaced with machines. Yang and Y.-K. Ng (1993) show that division of labor can increase the capacity of society to acquire information and speed up accumulation of knowledge. Subsection 2.3.4 will formalize these ideas. Section 2.4 explores the implication of endogenous cum exogenous comparative advantage for the existence of economies of division of labor.

It is not difficult to perceive the importance of specialization and division of labor for economic development. In the absence of social division of labor, you would have to produce all of the food, housing, furniture, cars, television sets, and airplanes whose services you wished to consume. What a crazy world it would be. Productivity in such a world would be as low as in an ancient society. Indeed productivity would be zero in the case of such technologically complex items as cars, TV sets, and airplanes, which could not be produced by one person. The most important difference between a developed economy and a less developed economy is that the former has a much higher level of division of labor than the latter. This implies that in a developed economy, most individuals are more "professional" or more specialized than their counterparts in a less developed country.

The degree of commercialization (ratio of consumption purchased from the market to total consumption including self-provided consumption) is higher in the former than in the latter. For instance, this degree was 0.3 in prior-reform rural China and is now higher than 0.8 in rural China (see Yang, Wang, and Wills, 1992). The ratio of transaction volume to income was 0.2 in 1869, and was 9.28 in 1997 in the US (US Department of Commerce, 1975, 1998).[2] This implies that an average American must conduct $0.2 business transactions to get $1 income in 1869, and this figure increased to $9.28 in 1998. This increase in the ratio certainly reflects an increase in division of labor, which generates a faster increase in transaction volume than in income. This phenomenon is called by trade economists the "gravity law."

Also, in a less developed economy, the diversity of different occupations is much smaller than in a developed economy. If you check the yellow pages of phone books of any state in the US in the past fifty years, you can see variety of occupations has been drastically increasing. Many new occupations, such as computer related occupations, emerge every year. When Kang Youwei, a leading reformist during China's reforms in Qian dynasty, visited Europe at the end of the nineteenth century, his first impression of the difference between industrialized Europe and less developed China was that each European individual bought much more and sold much more than her Chinese counterpart did; he was impressed by a very high degree of commercialization in European countries (see Kang, reprinted in 1980, pp. 12–13). In terms of Smith's academic jargon, the first difference that Kang perceived between developed and less developed economies is the difference in the level of division of labor.

In subsection 2.3.1, we define economies of specialization, then we define the level of division of labor in subsection 2.3.2. Economies of division of labor are then studied in subsections 2.3.3 and 2.3.4.

## 2.3.1 Economies of specialization

We can use the concept of a production function to define economies of specialization. According to classical thinking, economies of specialization derive from the narrowing down of the range of production activities of each individual, and can exist in the absence of the firm. Hence, we specify production functions for each consumer-producer.

### Example 2.3: a system of production with economies of specialization

Suppose that each individual can produce two goods. Her production functions for the goods are

$$x^p \equiv x + x^s = l x^a \qquad (2.3a)$$
$$y^p \equiv y + y^s = l y^a,$$

where $a > 1$ $x^p$ and $y^p$ are the output levels of the two goods, $x$ and $y$ are the amounts of the goods self-provided, and $x^s$ and $y^s$ are the amounts of the goods sold in the market. $l_i$ is the proportion of the individual's labor time allocated to producing good $i$. We define this as the individual's *level of specialization in producing good i*. $a$ is a parameter that represents the degree of economies of specialization. Since economies of specialization do not extend beyond the size of an individual's working-time, there is a working time constraint for each individual such that

$$l_x + l_y = 1 \tag{2.3b}$$

This states the obvious proposition that the total proportion of labor time to be allocated is 1. If we assume that an individual has one unit of work time, then (2.3b) is also an endowment constraint of time for the person, and $l_i$ is then the amount of time allocated to the production of good $i$. (2.3) is called *an individual's system of production*.

It is not difficult to show that

$$dx^p/dl_x = a l_x^{a-1} > 0, \qquad d^2 x^p/dl_x^2 = a(a-1) l_x^{a-2} > 0,$$
$$dy^p/dl_y = a l_y^{a-1} > 0, \qquad d^2 y^p/dl_y^2 = a(a-1) l_y^{a-2} > 0,$$

where marginal labor productivity of a good, $dx^p/dl_x$ or $dy^p/dl_y$ increases with the individual's level of specialization in its production. That is, the second-order derivative of output of a good with respect to the person's level of specialization in producing it is greater than 0. It is not difficult to verify that average labor productivity of a good $x^p/l_x$ or $y^p/l_y$ also increases with the person's level of specialization in producing the good. There are *economies of specialization* for a person in producing a particular good if her marginal (or average) labor productivity increases with her level of specialization in producing this good. More generally, we say there are economies of specialization for an individual in production if her production set

$$Y = \{x \in R_+^m \mid f(x) \le 0\}$$

is nonconvex, where $x$ is an $m$ dimension vector of outputs of goods and $f(x) \le 0$ is given by production functions of all goods and this person's endowment constraint of labor.

The system of production in (2.3) seems to exhibit economies of scale. That is, output is more than doubled when inputs are doubled. But economies of specialization differ from economies of scale for the following reasons.

First, economies of specialization are individual-specific and activity-specific. They cannot extend beyond an individual's maximum available working time. In other words, economies of specialization are localized increasing returns. This feature of localized increasing returns may be seen more clearly by considering the average labor-cost functions associated with the production system (2.3). Denote the respective average labor costs of the two goods $AC_x$ and $AC_y$; then if $l_i \le 1$,

$$AC_x = l_x/x^p = l_x^{1-a} > 0, \qquad dAC_x/dl_x = (1-a) l_x^{-a} < 0,$$
$$AC_y = l_y/y^p = l_y^{1-a} > 0, \qquad dAC_y/dl_y = (1-a) l_y^{-a} < 0,$$

From figure 2.2, it is clear that if $l_i \le 1$, the average labor cost of good $i$ monotonically decreases with the individual's level of specialization in producing good $i$. When $x_i > 1$ the average labor cost discontinuouly jumps to infinity, since an output level that is greater than 1 is infeasible due to the limited working time of the individual.

Second, as an individual increases her level of specialization in producing one good, her level of specialization in producing the other good must decrease, thereby narrowing down her scope of production activities. Hence, the individual-specific time constraint and individual-specific system of multiple production functions are essential for defining the concept of economies of specialization. However, we may define economies of scale for a firm, using a production function with a single output. One example is sufficient

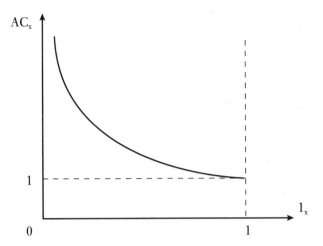

◆ **Figure 2.2:** Average labor cost

for illustrating the distinction between economies of specialization and economies of scale.

## Example 2.4

Suppose that a firm hires many workers, but each of the workers engages in many activities and the scope of activities is the same for each. If there are economies of scale, then the firm will be very productive. But if there are economies of specialization, the firm will have very low productivity.

This example implies that economies of scale can be achieved by pooling workers together even if each of them is not specialized. It is in this sense that Young (1928) argued that the concept of economies of scale misses the phenomenon of economies of division of labor and is therefore a misrepresentation of the classical notion of economies of specialization and division of labor. In order to well define level of specialization, each individual's range of production activities must be specified. This implies that a system of several production functions and a time constraint must be specified for each individual.

Another test of the distinction between economies of specialization and economies of scale is that the former can be specified for an individual in the absence of the firm, while the latter can be specified for a firm, in the absence of any specification of levels and patterns of specialization of individuals within the firm. Coase noted the implications of the distinction. He argued (1937) that the neoclassical black box of production function ignores the implication of the internal organization of the firm, leading the neoclassical theory of the firm to focus on interactions between quantities and prices. As a result, neoclassical economics cannot explain why and how the institution of the firm emerges from the division of labor, or what are the general equilibrium implications of the internal organization of the firm.

In chapters after part II, we will define the production function of the firm. In the new classical framework, the production function for the firm, and the existence of the firm itself, are a consequence of individuals' decisions in choosing the structure of transactions and residual rights; in this framework only *ex ante* players are individual consumer-producers. Hence, the new classical production function for the firm cannot be specified as part of the economic environment existing before individuals have made their decisions. In chapter 8, we will show that the production function for the firm will emerge from a combination of individuals' systems of production, as individuals choose trade of labor and the related asymmetric structure of residual rights to organize division of labor.

### 2.3.2 Division of labor

The concept of division of labor is related to but different from the concept of specialization. The level of division of labor is determined by all individuals' levels and patterns of specialization in producing all goods. Suppose $l_{ij}$ is person i's level of specialization in producing good j. *An individual's production pattern* is defined by $(l_{i1}, l_{i2}, \ldots l_{im})$, where m is the number goods and $l_{ij} \in [0, 1]$. For simplicity we assume that $m = M$, where M is population size. A *structure of production* of all individuals' production patterns can be defined by the matrix $L = \{l_{ij}\}$. The level and pattern of division of labor for society is determined by the features of the matrix L. The features of the matrix can be described by various indices, such as the Gini coefficient, which describes the degree of concentration of production, and the variance of $l_{ij}$. We may use the index

$$D = \sum_i \sum_j (l_{ij} - \bar{l}_j)^2 \tag{2.4}$$

to represent the *level of division of labor* for society, where

$$l_{ij} \in [0, 1], \quad \bar{l}_j = \sum_i l_{ij}/M.$$

The level of division of labor achieves its minimum $D = 0$ if $l_{ij}$ are equal for any i and j, or if every individual allocates the same share of working time to each activity. This structure of production is called *autarky*. The level of division of labor achieves its maximum $D = (M - 1)$, if each individual specializes in producing one good which is different from those produced by all other individuals. This pattern of division of labor is called *complete division of labor*. A feature of the measurement of level of division of labor is the lack of one-to-one correspondence between production structure and D. Later we will see that there may be several production structures for the same value of D.

In subsection 2.3.3, the concept of exogenous comparative advantage discussed by Ricardo, Heckscher, and Ohlin is formalized to show that economies of division of labor may exist in the absence of economies of scale and of economies of specialization. Subsection 2.3.4 draws the distinction between production schedules that are associated with different levels of division of labor and production possibility frontiers in the new classical framework.

### 2.3.3 Exogenous comparative advantage and economies of division of labor

Before David Ricardo, economists did not pay attention to the distinction between absolute and comparative advantage. An individual has *absolute advantage in producing good i* if her labor productivity in good i is greater than that of the other individual. Ricardo (1817) drew economists' attention to the distinction between this measure and the concept of comparative advantage. If person 2 is absolutely less productive than person 1 in producing both of goods x and y, but the ratio of productivities between the two individuals is greater for good y than for good x, then person 2 has a comparative advantage in producing good x since her absolute disadvantage is smaller in producing x than in producing y. Ricardo argued that as long as there exists such a comparative advantage, a country having no absolute advantage in producing any good nonetheless can gain from trade, as can the other country which enjoys absolute advantage in all lines of production. Let us formalize this idea in the following example.

### Example 2.5: a system of production involving two individuals with economies of division of labor based on exogenous technical comparative advantage

Denote the two individuals (or countries) by subscripts $i = 1, 2$ and the two goods by subscripts $j = x, y$. The production function and labor endowment constraints for the two individuals are (2.5a) and (2.5b), respectively.

$$x_1^p = a_{1x}l_{1x}, \quad y_1^p = a_{1y}l_{1y}, \quad l_{1x} + l_{1y} = 1 \tag{2.5a}$$

$$x_2^p = a_{2x}l_{2x}, \quad y_2^p = a_{2y}l_{2y}, \quad l_{2x} + l_{2y} = 1 \tag{2.5b}$$

where $a_{ij}$ is individual i's labor productivity in producing good j. We assume that $a_{1x} < a_{2x}$, $a_{1y} < a_{2y}$, $a_{1x}/a_{2x} > a_{1y}/a_{2y}$. That is, individual 2 has absolute advantage in producing both goods and individual 1 has a comparative advantage in producing good x. The individuals' transformation curves for $a_{1x} = 2$, $a_{2x} = 3$, $a_{1y} = 1$, $a_{2y} = 4$ are drawn in figure 2.3. AB is individual 2's transformation curve and CD is individual 1's transformation curve.

There are three patterns of production for each individual. Nonspecialization pattern $A_i$ implies that individual i produces both goods, or $l_{ix}$, $l_{iy} > 0$; Pattern $(x/y)_i$ implies that individual i produces only good x, that is $l_{ix} > 0$ and $l_{iy} = 0$; Pattern $(y/x)_i$ implies that individual i produces only good y, that is $l_{iy} > 0$ and $l_{ix} = 0$. $(x/y)_i$ and $(y/x)_i$ are referred to as specialization patterns. There are 7 structures of production for the two individuals. Autarky structure A consists of patterns $A_1$ and $A_2$ and satisfies $l_{1x} = l_{2x}$ and $l_{1y} = l_{2y}$. Using the two equations, and production functions and endowment constraints in (2.5), we can derive the maximum aggregate output schedule for this structure as follows.

$$Y \equiv y_1^p + y_2^p = (a_{1y} + a_{2y})[1 - X/(a_{1x} + a_{2x})] \tag{2.6}$$

where $X \equiv x_1^p + x_2^p$. This schedule is given by line EG in figure 2.3. The slope of the curve is $dY/dX = -(a_{1y} + a_{2y})/(a_{1x} + a_{2x})$, which is between $-a_{1y}/a_{1x}$ and $-a_{2y}/a_{2x}$. In other words, the line is flatter than line FG and is steeper than line EF. In chapter 12, we will show that the equilibrium production may occur on line EG if transaction costs outweigh gains from exogenous comparative advantage.

Structure EF consists of patterns $(y/x)_2$ and $A_1$. The maximum production schedule for this structure, EFD, can be obtained by moving individual 1's transformation curve CD up to point E on the vertical axis. Structure FG consists of patterns $(x/y)_1$ and $A_2$. The maximum production schedule for this structure, AFG, can be obtained by moving individual 2's transformation curve AB to the right to point G on the horizontal axis. The two structures represent partial division of labor with comparative advantage. Structure F, representing complete division of labor with comparative advantage, consists of patterns $(y/x)_2$ and $(x/y)_1$ and is associated with point F in figure 2.3.

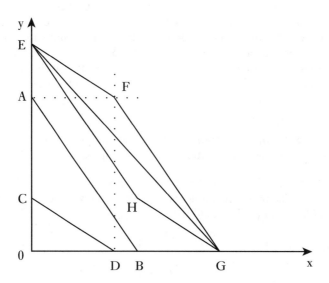

◆ **Figure 2.3:** Economies of division of labor based on exogenous technical comparative advantage

Structure EH consists of patterns $(y/x)_1$ and $A_2$. The maximum aggregate production schedule for this structure, EHB, can be obtained by moving individual 2's transformation curve AB up to point E on the vertical axis. Structure HG consists of patterns $(x/y)_2$ and $A_1$. The maximum aggregate production schedule for this structure, CHG, can be obtained by moving individual 1's transformation curve CD to the right to point G on the horizontal axis. These two structures represent partial division of labor with comparative disadvantage. Structure H, representing complete division of labor with comparative disadvantage, consists of patterns $(y/x)_1$ and $(x/y)_2$ and is associated with point H in figure 2.3.

For the two-individual-two-goods economy, we may define *division of labor* as a structure of production where at least one individual chooses a pattern of specialization and the two persons' patterns of production are not the same. This definition implies that specialization is not sufficient for the division of labor. Structure E, consisting of patterns $(y/x)_1$ and $(y/x)_2$, involves two individuals specializing in producing good y. But it is not associated with division of labor. Similarly structure G, consisting of $(x/y)_1$ and $(x/y)_2$, involves specialization, but no division of labor. For the simple Ricardian economy, according to the measure in (2.4), structure F displays a higher level of division of labor than structures EF and FG, which in turn display higher levels of division of labor than structure A. By the same measure, structure H has a higher level of division of labor than structures EH and HG.

Since the definition of level of division of labor, given in (2.4), implies that a particular level of division of labor may be associated with multiple production structures, we can see from figure 2.3 that structures F and H have the same level of division of labor, but different aggregate production schedules. We may define the maximum aggregate production schedule for a particular level of division of labor as the highest among all aggregate production schedules associated with this level of division of labor. It is obvious that division of labor with comparative advantage (structures EF, F, and FG) generate higher aggregate production schedules than autarky (structure A) and than division of labor with comparative disadvantage (structures EH, H, and HG).

The production possibility frontier (PPF) for the economy is the highest among all aggregate production schedules, which is EFG in figure 2.3. Since EFG is the highest production schedule for all structures with division of labor (structures EF, FG, F, EH, HG, H), the difference between EFG and line EG can then be defined as *economies of division of labor*. It is interesting to see that there exist economies of division of labor even if there are no economies of scale in the Ricardian economy. Also, in this Ricardian economy, production conditions display constant returns to specialization for all individuals. Hence, economies of division of labor may exist in the absence of economies of specialization. It is much more difficult to define economies of division of labor if there are more goods and more individuals than two, since we will then have more structures of production involving the same value of $D$ but generating different aggregate production schedules.

Also, it is interesting to see that the aggregate production set for the Ricardian economy is convex, despite the existence of economies of division of labor. The aggregate production set is the area enclosed by the vertical and horizontal axes, lines EF and FG and their boundaries. Certainly this set is convex.

Rosen (1978) calls economies of division of labor *superadditivity,* which is a kind of economy of interpersonal complementarity. It implies that aggregate productivity for society increases as individuals' levels of specialization and the diversity of different individuals' production patterns increase. Here, individuals' specialization and diversity of their production patterns are two aspects of the division of labor.

If we define comparative advantage that is based on *ex ante* differences of production conditions between individuals as *exogenous comparative advantage*, then the economies of division of labor in the Ricardian economy are generated by exogenous comparative advantage. As we have noted previously, in this text, *ex ante* means "before individuals choose patterns" and *ex post* means "after individuals have chosen patterns and made decisions, and the economy has settled down in equilibrium."

We call Ricardo's exogenous comparative advantage *exogenous comparative advantage in technology* since it is based on *ex ante* differences between individuals' production functions in producing different goods. Suppose the production functions are the same for the two individuals, but endowments of production factors are different between them. Then we may have *exogenous endowment comparative advantage*. In chapter 12, it will be shown that as the trade-off between economies of division of labor and transaction costs is introduced, the equilibrium production schedule will occur on the line EG if the transaction cost coefficient for each unit of traded goods is very large, while the equilibrium production schedule occurs on point F if this transaction cost coefficient is sufficiently small. Also, it will be shown that the equilibrium production schedule is Pareto optimal. Hence, as the transaction cost coefficient decreases, the equilibrium and Pareto optimum production schedule jumps from line EG to point F.

### Example 2.6: a system of production of two individuals with Heckscher–Ohlin exogenous endowment comparative advantage

Assume that the respective production functions of goods x and y for individual i are

$$x_i = L_{ix}{}^\alpha K_{ix}{}^{1-\alpha}, \qquad y_i = L_{iy}{}^\beta K_{iy}{}^{1-\beta}$$

and that her respective endowment constraints for labor and capital are

$$L_{ix} + L_{iy} = l_i \text{ and } K_{ix} + K_{iy} = k_i.$$

The production possibility frontier for individual 1, A, and that for individual 2, B, are shown in figure 2.4. The aggregate production schedule for autarky, as represented by curve C, can be obtained from the two persons' production functions, endowment constraints, and requirement for autarky $L_{1j} = L_{2j}$ and $K_{1j} = K_{2j}$ where $j = $ x, y. There are two aggregate production schedules for division of labor. One of them is represented by curve D in figure 2.4, which is lower than curve C, and the other is represented by curve E, which is higher than curve C. The difference between curve E and curve C represents economies of division of labor based on exogenous comparative advantage in endowments.

It is interesting to note that the aggregate production set in the Heckscher–Ohlin production system is nonconvex despite the absence of economies of scale. This implies that constant returns to scale technology do not necessarily imply a convex aggregate production set in a framework with no dichotomy between pure consumers and firms. Note that the concept of economies of division of labor is based solely on production conditions. It has nothing to do with individuals' preferences. But the notion of gains from trade involves both economies of division of labor and individuals' preferences. We will study gains from trade in the Ricardo model and in the Heckscher–Ohlin model in chapter 12.

Some readers may raise the following concern. The concept of economies of division of labor is *ad hoc* since a decrease in the level of division of labor measured by (2.4) implies that more constraints are imposed on aggregate production plan. This argument is incorrect since complete division of labor also imposes a constraint on production, that is, each individual is allowed to produce only one good. In exercise 13 you are asked to show that

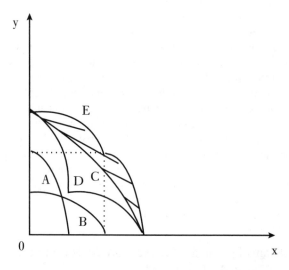

◆ **Figure 2.4:** Economies of division of labor based on exogenous comparative advantages in endowments

the following system of production transformation for individual i $= 1, 2$ displays diseconomies of division of labor: $y_i = 4 - 0.2x_i$ for $x_i \leq 4$ and $y_i = 10 - 0.6x_i$ for $x_i > 4$. For the aggregate production set based on the transformation functions, the aggregate PPF is associated with autarky, while the highest aggregate production schedule for the division of labor is lower than the PPF.

### 2.3.4 Endogenous absolute and comparative advantages

Some economists surmise that Ricardo's concept of exogenous comparative advantage is more general than Smith's concept of absolute advantage. However, Houthakker (1956) uses a graph to show that Smith's concept of endogenous absolute advantage may be more general than Ricardo's concept of exogenous comparative advantage. This subsection substantiates this proposition by specifying a simple system of production functions and time constraint for consumer-producers.

### Example 2.7: a system of production of two individuals with economies of division of labor based on endogenous comparative advantage

Suppose the subscripts i $= 1, 2$ denote two individuals, and the subscripts $j = x, y$ denote two goods. Then, the systems of production functions and time constraint for the two individuals are

$$x_1^p = l_{1x}^a, \qquad y_1^p = l_{1y}^a, \qquad l_{1x} + l_{1y} = 1 \tag{2.7a}$$

$$x_2^p = l_{2x}^a, \qquad y_2^p = l_{2y}^a, \qquad l_{1x} + l_{2y} = 1 \tag{2.7b}$$

where $x_i^p$ is individual i's output of good x, $y_i^p$ is individual i's output of good y, and $l_{ij}$ is individual i's level of specialization in producing good j. It is assumed that there are economies of specialization in producing each good, so that $a > 1$. Here, we assume that the two individuals are *ex ante* identical. They have the same production functions for every good, and the same endowment of working time. This implies that there is no exogenous comparative advantage. On the basis of (2.7), we work out the transformation function for individual i as follows.

$$(x_i^p)^{\frac{1}{a}} + (y_i^p)^{\frac{1}{a}} = 1$$

We can use this equation to express $y_i^p$ as a function of $x_i^p$.

$$y_i^p = [1 - (x_i^p)^{\frac{1}{a}}]^a, \qquad x_i^p, y_i^p \in [0,1] \tag{2.8}$$

The first- and second-order derivatives of $y_i^p$ with respect to $x_i^p$,

$$\frac{dy_i^p}{dx_i^p} = -[1 - (x_i^p)^{\frac{1}{a}}]^{a-1}(x_i^p)^{\frac{1}{a}-1} = [(x^p)^{-\frac{1}{a}} - 1]^{a-1} < 0 \tag{2.9a}$$

$$\frac{d\frac{dx_i^p}{dy_i^p}}{dx_i^p} \equiv \frac{d^2y_i^p}{d(x_i^p)^2} = \frac{a-1}{a}[(x^p)^{-\frac{1}{a}} - 1]^{a-2}(x^p)^{-\frac{1}{a}-1} > 0, \tag{2.9b}$$

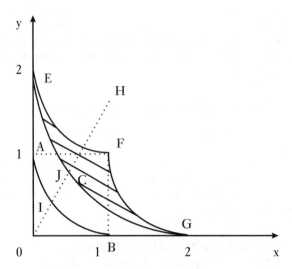

♦ **Figure 2.5:** Economies of division of labor based on endogenous absolute and comparative advantage

indicate that the individual transformation curve in the x–y coordinates is downward sloping and convex. The absolute value of (2.9a) is the marginal opportunity cost of $x_i^p$ in terms of $y_i^p$. Since $dy_i^p/dx_i^p$ is negative, the positive second-order derivative in (2.9b) implies that $dy_i^p/dx_i^p$ increases, or its absolute value $-dy_i^p/dx_i^p$ decreases (consider $-2 < -1$ implies $|-2| > |-1|$) as $x_i^p$ increases. Hence, (2.9b) implies a diminishing marginal opportunity cost of $x_i^p$ in terms of $y_i^p$, or an increasing marginal rate of transformation from $y_i^p$ to $x_i^p$. Hence, the transformation curve AB takes the shape shown in figure 2.5. You may let $x_i^p$ equal any values between 0 and 1, then calculate $y_i^p$ from (2.8) to draw the curve AB in the x–y coordinates.

Diminishing marginal opportunity costs and increasing marginal rate of transformation are the feature of increasing returns. It implies that amount by which y must be decreased for each marginal unit increase of x diminishes as x increases; alternatively, it implies that each unit of y can be transformed into increasingly larger increments of x.

Now let us draw the aggregate production schedules for the economy with two individuals. Again, the aggregate production schedules are structure dependent. Following the method adopted for structure A in the Ricardo model, the maximum aggregate production schedule for autarky, which is defined by the system of production functions and endowment constraint, together with $l_{1x} = l_{2x}$, $l_{1y} = l_{2y}$, in this model can be drawn as curve ECG in figure 2.5. Structure EF with partial division of labor in this model has the same definition as in the Ricardo model. Its aggregate production schedules is shown by curve EFB in figure 2.5. Similarly, we can work out the aggregate production schedules for structure FG with partial division of labor and for structure F with complete division of labor, as shown in figure 2.5. The aggregate transformation curve for the division of labor is then curve EFG. Economies of division of labor are then the difference between curve EFG and curve ECG, shown as the diagonally-shaded area in the figure.

Figure 2.5 provides a basis for defining *endogenous absolute and comparative advantage*. In this model, all individuals are *ex ante* identical, so that there is no *ex ante* difference in productivity or endowment between the two individuals. That is, there is no exogenous comparative advantage. If the two individuals are in autarky, then the production pattern must be the same for them. Therefore, their productivity of each good is the same. But if they choose complete division of labor (structure F), for instance individual 1 produces only x and individual 2 produces only y, then

$$x_1^p = 1, \qquad y_1^p = 0, \qquad x_2^p = 0, \qquad y_2^p = 1. \qquad (2.10a)$$

The two persons' average labor productivities in the two activities are thus

$$AL_{x1} = 1, \qquad AL_{y1} = 0, \qquad AL_{x2} = 0, \qquad AL_{y2} = 1. \qquad (2.10b)$$

This implies that the average labor productivity of the specialist of x in producing x is 1, higher than that of the specialist of y, which is 0, while the average labor productivity of the specialist of y in producing y is 1, higher than that of the specialist of x, which is 0. These *ex post* productivity differences between *ex ante* identical individuals result from their decisions to choose different production patterns. Such differences in productivity, arising from individuals' choices concerning patterns of specialization, represent *endogenous comparative advantage*. For this specific example, the endogenous comparative advantage is also endogenous absolute advantage.

In chapters 5 and 6 it will be shown that the equilibrium and Pareto optimum production schedule occurs on curve C if the transaction cost coefficient for each unit of goods purchased is large, and it occurs on point F if this coefficient is sufficiently small. Hence, as transaction conditions are improved, the aggregate production schedule jumps from a low to a high level, so that more economies of division of labor can be utilized.

The concepts of economies of division of labor and specialization can be used to clarify some confusion generated by the probably misleading concept of economies of scope. On the one hand, a person's economies of specialization in producing a good are positively related to diseconomies in her scope of activities. On the other hand, a firm's operation scope and its members' levels of specialization can increase at the same time if all individuals' levels of specialization, the number of different specialists, and the number of different specialties within the firm increase simultaneously. This implies that as the level of division of labor of a firm increases, the firm's scope of professional activities increases, and each of its employee's scope of activities narrows down, or their level of specialization increases. Here, the subtle distinction between a firm's scope of activities and an individual's scope of activities indicates that economies of division of labor is a more rigorous concept than economies of scope.

There is a particular class of production sets very common in reality, that are characterized by fixed learning cost. The concept of economies of division of labor is easier to define for these than for the production sets that we have so far considered. Houthakker (1956) uses a graph to illustrate the interesting features of the fixed learning cost production set.

## Example 2.8: production set with fixed learning cost

Assume that the system of production for individual j is

$$x_{ij}^{p} \equiv x_{ij} + x_{ij}^{s} = \text{Max } \{l_{ij} - A, 0\}$$

$$\sum_{i} l_{ij} = 1, \qquad i = 1, \ldots, m, j = 1, \ldots, M,$$

where $x_{ij}^{p}$ is person j's output level of good i, $l_{ij}$ is person j's level of specialization in producing good i, and $A$ is a fixed learning and training cost in producing each good. This cost includes the intellectual effort in figuring out the right way to produce a good, the costs caused by mistakes in a trial–error learning process, and some fixed labor input to start production. The output level is zero if $l_{ij} \leq A$. This system of production displays economies of specialization. For $l_{ij} > A$, average labor productivity $(x_{ij} + x_{ij}^{s})/l_{ij} = 1 - (A/l_{ij})$ increases at a diminishing rate as an individual's level of specialization in producing good i, $l_{ij}$, increases. The *ex ante* identical production conditions of all individuals exhibit economies of division of labor. To see this, let us consider the production sets of two individuals in producing two goods in figure 2.6.

An individual's transformation curve is EFGH in figure 2.6. The aggregate production schedule for the two persons when each of them produces two goods, with no division of labor, is segment DI. The aggregate transformation curve for the division of labor, which implies at least one person producing only one good, can be obtained in the following way.

Suppose that an individual (he) produces only good 1. His output level is represented by the vertical line KH. Assume that the other individual (she) can choose any production configuration, so that her transformation curve is still EFGH. By moving the individual transformation curve horizontally to the right by distance $1 - A$, the aggregate transformation curve for the two individuals can be then obtained as KBJL. Suppose now, alternatively, that he produces only good 2 instead of good 1, while she can still choose any production pattern. Now the aggregate transformation curve is MCAK. Therefore, in the simple two-good-two-person case, the aggregate transformation curve for the division of labor, where at least one individual produces only one good, is MCAKBJL.

It is obvious that the aggregate transformation curve for the division of labor is higher

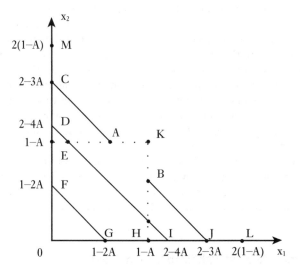

♦ **Figure 2.6**: Economies of division of labor generated by fixed learning costs

than the aggregate production schedule for autarky, even if the two persons are *ex ante*
identical or even if exogenous comparative advantage is absent. This is because each
individual's total learning cost is $2A$ if she produces both goods and her total learning cost
is reduced to $A$ if she produces only one good. That is, her time for production increases
from $1 - 2A$ to $1 - A$ as she reduces the number of goods produced from two to one, so
that her production possibility frontier extends as her level of specialization increases.
Hence, the total learning cost for the economy with two individuals is $4A$ in autarky, $3A$
for partial division of labor (segments CA and BJ), and $2A$ for complete division of labor
(point K). The economies of division of labor are represented by the difference between
the transformation curve (the PPF) for the division of labor, MCABJL, and the production schedule for autarky, DI.

Babbage (1832, pp. 170–4) noted this phenomenon more than a century ago, pointing
out that the division of labor can be used to save on fixed learning cost by avoiding
duplicated learning and training. Becker (1981), Barzel and Yu (1984), and Rosen (1983)
have formalized the idea that the division of labor can increase the utilization rate of a
fixed learning and training investment. Tamura (1992) and Yang (1996) have explored the
general equilibrium implication of the fixed learning cost for the endogenization of individuals' levels of specialization.

The economies of division of labor are, of course, generated by endogenous comparative
advantage. When *ex ante* identical individuals choose different levels of specialization in an
activity, a specialist endogenously acquires a higher productivity than a novice. Consider
the two-person-two-goods example in figure 2.6, where the two individuals choose complete division of labor. If person 1 specializes in producing good 1 (accordingly choosing $l_1$
= 1), her labor productivity in that good is $\text{Max}\{(l_1 - A)/l_1, 0\} = 1 - A$. For person 2,
specializing in good 2 (and thus choosing $l_1 = 0$), labor productivity in good 1 is $\text{Max}\{(l_1
- A)/l_1, 0\} = \text{Max}\{-\infty, 0\} = 0$. The difference in productivity between the specialist and
novice is endogenous comparative advantage.

The following story may provide a sense of the economies of division of labor generated
by fixed learning cost. Suppose there are two individuals: a professor (he) and a secretary
(she). If they do not have division of labor, then each of them must engage in both research
and secretarial support work. The first type of work needs education at Ph.D. level, while
the second type of work needs education in a secretarial school. Hence, each of them must
get two types of education to do the two kinds of job. If the professor specializes in
research and the secretary specializes in secretarial work, the professor can avoid the cost
of training at secretarial school and the secretary can avoid the cost of training for a Ph.D.
For each of them the utilization rate of the investment in specialized learning increases as
they spend more time in their specialties. The benefit of division of labor can be reaped by
both of them. The secretary starts her work at a younger age than when she has to take two
kinds of education, so that her lifetime income is increased. Similarly, specialization increases the professor's productivity in research and utilization rate of his learning investment in the Ph.D. program, and reduces his total fixed learning cost.

For the production set with fixed learning cost, economies of division of labor are
much easier to define. An autarkic production structure can be defined as $L = \{l_{ij}\}$ where
all $l_{ij}$ are positive. Here, equal $l_{ij}$ for any $i$ and $j$ are not needed for the definition of
autarky. As the number of zeros in the matrix L increases as to increase index D, defined
in (2.4), the level of division of labor increases. For each pair of production structures
with different numbers of zeros in the corresponding matrices Ls, the corresponding
maximum production schedules are different too. From figure 2.6, we can see that the

aggregate production schedule for autarky is the segment DI, even if two individuals' levels of specialization in producing two goods are not equal. The aggregate production schedule for the division of labor is MCAKBJL. Hence, as the number of zero-level activities increases, resulting in an increase in the level of division of labor, the aggregate production schedule expands.

This feature will not change if the production functions are nonlinear, as long as there is a fixed learning cost. Assume that individual j's production function of good i is $x_{ij}^p = \text{Max}\{g_{ij}(l_{ij} - A), 0\}$. Suppose that function $g_{ij}(.)$ is increasing and nonconcave, and that the inverse of $g_{ij}(.)$ is $f_{ij}(.)$, which is an increasing and concave function. Hence, the endowment constraint is $f_j(x_j^p) \equiv \Sigma_i \, f_{ij}(x_{ij}^p) = 1 - Am_j$, where $x_j^p$ is person j's $m_j$ dimension output vector and $m_j$ is her number of nonzero activities. Hence, we can define the aggregate production set of an economy with fixed learning costs in each production activity as

$$P = \{X \subset \Pi_j \, R_{++}^{m_j} : f_j(x_j^p) - (1 - m_j A) \leq 0, j = 1, \ldots, M\}, \qquad (2.11)$$

where $A$ is the fixed learning cost in each activity that an individual engages in, and $f_j(x_j^p) - (1 - m_j A) = 0$ is person j's transformation function. As the number of nonzero activities $m_j$ changes, the dimension of $x_j$ and the value of $m_j$ change. It follows that the aggregate production subset, which is associated with a structure of division of labor, will change as an individual's number of nonzero activities changes.

The production environment in examples 2.6 and 2.7 displays *global economies of division of labor*, since any production subset for division of labor is larger than the production subset for autarky. However, if $g_{ij}(.)$ is concave, then we may have *local economies of division of labor* since part of the aggregate production subset for division of labor is higher and part is lower than the production subset for autarky.

Figure 2.7(a) shows global economies of division of labor, which implies that the aggregate production schedule for the division of labor, LGHIJKM, is always higher than the aggregate production schedule for autarky, EF. Here, curve CABD is an individual's

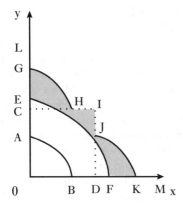

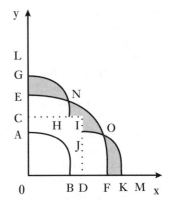

(a) Global economies of division of labor     (b) Local economies of division of labor

◆ **Figure 2.7:** Local vs. global economies of division of labor transformation curve when $g_{ij}(.)$ is concave and fixed learning cost is positive. Figure 2.7(b) shows local economies of division of labor. Parts of the aggregate production schedule for the division of labor, LGN and OKM, are higher than, and part, NHIJO, is lower than, the aggregate production schedule for autarky, ENOF. This case may be caused by a great curvature of an individual's PPF and a small fixed learning cost.

We now prove the following theorem.

**Theorem 2.1:** For the aggregate production set with fixed learning cost, there are at least local economies of division of labor.

*Proof:* According to the definition of economies of division of labor, we can see that the aggregate production set with fixed learning cost (2.11) displays economies of division of labor if the aggregate production subset is enlarged as $m_j$ decreases. Consider person j's transformation function $f_i(x_j^p) \equiv \sum_i f_{ij}(x_{ij}^p) - (1 - Am_j0)$ and $f_i(x_j^{p'}) \equiv \sum_i f_{ij}(x_{ij}^{p'}) - (1 - Am_j'0)$ where $m_j' = m_j - 1$, $x_{im_j}^{p'} = 0$. Because $f_{ij}(.)$ is an increasing function by assumption, $x_{im_j}^p$ must be negative if $x_{ij}^{p'} = x_{ij}^p$ for all $i = 1, 2, \ldots, m_j'$. This implies that individual j's production schedule is enlarged as her number of nonzero activities decreases from $m_j$ to $m_j' = m_j - 1$. This substantiates the claim that the aggregate production schedule is enlarged as person j's number of zero activity levels, $m_j$, increases, which is sufficient for establishing theorem 2.1. *Q.E.D.*

## ◆ 2.4 Endogenous cum Exogenous Comparative Advantage

### Example 2.9: endogenous comparative advantage in productivity vs. exogenous comparative advantage in capability

Suppose the production systems for individuals 1 and 2 are

$$x_1^p = l_{1x}^{a_1}, \qquad y_1^p = l_{1y}^{b_1}, \qquad l_{1x} + l_{1y} = 1$$
$$x_2^p = l_{2x}^{a_1}, \qquad y_2^p = l_{2y}^{b_1}, \qquad l_{2x} + l_{2y} = 1$$

Assume that $a_1 > a_2 > 1$ and $b_1 > b_2 > 1$; that is, person 1 is inherently smarter than person 2, so that she is more productive than person 2 if they have the same level of specialization in any activity. This is referred to as an *exogenous absolute advantage of capability* of person 1 over person 2. We can show that despite the exogenous absolute disadvantage of capability of person 2, she can gain endogenous absolute advantage of productivity in producing a good if her level of specialization in producing the good is sufficiently higher than that of the other. Person 1's respective labor productivities of the two goods are $l_{1x}^{a_1-1}$ and $l_{1y}^{b_1-1}$ and person 2's are $l_{2x}^{a_2-1}$ and $l_{2y}^{b_2-1}$. It is straightforward that person 1's productivities are higher than person 2's if $l_{1x} = l_{2x}$, $l_{1y} = l_{2y}$, $a_1 > a_2$, and $b_1 > b_2$. Hence, there is no absolute advantage in person 2's ability although there may be a comparative advantage in person 2's ability to learn by producing good $y$ if $a_1/a_2 > b_1/b_2$. However, person 2 may have the absolute advantage in productivity (rather than in the ability to learn by doing) of either good if she specializes in its production. A comparison between two persons' labor productivities of good x yields

$l_{2x}^{a_2-1} > l_{1x}^{a_1-1}$ if $l_{2x}/l_{1x}$ is sufficiently large.

This implies that for this system of production, if person 2's level of specialization in producing a good sufficiently exceeds that of person 1, her absolute labor productivity of this good will be greater than that of person 1 even though she has no absolute advantage in her ability to learn by producing. While there is no absolute advantage in favor of individual 2 in autarky where two persons have the same production pattern, with the division of labor in which the two persons specialize in producing different goods, such an absolute advantage will emerge. By contrast, for an economy with constant returns to scale, such an absolute advantage will never emerge from the division of labor if it does not exist in autarky. Again, we call the difference in productivity of a good between two individuals that is generated by their choices of patterns and levels of specialization *endogenous absolute advantage*. The feature that an individual with no exogenous advantage of capability may acquire endogenous advantage of productivity, further highlights the productivity implications of organization in the new classical framework.

It can be shown that for the Ricardian production set with exogenous comparative advantage, an individual who has no exogenous absolute advantage in producing any good, also will have no endogenous absolute advantage. On the other hand, as we have shown, if the production set displays endogenous comparative advantage, a person who initially has no absolute advantage in producing any good may acquire this through division of labor if her level of specialization in producing that good is sufficiently higher than that of an initially more capable person. Hence, an inherently incapable person may become more productive than a more capable person if the former is somehow involved in a very specialized pattern of production and the latter is not.

### Example 2.10: endogenous cum exogenous comparative advantage

Assume that individuals 1 and 2 have the following systems of production of goods x and y, respectively.

$$x_1^p = l_{1x}^2, \qquad y_1^p = l_{1y}, \qquad l_{1x} + l_{1y} = 2,$$
$$x_2^p = al_{2x}, \qquad y_2^p = l_{2y}^2, \qquad l_{2x} + l_{2y} = 2, \qquad a > 1$$

where $x_i^p$, $y_i^p$ are respective quantities of the two goods produced by person i, $l_{ij}$ is the amount of labor allocated to the production of good j by individual i. For this production environment, two individuals have *ex ante* different production functions. But also there are economies of specialization in producing one good for each individual. Hence, endogenous and exogenous comparative advantages coexist. Following the method used in example 2.5 and 2.7, we can draw two individuals' PPF as curves AB and CD respectively in figure 2.8. The aggregate production schedule in autarky is curve EGH. But the aggregate transformation for the division of labor is the curve EFH. The difference between EFH and EGH is economies of division of labor.

The general equilibrium implications of the coexistence of endogenous and exogenous comparative advantage will be explored in chapter 13.

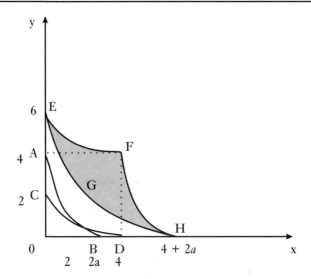

♦ **Figure 2.8:** Economies of division of labor based on endogenous and exogenous comparative advantage

## Key Terms and Review

Implications of mathematical formalism for economic research and the development of mainstream economics.

Features of the neoclassical and new classical framework and the differences between them.

An individual's level of specialization in producing a good.

Economies of specialization.

Economies of scale, constant returns to scale, decreasing returns to scale.

Relationship between economies of specialization and economies of scale.

Differences between the neoclassical concept of production function, based on the notion of economies of scale, and the new classical concept of production function, based on the notion of economies of specialization.

Marginal rate of transformation, marginal opportunity cost, marginal rate of substitution.

Level of division of labor for society.

Relationship between level of division of labor, individuals' levels of specialization, and diversity between different occupations.

Production possibility frontier (PPF), elasticity of substitution, factor elasticity of output, total factor productivity.

Distinction between production pattern and production structure.

Distinction between *ex ante* and *ex post* production functions.

Exogenous comparative and absolute advantage.

Endogenous comparative and absolute advantage.

Advantage in ability vs. advantage in productivity.

Global vs. local economies of division of labor.

## Further Reading

*Classical literature on economies of division of labor:* Anonymous (1701), West (1964), Babbage (1832), Durkheim (1933), Fawcett (1863), Groenewegen (1987), Schiller (1793), Senior (1836), Smith (1776), Marx (1867), Maxwell (1721), Meek and Skinner (1973), Cannan (1937), Campbell and Skinner (1976), Petty (1683, 1671), Fawcett (1863), Ruskin (1851–3), Nicholson (1893), Plato (380 BC), Rae (1834), Rashid (1986), Ricardo (1817), Walker (1874), Ure (1835), Say (1803), Tucker (1755, 1774), Turgot (1751), Stigler (1951, 1976), Houthakker (1956); *surveys on the literature of division of labor:* Yang and S. Ng (1998), Yang and Y.-K. Ng (1993, chs. 1, 2); *recent research on specialization and division of labor:* Buchanan (1994), Edwards and Starr (1987), Schultz (1993), Barzel and Yu (1984), Chandler (1990), Diamond, and Simon (1990), Lio (1996), Yang (1991, 1994, 1996), Borland and Yang (1992), Yang and Borland (1991), Baumgardner (1988), Kim (1989), Locay (1990), Becker (1981), Becker and Murphy (1992), Rosen (1978, 1983); *neoclassical theory of production condition:* Mas-Collell, Whinston, and Green (1995, chs. 2, 3, 5), Varian (1993, chs. 1, 3).

# QUESTIONS

1   Why did Young (1928) argue that the concept of economies of scale misses the phenomenon of economies of division of labor?

2   Why did Stigler (1976) claim: "specialization is not an integral part of the modern theory of production"?

3   Why can't the Herfindahl index of specialization, which is output share of the main industry of a city or a sector, reflect the level of division of labor of the city or sector? According to this index, many large American cities, such as Los Angeles, Chicago, San Francisco, and New York City have lower levels of specialization than Albany, Gary, and Norfolk (see Diamond and Simon 1990, pp. 180–3). But from casual observation, we can perceive that the four large cities have certainly a much higher level of division of labor than the three small cities because of their higher degree of diversity of occupations as well as the higher levels of specialization of many professionals. This is verified by Baumgardner's (1988b) empirical evidence that individuals in a larger city are more specialized than those in small towns.

4   According to Chandler (1990), the economic growth of the United States at the end of the nineteenth century and in the early twentieth century was generated by economies of scale and economies of scope. Clarify the statement, using the concept of economies of division of labor that you have learned in this chapter.

5   Economies of scope imply that a firm's productivity increases as the scope of activities of the firm increases. Suppose there are two firms, A and B. Firm A hires two workers. Each of them engages in two activities. Firm B hires 4 workers, so that its scale is larger than that of firm A. Each of the workers in firm B engages in an activity different from the activities of the others. Hence, firm B as a whole engages in 4 activities, with a greater scope than firm A. But also, each worker in firm B has a higher level of specialization than each worker in firm A. According to the definition of level of division of labor in this chapter, firm B has a higher level of division of labor than firm A. This implies that both the larger scale and the greater scope of firm B are two aspects of a higher level of division of labor. Use the example to discuss the distinction between economies of scale, economies of scope, economies of specialization, and economies of division of labor.

6   Marshall used the concept of external economies of scale to describe the economic phenomena that

relate to economies of division of labor. Assess the relevance of the concept to a real economy.

7   Specialization has many adverse effects on human life. It can lead to boredom and narrowing of the mind. It prevents full exploitation of economies of complementarity between different production activities (for instance, teaching economics generates benefits for economic research). Nevertheless we observe that the level of specialization still increases, and companies frequently use the slogan "We are professional" in their advertisements. Explain this phenomenon.

8   Some economists claim that economies of specialization are a special case of economies of scale, since economies of specialization reflect economies of scale of an individual's labor. Use the knowledge that you have learned in this chapter to assess this statement.

9   Some economists claim that the concept of comparative advantage is more general than the concept of absolute advantage. According to them, if each individual has an absolute advantage in at least one activity, then there will also be comparative advantages; whereas we can find cases where a person has comparative advantage but no absolute advantage. Use the distinction between exogenous comparative (and absolute) advantage and endogenous comparative (and absolute) advantage to comment on this claim.

10  Why is the concept of a nonconvex production set not necessary or sufficient for defining the concept of economies of division of labor?

11  Why can economies of division of labor exist in the absence of economies of specialization?

12  Define the following concepts and the distinctions and connections between them. Economies of specialization for an individual, economies of an individual's scale of labor in producing a good, diseconomies of scope of an individual's production activities. Economies of specialization for a firm, economies of operation scale of the firm in a single production activity, diseconomies of scope of production activities of the firm. Economies of scale for a firm. Economies of scope for a firm. Economies of variety of (final or intermediate) goods or economies of complementarity between final goods in raising utility (or between intermediate goods in raising productivity of a final good). Economies of complementarity between an individual's (or a firm's) production activities. Economies of division of labor (Buchanan: general increasing returns; Young: social increasing returns; Rosen: superadditivity; Marshall: external economies of scale), positive network effects of division of labor.

# EXERCISES

1   Calculate the output elasticity of each factor and the elasticity of substitution for the CES production function $y = (ax_1^\rho + bx_2^\rho)^{\alpha/\rho}$. Do so also for the production function $y = (x_1 - a)^\alpha(x_2 - b)^\beta$.

2   Show that the elasticity of scale $e(x) = \sum_i e_i(x)$, where $e_i(x)$, is the output elasticity of factor i.

3   A function $f(x)$ is *homogeneous to degree k* if $f(tx) = t^k f(x)$ for all $t > 0$. A function $f(x)$ is *homothetic* if $f(x) = g(h(x))$ where $g(.)$ is a strictly increasing function and $h(.)$ is homogeneous to degree 1. For a homothetic production function $f(x_1, x_2)$, show that its technical rate of substitution at $(x_1, x_2)$ equals its technical rate of substitution at $(tx_1, tx_2)$

4   Let $Y$ be a production set. We say that the technology is *additive* if $y$ in $Y$ and $y'$ in $Y$ implies that $y + y'$ is in $Y$. We say that the technology is *divisible* if $y$ in $Y$ and $t \in [0, 1]$

implies that $ty$ is in $Y$. Show that if a technology is both additive and divisible, then $Y$ must be convex and exhibit constant returns to scale.

5   Suppose that a firm's production function takes the form $y = [\alpha x_1{}^\rho + (1 - \alpha) x_2{}^\rho]^{1/\rho}$. This is known as a constant elasticity of substitution (or CES) production function. (a) Show that when $\rho = 1$, isoquants become linear. (b) Show that as $\rho \to 0$, this production function tends to become equivalent to the Cobb–Douglas technology $y = x_1{}^\alpha x_2{}^{1-\alpha}$. (c) Show that as $\rho \to -\infty$, this production function tends to become equivalent to the Leontief technology $y = \mathrm{Min}\{x_1, x_2\}$. Calculate elasticity of substitution, scale elasticity, and input elasticities of output for the three types of production function as special cases of the CES production function. Then calculate the three elasticities for a general form of the CES function.

6   Suppose $a < 1$ in the production functions (2.3). Draw the transformation curve for each individual, two individuals' aggregate transformation curves for autarky and for the division of labor in the x–y plane. Use the graphs to define diseconomies of division of labor.

7   Assume that $a = 1$ in the production functions (2.3). In the x–y plane, draw the transformation curve for each individual, and identify production schedules for the respective cases of autarky and division of labor. Use the graphs to define constant returns to division of labor.

8   Suppose $a \leq 1$ for good x and $a > 1$ for good y in the production functions (2.3). In the x–y plane, draw the transformation curve for each individual, and identify production schedules for the respective cases of autarky and division of labor. Use the graphs to identify the condition under which economies of division of labor exist.

9   Suppose that the endowment constraint for working time is $l_x + l_y = A > 1$. Draw transformation curves of the production system (2.3) for $a > 1$, $a = 1$, and $a < 1$ in the same graph. Compare this with the corresponding graph for $A < 1$. Discuss the implication of the value of $A$ compared with 1.

10   Use exercise (8) to demonstrate the following propositions for the case with *ex ante* identical individuals:
   i)    Economies of specialization in producing a good may be associated with the existence of local diseconomies of division of labor.
   ii)   Economies of division of labor cannot exist in the absence of economies of specialization in producing all goods.
   iii)  Local economies of division of labor exist if there are economies of specialization at least in producing a good.
   iv)   Global economies of division of labor must exist if economies of specialization exist in producing all goods.
   v)    Local economies of division of labor exist if there are economies of specialization in producing good y and diseconomies of specialization in producing x. In this case, economies of division of labor are external economies to the specialist producer of x. Show that external economies cannot exist if there are no economies of specialization in all sectors. Use your analysis to address the debate between Marshall, Young, and his student Frank Knight. Marshall argued that external economies of scale relate to the benefits of division of labor. Young argued that the concept of economies of scale is a misrepresentation of that benefit. Knight argued that economies of scale that are external to all firms constitute an empty box.

11   Assume that three individuals have the production system given in (2.3). Follow the method used in figure 2.3 to identify production schedules for autarky, for the case of two persons not completely specialized, for the case of one person completely specialized, and for the case of two persons completely specialized.

12 Calculate the level of division of labor for structures A, EF, FG, and F in examples 2.5 and 2.7. (Note that the level of division of labor in structure EF or FG is a function of labor allocation of the person choosing configuration A.)

13 Draw each individual's PPF for the following system of production transformation for individual i = 1, 2: $y_i = 4 - 0.2x_i$ for $x_i \leq 4$ and $y_i = 10 - 0.6x_i$ for $x_i > 4$. Show that this system of production displays diseconomies of division of labor, that is, the aggregate PPF is associated with autarky, while the highest aggregate production schedule for the division of labor is lower than the PPF.

14 Assume that the production functions in (2.3) are $x^p = \text{Max}\{l_x - a, 0\}$ and $y^p = \text{Max}\{l_y - b, 0\}$. Draw an individual's transformation curve and identify the two persons' aggregate production schedules for autarky and division of labor. Are there economies of division of labor if $b = 0$?

15 Assume that the production functions in (2.3) are $x^p = \text{Max}\{l_x^\alpha - a, 0\}$ and $y^p = \text{Max}\{l_y^\alpha - b, 0\}$. Draw an individual's transformation curve and identify the two persons' aggregate production schedules for autarky and division of labor. Analyze the difference between the case with $\alpha > 1$ and the case with $\alpha < 1$. Identify the condition for the existence of economies of division of labor.

16 Work out the aggregate production schedule for autarky in the Ricardo model and show that this is consistent with the graph in figure 2.3.

17 Use a graph to show that the following system of production for individuals 1 and 2 displays global economies of division of labor. $x_i^p = \text{Max}\{a_{ix}(l_{ix} - b), 0\}$, $y_i^p = \text{Max}\{a_{iy}(l_{iy} - b), 0\}$, $l_{ix} + l_{iy} = 1$.

18 (Becker, 1981; Rosen, 1983): An individual maximizes the difference between benefits and costs of learning, that is $V = w_1 k_1 t + w_2 k_2 (1 - t) - C(k_1, k_2)$, with respect to $t$, which is the time allocated to produce good 1, and $k_i$, which is learning and training level in activity i, where $C$ is the total learning and training cost, $1 - t$ is the amount of time allocated to produce good 2, and $w_i$ is a given benefit coefficient for activity i. Solve for two corner solutions with specialization and the interior solution with no specialization. Draw the distinction between technical complementarity ($\partial^2 C / \partial k_1 \partial k_2 > 0$) between two learning activities in producing two goods and social complementarity based on economies of specialization. Investigate the conditions under which economies of division of labor exist in the model with both technical and interpersonal complementarity.

## Notes

1 See Groenewegen (1987) and John Stuart Mill (1848, p. 13) for discussion on the transition from the notion of economies of specialization to the notion of economies of scale.

2 Transaction volume comprises domestic wholesale and retail trade, foreign trade, and financial transactions.

# part II

# THE NEOCLASSICAL
# FRAMEWORK

# chapter 3

# NEOCLASSICAL DECISION PROBLEMS

## ◆ 3.1 Budget Constraint and Dichotomy between Pure Consumers and Firms

In this chapter, we use nonlinear programming to describe a pure consumer's decision problem within the neoclassical framework. In section 3.1 we use the concept of budget constraint to specify the institutional environment in which the consumer's decisions are made. In section 3.2 a constrained utility maximization problem is used to investigate the consumer's self-interested behavior. Section 3.3 is devoted to the study of a dual expenditure minimization problem. Some important comparative statics of the decisions, such as compensated demand law, can then be identified. The relationship between the utility maximization problem and the expenditure minimization problem is also examined in that section. In section 3.4 we look at a pure consumer's expenditure minimization problem. In section 3.5 we address the question: how can we infer an intangible utility function from tangible demand functions? Finally, we consider the theory of revealed preference and a producer's decision problem in sections 3.6 and 3.7.

Because of the dichotomy between pure consumers and firms in neoclassical economics, the specification of the budget constraint differs from that in new classical economics. The budget constraint specified in neoclassical economics is referred to as a *Walrasian budget constraint*. It is associated with a *Walrasian budget set* $B = \{x \in X: px \leq I\}$, where $X$ is the consumption set defined in chapter 1, $p$ is an $m$ dimension row vector representing the prices of $m$ goods, $x$ is an $m$ dimension column vector representing a bundle of $m$ consumption goods, $px$ is the expenditure on $m$ goods, and $I$ is a parameter representing income. Income consists of earnings from selling endowments of goods and factors and earnings from ownership of firms, that is, $I = px^0 + w\alpha^0 + \pi$, where $x^0$ is an endowment column vector of $m$ goods, $\alpha^0$ is an endowment column vector of factors, $w$ is the price row vector of the factors, and $\pi$ is dividend earnings from ownership of firms. The graphical representation of equation $px = I$ for the case of two goods is shown in figure 3.1, where $I/x_i$ is the amount of good i that can be bought if all income $I$ is spent on it, and the arrow represents a move of the budget line caused by a fall of the price of good 2.

The Walrasian budget constraint has the following features. First, it implicitly describes the institutional environment, for it implies that there is a legal system that enforces

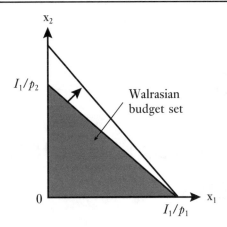

♦ **Figure 3.1:** Walrasian budget constraint

private property rights. It presupposes not only that stealing is disallowed, but also that private residual rights to firms are protected by the law. This kind of budget constraint is sometimes referred to as a *hard budget constraint*. Second, the Walrasian budget constraint assumes that the market is *competitive*. There are many buyers of each good and many sellers of each factor, so that prices are parameters not subject to the decision-maker's manipulation.

Since the endowments of goods and factors are given parameters too, income $I$ can be considered as a parameter. A *parameter* is between a variable and a constant. When we study a consumer's decision problem, the decision-maker takes the parameters as constants. When we study how the self-interested behavior changes in response to changes in parameters (as we do in comparative statics analysis), parameters are treated as variables rather than constants.

---

## Questions to Ask Yourself when Reading this Chapter

♦ What is the difference between marginal and inframarginal analyses of demand?

♦ What are the properties of an ordinary demand function and a compensated demand function?

♦ How can you derive an ordinary or a compensated demand function from a utility function? How can you derive an ordinary demand function from an indirect utility function? How can you derive a compensated demand function from an expenditure function?

♦ Under what conditions does the law of demand hold?

♦ How can you recover a utility function from an ordinary or a compensated demand function?

♦ What is the relationship between utility maximization and cost minimization problems?

## ◆ 3.2 A Pure Consumer's Constrained Utility Maximization Problem

Let us use an example to illustrate major concepts to be considered in this chapter.

### Example 3.1: a consumer's decision problem based on quasi-linear utility function

Suppose a pure consumer's preference can be represented by a quasi-linear utility function. Her *utility maximization problem* (*UMP*) is then

$$\text{Max: } u = x_1^{\alpha} + x_2, \quad \text{s.t. } px \leq I, \qquad (3.1a)$$
$$\scriptstyle x_1, x_2 \geq 0$$

where the decision variables are specified underneath the symbol for maximization, and $p$, $\alpha$, $I > 0$ are parameters. Those letters that do not denote decision variables are parameters. The difference between this UMP and the classical UMP is that here the decision variables are allowed to be zero, that is, corner solutions are allowed. The solution of the UMP is called a *Walrasian* or *ordinary demand function*, denoted $x(p, I) \in X$. It may be either a one-to-one function or a correspondence. The solution generates demand correspondence if the utility function is quasi-concave, but not strictly quasi-concave. It generates demand functions if the utility function is strictly quasi-concave. Using the assumption of nonsatiation, it is easy to show that the Walrasian demand function satisfies the condition that $px = I$, that is, the income will be exhausted by the utility maximization decision. This is referred to as *Walras's law*. But, $x_i(p, I)$ might be 0, for some $i$. Since any proportional changes in $p$ and $I$ add the same constants to the two sides of the semi-inequality in (3.1a) and the constants cancel each other, such changes will not alter the demand function. Hence, the Walrasian demand function is *homogeneous of degree 0* in $p$ and $I$.

The driving force for the decision problem is that there is a trade-off between amounts of different goods in raising utility subject to the budget constraint. If the consumer buys more of good 1, she must reduce the consumption of good 2 because of the budget constraint. The consumption of either good positively contributes to utility. The decision problem is to find an efficient trade-off that compromises between the two competing contributors to the consumer's utility.

Since it is not easy to deal with the constrained optimization problem directly, we first convert it to an equivalent nonconstrained maximization problem.

$$\text{Max: } R = u + \lambda(I - px) \qquad (3.1b)$$
$$\scriptstyle x_1, x_2, \lambda \geq 0$$

where $\lambda$ is a *Lagrange multiplier*. (3.1b) is equivalent to (3.1a) since $px = I$. The efficient trade-off is achieved if any marginal adjustment of the values of the decision variables $x_i$ and $\lambda$ would neither increase nor decrease the value of the objective function $R$. This implies that the derivative of $R$ with respect to $x_i$ and $\lambda$ should be 0 for the optimum. Hence, an *interior maximization decision*, which implies that the optimum values of all decision variables are positive, is given by the *first-order condition for classical mathematical programming*:

$$\partial R / \partial x_i = 0 \text{ and } \partial R / \partial \lambda = 0 \text{ or} \qquad (3.2a)$$

$\partial u/\partial x_1 = p_1\lambda$, $\partial u/\partial x_2 = p_2\lambda$, and $px = I$ (3.2b)

(3.2b) implies

$-dx_2/dx_1 = (\partial u/\partial x_1)/(\partial u/\partial x_2) = p_1/p_2$ and $px = I$ or (3.3a)

$(\partial u/\partial x_1)/p_1 = (\partial u/\partial x_2)/p_2$ and $px = I$. (3.3b)

The first equality in (3.3a) is derived from the *implicit function theorem*. (3.3a) implies that the efficient trade-off requires that the *relative marginal utility of two goods equals their relative price.* $-dx_2/dx_1$ is called *marginal rate of substitution* between the two goods. Thus (3.3a) implies also that the *marginal rate of substitution equals the relative price of the two goods.* This implies that the tangent line of the indifference curve coincides with the budget line, as shown in figure 3.2(a). A rearrangement of (3.3a) yields (3.3b), which is the well-known second Gossen's law: the efficient trade-off requires that an *equal marginal utility generated by the last dollar spent on each good.* If not, say $(\partial u/\partial x_1)/p_1 > (\partial u/\partial x_2)/p_2$, then the reallocation of a dollar from the consumption of good 2 to that of good 1 can raise total utility, since the marginal increase in utility due to the increase in $x_1$ is greater than the marginal decrease in utility due to the decrease in $x_2$. This implies that the optimum decision is yet to be achieved if $(\partial u/\partial x_1)/p_1 > (\partial u/\partial x_2)/p_2$.

(3.2) yields the *system of ordinary demand functions* and the optimum value of the Lagrange multiplier, which is called the *shadow price of a dollar*:

$x_1(p, I) = (\alpha p_2/p_1)^{1/(1-\alpha)}$,     $x_2(p, I) = (I/p_2) - (p_1/p_2)(\alpha p_2/p_1)^{1/(1-\alpha)}$ (3.4a)
$\lambda(p, I) = 1/[(I/p_2) - (p_1/p_2)(\alpha p_2/p_1)^{1/(1-\alpha)}]$

Plugging the demand functions back into the utility function yields the maximum value of utility function, which is called the *indirect utility function*.

$v(p, I) = u(x(p, I)) = 1 - \alpha(\alpha p_2/p_1)^{\alpha/(1-\alpha)} + (I/p_2)$ (3.4b)

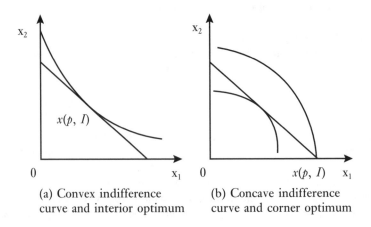

(a) Convex indifference
curve and interior optimum

(b) Concave indifference
curve and corner optimum

◆ **Figure 3.2:** Utility maximization solutions

Later, we shall show that the shadow price of a dollar $\lambda(p, I)$ is the derivative of the indirect utility function with respect to $I$.

The deduction of the efficient trade-off is referred to as *marginal analysis*, which is *classical mathematical programming for interior solutions*. However, the marginal analysis can be terribly wrong for the following two cases.

First, if the quasi-linear utility function is not quasi-concave, then we can see from figure 3.2(b) that the first-order condition of the marginal analysis gives the point of utility minimization rather than maximization on the budget line. This is intuitive. If the utility function is not quasi-concave, then it represents nonconvex preferences, which implies that the consumer desires specialized instead of diverse consumption. Hence, her utility maximization decision is to consume only one good. Applying the approach that you have learned in chapter 1 to check if a utility function is quasi-concave, you can find that the quasi-linear utility function is not strictly quasi-concave if $\alpha \geq 1$. We can therefore conclude that the first-order conditions of the marginal analysis give wrong answers to the decision problem if $\alpha \geq 1$. This is referred to as the *second-order condition for the interior maximum*, which requires a strictly quasi-concave utility function to ensure an interior maximum point for the constrained UMP.

Formally, the second-order condition for an interior maximum of the UMP is that the Hessian matrix of the Lagrange function bordered with the first-order derivatives of the constraint function is negative definite.

Although we know, from the second-order condition, that for $\alpha \geq 1$ the optimum decision is a corner solution, there is no standard procedure that can give the optimum corner solution in one step. A multiple-step procedure is used to sort out the optimum decision from multiple corner solutions. First, all possible profiles of zero and positive values of the decision variables are enumerated. Then, for each of the profiles, we can use marginal analysis to solve for the local maximization solution. We then compare indirect utility functions across the interior and corner solutions to identify the optimum solution. This multiple-step approach is referred to as *inframarginal analysis*. For $\alpha \geq 1$, the inframarginal analysis generates the ordinary demand functions, the shadow price of a dollar, and the indirect utility function as follows.

when $I/p_2 < (I/p_1)^\alpha$ (3.5a)
$x_1(p, I) = (I/p_1)^\alpha,$ $\quad x_2(p,I) = 0,$ $\quad \lambda(p,I) = \alpha/I^{1-\alpha}p_1{}^\alpha,$ and $v(p,I) = (I/p_1)^\alpha$

when $I/p_2 > (I/p_1)^\alpha$ (3.5b)
$x_1(p,I) = 0,$ $\quad x_2(p,I) = I/p_2,$ $\quad \lambda(p,I) = \alpha/I^{1-\alpha}p_1{}^\alpha,$ and $v(p,I) = I/p_2$

The demand functions are intuitive: if a consumer prefers specialized consumption, then she consumes only the cheaper good.

However, the second-order condition is still not enough for a consumer to ensure an interior optimum decision for the following case. Suppose that $\alpha < 1$, that is, the second-order condition for an interior maximum decision is satisfied. Then from (3.4a), we can see that the optimum decision cannot be an interior solution if

$$(I/p_2) \leq \alpha^{1/(1-\alpha)} (p_2/p_1)^{\alpha/(1-\alpha)}$$ (3.6)

which implies a nonpositive value of $x_2$ that is given by the first-order condition for an interior solution. For this case, we can use inframarginal analysis to show that the demand

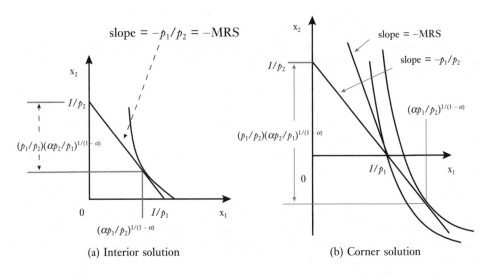

(a) Interior solution                                    (b) Corner solution

◆ **Figure 3.3:** Optimum decision based on a quasi-linear utility function that is strictly quasi-concave

function, shadow price of a dollar, and indirect utility function are given by (3.5a) instead of (3.4). Figure 3.3(b) gives a graphical illustration of the case. Note that for the corner solution, the marginal rate of substitution (or relative marginal utility) is not equal to relative price of goods.

The following *Kuhn–Tucker first-order condition for the nonlinear programming problem* in (3.1) applies to all interior and corner solutions.

$$x_i \geq 0 \text{ and } \partial R/\partial x_i = 0, \tag{3.7a}$$

$$x_i = 0 \text{ and } \partial R/\partial x_i < 0. \tag{3.7b}$$

The proof of the Kuhn–Tucker condition is straightforward. If the derivative of the objective function with respect to a decision variable is negative at the lower bound value (0) of the decision variable, then the optimum value must be 0. If the derivative at the maximum point is 0, then the maximum point is either an interior optimum, or is at a corner by coincidence. (3.7a, b) can be put together as

$$(\partial R/\partial x_i)x_i = 0, \ \partial R/\partial x_i \leq 0, \text{ and } x_i \geq 0. \tag{3.7c}$$

If the optimum values of all decision variables are interior, then (3.7) implies (3.3a). But for a quasi-linear utility function, if the optimum value of good i is 0 and that of good j is positive, then (3.7) implies

$$-dx_i/dx_j = (\partial u/\partial x_j)/(\partial u/\partial x_i) > p_j/p_i \tag{3.8}$$

Figure 3.3(b) shows the inequality for $i = 2$ and $j = 1$ (MRS stands for marginal rate of substitution, or $-dx_2/dx_1$). The Kuhn–Tucker condition is intuitive: if at the upper bound value of the amount of good 1 ($x_1 = I/p_1$ and $x_2 = 0$), the relative marginal utility of goods 1 to 2 is still greater than their relative price, then this implies that the marginal utility of a dollar spent on good 1 is greater than that of a dollar spent on good 2 at the corner. Hence, the consumer should spend all income on good 1.

In exercise 3, you are asked to check if all interior and corner solutions in (3.4) and (3.5) satisfy (3.7) for the relevant intervals of parameter values. If there are several interior extreme (maximum and/or minimum) points and a corner maximum is possible, then the Kuhn–Tucker condition is not enough for identifying the optimum decision from several corner and interior solutions. The second-order condition and inframarginal analysis are more essential for such a case. Our example for the quasi-linear utility function is such a case. The procedure that we follow is first to use the marginal condition to identify interior demand functions; and then to check the condition for $x_2$ to be nonpositive. This tells us the interval of parameter values for which the demand function is at a corner. Sometimes we need to work out the two corner solutions ($x_1 = 0$ and $x_2 > 0$ vs. $x_1 > 0$ and $x_2 = 0$). A comparison between the indirect utility functions of all corner solutions yields the interval of parameter values within which a particular corner solution is optimal. This inframarginal analysis is sufficient for us to sort out the optimum solution even if the Kuhn–Tucker condition is not used, provided the interior solution is not optimal.

Figure 3.4 illustrates a case where there are three *interior extreme points*. Point B is the *interior local minimum point*, point C is an *interior local* as well as *global maximum point*, while point D is the interior local as well as *global minimum point*. There are two corner solutions. One of them (point A) is the *global maximum point*. For that case, the first-order condition gives all interior local extreme points and the second-order condition distinguishes the interior local maximum points from the interior local minimum points. But the marginal analysis cannot tell which of the interior and corner solutions is the global optimum point. Only comparisons of indirect utility functions across all interior and corner solutions can sort out the global optimum decision. The comparison is referred to as *total cost–benefit analysis across corner and interior solutions*. The application of total cost–benefit analysis in addition to marginal analysis of each corner and interior solution is inframarginal analysis. The multiple interior solutions in this case arise from nonconvexity of preferences.

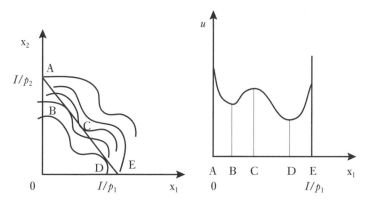

◆ **Figure 3.4:** Local and global interior extreme points, corner solutions, and the global optimum point

In part III, we will show that in new classical economics a consumer-producer's optimum decision is always a corner solution and that the interior solution is never optimal. In the new classical framework, the Kuhn–Tucker condition is essential for narrowing down the set of candidates for the optimum corner solution. Without the application of the Kuhn-Tucker condition, the number of possible corner solutions is too large to get the analysis going.

In neoclassical economics, by contrast, consumers' optimum decisions in most cases are interior solutions as long as the utility function is strictly quasi-concave. The exception is the quasi-linear utility function. If the utility function is quasi-linear, then the optimum decision is interior if good 2 in our example is not too expensive. If the utility function is not quasi-concave, then there is no trade-off. The optimum decision for the consumer is to go to the extreme and consume only one good. The compromise between the two consumption goods that is given by the marginal analysis is too conservative a decision. If the utility function is quasi-linear and strictly quasi-concave, but good 2 is too expensive, then the efficient trade-off is to consume only good 1. Otherwise, the efficient trade-off is to consume both goods and is given by the marginal condition (marginal rate of substitution equals relative price).

## ◆ 3.3 Comparative Statics of the Pure Consumer's Utility Maximization Problem

A central notion in neoclassical microeconomics is the law of demand, which concerns the relationship between the optimum consumption quantity of a good and its price. This law is deduced from the *comparative statics of the consumer's optimum decision*, which are about changes in the optimum decision in response to changes in parameters. Comparative statics provide a causal chain between endogenous variables and parameters, and thereby constitute the main source of explanatory power of economic theories.

Comparative static analysis is a kind of sensitivity analysis. It involves a comparison, between different goods, of the sensitivity of optimum quantities to changes in parameters. Economists use the concept of *elasticity*, rather than the concept of derivative, to measure this sensitivity. For instance, *own price elasticity of demand* is defined as ratio of the percentage change in quantity demanded of a good to a percentage change in the price of the good. The concept of elasticity avoids the impact of measurement unit on our measurement of sensitivity, enabling comparisons of sensitivities between different goods measured in different units.

The own price elasticity of demand is defined as

$$\frac{\partial x_i / x_i}{\partial p_i / p_i} = \frac{\partial x_i}{\partial p_i} \frac{p_i}{x_i}. \tag{3.9}$$

If the demand function for good 1 is the interior solution given in (3.4a), then the own price elasticity for that good 1 is $-1/(1 - \alpha)$. *Cross price elasticity of demand* is defined as

$$\frac{\partial x_i / x_i}{\partial p_j / p_j} = \frac{\partial x_i}{\partial p_j} \frac{p_j}{x_i}. \tag{3.10}$$

For the demand system in (3.4a), the cross price elasticities of demand for goods 1 and 2 are $1/(1 - \alpha)$ and $\alpha/(1 - \alpha)$, respectively. *Income elasticity of demand* is defined as

$$\frac{\partial x_i / x_i}{\partial I / I} = \frac{\partial x_i}{\partial I} \frac{I}{x_i}. \tag{3.11}$$

For the demand system in (3.4a), the income elasticities of demand for goods 1 and 2 are 0 and $1/x_2$, respectively, where $x_2$ is given in (3.4a).

It is important to note that as parameters change to reach certain critical values, the demand system generated by a quasi-linear or quasi-convex utility function will discontinuously jump between corner and interior solutions. Hence, comparative statics of the demand system will discontinuously jump too. We will study the features of discontinuous comparative statics in detail in part III.

Sometimes we are interested in the sensitivity of changes in the optimum relative consumption of two goods in response to changes of their relative price. We use the concept of *elasticity of substitution* to measure this sensitivity. The elasticity of substitution is defined as

$$E \equiv \frac{d \frac{x_2}{x_1} \Big/ \frac{x_2}{x_1}}{d \frac{p_1}{p_2} \Big/ \frac{p_1}{p_2}} \tag{3.12}$$

where the relative price $p_1/p_2 = (\partial u / \partial x_1)/(\partial u / \partial x_2)$ for the interior optimum decision according to the first-order condition. It is easy to show that the absolute value of $E$ does not change and only its sign changes if $p_1/p_2$ is replaced with $p_2/p_1$ in (3.12). Using the connection between relative price and relative marginal utility, we can calculate the elasticity of substitution for the quasi-linear utility function in (3.1) as follows.

$$E = (\alpha x_1^\alpha + x_2)/(1 - \alpha)x_2.$$

The elasticity of substitution tells us to what extent one good can be substituted for another good as relative price changes. Since the elasticity of substitution involves a derivative of derivatives, it relates to the curvature of indifference curves.

We now show that the optimum value of the Lagrange multiplier is the *shadow price of a dollar*, which is the derivative of the indirect utility function with respect to the income parameter. The concept of shadow price of a dollar is part of the comparative statics of the optimum decision, since it relates to how the maximum level of utility changes in response to a change in income. To show this we first note the definition of indirect utility function $v(p, I) \equiv u(x(p, I))$. Differentiation of the two sides of the identity with respect to $I$ yields

$$\frac{dv(p, I)}{dI} = \sum_i \frac{\partial u(x(p, I))}{\partial x_i} \frac{\partial x_i}{\partial I}, \tag{3.13a}$$

where $p$ is assumed to be constant and the differentiation rule for the chain function and the total differentiation rule are used. Because Walras's law holds for the optimum decision (the ordinary demand function), we have $px = I$. The differentiation of the two sides of the budget constraint with respect to $I$ yields

$$\sum_i p_i \frac{\partial x_i}{\partial I} = 1. \tag{3.13b}$$

(3.13a,b), together with the first order condition for the interior maximum $\partial u(p, I)/\partial x_i = p_i\lambda(p, I)$, yields

$$\lambda(p, I) = \frac{dv(p, I)}{dI}. \tag{3.13c}$$

This part of comparative statics relates to the welfare implication of changes in parameters, which is often the focus of economic analysis. A useful vehicle for analyzing this kind of comparative statics is the *envelope theorem*, which states that the total derivative of the optimum value of the objective function with respect to a parameter equals the partial derivative of the objective function with respect to that parameter. Suppose $p$ is fixed at a constant level and $R(x(p, I), \lambda(p, I), I) = u(x(p, I)) + \lambda(p, I)(I - px(p, I))$ is the optimum value of the Lagrange function. The total differentiation of $R$ with respect to $I$ yields

$$\frac{dR(p, I)}{dI} = \sum_i \frac{\partial R}{\partial x_i} \frac{\partial x_i}{\partial I} + \frac{\partial \lambda}{\partial I} (I - px) + \frac{\partial R}{\partial I} = \frac{\partial R}{\partial I},$$

where $\partial R/\partial x_i = 0$ and $I = px$ due to the first-order condition for an interior optimum. Using the envelope theorem, it is easy to prove that the optimum value of the Lagrange multiplier equals the derivative of the indirect utility function with respect to $I$. Because of the definition of the indirect utility function and Walras's law, $px = I$, $R(x(p, I), \lambda(p, I), I) = u(x(p, I)) + \lambda( p, I)(I - px) = v(p, I)$. Hence, $dR(x(p, I), \lambda(p, I), I)/dI = dv(p, I)/dI$. But according to the envelope theorem, $dR (x(p, I), \lambda(p, I), I)/dI = \partial R (x(p, I), \lambda(p, I), I)/\partial I = \lambda(p, I)$. We therefore obtain $dv(p, I)/dI = \lambda(p, I)$. This example shows that the envelope theorem can significantly simplify the analysis of the welfare implications of changes in parameters. We will repeatedly use the technique in this text.

Suppose that the interior demand function $x(p, I)$ and corresponding indirect utility function $v(p, I)$ are well defined, unique, and twice continuously differentiable. Then we may identify the ordinary demand function from an indirect utility function. *Roy's identity* helps us to do this. According to Roy's identity, if we know an indirect utility function $v(p, I)$, then the ordinary demand function $x_i(p, I) = -[\partial v(p, I)/\partial p_i]/[\partial v(p, I)/\partial I]$. To prove this, we first note that

$$\partial v(p, I)/\partial I = \lambda(p, I). \tag{3.14}$$

Note that here $p$ may change, so that $\partial v/\partial I$ is equivalent to $dv/dI$ in (3.13), where $p$ is a fixed constant. Then we know that $\partial v(p, I)/\partial p_i = \sum_i [\partial u(x(p, I))/\partial x_i][\partial x_i(p, I)/\partial p_i]$, where $\partial u(x(p, I))/\partial x_i = \lambda(p, I)p_i$ according to the first order condition for an interior optimum. Hence, $\partial v(p, I)/\partial p_i = \lambda(p, I) \sum_i [p_i\partial x_i (p, I)/\partial p_i]$. The differentiation of the budget constraint $px = I$ with respect to $p_i$ yields that $\sum_i p_i\partial x_i(p, I)/\partial p_i = -x_i$. Hence, $\partial v(p, I)/\partial p_i = -x_i \lambda(p, I)$. This, together with (3.14), establishes Roy's identity. Alternatively, we can use the envelope theorem to the Lagrange function $R(p, I)$ and to show that $\partial v(p, I)/\partial p_i = -\lambda(p, I) x_i(p, I)$. This, together with (3.14), can be used to establish Roy's identity as well.

In many cases, the optimum decisions cannot be solved analytically. Rather they are characterized only by the first- and second-order conditions. For such cases, we may identify the sign of the derivative of the optimum decision with respect to a parameter, using the first- and second-order conditions. The following example illustrates how this method works.

Suppose the solutions to the UMP, $x_1(p, I)$, $x_2(p, I)$, and $\lambda(p, I)$ are given by the first-order conditions

$$\partial u(x_1(p, I), x_2(p, I))/\partial x_1 - p_1\lambda(p, I) = 0,$$
$$\partial u(x_1(p, I), x_2(p, I))/\partial x_2 - p_2\lambda(p, I) = 0, \text{ and}$$
$$p_1 x_1(p, I) + p_2 x_2(p, I) - I = 0.$$

Differentiating with respect to $p_1$, and arranging in matrix form, we have

$$\begin{pmatrix} u_{11} & u_{12} & -p_1 \\ u_{12} & u_{22} & -p_2 \\ -p_1 & -p_2 & 0 \end{pmatrix} \begin{pmatrix} \partial x_1 / \partial p_1 \\ \partial x_2 / \partial p_1 \\ \partial\lambda / \partial p_1 \end{pmatrix} = \begin{pmatrix} \lambda \\ 0 \\ x_1 \end{pmatrix}$$

Solving for $\partial x_1/\partial p_1$ via Cramer's rule gives us

$$\frac{\partial x_1}{\partial p_1} = \begin{vmatrix} \lambda & u_{11} & -p_1 \\ 0 & u_{22} & -p_2 \\ x_1 & -p_2 & 0 \end{vmatrix} \div \begin{vmatrix} u_{11} & u_{12} & -p_1 \\ u_{12} & u_{22} & -p_2 \\ -p_1 & -p_2 & 0 \end{vmatrix} = \begin{vmatrix} \lambda & u_{11} & -p_1 \\ 0 & u_{22} & -p_2 \\ x_1 & -p_2 & 0 \end{vmatrix} \lambda^2 \div \begin{vmatrix} u_{11} & u_{12} & u_1 \\ u_{12} & u_{22} & u_2 \\ u_1 & u_2 & 0 \end{vmatrix},$$

where the bordered Hessian determinant is negative definite if the utility function is strictly quasi-concave. To obtain the second equality we have used the first-order conditions and the rule that when a row and a column of a determinant change their signs at the same time, the value of the determinant does not change. Denoting the bordered Hessian determinant $H$, we have $H > 0$ for a strictly quasi-concave utility function. Expanding the determinant in the numerator by cofactors on the first column, we have

$$\partial x_1/\partial p_1 = [-\lambda p_2{}^2 + (p_1 u_{11} - p_2 u_{12})x_1]\lambda^2/H.$$

If we know the utility function, we can use this method to identify the sign of all derivatives of the optimum decisions with respect to parameters.

## ♦ 3.4 A Pure Consumer's Expenditure Minimization Problem

In this section, we study the following *expenditure minimization problem* (EMP) for positive prices of all consumption goods.

$$\text{Min } px \quad \text{s.t. } u(x) \geq u \qquad (3.15)$$
$$x \geq 0$$

where $u(x)$ is a continuous utility function representing a nonsatiated preference relation, and $u$ is a given constant utility level. The solution of EMP $h(p, u)$ is called the *compensated* (or *Hicksian*) *demand function*. The minimum level of expenditure $e(p, u) \equiv ph(p, u)$ is called the *expenditure function*. The definitions of own price and cross price elasticities for a compensated demand system are the same as that for an ordinary demand system. But the compensated demand function does not involve nominal income. If we interpret utility as *real income*, then real income elasticity for a compensated demand function is the derivative of the compensated demand with respect to utility times the ratio of utility to the quantity demanded.

The second-order condition for an interior minimum of the EMP is that the Hessian matrix of the Lagrange function bordered with the first-order derivatives of the constraint function is positive definite. This condition is equivalent to a quasi-concave utility function (see Chiang, 1984).

For a continuous utility function representing a nonsatiated preference relation, it is not difficult to prove that

$$x(p, I) = h(p, v(p, I)) \text{ and } h(p, u) = x(p, e(p, u)). \tag{3.16}$$

The two equations allow us to make the following important connection between the expenditure function and the indirect utility function:

$$e(p, v(p, I)) = I \text{ and } v(p, e(p, u)) = u. \tag{3.17}$$

Hence, there is a direct correspondence between the properties of the expenditure function and the indirect utility function.

Also, $h(p, u)$ is homogeneous of degree 0 in $p$, since proportional changes in all prices would not alter the EMP. $h(p, u)$ satisfies no-excess-utility because of nonsatiated preference. It is not difficult to prove that the expenditure function $e(p, u)$ is strictly increasing in $u$ and nondecreasing in $p_i$ for all $i$, and homogeneous of degree one in $p$. It can be shown also that $e(p, u)$ is continuous in $p$ and $u$, though the proof is more difficult. The second-order condition for the EMP is that the Hessian matrix of the Lagrange function bordered by the first-order derivatives of the constraint $u(x) = u$,

$$\begin{pmatrix} L_{11} & L_{12} & -u_1 \\ L_{12} & L_{22} & -u_2 \\ -u_1 & -u_2 & 0 \end{pmatrix},$$

is positive definite. Here, $L = px + \lambda(u - u(x))$. It is not difficult to show that the second-order condition is satisfied if and only if the utility function is quasi-concave, or if and only if the marginal rates of substitution diminish (the indifference curves are convex; see Chiang, 1984).

We now prove that the expenditure function $e(p, u)$ is concave in $p$. This, together with Shephard's lemma (more below), will help us to establish the compensated demand law, which, together with the Slutsky equation, will help us to identify the condition under which the demand law holds. Fix utility level at $\bar{u}$ and let $p'' = \alpha p + (1 - \alpha)p'$ for $\alpha \in [0, 1]$. Suppose $x''$ is an optimal bundle in the EMP when prices are $p''$. Hence, $e(p'', \bar{u}) = p'' h(p'', \bar{u}) = \alpha p h(p'', \bar{u}) + (1 - \alpha)p' h(p'', \bar{u}) \geq \alpha e(p, \bar{u}) + (1 - \alpha) e(p', \bar{u})$. This implies that the expenditure function is concave. The last semi-equality follows because the definition of the expenditure function implies that $px'' \geq e(p, \bar{u}) = ph(p, \bar{u})$ and $p'x'' \geq e(p', \bar{u}) =$

$p'h(p', \bar{u})$. The intuition for a concave expenditure function is that as prices increase, the consumer will adjust quantities to minimize increased expenditure, so that the expenditure increases less than proportionally.

Following the method to show $dv(p, I)/dI = \lambda(p, I)$ and applying the envelope theorem to the Lagrange function for the EMP $px + \lambda(u - u(x))$, it can be shown that

$$de(p, u)/dp_i = \partial(ph(p, u))/\partial p_i = h_i(p, u). \tag{3.18}$$

This is referred to as *Shephard's lemma*, which is part of the comparative statics of the optimum solution of the EMP. Shephard's lemma establishes a direct connection between the expenditure function and the compensated demand function. Hence, we can use it to derive the compensated law of demand from concavity of the expenditure function. It can also be shown that the optimum value of the Lagrange multiplier for the EMP equals $de(p, u)/du$, which is the minimum amount of money the consumer has to pay for a marginal one-unit increase in utility.

For the concave expenditure function, we have

$$\partial^2 e(p, u)/\partial p_i^2 < 0 \text{ and } \partial^2 e(p, u)/\partial p_i \partial p_j = \partial^2 e(p, u)/\partial p_j \partial p_i \tag{3.19}$$

The second equation is owed to the Young theorem in mathematics. The two equations, together with Shephard's lemma, generate the *compensated law of demand*:

$$\partial h_i(p, u)/\partial p_i < 0 \text{ and} \tag{3.20}$$

*symmetry of the compensated demand system*:

$$\partial h_i(p, u)/\partial p_j = \partial h_j(p, u)/\partial p_i \tag{3.21}$$

The compensated law of demand, which is sometimes referred to as the *substitution effect* of a change in price, says that as the price of a good increases, its quantity demanded declines as far as the change in price is compensated by a change in income such that utility is not affected by the change in price.

We now identify the condition under which the law of demand holds, using the Slutsky equation and the compensated law of demand. From the duality in (3.16), we know that $h_i(p, u) = x_i(p, e(p, u))$ when $I$ is assumed to be equal to $e(p, u)$. Differentiation of the two sides of the equation with respect to $p_i$ yields

$$\partial h_i(p, u)/\partial p_i = \partial x_i(p, I)/\partial p_i + [\partial x_i(p, I)/\partial I][\partial e(p, u)/\partial p_i].$$

where $I$ is assumed to equal $e(p, u)$. Applying Shephard's lemma to the equation and using $h_i(p, u) = x_i(p, e(p, u))$ again yields the *Slutsky equation*

$$\partial h_i(p, u)/\partial p_i = \partial x_i(p, I)/\partial p_i + [\partial x_i(p, I)/\partial I]x_i(p, I). \tag{3.22}$$

where $\partial h_i(p, u)/\partial p_i < 0$ according to the compensated law of demand and $\partial x_i(p, I)/\partial I$ is positive if a good is a *normal good* and is negative if it is an *inferior good*. The term that includes $\partial x_i(p, I)/\partial I$ is referred to as the income effect of a change in price. Hence, we have

$\partial x_i(p, I)/\partial p_i < 0$ if good i is a normal good or
if good i is an inferior good and $|\partial h_i(p, I)/\partial p_i| > |\partial x_i(p, I)/\partial I|$;

$\partial x_i(p, I)/\partial p_i > 0$ if good i is an inferior good and $|\partial h_i(p, I)/\partial p_i| < |\partial x_i(p, I)/\partial I|$.

For the last case, where the amount demanded of the good increases as its price rises, good i is referred to as a *Giffin good*.

$\partial x_i(p, I)/\partial p_j + [\partial x_i(p, I)/\partial I] x_i (p, I)$ for all i and j constitutes a *Slutsky substitution matrix*, or simply *Slutsky matrix*, which satisfies the compensated law of demand and is symmetric. Since $e(p, u)$ is concave, its Hessian matrix consisting of all second-order derivatives of $e(p, u)$ is negative definite (see Chiang, 1984). (3.18) and (3.22) imply that the Slutsky matrix is the Hessian matrix of $e(p, u)$. This, together with (3.21), implies that the *Slutsky matrix is negative definite and symmetric*. The Slutsky equation and its properties impose two more requirements on a system of functions to be qualified as a system of ordinary demand functions. That is, it must have a Slutsky matrix that is negative definite and symmetric.

All dual relationships between the UMP and the EMP studied in this section are summarized in figure 3.5 (from Mas-Collell et al., 1995, ch. 3).

The solid arrows in figure 3.5 can be established from the duality shown in (3.16) and (3.17). According to (3.17), the indirect utility function can be worked out by using the compensated demand system and $ph(p, u) = I$. Also, the expenditure system can be worked out from the ordinary demand system by letting $I = e(p, u)$ and by using the Shephard's lemma which gives a system of partial differential equations of e and p. According to (3.17), the indirect utility function can be worked out from the expenditure function and $e(p, v(p, I)) = I$, and the expenditure function can be worked out from the indirect utility function and $v(p, e(p, u)) = u$.

Dual Problems

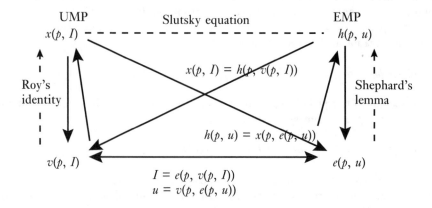

♦ **Figure 3.5:** Relationships between UMP and EMP

## ◆ 3.5 Recovering the Utility Function from a Demand System

Ultimately, we are more interested in inferring the intangible utility function from tangible demand functions. Suppose we have data that enables us to estimate a system of ordinary demand functions. Can we recover the utility function from the demand system? The answer is yes, provided the demand system has all properties required by the UMP. In this section, we first use an example to illustrate how this can be done. We then discuss the way to recover the utility function from the system of compensated demand functions, or from an expenditure function.

### Example 3.2: recover the utility function from a linear expenditure system

Suppose that we have the following demand system, which is called a *linear expenditure system*.

$$x = \alpha I/p_x \text{ and } y = (1 - \alpha)I/p_y$$

It is not difficult to verify that this demand system is homogeneous of degree zero in prices and income and that it satisfies Walras's law (the budget constraint is binding). Its Slutsky matrix is negative definite and symmetric, or its derivatives with respect to prices and income satisfy the compensated law of demand and are symmetric. Hence, we can use the first-order condition and the demand system to obtain a differential equation. Then integration of the differential equation will yield the underlying utility function. The first-order condition for the interior solution implies that the marginal rate of substitution equals relative price, or

$$-dy/dx = p_x/p_y \tag{3.23}$$

Because of homogeneity of the demand system, the relative price on the right hand side of the equation can be eliminated using the demand system. In other words, the demand system can be used to express the relative price as a function of $x$ and $y$. That is,

$$p_x/p_y = \alpha y/(1 - \alpha)x$$

Plugging this expression into (3.23) yields a differential equation of $x$ and $y$:

$$-(1 - \alpha)dy/y = \alpha dx/x$$

The solution of the differential equation is

$$u = (1 - \alpha)\ln y + \alpha \ln x \tag{3.24}$$

where $u$ is an integration constant, which relates to the fixed utility generated by an indifference curve. If we allow $u$ to change, then (3.24) is a utility function. Assume $u = \ln v$, then (3.24) becomes the Cobb–Douglas utility function

$$\nu = y^{1-\alpha}x^{\alpha} \tag{3.25}$$

The two utility functions represent the same preference relation because of the ordinal theory of utility. If you define the integration constant in different ways, you will find many other utility functions that represent the same preference relation. Essentially, then, the procedure to recover the utility function is to recover all indifference curves from a differential equation at the tangent point between the budget line and an indifference curve via integration.

As long as the ordinary demand system satisfies Walras's law, is homogeneous of degree zero in prices and income, and has a negative definite and symmetric Slutsky matrix, the demand system can be used to recover the utility function. This is referred to as the *integrability theorem*. For any ordinary demand system with $m$ ($>2$) goods, we need to construct a system of partial differential equations to recover the utility function from the ordinary demand system. First, we let $x(p, e(p, u)) = h(p, u)$. Then we can use Shephard's lemma to construct a system of partial differential equations $\partial e/\partial p_i = h_i(p, u)$ for all $i$. The solution of this system of equations gives the expenditure function. The integrability theorem says that the system of partial differential equations has a solution if and only if the Slutsky matrix of the demand system is negative definite and symmetric (see Mas-Collell, et al., 1995, sec. 3.H and Varian, 1992, secs. 8.5 and 26.12). The indirect utility function can then be recovered from the expenditure function and $e(p, v(p, I)) = I$. Eliminating relative prices by using the original ordinary demand system will then give the direct utility function.

We now consider another way to recover the utility function from an expenditure function or from a compensated demand system. Suppose the expenditure function is

$$e = (p_x/\alpha)^{\alpha}[p_y/(1-\alpha)]^{1-\alpha}u$$

It is not difficult to verify that the function is continuous, increasing in $p$ and $u$, homogeneous of degree one, and concave in $p$. This ensures that $e(.)$ is an expenditure function. We can then use Shephard's lemma to work out the compensated demand system from $e(.)$ as follows.

$$x = \partial e/\partial p_x = [\alpha p_y/p_x(1-\alpha)]^{1-\alpha}u \text{ and } y = \partial e/\partial p_y = [(1-\alpha)p_x/p_y\alpha]^{\alpha}u.$$

This system of compensated demand functions has a negative definite and symmetric Slutsky matrix. Because of homogeneity of degree zero in prices, we can use the system of two demand functions to eliminate the relative price by substitution. Then, we obtain the Cobb–Douglas utility function that generates the compensated demand system.

$$u = y^{1-\alpha}x^{\alpha}.$$

## ♦ 3.6 Revealed Preference

In our study of consumer behavior we have taken preferences as the primitive concept and derived the restrictions that the UMP or the EMP impose on the observed demand functions. These restrictions are basically that the Slutsky matrix based on demand functions be symmetric and negative definite. The other approach to investigating a consumer's behavior is to identify the restriction that utility maximization imposes on a list of observed prices and bundles of goods that are purchased in the absence of explicit demand functions.

We will say that a utility function *rationalizes* the observed behavior $(p, x)$ if $u(x) \geq u(x')$ for all $x'$ such that $px \geq px'$. That is, $u(x)$ rationalizes the observed behavior if it achieves its maximum value on the budget set at the chosen bundles. Suppose that the data were generated by such a maximization process of a non-satiated utility function. What observable restrictions must the observed choices satisfy? First, we note that if $px \geq px'$, then it must be the case that $u(x) \geq u(x')$. Since $x$ was chosen when $x'$ could have been chosen, the utility of $x$ must be at least as large as the utility of $x'$. In this case we will say that $x$ is *directly revealed preferred* to $x'$, and write $x \, R^D \, x'$. As a consequence of this definition and the assumption that the data were generated by utility maximization, we can conclude that $x \, R^D \, x'$ implies $u(x) \geq u(x')$.

Suppose that $px > px'$. Does it follow that $u(x) > u(x')$? It is not hard to show that nonsatiation implies this conclusion. For we know from the previous paragraph that $u(x) \geq u(x')$; if $u(x) = u(x')$, then by nonsatiation there would exist some other $x''$ so that $px > px''$ and $u(x'') > u(x)$. This contradicts the assumption of utility maximization.

If $px > px'$, we will say that $x$ is *strictly directly revealed preferred* to $x'$ and write $x \, P^D \, x'$.

Now suppose that we have a sequence of revealed preference comparisons such that $x \, R^D \, x^j \, R^D \, x^k, \ldots, x^n \, R^D \, x'$. In this case we will say that $x$ is *revealed preferred* to $x'$ and write $x \, R \, x'$. If we assume that the data were generated by utility maximization, it follows that $x \, R \, x'$ implies $u(x) \geq u(x')$. The following axiom is the primitive of the analysis of a consumer's behavior based on revealed preference.

**Generalized axiom of revealed preference (GARP):** $x \, R \, x'$ implies not $x' \, R^D \, x$. In other words, $x \, R \, x'$ implies $p'x \geq p'x'$.

If the data $(p, x)$ were generated by a utility-maximizing decision of a consumer with nonsatiated preferences, the data must satisfy GARP. Hence, GARP is an observable consequence of utility maximization. But does it express all the implications of that model? If some data satisfy this axiom, is it necessarily true that it must come from utility maximization, or at least be thought of in that way? Is GARP a sufficient condition for utility maximization?

It turns out that it is. If a finite set of data is consistent with GARP, then there exists a utility function that rationalizes the observed behavior. Hence, GARP exhausts the list of restrictions imposed by the utility maximization model. Afriat's theorem establishes the result (see Mas-Collell et al., 1995, ch. 3).

## ♦ 3.7 A Producer's Decision Problem in a Walrasian Regime

In the neoclassical framework, a pure producer's decision problem is much simpler than a pure consumer's decision problem; but it is also more flawed, because of the assumed dichotomy between pure consumers and firms. There are two methods of studying a producer's decision problem in neoclassical economics. First, we may assume that a producer minimizes production cost for a given output level. This problem is exactly the same as a consumer's EMP if the utility function in the EMP is interpreted as the production function, so that $u$ becomes the output level of a good and $x_i$ becomes the amount of factor i employed in production. After the producer has solved her cost minimization problem for a given output level, her expenditure function, which is referred to as *cost function* in the theory of production, gives the relationship between the minimum cost and output level, and the related Hicksian demand functions for factors. Suppose the producer's cost minimization problem

$$\underset{x \geq 0}{\text{Min}} \; wx \quad \text{s.t.} \; f(x) \geq y$$

yields the cost function $c(w, y)$ and the Hicksian demand function $x(w, y)$, where $w$ is a row vector of factor prices, $y$ is a given output level, $x$ is a column vector of factor input levels, and $f(.)$ is a production function. Using the cost function, the producer can construct the following profit maximization problem.

$$\underset{y \geq 0}{\text{Max}} \; \pi = py - c(w, y),$$

which generates the supply function $y(p, w)$, where $p$ is the price of the good. Inserting the supply function back into the Hicksian demand function $x(w, y)$ gives the demand functions for factors $x(w, p)$.

This two-step approach to solving the producer decision problem is equivalent to the following one-step producer's profit maximization problem (PMP):

$$\underset{x \geq 0}{\text{Max}} \; \pi = pf(x) - wx$$

The nonconstrained profit maximization problem is of course much simpler than the constrained utility maximization problem (UMP). A difference between constrained maximization and nonconstrained maximization is that for the latter the second-order condition for an interior maximum point is that the Hessian matrix of the objective function (instead of the bordered Hessian matrix of the Lagrange function) is negative definite. Hence, study of this kind of PMP involves only an application of what we have learned already from the UMP and EMP and from other nonconstrained optimization problems. For instance, if we interpret the marginal rate of substitution between goods in the EMP as the marginal rate of substitution between factors for a given output level, interpret the indifference curve for the UMP as an *isoquant*, and interpret the utility function as a production function, nothing is really new in substance. Hence, we consider the study of this kind of producer's decision problem as exercises and put them at the end of the chapter.

What is really new in the producer decision problem relates to some complicated cases concerning the second-order condition for the PMP. Let us consider the cases where the second-order condition for an interior optimum is not satisfied.

Suppose the production function $y = f(x)$ displays constant returns to scale or $f(tx) = tf(x)$. Then the PMP generates supply correspondence for goods and demand correspondence for factors, since the profit function in the PMP is neither strictly concave nor strictly convex. A correspondence is a multivalued function which may have multiple values of the dependent variable for a given value of the independent variable. This implies that the first-order conditions for an interior maximum generate zero profit and some requirements for market prices under which the firm can survive competition, but the optimum quantities of outputs and inputs are indeterminate. The following example of the Cobb–Douglas production function illustrates the implications of the constant returns to scale technology.

## Example 3.3: the decision of a firm with the Cobb–Douglas production function

Assume $y = Ax_1^{\alpha}x_2^{1-\alpha}$. Then the PMP becomes

$$\underset{x \geq 0}{\text{Max}} \ \pi = pAx_1^{\alpha}x_2^{1-\alpha} - w_1x_1 - w_2x_2,$$

where $w_i$ is the price of factor i and $p$ is the price of the good. The first-order conditions for the PMP generate

$$\alpha pA(x_2/x_1)^{1-\alpha} = w_1 \text{ and } (1-\alpha)pA(x_2/x_1)^{-\alpha} = w_2.$$

The two equations imply zero profit, on the one hand, and on the other hand that the equilibrium prices must satisfy the following condition if the firms facing this production function are to survive competition.[1]

$$p = (w_1/\alpha)^{\alpha}[w_2/(1-\alpha)]^{1-\alpha}/A.$$

If the market price is higher than the one given by the equation, the supply of the good and demand for factors are infinite, so that the equilibrium cannot be established. If the market price is lower, all firms with this production function will be out of the market because of negative profit. But if prices of goods and factors meet the condition, the quantity of good supplied and the quantities of factors demanded are indeterminate and they must be determined by the demand side. This indeterminacy of the optimum decision does not make trouble for the existence of general equilibrium. It just implies that the supply function is a correspondence rather than a one-to-one function. Since the first-order condition provides a basis for determining the equilibrium price, the market clearing condition (demand equals supply) can then be used to determine the equilibrium quantity. This somehow distinguishes neoclassical theory of production from neoclassical theory of consumption. For the theory of consumer's decision, it is exceptional for a one-to-one demand function not to exist. This occurs when at least part of the indifference curve is linear. But for a production function with constant returns to scale, non-existence of a one-to-one supply function is a rule rather than an exception.

We now consider a real problem of the theory of production with CRS. The zero profit condition for the production function with CRS implies that different production functions with CRS cannot simultaneously survive competition. This makes the theory of production very inflexible and very unrealistic. To see this point, assume that total factor productivity, parameter $A$, differs from firm to firm. Then the price at which the enterprise can survive is different from firm to firm. Hence, only the firm with the largest value of $A$ can survive, a situation implying monopoly which is incompatible with the Walrasian regime. In the real world we can see that total factor productivity differs from firm to firm. But we cannot see monopoly when constant returns to scale prevail.

If the elasticity of substitution between factors differs from firm to firm, we can also show that only one firm can survive. To see this, assume that all firms have the CES production function $y = (x_1^{\rho} + x_2^{\rho})^{1/\rho}$, but the parameter of elasticity of substitution

$\rho$ differs from firm to firm. Then the market price at which a firm can survive is $p = w_1 w_2 / \rho (w_1^{\rho/(1-\rho)} + w_2^{\rho/(1-\rho)})^{(1-\rho)/\rho}$, which changes with $\rho$. Since the minimum survival price changes from firm to firm when $\rho$ differs from firm to firm, only the firm with the lowest value of the price can survive, again a situation incompatible with the Walrasian regime.

For a convex production set with decreasing returns to scale, the second-order condition for an interior maximum of the PMP is satisfied. The first-order condition generates a well-defined supply function of goods and well-defined demand functions for factors. Also, the demand law holds for the demand functions and the supply law (the quantity of a good supplied increases with the price of the good) holds for the supply function of goods. However, the assumption of decreasing returns to scale is wildly at odds with empirical evidence. Also, we shall show in the next chapter that the production function with DRS generates a very peculiar general equilibrium implication, namely that equilibrium per capita real income for society as a whole is a monotonically increasing function of the number of firms. Hence, economists rarely make the assumption of DRS despite the high tractability of models with this property.

### Example 3.4: the decision problem with decreasing returns to scale technology

Consider a production function with DRS, $y = x^a$, where $a \in (0, 1)$. The PMP generates the demand function $x = (ap/w)^{1/(1-a)}$, where $x$ increases with the price of good y, $p$, and decreases with the price of factor x, $w$. It also generates the supply function $y = (ap/w)^{a/(1-a)}$, where $y$ increases with $p$ and decreases with $w$, and the *profit function* $\pi = w(1-a)(ap/w)^{1/(1-a)}/a$ which increases with $p$ and decreases with $w$.

Another problem with the assumption of a convex production set (DRS or CRS production technology) is the implausibility of its strong aggregation results. If each firm's production set is convex, then the aggregate production set for society is also convex. This implies that a central planner's optimizing decision to maximize all firms' total profit would give the same result as the aggregate outcome of decentralized optimizing decisions by the individual firms. This is inconsistent with our daily experience. From the failure of the Soviet-style economic system, we can see that such strong aggregation results do not exist in the real world.

Consider now the class of production functions with global increasing returns to scale (GIRS), $y = f(x)$, where $f(tx) > tf(x)$ for all $t > 0$. It is not difficult to show in this case that the second-order condition for an interior maximum in the PMP is not satisfied and that the maximum point is at the corner: $y, x = +\infty$. This is incompatible with market equilibrium because of limited supply of factors. Can we allow the demand side to determine quantity supplied and let the zero profit condition determine prices? The answer is no, since even if this were possible the global economies of scale imply that only one firm can survive competition, a situation incompatible with the Walrasian regime. Hence, economists do not assume GIRS in a Walrasian model.

The most realistic assumption about the characteristics of the production function in the neoclassical framework is that of local increasing returns to scale (LIRS).

### Example 3.5: the decision problem with LIRS technology

Let us consider a production function with LIRS: $y = bx^2$ for $x < x_0 \equiv a/(b + c)$ and $y = ax - cx^2$ for $x > x_0$, where $a, b, c > 0$. It is not difficult to show that the output level $y$ is an monotonically increasing function of the factor input level $x$. The function is convex for $x < x_0$ and is concave for $x > x_0$. This implies that there are local increasing returns to scale for $x < x_0$ and decreasing returns to scale for $x > x_0$. The optimum decision is $x^* = [a - (w/p)]/2c$ and the optimum profit is positive if $a > (w/p)$; however the optimum decision is $x^* = 0$ and profit is 0 if $a \leq (w/p)$.

Though the assumption of LIRS is most realistic, the model with LIRS is difficult to manage. For a model with LIRS, a positive quantity supplied implies positive profit, resulting in an infinite number of feedback loops between the supply function and consumers' income from dividends and positive profit. This creates difficulties in managing a general equilibrium model. Furthermore, when there are many production factors, even the supply function of goods and the demand functions for factors generated by production functions with LIRS are difficult to manage. The trade-off between tractability and realism of models explains why economists try to avoid models with LIRS despite the fact that these are much more realistic than models with CRS, GIRS, or DRS.

The most serious problem of the neoclassical theory of production is that it cannot explain why and how the institution of the firm emerges from the division of labor, and what are implications of the internal organization of the firm. Hence, the neoclassical theory in this section is referred to as the neoclassical theory of production, rather than the theory of the firm. As indicated by Coase (1937), the neoclassical theory of production is not a theory of the firm. The distinction between economies of division of labor and economies of scale characterizes the distinction between the neoclassical theory of production in this section and the new classical theory of production in part III, which embraces the theory of the firm. Economies of scale is a purely technical concept that has nothing to do with the productivity implications of network size of division of labor, whereas economies of division of labor relate to the network effect of division of labor.

## Key Terms and Review

Walrasian budget constraint.
Marginal rate of substitution.
Implicit function theorem.
Marginal decision rule of equal marginal rate of substitution (or relative marginal utility) and relative price.
Marginal decision rule of equal marginal utility of a dollar across goods.
Ordinary demand function and indirect utility function.
Compensated demand function and expenditure function.
Interior vs. corner solution and conditions for a corner solution to be the optimum decision.
Implications of the second-order condition for the analysis of decision problems.
Marginal vs. inframarginal analysis.
Comparative statics of the optimum decision.
Compensated law of demand.
Condition under which the demand law holds.
Walras's law and homogeneity of degree zero of an ordinary demand system.
Non-excess utility, compensated law of demand, and symmetry of a compensated demand system.
Own and cross price elasticity and income elasticity of demand.
Elasticity of substitution.
Slutsky equation.
Hessian matrix and bordered Hessian matrix.
Negative definite vs. positive definite matrix.
Shadow price of a dollar and shadow price of utility.

Envelope theorem.
Generalized axiom of revealed preference.
Elasticity of scale.
Output elasticity of a factor.
Economies of scale.
Increasing, decreasing, constant returns to scale.
Homogeneous and homothetic functions.
Factor demand function.
Supply function of goods.
Profit function.
Cost function.

## Further Reading

Mas-Collell et al. (1995, ch. 3), Varian (1992, chs. 7, 8, 9), Deaton and Muellbauer (1980), Debreu (1959), Samuelson (1947).

## QUESTIONS

1   How can one derive the ordinary demand system from a utility function?

2   How can one derive the compensated demand system from a utility function?

3   How can one derive the ordinary demand system from an indirect utility function?

4   How can one derive the compensated demand system from an expenditure function?

5   What properties of a system of functions are necessary and sufficient for it to be an ordinary demand system?

6   What properties of a system of functions are necessary and sufficient for it to be a compensated demand system?

7   What are the second-order conditions for constrained maximization and minimization problems?

8   How can one recover a utility function from an ordinary demand system?

9   How can one recover a utility function from a compensated demand system?

10  How can one find the ordinary demand system from an expenditure function?

11  Under what condition does the demand law hold for the ordinary demand system?

12  What properties of an indirect utility function are required by the underlying UMP?

13  What properties of an expenditure function are required by the underlying EMP?

14  What properties of a demand system ensure that a utility function can be recovered from the demand system?

15  Under what conditions are factor demand correspondence and good supply correspondence not one-to-one functions?

16　How can one derive factor demand and good supply functions, profit functions, and cost functions from the production function?

17　How can one derive factor demand and good supply functions from the profit function or cost function?

18　How can one derive a production function from the factor demand and good supply functions, or from the profit function or the cost function?

19　What are the second-order conditions for the UMP, the EMP, and the PMP? Why is it important to check these conditions?

# EXERCISES

1　Suppose that $u(x)$ is differentiable and strictly quasi-concave and that the ordinary demand function $x(p, I)$ is differentiable. Show the following.
  a)　If $u(x)$ is homogeneous of degree one, then the ordinary demand function $x(p, I)$ and the indirect utility function $v(p, I)$ are homogenous of degree one in $I$ and hence can be written in the form $x(p, I) = I\tilde{x}(p)$ and $v(p, I) = I\tilde{v}(p)$. What does this imply about the income elasticities of demand?
  b)　If $u(x)$ is strictly quasi-concave and $v(p, I)$ is homogeneous of degree one in $I$, then $u(x)$ must be homogeneous of degree one.

2　Assume that in a two goods world preferences are strictly convex and quasi-linear, represented by $u = x_1 + f(x_2)$.
  a)　Show that the ordinary demand function for good 2 is independent of income. What does this imply about the income effect?
  b)　Argue that the indirect utility function can be written in the form $v(p, I) = (I/p_1) + g(p)$.
  c)　When is the ordinary demand function for good 1 a corner solution? Calculate the income elasticity of demand.

3　Check if all interior and corner solutions in (3.4) and (3.5) satisfy (3.7) for the relevant intervals of parameter values.

4　Consider the CES utility function $u = (x_1^\rho + x_2^\rho)^{1/\rho}$.
  a)　Compute the ordinary demand and indirect utility functions for this utility function.
  b)　Verify that these two functions satisfy all the properties for the UMP.
  c)　Derive the ordinary demand correspondence and indirect utility functions for the case of linear utility and the case of Leontief utility. Show that the demand and indirect utility functions based on the CES utility function approach these as $\rho$ approaches 1 and $-\infty$, respectively.
  d)　Calculate the elasticities of substitution for the CES, linear, Leontief, and Cobb–Douglas utility functions

5　Consider the utility function $u = (x_1 - a)^\alpha (x_2 - b)^\beta$.
  a)　Why can you assume that $\alpha + \beta = 1$ without loss of generality? Do so for the rest of this exercise.
  b)　Write down the first-order conditions for the UMP, and derive the consumer's ordinary demand and indirect utility functions. This system of demand functions is known as the *linear expenditure system*.
  c)　Verify that these demand functions satisfy the properties for the MUP.

6  Suppose the utility function is $u = ax_1 + \ln x_2$.
   a)  Find the ordinary demand system and the indirect utility function.
   b)  Identify the conditions for the dividing line between corner and interior solutions.
   c)  Calculate the own and cross price elasticities of demand, the income elasticity of demand, and the elasticity of substitution.

7  Consider the CES utility function. Derive the compensated demand system and expenditure function. Verify the properties required by the EMP.

8  Suppose the utility function is $u = x_1^a + x_2$. Find the compensated demand system and expenditure function.
   a)  Identify the conditions for the dividing line between corner and interior solutions.
   b)  Calculate the own and cross price elasticities of demand, the real income (utility) elasticity of demand, and the elasticity of substitution.

9  A utility function $u(x)$ is *additively separable* if it has the form $u(x) = \sum_i u_i(x_i)$.
   a)  Show that additive separability is a cardinal property that is preserved only under linear transformations of the utility function.
   b)  Show that the ordinary and compensated demand functions generated by an additively separable utility function admit no inferior goods if the functions $u_i(.)$ are strictly concave, provided that the utility function is differentiable and generates an interior solution.

10  F. Fisher: A consumer in a three-good economy has demand functions for goods 1 and 2.

$$x_1 = 100 - 5(p_1/p_3) + \beta(p_2/p_3) + \delta(I/p_3)$$

$$x_2 = \alpha + \beta(p_1/p_3) + \gamma\,(p_2/p_3) + \delta(I/p_3)$$

where Greek letters are nonzero constants.
   a)  Indicate how to calculate the demand for good 3.
   b)  Are the demand functions for goods 1 and 2 appropriately homogeneous?
   c)  Calculate the restrictions on the numerical values of $\alpha$, $\beta$, $\gamma$, and $\delta$ implied by the UMP.
   d)  Given your results in (c), for a fixed $x_3$ draw the consumer's indifference curve in the $x_1$–$x_2$ plane.
   e)  What does your answer to (d) imply about the form of the consumer's utility function?

11  For a function of the Gorman form $v(p, I) = a(p) + b(p)I$, which properties will the functions $a(p)$ and $b(p)$ have to satisfy for $v(p, I)$ to qualify as an indirect utility function?

12  The matrix below records the ordinary demand substitution effects for a consumer endowed with rational preferences and consuming three goods at the prices $p_1 = 1$ and $p_2 = 2$, and $p_3 = 6$:

$$\begin{pmatrix} -10 & ? & ? \\ ? & -4 & ? \\ 3 & ? & ? \end{pmatrix}.$$

Supply the missing numbers. Does the resulting matrix possess all the properties for the UMP?

13  Consider the utility function $u = 2x_1^{1/2} + 4x_2^{1/2}$.
   a)  Find the ordinary demand and indirect utility functions. Check Roy's identity.
   b)  Find the compensated demand and expenditure functions. Check Shephard's lemma.

14  How would you recover $v(p, I)$ from $e(p, u)$?

15  Suppose you know the indirect utility function. How would you recover from it the expenditure function and the direct utility function?

16   Recover the utility function from the system of demand functions $x = (I - p_y y)/p_x$ and $y = \alpha p_x/p_y$.

17   Calculate the elasticity of substitution between goods x and y in generating a certain level of utility from the following demand system: $x = a(I - p_y b)/p_x$, $y = [(1 - a)I + ap_y b]/p_y$.

18   Is $E(p_x, p_y, u^0) = (p_x^2 + p_x p_y + p_y^2)u^0$ an expenditure function?

19   Is $V(p_x, p_y, I) = [p_x p_y/(p_x + p_y)] + (1/I)$ an indirect utility function?

20   Prove the *Euler theorem*, which says that $\sum_i \partial f(x)/\partial x_i = rf(x)$ if $f(.)$ is homogeneous of degree $r$, by differentiating $f(tx) = t^r f(tx)$ with respect to $t$ and letting $t = 1$.

21   Suppose that $c(w, y)$ is the cost function for a variable factor price $w$ and a given output level $y$. Prove scale elasticity $e(x^*) = [c(w, y)/y]/[\partial c(w, y)/\partial y]$, using the Euler theorem, the first-order condition for an interior optimum of the constrained cost minimization problem, and $\lambda = \partial c(w, y)/\partial y$, which can be shown from the envelope theorem.

22   Compute the cost function and profit function for the CES production function $y = (ax_1^p + bx_2^p)^{\alpha/p}$ and the Cobb–Douglas production function $y = x_1^\alpha x_2^\beta$. For what values of $\alpha$ and $\beta$ is there no profit function? Then find the demand function for factors from the cost function.

23   Compute the factor demand function, supply function of goods, and cost functions for the Leontief production function $y = \text{Min}\{ax_1, bx_2\}$ and the linear production function $y = ax_1 + x_2$.

24   Find the production function from the cost function $c = \text{Min}\{w_1, w_2\}y$.

25   Find the production function and factor demands from the cost function $c = (w_1 + w_2)y$.

26   Suppose the cost function is $c = w_1^a w_2^b$. What do we know about the values of $a$ and $b$?

## Notes

1 The Euler theorem (see exercise 20) implies that for a production function with CRS, the first order condition for the PMP is not independent of the zero profit condition.

# chapter 4

# GENERAL EQUILIBRIUM IN THE NEOCLASSICAL FRAMEWORK

## ♦ 4.1 General Equilibrium in a Walrasian Model

Roughly speaking, a *general equilibrium* is the outcome of interactions between self-interested behaviors. These interactions take place indirectly through the price system if the Walrasian regime (where all decision-makers are price takers) is specified, as in the last chapter. If a more general game rule than the price taking rule is specified, as in section 4.4, then it is direct interactions between self-interested decisions that generate the outcome. Since the interests of sellers and buyers of goods are in conflict (sellers wish to sell more and buyers to buy less as prices of goods go up), the equilibrium outcome involves a compromise which trades off the sellers' interests against those of the buyers. The price mechanism is the vehicle that coordinates and reconciles these conflicting interests to reach the efficient trade-off, which is of a higher order than the efficient trade-offs in individuals' decision-making.

In neoclassical economics, individuals choose quantities of goods that are produced, traded, and consumed for given prices, while equilibrium prices are determined as the aggregate outcome of those individuals' decisions. A general equilibrium is a consequence of the interactions between prices and quantities, which simultaneously determines both prices and quantities of goods and factors. Hence, in general equilibrium analysis, both prices and quantities demanded and supplied are endogenous variables. By contrast, in demand and supply analysis or analysis of decision-making (self-interested behavior), parameters of prices, tastes, endowments (including ownership of firms) and their initial distribution, and production conditions are exogenously given and they explain quantities demanded and supplied. The simple diagram below illustrates the differences between general equilibrium analysis and the analysis of decision-making. In the diagram, all variables on the left-hand side are exogenous and those on the right-hand side are endogenous. A variable is *endogenous* if its value is determined by decision-making or by interactions between self-interested decisions. A variable is *exogenous* if its value is specified as given to decision-makers or in equilibrium. For the analysis of an individual agent's behavior (decision), economists are concerned with how quantities demanded and supplied of goods and factors are determined by prices, tastes, technology, and endowments and their initial distribution, as illustrated by the following mapping:

Parameters of tastes, technology, prices,    $\Rightarrow$    Quantities of goods and factors
endowments and their initial distribution         demanded and supplied

The analysis of general equilibrium is concerned with how quantities demanded and supplied of goods and factors, and relative prices of goods and factors, are determined by the parameters of tastes, technology, endowments and their initial distribution. This is illustrated by the following mapping:

Parameters of tastes, technology,           Quantities of goods and factors demanded
endowments and their initial     $\Rightarrow$    and supplied, relative prices, resource
distribution                                allocation, and income distribution

In terms of daily language, 'mapping' means a causal relationship between explaining and explained variables. Prices are endogenous for general equilibrium analysis and are exogenous for the analysis of decision-making. It should be noted that in general equilibrium analysis the distribution of income is partly exogenously given by the initial distribution of endowments and partly endogenously determined by prices, since income is a product of initial endowments (which are exogenously given) and their prices (which are endogenously determined in equilibrium).

Many partial equilibrium models give students a misleading impression of economics. There are three types of partial equilibrium analysis. In *Type I partial equilibrium analysis*, which was popularized by Marshall, only the interactions between prices and quantities in one market are considered, and all other prices and quantities are assumed to be exogenously fixed.

Suppose that in a two-good (x and y) and one-factor (z) economy, the demand and supply functions are, respectively,

$$x^d(p_x, p_y, a, e), y^d(p_x, p_y, a, e), z^d(p_x, p_y, b),$$
$$x^s(p_x, b), y^s(p_y, b), z^s(p_x, p_y, a, e),$$

where z is assumed to be the *numéraire*, a is a parameter of consumers' tastes, e is a parameter of the initial distribution of consumers' endowments and ownership of firms, and b is a parameter of technology. Suppose that production functions display decreasing returns to scale, so that one-to-one market supply function of goods and demand function for factors are well defined. The general equilibrium (supposing that it exists) is determined by

$$x^d(p_x, p_y, a, e) = x^s(p_x, b), \qquad y^d(p_x, p_y, a, e) = y^s(p_y, b),$$

as shown in figure 4.1. Suppose now that the taste parameter a changes. A typical partial equilibrium analysis of the market for x predicts that this change will shift the demand curve for good x and therefore change the equilibrium price of x, as shown by the arrow in panel (a). However, a general equilibrium analysis will go beyond this first-round effect of the change in a, and recognize that the change of the price of x will in turn shift the demand curve for y and therefore change the price of y, as shown by the arrow in panel (b). This will shift the demand curve for x again. Indeed the initial change in a causes infinite interactions and feedback loops between changes in $p_x$ and $p_y$. The changes in $p_x$ and $p_y$ will also affect consumers' incomes, since profit and related income from ownership

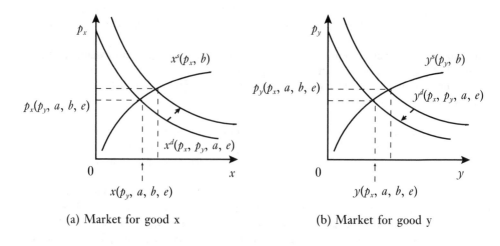

(a) Market for good x                              (b) Market for good y

◆ **Figure 4.1:** Type I partial equilibrium analysis

of firms is not zero. All of these changes will generate further interactions between the markets for goods and factors. This implies that the ultimate total effect, both on the economy and on the market for x, which includes all interactions and feedbacks between markets, is much more complicated than indicated by the partial equilibrium analysis. Example 4.1 in section 4.2 will show that partial equilibrium analysis usually gives wrong information about the consequences of changes in parameters.

In *Type II partial equilibrium analysis*, an attempt is made to consider the markets for all goods and interactions between them, but economic changes are not ultimately explained by changes in parameters that represent environment. Thus changes in prices in some markets are explained by changes in prices in one or more other markets. For instance, in the partial equilibrium analysis underlying the Stolper–Samuelson theorem, changes in prices of factors are explained by changes in prices of goods. As shown in exercise 7 in this chapter, and in chapter 12, this type of partial equilibrium analysis is often misleading too, since changes in the prices of goods are ultimately caused by changes in parameters. Thus, from a general equilibrium viewpoint, it is not legitimate to explain prices of factors by prices of goods, since all of them should be explained by parameters.

Hence, general equilibrium analysis suggests that any empirical works involving the regression of total quantities demanded in the market on prices are misleading, since what the data of quantities purchased reveal are equilibrium values of endogenous variables which should be explained by parameters. We should not explain endogenous variables by endogenous variables.

Another example of misunderstanding of the concept of general equilibrium is seen in the common statement that the quantity demanded is determined by income. This statement is wrong from a general equilibrium viewpoint, because (as we have seen earlier) income is itself an endogenous variable which, like demand, should be explained by parameters in a general equilibrium analysis. We can find many examples in our daily experience to verify not only that demand depends on income, but also that income and business revenue depend on how much firms can sell, which is determined by demand. Hence, demand and income are interdependent and must be simultaneously determined by a mechanism that explains both of them by some parameters.

*Type III partial equilibrium analysis* is illustrated by example 4.2 in section 4.3. In that example, as parameters reach certain critical values, individuals' optimum decisions discontinuously jump between interior and corner solutions. Type III partial equilibrium analysis does not take account of these discontinuous jumps. Instead, it applies marginal analysis to the interior solution and ignores all possible corner solutions. In other words, Type III partial equilibrium analysis, being preoccupied with marginal analysis, takes account only of interior local optima, whereas inframarginal analysis is essential for sorting out the global optimum from many local interior and corner optima. This requires a general equilibrium analysis that identifies each subspace of parameters within which one of the corner and interior solutions occurs at general equilibrium.

General equilibrium analysis studies the mechanism that simultaneously determines many endogenous variables through all of the interactions, interdepedencies, and feedback loops between individuals, between the markets for different goods and factors, and between prices and quantities. This analysis is carried out on the assumption that individual decision-makers are capable of doing the necessary inframarginal analysis. Because of the misinformation caused by partial equilibrium analysis, as illustrated above, we will focus in this textbook on general equilibrium analysis rather than on partial equilibrium analysis.

Since a general equilibrium is an outcome of interactions between self-interested behaviors, it may not necessarily imply market clearing (demand equals supply). As shown in some sequential equilibrium models (see Qian, 1994), which are dynamic game models with information asymmetry, direct interactions between strategies and information may generate a shortage of goods. General equilibrium does not necessarily imply unchanged static equilibrium. In parts IX and X of this text, we will present several dynamic general equilibrium models that generate spontaneous evolution of the outcome of interactions between self-interested decisions. General equilibrium may not be based on perfect rationality, deterministic optimization, or complete information. In chapter 24, a Walrasian sequential equilibrium model is used to show how interactions between adaptive self-interested behaviors based on bounded rationality generate concurrent evolution of economic organisms and knowledge of the organisms acquired by society through social experiments. Many challenges posed by nonlinear evolutionary economics (Nelson, 1995, Conlisk, 1996) and the Austrian School of economics (Kirzner, 1997) to the notion of equilibrium can indeed be absorbed into general equilibrium analysis.

In section 4.2, example 4.1 illustrates the notion of general equilibrium and the procedure for solving for it. Then an existence theorem of general equilibrium and its application are considered. In section 4.3, example 4.1 is further used to study comparative statics of general equilibrium. Then example 4.2 is used to explore the differences between marginal comparative statics and inframarginal comparative statics of neoclassical general equilibrium. Finally, example 4.3 is used to illustrate the trade-off between realism, tractability, and explaining power in specifying a general equilibrium model. In section 4.4 welfare analysis of general equilibrium is conducted. Neoclassical game models are considered in section 4.5.

---

## Questions to Ask Yourself when Reading this Chapter

♦ What are the differences between general equilibrium analysis and the three types of partial equilibrium analysis?

♦ What is the difference between the comparative statics of general equilibrium and the comparative statics of individual decisions?

♦ What is the difference between marginal and inframarginal comparative statics of general equilibrium?

♦ In specifying models, how can we achieve the efficient trade-offs between realism, tractability, generality, degree of endogenization, predictive power, and mathematical sophistication?

♦ What is the difference between indirect interactions between self-interested behaviors through prices and direct interactions between self-interested behaviors?

---

## ♦ 4.2 Neoclassical General Equilibrium Models

In this section, we first use an example to illustrate the concept of neoclassical general equilibrium, the procedure for solving for a general equilibrium, and problems that we may encounter in solving for an equilibrium. Then, we consider the existence theorem of equilibrium.

### Example 4.1: a neoclassical general equilibrium model

The environment of an economy is specified as follows. $M$ identical consumers have the Cobb–Douglas (C-D) utility function $u = x^\alpha y^\beta$, where $x$ and $y$ are the respective amounts of the two consumption goods, and the taste parameters satisfy the condition that $\alpha + \beta = 1$. Each consumer has $t$ units of time for working. Hence, her income from working is $wt$ at the wage rate per unit of work time, $w$. Ownership of all firms is assumed to be equally distributed among the $M$ consumers, so that each of them receives a dividend $\pi/M$, where $\pi$ is total profit of all firms. Each consumer is assumed to be endowed with $k$ units of capital. Therefore, each consumer's income is $I = wt + rk + \pi/M$, where $r$ is the interest rate. The expenditure is $p_x x + p_y y$, where $p_i$ is the price of good i.

We assume there are $N_x$ identical firms producing good x, each with the production function $x = K_x^a L_x^{1-a}$, where $K_x$ and $L_x$ are respective amounts of capital and labor employed to produce x. There are $N_y$ identical firms producing good y, each with the production function $y = L_y^b$, where $L_y$ is the amount of labor employed to produce y and $b \in (0,1)$. The Walrasian regime (characterized by competitive markets and private ownership of firms, goods, and factors) prevails in the economy.

The *ex ante* demand system for a consumer can be solved from her UMP:

$$x^d = \alpha I/p_x, \qquad y^d = \beta I/p_y, \qquad I = wt + rk + \pi/M. \tag{4.1}$$

Here, "*ex ante*" means that the consumer is yet to know the relationship between her dividend earnings and prices, that is, the optimum profit $\pi^*$ is yet to be solved.

The PMP of a firm producing y generates its demand function for labor, its supply function of y, and its profit function:

$$L_y^d = (bp_y/w)^{1/(1-b)}, \qquad y^s = (bp_y/w)^{b/(1-b)}, \qquad \pi_y = (1-b)p_y(bp_y/w)^{b/(1-b)}, \qquad (4.2)$$

where $\pi_y$ is the optimum profit of a firm producing y. Because of constant returns to scale in the production of x, the profit for firms producing x is 0 and the total profit of all firms is $\pi = N_y\pi_y$. Inserting the profit function back into each consumer's demand function yields the *ex post* demand system. It is interesting to note that the cross price elasticity of demand is 0 for the *ex ante* demand system and is not 0 for the *ex post* demand function for x. Own price elasticities and other properties are also different between the *ex ante* and *ex post* demand systems. The differences are relevant only if profit is positive, which can occur in a Walrasian regime only if technology displays global decreasing returns to scale or local increasing returns to scale.

The first-order conditions for the PMP of a firm producing x generate the following results (see example 3.3 in section 3.7):

$$L_x^d/K_x^d = (1-a)r/wa, \tag{4.3a}$$

$$p_x = (r/a)^a[w/(1-a)]^{1-a}, \tag{4.3b}$$

where the optimum input levels of labor and capital are indeterminate, and the first-order conditions impose a requirement for equilibrium relative prices. This, together with the constant returns-to-scale production function, implies that the quantity supplied of x is indeterminate also. Hence, demand and supply functions are not one-to-one functions, but rather correspondences, which implies that for a particular price level, multiple output levels are possible. However, such demand and supply correspondences are said to be *upper hemicontinuous*, that is, they are continuous lines in terms of two-dimensional graphs of horizontal supply and demand curves. Hence, the indeterminacy of quantities demanded and supplied would not preclude the existence of an intersection between demand and supply curves. It just means that the procedure for solving for general equilibrium prices and quantities differs between the model with constant returns to scale and the one with nonconstant returns to scale. For the former, the first-order conditions for the PMP give some conditions about equilibrium relative prices and relative quantities, while the equilibrium absolute quantities are given by the demand side for goods or the supply side for factors. This implies that the market clearing conditions are not enough to determine equilibrium relative prices and we need the first-order conditions for the PMP to sort these out, while the first-order conditions are not enough to determine equilibrium quantities and we need the market clearing condition to sort these out. Also, the technology of constant returns to scale in producing x implies that an equation to determine the equilibrium price of x can be obtained from the first-order conditions for the PMP without consideration of interdependency and feedback loops between production and consumption decisions.

We now consider the market clearing conditions

| | | |
|---|---|---|
| Market for labor: | $N_xL_x^d + N_yL_y^d = Mt,$ | (4.4a) |
| Market for capital: | $N_xK_x^d = Mk,$ | (4.4b) |
| Market for y: | $N_yy^s = My^d,$ | (4.4c) |
| Market for x: | $N_xx^s = Mx^d,$ | (4.4d) |

where the superscripts $s$ and $d$ represent the quantities demanded and supplied, respectively, by each decision-maker. If all individual decision-makers' budget constraints are added up, it can be shown that the aggregate revenue (income) equals aggregate expenditure before the optimum decisions are made or before the market is settled down in equilibrium. Summing up all consumers' budget constraints yields $M(p_x x^d + p_y y^d) = M(wt + rk) + \pi$, where total dividend equals total profit, that is, $\pi = N_x \pi_x + N_y \pi_y$, where $\pi_i$ is profit of a firm producing good $i$. The budget constraint for firms relates to their profit. Because of constant returns to scale in producing x, $\pi_x = 0$. Summing up profit $\pi_y$ yields $N_y \pi_y = N_y(p_y y^s - wL_y^d - rK_y^d)$. Inserting this into the aggregate budget constraint of consumers yields $M(p_x x^d + p_y y^d) = M(wt + rk) + N_y(p_y y^s - wL_y^d - rK_y^d)$. This equation establishes a relationship between quantities of goods and factors demanded and supplied before the economy reaches equilibrium. This implies that the four market clearing conditions in (4.4) are not independent of each other and that one of them can be expressed as a function of the others through the aggregate budget balance. This is referred to as *Walras's law*, according to which one of the four equations in (4.4) should be deleted in the process of solving for equilibrium because it is not independent of the other three equations. Since all demand and supply functions are homogeneous of degree zero in prices, the absolute levels of prices have no effect on equilibrium and only relative prices matter. We can thus assume any one of the goods and factors to be the *numeraire* and let its price be one. Accordingly we now delete any one of the four equations, say (4.4a).

The other three market clearing equations in (4.4), together with nine equations based on the first-order conditions in (4.1)–(4.3), constitute a system of 12 equations with 12 unknown endogenous variables $r/w$, $p_x/w$, $p_y/w$, $x^d$, $y^d$, $x^s$, $y^s$, $I$, $L_x$, $L_y$, $K_x$, and $\pi$. Denote all environment parameters of tastes ($\alpha$, $\beta = 1 - \alpha$), technology ($a$, $b$), endowments ($t$, $k$), population size ($M$), the numbers of firms ($N_x$, $N_y$), and the initial distribution of ownership of firms (each consumer owns $1/M$ of the shares of all firms) as a vector **A**. We can then solve for the general equilibrium values of the endogenous variables as functions of the parameter vector **A** from the system of equations. The solutions for the equilibrium relative prices, $x$, $y$, per capita income in terms of labor, and per capita real income (equilibrium utility) may be summarized as follows.

$$r/w = \alpha at/k[(1-a)\alpha - \beta b], \qquad p_y/w = \{\beta btM/N_y[(1-a)\alpha - \beta b]\}^{1-b}/b, \qquad (4.5a)$$
$$p_x/w = \{\alpha t/k[(1-a)\alpha - \beta b]\}^a/(1-a)^{(1-a)}$$

$$x = \{\alpha(1-a)t/[(1-a)\alpha - \beta b]\}^{1-a} k^a, \qquad\qquad\qquad\qquad (4.5b)$$
$$y = \{\beta bt/[(1-a)\alpha - \beta b]\}^b (N_y/M)^{1-b}, \qquad I/w = t/[(1-a)\alpha - \beta b],$$
$$u = [\alpha(1-a)^{1-a} k^a]^\alpha (\beta b)^{\beta b} \{t/[(1-a)\alpha - \beta b]\}^{(1-a)\alpha - \beta b} (N_y/M)^{\beta(1-b)}$$

The equilibrium values of other endogenous variables can then be solved from (4.1)–(4.5). Inserting the equilibrium values of all endogenous variables into (4.4a), we can check if the solution (4.5) is right, since according to Walras' law, (4.4a) must hold if (4.5a), given by (4.1)–(4.3) and (4.4b,c,d), is the right solution for equilibrium relative prices.

The decision problem is a mapping from the environment parameter vector **A** and the relative price vector $p$ to quantity vector of goods and factors $q$, $f : (\mathbf{A}, p) \rightarrow q$, while the equilibrating process is a mapping from quantities $q$ to relative prices $p$, $g : q \rightarrow p$. The two mappings $f$ and $g$ constitute a mapping $F : (\mathbf{A}, p) \rightarrow p$. If there exists a general equilibrium set of prices, $p(\mathbf{A})$, we say the mapping $F$ has a *fixed point*. The fixed point and mapping $f$ will generate a mapping $G: \mathbf{A} \rightarrow (q, p)$, which explains relative prices and quantities that are consumed and produced by the environment parameters (tastes, technology, endowments and their initial distribution, initial distribution of ownership of firms, the number and structure of firms, and population size).

Most times, a general equilibrium cannot be explicitly solved and comparative statics must be worked out from all equations for market equilibrium and optimum decisions. If, by inspecting the features of the specified environment in a model, we could know before we actually work with it whether or not the equations that characterize equilibrium have a solution, much research time could be saved. Hence, an existence theorem that identifies the features of a specified environment that are sufficient to guarantee the existence of general equilibrium for a very general class of models would seem to offer great value as an aid to research. The fixed point theorem represents just such a powerful tool. What an existence theorem does is to show that if the specification of environment (preferences, consumption sets, production sets, and initial distribution of endowments) satisfies certain conditions, then excess demand correspondences are upper hemicontinuous even if demand and supply functions are not one-to-one functions, so that an equilibrium with positive prices exists. For several reasons it is more powerful than the conventional approach of counting the number of market clearing conditions and the number of unknown prices to see if equilibrium exists.

First, with the existence theorem the conditions for the existence of equilibrium can be identified even if the functional forms of utility and production functions are not spelled out, as long as some properties of preferences and production sets are appropriately specified. Hence, the existence theorem can be applied to a class of very general models. Second, for the case of CRS technology, linear preferences, and other particular specifications of environment, the conditions for the existence of equilibrium can be identified even if the market clearing conditions are not enough for working out the equilibrium relative prices, and even if demand and supply functions are not one-to-one functions. Third, the existence theorem identifies the conditions for the specification of environment, whereas in the conventional analysis of existence of equilibrium, the conditions for existence are checked for *ad hoc* demand and supply functions which might have properties that are incompatible with utility or profit maximization behavior.

The usefulness of an existence theorem should not, however, be overstated. The conditions for the existence of equilibrium are sufficient but some of them may not be necessary. We can have a general equilibrium even if some conditions in the existence theorem do not hold. Moreover, our ultimate concern is with the explanatory power of a general equilibrium model that derives from the comparative statics of general equilibrium. For reasonably realistic models, the comparative statics of general equilibrium cannot be worked out without explicit specification of the models anyway. (See Sonnenschein, 1973, Mantel, 1974, Debreu, 1974, and Mas-Collell et al., 1995, ch. 17.) But once we have explicitly specified a model and solved it, then, it is not too difficult to see if equilibrium exists even if some of the conditions in the existence theorem are not satisfied. Experience in sorting out the efficient trade-offs among realism, generality, degree of endogenization, explaining power, tractability, and mathematical sophistication in specifying models through a trial-and-error process is much more important than memorizing and checking conditions in an existence theorem.

## Existence of an equilibrium

An equilibrium exists for an economy if the following conditions are satisified.

1) Each consumer's consumption set is closed, and bounded below.
2) Each consumer's preferences are continuous, nonsatiated, and convex.

3) Each consumer holds an initial endowment vector in the interior of her consumption set.
4) For each firm, no production is a choice in its production set.
5) The aggregate production set is closed and convex.
6) Production is irreversible in the sense that you cannot produce a net output vector and then turn around and use the outputs as inputs to produce all the inputs as outputs.
7) Firms can freely dispose of their outputs without costs.

Let us outline the proof of this theorem for the case that the excess demand functions are continuous. Assumptions (1) and (2) ensure the existence of a utility maximizing bundle. Assumptions (1) to (3) can be used to establish the continuity of the consumer's demand function. (5) ensures the continuity of firms' demand and supply functions. (6) can be used to guarantee that the feasible set of allocations is bounded. Hence, the excess demand functions are continuous, homogeneous of degree zero, and satisfy Walras's law. (7) ensures that the equilibrium prices are nonnegative. Then we can prove that for the excess demand system and strictly positive prices, there exists an equilibrium. The proof for nonnegative prices (some prices may be zero) is more difficult.

Because of the homogeneity of degree zero of the demand function we can restrict our search for an equilibrium to the unit simplex $\Delta = \{p \in R^m_+ : \Sigma_i p_i = 1\}$. Define on $\Delta$ the function $z^+(.)$ by $z_i^+(p) = \text{Max } \{z_i(p), 0\}$, where $z_i(p)$ is a continuous excess demand function for good i. Note that $z^+(.)$ is continuous and that $z^+(.) z_i^+(p) = 0$ implies $z(p) \leq 0$.

Denote $\alpha(p) = \Sigma_i [p_i + z_i^+(p)]$. We have $\alpha(p) \geq 1$ for all $p$. Define a continuous function $f(.)$ from the closed, convex set $\Delta$ into itself by $f(p) = [1/\alpha(p)][p + z^+(p)]$. Note that, corresponding to intuition, this fixed-point function tends to increase with the price of commodities in excess demand. By Brouwer's fixed-point theorem there is a $p^* \in \Delta$ such that $p^* = f(p^*)$.

We show that this implies that an equilibrium exists, that is, $z(p^*) \leq 0$. By Walras's law:
$0 = p^* z(p^*) = f(p^*) z(p^*) = [1/\alpha(p^*)] z^+(p^*) z(p^*)$. Therefore, $z^+(p^*) z(p^*) = 0$. But, as we have already pointed out, this implies $z(p^*) \leq 0$.

The proof of the theorem for the case that excess demand correspondences (rather than functions) are upper hemicontinuous needs Kakutani's fixed-point theorem (see Debreu, 1959) and is more difficult than the proof here.

It is not difficult to show that if utility functions are neither linear nor quasi-linear, equilibrium may exist even if assumption (3) in the existence theorem is not met. For instance, for a pure exchange economy with the identical Cobb–Douglas utility function for two representative consumers, equilibrium exists even if one of the consumers is endowed with all of the initial endowment of good 1 and the other is endowed with all of good 2, that is, even if condition (3) in the existence theorem is not met. But if some consumers' preferences are linear, condition (3) is essential for the continuity of the demand function and thereby essential for the existence of equilibrium. You are asked to verify this in exercise 6.

Also, we can easily find an example of the existence of equilibrium in a model with nonconvex preferences. Suppose a representative consumer has a quasi-linear utility function $u_1 = x_1^a + y_1$ and another representative consumer has a quasi-linear utility function $u_2 = x_2 + y_2^a$, where $a > 1$; this implies nonconvex preferences for the two consumers.

Assume that each consumer is endowed with one unit of labor, and that a representative firm producing x has technology $x = Al_x$ while a firm producing y has technology $y = l_y$. It can be shown that the equilibrium is $p_x/w = 1/A$, $p_y/w = 1$, $x_1 = A$, $y_1 = 0$, $x_2 = 0$, and $y_2 = 1$. This implies that equilibrium exists even if condition (2) in the existence theorem is not met. You are asked to further verify this in exercises 5 and 6. It will be seen also in part III of this text that there are many models with nonconvex production sets that generate well-defined Walrasian general equilibria if the set of individuals is a continuum.

The examples illustrate a trade-off between generality of the functional forms of models and generality of the structure of models covered by an existence theorem. With strong assumptions in the existence theorem, we can ensure existence of equilibrium for a class of general models. But the strong assumptions exclude many interesting models from consideration. In particular a class of models with nonconvex production sets are excluded from consideration despite their high explanatory power and interesting features. In chapter 13 we shall prove an existence theorem for a class of new classical models with nonconvex production sets.

You may ask how may an equilibrium not exist if it is the consequence of interactions between self-interested behaviors. It is perhaps hard to imagine non-existence of the consequences of interactions between self-interested behaviors. Mathematical reasons aside, the possibilities for non-existence of general equilibrium boil down to the limitations of the concept of Walrasian equilibrium, which is based on indirect interactions between self-interested behaviors through prices and does not involve direct interactions between them. Many game models show that game equilibrium can exist for an economy when the Walrasian equilibrium does not. Indeed, in a game model, we usually have too many possible equilibria and are rarely worried about non-existence of equilibrium. Hence, the nonexistence of a Walrasian equilibrium indicates a limitation of the concept of a Walrasian regime rather than the non-existence of consequences of interactions between self-interested behaviors.

## ◆ 4.3 Comparative Statics of Neoclassical General Equilibrium

### Example 4.1 (continued): the comparative statics of the equilibrium solved in section 4.2

If we differentiate the equilibrium values of the endogenous variables in (4.5) with respect to the parameters, we can analyze the comparative statics of general equilibrium, that is, how the equilibrium values of the endogenous variables change in response to changes in the environment. Table 4.1 summarizes the comparative statics of the equilibrium in example 4.1. In the table, "+" denotes a positive derivative of an endogenous variable with respect to a parameter, "−" denotes a negative derivative, and ? denotes that the sign of derivative is parameter value specific, dependent on the interval of parameter values. For instance, $\mathrm{d}(I/w)/\mathrm{d}\alpha > 0$ iff $a + b < 1$. The fact that $\alpha + \beta = 1$ is used in deriving the comparative statics.

We have several questions to raise about the results of the comparative statics of general equilibrium in table 4.1. First we ask whether we can get some results as general as the compensated demand law, based on a very general model specification such that no explicit functional forms of utility and production functions are specified; and only some

**Table 4.1:** Comparative statics of neoclassical general equilibrium

|        | $p_y/w$ | $p_x/w$ | $r/w$ | $x$ | $y$ | $I/w$ | $u$ |
|--------|---------|---------|-------|-----|-----|-------|-----|
| $\alpha$ | − | + | + | + | − | ? | ? |
| $\beta$  | + | − | − | − | + | ? | ? |
| $A$      | − | ? | + | ? | + | + | ? |
| $B$      | ? | − | − | − | ? | − | ? |
| $T$      | + | + | + | + | + | + | + |
| $K$      | 0 | − | − | + | 0 | 0 | + |
| $N_x$    | 0 | 0 | 0 | 0 | 0 | 0 | 0 |
| $N_y$    | − | 0 | 0 | 0 | + | 0 | + |
| $M$      | + | 0 | 0 | 0 | − | 0 | − |

general properties of the functions, such as quasi-concavity, are assumed. The answer is, unfortunately, negative.

Without the explicit specification of a model, there is nothing we can say about the comparative statics of a general equilibrium. This is realistic enough, since in a complicated economic system, there are no universal rules or regularities. The rules that are applicable to the relationship between endogenous variables and environment (comparative statics) are situation specific. Hence, economists do not claim that the comparative statics of any particular general equilibrium that they have worked out are in the nature of universal laws. They do, however, emphasize the method and the logical chain involved in sorting out the comparative statics. This point is compellingly shown in exercise 7 and in chapter 12.

The second question we ask is: how powerful or useful is this comparative statics approach to investigating the relationship between endogenous economic variables and environment parameters? The answer to the question is positive. We may substantiate our optimism by comparing the comparative statics of partial equilibrium, which are very close to common sense, to the comparative statics of general equilibrium, which are more complex and therefore less intuitively obvious.

Let us consider the comparative statics of the Marshallian Type I partial equilibrium in the market for good y. The market clearing condition (4.4c) yields

$$p_y/w = \{\beta M[t + (rk/w)]/[1 - \beta(1 - b)]\}^{1-b}b^b,$$

which indicates that as the per capita endowment of capital $k$ increases, each consumer's income increases, so that the demand for y increases (the demand curve for y shifts up and to the right) and the price of y in terms of labor rises. This seems consistent with our intuition and common sense. However, we have seen that the comparative statics of partial equilibrium can give misleading results. According to the comparative statics of general equilibrium in table 4.1, an increase in $k$ has no effect on the price of y in terms of labor, $p_y/w$. Where, then, have common-sense and the comparative statics of partial equilibrium gone wrong? The mistake comes from the neglect of interactions and feedback between the markets for all goods and factors. An increase in $k$ will indeed increase per capita income, thereby increasing the demand for y and its price. But this is only the first-round effect.

There are several second-round-effects. First, the rise of income will also increase the demand for x and its price, so that the price of y will be further affected by cross price elasticities. Second, an increase in $k$ will result in a change in the supply of capital and in the interest rate $r$, which will in turn affect the price of x and then the price of y. There are more third-round effects: a change in the price of x will affect profit, dividends, and income, which will affect demand for x and y, and so on. This process of deduction can continue without end, since there are infinite interactions and feedback loops between the markets for the two goods, capital, and labor. The comparative statics of general equilibrium takes account of all of the direct and indirect effects of a change in $k$ on $p_y/w$, which happen to offset each other completely, as reported in the entry of column 2 and row 7 of table 4.1. This result is far beyond what can be comprehended from common sense and intuition.

General equilibrium analysis ensures that what happens as a consequence of interactions between self-interested behaviors in the market must be logically consistent, while common sense and intuition are full of logical inconsistencies because of neglect of some links of the logical chain or of some feedback loops between variables. Hence, the comparative statics analysis of general equilibrium provides a rigorous method and a powerful network of logical chains which are much superior to common sense and intuition in sorting out the effects of a change in environment on endogenous economic variables.

The power of general equilibrium analysis comes from consistency of model specification, which takes account of all interactions and feedback loops between markets, between self-interested behaviors, and between prices and quantities. A well-specified model is called a *closed model*. A powerful test of whether a model is closed is to check if the conditions for equilibrium satisfy Walras's law. For instance, if the income of consumers in example 4.1 does not include the dividends from profit, the model is not closed in the sense that some source of income is not matched by the destination of the income. Hence, the equilibrium solution given by (4.4b,c,d) will not be consistent with (4.4a), that is, Walras's law will not hold. If an *ad hoc* demand function $x = a + bp$ is specified, the model based on it cannot be well closed since it is not generated by the UMP and it cannot ensure compliance with Walras's law. In other words, a model based on an *ad hoc* demand function cannot close the feedback loop between expenditure and income.

As shown in exercise 7 and in chapter 12, the flaw in the comparative statics of Type II partial equilibrium is similar to that in the comparative statics of Type I partial equilibrium. In the comparative statics of Type II partial equilibrium, the prices of factors are assumed either to be constants or to be explained by goods prices when all markets are considered. But the endogeneity of goods prices is ignored.

There are two ways to criticize the general equilibrium model in example 4.1. The first is to find some logical inconsistency within the model, and the second is to test empirically the hypotheses generated by the comparative statics results. One possible charge of logical inconsistency might be directed at the positive profits for firms producing y within a Walrasian regime which implies free entry into every sector. If the founding of a firm producing y can make positive profit, why are not more firms set up? You may suggest that this inconsistency could be avoided by assuming a zero profit condition. Unfortunately, this does not work since per capita real income is an increasing function of $N_y$, which is at odds with empirical evidence. We may try to defend the model by arguing that after the owners have taken dividends, pure profit is still zero. But the comparative statics in table 4.1 indicate that per capita real income (equilibrium utility) is a monotonically increasing function of $N_y$. If the number of firms is endogenous due to free entry, and utility increases with that number, why don't individuals set up more firms to produce y? A neoclassical answer to the question is that consumers cannot choose to set up firms and entrepreneurs are not specified in the model. Hence, as long as pure profit is zero (after distribution of dividends), nobody has an incentive to set up more firms.

The monotone positive relationship between the number of firms of the same type and per capita real income predicted by the comparative statics is, however, wildly at odds with the empirical evidence. This is why economists are reluctant to assume decreasing returns to scale technology, despite the high degree of tractability of models with DRS.

As discussed previously, another fatal flaw of the kind of model illustrated in example 4.1 is that only one firm with CRS can survive competition if total factor productivity differs from firm to firm. This prediction is also incompatible with empirical evidence. In particular, the neoclassical general equilibrium model cannot endogenize individuals' levels of specialization and the level of division of labor for society.

The next example is used to illustrate why inframarginal analysis is essential for a general equilibrium analysis and why the comparative statics of Type III partial equilibrium might be misleading.

### Example 4.2: a neoclassical general equilibrium model with corner solutions

An economy is specified as follows. A representative consumer has the utility function and demand function as given in (3.1), (3.4), and (3.5), and is endowed with one unit of labor and receives income from wages. A representative firm producing good 1 has the production function $x_1 = AL_1$ and a representative firm producing good 2 has the production function $x_2 = L_2$. For the economy with CRS technology, the general equilibrium relative prices are given by zero profit conditions for the two firms. Hence, $p_1/w = 1/A$ and $p_2/w = 1$. This, together with the inframarginal analysis that gives (3.4) and (3.5) in chapter 3, yields the following general equilibrium.

For $\alpha \geq 1$ and $A \geq 1$, the equilibrium is $p_1/w = 1/A$, $x_1 = A$, $x_2 = 0$;    (4.6a)

For $\alpha \geq 1$ and $A < 1$, the equilibrium is $p_2/w = 1$, $x_1 = 0$, $x_2 = 1$;    (4.6b)

For $\alpha < 1$ and $A \geq (1/\alpha)^{1/\alpha}$, the equilibrium is $p_1/w = 1/A$, $x_1 = A$, $x_2 = 0$    (4.6c)

For $\alpha < 1$ and $A < (1/\alpha)^{1/\alpha}$, the equilibrium is $p_1/w = 1/A$, $p_2/w = 1$,    (4.6d)
$$x_1 = (\alpha A)^{1/(1-\alpha)}, \quad x_2 = 1 - [\alpha(A)^{1/(1-\alpha)}/A].$$

There are two types of comparative statics of general equilibrium. The first is called *inframarginal comparative statics of general equilibrium*. For this type of comparative statics, the equilibrium values of endogenous variables discontinuously jump between corner and interior solutions as parameters reach certain critical values. For instance, as parameters $A$ and/or $\alpha$ change from $A \geq (1/\alpha)^{1/\alpha}$ to $A < (1/\alpha)^{1/\alpha}$, when $\alpha < 1$, the general equilibrium discontinuously jumps from (4.6c) to (4.6d). The second type of comparative statics is called *marginal comparative statics of general equilibrium*. For this type of comparative statics, endogenous variables continuously change in response to those changes in parameters that take place within the intervals demarcated by the inframarginal comparative statics of general equilibrium. For instance, if $\alpha < 1$ and $A < (1/\alpha)^{1/\alpha}$, the equilibrium value of $x_1$ increases and the equilibrium values of $p_1/w$ and $x_2$ decrease as parameter $A$ increases.

The values of all endogenous variables in each of (4.6a), (4.6b), (4.6c), (4.6d) constitute a partial equilibrium. A partial equilibrium is the general equilibrium only within particular intervals of parameter values. Comparative statics of Type III partial equilibrium are marginal comparative statics of partial equilibrium based on the first-order conditions for the interior solution, which relate to (4.6d). Hence, marginal comparative statics of partial equilibrium are misleading if values of the parameters are not within the relevant interval. Coase (1946, 1960) points out the flaw in Type III partial equilibrium analysis. Pigou's welfare analysis (see chapter 6) provides typical examples of Type I and Type III partial equilibrium analysis. It counts only the partial equilibrium based on interior solutions and completely ignores other partial equilibria based on corner solutions and discontinuous jumps of general equilibrium between the partial equilibria. According to Pigou, individual decision-makers are incapable of doing inframarginal analysis and naively stick to Pareto inefficient interior solutions.

Next, we use a general equilibrium model that is the most realistic and most difficult to handle among the neoclassical models to illustrate the trade-off between realism, explanatory power, and tractability in specifying a general equilibrium model.

## Example 4.3: a neoclassical general equilibrium model with local increasing returns to scale (LIRS)

A representative consumer has a Cobb-Douglas utility function with the taste parameters $\alpha$ and $1 - \alpha$, for goods 1 and 2 respectively. Each taste parameter represents the elasticity of utility with respect to the amount of the good consumed. The consumer is endowed with $t$ ($>4$) units of labor and owns all firms. The production function for a representative firm producing good 1 is $x_1 = AL_1$ and the production function for a representative firm producing good 2 is $x_2 = (2 + 0.01L_2)L_2$ if $L_2 \leq 4$ and is $x_2 = -2 + 3L_2 - 0.115L_2^2$ if $L_2 \geq 4$. The demand functions for the two goods are $x_1 = \alpha I/p_1$ and $x_2 = (1 - \alpha)I/p_2$, where $I = wt + \pi$, profit $\pi = p_2 x_2 - wL_2$, the supply of good 2 $x_2 = -2 + 3L_2 - 0.115L_2^2$, and the demand for labor $L_2 = (3 - w/p_2)/0.23$. The market clearing condition for good 2 yields $f(p_2/w, \alpha, t) = (2 - \alpha)(p_2/w)^2 + [(5.82 - 0.46t)\alpha - 5.71](p_2/w) + 8.08 = 0$ which gives $p_2/w$. The zero profit condition for good 1 yields $p_1/w = 1/A$. Using the implicit function theorem, the comparative statics of the equilibrium price of good 2 in terms of labor can be worked out as $d(p_2/w)/d\alpha = -(\partial f/\partial\alpha)/(\partial f/\partial(p_2/w))$ and $d(p_2/w)/dt = -(\partial f/\partial t)/(\partial f/\partial(p_2/w))$. They are positive in one interval of values of $t$ and $\alpha$ and negative in the other interval. This implies that the comparative statics of general equilibrium are dependent not only on the structure of the model and on specific functional forms, but also on intervals of parameter values for a given model structure and given functional forms.

The task of identifying the relevant intervals of parameter values is called *partitioning the parameter space into subspaces*. For any reasonably realistic model, the comparative statics of general equilibrium are structure specific, functional form specific, and parameter value specific. Usually, partitioning parameter space is a very challenging job for comparative statics analysis of general equilibrium. However, it is the richest source of the explanatory power of general equilibrium models.

In the model in example 4.3, the comparative statics analysis of the price of good 1 is relatively easy, that is, $d(p_1/w)/dA < 0$. This is a feature of the comparative statics of the price of goods with CRS in production. The easiness also implies a low explanatory power, since the comparative statics are not based on sophisticated interdependencies and feedback loops between production and consumption decisions. The *nonsubstitution theorem* (you can easily prove it on your own, or consult Varian, 1992, p. 354) shows that for a model with CRS technology and a single production factor, the general equilibrium prices of goods can be solved solely from the zero profit condition in production and are independent of the consumption environment. Of course, results of this kind are inconsistent with empirical evidence. The comparative statics of other endogenous variables in example 4.3 are more difficult to sign, but are more realistic.

Because of the nonhomogeneity of the production function with LIRS in example 4.3, it is difficult to work out the comparative statics, especially when more goods and more factors are specified, notwithstanding the well-behaved demand and supply functions and the realistic sophistication of this kind of model. The inconsistency between the existence of positive profit for a firm when there are LIRS and the Walrasian regime in this kind of model may also be open to criticism.

What we have learned from the three examples of general equilibrium model can be summarized as follows.

Production technology with DRS generates comparative statics of general equilibrium that are incompatible with empirical evidence although the general equilibrium of models with DRS technology is well behaved mathematically and is therefore easy to handle. In this kind of model, demand and supply functions are well defined and equilibrium relative prices are given by the market clearing conditions. Also, interesting interactions and feedbacks between markets, between consumption and production environments, and between individual decisions can be worked out through the positive profit that connects consumers' income to production decisions.

Production technology with CRS generates indeterminate quantities of goods supplied and factors demanded. Equilibrium relative prices are determined by the first-order conditions for the PMP rather than by the market clearing conditions. Though this kind of model is easy to handle, relative prices are solely determined by production conditions, whereas interactions and feedbacks between consumption and production decisions are blurred due to zero profit. This enables economists, to some degree, to isolate the analysis of prices from the analysis of consumers' behavior, thereby simplifying the algebra, though at the cost of realism and explanatory power.

Production technology with local economies of scale (or variable economies of scale) generates positive profit, which gives rise to complicated interactions and feedbacks between production and consumption decisions. Thus comparative statics of general equilibrium in these models are more consistent with empirical observations than other neoclassical models. However, this kind of model is very difficult to handle due to the nonhomogeneity of production functions.

If utility functions and/or production functions are linear, quasi-linear, or nonhomogeneous, the general equilibrium may discontinuously jump across multiple partial equilibria based on different corner and interior solutions as parameters shift between the parameter subspaces which demarcate those partial equilibria.

It is more important to understand the motivation for specifying a certain equilibrium model and the implications of the structure of that model for your motivation than to appreciate the above features of general equilibrium models. Usually, economists want to cook up some trade-offs in order to tell economic stories about how the efficient trade-offs between conflicting forces are explained by environmental parameters. For instance, in the three examples that we have examined, there are trade-offs between quantities of goods consumed in raising the utility of a consumer and between quantities of factors employed to raise a firm's output level. The efficient trade-off generates demand and supply, which are explained by prices, tastes, technology, and endowment. In addition to the trade-offs in decision-making, there are more complicated trade-offs in the marketplace. The efficient trade-off between conflicting interests in the marketplace is determined by tastes, technology, endowments, and the institutional environment.

Since the efficient trade-off achieved by the invisible hand involves infinite interactions and feedback loops between self-interested decisions, prices and quantities, and the markets for different goods and factors, we cannot appreciate it on the basis only of intuition and common sense. Hence, we need general equilibrium models in organizing thought experiments to make sure the models are well closed, so that all feedback loops and interdependencies are counted and logical consistency is maintained in analyzing the effects of changes of environmental parameters on endogenous variables (prices, quantities to consume and to produce, income distribution, and utility).

To cook up a right trade-off in the marketplace is much more complicated than cooking up trade-offs for decision-making. For the latter, we can check the Kuhn–Tucker condition and second-order condition to see if there is indeed a trade-off. If the conditions are not satisfied, the trade-off does not exist. The optimum decision is to go to the extreme, so that endogenous variables are explained by jumps of the optimum between corner solutions. For that case, we may cook up the trade-off in a more sophisticated way, as shown in part III of this text.

But it is not so simple to cook up an interesting trade-off in the marketplace because of the complicated interactions and feedback loops between self-interested behaviors, markets, prices, and quantities. Usually, we cannot tell if the marketplace trade-offs implied by our model specification are really interesting and really make sense to our motivation unless the model is explicitly specified and the general equilibrium implications of the structure of the model have been worked out. The following example illustrates the point.

### Example 4.4: a neoclassical general equilibrium model with an endogenous number of goods

Suppose that we are interested in using a general equilibrium model to figure out the mechanism that simultaneously explains quantities of goods that are consumed and produced, their prices, per capita real income (the equilibrium utility level), and the number of goods that are available from the market. We are interested also in how transaction costs affect the number of goods. We use the neoclassical general equilibrium framework, developed in this chapter, to conduct the thought experiment. Our purpose is to specify a trade-off to endogenize simultaneously the number, quantities, and prices of goods in general equilibrium. Since the number of goods can be a variable in the CES function, we assume a CES utility function for each of $M$ identical consumers, $u = (\Sigma_i x_i^\rho)^{1/\rho}$, where $x_i$ is the amount of good i that is consumed and $1/(1-\rho)$ is the elasticity of substitution. $1/\rho$ is the degree of complementarity between goods in raising utility since the elasticity of substitution is inversely related to economies of complementarity and positively related to $\rho$. Each consumer is endowed with one unit of labor, which is assumed to be the numeraire, and claims $1/M$ of ownership of all firms. A sales tax rate $t$ is assumed for each dollar of goods purchased, so that $(1 + t)p_i x_i$ is what a consumer pays for the purchase of $x_i$. All tax revenue is consumed by the government bureaucracy and never comes back to the economy.

We have some trade-off in specifying production conditions in the process of cooking up an interesting trade-off. If we assumed a quite realistic production function with LIRS, the model would be too complicated for us to work out any of the comparative statics in which we are interested, despite the attractive features of that production function as discussed in example 4.3. If we specify a DRS technology, the trade-off between quantities of goods in raising utility is easy to manage in order to endogenize relative prices and quantities of goods. However, an interesting trade-off in the marketplace for endogenizing the number of goods may not exist. If we specify a CRS technology, not only do the interesting feedback loops disappear, but also the equilibrium number of goods may be indeterminate. The most challenging job here is to find a no-nonsense trade-off to endogenize the number of goods.

Let us assume that each representative firm producing good i has DRS technology $X_i = L_i^a$, where $a \in (0, 1)$. We can then specify the UMP for a consumer and the PMP for a producer, and work out demand and supply functions for goods and labor. Note that the number of consumption goods $n$ is now a decision variable for a consumer. It can be shown that the optimum value of $n$ is as large as possible and this will be matched up by the largest possible number of different types of firms because of positive profit under DRS technology. Hence, the equilibrium $n$ is equal to the population size $M$ which is the upper bound of $n$. The general equilibrium can be solved from the market clearing condition as follows. $n = M$, $p_i = (t + a)^{a-1}a^{-a}$, $x_i = [a/(t + a)]^a/M$, per capita income is $(1 + t)/(t + a)$, per capita real income (equilibrium utility level) is $u = [a/(t + a)]^a M^{(1-\rho)/\rho}$. Certainly this is an uninteresting result. The equilibrium number of goods is at a corner and is explained solely by the population size because of the assumption of preferences for diverse consumption (utility monotonically increases with the number of goods) and the assumption of DRS. Also, the number of goods cannot be explained by the transaction cost parameter $t$. In other words, this model does not have a trade-off that can be used to endogenize the number of goods in an interesting way.

Let us now specify a CRS technology for each representative firm producing good i, $X_i = Al_i$. Also we assume that $t = 0$ and there is a fixed transaction cost, $c$, in sorting out the price of each good in terms of utility loss caused by the communication between the Walrasian auctioneer and each consumer. Hence, each consumer's utility function is $u = (1 - cn)(\Sigma_i x_i^\rho)^{1/\rho}$. We have now a real trade-off between preferences for diverse consumption and the transaction costs that are caused by greater variety in consumption. Hence, the general equilibrium is $n = (1 - \rho)/c$, $p_i = 1/A$, $x_i = Ac/(1 - \rho)$, $u = (A[(1 - \rho)/c])^{(1-\rho)/\rho}$. These results make sense to us: the equilibrium number of goods increases as the degree of complementarity between goods in raising utility $1/\rho$ rises and as the transaction cost coefficient $c$ falls; the equilibrium per capita consumption of each good increases with productivity $A$ and the transaction cost coefficient $c$, and decreases with the degree of economies of complementarity; and the equilibrium per capital real income increases as productivity $A$ rises and as the transaction cost coefficient $c$ falls.

We have successfully formalized the trade-off to endogenize the number of goods. But by assuming symmetry we have forgone the trade-offs that can be used to endogenize the relative prices and relative quantities of different goods. In the symmetric model, the two variables are 1 between each pair of goods. If we want to endogenize both the number of goods and relative prices, the model might be too complicated to get the comparative statics results that generate explanatory power. Similarly, if we want to specify a very general model without explicit functional forms, we may be compelled to sacrifice tractability of comparative statics and associated explanatory power.

The above model might be criticized on several grounds. It might be argued that the specification of coefficient $c$ is too *ad hoc*, or that the logic chain from the specification of the utility function to equilibrium implications of $c$ is too short and too straightforward, making the system short on roundaboutness and sophistication in its logical chains connecting the equilibrium values of the endogenous variables and the exogenous parameters. Or it might be argued that in any event the *degree of endogenization* of the model is not particularly high. The degree also increases with the number of endogenous variables specified in a model. Or, finally, it might be argued that the isolation of the determination of prices from consumers' decisions, because of CRS technology, makes the story relatively uninteresting. It would be possible to specify a model with local increasing returns to scale technology to cook up a trade-off to endogenize the number of goods through a mechanism involving more interactions and feedback loops between production and consumption decisions. But that would cause tractability problems. Again, we are faced with trade-offs.

Setting up a general equilibrium model to predict economic phenomena or to work out the implications of changes in the environment (including the policy environment represented by the transaction cost coefficient $c$) usually involves many complicated trade-offs among generality, tractability, explanatory power, realism, and degree of endogenization of the models. The efficient trade-off in the modeling process inevitably involves subjective weights that an economist assigns to the different features of a model. Hence, a positive analysis might not be completely positive in the sense that it is associated with the economist's subjective judgment of those weights. For instance, an economist whose command of high-powered mathematics is not strong may choose more readily than others to sacrifice some degree of endogenization and explanatory power in the interests of tractability. Awareness of the impossibility of isolating absolutely the positive and normative aspects of economic analysis is essential for maintaining a sharp sensitivity to innovative and critical thinking.

## ◆ 4.4 Welfare Implications of Neoclassical General Equilibrium

Because we have been concerned so far with positive economic analysis, we have not considered questions of what is good and what is bad for society as a whole, or what should be done. Our analysis has tried to figure out, through the comparative statics of general equilibrium, what will happen to the endogenous variables if the environment changes. We now turn our attention to normative questions, such as: is the outcome of interactions between the conflicting self-interested behaviors in a competitive market system based on private ownership, good for society as a whole? Analysis of the welfare implications of general equilibrium can be based on the comparative statics of general equilibrium. For instance, table 4.1 indicates that as the per capita endowment of capital or labor increases, per capita real income will increase. As shown in exercise 2, if a tax parameter is added to the budget constraint, the effect of the tax on the equilibrium level of per capita real income (utility) can be identified. However, the analysis based on the model in the previous section does not work if the utility function, initial endowments, and claims to ownership of firms differ from consumer to consumer. For instance, a change in tax may increase some consumers' utility at the cost of that of others. We need some concept of what is good for society as a whole to conduct welfare analysis for this situation.

There is a consensus among most economists that the notion of Pareto optimality establishes a bottom line for what is good for society as a whole. (An Austrian view that criticizes the usefulness of the notion of Pareto optimality is formalized in a sequential equilibrium model in chapter 24.) Let $x_i \in X_i \subset \mathbf{R}^m$ be a consumption bundle, $\omega_i \in \mathbf{R}^m$ be an endowment vector of consumer $i = 1, 2, \ldots, M$, and $y_j \in Y_j \subset \mathbf{R}^m$ be a production plan of firm $j = 1, 2, \ldots, N$. A feasible resource allocation $A$ is defined as

$$A = \{(x, y) \in X_1 \times \ldots \times X_M \times Y_1 \times \ldots \times Y_N : \textstyle\sum_i x_i = \omega + \sum_j y_j\} = \mathbf{R}^{m(M+N)}$$

A feasible allocation $(x, y)$ is *Pareto optimal* (or *Pareto efficient*) if there is no other allocation $(x', y') \in A$ that *Pareto dominates* it, that is, if there is no feasible allocation $(x', y')$ such that $x_i' \gtrsim_i x_i$ for all $i$ and $x_i' >_i x_i$ for some $i$. That is, an allocation is Pareto optimal if it is impossible to make any consumer strictly better off without making some other consumer worse off. Note that the Pareto optimality concept does not concern itself with income distribution issues.

A *competitive and private ownership economy* can be specified by

$$(\{(X_i, \gtrsim_i)\}_{i=1}^M, \{Y_j\}_{j=1}^N, \{(\omega_i, \theta_{i1}, \ldots, \theta_{iN})\}_{i=1}^M),$$

where $\theta_{ij} \in [0, 1]$ is the share of profit of firm $j$ claimed by consumer $i$. In this economy, an allocation $(x^*, y^*)$ and a price vector $p = (p_1, \ldots, p_m)$ constitute a *Walrasian (competitive) equilibrium* if: (i) for every $j$, $y_j^*$ maximizes profits in $Y_j$; that is, $py_j \leq py_j^*$ for all $y_j \in Y_j$; (ii) for every $i$, $x_i^* \gtrsim_i x_i$ in the budget set $\{x_i \in X_i : px_i \leq p\omega_i + \sum_j \theta_{ij} py_j^*\}$; and (iii) $\sum_i x_i^* = \omega + \sum_j y_j^*$.

**Proposition 4.1** (First Welfare Theorem): Any Walrasian equilibrium allocation is Pareto optimal.

*Proof*: Suppose not, and let $(x, y)$ be a Pareto dominating allocation. Then since consumers are maximizing utility we must have $px_i > \omega_i + \sum_j \theta_{ij} py_j^*$ for all $i = 1, \ldots, M$ due to the connection between revealed preference and utility maximizing choice (section 3.6 in chapter 3). Summing over all consumers $i = 1, \ldots, M$, we have

$$p\textstyle\sum_i x_i > \sum_i p\omega_i + \sum_j py_j^*. \tag{4.7}$$

Here we have used the fact that $\sum_i \theta_{ij} = 1$. Now we use the definition of feasibility of $x$ and replace $\sum_i x_i$ by $\sum_i \omega_i + \sum_j y_j$ and cancel $\sum_j p\omega_i$ in (4.7), so that $\sum_j py_j > \sum_j py_j^*$. But this says that aggregate profits for the production plans $(y_j)$ are greater than aggregate profits for the production plans $(y_j^*)$ which contradicts profit maximization by firms. *Q.E.D.*

The Second Welfare Theorem claims that a Pareto optimum resource allocation can be realized by a Walrasian equilibrium price set through a government endowment transfer scheme. In exercises 2, 3, and 4 you are asked to show that a government tax may cause distortions, so that any realistic income transfer scheme based on taxation may cause distortions. Exercise 9 asks you to endogenize the taxation rate in a model with the trade-off between the capacity of taxation to reduce the distortion caused by an externality, and the distortion that is caused by taxation.

The idea that taxation and related income transfers can be used to improve social welfare motivates, at least partially, the economics of public finance and the Second Welfare Theorem. We will apply inframarginal analysis to formalize this idea in a way that is substantially different from the Second Welfare Theorem and from the neoclassical analysis of externalities and public goods. As shown in chapters 10 and 17, the trade-off between endogenous and exogenous transaction costs can be used to justify taxation and other government institutions that can significantly reduce exogenous transaction costs, despite the endogenous transaction costs (distortions) caused by the tax. Chapter 16 endogenizes the degree of externality and the degree of competition by formulating a trade-off between the economies of division of labor and the coordination reliability of the network of division of labor. Chapter 15 formulates the trade-off between the positive network effect of public expenditure on transaction infrastructure and the negative effect of taxation on expansion of the network of division of labor. This will enable us to endogenize the public sector and explore the function of fair competition for rights to build infrastructure.

## ◆ 4.5 Equilibrium in Neoclassical Game Models

### 4.5.1 Game models

The Walrasian equilibrium model belongs to a special class of game models. In this class, it is a game rule that all players are price takers, that is, they do not directly pay attention to what other players are doing since they believe that all information about this is reflected in prices. Hence each player chooses the optimum quantities of goods and factors that are produced and used for given prices. The interactions between individuals' self-interested behaviors therefore take place indirectly, through prices, rather than directly. In this process, any player's attempt to manipulate prices is nullified by free entry and the ability of many other players to do the same. Therefore, there are no direct strategic interactions between self-interested behaviors. But for many economic games, the game rules are more general or more complicated than the price taking rule. In particular, if we want to understand how the price taking rule emerges from direct interactions between self-interested behaviors, the game rule at the beginning of the analysis must be much more general than the rule of price taking.

In this section, we study game models with more general game rules within the neoclassical framework. Game models within the new classical framework will be studied in chapter 9.

A game is defined by *game rules*, *players*, their *strategies*, *outcomes*, and players' *pay-off functions* on outcomes. The game rules specify who moves when, what they know when they move, what they can do, and when and how the game ends. The players are all the decision-makers who are involved in the game, and Nature, who randomly chooses whatever other players cannot choose when there are uncertainties in the game. A player's strategies are the actions that she can take when it is her turn to move. A profile of each and every players' chosen strategies generates an outcome of the game that affects players' well-being. Players' objective functions defined on outcomes of the game are called pay-off functions. In the next subsection, we use an example to illustrate all of these concepts.

### 4.5.2 Nash equilibrium

### Example 4.5: the Cournot model

Consider two firms in the market for good x. Since a game rule more general than the price taking rule makes the model much more difficult to manage, somehow generality and the degree of endogenization of other aspects of the model must be sacrificed. Hence, for this game with two players we adopt a partial equilibrium framework and assume an *ad hoc* total demand function for good x such that $x = (a - p)/b$, or $p = a - bx$. Suppose firm i's strategy is to choose its output level $x_i$ ($i = 1, 2$) and $x_1 + x_2 = x$. The game rules are that the two firms simultaneously choose their output levels for given opponent's output level. Firm i's pay-off function is its profit $\pi_i = px_i - c_ix_i$, where $c_i$ is firm i's marginal and average cost in producing x. Firm 1's self-interested behavior is to maximize its profit with respect to its output level for the given output level of firm 2; that is,

$$\underset{x_1}{\text{Max}} : \pi_1 = [a - b(x_1 + x_2)]x_1 - c_1x_1.$$

Its solution, $x_1 = (a - c_1 - bx_2)/2b$, is called the *reaction function* of firm 1. Similarly, firm 2's reaction function is $x_2 = (a - c_2 - bx_1)/2b$. The outcome of the direct interactions between the two firms' self-interested behaviors is determined by their reaction functions. Plugging firm 2's reaction function into that of firm 1, and combining this with the demand function, yields the outcome

$$x_1 = (a - 2c_1 + c_2)/3b, \; x_2 = (a - 2c_2 + c_1)/3b, \tag{4.8}$$
$$x = (2a - c_1 - c_2)/3b, \; p = (a + c_1 + c_2)/3$$

The outcome of direct interactions between the players' self-interested behaviors is called a *Nash equilibrium*. The Nash equilibrium in this particular game is also called a *Cournot equilibrium*. However if two firms' strategies are to choose prices rather than output levels, then the Nash equilibrium is called a *Bertrand equilibrium*.

Assume now that the two firms cooperate, or collude, with each other to maximize their joint profit $\pi = px - cx$, where $x = x_1 + x_2$, $p = a - bx$, and where, for simplicity, the cost coefficient c is assumed to be the same for the two firms. It is not difficult to show that here each firm's profit is greater than in the Nash equilibrium. However, each firm has an incentive to deviate from the collusion.

This can be shown from the *strategic form* of the game (see table 4.2), where, for each player, strategy M is to choose the optimum output level under the collusive agreement, and strategy C is to compete with the other player. Outcome MM is the result of collusion, CC is the Nash equilibrium, and MC is the outcome of firm 1 choosing the optimum output level for collusion while firm 2 competes with firm 1. MC implies that firm 2 maximizes its profit with respect to its output level, given firm 1's output at the optimum

Table 4.2: Strategic form of the game

|  |  | Player 2 | |
|---|---|---|---|
|  |  | M | C |
| Player 1 | M | $\dfrac{(a - c)^2}{8b} \, , \; \dfrac{(a - c)^2}{8b}$ | $\dfrac{3(a - c)^2}{32b} \, , \; \dfrac{9(a - c)^2}{64b}$ |
|  | C | $\dfrac{9(a - c)^2}{64b} \, , \; \dfrac{3(a - c)^2}{32b}$ | $\dfrac{(a - c)^2}{9b} \, , \; \dfrac{(a - c)^2}{9b}$ |

level under collusion. Outcome $CM$ is symmetric with $MC$. The first term in each entry is firm 1's profit and the second is firm 2's profit. It is easy to see that

$$\pi_1(CM) > \pi_1(MM), \; \pi_1(CC) > \pi_1(MC),$$
$$\pi_2(MC) > \pi_2(MM), \; \pi_2(CC) > \pi_2(CM).$$

This implies that each player has an incentive to deviate from the collusion unilaterally if the other produces the optimum output level for the collusion, and that each player has an incentive to choose a competitive strategy if the other does so too. In other words, the collusion cannot be a Nash equilibrium, despite a higher profit for each firm in the collusion than in the Nash equilibrium. This is called *coordination failure* due to all players' rational behaviors.

This type of game is sometimes called the prisoners' dilemma, indicating a situation in which, while two players can be better off by collusion, their rational behavior prevents them from choosing collusion. The term "coordination failure" might be misleading here; although there is a failure of coordination between the two firms as far as their profits are concerned, this is a coordination success as far as the welfare of society as a whole is concerned. Collusion is equivalent to monopoly, which generates a higher price and a lower total output than the Nash equilibrium, and accordingly lower utility for consumers. The coordination failure between the two firms leads to a competitive outcome (the Nash equilibrium) which generates a lower price and a higher total output level, so that consumers get more utility. In a later exercise you are asked to show this.

Also, you can specify a benevolent dictator's decision problem to maximize a consumer's utility subject to the transformation function between two goods and for a fixed utility of the other consumer in a general equilibrium model. Compare the first-order conditions for the optimum decision with the first-order condition for the monopolist's profit maximization problem. Then you can see that the monopoly entails a consumer's marginal rate of substitution that is not equal to the marginal rate of transformation between the good produced by the monopolist and a good produced by the other sector. But the Pareto optimum requires equality between MRS and MRT. Thus, the monopoly generates Pareto inefficient resource allocation. Further, the Nash equilibrium is Pareto superior to the collusive outcome because of the lower price and the higher output level than in monopoly. We can also show that the Nash equilibrium is Pareto inferior to the Walrasian equilibrium where the price of the good equals marginal cost $c$. It is not difficult to show that as the number of firms increases, the Nash equilibrium tends to the Walrasian equilibrium. In particular, for the special model, the Nash equilibrium is the Walrasian equilibrium if free entry is allowed. You are asked to show in exercise 20 that if firms' strategies are to choose prices in a Bertrand model, the Nash equilibrium is Pareto optimal. For many game models, it is shown that as the number of players increases, the Nash equilibrium converges to the Walrasian equilibrium (see Gale, 1986).

More generally, a strategy profile $s = (s_1, s_2, \ldots, s_N)$ of $N$ players constitutes a Nash equilibrium if for every $i = , 1, \ldots, N$,

$$u_i(s_i, s_{-i}) \geq u_i(s_i', s_{-i}) \text{ for all } s_i' \text{ that player i can choose;}$$

where $u_i(.)$ is player i's utility function and $s_{-i}$ is a strategy vector of all players except player i. In many games, there are multiple Nash equilibria. In order to enhance the predictive power of the theory, we may use various ways to narrow down the set of candidates for the game solution by refining the concept of equilibrium. One way is to allow players to choose a pure strategy with a particular probability. That is, players can choose *mixed strategies*. We will examine this kind of mixed strategy game in exercise 16 and in chapter 9. In the next subsection, we introduce the concept of subgame perfect equilibrium to refine the concept of Nash equilibrium.

### 4.5.3 Subgame perfect equilibrium
### Example 4.6: Stackleberg model

We now introduce a time dimension into the Nash game of the previous subsection. One of the two firms is the leader, who moves in period 1. The other is the follower, who moves in period 2. For simplicity, again we assume that the marginal cost coefficient $c$ is the same for the two firms. The rest of the structure of the game is the same as before. The *sequential move game* is described by the *extensive form* of the game in figure 4.2.

In the inverted tree graph, the root A denotes that the first mover chooses the output level $x_1$, which can be a high level $x_1^H$, a low level $x_1^L$, or any level in between. The nodes at the next layer denote that for any output level that the first mover has chosen in period 1, the second mover can choose a high level $x_2^H$, a low level $x_2^L$, or any level in between in period 2. Hereafter in this text, in any game with two players, for convenience we will call player 1 "he" and player 2 "she." The three broken ellipses denote that the second mover knows at which node she is located when it is her turn to move. This reflects the fact that this is a sequential move game. If it were a *simultaneous move game*, all nodes associated with the second player's moves would be shown within a single broken circle. The broken ellipses describe a player's *information set*. If she knows at which node she is located when it is her turn to move, we say she has *perfect information*. If she does not know, or knows only with some probability at which node she is located, we say she has *imperfect information*.

From each node at the second layer and below it, there is a *subgame*, represented by a span. The bottom layer is associated with the terminal period and gives outcomes, and pay-offs of the two players for each outcome, represented by a sequence of two lines.

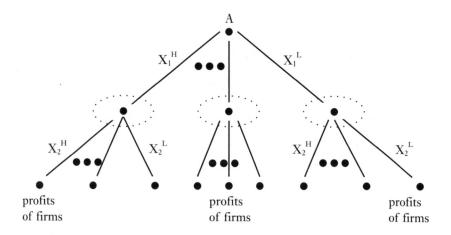

♦ **Figure 4.2:** Extensive form of a sequential move game

Roughly speaking, a *subgame perfect equilibrium* is a Nash equilibrium when players use dynamic programming (backward deduction) to choose their dynamic strategies on the basis of sequential rationality in a dynamic (sequential move) game. Here, *sequential rationality* implies that each player perfectly understands the other player's dynamic programming problem and the interactions between their dynamic decisions, and can recall all past plays.

Because of sequential rationality, the leader can put his feet in the follower's shoes to work out her optimum decision in the subgame of period 2 (the terminal period), which generates her reaction function $x_2 = (a - c - bx_1)/2b$. Then the leader plugs the reaction function back into his first-period profit maximization problem

$$\text{Max} : \pi_1 = [a - b(x_1 + x_2)]x_1 - cx_1 = (a - c - bx_1)x_1/2$$
$$\phantom{x}_{x_1}$$

to make money by fully exploiting the interactions between the two players' strategies. The solution of the problem yields the leader's optimum strategy in subgame perfect equilibrium $x_1 = (a - c)/2b$. Plugging the solution back into the follower's reaction function yields her optimum strategy in the subgame perfect equilibrium $x_2 = (a - c)/4b$. It is easy to show that in the subgame perfect equilibrium, the leader has an advantage. Relative to the follower, his market share is larger and his profit higher.

The next subsection shows that game models with information asymmetry may have significantly higher predictive power than the Walrasian model. More complicated dynamic games with an infinite decision horizon will be considered in exercise 14 and in chapter 9.

### 4.5.4. Bayes equilibrium

We now consider information asymmetry in a static Nash game. Again, we do not intend comprehensive coverage of this field of game theory. Instead, we use an example to illustrate the main concepts and this analytical approach to game models as one tool from our tool kit.

### Example 4.7: a Bayes equilibrium model

Consider again the Nash game in subsection 4.5.2. However, we now drop the assumption that the marginal cost coefficient $c$ is uniform across firms. We assume that firm 1's marginal cost $c_1$ is known to both firms, but firm 2's marginal cost $c_2$ has two possible states: a large value $\theta_h$ with probability $\rho$ and a small value $\theta_l$ with probability $1 - \rho$. This two-point distribution function of potential values of $c_2$ is common knowledge between the two firms. The actual, or realized value of $c_2$ is chosen by the third player, Nature. After Nature has chosen a state of $c_2$ according to the distribution function, player 2 is informed of the choice, but player 1 is not. Firm 2, then, has *complete information* about the realized value of $c_2$ and firm 1 has *incomplete information* about $c_2$. This is referred to as *information asymmetry* about the realized value of $c_2$ between the two firms.

A *Bayes equilibrium* is a Nash equilibrium in a simultaneous move game with information asymmetry, where the player with incomplete information maximizes his expected pay-off function for given uncertainties of types of his opponent. Here, *types* of the informed player are associated with states of marginal cost about which the other player does not have complete information.

Firm 2's reaction function is the same as in subsection 4.5.3 except that there are two reaction functions for two different states of $c_2$. Hence, we have the reaction function of player 2 (who is completely informed):

$$x_2(\theta_h) = (a - \theta_h - bx_1)/2b \text{ if } c_2 = \theta_h \text{ and } x_2(\theta_l) = (a - \theta_l - bx_1)/2b \text{ if } c_2 = \theta_l. \quad (4.9a)$$

Firm 1's decision problem is

$$\underset{x_1}{\text{Max}} : E\pi_1 = \rho\{a - c_1 - b[x_1 + x_2(\theta_h)]\}x_1 + (1 - \rho)\{a - c_1 - b[x_1 + x_2(\theta_l)]\}x_1$$

where E denotes expectation. The expected profit is a weighted average of two profit levels. The weights are the respective probabilities of the two profit levels. The reaction function of firm 1 is given by the first-order condition for the decision problem as follows.

$$x_1 = [a - c_1 - \rho bx_2(\theta_h) - (1 - \rho)bx_2(\theta_l)]/2b. \quad (4.9b)$$

(4.9) yields the Bayes equilibrium:

$$x_1{}^* = [a - 2c_1 + \rho\theta_h + (1 - \rho)\theta_l]/3b, \quad (4.10)$$
$$x_2{}^*(\theta_h) = [2(a + c_1) - (3 + \rho)\theta_h - (1 - \rho)\theta_l]/6b,$$
$$x_2{}^*(\theta_l) = [2(a + c_1) - \rho\theta_h - (4 - \rho)\theta_l]/6b.$$

This game model with information asymmetry involves interesting interactions between strategic interactions and information.

### 4.5.5 Sequential equilibrium

### Example 4.8: a sequential equilibrium model

If we introduce information asymmetry into a dynamic game, or introduce a time dimension into a Bayes game with information asymmetry, we will have an interesting type of game – a dynamic game with information asymmetry – which can generate significantly higher explanatory power than the Walrasian equilibrium model. The solution of this kind of game is referred to as *sequential equilibrium* or *perfect Bayes equilibrium*. For most dynamic game models with information asymmetry, perfect Bayes equilibrium, which is an extension of Bayes equilibrium to dynamic games, is equivalent to sequential equilibrium, which is a refinement of the notion of subgame perfect equilibrium to games with information asymmetry.

We use an example to illustrate the concept of sequential equilibrium in a dynamic game with information asymmetry, and its implication for economic analysis. This is a game between many managers and their potential clients. There are two types of managers: capable and incapable ones, denoted by subscripts $c$ and $n$, respectively. For a type $c$ manager, the profit she can make when a client has a deal with her is 20, which will be equally divided between her and her client. The capable manager's utility function is $u_c = (3 \times 0.5\theta_c\alpha_i - p_i)\alpha_i$ when she receives a half of the profit $\theta_c = 20$ that she makes, and consumes a car with quality $\alpha_i$ at price $p_i$. Here subscript $i$ denotes brand $i$ of car. There are three brands of cars. Brand 1 is a BMW with quality $\alpha_1 = 4$ and price $p_1 = 70$. Brand 2 is a Volvo with quality $\alpha_2 = 3$ and price $p_2 = 11$. Brand 3 is a Toyota with quality $\alpha_3 = 2$ and price $p_3 = 6$. For a type $n$ manager, the profit he can make when a client has a deal with him is 8, which will be equally divided between him and his client. His utility function is $u_n = (0.5\theta_n\alpha_i - p_i)\alpha_i$ when he receives a half of the profit $\theta_n = 8$ that he makes, and consumes a car with quality $\alpha_i$ at price $p_i$. For simplicity, we assume that a car can be used for two periods and the discount factor is 1 (or discount rate is 0).

A potential client has incomplete *prior information* about the type of a manager she meets. She knows in period 1 that, on average, type $c$ occurs with probability $\rho$ and type $n$ occurs with probability $1 - \rho$, where $\rho \in (0, 1)$ is the ratio of capable managers to the total population of managers. The client's utility function is $v = (\theta_i/2) - 5$, where $\theta_i$ is the profit made by the type i manager who gets the deal, of which the client gets a half. $\theta_c = 20$ when the capable manager gets the deal and $\theta_n = 8$ when the incapable manager gets the deal. For simplicity, we assume that a client's utility is 0 in period 1.

In period 1, the two types of managers choose the brands of cars that they drive, then in period 2 potential clients infer the managers' types from the brands of cars that they drive and decide with whom to deal. This story is interesting because of the complicated interactions between information and dynamic strategies. A client can infer that a capable manager will drive a Volvo since $u_c(\alpha_2, p_2) > u_c(\alpha_1, p_1)$, $u_c(\alpha_3, p_3)$ and an incapable manager will drive a Toyota since $u_n(\alpha_3, p_3) > u_n(\alpha_2, p_2)$ and $u_n(\alpha_1, p_1) = 0$. In other words, an incapable manager will drive a cheaper car and a capable manager will drive a more expensive Volvo. Then from the brands of cars the managers drive, the client can get complete information about their types, so that she would give a deal to a manager driving a Volvo and refuse to do business with a manager driving a Toyota.

But a rational manager will drive a Volvo even if he is incapable (check that $u_n(\alpha_2, p_2) > 0$, that is, an incapable manager can afford a Volvo, despite the fact that this is not a myopic utility maximizing choice), since if he drove a Toyota, he would get no business, so that his income would be 0 and he could not afford even a Toyota. But if all managers drive Volvo cars, the clients cannot tell their competence from their cars. They will not believe any manager claiming to be capable. Accordingly, if a capable manager wants to distinguish herself from an incapable one, she can drive a BMW, which an incapable manager cannot afford (check $u_n(\alpha_1, p_1) < 0$). In other words, what a client knows about a manager's type is dependent on which strategy the manager chooses. But the strategy that the manager sees as optimal is, in turn, dependent on the information known to the client, which affects the client's strategies. In a manner analogous to the interdependencies and feedback loops between quantities and prices in a Walrasian equilibrium model, there are infinite interactions and feedback loops between a client's information and her dynamic strategies, and between different players' dynamic strategies.

A *sequential equilibrium* is the outcome of all of the interactions between information and all players' dynamic strategies. Denoting the brand of car that a manager chooses in period 1 by $s$, then in period 2, from observing $s$, a client's *posterior probability* for a manager to be type $c$ is $\mu(s)$. This updated information may be different from the *prior probability*, $\rho$, for type c. Hence, a sequential equilibrium is defined by the following two conditions. (i) All players use dynamic programming (backward deduction) to solve for their optimum dynamic strategies for given information that they know; (ii) Each player's information in each period is updated according to the observed strategies of other players on the basis of the *Bayes updating rule*. The Bayes updating rule is illustrated in the following solution of the sequential equilibrium.

Let us now consider a client's decision problem. Her utility is 0 in period 1. In period 2 she has seen the brand $s$ of cars driven by managers and has updated her information $\mu(s)$. Hence, she can compute her expected utility as $E\nu = \mu(s)[(20/2) - 5] + [1 - \mu(s)][(8/2) - 5] = 6\mu(s) - 1$, which is greater than 0 iff $\mu(s) > 1/6$. Based on this solution, we can work out a *pooling equilibrium* by assuming $\mu(s) = \rho > 1/6$. A pooling equilibrium takes place when the client's prior and posterior information is the same or when $\mu(s) = \rho$. In the pooling equilibrium, all managers drive Volvo cars in period 1, and all clients cannot tell the capable managers from the incapable ones and do business with any managers in period 2.

We first check if a client's decision to do business with any manager is optimal for her updated information. Since in a pooling equilibrium $\mu(s) = \rho$ and we have assumed that $\rho > 1/6$, her expected utility is greater than 0. Therefore, her decision to do business with any manager is optimal. Though she has an incentive to know more information, we can show that provided the client is choosing to do business with any manager, a capable manager has no incentive to distinguish herself from an incapable manager, and that an incapable manager has an incentive to pretend to be a capable manager by driving a Volvo car. You can verify that a type $n$ manager can afford a Volvo, that his utility maximizing choice is a Toyota, and that he will lose business if he drives a Toyota. A $c$ type manager's total utility in the two periods is $-p_2\alpha_2 + 3 \times 0.5\theta_c\alpha_2^2 = (3 \times 0.5\theta_c\alpha_2 - p_2)\alpha_2 = 231$, which is greater than that for driving a BMW, which can distinguish her from an incapable manager. Note that in period 1, the manager receives no income and pays for a Volvo car and in period 2 she receives a half share of profit and uses the car without further payment. An $n$ type manager's total utility in the two periods is $-p_2\alpha_2 + 0.5\theta_c\alpha_2^2 = (0.5\theta_c\alpha_2 - p_2)\alpha_2 = 3$, which is greater than the zero pay-off when there is no business. Hence, all dynamic strategies are optimal for the updated information, and the information that is updated according to observed strategies is consistent with all players' dynamic strategies. This verifies that for $\rho > 1/6$, the pooling sequential equilibrium takes place. That is, if the likelihood for a manager to be capable is high (or capable managers sufficiently outnumber the incapable ones), a client will do business with any manager even if she cannot tell the capable from the incapable ones. Hence, the capable ones have no incentive to distinguish themselves from the incapable ones, so that the incapable can cheat by pretending to be capable. The confused client cannot get more information when the capable does not choose to distinguish herself from the incapable.

Suppose $\rho \leq 1/6$. We can show that there exists a *screening* or *separating sequential equilibrium*, in which all capable managers drive BMWs and all incapable managers cannot get any business. For this case, a client's expected utility is nonpositive if she cannot tell the capable from the incapable, so that she will not do any business unless she is convinced that a manager is capable. Hence, a capable manager has an incentive to distinguish herself from the incapable by driving a BMW, which an incapable manager cannot afford. Hence, the client can tell the capable from the incapable, so that she has business only with those who drive BMWs. Her posterior information is $\mu(s) = 1$ when she has seen a manager driving a BMW and is $\mu(s) = 0$ if she has seen a manager who does not drive a BMW. This process adjusts client's information about posterior probability according to observed strategy. It is called the *Bayes updating rule*. In other words, if incapable managers sufficiently outnumber capable ones, a client expects a nonpositive utility from doing business with any manager when she cannot tell who is who. Hence, she will not do any business unless she can establish who is who. This gives the capable managers an incentive to convince the clients by driving BMWs which the incapable managers cannot afford. Therefore, screening equilibrium results from complicated interactions between information and all players' dynamic strategies.

Let us now consider the endogenous transaction costs caused by information asymmetry in the model. Endogenous transaction costs cannot be identified before individual players have made their decisions and the economy has settled down in equilibrium. *Exogenous transaction costs* are those costs related to transactions that can be identified before individual players have made their decisions. If we define *endogenous transaction cost* as a departure of equilibrium from the Pareto optimum, there are two types of endogenous transaction cost in the sequential equilibrium model. *Type A endogenous transaction cost* is associated with the information distortion in the pooling equilibrium where the incapable managers successfully cheat the client by pretending to be capable. *Type B endogenous transaction cost* is a "convincing cost," incurred in the screening equilibrium in a situation in which the client may not believe the capable managers even if they tell the truth. The capable managers must sacrifice utility by driving BMWs in order to convince the client. The convincing cost would not be necessary if the incapable managers did not cheat; that is, if information asymmetry were absent. The concepts of perfect Bayes equilibrium and sequential equilibrium are useful vehicles for the analysis of endogenous transaction costs because information asymmetry creates scope for cheating and other opportunistic behaviors that cause endogenous transaction costs.

This sequential equilibrium model has a flavor of adverse selection (see chapter 9 for the definition of the concept) when the number of incapable managers is greater, it is more likely that information distortion may be avoided by a screening equilibrium; when the number is smaller, a pooling equilibrium with information distortion is more likely to take place. This model can be interpreted in various ways to suit specific applications. For instance, brands of cars can be interpreted as different levels of expenditure on advertisement that can be used by a producer to signal private information about his financial and production capacity, while a client can be interpreted as a potential buyer of his products. Hence, this model can be used to explain why advertisement expenditure is much higher than the level that is enough to transmit information about goods to the potential buyers. According to the model, if the advertisement expenditure is not high enough, then capable and incapable producers all can afford advertisement. Then the potential buyers cannot tell the capable from the incapable by observing the advertisement. Again, the high advertisement expenditure is a convincing cost. The client can also be interpreted as a banker who tries to distinguish the good investment projects from the bad ones or as an employer who wants to distinguish the capable candidates for the job from the incapable ones, while brands can be interpreted as education levels of the candidates.

This convincing mechanism in the screening equilibrium is sometimes called commitment mechanism. This kind of commitment game model has recently been applied to analyze endogenous transaction costs in economic transition from the socialist system to the capitalist one (see Dewatripont and Maskin's commitment game model in example 9.8 of chapter 9, and the surveys of Maskin and Xu, 1999 and Roland, 2000). Also, a model of this type can be used to show that the distortion caused by information asymmetry may offset the distortions caused by other opportunisms, such as that caused by monopoly (see exercise 19).

## Key Terms and Review

General equilibrium, the three types of partial equilibrium analysis.

Comparative statics of general equilibrium, and differences between this and the comparative statics of decisions and the comparative statics of the three types of partial equilibrium.

Equilibrium implications of production functions with CRS, DRS, and LIRS.

Sufficient conditions for the existence of equilibrium; why they may not be necessary.

Marginal vs. inframarginal comparative statics of general equilibrium.

Pareto optimality and the first welfare theorems.

Implications of Walras's law for general equilibrium analysis.

How we can make sure a general equilibrium model is closed, and why this is important.

Games, game rules, players, strategies, outcomes, pay-off functions.
The strategic form and extensive form of a game.
Perfect (imperfect) information vs. complete (incomplete) information.
Nash equilibrium, subgame perfect equilibrium, Bayes equilibrium, and sequential equilibrium.

## Further Reading

*General equilibrium analysis, comparative statics, and welfare implications*: Walras (1954), Mas-Collell et al. (1995, chs. 10, 15, 16, 17), Varian (1992, chs. 13, 17, 18), Debreu (1959); *Type I partial equilibrium analysis*: Marshall (1890), Mas-Collell et al. (1995); *Type II and Type III partial equilibrium analysis*: Dixit and Norman (1980), Mas-Collell et al. (1995, sec. 15.D); *the existence theorem*: Arrow and Debreu (1954), Debreu (1959); *the first welfare theorem*: Mas-Collell et al. (1995).

*A good introduction to game theory*: Dixit and Nalebuff (1991, pp. 7–84) and Gibbons (1992); *intermediate treatments of the Nash game and Nash equilibrium with pure strategies*: Kreps (1990, p. 328), Fudenberg and Tirole (1991, p. 14); *Nash equilibrium with mixed strategies*: Fudenberg and Tirole (1991, pp. 18–19), Kreps (1990, ch. 11), Fudenberg and Tirole (1991, ch. 2), Tirole (1989, ch. 11), Osborne and Rubinstein (1990); *Bayesian games*: Dixit and Nalebuff (1991, ch. 2), Tirole (1989, ch. 11), Kreps (1990, ch. 13), Fudenberg and Tirole (1991, ch. 6) (test: you should be able to duplicate the algebra of the model in Kreps, 1990, p. 468; see exercise 19, or Fundenberg and Tirole, 1991, p. 215); *subgame perfect equilibrium, or perfect equilibrium*: Dixit and Nalebuff (1991, chs. 6 and 11), Tirole (1989, ch. 11), Kreps (1990, secs. 12.7 and 15.3), Fudenberg and Tirole (1991, ch. 4) (test: you should be able to duplicate the algebra of the model in Kreps, 1990, p. 556, or in Tirole, 1989, pp. 430–1, Fudenberg and Tirole, 1991, Ch. 2); *Alternating-offer bargaining models*: Tirole (1989, p. 430), Osborne and Rubinstein (1990); *sequential equilibrium or perfect Bayesian equilibrium*: Tirole (1989, pp. 436–44), Kreps (1990, secs. 12.7 and 13.2), Fudenberg and Tirole (1991, Ch. 8) (Test: You should be able to duplicate the algebra of the model in Kreps, 1990, pp. 469–80, or exercise 19 in this chapter, or Tirole, 1989, pp. 439–41); *repeated game and reputation*: Fudenberg and Tirole (1991, sec. 4.3), ch. 9 of this text, Tirole (1989, sec. 6.3), Kreps (1990, sec. 14.2) (test: you should be able to duplicate the algebra of the model in Kreps, 1990, pp. 509–12, or in Tirole, 1989, pp. 247–51); *a proof of Nash's existence theorem of mixed strategy Nash equilibrium*: Fudenberg and Tirole (1991, sec. 1.3).

## QUESTIONS

1  What are the differences in procedure in solving for equilibrium in models with CRS, DRS, and LIRS technology?

2  What is the trade-off between generality of the functional forms and generality of model structure in the existence theorem?

3  Why is the analysis of comparative statics, welfare implications, and the existence of equilibrium based on an *ad hoc* system of excess demand functions misleading?

4  Some economists call a consumer's optimum decision "consumer's equilibrium." Analyze why this term might be misleading in connection with the difference between decisions and general equilibrium.

5  Since the first-order conditions for the PMP are enough to determine equilibrium-relative prices of goods and factors in a model with CRS technology, the relationship between the prices of goods and the

prices of factors can be sorted out without consideration of consumers' decisions. Stolper and Samuelson use this feature of the models with CRS technology to show that as the price of capital intensive goods increases, the price of capital will rise too. Discuss the flaws of Type II partial equilibrium analysis.

6   Because of the features of models with CRS technology discussed in Q1, Heckscher and Ohlin assume that the prices of factors are fixed at constant levels and then work out the comparative statics of Type II partial equilibrium from the first-order conditions for the PMP without consideration of consumers' decisions. Discuss the flaws of this comparative statics analysis.

7   Use example 4.1 to explain why the following statement is wrong from the point view of general equilibrium. If we have observed from the market equilibrium that the quantity demanded of good 1 increases as the price of good 2 falls, then the two goods are complements (cross price elasticity of the two goods is negative).

8   Use example 4.1 to explain why the following statement is wrong from the the the point of view of general equilibrium. If we have observed from the market equilibria that the quantity demanded of good 1 increases by 0.5 percent as its price falls by 1 percent, then the own price elasticity of substitution of this good is 0.5.

9   Why do the concepts of substitution effect and income effect make no sense for the analysis of comparative statics of general equilibrium (for instance, how do the price and the quantity demanded of a good and income in equilibrium change in response to a change in the taste parameter of that good)?

10   Why can rational behavior generate coordination failure? Why may a coordination failure between two players be a coordination success for society as a whole? Why may the Nash equilibrium in a noncooperative game converge to a Walrasian equilibrium if the number of players tends to infinity and free entry is allowed?

11   What is the trade-off between generality of game rules and generality of other aspects of a model in specifying an equilibrium model? Why do economists specify ad hoc demand functions and use misleading partial equilibrium analysis in game models?

12   Why can the Bayes equilibrium model and sequential equilibrium generate significantly higher explanatory power than the Walrasian equilibrium model?

13   What are the differences and connections between interplay of quantities and prices in a Walrasian equilibrium model, and interplay of information and dynamic strategies in a sequential equilibrium model?

# EXERCISES

1   Suppose a representative consumer's utility function is $u = a\ln x + (1 - a)\ln y$, where $a \in (0, 1)$, $x$ is the amount of a consumption good and $y$ is the amount of leisure. The consumer is endowed with one unit of time for working and leisure. A representative firm producing good x has the production function with DRS: $x = L^b$ where $b \in (0, 1)$. Find the equilibrium price of good x in terms of labor, and the equilibrium quantities of x and y. What are the effects of a change in the taste parameter $a$ or the productivity parameter $b$ on the equilibrium-relative price, quantities, incomes from labor and dividend, and per capita real income?

2   Suppose that in the model of exercise 1 a tax rate $t$ is imposed on each dollar received by the representative firm from sale of goods. Then the government transfers tax revenue to the

representative consumer. What are the effects of the tax on the equilibrium prices, quantity, and per capita real income? (Hint: the budget constraint for the consumer is $px = \pi + (1 - y) + R$, where $\pi$ is the dividend from ownership of the firm, $R = tpx$ is tax revenue that is transferred from the government to the consumer. The equilibrium price is $p/w = a^{1-b}/(1 - t)^b b^b[1 - a + ab(1 - t)]^{1-b}$, $x = \{ab(1 - t)/[1 - a + ab(1 - t)]\}^b$, $y = (1 - a)/[1 - a + ab(1 - t)]$, $R$ is exogenous to the consumer.) If the tax is imposed on each dollar of goods consumed and then the tax revenue goes to the producer, what are the effects of the tax? If the tax is imposed on the profit of firms and the tax revenue goes to the consumer, will your answer change? If it is imposed on the wage that the firm pays and the tax revenue goes to the consumer, will your answer change? The distortion caused by the tax is referred to as *dead weight*. Such a tax is like an income transfer imposed by a benevolent and absolutely efficient government (all tax revenue goes back to the consumers with no bureaucracy cost). Explain why this income transfer causes dead weights.

3   Consider a model with the same utility function as in exercise 2; but $y$ is the consumption quantity of another good and there is no trade-off between leisure and consumption. The production function for x is $x = bL_x$ and the production function for y is $y = L_y$. The representative consumer supplies one unit of labor. A tax rate $t$ is imposed on each dollar sold by the representative firms producing x and y, respectively, and all tax revenue goes to the consumer. Solve for the general equilibrium and analyze the impacts of the tax on all endogenous variables. Why will the tax not cause distortions in resource allocation? Suppose that the tax rate differs between the two goods: analyze the welfare implications of the tax. In some textbooks, a graph is used to show that a tax on firms with horizontal supply curves will not cause dead weight. Use the model with differential tax rates to show that partial equilibrium analysis based on the graph might be misleading. Use this example to discuss the limitation of conventional graphs used in economics textbooks. If a tax is imposed on the wage paid by firms, are the welfare implications of the tax different in the general equilibrium analysis?

4   Use the concept of Pareto optimality to analyze the welfare implications of all types of tax in exercises 2 and 3. Specify a benevolent dictator's decision problem that maximizes the consumer's utility subject to the transformation function with respect to $x$ and $y$. The problem yields the Pareto optimum resource allocation. Show that the Pareto optimum requires that the marginal rate of substitution between x and y in consumption equals the marginal rate of transformation in production. Compare your conclusion with the second welfare theorem which claims that for a Pareto efficient allocation in which each consumer is endowed with strictly positive amounts of each good, where preferences are convex, continuous, and nonsatiated, and where firms' production sets are convex, there exists an endowment transfer scheme through which the Pareto optimum allocation can be achieved by a Walrasian equilibrium price vector $p \neq 0$ (see Mas Collell et al., 1995, pp. 552–4, or Varian, 1992, p. 346).

5   The utility functions of consumers 1 and 2 are, respectively, $u_1 = a\ln x_1 + (1 - a)\ln y_1$ and $u_2 = \text{Min } \{x_2, by_2\}$. Consumer 1 is endowed with 1 unit of goods x and y, respectively, and consumer 2 is endowed with 2 units of good y. What is the general equilibrium and its comparative statics? Specify a constrained maximization problem: Max: $u_1$ s.t. $u_2 = u_0$, with respect to $x_i$ and $y_i$. The solution of this problem gives a Pareto optimum resource allocation for a given constant $u_0$. Show that the Pareto optimum requires that the marginal rate of substitution is equal for all consumers. Compare the first-order conditions for the problem with the conditions for the equilibrium to show that the equilibrium is Pareto optimal. If $u_1 = a\ln x_1 + (1 - a)\ln y_1 + c\ln y_2$ where $c$ is a jealousy parameter for $c < 0$ and a charity parameter for $c > 0$, show that the equilibrium is not Pareto optimal because of the externality in consumption.

6    Suppose that in the model in exercise 6, $u_1 = a\ln x_1 + y_1$. Solve for equilibrium and identify the interval of parameter values within which a corner equilibrium (consumer 1 consumes only one good) takes place. Assume now $u_1 = a\ln x_1$ and consumer 1 is endowed with 1 unit of good x. Show that Walrasian equilibrium does not exist. Which assumption for the existence of equilibrium is not met?

7    Consider an economy with $l$ consumers, two representative firms, two goods, and two factors. Each consumer has the Cobb–Douglas utility function $u = a\ln x + (1 - a)\ln y$ and is endowed with 1 unit of labor and $k/l$ units of capital. The firm producing good x has the production function $x = L_x^\alpha K_x^{1-\alpha}$ and the firm producing good y has the production function $y = L_y^\beta K_y^{1-\beta}$. Solve for the general equilibrium. Work out the comparative statics of the general equilibrium. Show that when $\alpha > \beta$ (the x sector is labor intensive) the relative price of goods $p_x/p_y$ and the relative price of factors $w/r$ fall and the relative output of the two goods $x/y$ goes up as $l/k$ rises. Jones (1965) has shown that $p_x/p_y$ increases as $l/k$ rises by assuming a fixed $r/w$. Use your comparative statics of the general equilibrium to show that $r/w$ cannot be a constant as $l/k$ changes even if all firms are price takers. Stolper and Samuelson have shown that $r/w$ increases as $p_x/p_y$ rises from the first-order conditions for firms' PMP. Use your comparative statics of the general equilibrium to show that $r/w$ rises and $p_x/p_y$ falls as $\beta$ rises if $\beta$ is sufficiently close to 0. Why have Stolper and Samuelson made an incorrect prediction for this case? Rybcszynski has shown that $x/y$ rises as $l/k$ increases by assuming fixed $p_x/p_y$ and $w/r$. Why is his analytical approach not correct from a general equilibrium view? Show that Rybcszynski's approach may generate a wrong prediction. Hint: the equilibrium is $p_x/p_y = A^{\alpha-\beta}B$, $w/r = A$, $x/y = a\,A^{\alpha-\beta}B/(1-a)$, where $A \equiv [\beta + a(\alpha - \beta)]k/[1 - \beta - a(\alpha - \beta)]l$ and $B \equiv (1 - \beta)^{1-\beta}\beta^\beta/(1 - \alpha)^{1-\alpha}\alpha^\alpha$. Consider inframarginal comparative statics of equilibrium and discuss why it is misleading to focus on marginal comparative statics.

8    Consider an economy with $M$ identical consumers equipped with utility function $u = x + a\ln y$, where $a$ is any positive constant, $x$ is the amount of the consumption good, and $y$ is the amount of time for leisure. Each consumer is endowed with 1 unit of time and 1 unit of capital. Each of $N$ identical firms has the production function $x = AL_x^\alpha K_x^{1-\alpha}$. Solve for equilibrium and its comparative statics. Discuss the equilibrium implications of the number of firms, $N$, population size, $M$, tastes for leisure, $a$, total factor productivity, $A$, and marginal productivity parameter of labor, $\alpha$, for equilibrium relative price, demand for goods, supply of labor, and per capita real income. Discuss the differences between inframarginal and marginal comparative statics of equilibrium and between general equilibrium analysis and Type III partial equilibrium analysis. Hint: There are several partial equilibria for different values of $a$. The general equilibrium discontinuously jumps between the partial equilibria as parameters reach some critical values. Review example 4.1 before trying to solve for the equilibrium.

9    Consider an economy with two consumers equipped with utility functions $u_1 = a\ln x_1 + (1 - a)\ln y_1 - \ln y_2$, $u_2 = a\ln x_2 + (1 - a)\ln y_2 - \ln y_1$, respectively, where $x_i$ and $y_i$ are the respective amounts of two consumption goods of consumer i. Each consumer is endowed with 1 unit of working time. The production function of a representative firm producing x is $X = bL_x$ and the production function of a representative firm producing y is $Y = L_y$. The government imposes a tax rate $t$ on each dollar of sales of good y and then evenly distributes returns $\beta tR$ to consumer 1, where $R$ is total tax revenue and $\beta \in (0,1)$ is a bureaucracy efficiency coefficient. Suppose that a democratic process forces the government to choose $t$ to maximize total utility of society. Find the Pareto optimum tax rate.

10   Consider an economy with $M$ identical consumers. Each of them has the utility function $u = x^a y^{1-a}$ and is endowed with one unit of labor and one unit of capital. A representative firm

producing x has the production function $x = L_x^\alpha K_x^{1-\alpha}$ and a representative firm producing y has the production function $y = L_y^\alpha K_y^{1-\alpha}$. If each consumer receives income from rent of capital $r$, what is the general equilibrium? If $K_x$ and $K_y$ are given constants and are possessed by firms, and each consumer has an equal share of each firm, what is the general equilibrium? What is the difference between the two ways of closing the model by specifying the initial distribution of endowments and ownership?

11 Consider an economy as in example 4.1. Now leisure is added to the model, so that the utility function is $u = x^\alpha y^\beta z^\gamma$, where $x$ and $y$ are the respective amounts of the two consumption goods, $z$ is the amount of time for leisure, and the taste parameters satisfy $\alpha + \beta + \gamma = 1$. Each consumer has $t$ units of time for work and leisure. Hence, her income from working is $w(t-z)$. Verify that the general equilibrium relative prices are: $r/w = \alpha at/k[1 - \alpha a - \beta(1 - b)]$, $p_y/w = \{\beta bt M/N_y[1 - \alpha a - \beta(1 - b)]\}^{1-b}/b$, $p_x/w = \{\alpha/[1 - \alpha a - \beta(1 - b)]\}^z/(1 - a)^{(1-a)}$. Solve for the equilibrium quantities and the comparative statics. Compare the comparative statics with Marshall's comparative statics of partial equilibrium and analyze why Marshall's partial equilibrium analysis is misleading. Analyze the impact of changes in parameters on the demand and supply of labor in equilibrium.

12 Consider a first-price sealed-bid auction of an object with two bidders. Each bidder $i$'s evaluation of the object is $v_i$, which is known to both bidders. The auction rules are that each player submits a bid in a sealed envelope. The envelopes are then opened, and the bidder who has submitted the highest bid gets the object and pays the auctioneer the amount of her bid. If the bidders submit the same bid, each gets the object with probability 0.5. Bids must be in dollar multiples (assume that valuations are also). Is there a Nash equilibrium? What is it? Is it unique?

13 Consider a bargaining situation in which two individuals are considering undertaking a business venture that will earn them 100 dollars in profit, but they must agree on how to split the 100 dollars. Bargaining works as follows: The two individuals each make a demand simultaneously. If their demands sum to more than 100 dollars, then they fail to agree, and each gets nothing. If their demands sum to less than 100 dollars, they do the project, each gets his demand, and the rest goes to charity. What is the pure strategy Nash equilibrium of this game?

14 In a Rubinstein alternating offer bargaining game with an infinite decision horizon, two players divide a dollar. Player 1 makes an offer $1 - x_1$ to player 2 (or he claims proportion $x_1$ of the dollar) in period 1, then player 2 decides if she takes this offer. If she does, the game ends and player 1 gets $x_1$ and player 2 gets $1 - x_1$. If she rejects the offer, she can make a counter-offer $x_2$ in period 2. Then player 1 decides if he takes the counter-offer. If he does not, he can make another offer in period 3, and so on. Each player's discount factor is $\delta$. Solve for the subgame perfect equilibrium in the bargaining game. Who gets more from the equilibrium and why? Suppose the discount factor $\delta$ differs between the two players. Who gets more under what conditions? Why?

15 Consider the first-price sealed-bid auction of exercise 12, but now suppose that each bidder $i$ observes only her own valuation $v_i$. This valuation is distributed uniformly and independently on $[0, \bar{v}]$ for each bidder. Derive a symmetric Bayesian Nash equilibrium for this auction. Bids can be any real number and an equilibrium bid of bidder $i$ is a linear function of her valuation.

16 Battle of the sexes. The two players wish to go to an event together, but disagree about whether to go to a football game or the ballet. Each player gets a utility of 2 if both go to his or her preferred event, a utility of 1 if both go to the other's preferred event, and 0 if the two are unable to agree and stay home or go out individually. Suppose the two players agree to

randomize their choices to make sure it is fair for both players to stay in the game. So he chooses the football game with probability $p_1$ such that her expected utility is indifferent between the choices of football game and ballet, and she chooses the ballet with probability $p_2$ such that his expected utility is indifferent between the two choices. Show that there are two pure strategy Nash equilibria and solve for the mixed strategy Nash equilibrium. Nash uses a fixed point argument to prove that for any mixed strategy Nash game, there exists a Nash equilibrium.

17  Suppose in the Nash (Cournot) equilibrium model in example 4.5, the demand function $p = a-bx$ involves uncertainties. With probability $\rho$, $a = \theta_h$ and with probability $1 - \rho$, $a = \theta_l$. Firm 2 has private information about the realized value of $a$ after Nature has chosen this. But firm 1 has only common knowledge about $a$. Solve for the Bayes equilibrium. If it is $b$ instead of $a$ that involves uncertainty, what is your answer?

18  Consider the Bayes game model in example 4.7 again. Assume that information asymmetry is symmetric between the two firms: $c_i$ involves uncertainties for $i = 1, 2$ and firm $i$ has complete information about $c_i$ but has incomplete information about $c_j$. The distribution function for $c_1$ and $c_2$ is the same as specified in example 4.7. Use the symmetry of information asymmetry to solve for the Bayes equilibrium.

19  The entry deterrence game from Kreps, 1990, and Milgrom and Roberts, 1982: In a dynamic game with information asymmetry, there are two players. Player 1 is an incumbent firm producing a good, called the insider. Player 2 is a potential entrant into the business, called the outsider. The inverse demand function of the good is $p = 9 - x$. The insider's cost function is $\theta x + 2.25$, where $\theta = 3$ with probability $\rho$ and $\theta = 1$ with probability $1 - \rho$. The insider knows the realization of $\theta$, but the outsider does not. The outsider's cost function, $3x + 2.25$, is common knowledge to all players. In period 1, the insider chooses an output level which will give the outsider some signal about the type of the insider, which will in turn affect the outsider's decision concerning entry in period 2. The outsider maximizes her expected profit in period 2 with respect to quantity to produce and decides whether to enter the sector for given information updated from observation of the insider's output in period 1. The insider maximizes total profit over the two periods with respect to his output levels in the two periods. He is the monopolist in period 1 and again in period 2 if the outsider does not get into the business then. The two firms have a Cournot equilibrium in period 2 if the outsider gets into the business in period 2. Find the two firms' output levels in the two periods, the posterior probability $\mu(p_1)$ for $\theta = 3$ when the outsider has seen the market price in period 1, $p_1$, the market prices over the two periods in the pooling equilibrium and screening equilibrium for the relevant interval of values of $\rho$. What is the outsider's decision concerning entry upon observation of the insider's output level in period 1? Analyze under what conditions and why information asymmetry may reduce distortions caused by monopoly when it generates endogenous transaction costs.

20  Suppose that the cost function and demand function in a Bertrand model are the same as in the Cournot model in example 4.5, but the two firms' strategies are to choose prices rather than quantities. Solve for the Nash equilibrium and prove that it is Pareto optimal.

# part III

# THE NEW CLASSICAL FRAMEWORK

# chapter 5

# Consumer-producers' Decisions to Choose the Optimum Level and Pattern of Specialization

♦ **5.1 The New Classical Framework and Transaction Costs**

Because the neoclassical framework does not endogenize individuals' levels of specialization, the size of the network of division of labor, and the degree of interpersonal dependency, the general equilibrium implications of transaction costs cannot be fully explored there. However, in the new classical framework with consumer-producers, economies of specialization, and transaction costs, the general equilibrium implication of transaction costs is a main theme. This theme is explored through an investigation of the trade-off between economies of specialization and transaction costs.

There are many ways to specify transaction costs. One general specification of transaction costs is to assume a delivery function of goods such that the amount of goods that arrives at the destination is a function of the amount of goods that departs from the origin, and of other inputs essential for the delivery (see Hahn, 1971 and Kurz, 1974). The delivery function describes the technical conditions governing transactions. The difference between the amounts of goods at the origin and at the destination, together with any inputs employed in the delivery process, can be considered as transaction costs. This specification of transaction costs involves a notoriously unmanageable set of indices of destinations and origins. This index set, compounded with corner solutions, makes it impossible to work out the comparative statics of general equilibrium. Thus the general equilibrium implications of transaction costs in the models with this otherwise appealing specification of transaction costs cannot be explored. Hence, a specification of so-called iceberg transaction cost is often used to work out the general equilibrium implications of transaction costs.

In a system involving iceberg transaction costs, an individual receives the fraction $k$ when she buys one unit of a good, or pays one dollar when she buys goods with value of

$k$ dollars, where $k \in [0, 1]$. If sellers of goods pay transaction costs, then they receive the fraction $k$ of each dollar paid by the buyers. These specifications imply that the fraction $1 - k$ of goods or their value disappears in transit because of transaction costs. These transaction costs can take the form, for example, of transportation costs, costs in implementing transactions, storage costs, and costs caused by nonpunctual delivery. However, the transaction cost coefficient $1 - k$ is considered an *exogenous transaction cost* that can be seen before individuals have made their decisions.

There are two common definitions of *endogenous transaction cost*. According to the more *general definition*, all transaction costs whose levels can be seen only after individuals have made their decisions are considered endogenous. In new classical models with iceberg transaction costs, although the transaction cost coefficient $1 - k$ is exogenous, the total transaction cost for each consumer-producer, and thus for society, is endogenous in terms of this general definition, since the number of transactions is endogenized in the new classical framework.

The second, narrower, definition of endogenous transaction cost relates to a *specific type of endogenous transaction costs*, namely those that are caused by a departure of general equilibrium from the Pareto optimum. Hereafter it is this second definition of endogenous transaction cost that we adopt unless otherwise indicated. Endogenous transaction cost is the focus of chapters 9, 12, and 17.

In Part III, we use a simple new classical model to explain some basic concepts and to illustrate our approach to inframarginal analysis. Consider an economy with a continuum of *ex ante* identical consumer-producers with mass $M$.[1] This specification, together with the further assumption of economies of specialization that are localized increasing returns, implies that a Walrasian regime prevails in the economy. All decision-makers are price takers, and equilibrium prices are sorted out by a Walrasian auction mechanism. The assumption that individuals are *ex ante* identical is a very strong assumption, since we rarely see two persons exactly the same in the real world. However, as Smith indicated, many differences between different specialists that look like *ex ante* differences are in fact *ex post* differences which are acquired as individuals choose different occupations.

The assumption that individuals are *ex ante* identical helps to highlight an important merit of the new classical framework. In neoclassical theory, if all individuals are *ex ante* identical in all aspects, the economic stories will be too trivial to make any sense to us. But we shall show that within the new classical framework, even if all individuals are *ex ante* identical in all aspects, *ex post* differences will emerge endogenously from the evolution of division of labor. This enables many interesting stories to be told that cannot be predicted by neoclassical economics, such as the emergence of professional middlemen, money, business cycles, unemployment, the firm, and a hierarchical structure of production and transactions. These all result from the evolution of division of labor, even in the absence of *ex ante* differences between individuals. The implications of *ex ante* and *ex post* differences between individuals for the equilibrium level of division of labor will be explored in chapters 12 and 13.

## Questions to Ask Yourself when Reading this Chapter

♦  Why is the decision problem to choose an occupation configuration and level of specialization much more complicated than the decision problem to allocate resources for a given occupation configuration?

---

♦ Why are demand and supply two sides of the division of labor?

♦ Why is it inappropriate to separate the analysis of demand and supply from the analysis of individuals' decision-making in choosing levels of specialization?

♦ What is the difference between marginal analysis of problems of resource allocation and inframarginal analysis of problems of organization?

♦ Why did Young claim that the extent of the market and level of division of labor are two sides of the same coin?

---

## ♦ 5.2 Configurations and Corner Solutions in the New Classical Framework

### Example 5.1: a simple new classical model

In this chapter, we assume that the set of consumer-producers is a continuum with mass $M$. This implies that the population size in the economy is very large. Hence, we will not have an integer problem of the numbers of different specialists, which may lead to non-existence of the equilibrium with the division of labor. Each consumer-producer has the following utility function.

$$u = (x + kx^d)(y + ky^d) \tag{5.1}$$

where $x$ and $y$ are respective amounts of goods x and y that are self-provided, $x^d$ and $y^d$ are respective amounts of the two goods that are purchased from the market, $1 - k$ is the iceberg transaction cost coefficient, or $k$ is an exogenous trading efficiency coefficient, which represents the conditions governing transactions. $k$ relates to infrastructure conditions, degree of urbanization, transportation conditions, and the general institutional environment.

Each consumer-producer's production functions and endowment constraint are

$$x + x^s = l_x^a, \qquad y + y^s = l_y^a, \qquad a > 1 \tag{5.2.a}$$

$$l_x + l_y = 1. \tag{5.2.b}$$

where $x^s$ and $y^s$ are respective amounts of the two goods sold, $l_i$ is an individual's share of labor allocated to the production of good i, and thus represents her *level of specialization* in producing good i. Her budget constraint is

$$p_x x^s + p_y y^s = p_x x^d + p_y y^d \tag{5.3}$$

where $p_i$ is the price of good i. Hence, the left-hand side of (5.3) is income from the market and the right-hand side is expenditure. Since corner solutions are allowed, we have the nonnegativity constraint

$$x, x^s, x^d, y, y^s, y^d, l_x, l_y \geq 0. \tag{5.4}$$

This constraint distinguishes the nonlinear programming from the classical mathematical programming. Each consumer-producer maximizes utility in (5.1) with respect to $x$, $x^s$, $x^d$, $y$, $y^s$, $y^d$, $l_x$, $l_y$ subject to the production conditions given by (5.2), the budget constraint (5.3), and the nonnegativity constraint (5.4). Since $l_x$ and $l_y$ are not independent of the values of the other decision variables, each of the 6 decision variables $x$, $x^s$, $x^d$, $y$, $y^s$, $y^d$ can take on 0 and positive values. When a decision variable takes on a value of 0, a *corner solution* is chosen.

Table 5.1 lists several possible profiles of zero and positive values of the 6 decision variables. The number of all possible profiles is $2^6 = 64$. Since the local optimum decisions are discontinuous across the profiles, there is no method that can be used to solve for the optimum decision in one step. A general procedure in solving for this kind of nonlinear programming problem is as follows. First, the Kuhn–Tucker theorem and other conditions for optimum decisions are used to rule out as many profiles as possible. Then, marginal analysis is applied to each of the remaining candidates for the optimum decision. Finally, the local maximum values of the objective function are compared across the candidates to identify the globally optimum decision. This is referred to as *inframarginal analysis*. Let us take the first step, which is to prove the following theorem.

**Theorem 5.1:** The optimum decision does not involve selling more than one good, does not involve selling and buying the same good, and does not involve buying and producing the same good.

This theorem is referred to as the *Wen theorem*. Though Yang (1988) is the first economist to have proved this theorem for some new classical general equilibrium models with specific utility and production functions, Wen proves this theorem for a class of new classical general equilibrium models with general utility and production functions (see Wen, 1998). A more general proof of the Wen theorem is provided in chapter 13. We will use the theorem frequently in this text.

*Proof Claim 1: The optimum decision does not involve selling and buying the same good.*
Substituting the budget constraint (5.3) for $x^s$ in (5.2a) and eliminating $x$ in (5.1) with (5.2a) yields

$$u = \{l_x^a - [x^d + p_y(y^d - y^s)/p_x] + kx^d\}(y + ky^d).$$

**Table 5.1:** Profiles of zero and positive values of the six decision variables

| $x$ | $x^d$ | $x^s$ | $y$ | $y^d$ | $y^s$ |
|-----|-------|-------|-----|-------|-------|
| + | + | + | + | + | + |
| 0 | + | + | 0 | + | + |
| 0 | + | 0 | 0 | + | + |
| + | 0 | 0 | 0 | + | + |
| • | • | • | • | • | • |
| + | 0 | 0 | 0 | 0 | + |
| 0 | 0 | 0 | 0 | 0 | + |

Differentiating this expression with respect to $x^d$ yields

$$\frac{\partial u}{\partial x^d} < 0 \ \forall \ x^d > 0.$$

According to the Kuhn–Tucker condition, this implies that when $x$, $x^s > 0$, the optimum value of $x^d$ is 0. Hence, $x^d$ and $x^s$ cannot be positive at the same time. Following the same deduction, but eliminating $y^s$ and $y$ instead of $x^s$ and $x$, it can be shown that $y^d$ and $y^s$ cannot be positive at the same time.

*Claim 2: The optimum decision does not involve buying and producing the same good.*
    Suppose $x^d > 0$. It follows from Claim 1 that $x^s = 0$. From the budget constraint, it follows that $y^s > 0$, if $x^s = 0$. We can then use Claim 1 again to obtain that $y^d = 0$, if $y^s > 0$. A positive utility requires $y > 0$. Now plugging the budget constraint and the production function of y into the utility function yields

$$u = \left\{ x + k \left[ \left( 1 - x^{\frac{1}{a}} \right)^a - y \right] \frac{p_y}{p_x} \right\} y$$

Differentiating $u$ twice yields

$$\frac{\partial^2 u}{\partial x^2} > 0 \ \forall \ x > 0.$$

This violates the second-order condition of the interior maximum point of $x$. Hence, the optimum $x$ is at a corner: either $x = 0$, or $x = l_x^a = 1$. $x = 1$ is incompatible with a positive $y$ which is required by a positive utility. Therefore, the optimum value of $x$ is zero if $x^d > 0$.

*Claim 3: An individual sells at most one good.*
    Let's use an argument of negation. Suppose Claim 3 does not hold. An individual sells two goods, that is $x^s$, $y^s > 0$. It follows from Claim 1 that $x^d = y^d = 0$. This violates the budget constraint since the individual sells, but does not buy. Therefore, it is impossible that $x^s$, $y^s > 0$.

Claims 1–3 suffice to establish Theorem 5.1. *Q.E.D.*

The Wen theorem is intuitive. Selling and buying the same good involves unnecessary transaction costs and therefore is inefficient. Selling two goods is also inefficient since it prevents the full exploitation of economies of specialization.
    The Wen theorem, together with the budget constraint and the requirement that utility be positive, can be used to reduce the number of candidates for the optimum decision radically from 64 to only 3. For instance, the first profile of zero and positive values of the 6 decision variables in table 5.1 is associated with the unique interior solution. This profile, which involves selling and buying the same good, obviously violates the Wen theorem. This implies that in the new classical framework, an interior solution cannot be optimal, so that the marginal analysis for the interior solution is not applicable. The second, third, and fourth profiles violate claim 1 in the Wen theorem, while the fifth and sixth profiles violate the budget constraint and the requirement for a positive utility level.

A profile of zero and positive values of the decision variables that is compatible with the Wen theorem is called *a decision configuration*. Note that the concept of decision configuration differs from the concept of production pattern. The former involves a profile of zero and positive values of quantities of goods that are self-provided, produced, sold, and purchased, while the latter involves only a profile of zero and positive values of quantities of different goods that are produced. The notion of occupation configuration can be virtualized from the *Dictionary of Occupational Titles*. In its 1939 edition, there were 17,500 occupational titles. In 1977, 2,100 occupational titles were added, and in 1996, 840 more were added. In 1991, a new section including many computer-related occupations was added. As population is divided among the occupation configurations, a certain structure of division of labor for society as a whole occurs.

The concepts of decision configuration and structure of decision configurations are essential for us to solve for a new classical equilibrium. For simplicity, hereafter we mean decision configuration when we say configuration. For each configuration, there is a corner solution. Each individual applies marginal analysis to solve for a corner solution in a configuration. Each corner solution gives the optimum resource allocation for a given level and pattern of specialization. Then each individual conducts total cost–benefit analysis across configurations to choose the optimum corner solution.

To choose the optimum configuration is to choose the optimum level and pattern of specialization. This involves the decision whether or not to engage in a certain activity. This is a decision about yes or no. The marginal analysis for each corner solution is to allocate resources between those activities that an individual has already decided to engage in. It is a decision about how much, after a person has already said "yes" to the first type of question. As your career develops, you will see that your peers will have very different lives according to their different occupations. To choose an occupation, and a level of specialization in that chosen occupation (that relates to how many activities and subactivities a person does not engage in) is to choose an configuration. This choice of configuration usually has much more important consequences on a person's future life than does the degree of commitment to a given occupation. From your university experience in choosing a major and the fields in the major chosen, you can see the importance of such inframarginal decisions.

## ◆ 5.3 The Optimum Resource Allocation for a Given Level and Pattern of Specialization

There are three configurations that an individual needs to consider.

i) Autarky, or configuration A, is defined by $x, y, l_x, l_y > 0$, $x^s = x^d = y^s = y^d = 0$.

This configuration implies that all quantities of goods that are self-provided are positive and all quantities of goods that are traded are zero. The decision problem for configuration A is

$$\text{Max} : u = xy \qquad\qquad\qquad (5.5a)$$
$$\scriptsize x,y,l_x,l_y$$

s.t. $x = l_x^a$, $\qquad y = l_y^a$, $\qquad l_x + l_y + 1$.

Here, we have used the production function and working time constraint in (5.2). Inserting all constraints into the utility function, (5.5a) can be converted to the following nonconstrained maximization problem.

$$\text{Max}_{l_x} : u = l_x^a (1 - l_x)^a \tag{5.5b}$$

Figure 5.1 shows that $x$ increases more than proportionally as $l_x$ increases, since $x = l_x^a$, $dx/dl_x = al_x^{a-1} > 0$ and $d^2x/dl_x^2 = a(a-1)l_x^{a-1} > 0$. Note the correspondence between the expression "increases more than proportionally" in natural language, a convex upward sloping curve in graphical terms, and the expression "$dx/dl_x = al_x^{a-1} > 0$ and $d^2 x/dl_x^2 = a(a-1) l_x^{a-2} > 0$" in mathematical language. You should repeatedly practice such translations between the three language systems until you get used to thinking economics in mathematical language without the need for such translations. Similarly, $y = (1 - l_x )^a$ is represented by a convex downward sloping curve in the graph, because $dy/dl_x = -a(1 - l_x)^{a-1} < 0$ and $d^2y/dl_x^2 = a(a-1)(1 - l_x)^{a-2} > 0$. Here, the positive second-order derivative $d^2y/dl_x^2$ implies that $dy/dl_x$ increases as $l_x$ increases or that $|dy/dl_x| = -dy/dl_x$ decreases as $l_x$ increases. This, together with $dy/dl_x < 0$, implies that "$y$ decreases less than proportionally as $l_x$ increases." The sign of the first-order derivative determines whether the curve is upward or downward sloping and the sign of the second-order derivative determines whether the curve is concave or convex. By now, you should be able to translate very quickly between "$y$ decreases less than proportionally as $l_x$ increases," "$dy/dl_x < 0$ and $d^2y/dl_x^2 > 0$," and "a convex downward sloping curve in the graph."

From the decision problem (5.5), we can see the trade-off between quantities of labor allocated to the production of x and y. As $l_x$ increases, utility increases through an increase in $x = l_x^a$, but decreases through a decrease in $y = (1 - l_x)^a$. This implies that $u = xy = l_x^a (1 - l_x)^a$ may not be monotone in $l_x$, or $du/dl_x$ might be positive in an interval of $l_x$ and negative in another interval. In between the two intervals, $du/dl_x$ might be zero, which gives an interior extreme value of $u$ or an extreme point of $l_x$. In terms of natural language, this

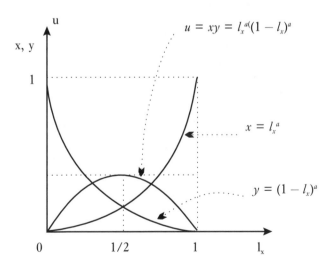

◆ **Figure 5.1**: The trade-off for maximization of utility

implies that there is a trade off in allocating labor between the production of x and the production of y.

In order to verify this, we totally differentiate $u$ with respect to $l_x$.

$$\frac{du}{dl_x} = \frac{\partial u}{\partial x}\frac{dx}{dl_x} + \frac{\partial u}{\partial y}\frac{dy}{dl_x} \tag{5.6}$$

where $\partial u/\partial x = y$ is the marginal utility of $x$, $\partial u/\partial y = x$ is the marginal utility of $y$, $dx/dl_x = al_x^{a-1}$ is marginal labor productivity in producing x, $dy/dl_x = -dy/dl_y = -al_y^{a-1} = -a(1-l_x)^{a-1}$, and $dy/dl_y$ is marginal labor productivity in producing y. Here, we have used the fact that a differentiation of the endowment constraint implies $dl_x = -dl_y$. $(\partial u/\partial x)(dx/dl_x)$, which can be considered as the marginal utility of labor allocated to the production of x, and $(\partial u/\partial y)(dy/dl_x) = -(\partial u/\partial y)(dy/dl_y)$, which can be considered as the negative of the marginal utility of labor allocated to the production of y. Let $du/dl_x$ in (5.6) equal zero. Then we obtain the first-order condition for interior maximization:

$$\frac{du}{dl_x} = \frac{\partial u}{\partial x}\frac{dx}{dl_x} + \frac{\partial u}{\partial y}\frac{dy}{dl_x} = \frac{\partial u}{\partial x}\frac{dx}{dl_x} - \frac{\partial u}{\partial y}\frac{dy}{dl_y} = 0, \quad \text{or} \tag{5.7a}$$

$$\frac{\partial u}{\partial x}\frac{dx}{dl_x} = \frac{\partial u}{\partial y}\frac{dy}{dl_y} \tag{5.7b}$$

Let us first figure out what is implied by $du/dl_x = 0$. From figure 5.2, it can be seen that this implies that $u$ is maximized when the tangent line of the curve representing the function $u = l_x^a(1-l_x)^a$ is horizontal. From $du/dl_x = al_x^{a-1}(1-l_x)^a - al_x^{a-1}(1-l_x)^{a-1} = 0$, it is straightforward that the optimum is $\frac{1}{2}$.

In terms of natural language, the marginal condition for the marginal analysis (3.7b) implies that the efficient trade-off is achieved when the marginal benefit in terms of the utility generated by an increase in the amount of labor allocated to the production of x, equals the marginal cost, measured by the utility sacrificed by the associated reduction in the amount of labor allocated to the production of y. Since the marginal utility of $l_x$ is $(\partial u/\partial x)(dx/dl_x) = y(dx/dl_x)$, which increases with $y$, and its marginal cost in terms of utility is $(\partial u/\partial y)(dy/dl_y) = x(dy/dl_y)$, which increases with $x$, or decreases with $y$ due to the endowment constraint, the marginal benefit of an increase in $l_x$ is greater than its marginal cost when $l_x$ and therefore $x$ is small ($y$ is large). Hence, an increase in $l_x$ can increase $u$. In terms of the graph in figure 5.2, the tangent line of the curve representing $u = l_x^a(1-l_x)^a$ is upward sloping when $l_x$ is small. Also, the marginal benefit of an increase in $l_x$ is smaller than its marginal cost when $l_x$ and therefore $x$ are large ($y$ is small). Hence, a decrease in $l_x$ can increase $u$. In terms of the graph, the tangent line of the curve representing $u$ is downward sloping when $l_x$ is large. When $l_x = \frac{1}{2}$, the marginal benefit equals the marginal cost and the tangent line of the curve representing $u$ is horizontal, any increase or decrease in $l_x$ would reduce $u$, so that $u$ is maximized at $l_x = \frac{1}{2}$.

The marginal analysis in terms of natural language is not efficient. As you get used to mathematical language, you can write down the first-order condition to sort out the efficient trade-off straight-way. But you should remember that the marginal analysis is relevant only if a configuration is given. It does not work for solving for the optimum configuration.

Inserting $l_x = \frac{1}{2}$ into $u = l_x^a(1 - l_x)^a$ yields the maximum value of utility that can be achieved in autarky, namely $u(A) = 2^{-2a}$, where $u(A)$ is called per capita real income in autarky. Economists often call utility real income.

The first-order condition tells you that $l_x = \frac{1}{2}$ is the interior extreme point, but does not tell you if it is the interior maximum or minimum point. If the curve of $u$ is convex, as shown by curve B in figure 5.2, rather than concave, then the first-order condition gives a minimum rather than a maximum point. For the nonconstrained maximization problem, the second-order condition is that at $l_x = \frac{1}{2}$, which is given by the first-order condition,

$$\frac{d^2u}{dl_x^2} = al_x^{a-1}(1 - l_x)^{a-1}\left[(a - 1)\left(\frac{1 - l_x}{l_x} + \frac{l_x}{1 - l_x}\right) - 2a\right] < 0.$$

This condition implies that the function $u = l_x^a (1 - l_x)^a$ is concave at $l_x = \frac{1}{2}$. It is easy to verify that the above inequality holds for $l_x = \frac{1}{2}$. If the utility function is associated with the convex curve B, then the second-order condition cannot hold. In terms of natural language, this means that there is no real trade-off for the decision problem. That is, the optimum decision is a corner solution, in which all labor should be allocated to the production of either x or y. In the real world, some resource allocation problems, for a given level and pattern of division of labor, do not actually involve a real trade-off, despite appearances to the contrary, because the second-order condition for the interior optimum is not satisfied. In this circumstance, the compromise between the conflicting forces that is given by the first-order condition is too conservative and is not efficient. For instance, an individual may achieve a higher productivity and utility if she chooses complete specialization $l_x = 0$, or $l_x = 1$. Hence, we consider the two configurations of specialization next.

The first configuration with specialization is (x/y), implying specialization in producing good x, selling x and buying y. It is defined by $x$, $x^s$, $y^d$, $l_x > 0$, $x^d = y^s = y = l_y = 0$. This

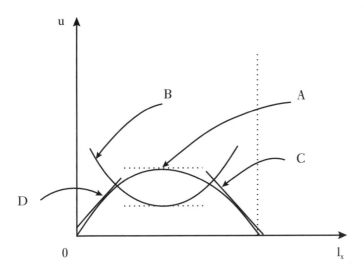

◆ **Figure 5.2:** The second-order condition of marginal analysis

definition, together with (5.1)–(5.4), can be used to specify the decision problem for this configuration.

$$\text{Max}_{x,x^s,x^d} : u = xky^d \tag{5.8}$$

s.t. $x + x^s = l_x^a, \qquad l_x = 1$     (production conditions)
$\qquad p_y y^d = p_x x^s$                 (budget constraint)

Plugging the constraints into the utility function to eliminate $l_x$, $x$, and $y^d$ yields the nonconstrained maximization problem

$$\text{Max}_{x^s} : u = (1 - x^s)k \frac{p_x x^s}{p_y} \tag{5.9}$$

The decision problem involves the trade-off between two opposite effects of an increase in $x^s$. The individual's utility increases with $x^s$ through an increase in revenue generated by the sale of good x, while her utility decreases with $x^s$ through a decrease in the self-provided quantity of good x. The optimum decision maximizes utility by efficiently trading off one against the other. The marginal analysis in terms of natural language that we used for configuration A is applicable to this configuration too. Since the natural language is quite inefficient, we will use mathematical language as you get used to it. However, you should keep in mind the intuition behind the mathematics: all mathematical conditions for the marginal analysis imply that the efficient allocation of resources is determined by the efficient trade-off between counteracting forces that optimizes the objective function. This allocation of resources is efficient only for a given configuration. The marginal analysis does not tell us which configuration is optimal. We need total benefit–cost analysis across configurations to sort out that problem.

As we have seen, the first-order condition for marginal analysis, $du/dx^s = 0$, gives the optimum decision $x^s = \frac{1}{2}$, which is *an individual's corner supply function* for good x. Inserting this into the budget constraint yields *an individual's corner demand function* for good y, $y^d = p_x/2p_y$. Inserting the corner supply and demand functions back into the utility function yields the *corner indirect utility function* $u_x = kp_x/4p_y$. The corner solution for configuration (x/y) is summarized as follows.

$$x^s = 0.5, \qquad y^d = p_x x^s/p_y = p_x/2p_y, \qquad u_x = kp_x/4p_y. \tag{5.10}$$

Here, the corner demand function is a decreasing function of the price of goods purchased and an increasing function of the price of goods sold. Also, demand is proportional to supply. This last feature of demand and supply is referred to by Young (1928) as the law of reciprocal demand, which implies that demand and supply are two sides of the division of labor. If individuals choose autarky, there is no demand and supply in the marketplace since self-demand is self-supply. If an individual chooses specialization in producing x, then she demands good y and supplies good x. Hence, when we consider problems related to unemployment and business cycles, and other problems involving inequality between demand and supply, we should look at the properties of the network of division of labor as a whole and investigate under what conditions coordination failure of the network arises. An analysis of demand that is separated from the analysis of supply is incompatible with the concept of general equilibrium and therefore is often misleading.

The second configuration of specialization (y/x), in which the individual sells good y and buys good x, is defined by $y, y^s, s^d, l_y > 0, y^d = x^s = x = l_x = 0$. The decision problem for this configuration is:

$$\underset{y,y^s,x^d}{\text{Max}};\ u = ykx^d \tag{5.11}$$

$$\text{s.t. } y + y^s = l_y^a = 1 \qquad\qquad \text{(production condition)}$$
$$p_y y^s = p_x x^d \qquad\qquad\qquad \text{(budget constraint)}$$

Following the procedure used in solving for the corner solution for configuration (x/y), the corner demand and supply functions and corner indirect utility function for configuration (y/x) is solved as follows.

$$y^s = 0.5, \qquad x^d = p_y/2p_x, \qquad u_y = kp_y/4p_x. \tag{5.12}$$

From (5.10), we have seen that the utility of a specialist producer of x increases with the price of x and decreases with the price of y. Similarly (5.12) indicates that the utility of a specialist producer of a good increases with the price of this good and decreases with the price of the good that she buys. This is referred to as the *law of specialization.*

## ◆ 5.4 The Optimum Level and Pattern of Specialization

### 5.4.1 Inframarginal analysis of demand and supply

According to mainstream classical economics, demand and supply are two sides of the division of labor (Young, 1928). In order to understand demand and supply, we must start from an investigation of individuals' decisions concerning their levels and patterns of specialization, which determine the level and structure of division of labor for society as a whole. In the previous section, we have studied corner demand and supply functions in each configuration. An individual's demand and supply functions are determined by her decision in choosing the optimum configuration. Since the local optimum decisions are discontinuous across configurations, an individual must compare locally maximum utility levels in all corner solutions to find the optimum corner solution. Table 5.2 summarizes the information of three corner solutions.

On the basis of this information, an individual compares utility levels across configurations. She will choose configuration (x/y), that is, specialization in x, iff

$u_x \geq u_A$ and $u_x \geq u_y$, that is, iff $p_x/p_y \geq 2^{2(1-a)}/k$ and $p_x/p_y \geq 1$.

She will choose configuration (y/x), that is specialization in y, iff

$u_y \geq u_A$ and $u_y \geq u_x$, that is, iff $p_x/p_y \leq 2^{-2(1-a)}k$ and $p_x/p_y \leq 1$.

The two conditions can hold simultaneously only if

$$k > k_0 \equiv 2^{2(1-a)} \text{ and } p_x/p_y = 1, \tag{5.13}$$

**Table 5.2:** Three corner solutions

| Configuration | Corner demand | Corner supply | Self-provided quantities | Level of specialization | Indirect utility function |
|---|---|---|---|---|---|
| A | 0 | 0 | $x = y = 0.5$ | $l_x = l_y = 0.5$ | $u_A = 2^{-2a}$ |
| (x/y) | $y^d = p_x/2p_y$ | $x^s = 0.5$ | $x = 0.5$ | $l_x = 1, l_y = 0$ | $u_x = kp_x/4p_y$ |
| (y/x) | $x^d = p_y/2p_x$ | $y^s = 0.5$ | $y = 0.5$ | $l_x = 0, l_y = 1$ | $u_y = kp_y/4p_x$ |

Since the division of labor can be realized only if both occupation configurations (x/y) and (y/x) are chosen and because of network effect of specialization, an individual will choose specialization only if (5.13) holds. When the relative price satisfies this condition, individuals are indifferent between the two configurations since utility would be the same in both. In equilibrium, utility equalization between different occupations must hold since individuals are *ex ante* identical in all aspects.

The individual will choose configuration A, that is, autarky, iff

$$u_x < u_A \text{ and } u_y < u_A \text{ which hold iff } p_x/p_y \in [2^{-2(1-a)}k, 2^{2(1-a)}/k]$$

which holds only if

$$k < k_0 \equiv 2^{2(1-a)} \tag{5.14}$$

(5.13) and (5.14) imply that there does not exist a relative price that generates higher utility for two occupations than in autarky if $k < k_0$. Therefore, individuals will choose autarky if the trading efficiency coefficient is smaller than the critical value $k_0$. They choose specialization if the trading efficiency coefficient $k$ is greater than the critical value, so that the market emerges from specialization.

(5.13) and (5.14) imply that specialization will be chosen if $p_x/p_y = 1$ and $k > k_0$ and autarky will be chosen if $k < k_0$. Here, we ignore *ex ante* differences in transaction and production conditions that generate unequal real incomes between individuals. We will consider this in chapters 12 and 13. However, the utility equalization condition is more realistic than it appears. Take a businessman and his secretary as an example. Nominal incomes between them are very unequal. Everybody knows that the businessman (if successful) can make more money, so that competition to get into business school is much more intensive than that for entry to a school for secretarial training. The more intensive competition generates intangible disutility as well as a greater financial burden (business schools rarely provide scholarships). More importantly, the businessman takes a considerable risk of bankruptcy, which may cause suicide (implying an infinitely large negative real income). If you count all of the tangible and intangible benefits and costs, the difference in expected real income between the businessman and his secretary is much smaller than seems to be.

If there is free entry into every occupation, utility equalization will hold. Later, we shall investigate the implications of free entry and entry barriers. Inserting $p_x/p_y = 1$ into the indirect utility function $u_x$ or $u_y$ yields

$$u_x = u_y = u_D = k/4$$

where $u_D$ is per capita real income for the division of labor, which depends on the trading efficiency parameter $k$, but does not depend on relative price. Each individual can compare $u_D$ with $u_A$, so that she will choose the division of labor if $k > k_0$ and will choose autarky if $k < k_0$. Hence, an individual's demand and supply functions are given by the corner solution in configuration A if $k < k_0$, and are given by the corner demand and supply functions in configuration (x/y) or (y/x) if $k > k_0$.

### 5.4.2 Inframarginal and marginal comparative statics of decisions

As $k$ increases from a value smaller than $k_0$ to a value greater than $k_0$, demand and supply discontinuously jump from 0 to positive levels as functions of relative prices, due to an increase in individuals' levels of specialization. This is referred to as the *new classical law of demand*, which is distinguished from the neoclassical law of demand (examined below). The analysis of the discontinuous shift of the optimum decisions between configurations in response to changes of parameters is called *inframarginal comparative statics of decision problems*, which is distinguished from marginal comparative statics of decisions. The inframarginal comparative statics of demand and supply are based on total benefit–cost analysis between corner solutions.

For a given configuration, marginal analysis generates marginal comparative statics of the decisions. For instance, in configuration (y/x), $dx^d/d(p_x/p_y) = -0.5(p_x/p_y)^{-2} < 0$. This implies that as the price of good x increases relative to that of good y, the quantity demanded of good x by each specialist in y falls. This is referred to as the *neoclassical law of demand*. The analysis of how the optimum decisions continuously change, within a given configuration, in response to changes in parameters is called *marginal comparative statics*. The marginal comparative statics of decisions are based on marginal analysis and are concerned with changes in efficient resource allocation for a given configuration of specialization in response to changes in parameters. The inframarginal comparative statics of the decisions relate to changes in the efficient configuration of specialization as parameters shift between the subspaces that demarcate the configurations. The marginal comparative statics relate to changes in the decisions in response to those changes of parameters within a given parameter subspace.

In summary, marginal comparative statics of decisions relate to marginal analysis, resource allocation, and disaggregate demand for a given configuration of specialization and given aggregate demand. In contrast, inframarginal comparative statics of decisions relate to inframarginal analysis of the level of specialization, which determines the extent of the market, the size of the network of division of labor, and aggregate demand, which will be defined later on.

## ◆ 5.5 Neoclassical and New Classical Laws of Supply and Elasticity of Substitution

In the previous sections, supply functions in configurations with specialization are independent of prices. This is because of the unitary elasticity of substitution of the C-D utility function. Unitary elasticity of substitution implies that the substitution effect and income effect cancel each other in a consumer-producer setting. In this section, we use a constant elasticity of substitution (CES) utility function to illustrate the implications of the elasticity of substitution for the law of supply.

**Example 5.2: A new classical model with the CES utility function**

The CES utility function is specified for each consumer-producer:

$$u = \left[(x^c)^\rho + (yc)^\rho\right]^{\frac{1}{\rho}}, \qquad x^c \equiv x + kx^d, \qquad y^c \equiv y + ky^d$$

where $\rho \in (0, 1)$ is a parameter of elasticity of substitution. The following features distinguish the CES utility function from the C-D utility function. For the C-D function, the quantity of each consumption good must be positive for maintaining a positive utility. For the CES function, utility is positive even if the quantity of a consumption good is 0, as long as the quantity of at least one of the other consumption goods is positive. According to the definition of elasticity of substitution in section 2.2, the elasticity of substitution of the CES function can be calculated as follows.

$$E = \frac{\left(\dfrac{\partial u / \partial y^c}{\partial u / \partial x^c}\right) d(x^c / y^c)}{(x^c / y^c) \, d\left(\dfrac{\partial u / \partial y^c}{\partial u / \partial x^c}\right)} = \frac{d \ln(x^c / y^c)}{d \ln\left(\dfrac{\partial u / \partial y^c}{\partial u / \partial x^c}\right)} = \frac{1}{1 - \rho},$$

which implies that relative quantities of the two goods consumed will decrease by $1/(1 - \rho)$ percent when the relative price of the two goods increases by one percent. Since the elasticity of substitution is an increasing function of $\rho$, or $dE/d\rho > 0$, the greater the value of $\rho$, the greater is the elasticity of substitution. Since an individual's desire for variety in consumption diminishes as the elasticity of substitution increases, the degree of desire for a variety in consumption can be defined by $1/\rho$. If we let $x^c = y^c$; it is not difficult to see that consumption of two goods always generates a greater level of utility than consumption of a single good. That is, $2^{1/\rho} x^c > x^c$. We need the assumption $\rho \in (0, 1)$ to ensure diverse consumption in equilibrium since $\rho < 0$ or $\rho > 1$ implies specialized consumption in autarky equilibrium.

Now that you are more familiar with the use of mathematical language in specifying economic models, we can quickly specify an individual's decision problem based on the CES utility function as follows.

Max: $u = \left[(x^c)^\rho + (y^c)^\rho\right]^{1/\rho}$        (utility function)

s.t.   $x^c \equiv x + kx^d \qquad y^c \equiv y + ky^d$     (definition of quantities to consume)
      $x + x^s = l_x^a \qquad\quad y + y^s = l_y^a$     (production function)
      $l_x + l_y = 1$                         (endowment constraint)
      $p_x x^s + p_y y^s = p_x x^d + p_y y^d$     (budget constraint)

where $x$, $x^s$, $x^d$, $y$, $y^s$, $y^d$, $l_x$, $l_y$ are decision variables and $p_x$, $p_y$, are price parameters. According to the Wen theorem, 5 configurations need to be considered. There are three autarky configurations: A1, in which one good is consumed; A2, in which two goods are consumed; and a third, which is symmetric to A1. The two configurations with specialization are (x/y) and (y/x). The optimum decisions in the various configurations are summarized in table 5.3, where $p \equiv p_y/p_x$ is the relative price. You should follow the procedure of the previous sections to solve for the optimum decisions in table 5.3, to make yourself familiar with inframarginal analysis.

**Table 5.3**: Corner solutions based on the CES utility function

| Configuration | Quantities self-provided | Corner supply functions | Corner demand functions | Corner indirect utility functions |
|---|---|---|---|---|
| A1 | $x = 1$ | 0 | 0 | 1 |
| A2 | $x = y = 0.5^a$ | 0 | 0 | $2(1 - pa)/\rho$ |
| (x/y) | $x = [1 + (k/p)^{\rho/(1-\rho)}]^{-1}$ | $x^s = [1 + (p/k)^{\rho/(1-\rho)}]^{-1}$ | $y^d = x^s/p$ | $[1 + (k/p)^{\rho/(1-\rho)}]^{(1-\rho)/\rho}$ |
| (y/x) | $y = [1 + (kp)^{\rho/1-\rho}]^{-1}$ | $y^s = [1 + (kp)^{-\rho/(1-\rho)}]^{-1}$ | $x^d = py^s$ | $[1 + (kp)^{\rho/(1-\rho)}]^{(1-\rho)/\rho}$ |

Where $p \equiv p_y/p_x$.

Let us consider first the marginal comparative statics of the decisions. For a given configuration of specialization, differentiation of the corner supply functions in table 5.3 yields $dx^s/d(p_x/p_y) > 0$ and $dy^s/d(p_y/p_x) > 0$. This is referred to as the neoclassical supply law, that is, the quantity of a good supplied increases with the price of the good. The neoclassical supply law implies also that the quantity of a good that is supplied decreases with the price of the good that is purchased by the specialist supplier. This is consistent with the feature of new classical demand and supply analysis: demand and supply are two sides of specialization. It is easy to verify from table 5.3 that neoclassical demand law holds for this model based on the CES utility function, that is, $dx^d/d(p_x/p_y) < 0$ and $dy^d/d(p_y/p_x) < 0$.

We next consider the inframarginal comparative statics of the decisions, which requires a comparison of per capita real income across configurations. It can be shown that both configurations of specialization will be chosen only if $p = 1$. For $p = 1$, a comparison between specialization and configuration $A_1$ implies that specialization is always better than $A_1$. Hence, $A_1$ will not be chosen. A comparison between specialization and configuration $A_2$ indicates that individuals will choose specialization if $k > k_1 \equiv [2^{(1-a\rho)/\rho} - 1]^{(1-\rho)/\rho}$ and will choose $A_2$ (autarky) if $k < k_1$. Hence, demand and supply will jump from autarky to configurations with specialization as $k$ increases from a value smaller than $k_1$ to that which is larger than $k_1$.

## Key Terms and Review

Configuration and corner solutions.
Implications of the Wen theorem for inframarginal analysis.
Trade-off in allocating resources for a given configuration of specialization vs. trade-off in choosing a configuration of specialization.
Marginal analysis of the problem of resource allocation vs. inframarginal analysis of the problem of economic organization.
Relationship between the trade-off in decision-making and the second-order condition.
Demand law, supply law, and law of specialization.
The difference between marginal and inframarginal analyses of demand and supply.
Marginal comparative statics vs. inframarginal comparative statics of decisions.

## Further Reading

*Inframarginal analysis*: Young (1928), Houthakker (1956), Rosen (1978, 1983), Becker (1981), Wen (1997a,b, 1998), Lio (1996, 1998), Sun (1999), Chu (1997), Chu and Wang (1998), Zhang (1997, 1998), Yang and Y.-K. Ng (1993, ch. 2), Yang (1991, 1996), Yang and S. Ng (1998); *marginal analysis of decision-making in choosing level of specialization*: Baumgardner (1988), Becker and Murphy (1992), Locay (1990), Kim (1989).

# QUESTIONS

1   In the last decade, many shops specializing in changing engine oil have emerged in the US. They are usually organized through franchise networks, which reduce transaction costs caused by a deep division of labor between the franchiser and the franchisees. The franchiser specializes in planning, advertising, designing the operation manual, choosing specialized equipment, and management, while the franchisee specializes in changing engine oil. Since the franchiser specializes in producing intangible intellectual properties, it is very easy for the franchisee to infringe upon the franchiser's property (for instance, the franchisee refuses to pay the franchise fee as soon as she has acquired the know-how from the operation manual provided by the franchiser). The franchise contract uses a hostage mechanism to restrict such opportunism. A typical franchise contract has a special clause that the franchiser can unilaterally terminate the contract if the franchisee does not pay a franchise fee which might be 9 percent of the sales revenue of the franchise. Within a certain period of time after the termination, the franchisee is not allowed to compete with the franchiser in specified territory and activities. This hostage mechanism significantly enhances the trading efficiency of intellectual properties of the franchiser. Use the model in this chapter to explain why this type of contract is essential for deepening the division of labor within the sector providing engine oil-change services, and between the sector and the rest of the economy.

2   Compare the new classical decision model in this chapter with the neoclassical decision model in chapter 3. Analyze why demand and supply can discontinuously jump in the absence of changes in parameters of tastes, production, and endowments in the new classical model, while such changes are essential for explaining changes in demand and supply in the neoclassical model.

3   A businessman found that many managers of hotels and restaurants need popular music tapes for their customers, but they do not have time to keep track of customers' constantly changing tastes. He then created a business to specialize in providing music to managers. He specialized in identifying the most popular music, adds a margin to the price of the tapes that he has chosen, and then sells to the managers. His business became very successful. Use the model in this chapter to explain how the businessman creates demand and supply for professional services by deepening the division of labor. If you use neoclassical analysis of demand and supply to consider this case, how would you explain the demand and supply of music tapes? Why can't that analysis predict created demand and supply based on an endogenous level of specialization, which is the most interesting feature of modern entrepreneurism?

4   When Lady Thatcher retired as Prime Minister of Britain, she was worried about whether her humble pension would be enough to support the very expensive lifestyle to which she had been accustomed. She was approached by an agency which specializes in cultivating public relations. The contract between her and the agent helped her to make so much money from public speaking throughout the world that she was able to earn much more than she made as Prime Minister. Explain why the division of labor between specialized agents and specialized movie stars, public figures, and singers occurs in the

marketplace. Explain why many writers in New York use agencies to find publishers and to sign publication contracts for their commercial books on their behalf, while the division of labor between academic writers and specialized publication agents is not common. In particular, why do academics never use professional publication agents for submitting research works to refereed journals on their behalf?

5   In the model in this chapter there are network effects of division of labor. This implies that the division of labor increases not only the productivity of a seller of good x, but also the productivity of a buyer of good x in producing good y. If all other individuals choose autarky, then an individual cannot choose specialization since she cannot sell her professional produce and cannot buy goods that she does not produce and that are essential for her consumption and production. In other words, a person's decision in choosing her level of specialization not only determines her productivity, but also determines the extent of the market for others' produce and therefore affects others' productivity and their decisions in choosing their levels of specialization. Use the model in this chapter to explain how individuals utilize the network effects of division of labor by trading it off against transaction costs through the price system. Why is inframarginal analysis essential for coordination between individuals' decisions in choosing their levels of specialization?

6   Before the 1830s, economists rarely used the concept of economies of scale. The notions that they used are benefits and costs of specialization and division of labor, which relate in essence to the economies of interpersonal complementarity and the network effect of division of labor. At the end of the nineteenth century, the notion of economies of scale became popular, partly due to the success of Marshall's principles textbook. Marshall was aware of the incompatibility between his marvellous marginal analysis of demand and supply and classical economic thinking about the implications of specialization and division of labor, so he created the distinction between internal economies of scale and external economies of scale. The latter is supposed to relate to economies of division of labor in the marketplace. However, as Allyn Young (1928, p. 531) argued, "the view of the nature of the processes of industrial progress which is implied in the distinction between internal and external economies is necessarily a partial view. Certain aspects of those processes are illuminated, while, for that very reason, certain other aspects, important in relation to other problems, are obscured." For instance, the notion of external economies of scale implies that distortions caused by external economies of scale generate coordination failure of division of labor in the marketplace. Hence, it seemed to Young that the concept of external economies of scale is a misrepresentation of the classical concept of economies of specialization and division of labor. Use the model in this chapter to illustrate why coordination failure caused by economies of scale disappears if the notion of economies of scale is replaced by the notion of economies of specialization and division of labor.

7   Use the model in this chapter to explain why Allyn Young claimed that demand and supply are two sides of division of labor and why we cannot understand what demand and supply are if we do not understand how individuals choose their levels and patterns of specialization.

8   Use the Wen theorem, which helps to keep inframarginal analysis tractable, to explain why, in the late nineteenth and the twentieth centuries, the analysis of demand and supply shifted from inframarginal analysis of decision-making in choosing a level of specialization to marginal analysis of resource allocation for a given level of specialization.

# EXERCISES

1   Assume that the production functions in (5.2) are $x + x^s = l_x - a, y + y^s = l_y - b$. Solve for the demand and supply functions and indirect utility function for configurations (x/y) and (y/x). Then solve for the corner solution in autarky.

2   Assume a decision problem that is the same as example 5.1, but that $k = 1$ and the government taxes each dollar of goods sold at the rate $t$, and then evenly distributes the tax revenue among the population. Solve for all corner solutions and identify the conditions under which each of them is the optimum decision. Use marginal and inframarginal comparative statics to analyze the effect of the tax.

3   Assume that the production functions in (5.2) are $x + x^s = l_x^a, y + y^s = l_y^b, a \neq b$. Solve for the corner solutions in three configurations.

4   Assume that in exercise 3 $k = 1$ and the government taxes each dollar of good x that is purchased, then evenly distributes the tax revenue among the buyers of good x. Use marginal and inframarginal comparative statics to analyze the effect of the tax on demand and supply. Compare your answer to that in exercise 2.

5   Assume that the utility function in (5.1) is $u = (x + kx^d)^\alpha (y + ky^d)^{1-\alpha}$. Solve for the corner solutions in three configurations.

6   Lio, 1998: Suppose that the utility function is the same as in (5.1) and the production functions are the same as in exercise 1. But there is a minimum consumption amount for good x, given by $x + kx^d \geq x_0, x_0 \in (0, 1 - a)$. How many configurations must we consider? Solve for the corner solution for each of them.

## Notes

1 The existence theorem of equilibrium for a general class of new classical models with a continuum of consumer-producers is established in chapter 13. Example 9.2 in chapter 9 will show that for a finite set of consumer-producers, the division of labor may never occur in the Walrasian equilibrium. In that chapter we shall investigate the function of Nash bargaining in eliminating endogenous transaction costs caused by the integer problem.

# chapter 6

# NEW CLASSICAL GENERAL EQUILIBRIUM AND ITS WELFARE IMPLICATIONS

## ◆ 6.1 Neoclassical vs. New Classical General Equilibrium

As in neoclassical economics, a general equilibrium in the new classical framework is the outcome of interactions between individuals' self-interested decisions which might be in conflict with each others. In neoclassical economics, individuals choose quantities of goods to be produced, traded, and consumed for given prices, while equilibrium prices are themselves determined by all individuals' decisions of quantities of goods and factors. A general equilibrium is a consequence of the interactions between prices and behaviors that simultaneously determines both prices and quantities of goods and factors. Because each individual's decision problem has multiple configurations, there are many possible combinations of all of these individual configurations. Hence, the new classical framework features multiple corner equilibria. Since each individual chooses only the optimal of the multiple corner solutions, the general equilibrium is one of multiple corner equilibria. The notion of general equilibrium in the new classical framework relates not only to all interactions between prices and quantities, between the markets for different goods and factors, and between individuals' self-interested decisions, but also to the mechanism that simultaneously determines the size of the network of division of labor, demand and supply as two aspects of that network, productivity, and per capita real incomes.

*Network effect* relates to the following phenomenon. In a system comprising many interdependent subsystems, the efficiency of the whole system is determined not only by each individual's productivity, but also by the number of participants in the network. Each individual's participation decision is dependent on the number of participants of the network, though this interdependence may occur indirectly through the price system. It is, indeed, the network effects of the division of labor that Smith and Young described in their classic works. Smith was more interested in the function of the invisible hand in coordinating the division of labor and in utilizing the network effects than in its function in allocating resources for a given structure of division of labor. Young emphasized several times that the benefits of division of labor are network effects rather than effects of the scale of a firm or a sector. The effects can be analyzed only by taking the division of labor as a whole. The economic analysis that separates the investigation of demand from that of supply does not help us in understanding the economic implications of division of labor.

From the model in the previous chapter, it can be seen that if each individual, as a consumer, prefers diverse consumption, and, as a producer, prefers specialized production, then the individual cannot specialize if all other individuals choose autarky. In this situation, the person cannot sell what she wants to sell and cannot buy consumption goods that she does not produce. This implies that each individual's level of specialization determines not only her own productivity, but also the extent of the market for the produce of others, thereby determining the others' productivities and levels of specialization. This is a typical network effect. The focus of the current chapter is on how the price system simultaneously sorts out the size of the network of division of labor, the extent of the market, prices, productivity, and per capita real income. In daily life, we hear many managers and other decision-markers state that demand is dependent on per capita real income. According to Young, this is a one-sided view that misses the nature of the network of division of labor. From a complete view of network effects, we can see that the extent of the market (effective demand) determines productivity and thereby per capita real income too. Certainly the question whether the extent of the market determines per capita income, or vice versa, is analogous to the question: did the egg generate the hen, or the hen the egg? The notion of general equilibrium is a powerful device for illuminating the mechanism that simultaneously determines all of the interdependent phenomena. New classical economics provides a framework within which the general equilibrium implications of the network effects of the division of labor can be understood. In this framework each individual's decision to choose her network size of trade is dependent on prices and the network size of division of labor, while the network size of division of labor and prices are determined by all individuals' decisions in choosing their levels of specialization. In addition, there are infinite feedback loops between quantities to produce and to consume, prices, and the network size of division of labor.

There is an extensive literature about coordination failure in the market where network effects exist (see the coordination game in subsection 4.4.2 of chapter 4). That literature might suggest to you that if, in the model in the previous chapter, all individuals choose to specialize in producing good x and nobody specializes in y, then it is an instance of coordination failure that prevents the realization of mutually beneficial division of labor. If the division of labor generates network effects, and all individuals are in autarky before they make decisions, then for society to choose the division of labor, all individuals must simultaneously jump to different occupations: some of them specializing in x and others specializing in y. But the question arises: if some individuals jump while others do not, how can we be so sure that the division of labor for society as a whole can be realized in the absence of a coordination mechanism involving the intervention of a visible hand?

The previous chapter has already provided some answers to this question. For instance, freedom of individual choice between different occupations and the price system establish a mechanism that successfully coordinates the division of labor and exploits positive network effects. Under this mechanism, if all individuals choose specialization in x and nobody specializes in y, then the demand for good y is great, but there is no supply of y. Similarly, the supply of x is great and demand for it is zero. This implies that the price of y increases relative to x, so that the indirect utility of specialists in y, which is an increasing function of the relative price of y to x, becomes greater than that for specialists in x. All individuals will choose specialization in y, so that the relative price of y to x falls. This negative feedback mechanism continues until the relative price equalizes utility levels between the two occupations. Therefore, the situation where all individuals specialize in x and nobody specializes in y could not take place under a free price system if $k > k_0$ (economies of division of labor outweigh total transaction costs). For $k < k_0$ (economies of division of labor are outweighed by transaction costs), there does not exist a relative price under which both professional occupations (x/y) and (y/x) are chosen. This implies that coordination failure of division of labor occurs in a decentralized market if and only if economies of division of labor are outweighed by transaction costs. This coordination failure is of course the success of the market (the invisible hand). In this chapter, we further study the function of the price mechanism in coordinating the division of labor and in exploiting network effects net of transaction costs.

From the concept of configuration, you may see that for society as a whole, combinations of configurations may generate many structures of division of labor. There is a corner equilibrium for each structure, and the general equilibrium is only one of them. Each corner equilibrium sorts out the resource allocation problems for a given structure of division of labor, while the new classical general equilibrium sorts out the efficient level and structure of division of labor. The distinction between corner equilibrium and general equilibrium based on corner solutions distinguishes the new classical from the neoclassical concept of equilibrium. It is this distinction that gives new classical economics much higher explanatory power.

---

### Questions to Ask Yourself when Reading this Chapter

♦ What are network effects of division of labor?

♦ How does the market coordinate the division of labor and utilize the network effects of the division of labor?

♦ What is the role of trading efficiency in the process by which general equilibrium achieves the production possibility frontier and reduces scarcity?

♦ Why are scarcity and productivity endogenous in new classical equilibrium models?

♦ What are the relationships among the level of division of labor, productivity, trade dependence, and trading efficiency?

♦ What is the distinction between the functions of the market in allocating resources and in determining the level of division of labor? What are the implications of the distinction for economic analysis?

---

## ♦ 6.2 How Does the Market Coordinate the Division of Labor and Utilize Network Effects?

Unless indicated otherwise, the analysis of the outcome of interactions between self-interested decisions in this chapter is based on the model specified in example 5.1 in chapter 5. In subsection 6.2.1, we examine how combinations of configurations generate many structures of organization and investigate corner equilibrium in each structure. In subsection 6.2.2, we study how the general equilibrium sorts out the level of division of labor for society as a whole to utilize network effects.

## 6.2.1 Structure, corner equilibrium, and resource allocation for a given structure of division of labor

In chapter 5, three corner solutions in three configurations have already been demonstrated. Combinations of the three configurations generate two *organization structures*, or *structures* for short. All individuals choosing configuration A (autarky) constitute a structure involving no market, no prices, no interdependence and no interaction between individuals. The division of $M$ individuals between configurations (x/y) and (y/x) constitutes a structure with division of labor, denoted D, where there are two markets for two goods sold by two types of specialists. Let the number (measure) of individuals choosing (x/y) be $M_x$ and the number choosing (y/x) be $M_y$.

To understand the distinction between occupation configuration and structure of division of labor, you may consider the university where you are studying. The first decision that you have to make when you enter university is to choose a major. If you choose economics as your major, then you do not go to classes in chemistry and physics, you take classes in microeconomics, macroeconomics, and econometrics. This decision chooses an occupation configuration. We call such a decision an inframarginal decision, since local optimum decisions are not continuous between occupation configurations. They discontinuously jump between 0 and a positive value as you shift between majors. After you have chosen a major, you allocate your limited time between the fields in this major. This decision of resource allocation for a given occupation configuration is called a marginal decision, since standard marginal analysis can be applied to this type of decision. The aggregate outcome of all students' choices of their majors in a university generates a division of students among majors and fields, which is equivalent to a structure of division of labor in our model.

There is a corner equilibrium for each structure. A *corner equilibrium* is defined by a relative price of the two traded goods $p_x/p_y$, and the numbers of the two types of specialists, $M_x$ and $M_y$, that satisfy the *market clearing condition* and *utility equalization condition* for a given structure. In a corner equilibrium individuals maximize their utility with respect to configurations and quantities of goods produced, traded, and consumed for the given structure and corner equilibrium relative price and numbers of individuals selling the two goods. The market clearing and utility equalization conditions are established by free choice between configurations and utility maximization behavior.

According to the definition of corner equilibrium, the corner solution in configuration A chosen by $M$ individuals is the corner equilibrium in structure A where the market clearing condition always holds, since self-demand and self-supply are two sides of self-provided quantities in the structure. In structure D, free choices between configurations (occupations) and utility maximizing behavior will establish the utility equalization condition. From table 5.2 it can be seen that the indirect utility function of a specialist in x is an increasing function of $p_x/p_y$ and the indirect utility function of a specialist in y is a decreasing function of $p_x/p_y$, as shown in figure 6.1.

Hence, the utility equalization condition is associated with the intersection point E in figure 6.1. The upward sloping straight line in the figure is an x specialist's indirect utility

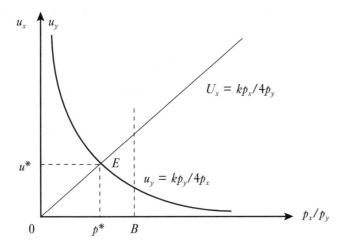

**◆ Figure 6.1:** Indirect utility functions and corner equilibrium relative price

function, which looks like a supply curve in neoclassical economics. The downward sloping curve is a y specialist's indirect utility function, which looks like a demand curve in
neoclassical economics. The corner equilibrium relative price in structure D is determined
by the intersection point between the two curves. If the relative price $p_x/p_y$ is at point B,
then the utility of a specialist in x is greater than that of a specialist in y, so that all
individuals will specialize in x and nobody in y. This implies that the corner equilibrium
in structure D cannot be established. Therefore, the utility equalization condition determines the corner equilibrium relative price of traded goods in structure D. That is

$$u_x = \frac{kp_y}{4p_y} = \frac{kp_y}{4p_x} = u_y \quad \text{or} \quad \frac{p_y}{p_x} = 1$$

Later, we will show that if the model is not symmetric, then the corner equilibrium
relative price is determined by relative tastes and relative production and transaction
conditions.

In structure D, the *market demand* for good x is

$$X^d \equiv M_y x^d = M_y p_y/2p_x ,$$

while the *market supply* of good x is

$$X^s \equiv M_x x^s = M_x/2$$

where $x^d = p_y/2p_x$ and $x^s = 1/2$ are given by table 5.2. The market demand function not
only exhibits the demand law (the quantity demanded of a good decreases as its price
increases relative to that of the good sold by the buyer), but is also an increasing function
of the number of specialists in y. The market supply function of x is an increasing function
of the number of specialists of x. If the C-D utility function is replaced with the CES

utility function, as shown in section 5.5, then the market supply function will exhibit the supply law (the quantity supplied of a good increases with the price of this good relative to that of the good bought by the seller).

The difference between market demand and market supply is called *excess demand*. In a Walrasian regime, prices are determined by a *Walrasian auction mechanism*. The *Walrasian auctioneer* calls a set of relative prices of all traded and nontraded goods. All individuals report to the auctioneer their optimum quantities of goods to be produced, traded, and consumed for the given set of prices. Then the auctioneer adjusts relative prices according to excess demands, raising or lowering the price of a good according to whether its excess demand is positive or negative. This *tâtonnement* process continues until the excess demands for all goods tend to 0. This is referred to as a *centralized pricing mechanism*. The Walrasian auction mechanism will establish the market clearing condition for good x:

$$X^d = M_y p_y / 2p_x = X^s = M_x / 2, \quad \text{or} \quad p_x / p_y = M_y / M_x$$

This equation implies that competition in the market and free choices of configurations establish an inverse relationship between the relative prices of goods x and y and the relative numbers of individuals selling goods x and y.

Free choice with respect to configurations (occupations), together with free choice of quantities to produce, trade, and consume, are the driving forces that establish a corner equilibrium.

From Walras's law, the market clearing condition for good y is not independent of that for good x. Hence, we do not need to consider that market clearing condition.

The market clearing condition for x, the utility equalization condition, and the population equation $M_x + M_y = M$ yield the corner equilibrium in structure D.

$$p_x / p_y = 1, \qquad M_x = M_y = M/2.$$

Inserting the corner equilibrium relative price of traded goods back into demand and supply functions and indirect utility functions yields the corner equilibrium quantities to produce, trade, and consume and the corner equilibrium utility level, which we call *per capita real income*, denoted by $u_D$. The corner equilibrium values of endogenous variables are no longer functions of prices. Due to symmetry, per capita real income depends only upon the parameter $k$.

$$x = y = x^s = y^s = x^d = y^d = \frac{1}{2}, \qquad u_D = k/4.$$

For an asymmetric model, all of the endogenous variables will depend upon the parameters of relative transaction and production conditions and relative tastes for the two goods. We call the corner equilibrium values of endogenous variables, including the relative price of traded goods and the numbers of individuals selling different goods, *a resource allocation for a given structure*.

A corner equilibrium sorts out resource allocation for a given structure. All information about the two corner equilibria in structures A and D is summarized in table 6.1.

We distinguish *per capita real income*, which is the corner equilibrium value of the indirect utility function in a structure, from the indirect utility function, which is the optimum value of utility for a configuration.

We now examine further the nature of the pricing mechanism in the Walrasian regime

**Table 6.1**: Two corner equilibria

| Structure | Relative price | Number of specialists | Quantities of goods | Per capita real income |
|---|---|---|---|---|
| A | $dy/dx = 1$ | | $x = y = 0.5^a$ | $2^{-2a}$ |
| D | $p_x/p_y = 1$ | $M_x = M_y = M/2$ | $x = y = x^s = y^s = x^d$ | $k/4$ |
| | | | $= y^d = \frac{1}{2},$ | |

in the new classical model. Though we use a Walrasian auction mechanism to describe the pricing mechanism, this centralized pricing mechanism is not essential in the new classical framework.

The *Walrasian pricing mechanism* in the new classical framework can be decentralized. In the new classical framework prices are determined by all individuals' self-interested decisions in choosing their occupation configurations. In principle, individuals are allowed to choose prices. But interactions between self-interested decisions in choosing occupation configurations will nullify any attempts to manipulate prices as long as nobody can manipulate the numbers of individuals choosing occupation configurations. To substantiate this claim, we first consider all individuals' budget constraints and the market clearing conditions.

The budget constraint for an individual choosing configuration (x/y) is $p_x x^s = p_y y^d$ and that for an individual choosing configuration (y/x) is $p_y y^s = p_x x^d$. The market clearing condition is $M_x x^s = M_y x^d$. The three equations imply

$$p_x/p_y = M_y y^s / M_x x^s. \tag{6.1}$$

This equation implies that the market relative price of the two traded goods is inversely determined by the corresponding relative number of individuals selling the two goods and the relative outputs of individual sellers. Since an individual's output level is trivial compared to the very large number of individuals who can choose any occupation configuration, the relative price cannot be manipulated by an individual's output level as long as the relative number of different specialist producers cannot be manipulated. This justifies the price-taking behavior for each individual despite the assumption that each individual is allowed to choose prices.

In the new classical economics the *tâtonnement* process, which is a negative feedback mechanism, differs slightly from that in the neoclassical framework. Suppose that the relative price $p_x/p_y$ is higher than the equilibrium one. Then it must be true $u_x > u_y$, so that individuals will shift from configuration (y/x) to configuration (x/y). This reduces $M_y/M_x$ and therefore reduces $p_x/p_y$ through (6.1). This adjustment will continue until the equilibrium is established.

In chapter 9, we will show that the decentralized Walrasian pricing mechanism can be justified by a Nash bargaining game in which an x specialist's utility is a threat point for a y specialist, since each player can always change occupation configuration. The Nash bargaining game establishes utility equalization conditions between *ex ante* identical consumer-producers, so that the Nash bargaining equilibrium coincides with the Walrasian equilibrium if direct interactions between prices and quantities are spelled out.

## 6.2.2 General equilibrium level and structure of division of labor – How does the market coordinate division of labor to utilize network effects?

A *general equilibrium* is defined by a set of relative prices of traded goods, a set of numbers of individuals choosing different configurations that constitute a structure, and individuals' quantities of goods produced, traded, and consumed that satisfy the following conditions. (i) Each individual's decision with regard to quantities and configurations maximizes her utility for the given equilibrium relative prices of traded goods and the given equilibrium numbers of individuals choosing different configurations; (ii) The set of relative prices of traded goods and numbers of individuals choosing different configurations enable market clearing for all traded goods.

It is straightforward that (i) implies equalization of all individuals' utilities in equilibrium. It is easy to see that a corner equilibrium satisfies the two conditions for a general equilibrium except that individuals' choices of configurations are confined within a given structure. Hence, the general equilibrium is the corner equilibrium in which each constituent configuration is preferred by those choosing it to alternative configurations. From (5.13) and (5.14), we can see that individuals prefer either of the two specialization configurations to autarky if $k > k_0$ and $p = 1$. Also, (5.13) and (5.14) imply that if $k < k_0$, there does not exist a relative price that ensures higher utility in both configurations of specialization than in autarky. Hence, it is impossible for the division of labor between two types of professional occupation to be coordinated via a relative price. This implies that the general equilibrium is autarky if $k < k_0$.

In summary, our two-step procedure to solve for a general equilibrium in the new classical model runs as follows. A corner equilibrium is first solved for each structure, then individuals' utilities under the corner equilibrium prices are compared between configurations to identify a parameter subspace within which each constituent configuration of this structure is at least as good as any other alternative configuration. Within this parameter subspace this corner equilibrium is a general equilibrium. As the parameter space is partitioned, we can identify within each of the parameter subspaces which corner equilibrium is the general equilibrium.

It can be seen that as the number of goods increases, the number of possible structures increases more than proportionally. As a result, the two-step approach to solving for general equilibrium becomes very cumbersome. Sun, Yao, and Yang (1999) have generalized this new classical model to the case with very general preferences and production and transaction conditions and developed a much simpler two-step approach to solving for general equilibrium. Their two-step procedure needs the concept of *Pareto optimum corner equilibrium* which is the corner equilibrium with the greatest per capita real income. They have shown that general equilibrium exists if the set of consumer-producers is a continuum and that a general equilibrium is the Pareto optimum corner equilibrium. Hence, we can solve for corner equilibrium for each feasible structure, then compare per capita real incomes between corner equilibria to identify the general equilibrium. The following theorem is the theoretical foundation of this two-step approach. Yang (1988) proves this theorem for a specific new classical model. Sun, Yang, and Yao have proved this theorem for a general class of new classical models with *ex ante* identical consumer-producers. For simplicity, we call it the Yao theorem.

**Theorem 6.1 (the Yao theorem):** For an economy with $m$ goods and a continuum of *ex ante* identical consumer-producers with rational and convex preferences, and production functions displaying economies of specialization, and individual specific limited labor, the Walrasian general equilibrium exists and it is the Pareto optimum corner equilibrium.

*Proof:* The proof of the existence of equilibrium will be outlined in chapter 13. We provide here only the proof of the second part of the Yao theorem (the general equilibrium is the Pareto optimum corner equilibrium) for the model. Without loss of generality we may assume that goods $\{1, \ldots, n\}$ are traded at any corner equilibrium. Denote this corner equilibrium $E$. Here, $n \leq m$ and $m$ is the number of all traded and nontraded goods. Assume that the values of prices for these traded goods are $(p_1, \ldots, p_n)$ in this corner equilibrium and the general equilibrium values of the prices are $(p_1^*, \ldots, p_n^*)$. Now without loss of generality, we may assume that

$$p_1^*/p_1 = \max_j \{p_j^*/p_j, j = 1, \ldots, n\}$$

which implies for $j = 1, \ldots, n$,

$$p_1^*/p_j^* \geq p_1/p_j. \tag{6.2}$$

The Wen theorem implies that an individual does not sell other goods if she sells good 1. Also, we have noted that the indirect utility function is an increasing function of the price of good sold and a decreasing function of the prices of goods purchased. This, together with (6.2), implies that the utility for selling good 1 under $p^*$ is not lower than that under $p$. Thus under $p^*$ an individual can do at least as well as those individuals selling good 1 at the corner equilibrium under $p$ if she chooses the same production and trade plan as theirs. It follows that

$$u_1(p^*) \geq u_1(p) = u(p), \tag{6.3}$$

where $u_1(p^*)$ is an individual's utility from a configuration in the corner equilibrium $E$ under the general equilibrium prices, $u_1(p)$ is her utility from this configuration under the corner equilibrium prices in $E$, and $u(p)$ is the per capita real income in the corner equilibrium $E$. The last equality in (6.3) is due to utility equalization in any corner equilibrium. But by the definition of general equilibrium any configuration chosen by any individual in general equilibrium generates at least the same utility as in any alternative configuration under the general equilibrium prices. This implies

$$u(p^*) \geq u_1(p^*) \tag{6.4}$$

where $u(p^*)$ is per capita real income in general equilibrium. (6.3) and (6.4) together imply $u(p^*) \geq u(p)$, that is, per capita real income in general equilibrium is not lower than in any corner equilibrium. In other words, the general equilibrium is the Pareto optimum corner equilibrium. *Q.E.D.*

We will use the Yao theorem very often in this text. The intuition behind the theorem is plausible. Suppose x is cloth and y is food. If all individuals are in autarky, each of them knows the shadow price of x in terms of y in autarky. If the shadow price is higher than the corner equilibrium one in D, she will have an incentive to try (x/y). If it is lower than in D, she will have an incentive to try (y/x). If D generates a higher per capita real income, then there must be a relative price such that both specialists of x and y are better off than in A. Hence, a person choosing (x/y) can always use the relative price to lure others to match up her configuration by choosing (y/x). If D generates a lower per capita real income, as shown in (5.14) such a relative price does not exist, so that individuals will choose autarky in a decentralized environment. There is difficulty in coordinating all individuals' choices of professional occupations if and only if economies of division of labor are outweighed by transaction costs. No such coordination difficulty in utilizing the network effects of division of labor exists if the positive network effects outweigh transaction costs.

## ◆ 6.3 Inframarginal Comparative Statics of New Classical General Equilibrium

### 6.3.1 Inframarginal vs. marginal comparative statics of new classical general equilibrium

For the model in this section, the Yao theorem implies the following inframarginal comparative statics.

**Proposition 6.1:** The general equilibrium is the corner equilibrium in structure D if $k > k_0 \equiv 2^{2(1-a)}$, and is the corner equilibrium in structure A if $k < k_0$.

Proposition 6.1. has partitioned a two-dimensional space of parameters $k$ and $a$ into two subspaces, as shown in figure 6.2. Since we assume $k \in [0, 1]$ and $a \geq 1$, the *feasible space of parameters* is the region below horizontal line $k = 1$, above the line $k = 0$, and on the right-hand side of the vertical line $a = 1$, including the boundaries of the region in figure 6.2. The curve $k = 2^{2(1-a)}$ partitions the parameter space into two subspaces, one of them is above the curve and the other is below the curve. If values of parameters are within the first subspace, the corner equilibrium in structure D is the general equilibrium; if values of parameters are within the second subspace, the corner equilibrium in autarky is the general equilibrium.

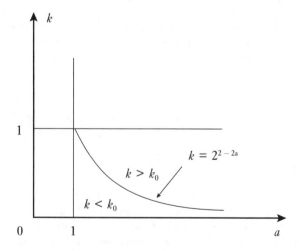

◆ **Figure 6.2:** Partition of parameter space

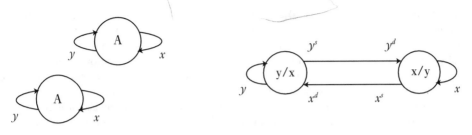

(a) Structure A, autarky    (b) Structure D, division of labor

◆ **Figure 6.3:** Autarky and division of labor

Figure 6.3 provides an intuitive illustration of proposition 6.1. Panel (a) denotes two representative individuals choosing autarky and panel (b) denotes two representative individuals choosing (x/y) and (y/x), respectively. The circles denote individuals, arrowed lines denote flows of goods. As trading efficiency $k$ increases from a value smaller than $k_0$ to a value larger than $k_0$, the general equilibrium jumps from autarky to the division of labor between two specialists. Such a jump generates discontinuous jumps of all endogenous variables, emergence of markets for two goods and demand and supply from the division of labor, and an increase in the size of the network of the market. We call this phenomenon *exogenous evolution in division of labor* since it never takes place in the absence of an exogenous change in parameters. An increase in individuals' specialization and an increase in diversity between different configurations are two sides of the evolution.

As a result of the evolution, aggregate demand jumps from 0 to a positive value, the total transaction cost for society jumps from 0 to $(1 - k)(M_x y^d + M_y x^d) = (1 - k)M/2$, the aggregate transformation curve jumps from a lower to a higher position, as indicated in figure 2.5, while the level of specialization of each individual increases from 0.5 to 1. An individual's labor productivity of the good sold increases from $0.5^{a-1}$ ($<1$) to 1 and her labor productivity of the good purchased decreases from $0.5^{a-1}$ to 0. But all individuals' productivities in each good are the same in autarky, which is the general equilibrium for $k < k_0$. This implies that productivity difference between *ex ante* identical individuals may emerge if they choose different levels of specialization in producing a good. Hence, we use the term *endogenous comparative and absolute advantage* to describe the difference in productivity between the buyer and seller of a good that is caused by the difference in their levels of specialization in producing a good. If the *ex ante* identical individuals choose the same level of specialization in producing a good, there is no endogenous comparative advantage. Of course, endogenous comparative advantage is not confined to cases involving *ex ante* identical individuals, as shown in chapter 2. The concept of endogenous comparative advantage formalizes Smith's idea (1776, p. 28) that differences in productivity between different specialists are consequences rather than the causes of the division of labor.

The exogenous evolution of division of labor is based on *inframarginal comparative statics of general equilibrium*. Inframarginal comparative statics of general equilibrium are analogous to the inframarginal comparative statics of individuals' decisions. That is, the general equilibrium discontinuously jumps between corner equilibria as values of parameters shift between parameter subspaces.

The difference between the inframarginal comparative statics of new classical general equilibrium and the inframarginal comparative statics of neoclassical general equilibrium, discussed in chapter 4, relates to the difference between new classical and neoclassical general equilibria. In the neoclassical framework, interior optimum decisions are common, and corner solutions are exceptional because of the neoclassical dichotomy between pure consumers and firms. But in the new classical framework, interior solutions never take place in equilibrium. Hence, corner solutions are the rule rather than the exception. It follows that we need inframarginal comparative statics analysis in neoclassical economics only for exceptional cases, such as for models with nonconvex preferences or with quasi-linear utility functions, as discussed in chapter 4. But inframarginal comparative statics analysis is the focus in new classical economics.

The *marginal comparative statics of general equilibrium* characterize changes of relative prices, of relative quantities of goods and factors, and of utility in response to those changes in parameters that take place within the subspace of parameters demarcated by the inframarginal comparative statics. For instance, if $k > k_0$, the general equilibrium is the corner equilibrium in D. If $k$ is increased, equilibrium per capita real income $u_D = k/4$ will increase. For $k < k_0$, the general equilibrium is the corner equilibrium in A. As $a$ is decreased, the equilibrium values of $x = y = 0.5^a$ will change. All such changes in the equilibrium values of endogenous variables are marginal comparative statics of general equilibrium. They are changes in equilibrium resource allocation in response to parameter changes for a given structure of division of labor, since each corner equilibrium determines resource allocation for a given structure. The inframarginal comparative statics of general equilibrium deal with changes in the structure of division of labor in response to parameter changes, since the general equilibrium determines the equilibrium structure. If there exists a parameter subspace within which a corner equilibrium is the general equilibrium, then within this parameter subspace the marginal comparative statics of general equilibrium is the comparative statics of the corner equilibrium.

We define a profile of quantities of goods produced, traded, and consumed by all consumer-producers for a given structure as *an allocation of resource for a given structure of division of labor*. In a sense, a corner equilibrium in the new classical framework is equivalent to a general equilibrium in the neoclassical framework. Both of them sort out resource allocation for a given structure of organization. Since problems of resource allocation relate to disaggregated demand and supply, the analysis of new classical corner equilibria relates to *microeconomic phenomena*. We define as a *problem of organization* the task of determining a structure of division of labor, which relates to all individuals' configurations of specialization, the size of the network of division of labor, variety between different configurations, and aggregate demand. The new classical general equilibrium sorts out problems of organization. Hence, the analysis of new classical general equilibria relates also to *macroeconomic phenomena*. Therefore, new classical theory represents a unified framework incorporating both microeconomics and macroeconomics as interrelated rather than separate levels of analysis. Microeconomic analysis relates to the marginal comparative statics of new classical general equilibrium, while macroeconomic analysis relates to the inframarginal comparative statics of new classical general equilibrium.

### Example 6.1: a new classical model with heterogeneous parameters of production and consumption

In the model we have discussed, there are too many symmetries. Hence, equilibrium values of endogenous variables are independent of relative tastes and relative production conditions. In this example, we examine the implications of relative tastes and relative production conditions for the equilibrium resource allocation and level of division of labor. Assume that all *ex ante* identical consumer-producers have the following utility and production functions:

$$u = (x + kx^d)^\alpha (y + ky^d)^{1-\alpha}, \qquad \alpha \in (0, 1)$$
$$x + x^s = l_x^a, \qquad y + y^s = l_y^b.$$

Then the corner equilibrium relative price in structure D is $p_y/p_x = k^{1-2\alpha}$. Its derivative with respect to $k$ is positive when $\alpha < \frac{1}{2}$ and is negative when $\alpha > \frac{1}{2}$. The corner equilibrium relative number of the two types of specialists is $M_x/M_y = \alpha k^{1-2\alpha}/(1 - \alpha)$. Its derivative with respect to $k$ has similar features. The general equilibrium is the division of labor if

$$k > k_2 \equiv \left( \frac{(\alpha a)^{\alpha a}[b(1 - \alpha)]^{b(1-\alpha)}}{[aa + (1 - a)b]^{\alpha a1(1-\alpha)b}\alpha^\alpha(1 - \alpha)^{1-\alpha}} \right)^{\frac{1}{2\alpha(1-\alpha)}}$$

and autarky if $k < k_2$. Equation $k = k_2$, which involves four parameters, partitions the four-dimensional space of parameters $a$, $b$, $\alpha$, and $k$ into the two subspaces. You should follow the procedure in the last and present chapters to solve for individuals' decisions, the marginal and inframarginal comparative statics of the decisions, the two corner equilibria, the general equilibrium, and finally for the marginal and inframarginal comparative statics of the general equilibrium.

## 6.3.2 Comparative statics of decisions vs. comparative statics of equilibrium

As the inframarginal comparative statics of general equilibrium indicate, the most important trade-off generated by interactions between self-interested decisions is the trade-off between economies of division of labor and transaction costs. If trading efficiency is low, then the positive network effects of division of labor are outweighed by transaction costs, so that the resulting efficient trade-off is associated with autarky. If trading efficiency is sufficiently high, the positive network effects outweigh transaction costs, so that the division of labor will be chosen. The efficient trade-off is not chosen by a central planner. It results rather from interactions between self-interested decisions in choosing occupation configurations. The comparative statics of general equilibrium describe how the consequences of these interactions change in response to changes in environment. It differs from the comparative statics of decisions that we investigated in chapter 5.

From the corner solutions in table 5.2, it can be seen that the decisions for a given configuration are functions of relative prices and parameters of production and transaction. For instance, the neoclassical demand law for a given configuration $dy^d/d(p_y/p_x) = -0.5$ $(p_x/p_y)^2$ is part of the marginal comparative statics of decisions. From the corner solution for a given configuration in example 6.1, we can see that the optimum decision, which is a corner solution in a configuration, is a function of parameters of tastes and production as well. If the maximum amount of working time is a parameter rather than a specific number, then the optimum decision is a function of the endowment parameter too. The inframarginal comparative statics are associated with discontinuous jumps of the optimum decisions between configurations as parameters of prices, tastes, endowments, and production and transaction conditions shift between the parameter subspaces that demarcate different configurations. Hence, the (marginal and inframarginal) comparative statics of decisions explain the optimum quantities of consumption, production and trade, and the optimum configuration of specialization, by parameters of prices, tastes, endowments, and production and transaction conditions.

Recalling table 6.1, we can see that the general equilibrium relative price, numbers of different specialists, and quantities of consumption, production, and trade are determined by parameters of tastes, endowments, population size, and production and transaction conditions. The marginal and inframarginal comparative statics of general equilibrium explain relative price, numbers of different specialists, structure of division of labor, per capita real income, and resource allocation by the parameters. In summary, the comparative statics of decisions may be represented by the following mapping:

Parameters of tastes, transaction             Quantities demanded and supplied,
and production conditions, endowments,  ⟹    resource allocation, utility,
prices, numbers of different specialists      configuration of specialization

The comparative statics of general equilibrium are summarized by a different mapping:

Parameters of tastes, endowment,              Quantities demanded and supplied,
production and transaction              ⟹    relative prices, numbers of specialists,
conditions, population size                   structure of division of labor

Hence, prices and numbers of individuals choosing different configurations are explaining parameters in the comparative statics of decisions, while in the comparative statics of general equilibrium, they are endogenous variables, themselves explained by parameters of tastes, endowments, production and transaction conditions, and population size. It should be noted that the comparative statics of decisions relate only to individuals' occupation configurations, since an individual cannot choose the structure of division of labor for society. The comparative statics of general equilibrium relate to the structure of division of labor for society as a whole, since the general equilibrium is the outcome of interactions among all individuals' optimizing decisions.

### 6.3.3 The inappropriateness of marginal cost pricing and the difference between neoclassical and new classical general equilibrium

It is interesting to note that the marginal cost pricing rule no longer holds in the equilibrium involving specialization. If $k > k_0$ in example 5.1, the general equilibrium is the division of labor. The transformation function for each individual is given by

$$\left(x^p\right)^{1/a} + \left(y^{pp}\right)^{1/a} = 1$$

where $x^p \equiv x + x^s$ and $y^p \equiv y + y^s$. The marginal opportunity cost of good x in terms of good y is

$$-\frac{dy^p}{dx^p} = \left(y^p/x^p\right)^{(a-1)/a}$$

This is 0 for a specialist in x, since for her $x^p = 1$ and $y^p = 0$. It is infinite for a specialist in y, since for her $x^p = 0$ and $y^p = 1$. But in the general equilibrium with division of labor the equilibrium price of good x in terms of good y is 1. This is a formal substantiation of Coase's argument (1946) against the marginal cost pricing rule. Coase shows that total benefit–cost analysis is necessary and marginal analysis is inappropriate for the pricing of goods with increasing returns in production. The marginal cost pricing rule is a fatal flaw of neoclassical economics. This rule makes a competitive market incompatible with increasing returns. In the real world, the price of goods with increasing returns in production is determined by total benefit–cost analysis. A break-even condition (total benefit equals total cost) determines the price. The break-even condition is similar to our utility equalization condition, which implies that shifting between configurations cannot make a decision-maker better off.

It is interesting to note the differences between neoclassical and new classical general equilibrium analysis. In neoclassical economics, the structures of production functions for firms are exogenously given. Economic phenomena in equilibrium are mainly explained by the exogenously specified structures of firms. For new classical economics, the structure of *ex post* production functions and firms are endogenously determined by the environment. This is analogous to the differences between a model based on an *ad hoc* demand and supply system and a properly closed general equilibrium model based on utility and production functions. In the former, equilibrium phenomena are determined by the nature of the *ad hoc* demand and supply systems, whereas in the latter case, equilibrium phenomena are ultimately determined by the specification of the environment (the degree of economies of specialization, transaction conditions, and tastes).

## ◆ 6.4 Efficiency of the Invisible Hand

Because of the central role of inframarginal analysis in new classical economics, there are two steps in welfare analysis. We first investigate whether a corner equilibrium is locally Pareto optimal for a given structure. The Yao theorem implies that, in a model with *ex ante* identical individuals, if each corner equilibrium is locally Pareto optimal for a given structure, then the general equilibrium must be globally Pareto optimal, since the general equilibrium is the Pareto optimum corner equilibrium according to the Yao theorem. Now let us prove that each corner equilibrium is locally Pareto optimal.

### 6.4.1 The first welfare theorem in the new classical framework

It is trivial to prove that the corner equilibrium in structure A is locally Pareto optimal, since the corner equilibrium is equivalent to the corner solution that maximizes each individual's utility in configuration A. Now we consider structure D. Let $X_i = \{x_i, x_i^s, y_i^d\}$ be the decision of individual i choosing configuration (x/y) and $Y_j = \{y_j, y_j^s, x_j^d\}$ be the decision of individual j choosing configuration (y/x). Denote the corner equilibrium values of $X_i$ and $Y_i$ as $X_i^*$ and $Y_i^*$, respectively, and the corner equilibrium price of good x in terms of good y as $p$. Now we use the argument of negation to establish the claim that the corner equilibrium in structure D is locally Pareto optimal. Suppose not. Then there exists an allocation $X_i$, $Y_i$ in structure D such that

$$u_i(X_i) \geq u_i(X_i^*) \text{ for all } i, \text{ and } u_i(X_i) > u_i(X_i^*) \text{ for some } i \quad (6.2a)$$

$$u_j(Y_j) \geq u_j(Y_j^*) \text{ for all } j. \quad (6.2b)$$

This implies that a benevolent central planner can increase at least one individual's utility without reducing all others' utilities by shifting the decisions from $\{X_i^*, Y_i^*\}$ to $\{X_i, Y_i\}$. That is, the corner equilibrium decisions $\{X_i^*, Y_i^*\}$ are not locally Pareto optimal.

Since utility is a strictly increasing function of consumption, the generalized axiom of revealed preference (see section 3.5 in chapter 3) and (6.2a) implies

$$p_x x_i^s \leq p_y y_i^d \text{ for all } i \text{ and } p_x x_i^s < p_y y_i^d \text{ for some } i \tag{6.3a}$$

and (6.2b) implies

$$p_y y_j^s \leq p_x x_j^d \text{ for all } j. \tag{6.3b}$$

Adding up the above inequalities for all individuals yields

$$p_x \sum_i x_i^s < p_y \sum_i y_i^d \text{ and } p_y \sum_j y_j^s \leq p_x \sum_j x_j^d \text{ or} \tag{6.4}$$

$$(p_x/p_y) \sum_i x_i^s < \sum_i y_i^d \text{ and } \sum_j y_j^s \leq (p_x/p_y) \sum_j x_j^d$$

(6.4), together with the market clearing condition for good y, $\sum_i y_i^d = \sum_j y_j$, yields

$$\sum_i x_i^s < \sum_j x_j^d$$

This violates the material balance condition for good x and therefore establishes the claim that the Pareto superior allocation $X_i$ and $Y_i$ are infeasible. Hence, the corner equilibrium in D, $X_i^*$ and $Y_i^*$ must be locally Pareto optimal.

This deduction, together with the Yao theorem, establishes theorem 6.2.

**Theorem 6.2 (the first welfare theorem):** In a new classical model with *ex ante* identical consumer-producers, each corner equilibrium is locally Pareto optimal for the given structure and the general equilibrium is globally Pareto optimal.

This theorem is applicable to all static new classical equilibrium models with *ex ante* identical individuals in this text, provided that preferences are nonsatiated and the relevant corner equilibrium exists. The existence theorem and the first welfare theorem for very general new classical models allowing *ex ante* differences between individuals is proved in chapter 13.

We describe the local Pareto optimum for a given structure as *efficient resource allocation*, and the global Pareto optimum as *efficient economic organism*, which includes efficient structure of division of labor and related efficient size of the market network. Theorem 6.2 implies that a corner equilibrium sorts out the efficient resource allocation for a given structure of division of labor, while the general equilibrium sorts out the efficient structure of division of labor and related efficient size of the market network as well as efficient resource allocation. Therefore, the first welfare theorem in the new classical framework implies that the most important function of the market is to determine the efficient structure of division of labor and efficient size of the market network. Its other function is to allocate resources efficiently. We describe an economy with an efficient structure of division of labor as *organization efficient*, and an economy with an efficient resource allocation for a given structure as *allocation efficient*. Certainly, each corner equilibrium is allocation efficient, but only the general equilibrium is organization efficient as well.

The implications of the first welfare theorem are different in the new classical and neoclassical frameworks not only because of the distinction between organization efficiency and allocation efficiency, but also because of the disparity between the production possibility frontier (PPF) and the Pareto optimum.

## 6.4.2 Economic development and disparity between the Pareto optimum and the PPF

From the neoclassical models in chapters 3 and 4, we know that the PPF is associated with the Pareto optimum. This is because the convex aggregate production set is a simple sum of convex individual production sets, and a central planner's solution for the maximization of total profit of all firms is equivalent to decentralized profit maximization of each individual firm. But in the new classical model in this chapter, we can see that the PPF may not be associated with the Pareto optimum. From theorems 6.1 and 6.2 and proposition 6.1, we know that the general equilibrium structure is A, which is Pareto optimal, if $k < k_0$. But the PPF is associated with structure D, not with structure A (recall figure 2.5). This is because in the new classical framework, there are multiple production schedules associated with different structures. The PPF is the highest of them. The trade-off between economies of division of labor and transaction costs implies that the Pareto optimum that is associated with the utility frontier is not the same as the production possibility frontier if trading efficiency is low. As trading efficiency is improved, the general equilibrium and the Pareto optimum get closer to the PPF. In other words, the equilibrium aggregate productivity is endogenized in the new classical model. This implies that the degree of scarcity is endogenized, while productivity is endogenously explained by individuals' decisions as to their levels of specialization, and is ultimately determined by trading efficiency.

Hence, problems of economic development occupy a central place in new classical economics. We do not need separate development economics to address these problems. Although the new classical model in the current chapter is a static model, the comparative statics of general equilibrium can explain not only productivity progress, increases in per capita real income and consumption, and other "growth phenomena"; they can also explain the emergence of the market, increases in diversification of economic structure and in the extent of the market, and other "development phenomena." We shall further investigate economic development and growth using dynamic general equilibrium models in chapters 22, 23, 24, 25, 27.

The disparity between the Pareto efficient production schedule and the PPF highlights an important difference between new classical economics and neoclassical economics. As shown in exercise 6 (see also Wen, 1997), if each consumer-producer maximizes production profit first and then maximizes utility for a given income, the resulting optimum production plan is not associated with the Pareto optimum in the new classical model. In other words, the dichotomy between the production decision and the consumption decision may generate Pareto inefficient decisions in a new classical model. As shown in chapters 3 and 4, such a dichotomy will not cause Pareto inefficient decisions in the neoclassical framework.

## 6.4.3 Interdependence and conflict between efficient resource allocation and efficient organization

### Example 6.2: effects of a tax on allocation and organization efficiencies

Consider the new classical model of example 5.1 with $k = 1$ and with taxation introduced. A benevolent and efficient government imposes a tax rate $t$ on each dollar of goods sold, and then evenly distributes the tax revenue among $M$ consumer-producers. Hence, the income transfer that each individual receives from the government is $r = t(M_x x^s + M_y y^s)/M$ if the structure D is the general equilibrium. Applying inframarginal analysis, and using the symmetry of the model, we can solve for the corner solutions in the three configurations A, (x/y), and (y/x). Then the utility equalization and market clearing condition in structure D yields the corner equilibrium in D, as follows.

$$p_x/p_y = 1, \quad M_x = M_y = M/2, \quad x = y = 1/(2 - t), \quad x^s = y^s = x^d = y^d =$$
$$(1 - t)/(2 - t), \quad u_D = (1 - t)/(2 - t)^2, \quad r = p_x(1 - t)t/(2 - t)$$

where $u_D$ is per capita real income in structure D, which is a monotonically decreasing function of the tax rate $t$. This implies that the tax causes a distortion resulting in a reduction of utility. The Pareto optimum tax rate is 0. But the corner equilibrium relative price in structure D is the same as in the equilibrium with no tax. Aggregate relative resources allocated to the production of the two goods, $M_x/M_y = 1$, and aggregate relative consumption and production of the two goods, $(M_x x + M_y x^d)/(M_x y^d + M_y y) = 1$, are Pareto optimal. However each individual's relative consumption of the two goods is not Pareto optimal. The relative consumption is $x/y^d = 1/(1 - t) > 1$ for an x specialist, and is $x^d/y = 1 - t < 1$ for a y specialist. Also, you can verify that each individual's resource allocation is inconsistent with the first-order condition for the Pareto optimum problem that maximizes the x specialist's utility for a constant utility of a y specialist. The tax encourages individuals to allocate too much resources for self-provided consumption and correspondingly discourages production for and consumption from the market. Hence, this allocation inefficiency may also cause organization inefficiency.

Since by definition autarky does not involve trade, no tax revenue can be collected in this case, so that per capita real income in autarky is the same as in example 5.1. The general equilibrium will be the corner equilibrium in structure D in the absence of tax when $k = 1$. But a sufficiently high tax rate will make $u_D$ smaller than per capita real income in autarky, $2^{-2a}$ even if $k = 1$. If $k < 1$, then we can show that the critical value of $k$ that ensures that division of labor will be the general equilibrium is smaller in the absence of tax than when the tax is imposed. Hence, if $k$ is between the two critical values, then the general equilibrium in the absence of tax is the division of labor, while the general equilibrium in the presence of tax is autarky. This example illustrates the interdependence between allocation efficiency and organization efficiency. The allocation inefficiency caused by the tax may also cause an inefficient general equilibrium level of division of labor. The model in exercise 3 shows that the imposition of unequal tax rates on different goods will cause distortions in relative price and aggregate resource allocation as well as in each individuals' resource allocation, thereby generating a higher likelihood of inefficient organization than in the case of a uniform tax rate. The next example illustrates the conflict between allocation efficiency and organization efficiency in a new classical model.

## Example 6.3: conflict between allocation efficiency and organization efficiency

Suppose that in the model in example 5.1 the utility function is $u = (x + kx^d)^\alpha (y + ky^d)^{1-\alpha}$. Then we can solve for corner equilibria in autarky and in structure D as follows.

$$u_A = [\alpha^\alpha(1 - \alpha)^{1-\alpha}]^a$$
$$u_D = [\alpha^\alpha(1 - \alpha)^{1-\alpha}]k^{2\alpha(1-\alpha)}, \quad p_x/p_y = k^{2\alpha-1},$$
$$M_x = (k^{1-2\alpha}M/(1 - \alpha + \alpha k^{1-2\alpha}), \quad M_y = (1 - \alpha)M/(1 - \alpha + \alpha k^{1-2\alpha})$$

The general equilibrium is the division of labor iff $k > k_1 \equiv [\alpha^\alpha(1 - \alpha)^{1-\alpha}]^{(a-1)/2\alpha(1-\alpha)}$. It is easy to show that the critical value $k_1$ is minimized with respect to $\alpha$ at $\alpha = \frac{1}{2}$ and that $M_x = M_y = M/2$ at $\alpha = \frac{1}{2}$. In other words, as the differential in tastes for different goods tends to 0, the general equilibrium is more likely to be the division of labor. This indicates a possible conflict between organization efficiency which relates to higher productivity and economic development, and efficiency of resource allocation, if a good is more preferred than the other good. Under this circumstance, in order to accommodate a taste differential, a high level of division of labor and related high productivity may have to be sacrificed. This is because for a larger $k_1$, $k$ is more likely to be smaller than $k_1$, so that autarky instead of the division of labor is more likely to occur in equilibrium.

## Example 6.4: free entry and free pricing

In new classical models, the power to manipulate the relative numbers of different specialists has a more crucial impact on allocation and organization efficiencies than does the power to manipulate relative prices. This result can be used to criticize Lange's theory of market socialism, which emphasizes the importance of price flexibility in achieving allocation efficiency. According to the theory of market socialism, the government adjusts prices according to excess demand and directs managers of state enterprises to choose profit maximizing quantities of outputs and inputs. Many economists have pointed out that self-interested government officials have no incentive to price commodities according to excess demand because of the absence of residual claimants of profits. According to our model in this chapter, even if a system of flexible prices clears the market, the self-interested government officials may still manipulate the relative numbers of different specialists, for instance by restricting free entry into the banking sector and entrepreneurial activities, such that market clearing prices of the services provided by the officials are high. This form of market socialism is not much better than the Soviet-style socialist system under which government-controlled prices do not clear the market and the great excess demand becomes the source of the power of the central planning authorities. The government officials gain a great deal of tangible and intangible benefit from that power.

## Key Terms and Review

Network effects of division of labor.
How the market coordinates division of labor and utilizes network effects of division of labor.
The connection between marginal analysis and coordination failure vs. connection between inframarginal analysis and coordination success in the market.
Structure based on configurations and corner equilibrium based on corner solutions.
General equilibrium vs. corner equilibrium.
Marginal vs. inframarginal comparative statics of general equilibrium.
Difference between an individual's demand and supply functions, total market demand and supply functions, and new classical aggregate demand and supply functions.
Implications of Walras's law for solving for a corner equilibrium.
Implications of free pricing and free choice between profession configurations for coordination of the network of division of labor.
Why marginal cost pricing may not work in a new classical general equilibrium.
Allocation efficiency vs. organization efficiency.
Implications of institution for the equilibrium level of division of labor through its effect on trading efficiency.

Why the Pareto optimum may not be associated with the production possibility frontier.

Implications of trading efficiency for the disparity between the Pareto optimum and the PPF and for reducing scarcity.

Implication of the trade-off between economies of division of labor and transaction costs for endogenizing productivity, network size of division of labor, and trade dependence.

What is the relationship between decisions in choosing an occupation configuration and the size of network of division of labor.

## Further Reading

*Network effects*: Buchanan and Stubblebine (1962), Farrell and Saloner (1985), Katz and Shapiro (1985, 1986), Liebowitz and Margolis (1994); *inframarginal analysis and rejection of marginal cost pricing*: Buchanan and Stubblebine (1962), Coase (1946, 1960), Rosen (1978, 1983), Yang and Ng (1993), Azariadis (1975), Baily (1974), Liebowitz and Margolis (1994), Tirole (1989); *neoclassical equilibrium models with endogenous specialization*: Baumgardner (1988), Kim (1989), Locay (1990), Tamura (1991); *neoclassical general equilibrium models with transaction costs and constant returns to scale technology*: Hahn (1971), Karman (1981), Kurz (1974), Schweizer (1986); *models with transaction costs and economies of scale*: Wong and Yang (1994, 1998), Krugman and Venables (1995), Fujita and Krugman (1995).

## QUESTIONS

1   What are network effects of division of labor? What is the difference between network effects of division of labor and economies of scale? How does this difference affect the explanatory power of economics? How can the market choose the efficient network size of division of labor? Why can we not really understand demand and supply if we do not understand the network effects of division of labor?

2   Why is the notion of general equilibrium a powerful vehicle in analyzing the network effects of division of labor? What is the difference between the interdependence between quantities of goods chosen by individuals for given prices and the market equilibrium prices that emerge as the consequence of all individuals' quantity decisions, and the interdependence between individuals' decisions in choosing their levels of specialization?

3   Suppose a student raises concerns about coordination failure in utilizing the network effects of division of labor in the model in this chapter. She suggests that if there is no central planner, the market cannot select the Pareto optimum corner equilibrium from the multiple corner equilibria. Analyze the coordination mechanism in the marketplace and address her concerns.

4   Use your daily experience to explain how the decentralized market coordinates individuals' decisions in choosing occupation configurations and levels of specialization to utility network effect of division of labor. If economies of division of labor outweigh transaction costs, but nobody is willing to choose some occupation configuration, how can the market sort out the coordination problem?

5   Many individuals prefer the occupation configurations of medical doctors, lawyers, and higher executive positions in large companies to those of doormen, cleaners, and garbage collectors. If all individuals refuse to choose occupation configurations in the latter category, then coordination failure of division of labor occurs. How can the market sort out this coordination problem? In neoclassical economics, the function of free pricing in equilibrating demand and supply is used to explain how the market coordinates conflicting self-interested decisions. In addition to free pricing, new classical economics empha-

sizes also free choice of occupation configurations in coordinating the division of labor, and inframarginal analysis across occupation configurations in coordinating the network effects of division of labor. Discuss the implications of the difference between the new classical and neoclassical frameworks for analyzing the coordination mechanism in the marketplace.

6   Many macroeconomists claim that coordination failure of the network of division of labor may generate an inefficient network of the market. For example, it is argued that if each individual wants to save money through reducing purchases, then each cannot sell much, so that per capita income is too low to afford many purchases; thus a self-fulfilling recession can generate coordination failure in the marketplace. Analyze why this argument may be misleading.

7   Network effect is a basic feature of division of labor. Smith and Young emphasized the function of the market in coordinating the network of division of labor, though they did not use the word network. Why didn't economists pay attention to this feature of the market and the function of the invisible hand in coordinating division of labor until recently? Why wasn't network effect the focus of economics in the nineteenth century and in most of the twentieth century?

8   Some economists state that neoclassical mainstream economics is not applicable to less developed countries where many markets are absent. Does this statement hold for new classical economics that formalizes the core of classical mainstream economics, which is about under what conditions the market emerges from the division of labor?

9   The Lewis model (1955) and the Fei and Ranis model (1964) are interpreted by some economists as explaining economic development as a process in which labor is transferred from the agricultural sector to the industrial sector. Compare this view of economic development to Lewis's original idea, formalized by the model in this chapter, that economic development is an evolutionary process of division of labor. Increases in each person's level of specialization and increases in the diversity of occupation configurations are two aspects of this evolution.

# EXERCISES

1   Suppose in example 5.1 the production functions are $x^p = l_x - a$ and $y^p = l_x - b$, and the utility function is $u = (x + kx^d)^\alpha (y + ky^d)^{1-\alpha}$ where $i^p$ is the output level of good i. Solve for the new classical general equilibrium and its inframarginal comparative statics.

2   Suppose in example 5.1 the utility function is of the CES type and the time endowment constraint is $l_x + l_y = 1 - c$ if an individual consumes one good and is $l_x + l_y = 1 - 2c$ if an individual consumes two goods. Solve for the new classical general equilibrium and its inframarginal comparative statics.

3   Suppose in example 5.1 a value tax rate $t$ is imposed on each dollar of good x that is purchased, and that the total tax revenue is evenly distributed among the sellers of x. Solve for the general equilibrium and its inframarginal comparative statics. Compare the results to the solutions in exercises 2, 3, and 4 in chapter 4. Discuss the different implications of tax and transaction costs in a neoclassical equilibrium model and in a new classical equilibrium model.

4   Assume in example 5.1 the trading efficiency coefficient for good i is $k_i$ and $1 > k_x > k_y > 0$. Solve for the general equilibrium and its inframarginal comparative statics. Analyze the implications of the difference in trading efficiency for the equilibrium relative price. Why is

the implication of the difference in trading efficiency different from the implication of the difference in tax rate for the equilibrium relative price in exercise 3?

5   Chu and Wang, 1998, Ng and Yang, 2000: Suppose that in exercise 1, $\alpha = 0.5$ and the production function of x is modified as $x^p = l_x - a - s \Sigma y^p$ where $s$ is an externality parameter. This specification implies that there is a negative externality of production of y on production of x. Suppose that the government taxes sales of good y at the tax rate $t$, then returns the tax revenue evenly to each buyer of y. Solve for the corner equilibrium for structure D, then solve for an individual's utility value when she chooses autarky (or specialization) and all other individuals choose D (or A). Then solve the corner equilibrium in a structure where the population is divided among autarky and specialization in x and y. Find general equilibrium and its inframarginal comparative statics. Show that within a certain parameter space, Pareto improving Pigouvian tax does not exist. Use your answer to justify Coase's claim that Pigou's marginal analysis of effects of tax on the distortions caused by externality is misleading and inframarginal analysis is essential for the analysis of the distortions.

6   Wen, 1997: Assume that in example 5.1 each consumer-producer maximizes production profit for given prices and then maximizes utility for a given income. Show that the optimum production plan based on such a dichotomy between the production decision and the consumption decision might not be Pareto optimal.

7   Solve for the inframarginal comparative statics of the model in exercise 6 in chapter 5.

## chapter 7

# TRADE PATTERN AND PROFESSIONAL MIDDLEMEN

◆ **7.1 Why Can Professional Middlemen Make Money? What Are the Determinants of Business Success?**

In all new classical models considered so far, trading efficiency has been exogenously given and specialization in trading has been disallowed. We have also focused on symmetric models. That is, in addition to identical utility functions and systems of production for all individuals, we have assumed that the parameters representing tastes, the degree of economies of specialization, and trading efficiency are the same for all goods. Under these conditions trade pattern makes no difference and only the number of traded goods matters. Even though we have considered some asymmetric models, the number of goods in those models has been restricted to two, so that the implications of asymmetry for inframarginal comparative statics could not be fully explored. In this chapter, we specify a production function for trading activities and allow for specialization in trading. Moreover, we assume that the preference parameters and the degrees of economies of specialization differ across three goods, although all individuals are *ex ante* identical in all aspects. We can thus investigate how professional middlemen emerge from the division of labor between productive activities and trading activities. The implications of relative preferences and relative degrees of economies of specialization for the pattern of trade can be investigated in this extended model. In addition, when we endogenize trading efficiency, we can specify an exogenous distance between each pair of neighbors, and show that all endogenous variables may be explained by that distance via comparative statics analysis of equilibrium. This will allow us to investigate the implications of urbanization for the development of division of labor and the progress of productivity.

The story in this chapter runs as follows. If individuals can choose their levels of specialization in transacting activities in which there are economies of specialization, then trading efficiency can be explained by the level of specialization in transacting activities. As trading efficiency is improved due to institutional changes, the development of urbanization, or as a better trading infrastructure is developed, the level of specialization in transacting activities will be increased. Thus trading efficiency is endogenously improved and accordingly the division of labor and productivity progress in production activities are promoted.

If not all goods are involved in the division of labor, then those with more significant economies of specialization in production and transacting, or those that are more desirable, become involved in trade earlier than other goods.

The asymmetry in the models in this chapter generates some complexities in solving for general equilibrium, which is one of many corner equilibria. Hence, we need to do more research on the method of inframarginal analysis.

---

### Questions to Ask Yourself when Reading this Chapter

♦ Why are there economies of specialization in transacting activities? What are their implications for the division of labor in production?

♦ What are network effects of division of labor? How can the market choose the efficient size of the network of division of labor and the related extent of the market?

♦ What are the determinants of the equilibrium structure of trade and of a successful business?

♦ What is the relationship between the division of labor in production and the division of labor in transacting activities?

♦ What are the implications for the division of labor in production and transacting activities of urbanization; *laissez-faire* policy; and a legal system that effectively protects and enforces private property rights?

---

## ♦ 7.2 A Model with Trading Activities and Heterogeneous Parameters

### Example 7.1: a new classical model with endogenous trading efficiency and endogenous specialization in transacting activities

Consider an economy with a continuum of *ex ante* identical consumer-producers of mass $M$ and three consumer goods. The self-provided amounts of these goods are $x$, $y$, and $z$, respectively. The amounts of these goods sold on the market are $x^s$, $y^s$, and $z^s$, respectively. The amounts of these goods purchased on the market are $x^d$, $y^d$, and $z^d$, respectively. The transaction cost coefficient is $1 - k$. Furthermore, we assume that $k$ depends on the quantity of labor used in transactions. $k$ can therefore be viewed as transaction service. Such services are categorized into self-provided ones and traded ones. Let $k = r + r^d$ where $r$ is the self-provided quantity of transaction service and $r^d$ is the quantity purchased of transaction service. The greater the transaction service $r + r^d$, the larger the portion of a purchase received by its buyer. Signifying the quantity sold of transaction service by $r^s$, transaction technology and production functions are thus given by

$$x + x^s = l_x^a \qquad y + y^s = l_y^b \qquad z + z^s = l_z^c \qquad r + r^s = l_r^h, \tag{7.1a}$$

where $x + x^s$, $y + y^s$, $z + z^s$, and $r + r^s$ are the respective output levels of four goods and

services, and $l_s$ is an individual's level of specialization in producing good (or service) $i$ where $i = x, y, z, r$. The endowment constraint of the specific labor for an individual is

$$l_x + l_y + l_z + l_r = 1, \qquad l_i \in [0,1], \qquad i = x, y, z, r. \tag{7.1b}$$

(7.1) is identical for all individuals.

Assume, further, that the transaction service $r$ (or $r^d$) relates only to the quantity traded, and that there are transaction costs related to the distance between a pair of trade partners; thus there is a location problem. Suppose that all individuals' residences are evenly spaced, so that the geographic distance between each pair of neighbors is a constant. The distance between a pair of trade partners may differ from the distance between a pair of neighbors. If all trade partners of an individual are located in a circle around her with radius $R$, it can be shown that the average distance between this individual and her trade partners is proportional to $R$ and that the number of trade partners $N$ is proportional to $R^2$. Hence, the average distance between this individual and her trade partners is proportional to $\sqrt{N}$. If all the trade partners supply different goods to this individual, the number of traded goods for her is $n = N + 1$. For simplicity, we assume that the number of trade partners of an individual, $N = n - 1$, where $n$ is the number of traded goods for her.

Assume that the transaction cost coefficient $1 - K$ characterizes the transaction cost related to the average distance between a pair of trade partners; then the fraction $1 - K$ of $(r + r^d)x^d$, $(r + r^d)y^d$, or $(r + r^d)z^d$ disappears on the way from a seller to a buyer. $1 - K$ is related to the number of trade partners of an individual, $N$, as given by

$$1 - K = s\sqrt{N} \tag{7.2}$$

where $s$ is a parameter depending on the distance between a pair of neighbors and $\pi$. If $1 - K$ is independent of $N$, equilibrium will be either autarky or the extreme division of labor. This implies that an intermediate level of partial division of labor never occurs in equilibrium. It follows that a gradual evolution of division of labor is impossible. Hence, (7.2) is essential for gradual evolution of division of labor. It implies that transaction cost increases more quickly than positive network effect of division of labor does as the number of traded goods increases. Taking (7.2) into account, the amounts consumed of the three goods are $x + Kkx^d$, $y + Kky^d$, and $z + Kkz^d$, respectively, where $k = r + r^d$. The utility function is identical for all individuals:

$$u = [x + K(r + r^d)x^d]^\alpha [\, y + K(r + r^d)y^d]^\beta [z + K(r + r^d)z^d]^\gamma \tag{7.3}$$

where $0 < \alpha, \beta, \gamma < 1$ and $\alpha + \beta + \gamma = 1$. Since each person's working time endowment is one, the maximum value of $r + r^d$ is always less than one in equilibrium.

The Walrasian regime is assumed.

## ◆ 7.3. The Decision to be a Professional Middleman

The individual decision problem is

$$\text{Max: } u = [x + K(r + r^d)x^d]^\alpha [\, y + K(r + r^d)y^d]^\beta [z + K(r + r^d)z^d]^\gamma \tag{7.4}$$

s.t. $x + x^s = l_x^a$  $y + y^s = l_y^b$  $z + z^s = l_z^c$          (production function)
    $r + r^s = l_r^h$                                      (transaction technology)
    $l_x + l_y + l_z + l_r = 1$                            (endowment constraint)
    $p_r(r^s - r^d) + p_x(x^s - x^d) + p_y(y^s - y^d) + p_z(z^s - z^d) = 0$   (budget constraint)

where $i$, $i^s$, $i^d$, and $l_i$ ($i = x, y, z, r$) are decision variables, which may take on zero or positive values. $p_i$ is the price of good (or service) $i$. There are $2^{12} = 4096$ combinations of zero and non zero variables. Following the same approach as in chapter 5, we can also establish the Wen theorem for the model in this chapter. The Wen theorem, combined with the budget constraint and positive utility constraint, implies that only 29 configurations of four general types need to be considered.

1) Autarky, denoted by A, i.e. an individual self-provides three goods. For this configuration

$$x^s = y^s = z^s = x^d = y^d = z^d = r = r^d = r^s = l_r = 0$$

In other words, the amounts sold and purchased of the three goods and transaction services are 0. This configuration is depicted in figure 7.1(a).

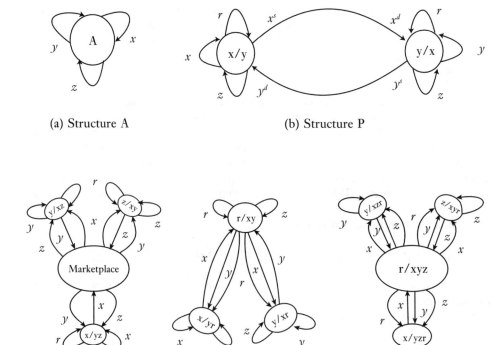

(a) Structure A                    (b) Structure P

(c) Structure C          (d) Structure PT          (e) Structure CT

◆ **Figure 7.1**: Configurations and structures

2) Configuration $(i/j)$, i.e. an individual sells good (or service) $i$ and purchases good (or service) j, where $i, j = x, y, z, r$. For such configurations

$$t^s = t^d = i^d = j = j^s = l_j = 0 \text{ for } t \neq i, j,$$

where the index $t$ denotes the goods other than goods $i$ and $j$. By 2 permutations of four factors, we obtain 12 configurations of this type: (x/y), (y/x), (x/z), (z/x), (y/z), (z/y), (r/x), (x/r), (r/y), (y/r), (r/z), and (z/r). Two configurations of this type, (x/y) and (y/x), are depicted in figure 7.1(b).

3) Configuration (i/jt), i.e. an individual sells good (or service) i and purchases goods (or services) j and t. i, j, t = x, y, z, r. For such configurations

$$o^s = o^d = i^d = j = t = j^s = t^s = l_j = l_t = 0 \text{ for } o \neq i, j, t,$$

where index o denote the goods other than goods $i, j,$ and $t$. There are 12 configurations of this type: (x/yz), (x/yr), (x/zr), (y/xz), (y/xr), (y/zr), (z/xy), (z/xr), (z/yr), (r/xy), (r/xz), and (r/yz). Configurations (x/yz), (y/xz), and (z/xy) are depicted in panel (c) of figure 7.1. Configurations (x/yr), (y/xr), and (r/xy) are depicted in panel (d) of Figure 7.1. A person choosing configuration (r/xy) is partially specialized in trading.

4) Configuration (i/jto), i.e. an individual sells good (or service) i and purchases goods (or services) j, t, and o, i, j, t, o = x, y, z, r. For such configurations

$$i^d = j = t = o = j^s = t^s = o^s = l_j = l_t = l_o = 0 \text{ for } j, t, o \neq i$$

There are four configurations of this type: (x/yzr), (y/xzr), (z/xyr), (r/xyz). A person choosing (r/xyz) is a completely specialized middleman. The four configurations are depicted in panel (e) of figure 7.1.

Letting the relevant variables in problem (7.4) take on a zero value, an individual can solve for her optimal decisions for each configuration, which generate individual supply and demand functions and an indirect utility function.

## ◆ 7.4. Market Structures and Corner Equilibria

### 7.4.1 Basic vs. nonbasic structures

There are many market structures, such as those shown in figures 7.1 and 7.2. Structure P in figure 7.1(b) consists of configuration (x/y) (an individual sells x and buys y, and self-provides z and r) and configuration (y/x) (an individual sells y and buys x, and self-provides z and r). Structure B in figure 7.2(a) consists of configuration (x/yz) (an individual sells x and buys y and z, and self-provides r), configuration (y/x), and configuration (z/x) (an individual sells z and buys x, and self-provides y and r). Note that some combinations of configurations cannot satisfy the market clearing condition, since demand for a certain good is not matched by supply of that good in each of those combinations. For instance, a combination of configurations (x/y) and (x/z) cannot constitute a structure because the supply of x is not matched by the demand for x, and the demand for y or z is not matched by the supply of y or z.

In the analysis of equilibrium, we will use the concept of a *basic structure*. A basic structure is defined as a structure for which one cannot obtain another structure by dropping one or more of its constituent configurations. All structures in figure 7.1 and structure in figure 7.2(a) are basic structures. However, a combination of configurations (x/yz), (x/y), (y/x) and (z/x), depicted in figure 7.2(b), is not a basic structure because we can obtain structure B in figure 7.2(a) by dropping configuration (x/y).

Many configurations can be combined with a basic structure to obtain a new, *non basic structure*. For example, by combining structure B with any of the other 6 configurations which do not involve trade in $r$ and are not in structure B we can obtain $\sum_{j=0}^{6} C_6^j = 2^6 = 64$ structures, where $C_6^j$ is $j$ combinations of 6 factors. For a basic structure, the number of traded goods equals the number of configurations. For a nonbasic structure, the number of traded goods is smaller than the number of configurations.

For any nonbasic structure, the following lemma is applicable to most new classical models in this text.

**Lemma 7.1**: Utility equalization conditions cannot hold for all configurations in any nonbasic structure.

*Proof:* For a nonbasic structure, there are $m$ configurations and $n$ traded goods, and $m > n$. According to the Wen theorem, in any optimal configuration an individual sells at most one type of good. This implies that the types of configurations selling the same type of good exceed one if $m > n$. Hence, there are $m - 1$ conditions of utility equalization that contain only $n - 1$ unknown relative prices. If these $m - 1$ equations are independent of each other, this system has no consistent solution since $m > n$. Therefore, lemma 7.1 has been established. *Q.E.D.*

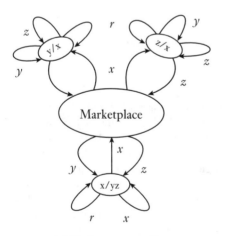

(a) Basic structure B

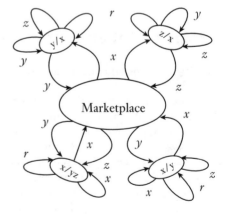

(b) A nonbasic structure

♦ **Figure 7.2:** Basic and nonbasic structures

## 7.4.2. Definitions of corner and general equilibria

A *general equilibrium* is a set of relative prices of all traded goods, a set of numbers of individuals selling different goods, a structure consisting of configurations chosen by all individuals, and quantities of goods produced, traded, and consumed by individuals that satisfy the following two conditions.

i) For the given relative prices of traded goods and numbers of individuals selling different goods in equilibrium, each individual's utility is maximized with respect to her choice of configuration and quantities of goods produced, traded, and consumed.

ii) For the given utility maximization decisions of all individuals, the relative prices of traded goods and number of individuals selling different goods equalize all individuals' utility levels and establish market clearing conditions for all goods.

The definition of *corner equilibrium* is the same as that for general equilibrium except that all individuals are allowed to choose only those configurations in a given structure, so that their utilities are maximized with respect to those configurations in the given structure, but not necessarily with respect to all configurations.

With these two concepts defined, the two-step approach to solving for the general equilibrium in this model is the same as in chapters 5 and 6. From the individual optimal decisions, the individual supply and demand functions for each configuration can be derived. Letting $M_i$ be the number of individuals selling good $i$, market clearing conditions can be specified for each basic structure. For example, for structure P, which is a division of $M$ individuals between configuration (x/y) and configuration (y/x), shown in Figure 7.1(b), there are the market clearing conditions.

$$M_x x^s = M_y x^d, \qquad M_x y^d = M_y y^s \tag{7.5a}$$

The individual budget constraints for the two constituent configurations are

$$p_{xy} x^s = y^d, \qquad p_{xy} x^d = y^s \tag{7.5b}$$

where $p_{xy} \equiv p_x/p_y$. One of these two equations implies the other due to Walras's law.
From (7.5), we can derive

$$p_{xy} = y^d/x^s = y^s/x^s M_{xy} \tag{7.6}$$

where $M_{xy} \equiv M_x/M_y$ is the ratio of the number of individuals choosing configuration (y/x) to those choosing configuration (x/y).

According to the individual optimal decisions, $x^s$ and $y^s$ are constants depending upon $a$, $b$, $c$, $\alpha$, $\beta$, $\gamma$, $s$, and $h$. Hence, (7.5b) implies, as in chapter 6, that $p_{xy}$ depends inversely on $M_{xy}$. The inverse relationship between the relative price of two traded goods and the relative number of individuals selling the two goods can be established for all basic structures in this model where each individual's supply function is independent of prices. For models in which individuals' supply functions are dependent on prices, this inverse relationship holds if the quantity of a good supplied increases with the price of this good relative to the prices of goods purchased, or if the supply law holds for each individual's supply function. Inserting (7.6) into the indirect utility functions for configurations (x/y) and (y/x), the utilities can be expressed as functions of $M_{xy}$. Setting $u(x/y) = u(y/x)$, we have

$$u(x/y) \equiv M_{xy}^{-\beta} G(x/y) = M_{xy}^{\alpha} G(y/x) \equiv u(y/x)$$

where $G$'s depend on $a$, $b$, $c$, $\alpha$, $\beta$, $\gamma$, $h$, and $s$. This equation yields a corner equilibrium value of $M_{xy}$. Inserting the value of $M_{xy}$ back into the indirect utility function for any constituent configuration gives a corner equilibrium utility $u^*$, which is real income as well as the real returns to labor in this structure because of the assumption that each person has one unit of labor. Since $u(x/y)$ is a decreasing function and $u(y/x)$ an increasing function of $M_{xy}$, they are analogues of neoclassical demand and supply functions, respectively. Hence, the corner equilibrium real income is determined by the intersection between the two functions, and represents the consequence of the interactions between different individuals in competition for a higher real income via choosing among different occupations.

According to the Yao theorem, we can compare per capita real incomes across basic structures to identify the Pareto optimum corner equilibrium as the general equilibrium. Since the general equilibrium jumps between structures as parameter values shift between parameter subspaces, this comparison also yields the inframarginal comparative statics of the general equilibrium.

In the new classical framework, each individual's decision in choosing a configuration determines the number of her transactions (or connections) with other individuals. All information describing the connections between individuals is called the *topological properties of an economic organism*. The most important of the topological properties is the size of the network of division of labor, which is referred to by some economists as the thickness of the market. The aggregate outcome of all individuals' decisions in choosing their configurations, and of the interactions between those decisions, determines the size of the network of division of labor for society as a whole. Graph theory and topology are powerful instruments for describing the network of division of labor. Chapter 13 considers formal definitions of the general equilibrium network of division of labor and its graph and reports some results with regard to the existence of the equilibrium network and its Pareto optimality.

The first welfare theorem is applicable to this model. This theorem and the Yao theorem are very important for us to appreciate the function of the market in utilizing network effect of division of labor. Some economists claim that the market cannot fully exploit network effects (they call it network externality). They ignore the fact that the market is a typical network with important network effects. The first welfare theorem and the Yao theorem show that the most important function of the market is to choose the efficient size of the market network and fully exploit the network effects of division of labor. In our new classical model, each individual's decision about how many goods to buy and to self-provide is dependent on prices. The equilibrium prices are determined by all individuals' decisions in choosing their numbers of traded goods. The interactions between these decisions also determine the network size of division of labor. But in this Walrasian equilibrium each individual's decision in choosing her network of trade partners does not directly depend on others' decisions in choosing their networks of trade. It is indirectly affected by these decisions via the interactions between them and prices. As each individual chooses a larger number of traded goods, she will have a larger network of anonymous trade partners. In this networking process, who trades with whom and who specializes in which activities are indeterminate. Sometimes, the network size of division of labor could be too large for any individual participant to comprehend even a trivial percentage of information about the network. But tremendous network effects of the division of labor can be utilized even if individuals are not aware of the functioning of the coordination mechanism.

## ◆ 7.5 The Equilibrium Size of the Network of Division of Labor

We now reconsider the model specified in (7.4). If it is assumed that $a = b = c = h$ and $\alpha = \beta = \gamma$, then it can be shown that per capita real incomes in the various structures are affected only by the number, and not by the composition, of traded goods and services. With this assumption, five distinct market structures are candidates for equilibrium and other structures are not distinguishable from these as far as per capita real income is concerned.

1. Autarky structure A, depicted in figure 7.1(a), consists of $M$ individuals choosing configuration A.
2. Structure P with partial division of labor in production, depicted in figure 7.1(b), consists of a division of $M$ individuals between configurations (x/y) and (y/x).
3. Structure C with complete division of labor in production, depicted in figure 7.1(c), is a division of $M$ individuals between configurations (x/yz), (y/xz) and (z/xy).
4. Structure PT with partial division of labor in production and transactions, depicted in panel (d), is a division of the population between (x/yr), (y/xr), and (r/xy).
5. Structure CT with complete division of labor in production and transactions, depicted in panel (e), is a division of the population between (x/yzr), (y/xzr), (z/xyr), and (r/xyz).

Following the approach devised in chapters 5 and 6, we can solve the corner equilibria in the five market structures for $a = b = c = h$ and $\alpha = \beta = \gamma$. The per capita real incomes and relative prices of traded goods for the five corner equilibria are summarized in table 7.1. In the table, $p_i$ is the price of traded good or service $i$, $M_r$ is the number of professional middlemen, and $M_i$ and $M_j$ are the numbers of producers of traded goods $i$ and $j$. Note that $K = 1 - s\sqrt{(n-1)}$ is used in computing the results in table 7.1, where $n - 1$ is the number of goods purchased by an individual and $s$ is an average distance parameter between each pair of neighbors. A comparison between $u(A)$, $u(P)$, and $u(C)$

**Table 7.1:** The five corner equilibria

| | | | Structure | | |
|---|---|---|---|---|---|
| | A | P | C | PT | CT |
| Relative price | | $p_x/p_y = 1$ | $p_x/p_y = p_z/p_y = 1$ | $p_r/p_x = p_r/p_y = 3^{a-1}2^{8/3}5^{5a/3}$ | $\dfrac{p_r}{p_x} = \dfrac{p_r}{p_y} = \dfrac{p_r}{p_z} = \dfrac{6^{1.2}}{5}$ |
| Number of specialists | | $M_x/M_y = 1$ | $M_x/M_y = M_z/M_y = 1$ | $\dfrac{M_r}{M_x} = \dfrac{M_r}{M_y} = .79\times.86^a$ | $\dfrac{M_r}{M_x} = \dfrac{M_r}{M_y} = \dfrac{M_r}{M_z} = 0.93$ |
| Real income | $\dfrac{1}{3^{3a}}$ | $\dfrac{1-s}{2^{2(3a+1)}}$ | $\dfrac{(1-s\sqrt{2})^2(3^32^2)^{a-1}}{5^{5a}}$ | $\dfrac{(1-s\sqrt{2})^2 3^{2(a-1)}2^{\frac{8(\alpha+1)}{3}}}{5^{\frac{5a}{3}}}$ | $\dfrac{(1-s\sqrt{2})^3}{6^{2.4}5^3}$ |

Table 7.2: General equilibrium and its inframarginal comparative statics

| $S$ | $> 0.71$ | $\in (.58, 0.71)$ | | $< .58$ | |
|---|---|---|---|---|---|
| $A$ | | $< 4.2$ | $> 4.2$ | $< 2.77$ | $> 2.77$ |
| Equilibrium structure | A | A | PT | A | CT |

indicates that $u(A) > u(P)$, $u(C)$ for $a > 1$. A comparison between $u(A)$, $u(PT)$, and $u(CT)$ yields table 7.2, which establishes proposition 7.3.

**Proposition 7.1:** Structures P and C cannot be equilibrium structures. The general equilibrium is structure A if the distance parameter $s > 0.71$; or if $0.71 > s > 0.58$ and the degree of economies of specialization $a < 4.20$; or if $s < 0.58$ and $a < 2.77$. The general equilibrium is structure PT if $0.71 > s > 0.58$ and $a > 4.20$. The general equilibrium is structure CT if $s < 0.58$ and $a > 2.77$.

Proposition 7.1 implies that the absolute sizes of parameters $s$ and $a$ determine which structure is the efficient pattern of economic organization. That is, the greater the degree of economies of specialization and/or the shorter the distance between each pair of neighbors, the higher is the equilibrium level of division of labor. For a sufficiently small distance between a pair of neighbors $s$, increasing economies of specialization will cause the equilibrium to evolve from autarky to complete division of labor in production and transactions (structure CT). For a sufficiently large $s$, equilibrium is autarky for any degree of increasing returns to specialization. For intermediate values of $s$, increasing economies of specialization will make equilibrium evolve from autarky to partial division of labor between production and transactions (structure PT). For sufficiently large economies of specialization, urbanization will shift the economy from autarky first to structure PT, then to structure CT by decreasing $s$.

The number of traded goods is determined by the absolute degree of economies of specialization and the average distance between a pair of neighbors. Yang (1990) shows that the composition of traded goods in this model is determined by the relative degree of economies of specialization, relative trading efficiency, and the relative preference for different goods. In example 7.2 we shall show this.

The Heckscher–Ohlin theory (Heckscher, 1919 and Ohlin, 1933) predicts that a country endowed with more labor relative to capital than its trade partners exports labor intensive goods in exchange for capital-intensive goods (see chapter 12). The model in this chapter predicts that in the absence of exogenous comparative advantages, the goods more likely to be traded are those which involve greater degrees of economies of specialization, higher trading efficiency, and/or are more preferred. Further, a sufficiently high degree of economies of specialization in production as well as in transactions is a necessary but not sufficient condition for the division of labor, while a sufficiently small $s$ is a necessary but not sufficient condition for the division of labor. Sufficient increases in $a$ as well as in $1/s$ (that is, an increase in the degree of economies of specialization and a decrease in the distance between a pair of neighbors) will produce a "take-off" of division of labor and productivity.

If the degree of economies of specialization in production as well as in transactions is a sufficiently large constant, then urbanization can decrease $s$, thereby producing a "take-off" of the equilibrium level of division of labor. This take-off will enhance trade dependence (the ratio of trade volume to income), the extent of the market (aggregate demand for traded goods), and per capita real income. In exercise 6 you are asked to work out the formula for the corner equilibrium values of these three variables in different structures to show that they are increasing when the structure evolves from autarky to the complete division of labor as $s$ decreases. Similar to the models in the previous chapters, this model can generate the following concurrent phenomena.

1   Self-sufficiency decreases as specialization develops.
2   Diversity of the economy increases as the number of traded goods and professional sectors increases.
3   The degree of concentration of production increases as the total output share of a traded good produced by one producer rises.
4   The degree of integration of the economy develops as the number of trade partners of each individual increases.
5   Trading efficiency increases and the ratio of the value of transaction service (or roundabout production) to the value of consumer goods increases as the division of labor evolves.

All these phenomena, some of them apparently contradictory, are different aspects of the evolution of division of labor. This evolution is caused by urbanization (a decrease in the distance between a pair of neighbors, $s$), and an increase in the degree of economies of specialization, $a$.

## ◆ 7.6 Emergence of Professional Middlemen and a Hierarchical Structure of Economic Organization

Consider the model in example 7.1. From figure 7.1, we can see that no transaction service is produced, and that therefore labor productivity of transaction service is 0 in autarky. As shown in table 7.2, semi-professional middlemen with labor productivity of transactions $(4/5)^{a-1}$ emerge from the partial division of labor between production and transactions if $a > 4.2$ and $0.71 > s > 0.58$. Completely specialized middlemen with labor productivity of 1, which is higher than $(4/5)^{a-1}$, emerge from the complete division of labor between production and transactions if $a > 2.77$ and $s < 0.58$. If urbanization is defined as a decrease in the distance between a pair of neighbors, then in the model in example 7.1 urbanization may generate concurrent increases in specialization in mediating activities, in trading efficiency, and in productivity of goods. From table 7.1, we can calculate the relative number of professional middlemen to producers. This relative number is 0 in autarky, $0.79 \times 0.86^a$ ($> 0$) in structure PT, and $0.93$ ($> 0.79 \times 0.86^a$) in structure CT if the model is symmetric across goods. This implies that the population share and income share of the professional transacting sector increases as division of labor evolves. From table 7.2 we can see that a decrease in $s$ raises the corner equilibrium utility levels in structures PT and CT. Hence, per capita real income increases as the division of labor evolves.

More interesting than this is that a hierarchical structure of transactions emerges as professional middlemen emerge from the division of labor. A comparison between panels of figure 7.1 indicates that the position of all individuals is symmetric in structures A, P, and C, but a professional middleman's position is not symmetric with a producer's position in structures PT and CT. In structure CT, producers do not trade directly with each other. Instead, they trade indirectly via professional middlemen. Hence, each middleman has relationships with three professions, while a specialized producer has a relationship only with the middleman. Hence, a professional middleman is in a central position and a professional producer is in a peripheral position in this hierarchical structure of transactions. In this simplest hierarchy of transactions, there are only two layers. At the bottom layer are several professional producers and at the top layer are several professional middlemen. The interesting feature of the story is that the asymmetry and the hierarchy can emerge from an *ex ante* homogeneous and symmetrical economy where all people are *ex ante* identical in all aspects. Moreover, the degree of asymmetry and heterogeneity and the number of layers of the hierarchy may also evolve. We will investigate in detail the endogenization of the number of layers of the hierarchy, and the implications of the hierarchical structure of transactions for efficient economic organization, in chapters 19 and 20. In exercise 7, you are asked to show in the model of example 7.2 (below) the concurrent evolution of division of labor, productivity, trading efficiency, and the hierarchical structure of transactions. This analysis leads us to:

**Proposition 7.2**: Increasing degree of economies of specialization and urbanization may cause concurrent increases in trading efficiency, the level of specialization in trading activity, the population and income shares of professional middlemen, and per capita real income. A hierarchical structure of transactions and professional middlemen will emerge from this evolution.

Baumgardner (1988b) provides empirical evidence for a positive correlation between urbanization and physicians' levels of specialization. North (1986) provides empirical evidence for a positive correlation between economic development and employment share of the transaction sector in the US in the nineteenth century.

## ♦ 7.7 Determinants of Trade Pattern and Successful Business

In this section, we are concerned with trade pattern when not all goods are traded. This problem of trade pattern in the new classical framework differs from the problems that relate to the topological properties of the network of division of labor (the network size of division of labor). For the former, we are concerned with the question: which goods are involved in trade for a given level of division of labor or a given number of traded goods? This question also differs from that of who specializes in producing which goods, which will be studied in chapters 12 and 13. The latter question is based on the notion of exogenous comparative advantage. In our new classical model in this chapter, there is no exogenous comparative advantage between *ex ante* identical individuals. Hence, it is not important who is specialized in which activities. For a model with endogenous comparative advantage, the important question about trade pattern is: which goods are traded if not all goods are traded, and what are the determinants of the relative sizes of different sectors and the relative prices of different traded goods?

## Example 7.2: a new classical model allowing for specialization in trading a particular good

In the previous sections we have assumed identical conditions of transacting activities for all goods, we were unable to consider the effects of differential trading efficiency on trade pattern. In order to explore this issue, we now specify a new model as follows.

$$\text{Max: } u = [x + (r_x + k_x r_x^d)x^d][y + (r_y + k_y r_y^d)y^d][z + (r_z + k_z r_z^d)z^d] \tag{7.20}$$

s.t. $x + x^s = \text{Max } \{l_x - a\}, \ y + y^s = \text{Max } \{l_y - a\},$
$z + z^s = \text{Max } \{l_z - a\}$     (production function)
$r_x + r_x^s = \text{Max } \{l_{rx} - a, 0\}, \ r_y + r_y^s = \text{Max } \{l_{ry} - a, 0\},$
$r_z + r_z^s = \text{Max } \{l_{rz} - a, 0\}$     (transaction technology)
$l_x + l_y + l_z + l_{rx} + l_{ry} + l_{rz} = 1$     (endowment constraint)
$p_{rx}(r_x^s - r_x^d) + p_{ry}(r_y^s - r_y^d) + p_{rz}(r_z^s - r_z^d) + p_x(x^s - x^d) +$
$p_y(y^s - y^d) + p_z(z^s - z^d) = 0$     (budget constraint)

where $a$ is a fixed learning or training cost in each production and transacting activity, transacting services r for different goods are distinguished by substript $i$ ($i = x,y,z$), $l_{ri}$ is labor allocated to the production of transaction service in delivering good i, $k_i$ is the trading efficiency coefficient for delivering transaction service for good i, and $p_{ri}$ is the price of transaction service in delivering good i. In this model, although trading efficiency for goods is endogenized, the trading efficiency coefficient for transaction services, $k_i$, is exogenously given. Hence, we can use $k_i$ to explain all endogenous variables in the absence of the transaction cost coefficient $s$, which relates to location, through comparative statics analysis of general equilibrium.

Following the two-step approach, we can solve for the corner equilibria in 5 structures A, P, PT, C, CT, as shown in table 7.3, where $p_{ri}$ is the price of transaction service for good i. Structures PT and CT slightly differ from their counterparts in example 7.1. Each middleman in the two structures here provides only transaction service for one good.

Comparisons between per capita real incomes in the five types of structure indicate that structures P and C cannot be equilibrium structures. If trading efficiency of transaction service is sufficiently low, autarky is the general equilibrium, whereas if that efficiency is sufficiently high the general equilibrium is the complete division of labor in production and transactions (structure CT) involving three types of middlemen. Each type of middlemen completely specializes in producing transaction services for one type of good. If the

**Table 7.3:** Corner equilibria in five structures with middlemen specialized in trading one good

| | | | | Structure | |
|---|---|---|---|---|---|
| | A | P | C | PT | CT |
| Relative price | $p_i/p_j = 1$ | $p_y/p_x = p_z/p_x$ $= 1$ | $p_z/p_x$ | $p_{ri}/p_{rj} = p_i/p_j = (k_i/k_j)^{1/4};$ $p_i/p_{ri} = [4^4(1-2a)/5^5]^{1/3}$ | $p_{ri}/p_{rj} = (k_i/k_j)^{1/6}$ $p_i/p_j = (k_j/k_i)^{1/6}$ $p_i/p_{ri} = 5(1-a)^{1/5}/6^{6/5}$ |
| Real income | $(1-3a)^3$ $\div 27$ | $(1-3a)^4$ $\div 4^4$ | $(1-3a)^5 \div 5^5$ | $(1-2a)^{13/3}(k_i k_j)^5 \div (5^{5/3}4^{8/3})$ | $(1-a)^{27/5}(k_x k_y k_z)^{2/3} \div (5^3 6^{12/5})$ |

trading efficiency of transaction service $k_i$ is neither too large nor too small, then the general equilibrium is structure PT, where only two goods are traded and transaction services for delivering each of the two goods are provided by middlemen. As indicated in table 7.3, the per capita real income for this structure is $u_{PT} = (1 - 2a)^{13/3}(k_i k_j)^{0.5}/5^{5/3}$ $4^{8/3}$, where $k_i$ and $k_j$ are the trading efficiency coefficients of transaction services for goods i and j, respectively. Hence, the corner equilibrium that trades the two goods with the larger trading efficiency coefficients of transaction services generates a greater per capita real income. According to the Yao theorem, this implies that if not all goods are traded in the general equilibrium, those will be traded that have the larger trading efficiency coefficients for transaction services.

Also, table 7.3 shows that the relative price of the two traded goods in the corner equilibrium trading only two goods is

$$p_i/p_j = (k_i/k_j)^{1/4},$$

where $k_i/k_j$ is the relative trading efficiency of transaction services for the two goods. Our results about the implications of relative trading efficiency for trade pattern are summarized in the following proposition.

**Proposition 7.3:** The general equilibrium includes as traded goods those with larger trading efficiency coefficients of transaction services if not all goods are traded. The equilibrium price of a good in terms of other goods is higher the higher is the trading efficiency of transaction service for this good. As trading efficiency for transaction services is improved, the general equilibrium evolves from autarky to the partial division of labor between production and transactions, followed by the complete division of labor between production and transactions.

This proposition implies that those goods that involve inferior trading efficiency may be excluded from the network of division of labor and related trade. Even if such a good is involved in trade, its equilibrium relative price will be lower than those of other goods with the same production and consumption conditions. This explains why the market price is lower for those houses that are subject to government renting and trading restrictions than for other similar houses that can be freely traded. This also explains why there is no market for some goods. For instance, no market exists for clear air because of the great transaction costs in trading this. In many textbooks, the absence of such markets is exogenously given. But in our new classical models, this is endogenously determined by the trade off between positive network effects of division of labor and transaction costs. In chapters 16 and 17, the existence of markets for different goods is endogenized by specifying more complicated trade offs among endogenous transaction costs, exogenous transaction costs, coordination reliability of the network of division of labor, and economies of division of labor.

Because of economies of specialization assumed in our models, proposition 7.3 also implies that productivities and equilibrium quantities produced and consumed are higher for the traded goods with the higher trading efficiency of transaction services than for the non-traded goods, even if production and consumption conditions are exactly the same for the two types of goods. This explains why the income share of the sectors manufacturing automobiles, refrigerators, and computers can dramatically increase despite the fact that they do not generate direct use value for final consumption. These sectors specialize in producing goods that can be used to improve trading efficiency, so that they can promote the division of labor in all sectors. This, in turn, enlarges the market for all goods, including those produced by these sectors.

In business practice, people very often underestimate the potential of those sectors that can improve trading efficiency. After you have studied chapter 22, you will better understand this. The essential point here is that the equilibrium level of division of labor depends on transaction cost, while the equilibrium total transaction cost depends on the level of division of labor that determines the number of transactions. Hence, we should use the notion of general equilibrium to figure out a mechanism that simultaneously determines the level of division of labor, the extent of the market, and total transaction costs, which are interdependent. As the inframarginal comparative statics of general equilibrium predicts, for instance, when trading efficiency is improved, the equilibrium levels of division of labor and productivity, the equilibrium extent of the market, and the equilibrium total transaction cost increase concurrently.

In exercises, you are asked to extend this example to prove the following proposition.

**Proposition 7.4:** The general equilibrium includes as traded goods those with larger preference parameters and with higher returns to specialization if not all goods are traded.

## Key Terms and Review

Economies of specialization in transacting activities; their implications for the division of labor in production.
How do the Yao theorem and the first welfare theorem help us to understand the function of the market in utilizing the network effects of the division of labor?
What are the determinants of the equilibrium structure of trade and of a successful business?
Why do markets not exist for some goods?
What are the implications of urbanization, policies, institutions, and a legal system that affect trading efficiency for the division of labor in production and transacting activities?

## Further Reading

*Endogenous pattern of division of labor*: Yang and Y.-K. Ng (1993, ch. 6), Yang (1991, 1994), Smith (1776), Young (1928). *Historical and empirical evidence for the theories in this chapter*: Chandler (1990), Braudel (1984), North (1958, 1986, 1990), Baumgardner (1988b).

## QUESTIONS

1   The level of division of labor in production is determined by trading efficiency, which is determined by the level of specialization in transacting activities. But the extent of the market for specialized transaction services is dependent on the level of division of labor in production. Use the models in this chapter to discuss why the notion of general equilibrium is a powerful vehicle for explaining the mechanism that simultaneously determines these interdependent variables.

2   The department store is an institution that emerged in the US around the time of the First World War. Analyze why the department store can generate higher transacting productivity than small stores and than direct trade between producers of goods such as in farmers' markets.

3    Under what conditions can the supermarket generate higher transacting productivity than the depart-
     ment store? Analyze the contribution to supermarket profitability of the finer division of labor between
     saleswomen specialized in cashiering, salesmen specialized in labeling prices, and other manage-
     ment. What are the effects on supermarket profitability of the finer division of labor involving the applica-
     tion of cashier machines and other specialized equipment that are produced by a high level of division
     of labor in a long, roundabout production chain? What are the implications of the popularization of
     automobiles for the profitability of supermarkets?

4    A development phenomenon noted by Naisbitt (1990) is rapid development of franchise networks in the
     US. He claims "franchising is the single most successful marketing concept ever." According to the
     International Franchise Association (1997), "More than 550,000 franchise businesses dot the American
     landscape, generating more than $800 billion in sales, with a new franchise business opening some-
     where in the US every 8 minutes each business day." Among three types of franchises – products
     franchise, brand name franchise, and business format franchise – the last grows much faster than the
     other two. In 1999, 4,177 business format franchises in the US were listed in *The Franchise Annual*.
     Most of them were franchised after 1960. One of them has 20 to 2,000 units. Most business format
     franchises (fast food franchise networks McDonald and Kentucky Fried Chicken are two of them) in-
     volve the division of labor between thinking and doing. The franchiser specializes in providing know-
     how (intangible intellectual property which is very commonly associated with an operations manual and
     training programs). The franchisee specializes in providing tangible goods or services, buying intangi-
     ble know-how from the franchiser. Sometimes a franchise network involves deep division of labor be-
     tween the sector providing roundabout productive equipment and the sector providing final services.
     For instance, the know-how (McDonalds bible) provided by the McDonalds franchiser includes pur-
     chase of very specialized cooking equipment that can utilize a high level of division of labor between the
     roundabout sector and the final sector to improve productivity. Also the know-how provided by the
     Precision Tune franchiser includes purchase of very specialized equipment for testing and fixing car
     engines. A hostage mechanism is developed to enhance trading efficiency of transaction services in
     many franchise networks (see question1 in ch. 5). Use the models in this chapter to explain the boom in
     franchise networks.

5    The high price of downtown land is supported by department stores, supermarkets, and other special-
     ized trade businesses. Explain how such trade businesses can make money even after paying the very
     high rents associated with downtown land.

6    Some building companies do not produce any goods, they get contracts from customers, then find
     specialist subcontractors to do the different jobs in building houses for those customers. For each of the
     goods and services provided by the subcontractors, the building companies charge a service fee. Why
     do the customers choose such building companies to build houses for them when they could do the
     same thing for themselves without paying the service fee? Why can the building companies make
     money in a competitive market by specializing in mediating transactions?

7    The US became a country on wheels within the first half of the twentieth century and the automobile
     industry became the most important part of the economy. Use the models in this chapter to analyze the
     rationale of the take-off of the automobile industry in the US. Why could the automobile industry, which
     has no direct connection to the consumption and production of consumption goods, become the lead-
     ing sector of economic development in the US in early twentieth century? Explain the implications of
     the development of automobiles, railroads, telecommunications, the internet, and refrigerators for in-
     dustrialization and economic development.

8    Having studied this chapter, what factors will you take into account in deciding on your future occupa-
     tion?

9   Analyze the input–output network associated with the production of a journal. Each contributor to the journal specializes in a topic and exchanges that specialized knowledge with each of the other contributors. There is also division of labor between the contributors and other readers of the journal, and between different professional journals. As George Stigler et al. (1995) observed, a hierarchical structure may emerge from the input–output network of journals. What are the determinants of the network size of division of labor and the features of the hierarchical structure, and how does the market utilize the network effects of journals?

10  In the model of this chapter, if all individuals are in structure A (no trade) or P (for instance with trade in goods x and y), then they do not know the prices of z and r in structure CT. Without this price information they cannot figure out per capita real income in CT. But their decisions in choosing configurations will determine whether the information about the prices in structure CT is available. If it takes one period of time for an individual to try one configuration and if pricing involves costs, then the interdependence between information about prices and decisions in choosing configuration may make a social experiment essential for the market to discover the efficient network size of division of labor. Use your daily experience to make a conjecture about how the market determines time sequence of structures that are experimented with. (See the sequential equilibrium model based on bounded rationality and adaptive behavior in chapter 24.)

11  According to Dicke's documentation (1992), the division of labor between a licenced manufacturing network and the invention of harvesting machine was crucial for the success of the McCormick Harvesting Machine Company. The division of labor between the dealer franchise network and the manufacturing of the Model T was critical for the success of the Ford Motor Company. Use the models in this chapter to explain these cases.

12  Use statistical data to verify the positive relationship between urbanization, economic development, and the increase in commercialization (the ratio of market-based income or consumption to total income or consumption), or the increase in trade dependence (the ratio of domestic and international transaction volume to income).

13  North (1958) has found empirical evidence of a negative relationship between freight rates and economic development during 1750–1913. Try to find other ways to test the evolution of division of labor. This might be measured by trade dependence (the ratio of total domestic and international transaction volume to income, which was 0.2 in 1869 and 9 in 1997 in the US); by degree of commercialization (the share of income from market transactions, which was smaller than 0.3 in rural China in the 1970s and more than 0.8 in the 1990s); or by other indices. Try to test also the evolution of productivity generated by improvements in trading efficiency or by a fall of transaction cost index for each ton-mile of goods transported.

14  In ancient Europe and China there was a debate about the role of commerce in comparison to production in determining the wealth of a nation. One side of the debate argued that commerce is nonproductive, and thus makes no positive contribution to the wealth of a nation. Hence, commerce should be restricted. The other side of the debate argued that commerce is a driving force of economic development which positively contributes to the wealth of the nation. Use the new classical models in this chapter, and the notion of the general equilibrium network of division of labor, to assess these views.

# EXERCISES

1   Assume that the production functions in (7.1) are replaced with $x + x^s = l_x - a$, $y + y^s = l_y - b$, $r + r^s = l_r - t$, and that there are only two goods x and y in the new model. Solve for general equilibrium and its marginal and inframarginal comparative statics.

2   Modify the model in example 7.1 as follows. The coefficient $s$ is now equal to 0. But the government taxes transaction services and/or the trade volume of goods and services. Hence, the difference between buyers' and sellers' prices is a tax rate $t_i$, where subscript $i = x, y, z, r$. Solve for the general equilibrium and its comparative statics. Compare the implications of absolute and relative tax rates for different goods and services for the equilibrium level and structure of division of labor.

3   Modify the model in example 7.1 as follows. The trading efficiency coefficients $k_i$ are now equal to 1. But the government taxes transaction services and/or trade volume. First, assume the tax rate is the same for all goods and services and total tax revenue is equally distributed among all individuals. Then assume different tax rates for different goods and services. Analyze the implications of absolute and relative tax rates for different goods and services for the equilibrium level and structure of division of labor.

4   Combine the model in example 7.1 with the model in chapter 8 to develop a model that can explain the emergence of firms that specialize in providing all kinds of transaction services.

5   Combine the model in example 7.2 with the model in chapter 8 to specify a model that can explain the emergence of firms that specialize in one type of transaction service.

6   Consider the model in example 7.1. Calculate and compare trade dependence, the extent of the market, the extent of endogenous comparative advantage and per capita real incomes in structures A, PT, and CT. Verify that these endogenous variables increase as division of labor evolves due to an increase in $a$ and/or a decrease in $s$.

7   Use the model in example 7.2 to show that as trading efficiency for transaction services is improved, a hierarchical structure of transactions emerges from division of labor between transacting and production activities. Show how trading efficiency, productivity of goods, and the extent of endogenous comparative advantage concurrently evolve as three aspects of evolution of division of labor.

8   Consider a model with $M$ *ex ante* identical consumer-producers. Each of them has the following utility function, production functions, and endowment constraint of labor. $u = (x + kx^d)(y + ky^d)(z + kz^d)$, $x + x^s = \text{Max } \{l_x - a, 0\}$, $y + y^s = \text{Max } \{l_y - b, 0\}$, $z + z^s = \text{Max } \{l_z - c, 0\}$, $l_x + l_y + l_z = e$, where $a$, $b$, and $c$ are fixed learning and training costs in producing goods x, y, and z, respectively. The trading efficiency coefficient for good i is $k_i$. It is assumed that $a > b > c$. Solve for general equilibrium and show that proposition 7.4 holds for this model.

9   Consider a model with $M$ *ex ante* identical consumer-producers. Each of them has the following utility function, production functions, and endowment constraint of labor. $u = (x + kx^d)^\alpha (y + ky^d)^\beta (z + kz^d)^\gamma$, $x + x^s = \text{Max } \{l_x - a, 0\}$, $y + y^s = \text{Max } \{l_y - a, 0\}$, $z + z^s = \text{Max } \{l_z - a, 0\}$, $l_x + l_y + l_z = e$. It is assumed that $\alpha > \beta > \gamma$ and $\alpha + \beta + \gamma = 1$. Solve for general equilibrium and show that proposition 7.4 holds for this model.

## chapter 8

# THE LABOR MARKET AND THE
# INSTITUTION OF THE FIRM

### ◆ 8.1. What is the Institution of the Firm?

In the new classical models of the previous three chapters, there is no labor trade, and there are no firms. You may wonder if this kind of model can only describe what was going on before the Industrial Revolution. But it is one of the advantages of the new classical framework over the neoclassical that the only *ex ante* players are consumer-producers, and there are no firms before individuals have made their decisions. The institution of the firm is a particular way of organizing transactions that are required by the division of labor. It may emerge from the division of labor only as a consequence of individuals' decisions in choosing their levels of specialization and the manner of organizing transactions. If the transaction cost coefficient for labor is smaller than that for goods, then the institution of the firm will be chosen to organize the division of labor as trade and pricing of goods are replaced by the corresponding trade and pricing of labor.

An example of the replacement of goods trade with labor trade is trade between a professor and his housekeeper. Outputs of services, which provided by housekeepers are prohibitively expensive to price because of a great variety of such services, which generates an extremely high cost in measuring quality and quantities of the services item by item. Hence, trade in labor that involves pricing of labor inputs of the housekeeper will substitute for trade in her outputs. The professor pays the housekeeper according to her working hours rather than to quantities and qualities of each and every service item that she provides. However, we do not take trade between the professor and the housekeeper to be associated with the institution of the firm. The division of labor between the professor and the housekeeper and the replacement of trade in housekeeping outputs with trade in her labor, are two necessary but not sufficient conditions for the emergence of the firm from the division of labor. Before we study the sufficient conditions for the existence of a firm, a rigorous definition for the institution of the firm is needed.

*The institution of the firm* is a structure of transactions based on division of labor that satisfy the following three conditions:

i) There are two types of trade partners associated with a firm: employers and employees. To save space, we call the employer "she" and the employee "he" in this chapter. There is an asymmetric distribution of *residual control rights* or authority. The employer has residual control rights to use the employee's labor. "Residual control" here implies that the employer may allow the employee to allocate his labor. But he must do what he is told to do, if she so demands. That is, the ultimate rights to use the employee's labor are owned by the employer, subject to the employee's freedom to quit the job and to other terms of the labor contract. In the Grossman and Hart model with incomplete contracts, the definition of residual control differs from our definition here. We will discuss the difference between the two definitions in chapter 10.

ii) The contract that is associated with the asymmetric relationship between the employer and the employee never specifies how much the employer receives from the relationship. It only specifies how much the employee receives from the relationship. The employer claims the *residual returns*, defined as the revenue of the firm net of the wage bill and other expenses. The employer is referred to as the owner of the firm. One of the most important components of the ownership of a modern firm is the entitlement to the business name of the firm. The exclusive rights to the business name are enforced through a business name search process when the firm is registered with the government and through recognition of the name in legal cases in the judicial process. The exclusive rights are also enforced through the laws of brand.

iii) A firm must involve a process that transforms employee labor into something that is sold in the market by the owner of the firm. In the process, what is produced by the employee is owned by the employer (residual returns).

The relationship between the professor and the housekeeper does not involve the institution of the firm since it does not involve such a resale process. The professor directly consumes what the housekeeper produces and never resells it to the market. If an individual hires a broker to conduct stock transactions, the relationship involves asymmetric rights to residual control and to residual returns. But the relationship does not involve the firm since it does not satisfy condition (iii).

Suppose that in the model in chapter 6, with only consumption goods, a specialist producer of x buys the labor of a specialist producer of y, directs that employee to specialize in producing y within the firm, and then sells y to the specialist producer of y in the market for y. Such roundabout transactions involve unnecessary transactions in labor. If the producer of y must buy his own produce from the market, why would he not directly sell y to the specialist producer of x in exchange for good x? The latter structure of transactions is exactly the same as the former except that the former involves more trade in labor and therefore creates unnecessary transaction costs. This implies that the institution of the firm will not be chosen if there are only consumption goods. In this chapter, we shall show that the institution of the firm may be used to save on transaction costs if there is division of labor between the production of the final goods and the production of the intermediate goods.

The rationale behind our story of the firm may not seem very plausible. Human society has been disturbed by the question of the fairness of asymmetric relationships between employer and employee. In a free enterprise system, employees have the freedom to become employers by using the free capital market and a legal system that protects free association. They also have the freedom to quit their jobs. Hence, an asymmetric relationship between the employer and the employee in a free market system differs from the relationship between a master and his slave or the feudal relationship between a lord and his servant. Notwithstanding this, many people (from Karl Marx to modern trade union activists) are still concerned with the following questions. Why must the employee do what he is told to do rather than what he likes to do? Why should the employee not have rights to the residual returns that may make a fortune for the employer? Such questions were at least partly responsible for the Russian Revolution in 1917 and the Chinese Revolution in 1949 that changed the lives of a billion people over the course of more than a half of the twentieth century.

Russia and East Europe have already abandoned the disastrous social experiments that were inspired by such questions, and China shows every prospect of doing so in the near future. However, we are still concerned with questions of the following kind. Why is there a continuous decrease in the number of family doctors? Why do large hospital networks develop through the merging of smaller clinics? Why is the average size of firms in many developed economies declining over time? What are the determinants of the size of the firm? What is the economic rationale for the existence of an asymmetric relationship between the employer and the employee?

This chapter will address such questions.

---

### Question to Ask Yourself when Reading this Chapter

♦ What is a firm?

♦ What are the necessary and sufficient conditions for the emergence of a firm?

♦ What is the function of the institution of the firm and what are the implications of its internal organization for the equilibrium level of division of labor and productivity?

---

## ♦ 8.2 Is It Fair to have an Asymmetric Relationship between Boss and Employees? – The Story behind the Model

We will outline the intuition behind the formal model by telling a story on the functioning of the institution of the firm, before you become mired in the algebra of the model and lose your capacity for economic thinking. Our story of the firm runs as follows.

Each individual as a consumer must consume a final good, called cloth, the production of which requires an intermediate good, called management service, as an input. There is a trade-off between economies of specialization and transaction costs. If transaction efficiency is high, then division of labor will occur at equilibrium. Otherwise autarky will be chosen as the equilibrium. There are three different structures of residual rights which can be used to organize transactions required by the division of labor. Structure D, shown in figure 8.1b, comprises markets for cloth and management services. Specialist producers of cloth exchange that product for the specialist services of management. For this market structure, residual rights to returns and control are symmetrically distributed between the trade partners, and no firms or labor market exist. Structure E, shown in figure 8.1c, comprises the market for cloth and the market for labor hired to produce the management service within a firm. The producer of cloth is the owner of the firm and specialist producers of management services are employees. Control rights over employees' labor and rights to the firm's residual returns are asymmetrically distributed between the employer and her employees. The employer claims the difference between revenue and the wage bill, has residual control rights over her employees' labor, and sells goods that are produced from employees' labor. Structure F, shown in figure 8.1d comprises the market for cloth and the market for labor hired to produce cloth within a firm. The professional manager is the owner of the firm and specialist producers of cloth are employees. For the final two structures of residual rights, the firm emerges from the division of labor. Compared with structure D, these involve a labor market but not a market for management services. As Cheung (1983) argues, the firm replaces the market for intermediate goods with the market for labor. Although both structures E and F involve a firm and an asymmetric structure of residual rights, they entail different firm ownership structures.

Suppose that transaction efficiency is much lower for management service than for labor. This is very likely to be the case in the real world, since the quality and quantity of the intangible entrepreneurial ideas are prohibitively expensive to measure. Potential buyers of the intellectual property in entrepreneurial ideas may refuse to pay by claiming that these are worthless as soon as they are acquired from their specialist producer. Under this circumstance, the institution of the firm can be used to organize the division of labor more efficiently because it avoids trade in intangible intellectual property.

Suppose further that transaction efficiency for labor hired to produce management services is much lower than for labor hired to produce cloth because it is prohibitively expensive to measure the efforts exerted in producing intangible management services (can you tell if a manager sitting in the office is pondering business management or her boyfriend?). Then the division of labor can be more efficiently organized in structure F than in structure E. This is because structure F involves trade in cloth and in labor hired to produce cloth but not trade in management services or in labor hired to produce management services, while structure E involves trade in cloth and in labor hired to produce management services. Hence, structure F will occur at equilibrium if the transaction

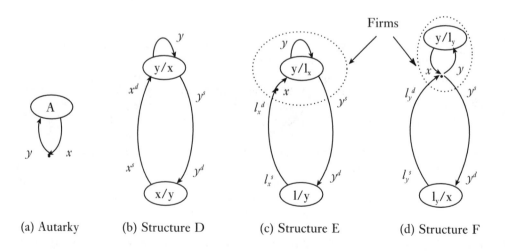

| (a) Autarky | (b) Structure D | (c) Structure E | (d) Structure F |

♦ **Figure 8.1:** Emergence of the firm from the division of labor efficiencies for labor hired to produce cloth and for cloth are sufficiently high. The claim to the residual return of the firm by the manager is the indirect price of management services. Therefore, the *function of the asymmetric structure of residual rights* is to get the activity with the lowest transaction efficiency involved in the division of labor while avoiding direct pricing and marketing of the output and input of that activity, thus promoting the division of labor and productivity. In a sense, the function of the asymmetric structure of residual rights is similar to that of a patent law which enforces rights to intangible intellectual property, thereby promoting the division of labor in producing the intangible. However, the asymmetric structure of residual rights to returns and control can indirectly price those intangible intellectual properties which are prohibitively expensive to price even through a patent law.

Intuitively, there are two ways to do business if an individual has an idea for making money. The first is to sell the entrepreneurial idea in the market. This is very likely to create a situation in which everybody can steal the idea and refuse to pay for its use. The second way of proceeding is for the entrepreneur to hire workers to realize the idea, while keeping the idea to herself as a business secret. Then she can claim as her reward the residual returns to the firm, which represent the difference between revenue and the wage bill. If the idea is a good one, then the entrepreneur will make a fortune. If the idea is a bad one, she will become bankrupt. The residual return is the precise price of the idea and the entrepreneur gets what she deserves, so that stealing and over- or underpricing of intellectual property is avoided.

This theory is referred to as the *theory of indirect pricing*, which is formalized by the Yang–Ng model (1995). It also formalizes the Coase–Cheung theory of the firm (Coase, 1937 and Cheung, 1983), such that the institution of the firm can save on transaction costs by replacing trade in intermediate goods with trade in labor if the former involves higher transaction costs than the latter. The model does not endogenize transaction costs if these are defined as a departure from the Pareto optimum. However, if endogenous transaction costs are defined as those transaction costs whose value is endogenously determined by individuals' decisions and the equilibrium process, then the Yang–Ng model has endogenized transaction costs. This is because the number of transactions for individuals and for the economy as a whole is endogenized in this model, due to the trade-off between economies of specialization and transaction costs. In chapter 10, we shall introduce moral hazard into the Yang–Ng model to simultaneously endogenize transaction costs and the emergence of the firm from the division of labor. In chapter 23, we shall consider a dynamic version with the CES production function of the Yang–Ng model.

This theory has an interesting empirical implication. It predicts that the equilibrium size of the firm may decrease as division of labor evolves if the transaction conditions are improved in such a way that the transaction cost coefficient of goods is larger than that of labor (see exercise 10). Empirical evidence to support the hypothesis can be found in Liu and Yang (2000), who show that productivity, level of division of labor, and per capita real income increase and the average size of firms declines concurrently as transaction conditions are improved so as to keep the transaction conditions for goods more favorable than those for labor.

## ◆ 8.3 Emergence of the Firm from the Division of Labor

In subsection 8.3.1 the model is elaborated and the concept of economies of roundabout production is defined. In subsection 8.3.2 the corner equilibria in all structures of organization and transaction are solved for. Finally, the general equilibrium and its comparative statics are solved in subsection 8.3.3.

### 8.3.1 Economies of roundabout production

### Example 8.1: a new classical model of the institution of the firm

As discussed in section 8.1, the existence of intermediate goods is essential for explaining the emergence of the firm from the division of labor. Here, *intermediate goods* or *producer goods* are goods that are not consumed, but used to produce other goods. People produce intermediate goods because they may be used to improve the productivity of the final goods. There are *economies of roundabout production* if the productivity of a good can be improved by employing intermediate goods. There are three types of economies of roundabout production. Type A relates to the quantity of an intermediate good that is employed to produce the final goods. Type B relates to the number of intermediate goods at a link of the roundabout production chain. Type C relates to the number of links in the roundabout production chain. In this chapter we study Type A economies of roundabout production. Types B and C will be investigated in chapters 18 and 19. The development of division of labor since the Industrial Revolution has been taking place mainly in roundabout production of these three types.

In the model in this chapter, each consumer-producer has the following system of production involving economies of roundabout production.

$$y + y^s = (x + tx^d)^c l_y^a,$$  (8.1a),

$$x + x^s = l_x^b$$  (8.1b)

$$l_x + l_y = 1 \qquad y, y^s, x, xd, x^s, l_x, l_y \geq 0;$$  (8.1c)

where $l_i$ is an individual's level of specialization as well as her amount of labor allocated to the production of good i; $x$ and $y$ are respective quantities of the intermediate and consumption goods self-provided, $x^s$ and $y^s$ are respective quantities of the two goods that are sold, $x^d$ is the quantity of the intermediate goods that is bought, $t$ is the transaction efficiency coefficient for the intermediate goods, and $a$ and $b$ are parameters of production conditions; $x + tx^d$ is the quantity of the intermediate good that is employed to produce the final good. The exponentially weighted average of this quantity and the amount of labor employed, $(x + tx^d)^{c/(c+a)} l_y^{a/(c+a)}$, is called the *total factor input* in producing good y. The ratio of output $y + y^s$ to total factor input is called *total factor productivity* (TFP), given by TFP = $[(x + tx^d)^c l_y^a]^{(a+c-1)/(a+c)}$. The TFP increases with an individual's level of specialization in producing y if $a + c > 1$. A production function of a good with two inputs displays *economies of specialization* if the total factor productivity increases with an individual's level of specialization in producing the good. A production function of a good displays *type A economies of roundabout production* if the total factor productivity of the good increases with the quantity of the intermediate good employed. In this chapter the parameter $c(a + c - 1)/(a + c)$ can be considered as the *degree of type A economies of roundabout production* and parameter $a(a + c - 1)/(a + c)$ can be considered as the degree of economies of specialization in producing the final good. We assume that $a = c$ for simplicity in the rest of the chapter, so that TFP increases with the quantity of the intermediate good employed and with the level of specialization in producing good y if $a > 0.5$. Hence, $a$ can be considered the degree of economies of roundaboutness as well as the degree of economies of specialization in producing y.

A production function of a good displays *Type B economies of roundabout production* if the total factor productivity increases with the number of different types of intermediate goods employed. Type B economies of roundabout production will be investigated in chapter 18. The concept of *Type C economies of roundabout production*, which relates to the number of links of a roundabout production chain, is not easy to define. In chapter 19 we will define it for a simple general equilibrium model with an endogenous number of links of a roundabout production chain.

Suppose that the transaction efficiency coefficient for the final good y is $k$, and that all *ex ante* identical consumer-producers have the following utility function:

$$u = y + ky^d. \tag{8.2}$$

### 8.3.2 The corner equilibria in four structures

The Wen theorem can be reestablished and refined for a model with intermediate goods.

**Lemma 8.1:** An individual sells at most one good and does not buy and self-provide the same good. She self-provides the consumer good if she sells it. If $b > 1$ and $a \in (.5, 1)$, she does not self-provide the intermediate good unless she produces the final good.

*Proof:* The procedure for proving the first two claims in lemma 8.1 is the same as that for proving the Wen theorem in chapter 5. The final claim of lemma 8.1, however, differs from the Wen theorem. Suppose the first two claims are true; then there are three possible configurations: autarky where $x^d = x^s = y^s = y^d = 0$; (x/y) where $x^d = y^s = 0$, $x^s$, $y^d > 0$; and (y/x) where $x^d$, $y^s$, $y > 0$, $x^s = y^d = 0$. To establish the final claim it is sufficient to prove that $x = l_y = 0$ for configuration (x/y) and $x = 0$ for (y/x). Assume that $x, l_y > 0$ for configuration (x/y) where $x^d = y^s = 0$, $x^s$, $y^d > 0$. Replacing y in the utility function with its equivalent from the production function for good y and replacing $y^d$ in the utility function with its equivalent from the budget constraint yields

$$u = (xl_y)^a + k[(1 - l_y)^b - x]/p.$$

Assume the optimal $x > 0$; then that optimal value of $x$ is characterized by

$$\partial u(x, l_y)/\partial x = 0.$$

Inserting this optimum value of $x$ into the utility function and differentiating $u$ with respect to $l_y$ yields

$\mathrm{d}\{\partial u[l_y,\, x(l_y)]/\partial l_y\}/\mathrm{d}l_y > 0$

if $\partial u(x,\, l_y)/\partial l_y = 0$ and $a \in (.5,\, 1)$ and $b > 1$

where $x(l_y)$ is given by the first order condition $\partial u(x,\, l_y)/\partial x = 0$. It can be shown that

$\mathrm{d}\{\partial u[l_y,\, x(l_y)]/\partial l_y\}/\mathrm{d}l_y > 0$

iff the Hessian of $u(x,\, l_y)$ is negative definite.

This result, together with the first-order condition, implies that the interior extreme of $l_y$ is not the maximum and the optimum $l_y$ must be at a corner, i.e. either $l_y = 0$ or $l_y = 1$ if $x > 0$, $a \in (.5,\, 1)$, and $b > 1$. Since $l_y = 1$, i.e. $l_x = 0$ contradicts the assumption of $x^s > 0$, it follows that

the optimum $l_y = 0$ if $x > 0$ for configuration (x/y).                          (8.3)

Since for configuration (x/y) we have

$\partial u/\partial x < 0 \;\forall\; x > 0$ if $l_y = 0$,

the optimum $x$ is zero if $l_y = 0$. This contradicts expression (8.3). Hence a positive optimum value of $x$ is impossible for configuration (x/y). Assume that $x = 0$; it is easy to see that the optimum $l_y = 0$ because $\partial u/\partial l_y < 0 \;\forall\; l_y > 0$. Hence, we have established the claim

$l_y = x = 0$ for configuration (x/y) if $b > 1$ and $a \in (.5,\, 1)$.

The above deduction is sufficient to establish the final claim in lemma 8.1. *Q.E.D.*

In this chapter, it is assumed that $b > 1$ and $a \in (.5,\, 1)$. Having considered lemma 8.1 and the possibility of establishing firms, we propose that there are 4 structures of organization and transactions: A, D, E, F, as shown in figure 8.1. Let us examine the structures one by one.

*Structure A (autarky)*, where each individual chooses a configuration with $x^s = y^s = x^d = y^d = 0$, as shown in figure 6.1a. The decision problem for each individual in this structure is:

Max: $u = y = x^a l_y^a = l_x^{ab}(1 - l_x)^a$

and its solution is:

$l_x = b/(1 + b), \qquad l_y + 1/(1 + b), \qquad x = [b/(1 + b)]^b$
$u_A = y = [b^b/(1 + b)^{1+b}]^a,$

where per capita real income in structure A, $u_A$, is per capita output of the consumption good as well.

*Structure D*, comprising configurations (x/y) and (y/x), as shown in figure 8.1b. There is no asymmetric distribution of residual rights in this structure. Individuals exchange goods for goods in the absence of the institution of the firm and a related labor market. Configuration (x/y) is defined by and $x = y = y^s = l_y = 0$ and $x^s, l_x, y^d > 0$. Inserting the

values of the variables and the budget constraint into the utility function yields the decision for this configuration. Indeed, there is no scope for adjusting values of the decision
variables, which are fixed by the definition of the configuration and the budget constraint.
Here, the specialist producer of good x does not self-provide x which is not a consumption
good. Configuration (y/x) is defined by $x = x^s = y^d = l_x = 0$ and $x^d, y, y^s, l_y > 0$.
Marginal analysis of the configuration yields the corner solution. The corner solutions for
the two configurations are summarized as follows.

$$(x/y): x^s = 1, \qquad y^d = p_x/p_y, \qquad u_x = kp_x/p_y$$

$$(y/x): x^d = (at^a p_y/p_x)^{\frac{1}{1-a}}, \qquad y^s = (at^a p_y/p_x)^{\frac{1}{1-a}} p_x/p_y$$

$$u_y = (at p_y/p_x)^{\frac{a}{1-a}}(1-a),$$

where $u_i$ is the indirect utility function of an individual selling good i.

Having considered the market clearing and utility equalization conditions and the population size equation $M_x + M_y = M$ in structure D, we can solve for the corner equilibrium
in that structure as follows.

$$p_y/p_x = [k/(1-a)]^{1-a}/(at)^a, \qquad u_D = a^a(1-a)^{1-a}(tk)^a$$

$$M_x = \frac{akM}{1-a+ak}, \qquad M_y = \frac{(1-a)M}{1-a+ak}$$

where $M_i$ is the number of individuals selling good i, and $u_D$ is the per capita real income
in structure D. Per capita real income is per capita consumption of the final good, and its
reciprocal is the absolute price of labor, which includes labor allocated to the production of
both final and intermediate goods.

*Structure E*, comprising configurations $(l_x/y)$ and $(y/l_x)$, as shown in figure 6.1c. $(y/l_x)$
denotes a specialist producer of y who hires workers and directs them to specialize in
producing x within the firm. $(l_x/y)$ denotes a worker who is hired to produce the intermediate good and who buys the final good. The decision problem of the employer choosing
$(y/l_x)$ is:

Max: $u_y = y$

s.t. $y + y^s = (x^d l_y)^a$,     $l_y = 1$,        (production conditions for specialist of y)

     $x^s = (sl_x)^b$,       $l_x = 1$,        (production conditions for specialist of x)

     $x^d = Nx^s$            (equality between quantities of x produced and employed)

     $p_y y^s = wNl_x = wN$        (budget constraint);

where $N$ is the number of workers hired by the employer, $w$ is the wage rate, and $1 - s$ is
the transaction cost coefficient for each unit of labor hired. The quantity of labor employed in production is thus $sl_x$. $Nl_x$ is the employer's demand for labor. Each worker in
the firm produces $x^s = (sl_x)^b = s^b$ when he is directed to specialize in producing x ($l_x = 1$).
Hence, the employer receives intermediate good $x^d = Nx^s$. Superscripts s and d denote

supply and demand for inputs and outputs within the firm. Note that $l_x$ is an employee's quantity of labor, but is the employer's decision variable. This is what we mean by residual control rights or asymmetric distribution of authority. However, the employee has always the right to quit the job and to find another employer. More important than this, he can use the free markets for capital, labor and goods to choose to become an employer and to found his own enterprise. This distinguishes the asymmetric relationship between employer and employee in a capitalist firm from the asymmetric relationship between a master and his slave and from the feudal relationship between a lord and his servant.

The employer's rights to residual returns relate to the difference between the output level of y within the firm and the quantity of y that is sold by the firm. Note that the production function of good x is still specified for each worker. It displays economies of specialization for each worker rather than economies of the scale of labor in the firm. All individual workers and production functions, and the employer's production function, are aggregated as the *production function for the firm*, which is $y + y^s = (x^d l_y)^a = (N s^b l_y)^a$. This production function does not display economies of scale of labor hired by the firm, $N$, because of the assumption $a \in (.5, 1)$, despite the existence of economies of specialization in producing y for the employer and in producing x for each worker. It displays local economies of scale in the total factor productivity. Note that the total factor is $(x^d)^{0.5} l_y^{0.5}$. This formalizes the distinction between economies of scale generated by pooling labor together within a firm and economies of specialization, drawn by Young (1928).

The solution of the decision problem for configuration $(y/l_x)$ is

$$N = (s^{ab} a p_y/w)^{1/(1-a)}, \qquad y^s = (s^{ab} a)^{\frac{1}{1-a}} (p_y/w)^{a/(1-a)}$$

$$u_y = y = (1-a)(s^b a p_y/w)^{a/(1-a)}$$

where $u_y$ is the employer's indirect utility function. Note that the interior solution of $N$ is relevant only for $a < 1$.

Each worker's decision is simple. He sells all his labor, so that the budget constraint is $p_y y^d = w l_x^s$, where $l_x^s = 1$ is supply of labor. The worker's utility is thus

$$u_x = k y^d = k w / p_y$$

Let the number of individuals choosing $(y/l_x)$ be $M_y$; then the market supply of good y is $M_y y^s$ and the market demand for labor is $M_y N$. Let the number of individuals choosing $(l_x/y)$ be $M_x$; then the market demand for good y is $M_x y^d$ and the market supply of labor is $M_x$. The market clearing conditions for good y and for labor are equivalent to each other due to Walras's law. Hence, we consider only one of them. Together with the utility equalization condition and two corner solutions, we have

$$M_x y^s = M_y y^d, \qquad y^s = (s^{ab} a)^{\frac{1}{1-a}} (p_y/w)^{a/(1-a)}, \qquad y^d = w/p_y$$

$$u_x = u_y \text{ or } k w / p_y = (1-a)(s^b a p_y/w)^{a/(1-a)}$$

This yields the corner equilibrium in structure E as follows.

$$N = M_x/M_y = \frac{ak}{1-a} \qquad w/p_y = [(1-a)/k]^{1-a}(s^b a)^a$$

$$u_E = (s^b k a)^a (1-a)^{1-a}$$

where $u_E$ is the per capita real income in structure E. Its reciprocal is also the absolute labor price of the final good.

*Structure F*, comprising configurations ($l_y/x$) and ($x/l_y$), as shown in figure 6.1d. ($x/l_y$), denotes a specialist producer of x who hires workers and directs them to specialize in producing y using her produce x within the firm. ($l_y/x$) denotes a worker who is hired to produce the final good, using the intermediate good, and who buys the final good. The decision problem of the employer choosing ($x/l_y$) is:

Max: $u_x = Y$

| | |
|---|---|
| $Y + Ys \equiv Ny^s$ | (total output of y for a firm) |
| $y^s = (x^d r l_y)^a, \quad l_y = 1$ | (production condition for each employee) |
| $x^d = x^s/N$ | (quantity of x employed by each employee) |
| $x^s = l_x^b, \quad l_x = 1$ | (production condition of employer) |
| $p_y Y^s = w l_y N = wN$ | (budget constraint); |

where the capitalized letters represent output levels for the firm, and the lower-cases represent quantities of goods for each individual. $Y + Y^s$ is total output of the final good for the firm, $Y$ is the residual return to the employer, $Y^s$ is total amount sold by the firm, $y^s$ is the output level of the final good produced by each employee, $x^d$ is amount of the intermediate good used by each employee to produce y, and $r$ is the transaction efficiency coefficient for the labor of employees. Because of the transaction cost of labor, the employer receives $r l_y$ when she buys $l_y$. $N$ is the number of workers hired by each employer and $x^s$ is amount of the intermediate good produced by the employer. The superscripts for the lower cases represent internal demand for inputs and supply of outputs within the firm, while the superscripts for the capitalized letters represent demand and supply in the market-place.

The solution of the decision problem is:

$$N = r[(1 - a)p_y/w]^{\frac{1}{a}}, \qquad Y^s = (p_y/w)^{(1-a)/a} r(1 - a)^{\frac{1}{a}},$$
$$u_x = Y = ar[(1 - a)p_y/w]^{(1-a)/a}$$

where $u_x$ is the employer's indirect utility function. The decision problem of a specialist worker producing y is simple. He sells all of his labor to exchange for good y. Hence, from the utility function $u_y = ky^d$ and the budget constraint $p_y y^d = w l_y = w$, we obtain his indirect utility function:

$$u_y = kw/p_y$$

The market clearing and utility equalization conditions yield the corner equilibrium in structure F:

$$w/p_y = (ar/k)^a(1 - a)^{1-a}, \qquad N = M_y/M_x = \frac{k(1 - a)}{a}$$
$$u_F = (ar)^a[k(1 - a)]^{1-a},$$

where $u_F$ is the per capita real income in this structure. Let us put all information relating to the four corner equilibria together in table 8.1.

### 8.3.3 The general equilibrium structure of transactions and residual rights

Per capita real incomes in the four structures are dependent on the transaction efficiency parameters $t$, $s$, $k$, the degree of economies of specialization $b$, and the degree of economies of roundabout production $a$. According to the Yao theorem, all we have to do in solving for the general equilibrium is to identify the Pareto optimum corner equilibrium from the four corner equilibria. Letting per capita real incomes in each pair of structures be equal, we will obtain several equations which partition the parameter space of five dimensions into several subspaces. Our job is then to identify which structure is the general equilibrium structure within each of the subspaces. Essentially, this is to solve for a system of simultaneous inequalities. There is no standard procedure for solving a system of simultaneous inequalities. Experience and skill in ruling out Pareto inefficient structures as far as possible through identifying incompatibility and contradictions between inequalities is crucial for finding the solution. From many models in this text, you will learn some skill in manipulating such systems of inequalities. For the current model, let us solve for the

**Table 8.1:** Corner equilibria in four structures

| | | | *Structure* | | |
|---|---|---|---|---|---|
| | A | D | E | F |
| Relative price | | $\dfrac{p_y}{p_x} = \left(\dfrac{k}{1-a}\right)^{1-a}(at)^{-a}$ | $\dfrac{w}{p_y} = \left(\dfrac{1-a}{k}\right)^{1-a}(as^b)^{-a}$ | $\dfrac{w}{p_y} = \left(\dfrac{ar}{k}\right)^{a}(1-a)^{1-a}$ |
| Number of specialists | | $M_x = \dfrac{akM}{1-a+ak}$ <br><br> $M_y = \dfrac{(1-a)M}{1-a+ak}$ | $M_x = \dfrac{akM}{1-a+ak}$ <br><br> $M_y = \dfrac{(1-a)M}{1-a+ak}$ | $M_x = \dfrac{aM}{(1-a)k+a}$ <br><br> $M_y = \dfrac{k(1-a)M}{(1-a)k+a}$ |
| Demand function | | $x^d = \left(at^a\dfrac{p_y}{p_x}\right)^{\frac{1}{1-a}}$ <br><br> $y^d = p_x/p_y$ | $N^d = \left(s^{ab}a\dfrac{p_y}{w}\right)^{\frac{1}{1-a}}$ <br><br> $y^d = w/p_y$ | $N^d = r\left(\dfrac{p_y(1-a)}{w}\right)^{\frac{1}{a}}$ <br><br> $y^d = w/p_y$ |
| Supply function | | $y^s = a^{\frac{1}{1-a}}\left(t\dfrac{p_y}{p_x}\right)^{\frac{a}{1-a}}$ <br><br> $x^s = 1$ | $y^s = a^{\frac{1}{1-a}}\left(\dfrac{s^b p_y}{w}\right)^{\frac{a}{1-a}}$ <br><br> $l_x^s = 1$ | $Y^s = (1-a)^{\frac{1}{a}}\left(\dfrac{p_y}{w}\right)^{\frac{1-a}{a}} r$ <br><br> $l_y^s = 1$ |
| Real income | $\left(\dfrac{b^b}{(1+b)^{1+b}}\right)^a$ | $(tka)^a(1-a)^{1-a}$ | $(s^b ka)^a(1-a)^{1-a}$ | $(ar)^a[k(1-a)]^{1-a}$ |

system of simultaneous inequalities in two steps. First, we compare per capita real incomes in structures D, E, and F. We have:

$$u_E > u_D \text{ iff } t < s^b \tag{8.4a}$$

$$u_E > u_F \text{ iff } k > k_8 \equiv (r/s^b)^{a/(2a-1)} \tag{8.4b}$$

$$u_D > u_F \text{ iff } k > k_7 \equiv (r/t)^{a/(2a-1)} \tag{8.4c}$$

A comparison between $k_7$ and $k_8$ indicates

$$k_8 > k_7 \text{ iff } t > s^b. \tag{8.4d}$$

(8.4d) can be used to partition the parameter space into two subspaces first. For $t < s^a$ or $k_8 < k_7$, information in (8.4) can be summarized in figure 8.2. This figure implies that for $t < s^b$ or $k_8 < k_7$, among the three structures with the division of labor,

Structure E generates the greatest per capita real income if $k > k_8$;
Structure F generates the greatest per capita real income if $k < k_8$;
Structure D cannot be general equilibrium since $u_D < u_E$ for any $k$.

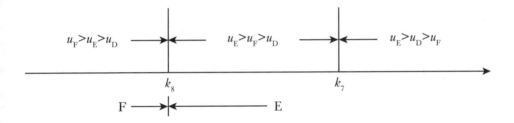

◆ **Figure 8.2:** Case with $t < s^b$ or $k_8 < k_7$

For the case with $t > s^b$ or $k_8 > k_7$, the information in (8.4) can be summarized as in the figure 8.3 This figure implies that for $t > s^b$ or $k_8 > k_7$, among the three structures with the division of labor,

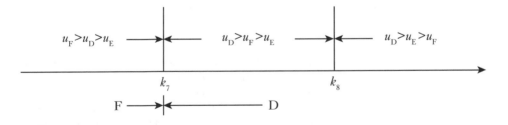

**Figure 8.3:** Case with $t > s^b$ or $k_8 > k_7$

Structure D generates the greatest per capita real income if $k > k_7$;
Structure F generates the greatest per capita real income if $k < k_7$;
Structure E cannot be general equilibrium since $u_E < u_D$ for any $k$ .

Putting the information together and considering per capita real income in autarky yields table 8.2.

**Table 8.2:** Candidates for equilibrium structure

| $t < s^b$ | | $t > s^b$ | |
|-----------|-----------|-----------|-----------|
| $k < k_8$ | $k > k_8$ | $k < k_7$ | $k > k_7$ |
| F, A      | E, A      | F, A      | D, A      |

Comparisons between per capita real incomes in each pair of structures for the parameter subspace in table 8.2 yield the results of the general equilibrium and its inframarginal comparative statics shown in table 8.3.

**Table 8.3:** General equilibrium and its inframarginal comparative statics

| Values of $t$ and $s$ | $t < s^b$ | | | | $t > s^b$ | | | |
|---|---|---|---|---|---|---|---|---|
| Value of $k$ relative to $r, t, s, a$ | $k < k_8$ | | $k > k_8$ | | $k < k_7$ | | $k > k_7$ | |
| | $< k_{11}$ | $> k_{11}$ | $< k_{10}$ | $> k_{10}$ | $< k_{11}$ | $> k_{11}$ | $< k_9$ | $k > k_9$ |
| Equilibrium structure | A | F | A | E | A | F | A | D |

where: $k_7 \equiv (r/t)^{a/(2a-1)}$ is given by $u_D = u_E$,
  $k_8 \equiv (r/s^b)^{a/(2a-1)}$ is given by $u_E = u_F$,
  $k_9 \equiv (1-a)^{(a-1)/a} b^b / ta(1+b)^{1+b}$ is given by $u_A = u_D$,
  $k_{10} \equiv (1-a)^{(a-1)/a} b^b / as^b (1+b)^{1+b}$ is given by $u_A = u_E$,
  $k_{11} \equiv [b^b/ar(1+b)^{1+b}]^{a/(1-a)}/(1-a)$ is given by $u_A = u_F$.

If you use the constraints that all critical values $k_i$ are between 0 and 1, you can partition the parameter space even further. We leave this as an exercise for you.

In terms of intuition, table 8.3 tells the following story.

I) The structure with division of labor and the producer of y as the employer (structure E) cannot be general equilibrium if the transaction efficiency for labor employed to produce the intermediate good ($s$) is low compared to that for the intermediate good ($t$), or if $t > s^a$, since structure E must trade labor employed to produce the intermediate good.

I.a) Under this circumstance, if the transaction efficiencies for the final and intermediate goods ($k$ and $t$) are sufficiently high, compared to the transaction efficiency for labor employed to produce the final good ($r$), or if $k > k_7$, the structure with the division of labor and the producer of x as the employer (structure F) cannot be general equilibrium either since F must trade labor employed to produce the final good. Note the relationship between this statement and the formula for $k_7$. Hence, only structures A and D are candidates for the equilibrium structure. If the transaction efficiencies for the final and intermediate goods are high, D is the equilibrium, otherwise A is the equilibrium.

I.b) If the transaction efficiency for the intermediate good ($t$) is low, compared to the transaction efficiency for labor employed to produce the final good ($r$), or if $k < k_7$, the structure with the division of labor and with no firms (structure D) cannot be general equilibrium since D must trade the intermediate good. Hence, only structures A and F are candidates for the equilibrium structure. If the transaction efficiencies for the final good and labor hired to produce the final good are high, F is the equilibrium, otherwise A is the equilibrium.

II) Structure D cannot be equilibrium if $t$ is small compared to $s$, or if $t < s^a$, since structure D must trade the intermediate good that involves a small $t$.

II.a) If $k$ and $s$ are sufficiently large compared to $r$, or if $k > k_8$, structure F cannot be equilibrium since F is associated with $r$. Hence, only structures A and E are candidates for the equilibrium structure. If $k$ and $s$ are sufficiently large (or $k > k_{10}$), E is the equilibrium, otherwise A is the equilibrium.

II.b) If $s$ is small compared to $r$, or if $k < k_8$, structure E cannot be equilibrium since E is associated with $s$. If $k$ and $r$ are sufficiently large, F is the equilibrium, otherwise A is the equilibrium.

The inframarginal comparative statics of general equilibrium are summarized in the following proposition.

**Proposition 8.1:** The general equilibrium is autarky if transaction efficiency is low and is the division of labor if transaction efficiency is high. The division of labor is coordinated through the institution of the firm and the labor market if the transaction efficiency for labor is higher than that for intermediate goods. Otherwise it is organized through the markets for the intermediate and final goods. When the general equilibrium is associated with the firm, the specialist of the final good is the owner of the firm if the transaction efficiency for labor employed to produce the intermediate good is higher than that for labor employed to produce the final good. Otherwise the specialist producer of the intermediate good is the owner of the firm. The institution of the firm can get the activity with the lowest transaction efficiency involved in the division of labor, while avoiding the direct pricing and marketing of the outputs and inputs of that activity. The residual returns claimed by the employer are the indirect price of her efforts.

The essence of the theory of indirect pricing can be summarized as follows. If individuals engage in division of labor in producing two goods x and y, trade in two of the four elements comprising outputs x, y, and inputs $l_x$, $l_y$ can be used to organize the division of labor. Hence, there are six possible structures of transactions (2 combinations of 4 elements) that can be used to organize the division of labor: x and y (structure D), y and $l_x$ (structure E), y and $l_y$ (structure F), x and $l_x$ (infeasible since a specialist of x who must consume y cannot buy y), x and $l_y$ (infeasible too), $l_y$ and $l_x$ (a structure that may be seen in some collective organization with direct exchange of labor but is rarely seen in the real world). Hence, individuals can at least consider three of the structures and choose one of them to avoid trade that involves the lowest transaction efficiency. Later, we shall show that as the number of traded goods and the level of division of labor increase, the number of possible structures of transactions increases more than proportionally. This implies that choice of transactions structure is increasingly more important than choice of production structure and resource allocation for a given structure of production as division of labor develops. This is why in a highly commercialized society (with a high level of division of labor) there are more opportunities for entrepreneurs to make fortunes from playing around with structures of transactions.

◆ 8.4 The Distinction between *ex ante* and *ex post* Production Functions and the New Classical Analysis of Demand and Supply

For inframarginal analysis, production functions discontinuously jump across production configurations (as discussed in chapter 2) as individuals shift between the production configurations. This feature of the new classical system of production generates important implications for endogenous productivity progress. Hence, it is important to draw the distinction between an *ex ante production function*, which is the production function that is specified before individuals have made their decisions, and an *ex post production function*, which can be seen only after individuals have chosen configurations and the economy is settled down in a structure.

The *ex ante* production functions are specified in (8.1). Since all decision variables are allowed to take on zero and positive values, there are multiple production configurations for different profiles of zero and positive values of decision variables. As individuals choose different configurations and the economy settles down in different structures, each individual's system of production differs from configuration to configuration and the system of production for society differs from structure to structure. If an individual chooses autarky $(x, y, l_x, l_y > 0, x^s, y^s, x^d, y^d = 0)$, then her *ex post* production function of y is

$$y = x^a l_y^a = l_x^{ab}(1 - l_x)^a = (1 - l_y)^{ab} l_y^a$$

where the endowment constraint is used. The marginal productivity of y and the derivative of the marginal productivity are

$$\frac{dy}{dl_y} = ay(bl_x^{-1} - l_y^{-1})$$

$$\frac{d^2y}{dl_y^2} < 0 \text{ when } \frac{dy}{dl_y} = 0.$$

This implies diminishing marginal labor productivity of y within the neighborhood of the corner solution in configuration A.

But if structure E is chosen, then the *ex post* production function of a firm in producing y is given in (8.7). It is

$$y + y^s = (x^d l_y)^a = (Ns^b)^a.$$

As discussed in the previous subsection, this *ex post* production function for the firm displays economies of specialization in producing y if $a > 0.5$ and exhibits global increasing returns to scale of labor, $N$, if $a > 1$ and local economies of scale if $0.5 < a < 1$. Hence, the *ex post* production function for the firm may emerge from the division of labor as the general equilibrium shifts from autarky to structure E. The *ex post* production function in E is not only different from the *ex post* production function in autarky, but also different from the *ex ante* production functions in (8.1), which does not involve the firm and economies of scale of the firm.

Rosen (1978) was the first economist to spell out the distinction between *ex ante* and *ex post* production functions. Stigler (1951) noted the discontinuous jumps of cost functions, which are based on the production function, as a result of changes in the level of specialization for the firm. In the new classical framework, the production function for the firm may emerge from individuals' decisions in choosing a certain structure of transactions required by the division of labor. In particular, the production function for a firm is a combination of many individuals' production functions. An owner of the firm combines her system of production with all employees' systems of production to get a system of production for the firm. This implies that in the new classical framework, the firm is no longer a black box represented by an *ad hoc* production function for the firm. The new classical theory of the firm in this chapter has spelled out how the production function for the firm emerges, and what are the general equilibrium implications of the internal organization of the firm.

It is very interesting to see that discontinuous shifts of demand and supply functions between structures, the emergence of a certain demand function, and the correlation between prices and quantities demanded which are generated by inframarginal comparative statics of general equilibrium all make the new classical analysis of demand and supply substantially differ from marginal comparative statics. From table 8.1 you can see that in this model, the demand law holds for individuals' demand functions for a given structure. However, as the transaction cost coefficients for labor and goods reach certain critical values, demand and supply functions emerge from a shift from A to a structure with the division of labor. Also, demand and supply functions for labor emerge from a shift to structures E or F from either A or D. Such shifts may change quantities demanded and prices at the same time. The correlation between the changes in quantities demanded and prices caused by such changes may or may not be compatible with the demand law.

## ◆ 8.5 Economies of Division of Labor and the Firm, and the Coase Theorem

Since each corner equilibrium is locally Pareto optimal for a given structure and there is only one consumption good in the model in this chapter, the corner equilibrium per capita output level of the final good in a structure represents the locally maximum productivity of the economy for that structure. Hence, *economies of division of labor* can be measured by the difference in per capita consumption of y between structures A and D when transaction cost is zero, that is:

$$u_D - u_A = a^a(1-a)^{1-a} - [b^b/(1+b)^{1+b}]^a,$$

where $u_D$ and $u_A$ are given in table 8.1. The economies of division of labor are positive if and only if

$$F \equiv a(1 - a)^{(1-a)/a}(1 + b)^{1+b}/b^b > 1. \tag{8.5}$$

It is obvious that $\partial F/\partial a > 0$ and $\partial F/\partial b > 0$, which implies that economies of division of labor increase with the degree of economies of roundabout production $a$, which is the degree of economies of specialization in producing y too, and with the degree of economies of specialization in producing the intermediate good $b$.

From (8.5), we can show that *economies of specialization in producing a single good are neither necessary nor sufficient for the existence of economies of division of labor for society as a whole*. Suppose $a < 0.5$, but is sufficiently close to 0.5. This implies that there are no economies of specialization in producing good y. But (8.5) indicates that for this case, there are economies of division of labor if $b$ is sufficiently large. You may verify this by plugging $a = 0.4$ and $b = 10$ into (8.5). Suppose $b < 1$, that is, there are no economies of specialization in producing x. But (8.5) indicates that there are economies of division of labor if $a$ is sufficiently large. You may verify this by plugging $a = b = 0.8$ into (8.5). This substantiates the claim that economies of specialization in producing a single good are not necessary for the existence of economies of division of labor. This implies that as long as economies of specialization in an activity are significant, we may have economies of division of labor even if there are no economies of specialization in the other activity. That is, economies of specialization can be transferred from one activity to the other through the input–output network of the division of labor. Hence, even if housekeeping or butlering do not exhibit many economies of specialization, individuals specialized in such activities can share economies of division of labor with specialists in other sectors, such as the automobile manufacturing sector, who enjoy significant economies of specialization. Here, economies of specialization in the automobile sector are external to a housekeeper. But we can show that economies of division of labor that are external to all individuals cannot exist.

Suppose, for instance, that $a < 0.5$ and $b < 1$, which implies that there are no economies of specialization in producing all goods, and that therefore there are no economies of division of labor as indicated by (8.4). This implies that economies of scale that are external to all firms are an "empty box" (Knight, 1925). This further justifies Allyn Young's view that the distinction between external economies of scale and internal economies of scale is misleading.

Now we substantiate the claim that economies of specialization in producing a single good are not sufficient for the existence of economies of division of labor for society as a whole. Suppose that $b = 2$ (there are economies of specialization in producing x) and that $a$ is sufficiently close to 0, for instance, $a = 0.1$. Then (8.5) indicates that there are no economies of division of labor. Assume that $a = 0.6$ (there are economies of specialization in producing y) and that $b = 0.6$. Then there are no economies of division of labor. However, if $a > 0.5$ and $b > 1$, then economies of division of labor must exist. That is, economies of specialization in producing all goods are sufficient for the existence of economies of division of labor for society as a whole.

If the maximum per capita consumption of the final good is greater in structure E or F than in structure D, then we say there are *economies of the institution of the firm*. From the discussion in the previous subsections, we can see that economies of division of labor are necessary but not sufficient for the existence of economies of the firm. This proposition was first proposed by Coase (1937). As Cheung (1983) argues, the other necessary condition for the existence of the firm is that the transaction efficiency for intermediate goods must be lower than that for labor employed to produce the intermediate goods. Cheung's theory refines Coase's idea about the firm. Coase (1937) indicates that the institution of the firm is used to replace the market with administration within the firm. According to Cheung, the institution of the firm replaces the market for intermediate goods with the market for labor, instead of replacing the market with a nonmarket institution.

Coase (1960) claims that the structure of ownership makes no difference to the efficiency of the market if transaction cost is zero, and that the market will choose a structure of ownership to maximize the benefit of division of labor, net of transaction costs (the Coase theorem). Our model substantiates the Coase theorem. From table 8.1, it is obvious that structures D, E, F generate the same per capita real income if $t = k = s = r = 1$ (no transaction costs). The structure of ownership of the firm makes a difference only if transaction costs are not zero. Also, proposition 8.1 implies the second statement of the Coase theorem that the market will choose the most efficient structure of ownership and property rights.

We have refined Coase's ideas about transaction costs. He claims that the institution of the firm can be used to reduce transaction costs. But our proposition 8.1 implies that as transaction efficiency is improved, total transaction costs will be increased as the general equilibrium shifts from autarky to structure E or F. Hence, the institution of the firm may increase transaction costs when it promotes division of labor as long as increased economies of division of labor outweigh the increased transaction costs.

From table 8.2, we can see that for $t < s^a$ and $k_9 > k > k_8$, $k_{10}$, the institution of the firm in structure E generates the highest per capita real income, while the division of labor in structure D generates a lower per capita real income than in autarky. Hence, if the institution of the firm is not allowed, the division of labor will not be chosen. If the institution of the firm is allowed, then individuals will choose the division of labor in structure E. Hence, the institution of the firm can promote the division of labor by reducing transaction costs compared to D and by increasing transaction costs compared to autarky.

Empirical evidence for the new classical theory of the firm in this chapter is relevant to *Type I scale effect*, the hypothesis that there is a positive correlation between productivity and average size of firms. Our new classical model of the firm predicts on the contrary that average size of firms decreases and each firm's productivity increases simultaneously if division of labor evolves between firms due to increases in relative transaction efficiency of goods to labor. In exercise 11, Liu and Yang's new classical model shows that if initial transaction efficiency for both labor and goods is low, then autarky is equilibrium. As transaction efficiency for labor is sufficiently improved, the equilibrium jumps to a low level of division of labor with small average size of firms. As transaction efficiency for labor and goods is further improved, the equilibrium jumps to an intermediate level of division of labor with a larger average size of firms. But if the transaction efficiency of goods is significantly improved further, then the average size of firms decreases and the level of division of labor and aggregate productivity increase. This formalizes Coase, Cheung, and Stigler's theory of irrelevance of the size of the firm. This theory states that if division of labor evolves within the firm, then the average size of firms and productivity increase side by side. But if division of labor evolves between firms, the average size of firms decreases, while productivity and level of division of labor increase. This theory rejects a monotonically positive correlation between average size of firms and productivity. Empirical evidence reported by Murakami, Liu, and Otsuka (1996), Y. Zhang (1999), and Liu and Yang (2000) supports this theory of the irrelevance of the size of firm and rejects Type I scale effect. Many neoclassical models with economies of scale, such as those we will look at in examples 11.4 and 11.5, predict Type I scale effects.

## Key Terms and Review

The institution of the firm.
Economies of specialization in producing a good require more than one input factor.
The relationship between economies of specialization in producing a good, economies of division of labor, and economies of the institution of the firm.
The distinction between *ex ante* and *ex post* production functions.
Necessary and sufficient conditions for the emergence of the firm from division of labor.
The function of the institution of the firm and implications of its internal organization for the equilibrium level of division of labor and productivity.
The relationship between individuals' production functions and the production function of a firm.
The difference between rights to residual returns and rights to residual control and the relationship between those residual rights and the function of the institution of the firm.
The role of freedom of choice of profession configuration and freedom of enterprise in enabling the institution of the firm to function.
The significance of a legal system that protects the residual rights of the owners of the firm in enabling the institution of the firm to function.
Type I scale effect.

## Further Reading

*Theory of the firm*: Cheung (1983), Coase (1937, 1991), Alchian and Demsetz (1972), Jensen and Meckling (1976), Knight (1921), Stigler (1951); *theory of incomplete contract*: Hart (1995), Grossman and Hart (1986), Hart and Moore (1990); *Theory of the firm and endogenous specialization*: Bolton and Dewatripont (1994), Carter (1995), Shi and Yang (1998), Yang and Y.-K. Ng (1993, ch. 9), Yang and Y.-K. Ng (1995), Borland and Yang (1995), Liu and Yang (2000); *models with the trade-off between incentive provision and measurement costs*: Bolton and Scharfstein (1998), Holmstrom and Milgrom (1995), Holmstrom and Roberts (1998); *theory of the firm and endogenous transaction costs*: Milgrom and Roberts (1990, 1992), Kreps (1990), Lewis and Sappington (1991), Maskin and Xiu (1999), Aghion and Tirole (1997), and Gibbons (1998); *theory of the firm and the commitment game*: Dewatripont and Maskin (1995), Dewatripont and Roland (1995), Dewatripont (1988), Qian (1994b); *empirical evidence against Type I scale effects*: Aiginger and Tichy (1991), Loveman and Sengenberger (1991), Liu and Yang (2000), Murakami, Liu, and Otsuka (1996), Berger and Ofek (1995), Bhagat, Shleifer, and Vishny (1990), Comment and Jarrell (1995), Fauver, Houston, and Naranjo (1998), Kaplan, and Weisbach (1992), Servaes (1996).

# QUESTIONS

1   Alchian and Demsetz (1972) indicate that the claim of the owner of the firm to its residual returns is the distinguishing feature of the capitalist firm. If the marginal productivities of the members of the production team are interdependent, then each member does not count the effect of her effort on others' productivity if her pay is determined by her marginal productivity in the market, thereby resulting in distortions. Hence, a monitor is essential to measure the efforts of the members and pay them according to their effects on the productivity of the entire team. But by what mechanism can the effort level of the monitor be efficiently determined? According to Alchian and Demsetz, the residual returns to the owner-monitor of the firm are the efficient institution for achieving this. Without a claim on the residual returns, nobody will have an incentive to ensure the efficient management of the firm. Hence, so-called X inefficiency, which means that productivity potential cannot be exploited even if it is technically easy to achieve, will emerge from the absence of claimants to the residual returns of the firm. This is why all state-owned firms, which have no individual residual rights claimants, are associated with significant X inefficiencies. Two criticisms of Alchian and Demsetz's theory may arise. One is proposed by Grossman and Hart (see ch. 10, below), who argue that the capitalist firm is distinguished not only by the asymmetric distribution of residual returns, but also by the asymmetric distribution of residual control, which implies that the owner of the firm has rights to dispose of the assets and labor of the firm. In chapter 10, the rationale for the asymmetric distribution of residual control rights will be investigated. The second criticism is that if the pricing of effort level of the monitor is highly efficient, the production team can pay the monitor according to her performance. Interdependence of the marginal productivities of members in a production team does not necessarily imply that residual returns are the only way to resolve the problem. It is because the pricing efficiency of the monitor's effort is even lower than the pricing efficiency of the efforts of the team members that the claim to residual returns emerges as an institution to indirectly price the effort level of the monitor. Comment on these criticisms of the Alchian–Demsetz argument.

2   John bought from James a copying shop at $110,000, which does not include the rental of the real estate and copy machines. Each year John can make up to $40,000 as profit net of all rents for real estate, copy machines, other equipment, and the wage bill for the machine keepers and for himself. James told John that the good will of the business, embodied in the client base that he had cultivated over the years, and his planning to put client base, the location of the shop, the machines, and other factors together in a right way are worth more than $110,000. This is verified by the fact that by his fourth year in the business John has repaid his investment of $110,000 and interest, and started to make a net profit. Use this case to analyze why the shop can make a net profit and why the intellectual property of James cannot be appropriately priced in the absence of the institution of the firm.

3   Use the model in this chapter to analyze increases in labor and capital indicated by statistical data. According to neoclassical economics, observed increases in labor and capital inputs are simply increases in production factors employed in production. But according to the new classical theory in this chapter, an increase in trade of labor is the result of the development of the institution of the firm, while an increase in trade of capital goods is the result of the development of division of labor in roundabout production between firms and individuals. The two phenomena can take place in the absence of increases in the total amounts of primary factors employed in production for society as a whole. Discuss the implications of the difference between these two interpretations of the data.

4   In the nineteenth century, France, Germany, and other major European countries followed Britain in enacting laws guaranteeing the right of free association. Analyze the implications of these laws, in conjunction with patent laws and laws that protect private property rights, for economic development and the evolution of division of labor. In Japan and China, such laws did not exist until the end of the

nineteenth century. Emperors were extremely sensitive to unofficial free associations and tended to infringe arbitrarily upon the residual rights of the owners of firms. Use that institutional feature, in relation to the theory in this chapter, to explain the following historical fact documented by Elvin (1973). Song China (960–1270 AD) possessed both the scientific knowledge and the mechanical ability to have experienced a full-fledged industrial revolution some four centuries before it occurred in Europe. The Chinese developed very elaborate contracts and sophisticated commercial organizations, but failed to have industrial revolution at that time.

5   Under a regime of free association, any individual can set up a firm by registering his firm with the local government. But in many less developed countries, a resident needs to apply for approval from the government to set up a firm. Many times, such as in the case of setting up a company engaging in foreign trade, a government licence is essential. Also, the government agency which has such approval power has vested interests in the business which relates to the application for setting up private firms. For instance, in each Chinese city, there is a government committee which has approval power for setting up wholesale and retail firms, while this committee is also the owner of the government monopolist wholesale and retail network in the city. Analyze the development implications of such an approval system in connection with the theory of the firm in this chapter.

6   Apply the theory of the firm in this chapter to analyze the role of multinational firms in economic development. Under what conditions can multinational firms more efficiently protect rights to intellectual property (know-how) than direct trade of the intellectual properties? In many developing countries, governments require that the foreign ownership share of firms cannot exceed a certain percentage. What are the effects of such regulation on economic development?

7   In all Soviet-style economies there are no laws that protect residual rights to firms. Due to Marx's ideology, in a Soviet-style socialist country such residual rights are considered to be a source of exploitation. Also, a Soviet-style government prohibits unofficial free association (including free enterprises) for political reasons. Apply the new classical theory of the firm to analyze the implications for economic development of these institutional features.

8   Apply the theory of indirect pricing in this chapter to analyze why it is the shareholders rather than the managers of a company who are the owners when the division of labor between portfolio management and production management emerges.

9   In the Soviet-style economic system, land cannot be owned privately or traded. Only pricing according to working effort is legitimate. Making income from the ownership of assets, including land and shares of a firm, is regarded as exploitation. Analyze why, under these institutional arrangements, intangible services in managing real estate will be underpriced and underprovided.

10  Many economists claim that the function of the institution of the firm is to internalize externalities. Coase also claims that the institution of the firm replaces market transactions with nonmarket arrangements with centralized planning within the firm. Apply the theory of indirect pricing to comment on this view. You may relate your discussion to Cheung's view that the institution of the firm replaces the market for intermediate goods with the labor market.

11  There were a lot of reports in media in the 1980s and 1990s (see, for instance, "Enterprise: How Entrepreneurs are Reshaping the Economy and What Big Companies Can Learn?" Business Week, Oct. 22, 1993, Special Issue, "Management Focus," The Economist, March 5, 1994, p. 79, and "Manufactures Use Supplies to Help Them Develop New Products," Wall Street Journal, Dec. 19, 1994, p. 1) about de-integration, focusing on core competence, increasing specialization, contracting out or outsourcing, which feature recent changes of company structure. Use the theory in this chapter to explain these phenomena.

**12**   Use the new classical theory of the firm to analyze the implications of minimum wage laws. Then compare your results to the neoclassical analysis of the effects of such laws.

**13**   Wang and Yang (1996) introduce pursuit of relative utility into a new classical model to explore the implications of pursuit of relative position for the equilibrium level of division of labor. Conduct a thought experiment to figure out if the level of division of labor will be promoted by individuals' pursuit of relative position, which implies that individuals would like to be the first mover into a new profession as far as relative position is concerned. Use the thought experiment to figure out the intuition behind the results of exercise 12. Then use the different values of taste parameter for relative position to explain why the average size of firms in Taiwan is smaller than in South Korea.

# EXERCISES

1   Assume that there is no transaction cost in the model in this chapter. But the government imposes a value tax rate $t$ on goods sold and then returns to the sellers of goods the tax revenue collected from them. Solve for the general equilibrium and its inframarginal comparative statics. Analyze the impact of the tax rate on the equilibrium level of division of labor and productivity and equilibrium structure of residual rights.

2   Assume that in the model in exercise 1, a fraction of tax revenue $1 - s$ is used to maintain the government bureaucratic apparatus, so that only the fraction $s$ of the tax revenue goes back to the sellers of goods. Solve for the general equilibrium and its inframarginal comparative statics again. Analyze the impact of the bureaucracy efficiency coefficient $s$ on the equilibrium level of division of labor and productivity.

3   Now suppose that in the model in exercise 1, the government imposes a value tax on the sale of labor instead of on the sale of goods. Then it returns all tax revenue to the sellers of labor. Solve for the general equilibrium and its inframarginal comparative statics. Analyze the impact of the tax on the equilibrium level of division of labor and productivity. Compare your answer here to that in exercise 1. Then analyze the impacts of different tax regimes on the equilibrium structure of transactions, residual rights, and ownership of the firm.

4   Assume that in the model in exercise 3, a fraction of tax revenue $1 - \theta$ is used to maintain the government bureaucratic apparatus, so that only the fraction $\theta$ of the tax revenue goes back to the sellers of labor. Solve for the general equilibrium and its inframarginal comparative statics again. Analyze the impact of the bureaucracy efficiency coefficient $\theta$ on the equilibrium level of division of labor and productivity. Compare your answer here to that in exercise 2. Then analyze the impacts of bureaucracy efficiency $\theta$ and different tax regimes on the equilibrium structure of transactions, residual rights, and ownership of the firm.

5   Analyze the impact of various tax regimes in exercises 1 and 3 on trade volume of labor and intermediate goods which can be observed from statistical data. Explain why within the new classical framework, an increase in labor trade implies the development of division of labor within the firm or the replacement of the market for intermediate goods with the institution of the firm as a vehicle to organize the division of labor, while an increase in capital trade may be associated with the development of division of labor in a roundabout production chain. Both phenomena can occur in the absence of changes of total endowments for society as a whole.

6   Suppose that transaction cost is 0 in the model in this chapter, but the government enforces a minimum wage law which requires the wage rate to be higher than a constant $\theta$. Analyze the general equilibrium implications of the minimum wage.

7   Assume that the production function in (8.1b) is replaced with $x + x^s = \text{Max}\{0, l_x - b\}$. Solve again for the general equilibrium and its inframarginal comparative statics.

8   Yang, 1988: Add one more consumption good to the model in this chapter, so that the utility function becomes $u = (y + ky^d)(z + kz^d)$, where z is the new consumption good. Solve for the general equilibrium and inframarginal comparative statics.

9   Assume that the production function (8.1a) is replaced with $y + y^s = \text{Min}\{l_y, x + tx^d\}$. Solve for the general equilibrium and inframarginal comparative statics. Add a fixed learning cost to the production function, so that $y + y^s = \text{Min}\{l_y - a, x + tx^d\}$. How will your answer change?

10  Yang and Ng, 1995: Assume that in the model in this chapter the transaction cost of labor is specified as a loss of goods produced by the employee in transit from the employee to the employer. The algebra can be significantly simplified. Solve for the general equilibrium and inframarginal comparative statics.

11  Consider the Liu and Yang model (2000) where each of $M$ ex ante identical consumer-producers has the utility function $u = z + kz^d$, where good z is food. Their system of production is $z + z^s = (x + rx^d)^{1/2}L_z$, $x + x^s = (y + ty^d)^{1/2}L_x$, $y + y^s = L_y^2$, $L_z + L_x + L_y = 1$, $L_i \in [0, 1]$, $i = z, x, y$. x is the hoe used to produce food and y is the steel used to produce the hoe. If we ignore differences in ownership structure of the firm, then there are 9 structures. Structure A is autarky. The structure with partial division of labor P(y) consists of configurations (zx/y), selling z, self-providing x, and buying y, and (y/z), selling y and buying z. The structure with partial division of labor P(x) consists of configurations (xy/z), selling x, self-providing y, and buying z, and (z/x), selling z and buying x. The structure with partial division of labor and the firm FP(y) consists of configurations (zx/L_y), selling z, self-providing x, and buying labor $L_y$, and (L_y/z), selling labor $L_y$ and buying z. The structure with partial division of labor and the firm FP(x) consists of configurations (L_x/z), selling labor $L_x$ and buying z, and (z/L_x), selling z and buying labor $L_x$. The structure with the complete division of labor C consists of configurations (z/x), (y/z), and (x/yz). The structure with the complete division of labor and the firm FC(y) consists of configurations (L_x/z), (y/z) and (z/L_xy) selling z and buying y and $L_x$. Another structure with the complete division of labor and the firm FCL consists of configurations (L_x/z), (L_y/z), and (z/L_xL_y), selling z and buying $L_x$ and $L_y$. Solve for the general equilibrium and its inframarginal comparative statics. Show that a complete division of labor structure with the producer of x hiring labor to produce y within the firm, and buying z from an independent specialist of z, cannot be a general equilibrium structure if $t < s$. Solve for eight corner equilibria, the general equilibrium, and its inframarginal comparative statics. Show that if the following evolutionary paths take place as transaction efficiency is improved over time, evolution in division of labor is associated with decreasing size of the firm: A⇒P(y)⇒FP(x)⇒C, A⇒P(y)⇒FP(x)⇒FC(y), A⇒FP(y)⇒FP(x)⇒C, A⇒FP(y)⇒FP(x)⇒FC(y). Under what conditions will trade of producer goods, which may be recorded as capital in statistical data, and trade of labor increase simultaneously in the absence of changes in the total amount of endowment for society as a whole? Use this model to formalize the argument of irrelevance of size of firms, proposed by Cheung, Coase, Young, and Stigler, which claims that the size of the firm may increase or decrease as division of labor evolves, dependent upon whether division of labor is developed via labor market or via goods market.

12  M. Liu, 1999: Consider the model in this chapter. Assume that each individual prefers to be boss over a configuration of the employees. Hence, the utility function becomes $u = (y + ky^d)E^\beta$ where $\beta \geq 1$ is a taste parameter for relative position, $E = \gamma > 1$ if an individual chooses a configuration of employer, $E = \rho < 1$ if she chooses a configuration of employee,

and $E = 1$ if she chooses a configuration involving no asymmetric relationship between an employer and an employee. Solve for the general equilibrium and its inframarginal comparative statics. The solution is the same as in example 8.1 if $\beta = 0$. Analyze the implications of the parameter of pursuit of relative position $\beta \geq 1$ for the equilibrium level of division of labor and the equilibrium structure of residual rights.

chapter 9

# PRICING MECHANISMS BASED ON BARGAINING

## ♦ 9.1. Bargaining Games, Strategic Behavior, Opportunistic Behavior

Individual specific prices, and pricing through bargaining, had existed long before the emergence of developed markets with impersonal common market prices and related pricing mechanisms. In less-developed markets, including those in Soviet-style economies, pricing is typically determined by bargains between trade partners. In order to understand how impersonal common market prices emerge from the prices that are different from player to player, we must study bargaining. Game theory is particularly useful in studying the bargaining process, since bargaining is characterized by direct interactions between players' self-interested decisions.

The concept of game also has special applicability to the analysis of endogenous transaction costs caused by competition for a greater share of gains from the division of labor between players.

There are three types of human behavior. The first, called *nonstrategic behavior*, has the feature that decision-makers do not react directly to others' decisions, but rather react only to prices. All behavior examined in chapters 3 and 5–8 is nonstrategic behavior. The second type of behavior, called *strategic behavior*, has the feature that all decision-makers directly react to others' decisions. This type of behavior can be classified into two subcategories: non-opportunistic behavior and opportunistic behavior. *Non-opportunistic strategic behavior* is distinguished by the characteristic that a player's interests are not pursued at the cost of other players' interests. The self-interested behavior in the Nash bargaining game in section 9.2 is non-opportunistic strategic behavior. *Opportunistic behavior* is that form of strategic behavior in which a player's interests are pursued at the cost of other players' interests. Endogenous transaction costs are caused by opportunistic behavior in competing for a greater share of the gains from the division of labor between players.

From the previous chapters we can appreciate the importance of transaction costs for the equilibrium level of division of labor and related productivity. The implications of endogenous transaction costs are more important than that of exogenous transaction cost for the equilibrium size of the network of division of labor, since endogenous transaction costs are determined by individuals' decisions and their choice of institutional and contractual arrangements. This chapter uses game models to explore implications for economic development of endogenous transaction costs.

In section 9.2, the role of Nash bargaining in reducing endogenous transaction costs and in promoting division of labor is explored. Section 9.3 introduces information asymmetry into the Nash bargaining game to study the endogenous transaction costs caused by information asymmetry. Section 9.4 presents a neoclassical alternating-offer bargaining model. The implication of alternating-offer bargaining for the network size of division of labor is investigated in section 9.5. In section 9.6, the new classical alternating-offer bargaining game is extended to endogenize the first mover and to investigate how competition for a larger share of the gains from division of labor causes endogenous transaction costs. Section 9.7 uses a repeated game model to show how consideration of reputation can reduce such endogenous transaction costs.

---

### Questions to Ask Yourself when Reading this Chapter

♦ What are the differences between endogenous and exogenous transaction costs?

♦ What are the implications of endogenous transaction costs caused by opportunistic behavior for the equilibrium network size of division of labor?

♦ Why will information asymmetry generate endogenous transaction costs?

♦ What is the function of Nash bargaining in promoting division of labor?

♦ How does the consideration of reputation in a repeated game result in reduction of endogenous transaction costs?

---

## ♦ 9.2 Nash Bargaining Games

### Example 9.1: a Nash bargaining game with endogenous specialization

In a *Nash bargaining game* there are two players who have complete information about their opponents' production and utility functions, transportation conditions, endowment constraints, and the *threat point* at which they will refuse to participate. Assume that the production and utility functions, endowment constraint, and transportation conditions for two *ex ante* identical consumer-producers are the same as in chapter 5. But they try to sort out terms of trade through bargaining. Each player knows that choosing specialization in producing x generates utility $u_x = (1 - x^s)ky^d$, choosing specialization in producing y generates utility $u_y = (1 - y^s)kx^d$, and choosing autarky generates utility $u_A = 2^{-2a}$. There are two threat points or *disagreement points* at which each player refuses to participate in trade. The first is the bottom line given by real income in autarky $u_A$. A player will refuse to participate in the division of labor if trade generates a lower utility than autarky.

Second, a player may use the utility for the occupation configuration in producing y as the threat point when choosing the occupation configuration of x, since she can always change occupation if the terms of trade are not fair or if one occupation generates more utility than the other. Because of the budget constraint, the terms of trade are $p_x/p_y = x^s/y^d = x^d/y^s$, where the first equality is given by the budget constraint for the specialist of x, $p_x x^s = p_y y^d$, and the second by the budget constraint for the specialist of y, $p_x x^d = p_y y^s$. Since market clearing is a constraint for the terms of trade, we have $x^d = x^s$ and $y^d = y^s$. For simplicity of notation, we use $X$ and $Y$ to represent equal quantities demanded and supplied for the two goods.

The net gain that an x specialist can receive from the division of labor is $V_x = (1 - X)kY - u_A$ and that for a specialist of y is $V_y = (1 - Y)kX - u_A$. The x specialist wants the relative price $p_x/p_y = Y/X$ to be as high as possible. But he has a trade-off. If $Y/X$ is large, his net gain $V_x$ is great, but his opponent's net gain $V_y$ is small, so that his opponent has little incentive to get involved in the division of labor. Accordingly, the probability of realizing the large value of $V_x$ is small if the bargaining process is subject to any stochastic disturbance. The disturbance may be caused by a quarrel that the opponent just had with her husband at home before coming to the bargaining meeting. In her resulting bad mood, the smallness of her net gain from the deal may cause her to refuse to participate in the division of labor.

If we consider $V_y$ as the probability that the x specialist can realize $V_x$, then the x specialist's expected net pay-off from the division of labor is

$$V = V_x V_y + 0 \times (1 - V_y) = V_x V_y$$

where $1 - V_y$ is the probability that the net pay-off cannot be realized, or that the net pay-off is 0. Nash has proved that in a noncooperative bargaining game with marginal stochastic disturbance, the *Nash product V* will be maximized by self-interested strategies. Hence, the *Nash bargaining equilibrium* is given by the following maximization problem.

$$\text{Max}_{X, Y} : V = V_x V_y = [(1 - X)kY - u_A][(1 - Y)kX - u_A]. \tag{9.1}$$

In a symmetric model with *ex ante* identical consumer-producers and symmetric tastes and production and transaction conditions, the Nash bargaining equilibrium defined in (9.1) is equivalent to the one defined by (9.2). If utility in an alternative occupation configuration is considered as a threat point, while utility in autarky is just a bottom line, the Nash product becomes

$$V = (u_x - u_y)(u_y - u_x) = -(u_x - u_y)^2, \tag{9.2}$$

where $u_x$ is the utility for specialization in x and $u_y$ is the utility for specialization in y. In a Nash bargaining game the x specialist threatens to choose specialization in producing y, while the specialist of y threatens to choose specialization in producing x if the terms of trade are unfair. Maximization of the Nash product, of course, implies the minimization of $(u_x - u_y)$. Hence, Nash bargaining will establish the utility equalization condition. The maximization of $V$ with respect to $X$ and $Y$ subject to utility equalization generates the Nash bargaining equilibrium.

The first-order condition for the constrained maximization problem yields the equilibrium terms of trade

$$X = Y = \frac{1}{2}, \quad u_x = u_y = \frac{k}{4}$$

which coincides with the Walrasian equilibrium with endogenous numbers of different specialists. The first order conditions for the problem in (9.1)

$$\partial V/\partial X = \partial V/\partial Y = 0 \text{ or } Y = 1 - X \text{ and } (1 - 2X)[X(1 - X)k + u_A] = 0$$

generate the same solution. However, if the consumption, production, and transportation conditions are asymmetric between the two goods, the solution for the maximization problem (9.1) differs from that for (9.2). For the case of asymmetric tastes and production and transaction conditions the Nash bargaining equilibrium may be different from the the Walrasian equilibrium, although both of them are Pareto optimal.

If all players are not *ex ante* identical, then the Walrasian equilibrium may generate very unequal distribution of gains from the division of labor. This creates an incentive to use collective actions such as tariffs imposed by the government that represents players who receive little gains from the division of labor in the Walrasian equilibrium to seek rents, while the Nash bargaining equilibrium may avoid incentives for such rent seeking. We shall investigate the function of Nash bargaining in reducing endogenous transaction costs caused by rent seeking in chapter 12. For a small number of consumer-producers, the set of individuals is finite instead of a continuum. Hence, the integer problem discussed in chapter 6 may generate endogenous transaction costs in a new classical model under the Walrasian regime. For this case, Nash bargaining can avoid such endogenous transaction costs. Let us use the following example to show this.

### Example 9.2: the function of Nash bargaining in reducing endogenous transaction costs caused by the Walrasian equilibrium in a new classical model with a finite set of consumer-producers

Consider the model in example 9.1. There are only two players (the set of players is not a continuum) and the utility function is $u = (x + kx^d)^{1/3}(y + ky^d)^{2/3}$. Hence, per capita real income in autarky is $(2^{2/3}/3)^a$ and the utility functions for configurations (x/y) and (y/x) are $u_x = (1 - x^s)^{1/3}(ky^d)^{2/3}$ and $u_y = (kx^d)^{1/3}(1 - y^s)^{2/3}$, respectively. Walrasian supply and demand functions for the two occupations are $x^s = 2/3$, $y^d = 2p/3$, $y^s = 1/3$, $x^d = 1/3p$, where $p$ is the price of x in terms of y. The indirect utility functions for the two occupa-tions are $u_x = (2kp)^{2/3}/3$ and $u_y = 2^{2/3}(k/p)^{1/3}/3$, respectively. The market clearing con-dition for x or y yields $p = 1/2$. But this relative price cannot be the equilibrium one since the two players will choose configuration (y/x) and nobody chooses (x/y) under this relative price. This implies that the market cannot clear (there is supply for y, but no demand for y). Hence, the Walrasian corner equilibrium for the division of labor does not exist or the Walrasian general equilibrium is always autarky for any $k \in [0, 1]$ and $a > 1$.

But it is easy to show that the Nash bargaining equilibrium is the division of labor and generates higher per capita real income than in autarky for sufficiently large values of $k$ and $a$. For instance, suppose $k = 1$. Then the Nash bargaining corner equilibrium for the division of labor is given by the following maximization problem:

$$\underset{X, Y}{\text{Max}} \ [(1 - X)^{1/3}Y^{2/3} - u_A][(1 - Y)^{2/3}X^{1/3} - u_A]$$

where $X = x^s = x^d$ and $Y = y^s = y^d$ are quantities demanded as well as supplied of the two goods and $u_A = (2^{2/3}/3)^a$ is per capita real income in autarky. The solution of the bargaining equilibrium is $Y = X = 1/2$. This Nash bargaining corner equilibrium generates per capita real income $1/2$ which is greater than in autarky iff $a > \ln2/(\ln3 - 2\ln2/3) \approx 1.09$. Hence, for a large value of $a$ and $k = 1$, the Walrasian equilibrium is autarky and the Nash bargaining equilibrium is the division of labor, and the latter is Pareto superior to the former. Since maximization of the Nash product is equivalent to the maximization of a social welfare function, it is straightforward that the Nash bargaining equilibrium is always Pareto optimal.

It is interesting to see a conflict between organization efficiency and allocation efficiency here. If coordination of division of labor is not concerned, the efficient resource allocation should be $l_x = 1/3$ and $l_y = 2/3$ since relative taste for goods x and y is $1/2$ and production conditions for the two goods are the same between the two persons. But this efficient resource allocation generates coordination difficulty of division of labor. Hence, the Pareto optimum which counts both organization and allocation efficiencies generates $l_x = l_y = 1/2$.

Our example shows that for finite consumer-producers in an asymmetric new classical model, the Walrasian equilibrium generates endogenous transaction costs that result in a Pareto inefficient level of division of labor, even if the Walrasian relative price and relative consumption and production are consistent with the Pareto optimum. In our example, asymmetric tastes for goods x and y imply that specialization in y receives more utility than specialization in x under the Walrasian market clearing prices, so that nobody specializes in x. In other words, the unfair distribution of gains from the division of labor between occupations might cause an inefficient level of division of labor in the Walrasian equilibrium with a finite number of consumer-producers.

In chapter 12, we shall show that even if the set of *ex ante* different players is a continuum, the Walrasian equilibrium may generate very unequal distribution of gains from the division of labor. This will generate incentives for those players who receive little gains to take collective actions for rent seeking. For instance, the government in the less developed country may have an incentive to impose an import tariff if all gains from the division of labor go to the developed country.

Though the gain from the division of labor is not always split between players in the Nash bargaining equilibrium, it is fairly distributed in the sense that the distribution of the gains tends to be equal as the gains converge to 0. This implies that it never occurs in the Nash bargaining equilibrium that one player wants to trade while the other does not. Hence, we call the terms of trade that are given by Nash bargaining *fair terms of trade*.

It is interesting to note that there might be a trade-off between the reduction of endogenous transaction costs through Nash bargaining and exogenous transaction costs caused by that bargaining. The Pareto optimality of the Nash bargaining solution is based on the assumption that all players know their opponents' utility and production functions and endowments, which is essential for each player to figure out the Nash bargaining solution. But the Walrasian equilibrium can be reached even if each player has no information about other players' utility and production functions and endowments. If collection of all of the information is very expensive, then there is the trade-off between endogenous transaction costs caused by trade conflict in the Walrasian regime with finite consumer-producers and exogenous cost in collecting information in the Nash bargaining game.

If players do not have complete information about opponents' utility and production functions, endowment, and transaction conditions as in the next section, Nash bargaining may generate endogenous transaction costs too. Therefore, there is a trade-off between endogenous transaction costs caused by unfair distribution of the gains from the division of labor in the Walrasian regime and endogenous transaction costs related to the information problem in the Nash bargaining game.

The Nash bargaining equilibrium looks like an outcome of a cooperative game which maximizes the Nash product that is equivalent to a social welfare function. However Nash (1950) has shown that this is a noncooperative game rather than a cooperative one if it is subject to marginal stochastic disturbance. But in the noncooperative game, each player will take care of the opponent's interest for the sake of her own self-interest. Intuitively, each player must ensure that the opponent receives sufficient net gains from the division of labor to secure the division of labor outcome. The efficient trade-off between each player's net gains from the division of labor and reliability of realizing them makes a cooperative outcome emerge from all players' noncooperative strategies. Hence, the Nash bargaining equilibrium is associated with non-opportunistic strategic behaviors. But the algebra of the Nash bargaining models is not easy to manage. The first-order conditions for the Nash bargaining solution usually involve polynomials with no analytical solutions.

The Nash bargaining game model in this section is a well closed general equilibrium game model where Walras's law holds. This feature can be used to endogenize the level of division of labor and to explore the implications of bargaining for the equilibrium size of the network of division of labor. It can be shown that the Nash bargaining equilibrium is the division of labor iff the Pareto optimum is the division of labor. In other words, if the exogenous transaction cost coefficient $1-k$ is sufficiently large, the equilibrium is autarky, and otherwise it is the division of labor. The conventional bargaining models cannot endogenize individuals' levels of specialization (see exercises 2, 3). The shortcoming of the Nash bargaining model is that it does not explicitly spell out uncertainties or a time dimension. In the next two sections the implications of information asymmetry and the time dimension will be examined.

## ◆ 9.3 Endogenous Transaction Costs caused by Information Asymmetry

If there is information asymmetry in a bargaining game, it will create scope for cheating (a form of opportunistic behavior). Because of possible cheating, players do not trust each other even if they tell the truth. This causes endogenous transaction costs that prevent the realization of mutually beneficial division of labor. For the division of labor, a specialist producer of a good certainly knows more about the production of that good than does the buyer, who is specialized in producing other goods. This information asymmetry is a driving force of economies of specialization as well as a source of endogenous transaction costs.

### Example 9.3: a Nash bargaining game with information asymmetry

Assume that in the bargaining model in example 9.1 y is a simple house-cleaning service which involves no information asymmetry between seller and buyer, so that a specialist producer does not know much more than a buyer about the production of y. Therefore, a y specialist's output level $y + y^s = 1$ is common knowledge to everybody. But suppose that good x is a sophisticated manufactured good whose production involves significant economies of specialized information, so that a specialist producer of x has more information about its production conditions than a novice buyer. Suppose that an x specialist's output level $\theta$ is 1.5 at probability 0.5 and is 0.5 with probability 0.5. Nature randomly chooses a value of $\theta$ and informs the specialist of x about the realized value of $\theta$. The specialist of y has only common knowledge about the distribution function of $\theta$. Assume that changing profession involves prohibitively high cost. This implies that utility for alternative occupations is not a threat point. Inserting the data into the model in example 9.1, we have the Nash product

$$V = V_x V_y = [(\theta - X)kY - u_A][(1 - Y)kX - u_A].$$

where utility in autarky $u_A = 2^{-2a}$ is the threat point. Suppose the specialist of x (he) tells the specialist of y (she) the realized value of $\theta$, and that she trusts what he says. The Nash bargaining equilibrium for the complete information case is

$$X = \theta/2, \qquad Y = 0.5, \qquad p_x/p_y = Y/X = 1/\theta, \qquad\qquad (9.3)$$

$$u_x = (\theta - X)kY = \theta k/4, \qquad u_y = (1 - Y)kX = \theta k/4.$$

This implies that the price of x in terms of y decreases as the output level $\theta$ increases. Suppose that the realized value of $\theta$ is 1.5, but the specialist of x claims that $\theta = 0.5$ and the specialist y trusts him. Then the equilibrium terms of trade are $X = \theta/2 = 1/4$, $Y = 0.5$, $p_x/p_y = Y/X = 1/\theta = 2$. But the realized utility of the specialist of x is $u_x = (\theta - X)kY = (1.5 - 0.25)k \times 0.5 = 5k/8$, which is greater than his realized utility when he tells the truth, $\theta k/4 = 1.5k/4 = 3k/8$. Therefore, the specialist of x has an incentive to understate his output level if the specialist of y has incomplete information about it. Since she is aware of the possibility of cheating, she would not trust him when he says $\theta = 0.5$, even if he is telling the truth.

If the specialist of y asks for the price that maximizes the expected Nash product based on her incomplete information, then the following problem generates a Nash bargaining solution.

$$\underset{XY}{\text{Max}} : EV = \tfrac{1}{2}[(\tfrac{3}{2} - X)kY - u_A][(1 - Y)kX - u_A] + \tfrac{1}{2}[(\tfrac{1}{2} - X)kY - u_A][1 - Y)kX - u_A]$$

The solution is $X = Y = 0.5$, $u_x = (\theta - 0.5)k \times 0.5$, $u_y = k/4$. But for $\theta = 0.5$, the x specialist's utility is nonpositive at the terms of trade. Hence, the deal can be done only if $\theta = 1.5$. The two players' perfect rationality implies that the Nash bargaining equilibrium terms of trade are given by (9.3), and the division of labor is chosen for $\theta = 1.5$ and $u_x = u_y = \theta k/4 = 3k/8 > u_A = 2^{-2a}$. The Nash bargaining equilibrium is autarky if $\theta = 0.5$ for any value of $k$.

Hence, for $\theta = 0.5$ and $k > 2^{3-2a}$ the Nash bargaining equilibrium in the game with information asymmetry generates the Pareto inefficient level of division of labor. Inserting $\theta = 0.5$ into (9.3) yields the Nash bargaining equilibrium for the game with no information asymmetry, which is $X = 0.25$, $Y = 0.5$ and $u_x = u_y = \theta k/4 = 3k/8 > u_A = 2^{-2a}$ for $k > 2^{3-2a}$. That is, the division of labor is chosen for $\theta = 0.5$ and $k > 2^{3-2a}$, if all players have complete information. But with information asymmetry, possible cheating makes players distrust each other, so that autarky is chosen for $\theta = 0.5$ and $k > 2^{3-2a}$. In other words, opportunistic behavior (cheating) causes endogenous transaction costs that prevent the realization of mutually beneficial division of labor.

A comparison between examples 9.2 and 9.3 indicates that there is a trade-off between endogenous transaction costs caused by Nash bargaining due to information asymmetry, and endogenous transaction costs caused by trade conflict in the Walrasian equilibrium. The trade-off can be used to endogenize trade regimes. If individuals are allowed to conduct inframarginal analysis between different trade regimes, then an extended model can show that if exogenous transaction efficiency in collecting information is high, the equilibrium trade regime is Nash bargaining (individual specific pricing), otherwise it is the Walrasian regime (impersonal pricing). You are asked to substantiate this conjecture in exercise 5.

In textbooks, this kind of endogenous transaction cost caused by information asymmetry is referred to as *adverse selection*. The early model of adverse selection was developed by Akerlof (1970), which is referred to as the lemon model. His story is similar to the one in this section. When buyers of second-hand cars do not have complete information about the quality of the cars, they can only accept the average price based on average quality. But the seller of high quality cars will ask for a price higher than the average. Hence, it is the high quality second hand cars that cannot be sold. This generates adverse selection in the sense that only low quality cars are sold in the market. In section 9.8, we will show that reality is much more sophisticated than predicted by the adverse selection model if individuals take into account interactions between information and strategies. Adverse selection is caused not only by information asymmetry, but also by the assumption that players are so naïve that they do not infer opponents' private information from observed strategies. The sequential equilibrium models in example 4.8 and exercise 19 of chapter 4 show that adverse selection would not be as serious as the model of adverse selection predicts if players are not so naive.

## ◆ 9.4 Alternating-offer Bargaining Games

One of the shortcoming of the Nash bargaining model is that it has not spelled out the dynamic nature of alternating offers sequentially made in the bargaining process. It looks like a simultaneous-move game which does not capture the feature that moves in a bargaining process are sequential. In this section, we examine a sequential-move game with alternating offers between players, proposed by Rubinstein (1982).

### Example 9.4: Rubinstein alternating offer bargaining model

The game is to divide a pie between two players. Nature randomly chooses a player as the first mover (he) who makes an offer in period 1. Player 2 (she) can accept the offer in period 1. This terminates the game, and the pie is divided according to his offer. But she may also reject his offer in period 1 and makes a counter-offer in period 2. He can then choose between acceptance and rejection of her counter-offer in the next round of bargaining. The game can go on to an infinite horizon. But the value of time provides players with incentives to conclude the deal as soon as possible. The value of time also creates the possibility of exploiting the opponent's impatience. This possibility ensures that a definite outcome emerges as the eqilibrium.

Assume that the value of time for a player can be represented by a subjective discount rate $\rho \in [0, 1]$. This may also be taken to be the interest rate. Since \$1 principal at $t = 0$ can generate principal plus interest of \$$(1 + \rho)$ at $t = 1$, \$1 at $t = 1$ is worth only \$$1/(1$

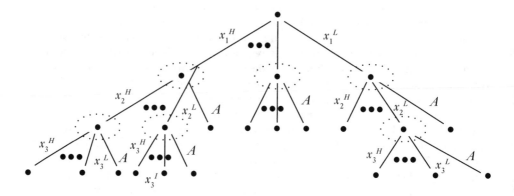

◆ **Figure 9.1:** Extensive form of alternating-offer bargaining game

$+ \rho$) at $t = 0$. In other words, the future value of $A$ dollars at $t = 0$ is $B = (1 + \rho)A$, or the present value of $B$ dollars at $t = 1$ is $A = B/(1 + \rho)$. $\delta \equiv 1/(1 + \rho)$ is called the *discount factor*, which is in between 0 and 1. The value of time, or a player's degree of impatience, increases as the discount factor $\delta$ tends to 0 or as the discount rate $\rho$ tends to infinity.

We now use the *extensive form* to describe the dynamic bargaining game (see figure 9.1). At the root of the inverted tree graph, player 1 makes an offer. He can ask for a large share of the pie, denoted by $x_1^H$, or a small share $x_1^L$, or any share in between. $x_1$ represents the share that player 1 asks for at period 1. At the nodes of the second layer, player 2 can choose $A$ (acceptance) for any offer that player 1 made in period 1. This terminates the game according to the terms of player 1. If she does not choose $A$, then she rejects the offer that player 1 made in period 1. She must then make a counter-offer, $x_2^H$, $x_2^L$, or anything in between, where $x_2$ represents the share that player 2 offers to player 1 in period 2. The dashed ovals denote that each player has perfect information about the node at which he is located when it is his or her turn to move. That is, this is a sequential-move game.

For each node, there is a branch of the tree, called a span, which represents a *subgame* below that node. If all players' dynamic strategies are Nash optimal, then in each subgame at any node, the players' strategies constitute a Nash equilibrium. That is, each player's sequence of moves must be dynamically optimal for given opponent's dynamic optimal strategy.

We now consider player 1's optimum dynamic decision. Suppose he asks for $x_1 \in [0, 1]$ in period 1. His principle for choosing $x_1$ is: (i) $x_1$ must be acceptable to player 2, since delay makes no sense in the model with no information asymmetry and with a discount factor between 0 and 1; (ii) $x_1$ should be as large as possible provided player 2 accepts it. Condition (i) can be achieved only if player 2's discounted pay-off from rejecting the offer is not more than her pay-off from the offer. She receives $1 - x_1$ if she takes the offer straight way. If she rejects $x_1$, then she can make a counter-offer $x_2$ in period 2, which yields discounted value to her $\delta(1 - x_2)$. Hence, (i) requires $1 - x_1 \geq \delta(1 - x_2)$. Condition (ii) requires that $x_1$ be as large as possible or the left-hand side of the semi-inequality be as small as possible, that is, $1 - x_1 = \delta(1 - x_2)$. For the same reason, player 2 will choose $x_2$

such that $x_2 = \delta x_3$ where $x_3$ is player 1's counter-counter offer in period 3. Consider the symmetry between bargaining situations in different rounds, we can see that in a steady equilibrium $x_1 = x_3 = x_5 \ldots$ and $x_2 = x_4 = x_6 \ldots$ Hence, the two players' optimum decisions in the first round summarize information in all rounds of bargains. Player 1 knows that player 2's optimum decision in period 2 is dependent on his optimum decision in period 1 because of $x_2 = \delta x_1$ if $x_1 = x_3$. He will put his feet in her shoes to calculate her optimum decision in period 2 according to the equation, then plug this equation back into the equation $1 - x_1 = \delta(1 - x_2)$ that gives his optimum decision in period 1 given her optimum decision in period 2. This backward deduction based on sequential rationality, which is called dynamic programming, thus yields the *subgame perfect equilibrium*. In other words the following system of equations gives the solution.

$$1 - x_1 = \delta(1 - x_2), \qquad x_2 = \delta x_1. \tag{9.4a}$$

The solution is

$$x_1{}^* = 1/(1 + \delta), \qquad x_2{}^* = \delta/(1 + \delta). \tag{9.4b}$$

Player 1 offers $x_1{}^*$ and player 2 accepts this in period 1; player 2's threatening counter-offer is $x_2{}^*$ if player 1's offer is not as good as $x_1{}^*$. The counter-offer threat is essential to restrain player 1's greediness.

You can easily verify that $x_1{}^* > 1 - x_1{}^*$, which means that the first mover has an advantage since he can hold up his opponent until period 2 to squeeze her, using her impatience. The first mover's advantage increases as the discount factor is reduced, or as a player's degree of impatience increases. Exercise 2 shows that if the discount factor differs from player to player, then a more patient player has an advantage too. The first mover advantage may be offset by his greater degree of impatience than the second mover if the advantage of the second mover's patience outweighs the first mover advantage.

## ◆ 9.5 Dynamic Bargaining Games and the Division of Labor

### Example 9.5: a new classical alternating offer bargaining model

Let us now introduce alternating-offer bargaining into the model in chapters 5 and 6 to study the implication of sequential bargaining for the size of the network of division of labor. Each consumer-producer can choose between specialization in x or y and autarky, so that utility in autarky is a threat point. Because of symmetry, there are two subgame perfect equilibria: one with the specialist of x as the first mover and the other with the specialist of y as the first mover. The two equilibria in which the first mover has the advantage are symmetric. Without loss of generality, we assume that the specialist of x is the first mover (referred to as player 1 or he) and the specialist of y is the second mover (referred to as player 2 or she). The two players have the same discount factor $\delta$.

We use subscripts to denote period. Suppose that player 1 offers $X_1$ (equivalent to $x^s$ in chapter 6) to exchange for $Y_1$ (equivalent to $y^d$ in chapter 6) in period 1. This implies that he offers the terms of trade $p_x/p_y = Y_1/X_1$ because of the market clearing conditions $x^s = x^d = X$ and $y^s = y^d = Y$, and the budget constraint $p_x/p_y = Y/X$. Player 1's decision rule is the same as in the preceding section. First, he must ensure that she will take the offer.

Second, he maximizes his utility subject to the acceptance constraint. Hence, his offer is given by the following problem.

$$\underset{X_2,Y_2}{\text{Max}} : u_{1x} = (1 - X_1)kY_1, \quad \text{s.t. } u_{1y} \equiv (1 - Y_1)kX_1 = \delta(1 - Y_2)kX_2 \equiv \delta u_{2y}, \quad (9.5a)$$

where $u_{1x}$ is the x specialist's utility under the terms of trade in period 1, $u_{1y}$ is the y specialist's utility under the terms of trade in period 1, and $u_{2y}$ is the y specialist's utility generated by her counter-offer in period 2. Similarly, the y specialist's counter-offer in period 2 is given by

$$\underset{X_2,Y_2}{\text{Max}} : u_{2y} = kX_2(1 - Y_2) \quad \text{s.t. } (1 - X_2)kY_2 = \delta(1 - X_1)kY_1 \quad (9.5b)$$

where we have used the fact that in a steady equilibrium $X_1 = X_3 = X_5 \ldots$, $Y_1 = Y_3 = Y_5 \ldots$, $X_2 = X_4 = X_6 \ldots$, and $Y_2 = Y_4 = Y_6 \ldots$ Player 1 can then use backward deduction to solve for the problem (9.5b) first, and then plug the solution back into the problem (9.5a). In other words, his sequential rationality implies that he knows player 2's optimum decision in period 2 is dependent on his decision in period 1, which is in turn dependent on her decision in period 2. He will fully use this interdependence to pursue his self-interest. (9.5b) yields

$$X_2 = 1 - Y_2, \quad Y_2 = \sqrt{\delta(1 - X_1)Y_1}. \quad (9.6a)$$

Inserting this into (9.5a) and then maximizing $u_{1x}$ with respect to $X_1$ and $Y_1$, we obtain the subgame perfect equilibrium terms of trade:

$$X_1 = \sqrt{\delta}/(1 + \sqrt{\delta}), \quad Y_1 = 1 - X_1 = 1/(1 + \sqrt{\delta}). \quad (9.6b)$$

Player 1 offers this term and player 2 accepts in period 1. Plugging this back into (9.6a) yields player 2's threatening counter-offer in period 2:

$$X_2 = 1/(1 + \sqrt{\delta}), \quad Y_2 = \sqrt{\delta}/(1 + \sqrt{\delta}). \quad (9.6c)$$

In this deduction, each player maximizes their utility for a given utility level of the opponent. Hence, the first-order conditions for the subgame perfect equilibrium are the same as those for a benevolent dictator's constrained maximization problem for the Pareto optimum. Hence, dynamic bargaining with complete information will not generate endogenous transaction costs. However, it does generate an unequal distribution of gains to trade. Inserting (9.6b) into the two players' utility functions yields the equilibrium real incomes

$$u_x = k/(1 + \sqrt{\delta})^2 > u_y = \delta k/(1 + \sqrt{\delta})^2 \text{ for } \delta \in (0,1) \quad (9.7a)$$
$$u_x = u_y \text{ for } \delta = 1$$

$$p_x/p_y = Y/X = 1/\sqrt{\delta} \text{ if } \delta \in (0,1); \ p_x/p_y = 1 \text{ if } \delta = 1. \quad (9.7b)$$

The equilibrium real incomes and relative price indicate that the first mover's advantage is greater as the discount factor falls (or as the degree of impatience increases). As the discount factor tends to 1 or as the time lag between offer and counter-offer shrinks, the two players' real incomes converge to the same level and the equilibrium terms of trade converge to the level of the impersonal market.

But the above deduction is relevant only if the gains from the division of labor, net of transaction costs, are great, since the threat to choose autarky is not credible in this case. Suppose $\delta \in (0, 1)$. If $k \leq k_1 \equiv 2^{-2a}(1 + \sqrt{\delta})^2/\delta$, then $u_y \leq u_A$ in the equilibrium given by (9.6). Player 2's threat to choose autarky is therefore credible. But so long as $k_1 > k > k_0 \equiv 2^{2(1-a)}$, the division of labor is still mutually beneficial. For this interval of parameter values, the subgame perfect equilibrium can be solved as follows.

We first solve for $X_2$ and $Y_2$ as functions of $X_1$ and $Y_1$ from (9.5b), then insert the solution into (9.5a) and replace the constraint in (9.5a) with $u_{1y} = (1 - Y_1)kX_1 = u_A = 2^{-2a}$. We can thus solve for the equilibrium values of $X_1$ and $Y_1$ from (9.5a). The equilibrium values of $X_2$ and $Y_2$ can be solved using the equilibrium values of $X_1$ and $Y_1$. The subgame perfect equilibrium for $k \leq k_1$ is summarized as follows.

$$X_1 = 1/2^a \sqrt{k}, \qquad Y_1 = 1 - (1/2^a \sqrt{\delta}), \qquad X_2 = 1/2^a \sqrt{k} \tag{9.8}$$

$$Y_2 = 1 - (1/2^a \sqrt{k}), \qquad u_x = k[1 - (1/2^a \sqrt{k})]^2, \qquad u_y = 2^{-2a}$$

If $k < k_0 \equiv 2^{2(1-a)}$, the solution in (9.8) implies $u_x < u_A = 2^{-2a}$. Hence, the subgame perfect equilibrium is autarky for $k < k_0$. It is given by (9.8) for $k \in (k_0, k_1)$ and is given by (9.5) for $k \in (k_1, 1)$. It is straightforward that the subgame perfect equilibrium is the division of labor iff the Nash bargaining equilibrium is the division of labor. That is, the alternating-offer bargaining generates the efficient level of division of labor. In other words, the subgame perfect equilibrium can successfully coordinate the division of labor as long as the division of labor is Pareto optimal.

The shortcoming of the dynamic bargaining model is that it cannot explain who is the first mover. All players know that the first mover has the advantage, so that they will compete for the first mover's position. This competition implies that the solution we have just obtained cannot be an equilibrium. In the next section, we shall show that such competition for a greater share of gains from the division of labor will generate endogenous transaction costs.

## ◆ 9.6 How Does Competition for a Greater Share of Gains from the Division of Labor Generate Endogenous Transaction Costs?

### Example 9.6: a new classical alternating-offer bargaining model generating endogenous transaction costs

We now allow players to compete for the first mover position. We add period 0 to the dynamic game in example 9.5. After period 0, the structure of the new game is the same as in example 9.5. Hence, the game in example 9.5 is a subgame within the new game. In period 0, the two players sort out who is the first mover. Consider the case $k \in (k_1, 1)$, which implies that the Nash bargaining equilibrium is the division of labor. Because of backward deduction, the subgame equilibrium from period 1 on is still given by (9.6) and (9.7). Assume that each player has two strategies: tough ($T$) and soft ($S$) in period 0. The tough strategy implies that a player insists on being the first mover, and will not accept any terms that give a lower utility than what the first mover receives. The soft strategy implies that a player accepts the second mover's position if the opponent is tough, and agrees to fair terms, as given by the Nash bargaining solution, if the opponent is soft too. The game in period 0 for a given subgame equilibrium in period 1 is described in table 9.1

The first term in an entry represents player 1's pay-off (utility) and the second represents that for player 2. $u_A = 2^{-2a}$ is the real income (utility) in autarky, $u_D = k/4$ is the real income for the division of labor given by a Nash bargaining solution. $u_H = k/(1 + \sqrt{\delta})^2$ is the first mover's real income in the subgame equilibrium in period 1, and $u_L = (k/(1 + \sqrt{\delta})^2$ is the second mover's real income in the subgame equilibrium. It is easy to see that $u_H > u_D > u_L > u_A$ for $k > k_1 > k_0$ and $\delta \in (0, 1)$.

From table 9.1, we can see that the two players receive real income in autarky if both of them choose a tough strategy, which means that no agreement can be achieved for the terms of trade. They receive real income for the division of labor outcome given by the Nash bargaining solution, and the gains from the division of labor are equally divided between them if both of them are soft. If one player is tough and the other is soft, then the tough one gets the greater gains; nevertheless, mutually beneficial gains from the division of labor are realized, despite the unequal distribution of income. The game in period 0, for a given subgame perfect equilibrium in period 1, is a typical Nash game which has two *pure strategy* Nash equilibria.

We first prove that outcomes $T$-$T$ and $S$-$S$ are not pure strategy Nash equilibria. We argue by negation. Suppose $T$-$T$ is a Nash equilibrium, so that we consider the upper-left entry in table 9.1. Assume that player 1's tough strategy is given. It is then clear that player 2 can increase her utility by deviating from $T$, which gives her $u_A$, to $S$, which shifts the outcome from $T$-$T$ to $T$-$S$ and brings $u_L$ ($> u_A$) to her. This implies that she has an incentive to deviate unilaterally from outcome $T$-$T$. This implies, by the definition of a Nash equilibrium, that $T$-$T$ cannot be a Nash equilibrium. Using similar reasoning, we can show that $S$-$S$ is not a Nash equilibrium either.

It can be seen that no player has an incentive to deviate unilaterally from an asymmetric equilibrium $S$-$T$ or $T$-$S$. For the Nash pure strategy game, the theory cannot predict which of the two Nash equilibria will take place. But if each player is allowed to choose a probability distribution for each and every pure strategy, we will have a unique *mixed strategy Nash equilibrium*. The probability distribution of pure strategies is called *mixed strategy*. Mixed strategy is a way to make sure that the game is fair and that all players still participate even if any pure strategy outcome must be unfair to some player. When family

Table 9.1: The strategic form of the game to compete for first mover advantage

|  |  | Player 2 | |
| --- | --- | --- | --- |
|  |  | $T$ | $S$ |
| Player 1 | $T$ | $u_A, u_A$ | $u_H, u_L$ |
|  | $S$ | $u_L, u_H$ | $u_D, u_D$ |

members have a disagreement about which TV channel should be on, a fair solution is to throw a coin and let the stochastic process sort out the conflict of interests.

Suppose player $i$ chooses the soft strategy with probability $q_i$ and chooses the tough strategy with probability $1 - q_i$. Since the purpose of a player's mixed strategy is to confuse his opponent, player 1 will choose $q_1$ such that player 2 feels indifferent between her choices of $T$ and $S$. For a given $q_1$, player 2's expected utility for her choice of $T$ is $(1 - q_1)u_A + q_1u_H$ and that for strategy $S$ is $(1 - q_1)u_L + q_1u_D$. The two utility levels are indifferent iff

$$q = (u_L - u_A)/(u_H - u_D + u_L - u_A) \text{ where} \tag{9.9a}$$

$$u_A = 2^{-2a}, \ u_D = k/4, \ u_L = \delta(k/(1 + \sqrt{\delta})^2, \text{ and } u_H = k/(1 + \sqrt{\delta})^2. \tag{9.9b}$$

Using the symmetry of the model, we can show that the mixed strategy of player 2, $q_2$, that makes player 1 feel indifferent between his choices of $T$ and $S$ is the same as (9.9a). It can be shown that

$$q \to 1/2 \text{ as } \delta \to 1; \quad q \to 0 \text{ as } \delta \to 0; \quad \text{and } \partial q/\partial \delta > 0. \tag{9.10}$$

where $1 - \delta$ can be considered as the *exogenous bargaining cost*, which is 0 for $\delta = 1$, and takes on its maximum value for $\delta = 0$. The fair Nash bargaining solution takes place with probability $q^2$ and the probability that the mutually beneficial gains from the division of labor cannot be realized is $(1 - q)^2$. Hence, $(1 - q)^2$ represents endogenous transaction costs. (9.10) indicates that in the competition for a greater share of the gains from the division of labor, endogenous transaction costs are not 0 even if exogenous transaction cost tends to 0, though the endogenous transaction cost falls as the exogenous transaction decreases.

We now consider the interval $k \in (k_0, k_1)$. For this case, since player 2 receives utility in autarky $u_A$, and so her threat to opt for autarky becomes credible, we must replace $u_L$ in table 9.1 with $u_A$. Also, $u_H$ in table 9.1 is now given by (9.8) instead by (9.7). Using this information, we can find player 1's expected utility

$$q_1q_2u_D + (1 - q_1)q_2u_H + (1 - q_2)q_1u_A + (1 - q_1)(1 - q_2)u_A$$
$$= q_1q_2u_D + (1 - q_1)q_2u_H + (1 - q_2)u_A,$$

which monotonically decreases with $q_1$ for a given $q_2$. Hence, the optimum value of $q_1$ is 0. Because of the symmetry, the optimum value of $q_2$ is also 0. This implies that for $k < k_1$ the equilibrium is autarky. Since $k_1 \equiv 2^{-2a}(1 + \sqrt{\delta})^2/\delta > k_0 \equiv 2^{2(1-a)}$, the subgame perfect equilibrium in the game to compete for a greater share of gains from the division of labor is autarky, while the Nash bargaining equilibrium, which is Pareto optimal, is the division of labor for $k_1 \in (k_0, k_1)$. In addition, the subgame perfect equilibrium is autarky with probability $(1 - q)^2$ for $k > k_1$, while the Nash bargaining equilibrium is the division of labor. Therefore, the competition for a greater share of the gains from the division of labor generates endogenous transaction costs that preclude realization of mutually beneficial division of labor. Compared to neoclassical game models that generate endogenous transaction costs, in the new classical bargaining model endogenous transaction costs cause not only inefficient resource allocation, but also an inefficient level of division of labor.

## ◆ 9.7 How Can Endogenous Transaction Costs be Eliminated by Consideration of Reputation?

### Example 9.7: a new classical model a of repeated game

If the pure strategy game in table 9.1 can be repeatedly played, then endogenous transaction costs may be eliminated due to consideration of reputation. Assume there are infinite periods $t = 1, 2, \ldots$ There is a *stage game* in each period, which is the same as the pure strategy game in table 9.1. Then in all periods, there is a *super-game*. In the super-game, each player chooses a series of pure strategies to maximize her total discounted utility. It can be shown that in the repeated game, there is at least a Nash equilibrium that makes a cooperative outcome emerge from noncooperative behavior, or that eliminates endogenous transaction costs.

We first consider a profile of two players' series of strategies. Player 1 announces that he always chooses a soft strategy as long as player 2 does so, but he will choose a tough strategy forever if player 2 chooses a tough strategy in the previous period. Player 2 can find that for this strategy of player 1 her total discounted utility for a soft strategy series is

$$u_D S = u_D(1 + \delta + \delta^2 \ldots + \delta^T) = \frac{1 - \delta^{T+1}}{1 - \delta} u_D \tag{9.11a}$$

where $S$ can be solved from $S - \delta S = (1 - \delta)S = 1 - \delta^{T+1}$. This total discounted utility converges to $u_D/(1 - \delta)$ as $T$ tends to infinity. If player 2 chooses a tough strategy in a period, her immediate utility is $u_H = \delta k/(1 + \sqrt{\delta})^2 > k/4$. But her utility afterwards is always $u_A$, because player 1 will refuse to cooperate. Hence, the total discounted utility for player 2 is

$$u_H + \delta(1 + \delta + \delta^2 + \ldots + \delta^{T-1})u_A = u_H + \delta u_A/(1 - \delta). \tag{9.11b}$$

It is easy to see that (9.11a) is greater than (9.11b) iff

$$u_D > (1 - \delta)u_H + \delta u_A \tag{9.12}$$

where $u_D = k/4 > u_A = 2^{-2a}$ for $k > k_0$. Also $u_H = k/(1 + \sqrt{\delta})^2 > u_D$. It can be shown that if $\delta > 0.5$, or if the discount rate is smaller than 100 percent, (9.12) becomes

$$k(4\sqrt{2} + 2) > k_0(3 + 2\sqrt{2})$$

which holds for $k > k_0$ because $2 + 4\sqrt{2} > 3 + 2\sqrt{2}$.

We may thus conclude that, provided players are not very impatient, the consideration of reputation can eliminate endogenous transaction costs, thereby making cooperation emerge from noncooperative strategic behavior. Here, long-run punishment for deviation from cooperation is the key to the result.

The Folk theorem in game theory shows that there are many other Nash equilibria in the super-game that can generate the same results, but with limited time for punishment of deviation. For instance, when a player chooses a tough strategy in the previous period, then her opponent chooses a tough strategy for three periods and then comes back to a soft strategy afterwards.

There are many institutional conditions that are essential for the reputation mechanism to work in eliminating endogenous transaction costs. Society must have a consensus about the moral code, and the legal regime must provide appropriate enforcement for punishment of deviant behavior. For instance if, in an ancient tribe, the "taking" of others' possession was not considered punishable as stealing (or if Iraq's invasion of Kuwait was not considered punishable), then the punishment for stealing (or invasion) could not be enforced. In a Soviet-style economic system, private rights to residual returns and control of firms are not protected by the law, so that nobody will care about reputation which generates residual returns. Again, if laws protecting business names and brands cannot be reasonably enforced, the reputation mechanism will not work either.

Our new classical model of repeated games shows that the consideration of reputation can reduce endogenous transaction costs caused by competition for a larger share of gains from division of labor, thereby increasing the equilibrium network size of division of labor and aggregate productivity.


## Key Terms and Review

The difference between endogenous and exogenous transaction costs and between general and specific endogenous transaction costs.
Nonstrategic and strategic behaviors, opportunistic behavior and its relationship with endogenous transaction costs.
Information asymmetry and endogenous transaction costs.
Subgame perfect equilibrium, sequential equilibrium, and alternating-offer bargaining games.
Effects on the equilibrium level of division of labor of the endogenous transaction costs caused by competition to get a greater share of gains from the division of labor.
The relationship between endogenous and exogenous transaction costs.
Super-games and stage games.


## Further Reading

*Nash bargaining games*: Nash (1950), Osborne and Rubinstein (1990), Gibbons (1992), Fudenberg and Tirole (1991), Kreps (1990), Tirole (1989), Dixit and Nalebuff (1991); *alternating offer bargaining games*: Rubinstein (1982, 1985), Kreps (1990), Fudenberg and Tirole (1991), Osborne and Rubinstein (1990), Binmore, Osborne, and Rubinstein (1992), Stahl (1972); *function of price*: Gale (1986), North (1987), Hayek (1945), S. Grossman (1989); *information efficiency of Walrasian equilibrium*: Hurwicz (1973); *super-games (repeated games)*: Fudenberg and Tirole (1991, sec. 4.3), Tirole (1989, sec. 6.3, pp. 247–51) and Kreps (1990, sec. 14.2, pp. 509–12).

## QUESTIONS

1  Why, for the sake of her own self-interest, must an individual ensure that her opponent receives a sufficiently large share of the gains from the division of labor?

2  Some economists claim that the Nash bargaining game is a cooperative game that does not capture the noncooperative nature of the bargaining process. Comment on this claim in relation to Nash's view about the connection between the nature of a Nash bargaining game and marginal disturbance.

3  Hurwicz (1973) shows that the Walrasian regime involves the lowest exogenous cost in collecting and transmitting information. But as we have shown in example 9.2, the Walrasian regime in an asymmetric new classical model with finite consumer-producers may generate trade conflict that results in endogenous transaction costs. Use the trade-off between endogenous transaction costs caused by trade conflict in the Walrasian equilibrium and endogenous and exogenous information costs in a Nash bargaining game to explain the phenomenon that impersonal pricing in the Walrasian regime becomes increasingly more important than individual specific pricing in bargaining as the network size of division of labor becomes increasingly larger (North, 1987).

4  Why does the Walrasian equilibrium model involve more information asymmetry than the sequential equilibrium model? Analyze the function of the invisible hand in promoting information asymmetry that generates economies of division of labor and in restricting endogenous transaction costs caused by information asymmetry in a new classical Walrasian equilibrium model with endogenous specialization.

5  Friedman uses the story of the manufacture of pencils to illustrate how the price system transmits information in such a way as to keep individuals away from what they need not know. When the price of timber increases, the manufacturer of pencils need not know if the rise of prices is caused by a devastating forest fire, by a change of consumers' tastes for furniture, or by some technical change in the other sector. If the level of division of labor is very high, exogenous transaction costs in collecting information about utility and production functions of trade partners, which is essential for bargaining, as described in examples 9.1 and 9.2, will be enormous. But impersonal pricing in the Walrasian regime can avoid all of these exogenous transaction costs. Use the example to illustrate how the invisible hand promotes information asymmetry and related economies of division of labor while restraining costs of information transmission.

6  Draw the distinction between fair pricing in the Nash bargaining game and equal income distribution, and discuss the implications of the distinction for the debate about "trade-off between efficiency and equity" (do we have such a trade-off at all?).

7  Analyze the significance of a legal system that protects residual rights of the owners of the firm, and of laws protecting brand and business names, in enabling the mechanism of reputation to play its role in reducing endogenous transaction costs.

# EXERCISES

1   Assume that player $i$'s utility in autarky is $a_i$ in the model in example 9.1. Solve for the Nash bargaining equilibrium and analyze the effects of the relative values of threat points on the relative bargaining power of a player.

2   Assume that player $i$'s discount factor is $\delta_i$ in the model in example 9.4. Solve for the subgame perfect equilibrium in the alternating offer bargaining game. Analyze the effects of relative degree of impatience (the relative value of $\delta_1$ and $\delta_2$) and first mover's advantage, on the relative bargaining power of a player.

3   In the following bargaining models, what are the determinants of the relative bargaining power of a player? (a) The bargaining model in exercise 1; (b) The bargaining model with information asymmetry in example 9.3; (c) The alternating offer bargaining game in exercise 2.

4   Consider the strategic form of the Nash game in the prisoners' dilemma model. Each of two criminals can choose the strategy "confess" or "not confess" when caught by police. Their pay-offs for four possible outcomes of the game are listed as follows.

|  |  | Prisoner 2 | | | |
|---|---|---|---|---|---|
|  |  | Confess | | Not confess | |
| Prisoner 1: | Confess | $-5$ | $-5$ | $1$ | $-10$ |
|  | Not confess | $-10$ | $1$ | $0$ | $0$ |

where the first figure in each entry is the pay-off to prisoner 1. Identify the Nash equilibrium.

5   Consider the model in example 9.2. Assume that players are allowed to conduct inframarginal analysis between the two trade regimes: Nash bargaining (individual specific pricing), and the Walrasian regime (impersonal pricing). Suppose that there is a cost coefficient $c$ in terms of utility loss caused by the collection of information that is essential for sorting out the Nash bargaining solution. Work out the critical value of $c$ below which the Nash bargaining solution is the general equilibrium.

6   Suppose that transportation efficiency $k$ is different for the two players in the model in example 9.2, so that the utility equalization condition does not hold. Solve for the Nash bargaining equilibrium and the Walrasian equilibrium, respectively. Identify the interval of parameter values in which the Nash bargaining equilibrium generates the Pareto efficient level of division of labor, but the Walrasian equilibrium does not.

# chapter 10

# ENDOGENOUS TRANSACTION COSTS AND THEORY OF CONTRACT, OWNERSHIP, AND RESIDUAL RIGHTS

## ♦ 10.1 Endogenous Transaction Costs and Moral Hazard

Barzel (1985) has raised the question: "Is transaction cost just cost?" This question draws our attention to the difference between endogenous and exogenous transaction costs. As we have shown, endogenous transaction costs are distortions caused by conflicts between self-interested decisions or by the incentive incompatibility problem. There are several neoclassical ways to study endogenous transaction costs. In many neoclassical models monopoly power, information asymmetry, public goods, and externality are all exogenously given. Then the distortions in equilibrium caused by these exogenous factors are analyzed. A more realistic approach is to endogenize the degree of monopoly power and externality by specifying some trade-offs. The degree of monopoly can be determined in the market as a consequence of interactions between conflicting self-interested behaviors. The Dixit–Stiglitz model (1977, see ch. 12) is such an example within the neoclassical framework. In the model, the trade-off between global economies of scale and distortions caused by monopoly power determines the equilibrium degree of monopoly and competition. In chapter 16, the trade-offs between economies of division of labor, reliability of the related network of the market, and transaction costs are specified in order to endogenize the degrees of competition and externality. As shown earlier, the new classical models can also be used to endogenize the network size of division of labor, and to explore the implications of endogenous transaction costs for the equilibrium network size of division of labor and productivity progress.

Another approach to investigating endogenous transaction costs is to specify information asymmetry, which causes endogenous transaction costs, as shown in chapters 4 and 9. In chapters 9 and 12, new classical game models and new classical Walrasian equilibrium models are also used to explore endogenous transaction costs caused by trade conflicts. In this chapter we study endogenous transaction costs that are caused by moral hazard. *Moral hazard* is the departure of equilibrium from the Pareto optimum caused by a special type of information asymmetry. In a model with moral hazard, the effort of one of two trade partners affects the risk of a bad outcome for the business, but the other partner cannot observe the effort level. This implies, for example, that a labor contract to pay the player according to her effort level is impossible; in other words, such a labor contract involves a prohibitively high exogenous transaction cost in measuring working effort. It is assumed that the direct effect of effort on the utility of the player choosing that effort is negative, so that if a pure or noncontingent single price is paid for the good or service that is provided, or if there is no contract, then the lowest effort level will be chosen. Hence, contingent contracted prices of goods or services become essential for reducing such endogenous transaction costs caused by moral hazard.

Usually, there are three periods in a model of moral hazard. In period 1, the outcome of the business is yet to be realized, but probabilities for bad and good outcomes, and the relationships between those probabilities and one party's effort levels, are common knowledge to all players. Two parties sign a contract in period 1 that determines terms of the deal after the realization of an outcome. In period 2, players choose effort levels for the given contractual terms. In period 3, Nature chooses an outcome according to the probabilities and players' effort levels. Then contractual terms are implemented and gains from the business are divided. Here, the assumption that the effort level must be chosen before the realization of an outcome, is essential to the story. This implies that the player who chooses her effort level has an incentive to cheat. Even though her real effort level may be low, and a bad outcome be partly attributable to this, she may claim that her effort level is high, and that the bad outcome is just a result of bad luck that is out of her control.

The driving force of the story of moral hazard is a trade-off between efficient incentive provision and efficient risk sharing. The two players should somehow share the risk of a bad outcome. But if one player cannot see the other player's effort levels, which affect the risk, then the effect of the low effort level on the risk cannot be distinguished from bad luck. Hence, there is a conflict between incentive provision and risk sharing. If a bad outcome occurs, the player who chooses the effort level should be penalized as far as incentive provision is concerned. But she should not be penalized too severely as far as risk sharing is concerned. Hence, a contract is used to minimize endogenous transaction cost by efficiently trading off risk sharing against incentive provision. In working out the contractual terms, each player should prepare for the worst that could result from the players' opportunistic behavior. This will ensure that both behave decently *ex post*. If a player behaves like a decent gentleman *ex ante*, without taking account of possible opportunistic behavior on each side, then he will behave very opportunistically *ex post*, so that a bad outcome is more likely to occur.

Since effort level is not an uncertain variable for the player who chooses the effort, information asymmetry in a model of moral hazard is different from that which we studied in chapters 4 and 9. Hence, information asymmetry is referred to as *hidden action* in a model of moral hazard, and as *hidden information* in the cases that we studied in chapters 4 and 9. Distortions caused by hidden information are referred to as endogenous transaction costs caused by adverse selection. In section 10.2 we study a neoclassical principal–agent model. Then in section 10.3 we study a new classical principal–agent model with endogenous principal–agent relationships. In section 10.4, we study the Holmstgrom–Migrom model with the trade-off between endogenous transaction costs caused by moral hazard and exogenous monitoring costs.

Sometimes, complete contractual terms are prohibitively expensive to specify and enforce. Hence, players can choose one of various structures of ownership and residual rights to minimize the endogenous and exogenous transaction costs. Section 10.5 studies the Grossman–Hart–Moore model (GHM) of optimum structure of ownership and incomplete contract. Finally, we use the Dewatripont and Maskin model to investigate commitment problems and soft-budget constraints that might cause endogenous transaction costs.

---

### Questions to Ask Yourself when Reading this Chapter

♦ What is meant by moral hazard and related endogenous transaction costs?

♦ What are the functions of contracts, ownership, and residual rights?

♦ Why can contingent contracts promote division of labor and productivity?

♦ How do incredible commitment and soft- budget constraint generate endogenous transaction costs?

---

## ♦ 10.2 Neoclassical Principal–Agent Models

Before specifying models, we need to learn some important concepts: expected utility function, risk aversion, and certainty equivalence.

Consider a random variable $x \sim N(\bar{x}, \sigma_x)$ where $\bar{x} = E(x) = \sum_{s \in S} p(s)x(s)$ is the expected value of $x$, $\sigma_x = \mathrm{Var}(x) = E[(x - \bar{x})^2] = \sum_{s \in S} p(s)(x(s) - \bar{x})^2$ is the variance of $x$, $p(s)$ is probability for state $s$. The theory of expected utility establishes conditions under which a decision-maker will rank risky prospects according to their associated *expected utilities*. Let $u$ be a function that assigns to each monetary outcome $x$ a utility $u(x)$. Then, representing prospects by random variables, the expected utility of prospect $x$ is $E[u(x)]$.

For simplicity of presentation, suppose that there are only two contingent states of an event, $x_1$ and $x_2$. An individual's utility function $f(x)$ is strictly concave, so that

$$f(\alpha x_1 + (1 - \alpha)x_2) > \alpha f(x_1) + (1 - \alpha)f(x_2) \tag{10.1}$$

where $\alpha \in (0, 1)$ and $x_1$ and $x_2$ are two different consumption bundles (vectors). If we interpret $\alpha$ as the probability for state $x_1$ and $1 - \alpha$ as the probability for state $x_2$, then the weighted average $\bar{x} = \alpha x_1 + (1 - \alpha)x_2$ is equivalent to an event with no uncertainty, or a consumption bundle that can be received through an insurance program which, by pooling risk, guarantees that the insured can receive the weighted average. Thus (10.1) implies that a person prefers the weighted average of the two contingent states, which does not involve risk, over the contingent event. Thus, we say that the person is risk averse. This implies that a person is *risk averse* iff her utility function is strictly concave in contingent variables. The person is *risk loving* if the inequality in (10.1) is reversed. The person is *risk neutral* if the inequality in (10.1) is made an equality. (10.1) is referred to as a *Jensen inequality*, which is illustrated by figure 10.1.

A function with two independent variables is strictly concave if and only if $\partial^2 f / \partial x_i^2 < 0$ and $(\partial^2 f / \partial x_1^2)(\partial^2 f / \partial x_2^2) - (\partial^2 f / \partial x_1 \partial x_2) > 0$.

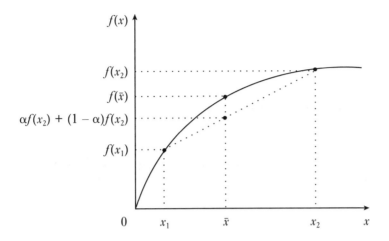

◆ **Figure 10.1:** Risk aversion and a strictly concave utility function

The concept of *certain equivalent wealth* is often used in the theory of contract. We now define this concept. Let us compare the expected utility of prospect $x$, $E[u(x)]$, with a certain prospect, that is, one that yields the payment $\hat{x}$ with probability 1. The certain prospect will be indifferent for the decision maker from the risky prospect $x$ if $u(\hat{x}) = E[u(x)]$. $\hat{x}$ is then called the *certain equivalent* of the prospect $x$.

Suppose that $u$ is three times continuously differentiable and that $u'(.) > 0$. Then, approximately, the certain equivalent is

$$\hat{x} \approx \bar{x} - 0.5r(\bar{x})\text{Var}(x) \tag{10.2}$$

where $r(\bar{x}) = -u''(\bar{x})/u'(\bar{x})$, which is called the *degree of risk aversion* at $\bar{x}$. We can use Taylor's theorem to prove this. According to this theorem, for any $z$, $u(z) = u(\bar{x}) + (z - \bar{x})u'(\bar{x}) + 0.5(z - \bar{x})^2 u''(\bar{x}) + R(z)$, where $R(z) = u'''(\hat{z})(z - \bar{x})^2/6$ for some $\hat{z} \in [\bar{x}, z]$ which is negligible. Hence, $u(z) \approx u(\bar{x}) + (z - \bar{x})u'(\bar{x}) + 0.5(z - \bar{x})^2 u''(\bar{x})$. Substituting $x$ for $z$ in this equation and computing the expectation, we find $E[u(x)] \approx u(\bar{x}) + E[x - \bar{x}]u'(\bar{x}) + 0.5E[(x - \bar{x})^2]u''(\bar{x})$, where $E[x - \bar{x}] = 0$. Therefore, we have

$$E[u(x)] \approx u(\bar{x}) + 0.5E[(x - \bar{x})^2]u''(\bar{x}).$$

Applying Taylor's theorem again to $u(\hat{x})$, where $\hat{x}$ is close to $\bar{x}$ yields $u(\hat{x}) = u(\bar{x}) + (\hat{x} - \bar{x})u'(\bar{x}) + Q(\hat{x})$, where $Q(\hat{x}) = 0.5[(\hat{x} - \bar{x})^2]u''(\hat{z})$, which is negligible for some $\hat{z} \in [\bar{x}, \hat{x}]$. Hence, we have

$$u(\hat{x}) = u(\bar{x}) + (\hat{x} - \bar{x})u'(\bar{x}).$$

For a certain equivalent, we have $u(\hat{x}) = E[u(x)]$. So, combining the above two equations, we have

$$(\hat{x} - \bar{x})u'(\bar{x}) \approx 0.5E[(x - \bar{x})^2]u''(\bar{x}).$$

Rearrangement of this equation yields (10.2).

On the basis of our definitions of expected utility, risk aversion, and certainty equivalence, we can now study models of moral hazard.

## Example 10.1: a neoclassical principal–agent model

There are two players in the model: principal and agent. The principal (he) cannot take care of his own business and must hire the agent to do the job. The agent (she) cannot have her own business and must work for others. The agent's utility function is $u_a = \sqrt{M} - e$, where $M$ is the payment that she receives from the job. Her effort level can be $e = 1$ or $e = 0$. If $e = 1$, the revenue of the project is

$$R = \begin{cases} 16 \text{ with probability } 3/4 \\ 4 \text{ with probability } 1/4 \end{cases}$$

If $e = 0$, then

$$R = \begin{cases} 16 \text{ with probability } 1/4 \\ 4 \text{ with probability } 3/4 \end{cases}$$

The principal's utility is $u_p = R - M$, which is linear in the contingent variable $R$. Hence, the principal is risk neutral. Suppose the principal can observe the agent's effort level. He can calculate his expected utility for different levels of effort. Assume that the agent can get utility 1 if she works elsewhere. Then the principal can see that if he pays her $M = 4$, she will be willing to choose $e = 1$ and to work for him because $u_a = (\sqrt{M}) - e = 1$ if $M = 4$ and $e = 1$. If $e = 1$ and he pays her $M = 4$, his expected utility is

$$Eu_p = \tfrac{3}{4}(16 - M) + \tfrac{1}{4}(4 - M)$$
$$= \tfrac{3}{4}(16 - 4) + \tfrac{1}{4}(4 - 4) = 9$$

If $e = 0$, the principal can pay the agent $M = 1$ to get her working for him, since her utility is $u_a = (\sqrt{M}) - e = 1$ if $e = 0$ and $M = 1$. Then, the principal's expected utility for $e = 0$ and $M = 1$ is

$$Eu_p = \tfrac{1}{4}(16 - 1) + \tfrac{3}{4}(4 - 1) = 6.$$

Certainly, the principal's expected utility is higher for $e = 1$ and $M = 4$ than that for $e = 0$ and $M = 1$ ($9 > 6$). Hence, the principal will pay $M = 4$ and get the agent to work for him with effort level $e = 1$.

But suppose the principal cannot observe the agent's effort level, or cannot verify this in the court if litigation should arise from a dispute about her effort level and corresponding pay. Then the principal must choose a contingent contract to facilitate an efficient trade-off between risk sharing and incentive provision. If pay is not contingent on outcome, then it is easy to see that the agent will always choose effort $e = 0$, since her utility $\sqrt{M} - e$ is always larger for $e = 0$ than for $e = 1$ for a noncontingent $M$. Suppose the principal pays

$M^H$ if the outcome is good or if $R = 16$ and pays $M^L$ if the outcome is bad or if $R = 4$, where $M^H > M^L$. Then the contingent contract will get the agent working for the principal with effort level $e = 1$ if the following two conditions hold.

The first condition is to ensure that the agent is not worse off than working elsewhere; that is, her expected utility, when she chooses effort level $e = 1$, should not be lower than her reservation pay 1, or

$$\tfrac{3}{4}(\sqrt{M^H} - 1) + \tfrac{1}{4}(\sqrt{M^L} - 1) \geq 1.$$

This is referred to as the *participation constraint*. The second condition is to ensure that the agent is not worse off when she chooses $e = 1$ than when she chooses $e = 0$; that is, her expected utility with effort $e = 1$ and $M^H$ should not be lower than her expected utility with effort $e = 0$ and $M^L$. That is,

$$\tfrac{3}{4}(\sqrt{M^H} - 1) + \tfrac{1}{4}(\sqrt{M^L} - 1) \geq \tfrac{1}{4}(\sqrt{M^H} - 0) + \tfrac{3}{4}(\sqrt{M^L} - 0).$$

This condition is referred to as the *incentive compatibility* condition. Since the principal's purpose is to maximize his expected utility, which is a decreasing function of $M$, he will choose $M^H$ and $M^L$ from the equalities in the two conditions. The two equations with two unknowns yield the efficient contingent contractual terms:

$$M^H = 6.25 \qquad M^L = 0.25$$

The efficient contract is the second best compared to the principal's expected utility when he can observe the agent's effort level. It is easy to compute that the principal's expected utility under the second-best contingent contract is

$$Eu_p = \tfrac{3}{4}(16 - 6.25) + \tfrac{1}{4}(4 - 0.25) = 8.25,$$

which is smaller than what can be obtained from the best labor contract, that is 9. The difference is *endogenous transaction cost caused by moral hazard*. In the best labor contract (pay $M = 4$ for effort $e = 1$ and pay $M = 1$ for effort $e = 0$), the principal takes all the risk and the agent receives her wage without risk. This contract yields efficient risk sharing in the sense that the risk neutral principal takes all the risk and the risk averse agent takes none. Or you may interpret this as a trade contract in risk, through which the agent sells all risk to the principal, or the agent is completely insured by the principal. The best labor contract also provides the right incentive for the agent to choose the right level of effort. This implies that if the principal can see the agent's effort level, there is no trade-off between efficient risk sharing and efficient incentive provision.

But when the principal cannot observe the agent's effort level, there is a trade-off between risk sharing and incentive provision. If the principal takes all the risk and pays a noncontingent $M$, which is equivalent to providing the agent with complete insurance, then the agent would not choose the right effort level. But if the principal rewards or penalizes the agent exactly according to the contingent outcome, they would not have efficient risk sharing. The pay to the agent will be greater, or the principal's profit be lower, because the risk is too high for the agent to take the job if the pay is not increased. Hence, the second-best contingent contract efficiently trades off risk sharing against incentive provision. Though the efficient trade-off has not achieved the best, and therefore is not Pareto optimal, it nonetheless maximizes the gains from trade net of the unavoidable endogenous transaction costs caused by moral hazard. When moral hazard exists, the best is an unachievable utopia. The second best is a realistically efficient contract. Hence, we call the contingent contract the *efficient contract* despite its Pareto inefficiency.

It is important to note, as Hart points out, that the contingent contract in the principal–agent model is not a labor contract. The contingent contract prices output rather than effort input, because the exact rationale for the contingent contract is that a labor contract for effort input is infeasible. Hence, it is misleading to call the principal–agent model a model of the firm. The principal–agent model cannot explain why and how firms emerge, or why we need asymmetric residual returns and residual control. The asymmetric relationship between employers and employees is not endogenized in the principal–agent model. Although the principal looks like an employer, we can show that he does not claim all residual returns, the agent claiming part of these through contingent pricing of outcome. For instance, if outcome $R = 16$ is realized, the agent gets $\sqrt{6.25} - 1 > 1$ where the prevailing market reservation pay is 1. Furthermore, in the principal–agent model, the principal has no residual control rights over the agent's effort level. What the agent can do (which level of effort she chooses) is completely up to her. But in a labor contract, what the employee does is up to the employer: she must do whatever she is told to do. The two main features of the institution of the firm and the related labor contract, namely, asymmetric distribution of residual returns and residual control rights, are absent in the principal–agent model.

The neoclassical principal–agent model is not a general equilibrium model. The principal–agent relationship is not endogenized, and reservation pay is exogenously given. Hence, the emergence of the principal–agent relationship from the division of labor cannot be investigated within the neoclassical model.

In the next section we develop a new classical principal–agent model which enables us to explore these issues.

## ◆ 10.3 A New Classical General Equilibrium Principal–Agent Model

In this section we use a new classical model of an endogenous principal–agent relationship to show that endogenous transaction costs caused by moral hazard might not be as serious as the neoclassical principal–agent model predicts if the principal–agent relationship is endogenized in a new classical general equilibrium model.

### Example 10.2: a new classical principal–agent model

Consider a model with $M$ *ex ante* identical consumer-producers, and two consumption goods x and y. Each person's utility function is specified as follows.

$$u = \ln[(x + k_x x^d)(y + k_y y^d)],$$

where $x$ and $y$ are the respective quantities of the two goods self-provided, and $x^d$ and $y^d$ are the respective quantities of the two goods purchased from the market. The trading efficiency coefficient $k_x$ is a random variable, given by the following condition.

$$\text{if } s \geq \beta, \text{ then } k_x = \begin{cases} k \text{ with probability } \rho \\ t \text{ with probability } 1 - \rho \end{cases}$$

$$\text{if } s < \beta, \text{ then } k_x = t$$

where $s$ is the effort level of a producer of x in avoiding the transaction risk and $\beta$ is a parameter between 0 and 1. It is assumed that $\rho \in (0, 1)$ and $1 > k > t$ and that $k_y = k$.

$k_x x^d$ and $k_y y^d$ are the respective quantities of the two goods that are received from the purchases of them. This strictly concave utility function represents a risk averse preference.

Each person is equipped with the same production functions for the two goods.

$$x + x^s = L_x - a$$
$$y + y^s = L_y - a$$

where $y^s$ and $x^s$ are respective quantities of the two goods sold, $L_i$ is an individual's level of specialization in producing good i. The production function displays economies of specialization.

Each individual is endowed with one unit of time, so that the endowment constraint for each person is

$$L_x + L_y + s = 1,$$

where $s$ is the time allocated for avoiding transaction risk. Finally, we assume

$$s, L_i \in [0, 1], x, x^s, x^d, y, y^s, y^d \geq 0.$$

Each individual's self-interested behavior is represented by a nonlinear programming problem that maximizes her expected utility with respect to $L_i$, $s$, $x$, $x^s$, $x^d$, $y$, $y^s$, $y^d$, subject to the production functions, endowment constraint, and nonnegative constraint.

Applying the Wen theorem to the model, we can show that a person never simultaneously buys and sells the same good, never simultaneously buys and self-provides the same good, and never sells more than one good. Taking account of the possibilities for pure and contingent pricing for goods, we can identify 10 configurations and 6 structures that need to be considered.

We assume a Walrasian regime where a representative pair of consumer–producers sort out their terms of trade and sign a contract in period 1. Then they decide on their quantities of goods to consume, to produce, and to trade, and Nature chooses a realization of $k_x$ according to the players' decisions and prior probabilities in period 2. Trade and consumption take place and the contract is implemented in period 3. In this regime, each person can observe $k_i$, but not the effort level $s$, of the other. We first identify all structures that need to be considered. Then all corner equilibria in the structures will be solved.

1) There is an autarky configuration, A, where there is no market or principal–agent relationship, and each individual self-provides all goods consumed. Structure A consists of $M$ individuals choosing configuration A, which implies a profile of decision variables with $L_x, L_y, x, y > 0$; $s = x^s = x^d = y^s = y^d = 0$. The decision problem for a person choosing configuration A is

Max: $U \equiv Eu = E(\ln x + \ln y)$             (utility function)        (10.3)

s.t. $x = L_x - a$, $y = L_y - a$             (production functions)

$L_x + L_y = 1$                          (endowment constraint)

where E denotes expectation, and $L_i$, $x$, $y$ are decision variables. The optimum solution for this problem, and the maximum expected utility for this configuration, are listed in table 10.1. Note that there are no transaction and related transaction risk in autarky.

2) There are two market structures with the division of labor and a unique relative price of the two goods. Structure $D_L$ is a division of population between configurations $(x/y)_D^L$ and $(y/x)_D^L$. Configuration $(x/y)_D^L$ implies that $x$, $x^s$, $y^d > 0$, $s = L_y = x^d = y = y^s = 0$, and an individual choosing this configuration specializes in producing x, chooses a low level of effort in avoiding transaction risk, and accepts only a single relative price of the two goods. Configuration $(y/x)_D^L$ implies that $L_y$, $y$, $y^s$, $x^d > 0$, $s = L_x = y^d = x = x^s = 0$, and an individual choosing this configuration specializes in producing y, and accepts only a single relative price of the two goods. Structure $D_H$ is a division of population between configurations $(x/y)_D^H$ and $(y/x)_D^H$. Configuration $(x/y)_D^H$ is the same as configuration $(x/y)_D^L$ except that an individual choosing this configuration chooses a high level of effort in avoiding transaction risk. Configuration $(y/x)_D^H$ is the same as configuration $(y/x)_D^L$ except her trading efficiency coefficient $k$ is determined by a high effort level of the specialist producer of x. Let us first consider individuals' decision problems in Structure $D_L$.

In this structure the decision problem for a person choosing configuration $(x/y)_D^L$ is

Max: $U_x \equiv Eu_x = E[\ln(ky^d) + \ln x]$

s.t. $y^d = px^s$                    (budget constraint)

$x + x^s = L_x - a$,            (production function)

$L_x = 1$                       (endowment constraint)

where $L_x$, $x^s$, $y^d$ are decision variables and $p \equiv p_x/p_y$ is the price of good x in terms of good y. Note that $s = 0$ for this configuration. The optimum decision for this configuration and the expected indirect utility function are listed in table 10.1.

The decision problem for configuration $(y/x)_D^L$ is

Max: $U_y \equiv Eu_y = E[\ln y + \ln(k_x x^d)]$

s.t. $y^s = px^d$                    (budget constraint)

$k_x = t$                        (transaction condition)

$y + y^s = L_y - a$              (production function)

$L_y = 1$                       (endowment constraint)

where $L_y$, $x^d$, $y^s$ are decision variables. The optimum decision for this configuration and the expected indirect utility function are listed in table 10.1.

The terms of trade in period 1 will be determined by the expected utility equalization condition: $U_x = U_y$ since individuals would keep changing occupation in period 1 if this condition were not satisfied. The market clearing condition $M_y y^s = M_x y^d$ or $M_x y^s = M_y x^d$, together with the population equation $M_x + M_y = M$, then determines the numbers of individuals choosing the two configurations. Plugging the corner equilibrium relative price

**Table 10.1:** Corner solutions in seven configurations

| Configuration | Self-provided quantities | Demand and supply | Expected indirect utility |
|---|---|---|---|
| A | $x = y = 0.5 - a$ | | $2\ln(0.5 - a)$ |
| $(x/y)_D{}^H$ | $s = \beta$ <br> $x = (1 - a - \beta)/2$ | $x^s = (1 - a - \beta)/2$ <br> $y^d = px^s$ | $\ln(pk) + 2[\ln(1 - a - \beta) - \ln 2]$ |
| $(y/x)_D{}^H$ | $y = (1 - a)/2$ | $x^d = y^s/p$ <br> $y^s = (1 - a)/2$ | $\rho\ln k + (1 - \rho)\ln t - \ln p +$ <br> $2[\ln(1 - a) - \ln 2]$ |
| $(x/y)_D{}^L$ | $s = 0$ <br> $x = (1 - a)/2$ | $x^s = (1 - a)/2$ <br> $y^d = px^s$ | $\ln(pk) + 2[\ln(1 - a) - \ln 2]$ |
| $(y/x)_D{}^L$ | $y = (1 - a)/2$ | $x^d = y^s/p$ <br> $y^s = (1 - a)/2$ | $\ln(t/p) + 2[\ln(1-a) - \ln 2]$ |
| $(x/y)_C$ | $s = \beta$ <br> $x = (1 - a - \beta)/2$ | $x^s = (1 - a - \beta)/2$ <br> $y^d = px^s$ | $\rho\ln(p_H k) + (1 - \rho)\ln(p_L t) +$ <br> $2[\ln(1 - a - \beta) - \ln 2]$ |
| $(y/x)_C$ | $y = (1 - a)/2$ | $x^d = x^s$ <br> $y^s = p$ | $\rho\ln(k_H/p_H) + (1 - \rho)\ln(k_L/p_L) +$ <br> $2[\ln(1 - a) - \ln 2]$ |

into the utility function yields the corner equilibrium expected real income in structure $D_L$. All of the information on this corner equilibrium is in table 10.2.

Assume that a single equilibrium relative price prevails. From table 10.1, it is clear that when $p_H = p_L = p$, an x specialist's expected utility is $\ln(pk) + 2[\ln(1 - a) - \ln 2]$ if she chooses a low effort level and is $2[\ln(1 - \alpha - \beta) - \ln 2] + \ln(kp)$ if she chooses a high effort level. A comparison between the two indirect utility functions implies that for a single relative price, an x specialist always chooses the low level of effort in avoiding transaction risk. Hence, structure $D_H$ never occurs in equilibrium.

3) Market Structure C is associated with the division of labor and with two contingent relative prices. This structure comprises a division of $M$ individuals between configurations $(x/y)_C$ and $(y/x)_C$. Configuration $(x/y)_C$ is the same as $(x/y)_D{}^H$ except that an individual choosing this configuration accepts the relative price $p_H$ when $k_x$ is $k$, and the relative price $p_L$ if $k_x$ is $t$. Configuration $(y/x)_C$ is the same as $(y/x)_D{}^H$ except that an individual choosing this configuration accepts the relative price $p_H$ when $k_x$ is $k$, and the relative price $p_L$ if $k_x$ is $t$.

The procedure for solving for this corner equilibrium is the same as that for structure $D_L$, except that the incentive compatibility condition is used, together with the utility equalization condition, to determine the two corner equilibrium relative prices. Assume that in Structure C the relative price is $p_H$ when $k_x$ is $k$ and that it is $p_L$ when $k_x$ is $t$. Assume that $p$ in configuration $(x/y)_D{}^L$ is $p_L$. Letting the expected utility of the specialist choosing $(x/y)_C$, given in table 10.1, equal the expected utility for $(x/y)_D{}^L$, the incentive compatibility condition for C can be derived as follows.

$$\ln(p_H/p_L) > 2[\ln(1 - a) - \ln(1 - a - \beta)]/\rho \tag{10.4}$$

This condition, together with an expected utility equalization condition between configurations $(x/y)_C$ and $(y/x)_C$, yields the corner equilibrium dual contingent relative prices in Structure C. Plugging the corner equilibrium prices back into the indirect utility function of either $(x/y)_C$ or $(y/x)_C$ then yields expected per capita real income (corner equilibrium utility) in Structure C.

All information on the four corner equilibria is summarized in table 10.2. Note that although per capita real incomes in structures $D_H$ and C are the same, individuals will not choose a single noncontingent relative price in $D_H$ if (10.4) is not satisfied because of moral hazard. Hence, (10.4) sets up a dividing line between Structures $D_H$ and C in addition to the dividing line between Structures $D_H$ and $D_L$.

General equilibrium satisfies the following conditions. (i) Each individual maximizes her expected utility with respect to configurations and quantities of each good produced, consumed, and traded for a given set of relative prices of traded goods; (ii) The set of relative prices of traded goods and numbers of individuals choosing different configurations clears the markets for goods subject to the incentive compatibility constraint. Since all individuals are *ex ante* identical, the relative prices will equalize expected utility for all individuals selling different goods.

Following inframarginal analysis, we can solve a corner equilibrium for each structure. We can identify the conditions under which each individual has no incentive to deviate from her configuration under the corner equilibrium prices in this structure. Alternatively, we can follow the procedure to prove the Yao theorem in chapter 5 to show that the general equilibrium is the corner equilibrium with the greatest expected per capita real income subject to the incentive compatibility condition. Hence, solving for the general equilibrium becomes a matter of identifying the corner equilibrium with the highest expected real income, subject to the incentive compatibility condition (10.4).

A comparison between per capita real incomes in Structures A, $D_L$, and C yields the inframarginal comparative statics of general equilibrium, summarized in table 10.3.

The bottom line in this table gives the equilibrium structure for each particular parameter subspace. Table 10.3 illustrates that as trading efficiency is improved the general equilibrium discontinuously jumps from autarky, where there is neither market nor principal–agent relationship, to a structure with the division of labor, where the reciprocal principal–agent relationships emerge from the division of labor and a market. It can be seen that the emergence of the principal–agent relationship will involve two contingent relative prices if the benefits $k/t$ of effort in reducing transaction risk are

Table 10.2: Corner equilibria in four structures

| Structure | Corner equilibrium relative price | Expected real income |
|---|---|---|
| A | | $2[\ln(1 - 2a) - \ln2]$ |
| $D_L$ | $p = (t/k)^{0.5}$ | $2[\ln(1 - a) - \ln2] + 0.5(\ln t + \ln k)$ |
| $D_H$ | $p = [(1 - a)/(1 - a - \beta)](t/k)^{0.5(1-\rho)}$ | $0.5[(1 + \rho)\ln k + (1 - \rho)\ln t] + \ln(1 - a) + \ln(1 - a - \beta) - 2\ln2$ |
| C | $p_L = (t/k)^{0.5(1-\rho)}[(1 - a - \beta)/(1 - a)]$, $p_H = p_L[(1 - a)/(1 - a - \beta)]^{2/\rho}$ | $0.5[(1 + \rho)\ln k + (1 - \rho)\ln t] + \ln(1 - a) + \ln(1 - a - \beta) - 2\ln2$ |

**Table 10.3:** General equilibrium and its inframarginal comparative statics

| $k/t < [(1-a)/(1-a-\beta)]^{a/\rho}$ | | $k/t > [(1-a)/(1-a-\beta)]^{a/\rho}$ | |
|---|---|---|---|
| $kt < [(1-2a)/(1-a)]^4$ | $kt > [(1-2a)/(1-a)]^4$ | $k^{1+\rho}t^{1-\rho} < B$ | $k^{1+\rho}t^{1-\rho} > B$ |
| A | C | A | C |

*where:* $B \equiv [(1-2a)^2/(1-a)(1-a-\beta)]^2$

great compared to its cost in terms of reduced production time, that is $\beta$. Otherwise, the emergence of the principal–agent relationship will involve a unique relative price of the two goods (D$_L$).

Since the production condition in this model can be represented by the graph in figure 11.1, a comparison between the comparative statics of general equilibrium in table 10.3 and figure 11.1 indicates that as transaction conditions are improved, the equilibrium production plan will discontinuously jump from the low line DI to the aggregate production possibility frontier MCAKBJL in figure 11.1. This explains why contingent contracts can be used to promote economic development.

Although this model can predict the function of contingent contracts in avoiding endogenous transaction costs caused by moral hazard, the general equilibrium is always Pareto optimal. Hence, a completely contingent contract can eliminate endogenous transaction costs caused by moral hazard.

## ◆ 10.4 The Trade-off between Endogenous Transaction Costs caused by Moral Hazard and Monitoring Cost

In this section, we use the Holmstrom and Milgrom model to show the function of contract in achieving the efficient trade off between endogenous transaction costs caused by moral hazard and monitoring cost in reducing moral hazard.

### Example 10.3: the Holmstrom–Milgrom model (1995)

The employer pays the employee a linear compensation $w = \alpha + \beta(z + \gamma y)$, where $z = e + x$ is observed outcome of the employee's effort $e$, and $x \sim N(\bar{x}, \sigma_x)$ is a random variable representing the firm-specific uncertainty, $y \sim N(\bar{y}, \sigma_y)$ is a random variable representing industry-wide or nation-wide uncertainty, the covariance between $x$ and $y$ is $\sigma_{xy} = \text{cov}(x, y) = E[(x - \bar{x})(y - \bar{y})] = \sum_{s \in S} p(s)[x(s) - \bar{x}][y(s) - \bar{y}]$, $e$ is the employee's effort level that affects the profit of the employer's business, but cannot be observed or verified by the employer, $\alpha$ is a fixed wage, and $\beta$ is the intensity coefficient of the contingent incentive payment. $N(\bar{x}, \sigma_x)$ is a normal probability distribution. $\sigma_y = \text{var}(y) = E[(y - \bar{y})^2] = \sum_{s \in S} p(s)[y(s) - \bar{y}]^2$. For simplicity, we assume that $\bar{x} = \bar{y} = 0$. The employee's certain equivalent wealth (CEW) is

$$CEW_e = \alpha + \beta e - C(e) - 0.5r\beta^2 V,$$

where $C(e)$ is disutility of effort and $C'(e) > 0$ and $C''(e) > 0$, $r$ is the degree of absolute risk aversion, and $V \equiv \text{Var}(x + \gamma y) = \sigma_x + \gamma^2 \sigma_y + 2\gamma\sigma_{xy}$. The employee maximizes this with her effort level $e$. The first-order condition yields

$$\beta = C'(e).$$

This is referred to as *incentive constraint*. The employer is risk neutral and her pay-off and its certain equivalent is

$$\text{CEW}_r = P(e) - (\alpha + \beta e),$$

where $P(e)$ is gross profit and $\alpha + \beta e$ is wage payment.

Assume that wealth distribution has no effect on productivity (a very strong assumption that abstracts the analysis from effects of transaction costs on productivity which has been the focus in all new classical models in this text). Then the efficient contract is determined by maximizing the total certain equivalent wealth of the employer and employee, which is

$$\text{CEW} = P(e) - C(e) - 0.5r\beta^2 V.$$

Maximizing this with respect to $e$, $\beta$, and $\gamma$, subject to the incentive constraint, yields the first-order condition for the efficient contingent incentive contract:

$$P'(e) - C'(e)[1 + rVC''(e)], \qquad \beta = C'(e), \qquad \gamma = -\sigma_{xy}/\sigma_y.$$

Suppose that $P(e) = ae$, $C(e) = ce^2$. Then $P'(e) = a$, $C'(e) = 2ce$, and $C''(e) = 2c$. For these specific functional forms, the efficient contract is

$$\gamma = -\sigma_{xy}/\sigma_y, \qquad e = a/2c(2crV + 1), \qquad \beta = 2ce = a/(2crV + 1).$$

The comparative statics of the efficient contract are

$$de/da > 0, \qquad de/dc < 0, \qquad d\beta/da > 0, \qquad d\beta/dc < 0.$$

This result indicates that as the benefit coefficient of effort, $a$, increases, or as the disutility coefficient of effort, $c$, decreases, the efficient incentive intensity $\beta$ increases, so that the efficient contract induces a higher level of effort, $e$. If the unobservable $x$ and observable $y$ are positively correlated, ($\sigma_{xy} > 0$), the efficient $\gamma$ is negative since good outcome is more likely to be caused by nation-wide contingence rather than by firm specific contingence. But if $\sigma_{xy} < 0$, the efficient $\gamma$ is positive.

This story shows that the trade-off between risk sharing and incentive provision implies that too great an incentive intensity may not be efficient. If we introduce the trade-off between monitoring cost and incentive provision into the model, this point becomes more obvious. Suppose $\text{Var}(x + \gamma y) = V$ is a decision variable. Assume that the monitoring cost $M(V)$ is an increasing function of $V$, or $M'(V) \geq 0$. Also, we assume that $M''(V) > 0$. The new total certain equivalent is now

$$\text{CEW} = P(e) - C(e) - 0.5r\beta^2 V - M(V).$$

The optimum contract is given by maximizing this CEW with respect to $e$, $V$, and $\beta$, subject to the incentive constraint.

In exercise 5 of chapter 16, Holmstrom and Milgrom introduce the trade-off between balanced incentives for two activities that the employee undertakes and strong incentive for each activity into the model in example 10.3. They have shown that the institution of the firm can more efficiently balance the trade-off by imposing some job restrictions and by providing weaker and more balanced incentives than in the market without firms. This kind of model shows that a realistic analysis of efficient contracts involves many-trade offs which are much more complicated than the simple trade-off between incentive provision and risk sharing in example 10.1.

Most of this kind of model are decision or partial equilibrium models that cannot figure out the mechanisms that simultaneously determine the network size of division of labor, the extent of the market, the number of transactions, total endogenous and exogenous transaction costs, and productivity.

## ◆ 10.5. The Grossman–Hart–Moore Model of Optimal Ownership Structure

### Example 10.4: the GHM model of optimum ownership structure

Consider a business venture between two players whose sales revenue may be high, $R = 40$, or low, $R = 10$, and whose operating costs may be high, $C = 30$, or low, $C = 10$. Player 1's effort level $x$ determines the probability of realizing the high level of sales revenue. Assume for simplicity that $x \in [0,1]$, and that the probability equals $x$. The probability of the low level of revenue, $R = 10$, is then $1 - x$. Player 2's effort level $y$ determines the probability of the business achieving the low level of operating costs, where $y \in [0,1]$, and we assume that this probability equals $y$. The probability of the high level of costs, $C = 30$, is then $1 - y$. Player 1 may be considered the salesman and player 2 the producer of goods, so that the profit of their business is jointly determined by the two players' effort levels.

There are four potential outcomes for the business. Their probabilities follow.

| $R$ | $C$ | $V$ | *Joint probability* |
|-----|-----|-----|---------------------|
| 40 | 10 | 30 | $xy$ |
| 40 | 30 | 10 | $x(1-y)$ |
| 20 | 10 | 10 | $(1-x)y$ |
| 20 | 30 | $-10$ | $(1-x)(1-y)$ |

Suppose, for simplicity, that the state of low revenue and high costs causes bankruptcy that yields zero profit. Then the expected profit of this joint venture is

$$V = y\,(40 - 10) + x\,(1 - y)(40 - 30) + (1 - x)y(20 - 10) + (1 - x)(1 - y)\,0$$
$$= 10\,(\,xy\; + \; x\; + y\,)$$

In order to illuminate the incentive problem and the related moral hazard, we assume that player 1's utility is $V_1 - \alpha x^2$, where $V_1$ is the part of the profit that he receives. Player 2's utility is $V_2 - 5x^2$, where $V_2$ is the part of the profit that she receives. If each player can see the other's effort level, so that there is no moral hazard, then they can work out their optimum effort levels from the following maximization problem and specify a contract that requires such effort levels in period 1.

Max: $W = V - \alpha x^2 - 5y^2 = 10(xy + x + y) - \alpha x^2 - 5y^2$

s.t. $x, y \in [0,1]$

where $W$ is the two players' total expected utility. Since $\partial W/\partial y = 10(1 + x - y) > 0$ for all $x, y \in [0, 1]$, the optimum value of $y$ is 1 according to the Kuhn–Tucker condition. The Kuhn–Tucker condition for maximizing $W$ with respect to $x$ then yields the optimum contractual terms, which are Pareto optimal, in the absence of moral hazard.

$$y^* = 1, \; x^* = \begin{cases} 1 \text{ for } \alpha \leq 10 \\ 10/\alpha \text{ for } \alpha > 10, \end{cases}$$

Then, the Pareto optimum total expected utility generated by the business can be computed as follows.

$$W^* = \begin{cases} 25 - \alpha \text{ if } \alpha \leq 10 \\ \dfrac{100}{\alpha} + 5 \text{ if } \alpha > 10 \end{cases}$$

For this case, the structure of ownership and residual rights makes no difference. Player 1 can claim all profit and then pay player 2 according to her effort level; or player 2 can claim all profit and then pay player 1 according to his effort level; or they can jointly claim the profit and then divide this according their effort levels. All three structures of ownership of profit will generate the same outcome in the absence of moral hazard. We assume now that each player cannot see the other's effort level, or cannot verify this in court when a dispute occurs. Hence, two-sided moral hazard exists. In addition, complete contingent pricing of the four outcome states is prohibitively expensive, so that *ex post* renegotiation will take place. An incomplete contract specifies the ownership structure of the business. Different structures of ownership will give different *ex post* bargaining power to a player.

We first consider a symmetric structure of ownership, D. In this structure, the two players are partners. They sort out the contractual terms through *ex post* Nash bargaining in period 2. The contractual terms between them provide for splitting the profit. For the given terms, each player maximizes her expected utility (which is her share of profit net of the disutility of her effort) in period 1, with respect to her effort level for a given effort level of the other party. Player 1's expected utility is

$$Eu_1 = (V/2) - \alpha x^2 = 5(xy + x + y) - \alpha x^2$$

and his optimum effort level, for the given effort level of player 2, is $x = 5(y + 1)/2\alpha$. Because of the absence of a complete contract, the interdependence between the two players' decisions is not fully taken into account in their self-interested decision-making. This uncounted interdependence looks like an externality. Player 2's decision problem in period 1 for given terms determined in *ex post* bargaining is

$$\text{Max: } Eu_2 = (V/2) - 5y^2 = 5(xy + x + y) - 5y^2$$

and her optimum effort level for the given effort level of player 1 is $y = (x + 1)/2$. The equilibrium is determined by the two optimum decisions. Considering possible corner solutions, the equilibrium is

$$x = 0, \quad y = 0 \text{ if } \alpha \in (0, 5/4)$$
$$x = y = 1 \text{ if } \alpha \in (5/4, 5)$$
$$x = 15/(4\alpha - 5), \quad y = (2\alpha + 5)/(4\alpha - 5) \text{ if } \alpha > 5$$

The total expected utility of the two players in Structure D is

$$W_D = V - \alpha x^2 - 5y^2 - 0 \text{ for } \alpha \in (0, 5/4)$$
$$W_D = 25 - \alpha \text{ for } \alpha \in (5/4, 5)$$
$$W_D = 10(xy + x + y) - \alpha x^2 - 5y^2 \text{ for } \alpha > 5$$

which is lower than the Pareto optimum level of total expected utility $W^*$ if $\alpha \in (0, 5/4)$ or $\alpha > 5$, and is the same as the Pareto optimum if $\alpha \in (5/4, 5)$. The difference represents the endogenous transaction costs caused by moral hazard and an incomplete contract.

There are two asymmetric structures of ownership and residual rights. In structure A, player 1 is the owner of the business and claims its residual returns via his *ex post* bargaining power. Player 2 receives a reservation pay, which is exogenously given in the partial equilibrium model. For simplicity, we assume that the reservation pay is 0, so that player 2 will choose $y = 0$. The owner's decision problem is

$$\text{Max: } Eu_1 = V - \alpha x^2 = 10x - \alpha x^2$$

The solution is $x^* = 5/\alpha$. The total utility of the two players is

$$W_A = 25/\alpha$$

which is smaller than in the Pareto optimum.

Similarly, we can solve for the corner equilibrium in the asymmetric structure B, where player 1 receives the reservation pay and player 2 is the owner of the business. The solution is

$$x = 0, y = 1, \text{ and } W_B = 5.$$

which again is smaller than in the Pareto optimum. Hence, each of the three structures of ownership and residual rights generates endogenous transaction costs. In Structure D, the two players partly free ride on their opponents' efforts, so that two-sided moral hazard causes endogenous transaction costs. These endogenous transaction costs are attributable to the moral hazard of player 2 in Structure A, and of player 1 in structure B. Considering all possible outcomes, two players can always use some side payment to choose the local equilibrium with the highest total utility in period 0.

An inframarginal analysis shows that for $\alpha \in (0, 5/4)$, $W_A > W_B > W_D$; for $\alpha \in (5/4, 5)$, $W_D > W_A > W_B$; for $\alpha \in (5, 43.2)$, $W_D > W_B, W_A$; for $\alpha > 43.1$, $W_B > W_D > W_A$. Hence, the equilibrium and its inframarginal comparative statics can be summarized in the following table.

| | $\alpha \in (0, 5/4)$ | $\alpha \in (5/4, 5)$ | $\alpha > 43.1$ |
|---|---|---|---|
| Equilibrium structure | A | D | B |

Since player 2's disutility coefficient of effort is fixed at 5, the disutility parameter of player 1's effort $\alpha$ represents the relative disutility of effort of the two players. Hence, the table implies that the relative disutility of effort between the two players determines which structure of ownership is the equilibrium. If player 1's disutility of effort is relatively small, then he will be the owner of the business (Structure A) in the equilibrium. If player 1's disutility of effort is relatively large, then player 2 will be the owner of the business (Structure B). If the disutilities of two players' efforts are close, then they will choose a symmetric relationship between partners (Structure D).

If the revenue and cost coefficients are parameterized too, it can be shown that the player whose effort has the more significant effects on profit and who has the relatively lower disutility will be the owner of the business. If the effects of the two players' efforts on profit and disutility are close, then a symmetric structure of ownership and residual rights will occur in the equilibrium. Hence, this model verifies the second part of the Coase theorem that contracts in the market will maximize the gains from trade net of endogenous transaction costs if those costs are unavoidable.

This model is a partial rather than a general equilibrium model. The player who receives reservation pay will minimize his effort level under the assumption of incomplete contract which implies that effort input as well as output cannot be priced. Hence, the risk of a bad outcome for the business is solely determined by the owner's effort level. This is defined as residual control rights in the GHM model. This definition of residual control is different from one in chapter 8, where for a labor contract, it is ultimately up to the employer how to use an employee's labor.

An owner's claims to residual rights, as described in the GHM model, can occur in the absence of a labor contract. For instance, in the market for automobiles, there are at least two structures of ownership. In one, ownership of a car is assigned to its driver and in the other, ownership is assigned to a car rental agent. An argument in favor of driver ownership is that the effort exerted in maintaining and carefully driving a car is expensive to contract out (expensive to verify or to distinguish from the consequence of uncertainty). However, for a driver who frequently travels long distances across states and countries, the costs of car ownership can be prohibitively high. If he travels those distances by air, the buying and selling of cars as required in each local market will generate high transaction costs; whereas if he drives everywhere the long distance driving will generate other costs. Thus for the case of frequent interstate or international travel, the costs of ownership of a car by its driver may outweigh the costs of its ownership by a car rental agent, so that the latter structure of ownership will be chosen. For a case without much long-distance travel, the former structure of ownership may be chosen.

Another story, about the ownership structure of housing, can be used to illustrate the theory behind the GHM model too. A house can be owned by its user or by the landlord who rents the house to a tenant. Since the tenant's effort in maintaining the house is not observable or verifiable, a rented house will tend to be less well kept than a house occupied by the owner. However, there are benefits in labor mobility for individuals who wish to keep moving around before settling down in a career. If these individuals insist that they must live in their own houses, then unless they are exceptionally wealthy they must frequently sell and buy houses as they move from one residence to another. If the transaction costs of such frequent selling and buying outweigh the endogenous transaction costs caused by tenants' moral hazard, then the ownership structure of tenant–landlord is better than that of owner–user. Both the car and housing stories are consistent with the GHM model. However, if car rental agents and landlords are independent players who do not hire any labor, then the stories have nothing to do with the institution of the firm. Therefore, Grossman and Hart's theory is a very good theory of the optimum structure of ownership or residual rights, rather than a theory of the firm.

## ◆ 10.6. Noncredible Commitment and Soft Budget Constraint

In this section we consider a simplest version of the Dewatripont and Maskin model (1995) of a commitment game and soft budget constraints.

### Example 10.5: the Dewatripont and Maskin model

Consider a game with two regimes. In one of them there is only a banker who is endowed with two units of capital and considers making a loan to a project proposed by an entrepreneur. We call this a centralized regime. In another regime there are two bankers, each with one unit of capital. We call this a decentralized regime. There is uncertainty of the project, which could be good or bad. In addition, information is asymmetric: only the entrepreneur knows if his project is good or bad. A banker knows this only after investment is made. There are two periods. If the project is the good one, it is completed within one period and the banker receives gross pay-off $R > 1$ or net pay-off $R - 1 > 0$ if she invests one unit capital in period 1. If the project is the bad one, it cannot be completed within one period and the banker must consider if she should refinance this project. If refinance takes place, the banker's gross pay-off is $r$ with probability $p$, and 0 with $1 - p$, where $p$ is a function of the banker's cost for monitoring the entrepreneur: $C = bp^2$ where $C$ is the total monitoring cost in period 1 and $b$ is a coefficient. We assume

$$b \in (r^2/8, \ r^2/4) \tag{10.5}$$

The entrepreneur always receives pay-off $A$ if the project is completed and pay-off $E$ if the project is not completed, regardless of whether the project is good or bad. It is assumed that $A > 0 > E$, which implies that the entrepreneur always has an incentive to get a loan and to complete the project.

We first consider the case of the good project which is completed in period 1 and generates net payoff $R - 1$ to the banker and $A$ to the entrepreneur regardless of regime. For a bad project, we can see that under a centralized system, the banker has an incentive to refinance this bad project if (10.5) holds. If she does not refinance in period 2 after one unit of loan has been made, her net pay-off is $-1$. If she refinances this project in period 2, she can maximize the expected net pay-off $pr - C - 2$ with respect to $p$ subject to $C = bp^2$. The optimum expected net payoff is thus $(r^2/4b) - 2$, which is greater than $-1$ if (10.5) holds. But if (10.5) holds, the bad project generates negative profit, or $(r^2/4b) - 2 < 0$. It is inefficient to undertake this project at all. This illustrates that due to information asymmetry and a centralized system, commitment not to refinance the bad project is not credible, so that the soft budget constraint (refinance) associated with this noncredible commitment generates endogenous transaction costs caused by refinancing the bad project.

Now we consider the case of two bankers, each with one unit of capital. Suppose that the project is bad, so that the first banker cannot refinance the project in period 2. In period 1, the first banker maximizes $\alpha pr - C - 1$ with respect to $p$ subject to $C = bp^2$. Here $\alpha \in (0, 1)$ is the fraction of gross pay-off generated by the completion of the project that the first banker receives, or $1 - \alpha$ is the fraction of gross pay-off received by the second banker who refinances this project. The optimum $p$ is $p^* = \alpha r/2b$. Here, we assume that the second banker cannot observe the first banker's monitoring intensity. The second banker will not refinance this project if her expected net pay-off $(1 - \alpha)pr - C - 1 < 0$, or if $(2 - 3\alpha)\alpha r^2 < 4b$, where $p = \alpha r/2b$. Hence, if $\alpha > 2/3$, the refinance will not take place. The entrepreneur who has the bad project will anticipate this, with his sequential rationality. Therefore, he will not ask for a loan from the outset if $\alpha > 2/3$. In other words, in a decentralized system, commitment not to refinance the bad project might be credible and thereby the budget constraint is hard. Hence, the bad project is more unlikely to occur in equilibrium. The commitment game model is a type of sequential equilibrium model. The equilibrium under a centralized regime is indeed a pooling equilibrium and the equilibrium under a decentralized regime is a screening equilibrium. The small capital size of each of the two banks is equivalent to the small prior probability of the capable businessmen in the sequential equilibrium model in example 4.8, or the low prior probability of the capable incumbent in exercise 19 (the Milgrom and Roberts model of entry deterrence) of chapter 4. Many such commitment game models have recently been developed to investigate endogenous transaction costs in economic transition (see the surveys listed in further readings).

## Key Terms and Review

Moral hazard and related endogenous transaction costs.
The difference between moral hazard and adverse selection.
Risk aversion, risk loving, and risk neutral preferences.
Jensen inequality.
Certain equivalent wealth.
Incentive compatibility and participation constraint.
Functions of the contract, ownership, and residual rights.
The difference between complete contracts and incomplete contracts and the implications of the difference for the role of ownership and residual rights.
The difference between symmetric and asymmetric structures of residual rights.
The difference between rights to residual returns and to residual control.
Functions of ownership and residual rights and the second part of the Coase theorem.
How can noncredible commitment and soft budget constraints cause endogenous transaction costs?

# Further Reading

*Surveys on principal–agent models and theory of contract*: Arrow (1985), Hart and Holmstrom (1987), Holmstrom and Roberts (1998), Bolton and Scharfstein (1998); *criticism of the principal–agent models*: Hart (1991); *the GHM model*: Hart and Moore (1990), Hart (1995), Grossman and Hart (1986); *criticism of the GHM model*: Holmstrom and Milgrom (1995), Holmstrom and Roberts (1998), Maskin and Tirole (1997), Hart and More (1999), Tirole (1989), Yang (1997); *new classical models of moral hazard*: Yang and Yeh (1996), Lio (1996), Yang (1997); *neoclassical models of moral hazard and adverse selection*: Mas–Collell, Whinston, and Green (1995, chs. 6, 13, 14), Varian (1992, ch. 8), Akerlof (1970); *the literature of transaction costs economics and economics of property rights without formal models*: Williamson (1985), Barzel (1982), Furubotn and Pejovich (1974), Buchanan (1975, 1989), Cheung (1970, 1983); *new political economy models with endogenous stealing*: Marcouiller and Young (1995), Skaperdas (1992); *general equilibrium models of moral hazard*: Helpman and Laffont (1975), Legros and Newman (1996), Kihlstrom and Laffont (1979); *two-sided moral hazard*: Bhattacharyya and Lafontaine (1995), Cooper and Ross (1985), Romano (1994); *models with endogenous specialization and endogenous transaction costs caused by information asymmetry*: Laffont and Tirole (1986), Lewis and Sappington (1991); *Coase theorem*: Coase (1960); *commitment games and soft budget constraints*: Dewatripont and Maskin (1995), Maskin (forthcoming), Qian (1994), Maskin and Xu (1999), Roland (2000).

# QUESTIONS

1. Consider the ownership structure in the equipment rental market. TV sets, video cameras, diggers, buckets, and other machines and equipment can be owned by their users, or be rented from other owners. Apply the theory of optimum ownership structure based on the GHM model to analyze the endogenous and exogenous transaction costs associated with the two structures of ownership. Identify the conditions under which each of the two structures occurs in equilibrium. Use the example to illustrate why the theory of optimum ownership may have nothing to do with the institution of the firm.

2. Why does Hart claim that the principal–agent model is not part of the formal theory of the institution of the firm?

3. Analyze the similarities and differences between the Yang–Ng model in chapter 8 and the GHM model in section 10.4.

4. John considers establishing with his Russian partner a business to publish a *Directory of American Businesses* in Russian. He hopes the business will make money from advertisements of American companies in the book and from sales revenue net of printing costs in Russia. Suppose that John approaches you to seek advice about which of the following three structures of ownership he should choose: (a) He hires the Russian partner to do the job in Russia and himself takes care of part of the business in the US. (b) He enters a joint venture with the partner. (c) He asks for a salary from his Russian partner to pay for the job that he takes care of, which must be done in the US. Outline your advice, which is of course dependent on specific business conditions about which you may make assumptions (for instance, the legal framework and enforcement of laws are not good in Russia, so that the Russian partner's special personal connections to government officials and related effort may be important for reducing the risk).

5. North (1958, 1986) has found empirical evidence of a negative correlation between freight rates and economic development and of concurrent evolution of the income share of the transaction sector and per capita real income. However, this empirical evidence is relevant only to exogenous transaction costs. Endogenous transaction costs are much more difficult to measure. Can you find a way to test the theories of endogenous transaction costs developed in this chapter against empirical observations?

# EXERCISES

1   Consider the model in example 10.1. Assume that the probability for $R = 16$ is $\theta > 0.5$ and that for $R = 4$ is $1 - \theta$ when effort level is high. The probability for $R = 4$ is $\theta$ and that for $R = 16$ is $1 - \theta$ when effort level is low. The agent's utility function is $\ln w - \ln e$. Solve for the equilibrium contract.

2   Consider the model in example 10.2. Assume that

$$\text{If } L_x = 16, \text{ then } x + x^s = \begin{cases} 4 \text{ with } 0.95 \\ 1 \text{ with } 0.05 \end{cases}$$

$$\text{If } L_x = 4, \text{ then } x + x^s = \begin{cases} 4 \text{ with } 0.01 \\ 1 \text{ with } 0.99 \end{cases}$$

$L_x + L_y + s = 20$. Solve for the general equilibrium and its inframarginal comparative statics

3   Consider a new classical principal–agent model with two consumer goods x and y. The structure of the model is the same as in chapter 5, but transaction efficiency $k$ is a contingent variable for good x. It is $\theta_h$ with probability $\rho$ and $\theta_l$ with probability $1 - \rho$ if the effort level in reducing transaction risk is $L_h$; and it is $\theta_l$ with probability $\rho$ and $\theta_h$ with probability $1 - \rho$ if effort level in reducing transaction risk is $L_l$, where $\theta_h > \theta_l$ and $\rho > 0.5$. Solve for the general equilibrium and its inframarginal comparative statics.

4   Stiglitz, 1974: Consider a simple sharecropping model where the landlord is the principal and the tenant is the agent. The production function is $y = \theta A L^a$ where $L$ is the tenant's input of labor in the production, $y$ is output level, $\theta$ is a random variable and its value is $\theta_L$ with probability $\rho$ and $\theta_H$ with probability $1 - \rho$, where $\theta_H > \theta_L$, and $a \in (0, 1)$ is the elasticity parameter of output with respect to labor input. We assume that the amount of land used in the production is fixed, so that it is included in parameter $A$. The tenant receives the share $\alpha$ of realized output and his expected utility is $u = \alpha E y + C - bL$, where $C$ is a side payment from the landlord to the tenant and $b$ is a disutility coefficient of working. The tenant's reservation utility is $u_0$. The landlord cannot observe or verify the labor input level of the tenant, so that the landlord's optimum contract with the tenant is given by his following decision problem. Max: $(1 - \alpha)Ey - C$ with respect to $\alpha$ and $C$ subject to the tenant's participation constraint: $u = \alpha E y + C - bL \geq u_0$ and the first-order condition for the tenant's utility maximization decision: $du/dL = 0$. The maximization of the landlord's pay-off implies that the equality in the tenant's participation constraint holds. Solve for the optimum share $\alpha$ and land rental $C$. Identify comparative statics $dC^*/du_0$, $dC^*/d\rho$, $d\alpha^*/d\rho$, and $\partial\alpha/\partial C < 0$. Interpret your results.

5   Consider the model in example 10.4. Assume that the parameters are modified as follows:

| R | C | V | Joint probability |
|---|---|---|---|
| 20 | 5 | 15 | $xy$ |
| 20 | 10 | 10 | $x(1 - y)$ |
| 10 | 5 | 5 | $(1 - x)y$ |
| 10 | 10 | 0 | $(1 - x)(1 - y)$ |

Solve for the general equilibrium and its inframarginal comparative statics.

6 Synthesize the theory of the firm in chapter 8 and the Holmstrom–Milgrom model in example 10.3 to explore the implications for the division of labor and productivity of the trade-off between endogenous and exogenous transaction costs.

7 Introduce two–sided moral hazard into the model in example 8.1. Assume that transaction efficiency coefficients are random variables, dependent on buyers' efforts in reducing transaction risk. The coefficients are structure-specific since monitoring efficiency differs between goods and labor. In Structure D (see figure 8.1), the transaction efficiency coefficient of good i, $k_i = \alpha_i$ with probability $s_i s_j$ and $k_i = 0$ with probability $1 - s_i s_j$ where $s_i$ is the effort level of a buyer of good $i = x, y$. In Structure E, the transaction efficiency coefficient of good y, $k_y = \alpha_y$ with probability $r_x s_y$ and $k_y = 0$ with probability $1 - r_x s_y$ where $r_i$ is the effort level of a buyer of labor used to produce good i in avoiding transaction risk. The transaction efficiency coefficient of labor used to produce good x, $t_x = \alpha_x$ with probability $r_x s_y$ and $t_x = 0$ with probability $1 - r_x s_y$. In structure F, $k_y = \theta_y$ with probability $r_y s_y$ and $k_y = 0$ with probability $1 - r_y s_y$. The transaction efficiency coefficient of labor used to produce good y, $t_y = \alpha_y$ with probability $r_y s_y$ and $t_x = 0$ with probability $1 - r_y s_y$. $\theta_i$ and $\mu_i$ are parameters for good i and for labor used to produce good i, respectively. Solve for the inframarginal comparative statics of equilibrium.

# part V

# TRADE THEORY AND MORE GENERAL NEW CLASSICAL MODELS

# chapter 11

# THE EMERGENCE OF INTERNATIONAL TRADE FROM DOMESTIC TRADE AND EMERGENCE OF NEW PRODUCTS

## ◆ 11.1 Endogenous Trade Theory and Endogenous Number of Consumer Goods

Adam Smith explained domestic and international trade by individuals' decisions in choosing their levels of specialization. Hence, the rationale for international and domestic trade is the same: economies of division of labor. But within the neoclassical framework, the dichotomy between pure consumers and firms implies that the rationale for domestic trade differs from that for international trade. Domestic trade is essential for pure consumers even if comparative advantage, economies of scale, and difference in tastes between individuals are absent, since they do not produce and will die from starvation in the absence of domestic trade between them and firms. However, international trade will not take place if these elements are not present, since each country has firms, so that each country is a consumer-producer. Hence, neoclassical trade theory cannot explain why and how international trade emerges from domestic trade.

The first purpose of this chapter is to develop a new classical trade theory referred to as *endogenous trade theory* (Smythe, 1994). This theory explains international and domestic trade by individuals' decisions in choosing their levels of specialization, and explains the emergence of international trade from domestic trade by evolution in division of labor and evolution in endogenous comparative advantage between *ex ante* identical individuals.

The previous two chapters investigated the relation between trade dependence, pattern of trade, and the division of labor. But the role of the development of division of labor in accounting for the emergence of new goods is yet to be explored. More than two centuries ago, Josiah Tucker (1755, 1774) noted that the development of division of labor creates the conditions for the emergence of new goods. Casual observations indicate that in an autarchic society without much division of labor, the variety of available goods is small, whereas in a developed economy with a high level of division of labor and specialization, the variety of available goods is large. Does this positive correlation between specialization and variety of available goods happen by coincidence? Or is it generated by some economic mechanism that is an essential aspect of division of labor? We may have a guess. Assume that there are economies of specialization, transaction costs, and economies of consumption variety, or economies of complementarity between consumption goods because of individuals' preferences for diverse consumption. Assume further that the calculation cost of the optimum decision increases with the number of consumption goods and accordingly counteracts the economies of consumption variety. Therefore, there are several trade-offs among four elements: economies of specialization, transaction costs, economies of consumption variety, and management costs of consumption variety. The efficient trade-offs are of course dependent on the parameters of trading efficiency, degree of economies of consumption variety, management cost of consumption variety, and degree of economies of specialization. For a sufficiently low trading efficiency, each person has to choose autarky. The narrow scope for trading off among economies of specialization, economies of consumption variety, and management cost of consumption variety, due to each individual's limited time endowment in autarky, may force individuals to produce a few goods. It would not be feasible in autarky for individuals to self-provide the cars, trains, airplanes, computers, television sets, telephones, and various detergents that they consume.

However, as trading efficiency is improved, the scope for trading off economies of specialization against transaction costs is enlarged, so that the level of division of labor is increased. The increased division of labor enlarges the scope for trading off economies and diseconomies of consumption variety, so that each individual's level of specialization and the number of available consumption goods can be simultaneously increased through a higher level of division of labor between specialists who produce different goods.

The endogenization of the number of goods is associated with the endogenization of emergence of new goods, which is considered by many economists as endogenous technical progress. Recalling the distinction between *ex ante* and *ex post* production functions examined in chapter 8, we can see that endogenous technical progress is associated with the emergence of some *ex post* production functions. This view of endogenous technical progress differs from the conventional view that attributes technical progress to investment in research and development. According to our view of endogenous technical progress, investment in R&D alone is not sufficient for emergence of new goods and related new production functions. It is essential for the emergence of new goods that the size of the network of division of labor and related extent of the market are sufficiently large to create the condition for the commercialization of new technology. A sufficiently high trading efficiency is then essential for a large size of the network of division of labor.

The Cobb–Douglas (C-D) utility function used in the previous chapters is not suitable for formalizing this story. For a general equilibrium model based on the C-D utility function, the number of consumption goods cannot be endogenized since utility is zero if the quantity of any single consumption good is zero. However the CES utility function examined in section 5.5 can be used to endogenize the number of consumption goods, since for this type of utility function, utility can be positive even if the quantity of a good consumed is zero, as long as the quantity of at least one of the other consumption goods is positive. In other words, consumption goods in the CES utility function are not necessities individually. Thus in a new classical model with the CES utility function the number of consumption goods and the level of division of labor can be simultaneously endogenized if a trade-off between economies and diseconomies of consumption variety is specified in addition to the trade-off between economies of specialization and transaction costs. This will be done in section 11.8.

In section 11.9, we consider the Becker–Murphy model with the trade-off between economies of specialization and coordination costs. This model confirms the principle of the efficient level of division of labor (Yang, 1984) which states that this efficient level is determined by equalization between marginal benefit of division of labor and marginal coordination of transaction costs. Also, this model shows that even if the population size is fixed, improvements in coordination efficiency can raise the efficient level of division of labor. It verifies the irrelevance argument of the size of the firm proposed by Cheung, Coase, Stigler, and Young (see chapter 9).

Dixit and Stiglitz (D-S, 1977) developed the first neoclassical general equilibrium model with an endogenous number of consumption goods. They assumed economies of scale, instead of economies of division of labor, and a dichotomy between pure consumers and firms, instead of the new classical framework with consumer-producers. The CES utility function is used to represent consumers' preferences for diverse consumption. The trade-off between economies of scale and consumption variety is specified to endogenize the number of consumption goods and productivity. A large number of goods implies a greater direct positive contribution to utility on the one hand, and on the other hand an indirect negative effect on utility due to a smaller operation scale in producing each good and associated higher prices. As the scale of an economy is increased, the scope for trading off economies of scale against consumption variety is enlarged, so that the number of consumption goods and productivity may increase concurrently. The story is formalized in section 11.10, and the differences between the new classical and neoclassical approaches to endogenizing the number of goods will be further discussed.

In section 11.11, we introduce transaction costs into the the Murphy–Shleifer–Vishny (MSV) model of industrialization to endogenize the duality between the modern sector with economies of scale and the traditional sector with constant returns to scale technology.

---

## Questions to Ask Yourself when Reading this Chapter

♦ What are the differences between the neoclassical and new classical theories of demand?

♦ What are the differences between neoclassical trade theory and new classical trade theory?

♦ Why does evolution in division of labor generate concurrent increases in the following variables: the degree of commercialization; trade dependence; the degree of interpersonal dependence; the extent of the market; the number of types of markets; productivity; the extent of endogenous comparative advantage; the degree of diversity of economic structure; individuals' levels of specialization; the degree of production concentration; and the degree of market integration?

♦ How does international trade emerge from domestic trade?

♦ Why does the development of division of labor create conditions for a greater consumption variety and the emergence of new goods?

♦ What are the differences between neoclassical and new classical approaches to endogenizing the number of goods?

## ◆ 11.2 A New Classical Trade Model with Fixed Learning Costs

### Example 11.1: a new classical trade model with fixed learning cost (Yang, 1996)

As shown in example 9.2 in chapter 9, general equilibrium with the division of labor may not exist if the set of consumer-producers is finite. Hence, we need the assumption that the set of consumer-producers is a continuum. The set of consumer goods is $\{1, 2, ..., m\}$, which is finite. We may assume that the set is a continuum with mass $m$. As will be shown in chapter 13, the assumption of a continuum of goods is not essential for the existence of equilibrium in this kind of model, though it may simplify the algebra of a symmetric model by avoiding integer problems. If the set of goods is considered as a continuum, then symbols $\Sigma$ and $\Pi$ should be considered as integration. If the set of goods is finite, then all derivatives with respect to the number of goods in the first-order condition for maximization should be considered as the approximation of the first-order condition for an integer programming.

Consider an economy with a continuum of *ex ante* identical consumer-producers of mass $M$. The self-provided amount of good i is $x_i$. The amount of good i sold in the market is $x_i^s$. The amount of good i purchased in the market is $x_i^d$. The transaction cost coefficient for a unit of goods bought is $1 - k$. Thus, $kx_i^d$ is the amount an individual obtains when he purchases $x_i^d$. The amount consumed of good i is thus $x_i^c \equiv x_i + kx_i^d$. The utility function is identical for all individuals:

$$u = \prod_{i=1}^{m} x_i^c \tag{11.1}$$

The system of production for each consumer-producer is

$$x_i^p \equiv x_i + x_i^s = \text{Max } \{L_i - A, 0\} \qquad i = 1, ..., m \tag{11.2a}$$

$$\sum_i L_i = 1 \tag{11.2b}$$

where $x_i^p$ is the output level of good i, $L_i$ is an individual's level of specialization in producing good i and $A$ is a fixed learning and training cost in producing each good. This system of production displays economies of specialization for each individual in producing each good. For $L_i > A$, the average labor productivity, $(x_i + x_i^s)/L_i = 1 - (A/L_i)$, increases with an individual's level of specialization in producing good i, $L_i$. All individuals' production conditions exhibit economies of division of labor as shown in chapter 2.

The next subsection investigates how the market sorts out the efficient trade-off between transaction costs and economies of division of labor based on the fixed learning cost.

## ◆ 11.3 How are Demand and Supply Functions Determined by Individuals' Levels of Specialization?

According to the Wen theorem an individual does not simultaneously buy and sell the same good; nor simultaneously buy and self-provide the same good; and she sells at most one good. This implies that the decision configuration of each consumer-producer who sells good i satisfies the following conditions.

$$x_i > 0,\ x_i^s > 0,\ x_i^d > 0,\ L_i > 0 \tag{11.3}$$
$$x_r = x_r^s = L_r = 0,\ x_r^d > 0,\ \forall\ r \in R,$$
$$x_j,\ L_j > 0,\ x_j^s = x_j^d = 0,\ \forall\ j \in J$$

where $R$ is the set of $n-1$ goods that are purchased from the market, and $J$ is the set of $m$-$n$ nontraded goods. In words, the conditions imply the following propositions: for good i that is sold, its self-provided quantity, its quantity for sale, and the level of specialization in producing it are positive while its quantity purchased is 0; for each good r that is purchased, its self-provided quantity, its quantity for sale, and the level of specialization in producing it are 0, while its quantity purchased is positive; for each nontraded good j, its quantity self-provided and amount of labor allocated to produce it are positive, while its quantities sold and bought are 0. According to these conditions, the decision problem of an individual selling good i can be specified as follows.

$$\text{Max: } u_i = x_i^c \prod_{r \in R} x_r^c \prod_{j \in J} x_j^c = x_i \prod_{r \in R} kx_r^d \prod_{j \in J} x_j$$

$$\text{s.t. } x_i^p \equiv x_i + x_i^s = \text{Max}\ \{L_i - A,\ 0\}, \qquad \text{(production function for good i)}$$
$$x_j = x_j^p \equiv x_j = \text{Max}\ \{L_j - A,\ 0\},\ \forall\ j \in J \quad \text{(production function for good j)}$$
$$L_i = \sum_{j \in J} L_j = 1 \qquad\qquad\qquad \text{(endowment constraint for time)}$$
$$p_i x_i^s = \sum_{r \in R} p_r x_r^d \qquad\qquad\qquad \text{(budget constraint)}$$

where $p_i$ is the price of good i, $x_r^c \equiv kx_r^d$ and $x_i^c \equiv x_i$ are respective quantities of goods r and i that are consumed, $x_i,\ x_i^s,\ x_r^d,\ L_i,\ x_j,\ L_j,\ n$ are decision variables. Having inserted all constraints into $u_i$, we can express $u_i$ as a function of $L_i,\ L_j,\ x_i^s,\ x_r^d$, and $n$. One of all $x_r^d$ can be eliminated using the budget constraint, and one of all $L_j$ can be eliminated using the endowment constraint for time. Hence, we can convert the original constrained maximization problem to a nonconstrained maximization problem.

$$\text{Max: } u_i = x_i^c x_s^c \prod_r x_r^c \prod_j x_j^c = x_i kx_s^d (\prod_r kx_r^d)(L_t - A)\prod_j(L_j - A) \tag{11.4}$$

where $x_i^c = x_i = \text{Max}\ [L_i - A,\ 0\} - x_i^s$
$$x_s^d = (p_i x_i^s - \sum_r p_r x_r^d)/p_s \qquad s,\ r \in R,\ s \neq r$$
$$L_i = 1 - Li - \sum_j L_j \qquad t,\ j \in J,\ t \neq j$$

The first-order conditions for problem (11.4) are

$$\partial u_i/\partial x_r^d = 0 \tag{11.5a}$$
$$\partial u_i/\partial x_i^s = 0 \tag{11.5b}$$
$$\partial u_i/\partial L_j = 0 \tag{11.5c}$$
$$\partial u_i/\partial L_i = 0 \tag{11.5d}$$
$$\partial u_i/\partial n = 0 \tag{11.5e}$$

Let us look at (11.5a) first. It implies

$$(\partial u_i/\partial x_s^c)/p_s = (\partial u_i/\partial x_r^c)/p_r \qquad \forall\ s,\ r \in R \tag{11.6a}$$

This is the rule of equal marginal utility of each dollar spent on different consumption goods.

Rearranging the equation yields the equivalent rule that the marginal rate of substitution between goods s and r equals their relative price, or the rule that the relative marginal utility of good r to good s equals their relative price.

$$-(dx_s^c/dx_r^c) = (\partial u_i/\partial x_r^c)/(\partial u_i/\partial x_s^c) = p_r/p_s$$

where the implicit function theorem is used.

Let us next consider the first-order condition (11.5b), which implies

$$(\partial u_i/\partial x_i^c)/p_i = k(\partial u_i/\partial x_r^c)/p_r \tag{11.6b}$$

This in turn implies that the relation (11.6a) does not hold between the good purchased and the good sold since the former involves transaction cost. Hence, (11.6b) is the rule of equal marginal utility of each dollar after transaction cost is deducted.

Next, let us look at (11.5c), which implies

$$(\partial u_i/\partial x_i^c)(dx_i^p/dL_i) = (\partial u_i/\partial x_j^c)(dx_j^p/dL_j), \tag{11.6c}$$

where superscript $p$ stands for the quantity produced and superscript $c$ stands for the quantity consumed. The identities in (11.1) and (11.2), which establish the connections between the quantities produced, self-provided, sold, bought, and consumed, are also used to obtain (11.6c). Let the quantities of labor allocated to the production of goods other than i and j be fixed. Then total differentiation of the time endowment constraint yields $dL_i = -dL_j$. Inserting this into (11.6c) yields

$$-dx_j^c/dx_i^c = (\partial u_i/\partial x_i^c)/(\partial u_i/\partial x_j^c) = -dx_j^p/dx_i^p,$$

where the extreme left end of the equation is the marginal rate of substitution between consumption of goods j and i for a fixed utility level, and the extreme right end of the equation is the marginal rate of transformation between outputs of the two goods for a fixed labor input. Hence, we can interpret (11.6c) as that the marginal rate of substitution in consumption equals the marginal rate of transformation in production.

(11.5d) implies that this decision rule holds not only between good i (sold) and good j (nontraded), but also between different non-traded goods. Since (11.5a) and (11.5d) hold for all $r \in R$ and for all $j \in J$, they can be used to prove that $p_r x_r^d$ is the same for any $r \in R$ and that $x_j$ is the same for any $j \in J$. Using this result, all first-order conditions yield

$$L_i = A + n[1 - (m - n - 1)A]/m \qquad x_i^s = (n - 1)[1 - (m - n - 1)A]/m \tag{11.7a}$$

$$x_i = x_j = [1 - (m - n - 1)A]/m, \qquad L_j = [1 - (m - n + 1)A]/m,$$

$$x_r^d = p_{ir}x_i^s/(n - 1) = p_{ir}[1 - (m - n - 1)A]/m, \ \forall \ r \in R$$

where $p_{ir} \equiv p_i/p_r$. As indicated in chapter 5, the neoclassical supply function in (11.7a) is independent of prices because of the unitary elasticity of substitution of the Cobb–Douglas utility function in this model. Inserting the solution into (11.4) yields the indirect utility function

$$u_i = \alpha\beta = u_i\,(n,\,A,\,k,\,p_{ir}), \tag{11.7b}$$

where $\alpha \equiv \{[1 - (m - n + 1)A]/m\}^m$, $\beta \equiv (kp_i)^{n-1}\,(\Pi_{r\in R}p_r^{-1})$. (11.7) are *neoclassical optimum decisions for a given level of specialization*. Here, an individual's level of specialization in producing the good sold is uniquely determined by the number of traded goods $n$. The neoclassical optimum decision sorts out resource allocation for given prices and a given number of traded goods $n$.

In (11.7), $[1 - (m - n + 1)A]/m$ is per capita output of each good, where $1 - (m - n + 1)A$ is the amount of time allocated for production after total fixed learning cost $(m - n + 1)A$ is deducted. This amount of time is allocated to produce $m - n$ nontraded goods and one good that is sold in exchange for $n - 1$ goods purchased. Hence, this amount is ultimately used to obtain $m$ consumption goods. Since marginal labor productivity of each good is 1, the total output of $m$ goods produced out of the amount of time is $1 - (m - n + 1)A$. Thus, per capita consumption of each good, which equals per capita output of each good, is $[1 - (m - n + 1)A]/m$. As the number of traded goods $n$ increases, the total learning cost incurred in producing $m - n$ nontraded goods, $(m - n)A$, will be reduced, so that the amount of time available for production increases and therefore per capita consumption of each good increases.

$\alpha$ in $u_i$ can be considered as the product of the per capita consumption of all goods, which is an increasing function of $n$, which determines an individual's level of specialization. $k^{n-1}$ in $\beta$ decreases as $n$ increases, since $k$ is between 0 and 1. $\beta$ can then be considered as a term through which utility is reduced by an increase in the number of transactions and related transaction costs.

Since the new classical optimum decision sorts out the optimum level of specialization that relates to $n$, the new classical optimum decisions are given by (11.7) and the following condition

$$(\partial u_i/\partial\alpha)(d\alpha/dn) = -(\partial u_i/\partial\beta)(d\beta/dn) \tag{11.8}$$

Since $n$ can represent an individual's level of specialization in the symmetric model, the left-hand side of the equation is the marginal utility of an individual's level of specialization. The right-hand side is marginal transaction cost in terms of utility loss caused by an increase in an individual's level of specialization. Hence, (11.8) implies that the optimum level of specialization is determined by *equality between marginal benefit of specialization and marginal transaction cost*. This condition for the optimum level of specialization was first proved by Yang (1984) and later confirmed by Becker and Murphy (1992). It is the distinguishing feature of new classical economics. Plugging the optimum value of $n$, given by (11.8), back into (11.7) yields the new classical optimum resource allocation. Hence, (11.7) and (11.8) give the complete new classical optimum decisions, which sort out optimum organization as well as optimum resource allocation.

It should be noted that although (11.8) looks like a marginal condition for an interior solution, it is only an approximation of realistic inframarginal analysis. Strictly speaking, when the set of goods is finite rather than a continuum we need integer programming to solve for the optimum $n$. As $n$ jumps between the integers, all endogenous variables discontinuously jump. More importantly, if the model is asymmetric, we must use marginal analysis to solve for many corner equilibria, and then use total benefit–cost analysis to identify the general equilibrium from among them. If a symmetric model is assumed, a decision to choose one from many configurations, and a procedure to identify one from many structures, turns out to be equivalent to choosing a value of $n$. There are two integer values of $n$, $n_1$ and $n_2$, such that $n_1 < n' < n_2$, where $n'$ is the value of $n$ that is given by (11.8). The optimum value of $n^*$ of the integer programming is determined by Max $\{u(n_1), u(n_2)\}$. But for a large value of $m$, $n'$ is a good approximation of $n^*$. In this text, we will use $n'$ to represent $n^*$ in all symmetric models.

Since all of $n$ traded goods are produced only if all occupations generate the same utility level for the *ex ante* identical individuals, the inframarginal analysis between configurations establishes the utility equalization conditions

$$u_1 = u_2 = u_3 = \ldots = u_n \tag{11.9}$$

(11.8) and (11.9) are completely symmetric between configurations selling different goods. Hence, they hold at the same time only if

$$p_i = p_r \qquad \forall\, i, r = 1, 2, \ldots, n \tag{11.10}$$

and $n$ is the same for all individuals. Using the information about the equilibrium relative prices of traded goods and the equilibrium number of traded goods, each individual's optimum decision can be solved as follows.

$$
\begin{aligned}
n &= m + 1 - (1/A) - [m/\ln(k p_{ir})] \\
L_i &= [1 - (\ln k p_{ir})^{-1} + (A - 1)mA]/(-\ln k p_{ir}) \\
x_i^s &= A[m - (1/A) - (m/\ln k p_{ir})]/(-\ln k p_{ir}) \\
x_i &= x_j = -A/(\ln k p_{ir}) \qquad j \in J \\
x_r^d &= p_{ir}A/(-\ln k p_{ir}) \;\forall\; r \in J \\
u_i &= (k p_{ir})^{m - (1/A) - (m/\ln k p_{ir})}[1 + (1/A) + (m/\ln k p_{ir})]/m
\end{aligned}
\tag{11.11}
$$

where $p_{ir} \equiv p_i/p_r$ is the price of a good sold in terms of a good purchased. Since the optimum values of all decision variables are no longer functions of $n$, we call them *new classical optimum decisions*, which differ from the neoclassical optimum decisions in (11.7). The distinction between the neoclassical decisions and the new classical decisions formalizes Young's idea that demand and supply are two sides of specialization. The optimum decisions that generate individuals' demand and supply are ultimately determined by the optimum level of specialization, $L_i$, which relates to $n$.

## ◆ 11.4 Inframarginal Comparative Statics of Optimum Decisions

As discussed in chapter 4, marginal comparative statics differ from inframarginal comparative statics of optimum decisions. From the neoclassical optimum decisions in (11.7), you can see that the optimum level of specialization $L_i$ and the neoclassical supply function are independent of relative prices. But the new classical optimum level of specialization and the new classical supply function are dependent on prices. The distinction between the decisions before and after the level of specialization is chosen was first noted by Stigler (1951) and received attention later from Rosen (1978).

Suppose that parameters $m$, $A$, and $k$ are fixed. Differentiation of the new classical optimum decisions with respect to the relative price $p_{ir}$ yields

$$dn/dp_{ir} > 0 \qquad dL_i/dp_{ir} > 0 \qquad\qquad\qquad (11.12a)$$

$$dx_i^s/dp_{ir} > 0 \qquad\qquad\qquad\qquad\qquad\qquad\qquad (11.12b)$$

$$dx_i/dp_{ir} = dx_j/dp_{ir} > 0 \qquad\qquad\qquad\qquad\qquad (11.12c)$$

$$dx_i^d/dp_{ir} < 0 \qquad\qquad\qquad\qquad\qquad\qquad\qquad (11.12d)$$

where (11.12b) is called the law of supply, and (11.12d) is called the law of demand. Certainly, the comparative statics of the new classical optimum decisions differ from the comparative statics of the neoclassical optimum decisions given in (11.7). The distinction between the marginal and inframarginal comparative statics of the optimum decisions highlights the point that we cannot really understand demand and supply, if we do not understand individuals' decisions in choosing their levels of specialization. The neoclassical demand and supply functions, and their marginal comparative statics for a given value of $n$, are only a halfway house.

## ◆ 11.5 How is the Level of Division of Labor in Society Determined in the Market?

Assume that the numbers of individuals selling goods i and r are respectively $M_i$ and $M_r$. The *total market supply* of good i is $M_i x_i^s$. The market demand for good r by individuals selling good r is $M_r x_i^d$. The *total market demand* for good i is then $\Sigma_{r \in R} M_r x_i^d$. The market clearing conditions are thus

$$M_i x_i^s = \Sigma_{r \in R} M_r x_i^d, \qquad i = 1, 2, ..., n \qquad\qquad (11.13)$$

This system comprises $n$ equations. One of them is independent of the other $n - 1$ due to Walras's law. The $n - 1$ equations and the population equation $\Sigma_i M_i = M$ determine the numbers of individuals selling $n$ traded goods. The market clearing conditions, together with the utility equalization condition (11.9), yield the final solution of the general equilibrium

$$L_i = [1 - (\ln k)^{-1} + (A - 1)/m]mA/(-\ln k), \qquad\qquad (11.14)$$
$$x_i^s = aA[m - (1/A) - (m/\ln k)]/(-\ln k),$$
$$x_i = x_r^d = x_j = -aA/\ln k, \ \forall \ r \in R, \ \forall \ j \in J$$
$$p_{ir} = 1, \ M_r = M/n, \text{ for } r = 1, ..., n$$
$$u_i = k^{n-1}a[1 - (m - n + 1)A]/m, \text{ for } i=1, ..., n$$
$$n = m + 1 - (1/A) - (m/\ln k)$$

where $i = 1, 2, ..., n$. The equilibrium value of utility can be considered as the *absolute price of labor*. We call $u_i(n)$ in (11.14) the *organization utility function*, which is a function of the number of traded goods, and which relates to an individual's level of specialization and the level of division of labor for society. The organization utility function differs from the indirect utility function since the former is not a function of prices, whereas the latter is a function of the prices of traded goods. Usually, we can work out the analytical expression of the organization utility function only for a completely symmetric model. For asymmetric models, we can only work out the corner equilibrium per capita real income in each structure, where the level and pattern of division of labor, equivalent to $n$ here, is exogenously fixed. Then a total benefit–cost analysis can sort out the equilibrium level and pattern of division of labor. The absolute price of labor is associated with the equilibrium level of division of labor. But the relative prices of traded goods, and the relative numbers of individuals choosing different configurations, are determined by relative tastes and relative production and transaction conditions. A corner equilibrium sorts out resource allocation, relative prices, and numbers of different specialists, while the general equilibrium sorts out the absolute price of labor and the level of division of labor.

Now we assume that individuals' residence locations are exogenously given. They reside at vertices of a grid of triangles with equal sides, as shown in figure 11.1. In order to save transaction costs, each individual will trade first with those closest. But as the number of each individual's traded goods increases, she will trade with those who are further away. Because of symmetry, the number of traded goods, $n$, is the same for all individuals and for society. Thus, there is a local business community around each individual. The members of the local community are trade partners of the individual who sells a good to and buys a good from each of them. Therefore, for $n$ traded goods, each individual has $n - 1$ trade partners, while there are $n$ members of the community.

If the local communities do not overlap, then $M$ individuals will be divided among $N = M/n$ local communities. If the local communities overlap, $N$ is the number of producers of each traded goods and can be considered as a measure of the fragmentation of the economy, since there is no trade between individuals who sell the same good or choose the same configuration (occupation). We may say that Structure B has a higher *level of division of labor* than structure A, if the levels of specialization of all individuals are higher in B than in A and the number of distinct configurations in B is larger than in A. Later, we shall

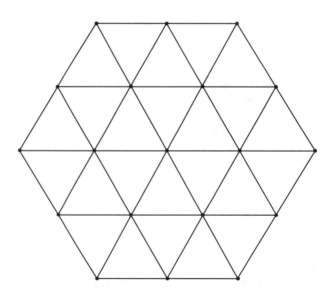

◆ **Figure 11.1:** Evenly dispersed residence location of individuals

show that in the model each individual's optimum level of specialization is an increasing function of her number of traded goods $n$. Also, the number of traded goods is positively related to the number of distinct configurations in a structure. Hence, $n$ represents the level of division of labor for the symmetric model.

Following the approach developed in chapter 6, it can be shown that the general equilibrium is Pareto optimal. For a given value of $n$, a corner equilibrium is allocation efficient, while the general equilibrium is both allocation efficient and organization efficient.

Two points need more attention. It is not difficult to show that the second-order condition for the optimum $n$ is satisfied. That is, the second order derivative of $u_i$ in (11.4) with respect to $n$ is negative. Also, it can be shown that the partial derivative of $u_i$ with respect to $n$ is always negative for any positive $n$ if $k$ is sufficiently close to 0. According to the Kuhn–Tucker theorem, this implies that the equilibrium level of division of labor will be its minimum value, $n = 1$, which means that the number of goods purchased $n - 1 = 0$ (autarky), if $k$ is sufficiently close to 0.

The second point to note is the problem of multiple equilibria. Because of symmetry, which bundle of goods to be traded is indeterminate in equilibrium. Hence, $n$ combinations of $m$ factors generate many general equilibria with the same per capita real income and the same value of $n$ but with different bundles of traded goods. There are still more possible general equilibria, since who specializes in producing which good is indeterminate too. Exchanges of choices of configurations between each pair of different specialists will generate more general equilibria with the same value of $n$ and the same per capita real income, but with different choices of configuration by each individual. Finally, the case in which the number of traded goods for society does not equal each individual's number of traded goods may incur more general equilibria with the same per capita real income. Figure 11.2a shows an example of the case where individual 1 sells good 1 to individual 2 who sells good 2 to individual 3 who sells good 3 to individual 1. Each individual in this structure trades two goods, but the whole society trades three goods. For the symmetric model, the equilibrium in this structure generates the same per capita real income as does the structure in figure 11.2b.

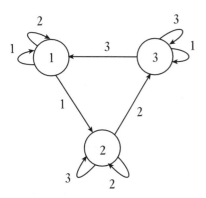

(a) Different individuals trade
different bundles of goods

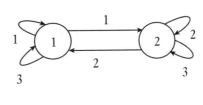

(b) All individuals trade
the same bundle of goods

◆ **Figure 11.2:** Multiple general equilibria

For the symmetric static model, the two types of structures have symmetric properties of equilibrium except that in the case of figure 11.2a the number of traded goods for an individual is smaller than that for society. Since the comparative statics of general equilibrium is easier to handle for those structures with an equal number of traded goods for each individual and for society, we focus on this type of structure. A slight difference in tastes or in production and transaction conditions between different goods will rule out the first type and third type of multiplicity of general equilibrium. A slight difference in taste and/ or production and transaction conditions between individuals will rule out the second type of multiplicity of general equilibrium.

## ◆ 11.6 Inframarginal Comparative Statics of General Equilibrium and Many Concurrent Economic Phenomena

Since to choose a structure of division of labor is also to choose a certain network of transactions, many economic phenomena can be generated by inframarginal comparative statics of the general equilibrium as different aspects of the size and structural features of the network of division of labor. Hence, we first examine the change in the equilibrium level of division of labor, $n$, in response to changes in trading efficiency, $k$, and in fixed learning cost, $A$. Differentiation of the equilibrium value of $n$ in (11.14) yields

$$\mathrm{d}n/\mathrm{d}k > 0 \qquad \mathrm{d}n/\mathrm{d}A > 0. \qquad (11.15)$$

This implies that the equilibrium level of division of labor increases as trading efficiency is improved or as the fixed learning cost increases.

Applying the envelope theorem (see section 3.3 in chapter 3) to $u$ in (11.4) with respect to parameters $k$ and $A$ yields

$$\mathrm{d}u/\mathrm{d}k = \partial u/\partial k > 0, \qquad \mathrm{d}u/\mathrm{d}A = \partial u/\partial A < 0. \qquad (11.16)$$

(11.15) implies that there are two different ways to increase the equilibrium level of division of labor. The first is to improve trading efficiency and the second is to increase the fixed learning cost of each activity. 11.16 first approach increases while the second decreases per capita real income as they raise the level of division of labor. You may relate the first method to the development of an efficient banking system, improvement of the legal system, government liberalization policies, and urbanization, all of which reduce the transaction costs coefficient $1 - k$. You may relate the second method to a stiff licence fee and other entry barriers that decrease per capita real income and increase the equilibrium level of division of labor.

Figure 11.3 gives an intuitive illustration of the inframarginal comparative statics of general equilibrium where the number of goods and the population are assumed to be 4. The lines denote goods flows. The small arrows indicate the directions of goods flows. The numbers beside the lines signify the goods involved. A circle with the number i denotes a person selling good i. Panel (a) illustrates the case of autarky, where each person self-provides 4 goods, due to an extremely low trading efficiency. Panel (b) shows how an improvement in trading efficiency leads to partial division of labor, where each person sells

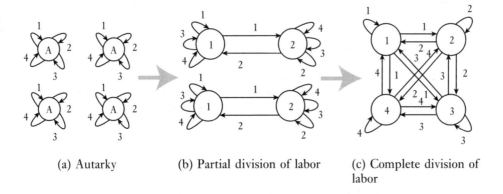

(a) Autarky            (b) Partial division of labor          (c) Complete division of
labor

♦ **Figure 11.3**: Exogenous evolution in division of labor

one good, buys one good, trades two goods, and self-provides three goods. Panel (c) shows
how a very high trading efficiency results in complete division of labor, where each person
sells and self-provides one good, buys three goods, and trades four goods.

If we suppose that the trading efficiency coefficient $k$ continuously and exogenously
evolves from 0 to 1, then the inframarginal comparative statics of general equilibrium
predict that the equilibrium level of division of labor will evolve as illustrated in figure
11.3. This exogenous evolution in division of labor differs from the exogenous evolution of
productivity and per capita real income generated by an exogenous change in the total
factor productivity parameter in the Solow model (1956), which is a state equation that
does not involve individual decision-making. In our model the exogenous evolution in
division of labor is based on individuals' decisions in choosing their levels of specialization
and on interactions between those decisions. Also, this evolution generates the following
concurrent development phenomena and structural changes:

## Concurrent increases in each person's level of specialization, degree of commercialization, and trade dependence, and a decrease in the degree of self-sufficiency, as results of an increase in the level of division of labor.

Each individual's level of specialization, $L_i$ is given in (11.7) and (11.14). It is not difficult
to see that

$$dL_i/dk = (dL_i/dn)(dn/dk) > 0, \tag{11.17}$$

where $dL_i/dn = [1 - (m - 2n + 1)A]/m > [1 - (m - n + 1)A]/m > 0$. The last inequality
can be obtained by inserting the equilibrium value of $n$ into the expression of the derivative. $dn/dk > 0$ is given by (11.16a).

In this simple model, the amount of labor allocated to producing a good can be considered as the price of the good in terms of labor. Hence, the equilibrium value of $L_i$ is a
measure not only of each individual's level of specialization, but also of the value, in terms
of labor, of commercialized consumption, which equals her income from the market. The
total value of consumption, including self-provided consumption and consumption from

the market, in terms of labor is 1. Thus, the ratio of commercialized consumption to total consumption, which is called the *degree of commercialization*, is $L_i/1 = L_i$. Also, *trade dependence* can be defined by total trade volume divided by total income including commercialized and self-provided income. It is not difficult to see that the degree of trade dependence equals two times the degree of commercialization in the simple model, since trade volume equals double commercialized income. (11.17) implies that the degrees of commercialization and trade dependence increase as an improvement in trading efficiency raises the level of division of labor. $(1 - L_i)/1 = 1 - L_i$ is the *degree of self-sufficiency*, which is defined as the ratio of the value of self-provided income to total income. Thus (11.17) shows the negative relationship between the degree of self-sufficiency and trading efficiency.

### The extent of the market and the level of division of labor are two sides of the same coin (Young, 1928).

Let $E$ denote the *extent of the market*; then $E$ equals the product of population size and per capita aggregate demand. *An individual's aggregate demand* is the total demand of that individual for all traded goods. *Market aggregate demand* is the sum of all individuals' aggregate demand for all traded goods. It is what we call the extent of the market and it differs from total market demand for a particular good. Total market demand for a good is a microeconomic or disaggregated concept, while market aggregate demand is a macroeconomic concept, which relates to the level of division of labor and the related size of the market network. From (11.7) and (11.14), the extent of the market can be calculated as follows.

$$E = Mx_i^s = M(n - 1)[1 - (m - n + 1)A]/m \qquad (11.18)$$
$$dE/dk = (dE/dn)(dn/dk) > 0$$

(11.15) and (11.18) imply that the equilibrium extent of the market and the equilibrium level of division of labor increase concurrently as trading efficiency is improved. Smith (1776) proposed the conjecture that the level of division of labor is determined by the extent of the market, which is in turn determined by trading efficiency. Some economists have misinterpreted this as meaning that division of labor is determined by the size of an economy (population size or resource size). Young (1928) criticized this interpretation. According to him, the extent of the market is determined not only by population size, but also by per capita effective demand, which is determined by income, which is determined by productivity, which is in turn determined by the level of division of labor. The interdependence between the level of division of labor and the extent of the market is analogous to the interdependence between prices and quantities demanded and supplied. The notion of general equilibrium is a powerful vehicle to sort out the mechanism that simultaneously determines the interdependent endogenous variables. In our new classical general equilibrium model, the equilibrium level of division of labor and the equilibrium extent of the market are two sides of the equilibrium size of the market network. They are simultaneously determined by trading efficiency. The driving force of the mechanism is, of course, the trade-off between economies of division of labor and transaction costs. Later, we shall use dynamic general equilibrium models to show that a dynamic mechanism may generate endogenous evolution in division of labor in the absence of exogenous changes in parameters.

## Productivity progress

The labor productivity of traded and nontraded goods, $x_i^s/L_i$ and $x_j^s/L_j$, can be worked out from (11.14). It can be shown that

$$d(x_i^s/L_i)/dk > 0, \qquad d(x_j/L_j)/dk > 0. \tag{11.19}$$

This implies that labor productivity increases as improvements in trading efficiency drive the evolution of division of labor. This formalizes Smith's thought that productivity progress and national wealth are generated by evolution in division of labor. The productivity implications of division of labor should be at the core of mainstream economics. Hence, if we formalize classical economic thought about the implications of division of labor within the new classical framework, then trade theory, which is concerned with trade dependence, and growth theory, which is concerned with productivity progress, are two aspects of the core of economics.

## Evolution in endogenous comparative advantage.

We define the *extent of endogenous comparative advantage* as the difference in productivity of a good between its sellers and its buyers. Since in our model the buyer of a good stops producing it, her labor productivity of that good is zero. But a seller's labor productivity of the good increases as trading efficiency is improved, as indicated in (11.19). Hence, the extent of endogenous comparative advantage increases as improvements in trading efficiency drive division of labor to evolve. This has formalized Smith's idea that the difference in productivity between a specialist and a novice is a consequence rather than the cause of division of labor.

## Development of diversity of economic structure and of interpersonal dependence.

From the foregoing comparative statics of general equilibrium, you can see that when individuals choose autarky, all individuals' configurations of production and consumption are the same, their productivities in all activities are the same, and thus there is no diversity of economic structure. As improvements in trading efficiency drive division of labor to evolve, the number of distinct configurations (occupations) and kinds of markets increase. As the degree of self-sufficiency falls, each pair of different specialists share a progressively smaller number of common self-provided production activities, so that the degree of difference between each pair of individuals choosing different configurations increases. We define the *degree of diversity* by reference to the degree of this difference and the number of different traded goods, $n$. We define the *degree of interpersonal dependence* as the number of trading partners for each individual, which is $n - 1$. Hence both the degree of diversity of economic structure and the degree of interpersonal dependence increase as division of labor evolves.

## Increases in the degree of production concentration and in the degree of market integration.

In the symmetric model, the number of producers of each traded good is $N = M/n$, where $M$ is population size and $n$ is the number of traded goods. The number of separate local business communities is also $N = M/n$. The *degree of production concentration* can then be defined as $1/N = n/M$. The *degree of market integration* can also be defined by $1/N$. Hence, the degrees of production concentration and market integration increase as improvements in trading efficiency raise the equilibrium level of division of labor $n$.

The inframarginal comparative statics of general equilibrium can be summarized in the following proposition

**Proposition 11.1:** As trading efficiency is improved, the level of division of labor increases. The following concurrent phenomena are different aspects of the evolution in division of labor. Each individual's levels of specialization, productivity, and trade dependence increase. The degree of commercialization, the extent of endogenous comparative advantage, the degrees of production concentration and market integration, and the degree of diversity of economic structure all increase. The number of traded goods and the number of markets increase, while the degree of self-sufficiency falls.

## ◆ 11.7 Emergence of International Trade from Domestic Trade

Now we use our model to address the question: Why and how does international trade emerge from domestic trade and what is the distinctive contribution of our framework to trade theory? Suppose there are 100 countries in the world and the population size of each country is 10 million. Assume further that the number of goods $m$ and the population size of the world are both one billion, and that trading efficiency is infinitesimally greater for trade within the same country than for trade across countries. Then our theory tells a story of trade as follows. If trading efficiency is extremely low, then autarky for each person is equilibrium and therefore domestic and international trade are not needed. If trading efficiency is improved such that the equilibrium $n = 1,000$, then 10,000 local markets emerge from the division of labor in each country. The equilibrium number of business communities is $M/n$ where $M$ is the population size of the economy and $n$ is the number of traded goods as well as the population size of a local business community. Each member of a local business community sells one traded good to the other 999 individuals and buys one traded good from each of them. Under the assumption that trade occurs first with those closest, there is no trade between the local communities and therefore a national market does not exist. Suppose that trading efficiency is further improved such that $n^* = 10,000,000$. Then the national market emerges from the higher level of division of labor, but international trade does not exist. As $n^*$ increases to 100 million due to an improvement in trading efficiency, such as caused by the innovation of the steam engine, the world will be divided into ten common markets. In each of these, ten countries have an integrated market and international trade emerges from domestic trade, but no trade occurs between the ten common markets. However, if trading efficiency becomes extremely high, then an integrated world market will emerge from the complete division of labor.

The difference between this story and the one from neoclassical theory is obvious. For a neoclassical model with constant returns to scale, international trade instead of autarky is the equilibrium in the absence of government intervention if exogenous comparative advantages exist. For the Dixit–Stiglitz model with economies of scale, international trade instead of autarky is always the equilibrium in the absence of government intervention. But for our model autarky for each individual or for each country may be the equilibrium in the absence of government intervention. In other words, in neoclassical theory the gains from international trade are exogenously given either by exogenous comparative advantages or by economies of scale, whereas in our model the gains from international trade, and the degree of involvement in international trade, are endogenized.

## ◆ 11.8 Co-movement of Division of Labor and Consumption Variety

This section uses a new classical model with an endogenous number of consumer goods and fixed learning costs to illustrate the general equilibrium mechanism that simultaneously determines the network size of division of labor, the number of traded goods, and the number of all goods (including nontraded ones).

### Example 11.2: a new classical model with the CES utility function (Yang, 1996)

The production functions and time endowment constraint for each consumer-producer are the same as in the previous sections.

$$x_i^p \equiv x_i + x_i^s = \text{Max } \{l_i - A,0\} \qquad i = 1, 2, ..., m \qquad (11.20)$$
$$\sum_{i=1}^{m} l_i = 1 \qquad l_i \in [0,1]$$

where $l_i$ is an individual's level of specialization in producing good i. Different from the previous sections, m, the number of consumption goods, is each individual's decision variable rather than a given parameter.

We assume that the calculation of the optimum decision will generate more disutility as the number of first-order conditions for the optimum decision increases with the number of consumption goods m. This disutility is referred to as the *management cost of consumption variety*. Let c be the management cost coefficient of a particular consumption good, measured as a fraction of utility that is lost. The total management cost of m consumption goods in terms of the fraction of utility that is lost is then cm. This implies that the fraction of utility that is ultimately enjoyed from the consumption of m goods is $(1 - cm)$. Hence, each individual's utility function is:

$$V = (1 - cm)u, \qquad u = \left[ \sum_{i=1}^{m} (x_i^c)^\rho \right]^{\frac{1}{\rho}} \qquad (11.21)$$

where $x_i^c \equiv x_i + kx_i^d$. Following the method introduced in subsection 5.5, we can calculate the elasticity of substitution between any pair of consumption goods as $1/(1 - \rho)$. $1/\rho$ represents the degree of economies of complementarity between each pair of consumption goods, or the degree of economies of consumption variety. Taking account of the Wen theorem and the budget constraint, each consumer-producer's decision problem is

$$\text{Max: } V_i = (1 - cm)u_i, \qquad u_i = \left[ x_i^p + \sum_{r \in R} (kx_r^d)^\rho + \sum_{j \in J} x_j^\rho \right]^{\frac{1}{\rho}} \qquad (11.22)$$

s.t. $x_i + x_i^s = \text{Max } \{l_i - A,0\}, \; x_j = \text{Max } \{l_j - A,0\} \; \forall \, j \in J$  (production function)
$\quad l_i + \sum_{j \in J} l_j = 1$  (endowment constraint)
$\quad p_i x_i^s = \sum_{r \in R} p_r x_r^d$  (budget constraint)

where $p_i$ is the price of good i, and $x_i$, $s_i^s$, $x_r^d$, $l_i$, $x_j$, $l_j$, $n$, $m$ are decision variables. Each decision variable can be zero or a positive value. $R$ is the set of goods purchased and $J$ is the set of nontraded goods. From the decision problem the individual's level of specialization, her demand and supply functions, and her indirect utility function can be solved as follows.

$$l_i = \{(n-1)[1 - A(m-n)] + K\}/[n - 1 + (m - n + 1)K] \tag{11.23}$$
$$x_i^s = (n-1)[1 - A(m-n+1)]/[n - 1 + K(m-n+1)]$$
$$x_i = x_r^d = x_j = K[1 - A(m - n + 1)]/[n - 1 + K(m - n + 1)], \ \forall \ r \in R, \ \forall \ j \in J$$
$$n = 1 + \{(A - c)(1 - K) + \rho[A - (1 - K^2)^2]\}/cA(1 + \rho)(1 - K)$$
$$m = [A + c\rho(1 - K)]/c(1 + \rho)$$
$$V_i = (1 - cm)(akp_i/p_r)[1 - A(m - n + 1)][n - 1 + K(m - n + 1)]^{(1-\rho)/\rho}$$

where $K \equiv (p_r/kp_i)^{\rho/(1-\rho)}$ is a decreasing function of $p_i$ and $k$ and an increasing function of $p_r$, good i is sold and good r is purchased. Note that the demand and supply functions in (11.23) are neoclassical demand and supply functions if $n$ is exogenously given, but are new classical demand and supply functions if $n$ is endogenized. In exercise 1, you are asked to work out the own-price elasticity of the neoclassical and new classical demand and supply functions, and to examine the differences between these functions.

The utility equalization and market clearing conditions

$$V_1 = V_2 = \cdots V_n$$
$$M_i x_i^s = \Sigma_{r \in R} M_r x_i^d \text{ for all } i = 2, 3, \cdots, n$$

and the population equation $\Sigma_i M_i = M$ yield:

$$p_i/p_r = 1 \qquad i, r = 1, 2, \cdots, n$$
$$M_i = M_r = M/n, \qquad i, r = 1, 2, \cdots, n.$$

Inserting the equilibrium values of the relative prices of traded goods into the optimum decision (11.23) yields the equilibrium values of the endogenous variables. Let $K = (p_r/kp_i)^{\rho/(1-\rho)} = k^{\rho/(\rho-1)}$ in (11.23). Then (11.23) becomes the equilibrium values of an individual's optimum decisions.

Differentiation of the equilibrium values of the number of consumption goods $m$ and the number of traded goods $n$ (which represents the level of division of labor) with respect to transaction efficiency $k$ and the management cost coefficient of consumption variety $c$ yields the main results of the inframarginal comparative statics of general equilibrium.

$$dn^*/dk > 0, \qquad dn^*/dc < 0 \tag{11.24a}$$
$$dm^*/dk > 0, \qquad dm^*/dc < 0, \qquad dm/d\rho < 0, \tag{11.24b}$$
$$d(m^* - n^*)/dk < 0, \qquad d(m^* - n^*)/dc > 0, \tag{11.24c}$$
$$d(cm^*)/dk > 0, \qquad d(cm^*)/dc < 0, \tag{11.24d}$$

where $cm^*$ is the fraction of utility that is lost because of the management costs of consumption variety. It is an interesting result that total management cost $cm^*$ increases as the management cost coefficient $c$ decreases. This implies that management cost as a proportion of real income increases as management efficiency is improved.

(11.24a,b) implies that the equilibrium number of traded goods (or the level of division of labor), $n$, and the equilibrium number of all consumption goods, $m$, increase concurrently as transaction efficiency, $k$, and/or management efficiency, $1/c$, is improved. (11.24c) implies that $n$ increases more quickly than $m$ does, so that the number of traded goods will eventually equal the number of all consumption goods; that is, all goods are eventually involved in the division of labor as transaction efficiency and/or management efficiency are continuously improved.

Let us now consider the second-order conditions for the interior solutions of $n$ and $m$. The second-order condition for a non-constrained maximization problem (see chapter 3 or Chiang, 1984) is:

$$\partial^2 V / \partial n^2 < 0, \qquad \partial^2 V / \partial m^2 < 0, \tag{11.25a}$$

$$(\partial^2 V / \partial n^2)(\partial^2 V / \partial m^2) - (\partial^2 V / \partial n \partial m) > 0, \tag{11.25b}$$

where $m$ and $n$ are valued at their equilibrium values. Let $p_i/p_r = 1$ in (11.23); then differentiation of $V$ with respect to $n$ and $m$ indicates that (11.25a) holds when $m$ and $n$ equal their equilibrium values. But, for $p_i/p_r = 1$ and the equilibrium values of $m$ and $n$, (11.25b) holds if and only if

$$f(k, \rho) \equiv k - [\rho/(1 + \rho - \rho^2)]^{(1+\rho)2\rho} > 0 \tag{11.26}$$

where $\partial f / \partial \rho < 0$. This implies that the second-order condition holds only if the degree of economies of consumption variety (or of complementarity between consumption goods), $1/\rho$, is sufficiently great in comparison with transaction efficiency. If economies of consumption variety are not significant, then the equilibrium $m$ takes on one of the two corner values, either $m = n$ or $m = \infty$. Since $m = \infty$ is incompatible with the endowment constraint, the general equilibrium entails $m = n$ if economies of consumption variety are not significant, or if the second-order condition is not satisfied.

If $m = n$, then (11.23) and (11.24) become irrelevant. For this case, in order to determine the general equilibrium and its comparative statics, we should first let $m = n$ in each individual's decision problem, and then solve for each individual's optimum decision. It can be shown that if (11.26) does not hold, or if economies of consumption variety are not significant in comparison to transaction efficiency, then the general equilibrium and its inframarginal comparative statics are given as follows:

$$m^* = n^* = [(1 - \rho)/c] + \rho(1 - k^{\rho/(\rho-1)}) \tag{11.27}$$
$$dm^*/dk > 0, \qquad dm^*/dc < 0.$$

(11.24), (11.26), and (11.27) together imply that as transaction efficiency $k$ and/or management efficiency $1/c$ are improved, the equilibrium level of division of labor, $n$, and the equilibrium number of all consumption goods, $m$, increase concurrently, with the former increasing more quickly than the latter, so that all goods are eventually traded and the complete division of labor will be achieved. If economies of consumption variety are not significant in comparison to transaction efficiency, the number of traded goods always equals the number of all consumption goods. They simultaneously increase as transaction efficiency and management efficiency are improved.

Figure 11.4 gives an intuitive illustration of the inframarginal comparative statics of general equilibrium.

(a) Autarky, $n = 1$, $m = 2$                    (b) Partial division of labor with $n = 2$, $m = 3$

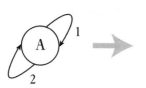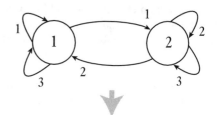

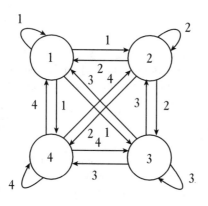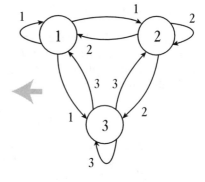

(d) Complete division of labor                (c) Complete division of labor
with $n = m = 4$                              with $n = m = 3$

◆ **Figure 11.4:** Emergence of new technology and new consumption goods

## ◆ 11.9 Trade-off between Economies of Specialization and Coordination Costs

### Example 11.3: the Becker–Murphy model of endogenous specialization (1992)

Consider a production team consisting of $n$ *ex ante* identical agents. This team undertakes a continuum of activities with mass 1 to produce good y. The production function of y is

$$Y = \text{Min}_{s \in [0, 1]} \ Y(s), \tag{11.28a}$$

where $Y(s)$ is the contribution of activity $s$ to the final output $Y$. The Leontief relationship between $Y$ and $Y(s)$ implies that each activity is essential for obtaining the final output. Each team member has a production function in activity $s$

$$Y(s) = A T_h^{\theta}(s) T_w^{1-\theta}(s), \tag{11.28b}$$

where $T_h(s)$ is her total amount of time devoted to acquiring activity-specific skills and $T_w(s)$ is that devoted to the production in activity $s$. Each agent is endowed with one unit of time. This implies that if each agent disperses her limited time among many activities, duplicated investment in acquiring activity-specific skills will generate inefficient aggregate output. Hence, in an efficient team, each team member specializes in a certain range of activities that are different from other members' activities. Suppose that the number of agents in the team is $n$, then each member undertakes a range of activities with measure $1/n$. Therefore (11.28b) is the production function of the agent who specializes in activity s as well as the team's aggregate production function in this activity.

Let each agent's total amount of time allocated to learning and production in each activity be $T(s)$. Then each person's time endowment constraint is $(1/n)T(s) = 1$, where $1/n$ is her range of activities. This implies that $T(s) = n$. Hence, each agent will maximize (11.28b) subject to the time endowment constraint $T_h(s) + T_w(s) = T(s) = n$. The optimum solution of this decision problem, together with the production function (11.28a) yields

$$Y^* = B(n) \equiv An\theta^\theta(1 - \theta)^{1-\theta}. \tag{11.29}$$

Hence, the optimum aggregate final output of the team is an increasing function of the team size $n$. But a larger team size generates greater coordination cost. Assume that the coordination cost in terms of final output among team members is

$$C(n), \qquad C'(.) > 0, \qquad C''(n) > 0, \tag{11.30}$$

Then the optimum team size can be determined by maximizing the net output $B(n) - C(n)$. The first-order condition is

$$dB(n)/dn = dC(n)/dn; \tag{11.31}$$

that is, the marginal benefit of division of labor equals the marginal coordination cost. Here, $1/n$ is the scope of each team member's activities and $n$ can be interpreted as each team member's level of specialization as well as the level of division of labor within the team. Suppose $C(n) = cn^2$. The efficient team size given by (11.31) is $n = \alpha/2c$, where $\alpha \equiv A\theta^\theta(1 - \theta)^{1-\theta}$. This result implies that even if the population size for the society is fixed, the level of division of labor increases as transaction condition is improved ($c$ decreases). Suppose the population size is $M$. Then for a very large $c$, the efficient team size $n = \alpha/2c$ is small, so that the economy is divided as a large number ($M/n$) of separated teams. There is no connection between the teams. As $c$ decreases, the efficient team size increases and the separate teams merge into an increasingly integrated coordination network. As Becker and Murphy (1992) indicate, the relationships between the members within the same team could be either relationships within a firm or market relationships between firms. Dynamic versions of this model of endogenous specialization can be found in Tamura (1991, 1992).

### ◆ 11.10 A Neoclassical Model Endogenizing the Number of Consumption Goods on the Basis of the Trade-off between Economies of Scale and Consumption Variety

The Dixit and Stiglitz (D-S) model (1977) is the first neoclassical general equilibrium model that endogenizes the number of consumption goods on the basis of the trade-off between economies of scale and consumption variety. The story behind this kind of model can be told as follows. Consider an economy in which pure consumers prefer diverse consumption, while there are global economies of scale for pure producers (firms) in the production of each good. With the CES utility function, each good is not a necessity individually, so that the number of consumption goods is endogenized in equilibrium despite the fact that each pure consumer will choose as many consumption goods as possible. A larger number of consumption goods implies, on the one hand, a higher level of direct utility because of the preference for diverse consumption; but on the other hand it may imply a lower level of indirect utility because of the higher prices of goods that are associated with smaller scales of production. The trade off between economies of scale and consumption variety can be used to endogenize the number of consumption goods. As the size of the economy is increased, the scope for the market to trade off economies of scale against consumption variety is enlarged, so that the number of goods and per capita real income may increase concurrently.

If the increase in the size of the economy is interpreted as the merging of two countries into an integrated market, or as the *ad hoc* opening of international trade between the two countries, then the comparative statics of the neoclassical general equilibrium can be used to explore the implications of international trade for welfare and consumption variety. We now use the following figure to illustrate the story.

In figure 11.5 there are two countries: Japan and the US. In each country, there are two individuals. Circles 1 and 2 are two Japanese and circles 3 and 4 are two Americans. In panel (a), there is no international trade between the two countries, and in each country there are two firms producing goods x and y, respectively. Each of the two firms sells its produce to each and every domestic consumer, and hires one worker. In panel (b), the two countries have merged to form an integrated market where a Japanese firm sells good x to each and every consumer in both countries, an American firm sells good y to each and every consumer in both countries, and a multi-national firm sells a new good z to each and every consumer in both countries. Firm x hires 4/3 Japanese, firm y hires 4/3 Americans, and firm z hires 2/3 Japanese and 2/3 Americans. Hence, the average size of the firm in panel (b) is larger than in panel (a). This implies that the productivity of each firm in panel (b) is higher than in panel (a) because of global economies of scale in production. Also, each consumer in panel (b) consumes three goods, while each consumer in panel (a) consumes only two goods. Hence, international trade may increase per capita real income through two possible channels. It may increase the number of consumption goods for each consumer, and it may improve productivity and thereby reduce prices of all goods through the utilization of economies of scale.

Gains from trade can arise between two *ex ante* identical countries in the absence of exogenous comparative advantage in technology and in endowments, and in the absence of differences in tastes between them. However, in order to realize those gains from trade, the two countries have to accept the shifting of workers between different sectors, which may cause temporary unemployment in the transitional period. For instance, a Japanese who, in

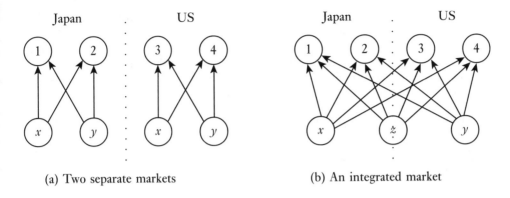

(a) Two separate markets                    (b) An integrated market

◆ **Figure 11.5:** Endogenous number of consumption goods and economies of scale

panel (a), produces good y before international trade is opened up, will lose her job as a producer of good y and take a new job in producing good z or x after international trade is opened up in panel (b). Symmetrically, an American who produces good x before the opening of international trade will lose her job as a producer of good x and take a new job to produce good z or y after the opening of international trade. Suppose the government, or some interest group, does not want to see the emergence of the new sector, and the associated reallocation of labor, because it generates temporary unemployment in the transitional period. If the Japanese government implements an interventionist policy to protect the firm producing good y from bankruptcy caused by international trade, or if an American interest group successfully lobbies the congress to implement a similar policy, then coordination failure in utilizing the gains from international trade will take place. The function of the market, and of a liberalization policy that allows the market fully to play its role, is to avoid such coordination failure.

### Example 11.4 (Yang, 1994): an extended Dixit–Stiglitz (D-S) model with transaction costs

Consider an economy with $M$ identical consumers. Each of them has the following neoclassical decision problem for consumption.

Max: $u = (\sum_{i=1}^{n} x_i^{\rho})^{1/\rho}$                    (utility function)

s.t. $\sum_{i=1}^{n} (1 + t)p_i x_i = 1$                    (budget constraint)

where $p_i$ is the price of good i in terms of labor, $x_i$ is the amount of good i that is consumed, $t$ is an *ad valorem* tax rate for goods purchased, which can be considered as a transaction cost coefficient, $n$ is the number of consumption goods, $\rho \in (0, 1)$ is the parameter of elasticity of substitution between each pair of consumption goods, and $u$ is utility level. It is assumed that each consumer is endowed with one unit of labor, which is the *numéraire*. Hence, each consumer's income from selling one unit of labor is 1, her expenditure on good i is $p_i x_i$, and her total expenditure is $\sum_{i=1}^{n} (1 + t)p_i x_i$. Each consumer is a price taker and her decision variable is $x_i$. It is assumed that the elasticity of substitution

$1/(1-\rho) > 1$. It is easy to see that if the quantity of each good consumed is the same, then utility is an increasing function of the number of consumption goods. That is, $u = (nx_i^\rho)^{1/\rho}$ and $du/dn = (1/\rho)n^{(1-\rho)/\rho}x_i > 0$. We need the assumption $\rho \in (0, 1)$ since for $\rho < 0$ which implies $1/(1-\rho) < 1$, utility will be a decreasing function of the number of consumption goods, indicating that individuals do not prefer diverse consumption. The first-order conditions for the consumer's decision problem are:

$$(\partial u/\partial x_i)/(\partial u/\partial x_j) = p_i/p_j \text{ and} \tag{11.32a}$$

$$\sum_{i=1}^{n}(1 + t)p_i x_i = 1. \tag{11.32b}$$

Concretely, (11.32a) is:

$$p_i x_i = p_j^{1/(1-\rho)}x_j p_i^{-\rho/(1-\rho)}.$$

Summing up the two sides of the equation with respect to $i$, and using the budget constraint (11.32b), yields

$$1/(1 + t) = \sum_i p_i x_i = p_j^{1/(1-\rho)}x_j \sum_i p_i^{-\rho/(1-\rho)}.$$

From this equation, the demand function for good $j$ can then be solved.

$$x_j = 1/(1 + t)[p_j^{1/(1-\rho)}\sum_i p_i^{\rho/(\rho-1)}] = 1/np(1 + t), \tag{11.33}$$

where the second equation is obtained by using the symmetry condition $p_j = p_i$ for all $i, j = 1, 2, ..., n$. This can be expressed as

$$\ln x_j = -[\ln p_j/(1 - \rho)] - \ln\sum_i p_i^{\rho/(\rho-1)} - \ln(1 + t). \tag{11.33b}$$

Hence, the own price elasticity of demand for good j is

$$\partial \ln x_j/\partial \ln p_j = -[1/(1 - \rho] - \partial \ln\sum_i p_i^{\rho/(\rho-1)}/\partial \ln p_j$$
$$= -[1/(1-\rho)] - \{[\rho/(\rho - 1)]p_j^{1/(\rho-1)}/\sum_i p_i^{\rho/(\rho-1)}\},$$

where $\sum_i p_i^{\rho/(\rho-1)}$ includes one $p_j$. Using the symmetry condition $p_j = p_i$ for all $i, j = 1, 2, ..., n$ again, we obtain the Yang–Heijdra (1993) formula for the own price elasticity of demand in the D-S model:

$$\partial \ln x_i/\partial \ln p_i = -[1/(1-\rho)] + [\rho/(1 - \rho)n] = -(n - \rho)/(1 - \rho)n. \tag{11.34}$$

Dixit–Stiglitz (1977) made an *ad hoc* assumption that the number of goods is infinitely large and accordingly ignored the term $\rho/(1 - \rho)n$, so that their expression for the elasticity is $-1/(1 - \rho)$. This assumption is not legitimate since the number of goods in this model is endogenous and it is very large only for a certain range of parameter values. With their formula for the own price elasticity of demand, the negative effect of international trade on prices cannot be figured out.

Next, we consider the pure producers' decision problems. Because of global increasing returns to scale, only one firm can survive in the market for a good. If there are two firms producing the same good, one of them can always increase output to reduce price by utilizing further economies of scale, thereby driving the other firm out of the market. Therefore, the monopolist can manipulate the interaction between quantity and price to choose a profit maximizing price. Free entry into each sector is however assumed. Free entry will drive to zero the profit of a marginal firm that has the lowest profit. Any positive profit of the marginal firm will invite a potential entrepreneur to set up a new firm to produce a differentiated good. For a symmetric model, this condition implies zero profit for all firms. This significantly simplifies the algebra and makes the D-S model popular.

Assume that the production function of good j is

$$X_j = (L_j - a)/b,$$

so that the labor cost function of good j is

$$L_j = bX_j + a \tag{11.35}$$

The first-order condition for the monopolist to maximize profit with respect to output level and price implies that

$$MR = p_j[1 + 1/(\partial \ln x_i/\partial \ln p_i)] = MC = b$$

where MR and MC stand for marginal revenue and marginal cost, respectively. Inserting the expression for the own price elasticity of demand $\partial \ln x_i/\partial \ln p_i$, given in (11.34), into the first-order condition yields

$$p_j = b/\rho(n - 1)(n - \rho). \tag{11.36a}$$

The zero profit condition implies

$$p_j = bX_j + a \tag{11.36b}$$

The general equilibrium is given by (11.33a), (11.34), (11.36), and the market clearing condition $Mx = X$, which involve the unknowns $p$, $n$, $x$, $X$. Here, the subscripts of variables are skipped because of symmetry. Hence, the general equilibrium and its comparative statics are

$$n = \rho + [M(1 - \rho)/(1 + t)a], \quad dn/dM > 0, \quad dn/dt < 0$$
$$p = bM/\rho[M - a(1 + t)], \quad dp/dM < 0, \quad dp/dt > 0$$
$$x = \rho[M - a(1 + t)]/bM[(1 - \rho)M + (1 + t)\rho], \quad dx/dt < 0$$
$$X = Mx, \quad dX/dM > 0, \quad dX/dt < 0$$
$$u = \rho\{[(1 - \rho)M/(1 + t)a] + \rho\}^{(1-\rho)/\rho}[M - a(1 + t)]/bM(1 + t),$$
$$du/dM > 0, \quad du/dt < 0$$

It can be shown that the equilibrium labor productivity of each good is the reciprocal of the equilibrium price of each good. The comparative statics substantiate the story presented in the previous subsection. That is, the equilibrium number of consumption goods, productivity of each good, and per capita real income increase and the price of each good falls as the size of the economy is enlarged or as the transaction cost coefficient falls.

Now let us compare the D-S model with neoclassical models with constant returns to scale and with new classical trade models. First, the D-S model can generate gains from trade even if all countries are *ex ante* identical, or even if exogenous comparative advantage is absent. The gains from trade based on economies of scale are referred to as *acquired comparative advantage* by Grossman and Helpman (1991). Hence, the D-S model can be used to explain the Linder pattern of trade, which suggests that trade volume between *ex ante* similar developed countries is much greater than that between *ex ante* different developed and less-developed economies. The Linder pattern of trade is inconsistent with the neoclassical trade model with constant returns to scale and with exogenous comparative advantage, which predicts that trade volume is greater between *ex ante* different countries than between similar countries.

Second, the D-S model predicts that an increase in population size has positive implications for economic development because of economies of scale. This prediction is referred to as *Type II scale effect*. Type II scale effect is consistent with the data of the early economic development of the US, Australia, and New Zealand, and with Hong Kong's data after the Second World War. In contrast, Solow's neoclassical growth model and other neoclassical models with constant returns to scale predict that an increase in population will have a negative impact on economic growth and productivity progress. This prediction is consistent with the data of many African countries and with the pre-reform data in China and India. National Research Council (1986) and other empirical evidence reviewed by Dasgupta (1995) reject the Type II scale effect on the grounds of empirical evidence (see chapters 21 and 22 for more discussion).

The D-S model can simultaneously explain the equilibrium number of goods and per capita real income by the size of an economy. It has more explanatory power than many neoclassical models with a fixed number of goods. If we define the extent of the market as the product of per capita aggregate market demand for all goods and population size, the D-S model has endogenized the extent of the market. Since each pure consumer's aggregate demand for all goods is determined by the number of goods, the D-S model has endogenized the extent of the market by endogenizing the number of goods. Many economists use this feature of the D-S model to explain aggregate demand and related macroeconomic phenomena. If we define the level of division of labor by each individual's level of specialization, the number of traded goods in society, and the degree of production roundaboutness, then the D–S model has endogenized one aspect of division of labor: the number of traded goods. However, it has not endogenized individuals' levels of specialization and production roundaboutness.

Let us examine the implications of the difference between the D-S model and the new classical model. Assume, in figure 11.5a, that each of consumers 1 and 2 sells half of her labor to each of the two Japanese firms. Since obviously this implies that each individual is not specialized, we call this allocation of labor a pattern of nonspecialization. Suppose, alternatively, that each of the two consumers sells all of her labor to a firm. Since now each individual is completely specialized, we call this allocation of labor a pattern of complete specialization. In the general equilibrium of the D-S model, the two patterns of labor allocation generate the same values of all endogenous variables (relative prices, output levels, productivity of each good, and consumption of each good by each person) since the two patterns of division of labor generate the same scale for each firm. In other words, individuals' levels of specialization in equilibrium are not well defined, so that individuals' levels of specialization have no productivity implications if the scale of firms is not changed, since productivity is determined by the scale of firms rather than by individuals' levels of specialization. Hence, the D-S model cannot explain individuals' levels of specialization by transaction efficiency. As a result, many interesting economic phenomena that are explained by new classical models, such as evolution in division of labor and specialization and the emergence of the firm, money, and business cycles, cannot be predicted by the D-S model.

In the D-S model, separate markets, as indicated in figure 11.5a, can never exist in equilibrium if transaction conditions are the same between all individuals because of the positive effect of population size on per capita real income, and because of the fact that each pure consumer will buy all goods that are produced. Hence, the D-S model cannot endogenize the degree of market integration. In contrast, the new classical model in section 11.8 has endogenized the degree of market integration and the emergence of international trade from domestic trade. Therefore, the new classical model is referred to by Smythe (1994) as endogenous trade theory, while the D-S model is an exogenous trade theory which cannot predict the emergence of international trade from domestic trade.

Moreover, the population size does not play an active and positive role in promoting productivity in a new classical model where productivity is determined by the level of division of labor, which is determined by transaction efficiency. Hence, high transaction efficiency, due to a good legal system, explains productivity progress in Hong Kong, the US, and Australia, where population growth passively provides more scope for evolution in division of labor (the number of different occupations cannot exceed population size). The low transaction efficiency in many African countries explains the low growth rate of per capita real income that coexists with high population growth. The new classical theory about the relationship between population growth, transaction efficiency, and growth in per capita real income and productivity fits empirical observations much better than the D-S model does.

In a new classical model, productivity progress and the emergence of new goods and technology in equilibrium can be achieved by the merging of many separate local communities into an increasingly integrated network of division of labor, even if the population size is fixed. Hence, new classical models do not have a scale effect, which is rejected by empirical evidence. But they do have network effects which are supported by empirical evidence (Kelly, 1997 and Chen, Lin, and Yang, 1999). The D-S model also predicts Type I scale effect: productivity goes up if and only if the average size of firms increases.

Murphy, Shleifer, and Vishny (MSV, 1989) have developed general equilibrium with compatibility between global economies of scale and competitive markets. The following example introduces transaction costs into the MSV model to endogenize the degree of duality between the modern sector with economies of scale and the traditional sector with constant returns to scale technology.

### ◆ 11.11. An Extended Murphy–Shleifer–Vishny Model with Compatibility between Economies of Scale and Competitive Markets

**Example 11.5 (Sachs and Yang, 1999): an extended MSV model (1989) with transaction costs and endogenous degree of duality**

Following MSV, we assume that the set of consumption goods is a continuum with mass $m$. Each of $L$ consumer-worker-owners has the same CES utility function. Her decision problem is:

Max: $u = [\int_0^m x(j)^\rho dj]^{1/\rho}$,        s.t. $\int_0^m p(j)x(j)dj = I = (\pi + w)$.

where $j \in [0, m]$ is a good, $x(j)$ is the quantity of good j consumed, $p(j)$ is the price of good j. (The assumption of a continuum of goods can avoid the integer problem. Integration based on a continuum of goods can be considered as summation based on a discrete number of goods for the symmetric model.) Each consumer endowed with one unit of labor has income $I$ which consists of dividend earning $\pi$ and wage income $w$. Labor is assumed to be the *numéraire*, so that $w = 1$. Ownership of all firms is equally shared by all consumers. For each good, there are two available technologies. The modern one exhibits economies of scale and the traditional one displays constant returns to scale. Because of the existence of the traditional technology, $p(j) = 1$ for all j in equilibrium, so that the quantity demanded is the same for all goods. Using the symmetry, the solution to the consumer's decision problem can be found as follows.

$x = I/m.$

The total market demand is:

$$X^d = IL/m = (\Pi + L)/m, \qquad \Pi = \pi L, \tag{11.38}$$

where $\Pi$ is total dividend earning which is equal to total profit.

The production function of the modern sector producing good j is

$$x_j = (L_j - F_j)/b, \qquad F_0 = \delta, \qquad F_j = \gamma j > \delta \text{ for } j \in (0, m]. \tag{11.39}$$

where $x_j$ is the quantity supplied, $L_j$ is the amount of labor allocated to the production of good j, and $F_j$ is the fixed production cost of good j. We assume that the fixed cost differs across modern sectors and that the goods are indexed according to their fixed costs. Good 0 has the smallest fixed cost $\delta$, which is a very small positive number, good $m$ has the largest fixed cost $\gamma m$, and for $j \in (0, m]$, $F_j = \gamma j \in (\delta, \gamma m]$. Here, $\gamma$ can be considered as a general production condition parameter. As $\gamma$ decreases, the fixed cost for any modern sector j decreases. Also, $F_j$ can be interpreted as the degree of capital intensity. A large value of $F_j$ implies that the modern sector j needs a high investment in fixed cost before a positive output can be produced. Hence, index j can be considered as an index of capital intensity of the modern sectors.

We assume further that there is a variable transaction cost for each modern firm. The transaction condition differs across countries. The transaction cost incurred to a modern firm in country i is

$$C_i = c_i x_j, \qquad c_1 = s, \qquad c_i = \mu i > s \text{ for } i = 2, 3, ..., M, \tag{11.40}$$

where $i = 1, 2, ..., M$ is an index of countries, $s$, a very small positive number, is the transaction cost coefficient for country 1, and $x_j$ is the output level of modern sector j which is the same in any country and in any sector as we have shown. The specification implies that two factors determine the transaction cost coefficient: a general transaction condition $\mu$ and country-specific transaction condition represented by index i. For a larger i, the transaction cost coefficient $c_i$ is larger. A country's geographical condition and institutional and cultural tradition determines its ranking index i. For any given i, the transaction cost coefficient $c_i$ decreases as $\mu$ decreases. A decrease in $\mu$ can be caused by world-wide changes in transportation technology or institutions. We may consider country 1 as the most developed country and $M$ as the most underdeveloped country. The profit of firm j in country i is

$$\pi_{ij} = x_j - L_j - c_i x_j = (1 - \mu i - b)x_j - \gamma j, \qquad (11.41)$$

where $x_j = X^d$ is determined by the demand function given in (11.38). Total dividend earning is equal to total profit of $n$ active modern firms:

$$\Pi = \int_0^n \pi_{ij} dj \qquad (11.42)$$

where $n \in [0, m]$ is endogenously determined. Plugging this expression for total dividend earning into (11.38), and considering demand caused by transaction cost, total market demand for the good produced by modern firm j can be found as

$$x_j = (\Pi + L)/m(1 - c_i) \qquad (11.43)$$

where the number of all goods is $m$, the number of active traditional sectors is $m - n$. (11.42) and (11.43) nicely capture the feedback loop between income, demand, and production conditions. It also captures the idea of big-push industrialization. If the transaction cost is 0, as more modern firms operate ($n$ increases), dividend earning and income increase, and demand increases, which makes more modern firms profitable. Hence, as the population size reaches a threshold level, the equilibrium number of modern sectors, $n$, jumps from 0 to its upper bound $m$. But in our model, transaction costs counteract the positive feedback between the extent of the market and economies of scale that can be exploited, so that industrialization may occur gradually as the transaction conditions are improved.

Inserting (11.43) into (11.42), then inserting the resulting expression into (11.42), we can conduct integration and then express total income $\Pi + L$ as a function of $n$.

$$\Pi + L = (L - 0.5\gamma n^2)m/\{m - n[1 - b/(1 - \mu i)]\} \qquad (11.44)$$

where $L - 0.5\gamma n^2 > 0$ and $m - n[1 - b/(1 - i)] > 0$ are required by positive income. We now consider the zero profit condition for the most capital intensive active modern sector $n$. Letting j equal $n$ in (11.41) and $\pi_n = 0$, we get the zero profit condition, $\pi_n = (1 - b - \mu i)x_j - \gamma n = 0$. Inserting the demand function, given in (11.43), into the zero profit condition for the marginal active modern firm generates another expression of $\Pi + L$:

$$\Pi + L = \gamma mn(1 - \mu i)/(1 - b - \mu i), \qquad (11.45)$$

where $1 - b - \mu i > 0$ is required by positive income. (11.44) and (11.45) together give the equilibrium number of active modern firms $n$ as a function of parameters $\gamma$, $\mu$, $L$, $b$, $i$.

$$f(n, \gamma, \mu, L, b, i) = f(n) = An^2 - Bn + D = 0. \qquad (11.46)$$

where $A \equiv 0.5\alpha\gamma[1 - b/(1 - \mu i)]$, $B \equiv m\gamma$, $D \equiv \alpha L[1 - b/(1 - \mu i)]$ are positive. The graph of this quadratic equation in the first and fourth quadrants of the n–f coordinates is a convex curve cutting the vertical axis above the horizontal axis since $f(0) = D > 0, f'(0)$ $= -B < 0, f''(n) = 2A > 0$. The unique minimum point $n = B/2A > 0$ of this curve is given by $f'(n) = 0$. Hence, this curve may have two cutting points of the right-half horizontal axis, which means two equilibria, given by $f(n^*) = 0$. Call the two solutions of $f(n) = 0$, $n_1$ and $n_2$, respectively, and assume $n_2 > n_1$. Hence, we can see that $f'(n_1) < 0$ and $f'(n_2) > 0$ for a convex curve with the unique minimum point that is below the horizontal axis. But we can show that for a positive income, $\partial f / \partial n = (\alpha/n)[1 - b/(1 - \mu i)](0.5\gamma n^2 - L) < 0$ must hold since positive income in (11.44) requires $1 - b(1 - \mu i) > 0$ and $0.5\gamma n^2 - L < 0$. This implies that $n_2$ cannot be an equilibrium. We have then established the claim that there is only one equilibrium in this model.

Differentiating (11.46) and using the implicit function theorem, we can identify the comparative statics of the equilibrium number of active modern firms.

$$\mathrm{d}n/\mathrm{d}L = -(\partial f/\partial L)/(\partial f/\partial n) > 0, \qquad \mathrm{d}n/\mathrm{d}\mu = -(\partial f/\partial \mu)/(\partial f/\partial n) < 0, \qquad (11.47)$$
$$\mathrm{d}n/\mathrm{d}b = -(\partial f/\partial b)/(\partial f/\partial n) < 0, \qquad \mathrm{d}n/\mathrm{d}i = -(\partial f/\partial i)/(\partial f/\partial n) < 0.$$

where $\partial f / \partial n = (\alpha/n)[1 - b/(1 - \mu i)](0.5\gamma n^2 - L) < 0$ and $\partial f/\partial \gamma = 0.5n^2(1 - b - \mu i) - mn < 0$ if (11.44) holds, $\partial f/\partial b, \partial f/\partial i, \partial f/\partial \mu < 0, \partial f/\partial L > 0$. (11.47) implies that there is substitution between transaction conditions and population size in promoting industrialization. For a given $\mu$, a larger population size generates a higher degree of industrialization. For a given $L$, better general transaction conditions generate a higher degree of industrialization. $\mathrm{d}n/\mathrm{d}i < 0$ implies that the degree of industrialization is lower for a country with a larger transaction cost coefficient, which implies a larger $i$. This implies that a large country may have low degree of industrialization if its transaction conditions are very bad.

Using comparative statics, we can show that as population size increases and/or as general transaction conditions are improved, the equilibrium number of active modern sectors, degree of capital intensity of active modern firms, productivity, and per capita real income increase. For a given general transaction condition and population size, the country with better country-specific transaction conditions has a higher degree of industrialization than other countries.

Like the D-S model, this model cannot endogenize market integration and level of division of labor, although it endogenizes aggregate productivity and dual structure. Also, it generates scale effects.

## Key Terms and Review

Economies of division of labor generated by fixed learning costs.

Differences between the decision rules in choosing the optimum resource allocation for a given configuration and the decision rules in choosing the optimum configuration of specialization.

Differences between neoclassical and new classical demand and supply functions.

The relationship between resource allocation and relative prices of traded goods vs. the relationship between the level of division of labor and the absolute price of labor.

Young theorem: demand and supply are two sides of the division of labor; the extent of the market and the level of division of labor are two sides of the same coin.

The distinction between total market demand for a good and aggregate demand (the extent of the market).

The difference between effects of an increase in transaction efficiency and an increase in fixed learning cost on the level of division of labor.

The mechanism that generates the following concurrent phenomena: increases in the degree of commercialization, in trade dependence, in the degree of interpersonal dependence, in the extent of the market, in the number of types of markets, in productivity, in the extent of endogenous comparative advantage, in the degree of diversity of economic structure, in individuals' levels of specialization, in the degree of production concentration, and in the degree of market integration.

The mechanism generating the Linda pattern of trade.

The relationship between evolution of division of labor, an increase in consumption variety, and emergence of new goods, endogenous technical progress.

Economies of consumption variety.

How the D-S model explains the number of goods and productivity by specifying the trade-off between economies of scale and consumption variety within the neoclassical framework.

Differences between the new classical and neoclassical approaches to endogenizing the number of goods and aggregate productivity.

## Further Reading

*New classical models*: Houthakker (1956), Wen (1997), Yang and Y.-K. Ng (1993, chs. 5, 8), Smith (1776), Yang (1991, 1994, 1996), Yang and S. Ng (1998), S. Ng (1995), Rosen (1983), Becker (1981), Barzel and Yu (1984), Young (1928), Sun and Lio (1997), Yang and Shi (1992); *neoclassical equilibrium models with economies of scale*: Dixit and Stiglitz (1977), Ethier (1982), Krugman (1979, 1980, 1981), Wong and Yang (1994, 1998), Yang and Heijdra (1993), Murphy, Shleifer, and Vishny (1989), Kelly (1997), Sachs and Yang (1999).

# QUESTIONS

1   In the early part of this century, Ford pioneered the use of mass production techniques featuring production lines. The new method of management and production substantially reduced the prices of automobiles and drastically increased demand for and supply of them. This made the US the first country "on wheels." Not only did the income share of the automobile industry and related sectors drastically increase, but also many new specialized sectors emerged from the better transportation conditions provided by cheap automobiles. (For instance, the supermarket may not be associated with Pareto efficient corner equilibrium in the absence of cheap automobiles.) Many economists call this phenomenon "economies of scale and economies of scope" (Chandler, 1990). However, Allyn Young claimed that the notion of economies of scale misses the phenomenon of division of labor, and in particular misses the qualitative aspect of division of labor. Use the notion of positive network effect of division of labor and the trade-off between economies of division of labor and transaction costs to explain the phenomenon. Discuss the implications of the production line, the geographical concentration of production of automobiles, and the standardization of parts for reducing coordination costs and for increasing the efficient level of division of labor within the automobile industry. Then analyze the implications of cheap automobiles for an increase in the level of division of labor for society as a whole and for the extent of the market for automobiles. Use the notion of general equilibrium to figure out the mechanisms that simultaneously determine all of these interdependent phenomena.

2   Use Marshall's idea, that a finer division of labor in production creates more scope for the division of labor in management, to explain the emergence of Taylor's scientific approach to management from mass production and industrialization. How does the market simultaneously determine the demand and supply of management services as two aspects of the division of labor between production and management?

3   Many economists cite the Smith theorem that division of labor is dependent upon the extent of the market to argue that population size determines the extent of the market, which determines the level of division of labor. Use the Young theorem to critically assess the statement. Allyn Young argued that the approach that separates the analysis of demand from the analysis of individuals' decisions in choosing their levels of specialization is misleading. The Young theorem (1928, pp. 539, 534) consists of three statements. (a) Not only is the level of division of labor dependent upon the extent of the market, but also the extent of the market is determined by the level of division of labor, so that the extent of the market and the level of division of labor are two sides of the same coin; (b) Demand and supply are two aspects of division of labor from a general equilibrium view; (c) The securing of increasing returns depends on the progressive division of labor. Use the new classical models in this chapter to explain the Young theorem.

4   Smith claimed that the extent of the market is determined by transportation efficiency (1776, pp. 31–2) and that the division of labor is limited by the extent of the market (1776, ch. 3 of book I). Use the new classical models in this chapter to formalize the Smith theorem in connection with the Young theorem.

5   Discuss the differences between the implications of transaction costs in the new classical and neoclassical frameworks in relation to the new classical propositions that: (a) the number of transactions, related transaction costs, and the income share of transaction costs will increase through the evolution of division of labor caused by improvements in transaction efficiency; and (b) the degree of market integration will increase through the merging of many separate local business communities into an increasingly integrated market as division of labor evolves.

6   Transaction costs in the new classical models can be interpreted as costs caused by unpunctual delivery of traded goods and unpunctual transmission of information. It follows that, according to new classical economics, such developments as the watch, the refrigerator, the automobile, the computer, the Internet, inventories of goods, and the standardization of goods and services have very important influences on the general equilibrium network size of division of labor. Use statistical data on the income shares of all sectors that are directly and indirectly related to transaction conditions to verify this theory.

7   Consider the new classical model with an endogenous number of consumption goods in example 11.2. Assume that there are job shifting costs, so that an individual who has just changed jobs is not as productive, at least for a time, as a person who has not changed jobs. Suppose that the oil crisis has suddenly reduced transaction efficiency. Analyze what will happen to the equilibrium network size of division of labor and the equilibrium number of goods. Then discuss the possible effects on short-run unemployment, which some economists (such as Friedman) call natural unemployment and other economists call structural unemployment. Analyze the intimate relationship between the equilibrium network size of division of labor before such a shock and the unemployment rate after the shock.

8   It is said that specialization should be restricted because this conflicts with diversification, which is good for society. Marx and other economists argued that specialization makes individuals dumb and bored, which is uncivilized, so that specialization should be restricted. Managers of Japanese companies emphasize the diversified experience of their employees rather than specialization. In contrast, American managers have paid more attention to specialization since Taylor's scientific approach to management was invented. Similarly, American universities emphasize the diversity of undergraduate education, while fine specialization occurs at the level of graduate education. In contrast, the German technical training system and the Russian tertiary education system introduce specialization at quite early stages of education. Analyze these cases to identify the conditions for different efficient balance points between specialization and diversification. Draw the distinction between the following two kinds of economy of diversity in your analysis. One is an economy with a variety of inputs, which is considered

in this chapter and in chapters 18 and 19. The diversity of each person's inputs and the specialization of each person's output can increase side by side as the network size of division of labor evolves, as shown in this chapter and in chapters 18 and 19. The other type of economy of diversity is a certain technical complementarity between activities that a person engages in. For instance, a person's teaching experience in economics may help her research in economics. This kind of technical complementarity is not considered in this chapter. Do some thought experiments about the possible general equilibrium implications of this kind of technical complementarity in the new classical framework. You are referred to Rosen (1983) for an analysis of the trade-off between economies of specialization and this type of economy of technical complementarity.

9   In the new classical models in this chapter, as transaction efficiency is improved, the production functions of some new goods emerge from evolution of division of labor. This looks like endogenous technical progress. Analyze the difference between this approach to explaining endogenous technical progress, which is dependent on a large market network and on the merging of separate local business communities into an increasingly integrated market, and the neoclassical approach to explaining technical progress by investment, which is independent of the evolution of the network size of division of labor.

10  Yang, Wang, and Wills (1992) have tested the concurrent evolution of the degree of commercialization (one aspect of division of labor) and per capita real income, generated by improvements in a transaction efficiency index, which is determined by institutional changes, against China's data. Find other ways to test the theory developed in this chapter. For instance, you may test concurrent evolution in division of labor and in the number of available goods or concurrent evolution in division of labor and in the degree of market integration and production concentration.

11  Causal observations indicate that individuals in a very developed and highly commercialized economy are often frustrated by the disutility caused by management of a great variety of goods and services. Use the statistical data of cases of psychosis caused by complexity in managing a great variety of goods in a highly commercialized society to test the theory developed in example 11.2.

12  Design a method to test, against empirical data, the model in example 11.2 which predicts a neutral role for population size in promoting per capita real income, vs. the D-S model with transaction costs in example 11.4, which predicts a positive effect of population size on per capita real income.

13  From our daily experience we can perceive that coordination costs for specialization are increasingly more significant as specialization is increased. For instance, an expert on the Russian military system can provide professional knowledge that nobody else can provide. But the value of her professional knowledge is very low in peace-time, though she may become a star in TV shows when there is a possibility of war between Russia and the US. Smith noted the trade-off between coordination costs and economies of division of labor. How does the market sort out the efficient balance of this trade-off? How should you find the efficient trade-off when you choose your future professional career?

14  Compare the four approaches to endogenizing the level of division of labor and number of goods in examples 11.2–11.5.

# Exercises

1   Let the equilibrium number of traded goods in the model in example 11.1 be $n \geq 1$. Then identify the parameter space within which the solution given by the first order condition is relevant. If the parameter values are not within this subspace, what is going to happen to general equilibrium and its inframarginal comparative statics? Do the same analysis for the case of $n \leq m$. Check the second-order condition for maximizing organization utility with respect to $n$ and discuss the features of the general equilibrium when the second-order condition is not satisfied.

2   Siang Ng, 1995: Consider the model in example 11.1 with $m = 3$. Suppose that there are two countries. Each of them has $M$ citizens and transaction efficiency $k$ differs from country to country, so that utility equalization may not hold. Solve for the general equilibrium and analyze under what condition international trade emerges from domestic trade. Suppose $k$ is the same between the two countries, but is larger for domestic trade than for international trade. Identify the condition for international trade emerging from domestic trade and trade pattern.

3   Suppose there are two countries and only two goods in the model in example 11.1. The utility function is $u = (x^c)^\alpha (y^c)^{1-\alpha}$. The population size for each country is $M$, which is an integer. Identify the condition for international trade to emerge from domestic trade.

4   Show that the Nash bargaining equilibrium in example 11.1 or 11.2 is the same as the Walrasian equilibrium.

5   Suppose that the government taxes each dollar that is sold at rate $t$ and then equally distributes the tax revenue among individuals in the model in example 11.1. Solve for the general equilibrium and its inframarginal comparative statics, and analyze the implications of the tax for the equilibrium network size of division of labor and other related variables.

6   Yang and Ng, 1993, ch. 5: Assume that the production function in (11.1) is $x_i^p = l_i^a$, $a > 1$. Solve for the general equilibrium and its inframarginal comparative statics. Check the second-order condition where the equilibrium number of traded goods is $n \in (1, m)$, and analyze the implications of the second-order condition. Then work out the general equilibrium and inframarginal comparative statics when the second-order condition is not satisfied.

7   Yang and Shi, 1992: Assume that the production function in (11.20) is $x_i^p = l_i^a$, $a > 1$. Solve for the general equilibrium and its inframarginal comparative statics. Check the second-order condition where the equilibrium number of traded goods is $n \in (1, m)$, and analyze the implications of the second-order condition. Then work out the general equilibrium and inframarginal comparative statics when the second-order condition is not satisfied.

8   Assume that in the model in example 11.2 transaction efficiency $k = 1$, but the government imposes a tax rate $t$ on each dollar of sales, then equally distributes the tax revenue among all individuals. Solve for general equilibrium and its comparative statics. Analyze the implications of the tax for the equilibrium network size of division of labor and number of available goods.

9   Assume that the economy in example 11.2 is initially in equilibrium. An oil crisis reduces transaction efficiency from $k_1$ to $k_2$, so that the equilibrium number of goods decreases. Assume that as the equilibrium shifts from a corner equilibrium to another corner equilibrium there is a job shifting cost when individuals change jobs, so that those who lose their jobs are not as competitive as those who do not change jobs. Thus unemployment will take place. Compute the unemployment rate caused by the oil crisis.

10 Replacing the production function in example 11.4 with $X_j = L_j^a$, solve for equilibrium and its comparative statics. If the D-S formula for the own price elasticity of demand $-1/(1 - \rho)$ is used in this new model, what is going to happen? If the production function is still $X_j = (L_j - a)/b$, what is the solution based on the D-S formula for the own price elasticity of demand? Analyze the results based on the D-S formula in comparison to the results based on the YH formula.

11 Using all conditions for equilibrium except the condition that marginal revenue equals marginal cost, we can express utility as functions of the number of goods $n$. Maximizing the utility with respect to $n$ yields the Pareto optimum number of traded goods. Compare the Pareto optimum number of goods with the one in equilibrium to identify the condition under which the equilibrium number of goods is smaller than the Pareto optimum one for production functions $X_j = (L_j - a)/b$ and $X_j = L_j^a$, respectively.

12 Wong and Yang, 1994: Suppose that in the D-S model in example 11.4, the tax rate $t$ is imposed on sales rather than on consumption. Solve for equilibrium and its comparative statics. Then replace the production function with $X_j = L_j^a$ and solve for equilibrium and its comparative statics. Analyze the sensitivity of the results to the specification of who is paying the transaction costs.

13 Ethier, 1982 and Wong and Yang, 1998: Assume that in a modified version of the model in example 11.4, each consumer's utility function is $u = yz$ where $y$ and $z$ are two consumption goods. The production function for a representative firm producing good z is $Z = AL_z$ where $L_z$ is the amount of labor employed to produce good z. The production function for the representative firm producing good y is $Y = L_y^\alpha (\sum_{i=1}^n x_i^\rho)^{(1-\alpha)/\rho}$. The production function for the monopolist producing the intermediate good i is the same as in the D-S model in example 11.4. Solve for equilibrium and its comparative statics. What is the implication of the population size $M$ for the equilibrium number of intermediate goods, the prices of y and the intermediate goods, and per capita real income?

14 Specify transaction costs or tax in the model in the last exercise. Then solve for equilibrium and its comparative statics. Analyze the impact of the transaction cost coefficient or tax rate on the equilibrium number of intermediate goods, the prices of goods, and per capita real income (Wong and Yang, 1998).

15 Suppose that in example 11.4 parameters $a$, $b$, $t$, or $M$ change. Show that the equilibrium average size of firms and labor productivity of each good in the D-S model will change in the same direction in response to each of these changes in parameters. Use your analysis to establish the claim that the D-S model will be rejected if data show a negative correlation between average size of firms and productivity. Use data to test the hypothesis based on the D-S model. Why can Liu and Yang's new classical model in exercise 11 of chapter 8 allow a negative correlation between the average size of firms and productivity?

16 Calculate the relative income share of the modern to traditional sector in the MSV model. Identify if it increases or decreases as the transaction cost coefficient $c$ decreases or as population size $L$ increases. Suppose the variable cost coefficient $b$ decreases or the fixed production cost $F$ decreases, what will happen to the equilibrium size of the modern sector $n$?

17 Assume that in example 11.5, each consumer's utility function is $u = yz$ where $y$ and $z$ are two consumption goods. The production function for a representative firm producing good z is $Z = AL_z$ where $L_z$ is the amount of labor employed to produce good z. The production function for the representative firm producing good y is $Y = L_y^\alpha (\sum_{i=1}^n x_i^\rho)^{(1-\alpha)/\rho}$. The production functions for good x are the same as in example 11.5. Solve for equilibrium and its comparative statics. Then analyze the relationship between industrialization and outsourcing trade.

chapter 12

# Exogenous Comparative Advantages in Technology and Endowment, Division of Labor, and Trade

## ◆ 12.1 Endogenous vs. Exogenous Comparative Advantage

So far we have not studied exogenous comparative advantage and its implications for the equilibrium level of division of labor and productivity within the new classical framework. We assume in the new classical models in the previous chapters that all individuals are *ex ante* identical in all aspects. The exogenous comparative advantage has at least two important implications for economic analysis.

First, as we show in chapter 2, economies of division of labor may exist in the absence of endogenous comparative advantage if exogenous advantage is present. This implication of exogenous comparative advantage is studied by neoclassical trade theory. However, the implication may be more important than neoclassical trade theory suggests if we have paid attention to the implications of the inframarginal analysis of comparative advantages when dichotomy between pure consumers and firms is absent. In the Ricardo and Heckscher–Ohlin (HO) models, each country is a consumer as well as a producer, so that there is no dichotomy between pure consumers and firms at the level of countries. Each country can be completely self-sufficient in the absence of international trade. We shall show that this implies that there are many corner equilibria in many structures based on countries' corner solutions. The general equilibrium may discontinuously jump between corner equilibira in response to changes in parameters.

This implies that marginal analysis does not work and inframarginal analysis is essential for managing the Ricardo and HO models. But trade economists have shown remarkable insistence in marginal analysis. When they prove the HO theorem and other core theorems in trade theory, they focus on interior solutions and do not pay sufficient attention to corner solutions and discontinuous jumps of equilibrium across corner equilibria. In other words, Type III partial equilibrium analysis dominates neoclassical trade theory. Some economists use Type II partial equilibrium analysis to prove core trade theorems by assuming exogenous prices of goods or factors.

The first purpose of this chapter is to apply inframarginal general equilibrium analysis to the Ricardo and HO models and to explore the implications of exogenous comparative advantage in the absence of a dichotomy between pure consumers and producers for network size of division of labor. We shall show that several existing trade theorems based on marginal analysis and Types II and III partial equilibrium analysis need to be refined. We shall show that discontinuous changes of trade structure based on inframarginal comparative statics of general equilibrium are much more important than marginal comparative statics.

The second purpose of this chapter is to introduce government tariffs into the Ricardo model to identify a general equilibrium mechanism that simultaneously determines interdependent policy regimes and trade patters. We shall show that not only are trade pattern and level of division of labor dependent on government trade policy, but also policy regime is endogenously determined by the level of division of labor. It will be shown that as trading efficiency is improved, equilibrium jumps from autarky first to the partial division of labor, then to the complete division of labor. In the transitional stage, a unilateral protection tariff in the country producing two goods, and *a laissez-faire* policy in the country that completely specializes, coexist. The former has no incentive to participate in Nash tariff negotiations which may generate a Pareto improving outcome. When each country completely specializes in equilibrium, both countries have incentives to participate in Nash tariff negotiation which leads to free trade. We will extend this analysis to the case with three countries to show that the country that has the lowest trading efficiency and/ or does not have comparative advantage to both potential partners in producing any single good may be excluded from trade despite the existence of comparative advantage between this country and another single country. This result can be used to substantiate the claim that competitiveness matters.

The third purpose of this chapter is to use the HO model as an example to illustrate the difference between neoclassical trade theory and new classical trade theory. In the HO model there are two countries, two goods (x and y), and two factors (capital K and labor L). There is the dichotomy between pure consumers and firms in each country. But each country is a consumer as well as a producer. Hence, each country can choose from several corner and interior solutions (producing x only, producing y only, and producing both x and y). Therefore, there are several corner and interior equilibria in structures based on combinations of the corner and interior solutions. The general equilibrium is one of them. We will work out an inframarginal comparative statics of general equilibrium. This is similar to a new classical model.

We consider the inframarginal analysis of the Ricardo model in sections 12.2 and 12.3. Then we introduce tariff policy into the model in section 12.4. We shall explicitly introduce transaction costs into the HO model to refine the core theorems of neoclassical trade theory in section 12.5.

**Questions to Ask Yourself when Reading this Chapter**

♦ What are differences between endogenous comparative advantage, exogenous comparative tech-
    nology advantage, and exogenous comparative endowment advantage?

♦ Why may unilateral protection tariff and unilateral *laissez-faire* polity coexist in the transitional stage
    of economic development?

♦ Under what conditions does the government have an incentive to participate in the Nash tariff nego-
    tiation which is essential for realizing free trade?

♦ What are the differences between new classical models and neoclassical trade models and between
    general equilibrium analysis and Types II and III partial equilibrium analysis? What are the implica-
    tions of the differences for economic analysis?

## ♦ 12.2. A Ricardian Model with Exogenous Comparative Technological Advantage and Transaction Costs

Before David Ricardo, economists did not pay attention to the distinction between
absolute and comparative advantages. An individual has *absolute advantage in producing
good i* if her labor productivity in good i is greater than that of the other individual.
Ricardo (1817) drew economists' attention to the distinction between this measure and
the concept of comparative advantage. If person 2 is absolutely less productive than
person 1 in producing both of goods x and y, but the ratio of productivities between the
two individuals is greater for good y than for good x, then person 2 has a *comparative
advantage* in producing good x since her absolute disadvantage is relatively smaller in
producing x than in producing y. Ricardo argued that as long as there exists such a
comparative advantage, a country having no absolute advantage in producing any good
nonetheless can gain from trade, as can the other country which enjoys absolute advantage in all lines of production.

Ricardo's theory of comparative advantage is regarded as the foundation of modern
trade theory. However, the Ricardian model has not attracted the attention it deserves.
This lack of attention is attributable to the fact that conventional marginal analysis is not
applicable to the Ricardian model because of corner solutions. There are two ways to
specify the Ricardo model. One is to specify the dichotomy between pure consumers and
firms. However, in the Ricardo model each country is a consumer as well as a producer.
Hence, corner solutions may be chosen by a country. This specification will entail multiple
general equilibria based on several structures of corner and interior solutions of countries.
Since in the Walrasian regime, firms' profit is always zero in each and every structure,
firms do not care about choice of structure. Pure consumers cannot choose the structure of
production. Therefore, local equilibrium in each structure can be a general equilibrium.
This multiplicity of general equilibria renders comparative statics analysis of general equilibrium impossible (see Dixit and Norman, 1980, p. 38 and Gomory, 1994).

The second way to specify the Ricardo model is to use a framework of consumer-
producers and transaction costs. In this framework, the general equilibrium is one of
several corner equilibria, which efficiently trades off economies of division of labor generated by exogenous technological comparative advantage against transaction costs. Hence,

inframarginal comparative statics of general equilibrium will generate very rich and interesting stories about economic development and trade.

The framework of consumer-producers not only avoids multiple equilibria, but also allows the model to explain international trade by individuals' choices of their patterns of specialization. Within this framework, even when the domestic and international transaction cost coefficients are the same, individuals still choose whether or not to engage in international trade, and autarky can be the unique general equilibrium structure when the transaction cost coefficient is large.

## Example 12.1: the Ricardian model with exogenous comparative technology advantage and transaction costs

Consider a world consisting of country 1 and country 2. In country i, a continuum of consumer-producers has mass $M_i$ ($i = 1, 2$). The individuals within a country are assumed to be identical. Hence, two countries may be considered as two groups of *ex ante* different individuals. As consumer-producers, the individuals consume two goods, x and y, and decide their own configurations of production and trade activities.

The utility function for individuals of group i or in country i is

$$U_i = (x_i + kx_i^d)^\beta (y_i + ky_i^d)^{1-\beta} \qquad (12.1)$$

where $x_i$, $y_i$ are quantities of goods x and y self-provided, $x_i^d$, $y_i^d$ are quantities of the goods bought from the market, and $k$ is the trading efficiency coefficient. Assume that the production functions for a consumer-producer in country i are

$$x_i^p \equiv x_i + x_i^s + a_{ix}l_{ix} \text{ and } y_i^p \equiv y_i + y_i^s = a_{iy}l_{iy} \qquad (12.2)$$

where $x_i^p$ and $y_i^p$ are respective output levels of the two goods produced by a person in country i and $l_{ij}$ is a type i individual's amount of labor allocated in producing good j or the level of specialization of a type i individual in producing good j. $a_{ij}$ is a type i individual's labor productivity in producing good j. The labor endowment constraint for a person in country i is $l_{ix} + l_{iy} = 1$. Let country 1 have comparative advantage in producing good x, thus

$$\frac{a_{1x}}{a_{1y}} > \frac{a_{2x}}{a_{2y}} \qquad (12.3)$$

The individuals' transformation curves for $a_{1x} = 3$, $a_{1y} = 4$, $a_{2x} = 2$, $a_{2y} = 1$ are drawn in figure 12.1, which is a duplicate of figure 2.3. CD is the transformation curve of an individual in country 1 and AB is the transformation curve of an individual in country 2. Here, an individual in country 2 has absolute advantage in producing both goods.

The consumption, production and trade decisions for an individual in country i involve choosing six variables $x_i$, $x_i^s$, $x_i^d$, $y_i$, $y_i^s$, $y_i^d \geq 0$. Since zero values are allowed, there are $2^6$ = 64 combinations of zero and positive values of the 6 variables. Since buying and selling the same good incur unnecessary transaction costs, $x_i^s$ and $x_i^d$ cannot both be positive, and $y_i^s$ and $y_i^d$ cannot both be positive. Thus, the budget constraint is either $p_x x_i^s = p_y y_i^d$ or $p_x x_i^d = p_y y_i^s$. Hence, we first rule out the 48 combinations which satisfy any of the following conditions, which violate the budget constraint: $x_i^s = 0$ and $y_i^d > 0$; $x_i^s > 0$ and $y_i^d = 0$; $x_i^d$

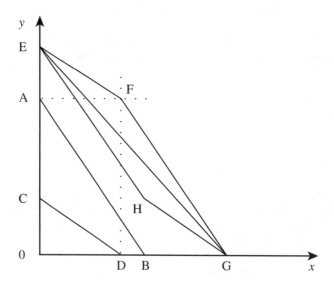

◆ **Figure 12.1:** Economies of division of labor based on exogenous technical comparative advantage

$= 0$ and $y_i^s > 0$ or $x_i^d > 0$ and $y_i^s = 0$. Four more combinations that involve selling and buying the same good can be ruled out. Then from the remaining 12 combinations, we use the positive utility constraint ($U_i = (x_i + kx_i^d)^\beta (y_i + ky_i^d)^{1-\beta} > 0$) to rule out 7 combinations that involve $x_i = x_i^d = 0$ or $y_i = y_i^d = 0$. We will show later that 2 combinations that involve specialization in an individual's comparative disadvantage good cannot occur in general equilibrium. Now we are left with 3 types of configuration, listed as follows:

1) Configuration $A_i$ (autarky) is shown in figure 12.2. This configuration is defined by $x_i, y_i > 0$, $x_i^s = x_i^d = y_i^s = y_i^d = 0$, $i = 1, 2$. In Structure A all individuals choose configuration A.

2) Configuration of partial specialization in the comparative advantage good, denoted by $(xy/y)_1$ and $(xy/x)_2$, is shown in figure 12.2, Configuration $(xy/y)_1$ is relevant for individuals in country 1 and is defined by $x_1, y_1, x_1^s, y_1^d > 0$, $x_1^d = y_1^s = 0$; configuration $(xy/x)_2$ is relevant to individuals in country 2 and is defined by $x_2, y_2, x_2^d, y_2^s = y_2^d = 0$.

3) Configuration of complete specialization in the comparative advantage good, denoted by $(x/y)_1$ and $(y/x)_2$, shown in figure 12.2. Configuration $(x/y)_1$ is defined by $x_1, x_1^s, y_1^d > 0$, $x_1^d = y_1 \, y_1^s = 0$; configuration $(y/x)_2$ is defined by $y_2, y_2^s, x_2^d > 0$, $y_2^d = x_2 = x_2^s = 0$.

There are two structures involving partial division of labor. Structure Ba consists of $(xy/y)_1$ and $(y/x)_2$ and structure Bb is composed of $(x/y)_1$ and $(xy/x)_2$. The structure of complete division of labor, C, consists of configurations $(x/y)_1$ and $(y/x)_2$.

Suppose there is only one person in each country. The aggregate production schedules for the four structures are shown in figure 12.1. We will show later that if autarky occurs in equilibrium, the aggregate production schedule is on the line EG.

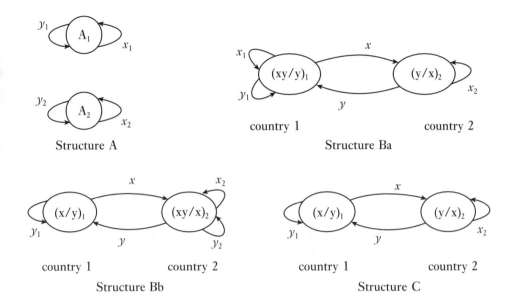

◆ **Figure 12.2:** Configurations and structures

For structure Ba, an individual in country 1 completely specializes in producing x and an individual in country 2 produces two goods. The aggregate transformation curve for this structure is the segment FG in figure 12.1. The aggregate transformation curve for structure Bb is EF. The aggregate production for structure C is point F in figure 12.1.

Production schedule EHG is associated with the division of labor with comparative disadvantage. Later we will show this production schedule never takes place in equilibrium.

The general equilibrium of the world economy is defined as a resource allocation and a trade network structure that satisfy these stipulations (1) each individual maximizes utility at a given set of prices with respect to configurations and quantities of production, trade, and consumption; (2) the set of prices clears the market. The individuals make their utility maximization decisions based on the inframarginal analysis. There is a partial or corner equilibrium for a given structure and the general equilibrium is one of the four corner equilibria.

We first apply nonlinear programming to solve the individuals' utility maximization problem and use the market clearing condition to find the partial equilibrium for each of the four structures. We then use total benefit–cost analysis to identify the general equilibrium.

For instance, given structure Ba, the decision problem for individuals choosing configuration $(xy/y)_1$ in country 1 is :

$$\underset{x_1,x_1^s,y_1,y_1^d,l_{1x},l_{1y}}{\text{Max}} \quad U_1 = x_1^\beta (y_1 + k y_1^d)^{1-\beta}$$

$$\text{s.t. } x_1 + x_1^s = a_{1x} l_{1x}, \quad y_1 = a_{1y} l_{1y}$$
$$y_1^d = p\, x_1^s, \quad l_{1x} + l_{1y} = 1$$

where all decision variables can be positive or zero and $p \equiv p_x/p_y$ is the price of x in terms of y. Inserting all constraints into the utility function to eliminate $x_1$, $y_1$, $y_1^d$, $l_{1x}$ yields

$$U_1 = (a_{1x} \, l_{1x} - x_1^s)^\beta [a_{1y} \, (1 - l_{1x-}) + kpx_1^s]^{1-\beta}.$$

It is not difficult to see that $\partial U_1/\partial l_{1x} > 0$ for any positive $l_{1x}$ if $p > a_{1y}/ka_{1x}$ and if the optimum value of $x_1^s$ is given by $\partial U_1/\partial x_1^s = 0$. This implies that the utility can always be increased by increasing $l_{1x}$ if $p > a_{1y}/ka_{1x}$. Or the optimum value of $l_{1x}$ is at its maximum. Due to the endowment constraint of working time, this implies that an individual should not produce y and should specialize in producing x if $p > a_{1y}/ka_{1x}$. That is, individuals in country 1 should choose configuration $(x/y)_1$ instead of configuration $(xy/y)_1$ if $p > a_{1y}/ka_{1x}$. Following a similar reasoning, it can be shown that individuals in country 1 will choose configuration $A_1$ instead of $(xy/y)$ if $p < a_{1y}/ka_{1x}$. Hence, individuals in country 1 will choose $(xy/y)_1$ only if the market relative price satisfies $p = a_{1y}/ka_{1x}$. This condition is analogous to the zero profit condition in a standard general equilibrium model with constant returns to scale. With the condition, the first order condition $\partial U_1/\partial x_1^s = 0$ yields the optimum value of $x_1^s$ as a function of $l_{1x}$. Inserting it into the constraints in the original decision problem yields the optimum decision:

$$p = a_{1y}/ka_{1x}, \qquad x_1 = \beta a_{1x}, \qquad x_1^s = a_{1x}(l_{1x} - \beta),$$
$$y_1 = a_{1y}(1 - l_{1x}), \qquad y_1^d = a_{1y}(l_{1x} - \beta)/k,$$

Let us figure out the intuition behind this nonlinear programming. If the price of x in terms of y, discounted by transaction cost in the world market, is lower than a type 1 individual's marginal rate of transformation $a_{1y}/a_{1x}$ in autarky, then the optimum decision is to choose autarky, producing both x and y. If $p > a_{1y}/ka_{1x}$, then marginal utility of $l_{1x}$ always increases as $l_{1x}$ increases. Hence, the optimum decision is to specialize in producing x. But for $p = a_{1y}/ka_{1x}$, the individual is indifferent between autarky and configuration $(xy/y)_1$. Hence, configuration $(xy/y)_1$ will be chosen if the market clearing condition in equilibrium ensures that demand and supply of occupation configuration $(xy/y)_1$ can be realized. In configuration $(xy/y)_1$ there is a trade-off between the quantity of x self-provided $x_1$ and quantity sold $x_1^s$. The former directly contributes to utility and the latter indirectly increases utility by increasing more good y that is exchanged from $x_1^s$. The efficient balance of the trade-off is determined by the first-order condition which implies that the marginal direct utility cost of $x_1^s$ equals marginal indirect utility of $x_1^s$.

In this solution, the optimum value of $l_{1x}$ is indeterminate. It will be determined by the market clearing condition. This is analogous to a standard equilibrium model where the zero profit condition determines prices, and the market clearing condition, together with demand functions, determine equilibrium quantities.

The decision problem for individuals in country 2 is

$$\underset{x_2^d, y_2, y_2^s}{\text{Max}} \; U_2 = (kx_2^d)^\beta y_2^{1-\beta}$$

$$\text{s.t.} \; y_2 + y_2^s = a_{2y}, \qquad y_2^s = p \, x_2^d$$

The first-order conditions imply:

**Table 12.1:** Four corner equilibria in the Ricardo model

| Structures | Relative price $(p_x/p_y)$ | Relevant parameter interval | Per capita real income (utility) | |
|---|---|---|---|---|
| | | | Country 1 | Country 2 |
| A | n.a. | | $U_1(A) \equiv (\beta a_{1x})^\beta$ $[(1-\beta)a_{1y}]^{1-\beta}$ | $U_2(A) \equiv (\beta a_{2x})^\beta$ $[(1-\beta)a_{2y}]^{2-\beta}$ |
| Ba | $a_{1y}/ka_{1x}$ | $k < k_1 \equiv$ $M_1 a_{1y}(1-\beta)/\beta M_2 a_{2y} < 1$ | $U_1(A)$ | $U_2(A)$ $(k^2 a_{2y} a_{1x}/a_{2x} a_{1y})^\beta$ |
| Bb | $ka_{2y}/a_{2x}$ | $k < k_2 \equiv$ $M_2 a_{2x}\beta/(1-\beta)M_1 a_{1x} < 1$ | $U_1 A$ $(k^2 a_{2y} a_{1x}/a_{2x} a_{1y})^{1-\beta}$ | $U_2 A$ |
| C | $\beta M_2 a_{2y}$ $\div M_1 a_{1x}(1-\beta)$ | | $U_1(A)[\beta k M_2 a_{2y}$ $\div M_1 a_{1y}(1-\beta)]^{1-\beta}$ | $U_2(A)[(1-\beta)$ $k M_1 a_{1x} \div M_2 a_{2x}\beta]^\beta$ |

$$x_2^d = \frac{ka_{2y}a_{1x}}{a_{1y}}\beta, \qquad y_2 = (1-\beta)a_{2y}, \qquad y_2^s = px_2^d = \beta a_{2y}$$

where $p = a_{1y}/k\,a_{1x}$ is the equilibrium price of good x in terms of good y.

From the market clearing condition $M_1 x_1^s = M_2 x_2^d$, we obtain: $l_{1x} = (ka_{2y}M_2\beta/a_{1y}M_1)$ $+ \beta$, which is less than 1 (the endowment of labor) if and only if (or iff for short) $a_{2y}/a_{1y}$ $< M_1(1-\beta)/M_2\beta k$. That is, structure Ba can be chosen iff $a_{2y}/a_{1y} < M_1(1-\beta)/M_2\beta k$. Using the same approach as above, we can find the corner equilibria for structures A, Bb, and C. The results are summarized in table 12.1.

## ◆ 12.3 Analysis of Decisions vs. Analysis of Equilibrium

There is a corner equilibrium for each of four structures. A general equilibrium is a corner equilibrium in which no individual has incentive to deviate from the configuration that she chooses under the corner equilibrium relative prices. Now, we apply the total benefit–cost analysis and the definition of general equilibrium to prove that a structure where the countries export their comparative disadvantage good cannot be a general equilibrium structure. Consider the structure where individuals in both countries completely specialize in their comparative disadvantage good, i.e., individuals in country 1 export good y (choose configuration $(y/x)_1$), and individuals in country 2 export good x (choose configuration $(x/y)_2$). For this structure to occur in general equilibrium, configuration $(y/x)_1$ must be most preferred by individuals in country 1, and configuration $(x/y)_2$ most preferred by individuals in country 2, that is, the following conditions must hold:

$U_1(y/x) > U_1(x/y)$ which holds iff $p < (a_{1y}/a_{1x})k^{2\beta-1}$ and

$U_2(x/y) > U_2(y/x)$ which holds iff $p > (a_{2y}/a_{2x})k^{2\beta-1}$.

The two inequalities jointly imply $(a_{2x}/a_{2y}) > (a_{1x}/a_{1y})$, which contradicts the assumption $(a_{2x}/a_{2y}) < (a_{1x}/a_{1y})$. Similarly, it can be shown that other structures involving specialization in comparative disadvantage goods cannot occur in general equilibrium.

Next, we apply the total benefit–cost analysis to find out under what conditions each of the structures listed in table 12.1 occurs in general equilibrium. Consider structure Ba first. Structure Ba is the general equilibrium structure if the following three conditions hold. First, under the corner equilibrium relative price in this structure $p = a_{1y}/ka_{1x}$, individuals in country 2 prefer specialization in y (configuration (y/x)) to the alternatives, namely autarky (configuration A) and specialization in x (configuration (x/y)). In other words, the following conditions hold:

$$U_2(y/x) \geq U_2(A) \text{ which holds iff } k \geq k_0 \equiv [(a_{2x}/a_{2y})/(a_{1x}/a_{1y})]^{0.5}, \tag{12.4a}$$

$$U_2(y/x) \geq U_2(x/y) \text{ which holds iff } k \geq k_3 \equiv [(a_{2x}/a_{2y})/(a_{1x}/a_{1y})]^{0.5/\beta}. \tag{12.4b}$$

Second, general equilibrium requires that all individuals in country 1 prefer configuration (xy/y) to the alternatives, that is,

$$U_1(xy/y) \geq U_1(x/y) \text{ which holds iff } a_{1y}/a_{1x} \geq kp = a_{1y}/a_{1x}, \tag{12.5a}$$

$$U_1(xy/y) \geq U_1(y/x) \text{ which holds iff } 1 \geq k. \tag{12.5b}$$

Third, no individual in country 1 is completely specialized in x, i.e.,

$$l_{1x} < 1, \text{ which holds iff } k < k_1 \equiv a_{1y}M_1(1 - \beta)/a_{2y}M_2\beta. \tag{12.6}$$

As $k_3 \leq k_0$, it follows that conditions (12.4)–(12.6) hold if $k \in (k_0, k_1)$. Since $k_0 < k_1$ holds iff $M_1(1 - \beta)/M_2\beta > [(a_{2x}a_{2y})/(a_{1x}a_{1y})]^{0.5}$, the corner equilibrium in structure Ba is the general equilibrium if $k \in (k_0, k_1)$ and $M_1(1 - \beta)/M_2\beta > [(a_{2x}a_{2y})/(a_{1x}a_{1y})]^{0.5}$, where $k_1 \equiv a_{1y}M_1(1 - \beta)/a_{2y}M_2\beta$.

Similarly, we can identify the conditions for other structures to occur in general equilibrium. These conditions are summarized in table 12.2, which reads that if $k < k_0$, the general equilibrium structure is autarky (structure A). If $k > k_0$ and $M_1/M_2 > (a_{2x}a_{2y}/a_{1x}a_{1y})^{0.5}\beta/(1 - \beta)$, the general equilibrium occurs in structure Ba if $k < k_1$, and in structure C if $k > k_1$. If $k > k_0$ and $M_1/M_2 < (a_{2x}a_{2y}/a_{1x}a_{1y})^{0.5}\beta/(1 - \beta)$, the general equilibrium occurs in structure Bb if $k < k_2$, and in structure C if $k > k_2$. It is important to note that the structures are compared within relevant intervals. For instance, structure Ba can be chosen only if $M_1/M_2 < (a_{2y}/a_{1y})\beta/(1 - \beta)$.

Table 12.2 implies that as the trading efficiency coefficient increases from a low value to $k_0$, and then to $k_1$ or $k_2$, the general equilibrium jumps from autarky to partial division of labor, then to complete division of labor. Whether the transitional structure is Ba or Bb depends on the relative size of the two countries compared to relative tastes and relative productivity. Since we assume $(a_{1x}/a_{2x}) > (a_{1y}/a_{2y})$ or country 1 has comparative advantage in producing good x, we can take $r = r_1r_2 \equiv (a_{1x}/a_{2x})(a_{2y}/a_{1y})$ as a measure of the degree of exogenous technical comparative advantage. A derivative of $k_0$, $k_1$, $k_2$ with respect to $r_1$ and $r_2$ yields

$$\partial k_0/\partial r_1, \partial k_0/\partial r_2, \partial k_1/\partial r_2, \partial k_2/\partial r_1 < 0.$$

This implies that for a given value of $k$, the greater the degree of comparative advantage, the more likely $k > k_i$ ($i = 0, 1, 2$) or the more likely the equilibrium level of division of labor is higher.

A close examination of all conditions for structure C to be the general equilibrium

**Table 12.2:** General equilibrium and its inframarginal comparative statics of the Ricardo model

| Parameter intervals: | $k < k_0$ | $k > k_0$ | | | |
|---|---|---|---|---|---|
| | | $M_1/M_2 >$ $(a_{2x}a_{2y}/a_{1x}a_{1y})^{0.5}\beta/(1-\beta),$ | | $M_1/M_2 <$ $(a_{2x}a_{2y}/a_{1x}a_{1y})^{0.5}\beta/(1-\beta),$ | |
| | | $k \in (k_0, k_1)$ | $k \in (k_1, 1)$ | $k \in (k_0, k_2)$ | $k \in (k_2, 1)$ |
| Equilibrium structure: | A | Ba | C | Bb | C |

*where:* $k_0 \equiv (a_{2x}a_{1y}/a_{1x}a_{2y})^{0.5}$, $k_1 \equiv (1-\beta)a_{1y}M_1/\beta a_{2y}M_2$, $k_2 \equiv \beta a_{2x}M_2/(1-\beta)a_{1x}M_1$.

indicates that they require either that $1 > k_1$ and $M_1/M_2 > (a_{2x}a_{2y}/a_{1x}a_{1y})^{0.5}\beta/(1-\beta)$, or that $1 > k_2$ and $M_1/M_2 < (a_{2x}a_{2y}/a_{1x}a_{1y})^{0.5}\beta/(1-\beta)$. The two conditions imply that the requirement for C to be equilibrium is either

$$(a_{2y}/a_{1y})\beta/(1-\beta) > M_1/M_2 > (a_{2x}a_{2y}/a_{1x}a_{1y})^{0.5}\beta/(1-\beta), \text{ or}$$

$$(a_{2y}/a_{1y})\beta/(1-\beta) < M_1/M_2 < (a_{2x}a_{2y}/a_{1x}a_{1y})^{0.5}\beta/(1-\beta).$$

Since individuals in one country have a higher level of specialization in structure C than in structures Ba or Bb, structure C has a higher level of division of labor than structure Ba or Bb. Our result implies that the more relative population size is in balance with relative tastes and relative productivity, the more likely the equilibrium level of division of labor is higher.

Now we consider the implications of inframarginal comparative statics for development economics. To this end, we need to work out the production schedule in autarky. If autarky is the general equilibrium, then the marginal rate of substitution equals marginal rate of transformation for each individual. This implies

$$\beta y_i/(1-\beta)x_i = a_{iy}/a_{ix} \text{ or } (x_1/a_{1x})/(y_1/a_{1y}) = \beta/(1-\beta) = (x_2/a_{2x})/(y_2/a_{2y})$$

where the subscript i represents country i. This, together with the production functions $x_i = a_{ix}l_{iy}$, $y_i = a_{iy}l_{iy}$ and the endowment constraint $l_{ix} + l_{iy} = 1$ implies that $l_{1x} = l_{2x} = \beta$, $l_{1y} = l_{2y} = 1 - \beta$. Using all of the conditions to eliminate taste parameter $\beta$, or using the production functions, the endowment constraints, and the conditions $l_{1x} = l_{2x}$ and $l_{1y} = l_{2y}$ we can then show that the equilibrium aggregate production schedule for two *ex ante* different individuals in autarky must satisfy

$$Y_i \equiv y_1 + y_2 = (a_{1y} + a_{2y})[1 - X/(a_{1y} + a_{2x})], \text{ where } X \equiv x_1 + x_2.$$

This is line EG in figure 12.1. The slope of this line is $dY/dX = -(a_{1y} + a_{2y})/(a_{1x} + a_{2x})$, which is between $-a_{1y}/a_{1x}$ and $-a_{2y}/a_{2x}$. In other words, this line is flatter than line FG and steeper than line EF in figure 12.1. Hence, production takes place at a point on EG if autarky is the general equilibrium. The exact position of the equilibrium production schedule on EG is dependent on the value of taste parameter $\beta$. Since line EG is lower than the PPF, the aggregate productivity in autarky is lower than for the division of labor which is associated with the PPF. As trading efficiency is improved, the equilibrium aggregate productivity will discontinuously jump from line EG to the PPF (EFG in figure 12.1). The difference between EFG and line EG can then be defined as *economies of division of labor*.

It is interesting to see that there exist economies of division of labor even if there are no economies of scale or the aggregate production set is convex in the Ricardian economy. This implies productivity chosen by the decision-makers in the equilibrium will endogenously increase as trading efficiency is improved. If trading efficiency is low, then the high productivity associated with the PPF is not Pareto efficient because of the trade-off between economies of division of labor and transaction costs.

Rosen (1978) calls economies of division of labor *superadditivity*, which is a kind of economies of interpersonal complementarity. It implies that equilibrium aggregate productivity for society increases as the equilibrium network size of division of labor increases. Buchanan (1994) calls this "generalized increasing returns" and Allyn Young (1928) calls it "social increasing returns" which may exist in the absence of economies of scale. Individuals' levels of specialization and the diversity of individuals' occupation configurations are two aspects of the network.

The inframarginal comparative statics of general equilibrium provides a general equilibrium mechanism for economic development and changes in trade dependence. In this mechanism, exogenous comparative advantage and trading efficiency are driving forces of economic development and increases in trade dependence. Exogenous changes in production functions or endowments are not needed for the economic development if trading efficiency is improved. Also, exogenous changes in tastes are not needed for structural changes in this economic development process.

We now consider the common wisdom that as terms of trade of a country deteriorate, the gains that this country receives from trade will fall. Many development economists regard worsening terms of trade as a cause of underdevelopment. The inframarginal comparative statics of our model show that this is not a general equilibrium view and might be misleading. Consider tables 12.1 and 12.2. Suppose that $M_1/M_2 > (a_{2x} a_{2y}/a_{1x} a_{1y})^{0.5}\beta/(1 - \beta)$ and the initial value of $k$ is $k' \in ((a_{2x} a_{1y}/a_{1x} a_{2y})^{0.5}, (M_1/M_2)(a_{1y}/a_{2y})\beta/(1 - \beta))$. Hence, the equilibrium structure is Ba where country 1 exports x and imports y at the relative price $p_x/p_y = a_{1y}/k' a_{2y}$. Assume now that the trading efficiency is improved, so that the value of $k$ is $k'' > (M_1/M_2)(a_{1y}/a_{2y})\beta/(1 - \beta)$, which is greater than $k'$. Hence, the equilibrium jumps to structure C where the relative price is $(M_2/M_1)(a_{2y}/a_{1x})\beta/(1 - \beta)$. This implies that country 1's terms of trade deteriorate as the improvement in trading efficiency drives the equilibrium to jump from Ba to C, if $k' < (M_1/M_2)(a_{1y}/a_{2y})(1 - \beta)/\beta$. It is straightforward that the parameter subspace for such a structural change is not empty. Therefore, as trading efficiency is improved within this parameter subspace, country 1's per capita real income increases despite deteriorated terms of trade.

The inframarginal comparative statics of the general equilibrium can be summarized in the following proposition.

**Proposition 12.1:** The general equilibrium structure is determined by the two countries' relative productivity, relative preference, relative population size, and the level of trading efficiency. Given other parameters, improvements in trading efficiency can make the general equilibrium structure jump from autarky to partial division of labor and then to complete division of labor. For given transaction conditions, relative population size, and relative tastes for the two goods, the greater the degree of comparative advantage, the more likely the equilibrium level of division of labor is higher. For given transaction conditions, the more the relative population size is in balance with relative tastes and relative productivity, the more likely the equilibrium level of division of labor is higher. As the equilibrium level of division of labor increases, the equilibrium aggregate productivity for society as a whole increases. In the process of moving to a high level of division of labor, a country may receive more gains from trade even if its terms of trade deteriorate.

As in example 5.1, the general equilibrium market price may not be determined by the conventional marginal cost pricing rule in the model with exogenous comparative advantage. When structure Ba (or Bb) is the general equilibrium, the market price of good x in terms of y equals country 1's (or country 2's) marginal opportunity cost including (or excluding) transaction cost. When structure C is the general equilibrium, the market price of x in terms of y is determined by the total demand and supply in both countries and does not equal either country's marginal opportunity cost of producing x. Rosen (1978) notes this feature of the model of endogenous specialization. He extends the analysis in this chapter to the case with many goods by applying linear programming to a firm's decision problem of job assignment.

As in example 5.1, in the Ricardo model, an increase in $k$ (or a decrease in transaction cost coefficient $1 - k$) can increase total transaction costs because the increase in $k$ can generate a jump of the general equilibrium from a low level to a high level of division of labor and increase the number of transactions. This implication of transaction costs can be used to explain why the income share of transaction costs increases as trading efficiency is improved. North (1986) has found empirical evidence for this phenomenon.

Zhou, Sun, and Yang (1998; see chapter 13 below) have proved an existence theorem of general equilibrium for a general class of models of endogenous specialization. In their model the set of *ex ante* different consumer-producers is a continuum, preferences are rational and increasing, both constant returns and local increasing returns are allowed in production. The Ricardian model in this chapter and the new classical models with economies of specialization in chapters 7, and 11 are just special cases of their model. They have also established the first welfare theorem and the equivalence between the set of competitive equilibria and economic core in this general class of models of endogenous specialization. The results imply that if transaction costs outweigh exogenous comparative advantage in a structure or if the corner equilibrium in this structure is not Pareto optimal, then there is coordination difficulty to get self-interested decision makers to choose the occupation configurations in this structure. This is because there does not exist a set of relative prices that can support individuals' Walrasian decisions to choose constituent occupation configurations in this structure.

Following the method used in section 9.2, it can be shown that for the model of endogenous specialization, general equilibrium may not exist if the number of individuals is finite because of integer problems.

## ♦ 12.4 Economic Development and Trade Policy

In early stage of economic development in the sixteenth century, the governments in some European countries used protection tariffs as a vehicle for rent seeking in international trade (see for instance Ekelund and Tollison, 1981). This mercantilism was replaced by free trade policy regime in some European countries in the eighteenth and nineteenth centuries. According to Smith (1776), *laissez-faire* regime is more conducive to economic development than protection tariffs. But after the Second World War, many governments in developing countries still used protection tariffs as a means to increase their share of gains from trade by manipulating terms of trade. This trade policy is sometimes referred to as an import substitution strategy. But governments in Hong Kong, Taiwan, and other developing countries use tax holidays, export-processing zones, and other policy instruments to reduce tariffs. This trade liberalization policy is sometimes referred to as export-oriented development strategy. Many economists argue that the trade liberalization which involves tariff reduction is a powerful engine of economic development (Krueger 1997, World Bank, 1997). Recently, bilateral and multilateral tariff negotiations have become a driving force of trade liberalization. The question is why is free trade difficult to realize and trade negotiation essential for trade liberalization if free trade is mutually beneficial? Why do some governments choose unilateral protection tariffs and others choose unilateral *laissez-faire* regimes at the same time? How can we use general equilibrium models to explain government policy shifts from protection tariffs to free trade or to tariff negotiation that leads to trade liberalization? This section will introduce government tariffs into the Ricardian model to address these questions.

### Example 12.2: a Ricardo model with an endogenous trade regime

Based on the model in section 12.2, suppose that the government in country i ($i = 1, 2$) imposes an *ad valorem* tariff of rate $t_i$, and transfers all tariff revenue equally to all individuals in country i. In this case, individuals' budget constraint, for instance for configuration (x/y), changes from $p_x x^s = p_y y^d$ to $p_x x^s + R_i = (1 + t_i) p_y y^d$, where $t_i$ is the tariff rate in country i and $R_i$ is tariff revenue received by each resident in country i. Individuals take the amount of transfer as given. At equilibrium, the total transfer equals total tariff revenue. Also, we assume that the trading efficiency coefficient for country i is $k_i$, which may be different between countries.

Using the same procedure as in section 12.3, we can solve for the corner equilibrium for each structure, as presented in table 12.3.

It is easy to see that if $t_1 = t_2 = 0$ and $k_1 = k_2$, table 12.3 reduces to table 12.1. If $t_1 = t_2 = 0$, the Ricardian model predicts that the "large" country which produces both goods does not get any gains from trade. This result can be clearly seen from table 12.1 – when the general equilibrium occurs in structure Ba (or Bb), individuals in country 1 (or country 2), which produces both goods x and y get the same level of utility as they do in autarky.

The story is different when tariff is introduced. Refer to table 12.3: if the general equilibrium occurs in structure Ba (or Bb), individuals in the country producing both goods get a higher utility than they do in autarky. Moreover, in structure Ba, $\partial U_1 / \partial t_1 > 0$ (or in structure Bb, $\partial U_2 / \partial t_2 > 0$), that is, given the tariff rate of the country producing one good, the country producing two goods can improve its own welfare by raising its tariff rate. This is because the latter country determines the terms of trade, and it can improve its terms of trade by imposing a tariff, thereby obtaining a larger share of the gains from trade. The gain of the country producing two goods is at the expense of its trading partner; it can be shown that $\partial U_2 / \partial t_1 < 0$ in structure Ba and $\partial U_1 / \partial t_2 < 0$ in structure Bb. If the country producing two goods imposes a sufficiently high tariff, the other country may want to withdraw from trade, in which case both countries are hurt.

**Table 12.3: Corner equilibrium solutions**

| Structure | Price $p_x/p_y$ | Relevant parameter subspace | Individual utility Country 1 | Country 2 |
|---|---|---|---|---|
| A | n.a. | | $(\beta a_{1x})^\beta[(1-\beta)a_{1y}]^{1-\beta}$ $\equiv U_1(A)$ | $(\beta a_{2x})^\beta[(1-\beta)a_{2y}]^{1-\beta}$ $\equiv U_2(A)$ |
| Ba | $a_{1y}(1+t_1)/k_1 a_{2x}$ | $k_1 < D_1(1-\beta)$ $a_{1y}M_1 \div \beta a_{2y}M_2$ | $[(1 + L_{1x}\, t_1)/(1 + \beta)t_1]$ $U_1(A)$ | $[k_1 k_2(a_{1x}a_{2y}) \div$ $(a_{1y}a_{2x})]^\beta T_1^\beta U_2(A)$ |
| Bb | $k_2 a_{2y}/(1+t_2)a_{2x}$ | $k_2 < D_2\beta a_{2x}M_2$ $\div (1-\beta)a_{1x}M_1$ | $[k_1 k_2(a_{1x}a_{2y}) \div$ $(a_{1y}a_{2x})]^{1-\beta}T_2^{1-\beta}$ $U_1(A)$ | $U_2(A)[1 + (1 - L_{2x})t_2] \div$ $[(1 - \beta)t_2]$ |
| C | $(1 + \beta t_1)\beta a_{2y}M_2$ $\div (1-\beta)[1 +$ $(1 - \beta t_2)]a_{1x}M_1$ | | $[k_1 T_3 \beta a_{2y}M_2/(1-\beta)$ $a_{1y}M_1]^{1-\beta}U_1(A)$ | $[k_2 T_4(1-\beta)a_{1x}M_1 \div$ $\beta a_{2x}M_2]^\beta U_2(A)$ |

*where*: $D_1 \equiv (1 + t_1)[(1-\beta)t_2]/(1 + \beta t_1)$, $D_2 \equiv (1 + \beta t_1)(1 + t_2)/[1 + (1-\beta)t_2]$,
$L_{1x} \equiv \beta + (1 + \beta t_1)k_1\beta a_{2y}M_1/a_{1y}M_2[1 + (1 - \beta t_2)] > \beta$,
$T_1 \equiv \{(1 + t_2)/[1 + (1-\beta)t_2]\}^{(1-\beta)/\beta}/(1 + t_1)[1 + (1-\beta)t_2)]$,
$L_{2x} \equiv \beta - [1 + (1-\beta)t_2]k_2(1-\beta)a_{2x}M_1/a_{1x}M_2(1 + t_2)(1 + \beta t_1)] < \beta$,
$T_2 \equiv [(1 + t_1)/(1 + \beta t_1)]^{\beta/(1-\beta)}/(1 + t_2)(1 + \beta t_1)$, $T_3 \equiv [(1 + t_1)/(1 + \beta t_1)]^{\beta/(1-\beta)}/[1 + (1-\beta)t_2)]$,
$T_4 \equiv \{(1 + t_2)/[1 + (1-\beta)t_2]\}^{(1-\beta)/\beta}/(1 + t_1)(1 + \beta t_1)$.

In contrast to the country producing two goods, the completely specialized country has no influence on the terms of trade. As a result, it only hurts itself by imposing a tariff, as can be derived from table 12.3, $\partial U_2/\partial t_2 < 0$ in structure Ba and $\partial U_1/\partial t_1 < 0$ in structure Bb.

If both countries can influence the terms of trade (as in structure C), then the gains of trade are shared between the two countries. However, since $\partial U_1/\partial t_1 > 0$ and $\partial U_2/\partial t_2 > 0$ in structure C, i.e., each country can benefit from raising its own tariff given the other country's tariff rate, each country will be tempted to raise its own tariff as much as possible. But if they both raise tariffs, both can be worse off, since in structure C $\partial U_1/\partial t_2 < 0$ and $\partial U_2/\partial t_1 < 0$. Also $U_1$ converges to 0 as $t_2$ tends to infinity and $U_2$ converges to 0 as $t_1$ tends to infinity. This implies that as a country sufficiently increases its tariff, the other country will not only be marginally worse off, but also discontinuously (inframarginally) jump from trade to autarky.

The above analysis is conducted within the Walrasian regime. To analyze the behavior of the governments in the two countries, we examine two other regimes: a Nash game and a Nash tariff bargaining game.

First, suppose the governments in the two countries play a Nash game. Each government chooses its own tariff rate to maximize home residents' utility, taking as given the tariff rate in the foreign country and the Walrasian decisions of all individuals. For each structure (A, Ba, Bb, or C), a Nash corner equilibrium can be calculated. The Nash general equilibrium is one of four Nash corner equilibria. Consider structure Ba first.

Since $\partial U_2 / \partial t_2 < 0$ in this structure, the equilibrium strategy of country 2's government is to impose a zero tariff. Since $\partial U_1 / \partial t_1 > 0$ and $\partial U_2 / \partial t_1 < 0$, the equilibrium strategy of country 1's government is to impose a tariff as high as possible provided each individual in country 2 will not deviate from configuration (y/x). If the Nash corner equilibrium in structure Ba is the Nash general equilibrium, each individual in country 2 is slightly better off than in autarky and most gains from trade go to country 1. In other words, the Nash corner equilibrium in the tariff game in this structure generates a distribution pattern of gains from trade that is opposite to the distribution in the absence of a tariff where all the gains go to country 2.

This Nash corner equilibrium is not Pareto optimal because of the deadweight loss caused by a tariff. But the distortion caused by the tariff converges to zero as gains from trade net of transaction costs go to zero. If each government can choose any level of tariff (including zero tariff), the Walrasian equilibrium with no tariff will not occur when Structure Ba is chosen in general equilibrium because country 1's government has an incentive to deviate from that "equilibrium" by increasing its tariff.

Since structure Bb is symmetric to Ba, we can obtain a similar result: a tariff game will reverse the distribution pattern of gains from trade and generate distortions.

Now consider structure C. Since $\partial U_1 / \partial t_1 > 0$, $\partial U_2 / \partial t_1 < 0$, $\partial U_1 / \partial t_2 < 0$, $\partial U_2 / \partial t_2 > 0$ in this structure, the Nash corner equilibrium strategy of each government in this structure is to impose a tariff as high as possible provided the individuals in the other country will not deviate from their configurations in this structure. This implies that the gains from the complete division of labor in this structure will be almost exhausted by the deadweight loss caused by the tariff war. If the Nash general equilibrium occurs in this structure, this equilibrium may generate very significant welfare loss to both countries. This is a typical prisoners' dilemma: mutual beneficial gains cannot be realized because of coordination difficulty between self-interested rational decisions (see chapters 4, 9 above).

Now suppose the two governments play a Nash tariff bargaining game. This game maximizes a Nash product of the net gains of the two countries with respect to tariff rates of the two countries. Each country's net gain is the difference between each individual's realized utility and her utility at a disagreement point. The Nash tariff negotiation equilibrium can be solved in two steps: (1) a restricted Nash bargaining game is solved for a given structure, taking another structure as a disagreement point; (2) the two governments bargain over choice of structure.

The Nash product in structure C is

$$V = V_1 V_2 = [U_1(C) - U_1(A)] \, [U_2(C) - U_2(A)]$$

where $U_i(C)$ and $U_i(A)$ are given in table 12.3. The Nash bargaining corner equilibrium in structure C is given by maximizing $V$ with respect to $t_1$ and $t_2$. The two first-order conditions $\partial V / \partial t_1 = \partial V / \partial t_2 = 0$ generate $(1 + t_1)(1 + t_2) = 1$. Hence, the solution of the Nash tariff negotiation game is $t_1^* = t_2^* = 0$. This implies that the Nash tariff negotiation will generate a bilateral *laissez-faire* regime. But this *laissez-faire* regime cannot be achieved in the absence of tariff negotiation because of interest conflict.

Although in this Nash bargaining game no risk is specified, the players' attitudes towards risk "plays a central role" (Osborne and Rubinstein, 1990, p. 10). As long as there exists uncertainty about other players' behavior, there is a chance that the negotiations will break down. Thus each government intends to maximize its expected utility gain in the negotiation. In fact, the Nash product can be interpreted as a player's expected utility gain, with the probability of reaching an agreement being approximated by the utility gain(s) of the other player(s). According to this view of Nash (1950), the Nash bargaining solution is the outcome of a noncooperative game despite the fact that the gains are shared fairly among players.

If each government can decide whether or not to participate in a tariff negotiation game, then it is clear that when structure Ba or Bb occur in general equilibrium, it must be a Nash equilibrium with no tariff negotiation since the country producing two goods can get most of the gains from a unilateral tariff. When structure C occurs in general equilibrium, the general equilibrium must involve tariff negotiation since both governments prefer tariff negotiation to tariff war – clearly, the two countries receive more net gains in the tariff negotiation game than in the tariff war since the Nash tariff bargaining equilibrium, which coincides with the Walrasian equilibrium with no tariff, is Pareto optimal.

This result explains why it is difficult to realize a *laissez-faire* regime even if it is good for all countries. When the sovereignty of a country can be used to seek rent in international trade via taxation power, coordination difficulty in a prisoners' dilemma makes tariff negotiation essential for fully exploiting mutually beneficial gains from trade. Following the method in the previous section, we can show that in the model with endogenous choice of regimes, the general equilibrium discontinuously jumps from autarky to structures Ba or Bb, then to structure C as the trading efficiency coefficient $k$ increases. From the relevant parameter subspace column in table 12.3, we can see that in the transitional stage from A to C, the country with low trading efficiency and/or large population size produces two goods.

Summarizing the above analysis, we have:

**Proposition 12.2:** In a model with the two governments which can choose tariff level and decide whether or not to participate in tariff negotiations, if partial division of labor occurs in equilibrium, it is a Nash tariff equilibrium with no tariff negotiation. Most gains from trade go to the country producing both goods and having lower trading efficiency or a larger population size. If complete division of labor occurs in equilibrium, it is a Nash tariff negotiation equilibrium which generates a bilateral *laissez-faire* regime.

Proposition 12.2 may be used to explain two phenomena. First, despite the distortions caused by tariffs, tariffs may be used by a government in a less-developed economy with low trading efficiency to get a larger share of gains from trade, since the Walrasian equilibrium with no tariff may divide gains to trade very unequally between countries. Second, when trading efficiency is not very high so that the equilibrium is associated with an intermediate level of division of labor, some countries (which have low trading efficiency and do not completely specialize) may prefer a unilateral tariff, whereas other countries (which have higher trading efficiency and completely specialize) may prefer a unilateral *laissez-faire* regime. But as trading efficiency is improved, all countries may prefer tariff negotiations to a unilateral tariff or to a unilateral *laissez-faire* regime.

In the sixteenth and seventeenth centuries, unilateral tariffs were advocated by mercantilists as a means of rent seeking in international trade. It gave way to trade liberalization in the eighteenth and nineteenth centuries in some European countries. However, even after the Second World War, many governments in developing countries still adopted unilateral tariff protection. More recently, tariff negotiations have become increasingly prevalent. Some economists use the Walrasian model to explain the emergence of *laissez-faire* regimes, but the model cannot explain why other trade regimes persisted in many countries for a long period of time. Other economists use the theory of import and export substitution to explain the transition from unilateral tariff to trade liberalization (see, for instance, Balassa, 1986), but the theory cannot explain why a *laissez-faire* regime was unstable even between developed countries; why a unilateral protection tariff and a *laissez-faire* regime may coexist; and why tariff negotiations may be necessary for free trade and for the exploitation of the gains from trade. Proposition 12.2 in this chapter seems to offer a more plausible explanation as to why unilateral tariffs prevailed in the early stage of economic development; why trade liberalization is preferred in later stages of economic development; and the above questions.

In the next example, we extend the simple $2 \times 2$ Ricardian model to include a third country, to show that a country may be excluded from trade despite the existence of comparative advantage between it and another country.

## Example 12.3: a Ricardo model with three countries

It is assumed that trading efficiency is different from country to country such that $k_1, k_3 > k_2$, where $k_i$ is the trading efficiency coefficient in country i. We intend to show that a country which does not have a comparative advantage to the other two countries and/or which has low trading efficiency can be excluded from trade.

Suppose that the production functions in country i ($i = 1, 2, 3$) are the same as in (12.2) and that $(a_{3x}/a_{3y}) < (a_{2x}/a_{2y}) < (a_{1x}/a_{1y})$, i.e., country 1 has a comparative advantage in producing good x to the other two countries, country 2 has a comparative advantage in producing x relative to country 3, and a comparative advantage in producing good y relative to country 1; and country 3 has a comparative advantage in producing y to the other two countries.

We consider only the case where the trading countries are completely specialized. For reasons similar to those discussed in example 12.2, all structures involving trade in comparative disadvantage goods cannot occur in general equilibrium. We now prove that if a structure involves trade between only two of the three countries, the two trading countries must be country 1 and country 3. In other words, the country which has the lowest trading efficiency and/or has no comparative advantage to the other two countries may be excluded from trade.

We first prove that it is impossible that only county 1 and country 2 trade or only country 2 and country 3 trade. We use argument of negation. Suppose only country 1 and country 2 trade. This can occur in general equilibrium only if individuals in country 2 prefer specialization in y (or configuration (y/x)) to autarky and individuals in country 3 prefer autarky to specialization in y. That is, the following inequalities hold:

$U_2(y/x) > U_2(A)$ which holds iff $p < (a_{2y}/a_{2x})k_2$ and

$U_3(y/x) < U_3(A)$ which holds iff $p > (a_{3y}/a_{3x})k_3$.

where the indirect utility functions for different configurations are from table 12.1. The two inequalities jointly imply $(a_{2x}/a_{2y}k_2) < (a_{3x}/a_{3y}k_3)$, which contradicts the assumption $(a_{2x}/a_{2y}) > (a_{3x}/a_{3y})$ and $k_2 < k_3$.

Suppose instead only country 2 and country 3 trade. This can occur in general equilibrium only if

$U_2(x/y) > U_2(A)$ which holds iff $p > a_{2y}/a_{2x}k_2$ and

$U_1(x/y) < U_1(A)$ which holds iff $p < a_{1y}/a_{1x}k_1$.

The two inequalities jointly imply $(a_{1y}/a_{1x}k_1) > (a_{2y}/a_{2x}k_2)$ which contradicts the assumptions $(a_{1x}/a_{1y}) > (a_{2x}/a_{2y})$ and $k_2 < k_1$. Hence, if only two countries trade, they must be country 1 and country 3.

Next we examine the conditions under which the structure involving trade only between country 1 and country 3 occurs in general equilibrium. The conditions are:

$U_1(x/y) > U_1(y/x)$ which holds iff $p > (a_{1y}/a_{1x})k_1^{2\beta-1}$,

$U_1(x/y) > U_1(A)$ which holds iff $p > a_{1y}/a_{1x}k_1$,

$U_2(x/y) < U_2(A)$ which holds iff $p < a_{2y}/a_{2x}k_2$,

$U_2(y/x) < U_2(A)$ which holds iff $p > (a_{2y}/a_{2x})k_2$,

$U_3(y/x) > U_3(A)$ which holds iff $p < (a_{3y}/a_{3x})k_3$,

$U_3(y/x) > U_3(x/y)$ which holds iff $p < (a_{3y}/a_{3x})k_3^{2\beta-1}$,

where $p = a_{3y}M_3\beta/a_{1x}M_1(1-\beta)$ is the corner equilibrium relative price in this structure. The six inequalities together imply $\text{Min}\{a_{2y}/a_{2x}k_2, (a_{3y}/a_{3x})k_3\} > a_{3y}M_3\beta/a_{1x}M_1(1-\beta) > \text{Max}\{a_{1y}/a_{1x}k_1, (a_{2y}/a_{2x})k_2\}$. The parameter subspace satisfying this condition is certainly not empty. For instance, if $k_2$ is sufficiently close to 0 and $k_1$ and $k_3$ are sufficiently close to 1, then the above condition becomes $(a_{3y}/a_{3x})k_3 > a_{3y}M_3\beta/a_{1x}M_1(1-\beta) > a_{1y}/a_{1x}k_1$, or $(a_{1x}/a_{3x})k_3 > M_3\beta/M_1(1-\beta) > a_{1y}/a_{3y}k_1$, which holds only if $k_3k_1[(a_{1x}/a_{1y})/(a_{3x}/a_{3y})] > 1$. This condition can be satisfied if the relative population size is not too far away from a balance with relative tastes, the two countries' trading efficiency is sufficiently high, and the degree of comparative advantage (measured by $(a_{1x}/a_{3x})(a_{3y}/a_{1y})$) between the two countries is great.

Summarizing the above analysis, we obtain:

**Proposition 12.3:** In a $3 \times 2$ Ricardian model within a certain parameter subspace, it is possible that the country that has no comparative advantage in producing any good over both of its potential trading partners and/or that has very low trading efficiency will be excluded from trade.

This proposition can accommodate opinions on both sides of a recent debate on international competitiveness. Krugman (1994a,b) argued that a nation should focus on promoting free trade and that the emphasis on international competitiveness can be "a dangerous obsession." Sachs (1996a,b) and Prestowitz et al. (1994), on the other hand, contended that international competitiveness plays an essential role in improving national welfare. If international competitiveness is measured by a country's trading efficiency, then proposition 12.3 confirms that competitiveness matters. Proposition 12.3 implies that comparative advantage is not enough for realizing gains from trade. A country can be excluded from trade even if it has comparative advantage to another single country when its trading efficiency is low or/and it has no comparative advantage to both of the other potential partners. However, the proposition also supports Krugman's argument that a country should focus on promoting free trade and improving trading efficiency. In our model, the promotion of free trade can be done through reducing tariff and nontariff barriers to trade so as to improve trading efficiency $k$. If $k$ is extremely low, no trade occurs and absolute and comparative advantage does not do good for trade. Since in our model the improvement of the trading efficiency coefficient through trade liberalization policies can generate a jump of general equilibrium from a low to a high level of division of labor, the argument for free trade is even stronger than the conventional marginal analysis suggests. Therefore, international competitiveness and free trade are important factors contributing to a country's welfare. And Krugman's emphasis on trade liberalization is particularly relevant if the pursuit of international competitiveness is used as an excuse for impeding free trade.

Introducing tariff into the model in this section, it can be shown that when all governments are allowed to choose a tariff level and when the partial division of labor occurs in general equilibrium, the country with a higher tariff and/or worse transaction condition (a small value of $k$) will be excluded from trade. Hence, in a world economy with many governments, each country will reduce tariffs to avoid such exclusion. This implies that even in a partial division of labor, tariff rates will be reduced by competition between governments in similar countries.

On the other hand, since a greater value of $k$ will increase the number of countries that are involved in international trade, which will in turn ensure a multilateral free trade regime even if the partial division of labor occurs in general equilibrium, a sufficiently great increase in $k$ in the country that was excluded from trade can then ensure a zero tariff rate for all countries even if the general equilibrium is associated with the partial division of labor. This result implies that there are two possible explanations for a shift of trade regime from protection tariff to trade liberalization. The first is to attribute such a shift to the increase in the level of division of labor (a shift from the partial division of labor to the complete division of labor), which is caused by improvements in transaction conditions. The second is to attribute such a shift to the increase in the number of countries that are involved in international trade, which is caused by improvements of the transaction conditions in those countries which used to be excluded from trade. Since an increase in $k$ can be generated either by improvements in transportation conditions (the emergence of new transportation technology or the development of transportation infrastructure) or by institutional changes (the emergence of a legal system that more effectively protects property rights or a more competitive and efficient banking system), we can explain this shift of trade regime by improvements of transportation and institution environment.

## ♦ 12.5 Comparative Endowment Advantage and Trading Efficiency

In this section, we develop a Heckscher–Ohlin (HO) model with two countries differing in endowments and transaction conditions. The HO model can be used to show that in the absence of Ricardo's technological comparative advantage, economies of division of labor may arise from exogenous differences in endowment between countries. Based on the HO model, some core neoclassical trade theorems are developed. In this section, we work out the inframarginal as well as marginal comparative statics of general equilibrium of the HO model to show that as transaction conditions are improved, the equilibrium levels of division of labor and productivity increase. In particular, comparative statics that relate to the Heckscher–Ohlin (HO) theorem, the Stolper–Samuelson (SS) theorem, and the factor price equalization (FPE) theorem are examined.

## Example 12.4: the HO model with transaction costs

Consider the HO model with comparative endowment advantages between two countries and with transaction costs. Perfect competition prevails in both goods and factor markets, and factors are mobile within a country but immobile between countries.

Country i ($i = 1, 2$) is endowed with labor $L_i$ and capital $K_i$, which can be used to produce two consumer goods x and y. The decision problem of a representative consumer in country i is

$$\text{Max: } U_i = X_i^\theta Y_i^{1-\theta},$$

$$\text{s.t. } p_{ix} x_i + p_{jx} x_{ji} + p_{iy} y_i + p_{jy} y_{ji} = w_i L_i + r_i K_i$$

where $X_i \equiv x_i + k_i x_{ji}$ and $Y_i \equiv y_i + k_i y_{ji}$ are respective amounts of the two goods consumed, $p_{st}$ is the price of good t in country s, $x_i$ and $y_i$ are respective amounts of the two goods purchased from domestic market in country i, $x_{ji}$ and $y_{ji}$ are respective amounts of the two goods, purchased from a foreign country, or delivered from country j to country i, $w_i$ and $r_i$ are wage rate and rental of capital in country i, respectively. $x_i, x_{ji}, y_i, y_{ji}$, may be 0, or corner solutions are allowed. Because of transaction costs, the prices of the same good may differ between the two countries. Since corner solutions are allowed, a consumer's decision is configuration-dependent as in previous sections.

In addition to autarky, there are 8 different trade structures in the HO model. Using the first letter to denote goods produced by country 1, the second letter to denote goods produced by country 2, and the subscript i to denote country i, we have the following structures, as shown in figure 12.3: $x_1 y_2$ (country 1 produces x and country 2 produces y); $y_1 x_2$ (country 1 produces y and country 2 produces x); $xy_1 y_2$ (country 1 produces both goods and country 2 produces y); $xy_1 x_2, x_1 xy_2, y_1 xy_2, yx_1 xy_2$ (each country produces two goods and country 1 exports x and imports y); $xy_1 yx_2$ (each country produces two goods and country 1 exports y and imports x). The last two structures are referred to as interior structures, since they are based on interior solutions for each country. The first six structures involve the corner solutions of at least one country, and are thus referred to as corner structures. Our concept of interior structure relates to the concept of the diversification cone, developed in the 1950s (see Lerner, 1952, and McKenzie, 1955). The difference is that the latter is defined as the range of factor endowments within which a country produces both goods for given prices, but the former occurs in equilibrium within a particular parameter subspace, as shown later.

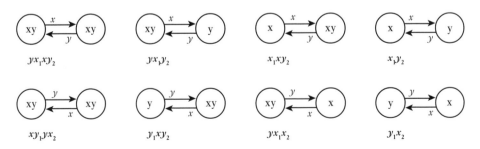

Figure 12.3: Possible trade structures

We first consider structure $yx_1xy_2$ where $x_{21} = y_{12} = 0$. The first-order conditions for the decision problems of representative consumers in the two countries yield: $p_{2y} = k_1 p_{1y} = k_1$, $p_{1x} = k_2 p_{2x}$. We assume that good y produced in country 1 is the *numéraire*, so that $p_{1y} = 1$ and denote $p = p_{1x}$, so that $p_{2x} = p/k_2$ and $p_{2y} = k_1$.

Assume that the production functions for x and y in country i are:

$$x_i^s = L_{ix}^\alpha K_{ix}^{1-\alpha}; \quad y_i^s = L_{iy}^\beta K_{iy}^{1-\beta}$$

where $x_i^s$ and $y_i^s$ are the respective output levels of the two goods, $L_{ij}$ ($i = 1, 2; j = x, y$) is the amount of labor and $K_{ij}$ is the amount of capital allocated to produce good j in country i. Constrained by the production technology, the representative firm producing x in country i maximizes its profit, i.e.,

$$\underset{L_{ix}, K_{ix}}{\text{Max}} \; \pi_{ix} = p_{ix} x_i^s - w_i L_{ix} - r_i K_{ix} = p_{ix} L_{ix}^\alpha K_{ix}^{1-\alpha} - w_i L_{ix} - r_i K_{ix}.$$

The decision problem for the representative firm producing y is similar. Because of the constant returns to scale, the optimum quantities of goods supplied and the optimum quantities of factors demanded are indeterminate. But the first-order conditions for the four decision problems of the two types of firms in the two countries can be used to express factor prices and relative factor allocation as functions of relative prices of goods. The market clearing conditions for factors in each country can then be used to solve resource allocations also as functions of the relative prices of goods. The world market clearing condition for goods x or y then determines the equilibrium relative prices of goods.

Without loss of generality, we assume that $\beta > \alpha$. It is easy to show that in the equilibrium $K_{ix}/L_{ix} > K_{iy}/L_{iy}$ if and only if $\beta > \alpha$. Hence, the assumption implies that the x industry is capital-intensive and the y industry is labor-intensive. We assume also that country 1 is relatively capital abundant, or $K_2/L_2 < K_1/L_1$.

We first consider the world equilibrium in structure $yx_1xy_2$, then consider structure $xy_1yx_2$ and identify the parameter subspaces for autarky and corner structures to be general equilibrium. The interior equilibrium in structure $yx_1xy_2$ is summarized as follows.

$$
\begin{aligned}
X_i &= A[\beta K_i - (1 - \beta)L_i/\gamma]\gamma^\alpha/(\beta - \alpha), \\
Y_i &= B[(1 - \alpha)(L_i/\gamma) - \alpha K_i]\gamma^\beta/(\beta - \alpha), \\
L_{ix} &= [\alpha/(\beta - \alpha)][\beta K_i \gamma - (1 - \beta)L_i], \\
L_{iy} &= [\beta/(\beta - \alpha)][(1 - \alpha)L_i - \alpha K_i \gamma], \\
K_{ix} &= (1 - \alpha)L_{ix} w_i/r_i \alpha, \qquad K_{iy} = (1 - \beta)L_{iy} w_i/r_i \beta, \\
p &= B\gamma^{(\beta-\alpha)}/A, \quad r_1/w_1 = (Ap/B)^{1/(\beta-\alpha)}, \quad r_2/w_2 = (Ap/k_1 k_2 B)^{1/(\beta-\alpha)},
\end{aligned}
$$

(12.7a)

where $A \equiv \alpha^\alpha(1 - \alpha)^{1-\alpha}$, $B \equiv \beta^\beta(1 - \beta)^{1-\beta}$,

$$\gamma \equiv \frac{[1 - \beta + (\beta - \alpha)\theta]L_1 + [1 - \beta + (\beta - \alpha)\theta/k_2](k_1 k_2)^{(1-\alpha)/(\beta-\alpha)}L_2}{[\beta(1 - \theta) + \alpha\theta]K_1 + [\beta - (\beta - \alpha)\theta/k_2](k_1 k_2)^{(1-\alpha)/(\beta-\alpha)}K_2},$$

(12.7b)

$X_i$ and $Y_i$ are respective amounts of the two goods consumed by the representative consumer in country i.

The HO theorem (Heckscher, 1919 and Ohlin, 1933) states that a country exports the goods whose production uses its abundant factor intensively. In terms of the model in this section, the HO theorem, together with the assumption that $\beta > \alpha$ (the x sector is capital intensive), implies that country 1 exports good x and imports y if $K_1/L_1 > K_2/L_2$. Considering all possible structures, this implies that structure $yx_1xy_2$, $xy_1y_2$, $x_1xy_2$, or $x_1y_2$, as shown in figure 12.3, occurs at general equilibrium.

Letting the equilibrium values of $L_{ix}$ and $L_{iy}$ be greater than or equal to 0, we can partition the nine-dimensional space of parameters $\beta$, $\alpha$, $\theta$, $K_i$, $L_i$, $k_i$ into subspaces. For instance, letting $L_{ix}$, $L_{iy} > 0$ for i = 1, 2, we can identify the parameter subspace for an interior structure to be the general equilibrium structure, and letting $L_{ix}$, $L_{1y} > 0$ and $L_{2y} = 0$, we can identify the parameter subspace for structure $xy_1x_2$ to be the general equilibrium structure. All possible trade structures are illustrated in figure 12.3, where the left circle in each panel represents country 1 and the right circle represents country 2; lines between circles represent goods flows. In figure 12.3, the distinction is drawn between the interior structure $xy_1yx_2$, in which country 1 exports y and country 2 exports x, and the structure $yx_1xy_2$, in which country 1 exports x and country 2 exports y. The two structures are interior structures, but the former is inconsistent with the HO theorem.

Structures $xy_1x_2$, $y_1xy_2$, $y_1x_2$ are incompatible with the HO theorem; in those cases the capital abundant country 1 exports the labor-intensive good y. We first identify the condition under which the parameter subspaces that enable the three structures to be general equilibrium structures are empty. Let $L_{ix}$, $L_{1y} > 0$ and $L_{2y} \leq 0$ in (12.7a), we can see that structure $xy_1x$ will be chosen only if $K_2/L_2 > K_1/L_1$. Hence, we can see that the parameter subspace for structure $xy_1x_2$ to be chosen is empty if

$$K_2/L_2 < K_1/L_1 \text{ and } \beta > \alpha \tag{12.8}$$

Similarly, we can prove that structures $y_1xy_2$, $y_1x_2$, which are incompatible with the HO theorem, cannot be general equilibrium structures if (12.8) holds. We can also show that the parameter subspaces for other structures to be equilibrium structures are not empty if (12.8) holds.

For an interior structure to occur in equilibrium, it must be true that $L_1x > 0$; $L_1y > 0$; $L_{2x} > 0$; $L_{2y} > 0$. These conditions are equivalent to

$$\gamma \in ((1-\beta)L_1/\beta K_1, (1-\alpha)L_1/\alpha K_1), \text{ which holds only if } \beta > \alpha \tag{12.9a}$$

$$\gamma/(k_1k_2) \in ((1-\beta)L_2/\beta K_2, (1-\alpha)L_2/\alpha K_2), \text{ which holds only if } \beta > \alpha. \tag{12.9b}$$

$$\gamma \in ((k_1k_2)^{1/(\beta-\alpha)}(1-\beta)L_2/\beta K_2, (1-\alpha)L_1/\alpha K_1), \text{ which holds only if} \tag{12.9c}$$
$$(1-\alpha)L_1/\alpha K_1 > (k_1k_2)^{1/(\beta-\alpha)}(1-\beta)L_2/\beta K_2$$

$$\gamma \in ((1-\beta)L_1/\beta K_1, (k_1k_2)^{1/(\beta-\alpha)}(1-\alpha)L_2/\alpha K_2), \text{ which holds only if} \tag{12.9d}$$
$$(k_1k_2)^{1/(\beta-\alpha)}(1-\alpha)L_2/\alpha K_2 > (1-\beta)L_1/\beta K_1$$

where $\gamma$ is given in (12.7) and $\partial\gamma/\partial k_1 > 0$ and $\partial[\gamma/(k_1k_2)]/\partial k_2 < 0$. (12.9a) implies that $k_1$ is neither too great nor too small, (12.9b) implies that $k_2$ is neither too great nor too small. (12.9c) implies that trading efficiencies in two countries $(k_1k_2)$ are not great and endowment comparative advantage $K_1L_2/L_1K_2$ is not too great compared to other parameters. (12.9d) implies that trading efficiency $(k_1k_2)$ is not small and endowment comparative advantage $K_1L_2/L_1K_2$ is not small. Hence, structure $yx_1xy_2$ occurs in equilibrium if trading efficiencies in two countries are neither too great nor too small and endowment comparative advantages are neither too significant nor too trivial.

Now we consider the dividing line between structure $yx_1xy_2$ and autarky. Since both structures satisfy $L_{ij} > 0$ for $i = 1, 2$ and $j = x, y$, we have to calculate the domestic excess demand for x and y to identify the dividing line. Inserting the equilibrium prices into the domestic demand and supply functions for goods yields:

$$x_1^s \geq X_1^d \text{ iff } \gamma \geq \gamma_1 \equiv [(\beta - \alpha)\theta + 1 - \beta]L_1/K_1[\beta(1 - \theta) + \alpha\theta] \tag{12.10a}$$

$$y_2^s \geq Y_2^d \text{ iff } \gamma \leq \gamma_2 \equiv [(\beta - \alpha)\theta + 1 - \beta](k_1k_2)^{1/(\beta-\alpha)}L_2/K_2[\beta(1 - \theta) + \alpha\theta]. \tag{12.10b}$$

The two semi-inequalities imply that

$$\gamma_2 \geq \gamma \geq \gamma_1 \text{ which holds only if } \gamma_2 \geq \gamma_1 . \tag{12.11}$$

It is not difficult to see that $\gamma_2 > \gamma_1$ if and only if

$$\eta \equiv (k_1k_2)^{1/(\beta-\alpha)}\mu = (k_1k_2)^{1/(\beta-\alpha)}(K_1L_2/K_2L_1) > 1, \tag{12.12}$$

where $\eta$ is a product of trading efficiencies in the two countries and comparative endowment advantage and $\mu$ represents the degree of comparative endowment advantage. It is obvious for $k_1k_2 = 1$, $\gamma_2 > \gamma_1$ if and only if (12.8) holds. Hence, if (12.8) holds and transaction costs in two countries do not outweigh comparative endowment advantage, then autarky will not be chosen and $yx_1xy_2$ is a candidate for equilibrium structure.

As $k_1$ and $k_2$ decrease from 1, $\gamma_2$ tends to $\gamma_1$ and $\eta$ tends to 1. If $k_1$ and $k_2$ are sufficiently small, it will be true that $\gamma_2 = \gamma_1$ and $\eta = 1$ which implies that the domestic excess demand in both countries is 0, or autarky occurs in equilibrium. Hence, the dividing line between structure $yx_1xy_2$ and autarky is

$$\eta = (k_1k_2)^{1/(\beta-\alpha)}(K_1L_2/K_2L_1) = 1.$$

For $\eta \leq 1$, autarky occurs in equilibrium. (12.12), together with (12.9c), implies that structure $yx_1xy_2$ occurs in equilibrium only if $\beta(1 - \alpha)/\alpha(1 - \beta) > \eta > 1$.

Alternatively, we can verify that autarky occurs in equilibrium if trading efficiency in either country is sufficiently low. First, note the fact that $d\gamma/dk_1 > 0$ and for $k_1k_2 = 1$, $\gamma > \gamma_1$. This implies that as $k_1$ decreases from 1 to 0, $\gamma$ monotonously decreases from a value greater than $\gamma_1$ toward $\gamma_1$. As $\gamma$ has reached $\gamma_1$, the equilibrium price in structure $yx_1xy_2$ becomes the same as that in autarky. Hence, as $k_1$ becomes sufficiently close to 0, country 1 chooses autarky and therefore the general equilibrium is autarky. Similarly, we can prove that as $k_2$ becomes sufficiently close to 0, country 2 chooses autarky and therefore the general equilibrium is autarky. Therefore, if trading efficiency in either country is too low, the general equilibrium will be autarky. As trading efficiencies increase, the general equilibrium jumps from autarky to a structure with trade.

In order to rule out structure $xy_1yx_2$, we assume $x_{12}, y_{21} = 0$ and $x_{21}, y_{12} > 0$ in the consumer's decision problem. Following the same procedure for solving for the local equilibrium in structure $yx_1xy_2$ we can show that the equilibrium prices in this structure are $p_{1y} = 1, p_{1x} = p, p_{2x} = k_2, p_{2y} = k_1p$ and that domestic excess demand for x in country 1 and that for y in country 2 are positive only if

$$\mu = (K_1 L_2 / K_2 L_1) < (k_1 k_2)^{1/(\beta-\alpha)},$$

which is incompatible with the assumption (12.8) for $k_i \in [0, 1]$ and $\beta > \alpha$. This implies that the parameter subspace for structure $xy_1yx_2$ to occur in equilibrium is empty or this structure is ruled out from the set of candidates for equilibrium structures.

Following this method, we can show that the parameter subspace for structure $x_1xy_2$ to occur in equilibrium is given by

$$(1 - \alpha)L_1 / \alpha K_1 < \gamma < (1 - \alpha)L_2(k_1 k_2)^{1/(\beta-\alpha)} / \alpha K_2 \text{ and} \tag{12.13a}$$

$$(1 - \alpha)L_2 / \alpha K_2 > \gamma / (k_1 k_2)^{1/(\beta-\alpha)} > (1 - \beta)L_2 / \beta K_2. \tag{12.13b}$$

(12.13a) holds only if $k_1 k_2$ is sufficiently large and the degree of comparative endowment advantage, $K_1 L_2 / L_1 K_2$, is not too great, compared to other parameters. Since $d[\gamma / (k_1 k_2)^{1/(\beta-\alpha)}] / dk_2 < 0$, (12.13b) implies that $k_2$ is neither too great nor too small and the degree of comparative endowment advantage, $K_1 L_2 / L_1 K_2$, is not too small, compared to other parameters. Hence, the general equilibrium occurs in structure $x_1xy_2$ if trading efficiency in country 2 and comparative advantage are neither too high nor too low, while the trading efficiency is great in country 1. In other words, country 1 completely specializes and country 2 produces two goods if $k_1$ is great compared to $k_2$. Since international terms of trade are determined by the domestic terms of trade in country 2 in this structure, most gains from trade go to the country producing one good.

The parameter subspace for structure $xy_1y_2$ to occur in equilibrium is given by

$$(1 - \beta)L_1 / \beta K_1 < \gamma < (1 - \alpha)L_1 / \alpha K_1 \text{ and} \tag{12.14a}$$

$$(1 - \alpha)L_2(k_1 k_2)^{1/(\beta-\alpha)} / \alpha K_2 > \gamma > (1 - \beta)L_1 / \beta K_1. \tag{12.14b}$$

(12.14b) holds only if $k_1 k_2$ is sufficiently large and the degree of comparative endowment advantage, $K_1 L_2 / L_1 K_2$, is not too small. Since $d\gamma / dk_1 > 0$, (12.14a) implies that $k_1$ is neither too great nor too small, and the degree of comparative endowment advantage, $K_1 L_2 / L_1 K_2$, is not too great. Hence, the general equilibrium occurs in structure $xy_1y_2$ if the trading efficiency in country 1 and comparative advantage are neither too high nor too low, while the trading efficiency is great in country 2. In other words, country 1 produces two goods and country 2 completely specializes if $k_2$ is great compared to $k_1$.

Following this method, we can identify the parameter subspace for each structure to be

Table 12.4: General equilibrium and its inframarginal comparative statics

| $\eta$ | $k$ | Equilibrium structure |
|---|---|---|
| $< 1$ | $k_1$ and/or $k_2$ are small | Autarky |
| $\in [1, \beta(1 - \alpha)/\alpha(1 - \beta)]$ | $k_1$ is great, $k_2$ is neither great nor small | $x_1xy_2$ |
| | $k_1$ and $k_2$ are neither great nor small | $yx_1xy_2$ |
| | $k_2$ is great, $k_1$ is neither great nor small | $yx_1y_2$ |
| $> \beta(1 - \alpha)/\alpha(1 - \beta)$ | $k_1$ is great, $k_2$ is neither great nor small | $x_1xy_2$ |
| | $k_1$ and $k_2$ are great | $x_1y_2$ |
| | $k_2$ is great, $k_1$ is neither great nor small | $yx_1y_2$ |

an equilibrium structure, as summarized in table 12.4, where $\eta \equiv (k_1 k_2)^{1/(\beta-\alpha)}\mu$ $= (k_1 k_2)^{1/(\beta-\alpha)}(K_1 L_2/K_2 L_1)$, and $\beta(1-\alpha)/\alpha(1-\beta) > 1 > \alpha(1-\beta)/\beta(1-\alpha) > 0$. $\eta$ is a product of trading efficiencies in the two countries and comparative endowment advantages and $\mu$ represents the degree of comparative endowment advantage.

Table 12.4 indicates that under our assumption (12.8), autarky and four different trade patterns can occur in equilibrium depending on parameter values. All of the four trade patterns feature country 1 exporting good x. (It can be shown that if we reverse our assumption (12.8), the other four trade patterns will occur in equilibrium each featuring country 1 exporting good y.)

All corner structures in table 12.4 are consistent with the HO theorem. For instance, in structure $xy_1 y_2$, the capital-abundant country 1 exports the capital-intensive good x and the labor-abundant country 2 exports labor-intensive good y, as shown in figure 12.3. We can see that for each corner structure, the market clearing condition ensures a trade pattern that is unambiguous about which country exports which good. This implies that the HO theorem holds for all corner structures in table 12.4, even if parameter values shift between the parameter subspaces that demarcate the structures.

Following the same approach to analyzing the Ricardo model in the previous sections, it can be shown that the equilibrium production schedule in autarky is lower than the PPF, as shown in figure 2.4, since autarky imposes the constraint that marginal rate of substitution and marginal rate of transformation must be equalized within each country. Hence, as transaction conditions are improved, the aggregate productivity jumps as a result of an increase in the equilibrium levels of division of labor and trade. This is another general equilibrium mechanism for economic development: as transaction conditions are improved, the equilibrium productivity increases due to exploitation of more comparative endowment advantages between countries or between different groups of individuals. You are asked in exercise 10 to introduce comparative technological advantages into the HO model to refine proposition 12.4 and to prove that the HO theorem may not hold in the model with comparative technological and endowment advantages.

The inframarginal comparative statics are summarized as follows.

**Proposition 12.4:** If trading efficiency is sufficiently low in any country and/or comparative endowment advantage is small, autarky occurs in equilibrium. As trading efficiencies in two countries are slightly improved and/or the degree of comparative advantage slightly increases, the equilibrium shifts to a low level of division of labor with each country producing two goods. If the trading efficiency is further improved in one country and/or the degree of comparative advantage increases further, the equilibrium shifts to a dual structure where this country completely specializes and gets most gains from trade, while the other country produces two goods. As trading efficiencies in two countries and/or the degree of comparative advantage are sufficiently increased, the equilibrium jumps to a high level of division of labor where each country produces only one good and gains from trade are shared by the two countries. This evolution in division of labor and trade dependence increases the equilibrium aggregate productivity.

Table 12.4 and (12.7) show that for $k_1 = k_2 = 1$, international trade will make factor prices in the trading countries equalize even though the factors themselves are immobile across countries (Samuelson, 1948), if the endowment comparative advantage and trading efficiencies in the two countries are neither great nor small, or if the interior structure $yx_1 xy_2$ occurs in equilibrium. It is easy to show that the factor price equalization does not hold if $k_1$ and

$k_2$ are not 1 (transaction cost is not zero). In addition, the factor price may not be equal if a corner structure occurs at equilibrium or if trading efficiency in any country and/or comparative endowment advantage are too great or too small. In exercise 10 you are asked to show that if total factor productivity is different from country to country and from good to good, then relative factor price may be different even in the interior structure $yx_1xy_2$ in the absence of transaction costs.

The SS theorem was derived from an interior structure in the HO model in which both countries produce both goods, and the commodity price is assumed to be exogenous. The theorem states that if the price of the capital-intensive (or labor-intensive) good rises, the price of capital (or labor) rises, and in greater proportion to the commodity price increase; while the price of labor falls (or of capital rises), but necessarily in greater proportion to the commodity price increase (Stolper and Samuelson, 1941). The theorem is wildly at odds with empirical evidence. (Grossman and Levinsohn (1989) show that the specific factors model captures reality more closely than the SS theorem for many US industries.) Since the price of a country's comparative advantage good rises with the opening–up of international trade, a corollary of the SS theorem is that international trade benefits a country's abundant factor and hurts its scarce factor, so that a tariff benefits a country's scarce factor. This prediction is inconsistent with the common sense that the protection of labor-intensive industries may shift the distribution of income marginally in favor of workers, but will lower overall income and on balance, therefore, will normally hurt them. On this view, the SS theorem provides a theory to explain the income distribution effect of international trade. The inframarginal comparative statics in table 12.4 implies that common sense might be closer to reality than the SS theorem.

Our iceberg transaction cost is equivalent to a tax system that uses all tax revenue to pay bureaucrats who collect tax. Hence, our model can be used to analyze effects of a tariff that incurs significant bureaucracy cost. The SS theorem ignores possible inframarginal effects of tariff and transaction costs on a discontinuous shift of trade structure. As shown in table 12.4, tariff and associated transaction costs may generate jumps between autarky and structures $x_1y_2$, and $yx_1xy_2$ that may be inconsistent with the SS theorem.

Second, proposition 12.4 implies that as the trading efficiency in a country unilaterally decreases compared to another country, the general equilibrium may shift from structure $x_1y_2$ to an asymmetric structure where this country produces two goods and most of the gains from trade go to the other country. This is because in an asymmetric structure, terms of international trade are determined by terms of domestic trade in the country producing two goods. This formalizes the common sense that even if tariff may marginally change terms of trade and increase income of scarce factors, it may inframarginally hurt all home residents by reducing level of trade and associated gains.

Finally, we prove that even within the interior structure, the SS theorem may not hold if price movements are caused by changes in transaction conditions. Suppose that the equilibrium occurs in structure $yx_1xy_2$, so that the equilibrium prices are given by (12.7). Country 2's terms of trade is $P \equiv p_{2y}/p_{1x} = k_1/p$, where $p_{2y}$ is the price of good y in country 2 in terms of good y in country 1, $p \equiv p_{1x}$ is the price of good x in terms of good y in country 1. The differentiation of the expression of $r_2/w_2$, given in (12.7a), yields

$$d(r_2/w_2)/dk_2 = \partial(r_2/w_2)/\partial k_2 + [\partial(r_2/w_2)\partial P](dP/dk_2)$$

where $\partial(r_2/w_2)/\partial k_2 < 0$, $\partial(r_2/w_2)/\partial P < 0$, and $dP/dk_2 = -k_1 dp/p^2 dk_2$ is ambiguous since $dp/dk_2$ is positive within a parameter subspace and negative within the other subspace. If

$dp/dk_2 > 0$, the sign of $\partial(r_2/w_2)/\partial k_2$ is opposite to that of $[\partial(r_2/w_2)/\partial P](dP/dk_2)$. Therefore, the SS theorem may not hold if the indirect effect of a change in $k_2$ on $r_2/w_2$ dominates direct effect. The prediction of the SS theorem even within the diversification cone may be wrong if price movements are caused by changes in transaction conditions because some feedback loops between price differentials, transaction conditions, and production and consumption in the two countries are ignored by the SS theorem.

In exercises 11–15 you are asked to prove that the SS theorem may not hold if price movements are caused by changes in nonneutral technological changes even within the diversification cone in the original HO model without transaction costs, or by changes in total factor productivity in a model with comparative technology and endowment advantages. Also, you are asked to verify that the SS theorem may not hold in a corner structure and it may not hold if price movements are caused by inframarginal shifts of trade structure. The lesson that you may learn from the exercises is summarized in the anything-possible theorem of Debreu (1974), Mantel (1974), and Sonnenschein (1973). This theorem establishes that in the absence of an explicitly specified model, it is impossible to identify the comparative statics of general equilibrium. Hence, all comparative statics of general equilibrium are not only model-structure specific, but also functional-form specific and parameter-value specific. Hence, when economists make any policy suggestions based on the comparative statics of general equilibrium of a particular model, they must be very cautious of the limited policy implications of the comparative statics. Also, obsession with the comparative statics of very general models may generate misleading results.

## Key Terms and Review

Absolute vs. comparative advantages.
Level of specialization and level of division of labor.
Economies of division of labor generated by exogenous comparative productivity and endowment advantages.
Comparative statics of decisions vs. comparative statics of general equilibrium.
Marginal comparative statics vs. inframarginal comparative statics.
Types I, II, III partial equilibrium analyses.
Why a country may receive more gains from trade even if its terms of trade deteriorate.
Implications of inframarginal analysis of the Ricardo model and the HO model.
The HO theorem, the SS theorem, the factor price equalization theorem, and the RY theorem, the conditions under which these hold.

## Further Reading

*Ricardo model:* Dixit and Norman (1980), Ethier (1988), Gomory (1994). *mercantilism, import substitution and export-oriented development:* Ekelund and Tollison (1981), Balassa (1986) and Bruton (1998) and references there; *theory of dependence and underdevelopment:* Palma (1978), Meier (1995), and references there; *Neoclassical trade theory and (HO, SS, RY, FPE) core theorems:* Dixit and Norman (1980), Dornbusch and Samuelson (1977), Ethier (1988), Deardorff and Stern, eds (1994), Jones (1965), Heckscher (1919), Mayer (1984), McKenzie (1955), Lerner (1952), Ohlin (1933), Rybczynski (1955), Samuelson (1948, 1955), Stolper and Sammuelson (1941), Uzawa (1959); *Ricardo model with economies of scale:* Gomory (1994); *debate about competitiveness:* Krugman (1994a,b), Prestowitz et al. (1994), Sachs (1996a,b); *political economics of trade policy, and strategic trade models:* Krueger (1974, 1997), World Bank (1996, 1997), Conybeare (1987), Grossman and Richardson (1986), Grossman and Helpman (1995a,b), Johnson (1954),

Pincus (1975), Riezman (1982); *Nash bargaining game*: Nash (1950), Osborne and Rubinstein (1990*); trade policy and dual structures*: Murphy, Shleifer, and Vishny (1989), Yang (1990, 1994, 1996), Cheng, Sachs, and Yang (1999, 2000); *deteriorated terms of trade and development*: Sen (1998), Morgan (1970), Kohli and Werner (1998); *Empirical tests of the core trade theorems*: Bowen, Leamer and Sveikauskas (1987), Trefler (1993, 1995), Grossman and Levinsohn (1989), Leamer (1984), Leontief (1956); *anything-possible theorem*: Debreu (1974), Mantel (1974), Sonnenschein (1973), or see Mas-Collel et al. (1995, ch. 17).

# QUESTIONS

1   An economics student claims that the extent of the market and demand are determined by income. Why did Allyn Young criticize this as a partial view? Why did he argue that not only division of labor depends upon the extent of the market, but also the extent of the market depends on the level of division of labor? What is the relationship between the Young theorem and the notion of network effect, and why is the notion of general equilibrium essential for formalizing the Young theorem?

2   Use the Ricardo model in example 12.1 to discuss why economies of division of labor may exist in the absence of economies of scale. What is network effect of division of labor? Why is the concept of a nonconvex production set neither sufficient nor necessary for defining the concept of economies of division of labor?

3   Lewis (1955) and Fei and Renis (1964) consider economic development as a process in which labor is transferred from the agricultural sector to the industrial sector. Compare this view of economic development to the Ricardo model in this chapter which formalizes Lewis's original view that economic development is an evolutionary process of commercialization. Increase in each person's level of specialization and increase in the diversity of occupation configurations are two aspects of this evolution.

4   There was a debate about international competitiveness of countries between Krugman (1994a,b) and Prestowitz et al. (1994) (see also Sachs, 1996a, b). One side of the debate argues that according to Ricardo's theory of comparative advantage, competitiveness which relates to absolute advantage does not matter for exploiting gains from trade. Assume in example 12.1, $(1 - \beta)M_1/\beta M_2 = 1$, show that Structure C cannot be general equilibrium if one country has no absolute advantage, even if $k = 1$ (there is no transaction cost). Under this condition, Ba or Bb is the equilibrium where one country obtains no gains from trade. Discuss possible trade conflicts and related distortions, and implications of absolute advantage for avoiding such endogenous transaction costs.

5   According to E. Jones (1981, pp. 226–7) political variety and Europe's very considerable geological, climatic and topographical variety endowed it with a dispersed portfolio of resources. This conduced to long-distance, multilateral trade in bulk loads of utilitarian goods. Taxing these was more rewarding than appropriating them. Bulk trade was also favored by an abnormally high ration of navigable routeways to surface area. Use the model in this chapter to explain the historical facts.

6   According to Mokyr (1990, p. 254, 1993, p. 34), Britain had a comparative advantage in entrepreneurs and skilled workers, and thus imported inventions and inventors and exported entrepreneurs and technicians to the industrializing enclaves of the Continent in the eighteenth and nineteenth centuries. In addition to the inventions that Britain imported from the Continent, it imported some inventors, including Mard Brunel, Friedrich Koenig, and the Swiss engineer J. G. Bodmer. E. Jones (1981) and Baechler (1976) indicate that the comparative advantage of British entrepreneurs was created by a variety of political systems in Europe. Some of them encouraged entrepreneurial activities and the others encouraged sciences. The created comparative advantage is called endogenous comparative advantage (see

chapters 5 and 6). The comparative advantage studied in this chapter is exogenous comparative advantage. Give some examples that some comparative advantages look like exogenous, but may be endogenously created by variety of institution and culture.

7   One way to specify increasing returns to scale based on the neoclassical dichotomy between consumers and firms in the Ricardo model can be found in Gomory (1994). That specification causes multiple general equilibria even if the multiple equilibria can be Pareto ranked, since pure consumers cannot choose between corner production patterns, while pure producers do not care about the choice because of zero profit in all structures. Discuss further the implications for trade theory of the difference between the new classical and neoclassical frameworks.

8   Some economists argue that the statement that improvements in trading efficiency can increase trade sounds like tautology. Use the model in this chapter to show that exact formula for substitution between relative population size, relative tastes, relative productivity, and trading efficiency in raising the equilibrium level of division of labor and productivity can be worked out from inframarginal comparative statics of the general equilibrium model with comparative advantage and transaction costs. Also, use the fact that improvements in trading efficiency may increase total transaction costs to comment on the above argument.

9   Conduct the following thought experiment. Suppose many goods are introduced into the Ricardian model in example 12.1. Each of the two countries has two types of individuals. Under what conditions may international trade emerge from domestic trade?

10  Baran (1957), see Palma (1978), argued that the integration of developing economies into the world economy is necessarily achieved through an interminable metropolis–satellite chain, in which the surplus generated at each stage is successively drawn off toward the center. "If it is satellite status which generates underdevelopment, then a weaker or lesser degree of metropolis-satellite relations may generate less deep structural underdevelopment and/or allow for more possibility of local development." Use the evolution of division of labor from autarky to the partial division of labor where gains from trade go to one country, then to the complete division of labor in the model in this chapter, to predict underdevelopment phenomenon, which implies divergence of income difference between countries, in transitional stage. Use the prediction to comment on the theory of dependence and underdevelopment. Recently, North uses the difference in institutions and policies between North America and Latin America to explain the difference of development performance between the two regions. You may use the cases of Taiwan, Australia, New Zealand in connection to the Ricardo model and HO model to explain why peripheral position may be associated with successful economic development based on globalization and liberalization.

11  In the sixteenth and seventeenth centuries, Britain and France were developing economies. In the eighteenth and nineteenth centuries, the US, Australia, Canada, and New Zealand were less-developed economies in a peripheral position compared to Britain and France. What are their development experiences? Are they applicable to currently less developed economies? Why do many development economists ignore these development experiences?

12  Assume that in the models in this chapter, two types of individuals are in a country. Use the model to explain dual structure, and sequential divergence and convergence of income distribution between the two types of individuals in economic development process. Compare this explanation to the theory of labor surplus (Lewis, 1955) which explains dual structure by labor market disequilibrium caused by exogenous institutional factors in connection to Lewis's original idea about a dual structure between the commercialized and noncommercialized sectors.

13  The Indian and Chinese governments carried out the following import substitution strategy in the 1950s and 1960s. It imposes a high tariff on imported manufactured consumption goods, manipulates terms of

trade using trade quotas, trade licences, and government monopoly on foreign trade, and overvalues local currency in favor of importing capital goods and exporting primary goods. The government restricts the role of the market in facilitating economic development through various regulations, government planning, state ownership of firms, monopoly of firms owned or backed by the government in many important businesses. Japanese government carried out an export promotion policy before the Second World War. It manipulated tariffs and the exchange rate of local currency in favor of importing producer goods and of exporting manufactured consumption goods. South Korea followed this so-called export-oriented development strategy in the 1960s and 1970s. This policy regime is very similar to mercantilism in sixteenth-century Europe. The Hong Kong government followed a *laissez-faire* policy which is very similar to the British government policy regime in the eighteenth century. The Taiwan government instituted various policies, such as tax holidays, and duty free and tariff exemption processing zones, to promote export of manufactured goods and import of related inputs. Use the models that you have learned from this chapter to assess benefits and costs of these different strategies for economic development. Analyze the role of policy and institutional experimentation and of competition between different governments in discovering policies and institutions that are conducive to economic development.

14  According to the models in this chapter, economic development is a process of evolution of the market network and the emergence of new markets for new traded goods. Use the models to comment on the following statement: In developing economies there is no perfect market system, so that development experiences in market economies in West Europe and the US are not applicable to the developing economies. Use the Ricardian model to explain why new markets emerged and the market system evolved in eighteenth and nineteenth century Britain and why expansion of the market is not easy in some Sub-Saharan economies. Summers (1992) and North and Weingast (1989) explain differences in transaction conditions between England in the eighteenth century and Sub-Saharan Africa in the twentieth century by institutional differences between them. Use their observation to critically comment on the specification of exogenous transaction conditions and exogenous evolution in the market network in this chapter (see chapters 9 and 10 for endogenous transaction costs and endogenous evolution of the market network).

15  Some economists claim that the concept of comparative advantage is more general than the concept of absolute advantage. According to them, if each individual has an absolute advantage in at least one activity, then there will also be comparative advantages; whereas we can find cases where a person has comparative advantage but no absolute advantage. Use the distinction between exogenous comparative (and absolute) advantage and endogenous comparative (and absolute) advantage to comment on this claim.

16  Sometimes (Jones, 1965, Dixit and Norman, 1980) the HO theorem is proved under the assumptions that the interior structure is the general equilibrium and factor prices are exogenously given. The first assumption is inconsistent with a general equilibrium analysis, since it ignores corner solutions and related corner structures. Discuss legitimacy of the second assumptions in a general equilibrium analysis.

17  Although we can prove that the SS theorem may not hold even if each country produces two goods, our proof is based on a specific version of the HO model with Cobb–Douglas utility and production functions. Use the everything-possible theorem, which states that it is impossible to identify comparative statics of general equilibrium in the absence of an explicitly specified model (Sonnenschein, 1973, Mantel, 1974, and Debreu, 1991), to discuss the trade-off between generality of functional forms and predictive power of a model that is based on comparative statics of general equilibrium.

18  Use the HO model to analyze dual structure in a transitional period from autarky to a trade structure with complete specialization of each country. Can the feature of the transitional dual structure be used to explain so-called underdevelopment phenomena which imply that the relative position of less-developed countries has deteriorated as international trade and productivity increase?

# EXERCISES

1 Prove that the equilibrium production schedule in autarky equilibrium occurs on line EG in figure 12.1.

2 Assume a dichotomy between pure consumers and firms in each country in the Ricardo model in example 12.1. Then solve for equilibrium. Discuss the implications of this specification for multiple general equilibria. Identify the conditions under which the Pareto optimum equilibrium is the same as the general equilibrium in the Ricardo model in example 12.1.

3 Assume that trading efficiency differs between the two countries in example 12.1. Solve for inframarginal comparative statics of general equilibrium. Show that the country with lower trading efficiency receives no gains from trade in a structure with the partial division of labor. Identify parameter subspace within which improvements in transaction conditions may generate concurrence of deteriorated terms of trade of a country and an increase in gains that this country receives from trade.

4 Assume that the utility function in example 12.1 is $U = (x + kx^d) + \ln(y + ky^d)$. Solve for the general equilibrium and its inframarginal comparative statics. Analyze the impact of transaction conditions on the equilibrium level of division of labor and productivity.

5 Assume that $k_1 = k_2$, $a_{1x} = 2$, $a_{1y} = a_{2x} = a_{1y} = M_1/M_2 = \beta/(1 - \beta) = 1$ in the model in example 12.2. Explicitly solve for inframarginal comparative statics of general equilibrium. Analyze the impact of the interplay between governments' decisions and the market on the equilibrium level of division of labor and welfare.

6 Assume that $k = 1$ in the model in example 12.4, but the government taxes each dollar used to import goods from the foreign country and then distributes the tariff revenue equally among all domestic residents. Solve for the general equilibrium and its inframarginal comparative statics. Analyze the impact of the tax on the equilibrium level of division of labor, productivity, and welfare.

7 Assume that in the HO model the production functions and endowment constraints are specified for each consumer-producer and trading efficiency coefficients are the same between domestic and international trade. Solve for the general equilibrium and its marginal and inframarginal comparative statics. Analyze the implications of the difference between this specification and the original specification of the HO model.

8 Consider the HO model in section 12.4. Assume that $K_{ij}$ is a sector j specific factor in country i and its amount is a given constant. Solve for the general equilibrium of the specific factor model and its inframarginal comparative statics.

9 Use the model in example 12.4 to show that the SS theorem, which states that if the price of the capital-intensive (or labor-intensive) good rises, the price of capital (or labor) rises, holds within the diversification cone if the changes in prices are caused by changes in taste or endowment parameters.

10 Suppose $k_i = 1$ and $a_{ij}$ is the total factor productivity of good j in country i in example 12.4. Verify the solutions of local equilibria in several structures: Autarky: $p_i = (a_{iy}/a_{ix})(r_i/w_i)^{\beta-\alpha}$ $/A$, $r_i/w_i = L_i\mu /K_i$, $x_i = a_{ix}A(\beta\mu - 1 + \beta)L_i^\alpha K_i^{1-\alpha}/(\beta - \alpha)\mu$, $y_i = a_{iy}B(1 - \alpha - \alpha\mu)L_i^\beta$ $K_i^{1-\beta}/(\beta - \alpha)\mu$, $K_{ix} = (1 - \alpha)(\beta\mu - 1 + \beta)K_i/(\beta - \alpha)\mu$, $K_{iy} = (1 - \beta)(1 - \alpha - \alpha\mu)K_i/(\beta - \alpha)\mu$, $L_{ix} = \alpha K_{ix} r_i/w_i(1 - \alpha)$, $L_{iy} = \beta K_{iy} r_i/w_i(1 - \beta)$; Structure $x_1y_2$: $p = \theta a_{2y}L_2^\beta K_2^{1-\beta}/$ $a_{1x}L_1^\alpha K_2^{1-\alpha}(1 - \theta)$, $r_1/w_1 = (1 - \alpha)L_1/\alpha K_1$, $w_1 = \alpha\theta a_{2y}L_2^\beta K_2^{1-\beta}/L_1(1 - \theta)$, $r_2/w_2 = (1 - \beta)L_2/\beta K_2$, $w_2 = \beta a_{2y}(K_2/L_2)^{1-\beta}$, $x_1 = a_{1x}L_1^\alpha K_1^{1-\alpha}$, $y_2 = a_{2y}L_2^\beta K_2^{1-\beta}$, Structure $xy_1y_2$: $p$ is given by $F \equiv (a_{1y}B)^{-\alpha/(\beta-\alpha)}K_1(a_{1x}Ap)^{(\beta/\beta-\alpha)} - (1/\mu)(a_{1y}B)^{(1-\alpha)/(\beta-\alpha)}L_1(a_{1x}Ap)^{(\beta-1)/(\beta-\alpha)} - \{\theta(\beta$

$-\alpha)/[\beta - \theta(\beta - \alpha)]\}a_{2y}L_2^{\beta}K_2^{1-\beta} = 0$, $r_1/w_1 = (a_{1x}Ap/a_{1y}B)^{1/(\beta-\alpha)}$, $w_1 = a_{1x}Ap(a_{1y}B/a_{1x}Ap)^{(1-\alpha)/(\beta-\alpha)}$, $r_2/w_2 = (1-\beta)L_2/K_2\beta$, $w_2 = a_{2y}B[\beta K_2/L_2(1-\beta)]^{1-\beta}$. Also in Structure $xy_1y_2$, it can be shown that $\partial F/\partial p > 0$, $\partial F/\partial \theta > 0$, $\partial F/\partial a_{1x} > 0$, $\partial F/\partial a_{1y} < 0$, $\partial F/\partial a_{2y} < 0$, $dp/d\theta = -(\partial F/\partial \theta)/(\partial F/\partial p) < 0$, $dp/da_{1x} = -(\partial F/\partial a_{1x})/(\partial F/\partial p) < 0$, $dp/da_{1y} = -(\partial F/\partial a_{1y})/(\partial F/\partial p) > 0$, $dp/da_{2y} = -(\partial F/\partial a_{2y})/(\partial F/\partial p) > 0$, $dp/dK_i < 0$, $dp/dL_i > 0$ for $i = 1, 2$. Here, $\mu \equiv [(\beta - \alpha)\theta + 1 - \beta]/[\beta - \theta(\beta - \alpha)] > 0$, and $A \equiv \alpha^{\alpha}(1-\alpha)^{1-\alpha}$ and $B \equiv \beta^{\beta}(1-\beta)^{1-\beta}$. Show that the HO theorem holds if country 1 has both comparative technological and endowment advantage in producing good x or its comparative endowment advantage dominates its comparative technological disadvantage. Use your results to analyze why the prediction of the HO theorem is inconsistent with empirical findings 50 percent of the time (Trefler, 1993). Use the model to check the theorem of factor price equalization.

11 Based on the result in previous exercises prove that for $k_i = 1$ and $a_{ij} = 1$ the SS theorem may not hold within the interior structure if changes in prices are caused by a change in $\alpha$. Then for $a_{ij} \neq 1$ prove that the SS theorem may not hold within the interior structure if price movements are caused by changes in $a_{ij}$.

12 Prove that for $k_i = 1$ the SS theorem may not hold when equilibrium jumps from autarky to structure $x_1y_2$ with specialization of each country or from structure $yx_1xy_2$ to structure $x_1y_2$, but the SS theorem always holds when equilibrium jumps from autarky to the interior structure with partial international division of labor.

13 Prove that if a corner equilibrium with complete specialization of each country is the general equilibrium, then changes in parameters of tastes, production, and endowments can generate movements of prices that are inconsistent with the SS theorem. If an asymmetric corner equilibrium is the general equilibrium, then changes in the relative factor price in the country producing both goods and in the relative commodity price that are caused by changes in the taste parameter are consistent with the SS theorem. But the corresponding unchanged relative factor price in the specialized country is inconsistent with the SS theorem. There exists a parameter subspace such that changes in production parameters and endowments will generate movements of prices within this corner structure that are inconsistent with the SS theorem.

14 The Rybczynski (RY) theorem is derived within the interior structure (diversification cone) and with the assumption of exogenous commodity prices. It states that, at given commodity prices, if the endowment of some resources increases, the industry that uses that resource most intensively will increase its output, while the other industry reduces its output (Rybczynski, 1955). Assume $k_i = 1$ in the HO model in example 12.4. Prove that the RY theorem does not hold in the interior structure and that the output of both industries can increase in response to an increase in the endowment of some resource.

15 Marshall's partial equilibrium analysis of the market for one good is called Type I partial equilibrium analysis. Type II partial equilibrium analysis assumes exogenous prices of goods (or factors) and investigates changes in prices of factors (or output) in response to changes in prices of goods (or endowment parameters). Type III partial equilibrium analysis considers only the interior structure and ignores discontinuous jumps of general equilibrium between different trade patterns. Use your answers in the previous exercises to analyze why Type II and Type III partial equilibrium analysis could be misleading. Why has the shortcoming of Type I partial equilibrium analysis received more attention than that of Type II and Type III?

16 Bhagwati and Dehejia, 1994, factor reversal theorem: Assume that the production functions in example 12.4 are $x_i^s = (L_{ix}^{\alpha} + K_{ix}^{\alpha})^{1/\alpha}$ and $y_i^s = (L_{iy}^{\alpha} + K_{iy}^{\alpha})^{1/\alpha}$. Show that the equilibrium-relative factor in producing a good may be reversed (changes from capital-intensive to labor-intensive) as relative price of goods changes.

# chapter 13

# MORE GENERAL NEW CLASSICAL MODELS

## ♦ 13.1 The Theoretical Foundation of New Classical Economics

The purpose of this chapter is threefold. First, we specify a general new classical model with no explicit specification of utility and production functions. It allows the coexistence of endogenous and exogenous comparative advantages. Hence, individual decision-makers might have *ex ante* different characteristics. The existence theorem of general equilibrium is then established. This makes inframarginal analysis applicable to a large family of models. Also, a stronger version of the Wen theorem and the first welfare theorem are proved for this very general class of new classical models. This will establish a sound theoretical foundation for new classical economics.

Second, we use graph theory and the notion of organism to study *Walrasian networking decisions* in this general class of new classical models. Walrasian networking decisions are those impersonal networking decisions which concern the degree of connectedness rather than with whom the connections are established. As North (1987, 1990) has pointed out, the institution of impersonal trading is essential for reducing transaction costs and for economic development. Many marketing decisions are such impersonal networking decisions. For instance, when a salesman tries to sell his goods, he does not care what the buyer's name is or if he or she is good looking, as long as the good is sold. From the new classical models so far studied in this text, we can see that each individual's decision on how many goods are purchased and how many self-provided will determine the extent of the market, the degree of interpersonal dependence, and the degree of market integration, which relate to the degree of connectedness. For such networking decisions, each person is concerned with the number of traded goods rather than whom she trades with, though the market will sort out who is matched with whom in an anonymous way (the invisible hand). Also, impersonal networking decisions are not associated with monopoly power in pricing and in manipulating the numbers of individuals choosing different occupation configurations. *Connectedness* is a so-called *topological property* of organisms. How much of a good that a person sells to another person is a *nontopological property*, but whether a person has a trade connection with the other person is a topological property of an organism.

Marshall might be the first economist who used the word "organism" to describe the topological properties of networks of division of labor. He pointed out (Marshall, 1890, p. 241) that "the development of the organism, whether social or physical, involves an increasing subdivision of functions between its separate parts on the one hand, and on the other a more intimate connection between them. Each part gets to be less and less self-sufficient, to depend for its well-being more and more on other parts, so that any disorder in any part of a highly-developed organism will affect other parts also. This increased subdivision of functions, or 'differentiation,' as it is called, manifests itself with regard to industry in such forms as the division of labor, and the development of specialized skills, knowledge and machinery: while 'integration,' that is, a growing intimacy and firmness of the connections between the separate parts of the industrial organism, shows itself in such forms as the increase of security of commercial credit, and of the means and habits of communication by sea and by road, by railway and telegraph, by post and printing-press." Here, the degrees of integration, of differentiation, of intimacy, and of firmness of connections, and asymmetry between the core and periphery of a network, are topological properties of an organism. They can be rigorously described by directed graphs, connection matrices, and a spectrum of graphs (see Roberts, 1989, Rouvray, 1990, Yang and Yeh, 1993). The concept of extent (or thickness) of the market relates to both topological and nontopological properties of the network of division of labor. The extent of the market is determined by trade volume of each transaction connection, which is a nontopological property of the network, and degree of connectedness of the network, which is a topological property.

In the emerging literature on general equilibrium networks, graph theory is used to describe trade networks (see Jackson and Wolinsky, 1996, Dutta and Mutuswami, 1997, Sun, Yang, and Yao, 1999, and Zhou, Sun, and Yang, 1998). In this chapter we will define a general equilibrium organism which is composed of a network structure of division of labor (represented by a directed graph) and resource allocation (represented by weights attached to arcs in the digraph). Hence, the Arrow–Debreu general equilibrium model of resource allocation (see chapters 3 and 4) and recent general equilibrium connection network models can be synthesized in the new classical framework.

Third, we explicitly specify a new classical model with both endogenous and exogenous comparative advantages to investigate trade and economic development patterns. We shall show that this kind of model is more powerful than models with *ex ante* identical individuals for investigating many interesting phenomena of trade and economic development.

In sections 13.2, 13.3., and 13.4 we consider a general model of an endogenous network of division of labor with *ex ante* different consumer-producers. Since these sections cover quite advanced materials, those readers who are interested more in applied theories than in pure theories may skip this section. Sections 13.5 and 13.6 return to applied theories by investigating inframarginal comparative statics of equilibrium in a new classical model with endogenous and exogenous comparative advantages.

---

### Questions to Ask Yourself when Reading this Chapter

- ◆ What is an economic organism?

- ◆ What is the distinction between topological and nontopological properties of an economic organism?

- ◆ What are the conditions for the existence of a general equilibrium organism?

- ◆ Why is the general equilibrium network of division of labor in a competitive market Pareto efficient?

- ◆ What are the implications for economic development of the coexistence of endogenous and exogenous comparative advantages?

---

## ◆ 13.2 A General New Classical Model with *ex ante* Different Consumer-producers

As shown in example 9.2, a Walrasian equilibrium may not exist in a new classical model with a finite set of consumer-producers (see exercise 1 below). This is true even if all individuals' production sets are convex. Hence, we consider a new classical model with a continuum of consumer-producers, represented by a complete atomless measure space ($\Omega$, $\mu$). The commodity space is taken as $R^m{}_+$. Each individual $\omega$ has rational, continuous, and strictly increasing preferences which can be represented by a continuous and strictly increasing utility function $u_\omega$ on $R^m{}_+$.

Each individual $\omega$ is endowed with one unit of labor, which she can use to produce different goods according to a set of production functions $f_\omega = (f_{\omega 1}, ..., f_{\omega m})$. Every $f_{\omega i}$ is continuous and weakly convex on $[0, 1]$, though it may or may not exhibit increasing return to specialization. If $\omega$'s labor allocation to the production of $m$ goods is $l = (l_1, ..., l_m)$, then her production is $f_\omega(l) = (f_{\omega 1}(l_1), ..., f_{\omega m}(l_m))$. The production set is denoted by

$$\Pi(f_\omega) = \{y \in R^m{}_+ \mid y = f_\omega(l) \text{ for some } l \in R^m{}_+ \text{ with } \sum_{i=1}^{i=m} l_i = 1\}.$$

In addition to her own production, $\omega$ also trades with other individuals via markets, buying and selling under market prices $p = (p_1, ..., p_m) \gg 0$. Assume that there are transaction costs associated with trading and all transaction costs are borne by buyers. Each individual $\omega$ has a set of transaction functions $g_\omega = (g_{\omega 1}, ..., g_{\omega m})$. If $t_i (> 0)$ units of good $i$ is bought, only $g_{\omega i}(t_i)$ units are available for her consumption. Every $g_{\omega i}$ is continuous and weakly increasing on $(0, \infty)$, and it satisfies (a) $0 < g_{\omega i}(s) \leq s$ and (b) $g_{\omega i}(s) \to \infty$ as $s \to \infty$. For any function $g$ on $(0, \infty)$, if we define $h_g$ as:

$$h_g(s) = \begin{cases} g(s), & s > 0, \\ s, & s \leq 0 \end{cases}$$

then the set of goods obtainable from $\omega$'s trades can be expressed as

$$\Theta(g_\omega, p) = \{z \in R^m{}_+ \mid z_i = h_{g_{\omega i}}(t_i) \text{ for some } (t_i, ..., t_n) \in R^l{}_+$$

with $\sum_{i=1}^{i=l} p_i t_i = 0\}.$

Together, these production and transaction functions, as well as the market prices, determine the set of goods that are feasible for individual $\omega$ to consume:

$$\Psi(f_\omega, g_\omega, p) = \{x \in R^m_+ \mid x \le y + z \text{ with } y \in \Pi(f_\omega) \text{ and } z \in \Theta(g_\omega, p)\}.$$

A competitive equilibrium is a triple $(p, (l(\omega))_{\omega \in \Omega}, (t(\omega))_{\omega \in \Omega})$, in which $p \in R^m_{++}$ is a price vector, $(l(\omega))_{\omega \in \Omega}$ is a list of the labor allocation for all individuals, and $(t(\omega))_{\omega \in \Omega}$ a list of the net trade for all individuals, such that

a)   each individual maximizes her utility, i.e., for $\mu$-almost every individual $\omega$, $x(\omega)(\equiv f_\omega(l(\omega)) + h_{g_\omega}(t(\omega)))$, the consumption bundle generated by $l(\omega)$ and $t(\omega)$, maximizes her utility function $u_\omega$ over $\Psi(f_\omega, g_\omega, p)$;
b)   all markets clear, i.e., the trade mapping $(t(\omega))_{\omega \in \Omega}$ is an integrable mapping from $(\Omega, \mu)$ to $R^m_+$, and

$$\int t(\omega)\mu(d\omega) = 0.$$

In the definition of a competitive equilibrium, the trade mapping is required to be integrable. We need to impose measurability conditions concerning the characteristics of the individuals in order to demonstrate the existence of a competitive equilibrium. Let us consider the following three spaces.

**The space of utility functions**   Let $U$ contain all utility functions $u$ on $R^m_+$ that are continuous, strictly increasing, and are normalized such that $u(\alpha, \ldots, \alpha) = \alpha$ for all $\alpha \ge 0$. Also, $U$ contains all Cobb–Douglas functions.

**The space of production functions**   Let $F$ contain all functions $f$ on $[0,1]$ that are continuous and weakly increasing.

**The space of transaction functions**   Let $G$ contain all functions $g$ on $[0, \infty]$ that are continuous and weakly increasing, and satisfy (a) $0 \le g(s) \le s$ for all $s$, (b) $g(s) \to \infty$ as $s \to \infty$, and no fixed transaction cost is present.[1]

We shall endow all three spaces with the compact-open topology (a sequence of functions converges in the compact-open topology if and only if the sequence converges uniformly on every compact set). We shall also consider these three spaces as measurable spaces by endowing them with the Borel algebras generated by their compact-open topologies.[2]
     Let us denote by $N_U \colon \Omega \to U^m$, $N_F \colon \Omega \to F^m$, and $N_G \colon \Omega \to G^m$, the mappings that associate all individuals with their characteristics, i.e., $N_U(\omega) = u_\omega$, $N_F(\omega) = f_\omega$ and $N_G(\omega) = g_\omega$ for every individual $\omega$.

**Assumption 13.1:** All three characteristic mappings, $N_U$, $N_F$, and $N_G$, are measurable.

The next assumption concerns with the aggregate production: Every good can be produced but none can produce an infinite amount.

**Assumption 13.2:** For every good $i$, $0 < \int f_{\omega i}(1)\mu(d\omega) < \infty$.

## ◆ 13.3 The Existence of a Competitive Equilibrium

In this section we adopt Hildenbrand's powerful approach to "excess demand" in a large economy and outline the proof of the existence of a competitive equilibrium for the large economy. The full proof can be found in Zhou, Sun, and Yang (1998). The proof proceeds as follows. Let

$$P = \{p \in R^m_+ \mid p_i > 0 \text{ for all } i \text{ and } \textstyle\sum_{i=1}^{i=m} p_i = 1\}.$$

For any $p \in P$, each individual $\omega$ chooses some labor allocation $l(\omega, p)$ and some trade vector $t(\omega, p)$ that lead to a consumption plan $x(\omega, p)$ ($\equiv f_\omega(l(\omega, p)) + h_{g_\omega} t(\omega, p))$) which maximizes $u_\omega$ on $\Psi(f_\omega, g_\omega, p)$. Then, individual trade vectors $t(\omega, p)$ are integrated over $\Omega$ to obtain the aggregate trade $T(p) = \int t(\omega, p)\mu(d\omega)$. The existence of a competitive equilibrium is established by showing that there is some $p^* \in P$ with $T(p^*) = 0.$[3]

Both the optimal trade $t(\omega, p)$ and the optimal consumption $x(\omega, p)$ are derived as a result of the maximization of $u_\omega$. To show that $t(\omega, p)$ is integrable, we need to study the utility maximization problem more closely.

The basic utility maximization problem is defined on the product space $U \times F^m \times G^m \times P$. Let us denote $f = (f_1, ..., f_m) \in F^m$, and $g = (g_1, ..., g_m) \in G^m$. For each $(u, f, g, p) \in U \times F^m \times G^m \times P$, the set of all feasible consumption goods is:

$$\Psi(u, f, g, p) = \{x \in R^m_+ \mid x \leq y + z \text{ with } y \in \Pi(f) \text{ and } z \in \Theta(g, p)\}.$$

Obviously, this defines a correspondence $\Psi$ from to $U \times F^m \times G^m \times P$ to $R^m_+$. Notice, though, that $\Psi$ does not depend on $u$ explicitly. We now show that $\Psi$ is continuous.

**Lemma 13.1:** $\Psi$ is continuous.

The complete proof of this lemma can be found in Zhou, Sun, and Yang (1998). Here is a brief outline of the proof:

Since correspondence $\Psi$ may not be a one-to-one function, we have to show that $\Psi$ is upper-hemicontinuous as well as lower-hemicontinuous. The upper and lower hemicontinuity properties for correspondence are a natural generalization of the notion of continuity for functions. A correspondence $\Psi: A \to Y$, $A \subset R^n$ and $Y \subset R^m$, is *upper hemicontinuous* if it has a closed graph and the images of compact sets are bounded, that is, for every compact set $B \subset A$, the set $\Psi(B) = \{y \in Y: y \in \Psi(x) \text{ for some } x \in B\}$ is bounded. Since $\Psi$ is bounded in a compact neighborhood of any $(f, g, p)$, we only need to show that $\Psi$ is closed to establish upper hemicontinuity. A correspondence $\Psi: A \to Y$, given $A \subset R^n$ and a compact set $Y \subset R^m$, is *lower hemicontinuous* if for every sequence $x^m \to x \in A$ with $x^m \in A$ for all $m$, and every $y \in \Psi(x)$, we can find a sequence $y^m \to y$ and an integer $M$ such that $y^m \in \Psi(x^m)$ for $m > M$.

We now consider the optimal consumption correspondence $\Gamma$ and the optimal trade correspondence $T$, both of which are defined from $U \times F^m \times G^m \times P$ to $R^m$:

$$\Gamma(u, f, g, p) = \{x \in \Psi(f, g, p) \mid u(x) \geq u(y) \text{ for all } y \in \Psi(f, g, p)\},$$

$$T(u, f, g, p) = \{t \in R^m \mid \textstyle\sum_{i=1}^{i=l} p_i t_i = 0, \text{ and there exist } x \in \Gamma(u, f, g, p) \text{ and}$$

$$l \in R^m_+ \text{ with } \textstyle\sum_{i=1}^{i=m} l_i = 1 \text{ such that } x = f(l) + h_g(t)\}.$$

**Lemma 13.2:** Both $\Gamma$ and $T$ are upper-hemicontinuous.

*Proof:* See Zhou, Sun, and Yang (1998).

$\Gamma$ is upper-hemi-continuous according to the Berge theorem (theorem 3, Hildenbrand, 1974, p. 29). It can be shown that for any $(u, f, g, p)$, $T$ is bounded in a small neighborhood of $(u, f, g, p)$. Hence, we only need to show that $T$ is closed.

Let us now consider the correspondence $T \circ N$ from $\Omega \times P$ to $R^m$, which is the composite of the optimal trade correspondence $T$ and the characteristic mappings $N$:

$$T \circ N (\omega, p) = T(m_U(\omega), m_F(\omega), m_G(\omega), p).$$

For every $p \in P$, $N$ is a function of $\omega$ only. Since, by lemma 13.2, $T$ is upper-hemicontinuous, $T$ is also measurable (proposition 4, Hildenbrand p. 61). Then, since mappings $N_U$, $N_F$, and $N_G$ are also measurable by assumption 1, the composite mapping $T \circ N$ is also measurable (proposition 1, Hildenbrand, p. 59). Let us integrate $T \circ N$ over $\Omega$ to obtain the aggregate trade:

$$T(p) = \int T(N_U(\omega), N_F(\omega), N_G(\omega), p)\mu(d\omega).$$

We summarize some properties of $T$ in lemma 13.3.

**Lemma 13.3:**
   i)   $T(p)$ is non-empty and compact for every $p \in P$. In Zhou, Sun, and Yang's proof of lemma 13.1, they show that the correspondence $T \circ N$ is bounded from below by

$$-\sum_{i=1}^{i=m} f_{\omega i} \ (1)$$

and bounded above by

$$\frac{\sum_{i=1}^{i=m} f_{\omega i}(1)}{\min_{1 \leq i \leq m} p_i}.$$

Since both bounds are integrable by assumption 13.2, $T(p)$ is non-empty and compact (proposition 7, Hildenbrand p. 73).
   ii)  $T(p)$ is convex for every $p \in P$. Since the measure space is atomless, this follows from the Lyapunov theorem (theorem 3, Hildenbrand p. 62).
   iii) $T$ is upper-hemicontinuous in $p \in P$. Given lemma 13.2, $T \circ M$ is upper-hemicontinuous in $p$. Since integration preserves upper-hemicontinuity (proposition 8, Hildenbrand, p. 73), $T$ is upper-hemicontinuous in $p$.
   iv)  Finally, if a sequence $\{p^k\}$ of strictly positive prices converges to a price $p$ that is not strictly positive, then

$$\lim \inf \left\{ \min \left[ \sum_{i=1}^{i=m} t_i \mid t \in T(p^k) \right] \right\} = \infty.$$

*Proof of (iv):* See Zhou, Sun, and Yang (1998).

As an immediate consequence of the above properties of the excess demand $T$, we can now establish the following existence result.

**Theorem 13.1 (the Existence Theorem):** Any atomless economy that satisfies assumptions 13.1 and 13.2 has at least one competitive equilibrium.

*Proof:* Now that $T$ satisfies the four properties in lemma 13.3, there must exist at least one $p^* \in P$ such that $0 \in T(p^*)$ (lemma 1, Hildenbrand p. 150). *Q.E.D*

A much simpler proof of the existence theorem for the model with *ex ante* identical individuals can be found in Sun, Yang, and Yao (1999). We now prove a strong version of the Wen theorem for the general class of models specified in the previous section. Exercise 2 shows that an individual's optimum decision may involve selling more than one good if production functions are linear. Hence, we need a general version of the Wen theorem to keep the model tractable. We will show that the result of the original Wen theorem remains valid as far as the strict convexity of the production functions holds; whether or not these functions are differentiable is not really important.

A function $f: [0,1] \rightarrow R$ is weakly convex if for any $x, x' \in [0,1]$, $x < x'$ and any $\lambda \in (0,1), f(\lambda x + (1 - \lambda)x') \leq \lambda f(x) + (1 - \lambda)f(x')$. $f$ is said to be strictly convex if in the above inequality $\leq$ is replaced with $<$. We first establish the following lemma.

**Lemma 13.4:** Assume that $f: [0, 1] \rightarrow R$ is weakly convex. Then for any $x \in [0,1], \Delta x > 0, a > 0$ such that $x + a + \Delta x \leq 1$, it holds that

$$\frac{f(x + a + \Delta x) - f(x + a)}{\Delta x} \geq \frac{f(x + a) - f(x)}{a} \tag{13.1}$$

If $f: [0, 1] \rightarrow R$ is strictly convex, then the above inequality holds with "$\geq$" being replaced by "$>$".

*Proof:* Let $\lambda = \dfrac{\Delta x}{a + \Delta x}$. Then $1 - \lambda = \dfrac{a}{a + \Delta x}$ and $\lambda x + (1 - \lambda)(x + a + \Delta x) = x + a$. From the definition of a weakly convex function we have

$$f(x + a) \leq \frac{\Delta x}{a + \Delta x} f(x) + \frac{a}{a + \Delta x} f(x + a + \Delta x)$$

Multiplying $(a + \Delta x)$ to both sides of the above semi-inequality and then rearranging it, one obtains:

$$a[f(x + a + \Delta x) - f(x + a)] \geq \Delta x[f(x + a) - f(x)] \tag{13.2}$$

Dividing each side of (13.2) by $a\Delta x$, we obtain (13.1). *Q.E.D.*

We now consider the decision of an individual in a Walrasian market with $m$ goods under a given price vector $p$. Assume that she is endowed with 1 unit of labor. Her decision consists of $3m$ decision variables: $l_j, \Delta x_j, \Delta y_j, j = 1, \ldots, m$. Here $l_j$ is the amount of labor allocated for good $j$'s production, $\Delta x_j$ is the amount of good $j$ she sells, and $\Delta y_j$ is the amount of good $j$ she purchases. We will denote by $f_j$ her production function for good $j$, and denote by $g_j$ the transaction function for good $j, j = 1, \ldots, m$.

We want to establish

**Theorem 13.2:** Consider a Walrasian market with $m$ goods with or without transaction costs. Assume that an individual is endowed with one unit of labor and that she has a continuous utility function $u(x_1, \ldots, x_m)$ which is non-decreasing in each of the variables. Assume that she has a set of weakly convex production functions $f_j: [0, 1] \to R_+, j = 1, \ldots, m$. Then given any price vector $p$ for these $m$ goods, the maximal utility $u(p)$ for this individual always *can be achieved* by a decision selling no more than one good. If $u$ is strictly increasing in each variable and all the $f_j$ are strictly convex, then any utility maximization decision *must* have no more than one good being sold.

*Proof*: First consider the case that $u$ is nondecreasing and the $f_j: [0, 1] \to R_+$ are weakly convex. Assume that $u$ is maximized at a decision in which there are two or more goods being sold. It suffices to show that this individual can reduce the number of goods sold and still achieve the same maximal utility.

Let goods 1 and 2 be sold originally. Let $L_1$ and $L_2$, respectively, be the units of labor allocated for the production of these two goods. Let $x_1$ and $x_2$, respectively, be the amounts of these two goods produced. Let $\Delta x_1$ and $\Delta x_2$, respectively be the amounts of them being sold. Let $l_j$ be the amounts of labor satisfying $f_j(l_j) = x_j - \Delta x_j, j = 1, 2$. Let $\Delta l_j = L_j - l_j$. Then we have

$$\Delta x_j = f_j(l_j + \Delta l_j) - f_j(l_j), j = 1, 2.$$

Let $p_j$ be the market price of good $j, j = 1, 2$. Then the contribution to the budget by selling these two goods is

$$p_1[f_1(l_1 + \Delta l_1) - f_1(l_1)] + p_2[f_2(l_2 + \Delta l_2) - f_2(l_2)].$$

To prove the first part of the theorem, it suffices to show that, by selling just one of these two goods but not changing the self-consumed amounts of them and not changing any other decision, this individual can achieve a better or at least the same budget. Define $k_1$ and $k_2$ by

$$k_1 = \frac{p_1[f_1(l_1 + \Delta l_1) - f_1(l_1)]}{\Delta l_1}, \quad k_2 = \frac{p_2[f_2(l_2 + \Delta l_2) - f_2(l_2)]}{\Delta l_2}.$$

Note that we have

$$p_1[f_1(l_1 + \Delta l_1) - f_1(l_1)] + p_2[f_2(l_2 + \Delta l_2) - f_2(l_2)] = k_1 \Delta l_1 + k_2 \Delta l_2.$$

Without loss of generality we may assume that $k_1 \leq k_2$. Then we obtain:

$$p_2[f_2(l_2 + \Delta l_2 + \Delta l_1) - f_2(l_2)] = \tag{13.3}$$
$$p_2[f_2(l_2 + \Delta l_2 + \Delta l_1) - f_2(l_2 + \Delta l_2)] + p_2[f_2(l_2 + \Delta l_2) - f_2(l_2)] =$$
$$\Delta l_1 \cdot p_2 \cdot \frac{f_2(l_2 + \Delta l_2 + \Delta l_1) - f_2(l_2 + \Delta l_2)}{\Delta l_1} + \Delta l_2 \cdot p_2 \cdot \frac{f_2(l_2 + \Delta l_2) - f_2(l_2)}{\Delta l_2} \geq$$
$$(\Delta l_1 + \Delta l_2)k_2 \geq k_1 \Delta l_1 + k_2 \Delta l_2.$$

Here we have applied lemma 13.4 to get:

$$\frac{f_2(l_2 + \Delta l_2 + \Delta l_1) - f_2(l_2 + \Delta l_2)}{\Delta l_1} \geq \frac{f_2(l_2 + \Delta l_2) - f_2(l_2)}{\Delta l_2}. \tag{13.4}$$

The implication of (13.3) is: if this individual sells good 2 only[4] while maintaining the self-consumed amounts of good 1 and good 2 not changed, then she either has a looser budget constraint, or at least her budget is not tighter than before, and, consequently she can achieve a higher or at least the same utility as before.

If, in addition, the utility function is strictly increasing in each variable and the production functions are all strictly convex, then (13.4) becomes a strict inequality as well as (13.3), which means that by reducing the number of goods sold, the individual can achieve a higher budget. She can always increase the consumption amount of one of the goods without reducing the consumption amounts of the others. As a result she can get a higher utility. $Q.E.D.$

**Theorem 13.3:** Consider a Walrasian market with $m$ goods with or without transaction costs. Assume that an individual is endowed with one unit of labor and that she has a continuous utility function $u(x_1, \ldots, x_m)$ which is nondecreasing in each of the variables. Assume that she has a set of weakly convex production functions $f_j: [0, 1] \rightarrow R_+$, $j = 1, \ldots, m$. Assume that all the transaction functions $g_j$ are linear. Then given any price vector $p$ for these $m$ goods, the maximal utility $u(p)$ for this individual always *can be achieved* by a decision not simultaneously producing and purchasing the same good. If $u$ is strictly increasing in each variable and all the $f_j$ are strictly convex, then any utility maximization decision *must* have no good being simultaneously produced and purchased.

*Proof:* Assume that $u$ is nondecreasing and the production functions are weakly convex. Assume that in a utility maximization decision an individual produces and purchases goods 1 and 2 simultaneously. According to theorem 13.2, she can achieve the same maximal utility by selling just one good. Thus we may assume that she sells good 2 only.

We let $p_1$, $p_2$ be the prices of these two goods. Let $g_1: R_+ \rightarrow R_+$ be the transaction function of good 1. Let $x_1 = f_1(l_1)$ be the quantity of good 1 she produces for herself. Let $y_1$ be the amount of good 1 purchased. Let $x_2 = f_2(l_2 + \Delta l_2)$ be the total amount of good 2 produced. Let $x_2 - \Delta x_2 = f_2(l_2)$ be the amount of good 2 she would just require if she had no need to purchase good 1. Here $\Delta l_2$ is the amount of labor she could have saved from the production of good 2 if she would no longer purchase good 1. We have $y_1 = (p_2/p_1)[f_2(l_2 + \Delta l_2) - f_2(l_2)]$. And the amount of good 1 she actually receives (excluding the transaction costs) is $g_1\{(p_2/p_1)[f_2(l_2 + \Delta l_2) - f_2(l_2)]\}$.

From the linearity of $g_i$, we have

$$g_1\{(p_2/p_1)[f_2(l_2 + \Delta l_2) - f_2(l_2)]\} =$$
$$(p_2/p_1)g_1 \circ f_2(l_2 + \Delta l_2) - (p_2/p_1)g_1 \circ f_2(l_2) =$$
$$h(l_2 + \Delta l_2) - h(l_2),$$

where $h = (p_2/p_1)g_1 \circ f_2$ is also weakly convex.

On the other hand, if she saves $\Delta l_2$ for good 1's production, she can produce a total amount of $f_1(l_1 + \Delta l_2)$. And if she does not produce good 1 at all and saves $l_1$ for good 2's production, spending all the increment to purchase good 1, she will receive an amount of good 1 of $h(l_2 + \Delta l_2 + l_1) - h(l_2)$. Thus we need only show that one of $f_1(l_i + \Delta l_2)$ and $h(l_2 + \Delta l_2 + l_1) - h(l_2)$ must be greater than or equal to $f_1(l_1) + h(l_2 + \Delta l_2) - h(l_2)$. We have a very much similar situation as in the proof of theorem 13.2. Define

$$k_1 = \frac{f_1(l_1)}{l_1}, \qquad k_2 = \frac{h(l_2 + \Delta l_2) - h(l_2)}{\Delta l_2}.$$

Without loss of generality we may assume that $k_1 \geq k_2$. But then by (13.3) we have

$$f_1(l_1 + \Delta l_2) = \frac{f_1(l_1 + \Delta l_2) - f(l_1)}{\Delta l_2} \Delta l_2 + \frac{f_1(l_1)}{l_1} l_1 \geq k_1(\Delta l_2 + l_1) \geq k_1 l_1 + k_2 \Delta l_2 =$$

$$f_1(l_1) + h(l_2 + \Delta l_2) - h(l_2)$$

which means by producing but not buying good 1, this individual can do at least as good as before. The first part of theorem 13.3 is proved.

To verify the second part, we need only to note that the strict convexity of the production functions implies the strict convexity of $f_1$ and $h$. Q.E.D.

Theorems 13.1, 13.2, and 13.3 are applicable to all new classical models without producer goods in this text. Sun (1999) has proved the existence theorem for a general class of new classical models with consumption goods as well as producer goods. His approach is similar to the one used in this chapter.

## ◆ 13.4 An Equilibrium Organism and the Efficiency of the Invisible Hand in Coordinating Division of Labor

In this section we first use the notion of a weighted digraph to describe an equilibrium organism in the general class of new classical models specified in the previous sections. An economic organism consists of a digraph and a system of weights associated with the digraph. A digraph represents a network of division of labor. The system of weights represents the resource allocation that is associated with a given digraph. We then establish the first welfare theorem for the general class of new classical models.

∀    Because of the Wen theorem, we can categorize individuals in such a way, $V_i \equiv \{\omega \,|\, x_i(\omega) > 0\}$, $\forall\, i \in I$ and $V_0 \equiv \{\omega \,|\, x_i(\omega) = 0, \forall\, i \in I\}$, i.e., all the individuals selling the same good form a category and those who choose autarky in the equilibrium form a separate one. Clearly, this classification is both exclusive and exhaustive. We can then construct a weighted digraph with $(n + 1)$ vertices, where $n$ ($\leq m$) is the number of traded goods. Define

$$\phi_{ij} = \int_{\omega \in V_j} y_i(\omega)\mu(d\omega), \quad \forall\, i \neq j \quad \text{and} \quad \phi_{ii} = \int_{\omega \in V_j} [f_i(l_i(\omega)) - x_i(\omega)]\mu(d\omega), \quad \forall\, i \in I.$$

If $\phi_{ij} \neq 0$, we draw a *directed arc ij* from vertex $i$ to $j$ and attach *weight* $\phi_{ij}$ to the arc $ij$, $i, j \in I$. Denote by $A$ the *arc set* and by $V$ the *vertex set*. We call the *weighted digraph* $G(V, A, \phi, p)$ the *economic organism* corresponding to the general equilibrium $(p, (l(\omega))_{\omega \in I}, (x(\omega))_{\omega \in I}, (y(\omega))_{\omega \in I}$. The directed graph is referred to as *network of division of labor* and the system of weights is referred to as *resource allocation* for the given network of division of labor. Clearly,

$$\sum_{s \in \underline{n}} p_s \phi_{si} = \sum_{r \in \underline{n}} p_r \phi_{ir}.$$

The equilibrium uniquely determines an economic organism defined in the above manner.

Once we establish the network of division of labor from general equilibrium, the concepts of component, spectrum, and connectedness of a network of division of labor could be defined in the same way as in graph theory (see e.g. Dondran and Minoux, 1984, Roberts, 1989, Rouvray, 1990). By doing so, we may get some new perspectives on the division of labor and economic development. For example, the concept of connectedness in graph theory could be used to describe the extent of market integration of the equilibrium organism. The concept of spectrum of a network of division of labor can be used to describe degree of asymmetry between the center and periphery and other characteristics of the network (see Yang and Yeh, 1993).

Finally, we show that any competitive equilibrium is efficient despite the presence of transaction costs and local increasing returns. This holds because each individual chooses her production and consumption plans jointly to maximize her utility. If the production plan is made to maximize the profit before the consumption plan is made, then the final allocation may not be efficient in general.

A labor-trade plan $((l(\omega))_{\omega \in \Omega}, (t(\omega))_{\omega \in \Omega})$ is said to be feasible if both $l$ and $t$ are measurable, $l(\omega) \geq 0$ and $\sum_{i=1}^{i=m} l_i(\omega) = 1$ for almost all $\omega$, and $\int t(\omega)\mu(d\omega) = 0$. A feasible labor-trade plan $((l(\omega))_{\omega \in \Omega}, (t(\omega))_{\omega \in \Omega})$ is efficient if there is no other feasible labor-trade plan $((\tilde{l}(\omega))_{\omega \in \Omega}, (\tilde{t}(\omega))_{\omega \in \Omega})$ such that

a) $u_\omega(f(\tilde{l}_\omega(\omega)) + h_{g_\omega}(\tilde{t}(\omega))) \geq u_\omega(f(l_\omega(\omega)) + h_{g_\omega}(t(\omega)))$ for almost all $\omega$, and
b) $u_\omega(f(\tilde{l}_\omega(\omega)) + h_{g_\omega}(\tilde{t}(\omega))) > u_\omega(f(l_\omega(\omega)) + h_{g_\omega}(t(\omega)))$ for all $\omega \in A$ for some $A$ with $\mu(A) > 0$.

**Theorem 13.4 (the First Welfare Theorem):** Every competitive equilibrium organism is Pareto efficient.

*Proof:* Let $(p, (l(\omega))_{\omega \in \Omega}, (t(\omega))_{\omega \in \Omega})$ be a competitive equilibrium. Suppose that it is not efficient, then there exists an alternative labor-trade plan $((\tilde{l}(\omega))_{\omega \in \Omega}, (\tilde{t}(\omega))_{\omega \in \Omega})$ such that

a) for $\mu$-almost every $\omega$, $\tilde{l}(\omega) \geq 0$ and $\sum_{i=1}^{i=m} \tilde{l}_i(\omega) = 1$,
b) $\int \tilde{t}(\omega)\mu(d\omega) = 0$,
c) $u_\omega(f(\tilde{l}_\omega(\omega)) + h_{g_\omega}(\tilde{t}(\omega))) \geq u_\omega(f(l_\omega(\omega)) + h_{g_\omega}(t(\omega)))$ for almost all $\omega$, and
   $u_\omega(f(\tilde{l}_\omega(\omega)) + h_{g_\omega}(\tilde{t}(\omega))) > u_\omega(f(l_\omega(\omega)) + h_{g_\omega}(t(\omega)))$ for all $\omega \in A$ for some $A$ with $\mu(A) > 0$.

For every individual $\omega$, if $p \cdot \tilde{t}(\omega) < 0$, then we can find another trade plan $\tilde{\tilde{t}}(\omega)$ in which $\omega$ sells less of whatever she sells at $\tilde{t}(\omega)$ and still keeps the budget balanced $p \cdot \tilde{\tilde{t}}(\omega) < 0$. In this case, $u_\omega(f(\tilde{l}_\omega(\omega)) + h_{g_\omega}(\tilde{\tilde{t}}(\omega))) > u_\omega(f(\tilde{l}_\omega(\omega)) + h_{g_\omega}(\tilde{t}(\omega))) \geq u_\omega(f(l_\omega(\omega)) + h_{g_\omega}(t(\omega)))$. But this contradicts that $f_\omega(l(\omega)) + h_{g_\omega}(t(\omega))$ maximizes $u_\omega$ over $\Psi(f_\omega, g_\omega, p)$. Hence,

$p \cdot \tilde{t}(\omega) \geq 0$ for all $\omega$.

Moreover, for any individual $\omega \in A$, we must have

$p \cdot \tilde{t}(\omega) > 0$.

Integrating the above inequalities over $\Omega$ leads to $\int p \cdot \tilde{t}(\omega)\mu(d\omega) > 0$, which contradicts (b). *Q.E.D.*

Since the notion of general equilibrium implies utility equalization in a new classical model with *ex ante* identical consumer-producers, the first welfare theorem implies that the Yao theorem holds if consumer-producers are *ex ante* identical in our general new classical model.

Zhou, Sun, and Yang (1998) have established the second welfare theorem for the general class of new classical models specified in the previous sections. In addition to the first and second welfare theorems, the core equivalence also holds in our model. A feasible allocation is a *core allocation* if no coalition of individuals can rearrange labor allocations and trades among themselves to improve the welfare of all members of the coalition. An argument similar to the proof of the first welfare theorem has shown that every competitive equilibrium allocation is a core allocation. A modification of the proof of the second welfare theorem shows that every core allocation is a competitive equilibrium allocation. One only needs to apply the separation argument in the proof to the negative orthant of $R^m$ and the collection of integrals of $F$ on all measurable subsets of $\Omega$. Hence, we can establish that the set of competitive equilibrium allocations coincides with the set of core allocations.

These results imply that the most important function of the invisible hand is to coordinate all individuals' networking decisions in choosing their patterns and levels of specialization and to utilize the positive network effect of division of labor net of transaction costs. We have thereby established a sound theoretical foundation for classical economic thinking. Note that our general models involve more information asymmetry than in any neoclassical models of information asymmetry. In our models, each individual does not know others' utility and production functions, transaction conditions, and endowment constraints. She even does not know the distribution functions of these characteristics. Each individual has complete information only about her own characteristics. As Hurwicz (1973) shows that the Walrasian mechanism is the one among all possible mechanisms that needs the least information to utilize all information in the market. Since evolution of division of labor will increase equilibrium degree of asymmetry between production structures of different occupations, the function of the market looks like to utilize increasingly more asymmetric information while keeping the information that each individual specialist has to know at the minimum level.

## ◆ 13.5 A New Classical Model with both Endogenous and Exogenous Comparative Advantages

### Example 13.1: a model (Sachs, Yang, and Zhang, 1999a,b) with endogenous and exogenous comparative advantages

Consider a world consisting of country 1 and country 2, each with a continuum of $M_i$ ($i = 1, 2$) consumer-producers. The individuals within a country are assumed to be identical. The utility function for individuals in country i is

$$u_i = (x_i + k_i x_i^d)^{0.5}(y_i + k_i y_i^d)^{0.5}$$

where $k_i$ is the trading efficiency coefficient in country i.

The production functions for a consumer-producer in country i are

$$x_1 + x_1^s = L_{1x}^b, \qquad y_1 + y_1^s = L_{1y}, \tag{13.7a}$$

$$x_2 + x_2^s = aL_{2x}, \qquad y_2 + y_2^s = L_{2y}^c, \tag{13.7b}$$

where $L_{ij}$ is the amount of labor allocated to the production of good j by an individual in country i, and $L_{ix} + L_{iy} = B > 1$. For simplicity, we assume that $B = 2$. It is assumed that $a$, $b$, $c > 1$. This system of production functions and endowment constraint displays economies of specialization in producing good x for an individual in country 1 and in producing good y for an individual in country 2. It exhibits constant returns to specialization for an individual in country 1 to produce good y and for an individual in country 2 to produce good x. But an individual in country 2 has a higher productivity in producing good x than an individual in country 1 in producing good y.

Suppose that $b = c = 1$. If all individuals allocate the same amount of labor to the production of each goods, then an individual in country 1 has the same average labor productivity of good x and y as an individual in country 2 in producing good y. But the average labor productivity of good x for an individual in country 2 is higher. This is similar to the situation in a Ricardian model with exogenous comparative advantage. Country 1's productivities are not higher than country 2 in producing all goods, but may have exogenous comparative advantage in producing good y. For $b = c = 2$ an individual in country 1 has endogenous comparative advantage in producing x and an individual in country 2 has endogenous comparative advantage in producing good y. But an individual in country 1 has no endogenous comparative advantage in producing good y and an individual in country 2 has no endogenous comparative advantage in producing good x, since respective productivities never change, independent of their labor allocation.

There are three configurations from which the individuals can choose. Configurations A, (x/y), and (y/x) are the same as in the Ricardo model in example 12.1. But in the model with both endogenous and exogenous comparative advantages, the number of possible structures is much more than in the model with only exogenous comparative advantage in example 12.1 or in the model with only endogenous comparative advantage in example 5.1. There are 13 feasible structures that may satisfy market clearing and other conditions for a general equilibrium.

Structure AA, as shown in panel (1) of figure 13.1, is an autarky structure where individuals in both countries choose self-sufficiency (configuration A). Structure AD, shown in panel (2) of figure 13.1, is asymmetric between the two countries: all individuals in country 1 choose autarky configuration A, while some individuals in country 2 choose configuration (x/y) and others choose configuration (y/x). Hence, there is domestic division of labor and related domestic trade in country 2, but no international division of labor and related international trade. Structure DA is symmetric to structure AD: country 1 has domestic division of labor and country 2 is in autarky. This structure involves a *Type I dual structure* between countries.

Structure $PC_+$, shown in panel (4), involves a *Type II dual structure* between the two countries as well as in country 1. Some individuals in country 1 choose configuration (x/y), the rest of the population choose autarky, and all individuals in country 2 choose configuration (y/x). There is a dual structure between professional individuals choosing (x/y) and self-sufficient individuals in country 1 despite their *ex ante* identical characteristics. The professional individuals in country 1 are involved in international trade with country 2. Structure $CP_+$ is symmetric to structure $PC_+$.

Structure $PC_-$, shown in panel (6), is the same as structure $PC_+$ except that professional individuals in country 1 choose configuration (y/x) instead of (x/y) and individuals in

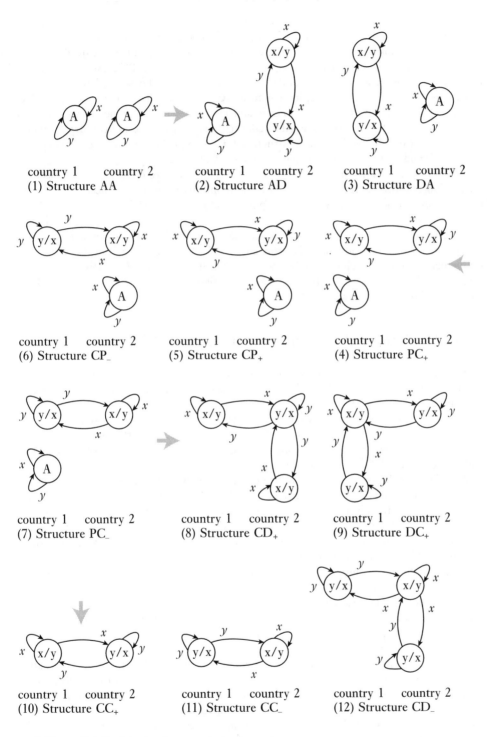

country 1     country 2
(1) Structure AA

country 1     country 2
(2) Structure AD

country 1     country 2
(3) Structure DA

country 1     country 2
(6) Structure CP_

country 1     country 2
(5) Structure CP_+

country 1     country 2
(4) Structure PC_+

country 1     country 2
(7) Structure PC_

country 1     country 2
(8) Structure CD_+

country 1     country 2
(9) Structure DC_+

country 1     country 2
(10) Structure CC_+

country 1     country 2
(11) Structure CC_

country 1     country 2
(12) Structure CD_

◆ **Figure 13.1:** Dual structure in economic development

country 2 choose configuration (x/y) instead of (y/x). Structure CP_ is the same as structure CP_+ except that individuals in country 1 choose configuration (y/x) instead of (x/y) and professional individuals in country 2 choose configuration (x/y) instead of (y/x).

Structure DC_+, shown in panel (9), is the same as structure PC_+ except that those individuals choosing autarky in country 1 in structure PC_+ choose configuration (y/x) instead in structure DC_+. Hence, in structure DC_+ all individuals completely specialize, but country 1 is involved in both domestic and international trade, whereas country 2 is involved only in international trade. Also, country 1 exports good x and country 2 exports good y. Structure DC_ is the same as structure DC_+ except that country 1 exports good y instead of good x and country 2 exports good x instead of good y.

Structure CD_+, shown in panel (8), is symmetric to structure DC_+: country 1 has only international trade whereas country 2 has both international and domestic trade, and country 1 exports good x and country 2 exports good y. Structure CD_ is the same as CD_+ except that country 1 exports good y instead of x; country 2 exports good x instead of y.

Structure CC_+, shown in panel (10), is international complete division of labor between two countries in which all individuals in country 1 choose configuration (x/y) and all individuals in country 2 choose configuration (y/x). Structure CC_ is symmetric to structure CC_+: all individuals in country 1 choose configuration (y/x) and all individuals in country 2 choose configuration (x/y).

## ◆ 13.6 Trade Pattern and Income Distribution

According to the existence theorem in section 13.4, a general equilibrium exists and is Pareto optimal for the new classical model with endogenous and exogenous comparative advantages in example 13.1.

We assume that the measure of type 1 persons is $M_1$, that of type 2 persons is $M_2$, and $M_1 + M_2 = 1$. For simplicity, let $M_1 = M_2 = 0.5$ and $\beta = 0.5$. Let the number (measure) of individuals in country i choosing configuration (x/y) be $M_{ix}$, that choosing (y/x) be $M_{iy}$, and that choosing A be $M_{iA}$.

We follow the two-step approach to inframarginal analysis developed in previous chapters. In the first step, we consider a structure. Each individual's utility maximizing decision is solved for the given structure. Utility equalization conditions between individuals choosing different configurations in the same country, and market clearing conditions are used to solve the corner equilibrium relative price of traded goods and numbers (measure) of individuals choosing different configurations.

According to the definition, a general equilibrium is a corner equilibrium in which all individuals have no incentive to deviate, under the corner equilibrium relative price, from their chosen configurations. Hence, in the second step, we can plug the corner equilibrium relative price into the indirect utility function for each constituent configuration in this structure, then compare corner equilibrium values of utility across configurations. The total cost–benefit analysis yields the conditions under which the corner equilibrium utility in each constituent configuration of this structure is not smaller than any alternative configuration. This system of inequalities can thus be used to identify a subspace of parameter space within which this corner equilibrium is a general equilibrium. We can completely partition the parameter space into subspaces, within each of which the corner equilibrium in a structure is a general equilibrium. As parameter values shift between the subspaces, the general equilibrium will discontinuously jump between structures.

We now take the first step of the inframarginal analysis. As an example, we consider structure $CP_+$. Assume that in this structure, $M_{2y}$ individuals choose configuration (y/x) and $M_{2A}$ individuals choose autarky in country 2, where $M_{2y} + M_{2A} = M_2 = 0.5$. $M_1 = 0.5$ individuals in country 1 choose configuration (x/y). Since all individuals in the same country are *ex ante* identical in all aspects (the same utility and production functions, the same transaction condition, and the same endowment), the maximum utilities in configurations A and (y/x) must be the same in country 2 in equilibrium. Marginal analysis of the decision problem for an individual in country 2 choosing autarky yields the maximum utility in configuration A: $u_{2A} = (a2^{c+1}\gamma)^{0.5}$, where $\gamma \equiv c^c/(c + 1)^{c+1}$. Marginal analysis of the decision problem for an individual in country 2 choosing configuration (y/x) yields the demand function $x_2^d = 2^{c-1}/p$ the supply function $y_2^s = 2^{c-1}$ and indirect utility function: $u_{2y} = 2^{c-1}(k_2/p)^{0.5}$. The utility equalization condition $u_{2y} = u_{2A}$ yields $p \equiv p_x/p_y = k_2 2^{c-3}/a\gamma$. Similarly, the marginal analysis of the decision problem of an individual choosing configuration (x/y) in country 1 yields the demand function, $y_1^d = 2^{b-1}/p$, the supply function $x_1^s = 2^{b-1}$, and indirect utility function: $u_{1x} = 2^{b-1}(k_1p)^{0.5}$. Inserting the corner equilibrium relative price into the market clearing condition for good x, $M_1 x_1^s = M_{2y} x_2^d$, yields the number of individuals selling good y, $M_{2y} = 0.5 k_2/2^{3-c}a\gamma$, where $M_1 = 0.5$ by assumption. Indirect utility functions for individuals choosing various configurations in the two countries are listed in table 13.1.

Following this procedure, we can solve for corner equilibrium in each structure. The solutions of all corner equilibria are summarized in table 13.2. Then we can take the second step to carry out total cost–benefit analysis for each corner equilibrium and to identify the parameter subspace within which the corner equilibrium is a general equilibrium. Consider the corner equilibrium in structure $CP_+$ as an example again.

In this structure $M_1$ individuals choose configuration (x/y) in country 1, and $M_{2y}$ individuals choose configuration (y/x) and $M_{2A}$ individuals choose autarky in country 2. For an individual in country 1, equilibrium requires that her utility in configuration (x/y) is not smaller than in configurations (y/x) and A under the corner equilibrium relative price in structure $CP_+$. Also equilibrium requires that all individuals in country 2 are indifferent between configurations (y/x) and A and receive a utility level that is not lower than in configuration (x/y). In addition, this structure occurs in equilibrium only if $M_{2y} \in (0, 0.5)$. All the conditions imply

$$u_{1x} \geq u_{1y}, \qquad u_{1x} \geq u_{1A}, \qquad u_{2A} = u_{2y} \geq u_{2x}, \qquad M_{2y} \in (0, 0.5),$$

where indirect utility functions in different configurations and the corner equilibrium relative price are given in tables 13.1 and 13.2. The conditions define a parameter subspace:

**Table 13.1: Indirect utility functions**

|  | *Indirect utility functions* | | |
| --- | --- | --- | --- |
| Configurations | (x/y) | (y/x) | A |
| Country 1 | $u_{1x} = 2^{b-1}(k_1p)^{0.5}$ | $u_{1y} = (k_1/p)^{0.5}$ | $u_{1A} = (2^{b+1}\alpha\gamma)^{0.5}$ |
| Country 2 | $u_{2x} = a(k_2p)^{0.5}$ | $u_{2y} = 2^{c-1}(k_2/p)^{0.5}$ | $u_{2A} = (2^{c+1}a\gamma)^{0.5}$ |

*where $\alpha \equiv b^b/(1 + b)^{b+1}$, $\gamma \equiv c^c/(1 + c)^{c+1}$.*

$$k_1 k_2 \geq 2^{6-b-c} a\alpha\gamma, \; k_2 \in (2^{4-b-c} a\gamma, \; \text{Min} \; \{4\gamma, \; a\gamma 2^{3-b}\}),$$

$$a < 2^{4+b-c}, \; k_1 > \text{Max} \; \{2^{4-b-c} a\alpha, \; \alpha 2^{3-c}\},$$

where $\alpha \equiv b^b/(1 + b)^{b+1}$ and $\gamma \equiv c^c/(c + 1)^{c+1}$. Within this parameter subspace, the corner equilibrium in structure $CP_+$ is the general equilibrium. Following this procedure, we can do total cost–benefit analysis for each structure. The total cost–benefit analysis in the second step and marginal analysis of each corner equilibrium in the first step yields an inframarginal comparative statics of general equilibrium, summarized in table 13.3. From this table, we can see that the parameter subspace for structure $DC_+$, $DC_-$, or $CC_-$ to occur in general equilibrium is empty.

In table 13.3, C stands for complete specialization in a country, D stands for the domestic division of labor in a country, A stands for autarky in a country, P stands for the partial division of labor where the population is divided between autarky and specialization in a country, subscript + stands for a pattern of trade in which country 1 exports good x and imports good y, and subscript − stands for a trade pattern in which country 1 exports good y and imports good x. Hence, structure AA involves autarky in both countries, structures AD and DA involve autarky in one country and division of labor in the other, structures PC and CP involve complete specialization in one country and coexistence of autarky and complete specialization in the other. The country with the lower trading efficiency in this structure looks underdeveloped in the sense that it receives none of the gains from trade, and the income differential between it and the other country with higher trading efficiency increases as a result of a shift of equilibrium from autarky to this structure. Also, *ex ante* identical individuals in the less-developed country in this structure are divided between a professional occupation that trades with the foreign country and those who are self-sufficient and not involved in commercialized production. These self-sufficient individuals look underemployed, since they cannot find a job to work for the market. All individuals completely specialize in structures CD and CC. But CC involves complete specialization of both countries in the absence of domestic trade, whereas CD involves complete specialization in country 1 and domestic division of labor in country 2. Figure 13.1 illustrates the equilibrium structures.[5] We say the level of division of labor increase in a structure if occurrence of letters A or P decreases or the occurrence of letters D or C increases.

Table 13.2: Corner equilibria

| Structure | Relative price of x to y | Numbers of individuals choosing configurations |
|---|---|---|
| AA | | $M_{1A} = M_{2A} = 0.5$ |
| AD | $2^{c-1}/a$ | $M_{1A} = 0.5, \; M_{2x} = M_{2y} = 0.25$ |
| DA | $2^{1-b}$ | $M_{2A} = 0.5, \; M_{1x} = M_{1y} = 0.25$ |
| $PC_+$ | $2^{3-b}\alpha/k_1$ | $M_{2y} = 0.5, \; M_{1A} = 0.5(1 - k_1 2^{c-3}/\alpha), \; M_{1x} = 0.5 k_1 2^{c-3}/\alpha$ |
| $CP_+$ | $2^{c-3}k_2/\gamma a$ | $M_{1x} = 0.5, \; M_{2A} = 0.5(1 - k_2 2^{b-3}/\gamma a), \; M_{2y} = 0.5 k_2 2^{b-3}/\gamma a$ |
| $CP_-$ | $2^{c+1}\gamma/ak_2$ | $M_{1y} = 0.5, \; M_{2x} = 0.5 k_2 2^{-c-1}/\gamma, \; M_{2A} = 0.5(1 - k_2 2^{-c-1}/\gamma)$ |
| $CC_+$ | $2^{c-b}$ | $M_{1x} = M_{2y} = 0.5$ |
| $CD_+$ | $2^{c-1}/a$ | $M_{1x} = 0.5, \; M_{2y} = (1 + 2^{b-1}/a)/4, \; M_{2x} = (1 - 2^{b-1}/a)4$ |
| $CD_-$ | $2^{c-1}/a$ | $M_{1y} = 0.5, \; M_{2x} = 0.25 + 2^{-c-1}, \; M_{2y} = 0.25 - 2^{-c-1}$ |

In order to accurately describe the inframarginal comparative statics, we define endogenous comparative advantage as productivity difference between individuals that is caused by individuals' labor allocations; and we define exogenous comparative advantage as productivity difference between individuals that is independent of labor allocation. Since marginal and average productivity never changes as labor allocation alters for a production function with constant returns to scale, these definitions imply that endogenous comparative advantages come from economies of specialization and exogenous comparative advantages come from exogenous differences of production conditions with constant returns. Parameter $b$ represents the degree of endogenous comparative advantage for a person in country 1 producing good x, since as $b$ increases, increases in productivity become more responsive to an increase in the amount of labor allocated to its production. Similarly, $c$ represents the degree of endogenous comparative advantage for a person in country 2 producing good y.

If $b = c = 1$, then country 2 has exogenous absolute and comparative advantage in producing good x and country 1 has exogenous comparative advantage in producing good y, since $a > 1$ in (13.2). This implies that $a$ represents the degree of exogenous comparative advantage.

With the definitions, we can now closely examine table 13.3, which consists of four blocks. The northwest block is associated with low trading efficiencies in both countries. The northeast block is associated with low trading efficiency in country 1 and high trading efficiency in country 2. The southwest block is associated with low trading efficiency in country 2 and high trading efficiency in country 1. The southeast block is associated with high trading

Table 13.3: General equilibrium structure: inframarginal comparative statics

| | $k_2 \in (0, 4\gamma)$ | | | $k_2 \in (4\gamma, 1)$ | | | |
|---|---|---|---|---|---|---|---|
| $k_1 \in$ $(0, 4\alpha)$ | $a > 2^{b+c-2}$ | | | $a < 2^{b+c-2}$ | $a > 2^{b+c-2}$ | | |
| | $k_1 k_2 < a\alpha\gamma 2^{6-b-c}$ | $k_1 k_2 > a\alpha\gamma 2^{6-b-c}$ | | $k_1 k_2 < \alpha\gamma 2^{b+c+2}/a$ | $a < 2^{b-1}$ | $a > 2^{b-1}$ | $k_1 < \alpha 2^{b+c}/a$ |
| | AA | $a < 2^{b-1}$ | $a > 2^{b-1}$ | AA | $k_1 < a\alpha 2^{4+b-c}$  AD | AD | AD |
| | | $k_1 < \alpha 2^{3-c}$  PC$_+$ | CP$_+$ | $k_1 k_2 > \alpha\gamma 2^{b+c+2}/a$ | $k_1 \in (a\alpha 2^{4+b-c}, \alpha 2^{3-c})$  PC$_+$ | $k_1 > a\alpha 2^{4+b-c}$  CD$_+$ | $k_1 \in (\alpha 2^{b+c}/a, 4\alpha)$  CD$_-$ |
| | | $k_2 < a\gamma 2^{3-b}$  CP$_+$ | | CP$_-$ | $k_1 > \alpha 2^{3-c}$  CC$_+$ | | |
| | | $k_1 > \alpha 2^{3-c}$ $k_2 > a\gamma 2^{3-b}$  CC$_+$ | | | | | |
| $k_1 \in$ $(4\alpha, 1)$ | $a < 2^{b-1}$ | $a > 2^{b-1}$ | | $k_2 < \gamma 2^{b+c}/a$ | $a < 2^{b-1}$ | $a > 2^{b-1}$ | |
| | $k_2 < a\gamma 2^{4+b-c}$  DA | DA | | DA | CC$_+$ | CD$_+$ | CD$_-$ |
| | $k_2 \in (a\gamma 2^{4+b-c}, a\gamma 2^{3-b})$  CP$_+$ | $k_2 > a\gamma 2^{4+b-c}$  CP$_+$ | | $k_2 > \gamma 2^{b+c}/a$  CD$_-$ | | | |
| | $k_2 > a\gamma 2^{3-b}$  CC$_+$ | | | | | | |

*where* $\alpha \equiv b^b/(1 + b)^{b+1}$, $\gamma \equiv c^c/(1 + c)^{c+1}$.

efficiencies in both countries. As parameter values move from the northwest toward the southeast, the occurrence of letter A, representing autarky, and letter P, representing partial division of labor, decreases, and the occurrence of letters D and C, representing complete division of labor, increases. Hence, as transaction conditions are improved, the level of domestic and international division of labor increases because of the trade-off between transaction costs and economies of division of labor generated by endogenous and exogenous comparative advantages. If the trading efficiency is low in one country and high in the other (the northeast or southwest blocks), the country with the lower trading efficiency has a dual structure (P) or is in autarky (A) in a structure with asymmetric division of labor between countries (AD, DA, PC, or CP). If the trading efficiencies are high in both countries, then complete division of labor occurs and dual structure disappears in equilibrium.

Each block consists of three sections. If the degree of exogenous comparative advantage $a$ is small compared to the degree of endogenous comparative advantage ($b$, $c$), each country exports the good with economies of specialization in production. This is denoted by subscript $+$. Otherwise, a country exports the good with constant returns and exogenous comparative advantage.

All the results on evolution of division of labor, dual structure, and trade pattern are summarized in the following proposition, illustrated in figure 13.1, where large arrows indicate the direction of the evolution in division of labor.

**Proposition 13.1:** As trading efficiency increases from a very low to a very high level, the equilibrium level of domestic and international division of labor increases from complete autarky in both countries to the complete division of labor in both countries. In the transitional stage, two types of dual structure may occur. In a Type 1 dual structure the country with the lower trading efficiency is in autarky and the other has domestic division of labor and higher productivity and per capita real income. In a Type 2 dual structure, the country with higher trading efficiency completely specializes and obtains all of the gains from trade, while the other country has a domestic dual structure between commercialized sector and self-sufficient sector (autarky) which suggests underemployment. The dual structures of two types disappear as individuals in all countries are involved in international and domestic division of labor. Each country exports goods of exogenous comparative advantage if exogenous comparative advantage dominates endogenous comparative advantage in producing this good. Otherwise, each country exports goods with endogenous comparative advantage and exogenous comparative disadvantage.

The inframarginal comparative statics of general equilibrium can be used to establish two corollaries. The first is that evolution in division of labor generated by improvements in transaction conditions will raise equilibrium aggregate productivity. You are asked to substantiate this corollary in exercise 4.

The second corollary is that deterioration of a country's terms of trade and increase of gains received by this country from trade may concur. Suppose that the initial values of parameters satisfy $k_1 \in (0, 4\alpha)$, $k_2 \in (0, 4\gamma)$, and $k_1 k_2 > a\gamma\alpha 2^{6-b-c}$, which implies, from table 13.3, that we are considering the northwest block. Suppose that the initial value of $k_2$ satisfies $k_2' < a\gamma 2^{3-c}$, so that the equilibrium structure is $CP_+$ in which country 2 exports y and imports x and its terms of trade, from table 13.2, is $1/p = 2^{c-3} a\gamma/k_2'$. Now, the value of $k_2$ increases to $k_2'' > a\gamma 2^{3-c}$, which implies, from table 13.3, that the general equilibrium jumps from $CP_+$ to structure $CC_+$ in which country 2's terms of trade, from table 13.2, is $2^{b-c}$. It can then be shown that country 2's terms of trade deteriorate as a result of the change in $k_2$. But this shift of the equilibrium from $CP_+$ to $CC_+$ increases the utility of each individual in country 2 from autarky level. This has established the claim that the deterioration of a country's terms of trade may concur with an increase of the gains that it receives from trade. There are other parameter subspaces within which changes in parameters may generate concurrence of the deterioration of one country's terms of trade and an increase in its gains from trade.

Although an equilibrium in this model is always Pareto optimal, it generates interesting implications of economic development and trade for income distribution. It is straightforward that as the equilibrium jumps from a structure in which at least some individuals in a country are in autarky (structure AD, DA, PC, CP) to a structure in which all individuals are involved in trade and division of labor, all individuals' utilities in this country will be increased. Hence, in our model evolution in division of labor will not reduce per capita real income in a less-developed economy. As the equilibrium jumps from autarky to the partial division of labor (AD, DA, PC, or CP), the developed country gets all gains from trade and development. But as the equilibrium jumps, say from $PC_+$ to $CC_+$, it is possible that the utility of a person in the developed country may decline. It can be shown that this takes place within the parameter subspace in the southwest block in table 13.3. This prediction is consistent with the fact, documented in Krugman and Venables (1995, pp. 857–8), that in the 1970s the general view was that integration of world markets produced a rise in the living standards of rich nations at the expense of the poor, but in the 1990s, it is believed that the rise of Third World manufacturing nations has serious adverse impacts on developed economies. But according to our model, this reversal of the tide is just compensation to less-developed economies which did not receive much gain from trade in the early development stage. Also, in our model there exists some parameter subspace within which such immiserizing development never occurs. This is the case when the improvements in the trading efficiency of the developed country keep pace with the improvements of the trading efficiency of the less-developed country (for instance, in the northeast block of table 13.3).

Since the inframarginal comparative statics change with the specification of the system of production functions, we report the sensitivity analysis of our result.

### Example 13.2: a model with economies of specialization in one activity for all individuals

The system of production functions in (13.7) displays economies of specialization in producing good x by a person in country 1 and in producing good y by a person in country 2. We now assume that there are economies of specialization for all individuals in producing x, but constant returns prevail in the production of good y. Hence, the system of production functions in (13.7) is replaced by

$$x_1 + x_1^s = L_{1x}^b, \qquad y_1 + y_1^s = L_{1y},$$
$$x_2 + x_2^s = L_{2x}^c, \qquad y_2 + y_2^s = aL_{2y},$$

Then the inframarginal comparative statics of general equilibrium are summarized in table 13.4 and proposition 13.2.

**Proposition 13.2**: As trading efficiency is improved, the equilibrium level of division of labor and aggregate productivity increase. The country with lower trading efficiency and/

or insignificant economies of specialization has a dual structure with underemployment in the transitional stage of economic development. If a country has endogenous comparative advantage and exogenous comparative disadvantage in producing a good, it exports this good if the former dominates the latter. Otherwise it imports this good.

The results of table 13.4 yield the following proposition. In exercise 7, you are asked to replace the production functions in (13.6) with the one displaying economies of specialization for individuals in one country and constant returns for individuals in the other country. Then you can show that the essence of propositions 13.1 and 13.2 would not be changed.

This analysis is different from those of Krugman (1980), Fujita and Krugman (1995), and Yang (1991, see example 7.1), who explain economic development, structural changes, and trade pattern by economic changes in the absence of *ex ante* differences between decision-makers. It is different from conventional trade theory and development economics concerning only exogenous comparative advantages. We explain complicated development and trade phenomena by the coexistence of endogenous and exogenous comparative advantages.

**Table 13.4:** Equilibrium structure (economies of specialization in producing one good for all countries)

| | $k_2 \in (0, 4\gamma)$ | | | $k_2 \in (4\gamma, 1)$ | | |
|---|---|---|---|---|---|---|
| $k_1 \in (0, 4\alpha)$ | $a > 2^{c-b}$ | | $a < 2^{c-b}$ | $a > 2^{c-b}$ | | $a < 2^{c-b}$ |
| | $k_1k_2 < \alpha\gamma2^{c-b+4}/a$ <br> AA | $k_1k_2 > \alpha\gamma2^{c-b+4}/a$ <br> CP$_+$ | $k_1k_2 < a\alpha\gamma2^{4+b-c}$   AA <br><br> $k_1k_2 > a\alpha\gamma2^{4+b+c}$   CP$_-$ | $2^{c-b} > 1$ <br> $k_1 < \alpha2^{2+c-b}/a$   AD <br> $k_1 > \alpha2^{2+c+b}/a$   CD$_+$ | $2^{c-b} < 1$ <br> AD <br> $k_1 < \alpha2^{2+c+b}/a$   CC$_+$ | $k_1 < a\alpha2^{2+b-c}$   AD <br><br> $k_1 > a\alpha2^{2+b-c}$   CD$_-$ |
| $k_1 \in (4\alpha, 1)$ | $k_2 < \gamma2^{2+b+c}/a$   DA <br> $k_2 > \gamma2^{2+b+c}/a$   CP$_+$ | | $k_2 < a\gamma2^{2+b+c}$   DA <br> $k_2 > a\gamma2^{2+b+c}$   CP$_-$ | $2^{c-b} > 1$ <br> CD$_+$ | $2^{c-b} < 1$ <br> CC$_+$ | CD$_-$ |

*where* $\alpha \equiv b^b/(1 + b)^{b+1}$, $\gamma \equiv c^c/(1 + c)^{c+1}$.

## Key Terms and Review

Networks of division of labor and digraphs.
Resource allocation and weights to vertices and arcs.
Organisms.
Conditions for the existence of a decision problem in choosing pattern of specialization and resource allocation.
Conditions for the existence of a general equilibrium organism.
Dual structure between the industrial and agricultural sectors, dual structure with unequal distribution of gains from trade, and dual structure between commercialized and self-sufficient sectors.

Dual structure caused by disequilibrium in labor market vs. dual structure in the transitional stage of evolution of division of labor.

Effects of coexistence of endogenous and exogenous comparative advantages on emergence, evolution, and disappearance of dual structure.

Underdevelopment and dual structure with underemployment.

Why the deterioration of terms of trade of a country may concur with increases in the gains it receives from trade.

The relationship between inequality of income distribution, economic development, trade, and evolution in division of labor.

## Further Reading

*Existence of equilibrium network of division of labor*: Border (1985), Dondran and Minoux (1984), Dutta and Mutuswami (1997), Jackson and Wolinsky (1996), Marshall (1890), Wen (1998), Spanjers (1992), Gilles (1990), Sun, Yang, and Yao (1999), Zhou, Sun, and Yang (1998); *graph theory and combinatorics*: Dondran and Minoux (1984), Roberts (1989), Rouvray (1990); *models with both endogenous and exogenous comparative advantages*: Gomory (1994), Liu (1998), Cheng, Liu, and Yang (2000), Sachs, Yang, and Zhang (1999), Yang and Zhang (1999); *underdevelopment*: Myrdal (1957), Nelson (1956), Palma (1978); *dual economy and structural changes*: Ranis (1988), Lewis (1955), Fei and Ranis (1964), Chenery (1979), Khandker and Rashid (1995); *equilibrium models of dual economy and economies of scale*: Din (1996), Murphy, Shleifer, and Vishny (1989), Gans (1998), Kelly (1997), Fujita and Krugman (1995), Baldwin and Venables (1995), Puga and Venables (1998), Krugman and Venables (1995); *deteriorated terms of trade*: Sen (1998), Cypher and Dietz (1998), Kohli and Werner (1998), Morgan (1970), Sapsford (1985).

# QUESTIONS

1   Why do we need an existence theorem of equilibrium organism for models without explicitly specified functional forms?

2   Why are the concepts of a weighted digraph and an equilibrium organism powerful vehicles to describe the network of division of labor and the extent of the market?

3   Compare the proof of the Wen theorem in chapter 5 to the proof in this chapter, and identify the advantage of the latter over the former in connection with the fact that an increasing convex function is differentiable almost everywhere, but not necessarily differentiable at every point in the domain.

4   Suppose in example 13.1 there is a dual structure where *ex ante* identical individuals in the same country are divided between specialization and autarky is not allowed. Show that interest conflict may occur: that some individuals prefer Structure A to Structure B and others prefer B to A. Use your cases to explain why such a dual structure emerges from the coexistence of endogenous and exogenous comparative advantages in new classical models.

5   There are several different definitions of dual economy. Lewis (1955) and Fei and Ranis (1964) take dual economy as a structure with division of population between modern industrial and traditional agricultural sectors. In example 12.1, we consider a structure with unequal gains from trade between two groups of *ex ante* different individuals as a dual structure. Compare the dual structure in example 13.1 to these definitions, and discuss effects of the coexistence of endogenous and exogenous comparative advantage on dual structure. Relate your discussion to the notions of underemployment and underdevelopment.

6   Emmanuel (1972) argued that international trade transfers wealth from the poor countries to the rich ones. Use the models in this chapter to assess the argument.

7   John Stuart Mill (1848) emphasized the importance of "the tendency of every extension of the market to improve the processes of production." He argued that "a country which produces for a larger market than its own, can introduce a more extended division of labour, can make greater use of machinery, and is more likely to make inventions and improvements in the processes of production." Use the models in this chapter to formalize his ideas.

8   Lewis (1955, p. 118) and other economists argue, based on the measurement of prices of the United Kingdom's commodity terms of trade or the terms of trade between primary products and manufactured products, that international market forces have transferred income from poor to rich nations through a deterioration in the terms of trade of the less developed countries. Meier (1995, pp. 390–2) argues that this does not provide a sufficiently strong statistical foundation for any adequate generalization about the terms of trade of poor countries. The import price index conceals the heterogeneous price movements within and among broad categories of foodstuffs, raw materials, and minerals; no allowance is made for changes in the quality of exports and imports; there is inadequate consideration of new commodities; and the recorded terms of trade are not corrected for the substantial decline in transportation costs. The introduction of new products and qualitative improvements has been more extensive in manufactured than in primary products, and a large proportion of the fall in British prices of primary products can be attributed to the great decline in inward freight rates. Even if it were true that the less-developed countries experienced a secular deterioration in their commodity terms of trade, this deterioration may be caused by productivity progress in the export sector. Hence, as long as productivity in export industries is increasing more rapidly than export prices are falling, the single-factor terms of trade (commodity terms corrected for changes in productivity in producing exports) may increase, and the country's real income can rise despite the deterioration in the commodity terms of trade. Use the model in example 13.1 to formalize this analysis.

9   Many economists argue that the deterioration of terms of trade for less-developed countries hinders economic development in these countries. Other economists try to find empirical evidence for or against the worsening or to measure adverse effects of the worsening on economic development (see, for example, Morgan, 1970, and Kohli and Werner, 1998). Sen (1998) reports that from 1990 to 1995 Thailand's GDP increased by 49%, its export prices increased by 18% and import prices by 21%. During the same period Singapore's GDP increased by 49%, its export price decreased by 18%, and import price decreased by 9%. Use the model in example 13.1 to explain the facts in connection to previous empirical studies.

10  Murphy, Shleifer, and Vishny (1989) show that if income distribution is very unequal, a limited market will adversely affect economic development. Compare this theory on the relationship between dual structure and economic development to the new classical mechanism for economic development in example 13.1.

11  Lewis (1955) argues that an exogenously fixed wage rate that is higher than the market clearing level generates labor surplus in the traditional agricultural sector. As capital accumulates in the modern industrial sector over time, marginal productivity of labor relative to capital in the industrial sector increases, so that this sector can absorb surplus labor and grow at no cost to the agricultural sector. Compare this mechanism of development and dual economy to the new classical mechanisms in examples 13.1 and 13.2. Find empirical evidence to test one against the other.

12  Chenery (1979) uses models with disequilibrium and changes of taste to explain structural changes in an economy. According to him, "given imperfect foresight and limits to factor mobility, structural changes are most likely to occur under conditions of disequilibrium; this is particularly true in factor markets.

Thus a shift of labor and capital from less productive to more productive sectors can accelerate growth." Use the equilibrium models in this and previous chapters to explain structural changes and dual structure and discuss the differences between the two approaches. Which of them is analytically more powerful and why?

13  Chenery (1979) emphasized effects of changes in the demand side on structural changes in the economic development process. For instance, he argued that changes in preferences and in income alter expenditure share of agricultural goods. Other economists pay more attention to the effects of supply-side or structural changes. For instance, changes in technology alter income share of industrial output. Use the general equilibrium analysis in this text to explain why the separation between demand and supply analyses is inconsistent with the notion of general equilibrium. For example, income is determined by productivity and network size of division of labor which cannot be determined only by preferences. Also, use models in this chapter to explain why economic structure may change endogenously in the absence of changes in production functions and preferences.

14  Compare the policy implications of the model in example 13.1 with the view that underdevelopment is caused by the exploitation of less-developed economies by capitalist developed economies (Myrdal, 1957, Nelson, 1956, Palma, 1978). Use this model to assess the statement that a country's competitiveness makes a difference for a country's development performance (Sachs, 1996a,b).

15  Use the inframarginal comparative statics in table 13.3 to analyze a recent debate on competitiveness. Show that a country with low trading efficiency cannot receive gains from trade in the transitional stage of economic development. Verify the following statements. From the northwest block of table 13.3, we can see that if the degree of economies of specialization in country 1, $b$, which negatively relates to $\alpha$, is small, relative to $c$, which negatively relates to $\gamma$, or $k_1 < \alpha 2^{3-c}$, structure PC is the equilibrium where this country is in an inferior position in the transitional stage. If $c$ is small relative to $b$, or $k_2 < a\gamma 2^{3-b}$, Structure CP occurs in equilibrium where country 2 is in an inferior position in the transitional state. You may interpret as degree of competitiveness absolute level of trading efficiency and degree of economies of specialization for a country in producing a good.

16  Ram (1997) provides empirical evidence for an uninverted-U pattern in the developed countries, taking into account data since World War II. Jones (1998, p. 65) also finds that the ratio of GDP per worker in the 5th-richest country to GDP per worker in the 5th-poorest country fluctuated from 1960 to 1990. A new data set in Deininger and Squire (1996) shows that inequality fluctuates as an economy develops. Yang and Zhang (1999) specify different types of individuals in each country in example 13.1 and show that inequality of income distribution fluctuates as different groups are sequentially involved in increasingly higher level of division of labor. This theory invalidates the conjecture that the relationship between inequality and economic development is monotonically negative (Alesina and Rodrik, 1994, Galor and Zeira, 1993, Thompson, 1995, Fei, Ranis, and Kuo, 1979, Balassa, 1986) or monotonically positive (Banerjee and Newman, 1993, Lewis, 1955, Palma, 1978, Li and Zou, 1998, Grossman, 1998, Murphy and Welch, 1991, Borjas, Freeman, and Katz, 1992, Karoly and Klerman, 1994, Sachs and Shartz, 1994) or that this relationship is an inverted U-curve (Kuznets, 1955, Krugman and Venables, 1995, Greenwood and Jovanovic, 1990).

# EXERCISES

1  Show that for an economy with a finite set $I = \{1, 2\}$, $M = \{1, 2\}$, the production functions $f_j(l_j) = \max\{0, l_j - 0.5\}$, and the utility function $u = x_1 x_2^2$, an equilibrium organism does not exist in the absence of transaction costs. Will your answer change if $f_j(l_j) = al_j$? Explain your answer.

2  In an economy there are four goods and a set of consumer-producers. Consider a consumer-producer having a utility function $u = x_1 x_2 x_3 x_4$, where $x_i$ is the quantity of good i she consumes. Assume that she is endowed with 1 unit of labor. Assume that she has production functions $q^1 j = \max\{0, L^1 j - 0.1\}$, $j = 1, 2$, and $q^1{}_k = \max\{0, L^1{}_k - 0.6\}$, $k = 3, 4$. Assume that when amount $y$ of any good is purchased by her, the amount she actually receives is equal to $0.6y$ because of transaction costs. Consider her decision in a Walrasian market when a price vector of $p = (2, 2, 1, 1)$ is given. If she chooses autarky, her maximal utility is 0. On the other hand, from the production functions and the given prices, it is easy to see that, for utility maximization, she should not allocate any amount of labor for the production of good 3 or good 4. Show that her optimal strategy is *either* selling only one of good 1 and good 2 *or* selling both goods.

3  Let us consider an economy with a continuum $[0, 1]$ of individuals and two goods $\{1, 2\}$. Assume that each individual is endowed with 1 unit of labor, and that the utility function for every individual is given by $u = x_1 x_2$, where $x_i$ is the amount of good i consumed. Assume that the trading efficiency coefficient is $k \in (0, 1)$. Assume that the production functions for every individual are given by $f_1 = 2l_1, f_2 = \text{Max}\{0, l_2 - 0.5\}$. Show that for the equilibrium price vector $(1, p)$, every individual *can achieve* her maximal utility either through an autarky or by producing one good, selling part of them and purchasing another good; i.e., through a complete specialization.

4  Consider the model in example 13.1 and assume that $b = c = 2$. Following the method used in chapter 2 to draw the PPF for an individual from country 1 and that for a person from country 2. Then draw the aggregate PPF for the two individuals. Draw the equilibrium production schedule when autarky occurs in equilibrium. Mark economies of division of labor in your graph and show how more economies of division of labor will be exploited as transaction conditions are improved.

5  Suppose that $b = c = 2$ in example 13.1. Show that inframarginal comparative statics are given by the following table 13.5. Interpret the results.

Table 13.5

| | $0 < k_1 \leq 16/27$ | | | | $16/27 < k_1 \leq 1$ | | |
|---|---|---|---|---|---|---|---|
| $0 < k_2 \leq$ 16/27 | $k_1 k_2 <$ $4a(2/3)^6$ | $k_1 k_2 > 4a(2/3)^6$ | | | $k_1 <$ $4a/27$ | $k_1 \in$ $(4a/27, 8/27)$ | $k_1 > 8/27$ |
| | | $k_1 < 8/27$ | $k_2 <$ $8a/27$: | $k_1 < 8/27,$ $k_2 < 8a/27$: | | | |
| | AA | PC | CP | CC | AC | PC | CC |
| $16/27 \leq k_2 < 1$ | $k_2 < 4a/27$ | $k_2 \in$ $(4a/27, 8/27)$: | $k_2 > 8/27$ | | Structure CC | | |
| | CA | CP | CC | | | | |

6  Show that in exercise 4 if $k_2'' > k_2'$, $k_2' \in (4a/27, 16/27)$, $k_1 \in (16/27, 1)$, $a < 4$, $k_2'' \in (16/27, 1)$ and if $k_2' < 8/27$, then as $k_2$ increases from $k_2'$ to $k_2''$, country 2's terms of trade

deteriorate, meanwhile utility of each individual in country 2 increases from autarky level to a higher level.

7   If we assume that there are economies of specialization only for individuals in country 1 in producing two goods, whereas constant returns prevail in country 2 in producing the two goods, the system of production functions is then:

$$x_1 + x_1^s = L_{1x}^b, \qquad y_1 + y_1^s = L_{1y}^c,$$
$$x_2 + x_2^s = aL_{2x}, \qquad y_2 + y_2^s = L_{2y},$$

Draw individual PPFs, the aggregate production schedule for autarky, and the aggregate PPF. Show that the inframarginal comparative statics of general equilibrium are given in table 13.6.

Table 13.6

| | $k_2 < 1$ | | | | $k_2 = 1$ | | | |
|---|---|---|---|---|---|---|---|---|
| $k_1 \in$ | $a > 2^{b-c}$ | | | $a < 2^{b-c}$ | $a > 2^{b-c}$ | | | $a < 2^{b-c}$ |
| (0, 4θ) | $k_1k_2 < \theta 2^{b-c+2}/a$ | $k_1k_2 > \theta 2^{b-c+2}/a$ | | $k_1k_2 < a\theta 2^{c-b+2}$ | $a > 2^{b-1}$ | $a < 2^{b-1}$ | | $k_1 < a\theta 2^{c-b+2}$ |
| | | $a > 2^{b-1}$ : $k_1 < \theta 2^{b+1}/a$ PC₋ ; $k_2 < 2^{1-c}$ CP₋ ; $k_1 > \theta 2^{b+1}/a$, $k_2 > 2^{1-c}$ CC₋ | $a < 2^{b-1}$ : CP₊ | AA | $k_1 < \theta 2^{c-b+2}/a$ AD ; $k_1 \in (\theta 2^{c-b+2}/a, \theta 2^{b+1}/a)$ PC₋ ; $k_1 > \theta 2^{b+1}/a$ CC₋ | $k_1 > \theta 2^{c-b+2}/a$ PC₋ | AD | $k_1 > a\theta 2^{c-b+2}$ PC₊ |
| | AA | | | $k_1k_2 > a\theta 2^{c-b+2}$ PC₊ | AD | | | |
| $k_1 \in$ (4θ, 1) | $a > 2^{b-1}$ | $a < 2^{b-1}$ | | $k_2 < a2^{c-b}$ DA ; $k_2 > a2^{c-b}$ DC₊ | $a > 2^{b-1}$ | $a < 2^{b-1}$ | | |
| | $k_2 < 2^{b-c}/a$ DA ; $k_2 \in (2^{b-c}/a, 2^{1-c})$ CD₋ ; $k_2 > 2^{1-c}$ CC₋ | $k_2 > 2^{b-c}/a$ DC₋ ; DA | | | CC₋ | DC₋ | | DC₊ |

where $\theta \equiv b^b c^c / (b + c)^{b+c}$.

8   Suppose that in the model in example 13.1 a value tax rate $t$ is imposed on each dollar of imported goods, and that the total tax revenue is evenly distributed among the buyers of the goods. Solve for the general equilibrium and its inframarginal comparative statics. Compare the results to the solutions in exercises 2, 3, and 4 in chapter 4. Discuss the different implications of tax and transaction costs in a neoclassical equilibrium model and in a new classical equilibrium model.

9   Liu, 1999: Consider the Ricardian model with endogenous cum exogenous comparative advantage in which the number of type 1 persons is $M_1$ and the number of type 2 persons is $M_2$. Assume that all individuals have the same Cobb–Douglas utility function with the same taste for the two goods. The production functions for type i persons are

$$x_i + x_i^s = \text{Max } \{l_{ix} - b_{ix}, 0\}$$

$$y_i + y_i^s = \text{Max } \{l_{iy} - b_{iy}, 0\}$$

Solve for the Walrasian general equilibrium and its inframarginal comparative statics. Use your results to analyze the relationship between international and domestic trade and dual structure in the transitional period from autarky to a high level of division of labor.

10   Suppose the production functions in example 13.1 are

$$x_i + x_i^s = \text{Max } \{a_{ix}(l_{ix} - b), 0\}$$

$$y_i + y_i^s = \text{Max } \{a_{ix}(l_{iy} - b), 0\}$$

Solve for the Walrasian general equilibrium and its inframarginal comparative statics.

11   Suppose the production functions in example 13.1 are

$$x_1 + x_1^s = \text{Max } \{l_{ix} - b, 0\}, \ x_2 + x_2^s = \text{Max } \{l_{2x} - c, 0\},$$

$$y_1 + y_1^s = l_{iy}, \ y_2 + y_2^s = al_{2y}.$$

Solve for the Walrasian general equilibrium and its inframarginal comparative statics. Use the model to explain pattern of trade by transaction and production conditions in two countries.

12   Draw the equilibrium production schedule in autarky and the PPF and identify economies of division of labor in example 13.1. Find the parameter subspace within which a country's terms of trade deteriorate and its gains from trade increase as the equilibrium shifts from Structure PC to Structure CC in example 13.1.

13   Liu (1998) introduces intermediate goods and tariffs into the new classical model in example 13.1 to analyze the development patterns of import and export substitution. Design such a model and examine the different implications of this model and the Ethier model for the analysis of development pattern.

14   Zhang, 1999: Introduce tariffs into the model in example 13.1 and allow a Nash tariff game and Nash tariff negotiations (see chapter 12 for the two regimes). Analyze under what conditions unilateral protection tariffs and unilateral *laissez-fairism* coexist and under what condition Nash tariff negotiation occurs in equilibrium.

15   Yang and Zhang, 1999: Assume that in the model in example 13.1 there are two types of individuals in country 1. Type a persons and type b persons are distinguished by their transaction conditions. We assume that $k_a = k$, $k_b = t$, and $k > t$. In other words, each Type a person has higher trading efficiency than each Type b person. Also, we assume that in country 2 $k_2 = k$. This implies that country 2 is a developed country which has better transaction conditions. Country 1 is a less-developed country where some residents (who might be urban or coastal residents) have the same transaction condition as in a developed country, but the rest of the population have lower trading efficiency. The production conditions are the same for all individuals in the same country, but different between the countries. Hence, the production functions for a type i consumer-producer are $x_j + x_j^s = L_{jx}^c$, $y_j + y_j^s = L_{jy}$, $j = a, b$. $x_2 + x_2^s = L_{2x}^c$, $y_2 + y_2^s = rL_{2y}$, where $x_i^s$, $y_i^s$ are respective quantities of the two goods sold by a type i person; $L_{is}$ is the amount of labor allocated to the production of good s (= x, y) by a type i person, and $L_{ix} + L_{iy} = B > 1$. For simplicity, we assume that $B = 2$. It is assumed that $r, c > 1$. Solve for equilibrium and its inframarginal comparative statics. Show that as trading efficiencies are improved the level of division of labor increases and inequality of income distribution in the less-developed country fluctuates. Use this model to invalidate the monotonic positive or negative correlation between inequality and economic development and the conjecture of an inverted U-curve of inequality and per capita income.

16  Yang and Zhang, 1999: Assume that in exercise 15 the developed country has two types of individuals too. Show that as more individuals are involved in the division of labor sequentially, some individuals achieve a higher level of specialization before others do. This increases inequality. As the latecomers catch up, inequality decreases. As the leading group goes to an even higher level of specialization, leaving others behind, inequality increases again. Show how such a ratcheting process generates inequality fluctuation.

## Notes

1 If fixed transaction cost is allowed, then the Cobb–Douglas utility function is not allowed for the existence theorem. If both fixed transaction cost and the Cobb–Douglas utility function are allowed, then we must assume that each individual can produce all goods in autarky in order to secure a boundary condition that is essential for establishing the existence theorem of equilibrium.

2 The Borel algebra of a topological space is the smallest $\sigma$-algebra generated by its open sets.

3 Of course, the relevant mappings are generally multivalued.

4 In case $k_1 \geq k_2$, she should consider the option of selling good 1 only.

5 It can be shown that there are multiple equilibria in some razor edge cases. For instance, if $2^{b-1} > a$, $0 < k_1 < 4\alpha$, $k_1 < a\alpha 2^{2+b-c}$, $k_2 = 4\gamma$, multiple equilibria occur.

# part VI

# Urbanization, Population, and the Trade-off between Working and Leisure

# chapter 14

# URBANIZATION, THE DUAL STRUCTURE BETWEEN URBAN AND RURAL AREAS, AND THE DIVISION OF LABOR

## ♦ 14.1 Why and How Cities Emerge from the Division of Labor

Xenopnon (see Gordon, 1975, p. 41) and William Petty (1683, p. 947) recognized the intrinsic connection between division of labor and the emergence of cities. Yang (1991; see ch. 7) uses a general equilibrium model to investigate the relationship between urbanization and evolution in division of labor. That model predicts that if all individuals reside together within a small area to form a city, then trading efficiency can be improved by reducing the distance between each pair of trade partners, so that the level of division of labor and productivity can be raised. But since the logic of that model suggests that all individuals should reside together, it cannot predict the emergence of a dichotomy between rural and urban areas. Yang and Rice (1994) have developed the first new classical general equilibrium model that can predict the emergence of cities, and the dichotomy between urban and rural areas, as consequences of the evolution of division of labor.

The story behind the model may be outlined as follows. Suppose the production of food is land intensive. The production of many manufactured goods is not land intensive. There are economies of specialization in producing each good, and trade generates transaction costs. Hence, there is a trade-off between economies of specialization and transaction costs. If trading efficiency is low, individuals will choose autarky where no market and city exist. As trading efficiency is slightly improved, the division of labor between partially specialized farmers and partially specialized cloth-makers emerges as a consequence of the efficient trade-off between economies of specialization and transaction costs. Since farming is land intensive and cloth-making is not, farmers will have dispersed residences while each cloth-maker will reside near a farm to reduce the transaction costs caused by the division of labor. Hence, the low level of division of labor between farming and cloth-making does not generate cities. As trading efficiency is further improved, the division of labor between cloth-makers, house-builders, and furniture-makers emerges in addition to the division of labor between farmers and manufacturers. The manufacturers can have dispersed residences or reside together in a city since their production is not land intensive. In order to save on the transaction costs caused by the division of labor and related transactions among manufacturers, they will reside in a city. Hence, a city and a dichotomy between urban and rural sectors emerge from a high level of division of labor between specialist manufacturers and between professional manufacturers and farmers. Here, the benefits of the concentrated residences of urban residents are referred to as *Type I economies of agglomeration*.

In this story, if different specialist manufactures reside in the city, the transaction cost coefficient for trade between manufacturers (urban residents) is much smaller than that for trade between farmers (rural residents) and urban residents. This trading efficiency differential, due to the different degrees of land intensity, is a driving force behind the emergence of the city from the division of labor.

In the development of urbanization and division of labor, urban residents' levels of specialization and productivity increase more quickly than rural residents', since the short distance between each pair of urban residents ensures higher trading efficiency in the urban area than in the rural area. The dual structure, in terms of differences in productivity and in commercialized income between the urban and rural areas, emerges in the transitional phase as the economy moves from a low to a high level of division of labor. However, free migration between areas, and between occupations, will equalize the per capita real incomes of urban and rural residents, despite the inequality of their per capita commercialized incomes. As trading efficiency is continuously improved, the economy will evolve to a state of complete division of labor. Then the dual structure will disappear and productivity, the degree of commercialization, and commercialized incomes will be equalized between the two areas. Section 14.2 uses a simplified version of the Yang–Rice model (1994) to formalize the story.

There is another way to explain the relationship between urbanization and evolution of division of labor in the absence of a differential of trading efficiency between agricultural and industrial goods. This explains urbanization by exploring the general equilibrium implications of interactions between the positive network effects of the division of labor and the geographical concentration of transactions that are required by a large network of division of labor. Because of the positive network effect of the division of labor, the geographical concentration of transactions required by a large network of division of labor can save on transaction costs by reducing total traveling distance for each individual. Hence, urbanization can promote division of labor by concentrating a large network of transactions in a city to reduce transaction costs, even if many individuals do not reside in cities. This effect of urbanization on the level of division of labor is referred to as *Type II economies of agglomeration*. It is interesting to note the interdependence among equilibrium trading efficiency, the equilibrium level of division of labor, and the equilibrium geographical pattern of transactions in this story. The concept of general equilibrium is a powerful vehicle to formalize the simultaneous determination of the interdependent variables. Section 14.3 will formalize the story of general equilibrium.

In section 14.4, we extend this story to simultaneously endogenize the land price differential between the rural and urban areas, the level of division of labor, and the population density in the urban area. This is done by introducing the consumption level of land into the utility function. In addition to the trade-off between economies of division of labor and transaction costs, there is a trade-off between high trading efficiency for urban residents and congestion in the city. Equilibrium is associated with the efficient trade-off that generates the following phenomenon. As trading efficiency is improved, division of labor evolves. This generates increasingly significant economies of agglomeration (trading efficiency increasing with the degree of geographical concentration of transactions), so that more individuals are willing to reside in the city. This drives up the land price in the urban area, resulting in a fall in the per capita consumption of land by urban residents, compared to rural residents. The potential for the rise of land prices in the urban area is determined by the potential for evolution of division of labor.

In section 14.5, we use a simplified version of the Fujita–Krugman model (1995) to illustrate the differences between the neoclassical equilibrium model of urbanization based on economies of scale and the new classical equilibrium model of urbanization based on economies of division of labor.

---

## Questions to Ask Yourself when Reading this Chapter

◆ What is the relationship between the emergence and development of cities, the level of division of labor, and trading efficiency?

◆ Why do the different land requirements of agricultural and industrial production generate a dual structure between urban areas with a high population density and rural areas with a low population density?

◆ What are the effects of free migration and the absence of free migration on urbanization and evolution in division of labor?

◆ Why are trading efficiency, the geographical pattern of transactions, and the level of division of labor interdependent? How are they simultaneously determined in the marketplace?

◆ Why is the price of land in the urban area higher than in the rural area? What are the main economic determinants of the potential for the increase in urban land prices in the development process?

---

## ◆ 14.2 The Emergence of Cities and of the Dual Structure between Urban and Rural Areas

### Example 14.1: a simplified version of the Yang–Rice model

We consider a simplified version of the Yang–Rice model (1994) that has been solved by Monchi Lio. The model is similar to those in chapter 11. There are three goods: cloth (good 1), furniture (good 2), and food (good 3). Goods 1 and 2 are industrial goods requiring little land for production. Hence, the residences of producers of these two goods can either be dispersed over a large area or be concentrated in a small area. Good 3, food, is land intensive. The residences of the farmers must be dispersed over a large area. Though all $M$ consumer-producers are *ex ante* identical, they can choose to specialize in producing different goods and thus choose their residence location pattern (far away from or close to neighbors). We call those individuals who choose to produce only industrial goods C-type persons and those who choose to produce agricultural goods R-type persons. The transaction cost coefficient for a unit of goods purchased is $1-K$, or the trading efficiency coefficient is $K$. But $K$ differs between different types of persons and is dependent on individuals' decisions concerning the geographic pattern of their residence. If C-type persons reside together within a small area, the trading efficiency coefficient $K = k$ between a pair of C-type persons. The trading efficiency coefficient $K = r$ between a pair of R-type persons and $K = s$ between a C-type person and an R-type person. We assume that $k > s > r$. The first inequality is easy to understand since the average distance between a pair of C-type persons who reside together is shorter than the average distance between an R-type person who must occupy a quite large area of land, and a C-type person. Suppose that an R-type person resides at the center of her farm, which has the shape of a circle with radius 1. Since a C-type person can minimize transaction costs by residing on the boundary of the farm if she trades with the farmer, the minimum distance between the R-type and C-type persons is 1. But the distance between two R-type persons who reside at the respective centers of their farms with radius 1 is 2. This is why trading efficiency is higher between an R-type person and a C-type person than between a pair of R-type persons, or why $s > r$.

As in the previous chapters, each consumer-producer's utility function is

$$u = \sum_{i=1}^{3} (x_i + Kx_i^d). \tag{14.1}$$

Each consumer-producer has the following production functions and endowment constraint for working time.

$$x_i + x_i^s = \text{Max}\{l_i - \alpha, 0\}, \; l_1 + l_2 + l_3 = 1, \; \alpha \in (0,1), \; l_i \in [0,1], \; i = 1, 2, 3. \tag{14.2}$$

$\alpha$ is a fixed learning or training cost in producing a good, $l_i$ is an individual's level of specialization in producing good i, subscript $i$ stands for good $i$, superscript $s$ stands for the quantity sold (supplied), and superscript $d$ stands for the quantity purchased (demanded).

According to the Wen theorem, there are three types of configurations: Autarky (denoted A), as shown in figure 14.1(a), selling good i and buying good j, denoted (i/j), and selling good i and buying goods j and t, denoted (i/jt), There are six of the second type of configuration: (1/2), (2/1), (1/3), (3/1), (2/3), and (3/1), as shown in figure 14.1(b). There are three of the third type of configuration: (1/23), (2/13), and (3/12), as shown in figure 14.1(c).

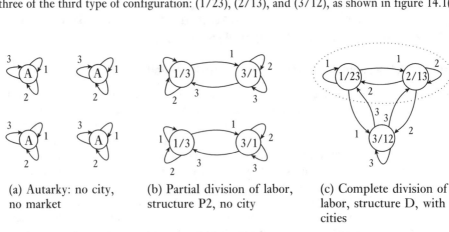

(a) Autarky: no city, no market

(b) Partial division of labor, structure P2, no city

(c) Complete division of labor, structure D, with cities

♦ **Figure 14.1:** The emergence of cities from the evolution of division of labor

**Table 14.1:** Eight corner solutions

| Configuration | Self-provided quantity | Level of specialization | Supply | Demand | Indirect utility function |
|---|---|---|---|---|---|
| A | $x_i = (1-3\alpha)/3$ | $l_i = 1/3$ | | | $[(1-3\alpha)/3]^3$ |
| (1/2) | $x_1 = x_3 =$ $(1-2\alpha)/3$ | $l_1 = (2-\alpha)/3$ | $x_1^s = (1-2\alpha)/3$ | $x_2^d = p_1 x_1^s/p_2$ | $[(1-2\alpha)/3]^3 r p_1/p_2$ |
| (2/1) | $x_2 = x_3 =$ $(1-2\alpha)/3$ | $l_2 = (2-\alpha)/3$ | $x_2^s = (1-2\alpha)/3$ | $x_1^d = p_2 x_2^s/p_1$ | $[(1-2\alpha)/3]^3 r p_2/p_1$ |
| (1/3) | $x_1 = x_2 =$ $(1-2\alpha)/3$ | $l_1 = (2-\alpha)/3$ | $x_1^s = (1-2\alpha)/3$ | $x_3^d = p_1 x_1^s/p_3$ | $[(1-2\alpha)/3]^3 s p_1/p_3$ |
| (3/1) | $x_3 = x_2 =$ $(1-2\alpha)/3$ | $l_3 = (2-\alpha)/3$ | $x_3^s = (1-2\alpha)/3$ | $x_1^d = p_3 x_3^s/p_1$ | $[(1-2\alpha)/3]^3 s p_3/p_1$ |
| (1/23) | $x_1 =$ $(1-\alpha)/3$ | $l_1 = 1$ | $x_1^s = 2(1-\alpha)/3$ | $x_i^d =$ $p_1(1-\alpha)/3p_i$ | $[(1-\alpha)/3]^3 k s p_1^2/p_2 p_3$ |
| (2/13) | $x_2 =$ $(1-\alpha)/3$ | $l_2 = 1$ | $x_2^s = 2(1-\alpha)/3$ | $x_i^d =$ $p_2(1-\alpha)/3p_i$ | $[(1-\alpha)/3]^3 k s p_2^2/p_1 p_3$ |
| (3/12) | $x_3 =$ $(1-\alpha)/3$ | $l_3 = 1$ | $x_3^s = 2(1-\alpha)/3$ | $x_i^d =$ $p_3(1-\alpha)/3p_i$ | $[(1-\alpha)/3]^3 s^2 p_3^2/p_2 p_1$ |

Combinations of these configurations yield four structures. $M$ individuals choosing configuration A constitute an autarky structure. A division of $M$ individuals between configurations (1/2) and (2/1) constitutes a partial division of labor structure P1. A division of the population between configurations (1/3) and (3/1) constitutes structure P2, as shown in figure 14.1b. Since a structure based on configurations (2/3) and (3/2) is symmetric to structure P2, and yields the same per capita real income as P2, we omit it. A division of individuals between the other configurations (1/23), (2/13), (3/12) constitutes the complete division of labor structure D, as shown in figure 14.1c.

Following the inframarginal analysis developed in the previous chapters, we can solve for the corner solutions in the eight configurations, as shown in table 14.1. From the utility equalization and market clearing conditions, we can solve for the corner equilibria in the four structures, as shown in table 14.2.

Comparisons of per capita real incomes in the four corner equilibria, together with the Yao theorem, yield the results shown in table 14.3, about the general equilibrium and its inframarginal comparative statics.

A comparison between structures P1 and P2 indicates that structure P2 always yields greater per capita real income than does P1. That is, under partial division of labor, it is impossible that two types of individuals exchange industrial goods and self-provide agricultural goods, since in this pattern of partial division of labor all individuals are of R-type (producing food), and have a larger transaction cost coefficient than that between R-type persons and C-type persons in structure P2. But structures P1 and P2 can exploit the same economies of division of labor (due to the symmetry of the model). Note that trading efficiency between two R-type persons, $r$, is lower than that between a C-type person and

**Table 14.2:** Corner equilibria in four structures

| Structure | Relative price | Number of individuals selling different goods | Per capita real income |
|---|---|---|---|
| A | | | $[(1 - 3\alpha)/3]^3$ |
| P1 | $p_1 p_2 = 1$ | $M_1 = M_2 = M/2$ | $[(1 - 2\alpha)/3]^3 r$ |
| P2 | $p_1 p_3 = 1$ | $M_1 = M_3 = M/2$ | $[(1 - 2\alpha)/3]^3 s$ |
| D | $p_2/p_1 = 1,$ | $M_1 = M_2 = M/[2 + (s/k)^{1/3}]$ | $[(1 - \alpha)/3]^3 (s^4/k^2)^{1/3}$ |
| | $p_3/p_1 = (k/s)^{1/3}$ | $M_3 = (s/k)^{1/3} M/[2 + (s/k)^{1/3}]$ | |

**Table 14.3:** General equilibrium and its inframarginal comparative statics

| $k < k_0$ | | $s < s_0$ | $s \in (s_0, s_1)$ | $s > s_1$ | $k > k_0$ | $s < s_2$ | $s > s_2$ |
|---|---|---|---|---|---|---|---|
| Equilibrium structure | | A | P2 | D | | A | D |

*where* $s_0 \equiv [(1 - 3\alpha)/(1 - 2\alpha)]^3 < s_1 \equiv [(1 - 2\alpha)/(1 - \alpha)]^9/k^2$ *iff* $k < k_0$.
$s_2 \equiv [(1 - 3\alpha)/(1 - \alpha)]^{9/4}/k^{0.5}$.

an R-type person by assumption. Hence, the set of candidates for the equilibrium structure consists of A, P2, and D.

Comparisons of per capita real incomes across structures A, P2, and D indicate that P2 is better than A iff $s > s_0$, D is better than P2 iff $s > s_1$. A comparison between $s_1$ and $s_0$ indicates that $s_1 > s_0$ iff $k < k_0 \equiv [(1 - 2\alpha)^4/(1 - \alpha)^3(1 - 3\alpha)]^{1.5}$. This implies that the general equilibrium structure is A if $s < s_0$, is P2 if $s$ is between $s_0$ and $s_1$, and is D if $s > s_1$. For $k > k_0$, $p_2$ is inferior to either A or D. Hence, A is equilibrium if $s > s_2$ and D is equilibrium if $s > s_2 \equiv [(1 - 3\alpha)/(1 - \alpha)]^{9/4}/k^{0.5}$, which is given by $u(A) = u(D)$.

Note that in structure P2, no individual selling an industrial good produces the agricultural good, so that she can either reside far away from her trade partner-farmer or reside on the boundary of the farmer. She will choose the latter geographical pattern of residence to save on transaction costs. This implies that for $k < k_0$ each partially specialized seller of an industrial good will reside next to a partially specialized farmer. Therefore, there is no city in structure P2, despite the division of labor between farmers and manufacturers of industrial goods. This establishes the statement that the division of labor is necessary, but not sufficient for the emergence of cities. For structure D, the division of labor between completely specialized manufacturers of industrial goods 1 and 2 can be organized in such a way as to save on transaction costs by all specialist manufacturers residing in cities. If two manufacturers reside in a city, trading efficiency is $k$ between them. If they have dispersed residences, trading efficiency is $s$, which is smaller than $k$.

As trading efficiency increases from a low to a high level, the general equilibrium evolves from autarky (A) to the partial division of labor between farmers and manufacturers of industrial goods (P2) where no cities exist, followed by the complete division of labor between specialist manufacturers of industrial goods and between professional farmers and the manufacturers (D). Cities emerge from this high level of division of labor between manufacturers of industrial goods and between farmers and the manufacturers. Hence, a sufficient condition for the emergence of cities from the division of labor is a sufficiently high level of division of labor in producing industrial goods which are not land intensive.

Figure 14.1 gives an intuitive illustration of the story based on the formal model. Panel (a) is autarky where there are no transactions nor cities, panel (b) is the partial division of labor without cities (P2), and panel (c) is the complete division of labor with cities, where two specialist manufacturers reside in a city denoted by the dashed circle. The geographical distance between the residences of the two manufacturers is much shorter than that between a manufacturer and a farmer. In panel (c) only a local community is used to illustrate structure D. In structure D, there are $M/[2 + (s/k)^{1/3}]$ such local communities and $M_1 + M_2$ urban residents who are specialist manufacturers and $M_3$ professional farmers, where the equilibrium values of $M_i$ are given in table 14.2. In each of the local communities 2 manufacturers reside in a city and $(s/k)^{1/3}$ farmers reside in countryside. In order to save on transaction costs, individuals will trade with those closest. Hence, there is no trade between different local communities. In structure D there are $M/[2 + (s/k)^{1/3}]$ cities.

If we introduce many goods into the model, it is not difficult to show that the number of local communities and the number of cities decreases and the size of each city increases as continuous improvement in trading efficiency raises the equilibrium level of division of labor. Yang and Rice (1994) extend the simple model in this section to the case with 4 goods and nonlinear production functions. They draw the distinction between a dual structure between the urban and rural areas in terms of the differential of population density, and a dual structure between the urban and rural sectors in terms of the differential of level of specialization and productivity between the two sectors. They show that as trading efficiency is improved there will be a transitional stage of unbalanced division of labor as the economy evolves from a low level of balanced division of labor to a high level of balanced division of labor. During that stage urban residents will have higher levels of specialization and productivity, and higher levels of per capita commercialized income and commercialization. This is because in the transitional stage, the levels of specialization cannot be the same between rural and urban residents, while a higher level of specialization for urban residents is better than a higher level of specialization for rural residents because of the higher trading efficiency for urban residents. However, free migration will ensure that per capita real incomes become the same between urban and rural residents despite their unequal commercialized incomes. As trading efficiency is further improved, such a dual structure in terms of a differential in productivity and level of specialization will disappear as it is replaced by complete and balanced division of labor, where levels of specialization and productivity in the two sectors converge.

## ♦ 14.3 Why Geographical Concentration of Transactions Can Improve Trading Efficiency

The method to explain the emergence of cities from evolution of division of labor in the preceding section relates to *Type I economies of agglomeration*, which occur as manufacturers' residences are concentrated giving dispersed farmers' residences. The other way to explain the emergence of cities from evolution in division of labor relates to *Type II economies of agglomeration* that are associated with the network effects of division of labor and concentrated location pattern of transactions. If the geographical pattern of individuals' residences is fixed and each pair of trade partners trade in the geographical midpoint of their residences, total travel distance and related cost will increase more than proportionally as the network of transactions required by a particular level of division of labor is enlarged. If all individuals conduct their transactions at a central place, the large network of transactions can be geographically shrunk and be concentrated in that central place to significantly reduce the total travel distance of all individuals. The economies of agglomeration differ from economies of scale. Some economists call them positive externalities of cities. Indeed, they are generated by interactions between the positive network effects of division of labor and the effects of the geographical concentration of transactions. In other words, not only do the equilibrium topological properties of economic organisms depend on the pattern of resource allocation (quantities of flows of goods and factors or nontopological properties of economic organisms), but also they depend on the geographical properties of economic organisms (which are also nontopological properties of those organisms).

One of the implications of the interplay between topological and nontopological properties of economic organisms relates to the potential for a rise of land price in the urban area. If we do not understand this implication, we will not be able to explain why the price of land of Hong Kong, Tokyo, and Taipei has increased by more than 40 times since the Second World War. The most important determinant of the land price of a city is the size of the network of division of labor that is associated with the city as its center of transactions. While that size is determined by trading efficiency, this itself depends on the geographical pattern of transactions. The effect of the geographical pattern is in turn determined by the level of division of labor. Hence, trading efficiency, geographical pattern of transactions, and level of division of labor are interdependent and should be simultaneously determined in general equilibrium. The notion of general equilibrium is a powerful vehicle to explore a mechanism that simultaneously determines all of the variables. We first use a simple example to illustrate why geographical concentration of transactions can improve trading efficiency through network effects of division of labor.

### Example 14.2: a general equilibrium model endogenizing the geographical pattern of transactions, trading efficiency, and network size of division of labor

Let us look at the case with $n = 7$ in figure 14.2. Panels (a) and (b) represent a local community with 7 traded goods in a symmetric model as in chapter 11. Seven *ex ante* identical consumer-producers reside at 7 vertices of a grid of triangles with equal sides, which are represented by 7 points. The distance between each pair of neighbors is assumed to be 1. Due to symmetry, each individual sells a good to and buys a good from each of other six individuals in equilibrium. In panel (a), each pair of individuals trades at the geographical middle point of their residences, which is represented by a small circle. In panel (b), all individuals go to the center of the local community, represented by the small circle, which is the residence of an individual, to trade with each other. Suppose that exogenous transaction costs are proportional to the travel distance of individuals in conducting the transactions required by the division of labor. This assumption implies that there are increasing returns in transactions. Transaction costs are independent of the quantity of goods traded. You may imagine that within a certain quantity range of goods that you purchase, transportation cost is proportional to the quantity of gas that you use for your car, which is proportional to the driving distance but independent of the quantity that you buy. That is, your car is large enough to generate increasing returns in transportation. In the next section this assumption is relaxed and variable transaction costs are specified as an increasing function of the quantity of goods traded. The relaxation will not change the essence of our result as long as increasing returns in transactions are sufficiently significant. Moreover, we assume that one unit of travel distance costs $1.

Let us now calculate total transaction costs for the two geographical patterns of transactions. In panel (a), each of the six individuals residing at the periphery of the community has a farthest trade partner. She travels to the center, which is the middle point between her and the partner, to trade with the partner. She can trade with the person at the center by way of the trip. The travel distance for the return trip cost $2. She has two other neighboring trade partners; it costs her $1 to trade with each of them. The distance between her and each of the other two trade partners is $\sqrt{3}$. A return trip to the middle point between her and each of them is thus $\sqrt{3}$. Hence, it cost her $2\sqrt{3}$ to trade with the two trade partners. Her transaction costs with six trade partners then total $(2 + 2 + 2\sqrt{3})$ = $7.46. For the person at the center, transaction costs are zero, since all other individuals will trade with her at the center as they stop by there to trade with their farthest partners.

In the geographical pattern of panel (b), all individuals not residing at the center bring their goods there to trade. Total transaction cost for each of them is $2. A comparison of transaction costs between panels (a) and (b) indicates that geographical concentration of transactions can save on transaction costs if the size of the network of division of labor is sufficiently large. Williamson refers to the pattern of transactions in panel (b) as the pattern of the wheel, and that in panel (a) as the pattern of all channels. If the purpose of traveling is to obtain information about products, prices, and partners, then increasing returns to the geographical concentration of transactions will be more significant. However, if geographical concentration of transactions (or exchanges) generates congestion problems for vehicles, and if new computer technology can significantly improve the transmission cost of information, then economies may generate geographical concentration of information exchange, as occurs in the information superhighway, rather than geographical concentration of the physical appearance of individuals and vehicles associated with the relevant exchanges.[1] If the fixed construction cost of highways is considered, the increasing returns in transactions will be more plausible.

We may define a *central marketplace* as a geographical location where many trade partners conduct transactions. This definition implies a corresponding geographical concentration of transactions. Geographically dispersed bilateral transactions are not associated with the market according to this definition. It can be shown that the market is not needed if the level of division of labor is low. Consider, for instance, a symmetric model in which there are two traded goods and a community of seven individuals. It can be shown that if the geographical pattern of transactions is such that each pair of trade partners trades at the midpoint between their residences, as shown in the case with $n = 2$ in figure 14.2, the transaction cost to each of them is only $1. But if all individuals go to the central marketplace to trade, as shown in figure 14.2, panel (b), for the case with $n = 7$, then each individual's transaction cost is $2. This illustrates that for a low level of division of labor, geographically concentrated transactions will generate unnecessary transaction costs.

Thus, the capacity of a geographically concentrated pattern of transactions to save on transaction costs depends on the level of division of labor. In other words, trading efficiency is dependent not only on the geographical pattern of transactions, but also on the level of division of labor. But, as shown in the previous chapters, the level of division of labor is itself determined by trading efficiency. This interdependence among the level of division of labor, the geographical pattern of transactions, and trading efficiency implies that the three variables are simultaneously determined in a general equilibrium environment. It is analogous to the interdependence between the prices and quantities of goods that are consumed and produced in the neoclassical general equilibrium model, where the optimum quantities of goods consumed and produced are dependent on prices, while the

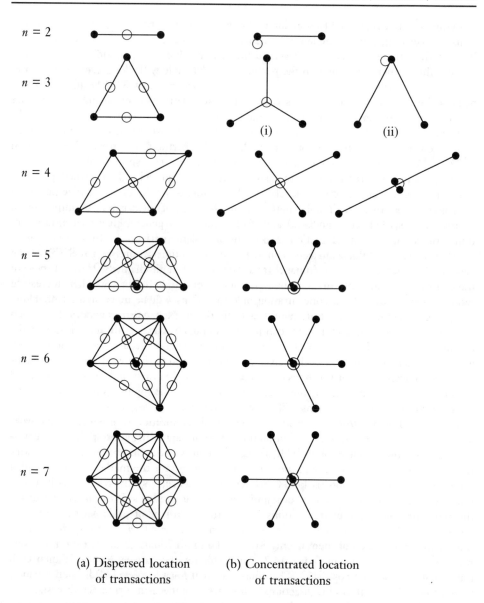

(a) Dispersed location          (b) Concentrated location
   of transactions                of transactions

◆ **Figure 14.2:** Dispersed vs. concentrated location patterns of transactions

equilibrium prices are themselves determined by individual agents' decisions on the optimum quantities.

Now we introduce the geographical pattern of transactions into the new classical model in section 11.2 of chapter 11 to illustrate how the level of division of labor, trading efficiency, and geographical pattern of transactions are simultaneously determined in general equilibrium. From (11.14) in chapter 11, we can see that the level of division of labor, $n$, is a function of trading efficiency $k$, that is

$$n = m + 1 - (1/A) - (m/\ln k) \tag{14.3}$$

where $m$ is the number of all consumer goods and $A$ is the fixed learning cost in each production activity. Assume now that

$$k = \beta/d \tag{14.4}$$

where $\beta$ is a parameter that reflects transportation conditions and $d$ is the average traveling distance for each individual to trade with her trade partners, which obviously is related to the geographical pattern of transactions. For simplicity, we consider only the cases with $n = 1, 2, 3, 4, 5, 6, 7$. We first assume a given value of $n$, then for the given $n$, compare values of $d$ for different geographical patterns of transactions as shown in figure 14.2. According the Yao theorem, it can be shown that in equilibrium individuals will choose a geographical pattern of transactions that has the lowest value of $d$ in order to minimize transaction costs for any given $n$. Thus we can use (14.3) and (14.4) to calculate the critical value of $\beta$ that ensures that values of the level of division of labor, $n$, trading efficiency, $k$, and geographical pattern of transactions, reflected by $d$, are consistent with each other in equilibrium. Let us start with $n = 2$ to use the iterative approach to solving for general equilibrium.

As discussed previously, and indicated in figure 14.2, where $n = 2$ each individual's traveling distance $d$ is 1 and transactions are dispersed at the midpoints between each pair of trade partners. Other geographical patterns generate longer traveling distances and higher transaction costs for this level of division of labor. For society as a whole with this level of division of labor, there are $M/2$ local business communities. If we define an *urban area* as a place where many transactions take place among many individuals at the residences of some of them, then there is no city associated with this pattern of transactions since all transactions are dispersed at many middle points of many pairs of trade partners. Here, the definition of an urban area overlaps with the definition of a central marketplace, but the distinction between them is that an urban area relates to the residences of some of the trade partners, while the definition of market is independent of individuals' residences.

Inserting $d = 1$ into (14.4), then inserting (14.4) into (14.3), we can solve for the critical value of $\beta$ for $n = 2$, which is $\beta_2 = e^{-mA/[1-(m-1)A]}$, where $A$ is the fixed learning cost in each production activity, $m$ is the number of all consumption goods, and $e \cong 2.718$ is the base of natural logarithm. The level of division of labor $n$ is at least 2 if $\beta \geq \beta_2$. In order to solve for the critical values of other levels of division of labor, let us look at figure 14.2. The graphs in the left column represent those geographical patterns of transactions which take place at the middle points of each pair of trade partners, whereas the graphs in the right column represent those geographical patterns of transactions which take place at the center of all trade partners. The solid dots denote consumer-producers and the circles denote the locations where transactions take place. Here, we follow that assumptions that all individuals reside at the vertices of a grid of triangles with equal sides, and that the distance between each pair of neighbors is 1. Hence, the values of $d$ for the different patterns of transactions that correspond to various levels of division of labor can be calculated from figure 14.2. All of the values of $d$, which are of course dependent on

**Table 14.4**: Interactions between geographical patterns of transactions, trading efficiency, and level of division of labor

| Level of division of labour | d for dispersed transactions | d for concentrated transactions | Trading efficiency k | Critical value of $\beta_n$ for a given n |
|---|---|---|---|---|
| $n = 2$ | 1 | 1 | $\beta$ | $e^{mA/[(m-1)A-1]}$ |
| $n = 3$ | $2/(n-1)$ | $(2\sqrt{3}) \div 2(n-1)$ | $2\beta/\sqrt{3}$ | $(\sqrt{3}/2)e^{mA/[(m-2)A-1]}$ |
| $n = 4$ | $(5+\sqrt{3}) \div 2(n-1)$ | $(1+\sqrt{3}) \div 2(n-1)$ | $6\beta \div (1+\sqrt{3})$ | $(1+\sqrt{3})e^{mA/[(m-3)A-1]}/6$ |
| $n = 5$ | $> 2$ | $2 \div (n-1)$ | $2\beta$ | $(1/2)e^{mA/[(m-4)A-1]}$ |
| $n = 6$ | $> 2$ | 2 | $5\beta/2$ | $(2/5)e^{mA/[(m-5)A-1]}$ |
| $n = 7$ | $> 2$ | 2 | $\beta/3$ | $(1/3)e^{mA/[(m-6)A-1]}$ |

geographical pattern of transactions as well as on the level of division of labor, are listed in table 14.4.

From figure 14.2, it can be seen that the best geographical pattern of transactions for $n$ = 2 is at the midpoints between each pair of trade partners, so that $d = 1$ for $n = 2$. For $n = 3$, there are two geographical patterns of transactions to choose. In one of them, each pair of partners trades at the geographical midpoint of their residences, so that all transactions in the economy take place at $M$ places. In the other, all partners in a local community where each person trades with each of the other two go to the geographical center of their residences to conduct all transactions between them, so that all transactions in the economy are implemented at $M/3$ places. For the latter pattern, it is not difficult to use basic geometry to show that $d = 0.5\sqrt{3} < 1$, whereas for the former $d = 2$. For the different geographical patterns of transactions that are associated with different values of $d$ but with the same value of $n$, there are several corresponding corner equilibria. According to the Yao theorem, individuals will choose the corner equilibrium with the greatest per capita real income that is associated with the smallest value of $d$ for a given $n$. Hence, the concentrated pattern of transactions with $d = 0.5\sqrt{3}$ will be chosen if the equilibrium value of $n$ is 3. There is no city despite the existence of a marketplace in this structure. Following the same procedure, it can be shown that those concentrated patterns of transactions in the right column of figure 14.2 yield the smallest value of $d$ for a given $n > 2$, and that the minimum value of $d$ for any given $n > 4$ is 2.

Inserting the minimum value of $d$ for a given $n$ back into (14.4) yields the values of trading efficiency $k$ for a given $n$, which are listed in column 4 of table 14.4. Plugging these values of $k$ back into (14.3), we can work out the critical values of $\beta_n$ for $n = 2, 3, 4, 5, 6, 7$, which are listed in column 5 of table 14.4. In fact, table 14.4 has already given

**Table 14.5**: General equilibrium and its inframarginal comparative statics

| Transaction condition $\beta$ | $< \beta_2$ | $\in (\beta_2, \beta_3)$ | $\in (\beta_3, \beta_4)$ | $\in (\beta_4, \beta_5)$ | $\in (\beta_5, \beta_6)$ | $\in (\beta_6, \beta_7)$ | $\beta > \beta_7$ |
|---|---|---|---|---|---|---|---|
| Equilibrium structure $n$ | 1 | 2 | 3 | 4 | 5 | 6 | 7 |

the general equilibrium and its inframarginal comparative statics, as summarized in table 14.5.

The table shows that the general equilibrium is autarky if $\beta < \beta_2$. If $\beta \in (\beta_2, \beta_3)$ the general equilibrium is partial division of labor with $n = 2$, with the geographical pattern as shown in the left column of figure 14.2, and with the trading efficiency $k$ as shown by the entry of row $n = 2$ and column 4 in table 14.4. If $\beta \in (\beta_3, \beta_4)$ the equilibrium is the division of labor with $n = 3$, with the geographic pattern as shown in the right column of figure 14.2, and with the trading efficiency $k$ as shown in the entry of row $n = 3$ and column 4 in table 14.4. If $\beta \in (\beta_4, \beta_5)$, general equilibrium is the division of labor with $n = 4$, with the geographic pattern as shown in the right column of figure 14.2, and with the trading efficiency $k$ as shown in the entry of row $n = 4$ and column 4 in table 14.4. If $\beta \in (\beta_5, \beta_6)$, the general equilibrium is the division of labor with $n = 5$, with the geographic pattern as shown in the right column of figure 14.2 for $n = 5$, and with the trading efficiency $k$ as shown in the entry of row $n = 5$ and column 4 in table 14.4. If $\beta \in (\beta_6, \beta_7)$, the equilibrium is the division of labor with $n = 6$, with the geographic pattern as shown in the right column of figure 14.2 for $n = 6$, and with the trading efficiency $k$ as shown in the entry of row $n = 6$ and column 4 in table 14.4. If $\beta > \beta_7$, the equilibrium is the division of labor with $n = 7$, with the geographic pattern as shown in the right column of figure 14.2 for $n = 7$, and with the trading efficiency $k$ as shown in the entry of row $n = 7$ and column 4 in table 14.4. Here, cities emerge from the division of labor with $n = 5, 6, 7$ and the number of cities is $M/n$. Marketplaces coincide with locations of the cities, and the number of marketplaces is the same as that of cities. There are no markets or cities in autarky. For $n = 2$, there are $M/n = M/2$ marketplaces with two trade partners for each, and no cities. For $n = 3, 4$, there are $M/n$ marketplaces with $n$ trade partners for each, and no cities exist.

The inframarginal comparative statics of general equilibrium indicate again that the division of labor is a necessary but not sufficient condition for the emergence of cities. For $n = 2, 3, 4$, there is division of labor and related marketplaces, but no cities. It is easy to see that the volume of trade that is executed in a marketplace or in a city increases with the equilibrium level of division of labor, which is determined by the transaction condition parameter $\beta$.

## ◆ 14.4 Simultaneous Endogenization of Level of Division of Labor, Location Pattern of Residences, Geographical Pattern of Transactions, and Land Prices

Although the equilibrium model in the previous section simultaneously endogenizes the level of division of labor, trading efficiency, and the geographical pattern of transactions, it has not endogenized the location pattern of individuals' residences and the differential of land price between the urban and rural areas, since we implicitly assume that $d$ is the same for urban and rural residents. But the average traveling distance for necessary transactions $d$ is much shorter for an urban resident than for a rural resident, since an urban resident can get all transactions done in the city where she resides without traveling around when all necessary transactions are concentrated in the city. In this section, we take into account the difference between traveling distances of urban and rural residents to develop a general equilibrium model with an endogenous geographical pattern of all individuals' residences and land price differential between the urban and rural areas.

### Example 14.3 (Sun and Yang, 1998): a new classical equilibrium model with endogenous residences of individuals and endogenous land prices

Consider a new classical model similar to that in example 11.1 of chapter 11. We assume that production, consumption, and transaction conditions are the same as in that example, except for the following two new features. Each consumer-producer's utility is a function of the amount of land consumed by her and of whether the city is a center of transactions because of the division of labor.

When a dual urban–rural structure occurs in equilibrium, the trading efficiency coefficient is $k_A$ for those who reside in the city and $k$ for those who reside in the rural area. The emergence of cities from a sufficiently high level of division of labor generates a transaction cost advantage for urban residents whose transaction cost coefficient is much smaller than that for rural residents. For simplicity, we assume that the relative trading efficiency coefficient of urban and rural residents is a constant greater than one,

$$k_A/k = \lambda > 1. \tag{14.5}$$

If free migration between the urban and rural areas is assumed, then the residential pattern must be endogenously determined rather than exogenously given. Free migration, together with the transaction cost advantage for urban residents and the positive contribution of land consumption to utility, generates a trade-off between Type II economies of agglomeration and per capita consumption of land in the urban area that will be reduced by competitive bidding up of urban land prices. The balance of this trade-off in the market will generate equilibrium location patterns of individuals' residences and of transactions, while the efficient trade-off between economies of specialization and transaction costs will determine the equilibrium network size of division of labor. Here, the location pattern of residences, the location pattern of transactions, the consumption pattern of land, the relative urban and rural land price, and the network size of division of labor are interdependent. Therefore, the concept of general equilibrium is a powerful vehicle for figuring out a mechanism that simultaneously determines all of the interdependent variables. For simiplicity, we assume that total land area for cities is a constant $A$ and that for rural areas is $B$.

It will be shown later that for $n \le 2$ the equilibrium location patterns of residences and transactions is trivial, that is, all individuals reside at vertices of the grid of triangles with equal sides, transactions take place at the midpoints between the residences of each pair of trade partners, and no cities exist. Hence, we first focus on the case with $n > 2$ where cities emerge from the division of labor. Later it will be shown that the equilibrium value of $n$ is greater than 2 if and only if trading efficiency $k$ is sufficiently large.

Denote the traded goods produced in the urban (or rural) area A-type goods (or B-type goods). Producers of A-type goods (B-type goods) have an incentive to reside in the urban (rural) area to save on commuting costs between their residences and their working places. Therefore, for each consumer-producer, the decision on residence location and occupation choice become independent: they choose to reside in the urban (rural) area if and only if they choose to produce A-type (B-type) goods. Thus, we can use symmetry to simplify the algebra significantly. We denote the number of goods produced in the urban (or rural) areas $n_A$ (or $n_B$), where $n_A + n_B = n$.

Since all individuals' choices of $n_A$, $n_B$, and $n$ determine the network size of division of labor and the location patterns of residences and transactions, their optimum values must be obtained from inframarginal analysis. A value profile of $n_A$, $n_B$, and $n$ is a structure.

First, all individuals' utility maximizing decisions are solved for given values of $n_A$, $n_B$, and $n$. Then the market clearing conditions and utility equalization conditions are used to solve for a corner equilibrium for a given structure. For different value profiles of $n_A$, $n_B$, and $n$ there are many corner equilibria. The general equilibrium is the corner equilibrium with the highest per capita real income.

The symmetry of the model implies that we need to consider only two types of decision problems. For an urban resident producing an A-type good, the decision problem is

$$\text{Max: } u_A = (x_A)(k_A x_A^d)^{n_A - 1}(k x_B^d)^{n_B} x_{jA}^{m-n} \cdot R_A \tag{14.6}$$

$$\text{s.t. } x_A + x_A^s = l_A - \alpha \qquad \text{(production function for a good sold)}$$
$$x_{jA} = l_{iA} - \alpha \qquad \text{(production function for a nontrade good)}$$
$$l_A + (m - n_A)l_{jA} = 1 \qquad \text{(endowment constraint for working time)}$$
$$p_A x_A^d (n_A - 1) + p_B n_B x_B^d + r_A R_A = p_A x_A^s + E_A \quad \text{(budget constraint)}$$

where $n_A$ ($n_B$) is her number of traded goods produced by the urban (rural) residents; $n \equiv n_A + n_B$ is the number of all traded goods that she purchases; $x_A$ is the quantity of the A-type good that she self-provides; $x_A^s$ is the amount of the A-type good that she sells to the market; $l_A$ is her level of specialization in producing this good; $x_A^d$ is the amount of the A-type good that she purchases from the market; $x_B^d$ is the amount of the B-type good that she purchases from the market; $x_{iA}$ is the amount of a nontraded good that she produces and consumes; and $l_{jA}$ is the quantity of labor that she allocates to the production of a nontraded good. Symmetry implies that $x_A^d$ is the same for $n_A - 1$ of A-type goods purchased, $x_B^d$ is the same for $n_A - 1$ of A-type goods purchased, $x_B^d$ is the same for $n_B$ of B-type goods purchased, and $l_{jA}$ is the same for $m - n$ nontraded goods. $p_A$ and $p_B$ are respectively the prices of A-type and B-type goods. $r_A$ and $r_B$ are respectively the prices of land in the urban and rural areas. $R_A$ is the lot size of each urban resident's house. $E_A = r_A A/M_A$ is the land rental, equally distributed to each urban resident, $M_A$ ($M_B$) is the number of urban (rural) residents. The decision variables are $x_A$, $x_A^s$, $l_A$, $x_{jA}$, $l_{iA}$, $x_A^d$, $x_B^d$, $R_A$, $n_A$, and $n$. The choice of $n_A$ and $n$, which determines $n_B$, determines how many goods an individual has to buy from the market and how many goods she self-provides.

The solution of the decision problem for given values of $n_A$, $n_B$, and $n$ in (14.6) is an individual's resource allocation for a given organizational pattern. Standard marginal analysis is applicable to such resource allocation problems. It yields the demand and supply functions and indirect utility function as follows.

$$x_A^s = \{np_A[1 - (m - n + 1)\alpha] - (m-n + 1)E_A\}/p_A(m + 1) \tag{14.7a}$$

$$l_A = [p_A(1 + n\alpha) + E_A]/p_A(m + 1),$$

$$x_A^d = \{p_A[1 - (m - n + 1)\alpha] + E_A\}/p_A(m + 1) \tag{14.7b}$$

$$x_B^d = \{p_A[1 - (m - n + 1)\alpha] + E_A\}/p_B(m + 1) \tag{14.7c}$$

$$R_A = \{p_A[1 - (m - n + 1)\alpha] + E_A\}/r_A(m + 1) \tag{14.7d}$$

$$u_A = \frac{k_A^{n-1}}{r_A p_A^m}(\frac{p_A}{p_B})^{n_B}\left[\frac{E_A + p_A[1 - (m - n + 1)\alpha]}{m + 1}\right]^{m+1}. \tag{14.7e}$$

The optimum decision for a rural resident is symmetric to (14.7), that is, it can be obtained by exchanging subscripts $A$ and $B$ in (14.7).

A corner equilibrium is determined by the market clearing conditions for land and goods, the utility equalization condition between urban and rural residents, and individuals' optimum decisions for given values of $n_A$, $n_B$, and $n$.

The land market clearing conditions are

$$M_A R_A = A, \qquad M_B R_B = B. \tag{14.8}$$

The market clearing condition for A-type goods (the traded goods produced in the urban area) yields

$$\frac{n p_A[1 - (m - n + 1)\alpha] - (m - n + 1)E_A}{(m + 1)p_A} \cdot \frac{M_A}{n_A} \tag{14.9}$$

$$= \frac{p_A[1 - (m - n + 1)\alpha] + E_A}{(m + 1)p_A} \cdot \frac{M_A}{n_A}(n_A - 1) + \frac{p_B[1 - (m - n + 1)\alpha\} + E_B}{(m + 1)p_A} \cdot M_B.$$

The market clearing condition for B-type goods is not independent of (14.8) and (14.9) because of Walras' law.

The utility equalization condition yields

$$\left(\frac{k_A}{k}\right)^{n-1} \left\{ \frac{E_A + p_A[1 - (m - n + 1)\alpha]}{E_B + p_B[1 - (m - n + 1)\alpha]} \right\}^{m+1} = \frac{r_A}{r_B}\left(\frac{p_A}{p_B}\right)^{m-n}. \tag{14.10}$$

(14.8)–(14.10), the population equation $M_A + M_B = M$, and the definitions $E_A \equiv r_A A/M_A$ and $E_B ( r_B B/M_B$ yield a corner equilibrium for a given structure defined by $n_A$, $n_B$, and $n$.

$$p \equiv \frac{p_A}{p_B} = \left(\frac{B\theta}{A(1 - \theta)}\right)^{\frac{1}{n}} \lambda^{\frac{1-n}{n}}, \tag{14.11}$$

$$l_A = l_B = \frac{1 + (n - 1)\alpha}{m}$$

$$r_A = \frac{[1 - (m - n + 1)\alpha]\theta M}{mA}, \; r_B = \frac{[1 - (m - n + 1)\alpha](1 - \theta)M}{mB},$$

$$M_A = \frac{n_A M}{n} = \theta M, \qquad M_B = \frac{n_B M}{n} = (1 - \theta)M,$$

$$\frac{R_A}{R_B} = \frac{AM_B}{BM_A} = \frac{A(1 - \theta)}{B\theta},$$

$$u_A = \frac{k_A^{n}{}^{-1}(1 + f)}{Mf^{(1-\theta)n+1}}\left(\frac{\theta}{1 - \theta}\right)^{(1-\theta)n}\left\{ \frac{[1 - (m - n + 1)\alpha]}{m} \right\}^m$$

$$\text{where } f \equiv \left[ \frac{A}{B} \cdot \lambda^{n-1} \cdot \left(\frac{\theta}{1 - \theta}\right)^n \right]^{n+1}$$

$\theta \equiv n_A/n$, $n_A + n_B = n$, and a B-type good is assumed to be the *numéraire*.

A general equilibrium has two components. The first consists of a set of relative prices of traded goods and of two types of land, and a set of numbers of individuals choosing different configurations of occupation and residence, a pattern of individuals' residences, and a location pattern of transactions that satisfy the market clearing and utility equalization conditions. The second component consists of each individual's choice of $n_A$ and $n$, or $n$ and $\theta$, and each individual's resource allocation that maximizes the decision-maker's utility.

Following a similar procedure to that used to prove the Yao theorem in chapter 6, we can prove that theorem for the model in this section. Therefore, the general equilibrium is the Pareto optimum corner equilibrium, and any Pareto inefficient corner equilibrium is not a general equilibrium. Or we may apply the first welfare theorem in chapter 13 to the model with *ex ante* identical consumer-producers to show that the Yao theorem holds for the Sun–Yang model, that is, any general equilibrium in this model is a corner equilibrium with utility equalization and the highest per capita real income.

The Yao theorem is pivotal to the results in this chapter, since it establishes the claim that a decentralized market can fully utilize the economies of agglomeration (which look like externalities) and the network effects of division of labor by choosing the Pareto efficient pattern of individuals' residences, the efficient location pattern of transactions, and the efficient network size of division of labor. This theorem also rules out multiple equilibria with different per capita real incomes, and shows that there is no coordination failure in a static general equilibrium model with network effects of division of labor and location pattern.[2] The very function of the market is to coordinate individuals' decisions in choosing the pattern and size of the network of division of labor and in choosing the location patterns of residences and transactions in order to fully utilize the network effects and the economies of agglomeration.

Maximization of $u_A$ in (14.7e) with respect to $n$ for a given $n_B$, and maximization of $u_B$, which is symmetric with $u_A$, with respect to $n$ for a given $n_A$, together with the market clearing and utility equalization conditions, will generate a corner equilibrium which is not the Pareto optimum corner equilibrium. According to the Yao theorem, that Pareto inefficient corner equilibrium is not general equilibrium. This corner equilibrium is based on individuals' Nash strategies in choosing trade patterns (an A type individual's choice of $n$ is dependent on a B type person's choice of $n_B$). According to the Yao theorem, that Pareto inefficient corner equilibrium partly based on Nash strategies is not a Walrasian general equilibrium. Using the Yao theorem we can prove the following proposition.

**Proposition 14.1:** In a symmetric model, the economy is divided into $M/n$ separate business communities. For $n \leq 2$, all individuals' residences are evenly located and all transactions (if any) are evenly dispersed. For $n > 2$ traded goods, all trade partners within a business community will choose to execute all transactions that are essential for the division of labor among them in the central marketplace of the community, even if some of them do not reside in the marketplace.

*Proof:* It is trivial to prove the first statement since each person needs only $n - 1$ trade partners and it will incur unnecessary transaction costs to trade with individuals other than $n - 1$ partners in the symmetric model. Hence, $n$ trade partners will form a local business community which does not trade with other local business communities. We now check whether residences are evenly located when the equilibrium value of $n$ is not greater than

2, and whether the dual urban–rural structure emerges from $n > 2$. Because all individuals are *ex ante* identical and have the same preference for consumption of land, in equilibrium each person must consume the same amount of land in autarky, and the price of land must be the same everywhere, which means residences must be evenly located. For $n = 2$, it is not difficult to show that residences are evenly located too because the *ex ante* identical individuals have the same tastes for land consumption. There are two possible location patterns of transactions. The pattern in figure 14.2a involves trade at the midpoint between two trade partners' residences, and pattern 14.2b involves trade at one person's residence (city). For the latter case the land price in the city is high enough to offset the transaction cost advantage of residing in the city. Hence, patterns (a) and (b) are equivalent. Let us assume that unequal land prices between the urban and rural areas generate infinitesimally small disutility for rural residents. Then (a) is Pareto superior to (b). According to the Yao theorem, (a) instead of (b) will occur in equilibrium for $n = 2$.

For $n = 3$, simple arithmetic shows that a location pattern (ii) of transactions, with one person's residence as a central marketplace, generates a lower total transaction cost than in (i) of panel (b), which generates a lower total transaction cost than in panel (a). Hence, a central marketplace will emerge from $n = 3$, which implies in turn that the transaction cost advantage of residing at the central market place will generate a land price differential, which implies that per capita land consumption is unequal between urban and rural residents and their residences cannot be evenly located in equilibrium.

For $n = 4$ in a symmetric model, the location pattern in (i) of panel (b) is better than that in (a). But in (i), two persons who reside more closely to the central marketplace certainly have a transaction cost advantage, so that land price cannot be the same for all residential lots. This implies that the initial even location pattern of residences cannot be sustained in equilibrium, since that even pattern occurs only if land price is the same for all localities. This implies that evenly dispersed residences cannot occur in equilibrium, so that the dual urban–rural structure, such as in (ii) where two persons reside in a city and the other two reside in the rural area with higher per capita consumption of land, may occur at equilibrium for $n = 4$. Following the same reasoning, we can show that the dual urban–rural structure occurs in equilibrium if and only if $n > 2$. *Q.E.D.*

With the Yao theorem and proposition 14.1, we can solve for the general equilibrium by maximizing the corner equilibrium per capita real income given in (14.11) with respect to $n_A$ and $n_B$. Since $n_A + n_B = n$, this is equivalent to maximizing per capita real income in (14.11) with respect to $n$ and $\theta \equiv n_A/n$. The first-order conditions for maximizing (14.11) with respect to $\theta$ and $n$ yield:

$$\ln\left[\frac{A(1-\theta)\lambda^{n-1}}{B\theta}\right] + \frac{1}{\theta} = \theta^{-2}\left\{\frac{1-\theta}{\theta} + \left[\frac{A(1-\theta)\lambda^{n-1}}{B\theta}\right]^{\frac{1}{n+1}}\right\}^{-1}. \qquad (14.12a)$$

$$\ln k + \frac{m\alpha}{1-(m-n+1)\alpha} = -\theta \ln \lambda. \qquad (14.12b)$$

(14.12) determines the general equilibrium values of $n$ and $\theta$ as functions of $k$, $\lambda$, $\alpha$, $m$, $A$, $B$, which characterize the size and pattern of the network of division of labor and the location pattern of individuals' residences and transactions.

Note that the left-hand side of (14.12a) is an increasing function while the right-hand side is a decreasing function of $\lambda^{n-1}A(1-\theta)/B\theta$, so that (14.12a) holds if and only if

$$\lambda^{n-1} = \frac{B}{A} \cdot \frac{\theta}{1 - \theta}. \tag{14.13}$$

Differentiation of (14.13) yields

$$[\ln \lambda]\partial n = \left[\frac{1}{\theta(1 - \theta)}\right]\partial\theta. \tag{14.14}$$

(14.14) implies that $\theta \equiv n_A/n$ increases with $n$, or the number of traded goods produced in the urban area increases more than proportionally as the network size of division of labor $n$ increases.

Using (14.11) and (14.13), we can also show that the general equilibrium relative price

$$p = 1. \tag{14.15}$$

We can show that the first-order conditions in (14.11), together with the second-order condition that requires a negative definite Hessian matrix ($D^2u(n, \theta) < 0$), lead to:

$$\frac{dn}{dk} = \left\{\frac{m\alpha^2}{[1 - (m - n + 1)\alpha]^2} - \theta(1 - \theta)(\ln \lambda)^2\right\}^{-1} > 0. \tag{14.16}$$

The second-order condition can be worked out as follows. Inserting (14.13) and (14.15) into the second-order derivative of $u^*$ in (14.11) with respect to $n$ and $\theta$ yields,

$$\frac{\partial^2 u}{\partial\theta^2} = -\frac{n(n + 2)}{(n + 1)^2} \cdot \frac{1}{\theta(1 - \theta)} \tag{14.17a}$$

$$\frac{\partial^2 u}{\partial\theta\partial n} = \frac{n(n + 2)}{(n + 1)^2} \cdot \ln \lambda \tag{14.17b}$$

$$\frac{\partial^2 u}{\partial n^2} = -\frac{m\alpha^2}{[1 - (m - n + 1)\alpha]^2} + \frac{\theta(1 - \theta)(\ln \lambda)^2}{(n + 1)^2} \tag{14.17c}$$

The negative definiteness of the Hessian matrix $D^2u(n, \theta) < 0$ requires that (14.17a) and (14.17c) be negative and

$$\frac{\partial^2 u}{\partial\theta^2} \cdot \frac{\partial^2 u}{\partial n^2} - \left(\frac{\partial^2 u}{\partial\theta\partial n}\right)^2 > 0. \tag{14.17d}$$

(14.17a) and (14.17c) are negative and (14.17d) holds if

$$\frac{m\alpha^2}{[1 - (m - n + 1)\alpha]^2} > \theta(1 - \theta)(\ln \lambda)^2. \tag{14.18}$$

Since (14.18) holds if and only if (14.16) holds, (14.16) holds if the second-order conditions for maximizing $u^*$ with respect to $n$ and $\theta$ are satisfied.

Since $k_A = \lambda k$ where $\lambda > 1$ is a constant, (14.16) implies also

$$\frac{dn}{dk_A} > 0. \tag{14.19}$$

This implies that the number of traded goods for each individual, as well as for society as a whole, increases with trading efficiency.

(14.14), (14.16), and (14.19) imply

$$\frac{d\theta}{dk_A}, \frac{d\theta}{dk} > 0 \tag{14.20}$$

where $\theta \equiv n_A/n$. This implies that the number of traded goods produced in the urban area increases more than proportionally as improvements in transaction conditions enlarge the equilibrium network of division of labor, $n$.

(14.16), (14.19), and (14.20) summarize the comparative statics of the general equilibrium network size of division of labor and the equilibrium location patterns of residences and transactions because of the correspondence between choices of residences and occupations. Since all endogenous variables are determined by $n$ and $\theta$, the comparative statics of the general equilibrium values of other endogenous variables can be worked out by using (14.16), (14.19), and (14.20). Differentiation of all corner equilibrium values of the endogenous variables in (14.11), together with (14.16), (14.19), and (14.20), yields the comparative statics of general equilibrium.

$n_A/n_B = M_A/M_B = \theta/(1 - \theta)$ increases with trading efficiency $k$ $\qquad$ (14.21)
$r_A = [1 - (m - n + 1)\alpha]\theta M/mA$ increases with trading efficiency $k$
$r_A/r_B = B\theta/A(1 - \theta)$ increases with trading efficiency $k$
$n$ increases with trading efficiency $k$
$n_A = \theta n$ increases with trading efficiency $k$
$R_A/R_B$ decreases with trading efficiency $k$
$l_i$ (an individual's level of specialization in producing the good sold) increases with
$\qquad$ trading efficiency $k$
$u^*$ (per capita real income) increases with trading efficiency $k$

To identify the positive effect of $k$ on $u^*$ in (14.21), we have applied the envelope theorem to $u^*$ in (14.11).

Following the analysis of chapter 11, we can also show all other aspects of evolution in division of labor discussed in chapter 11, such as increases in the degree of diversity of economic structure, the extent of the market, the degree of market integration, and individuals' levels of specialization. In addition, the number of separate communities, which is also the number of cities, rises as per capita real income and productivity of each good increase.

Now we consider the location patterns of residences and transactions that are associated with the general equilibrium values of division of labor, $n = 1$ and $n = 2$, respectively. If trading efficiency $k$ is sufficiently low, the transaction costs caused by a large network size of division of labor outweigh the positive network effects of the division of labor generated by fixed learning cost in each activity, so that the general equilibrium level of division of labor $n = 1$. This implies that each individual's number of goods purchased is $n - 1 = 0$, or autarky is chosen. According to proposition 14.2, all individuals' residences are evenly located. Each individual self-provides $m$ consumption goods, and no market or cities exist, as shown in figure 14.3a. Only four of $M$ self-sufficient consumer-producers are represented by four circles. Only four of $m$ self-provided goods are represented by four lines.

As trading efficiency $k$ is slightly improved, the equilibrium value of $n$ increases to 2. Each pair of individuals will establish a local business community in which each trade partner sells one good to and buys one good from the other. In order to save on transaction costs, according to proposition 14.1, two trade partners meet at the middle point between their residences to exchange goods 1 and 2. In order to maximize utility with respect to consumption of land, all individuals will reside at vertices of the grid of triangles with equal sides, so that the equilibrium price of land is equal for each residence. Hence, many local markets emerge from the low level of division of labor, but there is no central marketplace or city. All transactions are evenly dispersed at $M/2$ places, as shown in panel (b) where there is no division between the urban and rural areas. Only four of $m$ goods are represented by lines and only four of $M$ individuals are represented by four circles in (b).

As trading efficiency is further improved such that $n > 2$, then the central marketplace generates economies of agglomeration, according to proposition 14.2. In the symmetric model, each individual needs only $n - 1$ trade partners. In order to save on transaction costs, $n$ individuals will form a local business community where each person sells her produce to and buys one good from each of other $n - 1$ individuals. The good that she sells is different from the one sold by each of the other $n - 1$ members of the community. All of the $n$ members of the local community go to the central marketplace to trade with each other. As shown in figure 14.3c, $n_A$ of the $n$ individuals reside at the central marketplace which is a city, and $n_B$ of the $n$ individuals reside in the countryside. Population size of each local community is then $n$ and the number of such local communities is thus $M/n$. The urban land size of each local community is $An/M$ and the rural land size of each local community is $Bn/M$ because of the assumption of fixed respective total sizes of urban and rural areas. In panel (c), $M/n$ separate local business communities are represented by 4 medium squares and cities are denoted by small squares. All transactions in a community are executed at the city. The graph under (c) illustrates the network of transactions of all $n$ urban and rural residents that are executed at the city when $n = m = 4$ and $M = 16$.

Panel (e) represents a general equilibrium with a very high level of division of labor ($n = M$), where there is an integrated market and a single city. Big arrows denote the direction of the evolution of division of labor and the location patterns of residences and transactions caused by improvements of trading efficiency.

As division of labor evolves ($n$ increases) due to improved transaction conditions, the number of separate local communities (which is also the number of cities) decreases, the area size of each community, as well as its urban or rural area increases, the land price in the urban area increases absolutely as well as relative to that in the rural area, and relative per capita land consumption between the urban and rural areas declines.[3] The degree of concentration of residential location increases not only because the relative population size of urban and rural residents increases, but also because the average population size of each city and the population density of the urban area increase as division of labor evolves.

In summary, we have

**Proposition 14.2:** Improvements in transaction conditions will generate the following concurrent phenomena. The ratio of urban to rural land prices increases, the network of division of labor is enlarged, the number of traded goods for each individual as well as for society as a whole increases, the number of traded goods produced in the urban area

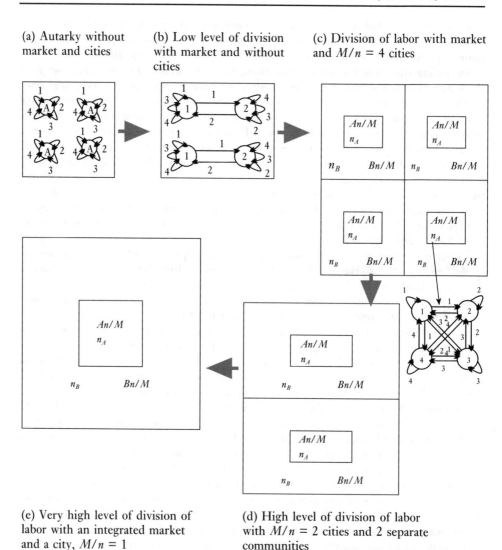

♦ **Figure 14.3:** Evolution of division of labor and location pattern of residences and transactions

increases absolutely as well as relatively to that in the rural area, the population ratio of urban to rural residents increases, each individual's level of specialization increases, the number of markets increases, the diversity of economic structure increases, the number of transactions for each individual, trade dependence and interdependence among individuals of different occupations increase, the extent of the market and the extent of endogenous comparative advantage increase, the degree of market integration and production concentration increase, and per capita real income and productivity of each good increase.

A distinguishing feature of the Type II economies of agglomeration in this model is that even if which $n_B$ out of $n$ traded goods to be produced in the rural area is indeterminate in equilibrium, a high level of division of labor will make the concentration of urban residences and all transactions in the urban area emerge from *ex ante* identical individuals with identical production conditions of all goods. The assumption made by Yang and Rice (1994, see sec. 14.2) and Fujita and Krugman (1995, see sec. 14.5), that land-intensive agricultural production must be dispersed in the rural area is not necessary for the existence of Type II economies of agglomeration. Also, a variety of manufactured goods that is not land intensive may be produced in the rural area because of the trade-off between economies of agglomeration and high land price in the city. This has a flavor of the theory of complexity: some phenomena that do not exist for each individual element of a system emerge from a complex structure of a collection of numerous identical individual elements. This is just like different DNA structures of the same molecules generating many species of animals.

## ◆ 14.5 The Fujita–Krugman Model of Urbanization

In this section we use the Fujita and Krugman model as an example to study general equilibrium models of economies of scale and urbanization.

### Example 14.4: (the Fujita–Krugman model, 1995):

The story behind the Fujita–Krugman model runs as follows. There are trade offs between global economies of scale, the utility benefit of consumption variety of manufactured goods, and transaction costs. An increase in population size or in trading efficiency will enlarge the scope for individuals to trade-off among these conflicting forces, thereby increasing productivity, per capita real income, and consumption variety. In addition, there is a trade-off between the reduction of transaction costs as residences of manufacturers are concentrated in a city and the increase in transaction costs between rural farmers and urban manufacturers resulting from that urban concentration. The increase in the number of manufactured goods, an aspect of division of labor, will move the efficient balance of this trade-off toward a more concentrated residential pattern of manufacturers, making a city more likely to emerge. The benefit of concentrated residences of manufactures caused by an increase in the number of manufactured goods is called Type I economies of agglomeration. As the comparative statics of the general equilibrium model predicts, a decrease in the unit transaction cost coefficient of agricultural goods or a larger population size will make a city more likely to emerge from a greater number of manufactured goods. But concurrent increases in the urban–rural land price differential, decreases in relative per capita consumption of land of urban and rural residents, the population size of urban residents as a share of total population, and increases of individuals' levels of specialization cannot be predicted by the model.

Consider an economy with $N$ identical consumers, an agricultural good, and $n$ manufactured goods, where $n$ is endogenous. It is assumed that the manufacturing activity needs no land. Hence, the central point of the geographic area is a city where all $N_M$ manufacturers reside. Suppose that $N_A = N - N_M$ farmers' residences are evenly located around the city. The area of land that is employed is endogenously determined in this model. Each rural resident has the following neoclassical decision problem.

Max: $u_A = z_A^{\alpha}[n(kx_A)^{\rho}]^{(1-\alpha)/\rho}$ (utility function) (14.22a)

s.t. $p z_A + nq x_A = w_A$ (budget constraint)

where $p$ is the price of the agricultural good, $q$ is the price of the manufactured goods, $z_A$ is the quantity of the agricultural good consumed by a rural resident, $n$ is the number of manufactured goods, and $x_A$ is the amount of a manufactured good consumed by the rural resident. Each consumer is endowed with one unit of labor, so that the income of a rural resident equals the rural wage rate $w_A$. $k \in (0, 1)$ is the trading efficiency coefficient for the manufactured goods. We assume that there is no transaction cost for a rural resident to buy the agricultural good from the local rural market. Hence, transaction costs are incurred only in buying the manufactured goods. Note that we have used symmetry to justify equal prices and quantities of all manufactured goods.

Each urban resident has the following neoclassical decision problem.

Max: $u_B = (tz_B)^{\alpha}[nx_B^{\rho}]^{(1-\alpha)/\rho}$ (utility function) (14.22b)

s.t. $pz_B + nq x_B = w_B$ (budget constraint)

where subscript $B$ stands for variables for an urban resident and $t \in (0, 1)$ is the trading efficiency coefficient for buying the agricultural good. If we assume that labor at the city is the *numéraire*, then $w_B = 1$. We assume that there is no transaction cost for an urban resident to buy manufactured goods from the local urban market. Hence, transaction costs are incurred by the urban resident only in buying the agricultural good.

The demand functions and indirect utility function and own price elasticity of demand for a consumer of type $i = A, B$ are:

$z_i = \alpha w_i / p_i ,$ $\qquad E = -(n - \rho)/(1 - \rho)n$ (14.23)

$x_i = (1 - \alpha)w_i / q_i n,$

$u_A = \alpha^{\alpha}(1 - \alpha)^{1-\alpha} n^{(1-\alpha)(1-\rho)/\rho} k^{(1-\alpha)} w_A / p_A^{\alpha} q_A^{1-\alpha}$

$u_B = \alpha^{\alpha}(1 - \alpha)^{1-\alpha} n^{(1-\alpha)(1-\rho)/\rho} t^{\alpha} w_B / p_B^{\alpha} q_B^{1-\alpha}$

where the own price elasticity of demand $E$ is calculated using the Yang–Heijdra formula (see section 11.9 of chapter 11).

The simple Leontief production function is assumed for the agricultural sector. So $a$ units of labor and one unit of land are required to produce one unit of z. For simplicity, it is assumed that each farming firm owns land that it uses for production. Hence, rental of land equals revenue from land for each farming firm. The zero profit condition in the agricultural sector yields

$p = aw_A$ (14.24)

Free migration between the urban and rural areas will establish utility equalization between the two areas. The condition $u_A = u_B$, together with (14.24), yields

$w_A = t^{\alpha}/k^{1-\alpha}, \qquad w_B = 1.$ (14.25)

A linear production function with a fixed cost is assumed for manufacturing a good. Hence, the amount of labor to produce output $Q_i$ is $f + bQ_i$. A monopolistically competitive regime prevails in the markets for manufactured goods. The condition that marginal revenue equals marginal cost and zero profit condition yields

$$nq(1 - \rho) = (n - \rho)(q - b), \quad (1 - \alpha)(q - b)(N_A w_A + N - N_A) = fnq \qquad (14.26)$$

where $N_A$ is the number of farmers, $N_B = N\text{-}N_A$ is the number of urban residents, and the equilibrium value of $w_A$ is given in (14.25).

(14.25) and (14.26), together with the market clearing condition for labor or for the manufactured goods, can then be used to determine $N_A$, $q$, $w_A$, and $n$. The equilibrium total output level of the agricultural good, $Z = zN$, can be obtained by plugging the equilibrium price into the demand function, $z_i = \alpha w_i / p_z$, where $z_i$ is given in (14.23). Therefore, the demand for labor from the agricultural sector is

$$N_A = aZ = a[(\alpha N_A/a) + (\alpha(N - N_A)/aw_A)] \text{ or}$$
$$N_A = \alpha k^{1-\alpha} N/[(1 - \alpha)t^\alpha + \alpha k^{1-\alpha}], \qquad (14.27)$$

where $w_A = t^\alpha / k^{1-\alpha}$ is given in (14.25). Inserting (14.27) into (14.26) yields the equilibrium value of the number of manufactured goods, which can be considered as the degree of industrialization.

$$n = \rho + (1 - \alpha)(1 - \rho)t^\alpha N/[(1 - \alpha)t^\alpha + \alpha k^{1-\alpha}]f. \qquad (14.28)$$

Differentiation of (14.27) and (14.28) yields

$$dn/dN > 0, \ dn/dt > 0, \text{ and } d(N_B/N)/dt > 0. \qquad (14.29)$$

$$dn/dk < 0, \text{ and } \quad d(N_B/N)/dk < 0.$$

This implies that as the population size and/or the trading efficiency for the agricultural good increase, the number of manufactured goods increases, or industrialization develops. Also, the comparative statics predict that as the transaction condition for the agricultural good is improved, the population share of urban residents increases, or urbanization develops. But the trading efficiency for the manufactured goods has the opposite effect. The equilibrium size of the rural area is the same as the output level of the agricultural good $z$, which increases as the population size rises, as the trading efficiency for the manufactured goods increases, or as the trading efficiency for the agricultural good declines.

In this chapter we have shown that one of the most important functions of the invisible hand (interactions between self-interested decisions) is to simultaneously sort out the efficient location patterns of transactions and individuals' residences, the related network size of division of labor, and trading efficiency. Our models predict that the potential for increases of land price in the large cities is determined by the potential for evolution of division of labor. As a large city becomes the central marketplace for an increasingly integrated large network of division of labor, land prices in the city can go up to a degree far beyond what the marginal analysis of demand and supply may predict.

Baumgardner (1988b) finds empirical evidence for the positive relationship between urbanization and individuals' levels of specialization. Colwell and Munneke (1997) provide empirical evidence for the negative relationship between land price and distance from the city (and per capita consumption of land). Simon and Nardinelli (1996) find empirical evidence, in a data set of English cities from 1861–1961, for a positive relationship between transaction conditions and city size, which is predicted by the Yang and Rice and by the Sun and Yang models in this chapter. They and Y. Zhang (1999) have also found empirical evidence against a positive relationship between the size of firms and city size, which is predicted by the Krugman and Fujita model in this chapter. They argue that the evidence indicates that external economies rather than internal economies of scale are a driving force of urbanization. Here, their notion of external economies of scale, from Marshall (1890), should be interpreted as the positive network effects of division of labor, since their data set shows a positive relationship between evolution of occupation diversity and urbanization. Also, their data set indicates a positive relationship between urbanization and evolution of the employment share of the transaction sector. More empirical work is needed for establishing a positive relationship between land price differentials in cities and rural areas, the degree of commercialization (level of division of labor), urbanization, and trading efficiency.

## Key Terms and Review

The conditions for cities to emerge from division of labor.

The relationship between urbanization, network size of division of labor, and trading efficiency.

The relationship between the difference of land intensity in producing agricultural and industrial goods, and the function of urbanization in promoting division of labor.

The general equilibrium mechanism that simultaneously determines network size of division of labor, location pattern of transactions, and trading efficiency.

The general equilibrium mechanism that simultaneously determines network size of division of labor, location pattern of individuals' residences, and land price differentials between urban and rural areas.

Type I and Type II economies of agglomeration.

The relationship between potential for rises of urban land prices and evolution of division of labor.

The roles of free migration, free choice of occupation configuration, and free pricing in enabling the market to sort out simultaneously the efficient location pattern of transactions, location pattern of individuals' residences, network size of division of labor, and trading efficiency.

## Further Reading

*Classical theory of the city*: Petty (1683), Wartenberg (1966); *division of labor and cities*: Scott (1988), Marshall (1890, ch. 11), Smith (1776, chs. 2, 3), Petty (1683, pp. 471–2); *models of the city and economies of scale*: Ben-Akiva, de Palma, and Thisse (1989), Krugman (1991, 1993, 1994), Fujita and Krugman (1994, 1995), Fujita, Krugman, and Venables (1999), Tabuchi (1998), Fujita (1988, 1989), Fujita and Mori (1997), Fujita and Thisse (1996), Quigley (1998), Krugman and Venables (1993), Page (1999); *hierarchical structure of cities*: Williamson (1985), Yang and Hogbin (1990), Yang and Ng (1993, ch. 13), Fujita and Krugman (1994); *new classical models of cities and economies of specialization*: Yang (1991), Yang and Rice (1994), Yang and Ng (1993, ch. 6), Sun and Yang (1998); *neoclassical models with constant returns to scale, transaction costs, cities*: Kelley and Williamson (1984), Hahn (1971), Karman (1981), Kurz (1974), Mills and Hamilton (1984), Schweizer (1986), Henderson (1996); *urban biased development*: Lipton (1977, 1984), Brown (1978), Sah and Stiglitz (1984), Sen (1977), Lin and Yang (1998); *economies of agglomeration, externality of cities, and size of cities*: Abdel-Rahman (1990), Arnott (1979), Fujita (1989), Henderson (1974), Mills (1967), *dual economies*: Murphy, Shleifer, and Vishny (1989a,b), Yang and Rice (1994); *land price of cities*: Colwell and Munneke (1997); *empirical evidence*: Simon and Nardinelli (1996), Baumgardner (1988), Y. Zhang (1999).

# QUESTIONS

1   North (1981, pp. 158–62) finds historical evidence for the following fact. "An urban world is a development that has occurred during the last hundred years and is associated not so much with the industrial city as with a dramatic decline in the costs of transportation, the increase in agricultural productivity, and the agglomerative benefits of central places for economic activity." Use the model in this chapter to explain the historical facts.

2   Consider an extended version of the model in example 14.2. In the extended model, the equilibrium number of traded goods might be as large as 49. Consider the following hierarchical structures of cities. $M$ consumer-producers are divided among $M/49$ local communities. In each of them each person sells one good to and buys one good from each of other 48 individuals. Each local community has one large central marketplace and 6 smaller central marketplaces. Each individual trades with her 6 neighboring trade partners through a small marketplace and goes to the large central market place to trade with the other 42 individuals. In other words, there is an hierarchical structure of cities. The large city is the central marketplace for the local community with 49 members as well as the trade center for 7 individuals who reside nearby the large city. Each of 6 small cities is a trade center among 7 individuals, similar to the one in figure 14.2b. Another location pattern of transactions is that all 49 individuals go to the center of the community to trade with each other. The third pattern is that each pair of trade partners can trade at the middle point between them. The fourth pattern is similar to that in figure 14.2b, that is, $M$ individuals are divided as $M/7$ separate local communities. Discuss under what conditions each of the four patterns occurs at general equilibrium. Analyze the difference in trade volume between the large and small cities in the first pattern.

3   Discuss the implications of a blend between the model in question 2 and the model in example 14.3 for a hierarchical structure of land prices between cities of different ranks. Use this model to predict the potential for increases in the land price of the large cities

4   Analyze the role of free migration, free choice of occupation configuration, and free trade and pricing of land in enabling the market to sort out the efficient pattern of urbanization and efficient geographical pattern of transactions.

5   Mills and Hamilton (1984) have found empirical evidence for concurrent evolution of per capita real income and of degree of urbanization. Design a method to test concurrent evolution of division of labor and the degree of urbanization against empirical observations. Find a way to test the theories developed in sections 14.3 and 14.4 against empirical observations.

6   Discuss the differences between the models in section 14.4 and that in section 14.5. Find empirical observations that can be used to test one model against the other. Show that the Fujita–Krugman model predicts a positive correlation between the degree of urbanization and the average size of industrialization.

# EXERCISES

1  Lio, 1996, 1998: extend the model in example 14.2 to the case with three industrial goods and one agricultural good. Solve for general equilibrium and its inframarginal comparative statics. Show that a dual economy, featuring an asymmetric structure of division of labor (urban residents have a higher level of specialization than rural residents), may occur during the transitional period from a low level of balanced division of labor (urban and rural residents have the same level of specialization and productivity) to a high level of balanced division of labor.

2  Yang and Rice, 1994: Assume that in the model in exercise 1, the production functions are the same as in chapter 5. Solve for the general equilibrium and its inframarginal comparative statics.

3  Extend the model in example 14.2 to a case with the number of traded goods $n \in [1, 49]$. Analyze the possible equilibrium hierarchical location pattern of transactions in which individuals trade with neighbors through a local marketplace, similar to that in figure 14.2b, with $n = 7$, and trade with non-neighbors through a larger central marketplace which may emerge from a large network size of division of labor with $n = 49$. The central marketplace looks like a large city which channels more transactions than each smaller market place. Discuss the possible evolution of the number of layers of the hierarchical system of cities if the level of division of labor is allowed to be $[1, m]$.

4  Assume that in the model in example 14.3 total land area is a fixed constant, but land areas for urban and rural areas are endogenous variables. Solve for the comparative statics of the general equilibrium. Analyze the effects of evolution of division of labor on the relative areas of cities and countryside.

5  Assume that in example 14.4. the agricultural good is the sole consumption good and all manufactured goods are employed to produce the agricultural good. Use the model to explain structural changes caused by industrialization. Compare your explanation to the conventional theory of labor surplus and structural changes (Lewis, 1955, and Fei and Ranis, 1964).

## Notes

1  Quigley (1998) considers benefits from intracity informational spillovers. Tabuchi (1998), by combining the methods of Henderson (1974) and Krugman (1991), considers the trade-off between Type I economies of agglomeration and the cost of intra-city congestion.

2  But because of indeterminacy about who specializes in which activity, which $n$ out of $m$ goods are traded, and which $n_A$ out of $n$ traded goods are produced in the urban area in equilibrium, we have multiple equilibria that generate the same per capita real income.

3  The result that the number of cities decreases as division of labor evolves can be changed either by endogenizing population size or by endogenizing the number of layers of city hierarchy, as discussed in question 2 and exercise 3, above.

# chapter 15

# THE TRADE-OFF BETWEEN WORKING AND LEISURE, AND THE EFFECTS OF RESOURCE SCARCITY AND POPULATION SIZE ON THE DIVISION OF LABOR

## ◆ 15.1 Why Can Division of Labor Enlarge the Scope for the Efficient Trade-off between Working and Leisure?

In the previous chapters, we have made the very strong assumption that each consumer-producer uses all of her time for working, and that accordingly there is no trade-off between working and leisure. From the neoclassical equilibrium model in exercise 1 of chapter 4, which does allow a trade-off between working and leisure, but excludes increasing returns, you can see that the trade-off has no implications for the equilibrium size of the network of division of labor and productivity progress. However, if that trade-off is introduced into the new classical framework, individuals will have very interesting trade-offs among leisure, working for the market, working for self-provided consumption, economies of specialization, and transaction costs. All these trade-offs may generate implications for the equilibrium network size of division of labor and for productivity progress.

Buchanan (1994) has conjectured that the adoption of a social moral code (such as that of Protestantism) which reduces individuals' desire for leisure and raises the equilibrium working time can lead to greater exploitation of economies of scale and therefore increased productivity. This is a conjecture on the comparative statics of general equilibrium (what will happen to the general equilibrium productivity if the parameter representing the taste for leisure is changed).

However our new classical models in this chapter will show that, under certain conditions, Buchanan's seemingly sensible conjecture is not right. One of these models, developed by Lio (1996), shows that if the utility function is of the Cobb–Douglas type an increase in individuals' desire for leisure can result in an increase in productivity. This is because as their time for working is reduced and their scope for trading-off working to self-provide consumption at home against working for the market is narrowed, they must raise the level of division of labor and related productivity to meet their desires for consumption and leisure by exploiting more economies of division of labor and related interpersonal complementarity. This implies that an increase in the desire for leisure may increase the level of division of labor and productivity. In other words, under certain conditions, a decrease in the desire for leisure will reduce the level of division of labor and productivity.

The inframarginal comparative statics of general equilibrium show also that per capita real income, individuals' levels of specialization, the level of division of labor and the related size of the market network, per capita working time for market vs. self-sufficient working time, per capita consumption of leisure, and per capita consumption of goods increase concurrently with improvements in trading efficiency that raise the equilibrium level of division of labor. These results are consistent with empirical observations documented in Lio (1996), which show that per capita leisure time, per capita consumption of goods, per capita real income, and productivity increase concurrently.

Lio (1996) uses a new classical equilibrium model incorporating the CES utility function and a trade-off between working and leisure to show that Buchanan's conjecture can be substantiated under a certain condition. According to the inframarginal comparative statics of general equilibrium in the model, if individuals' desires for consumption variety of physical goods are already very strong, then as their desires for leisure are increased the equilibrium level of division of labor and productivity increase; whereas if individuals' desires for variety of consumption goods are not strong, then as their desires for leisure increase the equilibrium level of division of labor and productivity fall. For the latter case, Buchanan's conjecture is right, that is, as the desire for leisure increases, productivity falls, provided the desire for consumption variety is not strong.

The intuition behind the story is illustrated as follows. As individuals' desires for leisure increases, the scope for trading off variety of consumption goods against leisure is narrowed. There are two methods to ease the tension between consumption variety and leisure. One of them is to raise the level of division of labor, thereby raising productivity to get more scope to take care of both. The other is to sacrifice consumption variety to meet the stronger desires for leisure. When the desire for consumption variety is not particularly strong, the second method is, of course, chosen. When the desire for consumption variety is strong, the first method will be chosen.

This story reminds us that as the parameters representing environment are changed, such that the scope for trading off one element against another is narrowed and social tension is increased, individuals may be compelled to choose a higher level of division of labor in order to exploit more interpersonal complementarities to alleviate the tension. This may involve the emergence of new opportunities and productivity progress from the crisis.

Lio (1998b; see exercise 5 at the end of this chapter) develops a new classical equilibrium model with a minimum level of consumption of goods that is essential for the survival of consumer-producers, to show that an increase in that minimum consumption will compel individuals to choose a higher level of division of labor, which yields a higher level of productivity. This explains why the Industrial Revolution took place in the northern hemisphere, where the minimum consumption level for survival in the harsh winter was much higher than in the tropical area. Hence, people in the northern hemisphere tended to exploit interpersonal complementarities and economies of division of labor in order to survive the harsh natural conditions.

Wen (1997b) has also developed a new classical equilibrium model incorporating endowment constraints on resources in addition to labor. She shows that as the population size increases or as the existing resources are depleted such that per capita endowment of resources declines, the equilibrium level of division of labor and productivity will be raised provided trading efficiency is sufficiently high. The inframarginal comparative statics of general equilibrium are consistent with the consequences of the first energy crisis caused by an increase in population coupled with the depletion of the forests in the eighteenth century. The wood shortage crisis created a new era of coal and steel that was followed by the Industrial Revolution. According to Wen's model, the network effects of division of labor are more fully exploited during such a crisis of resource scarcity to speed up the knowledge accumulation that creates new technology, new resources, and new energy sources. The Club of Rome's pessimistic description of growth limits certainly underestimates the growth potential that human society can achieve through utilizing the social network of division of labor to acquire new knowledge, new technology, new resources, and new energy.

Chu (1997) has developed another new classical equilibrium model to explore the implications of population size for the emergence of the infrastructure sector that specializes in improving trading efficiency, and for evolution in division of labor. In that model, trading efficiency, the level of division of labor, and the existence of the professional infrastructure sector are simultaneously endogenized in equilibrium. The productivity and existence of the professional infrastructure sector are determined by the size of the network of division of labor, which is determined by trading efficiency, which in turn is determined by the productivity and existence of the professional infrastructure sector. Chu shows that a larger population size will create more scope for the existence of the professional infrastructure sector, which improves trading efficiency and thus raises the equilibrium level of division of labor and productivity in the sectors producing goods. Since there are network effects of trading efficiency, Wen (1997a) and Zhang (1997) have developed two new classical dynamic general equilibrium models that explore the implications of governments' fiscal and monetary policies for the equilibrium aggregate demand. These models take account of the interdependencies between tax revenue, infrastructure expenditure, and the network effects of spontaneous (endogenous) evolution in division of labor.

In this chapter, we will use one of Lio's models incorporating the C-D utility function and a trade-off between working and leisure; Wen's static model; and Chu's model (1997) to illustrate the stories. We leave Wen's and Zhang's dynamic equilibrium models to exercises in chapter 22, from which you will learn the skills required for playing around with such models.

---

### Questions to Ask Yourself when Reading this Chapter

♦ What are the general equilibrium implications of a blend of trade-offs between economies of specialization and transaction costs and between working and leisure?

♦ Why is it possible that per capita consumption of each good and productivity increase as a result of increased desires for leisure?

♦ What are the conditions for concurrent increases in leisure time, working time for the market, productivity, and per capita consumption of each good?

♦ Why can an energy shortage crisis be a catalyst for evolution in division of labor and productivity progress under appropriate institutional conditions?

♦ Under what conditions can high population density promote the development of division of labor and productivity through saving on the per capita investment cost of infrastructure?

---

## ♦ 15.2 Why Leisure Time and Per Capita Consumption of Goods Increase as Division of Labor Develops

In this section, we use one of the Lio models (1996) to explain how evolution in division of labor can result in concurrent increases in leisure, per capita consumption of each good, and productivity.

### Example 15.1: the Lio model with trade-offs among economies of division of labor, transaction costs, working, and leisure

Each consumer–producer's utility function is specified as follows.

$$V = \ln u = \sum_{i=1}^{m} \ln(x_i + kx_i^d) + \beta \ln H \tag{15.1}$$

where $x_i$, $x_i^d$, and $k$ have the same meanings as in the previous chapters, $H = 1 - L$ is the amount of time allocated for leisure, $L$ is the amount of time allocated for the production of goods, and $\beta$ is a parameter representing the desire for leisure. It is assumed that the total amount of available time for each individual is 1, so that the production functions and the endowment constraint for time are

$$x_i + x_i^s = \text{Max}\{0, l_i - \alpha\} \qquad i = 1, \ldots, m \tag{15.2}$$

$$\sum_{i=1}^{m} l_i \equiv L \qquad L + H = 1$$

Using (15.1), (15.2), and the Wen theorem, the decision problem for an individual selling good i can be specified as follows.

$$\text{Max: } V = \ln x_i + \sum_{r \in R} \ln(kx_r^d) + \sum_{j \in J} \ln x_j + \beta \ln H \tag{15.3}$$

$$\text{s.t. } x_i + x_i^s = \text{Max }\{0, l_i - \alpha\}, \quad x_j = \text{Max }\{0, l_j - \alpha\},$$
$$\forall j \in J \qquad \text{(production function)}$$

$$l_i + \sum_{j \in J} l_j + H = 1 \qquad \text{(endowment constraint)}$$
$$p_i x_i^s = \sum_{r \in R} p_r x_r^d \qquad \text{(budget constraint)}$$

where $x_i$, $x_i^s$, $x_i^d$, $x_j$, $l_i$, $H$ are decision variables, $R$ is the set of $n - 1$ goods purchased, $J$ is the set of $m - n$ nontraded goods. The number of all consumption goods $m$ is fixed.

The symmetry of the model implies that the general equilibrium resource allocation is trivially simple and entails equal quantities of per capita consumption of each good, equal amounts of goods sold by each and every individual, and

$$p_i/p_r = 1, \qquad M_i = M_r = M/n, \qquad i, r = 1, 2, \cdots, n.$$

Using what we know about the equilibrium resource allocation, we can simplify the budget constraint as $x_i^s = (n - 1) x_i^d$ and simplify the endowment constraint as $l_i + (m - n)l_j + H = 1$. Inserting the simplified budget and endowment constraints into the original decision problem yields a nonconstrained maximization problem that maximizes

$$V = \ln(l_i - \alpha - x_i^s) + (n - 1) \ln[k x_i^s/(n - 1)] + (m - n) \ln(l_j - \alpha) + \beta \ln[1 - l_i - (m - n)l_j]$$

with respect to $x_i^s$, $l_j$, $n$. The first-order condition for the maximization problem yields the optimum decisions that include demand and supply functions and the indirect utility function.

$$\begin{aligned}
x_i &= x_j = x_r^d = [1 - (1 + m - n)\alpha]/(\beta + m) = -\alpha/\ln k \quad &(15.4a)\\
x_i^s &= (n + 1)[1 - (1 + m - n)\alpha]/(\beta + m)\\
&= (-1/\ln k)[1 - (1/\ln k)]\alpha m + (1/\ln k) + \beta\alpha/(\ln k)^2
\end{aligned}$$

$$\begin{aligned}
l_i &= [n + (n^2 - mn - n + \beta + m)\alpha]/(\beta + m) \quad &(15.4b)\\
&= (-1/\ln k)[1 - (1/\ln k)]\alpha m + 1/\ln k + \beta\alpha/(\ln k)^2 + [1 - (1/\ln k)]\alpha\\
l_j &= [1 + (n + \beta - 1)\alpha]/(\beta + m) = [1 - (1/\ln k)]\alpha\\
H &= \beta[1 - (1 + m - n)\alpha]/(\beta + m) = -\beta\alpha/\ln k
\end{aligned}$$

$$\begin{aligned}
n &= [1 - (1/\ln k)]m + [1 - (1/\alpha)] - \beta/\ln k \quad &(15.4c)\\
V &= (n - 1)\ln k + \beta\ln\beta + (\beta + m)\{\ln[1 - (1 + m - n)\alpha] - \ln(\beta + m)\}
\end{aligned}$$

Differentiation of the endogenous variables with respect to parameters $k$, $\beta$, and $\alpha$ yields the inframarginal comparative statics of the general equilibrium, summarized in table 15.1.

In table 15.1, the envelope theorem is used to obtain the total derivative of $u$ with

**Table 15.1:** Inframarginal comparative statics of the general equilibrium based on the trade-off between working and leisure

|   | $n$ | $V$ | $x_i^s$ | $x_i^d$ | $Mx_i^s$ | $L_i$ | $H$ | $(m - n)l_j$ |
|---|---|---|---|---|---|---|---|---|
| $k$ | + | + | + | + | + | + | + | − |
| $\beta$ | + | + | + | + | + | + | + | − |
| $\alpha$ | + | − | + | + | + | + | + | + |

respect to the three parameters. Here, the envelope theorem implies $dV(n^*, k)/dk = \partial V(n^*, k)/\partial k$, where $n^*$ is the optimum number of traded goods and $\partial V(n^*, k)/\partial n = 0$ due to the first-order condition for maximization. In table 15.1, "+" denotes a positive derivative of an endogenous variable with respect to a parameter. For instance, "+" in column $n$ and in row $k$ denotes $dV/dk > 0$, and "–" in column $V$ and in row $\alpha$ denotes $dV/d\alpha < 0$. $dV/d\beta$ does not make much sense since a change in $\beta$ is a change in the utility function $V$, and its effect on the utility level $V$ relates to a change in $V$ in response to a change in part of $V$.

In table 15.1, $x_i^s$ is the amount of good i sold to the market by an individual and therefore $Mx_i^s$ is the aggregate quantity sold by all individuals, that is, the extent of the market. $l_j$ is the amount of time allocated for the production of a nontraded good and therefore $(m - n)l_j$ is the total amount of time allocated to produce all nontraded and self-provided goods. $H$ is the amount of time for leisure.

From table 15.1, we can see that as trading efficiency $k$ is improved, there will be concurrent increases in the equilibrium level of division of labor, $n$, each individual's level of specialization $l_i$, the extent of the market, $Mx_i^s$, leisure, $H$, and per capita real income, $V$. An increase in the desire for leisure has similar results, since this puts more pressure on the limited time available for leisure and working. The pressure forces individuals to choose a higher level of division of labor to increase productivity, so that more time can be released to meet the stronger desire for leisure without reducing consumption of goods.

These results are interesting since an increase in trading efficiency or in the desire for leisure will simultaneously raise per capita working time for the market, $l_i$ (which is also a person's level of specialization) and the per capita amount of leisure time. Neoclassical economics, with its dichotomy between pure consumers and firms, cannot predict such phenomena, which are confirmed by empirical evidence (see Lio, 1996). In the neoclassical framework, each pure consumer must spend all of her working time in working for the market, since she is not allowed to self-provide goods. This implies that an increase in leisure time is necessarily a decrease in working time in the neoclassical framework. But in the new classical framework working time for the market and leisure time can be simultaneously increased by a decrease in the amount of time allocated to the self-provision of goods. Certainly, improvements in trading efficiency or an increase in the desire for leisure may generate such concurrent phenomena.

Lio (1996) extends this model to the case with the CES utility function. He also adds Becker's assumption that each individual must spend a certain amount of time to consume each good. Each consumer-producer's decision problem in that model is

$$\text{Max: } u_i = (1 - cm)[(x_i t_i^\beta)^\rho + \sum_{r \in R}(kx_r^d t_r^\beta)^\rho + \sum_{j \in J}(x_j t_j^\beta)^\rho]^{\frac{1}{\rho}} \tag{15.5}$$

$$\text{s.t. } x_i + x_i^s = l_i - \alpha, \qquad x_j = l_j - \alpha, \qquad \forall\, j \in J$$
$$l_i + \sum_{j \in J} l_j + t_i + \sum_{r \in R} t_r + \sum_{j \in J} t_j = 1$$
$$p_i x_i^s = \sum_{r \in R}(p_r x_r^d)$$

where $t_i$ is the amount of time required for the consumption of good i, $\beta$ is a parameter representing the effect of $t_i$ on utility or the degree of desire for direct consumption of time, $c$ is the management cost of each consumption good in terms of utility lost, $\rho$ is the parameter of elasticity of substitution, and $1/\rho$ is the degree of economies of consumption variety or of economies of complementarity between consumption goods. Following the procedure used already in this section, it is not difficult to solve for the general equilibrium and its inframarginal comparative statics of the extended model. The effects of an increase in $k$ are similar to those in table 15.1. But as the desire for leisure time, represented by $\beta$, increases, there are two different scenarios. When the degree of economies of consumption variety $1/\rho$ is large, the increase in $\beta$ has positive effects on all the endogenous variables listed in table 15.1. When $1/\rho$ is small, the increase has negative effects on the endogenous variables. That is, Buchanan's conjecture that an increase in the desire for leisure time will reduce productivity is right if the economies of consumption variety are not significant, or if the desire for diverse consumption is not very strong.

We leave the technical detail of obtaining the results to you as exercise 1 at the end of the chapter.

## ◆ 15.3 Why Can a Resource Shortage Crisis Promote Evolution in Division of Labor and Productivity?

This section is devoted to an investigation of the effects of a decline in per capita resource endowment, caused by an increase in population or by depletion of the existing resources, on the equilibrium level of division of labor and productivity. As suggested in the introductory section of this chapter, we can make some conjectures about the effects. As per capita resource endowment declines, production conditions tend to be less favorable. In order to meet their nonsatiated desire for consumption under these harsher conditions, individuals will be compelled to choose a higher level of division of labor, thereby raising their productivity by exploiting the interpersonal complementarity and social network effects of the division of labor. Wen (1997b) has developed a new classical general equilibrium model to formalize this idea. The model provides a new approach to explaining why labor surplus and the wood shortage crisis catalyzed the Industrial Revolution in Britain. This approach differs from the theory of Lewis (1955) and Fei and Ranis (1964), which also views labor surplus as a driving force of industrialization. Since the formal model of their theory is developed within the neoclassical framework, it cannot explore the intrinsic relationship between labor surplus, division of labor, and productivity progress. In particular, according to their model, exogenous technical progress in the industrial sector is essential to establishing the link between labor surplus, industrialization, and related productivity progress.

In this section, we shall use a simplified version of the Wen model to show that as trading efficiency is improved, the equilibrium level of division of labor and productivity may rise even if exogenous technical progress is absent. The Chicago School of economics is very critical of the pessimistic views often expressed on the population and energy crises. According to that school, not only can the market efficiently sort out any population and energy problems resulting from changes of natural conditions, but also the crises of population and energy turns out to be a driving force of productivity progress under favorable institutional conditions. The Wen model formalizes this idea within a new classical general equilibrium framework.

### Example 15.2: the Wen model with positive productivity implications of an energy crisis and labor surplus

Consider an economy with a continuum of $M$ *ex ante* identical consumer-producers. Each individual's utility is specified as a function of the quantities of two goods that are consumed.

$$u = (x + kx^d)(y + ky^d)$$

where all variables have the same meanings as in the previous chapters. Each individual has the following production functions for the two consumption goods.

$$x + x^s = (l_x - A)(s_x - B)$$
$$y + y^s = (l_y - A)(s_y - B)$$

where $l_i$ is the individual's level of specialization in producing good i, $s_i$ is the amount of primary resource allocated to produce good i, $A$ is a fixed learning cost in producing a good, and $B$ is a fixed amount of the resource that is essential for the production of each good. It is assumed also that the output level of a good is 0 if the labor input level is lower than the fixed learning cost, and/or the resource input level is lower than the fixed resource requirement. The fixed learning cost and the fixed resource amount are the sources of economies of specialization. Each individual's total factor input for good x is $l_x^{\frac{1}{2}}s_x^{\frac{1}{2}}$ and her total factor productivity for good x, $TFP_x = (x + x^s)/l_x^2 s_x^2$, is an increasing function of her level of specialization in producing good x.

Each individual's endowment constraints for working time and for the resource are

$$l_x + l_y = 1$$
$$s_x + s_y = s_0$$

where $s_0$ is each individual's initial endowment of the resource, which can be considered as coal, iron ore, or land.

There are two structures: autarky (A) and division of labor (D). We can apply the inframarginal analysis to solve for the general equilibrium. We start with autarky where each individual's decision problem is:

Max: $u = xy$

s.t. $x = (l_x - A)(s_x - B), \qquad y = (l_y - A)(s_y - B)$
$\qquad l_x + l_y = 1, \qquad s_x + s_y = s_0$

where $x$, $y$, $l_x$, $l_y$, $s_x$, $s_y$ are decision variables. The solution of this problem is:

$$l_x = l_y = A + [(1 - 2A)/2]$$
$$s_x = s_y = B + [(s_0 - 2B)/2]$$
$$x = y = (1 - 2A)(s_0 - 2B)/4$$
$$u_A = [(1 - 2A)(s_0 - 2B)4]^2$$

where $u_A$ is per capita real income in structure A. In structure D there are two configurations (x/y) and (y/x). The decision problem for configuration (x/y) is:

Max: $u = xky^d$

s.t. $x + x^s = (1 - A)(s_0 - B)$
$\qquad p_y y^d = p_x x^s$

where $x$, $x^s$, $y^d$ are decision variables. The solution of the decision problem is

$$x^s = (1 - A)(s_0 - B)/2, \qquad y^d = (1 - A)(s_0 - B)p_x/2p_y$$
$$u_x = [(1 - A)(s_0 - B)/2]^2 \, kp_x/p_y$$

where $u_x$ is the indirect utility function for configuration (x/y). The decision problem for configuration (y/x) is symmetric. Its solution is:

$$y^s = (1 - A)(s_0 - B)/2, \qquad x^d = (1 - A)(s_0 - B)p_y/2p_x$$
$$u_y = [(1 - A)(s_0 - B)/2]^2 \, kp_y/p_x$$

The market clearing and utility equalization conditions

$$M_x x^s = M_y y^d$$
$$u_x = u_y$$

yield the corner equilibrium relative price of the two traded goods, the numbers of individuals selling the two goods, and per capita real income in structure D.

$$p_x/p_y = 1, \qquad M_x = M_y = M/2$$
$$u_D = k[(1 - A)(s_0 - B)/2]^2$$

where $u_D$ is the per capita real income in structure D. A comparison between per capita real incomes in structures A and D, together with the Yao theorem, indicates that the general equilibrium structure is the division of labor (D) if $k > k_0$ and is autarky (A) if $k < k_0$. Here

$$k_0 \equiv [(1 - 2A)(s_0 - 2B)/2(1 - A)(s_0 - B)]^2.$$

Differentiation of $k_0$ with respect to $s_0$ yields

$$\partial k_0 / \partial s_0 > 0$$

This implies that as the per capita endowment of the resource $s_0$ falls, the critical value for the division of labor to be the general equilibrium structure becomes smaller. In other words, as $s_0$ falls, it is more likely that division of labor is the general equilibrium structure. In view of the positive relationship between the level of division of labor and productivity (due to economies of specialization), this result substantiates our conjecture that division of labor and related productivity progress may be promoted by a decrease in per capita endowment of resources, caused either by an increase in population and a related labor surplus, or by depletion of the existing resource base and a related energy (or other resource) shortage crisis.

It should be noted that the direct effect of a decrease in $s_0$ on utility is negative, even though it may raise the equilibrium level of division of labor and productivity. It is not difficult to show, using the envelope theorem, that the direct negative effect on utility dominates the positive effect of the increase in productivity. From the expressions of $u_A$ and $u_D$, it can be seen that the negative effect of a decrease in $s_0$ on $u_A$ is greater than its negative effect on $u_D$, so that as per capita resource endowment declines, it is more likely that the division of labor is better than autarky.

If we take into account the time dimension, a decrease in per capita resource endowment may generate a long-run effect on evolution in division of labor and productivity progress despite its negative effect on current utility. The long-run positive effect may outweigh the short-run negative effect. However, this scenario does not necessarily take place, since the critical condition for the division of labor to be better than autarky involves four parameters: $k$, $A$, $B$, and $s_0$. If trading efficiency $k$ is very low, due to a deficient legal system or a deficient transportation infrastructure and banking system (for the extreme case, $k = 0$), then no matter how small $s_0$ is, $k$ will be smaller than the critical value $k_0$ and the general equilibrium is always autarky. This establishes the conclusion that labor surplus or shortage of resources is not itself sufficient for the development of division of labor and productivity progress. We can find many examples, such as the Chinese economy during 1949–77 and the Indian economy during the same period, in which labor surplus did not generate significant economic development.

The model can be used also to show that a decline of per capita resource endowment, caused by labor surplus or resource shortage, is not necessary for economic development. From the expression of the critical value of trading efficiency, $k_0$, it is straightforward that for a given $s_0$, for sufficiently large values of $k$, $A$, and $B$, $k$ will be greater than $k_0$, or the division of labor will be the general equilibrium. This means that labor surplus and resource shortage are not necessary for economic development so long as trading efficiency is high and economies of specialization are significant. The experience of economic development in the US, Canada, and Australia provides evidence to support this statement. There was no labor surplus nor resource shortage in the early development stages of these three economies. However, in each case a good legal system and rapid improvements in transportation conditions provided high trading efficiency and generated impressive evolution in division of labor and productivity progress.

However, for Britain in the eighteenth century and for Japan in the twentieth century, labor surplus and the crisis of resource shortage were indeed a catalyst of economic development.

## ◆ 15.4 Implications of High Population Density for Evolution in Division of Labor through Its Effect on the Per Capita Investment Cost of Infrastructure

Many economists, such as Boserup (1975), have noted the fact that the per capita investment cost of a canal system, a railroad network, a freeway network, an airport system, and other infrastructure decreases with the population density, so that a high population density may be favorable for evolution in division of labor. Chu and Tsai (1998) and Chu (1997) have developed two new classical general equilibrium models to formalize the idea. In their model, trading efficiency, the level of division of labor that relates to the size of the market network, and the existence of a professional infrastructure sector are simultaneously endogenized. Trading efficiency is determined by the existence and size of the professional infrastructure sector, which are determined by the size of the network of division of labor, which is in turn determined by trading efficiency. The notion of general equilibrium is a powerful vehicle for analyzing the mechanism that simultaneously determines all of the interdependent variables. In this section we use the Chu model (1997) to study that mechanism.

### Example 15.3: the Chu model with positive implications for the division of labor of population size

Consider an economy with a continuum of $M$ *ex ante* identical consumer-producers. For an individual who does not produce infrastructure, the decision problem is:

$$\text{Max: } u = (x + kx^d)(y + ky^d) \qquad \text{(utility function)} \qquad (15.6)$$

$$\text{s.t. } x + x^s = \text{Max } \{0, 1 - \alpha\} \qquad \text{(production function of x)}$$
$$y + y^s = \text{Max } \{0, 1 - \alpha\} \qquad \text{(production function of y)}$$
$$L_x + L_y = 1 \qquad \text{(endowment constraint of time)}$$
$$k = \begin{cases} 1 - \frac{1}{M_k} \text{ if } M_k > 0 \\ k_0 \text{ if } M_k = 0 \end{cases} \qquad \text{(transaction condition)}$$
$$p_x x^s + p_y y^s = p_x x^d + p_y y^d + p_k \qquad \text{(budget constraint)}$$

where $x$ and $y$ are respective quantities of two goods that are self-provided, $x^d$ and $y^d$ are respective quantities of the two goods purchased from the market, $x^s$ and $y^s$ are respective quantities of the two goods sold, and $L_i$ is the individual's level of specialization in producing good i. $k$ is the trading efficiency coefficient, which is an increasing function of the number of individuals producing infrastructure, $M_k$. If the number is 0, that is, no professional infrastructure sector exists, then $k = k_0$. $p_i$ is the price of good i, and $p_k$ is a fee for use of infrastructure paid by each individual. It is assumed that individuals compete for the rights to construct infrastructure in an auction. The bidder who collects the lowest per capita fee will get the rights. If no infrastructure exists, that is, $M_k = 0$, then $p_k$ is irrelevant and $k = k_0$. Service $k$ provided by indivisible infrastructure is a public good, since all individuals can simultaneously consume $k$. This is referred to as *nonrivalry* of $k$. But if a certain fee collection institution is enforced, individuals can be excluded from using $k$. This is referred to as *exclusivity*. Nonrivalry is a technical characteristic of a service or good. It does not necessarily imply *non-exclusivity*, which is an institutional characteristic that relates to trade in the service or good.

For an individual choosing to be a specialist in the infrastructure sector, her decision problem is:

$$\text{Max: } u = kx^d ky^d \qquad (15.7)$$

$$\text{s.t. } p_x x^d + p_y y^d = p_k (M_x + M_y)/M_k$$

where $(M_x + M_y)/M_k$ is the ratio of the number of specialists producing goods to those producing infrastructure, so that $p_k(M_x + M_y)/M_k$ is the earnings that an infrastructure specialist receives from the production of infrastructure. Because of the assumptions that individuals are *ex ante* identical and that a competitive biding process determines distribution of the rights to produce infrastructure, the earnings must be the same between the infrastructure specialists. Here, trading efficiency $k$ is the same as in (15.6).

There are 6 configurations: autarky denoted A, specialization in producing x without an infrastructure sector, denoted (x/y), specialization in y without infrastructure, denoted (y/x), specialization in x with infrastructure, denoted (x/yk), specialization in y with infrastructure, denoted (y/xk), and specialization in producing infrastructure, denoted (k/xy). The corner solutions for the six configurations are summarized in table 15.2, where $p_{ij}$ is

**Table 15.2**: Corner solutions in six configurations

| Configuration | Self-sufficient quantity | Demand function | Suppy function | Indirect utility function |
|---|---|---|---|---|
| A | $x = y = (1 - 2\alpha)/2$ | 0 | 0 | $(1 - 2\alpha)^2/4$ |
| (x/y) | $x = (1 - \alpha)/2$ | $y^d = (1 - \alpha)p_{xy}/2$ | $x^s = (1 - \alpha)/2$ | $(1 - \alpha)^2 k_0 p_{xy}/4$ |
| (y/x) | $y = (1 - \alpha)/2$ | $x^d = (1 - \alpha)p_{yx}/2$ | $y^s = (1 - \alpha)/2$ | $(1 - \alpha)^2 k_0 p_{yx}/4$ |
| (x/yk) | $x = (1 - \alpha - p_{kx})/2$ | $y^d = [1 - \alpha)p_{xy} - p_{ky}]/2$ | $x^s = (1 - \alpha + p_{kx})/2$ | $(1 - \alpha - p_{kx})^2 k_0 p_{xy}/4$ |
| (y/xk) | $y = (1 - \alpha - p_{ky})/2$ | $x^d = [(1 - \alpha)p_{yx} - p_{kx}]/2$ | $y^s = (1 - \alpha + p_{ky})/2$ | $(1 - \alpha - p_{ky})^2 k_0 p_{yx}/4$ |
| (k/xy) | $k = 1 - (1/Mk)$ | $x^d = (M_{xk} - M_{yk})p_{kx}/2$ | $k = 1 - (1/M_k)$ | $0.5k^2(M_{xk} + M_{yk})$ |
|  |  | $y^d = (M_{xk} - M_{yk})p_{ky}/2$ |  | $p_{kx}p_{ky}$ |

the relative price of goods (or services) i to j, $M_{ij}$ is the relative number of individuals selling good i to those selling good j.

Combinations of the six configurations yield three structures: autarky structure A; structure D with the division of labor and without infrastructure, comprising configurations (x/y) and (y/x); and structure C with the division of labor and infrastructure, comprising configurations (x/yk), (y/xk), and (k/xy).

Competition will establish the market clearing conditions and utility equalization conditions between configurations. Here, the utility equalization condition between specialist producers of goods and specialist producers of infrastructure is equivalent to the zero profit condition for the infrastructure sector. The competitive bidding process for the rights to produce infrastructure and free choices between professions will establish the condition. All of the conditions for the corner equilibrium in structure C can be used to express per capita real income in that structure as a function of the number of specialist producers of infrastructure, $M_k$. Free choice between occupations and the competitive bidding process for rights to produce infrastructure will maximize the expression of per capita real income with respect to $M_k$. If utility can be raised by a change of jobs between the production sectors of goods and the infrastructure sector, which changes $M_k$, individuals will do so until utility is maximized with respect to $M_k$. From these conditions we can solve for the corner equilibria in the three structures, which are summarized in table 15.3, where $M_i$ is the number of individuals selling good i, and $k = 1 - (1/M_k)$. The corner equilibrium value of $M_k$ in structure C is given by the first-order condition for maximizing the per capita real income in C with respect to $M_k$, which is

**Table 15.3**: Corner equilibria in three structures

| Structure | Relative price | Number of specialists | Per capita real income |
|---|---|---|---|
| A |  |  | $(1 - 2\alpha)^2/4$ |
| D | $p_{xy} = 1$ | $M_x = M_y = M/2$ | $(1 - \alpha)^2 k_0/4$ |
| C | $p_{yx} = 1,$ | $M_x = M_y$ | $\left( \dfrac{0.5(1 - \alpha)}{\dfrac{M_k}{k(M - M_k)} + \dfrac{1}{\sqrt{k}}} \right)^2$ |
|  | $p_{kx} =$ | $= (M - M_k)/2$ |  |
|  | $(1 - \alpha)/\{1 + \sqrt{k}[(M/M_k) - 1]\}$ |  |  |

$$\frac{1}{(M - M_k)(M_k - 1)} + \frac{1}{2\sqrt{M_k(M_k - 1)}} = \frac{M}{(M - M_k)^2}. \tag{15.8}$$

Since per capita real income in structure C, given in table 15.3, is a function of $M_k$ and the per capita real income is maximized with respect to $M_k$, we can apply the envelope theorem to get

$$\frac{du(C)}{dM} = \frac{\partial u(C)}{\partial M} + \frac{\partial u(C)}{\partial M_k}\frac{dM_k}{dM} = \frac{\partial u(C)}{\partial M} > 0 \tag{15.9a}$$

where

$$u(C) = \left(\frac{1 - \alpha}{2}\right)^2 \left[\frac{Mk}{k(M - M_k)} + \frac{1}{\sqrt{k}}\right]^{-2}, \quad k = 1 - \frac{1}{M_k} \tag{15.9b}$$

is the corner equilibrium per capita real income in structure C, which is a function of $M$ and $M_k$. The maximization of $u(C)$ with respect to $M_k$ requires $\partial u(C)/\partial M_k = 0$. It is not difficult to see that $\partial u(C)/\partial M_k > 0$. (15.9) implies that the corner equilibrium per capita real income increases with the population size $M$. Therefore, when per capita real income in C is compared with that in D and in A, it is more likely that $u(C)$ is greater than $u(D)$ and $u(A)$ if $M$ is larger.

Comparisons of per capita real incomes in all corner equilibria, together with the Yao theorem, yield general equilibrium and its inframarginal comparative statics, as summarized in table 15.4, where $M_k$ is given by (15.8), $M_0$ is given by $u(A) = u(C)$, $M_1$ is given by $u(D) = u(C)$, and $u(A)$, $u(D)$, $u(C)$ are given in table 15.3. This table indicates that the larger the population size, the more likely is the professional infrastructure sector to emerge from equilibrium. It is not difficult to show that trading efficiency, per capita real income, and productivity are more likely to increase as the population size grows.

If we assume that the government collects tax from individuals and uses the tax revenue to construct infrastructure, then $p_k$ can be interpreted as a fee that the government charges each user of infrastructure. Zhang (1997) and Wen (1997a) have developed dynamic versions of the static new classical model. They show that trading efficiency, the network size of division of labor, and the positive network effect of expenditure on infrastructure are all interdependent in a dynamic general equilibrium. Hence, the efficient size of infrastructure and the optimum government expenditure on infrastructure evolve over time. The speed of evolution of division of labor, emergence and development of infrastructure, and trading efficiency are all determined by a government administration efficiency parameter. Also, the government's fiscal and monetary policies can affect aggregate demand through their effects on trading efficiency that generates network effects of division of labor.

**Table 15.4:** General equilibrium and its new classical comparative statics

| Statics | $k_0 < (\frac{1 - 2\alpha}{1 - \alpha})^2, M < M_0$ | $k_0 > (\frac{1 - 2\alpha}{1 - \alpha})^2, M < M_1$ | $M > \text{Max}\{M_0\ M_1\}$ |
|---|---|---|---|
| Equilibrium structure | A | D | C |

It must be noted, however, that the positive relationship between population size, trading efficiency, and the network size of division of labor is not an "if and only if" relationship, since $M_0$ and $M_1$ are functions of $\alpha$. If a transaction condition coefficient or a transformation coefficient from inputs to outputs of the infrastructure is specified as in the Wen model in exercise 3 of chapter 22, $M_0$ and $M_1$ are dependent on these parameters. Hence, even if the population size or density is great, but the legal system, the government bureaucracy system, or the banking system is not efficient, then the level of division of labor and productivity will be low. In this sense, the productivity implications of population size, based on the network effects of division of labor in the Chu and the Wen models, substantially differ from the Type II scale effects generated by the neoclassical trade and growth model with economies of scale (see chapters 11, 21, and 22).

## Key Terms and Review

General equilibrium implications of an interplay of the trade-off between economies of specialization and transaction costs and the trade-off between working and leisure.

Function of the market in sorting out the efficient allocation of time between working for the market, working to self-provide goods, and leisure.

Mechanism that generates concurrent evolution in per capita consumption of each good and productivity increase as a result of an increased desire for leisure.

Conditions for concurrent increases in time for leisure, in working time for the market, in productivity, and in per capita consumption of each good.

Why can the equilibrium level of division of labor and productivity increase as the per capita endowment of resource declines or as population increases?

Why can the crisis of energy shortage be a driving force for evolution in division of labor and productivity under appropriate institutional conditions?

Conditions under which high population density promotes the development of division of labor and productivity through saving on the per capita investment cost of infrastructure.

Conditions for the free market to provide an efficient infrastructure.

## Further Reading

*Population and division of labor*: Boserup (1975), Chu (1997), Chu and Tsai (1998), Chu and Wang (1998); *leisure and division of labor*: Lio (1996); *resource endowment, labor surplus, and division of labor*: Wen (1997b), Fei and Ranis (1964), Lewis (1955).

# QUESTIONS

1  The Hong Kong and Taiwan governments are considering the adoption of a five-day work week and the Chinese government has already converted from a six to a five work day system. According to some neoclassical models, this will decrease labor input and thereby reduce per capita income and its growth rate. Under what conditions is this prediction correct or incorrect?

2  Under what conditions does the frightening forecast of crises due to an energy shortage and a population explosion make sense, and under what conditions is the forecast just nonsense?

3 Mokyr (1993, p. 31) and other authors maintain that the challenge imposed by resource scarcities stimulates invention. Thus the deforestation of Britain is considered to have led to a rise in timber prices, triggering Britain into adopting a novel and ultimately far more efficient set of techniques using fossil fuels. Extend the models in this chapter to substantiate this conjecture.

4 Sachs and Warner (1999) explain the unsuccessful development experience of Latin American by abundant resources, and North and Weingast (1989) explain this by the deficient institutions that generate low trading efficiency. Use the models in this chapter to assess their analyses.

5 If each good is not a necessity individually (say the CES utility function is assumed), what will happen to the network size of division of labor, leisure time, productivity, and the number of available goods as trading efficiency is improved?

6 In the new classical models, the trading efficiency coefficient $k$ is equivalent to "public goods." According to Pigou and Samuelson, the output level of public goods is not Pareto efficient in the Walrasian regime with no government intervention. Use the Chu model to assess under what condition this claim is wrong in relation to the following facts. Early economic development in the US in the last century was driven by the development of infrastructure. But the infrastructure (canals, railroads, and early freeways) was developed largely by private companies. The development of freeways by private companies in Malaysia is much more successful than that in China, where the government monopolizes the construction of freeways. According to Coase (1960), the market and private sector are able to take care of so-called "public goods," and Pigou and Samuelson's notion of distortion caused by externality and public goods is misleading. Use the Chu model to assess Coase's view.

7 Analyze the difference between the implications of population size in the new classical models in examples 15.2 and 15.3 and scale effects in the D-S model in chapter 11.

8 North (1958) has found empirical evidence for a negative correlation between freight rates and economic development. Lio (1996) has found empirical evidence for concurrent increases in per capita real income, in leisure time, and in working time for the market. Find more empirical evidence that might support the theories developed in this chapter.

9 North (1986) has found empirical evidence for concurrent evolution of the income share of the transaction sector and per capita real income. Find empirical evidence for concurrent evolution of division of labor and the income share of infrastructure expenditure, which might support the model in example 15.3.

10 An economist predicts that in the end of the twenty-first century total income will be produced out of 20 percent of available labor in society. Use the new classical model in this chapter to assess this prediction.

# EXERCISES

1 Solve for the general equilibrium and inframarginal comparative statics of the Lio model, specified in (15.5), and identify the conditions under which an increase in the desire for leisure will decrease the equilibrium levels of division of labor and productivity.

2 Consider the model in example 15.1. Assume that fixed learning cost $\alpha_i$ differs from good to good and $m = 2$. Solve for general equilibrium and its inframarginal comparative statics.

3 Consider the model in example 15.1. Assume that trading efficiency $k_i$ differs from good to good and $m = 3$. Solve for general equilibrium and its inframarginal comparative statics.

4    Consider the model in example 15.2. Assume that all primary resources are owned by an individual who has the same utility function as others, but she does not produce. Solve for the inframarginal comparative statics of general equilibrium and analyze the implications of the shortage of resources or population size for the equilibrium level of division of labor and productivity

5    Solve for the inframarginal comparative statics of general equilibrium in the Lio model (1998b) where each of $M$ ex ante identical individuals has the following decision problem.

Max: $u = (x + kx^d)(y + ky^d)$

$x + x^s = \text{Max } \{0, L_x - \alpha\}, \quad y + y^s = \text{Max } \{0, L_y - \alpha\}$
$L_x + L_y = 1, \quad x + kx^d \geq \beta$
$p_x x^s + p_y y^s = p_x x^d + p_y y^d$

Show that as the minimum consumption level of good x, $\beta$, increases, the equilibrium level of division of labor and productivity will rise. Use your results to analyze why industrialization took place first in the northern hemisphere, where living conditions are much harsher than in warmer areas.

6    Consider the Chu model in example 15.3. Assume that the government taxes each dollar of goods that is bought and then uses the tax revenue to construct infrastructure. Hence, the budget constraints are specified as follows. For configuration (x/yk): $p_x x^s = (1 + t)p_y y^d$, for configurations (y/xk): $p_y y^s = (1 + t)p_x x^d$, for configuration (k/xy):

$[M_x p_y y_x^d + M_y p_x x_y^d + M_k(p_x x_k^d + p_y y_k^d)]t / M_k$

$= (1 + t)(p_x x_k^d + p_y y_k^d)$, or

$t(M_x p_x y_x^d + M_y p_x x_y^d) = M_k(p_x x_k^d + p_y y_k^d)$

where the subscripts i of $x^d$ and $y^d$ denote individuals selling good i. Solve for the inframarginal comparative statics of general equilibrium.

## chapter 16

# THE ECONOMICS OF PROPERTY RIGHTS AND THE DIVISION OF LABOR

### ◆ 16.1 Uncertainties in Transactions and the Economics of Property Rights

Though individuals' levels of specialization and the level of division of labor for society have been endogenized in the previous chapters, the question of the coordination reliability of the network of division of labor has not been investigated. This question relates to possible interactions between risk in transactions and the network effects of division of labor. The problem of coordination reliability is important in our daily decision-making process. It is because of this problem that many individuals do not want to specialize in a particular activity. As an individual increases her level of specialization, she becomes more dependent on other specialists whose products are essential for her consumption and production. Since the division of labor is associated with an input–output network which involves a series of many individual specialists, the whole network may fail to work if one of the links in the series connection fails to work. Therefore, the aggregate risk of coordination failure in the network of division of labor increases more than proportionally as the level of specialization and division of labor increase.

In the US, we can occasionally find some carpenter who engages in most of the activities involved in building a house, rather than relying on specialized subcontractors, in order to reduce risk of coordination failure caused by a high level of division of labor between specialized subcontractors. The Great Depression is another example illustrating the importance of the risk of coordination failure arising from division of labor. In the 1920s, as a result of successful industrialization in Western Europe and the US, a large network of domestic and international division of labor was developed. While on the one hand this raised productivity and created historically unprecedented prosperity, on the other hand it significantly increased the risk of coordination failure in the network. In a network, many very specialized sectors are connected in series, so that the whole network might fail to work when one of the professional sectors, such as the banking sector, fails to work, resulting in an episode such as the Great Depression and mass unemployment.

Although the Soviet Union did not develop a market system to coordinate the network of division of labor, it attempted to mimic the pattern of industrialization in the capitalist economies by developing a high level of division of labor through a central planning system. Each state or republic in the Soviet Union, or in the communist block of East Europe, was required to specialize in a particular sector. For instance, the Ukraine specialized in producing grain, Czechoslovakia specialized in producing locomotives, and Bulgaria specialized in producing fruit and vegetables. On the one hand, this high level of division of labor generated impressive industrialization in the 1930s and in the 1950s. But on the other hand it also significantly reduced the coordination reliability of the noncommercialized network of division of labor. Hence, the breakdown of some links in this large network of division of labor due to the breakup of the Eastern European block and the Soviet Union resulted in network coordination failure. This was the main reason for the negative growth rate of the Russian and East European economies in the 1990s.

No matter what causes the coordination failure of each transaction that is essential for the network of division of labor, the high level of division of labor and the associated large number of transactions will aggregate the risks in individual transactions into a much greater total risk of coordination failure for the whole network. The aggregate risk of coordination failure will be an exponential function of the number of transactions. Hence, as the level of division of labor and the related number of transactions increase, the aggregate risk of coordination failure will rise more than proportionally. This implies that the aggregate risk of coordination failure is a much more important constraint on the development of division of labor than exogenous transportation costs and other tangible transaction costs.

The simplest risk in transactions relates to all kinds of traffic accidents that may take place in the process of transporting goods. A more important risk of coordination failure relates to the specification of property rights and enforcement of contracts. For many business relationships, it is not easy to specify and enforce the rights of the participants involved. For instance, the rights of professors and their employers (university authorities) are not easy to specify and enforce because of the high cost of measuring the quality and quantity of the professors' teaching and research services. The inventor's rights to software are not easy to enforce even if they can be fully specified. Many users of such software have found some method of overcoming copyright protection, enabling them to infringe upon the rights of the patentees of the software without penalty. This makes the innovation of new software less profitable than it might otherwise be, thereby generating a coordination failure of division of labor between specialized research and specialized production of tangible goods.

The problem of coordination reliability in economics is analogous to the problem of reliability in the engineering literature. An extensive literature has developed to study problems of reliability of various engineering systems (see, for instance, Shooman, 1968). However, the problem of coordination reliability of division of labor is much more sophisticated than reliability problems in an engineering system. First, the costs caused by coordination failure must be traded off against the transaction costs incurred in raising the reliability of an economic system, whereas in an engineering system no such trade-off is considered, though different patterns of series cum parallel connection are compared to find a pattern with great reliability. Second, in economic analysis, interactions between the self-interested behavior of individuals must be considered, so that more complicated trade-offs may arise in the economic analysis of reliability problems.

Suppose that the risk of coordination failure for each transaction can be reduced by inputting resources. That risk then becomes an endogenous decision variable. The risk of coordination failure of division of labor can be reduced by allocating resources to the specification and enforcement of contractual terms at the cost of rising exogenous transaction costs in specifying and enforcing property rights. We may consider the welfare losses caused by the risk of coordination failure as endogenous transaction costs, or alternatively consider them as anticipated endogenous transaction costs that are caused by the opportunistic behavior examined in chapter 9. Thus we have a trade-off between the exogenous transaction costs of specifying and enforcing property rights and endogenous transaction costs. We can then see that the efficient trade-off between endogenous and exogenous transaction costs in the marketplace may involve imperfect specification and enforcement of property rights.

A monthly ticket for a train or bus is an example that illustrates the implications of this trade-off. A monthly ticket does not specify in detail the correspondence between the riding fee and the amount of transport services (number and distance of rides) provided, and it may encourage inefficient travel that generates endogenous transaction costs. However, it does not involve much exogenous transaction cost in collecting payment for each ride. Another example is the arrangements for financing construction of a bridge. There are different ways to finance a bridge. One is for the government to use tax revenue: under this arrangement some individuals who never use the bridge are compelled to pay the tax while others pay no more for frequent use of the bridge. This will generate distortions, which are endogenous transaction costs, so that, relative to the Pareto optimum, the output of the former type of individual is too little compared to that of the latter type. However, this arrangement does not involve much exogenous transaction costs in collecting fees from the users. The other way is to allow a private company to construct the bridge and to collect fees from the users of the bridge. This method avoids endogenous transaction costs at the expense of the exogenous transaction cost of collecting fees. The most efficient method is the one with the minimum sum of the two types of transaction cost.

If the exogenous transaction costs saved by financing the bridge through government taxes outweigh the endogenous transaction costs generated by the tax arrangement in comparison to the arrangement without the tax, then government finance can be used to promote division of labor and productivity progress, or to play a role in rectifying "market failure." Otherwise, the government tax may generate "government failure" and restrict the market from fulfilling its function. In many less-developed countries, the government did not know how to use public finance to develop an infrastructure that promotes evolution of division of labor and related urbanization. On the other hand, in the Soviet-style centrally planned economies, the governments extended public finance to such a degree that the market could not play its role in the development process. These two extreme cases illustrate that it is not easy to find an efficient trade-off between endogenous and exogenous transaction costs. In a world consisting of many countries, the efficient trade-off is achieved via rivalry between different governments which experiment with different institutions. War, economic and political competition, and free migration between countries then creates pressure to mimic competitive institutions.

One more example of the trade-off between endogenous and exogenous transaction costs in relation to coordination reliability is provided by a comparison of a piece rate wage system versus an hourly wage (Cheung, 1983, Milgrom and Roberts, 1992). If the quantity and quality of the job to be done can be precisely measured, a piece rate wage can be used to specify and enforce contractual terms and thereby reduce the risk of coordination failure of the network of division of labor. However, precise measurement of the quantity and quality of the job may involve prohibitively high exogenous transaction costs. If these costs are taken into account, an hourly wage with more vague contractual terms and with low exogenous transaction costs may be more efficient than a piece rate wage, despite the fact that the former generates much higher endogenous transaction costs than the latter.

In addition to the trade-off between the two types of transaction cost, there is also a trade-off between the benefits of competition and economies of division of labor. When the level of division of labor and the number of professions are increased, the number of specialist producers in each occupation declines for a given population size and therefore the extent of competition will decrease. The number of specialists positively contributes to the coordination reliability of division of labor. When there are many peer specialists in a profession, each buyer of the produce of the specialists can raise the coordination reliability of transactions by exploiting competition between the peer specialists. If coordination with a particular specialist seller failed, the buyer could shift to another peer specialist. As the development of division of labor reduces the number of peer specialists in each profession, the risk of coordination failure of division of labor rises. Therefore, there is a trade-off between economies of division of labor and the benefits of competition.

In this chapter we consider all of the interesting trade-offs and analyze how the market efficiently balances these through interactions between self-interested decisions. In section 16.2, we use a simplified version of the Yang–Wills model to study the trade-off between economies of division of labor and reliability. Then, we introduce the trade-off between endogenous and exogenous transaction costs in section 16.3. Finally, we consider the trade-offs between economies of division of labor and the benefit of competition, and between transaction costs incurred in broadening potential trade relationships and those incurred in deepening incumbent trade relations.

---

### *Questions to Ask Yourself when Reading this Chapter*

♦  What is the trade-off between endogenous and exogenous transaction costs?

♦  What is the trade-off between exogenous transaction costs in deepening incumbent relationships and exogenous transaction costs in expanding potential relationships?

♦  What are the implications of the trade-off between economies of division of labor and various transaction costs, in addition to the above two trade offs, for the equilibrium level of division of labor and productivity?

♦  Why can competition in the market substitute for precise specification and enforcement of property rights? Why might perfect competition and perfectly specified and enforced property rights not be efficient if the trade-offs among various endogenous and exogenous transaction costs and economies of division of labor are taken into account?

♦  How does the market sort out the efficient degree of competition, the efficient degree of vagueness in specifying and enforcing property rights, and the efficient level of division of labor?

## ◆ 16.2 Trade-offs among Economies of Division of Labor, Coordination Reliability, and the Benefits of Competition

We use a simplified version of the Yang–Wills model (1990) to tell the story discussed in the introductory section.

### Example 16.1: a simplified version of the Yang–Wills model

Consider the model in example 11.1. We now introduce a transaction risk for each good purchased. The decision problem for a person selling good i is:

$$\text{Max:} \quad V_i \equiv Eu_i = u_i P_i + (1 - P_i)0 = u_i P_i \qquad \text{(expected utility)} \qquad (16.1)$$

$$\text{s.t.} \quad u_i = x_i(kx_r^d)^{n-1} x_j^{m-n} \qquad \text{(utility function)}$$
$$P_i = (1 - q^N)^{n-1} \qquad \text{(reliability of } n - 1 \text{ transactions)}$$
$$x_i + x_i^s = \text{Max } \{0, l_i - \alpha\}, x_j = \text{Max } \{0, l_j - \alpha\} \qquad \text{(production function)}$$
$$l_i + (m - n)l_j = 1 \qquad \text{(endowment constraint of time)}$$
$$p_i x_i^s = (n - 1)p_r x_r^d (1 - q^N)/(1 - q) \qquad \text{(budget constraint)}$$

where $x_i$, $x_i^s$, $x_j$, $n$, $P_i$, $l_i$, $l_j$ are decision variables, $q$, $k$, $M$, $m$, are parameters, $N = M/n$ is the number of sellers of each traded good in the market, which is determined by the population size parameter $M$ and each person's number of traded goods $n$. $p_i$ is the price of good i, which is a parameter for the decision-maker in the Walrasian regime.

When uncertainty is present, a decision-maker maximizes her expected utility, $Eu_I$, which is a weighted average of $u_i$ and 0, where the weights are $P_i$ and $1 - P_i$, respectively. Let us examine the difference in specification between this model and the new classical models in the previous chapters.

The Cobb–Douglas utility function $u_i$ is the same as in the previous chapters. We have used the symmetry of that model, that is, tastes and production and transaction conditions are the same for all goods. Hence, the amounts of goods purchased, $x_r^d$, are the same for all $r$, the amounts of self-provided goods, $x_j$, and the amounts of labor allocated to the production of nontraded goods, $l_j$, are the same for all $j$. However, coordination reliability of division of labor $P_i$, which is the probability that all goods purchased by a person selling good i are received, is new. $q$ is the probability that the individual fails to receive a good from a purchase contract. The risk of coordination failure may be caused by traffic accidents or other stochastic events. That risk may also be caused by opportunistic behavior, as discussed in chapters 9 and 10. For this case, $q$ can be interpreted as the anticipated risk of coordination failure caused by opportunism. In the alternating-offer bargaining game of example 9.6, where players compete for the advantage of the first mover, there is a probability at which mutually beneficial gains to trade cannot be realized. The risk of coordination failure $q$ in this chapter can be interpreted as that probability as well.

$N$ is the number of individuals selling a traded good. In the symmetric model $N = M/n$, where $M$ is the population size and $n$ is the number of traded goods. Since the probability of an individual failing to receive a traded good from its seller is $q$, and since she can turn to any one of the $N$ sellers of the good, the probability of her failing to receive the traded good from all $N$ sellers is $q^N$. Therefore, $1 - q^N$ is the probability that at least one of the $N$ sellers delivers the good to the buyer. Here, the failure of a seller to deliver the good to the buyer is assumed to be an event that is independent of the failure of any of the other sellers to deliver. $q$ is assumed to be a given parameter. In the next section, $q$ is assumed to be a decision variable that is determined by the labor used to specify and enforce contractual terms.

The production functions in (16.1) are the same as in the previous chapters. $\alpha$ is a fixed learning cost in each activity, $l_i$ and $l_j$ are respectively the levels of specialization in producing the traded good i and the nontraded goods j.

The budget constraint in (16.1) differs from that of the models in the previous chapters. It is assumed that each buyer pays $p_r x_r^d$ according to the prevailing market price and the quantity that she orders. At probability $q$ she cannot receive the ordered quantity, so that she must turn to the second seller, where again the probability of failure is $q$, and again pay the amount $p_r x_r^d$. The expected payment is thus $q p_r x_r^d$. Hence, the buyer has to turn to the third seller at probability $q^2$, at which both the first and second sellers fail to deliver, and pays the same amount again. The expected payment is $q^2 p_r x_r^d$. Repeating this calculation, we can work out the buyer's expected total payment for a traded good that is sold by $N$ individuals

$$p_r x_r^d S = p_r x_r^d (1 + q + q^2 + \cdots + q^{N-1}) \tag{16.2}$$

where $S$ is calculated as follows. Multiplying the two sides of the identity $S \equiv 1 + q + q^2 + q^3 + \dots + q^{N-1}$ by $q$ yields $qS = q + q^2 + q^3 + \dots + q^N$. Abstracting $qS$ from $S$ yields $(1-q)S = 1 - q^N$ from which $S = (1 - q^N)/(1 - q)$ can be solved. Inserting the expression for $S$ back in (16.2), we can express the expected expenditure on a good purchased as $p_r x_r^d (1 - q^N)/(1 - q)$. The total expected expenditure on $n - 1$ goods that are purchased is therefore $(n - 1)p_r x_r^d (1 - q^N)/(1 - q)$. It is assumed that there is no risk on the side of seller, so that each seller can always receive payment for the goods ordered by a buyer and the individual, as a seller of good i, has income $p_i x_i^s$. Hence, the budget constraint is specified as in (16.2).

We call the budget constraint that takes account of the risk associated with payment the soft budget constraint. The degree of softness is determined by $(1 - q^N)/(1 - q)$. If the income risk were also specified, the soft budget constraint would be more realistic. The degree of softness decreases with the number of sellers of each traded good, $N = M/n$, or increases with the level of division of labor $n$. This implies that the budget constraint will be increasingly soft as the level of division of labor increases.

Assume that prices are sorted out through a Nash bargaining mechanism which generates the same utility between *ex ante* identical individuals who have the same disagreement point. This establishes the utility equalization conditions which, together with the market clearing conditions, will generate the same equilibrium as in a Walrasian regime. The equilibrium has equal prices of all traded goods and an equal number of sellers for each traded good, $N = M/n$, because of symmetry. With these results, the equilibrium values of decision variables can be solved as follows.

For any $i = 1, 2 \cdots, n$                   (16.3)

$x_i = x_r^d = x_j = [1 - \alpha(m - n + 1)]/m \qquad \forall\, r \in R, j \in J$

$x_i^s = (n - 1)[1 - \alpha(m - n + 1)]/m$

$l_i = \alpha + (n/m)[1 - \alpha(m - n + 1)]$

$P_i = (1 - q^N)^{n-1}$

$$V = Eu_i = \{1 - \alpha(m - n + 1)/m\}^m[k(1 - q)]^{n-1}$$
$$n = m + 1 - (1/\alpha)[k \ln(1 - q)]^{-1}.$$

If we define reliability of each transaction as $r \equiv 1 - q$, then the inframarginal comparative statics of the general equilibrium are:

$$dn/dr > 0, \quad dn/dq < 0, \quad dn/dk > 0 \tag{16.4a}$$
$$dP/dq = (\partial P/\partial q) + (\partial P/\partial n)(dn/dq) < 0, \text{ iff } \partial P/\partial q < |(\partial P/\partial n)(dn/dq)| \tag{16.4b}$$
$$dP/dk = (dP/dn)(dn/dk) < 0 \tag{16.4c}$$
$$dV/dr = \partial V/\partial r > 0, \quad dV/dk = \partial V/\partial k > 0. \tag{16.4d}$$
$$dl_i/dr = (dl_i/dn)(dn/dr) > 0, \quad dl_i/dk = (dl_i/dn)(dn/dk) > 0, \tag{16.4e}$$
$$dx_i^s/dr = (dx_i^s/dr)(dn/dr) > 0, \quad dx_i^s/dk = (dx_i^s/dn)(dn/dk) > 0 \tag{16.4f}$$
$$dN/dr = (dN/dn)(dn/dr) < 0, \quad dN/dk = (dN/dn)(dn/dk) > 0. \tag{16.4g}$$

(16.4a) implies that the equilibrium level of division of labor increases as the reliability of each transaction increases, or as the anticipated risk of coordination failure of each transaction caused by endogenous transaction costs falls. (16.4b) implies that as the risk of each transaction falls, total reliability $P$ would fall too if the negative effect of the fall in $q$, $\partial P/\partial q < 0$, outweighs its positive effect $(\partial P/\partial n)(\partial n/\partial q) > 0$. Otherwise, total reliability rises. Here, $\partial P/\partial n < 0$, $dn/dq < 0$. Since $1 - P$ can be considered as aggregate risk of coordination failure caused by anticipated endogenous transaction costs, (16.4b) can be interpreted in another way. It means that total endogenous transaction costs in terms of the aggregate risk increase as the endogenous transaction costs for each transaction fall, if the positive effect of the fall on the total endogenous transaction costs through its impact on the number of transactions outweigh its direct negative effect on total endogenous transaction costs. Otherwise, total endogenous transaction costs decrease with the endogenous transaction costs for each transaction. Because of the connection between total endogenous transaction costs and the degree of softness of the budget constraint, this result implies that the budget constraint may become increasingly soft as the endogenous transaction cost for each transaction falls.

(16.4c) implies that as the exogenous transaction cost coefficient, $1 - k$, is reduced, or as transaction efficiency $k$ rises, total endogenous transaction costs $1 - P$, or the risk of coordination failure, increase (or aggregate reliability $P$ falls). This is because, as exogenous transaction efficiency is improved, the benefit of increasing division of labor rises in comparison to increasing endogenous and exogenous transaction costs, so that total endogenous transaction costs may increase to the degree that the increased endogenous transaction cost is outweighed by the increased economies of division of labor that are exploited.

(16.4d) means that as endogenous transaction costs for each transaction fall (or as the coordination reliability for each transaction rises), or as exogenous transaction efficiency is improved, expected real income $V$ goes up. We have used the envelope theorem to get this result.

(16.4e) to (16.4g) imply that as the reliability of each transaction $r$ rises, or as exogenous transaction efficiency $k$ is improved, each individual's level of specialization and per capita trade volume all go up. Because of economies of specialization, the result implies that the labor productivity of each traded good goes up and the degree of self-sufficiency falls.

(16.4h) implies that as the reliability of each transaction $r$ goes up (or as the anticipated endogenous transaction costs for each transaction fall), or as exogenous transaction efficiency is improved, the number of sellers of each traded good, which represents the degree of competition, goes down. This results in a fall of aggregate reliability and a rise in total anticipated endogenous transaction costs.

The model can be used to criticize the notion of perfect competition and market failure. According to this model, the trade-off between utilization of economies of division of labor and utilization of the benefits of competition implies that perfect competition with an infinitely large $N$ is not efficient. An increase in $N$, the number of sellers of each traded good, will reduce total endogenous transaction costs $1 - P = 1 - (1 - q^N)^{n-1}$. If $N$ is infinitely large, $q^N = 0$, or $1 - q^N = 1$, $1 - P = 0$, which means that total endogenous transaction costs, or the aggregate risk of coordination failure, are 0. However, this is at the cost of decreasing the level of division of labor, $n = M/N$. The total endogenous transaction costs $1 - P$ relate to the distortions caused by externalities in the soft budget constraint, and public goods. Our model shows that the complete elimination of such "distortions" is not efficient since they can be completely eliminated only in autarky where economies of division of labor cannot be exploited.

The model can be used to explain why the efficient aggregate risk of coordination failure of division of labor rises as transaction efficiency is improved and division of labor evolves. There is a risk of mass unemployment too. $1 - P$ is the aggregate risk of coordination failure of the network of division of labor. As exogenous transaction efficiency $k$, or as anticipated endogenous transaction efficiency $r$, is improved, the equilibrium level of division of labor and related aggregate risk of coordination failure $1 - P$ go up. As soon as the coordination of the network of division of labor fails, each individual will be compelled to choose autarky with extremely low productivity, which looks like what happened in the Great Depression in the 1930s and in the depression in Russia in the early 1990s.

Figure 16.1 describes the trade-off between economies of division of labor and coordination reliability, where utility $u$ is converted to the expected utility $V$ through $n - 1$ links connected in series. That is, the expected utility is 0 if any of the links (consumption of a consumer good) is broken down. The reliability of each link, $1 - (1 - r)^N$, is an increasing function of $N = M/n$, while the aggregate reliability, $P = [1 - (1 - r)^N]^{n-1}$, is a decreasing function of $n$ and an increasing function of $r$, which is reliability for each transaction. For each link, there are $N$ sellers connected in parallel. The parallel connection (competition in each link) can raise total reliability of the series connection higher than the reliability of an individual transaction. That is, $1 - (1 - r)^N > r$ if $N > 1$. In the engineering literature, the parallel connection is used to raise the reliability of a system of series connections. The series connections will reduce aggregate reliability more than proportionally as the number of links rises.

In this chapter, we assume free choice between ocupation configurations, so that the

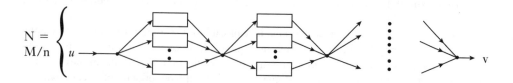

♦ **Figure 16.1:** Trade-off between economies of division of labor and coordination reliability in a system with series connection cum parallel connection

utility equalization conditions are established. We assume a free pricing system, so that the market clearing conditions are established. Under these assumptions, the degree of the softness of the budget constraint and the degree of competition are endogenously determined by interactions between self-interested decisions which result in efficient trade-offs among many conflicting forces. However, in a Soviet-style economy, individuals do not have freedom in choosing their occupation configurations and the pricing system is not free. The degree of competition and degree of the softness of the budget constraint are manipulated by a few government officials who pursue their own interest at the cost of society. They monopolize foreign trade, wholesale business, the distribution system, and the banking system and do not allow private entrepreneurs to enter the businesses. Hence, the resulting degree of softness of the budget constraint might be too great and the degree of competition might be too small compared to efficient levels.

This implies that the difference between a free market system and a Soviet-style economic system is a matter of how the degree of competition and the degree of softness of the budget constraint are determined, rather than a matter that the former has perfect competition and has no soft budget constraint while the latter has the opposite.

A more general version of the model with endogenous $q$ can be found in Yang and Wills (1990) or in Yang and Ng (1993, ch. 10). The endogenization of $q$ is a feature of the economic literature on the trade-off between economies of division of labor and coordination reliability that distinguishes this literature from the engineering literature on reliability.

## ◆ 16.3 Endogenization of Coordination Reliability in Each Transaction

### Example 16.2: the Yang and Wills model

In this section, we discuss the main results generated by the Yang and Wills model. The model has an endogenous degree of reliability of each transaction $r = 1 - q$, or an endogenous risk of coordination failure of each transaction, $q$, which can be interpreted as determined by anticipated endogenous transaction costs caused by opportunistic behavior. If an individual pays higher exogenous transaction costs in specifying and enforcing property rights and related contractual terms, the endogenous transaction costs and thereby the risk of coordination failure $q$ of each transaction can be reduced. Hence, $q$ becomes an individual's decision variable. From our experience of litigation (did you ever have such experience?), an increase in legal service fees paid to lawyers, a form of exogenous transaction costs, can raise the probability that our property rights are well protected. The damage caused by infringement of property rights can be considered a form of endogenous transaction cost. There is a trade-off between exogenous and endogenous transaction costs. The question of how the efficient trade-off between the two kinds of transaction costs can be achieved is the central question in the economics of property rights and institutional economics.

For instance, in a Soviet-style economy, the exogenous transaction costs associated with legal service fees are trivial. The income share of lawyers' earnings is very low. But endogenous transaction costs are extremely high because property rights are not well specified and enforced, so that individuals have no incentive to work hard, and the patterns of division of labor and resource allocation are distorted. Such endogenous transaction costs are not easy to measure directly. They can be indirectly measured from the long-run performance of the economy. In the US, the opposite situation prevails: exogenous transaction costs and the national income share of lawyers' earnings are high, whereas endogenous transaction costs are low because of much better specified and enforced property rights. In the US, individuals are more willing to work hard because of the much lower distortions in information transmission.

### 16.3.1 The Yang–Wills model endogenizing risk of coordination failure for each transaction

Because of the endogenization of $q$, the Yang and Wills model (1990) generates the following interesting results. As the parameter that represents efficiency in specifying and enforcing property rights is increased, the equilibrium level of division of labor and per capita real income go up, while the equilibrium degree of competition goes down. But two types of change in transaction reliability may take place in response to improvement in specification and enforcement efficiency. Individuals can either divert resources from specification and enforcement to raising the level of division of labor in production, or allocate the resources that are saved by the more effective specification and enforcement of rights to raising the degree of precision of the specification and enforcement of property rights in each transaction. These two responses are to some extent substitutes in raising per capita real income. If the first generates a greater net benefit than the second, an improvement in specification and enforcement efficiency will generate a lower reliability of each transaction and thereby a higher aggregate risk of coordination failure when it promotes division of labor. If the second method is better, then an improvement in specification and enforcement efficiency will raise the level of division of labor and the reliability of each transaction, meanwhile generating a higher or a lower aggregate risk of coordinate failure. Its effect on aggregate risk of coordination failure is parameter value dependent, since the positive effect of an increase in the number of transactions on the aggregate risk may or may not outweigh the negative effect of an increase in the reliability of each transaction.

In the model with endogenous risk of coordination failure of each transaction, if the transportation efficiency coefficient (which differs from the exogenous transaction efficiency coefficient in specifying and enforcing each contract) is increased, the equilibrium level of division of labor, productivity, and per capita real income all rise, while the equilibrium degree of reliability of each transaction and the degree of competition decrease. The inframarginal comparative statics of the general equilibrium explore very complicated relationships among the endogenous transaction costs of each transaction, exogenous transaction costs in specifying and enforcing property rights, exogenous transportation costs, aggregate endogenous transaction costs, and the level of division of labor. These sophisticated relationships imply that it is not efficient to entirely eliminate aggregate endogenous transaction costs that relate to distortions. The idea of eliminating all endogenous transaction costs is too naive to be realistic because it cannot explain why an hourly wage, which has a lower degree of precision in specifying and enforcing property rights than a piece rate wage, becomes more common than the piece rate wage as division of labor (commercialization) evolves.

It is impossible for the government to identify the efficient trade-offs among so many conflicting forces. It requires a *laissez-faire* regime, which allows individuals to choose freely among various structures of division of labor, institutions and contractual arrangements, to sort out the efficient trade-offs. The restriction of free choices among occupations and institutional configurations, and interference with free pricing, will paralyze the functioning of the market in sorting out the efficient trade offs.

## 16.3.2 The efficient extent of externalities

The results of the Yang–Wills model differ from the conventional wisdom of market failure which does not explain why markets do not exist for some commodities, for example, clean air and intangible information. The Yang–Wills model formalizes Cheung's argument (1983) that the determination of contractual forms is a matter of the degree of vagueness in specifying and enforcing property rights, or, in less illuminating words, the degree of externality. The difference between the externalities in buying a pound of oranges and buying clean air is a difference of degree rather than of substance. When people buy oranges, there are externalities resulting from vagueness in weighing oranges and in estimating their quality (Barzel, 1982). However, the equilibrium degree of vagueness in specifying and enforcing property rights is much lower for oranges than for clean air because there is much greater efficiency in specifying and enforcing property rights to oranges than to clean air.

The Yang–Wills model also formalizes Cheung's (1970) idea that a decentralized market based on a private property system will find an efficient extent of externality. According to Cheung, for some economic activities the costs of specifying and enforcing property rights are extremely high, so that the property rights cannot be practically delimited. Hence, no markets exist for such activities. The benefits and costs of such activities, not registered in markets, are commonly termed externalities. However, eliminating all such externalities is not efficient because of the costs of specifying and enforcing exclusive rights to property. The efficient extent of externality will balance the trade-off between the welfare loss caused by the absence of markets and the costs of specifying and enforcing the property rights required for markets.

Alternatively, a government may determine the appropriate trade-off between the welfare losses resulting from an externality and the costs of reducing it by a tax/subsidy scheme or by direct regulation. A positive economic analysis may compare the efficiencies of alternative economic systems in balancing this trade-off. Nevertheless, the role that the government can play in balancing the trade-off relates to political economics, constitutional economics, and the theory of public choice (Buchanan, 1975, 1989, 1991) which need more complicated new classical models to formalize. For instance, as Hayek argued, the government ownership of firms may create state opportunism because the government as the game rule maker, the referee, the rule enforcer, and a player cannot credibly commit to the rules because of interest conflict. Some historians argue that the absence of an overarching political power in Europe is essential for institutional experiments with the efficient balance of various complicated trade-offs. Intensive competition between governments of countries of nearly the same size in Europe, together with rivalry between the government and Church and free migration, creates pressure to enhance government capacity by striking an efficient balance of trade-offs and to mimic competitive institutions (Baechler, 1976, p. 79, McNeil, 1974, p.125, Hall, 1987, Mokyr, 1990, Jones, 1981, pp. 226–35, Braudel, 1984, pp. 128–9, Weber, quoted by MacFarlane, 1988, pp. 186–7, and Laslett, 1988, p. 235). This property rights approach to the problem of externalities is much more insightful than the theory of market failure, which attributes market inefficiencies to exogenously given externalities.

Efficiency in specifying and enforcing property rights is determined by both the legal system and technical conditions. For example, low efficiency in specifying and enforcing property rights in pre-reform China can be attributed to a legal system that restrained free trade in labor, land, and capital, while low efficiency in setting out and enforcing property rights to clean air is due to the high cost of the technology used to measure pollution.

### 16.3.3  Perfect competition is inefficient

The results of the Yang–Wills model formalize the trade-off between economies of specialization and transportation costs involved in additional transactions, the trade-off between economies of specialization and the use of labor to decrease vagueness in specifying and enforcing property rights in single transactions, and the trade-off between economies of specialization and the number of producers of each traded good, which contributes to the reliability of coordination in exchange. There are two kinds of cost of single transactions. The first is the cost borne by the buyer when the delivery fails to reach the destination. The second is the labor cost involved in less vague specification and enforcement of property rights. The first of these costs can be reduced either by increasing the number of sellers of each traded good, thereby sacrificing economies of specialization, or by less vague property rights, requiring an increase in the second type of cost.

A decentralized market will search for the efficient institutional arrangements defined by the degree of competition (related to the number of sellers of each traded good), the level of division of labor, the degree of risk of coordination failure of each transaction, and the aggregate risk of coordination failure of the entire network of division of labor in order to balance the trade-offs described above. Therefore, a decentralized market does not operate to completely eliminate the distortions which relate to $q$ and $1 - P$ and to maximize the number of sellers of each traded good, but rather determines the efficient numbers of sellers, so as to balance the trade-off between distortions and economies of specialization. Neoclassical microeconomics interprets Smith's invisible hand as a decentralized market that is capable of avoiding all distortions through so-called perfect competition (the number of sellers of each good is infinity) and a private property system in which there is no vagueness in specifying and enforcing property rights ($q = 1 - P = 0$). Yang and Wills have shown that this is a misinterpretation of Smith. The Yang–Wills model in this chapter can be used to provide a more appropriate interpretation of Smith. Conventional microeconomics formalizes the functions of a decentralized market in balancing two simple tradeoffs: a trade-off between quantities of different goods in raising utility and a trade-off between quantities of different factors in raising output or revenue. In the Yang–Wills model, the invisible hand balances trade-offs among increasing returns to specialization, distortions in trade, and transaction costs. It determines the efficient level of division of labor, the efficient distortion rate, the efficient degree of vagueness in specifying and enforcing property rights, and the efficient number of producers of each traded good. Here, the conjecture of the invisible hand is consistent with Smith's insight into the implications of the division of labor based on increasing returns to specialization for general welfare.

### 16.3.4  Risk of mass unemployment

Since an improvement in transaction efficiency will move the utility frontier closer to the production possibility frontier, a legal system that determines transaction efficiency has an impact on the equilibrium level of productivity. In terms of the comparative statics, there is a positive relationship between productivity progress and efficiency in specifying and enforcing property rights. However, the positive effects are not without costs. An increase in efficiency in specifying and enforcing property rights may increase both the equilibrium risk of coordination failure and productivity at the same time via raising the equilibrium level of division of labor. A high risk of coordination failure can be interpreted as a risk of mass unemployment, as all individuals will be forced to choose autarky when coordination of the division of labor breaks down. From (16.4) we can see that the equilibrium level of division of labor, $n$, and the equilibrium level of expected per capita real income, $V$, increase, and the equilibrium degree of aggregate reliability, $P$, decreases, as transaction efficiency increases. This implies that the probability of mass unemployment, productivity, and the level of division of labor may increase side by side as transaction efficiency is improved. The effective method of reducing the risk of mass unemployment is to increase the number of producers of each good. This method is analogous to increasing the number of elements in parallel connection to the working element in an electronic system with many components connected in series, which is in turn analogous to increasing the cash reserve rate in a federal reserve system. This method is not costless since such an increase will increase costs of parallel elements and decrease the level of specialization and productivity.

Yang (1984, pp. 394–413) conjectures that in a model with many final goods and intermediate sectors connected in series, a decentralized market will discover an efficient distribution of degrees of competition in different sectors. Yang used a simple example to argue that this distribution is crucial to the determination of the efficient balance of the trade-off between economies of specialization and coordination reliability in an economy with the division of labor in a long production chain. This conjecture may be verified by introducing into the model in this chapter many intermediate sectors connected in series. Models of this kind are useful for the analysis of a Soviet-style socialist economy where the central planner can manipulate the distribution of the degrees of competition in different sectors to pursue his interests at the cost of society. (Blanchard and Kremer (1997) provide an application of reliability theory to the analysis of transitional economies.) Such models may also be used to explain why competition is more intense in some sectors than in other sectors in a decentralized market. You might try to develop such a model.

### Example 16.3: a trade-off related to the institutions of the library and the university

The emergence of the institution of the university promotes a division of labor between the professional management of books (library) and the users of books (teachers and students). The emergence of professional libraries increases vagueness in specifying and enforcing rights to the knowledge generated by books. Before professional libraries were established, an individual had to buy a book if he wanted to utilize the knowledge in that book, since it was not easy to borrow many different books from other individuals. Since libraries have emerged, students can more easily borrow a book without any payment to its author. Even if students' tuition includes a payment for using a university library, the payment is not proportional to the frequency of book use, and does not go to the authors of the books. This implies that rights to authors' knowledge are more vaguely specified and enforced in a library system than in a book market without the institution of the library. However, the system with libraries will be the equilibrium as long as the benefits generated by the division of labor between professional libraries and other sectors outweigh the utility loss generated by the higher level of vagueness in specifying and enforcing the rights to intellectual property.

Nevertheless, a new institutional arrangement that charges for each use of a book in a library could be combined with copyright laws to increase the level of the division of labor and decrease the level of vagueness in specifying and enforcing rights to intellectual property at the same time, if magnetic cards and a computer system were effectively employed to monitor and collect the required payments. Such arrangements emerged in some North European countries in the 1980s. Intuitively, it would seem that the slight improvement in transaction efficiency due to the emergence of professional libraries increases both the equilibrium level of division of labor and the equilibrium degree of vagueness in specifying and enforcing property rights because this slight improvement is insufficient to allow both an increase in the level of division of labor and a decrease in vagueness at the same time. By contrast, the emergence of a system that charges for each use of a book, together with copyright laws, magnetic cards, and the computer system, will significantly improve transaction efficiency in specifying and enforcing authors' rights to knowledge in books, so that the level of division of labor increases and the degree of vagueness in specifying and enforcing property rights decreases, resulting in a significant increase in productivity and welfare.

### 16.3.5 The economics of property rights and the soft budget constraint

If the CES utility or production function is introduced, the evolution in the division of labor will be associated with the emergence of new goods and related new technology. As new technology emerges from the evolution of division of labor, the rights to use, transfer, and appropriate earnings from a property may be separable from the materials that carry the property. For instance, knowledge in a book is a property that can be separated from the book. An individual can use the property without paying for the knowledge if he borrows this book. Music in a tape is a property that can be separated from the tape. An individual can use and transfer the property without paying for it if he copies the tape from his friend or records the music from radio. As new technology develops enabling the separation of a property from the materials that carry it, trading of the rights to use, transfer, and appropriate that property is more important than trade in the related materials.

As defined by Furubotn and Pejovich (1974, ch. 1), the economics of property rights is the study of the trade in property rights rather than the trade in goods which carry property rights. The property rights approach would be similar to the traditional approach if a property could not be separated from the materials that carry it, since the trading of property rights is the same as the trading of the materials in this case. If the separation is possible, then the property rights approach will be substantially different from the traditional one. Traditional economics considers this kind of problem as one involving externalities resulting from non-exclusivity. But for the economics of property rights, the degree of "externalities" is not exogenous as in traditional economics, but rather is endogenously determined in an economic system. For instance, there were many "externalities" in activities that generated inventions prior to the introduction of patent laws. These laws have substantially reduced such "externalities." The extent of "externalities" is determined by property rights and related contractual arrangements, which can be chosen by individuals. There is a trade-off between the distortions generated by "externalities" and the costs of reducing them, so that eliminating all "externalities" is not efficient even though individuals can choose a level of "externality" or of vagueness of property rights.

Kornai (1980) surmises that economic development, which involves increases in productivity and in the level of division of labor, will in general make budget constraints increasingly soft, which means that they are increasingly less binding due to, for instance, more loans with soft terms. Since vagueness in specifying and enforcing property rights affects the real budget constraint, the concept of softness of the budget constraint is related to the concept of vagueness in specifying and enforcing property rights. If we interpret Kornai's concept of softness of the budget constraint as relating to the aggregate risk of losing property rights, or risk of coordination failure $1 - P$, Kornai's conjecture can be confirmed. (16.4) indicates that an increase in transaction efficiency $k$ will raise the level of division of labor, $n$, expected per capita real income, $V$, and the aggregate risk of losing property rights, $1 - P$. Yang and Wills (1990) have shown that as the risk of losing property rights in each transaction, $q$, is endogenized, Kornai's conjecture may not hold within some parameter subspace.

If transaction efficiency in specifying and enforcing property rights differs across goods, then both the number of traded goods and the composition of trade are important to determining equilibrium.

## Example 16.4: why markets for some goods do not exist

We consider the model in example 16.1 again. We now assume that there are only three goods ($m = 3$) and transaction risk is $q_i$ for good i. For simplicity, we abstract from effects of the number of sellers of a good on reliability. This is equivalent to the assumption $N = 1$ in example 16.1. Then only two out of the three goods are traded in equilibrium if transaction risk is neither too high nor too low. The expected utility for a person selling good i and buying good r is

$$V = x_i x_r^d x_j (1 - q_r).$$

She maximizes $x_i$, $x_r^d$, $x_j$, $q_r$, $x_i^s$, $l_i$, $l_j$, subject to $p_i x_i^s = p_r x_r^d$, $x_i + x_i^s = \text{Max}\{0, l_i - \alpha\}$, $x_j = \text{Max}\{0, l_j - \alpha\}$, $l_i + l_j = 1$, where good j is not traded, good i is sold, and good r is purchased. The budget constraint is different from the one in example 16.1. Here, we assume that a buyer does not pay for a good that she orders if she has not received it. The optimum decision is:

$$l_i = (2 - \alpha)/3, \qquad l_j = (1 + \alpha)/3, \qquad x_i = x_j = x_i^s = (1 - 2\alpha)/3,$$

$$x_r^d = p_i x_i^s / p_r, \qquad V_i = [(1 - 2\alpha)/3]^3 (1 - q_r) p_i / p_r.$$

Letting $V_i = V_r$, we can find the equilibrium relative price $p_i/p_r = [(1 - q_i)/(1 - q_r)]^{0.5}$ and expected per capita real income $V(ir) = [(1 - 2\alpha)/3]^3 (1 - q_r)^{0.5} (1 - q_i)^{0.5}$ when only goods i and r are traded. Similarly, we can show that the corner equilibrium expected real income in the complete division of labor is $V(irj) = [(1 - \alpha)/3]^3 (1 - q_r)^{1/3} (1 - q_i)^{1/3} (1 - q_j)^{1/3}$, which is smaller than $V(ir)$ if $q_j$ is sufficiently close to 0.

It is straightforward that the corner equilibrium per capita real income is greater when goods i and r are traded than when goods i and j or goods r and j are traded, if and only if $q_i$, $q_r < q_j$. According to the Yao theorem, this implies that it is goods i and r that are traded if only two out of the three goods are traded in equilibrium.

This establishes the proposition that the market for good j does not exist in equilibrium if the transaction risk for this good is too high, or if the transaction efficiency in specifying and enforcing property rights to this good is too low. In other words, the development of exchange for a certain good depends crucially on the efficiency in specifying and enforcing property rights to this good. Hence, the absence of the market for some goods is a consequence of the efficient trade-off between economies of division of labor and various transaction costs. Externality caused by the absence of the market is efficiently and endogenously determined in the market.

Here, the distinction should be drawn between non-exclusivity and nonrivalry of goods when we analyze endogenous externality. *Nonrivalry* is a technical property of goods. It implies that use of a good by a person does not prevent another person from using the same good. In other words, a good is nonrival if its production and/or consumption involves only fixed costs but no variable costs. A TV program is a nonrival good since the cost of its production and consumption do not increase with the number of its viewers. There is only a fixed production cost. Hence, nonrivalry implies significant increasing returns. This does not necessarily imply non-exclusivity, which is determined endogenously by institutions. If transaction efficiency in specifying and enforcing property rights to a nonrival good is very high, then in equilibrium, individuals will choose to specify in detail and enforce property rights, so that nonrivalry does not cause externality.

### Example 16.5: nonrivalry and non-exclusivity of TV programs

The example of a TV program illustrates the distinction between nonrivalry and non-exclusivity. A TV program is a commodity with nonrivalry. When a person watches a TV program at her home, it does not prevent others from watching the same program at their homes. The number of viewers of the same program can be very large. If the owner of the copyright of the TV program had very low costs for monitoring the consumption of the TV program at each person's home, she could extract a fee for each viewing of the program by each person. If somebody refused to pay, she could take legal action against him. But in reality, we never see such institutional arrangements, not because it is impossible, but because the monitoring costs are prohibitively high. Hence, the efficient trade-off between the transaction costs in specifying and enforcing property rights and the distortions caused by imprecise specification and enforcement results in free TV programs. This implies that TV programs are endogenously chosen as non-exclusive commodities. The *non-exclusivity* implies externality and related distortions. However, the degree of externality is endogenously chosen by individuals and the invisible hand (interactions between self-interested decisions).

The functioning of the market in handling distortions caused by externalities is much more sophisticated than described in neoclassical economics textbooks. For the case of the TV program, there is a multilateral trade among three parties: the owner of the copyright of the program, the viewers of the program who are buyers of other tangible goods, and the sellers of the tangible goods. A one-way trading chain may reduce the distortions caused by the non-exclusivity of the program. The sellers of the tangible goods make money by selling the goods to viewers of the program. The producer of the program makes money from selling advertising time to the sellers of the tangible goods, while the viewers obtain utility from freely viewing the program. This one-way trade triangle generates distortions by forcing viewers to watch advertisements that they may not want to see. But it saves on exogenous transaction costs for the producer of the TV program, who would otherwise have to directly collect payment from the viewers, thereby reducing externalities caused by the non-exclusivity of the program.

Compared to the cable TV system, the open TV system generates more distortions because of the inaccurate correspondence between the amount of payment of viewers and the amount of TV consumed by them, and by forcing viewers to see those advertisements that they do not like. The cable TV system causes much less endogenous transaction cost of this kind. But the open TV system saves on exogenous transaction costs caused by deploying cable and collecting fees. As discussed in chapter 10, the market will efficiently trade-off economies of division of labor against endogenous and exogenous transaction costs to determine the efficient degree of externality. If the total endogenous and exogenous transaction cost is nearly the same between the open TV system and the cable TV system, they may coexist in a competitive market.

The Yang–Wills model does not consider another trade-off, that between exogenous transaction costs in deepening the incumbent relationship and exogenous transaction costs in broadening potential relationships. This trade-off relates to the substitution between more precise specification and enforcement of incumbent contractual terms, and more competition pressure from potential partners. In the next section, a general equilibrium model is developed to explore the implications of this substitution.

## ◆ 16.4 Substitution between Precise Enforcement of Property Rights and Competition

In an economy with risk of coordination failure in each transaction, there are two ways to reduce such risk or to reduce the endogenous transaction costs in each transaction. The first is to allocate more resources to reducing the risk of coordination failure of each incumbent transaction. The second is to allocate more resources to cultivating more potential relationships which are in parallel connection with an incumbent relationship. This will increase the number of parallel connections for each incumbent transaction and reduce the risk of coordination failure of the transaction. In other words, extensive public relationships with many potential partners yields competitive pressure on the incumbent partner, so that the individual can turn to one of the potential partners when the incumbent one fails to deliver what the person needs. Mathematically, the reliability of each transaction $1 - q^N$ can be raised either by reducing the risk of coordination failure with the incumbent partner, $q \in (0, 1)$, or by increasing the number of potential partners, $N$. Here, $q^N$ is the total risk of coordination failure when there are potential trade partners.

However, there are exogenous transaction costs in keeping $N$ potential relationships. In the Yang–Wills model (1990), such transaction costs in cultivating and keeping the potential relationships are not considered, so that the number of incumbent and potential sellers of each good that a person keeps in touch with is the same as the number of all sellers of the good in the market. However, for a nontrivial transaction cost in keeping such a potential relationship, each person's efficient number of potential sellers of a good may be smaller than the number of all sellers of the good in the market. In this section, we develop a model that endogenizes the number of sellers of a good with whom a buyer keeps in touch.

### Example 16.6: a new classical equilibrium model with a trade-off between deepening the incumbent relationship and broadening potential relationships

The model is the same as in chapter 11 except that there are only two consumption goods and each buyer has a risk of failing to receive the good she buys. The risk may be caused by a transportation accident when the good she orders is delivered, or by some anticipated opportunistic behavior. If each of $M$ *ex ante* identical consumer-producers chooses autarky, then there is no risk of coordination failure. An individual's decision problem in autarky is

Max: $U = xy$ (utility function)

s.t. $x = $ Max $\{0, l_x - \alpha\}$ (production function of x)
$y = $ Max $\{0, l_y - \alpha\}$ (production function of y)
$l_x + l_y = 1$ (endowment constraint of time)

where $x, y, l_x,$ and $l_y$ are decision variables. The per capita real income in this structure is

$U_A = [(1 - 2\alpha)/2]^2.$

The decision problem for a specialist producer of good x is

Max: $Ux = xy^d P$ (utility function)

s.t. $x + x^s = $ Max $\{0, l_x - \alpha\}$ (production function)
$p_x x^s = p_y y^d$ (budget constraint)
$l_c = cN$ (labor cost of public relationship)
$l_s = sr$ (labor cost for each incumbent relation)
$l_x + l_c + l_s = 1$ (endowment constraint of time)
$P = 1 - (1 - r)^N$ (total coordination reliability)

where $x, x^s, y^d, N, P, l_x, l_c, l_s, r$ are decision variables. $c$ is the cost coefficient for the specialist of x to keep in touch with a seller of y. This may be interpreted as the cost of making a phone call to a potential seller to make sure of the availability of the required delivery, or as the cost of cultivating a relationship with the seller. A restriction on free choice of trade partners, such as those institutional arrangements in a Soviet-style economic system which prohibits individuals from trading land and capital goods, will increase $c$ to a very large value, so that the optimum choice of $N$ will be at its minimum, 1. Hence, $N$ represents the endogenous degree of competition and $l_c$ is the total labor cost of broadening public relationships.

  $s$ is the cost coefficient for the specialist producer of x to increase the degree of reliability of the incumbent relationship. This can be interpreted as the costs of specifying and enforcing contractual terms with the incumbent partner. Hence, $l_s$ is the total labor cost in deepening the incumbent relationship. For the models in the previous chapters, a small number of incumbent producers for each good does not necessarily incur distortions within our framework. However, uncertainties in trade may make the number of suppliers of a good an important determinant of the risk of coordination failure from the complex exchange interdependencies associated with the division of labor. To reduce such risk, a buyer of a good may maintain relationships with many suppliers, or alternatively she may increase the precision of the terms stipulated in a contract with the incumbent supplier. The former method of reducing a risk of coordination failure relates to transaction costs in delimiting rights to contracting, or $l_s$, and the latter relates to transaction costs in specifying and enforcing the terms of a contract, or $l_c$. If we draw the distinction between rights specified in a contract and rights to contracting, we may specify a trade-off between the two kinds of transaction costs and the substitution between increasing competition, which relates to $l_c$, and increasing accuracy in specifying and enforcing the terms of a contract, which relates to $l_s$.

An example is the decision problem faced by an assistant professor who holds a tenure track position. For her given ability and effort and the quality of the match with her incumbent employer, it is uncertain whether the employer will grant tenure to the employee even if she is qualified, and whether the employee will meet the terms of the contract even if the employer treats her fairly. To reduce the risk of being treated unfairly the employee may spend time negotiating and enforcing the terms of the contract. Alternatively, she may spend time keeping in touch with potential alternative employers in order to reduce the risk of losing her job. Similarly, the employer may hire several tenure track employees for one tenured position, or spend resources specifying and enforcing the terms of a contract. The question is: what is the efficient balance of the trade-off between the two alternative uses of resources to reduce the total risk of coordination failure? The efficient balance is crucial for the determination of the efficient level of division of labor that balances, in turn, the trade-off between economies of specialization and various transaction costs.

The trade-off between the two kinds of transaction cost relates to the trade-off, described by Williamson, between relational costs incurred in mitigating the hazards of opportunism and transaction costs incurred in stipulating detailed contingent contracts (Williamson, 1985). The public relations cost function, and the specification and enforcement cost function of each incumbent relationship in this section, formalize Williamson's idea. It will be clear later that for a small value of the relation cost coefficient, "classical contracts" associated with many potential trade partners (similar to perfect competition) may occur at equilibrium. For a large value of the relation cost coefficient, "relational contracts" without potentially alternative trade partners may occur at equilibrium.

Each buyer of good y receives that she orders from a seller of y. She keeps in touch with $N$ sellers of y and can turn to one of them if the incumbent seller fails to deliver the good according to the timing and quality that she requires. Reliability of each seller is $r$, or each seller has a risk of coordination failure $1 - r$. Hence, the total risk of the buyer failing to receive good y when she keeps in touch with $N$ incumbent and potential sellers is $(1 - r)^N$, or the aggregate reliability of her receiving $y^d$ is $P = 1 - (1 - r)^N$. You may interpret $P$ as the probability that the transaction efficiency coefficient is 1 and $1 - P = (1 - r)^N$ as the probability that the transaction efficiency coefficient is 0. The solution of the decision problem yields not only demand and supply functions for x and y, but also the optimum number of potential partners, $N$, with whom a buyer should keep in touch, the optimum risk of coordination failure of each relationship $1 - r$, and the optimum aggregate coordination reliability $P$ or optimum aggregate risk of coordination failure $1 - P$.

The decision problem for a specialist producer of y is symmetric to that for a specialist producer of x.

Max: $U_y = yx^dP$         (utility function)

s.t. $y + y^s = l_y - \alpha$         (production function of y)
    $p_y y^s = p_x x^d$         (budget constraint)
    $l_c = cN$         (labor cost of public relationship)
    $l_s = sr$         (labor cost of each incumbent relation)
    $l_y + l_c + l_s = 1$         (endowment constraint of time)
    $P = 1 - (1 - r)^N$         (aggregate coordination reliability)

where $y$, $x^d$, $y^s$, $N$, $P$, $l_y$, $l_c$, $l_s$, $r$ are decision variables.

Structure D is a division of $M$ individuals between the two occupations. Using the symmetry of the model, we can show that the corner equilibrium relative price of two goods $p_x/p_y = 1$ and the corner equilibrium numbers of two types of specialists are $M_x = M_y = M/2$ in Structure D. Also, in the corner equilibrium, the number of trade partners with whom each individual keeps in touch, $N$, the reliability of the incumbent relationship, $r$, and the labor allocation between broadening public relationships and deepening the incumbent relationship are all the same for the two types of specialists. Hence, the corner equilibrium expected utility is $(1 - cN - sr - \alpha - x^s)x^s P = (1 - cN - sr - \alpha - y^s)y^s P$, where the corner equilibrium values of $x^s$ and $y^s$ are $0.5(1 - cN - sr - \alpha)$. Therefore, the corner equilibrium $r$ and $N$ are given by maximizing $[1 - (1 - r)^N](1 - cN - sr - \alpha)^2/4$ with respect to $N$ and $r$. The first-order conditions yield

$$2c(1 - cN - sr - \alpha) = -(1 - r)^N \ln(1 - r) \tag{16.5a}$$

$$N = -\frac{s}{c}(1 - r)\ln(1 - r). \tag{16.5b}$$

There are multiple solutions of (16.5). Also (16.5) does not apply to the several possible corner solutions of $r$ and $N$. Hence, an analytical solution of the comparative statics of the corner equilibrium cannot be obtained.

Table 16.1 reports part of the computer simulation results of the comparative statics of the corner equilibrium reliability of each transaction, $r$, the number of trade partners with whom each person keeps in touch (degree of competition), $N$, and aggregate reliability $P$ in Structure D. It shows that if $s$ is sufficiently small, then the corner equilibrium value of $r$ is 1, its maximum, so that the equilibrium values of $N$ and $P$ are 1 too; if $c$ is too large, the corner equilibrium value of $N$ is 1, its minimum; as $s$ increases relative to $c$, the corner equilibrium value of $r$ falls and the corner equilibrium value of $N$ increases. This implies that as the cost of deepening the incumbent relationship increases in comparison to that in broadening potential relationships, the equilibrium degree of competition, $N$, increases and the equilibrium degree of reliability for the incumbent relationship, which relates to

**Table 16.1:** Equilibrium reliability and degree of competition

| $c$ | $s$ | $\alpha$ | $r$ | $N$ | $P$ |
|---|---|---|---|---|---|
|  | $\leq 0.05$ | 0.1 | 1 | 1 | 1 |
| 0.01 | 0.1 | 0.1 | 0.69 | 4 | 0.991 |
| $\geq 0.02$ | 0.1 | 0.1 | 1 | 1 | 1 |
| 0.01 | 0.2 | 0.1 | 0.43 | 6 | 0.966 |
| $\geq 0.02$ | 0.2 | 0.1 | 1 | 1 | 1 |
| 0.01 | 0.3 | 0.1 | 0.33 | 8 | 0.959 |
| 0.02 | 0.3 | 0.1 | 0.46 | 5 | 0.954 |
| 0.03 | 0.3 | 0.1 | 0.57 | 4 | 0.966 |
| 0.04 | 0.3 | 0.1 | 0.69 | 3 | 0.97 |
| $\geq 0.05$ | 0.3 | 0.1 | 1 | 1 | 1 |
|  | $\geq 0.4$ | 0.1 |  | 1 | $r$ |

the degree of precision of contractual terms, decreases. An increase in the transaction cost coefficient in broadening potential relationships, $c$, has the opposite effects, decreasing the equilibrium degree of competition and increasing the reliability of the incumbent relationship.

The expected per capita real income in the structure with the division of labor is

$$U_D = [(1 - \alpha)/2]^2[1 - (1 - r)^N] \tag{16.6}$$

where $r = l_s/s$ and $N = l_c/c$ are given by the labor cost functions in deepening the incumbent relationship and in broadening potential relationships, respectively. $l_s$ and $l_c$ are each individual's decision variables. Applying the envelope theorem to (16.6), we can show that

$$dU_D/ds = \partial U_D/\partial s < 0 \text{ and } dU_D/dc = \partial U_D/\partial c < 0. \tag{16.7}$$

Since per capita real income in autarky is independent of $s$ and $c$, (16.7) implies that as $s$ or $c$ falls, it is more likely that the corner equilibrium in Structure D will be Pareto superior to that in autarky. According to the Yao theorem, this implies that as $s$ and/or $c$ falls, the general equilibrium will jump from autarky to the division of labor.

It is interesting to see from (16.7) and table 16.1 that an increase in $c$ increases total reliability and reduces $U_D$ at the same time within the parameter subspace $c > 0.02$, $s = 0.3$, $\alpha = 0.1$. This implies that as $c$ increases (more expensive for broadening potential relationships), $N$ decreases (see table 16.1). In compensation for a decrease in $N$, more labor is allocated to increase $r$ away from production, so that $P$ increases and $U_D$ decreases.

Figure 16.2 gives an intuitive illustration of different patterns of equilibrium market structure. In panel (a), a large transaction cost coefficient for broadening potential relationships, $c$, relative to the transaction cost coefficient for deepening the incumbent relationship, $s$, generates the equilibrium $N = 1$ in an economy with 4 individuals, so that the economy is fragmented into two separated local communities. There is division of labor and transactions within each of the local communities, but no interactions between the communities. In panel (b), a small transaction cost coefficient for broadening potential relationships relative to the transaction cost coefficient for deepening the incumbent

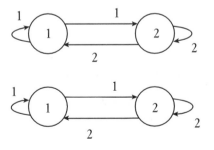

(a) Corner equilibrium $N = 1$

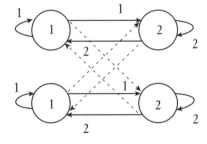

(b) Corner equilibrium $N = 2$

◆ **Figure 16.2:** Different degrees of competition in equilibrium relationship generates the equilibrium $N = 2$, so that each individual has one incumbent trade partner and keeps in touch with another potential partner to put pressure on the incumbent one. The economy is integrated as one market, though this degree of integration is not necessary for all incumbent trade relationships. Dashed lines denote possible trade between potential trade parners when the incumbent suppliers fail to deliver goods.

This model shows that there are two functions of the market. One is to execute exchanges. The other is to keep the pressure of competition on individuals in order to reduce the risk of coordination failure in exchanges. The second function may require a size of local market that is larger than required to complete all realized exchanges because each individual may keep in touch with some potential trade partners in order to put pressure on the incumbent trade partners, thereby reducing the risk of coordination failure. In the Yang and Wills model in the preceding section, the size of the market which relates to potential trade partners is the same as the size of the whole economy, although the size of a local community that is sufficient to accommodate all necessary exchanges between all local residents may be much smaller than the size of the whole economy. For instance, in that model if, due to a low transaction efficiency, the equilibrium number of traded goods is three, then three individuals can constitute a local community where each of them sells one good to and buys one good from each of the other individuals. But each individual may keep in touch with all other individuals in the economy in order to put pressure on her incumbent trade partners to reduce the risk of coordination failure. This market structure may not be efficient if the costs of maintaining contact with potential trade partners are nontrivial. The model developed in this section allows individuals to choose the number of potential trade partners such that the size of a local market which is defined by the number of incumbents as well as potential trade partners is endogenized.

One further aspect of economic organization is investigated in this chapter. It has been shown that the efficient number of potential and incumbent trade partners of each individual and the related degree of competition, the efficient degree of externality, and the extent of a local market will be chosen by the invisible hand which trades off economies of specialization against coordination reliability required by the network of division of labor and endogenous and exogenous transaction costs. Yang, Wang, and Wills (1992) test the theory in this chapter against China's data for 1979–87. The data set strongly supports the hypothesis that improvements in transaction efficiency in specifying and enforcing property rights will raise the level of division of labor and thereby increase productivity and per capita real income.

## Key Terms and Review

The trade-off between endogenous and exogenous transaction costs.

The trade-off between exogenous transaction costs in deepening the incumbent relationships and exogenous transaction costs in expanding potential relationships.

Implications of the trade-off between economies of division of labor and various transaction costs in addition to the above two trade-offs for the equilibrium level of division of labor and productivity.

Externality, public goods.

The relationships between nonrivalry, non-exclusivity, and public goods.

The difference between Pigou's marginal analysis of the distortions caused by externalities and public goods, and inframarginal analysis of those distortions (endogenous transaction costs).

Substitution between competition in the market and precise specification and enforcement of property rights.

Why perfect competition and perfectly specified and enforced property rights may not be efficient if the trade-offs among various endogenous and exogenous transaction costs and economies of division of labor are taken into account.

The connection between the softness of the budget constraint and vagueness in specifying and enforcing property rights.

The market mechanism to sort out the efficient degree of competition, the efficient degree of vagueness in specifying and enforcing property rights, and the efficient level of division of labor.

## Further Reading

*Trade-off between different kinds of transaction costs*: Cheung (1970, 1983), Milgrom and Roberts (1992), Yang and Y.-K. Ng (1993, chs. 10, 11), Yang and Wills (1990), Yang, Wang, and Wills (1992), Williamson (1967, 1985), Monteverde and Teece (1982); *economics of property rights and endogenous externality*: Chu and Wang (1998), Barzel (1989), Cheung (1969), Coase (1960), Demsetz (1967, 1988), Demsetz and Lehn (1985), Furubotn and Pejovich (1974), Manne (1975), North (1981), Buchanan (1975, 1989, 1991), North and Weingast (1989); *new political economy models with endogenous stealing*: Marcouiller and Young (1995), Skaperdas (1992); *soft budget constraint*: Kornai (1980, 1991), Qian (1994), Maskin and Xu (1999); *theory of reliability*: Shooman (1968), Sah and Stiglitz (1986, 1988, 1991), Sah (1991), Bazovsky (1961), Lange (1970), Blanchard and Kremer (1997), Kremer (1993); *historical evidence about the relationship between property rights and economic development*: MacFarlane (1988), E. Jones (1981), Baechler (1976), Rosenberg and Birdzell (1986), Mokyr (1990, 1993), Landes (1998); *empirical evidence for the relationship between better enforced property rights and economic development*: Barro (1997), Sachs and Warner (1995, 1997), Yang, Wang, and Wills (1992), Frye and Shleifer (1997).

# QUESTIONS

1   The automatic traffic light system can be used to save on the costs of hiring traffic policemen for manual control of traffic lights. But it causes endogenous transaction costs as well. The automatic traffic light system is not as flexible as a manually controlled system, so that it quite often wastes drivers' time in waiting for a green light. Technically, an ultrasound system for monitoring traffic conditions at each cross point can be used to reduce such endogenous transaction costs at the exogenous transaction costs of buying the ultrasound system. Discuss under what conditions (for instance, the salary of a policeman is low in a developing country, or technical progress could significantly reduce the price of the ultrasound system) acceptance of the endogenous transaction costs caused by the automatic traffic light system is efficient. Why is the term "externality" misleading for addressing endogenous transaction costs?

2   Before the patent laws were first introduced in Britain (Statute of Monopolies, 1624), invention of new technology involved substantial endogenous transaction costs in trading intellectual property. The patent laws significantly reduced such endogenous transaction costs at the cost of increasing the distortions caused by monopoly. Why are the terms "externality" and "spread-over effect of technical inventions" that are used to describe such endogenous transaction costs misleading?

3   In the earliest postal system in Britain, postal fees were accurately calculated according to the weight of the mail and the post distance in order to reduce the endogenous transaction costs caused by an inaccurate correspondence between fee and service provided. Analyze why that postal system was replaced with inaccurate measurement of the correspondence between fee and service based on postage stamps and pillar-boxes. Why is the term "externality" misleading for describing the various transaction costs involved in the postal system?

4    Use the new classical model of endogenous "externality" to formalize Coase's and Cheung's criticisms of Pigou's welfare analysis of externality and public goods. According to Cheung (1970, 1983) and Coase (1960), so-called externality is endogenously chosen by individuals in efficiently trading-off between endogenous and exogenous transaction costs, and if exogenous transaction costs in specifying and enforcing property rights are counted, keeping a certain degree of "externality" may be efficient. Also, inframarginal analysis across different structures of property rights is more appropriate than Pigou's marginal analysis of quantities and prices for a given economic structure. In other words, discontinuous jumps between corner solutions should be counted for a general equilibrium analysis of the trade-off between the benefits of trade and all kinds of transaction costs.

5    If the capital market is not developed, a government postal system can be used to develop the market for postal services. Why may the government postal system generate greater endogenous transaction costs than the market for private postal services if the capital market is developed? Some economists use the notion of network externality to justify a government monopoly in the market for postal services. Why may this notion be misleading?

6    The comparative statics of the equilibrium model in examples 16.6 can be used to identify the impact of the improvements in two kinds of transaction efficiency: efficiency in delimiting rights to contracting and efficiency in specifying and enforcing the terms of a contract. For instance, an improvement in transaction efficiency in delimiting rights to contracting may increase buyers' dependence on competition between peer suppliers of a good and reduce the equilibrium degree of precision in specifying and enforcing the terms of a contract. An improvement in efficiency in stipulating and enforcing a contract may have contrary effects, so that a buyer of a good will increase the precision of a contract rather than maintaining contacts with many potential suppliers of this good. Meanwhile, improvements in efficiency of either kind may enhance the equilibrium level of division of labor, trade dependence, and productivity. This model can also be used to analyze the structure of property rights in a Soviet-style economy. Economists are now realizing that equivocation in delimiting property rights under a state ownership system needs more attention than distorted prices for analyzing economic transition. Many Chinese economists believe the more precisely delimited property rights are better. Use the distinction between efficiency in delimiting rights to contracting and efficiency in specifying and enforcing the terms of a contract to comment on that view.

7    Restrictions which exist on the trading of labor, land, and capital in a Soviet-style economy will substantially reduce transaction efficiency in delimiting rights to contracting, thereby restricting institutional development and economic growth. Under such restraints, the scope for people to balance the two types of transaction cost is very limited. Use the model in example 16.6 to analyze the difference in transaction cost coefficients in specifying and enforcing rights to contracting and contractual terms between a state-run enterprise in a socialist country and a government owned firm in a free enterprise system, and the difference between a state-run enterprise in a socialist country and a private firm in a free market.

8    Use the following documentation of the differences between China and Europe to explain their different development performances in the seventeenth to nineteenth centuries. Landes (1998, pp. 34–6): "The concept of property rights went back to biblical times and was transmitted and transformed by Christian teaching." "Despotisms abounded in Europe, too, but they were mitigated by law, by territorial partition, and within states, by the division of power between the center (crown) and local seigneurial authority. Fragmentation gave rise to competition, and competition favored good care of good subjects. Treat them badly, and they might go elsewhere. Ecumenical empires did not fear flight, especially when, like China, they defined themselves as the center of the universe, the hearth and home of civilization, and everything outside as barbarian darkness. There was no other place to go, so that symbolic boundaries were enough, like the 'willow palisade,' a low wall that ran from the Great Wall to the sea

and separated China from the Mongol-Tartar lands to the north." Fairbank (1992): "Oriental societies, [were] organized under centralized monolithic governments in which the bureaucracy was dominant in almost all aspects of large-scale activity – administrative, military, religious, and economic – so that no sanction for private enterprise ever became established . . . " Imperial governments carried out the industrial policy of limiting commerce and promoting agriculture. Fairbank (1992, p. 179): "The merchant was kept in check by the official as an ally whose activities could be used and milked in the interest of either the officials personally or of the state. As Etienne Balazs pointed out, commercial transactions were always subject to the superintendence and taxation of the officials. Government monopolies of stable articles, like salt and iron in ancient times, or like tea, silk, tobacco, salt, and matches more recently, expressed the overriding economic prerogatives of the state. No merchant class had been allowed to rise independently and encroach upon these prerogatives. This was ensured in practice by the official disregard for private property. This meant that official patronage and support were necessary to protect any big commercial undertaking. The result was a close community of interest between the merchant and the official. . . . In short, capitalism failed to prosper in China because the merchant was never able to become established outside the control of the landlord gentry and their representatives in the bureaucracy. In feudal Europe the merchant class developed in the towns. Since the landed ruling class were settled in their manors upon the land, the European towns could grow up outside the feudal system instead of being integrated in it."

9   Yang, Wang, and Wills use meticulous documentation of institutional changes in China to estimate subindices of transaction efficiencies in specifying and enforcing rights to use, transfer, and appropriate earnings from land, goods, labor, and financial assets. Then the 12 subindices are used to estimate a comprehensive transaction efficiency index over 9 years. A regression of the per capita real income on the degree of commercialization (a measure of level of division of labor) and the transaction efficiency index, and a regression of the degree of commercialization on the index, show a significant positive relationship between per capita real income, level of division of labor, and transaction efficiency in specifying and enforcing property rights. Also, North and Weingast (1989) have documented that the institutional evolution in the seventeenth century that created a credible government commitment to a constitutional and legal framework that effectively protected private property rights, was the driving force for the Industrial Revolution and economic development. Derive more empirical implications, and find more empirical evidence for the theories developed in this chapter.

10  What are the differences between the new classical models in this chapter and the Holmstrom–Milgrom model (1995) in example 10.3 with the trade-off between moral hazard and monitoring costs?

# EXERCISES

1   Yang and Wills, 1990: Assume that $q$ in the model of example 16.1 is endogenously determined by labor effort in reducing transaction risk. Solve for general equilibrium and its inframarginal comparative statics.

2   Solve for the corner equilibrium with three traded goods in example 16.4 and the inframarginal comparative statics of general equilibrium. Identify the relationship between a corner equilibrium relative number of different specialists when only two goods are traded. Why is the price of a good with a higher transaction risk lower in equilibrium? Apply the analysis to explore the welfare implications of a public housing program. Use the model to explain why in many developing countries government institutions, including government funded universities, are reluctant to buy all kinds of services from the market. They tend to have their own guest houses instead of buying professional hotel services for their guests, to have their

own lawyers instead of buying professional law services from independent law firms, and so on. Analyze the implications of such a tendency to self-sufficiency for the equilibrium network size of division of labor and productivity.

3   Suppose good x in the model in example 16.6 is a producer good that is essential for the production of the consumption good y. Each consumer-producer's utility is a function of the consumption amount of good y. There is no transaction uncertainty for good y. Solve for the general equilibrium and its inframarginal comparative statics. (Yang and Ng, 1993, ch. 11.)

4   Introduce stealing into the new classical models in this chapter and assume that an individual can spend time in stealing the goods of trade partners in transactions. Also, each individual can spend time in protecting herself from theft. You may specify some stealing function, of which the right-hand side is time spent stealing and the left-hand side is goods that can be obtained without pay. Then you may specify a protection function on the negative relationship between the degree of theft and the effort spent protecting her property. Use such a new classical model to explore the implications of endogenous stealing for the equilibrium network size of division of labor. As Buchanan (1975) noted, criminal laws penalize stealing much more than the direct economic cost caused by stealing would suggest. Also, moral codes require responsible individuals to do more than suggested by a cold economic calculation of the cost and benefit of theft. What are the development implications of criminal laws and a moral code respecting private property which generate a much lower equilibrium stealing rate than alternative systems?

5   Holmstrom and Milgrom, 1991: The employer hires the employee to undertake two activities to generate profit. The employer's certain equivalent (see chapter 10 for the definition of this concept) is $P(e_1, e_2) - (\alpha + \beta_1 e_1 + \beta_2 e_2)$, where $e_i$ is the employee's effort level in activity i, $\beta_i$ is the incentive intensity coefficient for activity i, $P(e_1, e_2)$ is the expected gross profit, and $\alpha + \beta_1 e_1 + \beta_2 e_2$ is the expected wage payment. Contingent wage payment is $w = \alpha + \beta_1(e_1 + x_1) + \beta_2(e_2 + x_2)$, where $x_i \sim N(0, \sigma)$ is white noise in activity i and $x_1$ and $x_2$ are independent. The employee's certain equivalent wealth is $\alpha + \beta_1 e_1 + \beta_2 e_2 - C(e_1 + e_2) - 0.5r\text{var}(\beta_1 x_1 + \beta_2 x_2)$, where $C(e_1 + e_2)$ is the disutility of total effort, r is the employee's coefficient of absolute risk aversion, and $\text{var}(\beta_1 x_1 + \beta_2 x_2) = (\beta_1^2 + \beta_2^2)\sigma$. Find the optimum incentive intensity in each activity $\beta_i$ by maximizing the employer and employee's total certain equivalent wealth subject to the first-order condition for maximizing the employee's certain equivalent wealth. Show that the trade-off between balanced incentives for the two activities and benefit of strong incentives for each activity generates the optimum incentive payment structure that entails much weaker incentives than in the conventional principal–agent model. Holmstrom and Milgrom use this model to show that the institution of the firm can use such weak but balanced incentive contracts to get a particular activity going, whereas this activity may not occur in the market without the firm. Discuss the difference between this model and the model in example 16.6.

6   Sah and Stiglitz, 1986: Consider two patterns of decision-making process in which a project is assessed by two decision-makers. In pattern A (series connection), person 1 assesses a proposed project first. She accepts a proposal with probability p and rejects it with probability $1 - p$. A proposal that has been accepted by person 1 is then assessed by person 2, who accepts a proposal with $p \in (0, 1)$. In pattern B (parallel connection), each person assesses each proposal independently of the other's assessment. Assume that 50 percent of the proposals are good and the others are bad (should be rejected). What is the probability that a good proposal is rejected (Type I error) under each of the decision patterns? What is the probability that a bad proposal is accepted (type II error) under each of the decision patterns?

7   Kremer, 1993: The production function for a neoclassical firm is $y = k^{\alpha}q^{n}nB$, where $y$ is expected output level, $k$ is input level of capital, $\alpha \in (0, 1)$, $q$ is the probability that a worker does a job up to quality requirements, or $1 - q$ is the probability that this worker's job does not meet quality requirements, $n$ is the number of jobs that are essential for production, and $B$ is a parameter of contribution to output by each qualified job. Market wage is a function of $q$, which is positively related to quality of workers hired. Hence, $w = w(q)$. Interest rate is $r$. Suppose that good y is the *numéraire*. Specify the first-order conditions for maximizing profit with respect to $k$ and $q$ and identify the market relationship between wage rate and quality of workers $w(q)$. (Hint: insert the expression of the optimum $k$ into the first-order condition for the optimum $q$, then solve for the differential equation $dw/dq = f(q)$.)

chapter **17**

# INSURANCE AND RISK OF COORDINATION FAILURE OF THE NETWORK OF DIVISION OF LABOR

### ◆ 17.1 Uncertainty and Risk Aversion

In chapter 10, we learned the concepts of risk aversion and moral hazard. Let us review these concepts before developing new models utilizing them. In the presence of uncertainty, a decision-maker maximizes expected utility. If the decision-maker's utility function is strictly concave, she is risk averse. In other words, she prefers the value of the utility function at the weighted average of contingent states to the weighted average of utility values at contingent states. She prefers an outcome with no uncertainty to outcomes with uncertainty. If individuals have different degrees of risk aversion, they can all gain from trading in risk. An individual who is more risk averse than another can sell risk to the latter and both of them can be better off. This can be considered as the former buying insurance from the latter. The neoclassical principal–agent model in chapter 10 can be considered as a model with insurance where the agent buys insurance from the principal. The principal plays the role of an insurance company. That model shows that complete insurance will generate moral hazard if the principal cannot detect the agent's effort devoted to reducing risk. The efficient contract between the principal and agent entails incomplete insurance. That is, the payment to the agent is contingent: it is higher when the outcome is good than when the outcome is not good.

In this chapter, we investigate further the relationship between insurance, division of labor, and endogenous and exogenous transaction costs. The story in this chapter runs as follows.

Assume that there are risks in transactions in the model in chapter 11. In each transaction, transaction efficiency $k$ takes on a high value at probability $\theta$ and a low value at probability $1 - \theta$. The transaction risk may be caused by traffic accidents or by opportunistic behavior that takes place with a probability as shown in chapter 9. Moreover, we assume that all consumer-producers are risk averse to the same degree, or they have *ex ante* identical strictly concave utility functions. In the model there is a trade-off between economies of division of labor and coordination reliability in addition to a trade-off between economies of division of labor and exogenous transaction costs.

If an insurance company collects a premium from each individual and compensates them in the event of low transaction efficiency, each individual will be certain to have the weighted average of the two levels of transaction efficiency by pooling risk. Such an institution of insurance will certainly promote division of labor and productivity progress if all individuals are risk averse. It will promote many other structural changes associated with evolution in division of labor, which are discussed in the previous chapters. This story is formalized in section 17.2.

In section 17.3, we endogenize the risk in each transaction and individuals' effort levels in reducing transaction risk. It is assumed that the effort level is not observable to the insurance company, so that moral hazard may take place. We then investigate the function of incomplete insurance in promoting division of labor and productivity progress.

The implications of the trade-off between economies of division of labor and coordination reliability, and the relationship between insurance and endogenous transaction costs caused by moral hazard, are much more general than is immediately apparent. This is an important issue in comparative economics. In a Soviet-style economic system, there is complete insurance for each employee of a state enterprise. She can obtain complete medical insurance, she will never lose her job (a complete unemployment insurance), and she will receive a pension no matter what happens to her job, to her health condition, or to the enterprise that hired her (a complete insurance for pension payment). Also, each state enterprise is insured by the government through the soft-budget constraint against all kinds risk in business operation. In China such complete insurance is referred to as the iron rice bowl. It generates a great deal of endogenous transaction cost associated with moral hazard, on the one hand, and provides complete insurance that may maintain a reasonable coordination reliability of the network of division of labor, on the other. In Russia's reforms in the early 1990s, this form of complete insurance was abolished when an alternative insurance system had not yet been developed in the market. Hence, a breakdown of an enterprise, a sector, or of a link between two states, generated coordination failure of the whole network of division of labor. Over the period of the 1930s to the 1950s, the sophisticated network of division of labor of the capitalist market economies had been mimicked through a central planning system in the Soviet Union. The original model of this network in the free enterprise economies is coordinated through the market. The high risk of coordination failure generated by a high level of division of labor when complete insurance is abolished and the market for insurance is yet to be developed is the rationale behind the spectacular decline of the Russian economy in the 1990s.

**Questions to Ask Yourself when Reading this Chapter**

- What are the effects of transaction risk and the degree of risk aversion on the equilibrium level of division of labor, productivity, and size of the market network?

- Why can insurance promote division of labor?

- Why will complete insurance and moral hazard generate endogenous transaction costs?

- Under what condition will the market choose an economic structure with no insurance? Under what conditions, and why, is such a structure more efficient than a structure with insurance?

- Why do we have a trade-off between economies of division of labor and endogenous transaction costs? Under what conditions will Pareto optimum autarky with no endogenous transaction costs jump to the non-Pareto optimum division of labor with endogenous transaction costs? Why could such a jump be Pareto improving?

- How can we use the trade-off between economies of division of labor and endogenous transaction costs caused by moral hazard to explain simultaneous increases in moral hazard, per capita real income, and productivity?

## ◆ 17.2 A Model with Insurance and Endogenous Specialization in the Absence of Moral Hazard

### Example 17.1: the Lio model (1998a)

The structure of the model is similar to the one in chapter 11 except that transaction efficiency $k$ is a random variable. The decision problem for each consumer-producer selling good i is specified as follows.

$$\text{Max: } Eu_i = E\left\{x_i \Pi_{r \in R}(k_r x_r^d)\Pi_{j \in J} x_j\right\}^{\frac{1}{\rho}} \qquad \text{(expected utility)} \qquad (17.1)$$

$$\text{s.t. } x_i + x_i^s = \text{Max}\{0, l_i - \alpha\}, \quad x_j = \text{Max}\{0, l_j - \alpha\} \quad \text{(production functions)}$$
$$l_i + (m-n)l_j = 1 \qquad\qquad\qquad\qquad\qquad \text{(endowment constraint)}$$
$$p_i x_i^s = (n-1)p_r x_r^d \qquad\qquad\qquad\qquad\quad \text{(budget constraint)}$$

where $x_i$ is the amount of good i self-provided, $x_r^d$ is the amount of good r purchased, $k_r$ is the transaction efficiency coefficient for good r, $R$ is the set of $n-1$ goods purchased, $J$ is the set of $m-n$ nontraded goods, $n$ is the number of traded goods, $x_j$ is the self-provided amount of nontraded good j, $x_i^s$ is the amount of good i sold, $l_i$ and $l_j$ are respective levels of specialization in producing goods i and j, and $p_i$ and $p_r$ are respective prices of good i and r. It is assumed that each individual is endowed with one unit of non-leisure time. $\alpha$ is the fixed learning cost in each production activity. We will see later that parameter $\rho > 1$ relates to the degree of risk aversion. The larger the value of $\rho$, the more risk averse is the individual, since a larger value of $\rho$ implies a more concave utility function. The endowment constraint and the budget constraint in (17.1) are obtained using the symmetry.

The difference between this decision problem and the one in chapter 11 is characterized by the transaction efficiency coefficient.

$$k_r = \begin{cases} k_H \text{ with } \theta \\ k_L \text{ with } 1 - \theta \end{cases} \tag{17.2}$$

where $k_H > k_L$, $\theta \in (0, 1)$, $r \in R$. That is, there is transaction risk. We may note that the model in example 16.1 is a special case of the Lio model with $k_H = k$ and $k_L = 0$. Inserting all constraints into the utility function, the constrained maximization problem in (17.1) can be converted to a nonconstrained maximization problem.

$$\text{Max: } Eu_i = WE(\Pi_{r \in R} k_r)^{\frac{1}{\rho}} \tag{17.3a}$$

where $x_i^s$, $l_i$, and $n$ are decision variables and

$$W \equiv \{(l_i - \alpha - x_i^s)[x_i^s/(n-1)]^{n-1}[(1-l_i)/(m-n) - \alpha]^{m-n}\}^{\frac{1}{\rho}}. \tag{17.3b}$$

Also, it can be shown, using symmetry, that $p_i/p_r = 1$ in equilibrium. The procedure to solve for $x_i^s$ and $l_i$ is the same as in chapter 11. But the procedure to solve for $n$ differs from that in chapter 11 since the solution of equilibrium $n$ relates to the term with transaction risk $E(\Pi_r k_r)^{1/\rho}$. Let us have a close look at this term.

There are $n - 1$ $k_r$ for $r \in R$. $s$ of them take on value $k_H$ and $n - 1 - s$ of them take on value $k_L$, while $s$ can take on value from 1 to $n - 1$. Here, $k_H$ takes place with probability $\theta$ and $k_L$ takes place with probability $1 - \theta$. Therefore, the $n - 1$ of $k_r$ follows a binomial distribution. The probability for $n - s$ of $k_r$ to take on value $k_H$ and for $s - 1$ of $k_r$ to take on value $k_L$ is

$$P_s = C_{n-1}^{s-1} \theta^{n-s}(1-\theta)^{s-1} \tag{17.4}$$

where $C_{n-1}^{s-1}$ is $s - 1$ combinations of $n - 1$ elements. Following a binomial formula, it can be shown that

$$E(\Pi_{r \in R} k_r)^{\frac{1}{\rho}} = \sum_{s=1}^{n-1} P_s(k_H^{n-s} k_L^{s-1})^{\frac{1}{\rho}} \tag{17.5}$$

$$= C_{n-1}^0 \theta^{n-1} k_H^{(n-1)/\rho} + C_{n-1}^1 \theta^{n-2}(1-\theta)k_H^{(n-2)/\rho}k_L^{1/\rho} + \cdots$$

$$+ [C_{n-1}^{n-1}(1-\theta)^{n-1}k_L^{(n-1)/\rho}]$$

$$= [\theta k_H^{1/\rho} + (1-\theta)k_L^{1/\rho}]^{n-1}$$

where $P_s$ is given by (17.4) and the final equality in (17.5) is given by the binomial formula. Having inserted (17.5) into (17.3), we can express $Eu_i$ as a function of $l_i$, $x_i^s$, and $n$. Letting the derivatives of $Eu_i$ with respect to the three variables equal 0 yields the solutions for the corner equilibrium values of all endogenous variables when insurance is absent.

$$\begin{aligned}
l_i &= [n + \alpha(n^2 - mn + m - n)]/m \\
l_j &= [1 + \alpha(n-1)]/m \\
x_i &= x_r^d = x_j = [1 - \alpha(1 + m - n)]/m, \qquad x_i^s = (n-1)x_i/n \\
n &= (1 - \frac{1}{\alpha}) + m\{1 - 1/\ln[\theta k_H^{1/\rho} + (1-\theta)k_L^{1/\rho}]\} \\
Eu &= \{[1 - \alpha(1 + m - n)]/m\}^m[\theta k_H^{1/\rho} + (1-\theta)k_L^{1/\rho}]^{n-1} \\
P &= [\theta k_H^{1/\rho} + (1-\theta)k_L^{1/\rho}]^{n-1}.
\end{aligned} \tag{17.6}$$

Differentiation of the corner equilibrium values of the endogenous variables with respect to parameters $k_s$ ($s = H, L$), $\theta$, $\rho$ yields the inframarginal comparative statics of the corner equilibrium with no insurance:

$$dn/dk_s > 0, \qquad dn/d\theta > 0, \qquad dn/d\rho < 0 \tag{17.7a}$$

$$dl_i/dk_s > 0, \qquad dl_i/d\theta > 0, \qquad dl_i/d\rho < 0 \tag{17.7b}$$

$$d[M(n-1)x_r^d]/dk_s > 0, \qquad d[M(n-1)x^d]/d\theta > 0 \tag{17.7c}$$
$$d[M(n-1)x_r^d]/\alpha\rho < 0,$$

$$dEu/dk_s > 0, \qquad dEu/d\theta > 0 \tag{17.7d}$$

$$dP/dk_s = (\partial P/\partial k_s) + (\partial P/\partial n)(dn/dk_s) < 0, \text{ and} \tag{17.7e}$$
$$dP/d\theta = (\partial P/\partial\theta) + (\partial P/\partial n)(dn/d\theta) < 0$$

where $(n-1)x_r^d$ is each individual's aggregate purchase volume and $M(n-1)x_r^d$ is the aggregate demand for all goods in the market, which is the extent of the market. As in chapter 11, we have used the envelope theorem to obtain (17.7d). To obtain (17.7e), we have used the solution of $n$, given in (17.6), and the fact that $\alpha m < 1$ if the solution of $l_i$, given in (17.6), is between 0 and 1.

The comparative statics imply that as transaction efficiency $k_H$ and $k_L$ rises, or as the probability of a high transaction efficiency, $\theta$, increases (or as the risk of a low transaction efficiency decreases), or as the degree of risk aversion $\rho$ falls, the following concurrent phenomena take place.

The level of division of labor, $n$, increases. This implies increases in the number of markets for different goods, in diversity of structure, in market integration, and in production concentration. Aggregate coordination reliability of the network of division of labor, $P$, decreases, or aggregate risk for coordination failure of the network of division of labor increases. This is quite counter-intuitive: an increase in coordination reliability of each transaction or a decrease in transaction risk of each transaction will increase aggregate transaction risk! The logic behind this result is that as transaction conditions for each transaction, $k_s$, are improved, or as the risk of coordination failure of each transaction $1 - \theta$ decreases, the scope for trading off economies of division of labor against transaction risk is enlarged, so that individuals can expand the network of division of labor to exploit more economies of division of labor, so that they can afford more risk of coordination failure of the network of division of labor.

Each individual's level of specialization increases. This implies increases in productivity, in the extent of the market, in the extent of endogenous comparative advantage, in aggregate demand, and in per capita real income. An interesting interpretation of an increase in $k$ is a decrease in tax rate. Also an increase in $\theta$ can be interpreted as a more stable tax rate. Mokyr (1993, pp. 46–58) provides historical evidence that a stable and non-predatory tax system is essential for economic development. Sachs and Warner (1995, 1997) provide empirical evidence that economic development performance negatively relates to the transaction risk caused by institutional deficiency (they use an institution quality index to measure this).

Now we assume that there is an insurance company from which individuals can buy an insurance contract. No matter what the level of transaction efficiency, an individual buying insurance must pay a premium $\pi$. If transaction efficiency is low, or is $k_L$, the insurance company pays the individual $c$. Hence, the individual's expected utility is

$$Eu_i = W[\theta(k_H - \pi)^{1/\rho} + (1 - \theta)(k_L - \pi + c)^{1/\rho}]^{n-1} \tag{17.8}$$

where the nonrandom variable $W$ is given in (17.3). If the insurance is complete and the market for insurance is competitive, the insurance company's expected profit must be 0. The company receives premium $\pi$ at probability 1 from the individual and pays the individual $c$ at probability $1 - \theta$. Therefore, the complete insurance and 0 profit condition requires

$$\pi = (1 - \theta)c. \tag{17.9}$$

Inserting this expression into (17.8) and letting the derivative of $Eu_i$ with respect to $c$ equal 0 yields each individual's optimum insurance policy $c = k_H - k_L$. Plugging the optimum policy $c$ into (17.9) yields the optimum premium:

$$\pi^* = (1 - \theta)(k_H - k_L). \tag{17.10}$$

Inserting the optimum premium and policy back into (17.8) gives the expected utility in the presence of insurance:

$$Eu_i = W[\theta k_H + (1 - \theta)k_L]^{n-1/\rho} \tag{17.11}$$

It says that no matter what is the level of transaction efficiency, an insured person always gets the utility level at the weighted average of the high and low transaction efficiencies $\theta k_H + (1 - \theta)k_L$. That is, the insured individual avoids all risk. Such an insurance is called *complete insurance*. We now consider function $f(k) = k^{1/\rho}$ which is the part of the utility function that involves uncertainty. The function is concave in the random variable $k$ iff $\rho > 1$. A comparison between $Eu$ in (17.6) and $Eu$ in (17.11) indicates that an individual gets $f(Ek) = [\theta k_H + (1 - \theta)k_L]^{1/\rho}$ if she is insured, and she gets $Ef(k) = \theta k_H^{1/\rho} + (1 - \theta)k_L^{1/\rho}$ if she is not. Since for a strictly concave function $f(k)$, the value of the function at the weighted average of two contingent transaction efficiencies is greater than the weighted average of the values of the function at the two contingent transaction efficiencies, (17.11) is certainly greater than the expected utility in the absence of insurance. (Recall the discussion of this in section 10.3 of chapter 10.)

The first-order conditions for maximizing (17.11) are exactly the same as in (17.3), except the first-order condition for the equilibrium $n$. These conditions yield the corner equilibrium with insurance.

$$l_i = [n' + \alpha(n'^2 - mn' + m - n')]/m \tag{17.12}$$
$$l_j' = [1 + \alpha(n' - 1)]/m$$
$$x_i' = x_r^{d'} = x_j' = [1 - \alpha(1 + m - n')]/m, \qquad x_i^{s'} = (n' - 1)x_i'/n'$$
$$n' = (1 - 1/\alpha) + m\{1 - 1/\ln[\theta k_H + (1 - \theta)k_L]\}$$
$$Eu' - \{[1 - \alpha(1 + m - n')]/m\}^{m/\rho}[\theta k_H + (1 - \theta)k_L]^{(n'-1)/\rho}$$
$$P' = [\theta k_H = (1 - \theta)k_L]^{n-1/\rho}.$$

Primes of the variables indicate that they are corner equilibrium values with insurance. The differentiation of the corner equilibrium values of the endogenous variables with respect to parameters $k$, $\theta$, $\rho$ indicates that the comparative statics in (17.7) hold for the case with insurance. Comparisons between the two corner equilibria indicate

$$n' > n, \quad l_i' > l_i, \quad P' > P, \quad Eu' > Eu, \quad Mx_i^{s'} > Mx_i^s \tag{17.13a}$$

$$\mathrm{d}n'/\mathrm{d}k_s > 0, \quad \mathrm{d}n'/\mathrm{d}\theta > 0, \quad \mathrm{d}Eu'/\mathrm{d}k_s > 0, \quad \mathrm{d}Eu'/\mathrm{d}\theta < 0 \tag{17.13b}$$
$$\mathrm{d}P'/\mathrm{d}k_s < 0, \quad \mathrm{d}P'/\mathrm{d}\theta < 0.$$

This implies that the expected utility with insurance is greater than that with no insurance. Applying the Yao theorem, it can be shown that all individuals will choose insurance in a general equilibrium. The corner equilibrium with no insurance is not a general equilibrium. (17.13) implies also that the level of division of labor for society, individuals' levels of specialization, productivity, aggregate coordination reliability of the network of division of labor, and the extent of the market are all higher in the corner equilibrium with insurance than that in the corner equilibrium with no insurance.

The complete insurance in this model is equivalent to the complete insurance in a Soviet-style economy. But in this model, it is assumed that the risk of low transaction efficiency is exogenously given, independent of the effort devoted to reducing such risk. Hence, complete insurance does not generate the endogenous transaction costs that are associated with moral hazard. But we know that complete insurance in a Soviet-style economy indeed generates tremendous endogenous transaction costs and moral hazard problems. In the next section, we will endogenize the risk of a low transaction efficiency and investigate the relationships between the level of division of labor, incomplete insurance, and complete insurance that generates moral hazard and endogenous transaction costs.

## ◆ 17.3 The Division of Labor and Endogenous Transaction Costs caused by Complete Insurance

### Example 17.2: a simplified version of the Lio model (1996) with endogenous transaction costs caused by complete insurance

The difference between the Lio model (1996) and the Lio model (1998a) relates to the probabilities of different levels of transaction efficiency. Those probabilities are exogenously given in the last section, whereas here they are endogenously determined by an individual's effort devoted to reducing the risk of a low transaction efficiency. It is also assumed that that effort level not observable to others or not verifiable in the court when a dispute occurs, so that moral hazard may arise. Since the model with endogenous specialization and with moral hazard is much more difficult to manage than a model with endogenous specialization alone or with moral hazard alone, we assume there are only two goods in this section. Hence, each *ex ante* identical consumer-producer's decision problem is

$$\text{Max: } Eu = E[\ln(x + kx^d) + \ln(y + ky^d)] \qquad \text{(expected utility function)} \tag{17.14}$$

$$\text{s.t. } x + x^s = l_x - \alpha, \quad y + y^s = \text{Max } \{0, l_y - \alpha\} \qquad \text{(production functions)}$$
$$l_x + l_y + e = 1 \qquad \qquad \text{(endowment constraint)}$$

$$k = k_H \text{ with probability } \tfrac{2}{3} \atop k = k_L \text{ with probability } \tfrac{1}{3}\Big\} \text{ if } e = \tfrac{1}{3} \quad \text{(effect of effort on transaction risk)}$$

$$k = k_H \text{ with probability } 0 \atop k = k_H \text{ with probability } 1 \Big\} \text{ if } e = 0$$

$$p_x x^s + p_y y^s = p_x x^d + p_y y^d \qquad \text{(budget constraint)}$$

where it is assumed that $k_H > k_L$. Variable $e$ is the level of effort devoted to reducing the risk of a low transaction efficiency. It can be considered as effort devoted to transporting goods carefully or to protecting the goods from being stolen. For simplicity, we assume that there are only two levels of such effort. The high level of effort $e = 1/3$ generates a low probability $(1/3)$ of low transaction efficiency $(k = k_L)$ and the low level of effort $e = 0$ causes low transaction efficiency for sure.

Since the utility function is strictly concave in the quantities of the two goods consumed, all individuals are risk averse to the same degree. Also, an increase in the effort level devoted to reducing transaction risk will reduce the amount of labor allocated to the production of goods and thereby reduce income and utility. Hence, each individual has an incentive to choose the low level of effort in reducing transaction risk if complete insurance is available. This implies that complete insurance will generate moral hazard if the division of labor is chosen.

From the point of view of an insured, the insurance company cannot observe her effort level if she has complete insurance. Her optimum decision is thus to choose the lowest level of effort. The insurance company will go bankrupt if every one of the insured behaves similarly. Hence, the insurance company will provide an incomplete insurance to restrain moral hazard. Suppose that each consumer-producer chooses premium $\pi$ for a given policy of the insurance company, $c$. Then, the insurance company chooses the policy for a given $\pi$ according to the incentive compatibility condition. The second step to sort out the insurance contract terms is equivalent to choosing a parameter $\beta$ for a given $\pi$. The definition of $\beta$ is given as follows.

$$\beta = (2/3)\pi/(1/3)(c - \pi) \geq 1 \qquad (17.15)$$

where $1/3$ is the probability of a low transaction efficiency and $2/3$ is the probability of a high transaction efficiency, the denominator is the insurance company's expected net payout in the event of a low transaction efficiency and the numerator is its expected premium earnings in the event of a high transaction efficiency. Since $\beta$ is uniquely determined by $c$ for any given $\pi$, choosing $c$ for a given $\pi$ is equivalent to choosing $\beta$ for a given $\pi$. If $\beta = 1$, then the expected payout is the same as the expected premium, so that insurance is complete. If $\beta > 1$, the expected payout is smaller than the expected premium, so that insurance is incomplete and the insured must take part of transaction risks. Hence, parameter $\beta$ describes the completeness of the insurance contract for each transaction.

Using the definition of $\beta$, we can express the insurance company's payout net of premium in the event of low transaction efficiency as a function of $\beta$ and $\pi$ as well. We thus have

$$c - \pi = 2\pi/\beta \qquad (17.16)$$

Applying the Wen theorem to the model, there are 6 structures that we must consider. The first is autarky denoted as A. In this structure, there is no trade or transaction risk, so that it is easy to solve for the corner equilibrium in this structure.

The second class of structures features division of labor, but with no insurance, denoted as $B_i$, $i = L, M, H$. There are three structures in this class. In structure $B_L$, there are two types of specialist producers of the two goods and they choose the low level of effort in reducing transaction risk, that is $e = 0$. In structure $B_M$, the specialist producers of one good choose the high effort level $e = 1/3$ and the specialist producers of the other good choose $e = 0$. Because of symmetry, the outcome is unaffected by which specialist producers choose $e = 0$ and which choose $e = 1/3$. In structure $B_H$, both specialist producers of the two goods choose $e = 1/3$.

The third class of structures features division of labor with insurance, denoted $C_i$, $i = L, M, H$. Structure $C_L$ features complete insurance and $e = 0$. Since it is assumed in (17.7) that the probability of the low transaction efficiency is 1 if $e = 0$, the uncertainty disappears for this case, so that the insurance company cannot survive. This implies that the corner equilibrium for this structure does not exist. In structure $C_M$ with the division of labor and insurance, one type of specialist producer chooses $e = 1/3$ and the other type of specialist producers choose $e = 0$. Structure $C_H$ features division of labor, incomplete insurance, and $e = 1/3$ chosen by all individuals.

Let us first consider structure $C_H$. In this structure, the decision problem for a specialist producer of good x is:

$$\text{Max: } Eu_x = \ln x + \ln y^d + (\tfrac{2}{3})\ln(k_H - \pi) + (\tfrac{1}{3})\ln(k_L + c - \pi) \tag{17.17}$$

$$\text{s.t. } x + x_s = \text{Max } \{0, 1 - \alpha - e\}, \qquad e = \tfrac{1}{3} \qquad \text{(production condition)}$$
$$p_x x^s = p_y y^d \qquad \qquad \text{(budget constraint)}$$

We can use (17.15) and (17.16) to eliminate $c$, then solve for the optimum $x$, $x^s$, $y^d$. Inserting the solution back into (17.17) yields

$$\text{Max: } Eu_x = \ln(p_x/p_y) + 2\ln[2 - 3\alpha)/6] + (\tfrac{2}{3})\ln(k_H - \pi) + (\tfrac{1}{3})\ln[k_L + (2\pi/\beta)]. \tag{17.18}$$

Each specialist in x chooses premium $\pi$ to maximize $Eu_x$ for a given $\beta$. The optimum premium is

$$\pi = (\tfrac{1}{3})(k_H - \beta k_L). \tag{17.19}$$

Inserting (17.19) back into (17.18) yields the expected indirect utility function for a specialist in x.

$$Eu_x = \ln(p_x/p_y) + 2\ln(2 - 3\alpha) + \ln(2k_H + \beta k_L) - 3\ln 3 - (\ln\beta/3) - 2\ln 2. \tag{17.20a}$$

Following the same procedure, we can solve for the expected indirect utility function for a specialist in y.

$$Eu_y = \ln(p_y/p_x) + 2\ln(2 - 3\alpha) + \ln(2k_H + \beta k_L) - 3\ln 3 - (\ln\beta/3) - 2\ln 2. \tag{17.20b}$$

The expected utility equalization condition $Eu_x = Eu_y$ determines the corner equilibrium relative price of the two traded goods in structure $C_H$, that is $p_x/p_y = 1$. The market clearing condition $M_x x^s = M_y x^d$ and the population equation $M_x + M_y = M$, together with the corner equilibrium relative price, determine the corner equilibrium numbers of the two types of specialists $M_x = M_y = M/2$.

An insurance company will choose $\beta$ according to the incentive compatibility condition. This condition implies that the insured has a higher expected utility when she chooses $e = 1/3$ than when she chooses $e = 0$. Following the approach to calculating the expected indirect utility function, we can work out the expected indirect utility function for a specialist in x to choose $e = 0$. For this case $k = k_L$ is a certain event, so that the effect on utility of the expected payout net of premium is $\ln(k_L + c - \pi)$. After elimination of $c - \pi$ using (17.16), the expected indirect utility function for a specialist in x who chooses $e = 0$ is:

$$Eu_x = \ln(p_x/p_y) + 2\ln[(1 - \alpha)/2] + \ln(2k_H + \beta k_L) - \ln 3 - \ln\beta. \qquad (17.21)$$

Incentive compatibility implies that (17.20) is not smaller than (17.21), that is, the expected utility for a high effort level in reducing transaction risks is not lower than that for a low effort level. This inequality sets up a constraint for $\beta$:

$$\beta > [3(1 - \alpha)/(2 - 3\alpha)]^3. \qquad (17.22)$$

Further, a positive $\pi$ implies $k_H > k_H - \pi = (2k_H/3) + (\beta k_L/3)$, where we have used (17.19). This sets up another constraint on $\beta$:

$$\beta < k_H/k_L. \qquad (17.23)$$

The two constraints on $\beta$ imply that structure $C_H$ with insurance is equilibrium only if

$$k_H/k_L > [2(1 - \alpha)/(1 - 2\alpha)]^6. \qquad (17.24)$$

If this condition does not hold, the set of candidates for the equilibrium structure comprises only A, $B_L$, and $B_H$. If this condition is satisfied, the set comprises A, $B_L$, $B_H$, and $C_H$.

Following the procedure used in solving for the corner equilibrium in structure $C_H$, we can solve for all corner equilibria in the 7 structures, which are summarized in table 17.1.

Using the table, it can be shown that $Eu(B_M) < Eu(B_L)$, if $Eu(B_M) > Eu(B_H)$. This implies that either $Eu(B_M) < Eu(B_H)$ or $Eu(B_M) < Eu(B_L)$. According to the Yao theorem,

**Table 17.1:** Expected real income in seven structures

| Equilibrium structure | Expected corner equilibrium per capita real income |
|---|---|
| A | $2\ln[(1 - 2\alpha)/2]$ |
| $B_L$ | $2\ln[(1 - \alpha)/2] + \ln k_L$ |
| $B_M$ | $\ln(2 - 3\alpha) + \ln(1 - \alpha) - 2\ln 2 + (\ln k_H/3) + (2/3)\ln k_L - \ln 3$ |
| $B_H$ | $2\ln(2 - 3\alpha) - 2\ln 6 + (2/3)\ln k_H + (\ln k_L/3)$ |
| $C_L$ | No corner equilibrium exists |
| $C_M$ | $\ln[(2 - 3\alpha)/3] + \ln(1 - \alpha) - 2\ln 2 + 0.5\{\ln k_L - (\ln\beta/3) + \ln[2k_H/3) + (\beta k_H/3)]\}$ |
| $C_H$ | $2\ln(2 - 3\alpha) - 2\ln 6 + \ln[(2k_H/3) + (k_L\beta/3)] - (\ln\beta/3)$ |

it follows that structure $B_M$ cannot be an equilibrium structure. Similarly, we can prove that $B_H$ can be an equilibrium structure only if

$$\left(\frac{1-2\alpha}{1-\alpha}\right)^2 > k_L > 3^3 \beta^{2/3} \left(\frac{1-2\alpha}{2-3\alpha}\right)^2 k_H^{-2} \tag{17.25}$$

which holds only if $[(2-3\alpha)/3(1-\alpha)]^2 > 3\beta^{2/3}$ where $\beta > 1$. It is obvious that this inequality does not hold for $\alpha \in (0,1)$. Therefore, $B_H$ cannot be an equilibrium structure. Following a similar line of reasoning, it can be shown that $B_L$ cannot be an equilibrium structure if $k_H/k_L > [3(1-\alpha)/(2-3\alpha)]^3$. Taking into account all of the relevant information, comparisons of expected real incomes in all structures yield the general equilibrium and its inframarginal comparative statics, as summarized in table 17.2, where $\gamma \equiv 27[(1-2\alpha)/(2-3\alpha)]^2 \beta^{1/3}$, A is the autarky structure, $B_L$ is the structure with the division of labor and with no insurance, where individuals choose a low effort level in reducing transaction risks, $C_H$ is the structure with the division of labor and incomplete insurance where individuals choose a high effort level.

Table 17.2 implies that if the two values of transaction efficiency are sufficiently small, the general equilibrium is autarky where there is no market or transaction risk. As $k_H$ and $k_L$ increase, the general equilibrium jumps to the division of labor with transaction risks. When the ratio $k_H/k_L$ is not great, or the gains from a high effort in reducing risk of a low transaction efficiency are not great, insurance cannot survive moral hazard. Hence, the division of labor is not associated with insurance and individuals choose the low effort level in reducing transaction risk (structure $B_L$). When the gains are significant, insurance emerges from the division of labor and individuals choose the high effort level in reducing transaction risk (structure $C_H$).

Next, we show that for $k_H/k_L > [3(1-\alpha)/(2-3\alpha)]^3$, insurance can promote division of labor and productivity progress. Comparisons between corner equilibrium expected real incomes in structures A, $B_H$, and $C_H$, given in table 17.1, yield the following results:

$$Eu(B_H) > u(A) \text{ iff } \mu_1 \equiv k_H^{2/3} k_L^{1/3} > \mu_0 \equiv [3(1-2\alpha)/(2-3\alpha)]^2 \tag{17.25a}$$

$$Eu(C_H) > u(A) \text{ iff } \mu_2 \equiv (2k_H + \beta k_L)/3\beta^{1/3} > \mu_0 \tag{17.25b}$$

A close examination of $\mu_1$ and $\mu_2$ yields

$$\mu_2|_{\beta \to k_H \ k_L} = \mu_1 \text{ and} \tag{17.26a}$$

$$\partial\mu_2/\partial\beta < 0 \text{ if } \beta < k_H/k_L \text{ and } \partial\mu_2/\partial\beta > 0 \text{ if } \beta > k_H/k_L. \tag{17.26b}$$

**Table 17.2:** General equilibrium and its inframarginal comparative statics

| $k_H/k_L < [3(1-\alpha)/(2-3\alpha)]^3$ | | $k_H/k_L > [3(1-\alpha)/(2-3\alpha)]^3$ | |
|---|---|---|---|
| $k_L < [(1-2\alpha)/(1-\alpha)]^2$ | $k_L > [(1-2\alpha)/(1-\alpha)]^2$ | $2k_H + \beta k_L < \gamma$ | $2k_H + \beta k_L > \gamma$ |
| A | $B_L$ | A | $C_H$ |

(17.26b) implies that $\mu_2$ reaches its minimum at $\beta = k_H / k_L$. This, together with (17.26a), implies that $\mu_2 > \mu_1$. It follows that $Eu(B_H) < u(A)$ and $Eu(C_H) > u(A)$ if $\mu_0 \in (\mu_1, \mu_2)$. In other words, structure $C_H$ with insurance is better than autarky which is in turn better than structure $B_H$ with no insurance if $\mu_0 \in (\mu_1, \mu_2)$. This establishes the proposition that incomplete insurance in $C_H$ may promote division of labor and productivity progress.

Next, we show that such incomplete insurance cannot eliminate endogenous transaction costs caused by moral hazard, though it does reduce such endogenous transaction costs. To substantiate this claim, it suffices to prove that the corner equilibrium in structure $C_H$ is not locally Pareto optimal. It is easy to show that the corner equilibrium expected real income in $C_H$ increases as $\beta$ tends to 1. Indeed the local Pareto optimum for the division of labor can be calculated as the corner equilibrium in $C_H$ with $\beta = 1$. The locally Pareto optimum real income for the division of labor is

$$V = 2\ln(2 - 3\alpha) - 2\ln 6 - \ln 3 + \ln(2k_H + \beta k_L) - [(\ln\beta)/3] \text{ and} \tag{17.27}$$

$$V > u(A) \text{ iff } \mu_3 \equiv (2k_H + k_L)/3 > \mu_0.$$

A comparison between $\mu_3$ and $\mu_2$ indicates that $\mu_3 > \mu_2$. This implies that if the effort level in reducing transaction risks is observable, complete insurance can be given only to those who choose the high effort level, so that moral hazard is eliminated and the expected real income is higher than in structure $C_H$ that is associated with $\beta > 1$. In other words, the corner equilibrium in structure $C_H$ is not locally Pareto optimal. However, the Pareto optimum is an infeasible utopia when $C_H$ is the general equilibrium structure.

It is interesting to note four different cases of endogenous transaction costs caused by moral hazard.

1) Suppose $k_H/k_L > [3(1 - \alpha)/(2 - 3\alpha)]^3$ and $\mu_0 \in (\mu_2, \mu_3)$, which implies that the general equilibrium structure is A and the Pareto optimum is the division of labor with complete insurance and with no moral hazard. Hence, the division of labor and related welfare gains cannot be realized because of the positive equilibrium endogenous transaction costs. This kind of endogenous transaction cost is called *Type I endogenous transaction cost*, which is associated with the Pareto inefficient equilibrium levels of division of labor and productivity, and number of transactions.

2) Suppose $k_H/k_L > [3(1 - \alpha)/(2 - 3\alpha)]^3$ and $\mu_2 > \mu_0$, which implies that the general equilibrium structure is $C_H$ and is not Pareto optimal. Hence, the equilibrium resource allocation is not efficient (relative quantity and relative price of the two goods are not efficient) because of endogenous transaction costs caused by moral hazard, despite the efficient equilibrium level of division of labor. This kind of transaction cost is called *Type II endogenous transaction cost*.

3) Suppose $k_H/k_L < [3(1 - \alpha)/(2 - 3\alpha)]^3$ and $k_L > [(1 - 2\alpha)/(1 - \alpha)]^2$, which implies that the equilibrium structure is $B_L$, is not Pareto optimal, and has a low effort level in avoiding transaction risk. Hence, moral hazard generates endogenous transaction costs that are associated with a low effort level in avoiding transaction risk, despite the Pareto efficient level of division of labor. This is referred to as *Type III endogenous transaction cost*.

4) Suppose $k_H/k_L > [3(1 - \alpha)/(2 - 3\alpha)]^3$ and $\mu_0 > \mu_3 > \mu_2$, which implies that the equilibrium structure is A and is Pareto optimal. Assume now that transaction efficiency is improved such that $\mu_0 \in (\mu_2, \mu_3)$. This implies that the general equilibrium jumps from Structure A to Structure $C_H$ and the equilibrium endogenous transaction costs increase

from 0 to a positive level. In other words, concurrent increases in endogenous transaction costs, in productivity, and in the level of division of labor may take place as a result of reduced exogenous transaction costs (improved transaction efficiency). We call the kind of endogenous transaction cost that emerges from reduced exogenous transaction cost and increased productivity *Type IV endogenous transaction cost.*

Types I and III transactions are similar to X inefficiency, which causes low productivity or a low effort level. But Type I transaction cost causes organizational inefficiency (a Pareto inefficient level of division of labor) while Type III and Type II endogenous transaction costs result in allocative inefficiency. Type IV endogenous transaction cost is due both to a higher productivity which can be used to afford increased endogenous transaction costs and to moral hazard.

These results on endogenous transaction costs substantiate Coase's conjecture (1960) that if there exist endogenous transaction costs, the interactions between self-interested individuals will sort out contractual arrangements that maximize economies of division of labor net of endogenous and exogenous transaction cost rather than minimize a particular type of transaction cost.

In this section, the terms of an insurance contract $\beta$ are not finally determined, though they are subject to the incentive compatibility and positive premium constraints. If the market for insurance is competitive and the management cost for an insurance contract is $b$, then the expected profit for each insurance contract is $\pi - (c/3) = 0$. Free entry and competition will drive the profit down to 0. Hence, the equilibrium insurance contractual terms can be determined by the zero profit condition and equations (17.15), (17.16), (17.19). After manipulation of the equations, it can be shown that the equilibrium contractual terms are given by the following equations.

$\beta$ is given by $f(\beta, b, k_H, k_L) \equiv 2(\beta - 1)(k_H - \beta k_L) - 9b = 0$,

$c = 3b(2 + \beta)/2(\beta - 1), \qquad \pi = (c/3) + b.$

Then the equilibrium level of division of labor, endogenous transaction costs, and productivity are explained by the insurance management cost coefficient $b$. In this model, the efficient balance point (or efficient degree of incompleteness of insurance, $\beta$) of the trade-off between incentive provision and risk sharing is determined by the insurance management cost coefficient, $c$, the degree of risk that relates to $1 - \theta$, $k_H/k_L$, and $\rho$. Because of the connection between the degree of insurance completeness and the degree of softness of the budget constraint, the trade-off between risk sharing and incentive provision is equivalent to the trade-off between risk sharing and the softness of the budget constraint. This trade-off has much more general implications for the analysis of the relationship between economic development and institutions.

From the experience of the Asian financial crisis in 1997, we can see that it is not easy to identify the efficient balance point of the trade-off. When the IMF emphasized reforms of financial market as a precondition for financial assistance to alleviate the damage of the crisis, it paid more attention to incentive provision in reducing the risk of bad outcome. When Korea and Indonesia asked for prompt financial assistance from the IMF, they emphasized risk sharing. The bargaining between the two sides aims to find the efficient balance of the trade-off between incentive provision and risk sharing.

If the trade-off between measuring cost of effort level and moral hazard is introduced into the model with the trade-off between incentive provision and risk sharing, the story will be much more realistic and complicated. Milgrom and Roberts (1992, p. 336) survey several models that have the two types of trade-off. In one of the models, promotion according to seniority can reduce influencing (rent seeking) cost in a firm, encourage continuous accumulation of firm-specific human capital, and provide risk sharing between the employee and the employer. But it will cause endogenous transaction costs associated with inaccurate measurement of effort levels and prevent realization of productivity enhancing labor mobility. The effects of a promotion scheme according to performance are opposite. Hence, efficient promotion criteria must efficiently trade-off incentive provision against risk sharing, employment stability (or its reciprocal: labor mobility), and measurement costs.

### Example 17.3: application of the models in examples 17.1 and 17.2 to the analysis of the Asian financial crisis in 1997

There are two opposite views of the Asian financial crisis in 1997. According to one of them, the crisis was caused by moral hazard associated with cronyism and complete insurance of loans provided by the government. The other view (Radelet and Sachs, 1998, and Stiglitz, 1998) holds that as the network of trade expands, aggregate risk of coordination failure inevitably increases even if moral hazard is not that serious. Hence, policy missteps and hasty reactions by governments and international organizations may miss an efficient balance of the trade-off between insurance and incentive provision. For instance, the overemphasis on financial reform programs which reduce moral hazard when insurance should receive more attention added to the virulence of the banking panic. We can apply the models in examples 17.1 and 17.2 to assess the view. According to (17.7e) and (17.13b), it is obvious that even if moral hazard is absent, the aggregate risk of coordination failure $1 - P$ increases as transaction conditions are improved or as the risk of coordination failure for each transaction decreases. This is because as the risk of coordination failure for each transaction declines, the scope for trading off economies of division of labor against aggregate risk is enlarged, so that individuals can afford a higher risk. Hence, choosing a higher aggregate risk of coordination failure is associated with economic development generated by evolution of division of labor and it is efficient. This explains why a more successful developed economy has a higher risk of having an episode like the Great Depression than a less-developed economy. This is why Radelet and Sachs call the 1997 Asian financial crisis "crisis of success." The higher risk is efficiently chosen, just like choosing a higher risk of being killed by driving on the freeway.

This implies that moral hazard is not the whole story. This is why more moral hazard generated by complete insurance in China and in Soviet Union does not necessarily imply more risk of a financial crisis. The model in example 17.2 suggests that the efficient way to handle the Asian financial crisis is to balance the trade-off between incentive provision in reducing risk and risk sharing, rather than paying too much attention to one of them.

If the time lag between financial decisions and economic fundamentals is considered, we may have another trade-off between the strong incentive created by the sensitive feedback of financial decisions to market shocks, and the stability of the financial market. Financial reforms may increase sensitivity of the feedback mechanism. But overshot and overreactions are more likely to occur if feedback is too sensitive, leading to crisis. Aghion, Bacchetta, and Banerjee (1998) develop such a cobweb model. Policy-making aims to identify the efficient balance of trade-offs between insurance provision and moral hazard and between strong incentive, which makes feedback more sensitive, and stability.

## Key Terms and Review

The relationship between risk aversion and strictly concave utility functions.

Measuring degree of risk aversion.

Effects of transaction risk and the degree of risk aversion on the equilibrium level of division of labor, productivity, and size of the market network.

The effect of insurance on the equilibrium network size of division of labor.

Complete insurance, moral hazard, incomplete insurance, and endogenous transaction costs.

Why the Pareto optimum with complete insurance is a utopia when moral hazard is present.

Why incomplete insurance can reduce endogenous transaction costs, but cannot eliminate all endogenous transaction costs in the presence of moral hazard.

The trade-off between economies of division of labor and endogenous transaction costs.

Under what conditions will Pareto optimal autarky with no endogenous transaction costs jump to non-Pareto optimal division of labor with endogenous transaction costs? Why could such a jump be Pareto improving?

Under what conditions will the market choose an economic structure with no insurance? Under what conditions, and why, is such a structure more efficient than a structure with insurance?

What are the features of a Soviet-style economic system with complete insurance? Why does it have extremely high endogenous transaction costs? Why would productivity decline sharply if the complete insurance system were abolished before a developed market for insurance was available?

## Further Reading

*New classical models of endogenous risk and insurance*: Lio (1996, 1998a); *insurance and economic development*: Lio (1996), Dixit (1987, 1989); *risk and insurance*: Mas-Collell, Whinston, and Green (1995, chs. 6, 13, 14), Varian (1992, ch. 8), Milgrom and Roberts (1992*); general equilibrium models of moral hazard*: Legros and Newman (1996), Laffont and Tirole (1986, 1993), Helpman and Laffont (1975), Kihlstrom and Laffont (1979).

# QUESTIONS

1    Use the models in this chapter to analyze the function of the stock market in providing incomplete insurance for entrepreneurial activities.

2    Analyze the functions of unemployment insurance, medical insurance, and other insurance for promoting the network size of division of labor and productivity.

3    The Soviet-style economic system provides complete insurance for those specializing in some professions in the state sector. That complete insurance generates tremendous endogenous transaction costs because of moral hazard on the one hand, but is an essential condition for the operation of a large network size of division of labor on the other. Explain, using the models in this chapter, why the Russian economy drastically declined in the 1990s after the complete insurance system had been abolished.

4    Analyze why the new classical framework and the notion of the positive network effect of division of labor are essential for exploring the productivity implications of insurance.

5    A possible criticism of the Lio model in example 17.2 is that the insurance sector is not endogenized. Follow Dixit's approach (1987, 1989) to extend the Lio model to address this criticism (see exercise 5).

6 Use the new classical theory of insurance to explain the impact of the development of the insurance sector on the success of British commerce and the wealth of the nation in the eighteenth century.

7 A survey by *The Economist* (Sept. 5–11, 1998, pp. 4–7) documents an interesting situation phenomenon in the developed countries. This survey found that the probability that a motorist will get into traffic jams is higher in a US city with faster upgrading of its transportation infrastructure. Similarly, as communication technology is improved and the productivity of the computer sector increases, the income share of expenditure on computers and communications increases rather than decreases. Also, increasingly more time and resources are consumed in dealing with jargon and email files, and in searching and screening. Use the Lio model to analyze this modern development phenomenon.

8 Use empirical data to test for the concurrent evolution of division of labor and income share of insurance which is used to accommodate the increasing risk of coordination failure of a larger network of division of labor.

# EXERCISES

1 Assume that in the model of example 17.1 $m = 3$ and $\alpha_1 > \alpha_2 > \alpha_3$. Solve for the corner equilibria with and without insurance, and for the inframarginal comparative statics.

2 Assume that in the model of example 17.1 $m = 3$ and $k_H$ and $k_L$ differ from good to good. Solve for the corner equilibria with and without insurance, and for the inframarginal comparative statics. Analyze the implications of the difference in transaction risk across goods.

3 Assume that in the model in example 17.2 the utility function is $u = [(x + k_x x^d)(y + k_y y^d)]^{0.5}$. Solve for the inframarginal comparative statics.

4 Compare the model in example 17.2 and the model in example 10.2.

5 Develop a new classical general equilibrium model, on the basis of example 17.2, to endogenize the emergence of professional insurance agents from the evolution of division of labor. You may specify economies of specialization in estimating transaction risk. Discuss the possible implications of the economies of specialization which might be used to get results that are contrary to some insurance models which predict that the insured knows more about risk than the professional insurance company (adverse selection).

6 Assume that in example 17.2, the probability for $k = k_H$ is $e$, $k_H = 1$, and probability for $k = k_L = t$ is $1 - e$. There is no exogenous insurance company. Solve for the inframarginal comparative statics of general equilibrium in the extended model with endogenous trade of risk between two types of specialists.

# part VIII

# THE HIERARCHICAL STRUCTURE OF DIVISION OF LABOR

chapter **18**

# THE DIVISION OF LABOR IN ROUNDABOUT PRODUCTION AND EMERGENCE OF NEW MACHINES AND RELATED NEW TECHNOLOGY

## ◆ 18.1 New Classical vs. Neoclassical Views of the Emergence of New Producer Goods and Related New Technology

From as far back as Smith (1776, pp. 14, 105), Harris (1757), Tucker (1755, 1774), and Hegel (1821, p. 129), to Marshall (1890, p. 256) and Walker (1874, pp. 36–7), many economists have recognized that the emergence of new tools and machines, and the related invention of new technologies, are dependent on the development of division of labor. This classical mainstream view of invention and technology substantially differs from the neoclassical view. According to the neoclassical view, innovation is a matter of investment in research and development (R&D), regardless of the levels of specialization for individuals and the level of division of labor for society. According to the classical mainstream, in contrast, invention of new machines and technology is a matter of the size of the network of division of labor and the related extent of the market. If the network of division of labor is not sufficiently developed, not only can new technology not be invented, but even if it were invented, it would be a commercially nonviable luxury. That is why the invention of paper, the compass, printing technology, and metallurgical technology by the Chinese in the twelfth century could not generate industrialization, whereas the commercialization of these technologies through the development in division of labor in Europe promoted other inventions that led to the Industrial Revolution in the nineteenth century. However, all new classical models so far developed in the previous chapters cannot predict the emergence of new producer goods from the evolution in division of labor.

In order to formalize the classical ideas about the emergence of new producer goods from the evolution in division of labor, we shall extend the new classical model to endogenize the number of producer goods. A neoclassical approach to endogenizing the number of consumption goods developed by Dixit and Stiglitz (1977) is based on specification of the CES utility function. We have used that approach in chapter 11 to simultaneously endogenize individuals' levels of specialization and the number of consumption goods in a new classical model. Ethier (1982), Judd (1985), and Romer (1990) extend the Dixit–Stiglitz approach and develop neoclassical models with the CES production function to endogenize the number of producer goods. If we specify the CES production function in the new classical model of chapter 5, classical ideas about the intimate relationship between invention of new technology, the size of the network of division of labor, and the institution of the firm can be formalized. In chapter 25 we will investigate the relationships between invention of new producer goods, the division of labor, investment, and capital.

The story behind the formal model in this chapter runs as follows. There are economies of complementarity between various producer goods which suit different processes in producing a consumption good. These economies of complementarity can also be called economies of variety of producer goods. We shall use the two terms interchangeably in this text. Hence, an increase in the number of producer goods employed in producing consumption goods will raise the total factor productivity of the consumption goods. There are very complicated trade-offs among economies of complementarity, economies of specialization, and transaction costs. If each individual self-provides all goods that she needs, then there is a tension between economies of complementarity and economies of specialization, since if she produces many different producer goods, her level of specialization in producing each of them will be very low. However, if a large number of producer goods are produced through a high level of division of labor between different specialist producers, then both economies of division of labor and economies of complementarity between various producer goods can be utilized. But the high level of division of labor and the large number of producer goods would generate a high level of transaction costs. The sophisticated trade-offs imply that an improvement in transaction efficiency enlarges the scope for trading off economies of division of labor against transaction costs. This in turn enlarges the scope for trading off economies of division of labor against economies of variety of producer goods. Therefore, the improvement in transaction efficiency will generate concurrent evolution in division of labor and in the number of producer goods.

Intuitively it is clear that if transaction efficiency is extremely low, then individuals have to choose autarky where a narrow scope for trading off economies of specialization against economies of variety of producer goods entails a small equilibrium number of goods that directly relate to final consumption. Can you imagine an individual self-providing an automobile, the various machine tools that are employed to produce the automobile, and the steel and iron that are employed to produce the machine tools and automobile? As transaction efficiency is improved, each individual's level of specialization and the variety of available producer goods can simultaneously increase through a higher level of division of labor between different professions. In other words, a higher transaction efficiency increases society's capacity in acquiring knowledge in different professions through increasing the size of the network of division of labor and the related extent of the market. The network effects make new producer goods and related new technology become commercially viable.

The story of the invention of the steam engine by Boulton and Watt verifies our conjecture. Marshall (1890, p. 256) attributed this invention to a deep division of labor in the inventing activities. The high level of division of labor in inventing activities can be attributed to the improvement in transaction efficiency for trading intellectual properties brought about by the patent laws instituted in 1624 in Britain. The high transaction efficiency provided conditions for commercializing the invention of technology that are essential for the high level of division of labor in inventing activities. Also, residual rights based on the institution of the firm that were developed under common law could be used as a means of indirectly pricing Boulton and Watt's entrepreneurial activities (Mokyr, 1993). Finally, the British government's *laissez-faire* policy regime reduced transaction costs for trade across country boundaries. This promoted international division of labor and thereby enlarged the market network that was essential for the commercialization of the steam engine. According to North and Weingast (1989), the most important driving force for the successful industrialization in Britain was the fact that through the evolution of institutions in Britain in the seventeenth century the government's commitment to constitutions became credible. This significantly reduced state opportunism and therefore significantly reduced rent seeking in society and associated endogenous transaction costs.

In sections 18.2 to 18.7 a new classical model with a finite maximum number of intermediate goods is used to formalize classical economic thinking on the relationship between division of labor, the extent of the market, and technical progress. In section 18.8, this analysis is extended to a case with $m$ intermediate goods.

---

### *Questions to Ask Yourself when Reading this Chapter*

- What are economies of roundabout production?

- Under what conditions will it be profitable to produce producer goods that were not available previously from the market?

- What is the relationship between transaction efficiency, the level of division of labor, and the emergence of new machines and related new technology?

- What is the difference between the neoclassical view and the new classical view about invention of new technology?

- What are the implications of free pricing, free choice of occupation, and free enterprising for the invention of new machines and related new technology?

---

## ◆ 18.2 A Model with Endogenous Technical Progress, an Endogenous Number of Producer Goods, and Endogenous Specialization

### Example 18.1: a new classical model with an endogenous number of producer goods

Consider a model with a car as a consumption good. The car can be produced by employing two types of specialized machine tools and labor, or by employing one of the two types of machine tools and labor. Neither of the two types of machine tools is a necessity individually for the production of cars. But if both types of machine tools are employed, total factor productivity is higher since each is more productive in processing one subset of components of a car than the other subset.

The CES production functions of cars are *ex ante* identical for all consumer-producers.

$$z^p \equiv z + z^s = [(x + tx^d)^\rho + (y + ty^d)^\rho]^{\beta/\rho} l_z^\alpha, \quad \beta \in (0,1), \quad \rho \in (0,1) \tag{18.1}$$

where $x^d$ and $y^d$ are the respective amounts of the two intermediate goods purchased from the market, and $1 - t$ is their transaction cost coefficient. Hence, $tx^d$ or $ty^d$ is the amount an individual receives from the purchase of an intermediate good. The respective self-provided amounts of the two goods are $x$ and $y$, $l_z$ is a person's level of specialization in producing the consumer good, and $z + z^s$ is the output level of this consumer good. Taking $[(x + tx^d)^\rho + (y + ty^d)^\rho]^{1/\rho}$ to be a composite intermediate good with a variety of inputs, (18.1) is a Cobb–Douglas production function with the composite intermediate (or capital) good and labor $l_z$ as inputs. The total factor productivity of good z increases with the level of specialization in producing z if $\alpha + \beta > 1$ where $\alpha + \beta$ represents the degree of economies of specialization in producing the final goods. The composite intermediate good is produced with a CES production function with a variety of inputs. The elasticity of substitution between input varieties is $1/(1 - \rho)$. The degree of economies of complementarity between the two intermediate goods used in producing the final good is represented by $1/\rho$. $1/\rho$ represents the extent of the contribution of the number of intermediate goods to productivity of the final goods. A large $1/\rho$ indicates a high degree of difficulty in substituting one intermediate good for another, so that productivity of the final good is higher when the two intermediate goods are employed than when only one of them is employed. We assume $\beta \in (0,1)$, $\rho \in (0,1)$. The second-order condition for the interior optimum output level for a specialist of good z will not hold if $\beta > 1$. It can also be shown that if $\rho > 1$, total factor productivity is higher when only one intermediate good is employed than when the two intermediate goods are employed. There are Type A economies of roundabout production (productivity increases as the quantity of intermediate goods rises). $\beta$ can represent the degree of Type A economies of roundabout production, since it relates to the elasticity of the output level of the final good with respect to the input level of producer goods. There are Type B economies of roundabout production, which are economies of variety of producer goods. $1/\rho$ represents the degree of Type B economies of roundabout production. In the next chapter, we will study Type C economies of roundabout production that relate to the number of links of a roundabout production chain or the number of layers of a hierarchical structure of roundabout production.

The production functions for the intermediate goods are

$$x + x^s = l_x^a \quad \text{and} \quad y + y^s = l_y^a \tag{18.2}$$

where $x + x^s$ and $y + y^s$ are the respective output levels of the intermediate goods, and $l_x$ and $l_y$ are a person's respective levels of specialization in producing the two intermediate goods. The parameter $a$ represents the degree of economies of specialization in producing the intermediate goods. The productivity of labor in producing goods x and y increases with the levels of specialization in those production activities for $a > 1$.

The endowment constraint for labor is

$$l_z + l_x + l_y = 1, \quad l_i \in [0, 1], \quad i = z, x, y \tag{18.3}$$

The transaction cost coefficient for the final good is $1 - k$. Thus, $kz^d$ is the quantity an individual receives from the purchase of the consumer good. The amount consumed of the final good is $z + kz^d$. The utility function is *ex ante* identical for all individuals and given by

$$u = z + kz^d \tag{18.4}$$

As in the previous chapters, we assume a Walrasian regime.

## ◆ 18.3 The Efficient Number of Producer Goods and Level of Specialization

There are $2^9 = 512$ combinations of zero and nonzero values of $x$, $x^s$, $x^d$, $y$, $y^s$, $y^d$, $z$, $z^s$, $z^d$. Following the approach for proving lemma 8.1 in chapter 8, we can prove the following lemma to narrow down the set of candidates for the optimum decision.

**Lemma 18.1:** An individual sells at most one good and does not buy and sell or self-provide the same goods. She does not self-provide intermediate goods if she does not self-provide the final goods.
  *Proof:*

*Claim 1: An individual does not buy and sell the same goods*

Replacing $z$ in (18.4) with its equivalent from the production function of $z$, and $z^s$ with its equivalent from the budget constraint

$$p_x x^s + p_y y^s + p_z z^s = p_x x^d + p_y y^d + p_z z^d$$

A differentiation of $u$ with respect to $y^d$ yields that for $y^s > 0$

$$\partial u / \partial y^d < 0 \qquad \forall\, y^d > 0.$$

This implies that when $y^s > 0$, that is, when the individual sells good y, the optimum value of $y^d$ is always 0 according to the Kuhn–Tucker condition $(\partial u / \partial y^d) y^d = 0$ at the optimum. Replacing $z$ in (18.4) with its equivalent from the production function of $z$, and $z^d$ from the budget constraint, a differentiation of $u$ with respect to $y^s$ yields that for $y^d > 0$

$$\partial u / \partial y^s < 0 \qquad \forall\, y^s > 0.$$

This implies that when the individual buys good y, the optimum value of her quantity of good y sold is 0. Hence, claim 1 has been established.

*Claim 2: An individual sells one good at most; she does not self-provide intermediate goods if she sells the final good*

Assume $x^s$ and $z^s$ are positive at the same time, then claim 1 implies that $x^d = z^d = 0$. Replacing $x$ in (18.1) with its equivalent from the production function of $y$ with its equivalent from the endowment constraint of labor, and $z^s$ from the budget constraint and substituting (18.1) for $z$ in (18.4), a differentiation of $u$ with respect to $l_x$ yields

$\partial u / \partial l_x | l_{x=0} < 0$ and $\partial u / \partial l_x | l_{x=1} > 0$

This implies that there are at least three interior extreme points of $l_x$ if $l_x$ has an interior maximum point. As figure 18.1 illustrates, when $l_x$ increases from 0 at which $u$ declines with $l_x$, it must pass a minimum point, such as point $l_{x1}$ in figure 18.1a before it reaches the maximum point, such as point $l_{x2}$. Since $u$ rises at $l_x = 1$, $l_x$ must pass another minimum point, such as $l_{x3}$, as it increases from $l_{x2}$. Using the first-order conditions for interior extreme points of $x^s$, $y^d$, $l_x$, $l_z$ and the symmetry between $x$ and $y$, we can solve for a unique $l_x$. This implies that there does not exist an interior maximum point of $l_x$. The interior extreme of $l_x$ is a minimum point, as shown in figure 18.1b. Utility $u$ is maximized either at $l_x = 0$ (its lower bound) or at $l_x = 1$ (its upper bound). Suppose $z^s$, $l_z > 0$; then $l_x$ must be 0 because $l_x = 1$ contradicts $z^s > 0$ due to the endowment constraint. Suppose $l_x = 1$ and $x^s > 0$; then $z^s$, $l_z$, $l_y$, $y^s$ must be 0. We can thus conclude that $x^s$ and $z^s$ cannot be positive at the same time and $l_z = z^s = 0$ if $l_x$, $x^s > 0$, and $l_x = x = x^s = 0$ if $l_z$, $z^s > 0$. Similarly we can prove that $x^s$ and $y^s$, or $y^s$ and $z^s$ cannot be positive at the same time and that $l_y$, $y^s$ = 0 if $l_z$, $z^s > 0$ and $l_z$, $z^s = 0$ if $l_y$, $y^s > 0$. Claim 2 has been thus established.

*Q.E.D.*

*Claim 3: An individual does not self-provide intermediate goods if she does not produce the final good*

Since $x$ and $y$ have no positive contribution to $u$ if the final good is not produced by a person selling $x$ or $y$, $x = y = 0$ if $z = z^s = l_z = 0$.
 Claims 1–3 are sufficient to establish lemma 18.1.

## ◆ 18.4 The Corner Equilibria in Nine Structures

Taking into account lemma 18.1 and the possibility of setting up different organizational structures in production and transactions, there are nine market structures. We first solve for the corner equilibria in the nine structures, then identify the general equilibrium from

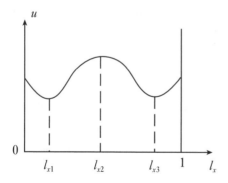

(a) Three interior solutions

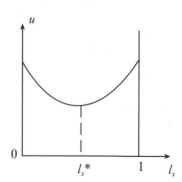

(b) The number of interior solutions is smaller than 3

◆ **Figure 18.1:** The interior extreme point of $l_x$ must be the minimum point these corner equilibria. The configurations and market structures are illustrated in figure 18.2.

Let us consider first three configurations in autarky. An autarky configuration implies $x^s = y^s = z^s = x^d = y^d = z^d = 0$. There are three configurations that meet the criterion: a configuration with zero quantities traded of all goods and $x$, $y$, $z > 0$, denoted A(xyz), a configuration with zero quantities traded of all goods, $x$, $z > 0$, and $y = 0$, denoted A(xz), and a configuration with zero quantities traded of all goods, $y$, $z > 0$, and $x = 0$, denoted A(yz). Since configuration A(xz) is symmetric with configuration A(yz), the corner solutions for the two configurations generate the same utility level. Let the quantities traded of all goods be 0 and $x$, $y$, $z > 0$ in (18.1)–(18.4) and insert (18.1)–(18.3) into (18.4); the per capita real income for configuration A(xyz) can then be solved as shown in table 18.1. Here the individual maximum utility equals the maximum output level of the final good per head. Also, the per capita real income is the same as the maximum labor productivity of the final good in an autarky configuration because the maximum quantity of labor per head is 1.

Let us then consider three structures with division of labor and without firms.

*Structure D(xyz)* consists of a division of $M$ individuals between configurations (x/z), (y/z), and (z/xy). Configuration (x/z) is defined by $x^s$, $z^d > 0$, $l_x = 1$, $x = x^d = y = y^s = y^d = l_y = z = z^s = l_z = 0$, configuration (y/z) is symmetric to (x/z), configuration (z/xy) is defined by $z^s$, $z$, $x^d$, $y^d > 0$, $l_z = 1$, $z^d = x = x^s = l_x = y = y^s = l_y = 0$. All configurations are shown in figure 18.2 and all corner solutions are summarized in table 18.1.

*Structure D(xz)* consists of configuration (x/z), which sells good x and buys good z, and (z/x), which sells good z and buys good x. *Structure D(yz)* is symmetric with structure D(xz).

Finally, let us consider the three structures with division of labor and firms

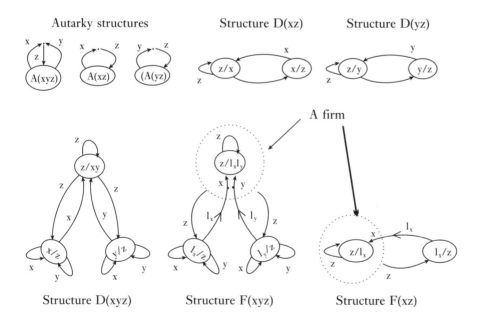

♦ **Figure 18.2:** Emergence of new producer goods and endogenous technical progress

**Table 18.1:** The corner solutions in nine distinct configurations

| Configuration | Supply function | Demand function | Utility |
|---|---|---|---|
| A(xyz) | | | $2^{(\beta/\rho)-a\beta}$ $(\alpha\beta)^{a\beta}\alpha^{\alpha}/(\alpha + a\beta)^{\alpha+a\beta}$ |
| A(xz) | | | $(\alpha\beta)^{a\beta}\alpha^{\alpha}/(\alpha + a\beta)^{\alpha+a\beta}$ |
| (z/xy) | $z^s = \{2^{\beta(1-\rho)/\rho}\beta(2p_z/p_x)^{\beta}\}^{1/(1-\beta)}$ | $x^d = p_z z^s/2p_x$ $y^d = p_z z^s/2p_y$ | $(1-\beta)\beta^{\beta/(1-\beta)}[2^{\beta(1-\rho)/\rho}(tp_z/p_x)^{\beta}]^{1/(1-\beta)}$ |
| (x/z) | $x^s = 1$ | $z^d = p_x/p_z$ | $kp_x/p_z$ |
| (y/z) | $y^s = 1$ | $z^d = p_y/p_z$ | $kp_y/p_z$ |
| (z/x) | $z^s = [\beta(tp_z/p_x)^{\beta}]^{1/(1-\beta)}$ | $x^d = p_z z^s/p_x$ | $(1-\beta)(\beta tp_z/p_x)^{\beta/(1-\beta)}$ |
| (z/l$_x$) | $z^s = [\beta(sp_z/w)^{\beta}]^{1/(1-\beta)}$ | $N_x = p_z z^s/w$ | $[\beta(sp_z/w)^{\beta}]^{1/(1-\beta)}$ |
| (l$_x$/z) | $l_x = 1$ | $z^d = w/p_z$ | $kw/p_z$ |
| (z/l$_x$l$_y$) | $z^s = 2N_x p_z/w$ | $N_x = N_y =$ $[2^{(\beta/\rho)-1}s^{\beta}\beta p_z/p_x]^{1/(1-\beta)}$ | $2^{\beta(1-\rho)(1-\beta)\rho}$ $(s\beta p_z/w)^{\beta/(1-\beta)}(1-\beta)$ |

*Structure F(xyz)* consists of $(z/l_x \, l_y)$ selling the final good and buying labor to produce the intermediate goods x, $(l_x/z)$ selling her labor, buying the final good, and producing intermediate good x, and $(l_y/z)$ selling labor, buying the final good, and producing intermediate good y. The individual decision problem for configuration $(z/l_x \, l_y)$ is

$$\underset{N_x, N_y}{\text{Max:}} \ u_z = z = l_z^{\alpha}[(sN_x)^{\rho} + (sN_y)^{\rho}]^{\beta/\rho} - (N_x + N_y)/p_z$$

$$\text{s.t.} \ z + z^s = l_z^{\alpha}[(sN_x)^{\rho} + (sN_y)^{\rho}]^{\beta/\rho}, \ l_z = 1 \quad \text{(production function of } z\text{)}$$
$$x^s = l_x^{a}, \quad l_x = 1, \quad \text{(production function of } x\text{)}$$
$$y^s = l_y^{a}, \quad l_y = 1, \quad \text{(production function of } y\text{)}$$
$$p_z z^s = w(N_x + N_y) \quad \text{(budget constraint)}$$

**Table 18.2:** Corner equilibria in four structures with division of labor

| Structure | Relative price | Number of specialists | Per capita real income |
|---|---|---|---|
| D(xyz) | $p_z/p_x = p_z/p_y =$ $2^{\beta(\rho-1)/\rho}(\beta t)^{-\beta}[k(1-\beta)]^{1-\beta}$ | $M_x/M_z = M_y/M_z =$ $\beta k/(1-\beta)$ | $[2^{(1-\rho)/\rho}t\beta k]^{\beta}$ $(1-\beta)^{1-\beta}$ |
| D(xz) | $p_z/p_x = (\beta t)^{-\beta}[k/(1-\beta)]^{1-\beta}$ | $M_x/M_z = (\beta kt)^{\beta}/(1-\beta)$ | $(t\beta k)^{\beta}(1-\beta)^{1-\beta}$ |
| F(xyz) | $p_z/w = (\beta s2^{(1-\rho)/\rho})^{-\beta}[k(1-\beta)]^{1-\beta}$ | $N_x = N_y = \beta k/(1-\beta)$ | $[2^{(1-\rho)/\rho}s\beta k]^{\beta}$ $(1-\beta)^{1-\beta}$ |
| F(xz) | $p_z/w = (\beta s)^{-\beta}[k/(1-\beta)]^{1-\beta}$ | $N_x = \beta ks/(1-\beta)$ | $(s\beta k)^{\beta}(1-\beta)^{1-\beta}$ |

where $z$ in the utility function is replaced with its equivalent from the production function and $z^s$ is replaced with its equivalent from the budget constraint. For simplicity, we assume that the transaction cost coefficient for labor trade $1 - s$ is in terms of loss of output produced by an employee in transit from the employee to the employer. This coefficient encompasses the supervision cost within a firm and transaction cost in the market for labor. $N_x$ is the number of workers hired to produce good x by an employer and $N_y$ is the number of workers hired to produce good y by the employer. The price of the final good is $p_z$ and the wage rate is $w$. The utility of an individual choosing $(z/l_x l_y)$ is denoted by $u_z$. In this structure, $l_z$ is the level of specialization of an individual choosing configuration $(z/l_x l_y)$ in producing the final good and $l_x$ (or $l_y$) is the level of specialization of an individual choosing configuration $(l_x/z)$ in producing good x (or configuration $(l_y/z)$ in producing good y). All of them are the employer's decision variables because of asymmetric distribution of residual control rights. The optimum decisions for a person choosing $(z/l_x l_y)$ are summarized in table 18.2.

For an individual choosing configuration $(l_x/z)$, all variables are fixed, given by

$$u_{lx} = kz^d = kw/p_z$$

$$p_z z^d = wl_x = w \qquad \text{(budget and endowment constraints)}$$

The decision in configuration $(l_y/z)$ is symmetric with that in configuration $(l_x/z)$.

Manipulating the market clearing and utility equalization conditions yields the corner equilibrium in structure F(xyz), given in table 18.2. The corner equilibrium is exactly the same as in structure D(xyz) except that the transaction efficiency coefficient in the market for intermediate goods, $t$, is replaced with the transaction efficiency coefficient in the market for labor, $s$. $M_{xz} \equiv M_x/M_y$ is the relative number of individuals choosing configuration $(l_x/z)$ to those choosing $(z/l_x l_y)$, $M_x$ is the total number of employees who produce x and $M_z$ is the total number of employers who produce z. It should be noted that an employer cannot manipulate $M_{xz}$ or $M_{yz}$ although she can choose $N_x$ and $N_y$ (the number of workers hired by an employer) and the corner equilibrium value of $N_x$ (or $N_y$) is the same as the corner equilibrium value of $M_{xz}$ (or $M_{yz}$) by coincidence. While more than one worker may be employed, economies of specialization in producing intermediate goods do not extend beyond a specific individual.

*Structure F(xz)* consists of $(z/l_x)$ producing and selling the final good and buying labor to produce the intermediate good x, and $(l_x/z)$. The difference between structures F(xyz) and F(xz) is that in the latter structure a smaller variety of inputs is produced. The corner equilibrium in structure F(xz) is exactly the same as in structure D(xz) except that the transaction efficiency coefficient in the market for intermediate goods, $t$, is replaced with the transaction efficiency coefficient in the market for labor, $s$. $M_{xz} \equiv M_x/M_z$ is the relative number of individuals choosing configuration $(l_x/z)$ to those choosing $(z/l_x)$, $M_x$ is the total number of employees who produce x and $M_z$ is the total number of employers who produce z.

*Structure F(yz)* is symmetric with structure F(xz).

Corresponding to structure D(xyz), there are more possible structures with firms. They all have the same structure of division of labor as in D(xyz) and F(xyz), but have different structures of transactions and residual rights. One of these structures is that a producer of good z hires labor to produce good x, but buys good y from the market. It can be shown that in the symmetric model, the corner equilibrium in this structure cannot be a general equilibrium since it generates a lower per capita real income than either structure F(xyz) or F(xz). Another of the structures is that the owner of a firm is the specialist producer of either good x or good y rather than the specialist producer of good z. Similarly, there are more structures with the same level and pattern of division of labor as in structure F(xz) or F(yz) but with different ownership arrangements for the firm. If we consider all of these structures the results will be richer. But the conclusion will be similar to those in chapter 8. That is, the general equilibrium structure is the corner equilibrium that involves the largest transaction efficiency coefficients and avoids the smallest transaction efficiency coefficients of goods and factors.

## ◆ 18.5 Concurrent Changes in the Level of Division of Labor, Productivity, and Input Diversity

Comparisons between the per capita real incomes in structures A(xyz), A(xz), A(yz), D(xyz), D(xz), D(yz), F(xyz), F(xz), and F(yz), together with the Yao theorem, generate the general equilibrium and its inframarginal comparative statics, summarized in table 18.3.

The inframarginal comparative statics of the general equilibrium implies that as transaction efficiency is improved, division of labor evolves. For instance, the general equilibrium shifts from an autarky structure A(xz) to the structure with division of labor D(xyz), as transaction efficiencies for final and intermediate goods $k$ and $t$ are increased to be greater than $Q2^{-1/\rho}$.

Whether such evolution is associated with the emergence of new producer goods and related new technology is determined by the degree of economies of variety of producer goods $1/\rho$ in comparison to the degree of economies of specialization in producing the producer goods $a$. If $1/\rho > a$, then the evolution in division of labor is not associated with the evolution in the number of producer goods. If the degree of economies of specialization in producing the producer goods dominates the degree of economies of variety of producer goods, that is, $1/\rho < a$, then new machines and related new technology emerge from the evolution in division of labor. For instance for $1/\rho > a$, autarky structure A(xyz), with two producer goods, shifts to the structure with division of labor D(xyz), with the two producer goods as transaction efficiencies for the final and intermediate goods are sufficiently improved. But if $1/\rho < a$, the equilibrium shifts from autarky structure A(xz), with one producer good, to the structure with division of labor D(xyz) and with two producer goods, as transaction efficiencies for the final and intermediate goods are suffi-

Table 18.3: General equilibrium and its inframarginal comparative statics

| | $1/\rho < a$ | | | | $1/\rho > a$ | | | |
|---|---|---|---|---|---|---|---|---|
| Transaction | $s < t$ | | $s > t$ | | $s < t$ | | $s > t$ | |
| Efficiency | $tk < Q2^{-1/\rho}$ | $tk > Q2^{-1/\rho}$ | $sk < Q2^{1/\rho}$ | $sk > Q2^{1/\rho}$ | $tk < Q2^{-a/\rho}$ | $tk > Q2^{-a/\rho}$ | $sk < Q2^{-a/\rho}$ | $sk > Q2^{-a/\rho}$ |
| Structure | A(xz) | D(xyz) | A(xz) | F(xyz) | A(xyz) | D(xyz) | A(xyz) | F(xyz) |

*where* $Q \equiv 2(a\beta)^{a\beta}\alpha^{\alpha/\beta}(1-\beta)^{(\beta-1)/\beta}\beta^{-1}(a\beta+\alpha)^{-(a\beta+\alpha)/\beta}$

ciently improved, thereby generating concurrent evolution in division of labor as well as in the number of producer goods.

Whether the division of labor is organized by the institution of the firm or by the markets for the final and intermediate goods is of course determined by the relative transaction efficiencies of the intermediate goods and labor. For instance, if the transaction efficiency for labor $s$ is smaller than that for intermediate good $t$, then the division of labor is organized by the markets for the intermediate and final goods (structure D(xyz), or D(xz)) in the absence of the institution of the firm and of a labor market. If the transaction efficiency for labor $s$ is greater than that for intermediate good $t$, then the division of labor is organized by the institution of the firm and the markets for labor and for the final good (structure F(xyz) or F(xz)). If we consider the difference in transaction efficiency between labor inputs employed to produce different goods, then we can prove, following the approach devised in chapter 8, that the question of which kind of specialist producers are the employers is determined by the relative sizes of the transaction efficiency coefficients of labor inputs employed to produce different goods. It can be shown that the institution of the firm can be used to get the activity with the lowest transaction efficiencies for both of its input and output involved in the division of labor, meanwhile avoiding their direct pricing and marketing.

Figure 18.2 gives an intuitive illustration of a shift of equilibrium from autarky to the division of labor (structure D or F) if $1/\rho < a$. In A(xz), each person self-provides the intermediate good x and uses it to self-provide the final good z because of low transaction efficiency. As the transaction efficiency of trading intermediate goods is sufficiently improved relative to the transaction efficiency of trading labor, the equilibrium shifts to structure D(xyz) where markets for intermediate goods and final goods emerge from the division of labor. If the transaction efficiency of labor is higher than that of intermediate goods, firms will emerge from the division of labor where the market for intermediate goods will be replaced by the market for labor. In structure D(xyz), people producing goods x and y exchange their products for good z. In structure F(xyz), workers exchange their labor for z and the employer selling good z has the authority to assign workers to produce different intermediate goods. Structure F(xyz) may improve transaction efficiency because residual rights to a firm can be used to indirectly price an activity that has a prohibitively low transaction efficiency. The model here shows that the function of the institution of the firm is not only to promote the division of labor, as shown in chapter 8, but also to bring out new producer goods which generate technical progress (an increase in productivity).

## ◆ 18.6 *Ex post* Production Functions, Emergence of New Machines, and Endogenous Technical Progress

Here, we would like to emphasize the distinction between the *ex ante production function* and the *ex post production function* again. (18.1) to (18.3) is a system of production functions that individuals can perceive before making their decisions. However, if transaction efficiency is low and $a > 1/\rho$, then only one intermediate good, for example good x, is produced in the general equilibrium which is autarky structure A(xz). Hence, the production function for good y is not observable in the market. We refer to a production function that is observable in the market equilibrium as an *ex post* production function. As shown in chapter 8, the structure of *ex post* production functions will change as the general equilibrium jumps from a corner equilibrium to another in response to parameter changes, despite the fixed structure and properties of the *ex ante* production functions.

The difference here is that such jumps may be associated with the emergence of new technology and related production functions. We define the emergence of a new *ex post* production function from the evolution of the division of labor as the *emergence of a new technology* or *endogenous technical progress*. According to this definition, the evolution of the division of labor will generate endogenous technical progress and a new technology will emerge from the evolution as transaction efficiency is improved, if economies of specialization dominate economies of complementarity.

When the transaction efficiency for intermediate goods is lower than that for labor employed to produce the intermediate goods, the asymmetric residual rights of the firm can be used to promote division of labor and endogenous technical progress and to bring about new machines. This is why the industrialization process is characterized by the concurrent emergence of new types of firms and new goods from evolution in division of labor. Most inventors of new machines and new technology, who made a fortune from their invention or innovation, used the institution of the firm to indirectly price their entrepreneurial effort. Thomas Edison organized a professional research institution with more than a hundred employees who specialized in different inventing activities (Josephson, 1959) and Boulton and Watt set up a firm and hired many individuals to invent the steam engine (their "condenser" was patented in 1769). However, all Chinese Emperors were extremely sensitive to unofficial free associations because dissidents tended to use such associations to develop underground antigovernment movements due to the characteristics of the dynasty cycle in Chinese history. Hence, there was no legal system that protected the residual rights of entrepreneurs to manufacturing firms. Instead, the government tended to infringe arbitrarily upon such residual rights. This explains the puzzle mentioned by Elvin (1973), that Song China (960–1270 AD) possessed both the scientific knowledge and the mechanical ability to have experienced a full-fledged industrial revolution four centuries before it occurred in Europe. It did not take place because the technology could not be commercialized through the institution of the firm. Also, the non-existence of patent law in China implies that transaction efficiency for intellectual property was low, so that inventors could not be specialized and the extent of the market for the invention was too thin to support sophisticated technology.

## ◆ 18.7 Changes in the Economic Structure and Topological Properties of Economic Organisms

Suppose that transaction efficiency changes within the parameter subspace that maintains F(xyz) or D(xyz) as equilibrium; it is then possible to analyze marginal comparative statics. If it is assumed that the final good is an agricultural product and the intermediate good is a capital good (equipment and machines used in producing the final good) produced by the manufacturing sector, $2M_{xz} \equiv (M_x + M_y)/M_z$ can measure the income ratio of the manufacturing sector to the agricultural sector in structure F(xyz) or D(xyz). Here, $M_x + M_y$ and $M_z$ are the respective quantities of labor allocated to the manufacturing and agricultural sectors. They can be considered as respective values of the sectors in terms of labor as well. Further, the value ratio of producer goods to consumer goods $2M_{xz}$ represents the relative importance of the roundabout productive sector to the final sector. From table 18.2, we know that $2M_{xz}$ in structures D($xyz$) and F($xyz$) is given by

$$2M_{xz} = 2kt\beta/(1 - \beta) \text{ in } D(xyz) \text{ and} \qquad (18.5a)$$

$$2M_{xz} = (N_x + N_y) = 2ks\beta/(1 - \beta) \text{ in } F(xyz) \qquad (18.5b)$$

This ratio is an increasing function of transaction efficiency $k$ and $t$ or $s$, and the degree of Type A economies of roundabout production which relates to $\beta$. Condition (18.5) implies that the greater the transaction efficiency and/or economies of roundabout production, the greater is the relative size of the roundabout productive sector. The manufacturing sector will be enlarged relative to the agricultural sector and the number of workers hired by an employer will increase if transaction efficiency and/or economies of roundabout production are increased. If we view people in autarky as traditional peasants, then a development from autarky to the division of labor will increase employment in the industrial sector, which is 0 in autarky and $M_x + M_y > 0$ with the division of labor. This development decreases the number of peasants, which is $M$ in autarky, and $M_z < M$ for the division of labor. However, this may be a misleading view of the economic development generated by the evolution of the division of labor. According to our model, the development from autarky to the division of labor is a process that involves the conversion of self-sufficient individuals to professional farmers and workers rather than a process that transfers labor from the agricultural sector to the industrial sector.

From table 18.2, it can be seen that the marginal comparative statics within structures $D(xyz)$ or $F(xyz)$ indicate that per capita real income and productivity also increase with transaction efficiency.

According to our model, the emergence of new producer (capital) goods and new technology and an increase in the quantity of intermediate goods (or capital goods) involved in the market is not a matter of changes in available resources and technology, but rather is a matter of the development of the division of labor in roundabout activities. The new classical framework can be used to endogenize technical progress in the sense of endogenizing the number of productive factors and productivity. The emergence of new capital goods related to new technology is determined by the equilibrium level of division of labor, which depends on transaction efficiency. The analysis in this section leads us to

**Proposition 18.1:** An improvement in transaction efficiency will shift an autarchic economy to the division of labor. Such a shift increases productivity, the extent of the market, trade dependence, the number of professional producers of intermediate goods, and per capita real income, and reduces the number of producers of final goods. It increases the diversity of inputs at the same time if economies of specialization dominate economies of complementarity. Firms emerge from this process if the trading of a producer good is less efficient than the trading of labor hired to produce the producer good. An improvement in transaction efficiency within a structure with the division of labor increases productivity and the income share of the intermediate sector relative to that of the final sector, and the size of a firm if firms emerge from the division of labor.

The model in this chapter has formalized the idea that available resources are ultimately constrained only by people's knowledge about their environment, while people's capacity for acquiring that knowledge is determined by the level of division of labor which is dictated by transaction efficiency in a static model and by a dynamic mechanism in a dynamic model (see chapter 22). For the model in this chapter, if economies of specialization dominate economies of complementarity, then only one producer good is used, and another producer good cannot be employed when transaction efficiency is so small that autarky is equilibrium. A sufficient improvement in transaction efficiency will bring out new producer goods and related new technology via a larger-sized network of division of labor.

## ◆ 18.8 Evolution in the Number of Producer Goods and Economic Development

For the model in example 18.1, the maximum number of producer goods is 2. In this section we use a model with $m \in (1, \infty)$ producer goods to study the relationship between industrialization, evolution of division of labor, and evolution of number of producer goods.

### Example 18.2: a simplified version of the Sun–Lio model of industrialization (1997)

Consider an economy with a continuum of *ex ante* identical consumer-producers of mass $M$. There is one consumer good, y, and $m$ types of intermediate goods, $i = 1, 2, \ldots, m$. For an individual, the self-provided quantities of the consumer good y and producer good $i$ are $y$ and $x_i$, respectively. The quantities sold of the consumer good y and producer goods $i$ are $y^s$ and $x_i^s$, respectively. The quantities purchased of the goods are $y^d$ and $x_i^d$, respectively.

An individual uses both labor and $m$ intermediate goods to produce the consumer good y. The consumer good is produced by a Cobb–Douglas production function with inputs $l_y$ and $V$, given by

$$y^p \equiv y + y^s = e^{-cm} V^\beta l_y^\alpha, \tag{18.6a}$$

$$V = \left[ \sum_{i=1}^{m} (x_i + kx_i^d)^\rho \right]^{1/\rho}, \qquad \alpha + \beta = 1, \qquad \alpha, \beta, \rho, k \in (0,1)$$

where $y^p$ is the output level of y. $l_y$ is the individual's amount of labor allocated to the production of y. $V$ can be considered as a composite intermediate good, which is a CES function of inputs of $m$ producer goods. The total factor productivity of y is an increasing function of the number of intermediate goods $m$, although the Cobb–Douglas function displays constant returns. It is assumed that $\alpha + \beta > 1$ in the original Sun–Lio model. Since that assumption makes the algebra cumbersome, we will consider that assumption later on. A producer of the consumer good can either self-provide or buy the intermediate goods used in the production process. The transaction efficiency coefficient is $k$. $e^{-cm}$ is the management cost of $m$ producer goods in terms of loss of the output of final goods. This management cost is caused by the calculation process of the optimum decision. It increases with the number of producer goods employed in producing the final goods, since the number of first-order conditions of the optimum decision increases with $m$. Here, we have the trade-off between economies of variety of producer goods and calculation costs.

The production function of intermediate good i exhibits economies of specialization, given by

$$x_i^p \equiv x_i + x_i^s = l_i^b, \qquad b > 1, \qquad i = 1, 2,\ldots, m \tag{18.6b}$$

where $x_i^p$ is the output level of good i. $l_i$ is an individual's level of specialization in producing good i. Parameter $b$ represents the degree of economies of specialization in producing the intermediate good. The endowment constraint for each individual is:

$$l_y + \sum_{i=1}^{m}(l_i = 1, \qquad l_y, l_i \in [0, 1].$$
(18.6c)

Each individual's utility function is

$$u = y + ky^d,$$
(18.6d)

where $k$ is the transaction efficiency coefficient.

The budget constraint for an individual is given by

$$y^d + \sum_{i=1}^{m}p_ix_i^d = y^s + \sum_{i=1}^{m}p_ix_i^s$$
(18.6e)

where $p_i$ is the price of good i in terms of the consumer good.

There are three types of structures. In autarky structure A, each individual self-provides $m$ producer goods and the final consumption good, as shown in figure 18.3a. In structure

(a) Autarky:
$m = 2, n - 1 = 0$

(b) Partial division of labor:
$m = 3, n = 2$

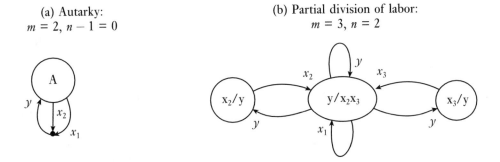

(c) Complete division of labor: $m = n = 4$

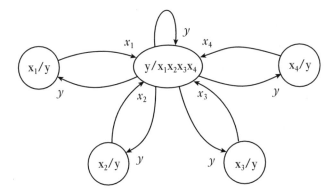

◆ **Figure 18.3:** Industrialization and evolution of division of labor in the Sun–Lio model

P, with partial division of labor, shown in 18.3b, population is divided between occupation configurations $(y/x_i)$ and $(x_i/y)$. A person choosing $(y/x_i)$ self-provides $m - n$ producer goods, buys $n$ producer goods, and sells the final good. A person choosing $(x_i/y)$ sells producer good i and buys the consumption good. In structure C, with complete division of labor, shown in 18.3c, population is divided between occupation configurations $(y/x_m)$ and $(x_i/y)$. A person choosing $(y/x_m)$ in C buys $m$ producer goods and sells the final good. Configuration $(x_i/y)$ in C is the same as in P.

Inserting $y^s = y^d = x_i^s = x_i^d = 0$ into an individual's decision problem, we can solve for the optimum decision and per capita real income in autarky as follows:

$$u_A = e^{-\beta(1-b\rho)/\rho}\alpha^{\alpha}(b\beta)^{b\beta}(\alpha + b\beta)^{-(\alpha+b\beta)}[\beta(1 - b\rho)/(c\rho)]^{\beta(1-b\rho)/\rho}, \tag{18.7}$$
$$l_y = \alpha/(\alpha + b\beta), \qquad m_A = \beta(1 - b\rho)/(c\rho)$$

where $u_A$ is the per capita real income and $m_A$ is the equilibrium number of intermediate goods in autarky. Since the solution of $m_A$ in (18.7) is negative for $b > 1/\rho$ but $m_A$ cannot be nonpositive, (18.7) implies that the corner equilibrium in autarky does not exist for $b > 1/\rho$. Differentiation of (18.7) yields $dm_A/d\beta > 0$, $dm_A/d\rho < 0$, $dm_A/dc < 0$, and $dm_A/db < 0$.

The decision problem for a person choosing configuration $(y/x_i)$ in structure P can be obtained by assuming that $y$, $y^s$, $l_y$, $l_j$, $x_j$, $x_r^d > 0$ and $y^d$, $l_r$, $x_j^s$, $x_j^d$, $x_r^s$, $x_r = 0$, where $r = 1$, 2, ..., $n$ denote producer goods purchased, and $j = n + 1, n + 2, ..., m$, denote producer goods self-provided. This decision problem is given as follows.

Max: $\displaystyle u_y = e^{-cm}[\sum_{j \in J} x_j^{\rho} + \sum_{r \in R}(kx_r^d)^{\rho}]^{\beta/\rho}l_y^{\alpha} - y^s$ \hfill (18.8)

s.t. $\displaystyle l_y + \sum_{j \in J} l_j = 1, \qquad y^s = \sum_{r \in R} p_r x_r^d$

where $u_y$ is the utility for configuration $(y/x)$, $R$ is the set of $n$ purchased intermediate goods, and $J$ is the set of self-provided intermediate goods. We can use the symmetry which implies that $\sum x_j^{\rho} = (m - n)x_j^{\rho}$, $\sum(kx_r^d)^{\rho} = n(kx_j^d)^{\rho}$, $\sum l_j = (m - n)l_j$, $\sum p_r x_r = np_r x_j$, to further simplify the decision problem in (18.8).

Using $y$, $y^s$, $l_y$, $l_j$, $x_j$, $x_r^d = 0$ and $y^d$, $l_r$, $y^d$, $x_r^s$, $> 0$, we have the decision problem for an individual choosing configuration $(x/y)$:

Max: $u_x = k_y y^d = k_y p_r$ \hfill (18.9)

s.t. $l_r = x_r^s = 1, \qquad y^d = p_r x_r^s = p_r$,

where $u_x$ is the utility for configuration $(x/y)$.

The solutions of the decision problems (18.8) and (18.9), together with utility equalization and market clearing conditions, determine the corner equilibrium in structure P. The corner equilibrium is summarized as follows.

$$p_i = p = e^{-cm}k\{1 + [(cb\rho s)/\alpha(1 - b\rho)]\}^{b(1-\beta)-\alpha}[\alpha(1 - b\rho)/(cb\rho)]^{b(1-\beta)} \tag{18.10}$$
$$[\beta(1 - b\rho)/\rho c]^{\beta/\rho}[\rho c/(1 - \rho)][(1 - \rho)/(1 - b\rho)]^{1/\rho},$$
$$l_y = 1/\{1 + (cb\rho s)/[\alpha(1 - b\rho)]\},$$
$$x^d = k[(1 - \beta)/(c\rho) + s/(1 - b\rho)]^{-1}(1 - \rho)^{-1},$$
$$m = [\beta(1 - b\rho)/(c\rho)] + [\rho(b - 1)/(1 - \rho)]n$$
$$= [\beta(1 - \rho)/(c\rho)] - [\rho(b - 1)/(1 - b\rho)]s,$$
$$n = m - s, \qquad M_y = M/(1 + nx^d), \qquad M_x = x^d M_y,$$

where the corner equilibrium value of $s$ is given by

$$f(s) \equiv [(1 - \beta)/(c\rho) + s/(1 - b\rho)]\{cb\rho/[\alpha(1 - b\rho) + cbs\rho]\}^b (1 - \rho)$$
$$[(1 - b\rho)/(1 - \rho)]^{1/\rho} - k^2 = 0 \qquad (18.11)$$

where $m$ is the corner equilibrium number of intermediate goods in structure P, $n$ is the corner equilibrium number of traded intermediate goods and represents the level of division of labor in equilibrium, and $s$ is the corner equilibrium number of self-provided intermediate goods and indicates the level of self-sufficiency. $M_x$ is the number of producers of a traded intermediate good and $M_y$ is the number of sellers of the final good.

(18.10) indicates that the corner equilibrium value of price $p_i$ is negative if $l_y$ is positive and if $b > 1/\rho$. This implies that the corner equilibrium in structure P does not exist for $b > 1/\rho$. A comparison between $m$ in (18.10) and $m_A$ in (18.7) suggests that the number of producer goods in structure P is always larger than in autarky. Differentiating (18.11) and then using the implicit function theorem, it can be shown

$$ds/dk = -(\partial f/\partial k)/(\partial f/\partial s) < 0 \qquad (18.12)$$

where $\partial f/\partial k, \partial f/\partial s < 0$ if $\alpha + \beta = 1$, $\rho \in (0, 1)$, and $b \in (1, 1/\rho)$. Therefore, if structure P is a general equilibrium structure, which means that $b < 1/\rho$, (18.12) must hold.

Manipulating (18.10)–(18.12) yields the comparative statics of the corner equilibrium in structure P:

$$dm/dk > 0, \qquad dn/dk > 0, \qquad (18.13a)$$

$$d(m - n)/dk < 0, \qquad dl_y/dk > 0, \qquad dx^d/dk > 0. \qquad (18.13b)$$

Using the envelope theorem, it can be shown that per capita real income in structure P increases as $k$ increases. Since the per capita real income in autarky is independent of transaction efficiency $k$, the per capita real income in structure P is more likely to be greater than in autarky as $k$ increases. This, together with the Yao theorem in chapter 6, implies that the general equilibrium will jump from autarky to structure P as transaction efficiency is improved. (18.13a) implies that the number of all available producer goods $m$ and the number of traded intermediate goods, $n$, increase concurrently, as transaction efficiency is improved. (18.13) implies that as transaction efficiency is improved, the number of traded intermediate goods, $n$, increases faster than the number of all intermediate goods, $m$, does. Hence, as transaction efficiency is sufficiently improved, the general equilibrium will jump from the partial division of labor to the complete division of labor (structure C). Also, (18.13b) implies that in this process, the level of specialization of each producer of the final good increases and her demand for each intermediate good increases.

Since some endogenous variables discontinuously jump as $n$ changes from a value smaller than $m$ to $m$, we cannot obtain the corner equilibrium values of some endogenous variables, such as relative prices, in structure C by simply letting $n = m$ in (18.10)–(18.15). But it is not difficult to solve for the corner equilibrium in structure C by following the same procedure for solving the corner equilibrium in structure P. The corner equilibrium and its comparative statics are given as follows.

$$m = \beta(1-\rho)/(\rho c), \qquad x^d = \rho ck/[(1-\rho)(1-\beta)] \tag{18.14}$$
$$p = k^{2\beta-1}e^{-\beta(1-\rho)/\rho}\beta^{\beta/\rho}(1-\beta)^{1-\beta}[\rho c/(1-\rho)]^{\beta}[(1-\rho)/(\rho c)]^{\beta/\rho},$$
$$u = k^{2\beta}e^{-\beta(1-\rho)/\rho}\beta^{\beta/\rho}(1-\beta)^{1-\beta}[\rho c/(1-\rho)]^{\beta}[(1-\rho)/(\rho c)]^{\beta/\rho},$$
$$dm/d\beta > 0, \qquad dm/d\rho < 0, \qquad dm/dc < 0, \qquad du/dk > 0,$$

where $m = n$ is the number of traded intermediate goods as well as the number of all available intermediate goods in the complete division of labor. Somehow the corner equilibrium in structure C is analogous to the general equilibrium in the Ethier model in exercise 13 of chapter 11. From this view, the Ethier model is a special case of the Sun–Lio model.

Figure 18.3 provides intuitive illustration of industrialization, structural changes, and evolution of division of labor in the Sun–Lio model. We first consider the parameter subspace $b < 1/\rho$. If transaction efficiency is very low, autarky is the general equilibrium where the number of available intermediate goods is very small and there is no market. As transaction efficiency is improved, the general equilibrium jumps to the partial division of labor in panel (b), where the *ex post* production functions of a new intermediate good and the markets for two intermediate goods and the final good emerge from the network of division of labor. As transaction efficiency is further improved, the general equilibrium jumps to the complete division of labor in panel (c), where one more new intermediate good and two more markets for intermediate goods emerge from evolution of network of division of labor and related transactions. The evolution of division of labor can continue as transaction conditions are improved, since there is no limit for the evolution of the number of goods which creates unlimited scope for the evolution of division of labor in roundabout production so long as the population size is not limited and $\rho$, $c$ are very small ($\beta(1-\rho)/c\rho$ is very large). For the parameter subspace $b > 1/\rho$ (economies of specialization dominate economies of complementarity), the general equilibrium is always associated with structure C. As the management cost coefficient $c$ declines, the equilibrium number of intermediate goods increases, but all individuals are always completely specialized. In other words, gradual evolution of specialization occurs only if economies of complementarity dominate economies of specialization.

Assume that the final good is the agricultural good and the intermediate goods are industrial goods (tractors, fertilizer, and other equipment) and that $b < 1/\rho$. Now we consider the relative population size of industrial and agricultural sectors. This ratio is

$$R = nM_x/M_y$$

where $n$ is the number of different occupation configurations selling $n$ intermediate goods, $M_x$ is the number of manufacturers selling one type of industrial good, and $M_y$ is the number of farmers. From the budget constraints in (18.8) and (18.9), it can be shown that $M_x/M_y = x^d$ (see (18.10)). Then from (18.10)–(18.13), it can be shown that $dx^d/dk = (dx^d/ds)(ds/dk) > 0$, where $dx^d/ds < 0$ from (18.10) and $ds/dk < 0$ from (18.12). Hence, we have

$$dR/dk = (\partial R/\partial x^d)(dx^d/dk) + (\partial R/\partial n)(dn/dk) > 0$$

where $dn/dk > 0$ due to (18.13). This result implies that as improvements in transaction conditions generate industrialization, the employment share in the industrial sector increases compared to the agricultural sector, even if the industrial sector does not produce any final goods.

Because of economies of specialization and economies of roundabout production in this model, productivities of all goods will increase as improvements in transaction efficiency drive division of labor to evolve in roundabout production. Also, the extent of the market, degree of endogenous comparative advantage, diversity of occupations and economic structure, production concentration, market integration all increase as division of labor evolves in roundabout production.

Sun and Lio (1996) have shown that the comparative statics of the general equilibrium in (18.12), (18.13), and (18.14) still hold even if $\alpha + \beta > 1$, which implies that there are economies of specialization in the agricultural sector. This distinguishes their model from the extended Ethier model in exercise 13 of chapter 11, where the agricultural sector has constant returns-to-scale technology. Lio and Sun solve for more corner equilibria with firms of this model, using the approach developed in chapter 8. They have shown that industrialization and declining average size of firms can concur if division of labor evolves between firms. Hence, possible empirical work to test the Sun–Lio model against the Ethier model can be conducted. If a negative correlation between the relative size of the industrial and agricultural sectors and the average size of firms is verified by empirical observation, then the Ehier model, which predicts positive correlation between the two variables, is rejected and the Sun–Lio model is affirmed.

One more aspect of economic organization has been studied in this chapter. We have shown that a function of a decentralized market is to find the efficient number of roundabout productive goods by trading off economies of specialization against transaction costs and economies of complementarity. In this process, the efficient structure of residual rights is chosen and endogenous technical progress is promoted by the invisible hand. Sun (1999) has established an existence theorem and the first welfare theorem for a class of general new classical models with producer goods. The models in this chapter are special cases of his general model, which provides a sound theoretical foundation for our results here.

## Key Terms and Review

Type A and Type B economies of roundabout production, economies of variety of producer goods, and economies of complementarity between different producer goods.

The difference between *ex ante* and *ex post* production functions, and implications of the difference for endogenization of technical progress.

The relationship between transaction efficiency, network size of division of labor, emergence of new machines from the evolution of division of labor, and related endogenous technical progress.

Implications of the CES function for endogenizing the number of producer goods.

The relationship between the degree of economies of complementarity between producer goods and the elasticity of substitution between producer goods.

Implications of free pricing, free choice of occupation configuration, free entry into any profession, and institutional arrangements in protecting residual rights to the firm for the emergence of new machines from evolution of division of labor in roundabout production.

Differences between neoclassical technology fundamentalism (or R&D investment fundamentalism) and the new classical view about the relationship between division of labor and technological progress.

## Further Reading

*New classical models of an endogenous number of producer goods*: Yang and Y.-K. Ng (1993, ch. 12), Sun and Lio (1996), Sun (1999), Liu (1999), Borland and Yang (1995), Young (1928), Yang and S. Ng (1998), Stigler (1951); *neoclassical models of an endogenous number of producer goods*: Ethier (1982), Krugman and Venables (1995); *evidence for the relationship between evolution of division of labor and technical progress*: Chandler (1990), Braudel (1984), Josephson (1959), Marshall (1890), Mokyr (1993), North (1981, 1990).

## QUESTIONS

1 Young (1928) and Marshall (1890) noted the network effect of division of labor in roundabout production. A change in the level of specialization in a sector changes the extent of the market for other sectors, thereby increasing the level of specialization in other sectors. The network effect is the most important driving force for technical progress. Marshall suggested using the notion of external economies of scale to describe the network effect of division of labor; Young indicated that the notion is misleading. Analyze the difference between this economic analysis of technical progress featuring the network effect of division of labor and the neoclassical analysis of technical progress featuring the notion of economies of scale and an *ad hoc* positive relationship between productivity and investment. Connect your discussion to the distinction between *ex ante* and *ex post* production functions and the notion of endogenous technical progress in this chapter.

2 Use historical evidence for the relationship between evolution of division of labor and technical progress provided by Chandler (1990), Braudel (1984), Josephson (1959), Mokyr (1993), North (1981), and Marshall (1890) to analyze the economic conditions for the Industrial Revolution which commercialized many technical inventions.

3 According to the model in this chapter, an increase in capital shown by statistical data is in essence an increase in the level of division of labor in roundabout production, while an increase in labor input level shown by statistical data indicates development of the institution of the firm which may be associated with an increase in the level of division of labor within firms. Use these ideas to discuss why the neoclassical view that explains technical progress by an increase in the size of capital or labor or by exogenous changes of production parameters might be misleading.

4 According to Mokyr (1990, pp. 235–50; 1993), violation of private property rights by the government, the absence of patent laws, more effective regulation by the government and guilds, a strong tradition of mercantilism which advocated protectionism in the European Continent explained why the Industrial Revolution did not take place first on the Continent. According to him, the following features of Chinese institutions explain why the Industrial Revolution could not occur in China before the nineteenth century. The state monopolized important industries and inventing activities and could arbitrarily infringe upon property rights and confiscate properties of private firms. The state monopolized trade, ideology, and provided incentive to elites only for political or military careers. Also the state carried out an active industrial policy to promote agriculture and to suppress commerce, and directly intervened in economic activities. There was no free city in China and the feudal system was replaced with a central government system after the first century, AD. Compare this analysis with North, Mokyr, and others' analyses of the conditions for the Industrial Revolution. Choose a developing country and examine if the conditions for the British Industrial Revolution are still essential for industrialization of this country and if obstacles for industrialization in eighteenth-century France and China are still obstacles for industrialization of this country.

5 Interpret the inframarginal comparative statics of general equilibrium in this chapter in connection to North's following observation (1981, p. 167): "The Industrial Revolution, as I perceive it, was initiated by increasing size of markets, which resulted in pressures to replace medieval and crown restrictions circumscribing entrepreneurs with better specified common laws. The growing size of the market also induced changes in organization, away from vertical integration as exemplified in home and handicraft production to specialization. With specialization came the increasing transaction costs of measuring the inputs and outputs. The resultant increased supervision and central monitoring of inputs to improve quality radically lowered the cost of devising new techniques. From handcraft to putting-out system to the factory system spans more than three centuries; the key to explaining the transformation is growth in the size of the market and problems of quality control (that is, measurement of the characteristics of the good)."

6 Marshall (1890, p. 241) described the relationship between network of division of labor, transaction conditions, and development of specialized machinery as follows. "The development of the organism, whether social or physical, involves an increasing subdivision of functions between its separate parts on the one hand, and on the other a more intimate connection between them. Each part gets to be less and less self-sufficient, to depend for its well-being more and more on other parts, so that any disorder in any part of a highly-developed organism will affect other parts also. This increased subdivision of functions, or 'differentiation,' as it is called, manifests itself with regard to industry in such forms as the division of labour, and the development of specialized skill, knowledge and machinery: while 'integration,' that is, a growing intimacy and firmness of the connections between the separate parts of the industrial organism, shows itself in such forms as the increase of security of commercial credit, and of the means and habits of communication by sea and by road, by railway and telegraph, by post and printing-press." Use the models in this chapter to formalize this description.

7 According to Mokyr (1993, p. 26), the positive feedback loop between transaction efficiency, technical inventions, and network size of division of labor was an important driving force for the British Industrial Revolution during 1750–1830. Use the Chu model in example 14.3 of chapter 14, which describes the feedback loop between transaction efficiency, the level of specialization in the transacting sector, and the extent of the market, and the model in this chapter to conduct a thought experiment to explain the historical facts.

8 Use the model in this chapter to explain why under certain conditions multinational firms are a better institution than the direct trade of know-how for efficiently pricing management and technical knowledge.

9 Identify the distinction between economies of complementarity in this chapter and economies of complementarity in chapter 11. The condition for a gradual evolution of the variety of consumer goods in chapter 11 is that economies of complementarity in consumption dominate economies of specialization in producing final goods, while the condition for a gradual evolution of the variety of producer goods in this chapter is that economies of complementarity between producer goods in producing final goods are dominated by economies of specialization in producing the producer goods. Discuss the results.

# EXERCISES

1  Replace the production functions of x and y in example 18.1 with $x^p \equiv x + x^s = \text{Max}\{0, l_x - \alpha\}, y^p \equiv y + y^s = \text{Max}\{0, l_y - \alpha\}$. Solve for the general equilibrium and its inframarginal comparative statics. Discuss the implications of fixed learning costs for the emergence of new machines and related new technology from evolution of division of labor.

2  Assume that in the model in example 18.1 $\beta = \rho = 0.5$ and $\alpha = 2$, but transaction efficiency $t$ differs between goods x and y. Solve for the general equilibrium and its infra-marginal comparative statics. Identify the condition under which one of the producer goods never emerges in the general equilibrium.

3  Assume that in the model in example 18.1 $\beta = \rho = 0.5$ and $\alpha = 2$, but transaction costs other than that caused by tax are absent. The government taxes each dollar of good x that is sold, then evenly distributes the tax revenue among the sellers of x. Solve for the general equilibrium and its inframarginal comparative statics. Analyze the impact of the tax on the equilibrium level of division of labor and emergence of new machines.

4  Consider the Sun and Lio model in example 18.2. We now assume that the production function for the intermediate good i is $x_i + x_i^s = \text{Max}\{0, l_x - b\}$. Solve for the equilibrium and its comparative statics. Use this model to analyze why many new machines emerged during the Industrial Revolution in Britain.

5  Assume in an extended version of the Sun–Lio model that there are two final goods, one of them needs intermediate goods in the production process and the other does not. Solve for the comparative statics of the general equilibrium. Then use your results to analyze the relationship between industrialization and evolution of division of labor.

6  Allow labor trade and setting up firms in example 18.2. Solve for the equilibrium and its comparative statics. Use this model to explore the relationship between evolution of the institution of the firm and evolution of division of labor in roundabout production.

7  Show that in the Sun–Lio model in example 18.2 the income share of agricultural goods (final goods) decreases as transaction conditions are improved. Some economists call this Engels' law and attribute it to changes in tastes and income. Why can the Engels' law hold in the absence of changes of tastes and production functions (or in the absence of changes on demand and supply sides)?

8  If intermediate goods in the Sun–Lio model are interpreted as capital goods, then as trans-action conditions are improved, the equilibrium degree of capital intensity will evolve. Assume that there are two countries with the same population size (or labor endowment) in the Sun–Lio model. Show that a country will export goods that are increasingly capital intensive even if the two countries have no exogenous endowment comparative advantage. Compare your results with the HO model in chapter 12 and discuss the essential differences in meaning of the notion of factor intensity between a neoclassical model with constant returns to scale and the new classical model with economies of specialization.

9  Liu, 1999: Replace the production function in the Sun–Lio model with $y + y^s = \{\sum_{i=1}^n [(kx_i^d + x_i)^\alpha (l_{yi} - F)^\rho\}^{1/\rho}$. Solve for equilibrium and its inframarginal comparative statics.

10  Liu, 1999: Consider an economy consisting of country 1 and country 2. There are $M_i$ ex ante identical consumer-producers in country i. Each individual consumes two final goods y and good z. Good z can be used as an intermediate good to produce good y as well. A person in country i has the utility function $u_i = (y_i + K_i y_i^d)(z_{1i} + K_i z_{1i}^d)$, where $z_1$ denotes good z used for final consumption and $z_2$ denotes that used as an intermediate good to produce final

good y. $K_i = k_i$ for domestic trade and $K_i = k_i\theta$ for international trade. The domestic transaction cost coefficient is $1-k_i$ in country i; $\theta \in (0, 1)$ is the transaction efficiency coefficient for international trade. The production functions for goods z and y are, respectively, $z_i + z_i^s = \text{Max}\{(L_{zi} - F), 0\}$, $F \in (0,L)$ and $y_i + y_i^s = \text{Max}\{(z_{2i} + K_i z_{2i}^d)^a(L_{yi} - F), (L_{yi} - F), 0\}$, $a \in (0,1)$, $i = 1,2$. The endowment constraint for an individual in country i is $L_{zi} + L_{yi} = L$. Solve for equilibrium and its inframarginal comparative statics.

11  Sun, 1999: Prove the existence theorem for a general class of the models in this chapter. Then establish the first welfare theorem. Discuss the implications of the two theorems for application of new classical economics. Sun does not consider the institution of the firm in his proof. You may explicitly consider the institution of the firm in your proof.

chapter **19**

# INDUSTRIALIZATION AND THE DIVISION OF LABOR IN ROUNDABOUT PRODUCTION

## ◆ 19.1 The Features of Industrialization

From the stories in the previous chapters about evolution in division of labor and related economic structure, and about the emergence of new machines and related new technology, we may be tempted to formalize the ideas about industrialization and industrial revolution proposed by Smith (1776), Young (1928), and other economists within the new classical framework. There are at least three models of industrialization. The first is the model of labor surplus and dual economy (Lewis, 1955, Fei and Ranis, 1964). In this model, the expansion of the industrial sector is explained by labor surplus and exogenous technical progress or capital accumulation in the industrial sector. As exogenous technical progress takes place or as capital accumulates in the industrial sector, which raises marginal productivity of labor, demand for labor increases. Because of the existence of labor surplus, the increasing demand would not raise the wage rate and cost of the expansion of the industrial sector. Hence, the industrial sector can be developed at a zero or low cost to the agricultural sector. Labor surplus in the model is caused by an *ad hoc* assumption that the price of labor is higher than the equilibrium level for some unspecified institutional reason. Since there is no trade-off between exploitation of exogenous comparative advantage and transaction costs in the model of labor surplus, this model cannot explain productivity progress in the absence of exogenous changes in production functions or in capital stock. As shown in chapter 12, we need to abandon the neoclassical dichotomy between pure consumers and firms to cook up the trade-off between exploitation of exogenous comparative advantage and transaction costs when constant returns-to-scale technology is specified.

The second type of theory of industrialization is called by Krugman (1995) "high development economics" and developed by Rosenstein-Rodan (1943), Nurkse (1953), Fleming (1955), and Hirschman (1958). Those authors did not use general equilibrium models to formalize their vague ideas. There are two ways to interpret their ideas. According to Krugman (1995), they imply that economies of scale are an important factor for industrialization. Krugman argues that the theory of labor surplus was more popular than high development economics because the former was easier to formulate in terms of the models with constant returns to scale, while economists did not know the right way to formalize the latter using the general equilibrium of economies of scale. Hence, the Dixit–Stiglitz model and the Ethier model in chapter 11 provide a technical vehicle to substantiate high development economics and the theory of industrialization.

However, most high development economists do not mention economies of scale. They talk about interdependencies of profitability in different industrial sectors, balanced vs. unbalanced industrialization, circular causation in the industrialization process, and external economies based on industrial linkage network. All of these notions are not difficult to formalize in a general equilibrium model. Circular causation is of course a notion of general equilibrium. In a standard neoclassical general equilibrium model each individual's decision in choosing her quantities demanded and supplied is dependent on prices, while the general equilibrium prices are determined by all individuals' decisions in choosing their quantities. This implies that all interdependent endogenous variables must be simultaneously determined by a general equilibrium mechanism. Comparative statics of general equilibrium is a powerful vehicle to substantiate the mechanism. Of course, we can use either static general equilibrium models and comparative statics of equilibrium, or dynamic general equilibrium models and dynamics and comparative dynamics of equilibrium to do the job. Explicit specification of time dimension can increase the degree of endogenization at the cost of tractability of models. But it is a matter of degree rather than a difference of substance. The substance here is the notions of general equilibrium and of a fixed point, and their power to substantiate mechanisms that simultaneously determine interdependent endogenous variables.

Hence, high development economics relates to the notion of general equilibrium. When economists are not familiar with the technical substance of general equilibrium models, they can only use vague words to address general equilibrium phenomena, such as circular causation, interdependent decisions in different industries, pecuniary externality of industrial linkage (external economies that can be exploited via the market price system), and so on.

However, there are three types of general equilibrium model. In a neoclassical general equilibrium model with constant returns to scale, circular causation is between quantities and prices and between individuals' decisions in different sectors. In a general equilibrium model with economies of scale and an endogenous number of goods (see chapter 11), circular causation is among quantities, prices, productivity, and the number of goods in addition to interdependencies among different markets and different individuals' decisions. In a new classical general equilibrium model (in chapters 5, 6, 8, 9, 11), there are interdependencies of the network size of division of labor, the extent of the market, productivity, trade dependence, diversity of economics structure, the number of goods, the degree of market integration, the degree of endogenous comparative advantage, and so on, in addition to the interdependencies among quantities, prices, different individuals' decisions, and different markets.

We have already studied the method to formalize high development economics using general equilibrium models with economies of scale in chapter 11. In this chapter we shall investigate the method to formalize high development economics using a new classical general equilibrium model.

In this chapter we predict a very important phenomenon of industrialization, noted by Allyn Young (1928), namely an increase in roundaboutness of production. The extended

Ethier model with economies of scale (exercise 13 in chapter 11) can predict concurrent increases in productivity, in the number of goods, and in the output share of the industrial sector. It cannot, however, predict concurrent evolution in individuals' levels of specialization, in productivity, and in the number of links of a roundabout production chain, although it endogenizes the number of goods at a single link of the chain. Industrialization is characterized by the following concurrent phenomena. Division of labor evolves and each individual's level of specialization increases, the degrees of commercialization and trade dependence rise, new producer goods and related new technology emerge from the evolution in division of labor, the degree of diversity of economic structure, the extent of endogenous comparative advantage, the degree of market integration, and the degree of production concentration all go up, and the institution of the firm and labor market emerge and develop as division of labor evolves. More importantly, the number of links in a long roundabout production chain, or the number of layers of a hierarchical structure in roundabout production, increases and some new links or new layers of the industrial structure emerge from the evolution in division of labor.

A general equilibrium model that describes industrialization must be able, at the minimum, to predict the following concurrent phenomena. Individuals' levels of specialization increase, the number of links in a roundabout production chain increases, the number of producer goods in each of the links increases, productivity and per capita real income increase, the size of the market network expands, and the institution of the firm emerges and develops in the process.

Let us first tell the story behind the formal model in this chapter. In the story there are many *ex ante* identical consumer-producers. Each of them could produce four types of good: food, hoes, tractors, and machine tools. Labor is essential in producing machine tools. Labor and machine tools are essential for the production of tractors. Labor is essential for the production of hoes. Each individual can either use labor, or hoes and labor, or tractors and labor, or both hoes and tractors together with labor to produce food. There are economies of complementarity between tractors and hoes in raising productivity of food. There are economies of specialization in producing each good. Trade will incur transaction costs. If hoes and tractors are not produced, there is only one link in production: labor is employed to produce food. If tractors are not produced, there are only two links in production: the production of hoes and the production of food. There is only one producer good in the upstream link. If tractors and hoes are produced, then machine tools, which are essential for the production of tractors, must be produced too. There are three links of roundabout production: the production of machine tools, the production of tractors and hoes, and the production of food, employing machine tools and hoes. There are two producer goods in the middle link of the roundabout production process. There are three types of economy of roundaboutness. The total factor productivity of the downstream goods increases with the quantities of upstream goods employed in producing the downstream goods (Type A economies of roundabout production); the total factor productivity of the downstream goods increases with the number of upstream goods (Type B economies of roundabout production); the total factor productivity of the final goods increases with the number of links of the roundabout production chain (Type C economies of roundabout production). Hence, the total factor productivity of food is the highest when all producer goods (hoes, tractors, and machine tools) are produced and is the lowest when none of them is produced. However, there is a trade-off between economies of roundabout production and economies of specialization, since each individual's level of specialization would be very low if she produced many goods. If she wants to keep her level of specialization as well as the degree of roundaboutness high at the same time, then she must trade with others, so that there are trade-offs between economies of specialization, economies of roundabout production, and transaction costs.

Suppose transaction efficiency is very low; then economies of specialization are outweighed by transaction costs, so that individuals have to choose autarky where the scope for trading off economies of specialization against economies of roundabout production is very narrow. Hence, only a few goods that directly relate to final consumption are produced in autarky. For instance, they may produce food with labor alone. As transaction efficiency is slightly improved, individuals can choose a larger network of division of labor, so that the scope for trading off economies of specialization against economies of roundabout production is enlarged. Therefore, the degree of roundaboutness and all individuals' levels of specialization can increase side by side through the division of labor between different specialists. For instance, the general equilibrium jumps from autarky with no producer goods to the division of labor between specialist manufacturers of hoes and professional farmers. As transaction efficiency is further improved, horizontal division of labor between the production of hoes and the production of tractors creates more scope for the vertical division of labor between the production of tractors and the production of machine tools, so that the number of links in roundabout production is further increased from 2 to 3. In this process, not only does a new link emerge from evolution in industrial structure, but also the number of producer goods in the existing upstream link increases.

If transaction efficiency for labor is higher than that for producer goods, then the evolution in division of labor will be associated with the emergence and development of the institution of the firm. Hence, improvements in transaction efficiency will generate the concurrent phenomena that are associated with industrialization and raise the income share of the roundabout production sector which is sometimes called the heavy industry sector.

Using this kind of model, we can formalize Smith's conjecture about a mechanism that decreases the income share of the agricultural sector. Smith explained the difference in productivity between the agricultural sector and industrial sector as determined by the relative difference in the benefits of specialization compared to the seasonal adjustment cost caused by specialization between the two sectors. This conjecture explains economic structure by the different balance points in trading off economies of division of labor against the coordination cost of the division of labor, instead of by tastes, income, or exogenous technical conditions. An extension of the theory implies that a decline in income share of the agricultural sector occurs not because of a change in tastes, in income, or in exogenous technical conditions, but because the agricultural sector has a higher coordination cost of division of labor compared to the benefits derived from the division of labor, and it can improve productivity only by importing an increasingly larger number of industrial goods. These goods are produced by a high level of division of labor in the manufacturing sector, where transaction costs are more likely to be outweighed by economies of division of labor.

Hence, Smith's conjecture implies that the increase in the income share of the industrial sector is due to relatively more significant economies of specialization compared to coordination costs in that sector than in the agricultural sector. In sections 19.2–19.4, we formalize the new classical story of industrialization. Sections 19.5 and 19.6 explore implications of the formal model.

---

### Questions to Ask Yourself when Reading this Chapter

◆ What is the driving mechanism of industrialization that is characterized by concurrent evolution of division of labor, of production roundaboutness, of the institution of the firm, of the income share of the industrial sector relative to the agricultural sector, and of the income share of the roundabout production sectors?

◆ What are the implications of private residual rights of the firm for the evolution of production roundaboutness?

◆ What are the implications of free pricing, free enterprising, and free choice between occupation configurations for the evolution of division of labor in roundabout production?

---

### ◆ 19.2 A General Equilibrium Model Endogenizing Production Roundaboutness

#### Example 19.1: a simplified version of the Shi–Yang model (1995)

Consider an economy with $M$ *ex ante* identical consumer-producers. Each consumer-producer's *ex ante* utility function is

$$u = z + kz^d \tag{19.1}$$

where $z$ is the self-provided quantity of food, $z^d$ is the amount of food purchased, $k$ is transaction efficiency. The *ex ante* production function of food is

$$z^p \equiv z + z^s = \mathrm{Max}\{l_z - \alpha, \ (y + ky^d)^{1/3}(l_z - \alpha), \ (x + kx^d)^{1/3}(l_z - \alpha)$$
$$(y + ky^d)^{1/3}(x + kx^d)^{1/3}(l_z - \alpha)\} \tag{19.2}$$

where $z^p$ is the output level of food, $z^s$ is the amount of food sold, $l_z$ is the amount of time allocated to the production of food, $y$ is the amount of hoes self-provided, $y^d$ is the amount of hoes purchased, $x$ is the amount of tractors self-provided, $x^d$ is the amount of tractors purchased, $k$ is transaction efficiency, and $\alpha$ is the fixed learning cost in each activity. The specification of the production function for food implies that there are four ways to produce food: using only labor, using hoes together with labor, using tractors together with labor, or using both hoes and tractors together with labor.

It is not difficult to see that if $y + ky^d > 1$, then $(y + ky^d)^{1/3}(l_z - \alpha) > l_z - \alpha$, which implies that it is more productive if hoes are employed than if they are not, even if the input level of labor is the same for the two cases. This means that there are *type C economies of roundabout production* of food. If we compare the total factor productivities of food for the two ways of production, we can see too that for $x + kx^d > 1$, total factor productivity is higher when hoes are employed. Similarly, it can be shown that the total factor productivity of food is higher when tractors, in addition to hoes, are employed than when they are not because of $(y + ky^d)^{1/3}(x + kx^d)^{1/3}(l_z - \alpha) > (y + ky^d)^{1/3}(l_z - \alpha)$. This means that there are type B economies of roundabout production of food. It can also be shown that the total factor productivity of food increases with the amount of tractors or hoes employed, that is, there are type A economies of roundabout production.

The *ex ante* production function for hoes is

$$y^p \equiv y + y^s = \text{Max}\{l_y - \alpha, 0\} \tag{19.3}$$

where $y^p$ is the output level of hoes, $y^s$ is the amount sold, $l_y$ is the amount of time allocated to the production of hoes, and $\alpha$ is the fixed learning cost in producing hoes.

The *ex ante* production function of tractors is

$$x^p \equiv x + x^s = \text{Max}\{(w + kw^d)^{1/2}(l_x - \alpha), 0\} \tag{19.4}$$

where $x^p$ is the output level of tractors, $x^s$ is the amount sold, $l_x$ is the amount of time allocated to the production of tractors, $w$ is the amount of machine tools self-provided, $w^d$ is the amount of machine tools purchased, and $\alpha$ is the fixed learning cost in producing tractors. You may interpret machine tools as steel essential for the production of tractors. The *ex ante* production function of machine tools is

$$w^p \equiv w + w^s = \text{Max}\{l_w - \alpha, 0\} \tag{19.5}$$

where $w^p$ is the output level of tractors, $w^s$ is the amount sold, $l_w$ is the amount of time allocated to the production of machine tools.

The endowment of nonleisure time is

$$l_x + l_y + l_z + l_w = 24. \tag{19.6}$$

$l_i \in [0, 24]$ can be considered as an individual's level of specialization in producing good i. It is not difficult to verify that the total factor productivity of food or tractors increases with an individual's level of specialization in producing the good, and that labor productivity of hoes or machine tools increases with an individual's level of specialization in producing the good. Hence, there are economies of specialization in producing each good. We draw the distinction between *emergence of a new industry* and *emergence of a new sector*. A new industry, which might comprise several sectors, emerges as a new link in the roundabout production chain emerges. A new sector producing a certain type of goods emerges if the number of goods at a certain link of the roundabout production chain increases. Hence, a new industry emerges from an increase in the number of links of the roundabout production chain and a new sector emerges from an increase in the number of producer goods at a particular link of the roundabout production chain. Here, a *link* is defined as the input–output relationship between an upstream and a downstream industry. The number of links is defined as the *degree of production roundaboutness*.

## ◆ 19.3 Corner Equilibria and the Emergence of New Industry

You are now familiar with the inframarginal analysis. Hence, we need not repeat the technical detail of the two-step approach to that analysis, but shall just define various structures, listed in figure 19.1. and summarize all corner equilibria in table 19.1.

There are 12 structures that we have to consider. Four of them are autarky structures. A(z) represents an autarky structure where only labor is employed to produce food and all producer goods are not produced. A(zy) represents an autarky structure where hoes are employed to produce food. A(zxw) represents an autarky structure where machine tools are employed to produce tractors which are employed to produce food. A(zxyw) is an autarky structure where all of three intermediate goods are employed to produce food. All of the four autarky structures except structure A(zxw) are shown in figure 19.1.

Structure C comprises a configuration producing only food and a configuration producing only hoes. Each individual is completely specialized, but the number of producer goods in upstream industry is small and the number of links in roundabout production is 2. Tractors and machine tools are not produced.

In structure D, all producer goods, hoes, tractors, and machine tools are produced. This structure comprises a configuration producing both food and hoes and a configuration producing both tractors and machine tools. Each individual produces two goods and has an intermediate level of specialization, but the degree of production roundaboutness and the variety of producer goods at the middle link of the roundabout production are great.

Structure E comprises three configurations. A professional farmer buys hoes and tractors and sells food. A completely specialized manufacturer of hoes sells hoes and buys food. The third configuration is not completely specialized. It produces both tractors and machine tools, sells tractors, and buys food.

Structure F is symmetric with structure E. The producers of tractors and machine tools are completely specialized but the third nonspecialized configuration produces both hoes and food.

Structure G is a structure with the complete division of labor, which implies not only that all individuals are completely specialized, but also that the degree of production roundaboutness and the number of producer goods at each link are greatest. There are four completely specialized configurations. Each of them produces only one good.

Each of the professional manufacturers of hoes, tractors, and machine tools buys food, each

**Table 19.1: Corner equilibria**

| Structure | Relative prices | Number of specialists | Per capita real income |
|---|---|---|---|
| A(z) | | | $24 - \alpha$ |
| A(zy) | | | $3[24 - 2\alpha)/4]^{4/3}$ |
| A(zxw) | | | $3[(24 - 3\alpha)/9]^{4/3}2^{4/3}$ |
| A(zxyw) | | | $3[24 - 4\alpha)/11]^{11/6}2^{5/3}$ |
| C | $p_y p_z = (1/3)2^{2/3}$ $[(24 - \alpha)/k]^{1/3}/3$ | $M_y/M_z = [(24 - \alpha)p_z/p_y 3]^{3/2}$ | $(24 - \alpha)^{4/3}(2k)^{2/3}/3$ |
| D | $p_x/p_z = 3[(24 - 2\alpha)/k]^{1/3}/2^{8/3}$ | $M_x/M_z = [k(12 - \alpha)]^{0.5}(3p_z/2p_x)^{3/2}$ | $(24 - 2\alpha)^{11/6}k^{2/3}/(3^{1/3}2^{5/3})$ |
| E | | | $[k(24 - \alpha)]^{4/3}[(24 - 2\alpha)/27]^{0.5}2^{1/3}$ |
| F | | | $(24 - \alpha)^{11/6}k^{5/6}/2^{7/3}$ |
| G | $p_x/p_z = 2^{2/3}(24 - \alpha)^{1/3}/3$ $p_y/p_z = p_w/p_z = (2k)^{0.5}(24 - \alpha)^{5/6}/3$ | $M_x/M_z = 2k(p_z/p_x)^3(24 - \alpha)p_w/27p_y$ $M_y/M_z = p_z^3[(24 - \alpha)k/p_y]^2/(27p_x)$ $M_w/M_x = [(24 - \alpha)k/4](p_x/p_w)^3$ | $(24 - \alpha)^{11/6}2^{0.5}k^{3/2}/3$ |

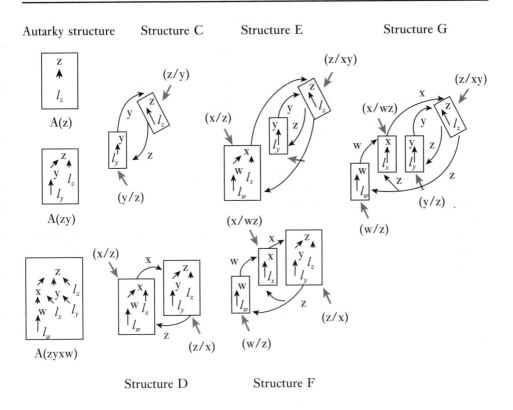

◆ **Figure 19.1:** Various industrial structures

professional farmer buys hoes and tractors, and each professional manufacturer of tractors also buys machine tools. All of the structures are shown in figure 19.1, where configurations are defined by letters in brackets, the letters before a slash denotes the good sold, and the letters after a slash denote those goods purchased. For instance, configuration (x/z) denotes that an individual produces both tractors and machine tools, sells tractors, x, and buys food, z; (z/xy) denotes a professional farmer selling food and buying tractors and hoes.

There are more structures that are not listed in figure 19.1. Structure H comprises a nonprofessional configuration that produces both food and tractors, sells food, and buys machine tools, and a professional configuration selling machine tools and buying food. In this structure, hoes are not produced. In structure I, which is symmetric with H, a professional farmer produces food, a nonprofessional manufacturer produces both tractors and machine tools, and hoes are not produced. Structure J is the same as structure G except that hoes are not produced.

If trade of intermediate goods is replaced with trade of labor, there are more structures with the institution of the firm. Some of them are shown in figure 19.2. Having applied inframarginal analysis, the corner equilibria in major structures are summarized in table 19.1.

From comparisons of per capita real incomes across structures, we can show that the set of candidates for the general equilibrium structure comprises A(z), A(zy), A(zxyw), C, D, G. Each of the other structures generates lower per capita real income than at least one of the above structures. Three methods are used to exclude these structures. If we compare per capita real income in a structure with those in two other similar structures, we can obtain two critical values of $k$. When the two structures to compare are appropriately chosen, the initial structure generates a higher per capita real income than both of the others only if $k$ is between the two critical values. For instance, structure F generates a higher per capita real income than structure D if and only if $k > k'$ and structure F generates a higher per capita real income than structure G if and only if $k < k''$. This implies that structure F is a candidate for the general equilibrium structure only if $k \in (k', k'')$. Here, the critical values $k'$, $k''$ can be obtained by comparing per capital real incomes in the three structures that are given in table 19.1. They are dependent on $\alpha$. But a comparison between $k''$ and $k'$ indicates that $k' > k''$, that is, the interval of $(k', k'')$, is empty. This implies that structure F generates a lower per capita real income than either structure D or structure G, or the per capita real income in F cannot be greater than that in structure D and G at the same time. According to the Yao theorem, this implies that the corner equilibrium in structure F cannot be a general equilibrium.

The second method that we have used is to compare the critical values of $k$ with 1. Since $k$ cannot be larger than 1, if a critical value of $k$ that makes a structure at least as good as another structure is greater than 1, then the former cannot be a candidate for the equilibrium structure. For instance, the per capita real income in structure G is greater than in structure C if and only if $k > k'''$. But it can be shown that $k''' > 1$ if and only if $\alpha$ is smaller than a constant. Hence, we can conclude that structure G cannot be a candidate for the general equilibrium structure if $\alpha$ is greater than that constant.

The third method that we have used is to identify the condition for per capita real income in each structure to be nonpositive. It is obvious from table 19.1, that if $\alpha$ is greater than a certain value, per capita real income in a particular structure is nonpositive. Repeatedly using the three methods, we can exclude structures A(zxw), E, F, H, I, J from the set of candidates for the general equilibrium structure. The results of course relate to some of our specific assumptions. For instance, we assume that each individual has 24 units of time available for production and that the elasticity parameters of outputs with respect to input levels of intermediate goods are specific numbers. In addition, we have assumed the Cobb–Douglas production function and that the fixed learning cost and transaction efficiency are the same for all goods. If we relax these assumptions, then each of the structures that we have outlined could be a general equilibrium structure within a certain parameter subspace. Shi and Yang (1995) have examined the effects of relaxing some of the assumptions. For example, they have assumed the CES production function with an elasticity of substitution that might not be 1. They have also assumed that the elasticity of output with respect to input is a parameter rather than a number. They have shown that within a certain parameter subspace, each of the structures could be a general equilibrium structure.

## ♦ 19.4 General Equilibrium and Industrialization

Comparisons of per capita real incomes across structures, together with the Yao theorem, yield the general equilibrium and its inframarginal comparative statics, summarized in table 19.2.

In order to compare topological properties between different structures, we define the

**Table 19.2:** Emergence of new industry and evolution in division of labor

| $\alpha$ | $\in (0, 0.92)$ | | | $\in (0.92, 3.57)$ | | |
|---|---|---|---|---|---|---|
| $k$ | $< k_1$ | $\in (k_1, k_2)$ | $> k_2$ | $< k_3$ | $\in (k_3, k_2)$ | $> k_2$ |
| Structure | A(zxyw) | D | G | A(zy) | D | G |

| $\alpha$ | $\in (3.57, 7.8)$ | | | $\in (7.8, 23.5)$ | | $(23.5, 24)$ | |
|---|---|---|---|---|---|---|---|
| $k$ | $< k_4$ | $\in (k_4, k_2)$ | $> k_2$ | $< k_5$ | $> k_5$ | $< k_6$ | $> k_6$ |
| Structure | A(z) | D | G | A(z) | C | A(z) | G |

where $k_1 \equiv 3^2 2^5 [(12 - 2\alpha)/11(12 - \alpha)]^{11/4}$; $k_2 \equiv (3^4/2^7)^{0.2} [(24 - 2\alpha)/(24 - \alpha)]^{11/5}$;
$k_3 \equiv 9(24 - 2\alpha)^{-3/4} 2^{-1.5}$; $k_4 \equiv 2^{2.5} 3^{0.5} (24 - \alpha)^{1.5}/(24 - 2\alpha)^{11/4}$; $k_5 \equiv 3^{1.5}/[2(24 - 2\alpha)^{0.5}]$;
$k_6 \equiv 3^{2/3}/[2^{1/3}(24 - \alpha)^{5/9}]$.

level of division of labor of an economy by three measures: each individual's level of specialization, the number of links in the roundabout production chain, and the number of goods at each link of the chain in a structure. According to this definition, structure C, in which each individual is completely specialized, the number of goods is 2 and the number of links is 2, has roughly the same level of division of labor as structure D, in which each individual has a lower level of specialization than in C, but the number of goods is 4 and the number of links of the roundabout production chain is 3.

We now read the results in table 19.2 in connection with the graphs in figure 19.1. There are 5 patterns of evolution in division of labor. Let us look the case with $\alpha \in (0, 0.92)$. Within this parameter subspace, if transaction efficiency is sufficiently low, autarky structure A(zxyw) is the general equilibrium, where each individual self-provides all of four goods and productivity and per capita real income are very low. As transaction efficiency is improved to greater than $k_1$, the general equilibrium jumps to structure D, where some individuals produce both food and hoes and others produce both tractors and machine tools. The number of goods produced by each individual is reduced from 4 to 2, so that each individual's level of specialization rises. As transaction efficiency is further improved to greater than $k_2$, the general equilibrium jumps to the complete division of labor, where each individual is completely specialized. For this pattern of evolution in division of labor, each individual's level of specialization evolves in the absence of evolution in the degree of production roundaboutness and in the variety of producer goods at each link. This is because the fixed learning cost $\alpha$ is very small, so that economies of specialization are not significant. Thus the tension between economies of specialization and economies of roundaboutness is not sufficiently great to induce evolution in production roundaboutness. As the fixed learning cost and accordingly economies of specialization increase, the correspondingly greater tension between economies of specialization and economies of roundaboutness will generate concurrent evolution both in individuals' levels of specialization and in production roundaboutness.

Suppose $\alpha \in (0.92, 3.57)$. If transaction efficiency is sufficiently low, autarky structure

A(zy) is the general equilibrium structure, where each individual self-provides food and hoes, each individual's level of specialization is not high, only two goods are produced, the number of links of roundabout production is 2, and the number of producer goods at the upstream industry is 1. Also, productivity and per capita real income are low and no market exists in autarky. As transaction efficiency is improved, the general equilibrium jumps to structure D, where a new link and two new producer goods emerge, although each individual's level of specialization remains unchanged. Productivity and per capita real income are higher than in A(zy) because more economies of roundabout production are exploited. As transaction efficiency is further improved, the general equilibrium jumps to structure G, where each individual's level of specialization is increased so that productivity, per capita real income, and the number of transactions are increased. This pattern of evolution in division of labor generates all concurrent phenomena that are associated with industrialization except evolution of the institution of the firm. Individuals' levels of specialization increase, the number of links in the roundabout production chain increases, the number of producer goods in each of the links increases, productivity and per capita real income increase, the size of the market network expands, the degree of market integration and production concentration increases, and the extent of endogenous comparative advantage rises. New *ex post* production functions and related new technology and new industries emerge from this process. This endogenous technical progress differs from the exogenous technical progress in the theory of labor surplus and dual economy.

Suppose the fixed learning cost is greater, so that $\alpha \in (3.57, 7.8)$. Then only one good will be produced in autarky because of a greater tension between economies of specialization and economies of roundaboutness. If transaction efficiency is extremely low, then the general equilibrium is structure A(z) where no producer goods are produced. As transaction efficiency is improved, the general equilibrium jumps to structure D, where a new link and two producer goods emerge despite a decline of each individual's level of specialization. As transaction efficiency is further improved, the general equilibrium jumps to structure G with the complete division of labor, generating evolution in each person's level of specialization. In this pattern of evolution of division of labor, each individual's level of specialization experiences nonmonotonic changes. It declines first and then increases. But the degree of production roundaboutness and the level of division of labor (involving each person's level of specialization, the degree of production roundaboutness, and variety of goods at each link) rise with the evolution of industrial structure.

Suppose $\alpha \in (7.8, 23.5)$, each individual's level of specialization and the degree of production roundaboutness increase concurrently as transaction efficiency is sufficiently improved, so that the general equilibrium jumps from structure A(z) to structure C. However, structure G with the complete division of labor cannot be the general equilibrium. You may see that if the elasticity of output of tractors with respect to input of machine tools is much larger than $1/3$, then the general equilibrium will jump from structure C to structure G as transaction efficiency $k$ tends to 1.

Suppose $\alpha \in (23.5, 24)$, each individual's level of specialization remains unchanged and the degree of production roundaboutness and variety of producer goods at the middle link increase concurrently as transaction efficiency is sufficiently improved, so that the general equilibrium jumps from structure A(z) to structure G with the complete division of labor. If the number of possible goods is much larger than four, then the story about industrialization will be much richer, so that concurrent evolution of the three aspects of the division of labor – individuals' levels of specialization, the number of links of the roundabout production chain, and the number of goods at each link of the chain – would be easier to see.

## ◆ 19.5 Changes in the Income Shares of the Industrial and Agricultural Sectors

From Tables 19.1 and 19.2, we can see that as transaction efficiency is improved and the general equilibrium jumps from autarky to the division of labor, say structure C or D, the number of professional farmers in the structure with division of labor is smaller than the number of individuals who self-provide either only food or all goods that they consume. This implies, on the one hand, that the number of individuals in the agricultural sector declines compared to the number of individuals in the industrial sector, and on the other hand that the income share of industrial goods rises due to both the increase in the number of producer goods and evolution in division of labor.

The structural changes caused by concurrent evolution in division of labor and in production roundaboutness can be verified by empirical data. The input and output tables of the US (Department of Commerce, 1975) indicate that the income share of the sector producing intermediate goods increases and the income share of the sector producing consumption goods declines over time. Shi and Yang (1995) extend the model in this chapter to the case with good v that is essential for the production of good y. They assume that goods y and v are intermediate goods or services (such as planting and harvesting) in the agricultural sector and that the transaction efficiency coefficients for the two goods are much smaller than that for goods x and w in the industrial sector. Then they show that as transaction efficiency is improved, division of labor will evolve only in the industrial sector, so that the income share of the industrial sector rises and the agricultural sector is increasingly dependent on importing the benefit of division of labor from the industrial sector. This substantiates Smith's conjecture that the increase in the income share of the industrial sector is due to relatively more significant economies of specialization compared to coordination costs in the industrial sector than in the agricultural sector. This approach to explaining structural changes, which are different aspects of evolution in division of labor, substantially differs from that of Kuznets. Kuznets (1966) explained structural changes by an increase in income and by exogenous changes in preferences or in technology. However, structural changes can take place in our model in the absence of exogenous changes in parameters of the production and utility functions. Explaining structural changes by changes in incomes is certainly not a general equilibrium view. In a general equilibrium model, per capita real income is endogenous. It should be explained either by parameters in static models (comparative statics of general equilibrium), or by a spontaneous mechanism in dynamic models. For instance, per capita real income in the model in this chapter is determined by the level of division of labor, which is in turn determined by transaction efficiency. Again, we can see that productivity progress in our model is generated by evolution in division of labor in the absence of changes in *ex ante* production functions. Hence, it can be considered as endogenous technical progress caused by institutional changes or urbanization that affect transaction efficiency. But the distinguishing feature of endogenous technical progress in our model in this chapter is that it is associated with the emergence of new industries and evolution in production roundaboutness.

The policy implications of the model enable us to identify fatal flaws in various industrial policies. Our model shows that one of the functions of the market is to sort out the efficient industrial structure and pattern of its evolution. If the model is asymmetric and has many possible goods and possible links, then it is impossible for any policy-maker to figure out what the efficient industrial structure is. However, the general equilibrium (unintended consequence of interactions between self-interested behaviors) can do so. Some historical examples may illustrate this point. In China prior to the nineteenth century, policy makers in the government and intellectuals advocated an industrial policy "promoting the agricultural sector and suppressing commerce." This industrial policy prevented ancient China from industrialization before Britain was industrialized under a *laissez-faire* regime. Similarly, the Japanese government had an industrial policy in the 1950s which restricted the development of the automobile industry. According to the Japanese government's judgment, Japan had no comparative advantage in manufacturing automobiles. But under a private rights and free enterprise system, the owners of private firms rather the government have the ultimate right to choose the industrial pattern. Hence, the industrial policy of the Japanese government was rejected by the market. From many such cases, we can see that it is those countries that have many complicated industrial policies which promote or protect some industries and ignore or suppress other industries that have shown poor performance in industrial development.

Shi and Yang have also shown that if the production function of food is of the CES type and its parameters are not fixed numbers, then structure F may be the general equilibrium in the transitional period as the economy evolves from autarky to the complete division of labor. Structure F is an asymmetric structure (see figure 19.1) in which producers of tractors and machine tools are completely specialized while producers of food and hoes are not completely specialized. Hence, a professional producer of machine tools or a professional producer of tractors has a higher productivity and a higher level of commercialized income than an individual self-providing hoes and selling food. This is referred to as a dual structure. The natural dual structure in a free market will generate equal per capita real income between the industrial and agricultural sectors, despite unequal nominal incomes. It emerges in the transitional period from a balanced low level of division of labor to a balanced high level of division of labor, and disappears as the complete division of labor has been reached.

If more goods are introduced into the model, the number of corner equilibria will increase more than proportionally. Many of these cannot be solved analytically. Hence, the inframarginal comparative statics of general equilibrium can be obtained only through numerical simulation on the computer. The complexity of calculation and variety of possible patterns of evolution of industrial structure imply that it is impossible for a central planning system to simulate what is going on in the market, and that the market is much more powerful than a decision-maker in sorting out the complex task of determining the efficient industrial structure.

## ♦ 19.6 The Number of Possible Structures of Transactions Increases More Than Proportionally as Division of Labor Evolves in Roundabout Production

As division of labor evolves in roundabout production, the possibilities for replacing trade in intermediate goods with trade in labor imply that the number of possible structures with firms increases more than proportionally. In particular, considering structures with different specialist producers being the employer of the firm, this point is even easier to see.

Let us look at figure 19.2 where possible structures with firms based on the complete division of labor (structure G) are drawn. In each of these structures, there are four types

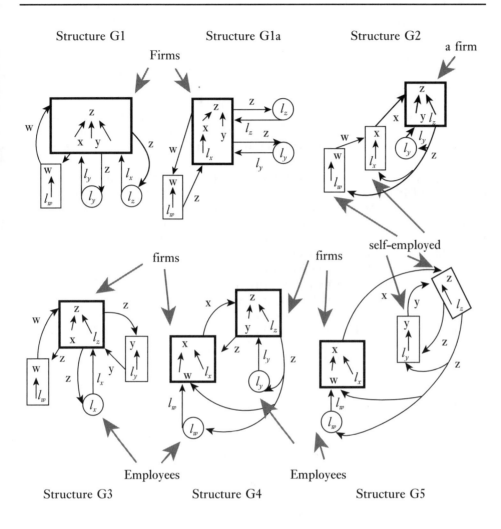

♦ **Figure 19.2:** Structures with firms based on the complete division of labor

of specialist producer of food (z), hoes (y), tractors (x), and machine tools (w). G1 represents a structure in which a specialist producer of food hires specialist producers of hoes and tractors, and buys machine tools from and sells food to independent specialist producers of machine tools. The rectangles with thick borders denote firms, circles denote employees, and the rectangles with thin borders denote independent specialist producers (or the self-employed). Structure G1a has the same structure of division of labor and transactions as structure G1, but has a different ownership structure of the firm. In structure G1a, it is the specialist producer of tractors instead of the specialist producer of food that owns the firm. There is another variant of structure G1 where the specialist producer of hoes is the owner of the firm.

The other parts of figure 19.2 represent other structures of the firm based on the same structure of division of labor as in structure G. For each of them, there are more variants with the same structure of transactions, but with different ownership structures. In fact, on the basis of the structure of division of labor in G, there are at least 13 different structures of transactions and ownership of the firm. It is not difficult to see that the number of possible structures increases more than proportionally as the level of division of labor evolves in the roundabout production chain. Hence, the potential for improving transaction efficiency and for promoting productivity increasingly comes from entrepreneurial activities that search for the efficient structure of transactions and ownership of the firm as division of labor evolves.

Although this chapter has explored how the market sorts out the efficient pattern of division of labor in a roundabout production chain through interactions between self-interested decisions, the functioning of the market in the real world is much more sophisticated than described in a simple model. For instance, in a simple model, we assume that the total factor productivity of the final goods monotonically increases with the number of links in the roundabout production chain. In the real world, such a monotonic relationship may not hold universally. In some industries, as the degree of production roundaboutness increases slightly, the total factor productivity of final goods may decline at first, and then rises as the roundaboutness is further increased. If dynamic economies of specialized learning by doing are explicitly considered (see chapter 22), it is possible that type C economies of roundabout production can be realized only if a sufficiently high degree of roundaboutness is maintained for a sufficiently long period of time.

Suppose that each of 1,000 sectors producing the final goods can have a long roundabout production chain. But only 100 of the 1,000 sectors have type C economies of roundabout production; the rest of the sectors have diseconomies of roundabout production. Also, the economies of roundabout production can be realized only if the roundaboutness in several of the 100 sectors simultaneously increases. For such a model, there are myriad possible structures. If account is taken of interdependency between information about relative prices and decisions in choosing one out of many corner solutions, as described in chapter 24, it may take a long time for society to search out the efficient industrial structure, despite the power of the market in performing this task.

What we can observe from the Industrial Revolution is a process through which an efficient industrial structure with the right pattern of division of labor in a long roundabout production chain has been sorted out by the market under a common law system that protects private residual rights to the firm and other private rights to various properties. Before the Industrial Revolution, many other industrial structures with long roundabout production chains had been experimented with. For instance, a quite long roundabout production method in producing a special vehicle out of wood was developed in the 3rd century AD in China. That roundabout production method could not stand the test of time, since it did not use durable material and could not provide more power than human and animal power. Hence, economies of roundabout production were too small to offset transaction costs and resource costs associated with roundabout production. In the Industrial Revolution the invention of the engine, the commercial use of steel and of all kinds of machines made out of steel and driven by engines, together with evolution in the division of labor in inventing activities and in roundabout production activities related to those inventions, brought about an efficient industrial structure that generated significant economies of roundaboutness. According to the model in this chapter, a high transaction efficiency provided by patent laws, a fair and adaptive common law system, and a *laissez-faire* regime were essential for the development of a large network of division of labor in the roundabout production which was in turn essential for the Industrial Revolution.

## Key Terms and Review

Type A, type B, and type C economies of roundabout production.

Conditions under which a business that creates a new link in the roundabout production chain can make money.

The relationships between transaction efficiency, the size of the market network, the size of the population or resource base, three types of economies of roundabout production, the equilibrium level of division of labor, and the equilibrium number of links in the roundabout production chain.

The mechanism that generates a decline of the income share of the agricultural sector and a rise in the income share of the industrial sector. The relationship between this phenomenon and the relative degree of economies of division of labor compared with transaction costs in the agricultural vs. industrial sector.

Why the scope for the development of the institution of the firm will be enlarged more than proportionally as division of labor in roundabout production evolves.

The significance of a firm's private residual rights to the firm for the evolution of production roundaboutness

Implications of free pricing, free enterprising, and free choice between profession configurations for the evolution of division of labor in roundabout production.

## Further Reading

*Industrial Revolution*: MacFarlane (1988), Jones (1981), Weber (1961), Baechler (1976), Braudel (1984), Rosenberg and Birdzell (1986), Mokyr (1990, 1993), Hartwell (1965), Hughes (1970), Hicks (1969), Reynolds (1985); *historical and empirical evidence for the theory in this chapter*: Olsen (1996), Kubo (1985), Chenery (1979), Kaldor (1967), Braudel (1984), Chandler (1990), Department of Commerce (1975), Liu and Yang (2000), Murakami, Liu, and Otsuka (1996); *classical and new classical theories of industrialization*: Smith (1776), Yang and Y.-K. Ng (1993, ch. 14), Young (1928), Shi and Yang (1995, 1998), Sun and Lio (1996); *high development economics and theory of industrialization*: Rosenstein-Rodan (1943), Nurkse (1953), Fleming (1955), Hirschman (1958), Krugman (1995); *the models of industrialization with economies of scale and an endogenous number of goods*: Murphy, Shleifer, and Vishny (1989a,b), Krugman and Venables (1995), Wong and Yang (1998), Kelly (1997).

## QUESTIONS

1   Smith (1776) explained the difference in productivity between the agricultural and industrial sectors as determined by the difference in the benefits of specialization compared to the seasonal adjustment costs caused by specialization between the two sectors. This theory explains economic structure by the different balance points in trading-off economies of division of labor against coordination cost, instead of by tastes, income, or exogenous technical conditions. An extension of the theory implies that a decline in the income share of the agricultural sector occurs not because of a change in tastes, in income, or in exogenous technical conditions, but because the agricultural sector has a higher coordination cost of the division of labor compared to the benefits derived from the division of labor, and it can improve productivity only by importing an increasingly large number of industrial goods, which is equivalent

to importing division of labor. These goods are produced by a high level of division of labor in the manufacturing sector, where transaction costs are more likely to be outweighed by economies of division of labor. Kaldor (1967) provided some empirical evidence for this conjecture. Extend the model in this chapter to formalize Smith's conjecture.

2    If all individuals would not buy roundabout productive machines because of the high prices of the machines, then for the sector producing the machines the extent of the market would be very small and the level of division of labor very low, so that the prices of the machines would indeed be high. Also, if a sector producing final goods increases its demand for steel, the extent of the market for steel will be enlarged and its price may decline due to a higher productivity generated by a higher level of division of labor within the sector producing steel. Hence, many other sectors may be able to afford the cheaper steel, so that a series of positive feedbacks may take place among many professional sectors. This implies that there are network effects of division of labor between roundabout production and the final sectors. Use the model in this section to explain how the market coordinates the division of labor and utilizes the network effects. Discuss the implications of free choice of occupation configurations, free pricing, and free enterprising for the market to utilize the network effects. Many economists call such network effects "linkage externality." Use the model in this chapter to analyze how the market utilizes such network effects.

3    According to Rosenberg and Birdzell (1986, p. 156), extensive use of steel, coal, and mechanical power was a feature of the Industrial Revolution. One interpretation of the use of steel in terms of the model in this chapter is as an increase of degree of type A economies of roundabout production. Durability of steel implies that the elasticity of output with respect to intermediate input is great. Hence, as transaction efficiency is improved, division of labor is more likely to evolve in producing steel and other sectors that use it. Use the model in this chapter to explain why many machines made of wood could not generate an industrial revolution in Song Dynasty China.

4    Many new growth models explain emergence of new producer goods by investment in the R&D sector. This kind of model cannot explain why producers in less-developed economies usually do not adopt the latest machinery and technology available at low cost (Olsen, 1996), and why numerous good-will attempts to introduce the newest production processes into less-developed countries meet with disappointing failure, as noted by Stigler (1951). Many peasants in less-developed countries do not use roundabout productive equipment and vehicles because a high level of division of labor is essential for producing the equipment at low prices. But the government monopoly in the sector producing these goods, and in the distribution system and banking system, causes very high transaction costs which make a high level of division of labor and sophisticated private organization nonviable. Also, use of some machines needs many very specialized services to provide cheap parts, instruments, and repair and transaction services. Due to the absence of a great variety of highly professional services, the peasants prefer very primitive tools with a low degree of roundaboutness. As Stigler (1951, p. 193) noted, the production process in the American industrialization model is usually too specialized for less-developed economies, as in them neither the vast network of auxiliary industries which producers in the United States can take for granted can be available, nor can the necessary narrowly specialized personnel be supplied. Benjamin Franklin, observing manufacturing in the United States, a backward economy at his time, also pointed out that: "Manufactures . . . are carried on by a multiplicity of hands, each of which is expert only in his own part, no one of them a master of the whole," so all the experts in the associated network of division of labor are needed to set up a manufacture in a foreign and underdeveloped land. But usually after "a complete set of good and skillful hands are collected and carried over, they find so much of the system imperfect, so many things wanting to carry on the trade to advantage, so many difficulties to overcome . . . the project vanishes into smoke" (cited by Stigler, 1951, p. 193). Use the models in this chapter to explain Stigler and Franklin's observation.

5    To the previous question, many economists may point to the purchasing power and income of peasants as the explanation for the low production roundaboutness in a developing country. But Young (1928) points out: "Taking a country's economic endowment as given, however, the most important single factor in determining the effectiveness of its industry appears to be the size of the market. But just what constitutes a large market. Not area or population alone, but buying power, the capacity to absorb a large annual output of goods. This trite observation, however, at once suggests another, equally trite, namely, that capacity to buy depends upon capacity to produce." But production capacity is dependent on the level of division of labor. Hence (1928, p. 533): "in the light of this broader conception of the market, Adam Smith's dictum amounts to the theorem that the division of labor depends in large part upon the division of labor . . . Even with a stationary population and in the absence of new discoveries in pure or applied science, there are no limits to the process of expansion except the limits beyond which demand is not elastic and returns do not increase." Use the models in this chapter to formalize Young's idea about the relationship between the extent of the market, division of labor, and roundabout production. See also Young's explanation of the Industrial Revolution, which "has come to be generally regarded, not as a cataclysm brought about by certain inspired improvements in industrial technique, but as a series of changes related in an orderly way to prior changes in organization and to the enlargement of markets" (p. 536).

6    McGuirk and Mundlak (1992) report evidence of the effect of transaction conditions on the choice of techniques of different degrees of roundaboutness. According to them, modern crop varieties (MVs) generate more output but require considerably more fertilizer per unit of land than do traditional varieties, which implies that MVs involve more roundabout production processes using more intermediate goods. The technique of MVs also has to compete with traditional ones for adoption. The adoption of MVs is positively and strongly influenced by the density of roads. The importance of roads therefore indicates that linking rural areas to markets, or in our terminology, the improvement in transaction conditions in these rural areas, strongly affects the adoption of more roundabout techniques, as hypothesized by our model. Find more empirical evidence for the models in this chapter.

7    North has suggested that we should recognize that differences in ability to make efficient use of available knowledge are a factor as preeminent as differences in knowledge state for explaining the widely disparate experience of national economies. The development of division of labor allows us to cross the gap between what has been known and what can be realized. If there is no well-developed network of division of labor to support high degrees of roundaboutness, then to heavily invest in R&D seems to be a recipe for lowering the average productivity of the knowledge stock rather than for rapid economic progress. Use the models in this chapter to substantiate North's conjecture.

8    An economist argues that since the population size of Australia is less than 20 million and that of the US is 200 million, the extent of the market in Australia is much smaller than in the US. Hence, all kinds of machines are much cheaper in the US than in Australia. The new endogenous growth models recently developed by Judd and Romer generate a similar prediction that larger economies will generate higher growth rates and levels of per capita income. Use the model in this chapter to comment on this view. In your analysis you might use the Smith theorem, that division of labor depends upon the extent of the market, and the extent of the market is determined by transaction conditions, to clarify the relationship between the extent of the market, population size, transaction efficiency, and the network size of division of labor.

9    As an economy develops, many families self-provide increasingly more household services, such as laundry using a washing machine at home rather than relying on a specialized laundry shop, and mowing the lawn using a mower rather than relying on specialized gardeners. Professors may use computers to do some jobs that used to be done by a secretary and professional publishing houses. However, the decrease in the level of specialization in the downstream sector usually concurs with the increase in

division of labor and specialization in the upstream sector specialized in producing washing machines, lawn mowers, or computers. Based on the model in this chapter, develop a new classical general equilibrium model to explain changes in the distribution of the degree of division of labor between upstream and downstream production activities. Explain why the increase in division of labor for society as a whole is an irreversible process, despite the changes that occur in the distribution of degree of division of labor.

10 Shi and Yang (1998) introduce additional goods into the model in this chapter to show that as transaction efficiency is improved, the level of division of labor in an increasingly longer roundabout production chain evolves, thereby creating more scope for finer division of labor between firms and within each firm. Hence, a hierarchical industrial structure between firms and a hierarchical structure within each firm may concurrently evolve. If transaction efficiency for labor and for intermediate goods is improved at different speeds, the equilibrium dividing line between the decentralized network hierarchy in the market and the centralized hierarchy within each firm may evolve too. Discuss the conditions under which the decentralized hierarchy in the market becomes increasingly less important than the centralized hierarchy within each firm, a phenomenon described by Chandler (1990).

11 Analyze why the potential to make money by playing around with choice of structure of residual rights increases as the level of division of labor in an increasingly longer roundabout production chain evolves.

12 It has been claimed that in a modern society, all individuals are completely specialized and buy all the goods they consume from the market, so that there is not much room for finer division of labor. Hence, models of endogenous specialization are not particularly relevant to a modern economy. Use examples, such as the emergence of the electronic toothbrush, to illustrate that the potential for further division of labor in producing consumption tools to replace existing self-provided consumption activities can never be exhausted, except for the limitations imposed by population size (the number of different professions cannot be larger than population size) and transaction costs. Then use examples, such as the finer division of labor in producing the more than 10,000 parts of an automobile, and the many subprocesses involved in producing each of them, to illustrate the infinitely many possibilities for finer division of labor in roundabout production.

13 From the input–output tables of eight countries, Kubo (1985) has found empirical evidence for concurrent increases in the output share of manufactured intermediate goods and in per capita real income. According to the input–output tables of the US, the output share of the roundabout production sector steadily increased from 0.44 in 1947, to 0.54 in 1958, 0.55 in 1961, 0.57 in 1963, and 0.62 in 1967 (see Department of Commerce, 1975). Kaldor (1967) also found empirical evidence for concurrent increases in the income share of the manufacturing sector and in per capita income. Try to find other methods to test the hypotheses generated by the model in this chapter against empirical observations.

14 Rosenstein-Rodan (1943) argues that an investment is likely to be unprofitable in isolation, but profitable if accompanied by similar investments in many other industries. Hirschman (1958) argues that an industry creates a backward linkage when its demand enables an upstream industry to be established at at least minimum economic scale. The strength of an industry's backward linkages is to be measured by the probability that it will in fact push other industries over the threshold of profitability. This is called effect of backward linkage. Forward linkage is also defined by Hirschman as involving an interaction between scale and market size. It involves the ability of an industry to reduce the costs of potential downstream users of its products and thus, again, push them over the threshold. Use the models in this chapter to formalize the vague ideas about industrialization and economic development.

15 Nurkse (1953) proposed a concept of virtuous circles of development, which implies that demand and supply of different sectors are interdependent. Use the general equilibrium model in this chapter to formalize his vague idea. Scitovsky (1954) made a clear distinction between technological and pecuni-

ary external economies, and the point that in competitive equilibrium it is actually efficient to ignore pecuniary external effects. Pecuniary external effects are those interdependencies between endogenous variables that are registered in price signals. Use the concept of general equilibrium to analyze how interactions between self-interested decisions in the market take into account the benefit of economies of scale and interdependencies between sectors. Most of those early development economists did not mention economies of scale. Use the model in chapters 5 and 6 to analyze why the network effect of industrial linkage can exist in the absence of economies of scale.

16  Fleming (1955) argues that the "horizontal" external economies of Rosenstein-Rodan were less important than the "vertical" external economies. His horizontal external economies relate to interdependency between the different sectors at the same link of a roundabout production chain, while vertical external economies relate to interdependency between different links. Use the distinction between the D–S model and the Ethier model to formalize the distinction between vertical and horizontal economies. You may relate your analysis to the model in this chapter.

17  According to Krugman (1995), it is because the vague ideas were not formalized by general equilibrium models that the sensible ideas about industrial interdependence and linkage of the 1950s have been abandoned. Use the models in this chapter to explain why formal general equilibrium models are more effective to communicate ideas than vague verbal description. Krugman also argues that the theory of labor surplus became popular because it was easier to formalize than the idea of big-push industrialization, although the latter seems to Krugman to be more sensible. Use this example to analyze the trade-off between realism and tractability in economic modeling.

# EXERCISES

1  Consider the model in this chapter. Assume the production function (19.2) is replaced with $z^p = \text{Max}\{\text{Min}\{l_z - \alpha, y + ky^d\}, x + kx^d\}$ and $x^p = \text{Min}\{l_x - \alpha, w + kw^d\}$. Solve for the inframarginal comparative statics of the general equilibrium.

2  Consider the model in this chapter. Assume that transaction efficiency $k$ differs from good to good. Identify the conditions under which the general equilibrium shifts from the autarky corner equilibrium producing goods x, y, z to the corner equilibrium with the complete division of labor with goods x, y, w produced. This implies that some goods may disappear as division of labor evolves.

3  Assume that in the model in this chapter the production function of good y is $y^p = \text{Min}\{l_y - \alpha, v + k_v v^d\}$ and $v^p \equiv v + v^s = l_v - \alpha$. Suppose that transaction efficiency $k_i$, $i = x, y, z, w, v$, differs from good to good, and that the endowment constraint for working time is $l_x + l_y + l_z + l_w + l_v = 1$. v is a producer good used to produce y. Solve for the inframarginal comparative statics of the general equilibrium. Show that if $k_v$, $k_y$ are significantly smaller than $k_z$, $k_x$, $k_w$, the division of labor evolves only in the sectors producing z, x, and y and does not evolve in the sectors producing y and z. If y is interpreted as harvesting and z is interpreted as sowing, then the model can explain why the development of division of labor in the agricultural sector is not as fast as in the industrial sector by the difference in transaction costs between the two sectors. Use the model to formalize Smith's conjecture on the rationale for the increasing income share of the industrial sector compared to the agricultural sector.

4  Assume that in the model in this chapter good w can be used to produce goods x and y, so that the production function of y is $y^p = \text{Min}\{l_y - \alpha, w + kw^d\}$. Solve for the inframarginal

comparative statics of the general equilibrium. Analyze the implications of the interdependencies between different production activities in the complicated input–output network for the equilibrium level of division of labor.

5   Shi–Yang model, 1995: assume that in example 19.1 the production function for tractors (19.2) is replaced with the CES function $z^\rho = [(x + kx^d)^\rho + (y + ky^d)^\rho]^{1/\rho} l_z^{0.5}$. Solve the general equilibrium and its inframarginal comparative statics. Note that some corner equilibria may not be solved analytically, and computer simulation is needed for solving the inframarginal comparative statics of general equilibrium.

# chapter 20

# THE HIERARCHICAL STRUCTURE OF THE NETWORK OF DIVISION OF LABOR AND RELATED TRANSACTIONS

## ◆ 20.1 The Theory of Hierarchy

A structural pattern of many elements is called a *hierarchy* if the individual elements are divided into several layers and the number of elements in each layer is related inversely to the rank of the layer. This definition implies that a hierarchy is characterized by series connections between layers, by parallel connections between the elements within each layer under the top, and by a pyramid structure of elements. Some authors – for instance Sah and Stiglitz (1988), MacLeod and Malcomson (1988) – refer to a system as a hierarchy where there are series connections between elements but no parallel connections and no pyramid structure.[1]

According to our definition, a series connection of elements is not sufficient for the existence of a hierarchy. The concept of hierarchy used here is referred to as "spanning" by Williamson (1967), Calvo and Wellisz (1978, 1979), Keren and Levhari (1979, 1982, 1989), and Rosen (1982). In graph theory, hierarchies are described by tree graphs.

Typical examples of hierarchies are a library catalog system, a dictionary, the system of cities, the wholesale and retail network, and the postal system. If we know that there is a book titled *French–English Dictionary* in a library with 1,000 books, there are two methods of picking out this book. We can check all the books on the shelves one by one. If it takes one minute to check an item, then the desired book will be found within 1,000 minutes. Another method is to look for the book by using the library's catalog system. Suppose that the system is divided into three layers. At the top layer, the 1,000 books are cataloged into ten categories, such as, "social science," "engineering," "reference books," and so on. Each of these categories is divided into ten subcategories; for example, "reference books" are cataloged into "social science reference books," "engineering reference books," "language reference books," and so on. Each of these subcategories comprises ten books such as *Chinese–English Dictionary*, *French–English Dictionary*, and so on. Using the catalog system, we can find the category "reference book" within ten minutes, the subcategory "language reference book" within another ten minutes, and *French–English Dictionary* within the final ten minutes. Therefore, it is possible to find this book within thirty minutes using the hierarchy of the catalogue system. The efficiency of the hierarchy is 1,000/30 times as great as that of a nonhierarchical system. Referring to this number as the efficiency multiplier, it is not difficult to see that the multiplier will change if this system is divided into two layers (categories and books) rather than three layers (categories, subcategories, and books). In other words, the efficiency multiplier of a hierarchy depends on the number of its layers. This example raises a question: how many layers of a hierarchy are optimal for the maximization of the efficiency multiplier? The theory of optimum hierarchy has been developed to address this question.

Hierarchical structures can be classified into two types. When a person uses a library catalog system to look for a book at the bottom layer of the system, she searches from the top layer, such as categories, to the bottom layer, such as books. We refer to such a hierarchy as a *one-way hierarchy* because the search process is in a single direction from top to bottom. Among other one-way hierarchies are the military command system, an English dictionary, a hierarchical screening process in a tournament involving many contestants, and the packaging system of some standard commodities. The top of the hierarchy of the dictionary is its user. The next layer is divided into the 26 letters used for the first letter of words. Each of the letters is divided into 26 letters used for the second letter of the words at the next layer, and so on. In the tournament a large number of groups of contestants have the first-round tournament within each group separately. The winners of the first round of the tournament then compete separately in a smaller number of groups in the second round, and so on. In the packaging system, goods are packaged in a large number of small boxes which are packaged in a smaller number of larger boxes which are put in a few containers, which are then carried by a cargo ship.

A postal system is a hierarchy based on a network. The bottom of the hierarchy consists of many people whose mail is delivered to one another through the higher layers of this hierarchy (postal centers in large cities and post offices in medium cities and small towns). The function of such a hierarchy is to improve the efficiency of each element at the bottom in communication with one another through the higher layers. We refer to such a hierarchy as a *network hierarchy* since communications are two-way, both from bottom to top and from top to bottom. Among other network hierarchies are the system of cities, the wholesale and retail network, the telephone network, and a management system in a large company.

Another way to classify hierarchies is to look at the structure of decision-making. If a decision-maker at the top of a hierarchy can choose the number of layers and other structural features of the hierarchy, then the hierarchy is referred to as a *centralized hierarchy*. The hierarchy in Qian's (1994) central planning economy is a centralized hierarchy where a central planner can choose the number of layers. Also, the management hierarchies studied by Williamson (1967), Calvo and Wellisz (1978, 1979), Keren and Levhari (1979, 1982), Rosen (1982), and Radner (1992), are all centralized hierarchies where a manager can choose the number of layers and the number of elements at each layer of a hierarchy. If no individual decision-maker can consciously choose the number of layers of a hierarchy, then it is referred to as a *decentralized hierarchy*. A hierarchical structure of cities and a wholesale and retail network in the market-place are typical decentralized hierarchies.

The study of hierarchies received the first serious attention from Tuck (1954), who draws a distinction between the problem of resource allocation studied in a standard microeconomics textbook and the problem of organization that relates to a hierarchical structure. The theory of one-way and centralized hierarchies is developed by Williamson (1967), Calvo and Wellisz (1978, 1979), Keren and Levhari (1979, 1982), Rosen (1982), and Yang (1984). Qian applies the calculus of variations to the analysis of this kind of hierarchy in connection with the decision problem of a central planner in a socialist economy. Radner (1992, 1993) extends the analysis to the case with asymmetric hierarchical structure. Yang and Hogbin (1990) develop a centralized network hierarchy model which is relevant to the analysis of those hierarchical structures of cities and wholesale and retail networks that can be commanded by a central planner. Yang (1994) has developed the first decentralized hierarchy model within the new classical framework.

From the model in chapter 7, we can see that professional middlemen will emerge from the division of labor between the production of goods and the production of transaction services. A hierarchical structure of the network of division of labor and related transactions is associated with professional middlemen. In that model, each middleman has connections with specialist producers of different goods while each specialist producer of goods has connections only with the middleman. This asymmetric relationship between the middleman and different specialist producers of goods generates a simple hierarchical structure in which the middleman is on the top and specialist producers of goods are on the bottom. Each specialist producer of a good trades indirectly with specialist producers of other goods through the middleman, which creates a local business community where each consumer-producer directly or indirectly trades with each of the others.

As shown in chapter 8, the hierarchical structure between the employer and her employees will emerge from the institution of the firm. As division of labor evolves within a firm, the number of layers of hierarchy within the firm increases. As division of labor evolves between firms, the number of upstream and downstream layers increases too. The hierarchical structure within a firm is associated with asymmetric distribution of residual returns and residual control. This asymmetric superior–subordinate relationship adds another feature to hierarchy.

From chapter 19, we can understand the intrinsic relationship between the hierarchical structure of transactions and the hierarchical structure of division of labor. As division of labor evolves into a longer, roundabout production chain with more goods at each link of the chain, the number of layers of the corresponding hierarchy of transactions will increase accordingly.

In section 20.2 we use simple, centralized hierarchy models to illustrate the relationship between division of labor and hierarchical structure. In sections 20.3, 20.4, and 20.5 Yang's decentralized hierarchy model (1994) is used to illustrate the intimate relationship between the number of layers of the hierarchical structure of transactions and the level of division of labor between transaction and production activities. In section 20.6, a network hierarchy model of cities is used to explain the relationship between the number of layers of hierarchical structure of cities and the level of division of labor.

## ◆ 20.2. One-way Centralized Hierarchy

We use two examples to illustrate *one-way centralized hierarchy*.

### Example 20.1. a centralized one-way hierarchy

Assume that in a library the number of books distinctive from one another is $n$; we refer to $n$ as the number of *basic elements* in a library catalogue system. A catalogue system consists of $m$ layers. An element at a layer is a category (or subcategory). Each category (or subcategory) is divided into $x$ subcategories at the lower layer. At the bottom of this catalogue system are $n$ books (basic elements). We refer to all categories, subcategories, and books as *elements* in a hierarchy. A catalog system with $n = 8$ (8 books), $m = 3$ (3 layers), $x = 2$ (2 channels or spans connecting an element with the elements at the lower layer) is shown in figure 20.1a. This is an analogue of a decision tree. The top layer is a tree root. At the next layer books are divided between two categories under each of which are four subcategories.

A degenerate catalog system with $n = 8$, $m = 1$, $x = 8$ is shown in figure 20.1b. In this system, a person must directly check each book. If layers of the tree are designated in order from bottom to top with the tree root as layer $m$ and the bottom as layer 0, then the bottom layer in figure 20.1a is layer 0, the top layer is layer 3. The two intermediate layers are layers 1 and 2 respectively. For a variable $m$, the number of elements at layer $m$ is 1, that at layer $m - 1$ is $x$, that at layer $m - 2$ is $x^2$, that at layer $i$ is $x^{m-i}$, and that at layer 0 (the bottom) is $x^m$. Since the number of elements at the bottom is the number of basic elements $n$, we have a simple relation between $x$, $m$, and $n$:

$$n = x^m, \text{ or } x = n^{1/m}. \tag{20.1}$$

Assume that the cost of checking an element (the title of a category, a subcategory, or a book) is a constant $c$; the cost of finding a certain element at a layer is $cx$ if a person uses the catalogue system. The hierarchy with the same cost of checking an element is referred to as symmetric hierarchy. Asymmetric hierarchy is studied by Radner (1992). For symmetric hierarchy, the total cost of finding a book through a catalog system with $m$ layers is

$$C = cmx = cmn^{1/m} \tag{20.2}$$

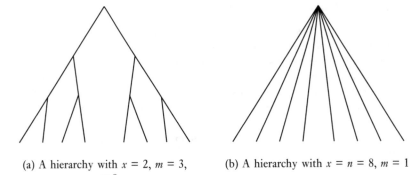

(a) A hierarchy with $x = 2$, $m = 3$, $n = 8$

(b) A hierarchy with $x = n = 8$, $m = 1$

♦ **Figure 20.1**: Hierarchical structures

where we have used (20.1). The optimum $m$ is given by minimizing $C$ with respect to $m$, or is given by

$$m^* = \log n \tag{20.3}$$

where log is the logarithm with $e$ as a base and hence $m^*$ increases less than proportionally with $n$.[2] The optimum $x$ and the minimum cost are given by

$$x^* = n^{1/\log n} \text{ and } C^* = cn^{1/\log n} \log n \tag{20.4}$$

respectively. If there is no catalogue system ($m = 1$ and $x = n$), a person must check each book in order to find the book she wants. The total cost is

$$C' = cn \tag{20.5}$$

The efficiency multiplier of the hierarchy, defined by the ratio of $C'$ to $C^*$, is:

$$E = C'/C^* = n^{1-1/\log n}/\log n, \tag{20.6}$$

where $E$ characterizes the efficiency of a hierarchy in comparison to a system without the hierarchy, $dE/dn > 0$, and $E > 1$ if $n > e$.

(20.3) and (20.6) may be summarized in the following proposition.

**Proposition 20.1**: The optimum number of layers in a hierarchy is a weakly increasing function of the number of basic elements in the system. A hierarchy is more efficient if the number of basic elements in the system is nontrivial. The efficiency of an optimum hierarchy compared to a nonhierarchical structure increases with the number of basic elements.[3]

It is not difficult to extend this analysis to a military command or a management system, as shown in the following example.

## Example 20.2: a management hierarchy

Assume that a manager has to supervise and coordinate the activities of $n$ workers who specialize in different professions. She can use a management hierarchy by hiring several division chiefs and letting them supervise their subordinates. Suppose that she supervises $x$ subordinates each of whom supervises $x$ subordinates, and so on. Assume, moreover, that this hierarchy has $m$ layers and its bottom consists of $n$ workers. The relationship between $x$, $n$, and $m$ is the same as in (20.1). If supervision quality decreases with the number of subordinates supervised by each manager, $x$, we may assume that the management cost related to low management quality is an increasing function of the number of subordinates supervised by each manager. Let the cost be $C_1$; then we have

$$C_1 = cx \tag{20.7}$$

where $c$ is a constant coefficient. Another type of management cost, namely the cost of employing managers, is an increasing function of the total number of managers. This number is

$$S = 1 + x + x^2 + \ldots + x^{m-1}. \tag{20.8}$$

Since $xS = x + x^2 + \ldots + x^m$, the difference between $S$ and $xS$ is $1 - x^m$. Hence,

$$S = (x^m - 1)/(x - 1) = (n - 1)/(x - 1)$$

where we have used (20.1). The management cost related to $S$ is

$$C_2 = tS = t(n - 1)/(x - 1) \tag{20.9}$$

where $t$ is a constant wage rate. The total management cost is

$$C = C_1 + C_2 = cx + t(n - 1)/(x - 1). \tag{20.10}$$

Minimizing $C$ with respect to $x$ gives the optimum hierarchy, characterized by

$$x^* = 1 + [t(n - 1)/c]^{.5}, \qquad m^* = \log n/\log x^* \tag{20.11}$$

where $x^*$ is the optimum number of subordinates supervised by each manager, $m^*$ is the optimum number of layers, $t$ is the salary rate of a manager, and $c$ characterizes the negative effects on management quality of an increasing number of subordinates supervised by a manager. $x^*$ increases with $n$, the number of workers, and $t$, and decreases with $c$. $m^*$ decreases with $t$ and increases with $c$ because of the negative relationship between $m^*$ and $x^*$ and between $x^*$ and $c$, and the positive relationship between $x^*$ and $t$.

## ◆ 20.3 A Decentralized Hierarchy of Transactions and the Division of Labor

In this section and sections 22.4 and 22.5, we use a new classical general equilibrium model to show how the equilibrium level of division of labor, the equilibrium number of layers of the hierarchical network of transactions, transaction efficiency, productivity in production, and the size of the market network are simultaneously determined in a decentralized market.

## Example 20.3 a decentralized network hierarchy

As before, we first outline the story behind the model. In the model to be considered there are four consumer goods, two types of transaction service, and many *ex ante* identical consumer-producers. Each good is essential in consumption. Each individual, as a consumer, prefers diverse consumption and, as a producer, prefers specialized production of goods and transaction services due to a fixed learning cost which generates economies of specialization in each activity. Moreover, trade will incur transaction costs. The trade-off between economies of specialization and transaction costs can be used to endogenize the level of division of labor. A low level of division of labor involves only trade between neighbors and a high level of division of labor will involve trade between non-neighbors as well as between neighbors. Assume that trade with a neighbor is a transacting activity that is distinct from trade with non-neighbors. Then, there are three possible levels of specialization in transacting activities if the level of division of labor in producing goods is sufficiently high: (i) Self-provision of two types of transaction service by producers of goods; (ii) Supply of one type of transaction service by partially specialized middlemen and self-provision of the other type of transaction service by each person; and (iii) Supply of each type of transaction service by completely specialized middlemen. For the third case, a middleman may specialize in mediating transactions between local middlemen who take care of trade between neighbors. This implies that the hierarchical structure of a wholesale and retail network may emerge from a high level of division of labor. In addition to the trade-off between economies of specialization in producing goods and transaction costs, a trade-off between economies of specialization in transacting activities and transaction costs in delivering transaction services can then be used to simultaneously endogenize the number of layers of a hierarchical structure of transactions and the level of division of labor in production and transaction activities. The first trade-off entails endogenization of each individual's level of specialization and the related number of her trade partners. Hence, as the number of trade partners increases with the level of specialization, a new transacting activity for trade between non-neighbors endogenously emerges and thereby creates scope for a hierarchical structure of transactions to emerge from the second trade-off.

Using inframarginal analysis, we can identify four types of market structure as candidates for the general equilibrium. The first is autarky where no market exists. The second is the partial division of labor where each partially specialized producer of goods self-provides transaction services. This structure of transactions is symmetric, and no hierarchy exists. The third is associated with the division of labor between partially specialized producers of goods and partially specialized producers of one type of transaction service where each middleman has two producers of goods as trade partners, but each producer of goods has only one trade partner. The simplest hierarchy of transactions with two layers emerges from a higher level of division of labor between the production of goods and the production of transaction services. The fourth is a complete division of labor where everybody trades all four goods and all types of transaction services, and each professional middleman specializes in a single transacting activity. A retail middleman specializes in local business between neighbors and a wholesale middleman specializes in trade between local communities. There are three layers of the hierarchy of transactions: the top consists of the wholesale middlemen; the middle layer consists of the retail middlemen; the bottom consists of specialist producers of goods. In the decentralized hierarchy of three layers the producers of goods are more peripheral than the retail middlemen who are more peripheral than the wholesale middlemen.

Applying inframarginal analysis, we prove that the equilibrium is autarky if the degree of economies of specialization is sufficiently small and if the transaction cost coefficient for a unit of transaction service is sufficiently large, since in this case transaction costs outweigh economies of specialization generated by the division of labor. As the transaction cost coefficient is slightly lowered and/or the degree of economies of specialization increases, the general equilibrium shifts to the partial division of labor with partially specialized producers of goods where there is no middleman. If the transaction cost coefficient is further lowered and/or the degree of economies of specialization further increases, the general equilibrium entails a hierarchical structure of transactions with two layers where there is a division of labor between producers and middlemen. If the transaction cost coefficient is extremely small and the degree of economies of specialization is great a hierarchy of three layers emerges from a high level of division of labor between wholesale and retail businesses and between producers and middlemen. As the transaction cost coefficient is reduced, the division of labor evolves, resulting in an increase in productivity, the extent of the market, the degree of endogenous comparative advantage, the degree of diversity of economic structure, and in trade dependence.

We turn now to the technical substance of the model. Consider an economy with a continuum of *ex ante* identical consumer-producers of mass $M$, and with four consumer goods. The amount of good i self-provided by each consumer-producer is $x_i$. The respective amounts of good i sold and purchased in the market are $x_i^s$ and $x_i^d$. The fraction $1 - T_i$ of a shipment of good i disappears in transit because of transaction costs. Thus, $T_i x_i^d$ is the amount a person receives from the purchase of good i.[4] An individual's consumption of good i is $x_i + T_i x_i^d$. The utility function is identical for all individuals:

$$U = \Pi^4_{i=1}(x_i + T_i x_i^d). \tag{20.12}$$

This function implies that utility is 0 if the amount of any goods consumed is nonpositive. For simplicity, we assume further that a local community consists of at most three types of occupation configurations. Two individuals who are in different communities are called non-neighbors.[5] Suppose the coefficient $T_i$ equals the quantity of the transaction service for delivering good i. $T_i$ consists of only $T_{in}$ if trade takes place between neighbors where $T_{in}$ denotes the quantity of the transaction service for delivering good i between neighbors. If trade takes place between non-neighbors in the absence of the division of labor between wholesale and retail middlemen, $T_i$ consists of two components, $T_{in}$ and $T_{io}$, where $T_{io}$ denotes the quantity of the transaction service for delivering good i between non-neighbors. If a seller of a good buys a good through both wholesale and retail businessmen from another community (see figure 12.3(4c)), two types of transaction service for neighbors will be needed. First the good purchased will be procured from an original seller by the local middleman who resides in the same community as the seller. Then the local middleman delivers the good to the wholesaler who then delivers the good to the retail middleman in the local community of the ultimate buyer. Let n denote a service for neighbors provided by the middleman in the community of the ultimate buyer and n' denote a service for neighbors provided by a middleman in the community of the original seller. $T_i$ consists of $T_{in}$, $T_{io}$, and $T_{in'}$ if a good is delivered by both wholesale and

retail middlemen between non-neighbors. Because of the assumption of the iceberg transaction cost coefficient, $T_i$ is a coefficient of receiving rate as well as the compounded
quantity of transaction services. With this assumption, a transfer of good from a middleman to the ultimate buyer can be considered as a delivery with an added transaction
service in the absence of resale of goods. This avoids the formidable problem of indices of
destinations and origins of a delivery.

Transaction services can be either self-provided or purchased. Each consumer-producer's
self-provided amount of transaction service of good i is $t_{ij}$, where j = n, n', o, letters n and
n' stand for neighbor and o stands for non-neighbor. The respective amounts of transaction service sold and purchased in the market are $t_{ij}^s$ and $t_{ij}^d$. The fraction $1 - k$ of a
delivery of transaction service purchased disappears in transit because of the transaction
costs of the services. Thus, $kt_{ij}^d$ is the amount a person receives from the purchase of
transaction service $t_{ij}^d$ and the definition for $T_i$ is given as follows.

$$T_i = T_{in} = (t_{in} + kt_{in}^d) \text{ if trade occurs between neighbors;} \qquad (20.13a)$$

$$T_i = T_{in}T_{io} = (t_{in} + kt_{in}^d)(t_{io} + kt_{io}^d) \text{ if trade occurs between non-neighbors}$$
in the absence of division of labor between wholesale and retail middlemen;   (20.13b)

$$T_i = T_{in}T_{io}T_{in'} = (t_{in} + kt_{in}^d)(t_{io} + kt_{io}^d)(t_{in'} + kt_{in'}^d) \text{ if trade occurs}$$
between non-neighbors through both wholesale and retail middlemen,        (20.13c)

where it is assumed that $k \in [0, 1]$. The transaction services n, o, and/or n' are connected
in series when trade occurs between non-neighbors, since the service will not be completed
if either the delivery of a good within a local community or its delivery between local
communities fails to complete. The production functions for the four goods and various
services and the endowment constraint are the same for each consumer-producer, given by

$$x_i + x_i^s = \text{Max}\{0, L_{ix} - A\}, \qquad A \in [0, 1) \qquad (20.14a)$$

$$t_{ij} + t_{ij}^s = \text{Max}\{0, L_{ij} - A\} \qquad (20.14b)$$

$$\Sigma_i L_{ix} + \Sigma_i \Sigma_j L_{ij} = 1, \qquad (20.14c)$$
$$L_{ix}, L_{ij} \in [0, 1], \text{ i} = 1, 2, 3, 4, \text{ j} = \text{n, o}$$

where $x_i + x_i^s$ is the output level of good i, $t_{ij} + t_{ij}^s$ is the output level of type j service for
good i, $L_{ix}$ is a person's level of specialization in producing good i. $L_{ij}$ is a person's level of
specialization in producing type j transaction service for good i. Each consumer-producer
is endowed with one unit of labor. Parameter A is a fixed learning cost in producing a good
or a type of service. A larger A is associated with a greater degree of economies of
specialization, since division of labor and specialization can avoid more duplicated fixed
learning cost as A increases.

The specification of the physical conditions of the model formalizes the following trade-
offs which give rise to the emergence of a hierarchy from a high level of division of labor.
If a person has a low level of specialization, so that she has not more than two types of
producers of goods as trade partners, then she needs to trade with only her neighbors.
If her level of specialization in producing goods is high, then she will need services both
for neighbors and non-neighbors. This implies that a higher level of specialization in

producing goods creates scope for a higher level of division of labor in producing two types of service.

Several subtle trade-offs, however, complicate the story. If there is a division of labor between producers of 3 goods, then 3 producers can constitute an integrated local business community where they trade only with neighbors. If there is a division of labor between producers and a local retail middleman, then the local community can contain only 2 producers in addition to the middleman. This implies that only two goods are traded between neighbors, and trading three goods will involve non-neighbors. This implies a trade-off between economies of specialization in production and economies of specialization in trading. That is, a middleman in a local community trading 3 goods can provide better transaction conditions for increasing a person's level of specialization in producing goods. But since the specialist producer now trades more goods, she must spend time on one additional transaction service for non-neighbors. This reduces her level of specialization. Also, each local middleman can buy at most two goods from neighbors and has to buy goods from non-neighbors if she trades 3 goods. Emergence of wholesale middlemen will enlarge the scope for trading off one against another among the conflicting forces. But a wholesaler has to buy all her consumption goods from non-neighboring producers of goods through local middlemen because her neighbors are retail middlemen who do not produce goods for sale. Each transfer of goods between different middlemen and between middlemen and original sellers or ultimate buyers involves transaction costs, and the division of labor between wholesale and retail middlemen increases the number of such transfers that are essential for a good to reach its ultimate consumer. Hence, another trade-off exists between economies of specialization in producing transaction services and the transaction cost in delivering such services. An improvement in transaction efficiency in delivering the services and/or an increase in the degree of economies of specialization will enlarge the scope for the market efficiently trading off one against others among the conflicting forces. Therefore, the level of division of labor and the number of layers of the hierarchy of transactions can be explained by the two parameters.

## ◆ 20.4 Configurations and Market Structures

In this section we investigate the relationship between individuals' decisions concerning their levels and patterns of specialization and the network pattern of transactions for society as a whole. Combinations of zero and nonzero values of 36 decision variables $x_i$, $x_i^s$, $x_i^d$, $t_{ij}$, $t_{ij}^s$, $t_{ij}^d$ (i = 1, 2, 3, 4 and j = n, o) generate $2^{36} = 68,719,476,736$ profiles of zero and non-zero variables and thereby one interior solution and $2^{36} - 1$ corner solutions. Because of the assumption of iceberg transaction cost, a delivery of goods from a middleman to a buyer does not involve resale of the good although it adds a transaction service factor to the good. This ensures the applicability of the Wen theorem to the model. Using the Wen theorem, the interior solution and many corner solutions can be ruled out from the set of candidates for the optimal decision, leaving only 9 structures that need to be considered.

1. Structure and configuration (1), depicted in figure 20.2(1), where a circle represents a consumer-producer and lines with arrows represent goods flows, is referred to as *autarky*. In structure (1), each individual self-provides all 4 goods.

2. Structure (2a) is depicted in figure 20.2(2a), where a symbol i in a circle represents good or service i sold by the circle, which denotes an occupation configuration. This structure consists of two different configurations. One configuration is denoted by the

circle with 1. A person choosing this configuration sells good 1, buys good 2, and self-provides goods 1, 3, and 4 and service n. Another configuration is denoted by the circle with 2. A person choosing this configuration sells good 2, buys good 1, and self-provides goods 2, 3, and 4 and service n. For this structure there is no middleman and each person produces 4 types of goods and services, trades 2 goods, and needs only one type of neighbor as her trade partner. Hence, no transaction services for non–neighbors are needed.

3. Structure (2b), depicted in figure 20.2(2b), consists of three different configurations. One configuration is denoted by the circle with 1. A person choosing this configuration sells good 1, buys good 2 and service n, and self-provides goods 1, 3 and 4. The second configuration is denoted by the circle with 2. A person choosing this configuration sells good 2, buys good 1 and service n, and self-provides goods 2, 3, and 4. The third configuration is denoted by the circle with n. A person choosing this configuration sells service n, buys goods 1 and 2, and self-provides goods 3 and 4 and service n. This structure is referred to as *low partial division of labor with a hierarchy of two layers*, where there is a division of labor between producers of goods and middlemen. A simple hierarchical structure of transactions emerges from the low level of division of labor where a middleman is the center of a local business community and producers of goods are peripheral and have to trade with each other through a middleman. Each person produces 3 goods and trades 3 types of goods and services. Each seller of goods has one type of neighboring producer of goods and a middleman has two types of producers of goods as trade partner(s). Hence, services for non–neighbors are not needed and the division of labor in producing different transaction services cannot take place.

4. Structure (3a) is depicted in Figure 20.2(3a), where a circle with i represents a configuration which sells good i, buys goods j and r, and self-provides goods i and s (s ≠ i, j, r). In this structure consisting of three configurations, each individual produces 3 types of goods and services, trades 3 goods, and has 2 types of neighboring sellers of goods as her trade partners. Hence, transaction services for non–neighbors are not needed. Note that there are at most three types of occupation configurations in a local community by assumption. This structure is referred to as *high partial division of labor in production without hierarchy*, where there is no division of labor between producers of goods and middlemen.

5. Structure (3b) is depicted in figure 20.2(3b), where a circle with i represents a configuration which sells good i, buys goods j and r and service n, self-provides goods i and s (s ≠ i, j r), and service o. A circle with letter n represents a middleman who sells service n, buys three goods, and self-provides one good and services o and n. In this structure, each person produces 3 types of goods and services and trades 4 types of goods and services. Two dashed circles in (3b) denote two local communities. Individuals in the same community are neighbors and they need transaction service for non–neighbors if they buy goods from another community. For this structure, there is a division of labor between producers of goods and middlemen but there is no division of labor in producing different transaction services. Here, the Wen theorem is used to exclude those configurations in which a middleman sells two types of services or a producer sells more than one good. Since the level of specialization of each producer of goods is higher than in structure (2b), each producer of goods produces one less good than in (2b) and she has a neighboring producer of goods, a neighboring middleman, and a non–neighboring seller of goods as her trade partners. Hence, services for both neighbors and non–neighbors are needed.

6. Structure (3c) is depicted in figure 20.2(3c), where a circle with i represents a

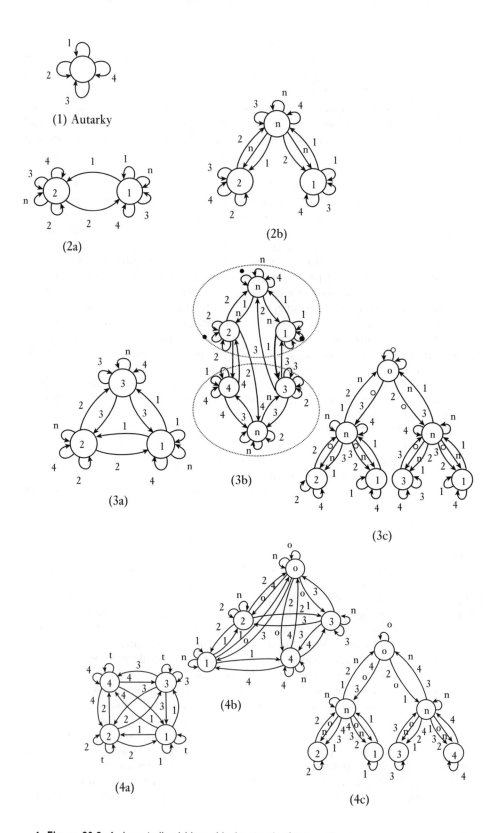

(1) Autarky

(2a)

(2b)

(3a)

(3b)

(3c)

(4a)

(4b)

(4c)

♦ **Figure 20.2:** A decentralized hierarchical network of transactions

configuration which sells good i, buys goods j and r and services n and o, self-provides goods i and 4. A circle with letter o represents a wholesale middleman who sells service o, buys goods 1, 2, and 3 and service n, and self-provides good 4 and service o. A circle with letter n represents a retail middleman who sells service n, buys goods 1, 2, and 3 and service o, and self-provides good 4 and service n. Here, a wholesale middleman trades goods and services indirectly with the producers of goods through the retail middlemen. Each producer of goods must buy a local retail middleman's service as well as a distant retail middleman's service if she buys goods from non-neighbors. In this structure, consisting of five configurations, each individual produces 2 types of goods and services and trades 5 types of goods and services. This structure is referred to as *high partial division of labor with a hierarchy of three layers*, where there is a division of labor between producers of goods and middlemen as well as between wholesale and retail middlemen, so that a hierarchical structure of transactions involves three layers. Since the level of specialization of each producer of goods is higher than in structures (2a), (2b), or (3b), each seller of goods has neighboring producer of goods and a non-neighboring producer of goods as her trade partners. Hence, services for both neighbors and non-neighbors are needed. This implies that a higher level of division of labor in producing goods creates more scope for a division of labor between middlemen (see Marshall, 1890, pp. 256, 264). It is interesting to see that specialization in producing transaction services is associated with diversity of goods flows handled by those professional middlemen.

7. Structure (4a), depicted in figure 20.2(4a), is analogous to (3a) except that each person buys good 4 from a specialist producer instead of self-providing it. There is no middleman in this structure.

8. Structure (4b), depicted in figure 20.2(4b), is analogous to (3b) except that each person buys all goods from specialist producers without self-provision of goods. This structure is referred to as *complete division of labor in production with a hierarchy of two layers*, where there is a complete division of labor between producers of goods with the assistance of partially specialized middlemen but there is no division of labor in producing different transaction services.

9. Structure (4c), depicted in figure 20.2(4c), is analogous to (3c) except that each person buys good 4 from a specialist producer instead of self-providing it. This structure is referred to as *complete division of labor in transactions and production with a hierarchy of three layers*

There are many symmetric structures which generate the same per capita real income as in the corresponding structures listed above. For instance, in a structure analogous to (2a), each individual has the same level of specialization as in structure (2a) but goods 1 and 3 instead of goods 1 and 2 are traded. We exclude those structures from consideration. We use structure (3c) as an example to show the algebra for solving for a corner equilibrium.

In structure (3c), there are six different configurations. The decision problem for a person who sells good 1, buys goods 2 and 3, and services n and o, and self-provides goods 1 and 4 is

$$\text{Max: } U_1 = x_1[(kt_{2n}^{\ d})x_2^{\ d}][(kt_{3n}^{\ d})(kt_{3o}^{\ d})(kt_{3n'}^{\ d})x_3^{\ d}]x_4$$

$$\text{s.t. } x_1 + x_1^{\ s} = \text{Max } \{0, L_1 - A\}, \quad x_4 = L_4 - A, \quad \text{(production functions of goods)}$$
$$L_1 + L_4 = 1 \quad \text{(endowment constraint)}$$
$$p_1 x_1^{\ s} = p_2 x_2^{\ d} + p_3 x_3^{\ d} + p_n(t_{2n}^{\ d} + t_{3n}^{\ d}) + p_{n'} t_{3n'}^{\ d} \quad \text{(budget constraint)}$$

where each $t_{ij}^d$ involves a transaction cost $(1 - k)t_{ij}^d$, n is the service bought from a local retail middleman and n' is the service transactions with non-neighbors bought from a retail middleman who is in another community. The solution is

$$L_1 = (7 - 6A)/8, \qquad L_4 = (1 + 6A)/8, \qquad x_1^s = 3(1 - 2A)/4$$

$$x_1 = x_4 = (1 - 2A)/8, \qquad x_2^d = p_1(1 - 2A)/8p_2, \qquad x_3^d = p_1(1 - 2A)/8p_3,$$

$$t_{2n}^d = t_{3n}^d = p_1(1 - 2A)/8p_n, \qquad t_{3n'}^d = p_1(1 - 2A)/8p_{n'},$$

$$t_{3o}^d = p_1(1 - 2A)/8p_o, \qquad U_1(p) = k^4 p_1^6[(1 - 2A)/8]^8/p_n^2 p_{n'} p_o p_2 p_3$$

where $U_1(p)$ is the indirect utility function for this configuration. The symmetry between services n and n' and the utility equalization condition imply $p_n = p_{n'}$. The decision problem for the configuration which sells good 2, buys goods 1 and 3, and services n and o, and self-provides good 4, and the configuration which sells good 3, buys goods 1 and 2, and services n and o, and self-provides good 4, are symmetric to the above decision. The symmetry and utility equalization conditions between the three symmetric configurations imply $p_1 = p_2 = p_3$.

The decision problem for a person who sells service n, buys goods 1, 2, and 3, and service o, and self-provides good 4 and service n is

Max: $U_n = (t_{1n}x_1^d)(t_{2n}x_2^d)[(kt_{3n}^d)(kt_{3o}^d)x_3^d]x_4$

s.t. $t_{1n} + t_{2n} + t_n^s = \text{Max } \{0, L_n - A\}, \quad x_4 =$      (production functions of
Max $\{0, L_4 - A\}$      services, goods)
$L_n + L_4 = 1$      (endowment constraint)
$p_n t_n^s = p_1 x_1^d + p_2 x_2^d + p_3 x_3^d + p_o t_{3o}^d + p_{n'} t_{3n'}^d$      (budget constraint)

The solution is

$$L_n = (7 - 6A)/8, \qquad\qquad L_4 = (1 + 6A)/8, \qquad t_n^s = 5(1 - 2A)/8$$

$$t_{1n} = t_{2n} = x_4 = (1 - 2A)/8, \quad x_1^d = p_n(1 - 2A)/8p_1 \qquad x_2^d = p_n(1 - 2A)/8p_2$$

$$x_3^d = p_n(1 - 2A)/8p_3, \qquad\qquad t_{3n'}^d = p_n(1 - 2A)/8p_{n'} \qquad t_{3o}^d = p_n(1 - 2A)/8p_o$$

$$U_n(p) = k^2 p_n^5[(1 - 2A)/8]^8/p_1 p_2 p_3 p_o p_{n'}$$

where $U_n(p)$ is the indirect utility function for this configuration.

The decision problem for a person who sells service o, buys goods 1, 2, and 3, and service n, and self-provides good 4 and service o is

Max: $U_o = [(kt_{1n}^d)t_{1o}^d x_1^d][(kt_{2n}^d)t_{2o}x_2^d][(kt_{3n}^d)t_{3o}x_3^d]x_4$

s.t. $t_{1o} + t_{2o} + t_{3o} + t_o^s = \text{Max } \{0, L_o - A\}, \quad x_4 =$      (production functions of
Max $\{0, L_4 - A\}$      services, goods)
$L_o + L_4 = 1$      (endowment constraint)
$p_o t_o^s = p_1 x_1^d + p_2 x_2^d + p_3 x_3^d + p_n(t_{1n}^d + t_{2n}^d + t_{3n}^d)$      (budget constraint)

The solution is

$$L_o = (9 - 8A)/10, \qquad L_4 = (1 + 8A)/10, \qquad t_o{}^s = 3(1 - 2A)/5$$

$$t_{1o} = t_{2o} = t_{3o} = x_4 = (1 - 2A)/10, \quad x_1{}^d = p_o(1 - 2A)/10p_1 \quad x_2{}^d = p_o(1 - 2A)/10p_2$$

$$x_3{}^d = p_o(1 - 2A)/10p_3, \qquad U_o(p) = k^3 p_o{}^6[(1 - 2A)/10]^{10}/p_1 p_2 p_3 p_n{}^3$$

where $U_o(p)$ is the indirect utility function for this configuration.

The market clearing and utility equalization conditions for structure (3c) are

$$M_1 x_1{}^s = M_2 x_1{}^d(2) + M_3 x_1{}^d(3) + M_n x_1{}^d(n) + M_o x_1{}^d(o),$$

$$M_2 x_2{}^s = M_1 x_2{}^d(1) + M_3 x_2{}^d(3) + M_n x_2{}^d(n) + M_o x_2{}^d(o),$$

$$M_3 x_3{}^s = M_1 x_3{}^d(1) + M_2 x_3{}^d(2) + M_n x_3{}^d(n) + M_o x_3{}^d(o),$$

$$M_n t_n{}^s = M_1[t_{2n}{}^d(1) + t_{3n}{}^d(1) + t_{3n'}{}^d(1)] + M_2[t_{1n}{}^d(2) + t_{3n}{}^d(2) + t_{3n'}{}^d(2)] +$$

$$M_3[t_{1n}{}^d(3) + t_{2n}{}^d(3) + t_{1n'}{}^d(3)] + M_o t_{3n}{}^d(o),$$

$$U_1(p) = U_2(p) = U_3(p) = U_n(p) = U_o(p),$$

where $M_i$ is the number of individuals selling good or service i. We denote the quantity of good i demanded by a person selling good j by (j) after $x_i{}^d$ or $t_{in}{}^d$. Due to Walras's law, the market clearing condition for service o is not independent of the above equations. Due to the symmetry between services n and n′, we do not draw the distinction between them, so that $M_n$ is the number of individuals who sell n and n′. The five equations give the corner equilibrium in structure (3c) as listed in table 20.1.

Repeating this procedure, we have solved for the corner equilibria in the other 8 structures. The per capita real income, relative prices, the numbers of individuals selling different goods and services, and level of specialization for individuals choosing different configurations are listed in table 20.1.

In table 20.1, $M_i$ is the number of individuals selling good or service i, $p_i$ is the price of good or service i, and $L_i$ is the level of specialization for a person selling good or service i, $i = 1, 2, 3, 4, n, o$. $M$ is the population size, $k$ is the transaction efficiency of transaction services, and $A$ is the fixed learning cost in each activity which relates to the degree of economies of specialization. In the notation for a structure ij (i = 1, 2, 3 4 and j = a, b, c), letter i represents a level of specialization in producing goods and letter j represents a level of specialization in producing transaction services and the related hierarchical structure of transactions. For instance structure 2b denotes that two goods are involved in trade and there are two layers in the hierarchical structure of transactions. Each individual does not trade if i = 1; she trades 2 goods if i = 2, trades 3 goods if i = 3, and trades 4 goods if i = 4. If j = a, there is a division of labor in producing goods but no division of labor exists between the production of goods and the production of transaction services, so that no hierarchical structure of organization exists. If j = b, there is a division of labor between the production of goods and the production of transaction services but no division of labor exists in producing different transaction services, so that the number of layers of

**Table 20.1:** Corner equilibria in nine market structures

| Structure | Per capita real income | Corner equilibrium relative prices | Number of different specialists | Level of specialization |
|---|---|---|---|---|
| (1) | $[(1-4A)/4]^4$ | | | |
| (2a) | $[(1-4A)/5]^5$ | $p_1/p_2 = 1$ | $M_1 = M_2 = M/2$ | $L_1 = L_2 = (3-7A)/5$ |
| (2b) | $k^{2/3}(1-3A)^{16/3}/5^{10/3}6^2$ | $p_1/p_n = (1-3A)^{1/6}5^{5/3}/36k^{1/3}$, $p_1/p_2 = 1$ | $M_n = M[1 + 12k^{1/3}/5^{2/3}(1-3a)^{1/6}]^{-1}$, $M_1 = M_2 = 6k^{1/3}M_n/[12k^{1/3} + 5^{2/3}(1-3A)^{1/6}]$ | $L_1 = L_2 = (3-4A)/5$, $L_n = (2-3A)/3$ |
| (3a) | $[(1-3A)/6]^6$ | $p_1/p_2 = p_1/p_3 = 1$ | $M_1 = M_2 = M_3 = M/3$ | $L_1 = L_2 = (1-A)/2$ |
| (3b) | $k^{3/4}[(1-3A)/9]^{9/4}$ $[(1-4A)/7]^{21/4}$ | | | |
| (3c) | $k^3(1-2A)^{58/7}8^{-48/7}10^{-10/7}$ | $p_1/p_2 = p_1/p_3 = 1$, $p_n/p_o = [8^8k(1-2A)^210^{-10}]^{1/7}$ $p_1/p_n = k^{-2/7}$ | $M_o = 5M/[5 + 12p_o(1/p_n + 1/p_1)]$ $M_1 = M_2 = M_3 = 4p_oM_o/5p_1$, $M_n = 12p_oM_o/5p_n$ | $L_1 = L_2 = L_3 = (6-5A)7$ $L_n = (7-6A)/8$, $L_o = (9-8A)/10$ |
| (4a) | $[(1-3A)/8]^8$ | $p_1/p_2 = p_1/p_3 = p_1/p_4 = 1$ | $M_1 = M_2 = M_3 = M_4 = M/4$ | $L_1 = L_2 = L_3 = L_4 = (1-A)/2$ |
| (4b) | $[k(1-24)^{11} \div 8^812^31]^{4/5}$ | $p_1/p_2 = p_1/p_3 = p_1/p_4 = 1$, $p_1/p_o = [(1-2A)^48^8/k12^3]^{1/5}$ | $M_o = M/[1 + 2^33^{7/5}/(1-2A)^{4/5}]$ $M_1 = M_2 = M_3 = M_4 = 3^{7/5}2k^{1/5}M_o/(1-2A)^{4/5}$ | $L_1 = L_2 = L_3 = L_4 = (5-2A)/8$ $L_o = (2-A)/3$ |
| (4c) | $k^{56/11}(1-A)^{592/55}10^{-48/11}$ $11^{-4}12^{-12/5}$ | $p_1/p_2 = p_1/p_3 = p_1/p_4 = 1$, $p_1/p_n = 11[k^3(1-A)10^{-10}]^{-1/11}$ $p_n/p_o = 10(1-A)^{1/5}12^{-6/5}$ | $M_o = M[1 + 5p_o(1/3p_1 + 4/11p_n)]^{-1}$, $M_1 = M_2 = M_3 = M_4 = 5p_oM_o/12p_1$ $M_n = 20p_oM_o/11p_n$ | $L_1 = L_2 = L_3 = L_4 = L_n = L_o = 1$ |

the hierarchy of transactions is 2. If $j = c$, there is a division of labor between the production of goods and the production of transaction services as well as between different transaction services, so that the number of layers of the hierarchy of transactions is 3.

In this model, the general equilibrium will determine not only the efficient network size of division of labor, but also the efficient number of layers of the network hierarchy of transactions.

## ♦ 20.5. The General Equilibrium and its Inframarginal Comparative Statics

By comparing per capita real incomes in all structures and using the Yao theorem, we can identify the general equilibrium and its inframarginal comparative statics, as shown in table 20.2, where $k_1 \equiv 164.79(1 - 4A)^6/(1 - 3A)^8$, $k_2 \equiv 5^5(1 - 3A)/6^6$, $k_3 \equiv 39.88(1 - 3A)^{16/7}/(1 - 2A)^{174/49}$, $k_4 \equiv .46(1 - 2A)^{18/77}$, $k_5 \equiv 47.10(1 - 2A)^{3.97}/(1 - A)^{5.15}$, $k_6 \equiv \{10^{48/11} 11^4[(1 - 2A)^{11}/8^8]^{4/5}/12^{24}(1 - A)^{592/55}\}^{55/236}$, $k_5 > k_4$ for $A \in (.40, .44)$, and $k_3 > k_2$ for $A \in (.32, .33)$. Structure (1) is autarky, structure (2b) is low partial division of labor in production and transactions with a hierarchy of two layers, (3a) is nonhierarchical high partial division of labor in production, (4b) is the complete division of labor in producing goods with a hierarchy of two layers, (3c) is high level of partial division of labor with a hierarchy of three layers, (4c) is the complete division of labor in production and transactions with a hierarchy of three layers. Note that the level of division of labor in producing goods is higher in (4b) where 4 goods are traded than in (3c) where 3 goods are traded, but the level of division of labor in producing transaction services is higher in (3c) where there is the division of labor between wholesale and retail middlemen, than in (4b) where there is only one type of middleman. The level of division of labor for the whole economy is roughly the same for the two structures since each person in both structures produces 2 types of goods and/or services. Also, the level of division of labor is roughly same in (2b) and (3a). (3a) has a higher level of division of labor in production but a lower level of division of labor in transactions than (2b). But the level of division of labor in (4c) is higher than in (4b) and (3c), which have higher levels of division of labor than (2b) and (3a), which have higher levels of division of labor than in structure (1).[6]

Table 20.2 implies that if the transaction efficiency coefficient $k$ is held constant, the level of division of labor and the number of layers of the hierarchy of transactions increases as the fixed learning cost $A$ increases. If $A$ is held constant, the level of division of labor and the number of layers of the hierarchy of transactions increases as transaction efficiency for delivering transaction services is improved.

The inframarginal comparative statics are summarized in the following proposition.

**Table 20.2:** General equilibrium and its inframarginal comparative statics

| $A \in$ | (0, .22) | (.22, .24) | | (.24, .32) | | (.32, .33) | | | (.33, .4) | | (.40, .44) | | | (.44, .5) | (.5, 1) |
|---|---|---|---|---|---|---|---|---|---|---|---|---|---|---|---|
| $k$ | | $<$ | $>$ | $<$ | $>$ | $<$ | $\in (k_2,$ | $>$ | $<$ | $>$ | $<$ | $\in (k_4,$ | $>$ | $<$ | $>$ |
| | | $k_1$ | $k_1$ | $k_2$ | $k_2$ | $k_2$ | $k_3)$ | $k_3$ | $k_4$ | $k_4$ | $k_4$ | $k_5)$ | $k_5$ | $k_6$ | $k_6$ |
| Structure | 1 | 2b | 3a | 2b | 3a | 2b | | 3c | 4b | 3c | 4b | | 4c | 4b | 4c |

**Proposition 20.2:** If the degree of economies of specialization in producing goods and transaction services is sufficiently small and the transaction cost coefficient for delivering transaction services is large, then the general equilibrium is autarky where no market and hierarchical pattern of organization exist. If the degree of economies of specialization and transaction efficiency are sufficiently great, then the general equilibrium is a hierarchical structure of transactions with three layers, which is based on the complete division of labor in producing various goods and transaction services. As the degree of economies of specialization increases and/or as the transaction cost coefficient for delivering transaction services falls, the level of division of labor and the number of layers of the hierarchy of transactions increase.

Proposition 20.2 is more intuitive if it is considered in relation to figure 20.2 and table 20.2.

Following an approach devised in chapter 6 for proving the first welfare theorem, it is not difficult to show that the general equilibrium is Pareto optimal because economies of specialization are individual-specific. This implies that a competitive market will sort out not only the efficient resource allocation for a given pattern of organization, but also the efficient network size of division of labor and the efficient hierarchical structure of transactions, through individuals' free horizontal and vertical mobility across occupations and across layers.

The evolution of division of labor and the number of layers of the hierarchy based on the comparative statics in this chapter is exogenous because it never occurs in the absence of the exogenous evolution of transaction efficiency and the degree of economies of specialization. If the approach to endogenizing evolution in division of labor developed in chapter 24 is applied to the model here, we can explain endogenous evolution in division of labor as well as in the number of layers of the network hierarchy of transactions. If the number of goods is 100 instead of 4, and/or if producer goods are introduced into the model, and/or parameters $k$ and $A$ are different across goods and services, then a much richer story of incessant evolution of division of labor and the hierarchical structure of the wholesale and retail network will be predicted by an extended version of the model. As the number of layers of the hierarchy becomes very large, a hierarchy within a firm which is part of the market hierarchy may emerge from a high level of division of labor. Then, a theory of centralized hierarchy in the firm, cum decentralized hierarchy in the market, is needed. Shi and Yang (1998) have developed a new classical equilibrium model to endogenize the dividing line between the hierarchy within the firm and the network hierarchy in the market (see exercise 3).

### ◆ 20.6 The Network Hierarchy of Cities and Division of Labor (Yang and Hogbin, 1990)

In this section, a market system consisting of many cities is taken to be another example of the decentralized network hierarchy. In subsection 20.6.1, we investigate the relationship between the number of cities and the number of layers in the hierarchy of cities. In subsection 20.6.2, we specify two types of transaction cost function in order to establish a trade-off between the transaction cost related to the number of cities and the transaction cost related to the average distance between a pair of trade partners. In subsection 20.6.3, the relationship between the optimal number of layers and the level of division of labor in production is considered.

## ◆ 20.6.1 Consumer-producers, cities, and layers of a hierarchy of cities

Consider an economy with $N$ *ex ante* identical consumer-producers. All have the same utility function, which represents a preference for diverse consumption, and a system of production and transactions that displays economies of specialization, similar to that in example 11.1 and in example 20.3. There are $M$ consumer goods where $M < N$. As in the model in previous sections, individuals can choose between self-providing and purchasing consumer goods and transaction services. In addition, consumer-producers can choose their home location and their professional jobs. If a market hierarchy consisting of cities can improve transaction efficiency in facilitating the division of labor, then a competitive market will drive people to move between cities, between occupations, and between localities until per capita real income is equalized across cities, across occupations, and across localities. As demonstrated in the previous sections, in this process, an optimum structure of the market hierarchy will be determined by the "invisible hand." As shown by the Yao theorem, solving for the equilibrium hierarchical structure of transactions based on the division of labor is equivalent to solving for the Pareto optimum with equal real income across consumer-producers. Accordingly, in order to simplify the algebra we adopt the approach of solving for the Pareto optimal structure of the market hierarchy that generates equal real income across consumer-producers.

As shown in chapters 7 and 11, competitive equilibrium has the following properties if transaction efficiency is neither too large nor too small. The economy is divided into several local business communities. There is no trade between communities. In each community there are $n$ consumer-producers and there are some professional middlemen in each city. We assume that residences of producers of goods are evenly located at the vertices of a grid of triangles with equal sides and that middlemen reside in cities. Each consumer-producer produces one traded good and $M - n$ nontraded goods and consumes $M$ goods. She sells one traded good to the other $n - 1$ consumer-producers in the same community through middlemen, and buys one traded good from each of the other local consumer-producers through middlemen. In a community, therefore, each consumer-producer must exchange her professional produce with each of the other local consumer-producers. Since the production and demand conditions are completely symmetric for all people who sell different goods, the trade volume between each pair of consumer-producers is identical. For simplicity, a consumer-producer is henceforth referred to as a producer. The economy may be a single integrated market (community) if $n$ is sufficiently large due to a sufficiently large transaction efficiency. For small values of $n$, the economy is divided into several local business communities. $n$ characterizes the level of division of labor in production as well as the size of a local business community.

In each community, the producers can either trade directly with one another, or trade through a hierarchy of cities. In a city within the hierarchy, there are several professional middlemen. The hierarchy is divided into several layers with large cities at the top, followed by medium cities and finally small towns. If the number of layers is large, then people can exchange with neighbors through small towns nearby and exchange with more distant consumer-producers through large cities and other medium and small cities. That is, a large number of layers will reduce the average distance between trade partners. This large number of layers will, however, increase the number of cities (this point will later be shown), so that the average size of cities and the welfare based on increasing returns to specialization in transactions are reduced. If this hierarchy of cities has only one layer, i.e. each consumer-producer exchanges her professional product with others through a supercity, then each consumer-producer has to go to the distant city in order to exchange even with her neighbors. Such an urban hierarchy will create great benefits based on a higher level of division of labor between professional middlemen, which is made possible by the large size of the supercity, at the cost, however, of increasing the average distance between a pair of producers. In the remainder of this section this trade-off between increasing returns to city size and the average distance between a pair of trade partners is formalized.

It is assumed that the hierarchy of cities in a community has $m$ layers. The top of this network is a city. The bottom layer consists of $n$ consumer-producers. At each other layer, there are some cities. For simplicity, it is assumed that at each city there are $x$ channels connecting a city with the elements (cities or producers) at the lower layer. A hierarchical structure of cities may be the same as in figure 20.1. In the real world $x$ may differ from city to city. In this hierarchy all producers are evenly located and the distance between any pair of neighbors is equal. With the assumption of equal $x$, the relation between the number of producers $n$, the number of layers $m$, and the number of channels or the size of a span $x$ at each city is the same as in (20.1), or

$$n = x^m \text{ or } x = n^{1/m} \tag{20.15}$$

where $n$ characterizes the level of division of labor in production as well as the number of producers in a community. The number of cities is 1 at layer $m$, $x$ at layer $m - 1$, ..., $x^{m-1}$ at layer 1. In general, where the number of cities at layer $i$ is $S_i$, then

$$S_i = x^{m-i} \tag{20.16a}$$

Let the total number of cities at all layers be $S$; $S$ is therefore given by

$$S = \sum_{i=1}^{m} S_i = 1 + x + x^2 + \ldots + x^{m-1} \tag{20.16b}$$
$$= (1 - x^m)/(1 - x) = (n - 1)/(n^{1/m} - 1)$$

where $m$ decreases with $x$ due to (20.15) and $S$ increases with $m$ or decreases with $x$ for a given $n$.

### 20.6.2 Two types of transaction cost

The total transaction cost $TC$ per head is assumed to consist of two components, $CN$ and $CI$. $CN$ depends inversely on the average size of cities and positively on the number of cities in a hierarchy of cities in a community, $S$. The greater the number of cities, the smaller the average size of the city, so that the greater is the transaction cost $CN$ (per capita). The number of cities is given by (20.16). Hence, the relation between transaction cost per capita and the number of cities is

$$CN = tS = t(n - 1)/(n^{1/m} - 1), \tag{20.17}$$

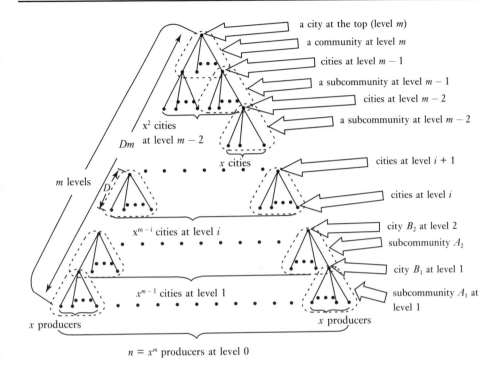

**♦ Figure 20.3:** A network hierarchy of cities

where $t$ is a parameter and hence $CN$ increases with $m$. Since $S$ is related inversely to the average size of cities, $CN$ is a decreasing function of the average size of cities. A greater $t$ implies a greater decrease in $CN$ for a one unit increase in city size. Therefore, $t$ represents the degree of economy of city size.

A smaller $S$ implies a longer average distance between a pair of trade partners, since an individual must go to a farther trade center in order to get even those goods produced by her neighbors. Consequently, a trade-off exists: the greater the number of layers (based on greater $S$), the smaller the transaction cost related to the average distance between a pair of trade partners, but the greater the transaction cost related to the number of cities.

$CI$ is related to the distance between trade partners and the trade volume. As shown in chapter 11, the trade volume between each pair of producers is identical for all producers in a community. Assume that this trade volume is $A$ and the sum of the distances between a producer and all other producers is $T$; we have a transportation moment $W$ and its unit is, for example, a kilogram-mile. $W$ is an analog of work in physics and is a product of $A$ and $T$. $CI$ is proportional to the transportation moment $W$, or

$$CI = cW = cTA \tag{20.18}$$

where $c$ is a parameter. As shown in chapter 11, $A$ depends positively on $n$ (that is, per capita trade volume of a good is an increasing function of the number of traded goods) because an increase in the level of division of labor can improve productivity, thereby raising the per capita trade volume of a traded good. In this chapter it is assumed that this relation takes the simple form

$$A = an \tag{20.19}$$

where $a$ is a parameter and $n$ is the number of traded goods per capita. If the distance between each pair of neighbors is equal, it is not difficult to show that the average travel distance for trade between a producer and other producers increases with the number of traded goods, $n$. Letting the furthest geographic distance between a producer and other producers be $d$; it is assumed that

$$d = b'n \tag{20.20}$$

where $b'$ is a constant. From figure 20.3, we can see that the furthest distance between producers is a sum of the length of the two sloped sides of the triangle describing a hierarchy of cities.[7] Let the geographic distance between two layers be $D$, then the length of a sloped side of that triangle is $Dm$, where $m$ is the number of layers in a hierarchy. Hence, $d$ can be alternatively represented as

$$d = 2Dm. \tag{20.21}$$

From (20.20) and (20.21) therefore

$$D = bn/m \tag{20.22}$$

where $b \equiv b'/2$.

In order to derive a sum of distances between a producer and her trade partners (all other producers in a community), $T$, let us carefully examine Figure 20.3, where a hierarchy of cities in a community has $m$ layers. At the bottom (layer 0), there are $n$ producers. The geographic distance between two layers is $D$. At each city, there are $x$ channels connecting with cities at the lower layer. The top (layer $m$) of this hierarchy is a city that is a center of a community. This community is divided into $x$ subcommunities at layer $m - 1$. There are $x$ cities at layer $m - 1$ as well. Each city at this layer is a member of the community and the center of a subcommunity at layer $m - 1$. A subcommunity at layer $m - 1$ is divided into $x$ subcommunities at layer $m - 2$. A city at layer $m - 2$ is a member of a subcommunity at layer $m - 1$ as well as the center of a subcommunity at layer $m - 2$. The number of cities at layer $m - 2$ is $x^2$. There are $x^{m-2}$ cities and $x^{m-2}$ subcommunities at layer 2. $A_2$ and $B_2$ are the subcommunity and city respectively on the right-hand side of this layer. $A_2$ is divided into $x$ subcommunities at layer 1. Among them the one on the right hand side is subcommunity $A_1$. Small town $B_1$ at layer 1 is a member of subcommunity $A_2$ as well as the center of subcommunity $A_1$. $A_1$ consists of $x$ producers at layer 0.

Let us consider a producer on the right-hand side at the bottom of the hierarchy. The town $B_1$ at layer 1 connects that producer with $x - 1$ neighboring producers in subcommunity $A_1$. The distance between this producer and any one from amongst the other $x - 1$ producers is $2D$; the total distance between this producer and the $x - 1$ producers is $2D(x - 1)$. At layer 2, small city $B_2$ connects this producer with other producers. Because this producer can reach $x - 1$ towns of $B_1$-type in subcommunity $A_2$ through city $B_2$ and each one of these towns connects with $x$ producers at layer 0, through city $B_2$ at layer 2 this producer can reach $(x - 1)x$ producers, who are inside subcommunity $A_2$ and outside subcommunity $A_1$. The distance between this producer and each one of those producers is $4D$. Thus, the total distance between this producer and the $(x - 1)x$ producers is $4D(x - 1)x$. Similarly, the total distance between this producer and the producers connected with her through a city at layer $i$ is $2Di(x - 1)x^{i-1}$ and the total distance between this producer and the producers connected to her through a city at layer $m$ is $2Dm(x - 1)x^{m-1}$. Therefore, the total distance between this producer and all other producers is

$$T = 2D(x - 1)(1 + 2x + 3x^2 + \ldots + mx^{m-1}). \tag{20.23}$$

The polynomial in the second parenthesis is the sum of an arithmetic-geometric series. According to a standard formula, this sum is given by

$$[1 - (m + 1)x^m + mx^{m+1}]/(x - 1)^2. \tag{20.24}$$

Substituting (20.24) for the sum in the second parenthesis in (20.23), we obtain

$$T = 2D[1 - (m + 1)x^m + mx^{m+1}]/(x - 1). \tag{20.25}$$

Hence, the total transaction cost related to the transportation moment for each producer is given by

$$CI = cW = cTA = 2abcn^{2m}[1 - m + 1)n + mn^{1+1/m}]/(n^{1/m} - 1), \tag{20.26}$$

$CI$ decreases with $m$

where we have used (20.17)–(20.25). $1/c$ is the transaction efficiency per unit of transportation moment. $CI$ decreases as the unit transaction efficiency increases.

### 20.6.3 The optimal number of layers in a hierarchical structure

As described in the previous subsection, the total transaction cost per capita is given by

$$TC = CN + CI, \tag{20.27}$$

where $CN$ is an increasing function of $m$ due to (20.17) and $CI$ is a decreasing function of $m$ due to (20.15). In other words, an increase in the number of layers will increase the transaction cost related to the number of cities and decrease the transaction cost related to the transportation moment.

As shown in the previous chapters, the general equilibrium maximizes per capita real income if each individual is a consumer-producer and increasing returns to specialization are specific to each individual and each activity. As far as the model in this section is concerned, this implies that free entry between layers at city hierarchy and between professional jobs will drive the difference in per capita real income across occupations to 0. Since the number of layers of the hierarchical structure of transactions affects per capita real income via its effects on the transaction costs per capita $TC$, competition will force people to shift between occupations and between cities at different layers until the number of layers $m$ maximizes per capita real income via minimizing $TC$. That is, a decentralized market will minimize $TC$ with respect to $m$ when $n$ is given. Using a numerical simulation, we can find the optimal $m$ that minimizes $TC$ for given values of $n$ and $t/abc$. The relationship between the values of $t/abc$ and $n$ and the optimal $m$ is summarized in table 20.3. The figures in the first row are the values of $n$. The first column is values of $t/abc$. Other entries are the optimal numbers of layers in the hierarchy, $m^*$.

A solution $m = 1$ implies that the hierarchy has only one layer. That is, all producers exchange their products through a single trade center. The minimum value of $m$ is 1. From table 20.3, it can be seen that if $n$ is not too large and/or $t/abc$ is large, then the optimum number of layers is 1. The entries with asterisks are the interior optimum numbers of layers. These numbers are greater than 1 and smaller than the maximum number of layers. This maximum number is determined by the minimum value of $x$ at a city. If $x = 1$, then (20.15) cannot hold for $n > 1$. Hence, $x$ must be greater than 1. Noting that $m$ and $x$ must be integers, we see that the minimum value of $x$ is 2 and the maximum $m$ is given by $\log n/\log x = \log n/\log 2$ due to (20.15). All other entries without asterisks and greater than 1 are the maximum values of $m$. Note that this maximum $m$ is an integer that is closest to $\log n/\log 2$. From this table, we can see that the optimal $m$ equals its maximum if $n$ is sufficiently large and/or $t/abc$ is sufficiently small. The optimum $x$ can be obtained by inserting the optimum $m$ given by table 20.3 into (20.15).

Table 20.3 shows that the optimum number of layers is an increasing step function of the level of division of labor $n$ and a decreasing step function of $t/abc$. Noting that $t$ characterizes the degree of economy of city size due to (20.17), and $1/c$ is transaction efficiency per unit of transportation moment shown by (20.16), we are led to

**Proposition 20.3**: The optimum number of layers in a market hierarchy consisting of cities in a community is an increasing step function of the level of division of labor in production and a decreasing step function of the degree of economy of city size and transaction efficiency per unit of transportation moment.

Since $S$ increases with $n$ and $m$, and $m$ increases with $n$, indicated by table 20.3, we have

$$S \text{ increases with } n. \tag{20.28}$$

**Table 20.3**: The optimal number of layers

| $t/abc$ $\quad$ $n$ | 10 | 20 | 30 | 40 | 50 | 60 | 70–120 |
|---|---|---|---|---|---|---|---|
| 10 | 3 | 4 | 4 | 5 | 5 | 5 | 6 |
| 20–30 | 2* | 4 | 4 | 5 | 5 | 5 | 6 |
| 40–60 | 1 | 3* | 4 | 5 | 5 | 5 | 6 |
| 80 | 1 | 2* | 4 | 5 | 5 | 5 | 6 |
| 100 | 1 | 2* | 3* | 5 | 5 | 5 | 6 |
| 120–140 | 1 | 2* | 3* | 4* | 5 | 5 | 6 |
| 160 | 1 | 1 | 3* | 4* | 5 | 5 | 6 |
| 180 | 1 | 1 | 2* | 3* | 5 | 5 | 6 |
| 200–260 | 1 | 1 | 2* | 3* | 4* | 5 | 6 |
| 280 | 1 | 1 | 2* | 3* | 4* | 4* | 6 |
| 300 | 1 | 1 | 2* | 3* | 3* | 4* | 6 |

Since $S$ is the number of cities in the hierarchy in a community, (20.28) means

**Corollary 20.1:** The number of cities in an integrated trade network increases as the division of labor in production evolves.

## Key Terms and Review

Hierarchy, relationship between hierarchy, series cum parallel connection, and residual control rights.
One-way hierarchy, network hierarchy, centralized hierarchy, decentralized hierarchy.
Why a hierarchical structure can be more efficient than a nonhierarchical structure.
Relationship between productivity implications of hierarchy and the level of division of labor.
Relationship between the efficient number of layers of a hierarchical network of transactions, transaction efficiency, productivity, and the level of division of labor.
Trade-off that determines the efficient number of layers of the hierarchical network of cities and determinants of the efficient hierarchical structure of cities.
Market mechanism to determine the efficient hierarchical network of transactions and cities.

## Further Reading

*Hierarchy*: Tuck (1954), Yang and Y.-K. Ng (1993, ch. 14); *survey of the literature of pyramidal hierarchy*: Borland and Eichberger (1998); *survey of the literature of multiple layers of principal–agent relationships*: Milgrom and Roberts (1992), Bolton and Scharfstein (1998), Gibbons (1998); *centralized hierarchy*: Yang and Y.-K. Ng (1993, ch. 14), Williamson (1967, 1985), Calvo and Wellisz (1978, 1979), Keren and Levhari (1979, 1982, 1989), MacLeod and Malcomson (1988), Qian (1994), Rosen (1982), Sah and Stiglitz (1988); *asymmetric hierarchy*: Radner (1992); *decentralized hierarchy*: Spanjers (1992),Yang (1994), Shi and Yang (1998), Y. Zhou (1996); *division of labor and network hierarchy*: Spanjers (1992), Yang and Hogbin (1990), Yang (1994), Carter (1995), Bolton and Dewatripont (1994); *Endogenous transaction costs and hierarchy*: Bac (1996), Bag (1997), Hart and Moore (1999), Aghion and Tirole (1997).

## QUESTIONS

1   It has been suggested that the hierarchical structure of government bureaucracy is the source of government failure in those economies with extensive government intervention or control of economic activities. Use the models in this chapter to comment on this suggestion. Why is free vertical mobility between layers of hierarchy and free mobility between occupation configurations essential to ensure the efficiency of a hierarchical organization structure? Discuss the connection between the failure of the Soviet-style economic system and its feature that the government monopolizes the designing of the economic system, the founding of firms, and the provision of planning and management services. What is the difference between the hierarchy in a Soviet-style economic system and the hierarchical network of transactions in the US, where planning power is freely traded through the franchise, the stock market, and other institutions, which are spontaneously formed as the unintended consequence of interactions between many individuals through fair competition?

2   Assume that in a model of hierarchy, each connection between a pair of individuals involves uncertainty, and that each individual's effort can affect the risk of coordination failure of her relationship with

each trade partner. Then, the impact of the effort of the person at the top of the hierarchy on the reliability of the hierarchy is certainly much more important than that of a person on the bottom of the hierarchy. Use this feature to explain why income distribution between layers of the hierarchy will be efficiently unequal in a free market system. Why may real income still be quite equal, even if there is unequal nominal income distribution, when account is taken of the disutility of intensive competition caused by free entry into the top layer, which may drive the person on the top to be a competitive animal. (See Rosen, 1982, for a model that formalizes this idea.)

3　As the hierarchical network of division of labor evolves, the structure of competition becomes hierarchical too. It may not be a good thing to have more competition or more cooperation when we take into account the complicated hierarchical structure of competition. For instance, in example 4.5, or in the story of the prisoners' dilemma in exercise 4 of chapter 9, coordination failure between two oligopolists in the market (or between two prisoners) is good news for consumers (or for the judge) and for society as a whole. Also, more intensive competition at the top of the hierarchy (for instance, between two presidential candidates in an election campaign) is good news for individuals at other layers, but is full of breathtaking pain for the rival candidates. Analyze what kind of distribution of degree of competition across layers of the hierarchical structure of an economy may emerge from equilibrium in a free market society. Discuss the welfare implications of the pattern of hierarchical structuring of competition. What is the most effective lever for an individual to affect the behavior of individuals who are at a higher layer in the hierarchy?

4　Analyze the roles of free migration, free choice of occupation configurations, free pricing, and free enterprising in the process by which the market sorts out the efficient hierarchical network of division of labor and cities.

# EXERCISES

1　Consider the Williamson model (1967), which is the same as in example 20.2 except that $x$ is a given parameter and $n$ and $m$ are endogenously determined. Solve for the optimum hierarchy in the model.

2　Consider the model in example 20.1. Now assume that the optimum hierarchy is given by the solution of that model. Suppose that parameter $n$ increases. The optimum number of layers $m$ must change accordingly. Assuming that there is an adjustment cost $b$ to add one more layer, calculate the optimum adjustment of the optimum hierarchy in response to the change in $n$. Now assume that there is one period time lag of changes in $m$ in response to changes in $n$, and $n$ is determined by search efficiency, $E(m)$, which is determined by the optimum number of layers. Work out the difference equation of evolution of a hierarchical structure and analyze the dynamics of the evolution for a given initial value of $n$.

3　Shi and Yang, 1998: Consider the model in example 20.3. Assume that individuals are allowed to set up firms. Analyze the implications of the institution of the firm for the evolution of a centralized hierarchy within the firm and decentralized hierarchy in the market. What are the major determinants for the dividing line between the two hierarchies?

4　Y. Zhou, 1997: Extend the model in example 20.3 to a case with one consumption good, one intermediate good, and two kinds of transaction service. Solve for the inframarginal comparative statics of general equilibrium.

5　Spanjers (1992) proves an existence theorem of general equilibrium in a decentralized

> network hierarchy. Prove an existence theorem for a general version of the model in example 20.3
>
> 6 Yang and Ng, 1993, chapter 14: Assume that in the model in section 20.6 there is a time lag between the number of layers $m$ and the level of division of labor $n$. Hence, a new dynamic version of that model is specified as follows. $n_t = f(TC_t), f'(.) < 0$, $TC_t = g(n_t, c_t)$, $dTC_t / dn_t = g_n \, \partial TC_t / \partial n_t > 0$ and $g_c \, \partial TC_t / \partial c_t > 0$. $c_t = k(S_t)$, $k'(.) < 0$, $m_{t+1} = h(n_t)$, $h'(.) > 0$. Solve for the difference equation of time path of $m$ or $n$. Analyze dynamics of coevolution of division of labor and number of layers of city hierarchy.

## Notes

1 Many models of hierarchies without a pyramid structure involve endogenous transaction costs. But most of the pyramid models do not involve endogenous transaction costs because of the trade-off between realism, degree of endogenization, and tractability of the models.

2 Strictly speaking, we should use integer programming to solve for the optimum $x$. However, we may use $x^*$ and $m^*$ in (20.3), (20.4), and (20.11) as approximations of integer solutions because $C$ is strictly convex in $m$ or $x$.

3 Here we do not take into account the costs of establishing and changing a hierarchy. You are asked to incorporate this cost in exercise 2.

4 Later, it will be clear that $T_i$ is always between 0 and 1 due to the assumption of unitary endowment of labor for each person.

5 If a more realistic assumption is made that each producer of goods has more than two neighbors, a much more complicated but intractable model is needed to endogenize the level of division of labor and the number of layers of hierarchy.

6 Structures (2a), (3b), or (4a) might be general equilibrium if the fixed learning cost is much smaller in producing transaction services than in producing goods.

7 In a real economy, the distance between the center of the community and a person located near the center is much shorter than the distance between the community center and a person located at the periphery of the community. This asymmetry renders the model intractable. Hence, for the sake of tractability of the model, we assume that the distances between layers are the same for all individuals.

# part IX

# ECONOMIC DEVELOPMENT AND ECONOMIC GROWTH

# chapter 21

# NEOCLASSICAL MODELS OF ECONOMIC GROWTH

## ♦ 21.1 Exogenous vs. Endogenous Growth

The Ramsey model (1928) is representative of the neoclassical growth models. In that model, saving can be used to raise per capita capital that contributes to the growth rate of per capita consumption in the future at the cost of current consumption. Ramsey used dynamic marginal analysis (calculus of variations) to solve for the efficient trade-off between current and future consumption, which determines the optimum time path of saving, production, and consumption. We define *endogenous growth* as long-run growth in per capita real income or in per capita consumption that has the following features. (i) The long-run growth can take place in the absence of any exogenous changes of parameters. (ii) The growth is based on individuals' intertemporal optimum decisions (dynamic self-interested behavior). The Ramsey model meets the second criterion since the optimum saving rate that maximizes total discounted utility in the model describes self-interested behavior. If the production function in the Ramsey model is linear (a so-called AK function), it meets the first criterion too. Hence, a specific AK version of the Ramsey model is the first endogenous growth model.

We define exogenous growth as growth that does not meet the foregoing two criteria. In the 1940s and 1950s, exogenous growth models (the Harrod–Domar model and the Solow model) were developed. The Harrod–Domar model is a system of state equations:

$$I_t = v(Y_{t+1} - Y_t),$$

$$S_t = I_t = sY_t,$$

where $v$ is a coefficient of investment requirement for each unit increase in income, $s$ is a fixed saving rate, $S_t$ is the aggregate saving level, $I_t$ is the aggregate investment level, and $Y_t$ is the aggregate income (and output) level at time $t$. The parameter $v$ is assumed to be greater than 1 since one period's output is typically less than the value of capital required to produce it. The system of equations, together with the idenity $Y_t \equiv S_t + C_t$, generates an explosive time path of demand for investment and consumption, characterized by the difference equation

$$Y_{t+1} = [(s + v)/v]Y_t = [(s + v)/v]^2 Y_{t-1} = [(s + v)/v]^t Y_0.$$

This equation does not have a steady state and generates an explosive increase in $Y$ at rate $s/v$ over time. Since no production function (supply side) is specified, the equilibrium growth cannot be quarantined by the equation. If the Leontief production function $Y_t = \mathrm{Min}\{K_t/v, L_t/a\}$, where $L_t$ is the amount of labor employed to produce $Y_t$, is specified, then the equilibrium growth is consistent with the above difference equation only if the initial labor supply is not less than $sK_0/v$, and labor supply increases at a rate not lower than $s/v$. Even if we ignore the problem of existence of equilibrium growth, the Harrod–Domar model is an exogenous growth model in the sense that no decision-making process of individuals is specified and the saving rate $s$ is exogenously given.

The Solow model (1956) specifies a Cobb–Douglas production function,

$$Y = AK^\beta L^{1-\beta},$$

in addition to the saving equation, income and investment identities, and the market clearing condition for investment:

$$S = sY, \qquad Y \equiv C + S, \qquad I = \dot{K}, \qquad S = I$$

where $Y, K, L, S, I, C$ are functions of time $t$ and $\dot{K} \equiv dK/dt$ is the change rate of capital. This system of equations yields a state equation in $k \equiv K/L$

$$\dot{k} = sAk^\beta - kn$$

where $n \equiv \dot{L}/L$ is an exogenously given parameter of the growth rate of population size. For simplicity, the labor force is assumed to be the same as the population size. Letting $\dot{k} = 0$, we obtain a *steady state* of $k$, which is a function of the parameters $s$, $A$, and $n$. The steady state is an analogue of static equilibrium. In the long run (as $t$ tends to infinity), $k$ and per capita income $y \equiv Y/L$ will converge to the steady state and stay there forever (growth stops) if the parameters are fixed. In this sense, the Solow model is an exogenous growth model since it cannot generate long-run growth in the absence of exogenous changes in parameters. Also, the growth in the Solow model does not meet the second criterion for endogenous growth, that is, in the Solow model the saving rate $s$ is exogenously given rather than endogenously determined by an intertemporal optimum decision (behavior).

In the 1960s, many growth models were developed. Most of them follow the Ramsey model in specifying a dynamic optimization problem. Hence, they meet the second criterion for an endogenous growth model. Some of them meet the first criterion too. The Uzawa model (1965) is representative of these.

All of the growth models mentioned are macroeconomic models which do not spell out the microeconomic mechanism for economic growth in the following sense. It is assumed that investment can raise productivity in the future through increasing per capita capital. From a Smith–Young point of view, an increase in capital is an increase in division of labor in the roundabout production chain. The neoclassical growth models do not explain why and how the increased capital per person can increase productivity.

A new wave of neoclassical growth models occurred in the 1980s. Judd (1985) develops a dynamic general equilibrium model, built on the Dixit–Stiglitz (DS) model (1977). The trade-off between current and future consumption is added to the trade-off between economies of scale and consumption variety to tell a story about endogenous growth and sponta-neous evolution in the number of goods. Romer (1990) develops a dynamic equilibrium model, built on the Ethier model (1982), to explain economic growth by spontaneous evolu-tion in the number of producer goods. Now, many of this kind of neoclassical endogenous growth model have been developed. Since the reduced form of many of the models can be considered a special version of the Ramsey model with a linear production function, referred to as the AK model, and many of the models involve endogenous research and development (R&D) decisions, the neoclassical endogenous growth models are called AK models or R&D-based models. In this text, we refer to them as *neoclassical endogenous growth models*.

The new growth models not only generate long-run endogenous growth on the basis of individuals' intertemporal optimum decisions in the absence of exogenous changes in parameters, but also explain the growth by interactions between self-interested dynamic decisions. They are dynamic microeconomic general equilibrium models which endogenize the relative prices of different goods and factors. They are, however, still neoclassical growth models in the sense that the neoclassical dichotomy between pure consumers and firms is retained, the neoclassical notion of economies of scale is used, and neoclassical (dynamic) marginal analysis is employed as the main analytical instrument. Many R&D-based models have formalized Allyn Young's ideas on spontaneous evolution in the number of producer goods, as a "qualitative aspect of division of labor." But the neoclassical endogenous growth models cannot explain endogenous evolution in the degree of market integration and in the levels of specialization of individuals.

Since economies of scale is the central notion used in the neoclassical endogenous growth models, the models generate scale effects. There are four types of scale effects. Type I scale effect exists if productivity or growth performance is positively correlated with average size of firm. Type II scale effect exists if the growth rate of per capita income or per capita consumption goes up as the size or growth rate of population increases. Type III scale effect exists if the growth rate of per capita income goes up as the size of the research and development sector increases. Type IV scale effect exists if the growth rate of per capita income goes up as the investment rate increases. All four types of scale effect are wildly at odds with empirical evidence. The AK model and R&D-based model have generated scale effects of Types II, III, and IV. The empirical work of C. Jones (1995a,b, 1998), Dasgupta (1995), and National Research Council (1986) has rejected the three types of scale effect. C. Jones (1995), Alwyn Young (1998), and Segerstrom (1998) suggest several ways to avoid Type III scale effect in the R&D-based model. But the modified models still have a Type-II scale effect. As Jones has shown, endogenous growth cannot be preserved in the neoclassical endogenous growth models in the absence of scale effect. On the grounds of the empirical evidence, it is concluded that the neoclassical endogenous growth models have not provided a convincing explanation of the driving mechanism of economic growth (Jones, 1995a, pp. 508–9).

In the next chapter, we will show that the new classical growth model can generate endogenous growth based on spontaneous evolution in division of labor in the absence of scale effects. Technically, the essential instrument to manage the neoclassical endogenous growth models is dynamic marginal analysis (calculus of variations). Control theory is not necessary for managing the models, though many authors use this. Dynamic inframarginal analysis (control theory and dynamic programming) is essential for managing the new classical endogenous growth model which will be studied in the next chapter.

Section 21.2 studies the Ramsey model and one of its special versions, the AK model. Section 21.3 studies the R&D-based model.

**Questions to Ask Yourself when Reading this Chapter**

♦ What is the driving mechanism of economic growth in neoclassical growth models?

♦ What is the difference between endogenous and exogenous growth?

♦ Why do neoclassical endogenous growth models generate scale effects that are rejected by empirical evidence?

## ♦ 21.2 The Ramsey and AK Models

First let's look at the story behind the Ramsey model. Each individual's utility at each point in time displays diminishing marginal utility and she gives value to time, so that each individual prefers a fairly even distribution of consumption over time and prefers current consumption to future consumption of the same amount of goods. It is assumed that saving and investment can be used to increase per capita capital, while per capita income in the future is an increasing function of per capita capital. This positive correlation between current saving rate and future productivity is referred to as *investment (saving) fundamentalism*. The microeconomic mechanism that links productivity and per capita capital is not elaborated. The tension between consumption and saving, together with the productivity implication of saving and the preference for current consumption and for a fairly even distribution of consumption over time, therefore generates a trade-off between current and future consumption. The optimum dynamic decision is to efficiently trade-off current consumption against future consumption in order to maximize total discounted utility over the decision horizon. The efficient trade-off will generate an optimum time path of savings, consumption, and production. The optimum saving rate is usually not a constant.

### Example 21.1: the Ramsey model with a Cobb–Douglas production function

Assume each individual's utility at time $t$ is

$$u = f(c) \tag{21.1}$$

where $c$ is her consumption level at time $t$. We may take a specific function, where $f(c) = (c^\alpha - 1)/\alpha$, $\alpha \in (0, 1)$. This utility function displays diminishing marginal utility, which implies that an individual does not prefer concentrating consumption at a point in time. This rules out the optimum decision that consumes nothing in the early stage, and saves all resources to increase per capita capital and concentrates consumption at a later stage. Assume that total population size is $L$ at time $t$, aggregate income at $t$ is $Y \equiv C + I$, where $C$ is aggregate consumption and $I$ is aggregate investment at time $t$. Assume aggregate capital at $t$ is $K$ and its change rate at $t$ is $\dot{K} \equiv dK/dt$. Since the change rate is caused by investment, in the absence of depreciation of capital, we have $I = \dot{K}$. Plugging this into the income identity yields

$$Y = C + I = C + \dot{K}.$$

If we divide all variables by the population $L$, which is assumed to be the same as the labor force for simplicity, we have $y \equiv Y/L$, $c \equiv C/L$, $k \equiv K/L$. Hence, the income identity in terms of per capita variables becomes

$$y = c + \dot{K}/L.$$

Since $\dot{k} = (\dot{K}/L) - (K\dot{L}/L^2)$, we have $\dot{K}/L = \dot{k} + kn$, where $n \equiv \dot{L}/L$ is an exogenously given growth rate of population. Inserting this back into the income identity, we have

$$y = c + \dot{k} + nk \text{ or } c = y - \dot{k} - nk. \tag{21.2}$$

Suppose per capita output is an increasing function of per capita capital, or $y = g(k)$ and $g'(.) > 0$ and $g''(.) < 0$. If the aggregate production function is of the Cobb–Douglas form, or $Y = AK^\beta L^{1-\beta}$, then

$$g(k) = Ak^\beta. \tag{21.3a}$$

If the production function is of the AK form, or $Y = AK$, then

$$g(k) = Ak. \tag{21.3b}$$

Inserting (21.3) into (21.2), then into (21.1), we can express utility at $t$ as a function of $k$ and $\dot{k}$. We now assume that an individual's utility over the decision horizon is a weighted average of utilities at each point in time within the horizon. The weight is a continuously compounded discount factor $e^{-\rho t}$, where $\rho$ is a *subjective discount rate*, which reflects the value of time for the individual, $e \approx 2.718$ is the base of the natural logarithm. To understand where the discount factor comes from, we need to tell the story of a banking deposit.

Suppose that you deposit $\$A$ in a bank at the beginning of the year. If interest is earned at rate $\rho$, the principal and interest at the end of the year is $A + \rho A = A(1 + \rho)$. Now suppose that you withdraw your principal and accrued interest from the bank in the middle of the year. At the interest rate for half a year, $\rho/2$, your total asset is $A + A\rho/2 = A(1 + \rho/2)$ in the end of June. Then you deposit the money (principal $A$ plus interest) in the bank again. The value of your asset at the end of the year will be

$$A(1 + \rho/2) + (\rho/2)A(1 + \rho/2) = A(1 + \rho/2)^2 = A(1 + \rho + \rho^2/4),$$

which is greater than $A(1 + \rho)$, the value of your asset with no withdrawal and re-deposit in the middle of the year. In general, if you do such withdrawals and re-deposits $m$ times each year, then the value of your asset will be $A[1 + (\rho/m)]^m$ at the end of the year. Suppose you do this for $t$ years, then the value of your asset at the end of year $t$ is $A[1 + (\rho/m)]^{mt} = A\{[1 + (\rho/m)]^{m/\rho}\}^{\rho t}$ The limit of the formula as $m$ tends to infinity is a well-known constant, which is $B = Ae^{\rho t}$. We call $B$ the future value of a present amount $\$A$, compounded continuously. Alternatively, we call $A = Be^{-\rho t}$ the present value of $\$B$ in the future with continuously compounded discounting. The value of $e^{-\rho t}$ is between 0 and 1 and is referred to as the *continuously compounded discount factor*. In practice, banks never pay continuously compounded interests. Instead, they pay interests at higher rates for long-term deposits than for short-term deposits. This practice uses different interest rates to approximate continuously compounding at the same rate.

Assume that each individual's objective is to maximize her total discounted utility over her decision horizon. The present value of utility at time $t$ is $F = u\,e^{-\rho t}$. Inserting (21.2) and (21.3) into $u$, we can express the present value of utility as $F(k, \dot{k}, t) = f[g(k) - \dot{k} - nk]e^{-\rho t}$. The total present value of utility over the decision horizon $T$ can be expressed as an integration of $F(k, \dot{k}, t)$ from $t = 0$ to $t = T$, where the decision horizon $T$ can be infinity. Hence, the individual's dynamic optimum decision at $t = 0$ is:

$$\text{Max:} \quad U(T) \equiv \int_0^T F(k, \dot{k}, t)dt = \int_0^T u\,e^{-\rho t}dt \tag{21.4}$$

where $u = f(c)$, $c = g(k) - \dot{k} - nk$ and the decision variables are $k$ and $\dot{k}$. Integration can be viewed as approximation of summation. The boundary conditions are $k = k_0$ for $t = 0$ and $k = k_T$ for $t = T$. This is a problem in the calculus of variations. $U(T)$ is called the objective functional, which is a function of $k$, which is in turn a function of $t$. But $U$ is not a function of $t$, $U$ is dependent on the terminal time, $T$. The trade-off in the problem is between current and future consumption. An increase in $k$ will increase future consumption through $g(k)$ and will reduce current consumption through $-\dot{k} - nk$ in $c = g(k) - \dot{k} - nk$. Here, $nk$ is capital allocated to all newly born babies and $\dot{k}$ is change in per capita capital of adults, each of the two terms has negative effect on current consumption. The efficient trade-off is given by the Euler equation which is a dynamic marginal condition equivalent to the static marginal condition that marginal benefit equals marginal cost. We will not prove the Euler equation here. Rather, we provide some economic intuition for the first-order condition for the intertemporal optimization problem.

Since dynamic marginal analysis is analogous to static marginal analysis, the efficient trade-off requires equal marginal benefit and marginal cost of investment. But in the dynamic marginal analysis, the marginal benefit generated by an investment lasts for a long time, since capital can be used for many years after it is formed. The marginal benefit at each point in time when investment has been made is $\partial F/\partial k$. The total marginal benefit after an investment is made is therefore $\int(\partial F/\partial k)dt$. The marginal cost of the investment is instant and does not last for a long time, since it reduces only current consumption through an increase in per capita saving which relates to $\dot{k}$. Hence, the marginal cost of investment is $\partial F/\partial \dot{k}$. If the total marginal benefit is greater than the instant marginal cost of the investment, then the total benefit net of cost can be increased by increasing investment. If the total marginal benefit is smaller than the instant marginal cost of the investment, then the total benefit net of cost can be increased by reducing investment. The efficient trade-off will be achieved if the total marginal benefit equals the instant marginal cost, or if

$$\int(\partial F/\partial k)dt = \partial F/\partial \dot{k}.$$

Differentiating two sides of the equation and noting that $d[\int \partial F/\partial k)dt]/dt = \int d[\partial F/\partial k)dt]/dt = \int d(\partial F/\partial k) = \partial F/\partial k$, we obtain the first-order condition for the efficient trade-off, which is referred to as the *Euler equation*:

$$\partial F/\partial k = d(\partial F/\partial \dot{k})/dt. \tag{21.5}$$

The Euler equation is usually a second-order differential equation in $k$. For the utility function $f(c) = (c^\alpha - 1)/\alpha$ and the production function $g(k) = Ak^\beta$, where $\beta \in (0, 1)$, the Euler equation is

$$\dot{c}/c = (A\beta k^{\beta-1} - n - \rho/(1 - \alpha) \qquad (21.6)$$

where $c = Ak^{\beta} - \dot{k} - nk$ and $\dot{c} = (A\beta k^{\beta-1} - n)\dot{k} - \ddot{k}$. This is a second-order nonlinear differential equation in $k$. We cannot obtain an analytical solution of the equilibrium that gives the optimum time path of per capita capital, $k$. But we can use a *phase diagram* to figure out qualitatively the dynamics of the optimum time path of $k$. To do so, we rearrange the first-order condition as a system of differential equations in $k$ and $c$:

$$\dot{c} = (A\beta k^{\beta-1} - n - \rho)c/(1 - \alpha) \qquad (21.7)$$

$$\dot{k} = Ak^{\beta} - nk - c.$$

Letting $\dot{c} = 0$, we obtain $k = [\beta/(n + r)]^{1/(1-\beta)}$, which is a vertical line in the phase diagram of $k$ and $c$ in figure 21.1, where the horizontal axis represents the value of $k$, the vertical axis represents value of $c$, and arrows represent the direction of movement of the two variables over time. If the system is in the region on the right-hand side of the vertical line, $\dot{c} < 0$, or $c$ decreases with time. This is denoted by downward arrows in regimes (2) and (3) in the phase diagram. If the system is in regions (1) and (4) in the phase diagram, $\dot{c} > 0$ or $c$ increases with time. This is denoted by upward arrows in regimes (1) and (4) in the phase diagram. Letting $\dot{k} = 0$, we obtain $c = Ak^{\beta} - nk$, which is a concave curve cutting the origin, whose maximum point is at $k = (A\beta/n)^{1/(1-\beta)}$.

If the system is in regions (1) and (2) below the curve, $\dot{k} > 0$, or $k$ increases with time. This is denoted by eastward arrows in regimes (1) and (2) in the phase diagram. If the system is in regions (3) and (4) in the phase diagram, $\dot{k} < 0$ or $k$ decreases with time. This is denoted by westward arrows in regimes (3) and (4) in the phase diagram. You can see

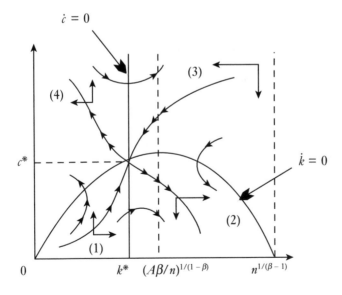

◆ **Figure 21.1:** A phase diagram of the Ramsey model

that the phase diagram uses a two-dimensional graph of $k$ and $c$ to describe a three-dimensional system of $k$, $c$, and $t$. The time dimension $t$ is implicitly given by an arrow-head. The steady state of the dynamic optimum decision is given by setting $\dot{k} = \dot{c} = 0$ or by the intersection between the two curves in the phase diagram:

$$k^* = [A\beta/(n + \rho)]^{1/(1-\beta)}, \quad c^* = A[A\beta/(n + \rho)]^{\beta/(1-\beta)}[1 - n\beta/(n + \rho)]. \tag{21.8}$$

(21.8) gives static optimum levels of per capita consumption $c$ and per capita capital $k$. Assume that the total factor productivity parameter $A$ exogenously evolves according to the rule $A = A_0 e^{bt}$, then $k^*$ and $c^*$ evolve at rate $\beta/(1 - \beta)$. This is referred to as a *steady growth rate*. The steady growth rate may depend also on the growth rate of population size and time preference parameter if population grows at a variable rate.

The dynamic optimum decision given by the Euler equation describes the conditions for optimum transitional dynamics from the initial state to the static optimum. The dynamics are characterized by stability of the static optimum or steady state. A steady state is *stable* if a deviation of the system from the steady state will generate movement of endogenous variables back toward it. Otherwise the steady state is unstable. It can be seen from the phase diagram in figure 21.1 that the steady state is stable in regions (1) and (3), but is unstable in regions (2) and (4). This feature of dynamics is referred to as *saddle-path stability*. If the economy starts from a point near the saddle path in region (1), it will evolve from that point toward the steady state, where it will remain forever thereafter. Hence, there is no long-run growth. All growth takes place as transitional dynamics. In the transitional period from the initial state to the steady state (static optimum), the trade-off is between the benefit and the cost of a faster move to the steady state. The Euler equation gives the condition for the efficient trade-off in the transitional process.

It can be seen that those time paths of $c$ and $k$ in region 2 are not optimal since they will ultimately cut the vertical axis, generating 0 per capita capital and thereby 0 per capita consumption. Also, those time paths in region 4 are not optimal since they generate lower per capita consumption than the saddle path from the same per capita capital at each point in time.

If the phase diagram is not used, we can use the following approach to analyzing the stability of the steady state. We first expand the system of differential equations in (21.7) as a Taylor series in the neighborhood of the steady state. We take the linear terms with the first-order derivatives in the series as the proxies of the original differential equations. By doing so, the original nonlinear differential equations are converted to linear differential equations. Then we can check the eigenvalues of the coefficient matrix of the system of linear differential equations. If the two eigenvalues are real and positive, then the system is unstable. If the two eigenvalues are real and negative, the system is stable. If the two eigenvalues are real with opposite signs, then the system is saddle-path stable. If the two eigenvalues are complex with negative real parts, then the system converges to the steady state in an oscillating manner. If the two eigenvalues are complex with positive real parts, the system is unstable and oscillating. If the two eigenvalues are complex with 0 real parts, the trajectories are then elliptical around the steady state.

This version of the Ramsey model is sometimes referred to as the neoclassical growth model, which cannot generate long-run endogenous growth in the absence of exogenous evolution in parameters. But if we assume that the parameter of total factor productivity, $A$, exogenously evolves over time, then this version of the Ramsey model will generate exogenous growth driven by exogenous technical progress. Such exogenous technical progress is not affected by individuals' decisions concerning economic organization and resource allocation. This view about exogenous technical progress being the driving force of economic development is referred to as *technology fundamentalism*.

The neoclassical growth model predicts a negative effect of the growth rate of population $n$ on the growth rate of per capita income and per capita consumption. From (21.6), it is clear that the optimum growth rate of per capita consumption $\dot{c}/c$ is a decreasing function of growth rate of population $n$. From the steady state, given in (21.8), it can be seen that as the growth rate of population increases, the steady state levels of per capita consumption and per capita capital decline.

The intuition behind the negative effect of the growth rate of population on economic growth runs as follows. If population increases, then part of savings must be used to equip newly born babies with capital (hospitals, free-ways, and other facilities), so that saving used to increase per capita capital is reduced. Since per capita output is an increasing function of per capita capital, this decrease in saving used to increase per capita capital will slow down economic growth. This intuition may not be compatible with observations of a positive correlation between economic growth and population growth in the early growth stages of the US, Australia, and New Zealand, though it shows some consistency with the negative correlation between economic growth and population growth found in some African and South Asian countries (Dasgupta, 1995).

As shown by the new classical models, scale effects (negative or positive) are not essential for economic development. If transaction efficiency is very low due to deficient institutional arrangements, a large and high-density population will be divided into many separate local markets with a low growth rate of per capita income. As transaction efficiency is improved, the local markets will merge into an increasingly more integrated market with a higher growth rate of per capita income.

### Example 21.2: the AK model [1]

Now we consider a special version of the Ramsey model: the AK model, where the production function is $Y = AK$, or $y = Ak$. We assume the growth rate of population is 0. For the AK model, the Euler equation becomes

$$\dot{c}/c = (A - \rho)/(1 - \alpha) \quad \text{or} \tag{21.9}$$

$$\ddot{k} + [\rho - (2 - \alpha)A]\dot{k}/(1 - \alpha) + (A - \rho)Ak/(1 - \alpha) = 0,$$

with the boundary conditions $k = k_0$ for $t = 0$ and $k = k_T$ for $t = T$. This is a linear second-order homogeneous differential equation in $k$. Its steady state is $k = 0$, which is not stable. This is a feature of long-run endogenous growth. The solution of the differential equation is:

$$k^* = B_1 e^{2At} + B_2 e^{2(A-\rho)t/(1-\alpha)} \tag{21.10}$$

where the integration constants $B_1$ and $B_2$ are given by the system of equations

$$k_0 = B_1 + B_2 \quad \text{and} \quad k_T = B_1 e^{2AT} + B_2 e^{2(A-\rho)T/(1-\alpha)}.$$

(21.10) and the production function $y = Ak$ yield the optimum time path of per capita income. The optimum growth rate of per capita consumption, given in (21.9), is a constant. But the optimum growth rates of per capita income and capital per person are not constants. The differentiation of (21.10) with respect to $t$ yields the optimum growth rate of per capita capital $\dot{k}/k$ and the optimum per capita saving rate $i = I/L = \dot{K}/L = \dot{k}$ if the growth rate of population is 0. This, together with the production function, yield the optimum growth rate of per capita income $\dot{y}/y = A\dot{k}/k$. From the production function $Y = AK$, it is obvious that $\dot{Y}/Y = A\dot{K}/Y = A(I/Y)$, that is, the growth rate of income is an increasing function of the investment rate. This Type IV scale effect is rejected by empirical evidence found by C. Jones (1995).

The growth rate of per capita consumption is always positive for $A > \rho$. Hence, long-run endogenous growth can take place in the absence of exogenous changes in parameters. However, a constant growth rate of per capita consumption is inconsistent with the take-off phenomenon in the industrialization process, which is associated with an accelerating growth (increasing growth rate) of per capita consumption and income, documented by Romer (1986) and Chen, Lin, and Yang (1999). It is also inconsistent with a slowing down of growth in the post industrialization era, documented by Chen, Lin, and Yang (1999). A test of the explanatory power of a growth model is to see if it can predict both accelerating and decelerating growth. Many authors introduce new features into the Ramsey model to enable it to tell more stories. For instance, the Uzawa–Lucas model in exercise 3 introduces externality and a trade-off between working and education to endogenize evolution in the income share of human capital.

An extensive empirical literature has been developed to test the two versions of the Ramsey model: the neoclassical version in example 21.1 and the AK version in example 21.2. It was claimed that the neoclassical version predicts conditional convergence, while the AK version would not predict this. *Absolute convergence* takes place when poorer areas grow faster than richer ones whatever their respective characteristics, represented by parameters of tastes, production conditions and population size and its growth, whereas there is *conditional convergence* when a country or a region grows faster the farther it is below its own steady state. The latter form of convergence is the weaker. Under certain conditions, conditional convergence even allows for rich countries to grow faster than poorer ones.

Transitional dynamics in example 21.1 are determined by a system of nonlinear differential equations in (21.7). Using simulation on a computer, it can be shown that sequential decelerating–accelerating–decelerating growth patterns are possible during transitional periods. Hence, the transitional dynamics of the Ramsey model in example 21.1 do not always predict conditional convergence. If the total factor productivity parameter $A$ in (21.8) evolves according the moving rule $A = A_0 e^{bt}$, the steady growth rates of $k$ and $y$ are $\beta/(1 - \beta)$ and they may depend on the growth rate of population and time preference parameter too if population grows at a variable rate. If the growth rate of population and parameters of time preference and production differ across countries and exogenous technical progress is present, the Ramsey model does not predict conditional convergence. Hence, all empirical work, such as Sala-i-Martin (1996) and Romer (1986), that confirms or rejects conditional convergence may not confirm or reject the Ramsey model.[2]

The real empirical distinction between the neoclassical and AK versions of the Ramsey model relates to Type II scale effect. For the former, the growth rate of per capita income decreases with the growth rate of population, whereas the growth rate of per capita income increases with population size (Type II scale effect) in the latter. Unfortunately, empirical evidence in Dasgupta (1995) and the National Research Council (1986) confirms neither of the predictions.

The second piece of empirical work is to find evidence for or against decreasing returns to capital. Romer (1987) has found evidence for a capital elasticity of output that is greater than one. But King and Levine (1994) find evidence for an elasticity that is smaller than one. In this literature, some interesting work entirely rejects the neoclassical prediction that the capital–labor ratio increases as an economy grows. Cho and Graham (1996) have found that many poor countries have been running down their capital–labor ratios over 1960–85. This reminds us that the neoclassical framework and concepts may not be appropriate for analyzing the real economic development process. According to Smith–Young's theory of economic development, an increase in capital shown by statistical data is an indirect reflection of a finer division of labor in roundabout production, or evolution of division of labor between firms (see the models in chapter 19), and an increase in labor in statistical data reflects the evolution of division of labor within firms (see the models in chapters 8, 18, and 19). It may have nothing to do with increasing or decreasing returns to capital. A declining capital–labor ratio in economic development may be associated with faster evolution of division of labor within firms than that between firms. Evolution of division of labor within firms will increase trade in labor and decrease trade in intermediate goods and services, while evolution of division of labor between firms have opposite effects. Hence, trade in labor increases faster than trade volume of goods.

Various versions of the Ramsey model share the feature that they are aggregate decision models. The relative prices of different goods, and interactions between self-interested decisions, are not endogenized. In the next section, we shall consider dynamic microeconomic equilibrium models which endogenize the consequence of interactions between self-interested intertemporal decisions.

## ♦ 21.3 R&D-based Endogenous Growth Models

R&D-based endogenous growth models have the following features. They are dynamic general equilibrium rather than decision models, so that they endogenize not only self-interested behavior, but also prices as the consequence of interactions between self-interested decisions. To endogenize evolution in the number of goods, the trade-off between economies of scale and economies of complementarity between goods in raising either utility or productivity are specified in the models. The CES function is a crucial vehicle for endogenizing the number of goods in the R&D-based growth models. We use Barro and Sala-i-Martin's extended version (1995) of the Romer model (1990) to illustrate these features.

### Example 21.3: Barro and Sala-i-Martin's extended version (1995) of the Romer model (1990)

The pure consumer's dynamic decision problem is

$$\text{Max:} \quad U(T) = \int_0^T [(c^\alpha - 1)/\alpha] e^{-\rho t} \mathrm{d}t \qquad \text{s.t.} \quad c + \dot{s} = rs + w$$

where $s$ is the saving level at time $t$, $r$ is market interest rate at time $t$, so that $rs$ is the level of interest earnings at time $t$, and $\dot{s}$ is the rate of change of saving. We assume that each consumer is endowed with 1 unit of labor and receives the wage rate $w$. Later we will see that perfect competition in the market for final goods and monopolistic competition in the markets for intermediate goods drive profit to 0. Hence, the consumer's income comes only from interest earnings and wages. $\alpha \in (0, 1)$ is a parameter of elasticity of substitution between consumption at different points in time since $\int[(c^{\alpha} - 1)/\alpha]e^{-\rho t} \, dt \approx \sum_s \{[c^{\alpha}(s) - 1]/\alpha\}e^{-\rho s}\Delta t_s$, which is a CES function of $c$. $\rho$ is a subjective discount rate. Using the budget constraint, we can express the function to be integrated as a function of $s$, $\dot{s}$, and $t$:

$$F \equiv [(rs + w - \dot{s})^{\alpha} - 1](1/\alpha)e^{-\rho t}$$

The Euler equation $\partial F/\partial s = d(\partial F/\partial \dot{s})/dt$ yields

$$\dot{c}/c = (r - \rho)/(1 - \alpha) \qquad (21.11)$$

where $c = rs + w - \dot{s}$. This is a second-order differential equation in $s$.

The production function of the final good is

$$y = AL_y^{1-\beta} \sum_{i=1}^{n} x_i^{\beta} \qquad (21.12)$$

where $\beta \in (0, 1)$, $y$ is the output level of the final good, $L_y$ is the amount of labor allocated to the production of the final good, $x_i$ is the amount of intermediate good i employed to produce the final good and $n$ is the number of intermediate goods. This production function displays constant returns to scale of $L_y$ and $x_i$. But it is a type of CES function in $x_i$, and total factor productivity is a monotonically increasing function of the number of intermediate goods. Hence, this function has external economies associated with the number of intermediate goods, which can generate endogenous productivity progress. The profit of the representative firm producing the final good is

$$\pi_y = y - wL_y - \sum_{i=1}^{n} p_i x_i$$

where the decision variables are $L_y$ and $x_i$. We assume the final good to be the *numéraire*, so its price is 1. $p_i$ is the price of intermediate good i in terms of the final good. The two first-order conditions, the zero profit condition, and the market clearing condition for labor yield

$$w = (1 - \beta)An(\beta A/p_i)^{\beta/(1-\beta)} \qquad (21.13a)$$

$$x_i = L(\beta A/p_i)^{1/(1-\beta)} \qquad (21.13b)$$

$$y = AnL(\beta A/p_i)^{\beta/(1-\beta)} \qquad (21.13c)$$

where the symmetry of the model is used and $L$ is labor supply as well as population size.

Next, we consider the firm producing intermediate good i. The firm spends $b$ units of final good to invent intermediate good i and gets a patent for it. Hence, the market for intermediate goods is monopolistically competitive. There is only one firm producing an intermediate good, so that the price of the good is the monopolist's decision variable. But free entry will drive pure profit to 0. Hence, total gross profit just breaks even with investment to invent the good.

If we assume that the production of good i employs labor, the decision problem for a firm producing good i which emerges at time $t$ will be asymmetric with the decision problem for the firm producing another good which emerges at time $t'$. This asymmetry renders the algebra intractable. Hence, we assume that only final goods are used as inputs to produce an intermediate good. Suppose the firm needs 1 unit of the final good to produce 1 unit of each intermediate good, so that gross profit in producing intermediate good i is $(p_i - 1)x_i$. Inserting the demand function for intermediate good i, given in (21.13b), into the gross profit formula, the gross profit for the firm is thus

$$\pi_i = (p_i - 1)L(\beta A/p_i)^{1/(1-\beta)}. \qquad (21.14)$$

The optimum price that maximizes the gross profit is then

$$p_i = 1/\beta > 1. \qquad (21.15)$$

This implies that the prices of all intermediate goods that are available from the market are the same at any point in time. This ensures the symmetry of the model. It can be verified that if labor is employed to produce the intermediate goods, the symmetry cannot be retained. Inserting the optimum price into (21.14), we can compute the total present value of gross profit from the time when the intermediate good becomes available to terminal time $T$. The total present value of gross profit is also the value of the firm in the market $V(t)$.

$$V(t) = \int_t^T (p_i - 1)x_i e^{-r(\tau - t)} d\tau. \qquad (21.16a)$$

$$= [L(\beta^2 A)^{1/(1-\beta)}/\beta] \int_t^T e^{-r(\tau - t)} d\tau.$$

Free entry and arbitrage will drive pure profit to 0, that is, the total present value of gross profit equals investment in inventing the good, or

$$V(t) = b. \qquad (21.16b)$$

With Sala-i-Martin's assumption of constant $r$, (21.16) yields the equilibrium interest rate

$$r = (L/b)(\beta^2 A)^{1/(1-\beta)}(1 - \beta)/\beta. \qquad (21.17)$$

Inserting the equilibrium price of the final good, given in (21.15), into (21.13b) yields the equilibrium wage rate. Hence, (21.13b), (21.15), and (21.17) give all information about the dynamic equilibrium prices of goods and factors. Plugging the equilibrium interest rate, given in (21.17), into (21.11) yields the equilibrium time path of the growth rate of per capita consumption:

$$\dot{c}/c = \{[(L/b)(\beta^2 A)^{1/(1-\beta)}(1 - \beta)/\beta] - \rho\}/(1 - \alpha). \qquad (21.18)$$

This growth rate is an increasing function of population size $L$. That is, the Romer model has a Type II scale effect, which means a country with a larger population size grows faster than a smaller country. This empirical implication is rejected by empirical evidence in Dasgupta (1995) and the National Research Council (1986). We can see that India did not have a high growth rate of per capita consumption until the recent reform period, despite its large population size. This was true too for pre-reform China.

Inserting the equilibrium price of the final good, given in (21.15), into the demand function for intermediate goods in (21.13b) yields the equilibrium quantity of each intermediate good

$$x_i = L(\beta^2 A)^{1/(1-\beta)}. \qquad (21.19)$$

Plugging this back into the production function of the final good, given in (21.12), and using the market clearing condition for labor, we can express the equilibrium quantity of the final good as a function of the number of intermediate goods, $n$:

$$y = (\beta^{2\beta}A)^{\frac{1}{(1-\beta)}}Ln. \tag{21.20}$$

Taking the logarithm of the two sides of the equation and then differentiating it with respect to $t$, we can see that the growth rate of output of the final goods is an increasing function of the growth rate of the number of intermediate goods, $\dot{n}/n$ and the growth rate of population $\dot{L}/L$. Noting that the size of the R&D sector is $b\dot{n}$, we can see that the growth rate of output of the final good is an increasing function of the size of the R&D sector. This is a Type III scale effect. This scale effect of the Romer model is rejected by empirical evidence in developed countries (C. Jones, 1995). The size of the R&D sector in the US increased by several times in the last several decades, but the growth rate of output was quite steady during the same period of time. Type III scale effect can be considered a combination of investment fundamentalism and technology fundamentalism.

In order to figure out the equilibrium dynamics of the model, we now consider the market clearing condition for the final good. Each consumer's demand for the final good is $c$, so that $L$ consumers' total demand for the final good is $Lc$. 1 unit of the final good is needed to produce 1 unit of each of $n$ intermediate goods that are available from the market at time $t$. Hence, total demand for the final goods from the $n$ sectors is $nx_i$. The number of new goods that emerges at time $t$ is $\dot{n}$. Each of them needs $b$ units of the final good to invent. Hence, the demand for the final good from the R&D sector at time $t$ is $b\dot{n}$. The market clearing condition for the final good is therefore:

$$y = cL + nx_i + b\dot{n}. \tag{21.21}$$

Inserting (21.20) into (21.21), we have, together with (21.11), a system of first-order linear differential equations:

$$\dot{c} = Dc \tag{21.22a}$$

$$\dot{n} = (L/b)\,(En - c) \tag{21.22b}$$

where $D \equiv [(A\beta^{1+\beta})^{1/(1-\beta)}(1 - \beta)(L/b) - \rho]/(1 - \alpha) > 0$ iff

$$(A\beta^{1+\beta})^{1/(1-\beta)}(1 - \beta)L > b\rho. \tag{21.22c}$$

Also, we have $E \equiv (\beta^{2\beta}A)^{\frac{1}{(1-\beta)}}(1 - \beta^2)$ and $\dot{n}$ is positive iff

$$En > c. \tag{21.22d}$$

We can thus use the phase diagram of figure 21.2 to describe the equilibrium dynamics of the Romer model.

From (21.22), we can see that the necessary condition for long-run growth is that the population size $L$ and total factor productivity of the final good $A$ are sufficiently large, compared to the invention cost coefficient $b$ and the subjective discount rate $\rho$. If this condition (21.22c) is satisfied, then the unique equilibrium steady state, given by $\dot{n} = \dot{c} = 0$, is $c = n = 0$, is of course unstable. This is a distinctive feature of long-run endogenous growth, which implies that as soon as the economy departs from the steady state, it never comes back. Suppose condition (21.22c) is met; then the condition for long-run growth that is associated with an increasing number of intermediate goods, given by (21.22d), is that the economy starts from a sufficiently large number of intermediate goods, compared to per capita consumption of the final good. This condition can be further illustrated by the phase diagram. Letting $\dot{n} = 0$, we obtain a straight line in the phase diagram, given by $n = c/E$. Underneath the line, the dynamic equilibrium number of intermediate goods keeps decreasing, while above the line, this number keeps increasing.

From (21.22a), we can see that $c$ always increases for a positive $c$ if the condition (21.22c) is met. Hence, if (21.22c) holds, there are only two regions in the phase diagram. Above the locus $\dot{n} = 0$, economic growth is characterized by simultaneous increases in per capita consumption and in the number of intermediate goods, while below the locus $\dot{n} = 0$, endogenous growth in per capita consumption is associated with decline in the number of intermediate goods. If the initial number of intermediate goods is sufficiently large, compared to per capita consumption, so that (21.22d) is met and the economy starts from a point above the locus $\dot{n} = 0$, then endogenous economic growth features spontaneous evolution in the number of intermediate goods or incessant emergence of new machines and related new technology.

It is not difficult to verify that the coefficient matrix of the system of constant coefficient differential equations in (21.22) has two positive real eigenvalues. This can be confirmed by $\partial \dot{c}/\partial c > 0$ and $\partial \dot{n}/\partial n > 0$. This implies that the steady state of the dynamic equilibrium is unstable, a feature of long-run endogenous economic growth.

The intuition behind the dynamic equilibrium runs as follows. If the population size $L$ and total factor productivity of the final good $A$ are sufficiently large, compared to the invention cost coefficient $b$ and the subjective discount rate $\rho$, and the initial number of intermediate goods is not small, then saving can be used to invent more new machines, which improve productivity and raise income. Hence, consumption and saving can increase side by side. This implies more investment in the R&D sector and more invention of new machines, which will improve productivity and raise income again. This positive feedback or

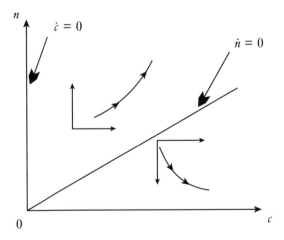

◆ **Figure 21.2:** A phase diagram of the Romer model

virtuous circle will generate incessant evolution in per capita consumption and in the number of intermediate goods. The intuition of the scale effect in the Romer model is that since the invention cost of a good b can be shared by more individuals as the population size increases, the per capita invention cost of each new good declines as the population expands.

Though the intuition of the scale effect seems to make sense, it might be misleading. In the Romer model, the neoclassical dichotomy between pure consumers and firms is assumed. This implies that the whole economy is always an integrated market and separate local markets never occur in dynamic equilibrium. Each consumer indirectly consumes all $n$ intermediate goods that are available from the integrated market at a particular point in time. This implies that the neoclassical endogenous growth models cannot endogenize the evolution of the degree of market integration or the network size of division of labor. The scale effect is based on this feature of the neoclassical endogenous growth models.

If we abandon the neoclassical dichotomy and adopt the new classical framework with endogenous specialization, then the economy may be divided into many separate local business communities which do not trade with each other when transaction efficiency is very low. Hence, a large population size is not sufficient for an integrated network of division of labor to emerge from equilibrium. In the absence of that network, each local community duplicates the invention cost or learning cost of other local communities and a large population size cannot fully utilize the positive network effect of division of labor between a professional R&D sector and the rest of the economy. Hence, from a Smith–Young point of view, whether positive network effects of the division of labor between the professional R&D sector and the rest of the economy can be exploited is determined by the equilibrium network size of division of labor, which is determined by transaction conditions rather than by the population size. As transaction conditions are improved, or as division of labor spontaneously evolves to a sufficiently high level (as shown in the next chapter), many separate local communities will merge into an increasingly more integrated market network, thereby generating endogenous growth and related development phenomena. This can take place in the absence of population growth and other scale effects.

When we talk about a large market, as in the US or China, what we really mean is that transaction conditions are good, rather than that the population size is large. We know the population size of Europe is comparable to that of the US. But different languages and cultures, different tariff and monetary systems, and fragmented media systems and distribution networks in Europe imply that transaction conditions are much inferior to those in the US. Hence, the same population size does not mean the same size of market. The population size in Taiwan (21 million) is much smaller than in mainland China (1.3 billion). But international and domestic trade volume for Taiwan was greater than that for mainland China in the 1970s and 1980s. When we say the Australian market is too small, what we really mean is that transaction efficiency for trade between this continent and other continents is too low due to Australia's isolated geographical position. This implies that a large population size does not necessarily imply a large size of market. The extent of the market, as we have shown in the new classical models, is determined by the equilibrium network size of division of labor, which is determined by transaction conditions in a static model or by endogenous evolution in division of labor in a dynamic equilibrium model.

If we understand the distinction between the network effect of division of labor and economies of scale, we will see that the intuition for scale effect is misleading. This is why scale effect is conclusively rejected by empirical evidence.

In the model in example 21.3, the dynamic equilibrium is not Pareto optimal since individual decision-makers do not take into account positive effect of the number of intermediate goods on the total factor productivity of the final good. As in other R&D-based growth models, the external economies and spillover effects that are not exploited by the price system make the equilibrium growth inefficient compared to the Pareto optimum. For some endogenous growth models, such as the Romer (1986) and Lucas (1988) models, no competitive equilibrium exists if external economies are internalized in individuals' decision-making.

Inserting the production functions of x and y and the endowment constraint of labor into the utility function of the representative consumer, the Pareto optimum in example 21.3 can be defined as the solution to the dynamic optimization problem maximizing the total discounted utility of the representative consumer. It can be shown that the Pareto optimum growth rate of per capita consumption is $[(A\beta^\beta)^{1/(1-\beta)}(1 - \beta)(L/b) - \rho]/(1 - \alpha)$, which is greater than the equilibrium growth rate of per capita consumption, given in (21.18), for $\beta \in (0, 1)$.

This implies that the external economies and spillover effects are not the driving force behind long-run economic growth in the R&D-based growth models. Rather they are obstacles to growth. Spillover effects are a source of endogenous transaction costs which impede economic growth by discouraging investment in intellectual property. China's experience before the twentieth century is a good example. Then there were no patent laws or other laws to protect the residual rights of owners of firms in China. Hence, there were substantial spillover effects from smart Chinese inventions. Since the inventors of the new technology and originators of entrepreneurial ideas could not appropriate incomes from their intellectual properties, the Chinese were reluctant to invest in intellectual property and entrepreneurial activities despite the high IQ of Chinese people. Hence, many Chinese inventions could not be commercialized and expanded to create an industrial revolution.

The real story of the economic growth process is that patent laws, laws that protect free association (including free enterprise) and private property, the de facto laissez-faire policies that prevailed in eighteenth- and nineteenth-century Britain, and other related institutions reduced significantly all kinds of endogenous transaction costs including those caused by spillover effects, so that evolution in division of labor between the production of intellectual properties and the production of tangible goods was significantly speeded up in those centuries in Britain and Western Europe (see Baechler, 1976, MacFarlane, 1988, Mokyr, 1993, North, 1981, and Rosenberg and Birdzell, 1986). The driving force of this process was not spillover effects, but rather the emergence of institutions that internalized these effects and reduced endogenous transaction costs caused by them.

## Key Terms and Review

Exogenous vs. endogenous growth.
The Ramsey model, the AK model, the R&D-based model.
Technology fundamentalism, investment (saving) fundamentalism.
Types I, II, III, IV scale effects.
Relationship between externality, spillover effect, and growth.
Dynamic marginal analysis and the Euler equation.
Dynamic general equilibrium mechanisms for spontaneous evolution in the number of producer or consumer goods.
Convergence and divergence hypotheses.

## Further Reading

*Dynamic optimization*: Seierstad and Sydsater (1987), Barro and Sala-i-Martin (1995, appendix), Chow (1975); *neoclassical growth models*: Barro (1991, 1997), Barro and Sala-i-Martin (1992, 1995), Rebelo (1991), Solow (1956); *R&D-based models and other endogenous growth models*: Judd (1985), Lucas (1988, 1993), Romer (1986, 1987, 1990), Grossman and Helpman (1989, 1990, 1991), Aghion and Howitt (1992), Alwyn Young (1998); *empirical evidence*: Sala-i-Martin (1996), Jones (1995a,b), Chen, Lin, and Yang (1999), National Research Council (1986), Dasgupta (1995), Cho and Graham (1996), King and Levine (1994), Mankiw, Romer, and Weil (1992), Romer (1987), Liu and Yang (2000), Temple (1999); *historical evidence*: Baechler (1976), Crafts (1997), MacFarlane (1988), Mokyr (1993), North (1981), Rosenberg and Birdzell (1986), Marshall (1890), Allyn Young (1928), Braudel (1984), Chandler (1990), Solow (1956), and Lucas (1988, 1993).

## QUESTIONS

1    What are the differences between the Ramsey model, the Harrod–Domar model, and the Solow model?

2    Romer (1986) and Lucas (1988) argue that the neoclassical growth model cannot predict the observed divergence of growth rates of per capita income between different countries. Use the distinction between the concepts of conditional and absolute convergence to show that the Ramsey model in example 21.1 may predict the conditional divergence of growth rates of per capita consumption. In your analysis, consider the following three cases. (i) transitional dynamics for a sufficiently large difference between the initial state and steady state; (ii) a steady state with exogenous evolution of $A = A_0 e^{-bt}$, (iii) population growth at variable rates.

3    What are the differences between the Ramsey model and the R&D-based model?

4    The driving force of the AK and R&D-based models are (internal or external) economies of scale, and the driving force of the new classical models in the previous chapters and the new classical growth models in chapters 22, 23, 24, 25 is the network effect of division of labor. The difference between the two approaches to explaining economic development originates in the debate between Allyn Young, who rejected the notion of economies of scale as a misrepresentation of economies of division of labor, his student Knight, who rejected the existence of any kinds of increasing returns, and Marshall, who used the notion of external economies of scale to represent economies of division of labor. Discuss the difference between the two approaches to explaining economic development.

5    In the Romer model (1986) and the Lucas model (1988), the key feature that ensures the existence of equilibrium is that economies of scale are external to firms or there exists externality of education. If the external economies are internalized by the market, what will happen to the equilibria in these two models? Suppose that a central planner solves for an optimum growth plan which takes into account all external economies of scale and externality. What will the optimum growth rates of per capita consumption be?

6    An economist argues that since the population of Australia is less than 20 million and that of the US is more than 200 million, the extent of the market in Australia is much smaller than in the US. Hence, all kinds of machines are much cheaper in the US than in Australia. The new endogenous growth models recently developed by Judd and Romer generate a similar prediction that larger economies will generate higher growth rates and levels of per capita income. Use the Smith–Young theorem about the relationship between division of labor and the extent of the market to comment on this view.

7   The driving force of economic growth in the models in this chapter is an *ad hoc* "if and only if" relation-
    ship between investment and productivity, which is called investment (saving) fundamentalism. Give
    some counter-examples to investment (saving) fundamentalism. According to Smith and Young, in-
    vestment creates economic growth because it promotes division of labor in roundabout production.
    Discuss the difference between investment (saving) fundamentalism and the classical way of explain-
    ing the wealth of the nation by division of labor (see chapter 25 for more about this).

# EXERCISES

1   Consider the Ramsey model in example 21.2. Assume the production function is $Y = AK^\beta L^{1-\beta}$ and the rate of change of capital is $\dot{K} = I - \gamma K$, where $\gamma$ is the depreciation rate of capital. Solve for the optimum growth rates of per capita consumption. Use a phase graph to describe the dynamics of per capita consumption and the capital–labor ratio.

2   Assume that in the model in exercise 1 the production function takes the AK form. Solve for the dynamics of optimum growth.

3   Consider the Uzawa–Lucas model, which is an extension of the Ramsey model. Redefine labor $L$ in the Ramsey model as $uH$, where $u \in (0, 1)$ is the fraction of total human capital that is devoted to the production of goods and $1 - u$ is the fraction devoted to education. Hence, the production function is $Y = AK^\beta(uH)^{1-\beta}$, where $H$ is total available human capital at each point in time. The growth rate $\dot{H}/H$ is a linear increasing function of $1 - u$. The rest of the model is the same as in the Ramsey model. Solve for the optimum growth plan. Use the trade-off between education and production and the trade-off between current and future consumption to tell the story behind your solution.

4   T. N. Srinivasan, 1964: Interpret $H$ in the Uzawa–Lucas model as population size and $1 - u$ as the fraction of human resources used to produce offspring. Discuss the implications of a model with endogenous population growth.

5   Romer, 1986: A representative consumer maximizes $U = \int_0^T ue^{-\rho t}dt$, subject to $u = (c^b - 1)/b$, $w + rs = (ds/dt) + c$, where $c$ is consumption, $w$ is wage rate, $s$ is saving level, and $r$ is interest rate. The population size is one. The income identity is $i + c = y$, where $i = dk/dt$, $y$ is given by the production function $y = Bk^\alpha l^{1-\alpha}$ for a representative firm. This production function displays constant returns to scale for each firm. But there are external economies of scale, given by $B = A(K/L)^\beta$, where $K$ is the total amount of capital employed and $L$ is the total amount of labor employed in production. In equilibrium, $K = k$ and $L = l = 1$ if the set of firms is a continuum of mass 1. It is assumed that $\alpha + \beta \geq 1$. Solve for the dynamic general equilibrium. Under what conditions is the solution of this model with external economies of scale the same as that of the AK model? Analyze the difference between this model and the AK model in connection to Pareto optimality of equilibrium. Suppose that a central planner takes into account the external economies of scale to maximize each consumer's total discounted utility. What is her optimum decision? Is the Pareto optimum growth rate higher than the equilibrium one? Use your answer to address the claim that the spillover effects caused by external economies of scale are the driving force of endogenous growth in the model.

6   Use the Ramsey model in 21.1 to show that the steady growth rates of per capita capital and per capita income are dependent on taste and production parameters $\alpha$ and $\beta$ when total factor productivity $A$ exogenously grows at rate $b$. Use your result to show that the Ramsey

model predicts conditional divergence, that is, the growth rates of two countries with different values of parameters $\alpha$ and $\beta$ never converge, even if exogenous technical progress is the same for them.

7   Aghion and Howitt, 1992: Consider an economy with a representative consumer consuming $y$. The representative firm producing y has the production function $y_s = A_s x_s^\alpha$, where $\alpha \in (0, 1)$, $x_s$ is the amount of intermediate good of generation s. In the market only one generation of good is produced. When a new generation of good emerges, it replaces the old generation and $A_s = \gamma A_{s-1}$ where $\gamma > 1$ looks like an exogenous technical progress coefficient. The probability for the emergence of a new generation of intermediate good is $\lambda n$ where $n$ is the amount of labor employed for invention. The production of each unit of intermediate good needs one unit of labor. The market for intermediate goods is monopolistically competitive. This implies that the producer of the available intermediate good can manipulate the interaction between price and quantity of the good to maximize profit. But free entry will establish the following asset equation which is analogous to a zero profit condition in static models: $rV_s = \pi_s - \lambda n_s V_s$ where $r$ is the interest rate, $V_s$ is the value of the firm producing good of generation s, $\pi_s$ is its profit, $\lambda n_s$ is the probability that this generation of good is replaced by the next generation of good, $\lambda n_s V_s$ is the expected loss of value of the firm if this replacement occurs, and $V_s$ is the discounted expected pay-off to the $s^{th}$ innovation. The population size and labor force is $L$. In the labor market, the wage rate for a worker producing the intermediate good must be the same as that for a researcher. The expected value of $n$ units of labor in research is $\lambda n V_s$, so that this arbitrage condition requires $w_s = \lambda n V_s / n = \lambda V_s$. The steady state is defined by $\omega_s = \omega_{s-1}$, where $\omega_s = w_s / A_s$. Show that the expected growth rate of $y$ is $\lambda n \ln \gamma$, which implies a Type III scale effect (growth rate of per capita income increases with the size of the R&D sector). Solve for the equilibrium and show that the probability of the emergence of new generation of goods $\lambda n$ is an increasing function of population size $L$, which implies Type II scale effect (growth rate of per capita income increases with the population size). Why are the Type II and Type III scale effects rejected by empirical evidence?

8   Mankiw, Romer, and Weil, 1992: Consider the neoclassical model in example 21.1, where output is given by $Y = (AL)^\alpha K^{1-\alpha}$. Technology parameter $A$ grows at rate $x$, the population at rate $n$, and the stock of capital depreciates at rate $\delta$. There is a constant saving rate, $s$. Find an expression for the rate of growth of income toward the steady state that depends on initial income. Use this model to analyze the convergence phenomenon and what the convergence is conditional on. Assume the production function is $Y = (AL)^{1-\alpha-\beta} K^\alpha H^\beta$, where $0 < \alpha + \beta < 1$ and $H$ is human capital, and that gross investment rates in the two types of capital are a fraction $s_k$ and $s_h$ of output, respectively. Is there unconditional convergence?

9   Barro and Sala-i-Martin, 1995: Assume that the saving rate is fixed at $s$ and population grows at $n$ in the neoclassical model in example 21.1. The output per work of firm j is $y_j = A^\beta k_j^\alpha$, where $A = A_0 \sum_j k_j / N$, where $N$ is the number of firms. Find the differential equation for $k$ when all firms are identical. Represent graphically the solutions to the model for the cases where the production function exhibits (i) diminishing returns to scale, $\beta + \alpha < 1$, (ii) constant returns, $\beta + \alpha = 1$, (iii) increasing returns, $\beta + \alpha > 1$. What is meant by the "razor-edge property" of the AK model?

10  Romer, 1990: Assume that a consumer' decision problem is the same as in example 21.3. Final output is produced using labor and intermediate goods. Labor can be used either in manufacturing the final good ($L_1$) or alternatively in research ($L_2$). Total endowment of labor is $L_1 + L_2 = B$. Research generates designs (or licences) for new intermediate inputs, and $n$ is the current number of designs or the current number of intermediate inputs. The production function of the final good is $Y = L_1^{1-\alpha} \int_0^n x_i^\alpha di$, where $x_i$ is the amount of

intermediate good i. Variety of intermediate inputs is a continuum. There is a sunk cost of producing $x$ units of a given intermediate input, namely the price $q$ for the corresponding design or license. The speed at which new designs are being generated depends on both the aggregate amount of research and the existing number of designs, according to $dn/dt = \delta n L_2$. The market for intermediate goods is monopolistically competitive. Show that the steady growth rate of output is equal to the growth rate of $n$ which is $\delta L_2$. This is a Type III scale effect: growth rate goes up as the size of the R&D sector increases. This type of scale effect is rejected by empirical evidence (Jones, 1995b). Then show that the steady growth rate of output increases with the population size $B$. This Type II scale effect is rejected by empirical evidence surveyed in Dasgupta (1995). Show that the equilibrium growth is slower than the Pareto optimum due to spillover effects. Use your results to analyze the claim that the spillover effect is the driving force of economic growth.

11   C. Jones, 1995b: Consider the Romer model in the preceding exercise. Now the production function of the R&D sector is $dn/dt = \delta n^{\beta} L_2^{\lambda}$ where $\lambda \in (0, 1)$. Show that a Type III scale effect is avoided and a Type II scale effect still exists. Show that the equilibrium growth is slower than the Pareto optimum due to spillover effects.

# Notes

1  Romer (1986) extends this version of the Ramsey model by specifying external economies of scale and interactions between self-interested decisions. Its reduced form is the same as the AK model.
2  Sala-i-Martin (1996) defines absolute $\beta$-convergence as the case in which poor economies tend to grow faster than rich ones, and defines $\sigma$-convergence as the case in which the dispersion of real per capita GDP levels of a group of economies tends to decrease over time. His empirical work shows that there was neither $\sigma$-convergence nor absolute $\beta$-convergence in the cross-country distribution of world GDP between 1960 and 1990, although the sample of OECD economies displys $\sigma$-convergence and so do the samples of regions within a country, such as the US, Japan, Germany, the UK, Frane, Italy, or Spain. Romer (1986) finds evidence for divergence from time series data.

# CHAPTER 22

# ECONOMIC GROWTH GENERATED BY ENDOGENOUS EVOLUTION IN DIVISION OF LABOR

## ◆ 22.1. Economies of Specialized Learning by Doing and Endogenous Evolution in Division of Labor

All new classical models of endogenous specialization so far analyzed have been static and the role of learning by doing has not been explicitly considered. The evolution of division of labor generated by comparative statics is exogenous, because it never occurs in the absence of the exogenous evolution of transaction efficiency and other parameters. Though transaction efficiency is endogenized in chapters 7 and 20, the evolution of division of labor in those two chapters is driven by exogenous evolution in a parameter representing average distance between neighbors (in chapter 7), or representing transaction efficiency of transaction services (in chapter 20). In this chapter, we explicitly spell out a process of learning by doing. The interaction between learning by doing, specialization, transaction costs, and accumulation of human capital may generate endogenous evolution of the division of labor in the absence of any exogenous changes in parameters. A dynamic general equilibrium mechanism may generate the spontaneous evolution of endogenous comparative advantage which is associated with economic growth and the evolution of trade dependence.

The model in this chapter is the same as in chapter 5, except that learning by doing is explicitly specified and the number of goods is $m$ instead of 2. The economies of division of labor come from the intimate relationship between knowledge commanded by society as a whole and the division of labor. Suppose that in the model in chapter 5 there are two individuals ($M = 2$), each having one unit of working time in each period. In addition to static economies of specialization, there are learning-by-doing effects. For simplicity, we consider only two periods. Each person's output level of good i ($= 1, 2$) in period $t$ is an increasing function of total labor input in producing good i over all periods up to $t$, or we may assume that $x_{it}^p = L_{it}^{1.5}$, where $L_{i1} = l_{i1}$, $L_{i2} = l_{i1} + l_{i2}$, $x_{it}^p$ is the output level of good i at time $t$, $l_{it}$ is the amount of time allocated to the production of good i at time $t$, and $L_{it}$ is the accumulated amount of time allocated to the production of good i at time $t$. This implies that productivity is dependent on experience that has been accumulated through learning by doing. The experience not only leads to avoidance of mistakes made in the past, but also can enhance the learning ability of society as a whole through division of labor based on specialized learning by doing.

If the two persons choose autarky and spend half of their time producing each good in each period, then each of them knows little of each activity and therefore output in each activity is $L_{i1}^{1.5} = 0.5^{1.5} = 0.354$ in period 1, and is $L_{i2}^{1.5} = (0.5 + 0.5)^{1.5} = 1$ in period 2 for each of them. Since two persons engage in the same activities, neither person's knowledge is more than the other's, and the total knowledge commanded by society as a whole is not more than that commanded by an individual. Hence, the aggregate transformation curve is a simple addition of individual transformation curves in each period, though a learning-by-doing effect raises each person's labor productivity over time. Such an effect diminishes over time. Each person's output of each good in period $t$ is $L_{it}^{1.5} = (0.5t)^{1.5}$, which increases at a diminishing rate as $t$ increases (the second-order derivative of output with respect to $t$ is negative).

If the two persons choose the division of labor where person 1 produces only good 1 and person 2 produces only good 2, then person 1 knows more about the production of good 1 than person 2 and also more than either of them in autarky. This is because she concentrates her time on the production of good 1, so that she can inquire into the finer details of this activity and acquire more experience from learning by doing. She can thus acquire more knowledge of the production of good 1 than person 2 and than a person in autarky. More knowledge implies a higher labor productivity. Per capita output of good 1 is $0.5L_{x1}^{1.5} = 0.5$ in period 1, and $0.5L_{x2}^{1.5} = 0.5 \times 2^{1.5} = 1.414$ in period 2, higher than person 2's labor productivity of good 1 at 0, and higher than per capita output of good 1 in autarky at $0.5^{1.5} = 0.354$ in period 1, and 1 in period 2. Similarly, person 2 has a higher labor productivity of good 2 than person 1 and than a person in autarky.

Since one person's knowledge differs from that of the other when they engage in division of labor, the total knowledge commanded by society is the sum of the two persons' knowledge, which is more than that commanded by each specialist producer who has more knowledge of her profession than each person in autarky. Hence, the division of labor increases the knowledge commanded by society and thereby increases aggregate productivity at each point in time. For our simple example of two persons, two goods, and two periods, per capita consumption of each good is 0.354 in period 1, and 1 in period 2, in autarky, while it is 1 in period 1 and $\sqrt{2} = 1.414$ for the division of labor.

In addition to the static network effect of division of labor, an expansion of the network size of division of labor over time generates compounded effects of learning by doing over time for each person, and effects of increasingly more specialized learning by doing of different specialists. This will speed up the accumulation of human capital (experience), and keep learning-by-doing effects from diminishing. Hence, evolution of the network size of division of labor may generate accelerating growth (take-off). The model in this chapter will show that learning by doing alone or division of labor alone may not be enough to generate accelerating growth of the kind that we have observed in the industrialization process. In the absence of evolution of division of labor, learning-by-doing effects or effects of specialized learning by doing may diminish.

Later we will show that if economies of specialized learning by doing are very significant, say the production function is $x_{it}^p = L_{it}^4$, then gradual evolution of division of labor is impossible, provided transaction conditions are not too bad. Dynamic equilibrium will jump to the complete division of labor from the outset. With the economies of specialized learning by doing and not too large value of parameter $a$, our story of endogenous evolution of division of labor runs as follows.

At any point in time there is a trade-off involved in an individual's decision on the optimum level of specialization. Choosing to specialize more in the current period has the benefit of generating higher productive capacity in future periods (because of economies of specialized learning by doing). However, because of the preference for diverse consumption, greater specialization must be accompanied by a greater number and higher quantity of goods purchased from other individuals. This higher level of trade will incur greater transaction costs, which is undesirable because of the individual's preference for current consumption.

One dynamic equilibrium of this model involves the evolution of the economy from autarky to a state in which there is a high degree of division of labor. This equilibrium will occur if in the early periods the discounted value of the benefits from specialized learning by doing is not significant compared to the associated utility losses that arise because of transaction costs. Later, the effects of learning by doing will enlarge an individual's scope for trading off the dynamic gains from specialization against the costs of forgone consumption, so that the efficient trade-off evolves over time, generating evolution of division of labor and other concurrent phenomena. The evolution of division of labor will increase the extent of the market, production concentration of each traded good, the diversity of different occupations, the extent of endogenous comparative advantage, the degree of market integration, each person's level of specialization, the income share of transaction cost, and each person's productivity in her occupation, and speed up the accumulation of human capital. As long as the division of labor has evolved to a sufficient degree and the potential for further division of labor remains, the rate of growth of per capita income will increase over time.

The intuition behind the model is quite straightforward. Suppose that there are transaction costs and productivity gains from specialized learning by doing and that consumer-producers prefer current diverse consumption. At $t = 0$ each person does not have much experience in producing each and every good, so her productivity is low and she cannot afford the transaction costs caused by specialization and division of labor. Autarky is thus chosen. As time goes by, each person builds up some experience (human capital) in producing every good, so that her productivity goes up slightly and she can afford a slightly higher transaction cost, and therefore will choose a slightly higher level of specialization. The specialized learning by doing will speed up the accumulation of professional experience. Consequently, each person's productivity in her professional activity increases further and therefore she can afford an even higher transaction cost and will choose an even higher level of specialization, and so on, until the potential for further evolution of division of labor has been exhausted. In the process, the growth rate of per capita real income declines initially due to a low level of division of labor, then increases (takes off) as the evolution in division of labor is speeded up by compounded effects of learning over time and increasingly specialized learning at each point in time, and finally declines again (but is always positive) as the potential for further evolution of division of labor has been exhausted and learning over time becomes the sole driving force of growth.

Section 22.2 details a new classical model of dynamic general equilibrium. Section 22.3 solves for the dynamics and comparative dynamics of general equilibrium. Section 22.4 shows several concurrent phenomena as different aspects of endogenous evolution in division of labor. Section 22.5 reports some empirical work to test new classical growth models and other endogenous growth models in connection with the puzzle of scale effect and the debate over convergence, which has motivated some rethinking of development economics and endogenous growth theory.

---

### Questions to Ask Yourself when Reading this Chapter

- ◆ What is the difference between endogenous and exogenous evolution of division of labor?

- ◆ What is the driving force behind economic growth that increases the wealth of nations?

- ◆ How does the difference between the notion of network effects of division of labor and the concept of economies of scale help us to understand the driving force of economic growth?

- ◆ What is the difference between specialized learning by doing through division of labor in new classical growth models, and learning by doing in neoclassical endogenous growth models?

---

## ◆ 22.2 A New Classical Dynamic Model with Learning by Doing

In this chapter we use a new classical dynamic general equilibrium model, developed by Yang and Borland (1991), to illustrate dynamic general equilibrium mechanisms of the endogenous evolution of division of labor. Other new classical dynamic general equilibrium models can be found in Borland and Yang (1995; chapter 23 of this text), Wen (1997; exercise 2 in this chapter), Yang and Ng (1993), and Zhang (1997; exercise 3 in this chapter).

### Example 22.1: the Yang–Borland (YB) model of endogenous evolution of division of labor

We consider an economy with a continuum of consumer-producers of mass $M$ and $m$ consumer goods. The self-provided amount of a good $i$ at time $t$ is $x_{it}$. The amounts sold and purchased of good i at that time are $x_{it}^{s}$ and $x_{it}^{d}$, respectively. The transaction cost coefficient is $1 - K_t$ so that $K_t x_{it}^{d}$ is the amount available for consumption after purchasing $x_{it}^{d}$ of good i. The total amount of good i consumed is therefore $x_{it} + K_t x_{it}^{d}$. The utility function at time $t$ for any individual is

$$u_t = \Pi^{m}_{i=1}(x_{it} + K_t x_{it}^{d}). \tag{22.1}$$

The coefficient $K_t$ is assumed to depend on the number of a person's trade partners; this number is $n_t - 1$. If all people reside at the vertices of a grid of triangles with equal sides, the average distance between a person and her trade partners will be an increasing function of the number of her trade partners and of the distance between a pair of neighbors (under the assumption that trade occurs first with those who are closest). If the transaction cost 1 $- K_t$ increases with the average distance between a person and her trade partners, then $K_t$ is a decreasing function of $n_t$. More specifically, it is assumed that

$$K_t = k/n_t, \quad 0 < k < 1 \tag{22.2}$$

where $k$ is a parameter that characterizes transaction conditions.

The second-order conditions for a dynamic equilibrium with $n_t \in (0, m)$ will not be satisfied if $K_t$ is independent of $n_t$. In other words, the dynamic equilibrium will be at a corner, either autarky or extreme specialization forever, so that no evolution of the division of labor will occur. This means that to secure a gradual evolution of the division of labor it is necessary that diseconomies of specialization increase more rapidly than economies of specialization as the level of division of labor increases. The static models of specialization have this feature as well. If the transaction cost coefficient in the static models in chapter 7 does not increase with the number of traded goods, an intermediate level of specialization between autarky and extreme specialization can never occur at equilibrium. But for the linear production function with a fixed learning cost, gradual evolution in division of labor is possible even if transaction efficiency $k$ is independent of the number of traded goods. This is due to the fact that for a linear production function with a fixed learning cost the marginal returns to specialization diminish as the level of specialization increases.

It is assumed that all trade in this economy is mediated through futures and spot market contracts signed at time $t = 0$. These contracts cannot be renegotiated at some later date. Assume that the futures' market horizon and an individual's decision horizon are infinity. The objective function for the individual's decision problem is therefore

$$U = \int_0^\infty u_t e^{-rt} dt \tag{22.3}$$

where $r$ is a subjective discount rate. This objective function represents a preference for diverse consumption and for current over future consumption.

The system of production for an individual is assumed to exhibit learning by doing and economies of specialization:

$$x_{it}^p \equiv x_{it} + x_{it}^s = L_{it}^a, \qquad a > 1 \tag{22.4}$$

$$\text{if } l_{it} > 0, \qquad \text{then } L_{it} \equiv \int_0^t l_{it} d\tau \qquad \text{or } l_{it} = dL_{it}/dt$$

$$\text{if } l_{it} = 0, \qquad \text{then } L_{it} = 0$$

where $x_{it}^p = x_{it} + x_{it}^s$ is a person's output level of good $i$ at time $t$, $l_{i\tau}$ is her labor spent producing good $i$ and her level of specialization for this good at time $\tau$, and $L_{it}$ is the labor accumulated in activity $i$ up to time $t$. Hence $L_{it} - l_{it}$ represents the level of experience, knowledge, or human capital accumulated in producing good $i$ up to $t$. The definition of $L_{it}$, given by the second and third lines of (22.4), implies that all previous experience in producing a good will be forgotten if a person ceases to produce this good at $t$. This assumption is too strong to be realistic, but it is necessary for keeping the model tractable based on control theory. In chapter 23, the assumption is relaxed, so control theory does not work and dynamic programming is needed in that chapter.

It is assumed that the total nonleisure hours for an individual at any time $t$ is 1, and these hours are individual-specific since learning by doing is individual-specific. Hence, there is an individual-specific endowment constraint for working time

$$\sum_{i=1}^{m} l_{it} = 1 \qquad l_{it} \in [0, 1]. \tag{22.5}$$

As described in section 22.1, this model features a trade-off between economies of specialized learning by doing and transaction costs, and a trade-off between current and future consumption. The next section spells out these trade-offs.

## ◆ 22.3 Optimum Speed of Learning by Doing and Evolution of Endogenous Comparative Advantage

### 22.3.1 The function of contracts

In a dynamic model without contracting at $t = 0$, learning by doing and economies of specialization create the scope for opportunistic behavior in the market, even in the absence of uncertainty and information asymmetries. Each person as a seller of a traded good will build up human capital in producing this good via learning by doing, while buyers of this good have ceased learning by producing the good and will be in an increasingly disadvantageous position. Hence, each person as a seller may seek to act as a monopolist and as a buyer may be exploited by other professional producers. Holding up and other opportunistic behavior as described in chapters 9 and 10, and by Williamson (1967, 1985), will generate endogenous transaction costs in the spot market at each point in time.

In the initial stage when the level of division of labor is low, there are many producers of each traded good. Hence, buyers can turn to any of the many sellers even though the buyers cannot compete with the professional producers in producing this good because the buyers have ceased accumulating human capital in its production. Therefore, a Walrasian regime prevails at each point in time. However, we will show that the economy described in the preceding section may evolve to a state with extreme division of labor where there are only a few professional producers of each good, and where each person as a seller of her professional produce has monopolist power, and as a buyer of other goods (or as a "novice") is not competitive with the professional producer, despite the fact that she as a consumer-producer may produce every good. Hence, monopoly power may generate endogenous transaction costs which may prevent full exploitation of economies of specialization and dynamic endogenous comparative advantages. (Strictly speaking, this argument is relevant only if the set of individuals is infinite.)

An institutional arrangement based on long-term contracts can be used to restrict opportunistic behavior and endogenous transaction costs. Suppose that all trade is negotiated through a contract system and a futures market. A Walrasian regime determines all long-term contracts at time $t = 0$. Those long-term contracts cannot be renegotiated at a later date. At time $t = 0$, all individuals are identical, and hence there are many potential competitive producers of each good. That is, no individual has experience in any production activity at $t = 0$, so that competition for the rights to produce a good in the future occurs between identical peers rather than between "experts" and "novices." Since all trade is entirely determined in a futures market that operates at $t = 0$ and via a contract system, although over time producers will gain monopoly power from learning by doing, at the time at which contracts are signed, no such monopoly power exists. Combined with the perfect foresight of all individuals, a Walrasian regime at time $t = 0$ can prevail. Hence, the function of a contract system is to eliminate endogenous transaction costs generated by opportunistic behavior that is unavoidable in the spot market at each $t$ when both learning by doing and economies of specialization exist.

For the existing theory of contract (see chapter 10), the contract system is an institutional arrangement that can avoid or reduce endogenous transaction costs generated by moral hazard, or information asymmetry. In our dynamic model, binding long-term contracts are necessary for eliminating endogenous transaction costs even if no uncertainty, information asymmetry, and related moral hazard and adverse selection exist.

Since the time derivatives of the quantities of goods do not appear in the intertemporal decision problem, the proof of the Wen theorem is similar to that for a static model. Hence, at any instant in the dynamic model an individual does not buy and sell the same good, she self-provides a good that is sold and sells one good at most.

## 22.3.2 An individual's dynamic decision problem

The Wen theorem implies that for an individual who sells good $i$ and trades $n_t$ goods at $t$ $(1 < n_t \leq m)$,

$$x_{it}, x_{it}^s, l_{it} > 0, x_{it}^d = 0, \tag{22.6}$$

$$x_{rt} = x_{rt}^s = l_{rt} = 0, x_{rt}^d > 0, \forall\, r \in R$$

$$x_{jt}, l_{jt} > 0, x_{jt}^s = x_{jt}^d = 0, \forall\, j \in J$$

where R is the set of $n_t - 1$ goods bought and J is the set of $m - n_t$ nontraded goods. Note that $n_t = 1$ or $n_t - 1 = 0$ implies autarky. The set of conditions in (22.6) means that this person sells and self-provides good $i$, buys $n_t - 1$ other traded goods, and self-provides $m - n_t$ nontraded goods. Let $u_{it}$ and $U_i$ denote, respectively, the utility of a person who sells good $i$, and her objective function. Then the decision problem for such an individual is

$$\text{Max} \quad U_i = \int_0^\infty u_{it}\, e^{-rt} dt \tag{22.7}$$

$$
\begin{aligned}
\text{s.t.} \quad & u_{it} = x_{it}[\Pi_{r \in R}(K_t x_{it}^d)](\Pi_{j \in J} x_{it}) && \text{(utility function at } t) \\
& x_{it} + x_{it}^s = L_{it}^a, \quad x_{jt} = L_{jt}^a, j \in J && \text{(production function)} \\
& l_{it} + \Sigma_{j \in J} l_{jt} = 1 && \text{(endowment constraint)} \\
& K_t = k/n_t && \text{(transaction technology)} \\
& p_{it} x_{it}^s = \Sigma_{r \in R} p_{rt} x_{rt}^d && \text{(budget constraint)} \\
& n_t|_{t=0} = 1, \quad L_{st}|_{t=0} = 0, \quad s = i, j, j \in J && \text{(boundary condition)} \\
& l_{st} = dL_{st}/dt, \quad l_{st} \in [0, 1] && \text{(state equation)}
\end{aligned}
$$

where $p_{st}$ is the price of good $s$ at time $t$ ($s = i, r$, where $r \in R$). It is assumed that an individual does not save or borrow, although all trading decisions are made at $t = 0$.

Hence, there is an instantaneous budget constraint. Replacing $x_{it}$ and $x_{jt}$ in $U_i$ with their equivalents in the production functions and one of $x_{rt}^d$ ($r \in R$) with its equivalent in the budget constraint, we can construct a Hamiltonian function

$$H_i = u_{it} + \lambda_t(1 - l_{it} - \sum_{j \in J} l_{jt}) + \sum_{j \in J} \gamma_{jt} l_{jt} + \gamma_{it} l_{it} \tag{22.8}$$

where $\lambda_t$ is the discounted dynamic shadow price of the labor endowment at time $t$, and $\gamma_{st}$ ($s = i, j$, where $j \in J$) is the discounted shadow price of the labor input to good $s$ at time $t$. The Hamiltonian $H_i$ is a function of state variable $L_{st}$; costate variables $\lambda_t$ and $\gamma_{st}$; and control variables $x_{it}^s$, $x_{rt}^d$, $l_{st}$, and $n_t$, where $r \in R$, $s = i, j$, and $j \in J$. Only $n_t - 2$ of the $x_{rt}^d$ are in $u_{it}$ because the other is eliminated using the budget constraint.

The first-order conditions for the control problem are given by the maximum principle in (22.12) (see appendix 22.1 below, about the relationship between the control theory and calculus variations). It is interesting to note that the calculus of variations cannot be used to solve this model because the optimum labor input for a good will jump to a corner solution from an interior solution as the number of traded goods increases. That is, we are solving a "bang-bang control problem" in which $l_{it}$ will jump to 1 from an interior solution and $l_{jt}$ will jump to 0 from an interior solution as $n_t$ tends to $m$. The optimum $n_t$, $L_{jt}$, $L_{it}$, $x_{it}^s$, and $x_{rt}^d$ depend on the dynamic prices of all traded goods and on $t$. Inserting these optimal $x_{it}^s$ and $x_{rt}^d$ into $U_i$, we can therefore express total utility as a function of the prices of traded goods.

### 22.3.3 Dynamic equilibrium

A dynamic equilibrium is characterized by a set of market clearing conditions and a set of utility equalization conditions. The market clearing conditions at time $t$ are

$$M_r x_{rt}^s = \sum_{i \neq r} M_i x_{irt}^d, \, r = 1, \ldots, m \tag{22.9}$$

where $M_i$ is the number of persons selling good i, $M_r x_{rt}^s$ is the total market supply of good r, $x_{irt}^d$ is the demand of a person selling good i for good r at time $t$, and hence $\sum_i M_i x_{irt}^d$ is the total market demand for good r. Later we shall show that $x_{irt}^d$ is identical for all $i = 1, \ldots, m$ except r. Hence $x_{irt}^d$ is the same as $x_{rt}^d$ in equation (22.7). Condition (22.9) consists of $m$ equations; however, by Walras's law, only $m - 1$ equations are independent.

The utility equalization conditions are

$$U_1 = U_2 = \ldots = U_m. \tag{22.10}$$

Condition (22.10) consists of $m - 1$ equations. (22.9) and (22.10), together with the population equation $\sum_j M_j = M$, determine the relative prices and the numbers (measure) of persons selling different goods that define the dynamic equilibrium.

At this stage, we turn to a discussion of the equilibrium structure of trade in the market. In one possible equilibrium, each person trades few goods in early periods but trades a progressively larger range of goods as time continues. In the early period there are many possible market structures. One of them, which we shall signify as A, involves all people trading the same bundle of goods. As the number of a person's traded goods increases over time, the number of sellers of each good previously involved in trade decreases, and some people change their occupations to specialize in producing the new traded goods. Another market structure, signified by F, involves a set of sellers (of mass $M/m$) of each good. People trade different bundles of goods but with the same number of traded goods for each person. As the number of a person's traded goods increases over time, she buys more goods and sells more of a good to a larger set of persons, but she will not change her occupation.

To illustrate this point, consider the example of $M = m = 4$ depicted in figure 22.1. Market structure A is shown in panel (a) and market structure F in panel (b). The lines signify the flow of goods. The arrows indicate the directions of flows of goods. The numbers beside the lines signify the goods involved. A circle with number $i$ signifies a person selling good $i$. In market A, each person trades goods 1 and 2 and self-provides goods 3 and 4. The number of traded goods for each person, as well as for the economy, is two. In market F, persons 1 and 2 trade goods 1 and 2, but persons 3 and 4 trade goods 3 and 4. Each person trades two goods, but four goods are traded in the economy.

It is not difficult to see that if all goods will eventually be traded, market F is Pareto superior to market A. There are two reasons: (1) Because of the complete symmetry of the model, the composition of trade has no effect on welfare in the initial periods; only the number of each person's traded goods matters. Thus individuals' welfare in the initial periods is the same for the two market structures. (2) However, individuals' welfare is greater in later periods in market F than in market A because more experience in producing goods 3 and 4 has been accumulated in market F. In market F, experience in producing goods 3 and 4 is accumulated from an earlier point in time, and hence the productivity of labor input to these goods is raised in the future. In market A, however, such experience is not accumulated in the early periods.

The Yao theorem can be established for the dynamic general equilibrium model with identical individuals. Hence, the corner equilibrium in structure A in panel (a) cannot be a general equilibrium model. The intuition is that there exist unexploited gains to trade in structure A that can be captured through the Walrasian regime that prevails at $t = 0$, and hence some individual will always have an incentive to deviate from this market structure. Suppose that there is a dynamic corner equilibrium of market A in which the market clearing conditions are satisfied. In this corner equilibrium, in the early period some individual sells good 1 and others sell good 2; at a later period, all goods are traded.

Consider the following deviation from market structure A: in the early period, some individual switches to selling good 3 at a price equivalent to those of goods 1 and 2 (this is made feasible by the symmetry properties of the model), and at a later stage sells good 3 at a marginally lower price than in market A (feasible because of learning by doing and increasing returns). With this deviation, both the seller and buyers of good 3 will have higher total utility than in market A. Therefore, an individual in market A would have an incentive to switch to selling good 3 from selling good 1 or 2 in the early period. By this argument, market A cannot constitute a dynamic equilibrium market structure.[1]

With similar reasoning or by directly applying the Yao theorem, it can be established that all other market structures are less efficient than market F and that a dynamic equilibrium does not exist for any market structure apart from F. Having considered the fact that individuals will trade first with those closest in order to save transaction costs, we have the following lemma.

**Lemma 22.1:** For $n_t \geq 2$, the equilibrium market structure is F, in which there are $m$ types of individual. The measure of sellers of every good is $M/m$; $m$ goods are traded in the economy although the number of any individual's purchased goods, $n_t - 1$, increases from 0 to $m - 1$ over time.[2]

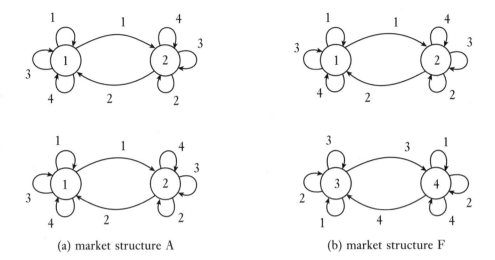

(a) market structure A  (b) market structure F

◆ **Figure 22.1:** Different market structures in an early development stage

In the equilibrium market structure described in lemma 22.1, the individual's decision problems are exactly symmetric. Combined with the symmetry of the market clearing conditions and the utility equalization conditions in (22.10), this implies that when trade occurs, $p_{it}/p_{st} = 1$ for all $i, s = 1, \ldots, m$. When we insert the equilibrium relative prices into (22.9), the first-order condition with respect to $x_{rt}^d$ for the control problem implies that $x_{rt}^d$ is identical $\forall\ r \in R$. With this information, the first-order condition with respect to $x_{it}^s$ gives

$$x_{it}^s = (n_t - 1)L_{it}^a/n_t, \tag{22.11a}$$

$$x_{rt}^d = L_{it}^a/n_t, \qquad \forall\ r \in R, \text{ for } i = 1, \ldots, m$$

Here we have used the budget constraint to derive $x_{rt}^d$. The complete symmetry of the necessary conditions for utility maximization of individuals selling different goods, the market clearing conditions, and utility equalization conditions imply that $x_{it}^s$, $L_{it}$, and $l_{it}$ are identical for $i = 1, \ldots, m$; $L_{jt}$ and $l_{jt}$ are identical for all people; $n_t$ is identical for all people; and

$$H_i = H = u_t + \lambda_t(1 - l_{it} - \sum_{j \in J} l_{jt}) + \sum_{j \in J} \gamma_{jt} l_{jt} + \gamma_{it} l_{it}, \text{ for } i = 1, \ldots, m \tag{22.11b}$$

$$u_t = k^{n_t-1}(n_t)^{1-2n_t}(L_{it})^{an_t}\pi_{j \in J}(L_{jt})^a, \text{ for } i = 1, \ldots, m.$$

The equilibrium $n_t$, $L_{it}$, and $L_{jt}$ are therefore determined by the first-order conditions

$$\partial H/\partial \gamma_{st} = dL_{st}/dt, \qquad s = i, j, j \in J \tag{22.12a}$$

or   $l_{st} = dL_{st}/dt$

$$\partial H/\partial L_{st} = r\gamma_{st} - d\gamma_{st}/dt, \qquad s = i, j, j \in J \tag{22.12b}$$
$$\text{or} \quad an_t u_t/L_{it} = r\gamma_{it} - d\gamma_{it}/dt, \qquad au_t/L_{jt} = r\gamma_{jt} - d\gamma_{jt}/dt,$$

Max $H$ with respect to integer $n_t$ or                                                           (22.12c)
(i)   $\partial H/\partial n_t = u_t B_t = 0$, for $n_t \in (1, m)$
(ii)  $n_t = 1 \; \forall \; t \in [0, \infty]$ if $H$ monotonically decreases $\forall \; n_t \in [1, m]$
(iii) $n_t = m \; \forall \; t \in [0, \infty]$ if $H$ monotonically increases $\forall \; n_t \in [1, m]$

Max $H$ with respect to $l_{st}$, $s = i, j, j \in J$ or                                            (22.12d)
(i)   $l_{st} = 1$ if $\gamma_{st} > \lambda_t$
(ii)  $l_{st} \in (0, 1)$ if $\gamma_{st} = \lambda_t$
(iii) $l_{st} = 0$ if $\gamma_{st} < \lambda_t$,

$$l_{it} + \sum_{j \in J} l_{jt} = 1 \tag{22.12e}$$

where $B_t \equiv \log(k) - 2[\log(n_t) + 1] + (1/n_t) + a\log(L_{it})$. Condition (22.12c) is equivalent to an instantaneous problem, Max $u_t$ with respect to integer $n_t$, since the rate of change of $n_t$ does not appear in $H$. The time path of $n_t$ that is given by

$$\partial u_t/\partial n_t = 0 \tag{22.12f}$$

is a good approximation of the optimum time path of $n_t$ if $m$ is very large because $u_t$ is strictly concave in $n_t$ if $n_t$ takes on a continuous interior value. Hence, we can approximate the optimum time path of $n_t$, which is solved from a dynamic integer programming problem by the time path of $n_t$ given by equation (22.12f). In what follows, $n_t$ is the approximation of the optimum $n_t$.

A careful examination of $B_t$ indicates that it tends to negative infinity as $k$ converges to 0 and $a$ converges to 1 for any $n_t \in [1, m]$ if $L_{it}$ is limited. Hence, $\partial H/\partial n_t$ is negative for any $n_t$ if $k$ and $a$ are too small. This, combined with (22.12c), implies that the equilibrium is $n_t = 1$ for all $t$. If $a$ and $k$ are sufficiently large that $B_t > 0$, then $\partial H/\partial n_t > 0$ for any positive $n_t \le m$. Therefore, the equilibrium $n_t$ is the maximum, $m$, for all $t$. This leads us to

$n_t = 1 \; \forall \; t \in [0, \infty]$ if $k$ and $a$ are sufficiently small                       (22.13)
$n_t = m \; \forall \; t \in [0, \infty]$ if $k$ and $a$ are sufficiently great
$n_t \in (1, m)$ for at least some $t$ if $k$ and $a$ are neither too large nor too small.

Since by the Wen theorem a person sells at most one good, expression (22.13) implies that $l_{it} = 1$ and $l_{jt} = 0$ iff $n_t = m$ and that $l_{it} = 0$ and $l_{jt} \in (0, 1)$ iff $n_t = 1$. Combined with the bang-bang control given in (22.12d), this implies that $l_{it}$ and $l_{jt}$ (for $j \in J$) are between 0 and 1 when $1 < n_t < m$. Hence, $\gamma_{it} = \gamma_{jt} = \lambda_t$ (for $j \in J$) iff $n_t \in (1, m)$.

The first-order condition for an interior $n_t$ given in (22.12c) entails $B_t = 0$. Differentiating this equation with respect to $t$ yields

$$\rho_n \equiv \frac{\dot{n}_t}{n_t} = \frac{a\rho_i}{2 + 1/n_t} > 0 \quad n_t \in (1, m), \tag{22.14}$$

where $\rho_i \equiv l_{it}/L_{it}$ is positive for $n_t > 1$. (22.13) and (22.14) imply that if $k$ and $a$ are neither too small nor too large, the equilibrium level of division of labor will evolve and $n_t$ will eventually reach $m$, and then the evolution in division of labor stops. Since (22.14) includes $\rho_i \equiv l_{it}/L_{it}$ that is yet to be solved, the dynamics of general equilibrium are yet to be figured out.

Assume that $k$ and $a$ are neither too small nor too large, so that $n_t \in (1, m)$ and evolution in division of labor occurs at equilibrium for some period of time. This implies $l_{it}, l_{jt} \in (0.1)$ when $n_t \in (1, m)$. Hence, $\gamma_{st} = \lambda_t$ according to (22.12d). Differentiation of this equation yields $d\gamma_{st}/dt = d\lambda_t/dt$. We can thus obtain $L_{it} = n_t L_{it}$ from (22.12b). The differentiation of this equation yields $\dot{l}_{it} = \dot{n}_t L_{jt} + l_{jt} \dot{n}_t$, which, together with $L_{it} = n_t L_{jt}$, implies

$$l_{jt} = (\dot{l}_{it} - \dot{n}L_{it}/n_t)/n_t. \tag{22.15}$$

This verifies that $l_{jt}$ is the same for any $j \in J$. Using this information, we can obtain

$$l_{jt} = (1 - l_{it})/(m - n_t) \tag{22.16}$$

from the time constraint (22.12e). Use (22.15) and (22.16) to eliminate $l_{jt}$, we have $l_{it} - \dot{n}_t L_{it}/n_t = n_t(1 - l_{it})/(m - n_t)$. Inserting (22.14) into this equation yields

$$l_{it} = \frac{n_t(2n_t + 1)}{m(2n_t + 1) - an_t(m - n_t)} \tag{22.17}$$

(22.17) tends to 1 as $n_t$ tends to $m$, since the upper bound of $l_{it}$ is 1. According to the bang-bang control in (22.12d), the value of some $l_{jt}$ must jump to 0 as $n_t$ increases (i.e., an individual must cease self-providing a good at the time that she starts to buy that good). Using $B_t = 0$ in (22.12c) again, we can express human capital $L_{it}$ as a function of $n_t$, that is,

$$L_{it} = [n_t^2 e^{2-(1/n_t)}/k]^{1/a} \text{ and } L_{jt} = L_{it}/n_t. \tag{22.18}$$

(22.17) and (22.18) can be used to express the growth rate of human capital $\rho_i \equiv l_{it}/L_{it}$ as a function of $n_t$. Using this function, we can finally express the growth rate of the level of division of labor as a function of the level of division of labor and the transaction condition parameter $k$.

$$\rho_n \equiv \frac{\dot{n}_t}{n_t} = \frac{an_t^{2(1-1/a)}k^{1/a}e^{\frac{1}{an_t}\frac{2}{a}}}{(2n_t + 1)m - an_t(m - n_t)} \quad \text{for } n_t \in (1, m). \tag{22.19}$$

This is a nonlinear differential equation in $n_t$ that, together with the transversality conditions $n_t|_{t=0} = 1$ and $dn_t/dt|_{n=m} = 0$, determines the dynamics and comparative dynamics of the general equilibrium for an interior $n_t$. Expression (22.19), together with (22.13), implies that $n_t = 1$ forever from $t = 0$ if $k$ and $a$ are sufficiently small, $n_t$ jumps to $m$ at $t = 0$ and stays there forever if $k$ and $a$ are sufficiently large, and $n_t$ increases over time until $n_t = m$ if $k$ and $a$ are neither too large nor too small. Also, expression (22.19) implies that the increase in $n_t$ is faster if $k$ is larger (i.e. the better the transaction condition, the faster the evolution of the division of labor) since $dn_t/dt$ in (22.19) increases with $k$ for $n_t < m$. The time paths of demand, supply, and other endogenous variables are determined by the time path of the level of division of labor $n_t$. But note that (22.19) does not apply to $n_t = m$ which is a corner solution. Autarky $n_t = 1$ is another corner solution to which (22.19) is not applicable either.

Taking the log of $u_t$ in (22.11b) and then differentiating it with respect to $t$ yields

$$\rho_u \equiv \frac{\dot{u}_t}{u_t} = a\,[n_t\rho_i + (m + n_t)\rho_j] \tag{22.20a}$$

$$= [(2n_t + 1)m - an_t(m - n_t)]\frac{\rho_n}{n_t} = an_t^{1-\frac{2}{a}}k^{1/a}e^{\frac{1-2n_t}{an_t}}$$

$$\frac{\dot{\rho}_u}{\rho_u} = \frac{[a - 2)n_t - 1]\rho_n}{an_t} \tag{22.20b}$$

where $\rho_u$ is the growth rate of per capita real income. (22.20a) indicates that there is no steady state of per capita real income, a feature shared with other endogenous growth models. Also, there is no steady growth rate of per capita real income. But rather, the growth rate of per capita real income keeps changing over time.

(22.17)–(22.20) can be used to identify several growth patterns and subpatterns. The expressions indicate that the growth rate of the level of division of labor, $\rho_n$, the growth rate of per capita real income, $\rho_u$ , and each individual's level of specialization, $l_{it}$, are positive if and only if

$$f(n_t) = (2n_t + 1)m - an_t(m - n_t) > 0 \tag{22.21}$$

Note that for an interior solution, $f(n_t)$ must be positive. The upper bound of $l_{it}$ is 1 due to the endowment constraint and its lower bound is 0 due to the non-negative constraint. (22.17) indicates $l_{it}$ takes on its upper bound, 1, when $f(n_t) = 0$ and takes on its lower bound, 0, when $f(n_t) < 0$. $f(n_t)$ can be used to identify three patterns of path of $n_t$. Having differentiated (22.21) with respect to $n$ twice, we can show that $f(n_t)$ is a nonmonotonous convex function with the minimum point $n \equiv (a - 2)m/2a$ as shown in figure 22.2. It is not difficult to see that for $a \leq 2$, the minimum value of $f(n_t)$ is positive, so that $f(n_t)$ is always positive. If $a > 2$, the curve associated with $f(n_t)$ cuts the horizontal axis at two points (a single point for $m = [2/(a - 2)^2 a]$. From $f(n_t) = 0$, the two cutting points can be solved as follows.

$$n' = \{(a - 2)m - [(a - 2)^2m^2 - 4am]^{1/2}\}/2a, \tag{22.22a}$$

$$n'' = \{(a - 2)m + [(a - 2)^2m^2 - 4am]^{1/2}\}/2a, \tag{22.12b}$$

where $n'' \geq. n'$. It is not difficult to show that $n' \geq 1$ if $a \in (2.3)$ and $n' < 1$ if $a > 3$. Since the minimum value of $n$ is 1, which means autarky, $n' < 1$ is impossible. Hence, for $a > 3$, $n'$ is irrelevant. This discussion generates three intervals of $a$ that are associated with three growth patterns, as shown in figure 22.2.

First we consider interval $a > 3$ in figure 22.2c. Since the initial condition is $n_t = 1$ for $t = 0$, the system starts from the point $n_t = 1$ which is on the right-hand side of the cutting point $n'$. At point $n'$, $f(n_t) = 0$ implies that $l_{it}$ tends to be as large as possible according to panel (c), but the upper bound of $l_{it}$ is 1 because of the endowment constraint

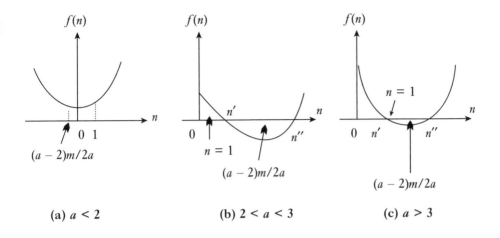

◆ **Figure 22.2:** Intervals of a that divide between various growth patterns

of time. The application of the maximum principle to the individual's decision of level of specialization yields $l_{it} = 1$. This implies that at $t = 0$, each individual jumps from autarky ($n_t = 1$) to complete specialization ($l_{it} = 1$ and $n_t = m$). Afterward, the level of division of labor stays there and the growth rate of per capita real income declines, although they are always positive. The paths of the level of division of labor and per capita real income for this growth pattern are shown in figure 22.3a. This pattern features a single big-push industrialization in the absence of a smooth take-off and smooth evolution in division of labor. We cannot observe the phenomenon of human society jumping to a completely commercialized state from autarky as soon as the society comes into existence. The lack of empirical evidence for this pattern of growth can be attributed to the fact that the degree of economies of specialization, $a$, in the real world is not larger than 3. Of course, the threshold value of $a$ would be much more complicated if the model were not symmetric.

Let us consider the case of $a \in (2, 3)$ in figure 22.2b. From (22.22), it can be shown that $1 < n' < n'' < m$ for this case. The dynamic equilibrium value of $n_t$ increases over time before $t = t_2$ or before $n_t = n'$ since $n_t < n'$ for $f(n_t) > 0$ which implies $\rho_n > 0$ according to equation (22.19). At $t = t_2$ or at $n_t = n'$, $f(n_t) = 0$, which implies $l_{it} = 1$ according to equation (22.17). Hence, the level of division of labor jumps from $n_t = n'$ to $n_t = m$ (complete division of labor) at this point in time. From equation (22.20b), it is obvious that there is a point $t_1$ before $t_2$. The growth rate of per capita real income decreases (although they are positive) before $t_1$ but increases between $t_1$ and $t_2$, as shown in figure 22.3b. The subgrowth pattern before $t_1$ is referred to as pre-industrialization growth which features a low level of division of labor and decreasing growth rate. The subgrowth pattern between $t_1$ and $t_2$ is referred to as smooth take-off, which features a smoothly increasing growth rate of per capita real income and increasing $n_t$. The subgrowth pattern at $t_2$ is referred to as big-push industrialization, which features a discontinuous jump of the level of division of labor (or the level of commercialization). At this point, the degree of commercialization and extent of the market suddenly jump up, and many separate local business communities suddenly merge into the integrated market. After the big jump, the economy has reached

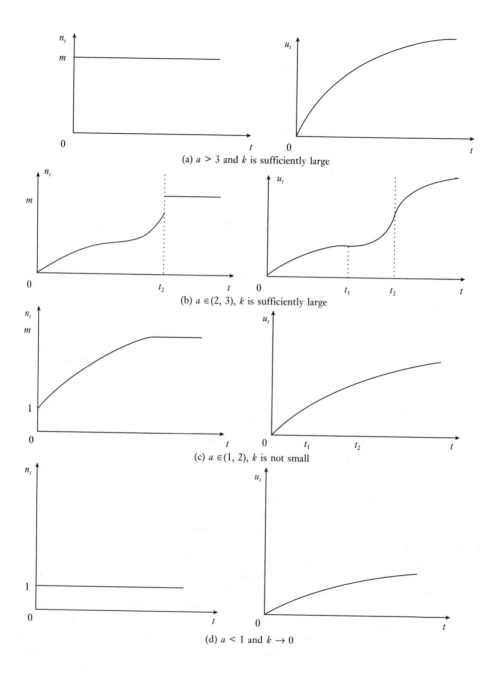

(a) $a > 3$ and $k$ is sufficiently large

(b) $a \in (2, 3)$, $k$ is sufficiently large

(c) $a \in (1, 2)$, $k$ is not small

(d) $a < 1$ and $k \to 0$

◆ **Figure 22.3:** Various growth patterns of $n_t$ and per capita real income

the complete division of labor and enters the mature growth stage, which features a decreasing growth rate of per capita real income and zero growth in the level of division of labor. The potential for further evolution in division of labor has been exhausted. The growth rate of per capita real income is determined solely by the growth rate of human capital in producing the traded good ($\rho_i$) which equals $1/L_i$ for $l_{it} = 1$. Though $\rho_i$ is always positive, it monotonically declines as human capital increases over time.

For $a \in (1, 2)$, equation (22.20b) indicates that the growth rate of per capita real income is always positive and declining if $n_t \in (1, m)$. Also, equations (22.19) and (22.21b) shows that the growth rate of the level of division of labor is always positive for $n_t \in (1, m)$ and $a < 2$. The pattern of evolution in division of labor and the growth pattern of per capita real income for this case are illustrated by figure 22.3c, which features decreasing growth rates of both per capita real income and the level of division of labor. Finally, expressions (22.15), (22.19), and (22.20) imply that the growth rate of the level of division of labor is 0 if parameter $k$ is close to 0. The application of the maximum principle to each individual's decision concerning the level of specialization indicates that the optimum value of $n_t$ is always at a corner $n_t = 1$ if $k$ is sufficiently close to 0. If $n_t = 1$ for all $t$, then the equilibrium is autarky and is characterized by:

$$\rho_u = am\rho_j = aml_j/L_j = am/t \tag{22.23}$$

which declines monotonically as $t$ increases.

This pattern of growth is illustrated in figure 22.3d, which features autarky and continuously decelerating growth. This pattern of growth is similar to the so-called growth trap. However, in the YB model such a growth trap is not an accidental outcome caused by multiple steady states for given parameters. But rather, it is based on comparative dynamics (changes in the dynamic equilibrium in response to changes in parameters) and generated by a small $k$ resulting from deficient institutional arrangements, a low degree of openness, high tariffs, underdeveloped transportation infrastructures, deficient banking and legal systems, and other unfavorable transaction conditions.

Intuitively, if economies of specialization are not significant ($a$ is close to 1) and transaction conditions are not good ($k$ is close to 0), then the equilibrium will be autarky forever. At the other extreme, suppose that $a$ is large and $k$ is close to 1. In this case the equilibrium will involve individuals completely specializing from time $t = 0$, since the benefits from the consequently higher volume of output outweigh transaction costs incurred in trade.

For intermediate values of $a$ and $k$, the equilibrium involves evolution of the division of labor. If in early periods the total discounted value of the benefits from specialization is outweighed by the current utility losses caused by such specialization due to transaction costs, then the level of specialization will be low. However, over time, learning by doing in production will raise the benefits from specializing relative to the costs of forgone consumption, and a greater degree of specialization will occur. In order for the level of specialization to increase over time, both learning by doing and economies of specialization are necessary. Without learning by doing, although specialization may occur, the optimal level of specialization is invariant over time. On the other hand, in the absence of economies of specialization and given a positive transaction cost, specialization will never be optimal.

**Proposition 22.1:** Dynamic equilibrium is autarky forever from $t = 0$ if transaction condition parameter $k$ and the degree of economies of specialization $a$ are sufficiently small, and is extreme specialization forever from $t = 0$ if $k$ and $a$ are sufficiently large. The division of labor will evolve until $n_t$ reaches $m$ if $k$ and $a$ are neither too large nor too small. For such intermediate values of $k$ and $a$, the better the transaction condition, the faster the evolution of the division of labor. For $a \in (2, 3)$, division of labor evolves over time. When $n_t \in [1, 1/(a-2)]$, growth rate of per capita real income declines. When $n_t \in (1/(a-2), n')$, growth rate of per capita real income increases (smooth take-off). At $n_t = n'$, big-push industrialization takes place and the economy jumps to the complete division of labor. Then, the economy enters a mature growth stage with positive and declining growth rate of per capita real income in the absence of evolution of division of labor.

Note that the driving force of economic growth is not growth in population size or exogenous changes in the transaction, production, or preference parameters. Rather, growth is generated by a spontaneous evolution in division of labor. An example of such an evolution is illustrated in figure 22.4 for the case of $m = 4$. In panel (a), each person self-provides all goods she needs. In panel (b), each person sells a good, buys a good, and self-provides three goods ($n_t = 2$). In panel (c), each person sells a good, buys two goods, and self-provides two goods ($n_t = 3$). In panel (d), each person sells and self-provides a good, buys three goods, and trades four goods ($n_t = 4$). The circles, lines, and numbers in Fig. 22.4 have the same interpretation as those in figure 22.1. The graphs provide a better illustration of the topological and graphical properties of the evolution in division of labor than figure 22.3 and the algebra do.

The dynamic equilibrium is Pareto optimal because of the Walrasian regime. In the models of Judd (1985), Romer (1986, 1990), Lucas (1988), and Grossman and Helpman (1989), the dynamic equilibrium is not Pareto optimal either, because increasing returns are external to agents or because of the existence of monopoly power.

As in static symmetric models there are multiple dynamic equilibria in the new classical dynamic equilibrium model, since it is indeterminate who is specialized in producing which good in the model with *ex ante* identical individuals. Also, possible one-way trade (person 1 sells good 1 to person 2 who sells good 2 to person 3 who sells good 3 to person 4 who sells good 4 to person 1 when $n_t = 2$) generates more possible dynamic equilibria. But if the assumption is made that there is neither a central clearing house nor money and related credit systems, then all of the structures with one-way trade (without double coincidence of demand and supply) cannot take place at equilibrium (see chapter 26 for the definition of double coincidence of demand and supply and the relationship between it, money, and central clearing houses). All of the multiple dynamic equilibria generate the same total present value of utility for each individual and have similar dynamics and comparative dynamics.

## ◆ 22.4 Endogenous Evolution of the Extent of the Market, Trade Dependence, Endogenous Comparative Advantages, and Economic Structure

In this section we consider some further implications of equilibria that involve evolution of the division of labor. Following the definitions of trade dependence and extent of the market given in chapter 11, we take the ratio of trade volume per head in terms of labor to total real income in terms of labor, $2(n_t - 1)(L_{it})^a/n_t$, to be the measure of trade dependence, where $(L_{it})^a$ is the output level of the good an individual produces for sale, and $(n_t - 1)/n_t$ is the portion of the good that is sold. The extent of the market $E$ is the product of

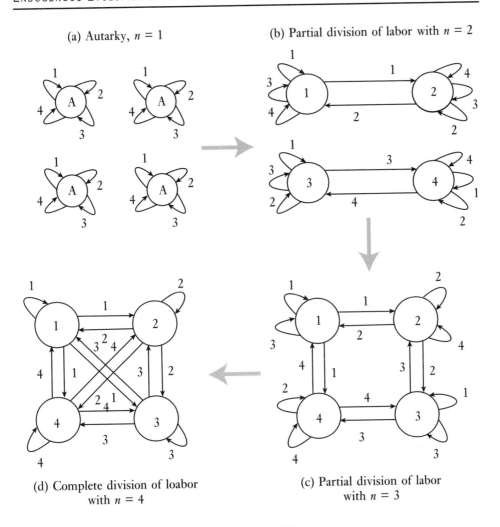

(a) Autarky, $n = 1$

(b) Partial division of labor with $n = 2$

(d) Complete division of loabor with $n = 4$

(c) Partial division of labor with $n = 3$

◆ **Figure 22.4**: Endogenous evolution in division of labor

population size $M$ and $(n_t - 1)(L_{it})^a/n_t$. Hence, $E = M(n_t - 1)(L_{it})^a/n_t$. Differentiating $E$ with respect to $t$ yields the growth rate of the extent of the market

$$\rho_E = \dot{E}/E > 0 \text{ iff } [\rho_n/(n_t - 1)] + a\rho_i + (\dot{M}/M) > 0. \qquad (22.24)$$

Here, $\rho_n/(n_t - 1)$, which is positive if $\rho_n > 0$ and $n_t \in (1, m)$ is the contribution of the evolution of the division of labor to the expansion of the market, $a\rho_i$ is the contribution of learning by doing, which is always positive, and $\dot{M}/M$ is the growth rate of population. Suppose the growth rate of population is zero. If the potential for further evolution of the division of labor has been exhausted ($n_t = m$), the first term tends to 0 and accordingly the rate of growth of the extent of the market is solely determined by the second term. The extent of the market is aggregate demand and supply as well. Hence, aggregate demand and supply will evolve as the division of labor evolves over time according to (22.24). This result substantiates Allyn Young's idea that the extent of the market can expand as division of labor evolves in the absence of changes in population size. Since trade dependence R = $2E/M = 2(n_t - 1)(L_{it})^a/n_t$, it evolves also as division of labor evolves.

The endogenous comparative advantage of a producer is characterized by the difference between a seller's per capita output of a good and a buyer's per capita output of that good. Denoting this difference by $D$, we have $D = [(L_{it})^a/n_t] - G$, where $G$ is the buyer's per capita output and its rate of change is 0, since the buyer ceases to produce the good, so that professional experience is forgotten. If we differentiate this difference, it is evident that

$$\rho_D \equiv \frac{\dot{D}}{D} > 0 \text{ if } a\rho_i > \rho_n. \tag{22.25}$$

From (22.14), $a\rho_i > \rho_n$ if $n_t \in (1, m)$. Hence, the comparative advantage of an expert over a novice increases endogenously as the division of labor evolves (even though there is no exogenous comparative advantage).

The income share of transaction costs, $S$, is equal to the ratio of the cost of bought goods lost in transit to nominal income. Since $p_{rt}x_{rt}^d$ is the same for all $r \in R$, therefore, $(1 - K_t)(n_t - 1)p_{rt}x_{rt}^d$ is the transaction cost and $(n_t - 1)p_{rt}x_{rt}^d = p_{rt}x_{rt}^s$ is per capita nominal income at time $t$. Hence

$$S \equiv \frac{(1 - K_t)(n_t - 1) p_{rt}x_{rt}^d}{(n_t - 1)p_{rt}x_{rt}^d} = 1 - \frac{k}{n_t} \tag{22.26a}$$

is the income share of the transaction cost. Differentiation of (22.26a) yields

$$\frac{\partial S}{\partial n_t} > 0, \frac{dS}{dk} = \frac{(kdn_t/n_tdk) - 1}{n_t} \text{ if } n_t < m \tag{22.26b}$$

Condition (22.26b) implies that the income share of transaction costs increases as the division of labor evolves and as transaction efficiency is improved (the latter result holds provided that the level of the division of labor is elastic with respect to transaction efficiency). Since transaction costs can be viewed as "nonproductive costs" or roundabout production costs, condition (22.26b) implies that the income share of the roundabout productive sector rises as the division of labor evolves.

It is interesting to note that transaction efficiency $K_t = k/n_t$ decreases as division of labor spontaneously evolves ($n_t$ increases). Since $\dot{K}_t/K_t = \dot{k}/k - \dot{n}_t/n_t$, it is possible that transaction efficiency $K_t$ declines as transaction condition parameter $k$ increases. This occurs when the increase in $n$ caused by an increase in $k$ dominates the increase in $k$ itself. This result is intuitive. As transaction conditions improve, the network of division of labor expands. Individuals must trade with more distant partners, so that transaction efficiency declines provided increases in division of labor are faster than increases in $k$. The results in this section are summarized in the following proposition.

**Proposition 22.2:** The extent of the market, trade dependence, the extent of endogenous comparative advantage of an expert relative to a novice, and the income share of transaction costs increase as the division of labor evolves over time.

## ◆ 22.5 Empirical Evidence and Rethinking Development Economics and Endogenous Growth Theory

The YB model in this chapter generates the following empirical implications. (1) The income share of the transaction sector increases as division of labor evolves and per capita real income increases. (2) Growth performance and speed of evolution of division of labor critically depend on transaction conditions. Hypothesis (1) is verified by North's empirical work (1986), which shows that the employment share of the transaction sector increased with economic development in the US in the past century. Hypothesis (2) is verified by historical evidences documented in North (1958) and North and Weingast (1989) and by empirical evidence provided in Barro (1997), Easton and Walker (1997), Frye and Shleifer (1997), Gallup and Sachs (1998), and Sachs and Warner (1997).

North shows that the continuous fall of ocean freight rates contributed significantly to early economic development in Europe. Yang, Wang, and Wills (1992) have found empirical evidence for the effects of institutions that affect transaction conditions on development performance and evolution of degree of commercialization (an aspect of division of labor).

Barro uses a data set of 100 countries in 1965–90 to establish a positive effect of an index of rule of law, which affects transaction conditions, on growth rates of per capita real GDP. Easton and Walker use cross-country data to show that growth performance is positively affected by an index of economic freedom. Frye and Shleifer use survey data from Poland and Russia to establish a negative correlation between growth performance and governments' violation of private property rights. Gallup and Sachs use cross-country data to show that the geographical conditions that affect transportation efficiency of a country, such as population share of coast region and distance from the major international market, have a very significant impact on per capita income. Sachs and Warner use a data set of 83 countries in 1965–90 to establish a positive correlation between growth performance and indices of openness and quality of institution that affect trading efficiency.

In addition, the YB model can be used to address the puzzle of scale effect and the debate over convergence in the literature of endogenous growth theory. Two classes of major endogenous growth models, the AK model and R&D-based model, discussed in chapter 21, have recently been tested against empirical data (see C. Jones, 1995a,b). The R&D-based model generates a Type III scale effect, which is a positive relationship between the growth rate in per capita GDP and the level of resources devoted to R&D.[3] Type III scale effect is rejected by empirical observation (Jones, 1995a,b). The AK model generates a Type IV scale effect, which is a positive relationship between the growth rate in per capita GDP and the investment rate.[4]

The YB model in this chapter has the following attractive features that can be used to address the puzzle of the scale effect. The driving force of economic growth in the YB model is the positive network effect of division of labor rather than economies of scale. Economies of division of labor differ from economies of scale as discussed in Allyn Young (1928) and in chapters 2, 5, and 11 above. Investment in terms of transaction costs and related loss of current consumption enlarges scope for specialized learning by doing which enhances social learning capacity and related network effects on aggregate productivity in future. This *implicit investment mechanism* can generate long-term endogenous growth in the absence of interpersonal loans and tangible saving.[5] It does not necessarily generate a positive correlation between a tangible savings rate (or investment rate) and growth rates of per capita real income. The endogenous evolution of each person's number of traded goods in the YB model is associated with endogenous evolution in the size of the network of division of labor. As the size of the network increases, many separate local communities merge into an increasingly more integrated market. This can take place in the absence of an increase in population size or in the R&D sector. Hence, the speed at which new traded goods emerge is determined by the speed of evolution of division of labor rather than by population size or the size of the R&D sector. In other words, in the R&D-based models, there is an "if and only if" relationship between investment in R&D and the number of new goods and related technology (investment and technology fundamentalism). But in the YB model, there is no such relationship. Endogenous technical progress is a matter of whether the network of division of labor evolves to a sufficiently large size to create a social learning capacity and to make new traded goods commercially viable. The individual-specific economies of specialized learning by doing distinguishes the YB model from the other models with learning by doing (Arrow, 1962, Lucas, 1988, Stokey, 1991, Alwyn Young, 1993, and others). In the YB model, the blend of individuals' specialized learning by doing and an increase in the size of the network of division of labor can generate network effects of social learning without a scale effect. By contrast, the learning by doing in the other models is independent of evolution of division of labor and generates a scale effect. The growth rates of level of division of labor and of per capita real income in (22.20) are independent of population size $M$. The population size plays a very passive role in this model. It sets up a limit to the evolution in division of labor: the number of professions cannot be larger than population size if the number of individuals must be an integer.

Let us now turn to the debate over convergence. The new theory of endogenous growth was motivated in part by criticism of the convergence theory based on the neoclassical growth model (Lucas, 1988, Romer, 1986). The absolute convergence hypothesis – per capita incomes of countries converge to one another in the long run independently of their initial conditions – has been rejected by empirical data (Barro, 1991). Some new endogenous growth models are developed to predict the divergence phenomenon, accommodating the empirical evidence. However, the new theoretical models are not only disturbed by the puzzle of scale effects; they are also challenged by the new evidence on convergence. Many slightly different concepts of convergence and divergence are proposed (see Sala-i-Martin, 1996, Galor, 1996). However, all of these concepts generate more confusion than clarification. They do not alter the fact that convergence and divergence, no matter how defined, may coexist, and that such coexistence has not received the attention it deserves.

One of the empirical implications of the YB model is a sequential pattern in divergence and convergence phenomena. The YB model implies that three stages of growth will take place sequentially: preindustrialization growth, accelerating growth and take-off, and mature growth. The growth rate first declines, then increases, and finally declines again. This is consistent with Rostow's (1960) description of the three historical stages of economic growth. As the transaction condition parameter $k$ increases, the growth rate of per capita real income rises, despite the fact that changes in $k$ are not necessary for accelerating growth and for endogenous evolution in division of labor. The result of this comparative dynamics can be used to explain cross-country growth differentials, since different tariff regimes and degrees of openness, different institutional arrangements, different legal systems and related property rights regimes, and different geographical conditions across countries all imply different values of $k$ across countries. Hence, those countries with a larger $k$ enter the take-off stage earlier.

The UK, for example, entered the take-off stage earlier than other countries since it is an island country, which implied a higher shipment efficiency in the UK than in hinter-land countries, such as Germany and China, when automobiles and trains were not avail-able. The UK was the first country to have a Statute of Monopolies (patent laws, 1624) which significantly improved transaction conditions in trading intellectual property (see North, 1981). Evolving common law and a *de facto laissez-faire* policy and deregulation started before Smith's advocacy for free trade significantly improved transaction condi-tions (Mokyr, 1993). As North and Weingast (1989) show, the most important driving force for the successful industrialization of Britain was the evolution of institutions, begin-ning in the seventeenth century, that made credible the government's commitment to constitutional stability. This significantly reduced state opportunism and therefore signifi-cantly reduced rent seeking in society and related endogenous transaction costs. On the other hand, because of their deficient legal systems, violations of private property rights, extreme protectionism (low level of openness), and political instability, all of which gener-ated a small $k$, France and China entered the take-off stage later than Britain (Landes, 1998, pp. 34–6, Fairbank, 1992, Mokyr, 1990, pp. 235–50, 1993).

In a sense our model in this chapter shares a feature with Alwyn Young's model (1993): learning speed and the growth rate of per capita real income decline over time if each individual's number of traded goods is fixed. As the number of traded goods increases, the network of division of labor expands, thereby creating more scope for specialized learning by producing a greater variety of traded goods in society. However, the difference between the two models is important. In the YB model, when an individual chooses her number of traded goods $n_t$, she chooses the number of types of her trade partners, which is $n_t - 1$ in a symmetric model. The aggregate outcome of all individuals' decisions in choosing their $n_t$ determines the size of the network of division of labor and the degree of connectedness of the network. Hence, in the YB model, the degree to which learning by producing new traded goods can promote growth is determined by the level of division of labor and the related size of the market network. The connection between the invention of new goods and division of labor was emphasized by Smith (1776) and many other classical econo-mists. But individuals' levels of specialization and the network size of division of labor are not endogenized in Alwyn Young's model.

It is obvious that for an economy that has experienced mature growth, the time path of the structure of division of labor and per capita real income are like those in figure 22.3b. As $t$ increases from its initial value towards infinity, the curve representing per capita real income is first concave, then convex, and finally concave again, if short-run fluctuation is eliminated. However, economies may differ in their parameter $k$ representing transaction conditions. We should therefore see that different countries enter the take-off stage at different points in time. Between each pair of economies that enter the take-off stage at different points in time, the difference in per capita real incomes should be an inverted U curve in the coordinates of time and per capita real income. That is, when the country that enters the take-off stage earlier starts accelerating growth, the latecomer is still in the decelerating growth stage. Their per capita real incomes and growth rates will diverge. As the latecomer ultimately enters the take-off stage and the leader reaches the mature growth stage, the differences in their per capita real incomes and growth rate diminish, and they experience convergence.

This sequential divergence and convergence is illustrated in figure 22.5, in which per capita real incomes between two economies (the UK and Germany) diverge before $t_1$ and converge thereafter. The convergence may be conditional, and different economies may not end up with the same income level and growth rate due to differences in $k$ between

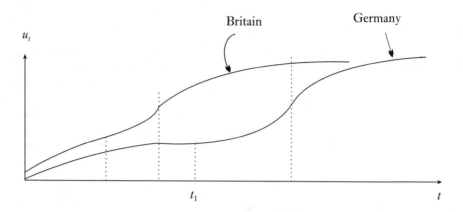

♦ **Figure 22.5**: Sequential divergence and convergence

them and possible changes in $k$ over time. The hypothesis to test is that for a pair of economies that have experienced mature growth, the time path of the per capita income differential between them should be an inverted U curve.

Chen, Lin, and Yang (1999) have tested the hypothesis against the data set of 15 OECD countries over the long period of 1870–1992, provided by Madison (1991) and Penn World Table 5.6 (Center for International Comparisons at the University of Pennsylvania, 1996). These countries are chosen because they all have experienced the stages of preindustrialization decelerating growth, take-off, and mature growth with a declining growth rate. The UK is taken to be the benchmark country for examining the sequential divergence and convergence phenomena, as the UK was the first country to experience a take-off. The data show that the differences in per capita real income between the UK and the other 14 countries are roughly inverted U curves.

Overall, the data set strongly supports the posited hypothesis: an inverted U relation exists for long-run per capita real income differentials between the UK and 13 out of 14 countries. It conclusively rejects the hypotheses of a monotonically increasing difference in per capita real income. Also, it conclusively rejects the hypothesis of a monotonically decreasing difference in per capita real income, except for Canada. The difference in per capita real income between the UK and Canada monotonically decreases over time because of missing data for divergence which occurred before 1879, the first year for which internationally comparable data are available.

Sala-i-Martin (1996) defines absolute β-convergence as the case in which poor economies tend to grow faster than rich ones. This concept relates to the Barro regression of average growth rate on the initial level of per capita real income. Since the focus of the Barro regression is average growth rates in a quite long period of time, it ignores possible sequential divergence and convergence.[6] The concept of convergence used in this chapter relates to Sala-i-Martin's σ-convergence, which occurs if the dispersion of real per capita GDP levels of a group of economies tends to decrease over time. His empirical work shows that there was neither σ-convergence nor absolute β-convergence in the cross-country distribution of world GDP between 1960 and 1990. His regression results show that the sample of OECD economies displays σ-convergence and so do the samples of regions within a country, such as the US, Japan, Germany, the UK, France, Italy, or Spain. Romer (1986) finds evidence for divergence from time series data are consistent with Chen, Lin, and Yang's results. It seems that the notion of σ-convergence is more relevant than the notion of β-convergence since we ultimately are concerned with differences in per capita real income between countries.

What differentiates new classical development and growth models from other endogenous growth models is that they make endogenous the level of specialization of individuals and the network size of division of labor. This feature substantiates Young's (1928, p. 539) insight that "the securing of increasing returns depends on the progressive division of labor." It also establishes a formal basis for his extension of Smith's famous proposition that not only does the division of labor depend on the extent of the market, "but the extent of the market also depends on the division of labor." In proposition 22.2 it was shown that as the division of labor evolves, the extent of the market will increase. Although the circular causation between the extent of the market and the level of division of labor in this dynamic general equilibrium model is similar to that in a new classical static general equilibrium model, co-movement of the extent of the market and network size of division of labor can take place in the absence of exogenous evolution of transaction conditions and other parameters in the dynamic model. In other words, the dynamic general equilibrium model has a higher degree of endogenization than the static general equilibrium model. The spirit of the model in this chapter is consistent with Young's insight that economic development is not only a process that involves increases in per capita real income, but also a process that is driven and characterized by the evolution of the network of division of labor.

The new classical growth model in this chapter is a dynamic version of the new classical trade model in chapters 5, 6, and 11, while the R&D-based models are dynamic versions of the DS and Ethier models in chapter 11. Hence, the differences between the new classical growth models and the R&D-based models are similar to those between the new classical trade models and the DS model. New classical growth models have endogenized individuals' levels of specialization, the degree of market integration, and the network size of division of labor. In the Romer model (1987, 1990) and Grossman and Helpman models (1989, 1990), the economy is always an integrated market and separate local markets never occur at equilibrium. There is an *ad hoc* "if and only if" relationship between an increase in investment and higher future productivity (investment fundamentalism). This, together with the notion of economies of scale, generates scale effects that are conclusively rejected by empirical evidence. We will investigate in chapter 25 why the *ad hoc* positive relationship between investment and future productivity does not capture the real driving force of economic development.

There are many different ways to specify a dynamic equilibrium model that can predict evolution in division of labor. For instance, a time lag between choosing the efficient hierarchical structure of transactions that determines transaction efficiency and choosing the efficient level of division of labor which depends on transaction efficiency can be used to explain the evolution of the division of labor and the hierarchical structure of cities and transactions, described in chapter 20. In chapter 24 we will construct a model that explains the evolution of the division of labor by a trade-off between economies of division of labor and costs in acquiring information on the efficient pattern of division of labor. In chapter 23, we will explain the evolution of the division of labor in terms of trade-offs between economies of specialized learning by doing, economies of complementarity, and transaction costs.

A common feature of all of the different methods for predicting the evolution of the division of labor is that more rapidly increasing diseconomies than economies of division of labor, as the level of division increases, are necessary to generate its gradual evolution.

The limitation of the method developed in this chapter is that it is not easy to apply to reasonably realistic asymmetric models. Symmetry is essential to keep this kind of dynamic general equilibrium model tractable. But symmetry cannot be preserved if the CES utility or production function are introduced into the model, since the decision problems for individuals producing new goods who must change occupation are asymmetric to those who do not change occupation. Hence, control theory does not work and dynamic programming is needed if the number of goods is an endogenous variable or if the parameters of tastes and of production and transaction conditions are not the same across goods in this kind of model. In chapter 23, we shall show that the algebra is cumbersome and results are very difficult to obtain even if dynamic programming is applied to asymmetric new classical growth models. In chapter 24, we will develop a new method based on the concept of Walrasian sequential equilibrium and show that it is easy to dynamize all static new classical models in this textbook by applying that approach.

If we introduce exogenous comparative advantages into the dynamic model, it can be shown that endogenous advantages may be used to offset exogenous disadvantages. Suppose, for instance, that person A is exogenously more productive than person B in producing good 1 at $t = 0$. However, if person B's level of specialization in producing good 1 is higher than person A's for a sufficiently long period of time, B's productivity of good 1 may be higher than A's. Hence, for this kind of dynamic model, in order to win in market competition it is much more important to get a person involved in a self-enforced evolutionary process than to rely on inherited genius. If a person overestimates the implications of her exogenous advantage, she may turn out to be a loser to an exogenously less capable person who can effectively get herself involved in a self-accelerated evolutionary process (via, for instance, a successful self-selling strategy or advertisement). In question 1 at the end of this chapter, you are asked to use new classical models to analyze a vicious circle between unemployment and endogenous disadvantage in accumulating professional human capital through learning by doing.

## ◆ Appendix 22.1: The Relationship between the Control Theory and Calculus of Variations

The intertemporal decision problem in (22.7) is equivalent to maximizing the following Lagrange function

$$F = ue^{-rt} + \alpha_i(l_i - \dot{L}_i) + \sum_j \alpha_j(l_j - \dot{L}_j) + \beta(1 - l_i - \sum_j l_j)$$

where $l_i = \dot{L}_i$, $l_j = \dot{L}_j$, and $u$ can be expressed as a function of $x_i^s$, $x_r^d$, $n$, $l_i$, $l_j$ using all constraints in (22.7), the symmetry, and equal prices of all goods. We have omitted the subscript of time for $x_i^s$, $x_r^d$, $n$, $u$, $\alpha_i$, $l_i$, $\beta$, $L_i$, $\beta$, $\alpha_j$, $\dot{L}_j$. $\alpha_i$ and $\alpha_j$ are the Lagrange multipliers for labor allocated to produce traded goods i and nontraded goods j, respectively. $\beta$ is the Lagrange multiplier for the labor endowment constraint. Since $l_s$ ($s = i, j$) may discontinuously jump between the interior and corner values, $F$ may not be differentiable with respect to $\dot{L}_s$, so that the calculus of variations, which requires continuous, $\dot{L}_s$ may not be applicable. In order to avoid this trouble, we specify a Hamiltonian function

$$H = u + \gamma_i l_I + \Sigma_j \gamma_j l_j + \lambda (1 - l_I - \Sigma_j l_j)$$

which does not directly contain $\dot{L}_s$, though $l_s = \dot{L}_s$. Here, $\lambda$ and $\gamma_s$ are dynamic shadow prices of labor endowment and labor allocated to the production of good s, respectively. They are called *costate variables* in the control theory. $l_s$, $n$, $x_i^s$, and $x_r^d$ are called *control variables*. $\beta = \lambda e^{-rt}$, $\alpha_s = \gamma_s e^{-rt}$ are the corresponding *discounted shadow prices*. Suppose that the control variables do not take on corner values. Then, the application of the Euler equation to the Lagrange function $F$ generates a set of the first-order conditions in terms of $H$:

$\partial F / \partial \alpha_s = d[\partial F / \partial(d\alpha_s/dt)]/dt = 0$, which is equivalent to (22.12a): $\partial H / \partial \gamma_{st} = dL_{st}/dt$,

$\partial F / \partial L_s = d(\partial F / \partial \dot{L}_s)/dt$, which is equivalent to (22.12b): $\partial H / \partial L_s = r\gamma_s - d\gamma_s/dt$,

$\partial F / \partial n = d[\partial F / \partial(dn/dt)]/dt = 0$, which is equivalent to (22.12c) (i): $\partial H / \partial n_t = 0$, for $n_t \in (1, m)$.

If the corner solutions are considered, then (ii) and (iii) in (22.12c) will be included in a general condition for maximizing $F$ or $H$ with respect to $n$. Maximization of $F$ with respect to $l_s$ generates the same first-order condition for the maximization of $H$ with respect to $l_s$ which is (22.12d): (i) $l_{st} = 1$ if $\gamma_{st} > \lambda_t$; (ii) $l_{st} \in (0, 1)$ if $\gamma_{st} = \lambda_t$; (iii) $l_{st} = 0$ if $\gamma_{st} < \lambda_t$. Maximization of $F$ with respect to $\alpha_s$ and $\beta$ is equivalent to the maximization of $H$ with respect to $\gamma_s$ and $\lambda$, which yield the constraint in (22.12e), $l_{it} + \Sigma_{j \in J} l_{jt} = 1$ and the definitions $l_s = \dot{L}_s$. Hence, by using $H$ instead of $F$, we can get the first-order condition in (22.12), while avoiding trouble caused by discontinuous jumps of control variables between corner and interior solutions.

It is obvious that the control theory is equivalent to the Euler equation if control variables do not discontinuously jump between corner and interior solutions. But the Euler equation is more straightforward. Hence, for the neoclassical endogenous growth models in chapter 21, the Euler equation is better than the control theory. But the Euler equation does not work for new classical endogenous growth models.

## Key Terms and Review

Endogenous vs. exogenous evolution of division of labor.
The difference between new classical endogenous growth models and neoclassical endogenous growth models (R&D-based models, AK models).
The relationship between the YB model and the Young theorem.
The difference between specialized learning by doing through division of labor in new classical growth models and learning by doing in neoclassical endogenous growth models.
Preindustrialization growth, smooth take-off, big-push industrialization, mature growth, growth trap.
Implications of compounded effects of learning by doing over time, and increasingly more specialized learning by doing.
Trade-offs between economies of specialized learning by doing, transaction costs, current and future consumption
Implications of transaction conditions for evolution of division of labor.
The relationship between evolution of the number of traded goods and evolution of the network size of division of labor.
Implicit investment that relates to transaction costs and economies of specialized learning by doing.
The difference between investment in neoclassical growth models and that in new classical growth models.
The advantage of the analysis of dynamics and comparative dynamics of general equilibrium over comparative statics analysis of static equilibrium.

Function of long-run contracts in reducing endogenous transaction costs.
Concurrent evolution of division of labor and income share of transaction costs.
Difference between growth phenomena and development phenomena.
State variable, control variable, and how one can be distinguished from the other.
Hamiltonian function, costate variable, and dynamic shadow price.
First-order conditions for the control problem.
The difference between dynamic marginal analysis and dynamic inframarginal analysis.
The difference between dynamics and comparative dynamics of dynamic equilibrium.
Theories of convergence, divergence, and sequential divergence and convergence.
Four types of scale effect and why they are rejected by empirical evidence.
Function of the market in sorting out the efficient speed of accumulation of human capital, and the efficient patterns of evolution of the network size of division of labor and economic growth.

## Further Reading

*Control theory*: Seierstad and Sydsater (1987), Barro and Sala-i-Martin (1995, appendix), Chow (1975); *neoclassical growth models*: Barro (1991), Barro and Sala-i-Martin (1992, 1995), Rebelo (1991), Solow (1956); *R&D-based models and other endogenous growth models*: Judd (1985), Lucas (1988, 1993), Romer (1986, 1987, 1990), Grossman and Helpman (1989, 1990, 1991), Aghion and Howitt (1992), Alwyn Young (1993); *new classical growth models*: Borland and Yang (1995), Yang and Y.-K. Ng (1993, chs. 7, 16), Yang and Borland (1991a,b), Wen (1997), Zhang (1997); *structural changes and development economics*: Lewis (1955), Fei and Ranis (1964), Stiglitz (1986), Chenery (1979), Kaldor (1967); *big-push industrialization*: Rosenstein-Rodan (1943), Fleming (1955), Nurkse (1953), Scitovsky (1954), Myrdal (1957), Hirschman (1958), Murphy, Shleifer, and Vishny (1989a); *growth and endogenous specialization*: Smith (1776), Allyn Young (1928), Schultz (1993), Lucas (1993), Rosen (1983), Tamura (1991, 1992); *surveys of evolutionary economics*: Nelson (1995), Kirzner (1997), Conlisk (1996); *learning by doing*: Stoke (1991), Alwyn Young (1993), Arrow (1962); *the puzzle of scale effect*: Chen, Lin, and Yang (1999), Jones (1995a,b, 1996), Bernard and Jones (1996), Young (1998), Segerstrom (1998); *the debate on convergence*: Chen, Lin, and Yang (1999), Baumol (1996), Delong (1988), Dowrick and Nguyen (1989), Sala-i-Martin (1996), Quah (1993, 1996), Galor (1996), Mankiw, Romer, and Weil (1992).

## QUESTIONS

1   Use the new classical model in this chapter to analyze the vicious circle between unemployment and disadvantage in accumulating human capital through learning by doing. Suggest a way in which the market can avoid this vicious circle through a market for loans and some retraining businesses which can make money by providing professional learning-by-doing opportunities for the unemployed who may borrow money to buy this kind of opportunity.

2   Analyze the function of division of labor in enhancing the capacity of society to accumulate knowledge. Use the tendency of divergence between professional languages documented in various professional dictionaries to explain how the market uses division of labor to speed up knowledge accumulation.

3   What are the implications of the difference between the notion of economies of scale and the concept of economies of division of labor for the explanatory power of the neoclassical endogenous growth models in the previous chapter and the new classical growth model in this chapter?

4   Analyze the equivalence between learning by engaging in many activities over a long time and learning by doing in one activity within a short period of time. If learning by doing through time and social learning by doing through division of labor occur simultaneously, what is the implication for society's capacity to acquire technical knowledge? What are the growth implications of these two types of learning by doing, compounded by evolution of division of labor?

5   Use some phenomena that you can observe from your daily experience to verify the evolution of division of labor. You may also find such phenomena discussed by Marshall (1890), Allyn Young (1928), Braudel (1984), Chandler (1990), Rostow (1960), North (1981), Mokyr (1990, 1993) and other economic history books.

6   Apply the model in this chapter to explain why division of labor evolved more quickly in Britain than in Germany in the eighteenth century and why division of labor evolved more quickly in Japan than in China at the end of the nineteenth century and in the twentieth century.

7   Explain why the following view might be misleading. Division of labor is determined by the extent of the market which is the size of the economy. Use the dynamic general equilibrium model in this chapter to formalize Allyn Young's idea that the extent of the market and the level of division of labor are interdependent from a dynamic general equilibrium viewpoint. They should be simultaneously determined by a dynamic mechanism that can generate spontaneous evolution of division of labor.

8   North (1986) has found empirical evidence of a positive correlation between evolution of the income share of the transaction sector and economic development from the data set of the US in 1870–1970. Find other ways to test the theory in this chapter against empirical observations. For instance, you may test concurrent evolution of division of labor, productivity, and the extent of endogenous comparative advantage.

9   Why can't neoclassical growth models explain evolution of the income share of transaction costs and evolution of individuals' levels of specialization?

# EXERCISES

1   Replace the utility function in example 22.1 with the CES utility function $u_t = [(x_t + kx_t^d)^\rho + (y_t + ky_t^d)^\rho]^{\frac{1}{\rho}}$. Solve for dynamic general equilibrium and its comparative dynamics and analyze the relationship between endogenous evolution of division of labor and emergence of new goods and related technology. Compare the model with neoclassical R&D-based endogenous growth models, studied in chapter 21, and discuss the difference in driving mechanism between the new classical model and neoclassical R&D-based models.

2   Wen, 1997: Assume that in the model in this chapter, the transaction efficiency coefficient $K_t = 1 - 1/\theta_t mx_{it}^s + \beta)$, where $m = M$ is the number of goods as well as the population size and $\theta mx_t^s$ is total sales tax revenue collected by the government and used to develop transaction infrastructure. $\beta = 1/(1 - K_0)$ is a constant related to the lower bound of transaction efficiency $K_0$ in the absence of expenditure on infrastructure. $\theta$ is a tax rate, which is a decision variable of the benevolent government which maximizes per capita total discounted utility over an infinite horizon. Because of symmetry, the equilibrium prices of all traded goods at each point in time are equal, so that the budget constraint at each point in time is $(1 - \theta_t)x_{it}^s = \sum_{r \in R} x_{rt}^d$. Work out the conditions for dynamic general equilibrium (analytical expressions for the equilibrium level of division of labor $n_t$ cannot be obtained) and then analyze the dynamics and comparative dynamics of general equilibrium.

3   Zhang, 1997: Consider the economy specified in section 22.2. The government taxes sale of goods. Hence, the budget constraint for each individual selling good i is the same as in the Wen model. But transaction conditions are characterized by $K = (k/n_i)s^b$, where $b > 0$ and $s$ is the tax rate. Solve the dynamic general equilibrium and analyze the effect of fiscal policy $s$ on the evolution of division of labor and economic development. According to Zhang, many macroeconomic models can be worked out to predict the effects of monetary and fiscal policies on aggregate variables which are determined by network size of division of labor, if the effects of the policies on $n$ via their effects on transaction conditions ($K$) can be appropriately specified. Try developing some new classical macroeconomic models based on this idea.

# Notes

1   This discussion of the market structure is relevant only in those cases in which trade will occur (i.e., obviously in autarky structure F could not arise).
2   If the returns to specialization, preference, and transaction cost parameters differ across goods, then the equilibrium market structure in the early stages may be A rather than F. The reason is that trading only those goods with a greater degree of increasing returns, lower transaction costs, or more desirability in the early periods is more efficient than trading other goods. However, introducing *ex ante* differences in these parameters across goods removes the symmetry between decision problems so that the dynamic model becomes intractable.
3   Judd (1985), Romer (1990), Grossman and Helpman (1990, 1991), and Aghion and Howitt (1992), among others, are along these lines.
4   According to C. Jones (1995a,b) and Barro and Sala-i-Martin (1995), the Romer model (1987), the Rebelo model (1991), the Barro model (1991), and the Benhabib and Joranovic model (1991) can be considered AK models since their reduced forms are the same as that of the AK model.
5   The relationship between interpersonal loans and division of labor will be investigated in chapter 25.
6   Quah (1993) argued that Barro regressions, using a negative coefficient on the initial level of per capita real income to infer convergence, have a spurious effect which turns out to be plagued by Galton's fallacy of regression towards the mean. Quah proposes a direct test on the cross-section distribution of output per worker over time using the four- or five-state fractile Markov chain models, and provides the evidence against the convergence.

# chapter 23

# CONCURRENT ENDOGENOUS EVOLUTION IN DIVISION OF LABOR, IN THE NUMBER OF GOODS, AND IN THE INSTITUTION OF THE FIRM

## ◆ 23.1 How Can We Simultaneously Endogenize Evolution in Division of Labor and in the Number of Producer Goods?

The concurrent evolution of specialization and variety of consumer goods which is modeled in chapter 11, and the concurrent evolution of specialization, variety of producer goods, and the institution of the firm modeled in chapters 18 and 19, are exogenous because they cannot occur in the absence of exogenous evolution of transaction efficiency. On the other hand, the endogenous evolution of the division of labor and productivity modeled in chapter 22 does not involve the evolution of product diversity and the institution of the firm because of the restriction to the Cobb–Douglas utility and production functions and the absence of producer goods in that model. A natural conjecture is that introduction of the CES production function and producer goods into the YB model presented in chapter 22 will allow concurrently endogenous evolution of specialization, product diversity, and the institution of the firm to be predicted. This chapter shall verify this conjecture.

The difference between the model examined here and the Yang–Borland (YB) model is similar to the difference between the Judd model (1985), which endogenizes the evolution of the number of consumer goods by specifying a CES utility function, and the Romer model (1990), which endogenizes the evolution of the number of producer goods by specifying a CES production function. The difference between our models and theirs is that their models do not endogenize the level of specialization and the emergence of firms while our models do.

The dynamic equilibrium model presented in this chapter can be used to explain how the endogenous evolution of the division of labor can bring forth new production factors and related new technology that improves productivity, and to explain how the evolution of the institution of the firm can facilitate this process. In this chapter we emphasize the role of specialization in speeding up learning by doing, and the distinction between learning by doing with and without the division of labor.

For the YB dynamic equilibrium model in chapter 22 the calculus of variations cannot be used to solve for equilibrium and the control theory is necessary for a so-called "bang-bang control problem" which is based on corner solutions. However, that approach is extremely difficult to apply to a model with a CES production function and the producer goods which can be used for the endogenization of the number of producer goods. It is impossible to obtain analytical results if the CES function or asymmetry is introduced into the dynamic model. The asymmetry between the decisions of specialist producers of consumer and intermediate goods is however, unavoidable as producer goods are introduced. In this chapter, this technical problem is solved by applying dynamic programming instead of the control theory. It is the ability of dynamic programming to tackle problems with discrete decision variables in a dynamic equilibrium model based on corner solutions that contributes to the approach's success. Dynamic programming techniques are more powerful than the control theory, which is more powerful than the calculus of variations, in handling the decision problem with complex combinatorics, which is a feature of endogenous specialization. However, this kind of dynamic general equilibrium model is still too complicated to manage. Its solution involves the analytical solution of dynamic programming, which does not yet have a well-developed supporting mathematical theory. Hence, the applicability of the approach developed in this chapter is in question until more powerful mathematical tools are developed. The next chapter will introduce a more applicable approach than can be used to extend all static new classical models in this volume to dynamic general equilibrium models very easily.

In section 23.2 we set out the dynamic general equilibrium model. Section 23.3 solves for the dynamic general equilibrium that may generate concurrent endogenous evolution in division of labor and in the number of producer goods. In section 23.4 we investigate the function of the evolution of the institution of the firm in facilitating evolution in division of labor and the emergence of new technology.

---

### Questions to Ask Yourself when Reading this Chapter

♦ What is endogenous technical progress that is generated by spontaneous evolution of division of labor and the institution of the firm?

♦ What is the difference between endogenous technical progress driven by evolution of division of labor and endogenous technical progress in the R&D-based models?

♦ What are the implications of the evolution of the institution of the firm for endogenous technical progress?

## ◆ 23.2 A Dynamic Equilibrium Model with Learning by Doing and an Endogenous Number of Producer Goods

### Example 23.1: the Borland–Yang model (1995)

We consider a finite horizon (two-period) economy with a continuum of producer-consumers of mass $M$. There is a single consumer good which has as inputs labor and either one or two intermediate goods. Individuals can self-provide any goods, or alternatively can purchase them in the market. The self-provided amounts of the consumer good and of the two intermediate goods in period $t$ are denoted respectively $z_t$, $x_t$, and $y_t$. The respective amounts of good z sold and purchased in period $t$ are $z_t s$ and $z_t^d$, those of good x are $x_t^s$ and $x_t^d$, and those of y are $y_t^s$ and $y_t^d$. The variable transaction efficiency coefficient for the consumer good is $k$ so that $kz_t^d$ is the amount available for consumption after purchasing $z_t^d$. The total amount of a good consumed is therefore $z_t + kz_t^d$. The variable transaction efficiency coefficient for an intermediate good is $s$ so that $sx_t^d$ or $sy_t^d$ is the amount available of the intermediate good after its purchase. The total amount of an intermediate good available is therefore $x_t + sx_t^d$ or $y_t + sy_t^d$. In addition, it is assumed that a fixed cost, $c$, is incurred in the period in which an individual first engages in trade. This fixed cost coefficient can be interpreted as the cost of creating a new market: for example, the investment cost of the facilities and instruments that are necessary to implement trade.[1] The utility function in period $t$ for any individual is therefore assumed to be equal to the amount of good z consumed net of the fixed transaction cost.

$$u_t = z_t + kz_t^d - c \tag{23.1}$$

where $c = 0$ if an individual has either engaged in trade prior to period $t$ or has never engaged in trade up to and including period $t$, and $c > 0$ if an individual engages in trade for the first time in period $t$.

As in chapter 22, it is assumed that all trade in this economy is mediated through contracts signed in futures and spot markets that operate in period 1. Assume further that the futures market horizon and an individual's decision horizon are for two periods. The objective function for an individual's decision problem is therefore total discounted utility, given by

$$U = u_1 + \delta u_2 \tag{23.2}$$

where $U$ is the total discounted utility and $\delta \in (0, 1)$ is the discount factor.

The system of production of an individual is assumed to exhibit learning by doing and increasing returns to specialization:

$$z_t + z_t^s = \beta^\alpha \gamma_z^{\alpha a}, \qquad x_t + x_t^s = \gamma_x^a, \tag{23.3}$$

$$y_t + y_t^s = \gamma_y^a, \qquad \alpha a > 1, \qquad a > 1$$

$$\beta \equiv [(x_t + sx_t^d)^\rho + (y_t + sy_t^d)^\rho]^{1/\rho} \text{ and } \gamma_1 \equiv L_{it}l_{it}$$

$$l_{zt} + l_{xt} + l_{yt} = 1, \qquad l_{it} \in [0, 1], \qquad L_{it} = L_{it} + l_{it-1}$$

where $l_{it}$ is a person's level of specialization in producing good i as well as her labor allocated to the production of good i in period $t$, and $L_{it}$ is the labor accumulated in producing good i prior to period $t$ which represents the level of experience or human capital accumulated in producing good i before period $t$. The production function for z is a Cobb–Douglas function of a composite intermediate input $\beta$ and a composite labor input $\gamma_z$. The elasticity of output with respect to the composite intermediate input is $\alpha \in (0, 1)$, and that with respect to current and accumulated labor is $\alpha a$. The composite intermediate input is produced using a CES production function with a variety of inputs; the elasticity of substitution between the intermediate goods is $1/(1 - \rho)$. Since the elasticity of substitution and degree of economies of complementarity between the intermediate goods are inversely related, $1/\rho$ can therefore be interpreted as the degree of economies of complementarity between producer goods. Current labor input in (23.3) is necessary for a person to produce a positive output for a good. The human capital in each previous period contributes to productivity, but is not a necessity individually for a positive output level of a good in period $t$.

This system of production displays economies of specialization since the total factor productivity of z, $(z_t + z_t^s)/\beta^\alpha \gamma_z^{1-\alpha}$ increases with the level of specialization in producing z, $l_z$, and the labor productivity of x and y increases with the level of specialization. The parameter $a$ represents the degree of economies of specialization. An identical value of $a$ across the three goods is assumed to simplify the algebra at the cost of generality. If $a$ differs across goods, then individuals' dynamic decisions and the dynamic equilibrium cannot be solved analytically, so that the comparative dynamics which generate the main results in this chapter cannot be identified. It is assumed that the total available working time for an individual in period $t$ is equal to 1 and that learning by doing and economies of specialization are specific to each individual and to each production activity.

In order to solve for an equilibrium in this dynamic model, it is necessary to specify initial values for the state variables $L_{it}$. It is assumed that

$$L_{i1} = 1, \, i = z, x, y \tag{23.4}$$

so that individual is able to produce a positive amount of each good in period 1, and begins with an equal endowment of human capital for undertaking each activity. Finally, it is assumed that no explicit savings and lending occur in this model.

## ◆ 23.3 Dynamic Equilibrium Level of Specialization and Input Variety

As in chapter 22, the assumption that all trade is determined in spot and futures markets that operate in period $t = 1$ is sufficient to ensure that a Walrasian regime prevails in period 1. Hence any dynamic equilibrium will be characterized by a set of market clearing conditions and a set of utility equalization conditions in a period in which trade occurs. Following the approach for proving lemma 8.1, appendix 23.1 (below) establishes lemma 23.1

**Lemma 23.1:** In any period, an individual does not buy and produce the same good. She self-provides the consumer good if she sells it, and does not self-provide any intermediate good if she does self-provide the consumer good. She sells at most one good although she may produce several goods.

Taking this lemma into account, there are only eight corner solutions for the eight configurations and six corner equilibria for the six market structures, depicted in figure 23.1, that need to be considered.

Three configurations A, A', and B, which are also structures, are autarky with $x^s = y^s - z^s = x^d = y^d = z^d = 0$. for configuration A the quantities traded of all goods are zero, $y = 0$ and $x, z > 0$ so that each individual self-provides a single intermediate good which is an input along with labor in production of the consumer good. Configuration A' is symmetric with configuration A, with $x = 0$ and $y, z > 0$. For configuration B, the quantities traded of all goods are zero, but $x, y, z > 0$. Panel (a) in figure 23.1 depicts the three autarchic configurations. A circle denotes a configuration chosen by a person; dots denote a process that transforms producer goods into consumer goods; and arrows denote the flow of goods.

The other five configurations, $(z/x)$, $(z/y)$, $(z/xy)$, $(x/z)$ and $(y/z)$, are associated with specialization. If a person chooses configuration $(z/x)$, she sells and self-provides z and buys x; she does not buy z and y and does not produce x and y. Configuration $(z/y)$ is symmetric to $(z/x)$. If a person chooses configuration $(x/z)$, she sells x and buys z; she does not buy x and y and does not produce y and z. Configuration $(y/z)$ is symmetric to $(x/z)$. If a person chooses configuration $(z/xy)$, she sells and self-provides z and buys x and y; she does not buy z and does not produce x and y.

Given these configurations, there are three market structures. Structure C, depicted in panel (b) of figure 23.1, consists of a division of the $M$ individuals between configurations $(x/z)$ and $(z/x)$. Structure C', symmetric to structure C, consists of $(z/y)$ and $(y/z)$. Structure C' can be obtained by replacing the letter x with the letter y in panel (b). Structure D, depicted in panel (c), consists of a division of the $M$ individuals between configurations $(z/xy)$, $(x/z)$, and $(y/z)$.

An individual's dynamic decision is defined as a choice from all feasible sequences of configurations over the two periods and a sequence of values of the quantities consumed, produced, and traded of goods over the two periods which are consistent with the chosen sequence of configurations. The intertemporal decision yields an individual's dynamic demand and supply functions and dynamic indirect utility function, which depend on the time path of the relative price. Note that the relative price is relevant only if trade occurs in the period concerned.

There is a formidable technical problem in solving for the equilibrium of this model. If equilibrium involves the evolution in division of labor, then each individual, in autarky, must spend more time in the activity that will be her professional occupation in future. This consideration generates transcendent equations as the first-order conditions for her dynamic optimal decision. Hence, her decision problem and therefore the dynamic equilibrium cannot be solved analytically. In order to get around this technical difficulty, we will solve the dynamic equilibrium in two steps. First, the dynamic equilibrium is solved under the following assumption A1. Then the effect of the relaxation of assumption A1 on the dynamic equilibrium is analyzed.

**Assumption A1:** In period 1, where an individual's production decision involves allocating labor between a number of production activities, an individual will choose the type of activities optimally with reference to her future behavior, but will choose the levels of those activities without reference to future behavior.

Since we are considering a two-period model, the assumption of partial myopia will affect the characterization of an individual's decision problem only in the initial period;

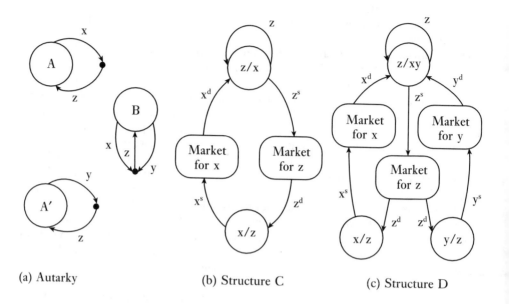

(a) Autarky                    (b) Structure C                    (c) Structure D

♦ **Figure 23.1:** Market structures without firms

optimal decisions in the terminal period are consistent with full dynamic optimization. As will be discussed in the next section, it is also possible to identify exactly those sequences of production and trade decisions (where an individual will allocate her labor between a number of activities) for which our solution method constrains total discounted utility below its optimal value, and hence to identify the direction of bias in the characterization of the dynamic equilibrium caused by assumption A1. The incorporation of assumption A1 is then justified by the increase in tractability, which is achieved without limiting our understanding of the factors which determine the dynamic equilibrium.

With assumption A1, a person's dynamic decision problem can be divided into two parts. The first part involves solving a static decision problem for a given configuration and given prices. The second part is to solve a dynamic programming problem which involves maximizing total discounted utility with respect to configuration sequences.

According to the Bellman optimality principle, a backward decision rule is followed by individuals. Hence, an individual's optimal decision in each period is a function of the state of human capital which is determined by previous decisions. And hence, equilibrium in each period can be defined as dependent solely on the state of human capital. Therefore, we can solve for equilibrium in each period by following a backward approach as individuals solve for their decisions by following the backward decision rule.

Since there are six possible corner equilibria in configurations A, A′, B, and market structures C, C′, and D, there are many possible sequences of corner equilibria over the two periods. A *dynamic equilibrium* is defined by the sequence of corner equilibria over the two periods that is consistent with all individuals' dynamic decisions based on price taking behavior.

With assumption A1, we can first solve for the corner solutions for all configurations as functions of the relative prices and the level of human capital. Then we establish the market clearing and utility equalization conditions for all market structures and solve for the relative prices and the relative numbers of different specialists in a period as functions of the level of human capital. Using the relative prices, each person can find her utility for different configurations in each period, and total discounted utility for different configuration sequences over the two periods. Each person can thus maximize her total discounted utility with respect to configuration sequence, using dynamic programming techniques. The dynamic equilibrium is then identified by using the solutions to the individual dynamic decision problems.

The optimum decision for configuration A in period $t$ is

$$l_{xt} = l_{zt} = 0.5, \qquad u_t(A) = (L_{xt}L_{zt}/4)^{\alpha a} \tag{23.5}$$

where $u_t(A)$ is the per capita real income, a function of human capital $L_{it}$, when an individual chooses configuration A in period $t$. The per capita real income for configuration A' is symmetric to that for A, given by

$$u_t(A') = (L_{yt}L_{zt}/4)^{\alpha a}. \tag{23.6}$$

The optimum decision for configuration B in period $t$ is

$$l_{xt} = 0.5 L_{yt}^{\ b}/(L_{xt}^{\ b} + L_{yt}^{\ b}), \qquad l_{yt} = 0.5\, L_{xt}^{\ b}/(L_{xt}^{\ b} + L_{yt}^{\ b}), \qquad l_{zt} = 1/2 \tag{23.7}$$

$$u_t(B) = (L_{xt}L_{yt}L_{xt}/4)^{\alpha a}(L_{xt}^{\ b} + Ly_t^{\ b})^{a(1-\rho a)/\rho}, \qquad b \equiv \rho a/(\rho a - 1).$$

Next, we consider market structure C which comprises configurations (z/x) and (x/z). The optimum decision in period $t$ for configuration (z/x), given the prices and human capital in period $t$, is

$$z_t^s = \alpha^{1/(1-\alpha)}(sL_{zt}^{\ a}/p_t)\alpha/(1 - \alpha), \qquad z_t = (1 - \alpha)(\alpha sL_{zt}^{\ a}/p_t)^{\alpha/(1-\alpha)} \tag{23.8}$$

$$p_t x_t^d = z_t^s, \qquad u_t(z/x) = z_t - c.$$

where $p_t$ is the price of x in terms of z in period $t$. The parameter $c$ is positive if a person engages in trade for the first time in this period, and is zero otherwise.

For configuration (x/z), we have

$$l_{xt} = 1, \qquad x_t^s = L_{xt}^{\ a}, \qquad z_t^d = p_t L_{xt}^{\ a}, \qquad u_t\,(x/z) = kp_t L_{xt}^{\ a} - c. \tag{23.9}$$

The corner equilibrium in market structure C is determined by the market clearing condition and utility equalization condition in period $t$ as

$$p_t = Q(sL_{zt}^{\ a})^{\alpha}(kL_{xt}^{\ a})^{\alpha-1} \qquad M_{zx} = z^s/z^d \tag{23.10}$$

$$u_t(C) - Q(sk)^{\alpha}(L_{xt}L_{zt})^{\alpha a} - c$$

where $Q \equiv \alpha^{\alpha}(1 - \alpha)^{1-\alpha}$, $u_t(C)$ is the per capita real income in market structure C, $L_{xt}$ is the human capital of a person choosing configuration (x/z), and $L_{zt}$ is the human capital of an individual choosing configuration (z/x) in period $t$. $M_{xz}$ is the relative number of individuals choosing configuration (x/z) to those choosing (z/x), and $z^s$ and $z^d$ are given in (23.8), (23.9), and the corner equilibrium value of $p_t$.

The corner equilibrium for structure C' in period $t$ is given by

$$q_t = Q(sL_{zt}^a)^\alpha(kL_{yt}^a)^{\alpha-1}, \qquad u_t(C') = Q(sk)^\alpha(L_{yt}L_{zt})^{\alpha a} - c \qquad (23.11)$$

where $q_t$ is the corner equilibrium price of good y in terms of z in period $t$. $u_t(C')$ is the per capita real income in market structure C', $L_{yt}$ is the human capital of a person choosing configuration (y/z), and $L_{zt}$ is the human capital of a person choosing configuration (z/y).

Following the two-step procedure for solving for the corner equilibrium in structure C, we can also solve for the corner equilibrium in structure D in period $t$ as a function of the level of human capital. The corner equilibrium is given by

$$p_t = Q(sL_{zt}^a/2)^\alpha(L_{xt}^{\alpha\rho} + L_{yt}^{\alpha\rho})^{\alpha/\rho}k^{\alpha-1}L_{xt}^{-a}, \qquad (23.12)$$

$$q_t = (L_{xt}/L_{yt})^a p_t, \qquad u_t(D) = Q(ksL_{zt}^a/2)^\alpha(L_{xt}^{\alpha\rho} + L_{yt}^{\alpha\rho})^{\alpha/\rho} - c$$

where $u_t(D)$ is the per capita real income in market structure D, $L_{xt}$ is the human capital of a person choosing configuration (x/z), $L_{yt}$ is the human capital of a person choosing configuration (y/z), and $L_{zt}$ is the human capital of a person choosing configuration (z/xy).

(23.5)–(23.12) give the optimum decisions and corresponding pay-offs for all configurations as functions of the level of human capital which in turn depends upon individuals' decisions on configuration sequences. With this information, each person can solve a dynamic programming problem in order to find her optimum sequential decision over the two periods. In each period, an individual can choose one out of A, A', B, (x/z), (y/z), (z/x), (z/y), and (z/xy).

The dynamic programming problem is specified as follows. The objective function is specified in (23.2), where the value of $u_t$ is given by (23.5) or (23.6) if configuration A or A' is chosen; given by (23.7) if configuration B is chosen; given by (23.10) if configurations (x/z) and (z/x) are chosen; given by (23.11) if configurations (y/z) and (z/y) are chosen; given by (23.12) if (z/xy), (x/z), and (y/z) are chosen in period $t$. As all values of quantities consumed, produced, and traded are solved for in (23.5)–(23.12), an individual can solve a dynamic programming problem by maximizing $U$ with respect to configuration sequences over the two periods.

There are $8^2 = 64$ patterns of possible configuration sequences over the two periods for an individual's dynamic decision problem. However, since it has been shown that all configurations in the same market structure generate the same real income, the distinction between configurations within the same market structure may be ignored, such as between (z/xy), (x/z), and (y/z) in market structure D, as well as between symmetric configurations and market structures such as A and A'. Taking this symmetry into account there are only $4^2 = 16$ distinct configuration sequences. Signifying the order of configurations chosen over the two periods by the order of the letters, the 16 patterns are AA, AB, AC, AD, BB, BA, BC, BD, CC, CA, CB, CD, DD, DA, DB, and DC, where, for example, AA denotes that an individual chooses autarky producing the consumption good with a single intermediate good in each period, and AD denotes that an individual chooses configuration A in period 1 and a constituent configuration of structure D, (x/z), (y/z), or (z/xy) in period 2.

With the information on the equilibrium relative price and real income for the different configurations, a solution is derived for each individual's dynamic programming problem in appendix 23 (below). The solution to the dynamic programming problem consists of one out of the 16 possible configuration sequences and the quantities consumed, produced, and traded for this configuration sequence. All individuals' optimal configuration sequences are either the same or symmetric, due to the symmetry of the model. Hence, the optimal sequence is the dynamic equilibrium sequence. The dynamic equilibrium relative prices of the goods and relative numbers of different specialists are given by (23.10), (23.11), and (23.12) if trade occurs. The dynamic equilibrium, given in proposition 23.1, is dependent on parameters $a$, $\alpha$, $\rho$, $c$, $r$.

As already described, individuals' labor allocation decisions within any configuration are made without reference to future behavior; however it should be emphasized that individuals' choice of configurations are assumed to be made taking into account future behavior. For example, in sequence DD if an individual chooses $(x/z)$ in period 2, that individual will choose the same configuration instead of $(z/x)$ in period 1, as this will allow them to exploit economies of specialized learning by doing. In sequence AD if an individual chooses $(x/z)$ in period 2, that individual will choose A instead of $A'$ in period 1, as this will allow the individual to accumulate human capital in period 1 in producing x, which is her professional activity in period 2.

It is shown in appendix 23.2 that since a market structure where each individual specializes in a single production activity avoids the trade-off between economies of complementarity and specialization, which is present in autarky, both intermediate goods are always produced in that market structure with specialization; hence a sequence of configurations with market structure C cannot constitute a dynamic equilibrium. It is also the case that the economy will not evolve from specialization to autarky. In the absence of transaction costs the economy would move immediately to specialization, since this allows economies of specialized learning by doing to be fully exploited; hence if the economies of specialization are sufficient to outweigh the transaction costs incurred through trade in period 1, specialization in production must also be optimal in period 2. A comparison of the remaining sequences of market structures in appendix 23.2 yields proposition 23.1.

**Proposition 23.1:** If transaction efficiency is sufficiently high the economy will move immediately to a market structure with the division of labor and two producer goods (DD is dynamic equilibrium). If transaction efficiency is sufficiently small, the economy remains in autarky forever with self-production of a single producer good if economies of specialization outweigh economies of complementarity (AA is dynamic equilibrium), or with self-production of two producer goods if economies of complementarity outweigh economies of specialization (BB is dynamic equilibrium). If transaction efficiency is at an intermediate level, the dynamic equilibrium involves evolution of the division of labor from autarky. This evolution involves an increase in the number of producer goods if economies of complementarity are not too large relative to economies of specialization (AD is dynamic equilibrium); otherwise this evolution involves no expansion in the range of producer goods used in production (BD is dynamic equilibrium). A dynamic equilibrium never involves structure C or devolution of the division of labor.

The dynamic equilibrium AD is most interesting due to its empirical implications. In reality, we can observe a gradual evolution of the division of labor, accompanied by an increase in the variety of available producer goods and progress in productivity. The concurrence of the evolution of the division of labor, the increase in the variety of available producer goods, and productivity progress is regarded as "technical progress." However, the economic mechanism behind "technical progress" is unclear to economists. Some economists, such as Solow (1956), attribute technical progress to exogenous factors that economics cannot explain. The model here provides an economic mechanism that can generate the concurrence of several phenomena which looks like technical progress. The intuition behind the dynamic equilibrium AD is as follows. It is better to shift to the division of labor in a later period because the fixed cost for individuals to shift to the division of labor from autarky is not too small, individuals prefer current consumption, and there is learning by doing. On the other hand, the economy will not stay in autarky forever, since the fixed transaction cost is also not too large and learning by doing has a positive effect on productivity. In autarky in period 1, the forgone economies of specialization outweigh the benefits from economies of complementarity between producer goods if an individual divides her limited time between three activities. Hence, she produces only one producer good in autarky.[2] As individuals shift to the division of labor in period 2, the level of specialization of each person can be increased, and in the meantime the variety of available producer goods used by each producer of the final good can be increased as individuals specialize in producing different goods. As in the model in chapter 22, such a gradual evolution of the division of labor and the variety of producer goods can occur even in the absence of any exogenous changes in values of the parameters.[3]

A further interesting implication of proposition 23.1 is that the emergence of professional education or professional research can be endogenized. If we interpret good x as knowledge about the production of good z, then good x is a special intermediate input in producing good z. An individual can acquire the knowledge by self-learning. In this self-education case, on-the-job training is adopted. Alternatively, a person may buy good x from the market; for instance, she buys professional education from a university. Suppose further that all conditions for the sequence AD to be dynamic equilibrium are satisfied and the transaction efficiency is higher for y than for x. Then our model may predict the emergence of professional education, represented by x. In period 1, individuals are in autarky and produce only the physical goods y and z. In period 2, the division of labor and professional education sector emerge simultaneously. If we interpret x as knowledge produced by a research activity, our model can predict the concurrence of the evolution of the division of labor and the emergence of professional research.

Similar to the model in chapter 22, the dynamic equilibrium AD generates concurrent increases in productivity, in endogenous comparative advantages, in the extent of the market (aggregate demand and supply), in the number of distinct professional sectors, and in trade dependence. Figure 23.1 provides an intuitive illustration of such an evolutionary path of division of labor.

An important issue is the effect of assumption A1 on the characterization of the dynamic equilibrium in proposition 23.1. If assumption A1 were to be relaxed, so that individuals took into account future behavior not only in deciding upon the choice of configuration in period 1, but also in their discretionary labor allocation decisions within any configuration, the effect would be to increase the relative likelihood that the dynamic equilibrium would be a configuration sequence involving the evolution of specialization or an increase in the variety of intermediate goods. That is, in any sequence of configurations which involves a choice of labor allocation between activities in period 1 (AB, AD, BD) the calculations of total discounted utility upon which proposition 23.1 are based understate the level of utility which would be achieved if the assumption of partial myopia were to be removed (since this can be interpreted as a reduction in the set of constraints on an individual's decision problem, its effect on utility is unambiguously non-negative). It should be noted, however, that removing assumption A1 would not enlarge the set of sequences of structures which can constitute a dynamic equilibrium. For instance, any sequence of structures involving structure C would still be dominated by a sequence replacing that structure with structure D. The above results are summarized in the following proposition, which is proved in appendix 23.3

**Proposition 23.2:** If individuals take into account not only the effects of choice of configuration, but also those of time allocation within a given configuration on accumulation of human capital (that is, if assumption A1 is not imposed), then the structure sequences that involve the evolution of the division of labor and/or an increase in the variety of producer goods are more likely than other structure sequences to be the dynamic equilibrium.

Following the approach developed in chapter 6, it is possible to show that the dynamic equilibrium is Pareto optimal if assumption A1 is not imposed.

# ♦ 23.4 Concurrent Evolution of Specialization, Variety of Producer Goods, and the Institution of the Firm

Allowing trade in labor and applying the approach developed in chapters 8, 18, and 19 to the model in this chapter, we can prove

**Proposition 23.3:** If transaction efficiency is lower in the market for a producer good than in the market for labor used to produce the producer good, then the institution of the firm will emerge from the endogenous evolution of the division of labor. Otherwise, the institution of the firm will not emerge. The equilibrium ownership structure of a firm gets the activity with the lowest transaction efficiency involved in the division of labor while avoiding direct pricing and trading of the outputs and inputs of that activity.

Suppose that trade in labor is allowed, then there are five more market structures: FC, FC′, FD(z), FD(xz), FD(yz). Let $(z/l_x)$ denote a configuration in which an individual sells the final good, buys labor, produces the final good, and employs workers to produce good x. Similarly, $(l_x/z)$ denotes a configuration in which an individual sells her labor and buys the final good, and she becomes a worker producing intermediate good x. Structure FC consists of configuration $(z/l_x)$ and configuration $(l_x/z)$. In this structure, the producer of z claims residual rights. Authority is asymmetrically distributed between the employer and the employees. It is easy to see that market structure FC is exactly the same as structure C as far as the level and pattern of the division of labor and the variety of producer goods are concerned. The only difference between structures FC and C is in the organizational structure of transactions. Structure FC involves the institution of the firm, the market for labor and the market for z, but does not involve a market for good x, while structure C involves markets for goods x and z, but does not involve the institution of the firm and the market for labor. In other words, this institution of the firm replaces the market for good x with a market for the labor used to produce good x. Market structures involving firms are depicted in figure 23.2. The dashed circle or rectangle represents a firm and the dot in

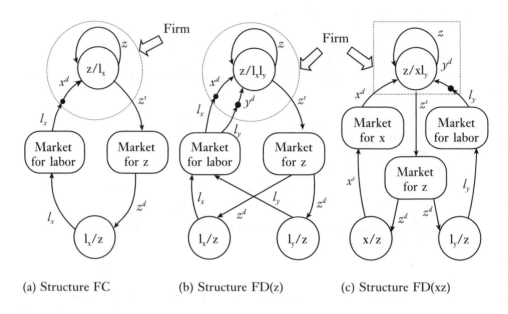

(a) Structure FC          (b) Structure FD(z)          (c) Structure FD(xz)

♦ **Figure 23.2:** Market structures with firms

the dashed circle represents a process that transforms labor into intermediate goods. Panel (a) depicts structure FC.

Structure FC′ is symmetric to structure FC. It consists of configurations $(z/l_y)$ and $(l_y/z)$, where $(z/l_y)$ denotes a configuration in which an individual sells the final good, buys labor, produces the final good, and employs workers to produce y; $(l_y/z)$ denotes a configuration in which an individual sells her labor, buys the final good, and becomes a worker producing intermediate good y. Replacing letter x with letter y, panel (a) in figure 23.2 depicts structure FC′.

Structure FD(z) consists of configurations $(z/l_x\, l_y)$, $(l_x/z)$, and $(l_y/z)$, where $(z/l_x l_y)$ denotes a configuration in which an individual sells the final good and buys labor, produces the final good, and employs workers to produce x and y. Configurations $(l_x/z)$ and $(l_y/z)$ are the same as in structures FC and FC′. Structure FD(z) is the same as structure D except that it replaces the markets for goods x and y with the market for labor. Structure FD(z) is depicted in panel (b).

Structure FD(xz) consists of configurations $(z/xl_y)$, $(x/z)$, and $(l_y/z)$, where $(z/xl_y)$ denotes a configuration in which an individual sells the final good and buys labor and x. She produces the final good and employs workers to produce y. Configuration $(x/z)$ is the same as in structure C or D and $(l_y/z)$ is the same as in structure FC′ or FD (z). Structure FD(xz) is the same as structure D except that it replaces the markets for y with the market for labor. Structure FD(xz) is depicted in panel (c).

Structure FD(yz) consists of configurations $(z/yl_x)$, $(y/z)$, and $(l_x/z)$, where $(z/yl_x)$ denotes a configuration in which an individual sells the final good and buys labor and y. She produces the final good and employs workers to produce x. Configuration $(y/z)$ is the same as in structure C' or D and $(lx/z)$ is the same as in structure FC or D. Structure FD(yz) is the same as structure D except it replaces the markets for x with the market for labor. Exchanging the places of letters x and y, panel (c) of figure 23.2 depicts structure FD(yz).

To distinguish between transaction cost coefficients for different market structures, let $1 - s_0$ and $c_0$ denote the variable and fixed transaction cost coefficients, respectively, in structure C, $1 - s_1$ and $c_1$ denote those in structure C', and $1 - s_2$ and $c_2$ denote those in structure D. Consider structure FC. The individual decision problem in period t for configuration $(z/l_x)$ can be derived from (23.1), (23.2), and (23.3) by noting the fact that configurations $(z/x)$ and $(z/l_x)$ have the same structure of human capital, consumption, and trade except that the method of transactions differs. The problem is

$$\text{Max: } u_t = z_t - c_3 \qquad (23.13a)$$
$$\scriptstyle N,\, z_t,\, z_t^s,\, x^d$$

$$\text{s.t. } z_t + z_t^s = (s_3 x_t^d)^\alpha (L_{zt} l_{zt})^{\alpha a}$$
$$= (s_3 N L_{xt}^a)^\alpha L_{zt}^\alpha, \qquad \text{(production function)}$$
$$l_{zt} = 1 \quad l_{xt} = 1 \qquad \text{(endowment constraint)}$$
$$p_z z^s = w N l_{xt} = w N \qquad \text{(budget constraint or trade balance)}$$

where $1 - s_3$ is the transaction cost coefficient of labor hired to produce the intermediate good. The fixed transaction cost coefficient for structure FD(z) is $c_3$. $N$ is the number of workers hired by an employer, $p_z$ is the price of the final good, $w$ is the wage rate, and $u_t$ is the utility of an individual choosing $(z/l_x)$. Here, $l_{zt}$ is the level of specialization of an individual choosing configuration $(z/l_x)$ in producing the final good and $l_{xt}$ is that of an individual choosing configuration $(l_x/z)$ in producing the intermediate good.

The optimum decisions are

$$z^s = w N/p_z, \qquad u_t(z/l_{xt}) = z = (s_3 N L_{xt}^a)^\alpha L_{zt}^{\alpha a} - (w N/p_z) - c_3 \qquad (23.13b)$$

$$N = (\alpha p_z/w)^{1/(1-\alpha)} [s_1 L_{xt} L_{zt}^a]^{\alpha/(1-\alpha)}$$

where $L_{xt}$ is an employee's human capital in producing the intermediate good, $L_{zt}$ is the employer's human capital in producing the final good, and $u_t (z/l_x)$ is the employer's indirect utility function.

For an individual choosing configuration $(l_x/z)$, all variables are fixed, given by

$$u_t(l_x/z) = kz^d - c_3 = (kw/p_z) - c_3 \qquad (23.14)$$

$$p_z z^d = w l_{xt} = w \qquad \text{(budget and endowment constraints)}$$

where $u_t(l_x/z)$ is an employee's indirect utility. Here, an individual sells one unit of labor.

Manipulating the market clearing and utility equalization conditions yields the corner equilibrium in structure FC in period $t$, given by

$$N = k\alpha/(1 - \alpha), \qquad p_z/w = [k/1 - \alpha]^{1-\alpha} [\alpha s_3 L_{xt} L_{zt}]^{-\alpha}, \qquad (23.15)$$
$$u_t(\text{FC}) = \alpha^\alpha (1 - \alpha)^{1-\alpha} [s_3 k L_{xt}^a]^\alpha - c_3$$

where $u_t(\text{FC})$ is the per capita real income in structure FC. $N$ is the number of workers hired by an employer as well as the relative number of individuals choosing configuration $(l_x/z)$ to those choosing $(z/l_x)$. The total number of employees and the total number of employers can be solved from $N$ and the population size $M$. It should be noted that an employer cannot manipulate the relative number of workers to employers for society as a whole, although she can choose $N$ and the equilibrium value of $N$ is the same as the equilibrium value of the relative number by coincidence. While more than one worker may be employed, economies of specialization do not extend beyond a single individual.

A comparison between $u_t$ (FC) given in (23.15) and $u_t$ (C) given in (23.10) in section 23.2 indicates that

$$u_t(\text{FC}) > u_t(\text{C}) \text{ iff } (s_3 \geq s_0 \text{ and/or } c_3 \leq c_0). \tag{23.16}$$

Following the two-step approach to solving for an equilibrium based on corner solutions, we can find the corner equilibria in structure FC′, FD(z), FD(xz), and FD(yz). FC′ is symmetric to FC Replacing $L_{xt}$ in (23.15) with $L_{yt}$ yields the corner equilibrium in FC′.

For structure FD(z), the corner equilibrium in period $t$ is given by

$$w/p_z = \alpha^\alpha[(1-\alpha)/k]^{1-\alpha}[(s_5/2)L_{zt}{}^a(L_{xt}{}^{a\rho} + L_{yt}{}^{a\rho})^{1/\rho}]^\alpha \tag{23.17}$$

$$u_t[\text{FD}(z)] = \alpha^\alpha(1-\alpha)^{1-\alpha}[(ks_5/2)L_{zt}{}^a(L_{xt}{}^{a\rho} + L_{yt}{}^{a\rho})^{1/\rho}]^\alpha - c_5$$

where $1 - s_5$ is the transaction cost coefficient of labor, $c_5$ is the fixed transaction cost coefficient in structure FD(z), and u[FD(z)] is the per capita real income in this structure. Here, we have used the symmetry and the fact that $L_{xt} = L_{yt}$ in equilibrium.

For structure FD(xz), corner equilibrium in period $t$ is given by

$$w/p_z = \alpha^\alpha[(1-\alpha)/k]^{1-\alpha}[(s_6/2)L_{zt}{}^a(L_{xt}{}^{a\rho} + L_{yt}{}^{a\rho})^{1/\rho}]^\alpha, \tag{23.18}$$

$$p_x/p_z = w/L_{xt}{}^a$$

$$u_t[\text{FD}(xz)] = \alpha^\alpha(1-\alpha)^{1-\alpha}[(ks_6/2)L_{zt}{}^a(L_{xt}{}^{a\rho} + L_{yt}{}^{a\rho})^{1/\rho}]^a - c_6$$

where $1 - s_6$ and $c_6$ are the variable and fixed transaction cost coefficients, respectively, in structure FD(xz). u [FD(xz)] is the per capita real income in this structure. Here, we have used the symmetry and the fact that $L_{xt} = L_{yt}$ in equilibrium. Replacing $p_x$ with $p_y$, (23.18) gives the corner equilibrium for structure FD(yz) which is symmetric to FD(xz).

A comparison between corner equilibria in structures C′, D, FD(z), FD(xz), and FD(yz) leads us to

$$u_t(\text{FC}') \geq u_t(\text{C}') \text{ iff } (s_4 \geq s_1 \text{ and/or } c_4 \leq c_1) \tag{23.19}$$

$$u_t[\text{FD}(z)] \geq u_t(\text{D}) \text{ iff } (s_5 \geq s_2 \text{ and/or } c_5 \leq c_2)$$

$$u_t[\text{FD}(xz)] \geq u_t(\text{D}) \text{ iff } (s_6 \geq s_2 \text{ and/or } c_6 \leq c_2)$$

$$u_t[\text{FD}(yz)] \geq u_t(\text{D}) \text{ iff } (s_7 \geq s_2 \text{ and/or } c_7 \leq c_2)$$

where $1 - s_4$ and $c_4$ are the variable and fixed transaction efficiency coefficients, respectively, in structure FC′, and $1 - s_7$ and $c_7$ are those in structure FD(yz).

(23.16) and (23.19) together with proposition 23.1 imply that all market structures that involve the division of labor in proposition 23.1 will be replaced by the corresponding structures with firms if the transaction efficiency for an intermediate good is lower than the transaction efficiency for the labor that is used to produce the intermediate good. This deduction yields proposition 23.3.

It is interesting to note that if the transaction efficiency of good y is lower than that for the labor hired to produce good y, but the transaction efficiency of good x is higher than that for the labor hired to produce good x, that is, $s_6 > s_i$ for $i = 5, 7$, then market structure FD(xz) emerges from the division of labor when the fixed transaction cost $c$ is sufficiently low. In this case, an employer hires labor to produce y within her firm and buys x from the goods market. The story for structure FD(yz) is symmetric to this one.

Taking into account the structure of ownership, and employing the approach developed in chapter 8, it can be shown that the structure of ownership of a firm that gets the activity with the lowest transaction efficiency involved in the division of labor, while avoiding the direct trading and pricing of the outputs and inputs of that activity, will emerge from the endogenous evolution of the division of labor.

If we introduce many consumer and producer goods and a long decision horizon, then the extended model may generate incessant evolution of the division of labor, of variety of producer goods, and of the institution of the firm. However, the studies of such models are restricted by available computer software. Since the dynamic equilibrium in such a model is path dependent, the number of terminal points, such as A, B, C, D in period 2, exponentially increases with the number of goods and the decision horizon. It is impossible to obtain an analytical solution from such a sophisticated model in the absence of software that can solve dynamic programming problems analytically.

## ◆ Appendix 23.1: Proof of Lemma 23.1

By assumption A1 an individual's allocation of labor within a given period is time independent. Hence the time subscript is omitted throughout this proof.

*Claim 1: z and $z^d$ cannot be positive at the same time.*

Suppose z, $z^d > 0$. We may then establish claim 1 by showing a contradiction. Replacing $z^d$ in the utility function with its equivalent in the budget constraint: $p_x(x^s - x^d) + p_y (y^s - y^d) = p_z(z^d - z^s)$, we have

$$u = z + kz^d = z + kz^s + k\{[p_x(x^s - x^d) + p_y(y^s - y^d)]/p_z\}. \tag{23.20}$$

Substituting for $z^s$ from the production function for good z, (23.20) becomes

$$u = (1 - k)z + k\{[p_x(x^s - x^d) + p_y(y^s y^d)]/p_z\} \tag{23.21}$$
$$+ k\{[(x + sx^d)^\rho + (y + sy^d)^\rho]^{a/\rho}(L_z l_z^{a\alpha})\}$$

Hence $\partial u/\partial z > 0 \; \forall \, z > 0$ so that the optimum value of z is as large as possible due to the Kuhn–Tucker theorem. From the endowment constraint, this implies $x^s = y^s = z^s = 0$. But zero values for these variables contradicts $z^d > 0$ due to the budget constraint, so that $z$ and $z^d$ cannot be positive at the same time.

*Claim 2: $x^s$ and $y^s$ are zero if $z$ and $z^s$ are positive.*

A positive value of $z$ implies $z^d = 0$ due to claim 1. Hence substituting from the production function for $z$ and the budget constraint yields

$$u = \{(x + sx^d)^{\rho r} + [y + s((p_x(x^s - x^d) + p_z z^s)/p_y) + y^s)]^\rho\}^{\alpha/\rho}(L_z l_z)^{\alpha a} - z^s \qquad (23.22)$$

where $y = (L_y l_y)^a - y^s$. From (23.22) we can see that $sgn\{\partial u/\partial y^s\} = sgn\{-1 + s\} < 0 \ \forall \ y^s > 0$. From the Kuhn–Tucker theorem this implies $y^s = 0$ if $z$, $z^s > 0$. By using the budget constraint to eliminate $x^d$ rather than $y^d$ from $u$, it is also possible to show that $x^s = 0$ if $z$, $z^s > 0$.

*Claim 3: If $z^d > 0$, then $x = y = z^s = x^d = y^d = 0$*

If $z^d > 0$, claim 1 implies $z = 0$, hence $u = kz^d$. Since $z^d$ and $z^s$ are quantities of the same good, due to the transaction cost incurred, if $z^d > 0$, $z^s = 0$. Substituting from the budget constraint and production functions for $x$ and $y$ yields

$$u = (k/p_z)\{p_x[(L_x l_x)^a - x - x^d] + p_y[L_y^a(1 - l_x)^a - y - y^d]\} \qquad (23.23)$$

Hence $\partial u/\partial x < 0 \ \forall \ x > 0$; $\partial u/\partial y < 0 \ \forall \ y > 0$; $\partial u/\partial x^d < 0 \ \forall \ x^d > 0$; and $\partial u/\partial y^d < 0 \ \forall \ y^d > 0$. Therefore $x = y = x^d = y^d = 0$.

*Claim 4: $x^s$ and $y^s$ cannot be positive at the same time if $z^d > 0$.*

From (23.23) we have

$$\partial u/\partial l_x < 0 \ \text{if} \ l_x = 0 \ \text{and} \ \partial u/\partial l_x > 0 \ \text{if} \ l_x = 1 \qquad (23.24)$$

and from $\partial u/\partial l_x = 0$ it is possible to derive the unique solution of $l_x$. (23.24) implies that an interior maximum point of $l_x$ exists only if there are at least three interior extremes. However, there is a unique interior extreme point. Hence the optimum $l_x$ is at either zero or one. But $l_x = 1$ implies $l_y = y^s = 0$. Hence $x^s$ and $y^s$ cannot be positive at the same time if $z^d > 0$.
Claims 1–4 are sufficient for establishing Lemma 23.1.

## ◆ Appendix 23.2: Proof of Proposition 23.1

Let $u_t(i)$ be a person's utility level in period $t$ when she chooses configuration $i$, and $v_t(i)$ be the maximum discounted value of $u_t(i)$ for given levels of human capital in producing goods. According to Bellman's optimality principle and her backward decision rule and assumption A1, $v_t(i)$ can be calculated using the solution to the decision problem for given human capital in each period. Using the solutions for an individual's decision problem and the relative prices given in (23.5)–(23.12), a person's total discounted utility level $U(ij)$ for sequence $ij$ can be calculated as follows:

$$U(Aj) = v_1(A) + \begin{cases} v_2(A) = \delta(3/4)^{2\alpha a}, & (23.25a) \\ v_2(B) = v_2(A)E^\alpha \\ v_2(C) = \delta[Q\beta^\alpha 1.5^{2\alpha a} - c], \\ v_2(D) = \delta[HQ\beta^\alpha 1.5^{2\alpha a} - c] > v_2(C) \text{ since } H > 1 \end{cases}$$

$$v_1(A) = 2^{-2\alpha a}$$

so that A maximizes $v_2$ if $\rho > 1/a$ and $[(c > c_1$ and $\beta > \beta_1)$ or $\beta < \beta_1]$, B maximizes $v_2$ if $\rho < 1/a$ and $[(c > c_4$ and $\beta < \beta_5)$ or $\beta < \beta_1]$, and D maximizes $v_2$ if $[c > \max(c_1, c_4)$ and $\beta > \max(\beta_1, \beta_5)]$ or if $\beta < \min(\beta_1, \beta_5)]$. The definitions of $Q$, $H$, $\beta$, $\beta$, $\beta$, $c_i$, and other notations are given below.

$$U(Bj) = v_1(B) + v_1(B) = 2^{\alpha/\rho}/3^{-2a} \quad \begin{cases} v_2(A) = \delta(2/3)^{2\alpha a}, \\ v_2(B) = \delta 2^{\alpha/\rho}(2/3)^{4\alpha a}, \\ v_2(C) = \delta[Q\beta^\alpha(4/3)^{2\alpha a} - c], \\ v_2(D) = \delta[HQ\beta^\alpha(4/3)^{2\alpha a} - c] > v_2(C) \text{ since } H > 1, \end{cases} \quad (23.25b)$$

so that A maximizes $v_2$ if $\rho > \rho_0$ and $[(c > c_2$ and $\beta > \beta_1)$ or $\beta > \beta_1]$, B maximizes $v_2$ if $\rho < \rho_0$, and $[(c > c_7$ and $\beta > \beta_8)$ or $\beta < \beta_8]$, D maximizes $v_2$ if $[c > \max(c_1, c_4)$ and $\beta > \max(\beta_1, \beta_5)]$ or if $\beta < \min(\beta_1, \beta_5)$. The value of $\rho_i$ is given below.

$$U(Cj) = v_1(C) + v_1(C) = Q\beta^\alpha - c \quad \begin{cases} v_2(A) = \delta 2^{-\alpha a}, \\ v_2(B) = \delta 2^{\alpha(1-2\rho a)/\rho}, \\ v_2(C) = \delta Q\beta^\alpha 2^{2\alpha a}, \\ v_2(D) = \delta HQ\beta^\alpha 2^{2\alpha a} > v_2(C) \text{ since } H > 1 \end{cases} \quad (23.25c)$$

$$U(Dj) = v_1(D) + v_1(D) = Q\beta^\alpha 2^{\alpha/\rho} - c \quad \begin{cases} v_2(A) = \delta 2^{-aa} < v_2(B) \\ v_2(B) = \delta 2^{\alpha(1-2\rho a)/\rho}, \\ v_2(C) = \delta Q\beta^\alpha 2^{2\alpha a}, \\ v_2(D) = \delta HQ\beta^\alpha 2^{2\alpha a} > v_2(C) \text{ since } H > 1. \end{cases} \quad (23.25d)$$

so that D maximizes $v_2$ if $\beta > S$, where

$\rho_0 \equiv \log 2/2(\log 3 - \log 2)a < 1/a,$

$c_1 \equiv Q\beta^\alpha 1.5^{2\alpha a}H - (3/4)^{2\alpha a}, \quad c_2 \equiv Q\beta^\alpha 2^{\alpha/\rho}[1 + \delta 2^{\alpha(2\alpha-1)}] - K,$

$c_3 \equiv [Q\beta^\alpha 2^{\alpha/\rho}(1 + \delta G) - 3^{-2\alpha a}]2^{\alpha/\rho}(1 - \delta)^{-1}, \quad c_4 \equiv Q\beta^\alpha 1.5^{2\alpha a}H - (3/4)2^{\alpha a}E^\alpha,$

$c_5 \equiv Q\beta^\alpha 2^{\alpha/\rho}J - 2^{-2\alpha a} - \delta(3/4)^{2\alpha a}E^\alpha, \quad c_6 \equiv [JQ\beta^\alpha - 3^{-2aa} - \delta(2/3)4^{\alpha a}]2^{\alpha/\rho},$

$c_7 \equiv Q\beta^\alpha(4/3)^{2\alpha a}H - (2/3)^{4\alpha/\rho}2^{\alpha/\rho}, \quad c_8 \equiv [Q\beta^\alpha(1 + \delta G) - 3^{-2\alpha a}]2^{\alpha/\rho}/(1 - \delta),$

$\beta \equiv sk, \quad \beta_1 \equiv 2^{1-2a-1/\rho}/Q^{1/\alpha},$

$\beta_2 \equiv 2^{-1/\rho}Q^{-1/\alpha}\{[(1 - \delta)(3/4)^{2\alpha a} - 2^{-2\alpha a}]/(1.5^{2\alpha a}2^{-\alpha} - 1 - 2^{-\alpha}\delta F)\}^{1/\alpha},$

$\beta_3 \equiv 2^{2a+1/\rho}Q^{-1/\alpha}(1 + 2^{-\alpha}\delta F)^{-1/\alpha}, \quad \beta_4 \equiv 2^{-1/\rho}(K/JQ)^{1/\alpha},$

$\beta_5 \equiv 2^{1-1/\rho-2a}Q^{-1/\alpha}E, \quad \beta_6 \equiv 2^{-2a-1/\rho}(JQ)^{-1/\alpha}(1 + 1.5^{-2\alpha a}\delta E^\alpha)^{1/\alpha},$

$\beta_7 \equiv \{[(1 - \delta)1.5^{2\alpha a}E^\alpha - 1]/(3^{2\alpha a}2^{-\alpha} - 2^{4\alpha a-\alpha-1}\delta)\}^{1/\alpha}, \quad \beta_8 \equiv 3^{-2\alpha}(2/Q)^{1/\alpha},$

$\beta_9 \equiv \{[3^{-2\alpha a} + \delta(2/3)^{4\alpha a}]/JQ\}^{1/\alpha}, \quad \beta_{10} \equiv 3^{-2a}[Q(1 + \delta G)]^{-1/\alpha}$

$\beta_{11} \equiv \{[1 - \delta)(2/3)^{4\alpha a} - 3^{-2\alpha a}]/Q[R(1 - \delta) - 1 - \delta G]\}^{1/\alpha},$

$\delta_1 \equiv 1 - (2/3)^{2\alpha a}, \quad \delta_2 \equiv (3/4)^{2\alpha a} - 2^{\alpha(1-2a)}$

$\delta_3 \equiv 1 - (2/3)^{2\alpha a}E^\alpha, \quad \delta_4 \equiv 1 - (3/4)^{2\alpha a},$

$\delta_5 \equiv (R - 1)/(R + G)$

$Q \equiv \alpha^\alpha(1 - \alpha)^{1-\alpha}, \quad S \equiv 2^{-4a-1}Q^{-1/\alpha}, \quad H \equiv 2^{\alpha(1-\rho)/\rho}$

$K \equiv 2^{-2\alpha a} + \delta(3/4)^{2\alpha a}, \quad G \equiv 2^{\alpha(2a-1)} - \delta(8/9)^\alpha, \quad J \equiv 1 + 2^{\alpha(2a-1)}\delta$

$E \equiv [1 + 1.5^{a\rho/(a\rho-1)}]^{-a+1/\rho}, \quad R \equiv (4/3)^{-2\alpha a}2^{-\alpha}$

Note that C, which denotes that a person chooses either $(x/z)$ or $(z/x)$ is symmetric with C' which denotes that a person chooses either $(y/z)$ or $(z/y)$. The four configurations generate the same real income for a person in C or C' due to the symmetry. D denotes that a person chooses either $(x/z)$ or $(y/x)$ or $(z/xy)$. The three configurations in D generate the same real income for a person due to the utility equalization condition.

According to the Bellman optimality principle, an individual can solve her dynamic decision using a backward decision rule. She first maximizes her discounted utility in period 2, which is the terminal period, with respect to configuration for given levels of human capital in producing the different goods. From (23.25), an individual can see that C cannot be the optimal choice in period 2 because $v_2(D) > v_2(C)$ irrespective of which configuration she chooses in period 1. Also, she can see that A cannot be an optimal choice in period 2 if she chooses B or D in period 1 because $v_2(B) > v_2(A)$ for the two cases. Hence, she excludes the relevant options in period 2 from consideration. Then she can identify a range of parameter values within which an option is optimal in period 2. For instance, A cannot be optimal in period 2 if $\rho < 1/a$ and B cannot be optimal in period 2 if $\rho > 1/a$. The relevant ranges are indicated in (23.25).

Then an individual examines pay-offs in period 1. It can be seen that the payoff for option D is always higher than that for option C in period 1. Also, each option in period 2 is not worse off if a person chooses D in period 1 than the same option in period 2 if she chooses C in period 1. That is, $v_2(i)$ in (23.25d) is not lower than $v_2(i)$ in (23.25c) for $i =$ A, B, C, D. Hence C cannot be the best choice in period 1. Therefore, a person can exclude four more configuration sequences from consideration. Remaining configuration sequences that have to be considered are AA, AB, AD, BB, BD, DB, and DD. A comparison between total discounted real incomes generated by the configuration sequences thus establishes the following results.

1) for $\rho a > 1$

   a)   AA is the dynamic equilibrium if $c > \max \{c_1, c_2\}$ and $\beta > \max \{\beta_1, \beta_2\}$, or if $\beta < \min \{\beta_1, \beta_2\}$;

   b)   AD is the dynamic equilibrium (*i*) if $c_1 > c > c_3$ and $\beta > \max \{\beta_1, \beta_3\}$, or if $c_1 > c$ and $\beta_1 < \beta < \beta_3$, and (*ii*) if $\delta < \delta_1$ and $\beta > \beta_2$, or if $\delta_2 > \delta > \delta_1$;

   c)   DD is the dynamic equilibrium if $c < \min \{c_2, c_3\}$ and $\beta > \max \{\beta_3, \beta_4\}$.

2) For $1 > \rho a > \log 2/2 \ (\log 3 - \log 2)$

   a)   AB is the dynamic equilibrium if $c > \max \{c_4, c_5\}$ and $\beta > \max \{\beta_5, \beta_6\}$, or if $\beta < \min \{\beta_5, \beta_6\}$;

   b)   AD is the dynamic equilibrium (*i*) if $c_4 > c > c_3$ and $\beta > \max \{\beta_5, \beta_3\}$, or if $c_4 > c$ and $\beta_5 < \beta < \beta_3$ and (*ii*) if $\delta < \delta_3$ and $\beta > \beta_7$, or if $\delta_2 > \delta > \delta_3$;

   c)   DD is the dynamic equilibrium if $c < \min \{c_3, c_6\}$ and $\beta > \max \{\beta_3, \beta_{10}\}$;

3) For $\log 2/2(\log 3 - \log 2) > \rho a$

   a)   BB is the dynamic equilibrium if $c > \max \{c_6, c_7\}$ and $\beta > \max \{\beta_8, \beta_9\}$, or if $\beta < \min \{\beta_8, \beta_9\}$; where

   b)   BD is the dynamic equilibrium (*i*) if $c_7 > c > c_8$ and $\beta > \max \{\beta_8, \beta_{10}\}$, or if $c_6 > c$ and $\beta_8 < \beta < \beta_{10}$, and (*ii*) if $\delta < \delta_5$ and $\beta < \delta_5$ and $\beta > \beta_{11}$, or if $\delta > \delta_4$ and $\beta < \beta_{11}$, where

   c)   DD is the dynamic equilibrium if $c < \min \{c_3, c_6\}$ and $\beta > \max \{\beta_3, \beta_6\}$.

(1)–(3) are sufficient for establishing proposition 23.1

## ◆ Appendix 23.3: Proof of Proposition 23.2

This appendix establishes proposition 23.2 which concerns the implications of assumption A1 for dynamic decisions. In this model only the accumulated value of $l_{it}$ appears. Moreover, the value of $l_{it}$ is variable only for configurations A, A', and B. Also, the specificiation of functional forms makes decisions on $l_{it}$ for configurations A, A′, and B time separable if a configuration sequence does not involve shifts between configurations over time. Hence, we are concerned only with configuration sequences that involve shifts between A, A′, B, and other configurations. Due to Bellman's backward decision rule, if A, A′, or B is chosen in the terminal period, then the decision on $l_{it}$ is still time separable in this period, so that full optimization solutions in the absence of assumption A1 for all configuration sequences that do not involve A, A′, or B in period 1 are indistinguishable from one solved in section 23.2. That is, we are concerned only with configuration sequences AB, AC, AD, BA, BC and BD when we examine the implications of assumption A1 for dynamic decisions. Suppose that assumption A1 is not imposed and that a person chooses A in period 1 and (z/x) in period 2. According to the Bellman backward decision rule, the decision and equilibrium in period 2 is given by (23.10), dependent on human capital which is determined by the allocation of time between production of goods x and z in period 1. Total discounted utility for sequence AC is

$$U(AC) = u_1(A) + \delta u_2(C) = z_1 + \delta[\alpha^\alpha(1-\alpha)^{1-\alpha}(sk)^\alpha(L_{z2}L_{x2}{}')^{\alpha a} - c] \tag{23.26}$$

$$= [L_{x1}L_{z1}l_{z1}(1-l_{z1})]^{\alpha a} + \delta\{\alpha^\alpha(1-\alpha)^{1-\alpha}(sk)^\alpha[((L_{z1} + l_{z1})L_{x2}{}')^{\alpha a} - c]\}$$

$$= [l_{z1}(1-l_{z1})]^{\alpha a} + \delta\{\alpha^\alpha(1-\alpha)^{1-\alpha}(sk)^\alpha[((1 + l_{z1})L_{x2}{}')^{\alpha a} - c]\}$$

where we have used (23.1)–(23.2), the initial condition $L_{i1} = 1$, the definition of $L_{i2} = L_{i1} + l_{i1}$, the definition of (z/x) that requires $l_{zt} = 1$ and $l_{xt} = 0$, and the endowment constraint $l_{xt} + l_{zt} = 1$. $L_{x2}{}'$ is the human capital of another individual who chooses (x/z) in period 2. Hence $L_{x2}{}'$ is independent of the decision of the individual choosing (z/x) in period 2.

It is easy to see that the optimum decision based on assumption A1 is $L_{x1} = L_{z1} = 0.5$ and the optimum decision in the absence of assumption A1 is $l_{z1} > 0.5$ because

$$\partial U(AC)/\partial l_{z1} > 0 \text{ if } l_{z1} = 0.5. \tag{23.27}$$

(23.27) implies that the optimum value of $U(AC)$ is greater when assumption A1 is not imposed. Similarly, we can prove that the maximum values of $U(AB)$, $U(AD)$, $U(BC)$, and $U(BD)$ are greater, relative to $U$ for other sequences, when assumption A1 is not imposed. Moreover, A cannot be the optimal choice in period 2 irrespective of assumption A1 due to the backward decision rule. Hence BA, which involves a decrease in product variety, can be excluded from consideration. Therefore, all sequences that involve the evolution of the division of labor and/or an increase in the variety of producer goods are more likely to be the dynamic equilibrium if assumption A1 is not imposed. This yields proposition 23.2.

## Key Terms and Review

Dynamic programming and the Bellman principle of optimality.

Endogenous technical progress.

Implications of spontaneous evolution of the network size of division of labor for endogenous technical progress.

Concurrent endogenous evolution of division of labor and of the institution of the firm.

The mechanism for emergence of new producer goods from spontaneous evolution of division of labor in roundabout production.

Implications of evolution of the institution of the firm for endogenous technical progress.

## Further Reading

Marshall (1890), Allyn Young (1928), Braudel (1984), Chandler (1990), Rostow (1960), Borland and Yang (1995), Yang and Y.-K. Ng (1993, chs. 7, 16).

# QUESTIONS

1  In the new classical growth model in this chapter there is implicit saving that is used to invest and speed up evolution of division of labor. This implicit saving represents a utility loss compared to the alternative autarky structure. What is the difference between this kind of investment, that determines the network size of division of labor, and investment in the neoclassical growth model in chapter 21? Why is this difference important for avoiding scale effects that are conclusively rejected by empirical evidence?

2  Conduct the following thought experiment on the basis of the model in this chapter. Evolution of international division of labor is a driving force for economic development. Multinational firms and foreign direct investment are used to develop division of labor between developed economies and developing economies. Assume that it takes a longer time for specialized learning by producing upstream producer goods to acquire competitive endogenous advantage than in producing final goods. Then the evolution of international division of labor may have the following feature. The developing country, say Taiwan, specializes in producing final goods to exchange for upstream producer goods with the developed country, say the US in the early stage of the evolution. Then more and more upstream production activities are gradually moved from the US to Taiwan, until Taiwan has caught up to the US in terms of per capita real income. Discuss the difference between this new classical view of economic development and the neoclassical theory of import substitution vs. export substitution.

3  Use evidences provided by Marshall (1890), Allyn Young, Braudel (1984), and Chandler (1990) to analyze the implications of the evolution of the network size of division of labor for endogenous technical progress. Why are expansion of the market, emergence of new machines, evolution of production roundaboutness, and the merging of many mutually isolated local communities into an increasingly more integrated market all different aspects of the evolution of network of division of labor?

4  What is the difference between evolution of the number of producer goods in the R&D-based models and evolution of the number of producer goods in the new classical model in this chapter? What is the connection between this difference and the difference between economies of division of labor and economies of scale?

5  Use the case of the invention of the steam engine by Boulton and Watt (see Marshall, 1899, p. 256), and the case of the invention of more than a hundred electronic devices by Edison's company (Josephson, 1959), to explain the function of the institution of the firm in promoting the division of labor in inventing activities. Use the theory in this chapter and the two cases to analyze why industrialization and the Industrial Revolution featured rapid development of the institution of the firm in all new industries. Discuss the connection between the role of patent laws in promoting invention, the function of the firm in indirectly pricing entrepreneurial activity, and the role of transaction efficiency in promoting evolution of division of labor which brought about new technology.

6  Why did Young (1928) claim that the concept of economies of scale misses qualitative aspects of division of labor? Use the model in this chapter to formalize Young's idea about evolution of division of labor in roundabout production that is associated with the evolution of the number of roundabout productive activities.

# EXERCISES

1   Yang and Borland, 1991b: Apply the approach developed in this chapter to extend the static model with the CES utility function in chapter 11. In order to keep the model tractable, you may assume that there are at most two consumption goods. The utility function at time $t$ is $u_t = [(x_t + kx_t^d)^\rho + (y_t + ky_t^d)^\rho]^{1/\rho}$. The production functions are $y_t + y_t^s = L_{yt}^a$, $x_t + x_t^s = L_{xt}^a$. The endowment constraint is $l_{xt} + l_{yt} = 1$, $l_{it} \in [0, 1]$, $L_{it} = L_{it-1} + l_{it-1}$. Identify the condition that generates concurrent endogenous evolution of specialization and consumption variety.

2   Consider the model in exercise 1. The production functions are respecified as

$$z_t + z_t^s = \beta^\alpha \gamma_z^{\alpha a}, \qquad x_t + x_t^s = \gamma_x^a,$$

$$y_t + y_t^s = \gamma_y^a, \qquad \alpha a > 1, \qquad a > 1$$

$$\beta \equiv \text{Max } \{[(x_t + sx_t^d)^\rho + (y_t + sy_t^d)^\rho]^{1/\rho}, \quad x_t + sx_t^d, y_t + sy_t^d, 0\} \text{ and } \gamma_i \equiv L_{it}$$

$$l_{zt} + l_{xt} + l_{yt} = 1, \qquad l_{it} \in [0, 1], L_{it} = L_{it-1} + l_{it-1}$$

Solve for the dynamic equilibrium.

3   Yang and Borland, 1992: Consider an economy with $M$ *ex ante* identical consumer-producers. The utility function at $t$ is $u_t = (x_t + kx_t^d)(y_t + ky_t^d) - c$, where $c$ is a fixed cost for trade caused by the first transactions. $c = 0$ at $t$ if an individual never trades or if she traded at $t-1$. $c$ is positive if she trades for the first time at $t$. The decision horizon is of three periods, so that total discounted utility over the three periods is $U = u_0 + \delta u_1 + \delta^2 u_2$, where $\delta \in (0, 1)$ is the discount factor. Each individual's production function is $x_t + x_t^s = (L_{xt} l_{xt})^a$, $y_t + y_t^s = (L_{yt} l_{yt})^b$, where $L_{it} = \sum_{\tau=0}^{t-1} l_{i\tau}$ is human capital at $t$ and $l_{it}$ is labor input at $t$. The time endowment constraint for each person is $l_{xt} + l_{yt} = 1$, where $l_{it} \in [0, 1]$. Enumerate all of each person's configurations in each period and all configuration sequences over the three periods. Then specify a dynamic programming problem that maximizes a person's total discounted utility with respect to choice of configuration sequence. Specify the market clearing condition in each period and the utility equalization conditions. Then solve for dynamic general equilibrium and its comparative dynamics.

## Notes

1   Introducing only the variable transaction cost without the fixed transaction cost will mean that the condition for a dynamic equilibrium with the gradual evolution of specialization will not be satisfied and the dynamic equilibrium will be at a corner, forever involving either autarky or specialization in production. Together with the discounting of future consumption, the fixed transaction cost introduces an efficient timing problem of when to shift from autarky to market exchange so that the gradual evolution of specialization may occur.

2   Note that the population is divided between configurations A and A′ in period 1 for the sequential equilibrium AD. This is because each individual has an incentive in period 1 to build up her human capital in an activity that will be her profession in period 2. Hence, those individuals who will specialize in producing good x in period 2 choose configuration A (self-providing goods x and z) in period 1, and those who will specialize in producing good y in period 2 choose configuration A′ (self-providing goods y and z) in period 1.

3   If the parameters of preference or production differ between goods, then sequence AD implies

that in autarky all individuals produce and consume the same good that is preferred more, or has a higher productivity. Thus the evolution of the division of labor involves not only an increase in the variety of producer goods used by each producer of the final good, but also in the number of goods produced by society as a whole. However, such a model with an asymmetry between goods x and y involves a complicated decision problem over the transitional period from autarky to the division of labor. The price of the good that was not produced in autarky must be higher than those goods produced in autarky over the transitional period in order to facilitate the transition. This asymmetry generates a tractability problem. Such more realistic and complicated models need analytical tools that will be developed in the next chapter.

# CHAPTER 24

# EXPERIMENTS WITH STRUCTURES OF DIVISION OF LABOR AND EVOLUTION IN ORGANIZATION INFORMATION ACQUIRED BY SOCIETY

## ◆ 24.1 How Does Organization Knowledge Acquired by Society Determine Economic Development?

From what we have learned in the previous chapters, we understand that the level of division of labor determines the speed of accumulation of professional knowledge of production (human capital) and the capacity of society to acquire knowledge, while individuals' knowledge about the efficient levels of specialization determines which level of division of labor will be chosen by society. But in the new classical framework, each individual must choose one from many corner solutions, and society must choose one from many corner equilibria. Because optimum decisions are not continuous between corner solutions and between corner equilibria, the optimum corner solution can be identified and the economy can settle down in the Pareto optimum corner equilibrium only after completion of a total benefit–cost analysis of all corner solutions in addition to a marginal analysis of each. If it takes time for an individual to calculate a corner solution and for society to sort out the corner equilibrium prices in a structure, and if the calculation and pricing processes cause nontrivial costs, then we may have a very interesting interdependency between individuals' dynamic decisions and the organization information that they have acquired.

Which configuration an individual chooses is dependent on corner equilibrium prices in different structures that she knows, since she needs the information about relative prices to calculate real incomes in different structures, to compare them, and then to tell which configuration should be chosen. However, the information on corner equilibrium relative prices that is available is in turn determined by which structure and which configurations are chosen by individuals. For instance, if all individuals choose the autarky configuration, then they never know the corner equilibrium relative prices in other structures involving division of labor, so that they cannot tell whether they should engage in division of labor or which pattern of division of labor they should choose. This interdependency between decision and information is analogous to the interdependence between quantities and prices in a Walrasian general equilibrium model. Hence, our job in this chapter is to investigate the mechanism that simultaneously determines both of them.

Suppose an individual decides to go to a public place (or the marketplace, as we call it) to meet somebody else, and through bargaining to sort out relative prices under which both parties agree to specialize in different occupations. If no mutually agreeable prices can be worked out, then at least the individual can come back to autarky. But if both parties can find mutually beneficial terms of division of labor, then both parties can be better off than in autarky. No matter which case occurs, the individual always has an expected information gain from the pricing process: she receives the autarky pay-off (not worse off than in autarky) with probability $\rho$, and receives a higher pay-off yielded by mutually beneficial division of labor with probability $1 - \rho$. However, the pricing process incurs bargaining costs between individuals or communication costs between the Walrasian auctioneer and individuals. Hence, there is a trade-off between expected information gains from a social experiment with a certain structure of division of labor and the related pricing process and pricing costs (experiment costs). The bargaining or Walrasian pricing mechanism becomes a vehicle to organize social experiments with various structures of division of labor.

The principal questions that we shall address in this chapter are: how do individuals' dynamic decisions about the price search process, or about an organization experiment, affect the evolution of the organization information that they acquire; and how does this information affect individuals' dynamic decisions? The interactions between acquisition of organization information and dynamic decisions in choosing a structure of division of labor are complex, since they involve a process of social experimentation in searching for the efficient network of division of labor. This is much more complex than a single decision-maker's search process, as studied in Aghion et al. (1991) and Morgan and Manning (1985). You might suggest using the notion of sequential equilibrium proposed by Selten (1975) and Kreps and Wilson (1982) to describe the interactions between dynamic decisions and evolution of information (see chapter 10).

But we have two problems in applying the notion of sequential equilibrium directly. The first is conceptual and the second is technical. The sequential equilibrium (or Bayes perfect equilibrium) model is based on information asymmetry. The focus of the model is on possible devolution of information asymmetry rather than increases in organization information acquired by *all* individuals. We must find a way to specify the trade-off between information gains and related costs in connection with possible concurrent evolution in the network of division of labor and in information about the efficient network of division of labor. We need some conceptual innovation here. The unbounded sequential rationality and complete information for one player (despite incomplete information for the other player) in Kreps' sequential equilibrium model does not work for our analysis. We need the notions of bounded rationality and adaptive behavior to describe the complex interactions between individuals' dynamic decisions, which affect social experiments, and organization information, which is acquired by society. Hence, we will develop the concept of Walrasian sequential equilibrium in this chapter. The following two features distinguish our notion of Walrasian sequential equilibrium from Selten's and Kreps' notion of sequential equilibrium.

First, in our Walrasian sequential equilibrium model, all individuals have no information at the outset, and the lack of information is symmetric between different individuals, whereas in the Kreps sequential equilibrium model asymmetric information between individuals is assumed. One player has complete information and the other has incomplete information. Though uncertainty exists in Kreps' sequential equilibrium model, each decision-maker's dynamic decision never changes over time for given parameter values, despite the fact that there are different dynamic decisions for different parameter subspaces (within some of them, screening equilibrium occurs, and within others, pooling equilibrium occurs). In our Walrasian sequential equilibrium model, evolution in organization information acquired by society generates adaptive decisions, so that each individual's dynamic programming problem in one period may be different from that in the next period. The whole decision problem, rather than merely a strategy, must be adjusted in response to updated information even if parameters are fixed. This makes our Walrasian sequential equilibrium model more sophisticated and more realistic than that of Kreps.

The increased sophistication of our approach has its cost. It is prohibitively difficult to simultaneously endogenize direct interactions between individuals' decisions, evolution in information, and evolution in division of labor. Only very simple sequential equilibrium models in game theory can be solved, and even completely symmetric models of endogenous evolution of division of labor are very difficult to manage. Hence we ignore direct interactions between individuals' decisions in our Walrasian sequential equilibrium model. However, individual decision-makers interact with each other indirectly through the Walrasian pricing mechanism. Hence, our Walrasian sequential equilibrium comprises a sequence of static Walrasian corner equilibria. This enables our models to have high explanatory power while remaining reasonably tractable. The information symmetry in our Walrasian sequential equilibrium model is a setback. This assumption is made to avoid the problem of coordination and mismatch in experiments with various patterns of division of labor, thereby keeping the model tractable at the cost of realism. If information asymmetry is introduced, the coordination problem may generate interesting implications for the role of entrepreneurship in experiments with economic organization (see question 2).

A technical advantage of the features of our approach is that all static new classical models covered in this text can be dynamized without much additional technical complexity. Also, this approach solves a well-known recursive paradox associated with the decision problem based on bounded rationality (see Conlisk, 1996 for the notion of recursive paradox and a recent comprehensive survey of the literature of bounded rationality). This paradox implies that a decision or equilibrium model cannot be well closed in the presence of bounded rationality. We will show that there is a way to satisfactorily close a dynamic decision problem and dynamic general equilibrium model in the presence of bounded rationality. Our Walrasian sequential equilibrium model also echoes the criticisms of the recent endogenous growth models of Judd (1985), Romer (1990, and see chapter 21 above), Grossman and Helpman (1989), and Yang and Borland (1991, and see chapter 22 above) which feature, very unrealistically, an infinite decision horizon, complete information, unbounded rationality, and deterministic dynamics. As Nelson (1995) points out, the real economic growth process is an evolutionary process that features uncertainties about the direction of the evolution and a certain tendency of the evolution. The Walrasian sequential equilibrium model in this chapter is characterized by these two features.

Two examples may help to motivate your study of the Walrasian sequential equilibrium model. The founding of the McDonalds restaurant network can be considered an experiment with a pattern of high-level division of labor between specialized production of management and specialized production of direct services within the franchise, and between specialized production of food and specialized production of other goods. Since demand and supply functions are discontinuous from corner solution to corner solution, marginal analysis based on interior solutions could not provide the founder (Ray Kroc) of this franchise with the information necessary for the right decisions. Instead he decided to use the market to experiment with a new pattern of business organization involving a higher level of division of labor within the franchise and between the franchise and the rest of the economy. Instead of adjusting prices at the margin, he tried pricing restaurant services at a much lower level than the prevailing price. According to his calculation, the higher level of division of labor would generate productivity gains (for instance, a high productivity generated by a high level of division of labor between the production of standardized cooking equipment and the production of food, and between specialized management and head office planning, and specialized production of restaurant services by franchisees) on the one hand, and more transaction costs on the other. McDonalds' franchise arrangements adopted a form of hostage mechanism, by which the great discretionary power of the franchiser and the intentionally great asset specificity of the franchisees would serve to protect the intangible intellectual property of the franchiser. It was hoped that these arrangements would reduce endogenous transaction costs to the extent that the benefit of the higher level of division of labor would outweigh its cost, so that the substantially lower price of services could stand the test of the social experiment. Though the subsequent success of the McDonalds chain has clearly substantiated this idea, the founder might have gone into bankruptcy if the social experimentation had proved the business to be inefficient compared to the prevailing pattern of organization. But such social experimentation through the price system is necessary for society to acquire information about the efficient pattern of division of labor, even if it may generate business failure because of the interdependency between decisions in choosing a pattern of organization and available information about prices, and because of discontinuity of locally optimum decisions between different patterns of division of labor.

The second example involves the business practice of large-scale experimenting in the production of a new product. A successful research and development project that invents the new product may not be able to stand the test of large-scale commercialized production. In order to tell to what degree the new product can generate economies of division of labor for society as a whole, a social experiment must be conducted. Without the experiment, potential buyers do not know the benefit of the product to them in comparison to its price, and the manufacturer does not know to what degree the average cost can be reduced to support a sufficiently low price based on a reasonable market. Without knowledge of the price of the product, potential buyers cannot make purchase decisions. But if the price is determined simply by the high average cost incurred in the R&D process, nobody will buy the product. Hence, the entrepreneur must make a guess about the possible corner equilibrium price in the new structure of division of labor between the production of the new product and the production of other goods. A promotion campaign may be initiated, and the price set at a level much lower than its current average production cost in the hope that potential buyers will give up the self-provision of substitutes for the new product and choose the new structure of division of labor. If the corner equilibrium in the new structure of division of labor is Pareto inferior to the prevailing corner equilibrium, then the entrepreneur will go bankrupt. If the new corner equilibrium is Pareto superior to the prevailing one, then she may make a fortune. The stock market can then be used to raise venture capital and to share the risk in the social experiments initiated by the entrepreneur. Also, the R&D process must involve experimentation with different structures of division of labor between different specialties in the R&D activities. The success of the invention itself is determined by these organizational experiments. Hence, a business success is more dependent on social experimentation with a new structure of division of labor than on technical conditions.

A striking feature of experiments with various structures of division of labor is that mistakes are not only unavoidable, but also necessary for distinguishing the efficient structure from inefficient ones. The first welfare theorem about the Pareto optimality of market equilibrium is incompatible with the notion of experimenting. An experiment with a Pareto inefficient structure of division of labor is certainly not Pareto optimal. But without experimenting with inefficient as well efficient structures, society can never know which structure is efficient and which is not. This is because of the discontinuity of locally optimum decisions across structures and the interdependence between information and decisions. It follows that because of bounded rationality, the Pareto optimum is a utopia, and the simple and direct method of pursuing the Pareto optimum is not efficient. A sophisticated pursuit of the Pareto optimum structure of division of labor should encourage experiments with Pareto inefficient as well as Pareto efficient structures. The simple and direct pursuit of the Pareto optimum may impede the efficient search, since such a pursuit is like asking a researcher to find the optimum design without experimenting with inefficient patterns.

Casual observation indicates that countries with many organizational inventions and innovations usually have relatively high rates of bankruptcy of firms. This view of bounded rationality helps us not to overestimate businesses which are successful by and large because of luck in their experiments with various structures of division of labor. It also helps us not to underestimate the value of the failed businesses which might be necessary for society to acquire information about the efficient pattern of division of labor.

In the model to be considered, there are many *ex ante* identical consumer-producers with preferences for diverse consumption and production functions displaying economies of specialization. Complicated interactions between economies of specialization and transaction costs in the market generate uncertainties about real income for different patterns of division of labor. Each person's optimal decision is a corner solution. Combinations of different corner solutions generate many corner equilibria. Individuals may experiment with each possible pattern of division of labor via a Walrasian auction mechanism at a point in time, and thereby eliminate uncertainties and acquire information about the efficient pattern of division of labor over time. However, the costs in discovering prices generate a trade-off between information gains and experiment costs in the information acquisition process. A decentralized market will trade-off gains from information acquisition against experiment costs to determine the equilibrium pattern of experiments with patterns of division of labor over time. In the process, individuals use Bayes' rule and dynamic programming to adjust their beliefs and behavior according to updated information. The determinants of the dynamics of the Walrasian sequential equilibrium are the transportation cost coefficient for trading one unit of goods, the degree of economies of specialization, the degree of economies of complementarity between two producer goods in producing the final good, the discount rate, and the pricing cost coefficient.

Suppose the transportation cost coefficient and the degrees of economies of specialization and complementarity are fixed. If pricing costs are high, then the market will not experiment with any sophisticated pattern of division of labor. If pricing costs are sufficiently low, all possible patterns of division of labor will be experimented with. In this process, simple patterns of division of labor are experimented with before the more complicated ones, so that a gradual evolution of division of labor may occur. For a fixed pricing cost coefficient, more patterns of division of labor will be experimented with as the transportation cost coefficient decreases and/or as the degree of economies of specialization increases.

Section 24.2 sets out a static new classical equilibrium model. Then in section 24.3 the time dimension and the information problem are introduced into the model. Section 24.4 solves for the Walrasian sequential equilibrium and its inframarginal comparative dynamics.

---

### Questions to Ask Yourself when Reading this Chapter

♦ Why are social experiments with various structures of division of labor a driving force of economic development in the presence of interdependency between organization information acquired by society and individuals' decisions in choosing occupation configurations?

♦ How does the price system coordinate social experiments with various structures of division of labor to facilitate acquisition of organization information?

♦ What is the difference between social experiments with various structures of division of labor and a decision-maker's search process for the efficient decision?

♦ How does the trade-off between the information gains of social experiments and their costs determine the pattern of evolution of division of labor?

♦ Why is an adaptive decision rule more efficient than a deterministic decision rule when individuals are short of information and have bounded rationality?

♦ How is the capacity of society to acquire information about production technology and to achieve high productivity determined by its capacity to acquire organization information?

---

## ♦ 24.2 A Static Model with an Endogenous Length, of Roundabout Production Chain and an Endogenous Division of Labor

### Example 24.1: a static new classical model with endogenous production roundaboutness

In this section, we consider a model where each consumer-producer has the following utility and production functions and endowment constraint:

$$u = y + ky^d \qquad \text{(utility function)}$$

$$y^p \equiv y + y^s = \text{Max} \{l_y^\alpha, \quad (x + kx^d)^{\frac{1}{2}} l_y^\alpha\} \quad \text{(production function of final good)}$$

$$x^p \equiv x + x^s = l_x^\beta \qquad \text{(production function of intermediate good)}$$

$$l_x + l_y = L, \qquad l_i \in [0, L] \qquad \text{(endowment constraint of working time)}$$

where $y$ and $x$ are respectively the amounts of the final good (called food) and the intermediate good (called hoes) that are self-provided, $y^s$ and $x^s$ are the amounts of the two goods sold, $y^d$ and $x^d$ are the amounts of the two goods purchased, $y^p$ and $x^p$ are the output levels of the two goods, $k$ is the transaction efficiency of goods, and $l_i$ is the individual's level of specialization in producing good i. Food can be produced either from labor or from labor and hoes. Each individual is endowed with $L$ units of working time. $\alpha$ is the degree of economies of specialization in producing food. When only labor is employed to produce food, there exist economies of specialization in producing food if $\alpha > 1$; when both labor and hoes are employed in producing food, there are economies of specialization if $\alpha > \frac{1}{2}$. The total factor input for the latter case is $\text{TF} = X^{0.5/(0.5+\alpha)} l_y^{\alpha/(0.5+\alpha)}$ where $X \equiv x + kx^d$. The total factor productivity is $\text{TFP} \equiv y^p/\text{TF} = X^{0.5(\alpha-0.5)/(\alpha+0.5)} l_y^{\alpha(\alpha-0.5)/(\alpha+0.5)}$ which increases as the level of specialization in producing y, $l_y$, rises if $\alpha > \frac{1}{2}$. The production function of hoes displays economies of specialization if $\beta > 1$. The system of production functions displays economies of division of labor if there are economies of specialization in producing both goods. If the production function of a good displays economies of specialization and the other displays diseconomies of specialization, the economies of division of labor exist when the economies of specialization dominate the diseconomies of specialization.

Applying inframarginal analysis, we can solve for the corner equilibria in three structures. The first autarky structure A is shown in figure 24.1a, where each individual self-provides food in the absence of hoes. The second autarky structure B is shown in figure 24.1b, where each individual self-provides both hoes and food. The structure with division of labor, C, is shown in figure 24.1c, where some individuals choose specialization in producing hoes, or configuration (x/y), and other individuals choose specialization in producing food, or configuration (y/x). All information about corner solutions in the four configurations and the corner equilibria in the three structures is summarized in table 24.1.

Comparisons of per capita real incomes in all structures, and application of the Yao theorem, yield the general equilibrium and its inframarginal comparative statics, summarized in table 24.2, where, $L_0 \equiv (1 + 2\alpha/\beta)(1 + \beta/2\alpha)^{2\alpha/\beta}$, $k_0 \equiv 2L^{-\beta/\alpha}$, $k_1 \equiv 2\alpha^\alpha(0.5\beta)^{0.5\beta}(0.5\beta + \alpha)^{-0.5\beta-\alpha}$. Since $dL_0/d(\alpha/\beta) > 0$, $L < L_0$ implies that relative degree of

**Table 24.1: Three corner equilibria**

| Configuration and structure | Corner solutions and corner equilibria |
|---|---|
| A | $l_x = 0,\ \ l_y = L,\ \ y = L^\alpha,\ \ u = L^\alpha$ |
| B | $l_x = \dfrac{0.5\beta L}{0.5\beta + \alpha},\ l_y = \dfrac{\alpha L}{0.5\beta + \alpha},\ x = l_x^\beta, y = x^{0.5} l_y^a, u = y$ |
| (x/y) | $l_x = L,\ l_y = 0,\ x^s = L^\beta,\ y^d = \dfrac{p_x L^\beta}{p_y},\ u = \dfrac{k p_x L^\beta}{p_y}$ |
| (yx) | $l_x = 0,\ l_y = L,\ y^s = \dfrac{k p_y L^{2\alpha}}{4 p_x},\ x^d = \dfrac{p_y y^s}{p_x},\ y = \dfrac{k p_y L^{2\alpha}}{4 p_x},\ u = y$ |
| C | $\dfrac{p_y}{p_x} = 2L^{0.5\beta-\alpha},\ M_y = \dfrac{M}{1 + 0.25k\left(\dfrac{p_y}{p_x}\right)^2 L^{2\alpha-\beta}},\ M_x = M - M_y$ |
| | $u = 0.5kL^{0.5\beta+\alpha}$ |

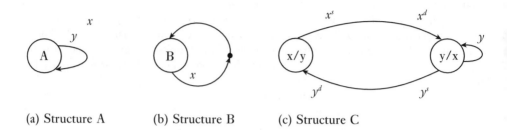

(a) Structure A                 (b) Structure B               (c) Structure C

◆ **Figure 24.1:** Configurations and structures in the static model

economies of specialization of food to hoes, $\alpha/\beta$, is sufficiently large, while $L > L_0$ implies that economies of specialization in producing food are not that significant in comparison to those in producing hoes ($\alpha/\beta$ is small). The results in table 24.2 imply that if economies of specialization in producing food are sufficiently more significant than in producing hoes, then individuals use labor alone to produce food and hoes are not produced in autarky. As transaction efficiency is improved, the general equilibrium jumps from autarky to the division of labor and a new intermediate good emerges from the exogenous evolution in division of labor. If economies of specialization in producing hoes are significant compared to food production, then the evolution in division of labor is not associated with evolution in the length of the roundabout production chain and emergence of new producer goods.

◆ **24.3 Interactions between Dynamic Decisions and Evolution in Organization Information**

### Example 24.2: a Walrasian sequential equilibrium model (Ng and Yang, 1997)

We now introduce the time dimension and the information problem into the static model. But we assume that there is no real dynamic learning by doing, nor uncertainty in production and consumption. This assumption is not highly realistic, but is essential for keeping the model tractable. The time dimension and information problem affect only what individuals know about corner solutions and corner equilibrium prices in different structures. There are 4 periods, $t = 0, 1, 2, 3$. In period 0, all individuals are in structure A and each of them knows her real income $u_A = L^\alpha$ (see table 24.1). She does not know per capita real

Table 24.2: Static general equilibrium and its inframarginal comparative statics

| Parameter | $L < L_0$ | | $L > L_0$ | |
|---|---|---|---|---|
| Subspace | $k < k_0$ | $k > k_0$ | $k < k_1$ | $k > k_1$ |
| Equilibrium structure | A | C | B | C |

incomes in structures B and C. If she wants to know real income in structure B, she must spend the time necessary to calculate the optimum decision in that structure and the real income yielded by the decision. This computation process not only needs time, but also causes disutility. Suppose the fraction $1 - s_B$ of expected utility disappears due to the computation cost. Then only the fraction $s_B$ of expected utility can be received if the individual carries out the computation. If she wants to know per capita real income in structure C, she must pay two kinds of experiment costs. First, she must bargain with another person to sort out the terms of trade required by the division of labor, or alternatively sort out prices through a Walrasian auction mechanism. Though the Nash bargaining and Walrasian mechanisms will generate the same terms of trade, either will incur a pricing cost. Second, she must compute the corner solutions of the two configurations in order to make a decision in choosing a profession. This computation causes disutility. If an individual wants to try a structure, she can always propose a relative price to attract others to get involved in bargaining. But bilateral bargaining is not sufficient to sort out the corner equilibrium numbers of different specialists. The corner equilibrium numbers, which relate to the corner equilibrium relative price, can be sorted out only if all individuals participate in the experiment with structure C. We shall show that all individuals' decisions about the experiment pattern are consistent. Otherwise, coordination difficulty may occur. Suppose the three types of experiment cost for structure C are summarized by the experiment efficiency coefficient $s_C$, which is smaller than $s_B$ due to pricing cost and more computation in C than in B. It is assumed that each individual's subjective discount factor is $\delta \in (0, 1)$.

We now consider each individual's information at $t = 0$ and the relationship between the available information and her decision about experimenting with configurations in B and C. In period 0, each individual does not know real incomes in structures B and C, nor the probability distribution function of those real incomes. But she knows there are 6 possible ranking orders of three per capita real income levels in the three structures. Let the order of letters A, B, C represent the ranking of per capita real incomes in structures A, B, C. The 6 possible rankings are: ABC, ACB, BAC, BCA, CAB, CBA, where, for instance, ABC denotes that the per capita real income in structure A is greater than that in B which is greater than that in structure C, and BAC denotes that the per capita real income in B is greater than that in A which is greater than that in C. We assume that each individual has no information about per capita real incomes in structures B and C in period 0. This implies that each of the 6 rankings occurs with probability $1/6$. Also, we assume that each individual knows the difference between two consecutive levels of per capita real incomes, which is an exogenously given parameter $b_0$ in period 0. She can update her information about $b$ according to a Bayes updating rule and observed differences between per capita real incomes in different structures, as shown later on. It is not difficult to show that the expected per capita real income in structure B or C based on the information in period 0 is $u_A$. That is, each individual knows only the real income in structure A, $u_A$. We call this structure of information at period 0 *lack of information*, which is different from incomplete information.

If an individual experiments with configuration B in period 1, then her expected utility in period 1, computed in period 0, is

$$E_0[u_1(B)] = s_B[0.5u_A + (1/3)(u_A + b_0) + (1/6)(u_A + 2b_0)] = s_B\delta(u_A + 2b_0/3) \quad (24.1)$$

The expected utility can be worked out as follows. According to what an individual knows in period 0, the probability that $u_A > u_B$ is 0.5 since ABC, ACB, CAB account for half of 6 rankings. If any of the three rankings proves correct, the individual will return to structure A after the experiment with structure B. Hence, based on what she knows in period 0, she expects to receive real income $u_A$ with probability 0.5 after the experiment with B. Since BAC and CBA account for 1/3 of the 6 rankings and $u_B = u_A + b_0$ for the two rankings, in period 0 the individual expects to receive $u_A + b_0$ with probability 1/3 after the experiment with B in period 1. Finally ranking BCA, which implies $u_B = u_A + 2b_0$, occurs with probability 1/6. The individual expects to receive $u_B = u_A + 2b_0$ after the experiment with B. This, together with the consideration of the experiment efficiency coefficient $s_B$, implies that in period 0 the individual's expected utility for the experiment with configuration B in period 1 is (24.1).

Following this procedure, we can compute the expected utility in period 0 for the experiment with structure j in period $t$, $E_0[u_t(j)]$. Assume that each individual's decision horizon consists of 2 periods. Then an individual's dynamic programming problem in period 0 can be described by figure 24.2, where individuals are in structure A in period 0. In period 1, each individual can choose any among 4 configurations: A, B, (x/y), (y/x). Since the dynamic programming process depends only on information that a person has in period 0, the discount factor $\rho$, experimental efficiency $s_i$, and $b_0$, are the same for every individual, all other individuals will choose either (x/y) or (y/x) if one chooses to experiment with (x/y) or (y/x) in period 1. Free choice between profession configurations and the Walrasian pricing mechanism (or Nash bargaining) will coordinate the division of $M$ individuals between configurations (x/y) and (y/x) as soon as one of them is chosen by somebody. This implies that structure C will be experimented with if an individual chooses to experiment with either configuration (x/y) or (y/x) in period 1. Therefore, as shown in figure 24.2, where $u \equiv u_A$, $v \equiv u_A + 2b/3$, $w \equiv u_A + b$, there are 3 nodes: A, B, C, in period 1.

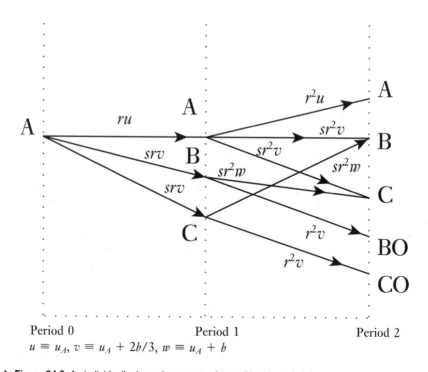

Period 0            Period 1            Period 2

$u \equiv u_A$, $v \equiv u_A + 2b/3$, $w \equiv u_A + b$

♦ **Figure 24.2:** An individual's dynamic programming problem in period 0

We assume that in each period each individual has perfect recall of the past history of the economy. This, together with the feature of path dependence of the dynamic equilibrium, implies that there are more nodes in period 2 than in period 1. Nodes A, B, C in period 2 are the same as in period 1. Node BO implies staying with the best between A and B with no more new experiments in period 2 after the experiment with B in period 1. Node CO implies staying with the best between A and C, with no more new experiments in period 2 after the experiment with C in period 1.

Each individual's dynamic decision in period 0 about the optimum pattern of experimental sequence in periods 1 and 2 is to maximize the following expected total discounted utility over periods 1 and 2:

$$\text{Max: } \sum_{t=1}^{2} \delta^t E_0[u_t(i)] \tag{24.2}$$

where nodes that can be chosen in period 1 are $i(1)$ = A, B, C and in period 2 are $i(2)$ = A, B, C, BO, CO. Following the method used to establish (24.1), we can prove that

$$E_0[u_t(A)] = u_A, \qquad E_0[u_1(B)] = s_B(u_A + 2b_0/3), \qquad E_0[u_1(C)] = s_C(u_A + 2b_0/3);$$

If A is chosen in period 1, $E_0[u_2(B)] = s_B(u_A + 2b_0/3)$, $E_0[u_2(C)] = s_C(u_A + 2b_0/3)$;
If B is experimented with in period 1, then $E_0[u_2(C)] = s_C(u_A + b_0)$;
If C is experimented with in period 1, then $E_0[u_2(B)] = s_B(u_A + b_0)]$ and $E_0[U_2(BO)] = E_0[u_2(CO)] = u_A + 2b_0/3$.

The essence of the dynamic programming problem is the trade-off between information gains from the experiments and the experiment costs. If each individual has an experiment with one configuration, the expected utility will increase from $u_A$ to $u_A + 2b_0/3$. If she has two experiments with 2 configurations in different structures, the expected utility $u_A + b_0$ is even higher. This is because she can always go back to the best configuration if the one experimented with is not as good as that arising from any previous experiment. The worst situation is at least as good as before. But the probability of a higher utility is nontrivial. This is the information gain from experimentation.

However, there is an experimental cost. The fraction $1 - s$ of the expected utility which includes information gains disappears because of the experimental cost. This cost is a one-off, but the associated information gains are perpetual. If an individual has experimented with configuration B in period 1, she pays the calculation cost in period 1 and enjoys the information gains forever, with no further experimental cost after period 1. Hence, the trade-off between the information gains and the experimental cost (or investment in information) is analogous to the trade-off between current consumption and future consumption that can be raised by investment in the conventional growth model. But the investment in our model is in organization information acquired by society rather than in production, R&D, education, or physical capital.

We call a pattern of structures that are experimented with over successive periods an *experimental sequence*, or *sequence* for short. From (24.2), we can see that the expected total discounted utility, in terms of the present value in period 1, generated by sequence CB is

$$U(CB) = s_C(u_A + 2b_0/3) + s_B\delta(u_A + b_0).$$

It is always smaller than the expected total discounted utility, in terms of the present value in period 1, generated by sequence BC, which is

$U(\text{BC}) = s_B (u_A + 2b_0/3) + s_C \delta(uA + b_0).$

To see this, we first note that if the experimental cost is ignored the two expected utility levels are the same, due to the lack of information in period 0. However if account is taken of the facts that the experiment cost is higher for C than for B because of a higher pricing cost in C, and that time has value, that is $\delta \in (0, 1)$, then it is better for individuals to try structure B with a lower experiment cost first if they have no information about which of B and C generates the higher per capita real income.

Similarly, we can show that sequence CO is not as good as BO. Hence, we can narrow down the set of candidates for the optimum sequence, which now comprises the 4 sequences AA, AB, BO, BC. Comparisons of expected total discounted utility levels in the 4 sequences yield the analytical solution of the dynamic programming problem, summarized in table 24.3.

The dynamic optimum decision and its comparative dynamics imply that if the experimental efficiency for structure B is too low, individuals will always stay in autarky with no experimentation. If the experimental efficiency is increased to the critical value $s_B^0$, but the experimental efficiency for structure C is not high, then structure B will be experimented with in period 1 and no further experimenting will take place in period 2, that is, sequence BO is chosen. If the experimental efficiency for structure C is increased to the critical value $s_C^0$, the optimum sequence is BC, which experiments with B in period 1 and with C in period 2. Since the dynamic optimum decision depends only on information in period 0, on real income in structure A, and on $u_A$, $b_0$, $s$, $\delta$, which are the same for all individuals, the dynamic optimum decision is the same for all individuals, so that there is no coordination difficulty. As shown in Ng and Yang (1997) and in Zhao (1999), the analytical solution of such a dynamic programming problem will become very complicated as the number of structures and decision horizons increases. Zhao (1999) has worked out the analytical solution to such a dynamic programming problem with any limited decision horizon and with 4 structures to experiment with. But to our knowledge, the analytical solution of a larger dynamic programming problem is too complicated to be tractable.

**Table 24.3:** Optimum dynamic decision in period 0

| $S$ | $s_B < s_B^0$ | $s_B > s_B^0, s_C < s_C^0$ | $s_C > s_C^0$ |
|---|---|---|---|
| Structure sequence | AA | BO | BC |

where: $s_B^0 \equiv \dfrac{L^\alpha - 2b_0\delta/3}{L^\alpha + 2b_0/3}$,  $s_C^0 \equiv \dfrac{L^\alpha + b_0}{L^\alpha + 2b_0/3}.$

♦ **24.4 Walrasian Sequential Equilibrium and Concurrent Evolution in Organization Information and Division of Labor**

We now consider information updating in period 1 and interactions between information and adjustment of dynamic decisions. If individuals try structure B in period 1, then their information will be changed by such experimentation after they have seen per capita real income in B. Hence, their optimum dynamic decision in period 0 is out of date. They must adjust their dynamic decisions about further experiments according to the updated information. We assume that the decision horizon for the new dynamic programming problem based on updated information in period 1 consists of two periods too. In each period in which a new structure is experimented with, the new dynamic programming problem for further experiments in the next two periods is different from the one in the last period. The recursively adjusted dynamic decision according to updated information is referred to as an *adaptive decision*, which distinguishes our notion of Walrasian sequential equilibrium from Kreps' concept of sequential equilibrium in game theory.

Suppose $s_B < s_B^0$. Then individuals will not try structures B and C. Their updated information in period 1 is the same as in period 0. Hence, their adjusted new dynamic programming problem in period 1 is the same as that in period 0, so that the optimum decision is to stay in autarky with no further experimentation. The recursive deduction shows that the sequential Walrasian equilibrium is a sequence of structure A over all periods.

Suppose $s_B > s_B^0$. Then individuals will try structure B in period 1. Two cases may take place. If $L < L_0$, individuals will find in period 1 that A is better than B, as shown in table 24.1. Hence, they will go back to A at the end of period 1. If $L > L_0$, they will find in period 1 that B is better than A and choose B at the end of period 1. No matter which case takes place, the experiment changes the information that an individual knows in period 1, so that her dynamic optimum decision in period 0 is out of date. She must reformulate a new dynamic programming problem for further experiments in periods 2 and 3.

Let us see what information an individual knows after she has tried B in period 1. Suppose $L < L_0$, so that A is better than B, which implies that BAC, BCA, and CBA are impossible. The set of possible rankings now comprises ABC, ACB, CAB. A is better than C with probability 2/3 and $u_C = u_A + b_1$ with probability 1/3. This method of updating information according to new observations is referred to as the *Bayes updating rule*. Here, $b_1$ needs to be updated according to any observed difference between $u_A$ and $u_B$ too. We assume that before individuals have observed two differences in per capita real incomes between structures, they believe $b$ is the same between each consecutive pair of real income levels. After they have tried B in period 1, they have seen $u_A - u_B \equiv \theta$. If $\theta$ is positive, individuals know that only rankings ABC, ACB, CAB are possible. With probability 1/3, ACB or $u_A - u_B = 2b$ occurs. That is, $\theta = 2b$ with probability 1/3. Also, $\theta = b$, or either of ABC and CAB occurs, with probability 2/3. Hence, the expected value of $\theta$ is $E\theta = (1/3)2b_1 + (2/3)b_1 = (4/3)b_1$. This implies that according to the Bayes updating rule the estimate of $b_1$ from observed $\theta$ is $b_1 = 3\theta/4 = 3(u_A - u_B)/4$, where the values of $u_A$ and $u_B$ can be found in table 24.1. If the individual chooses structure sequence AA, that is, to stay in A without experimenting with C in periods 2 and 3, her expected total discounted utility in periods 2 and 3 is $U(AA) = u_A(1 + \delta)$. According to her updated information in period 1, only ranking CAB among ABC, ACB, CAB entails a higher utility in C than in A. Hence, if she tries C in period 3, she expects to obtain $u_A + b_1$ with probability 1/3 and $u_A$ with probability 2/3. Therefore, if she chooses structure sequence AC, that is, to stay in A in period 2 and to try a configuration in C in period 3, her expected total discounted utility over the two periods is $U(AC) = u_A + \delta s_C[(u_A + b_1)/3 + 2u_A/3] = u_A + \delta s_C(u_A + b_1/3)$.

Now let us consider sequence CO in periods 2 and 3, which implies trying C in period 2 and staying with the better of A and C in period 3. Remember that we are concerned with an individual's decision in period 1 after she has tried B and knows A is better than B. Using the Bayes updating rule, we can find that the expected total discounted utility generated by sequence CO over periods 2 and 3 is

$$U(CO) = (u_A + b_1/3) \, (s_C + \delta).$$

Comparisons between $U(AA)$, $U(AC)$, $U(CO)$ yield

$$U(AC) > U(AA) \text{ iff } s_C > s_C^3 \equiv b_1 u_A/(u_A + b_1/3) \text{ and} \tag{24.3}$$

$$U(CO) > U(AC) \text{ iff } s_C > s_C^4 \equiv [u_A/(1 - \delta)(u_A + b_1/3)] - [\delta/(1 - \delta)].$$

It can be shown that $s_C^3 > s_C^4$. This implies that AC is worse than AA if $s < s_C^4 < s_C^3$, and AC is worse than CO if $s > s_C^4$. In other words, AC, which delays experimentation with C by one period, cannot be chosen, since it is better to try C earlier, if a person wants to try it, due to the perpetual value of information and the value of time. Otherwise, no experiment with C is better than a delayed experiment with it. This result is dependent on the assumption about the absence of dynamic learning by doing. If the dynamic learning by doing in chapter 22 is introduced, the result may be changed.

We now need to consider only sequences AA and CO. A comparison between $U(AA)$ and $U(CO)$ yields

$$U(CO) > U(AA) \text{ iff } s_C > s_C^1 \equiv [(u_A + 1 - \delta)/(u_A + b_1/3)] - \delta. \tag{24.4}$$

We have now finished the analysis for the case that $s_B > s_B^1$ and $L < L_0$. For this case, individuals will try structure B in period 1, and know that A is better than B at the end of period 1. Based on the new information, her adjusted new dynamic decision tells her that she should try C in period 2 if $s_C > s_C^1$. Otherwise she should stay in autarky forever.

Let us now consider the case in which $s_B > s_B^1$ and $L > L_0$. For this case, individuals try structure B, and know B is better than A by the end of period 1. Following the same procedure, we can show that, based on the updated information, individuals will find out by the end of period 1 that

$$U(CO) > U(BB) \text{ iff } s_C > s_C^2 \equiv [(u_B + 1 + \delta)/(u_B + b_1/3)] - \delta, \tag{24.5}$$

where $b_1$ can be estimated according to the Bayes updating rule in the same way as before.

All of the dynamic optimum decisions about further experiments over periods 2 and 3, made in period 1 according to updated information, are summarized in table 24.4, where AA denotes that an individual stays in A with no experimenting over periods 2 and 3. For $L < L_0$, CO denotes that an individual tries C in period 2, chooses the better of A and C at the end of period 2, and stays with it in period 3; for $L > L_0$, CO denotes that an individual tries C in period 2, chooses the better of B and C at the end of period 2, and

Table 24.4: Adjusted optimum dynamic decisions in period 1

| $L < L_0$;  A is chosen at $t = 1$ | | $L > L_0$;  B is chosen at $t = 1$ | |
|---|---|---|---|
| $s < s_B^1$ | $s > s_B^1$ | $s < s_C^2$ | $s > s_C^2$ |
| AA | CO | BB | CO |

stays with it in period 3; BB denotes that an individual stays in B with no experiment over periods 2 and 3.

Let us now consider dynamic general equilibrium in the marketplace, which is the consequence of interactions between all individuals' dynamic optimum decisions and between the dynamic decisions and information that individuals know. One of the differences between the Walrasian sequential equilibrium and Kreps' sequential equilibrium is that in the former individuals indirectly interact with each other through the Walrasian pricing mechanism. Also, the adaptive decision rule and the initial lack of information of all individuals in the former differ from the deterministic decision rule and the asymmetric and incomplete information in the latter. *Walrasian sequential equilibrium* is a sequence of sets of relative prices of traded goods, a sequence of numbers of individuals choosing various configurations, an evolutionary path of information that each individual knows, and all individuals' dynamic optimum decisions in choosing quantities of goods produced, consumed, and traded and in choosing an experimental sequence of configurations after experiments in each period. We call the combination of individuals' dynamic decisions, the time paths of prices, the number of different specialists, and information, a *dynamic organism*. The Walrasian sequential equilibrium is a dynamic organism that satisfies the following three conditions.

i) In each period each individual's dynamic optimum decision in choosing an experimental sequence of configurations in the future two periods maximizes her expected total discounted utility over the two periods for given information that she knows in this period. Her choice of configuration after experimenting in each period is optimal for given updated information generated by the experiment in this period. Her decision in allocating resources in a given structure that is realized in a period maximizes her utility in this period for given corner equilibrium relative prices of traded goods and for given numbers of individuals choosing different configurations in this period.

ii) Information is updated according to Bayes' rule, observed prices and numbers of different specialists on the basis of perfect recall of the past.

iii) The corner equilibrium relative price of traded goods and numbers of individuals choosing different configurations in the structure that is experimented with or is ultimately chosen in a period, equalize all individuals' utility and clear the markets for traded goods in this period.

Putting together information about static equilibrium in table 24.1 and information about dynamic decisions in periods 0 and 1 in tables 24.2 and 24.3, we can solve for the Walrasian sequential equilibrium, as summarized in figure 24.3.

In figure 24.3, $b_0$ is a given parameter,

$$s_B^0 \equiv \frac{L^\alpha - 2b_0\delta/3}{L^\alpha + 2b/3}, \quad s_C^0 \equiv \frac{L^\alpha + b_0}{L^\alpha + 2b_0/3},$$

$$L_0 = [1 + (2\alpha/\beta)][1 + (\beta/2\alpha)]^{2\alpha/\beta}, \quad s_C^2 \equiv \frac{u_A + 1 + \delta}{u_A + b_1/3} - \delta,$$

$$s_C^2 \equiv \frac{u_B + 1 + \delta}{u_B + b_1/3} - \delta, \quad b_1 \equiv \frac{3}{4}| u_A - u_B |, \quad k_0 \equiv \frac{2}{L^{\beta/\alpha}}$$

$$k_1 \equiv 2\alpha^\alpha(0.5\beta)^{0.5\beta}(0.5\beta + \alpha)^{-0.5\beta-\alpha}, \quad u_A = L^\alpha,$$

$$u_B = (0.5\beta)^{0.5\beta}\alpha^\alpha[L/(0.5\beta + \alpha)]^{0.5\beta+\alpha}$$

In figure 24.3, the capitalized letters in brackets denote structures that are experimented with, the capitalized letters without brackets denote structures that are finally chosen. Let's interpret the figure. Start from structure A in period 0. If $s_B < s_B^0$, then individuals stay in A forever. No additional information becomes available from which they can learn, so that posterior information is the same as the prior information; that is, they have no organization information at all. If $s_B > s_B^0$, individuals try structure B in period 1, denoted by (B) at the lower node in period 1. This can be verified by dynamic decision as shown in table 24.3. After the experiment with B, if $L < L_0$, individuals will go back to structure A, denoted by the node A in the middle, at the end of period 1, since tables 24.1 and 24.2 indicate that utility in A is greater than in B if $L < L_0$. If $L > L_0$, individuals will stay with B, denoted by the lower node B, at the end of period 1.

Suppose $L < L_0$, so that individuals have chosen A at the end of period 1. From their dynamic optimum decisions made in period 1 about structure sequence over the future two periods 2 and 3, given in table 24.4, we can see that if $s_C < s_C^1$, they will stay in A forever. Individuals have learned some organization information. They know now which is the better of A and B, but do not know which is the better of A and C or of B and C. If $s_C > s_C^1$, each individual will try a configuration in structure C in period 2. Since all individuals' dynamic decisions are the same, structure C will be tried out in period 2. At the end of period 2, individuals will go back to A if $k < k_0$ since table 24.2 indicates that A is better than C for $k < k_0$ and $L < L_0$. Note that the middle node A at the end of period 1 can be reached only if $L < L_0$. If $k > k_0$, then the static corner equilibrium in structure C, given in table 24.1, is realized at the end of period 2. No matter which of A and C is chosen at the end of period 2, individuals have acquired all available organization information after they have tried B and C.

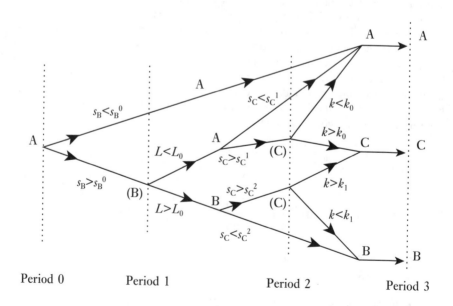

◆ **Figure 24.3:** Walrasian sequential equilibrium: interactions between evolution in division of labor and evolution of organization information

Table 24.5: Inframarginal comparative dynamics of Walrasian sequential equilibrium

| Parameter subspace | $s_B < s_B^0$ | $s_B > s_B^0$ | | | | | |
|---|---|---|---|---|---|---|---|
| | | $L < L_0$ | | | $L > L_0$ | | |
| | | $s_C < s_C^1$ | $s_C > s_C^1$ | | $s_C < s_C^2$ | $s_C > s_C^2$ | |
| | | | $k < k_0$ | $k > k_0$ | | $k < k_1$ | $k > k_1$ |
| Structure sequence tried | AAA | ABA | ABC | ABC | ABB | ABC | ABC |
| Structure series chosen | AAA | AAA | AAA | AAC | ABB | ABB | ABC |

Now we come back to the lower node B at the end of period 1, which will be reached if $s_B > s_B^0$ and $L > L_0$. Suppose $s_C < s_C^2$. From table 24.4, we can see that individuals' dynamic decisions at the end of period 1 are to stay in B in period 2 with no further experiments forever. This implies that individuals have learned part of the relevant organization information. If $s_C > s_C^2$, then individuals will try structure C in period 2 and learn all organization information. But for $k < k_1$, individuals will go back to structure B at the end of period 2, since table 24.2 indicates that B is better than C for $k < k_1$ and $L > L_0$. Note again that the experiment with C can take place in period 2 only if $L > L_0$. For $k > k_1$ and $L > L_0$, individuals will stay with C at the end of period 2 and afterward.

So far we have partitioned the parameter space into several subspaces. Within each of them the dynamic general equilibrium is determined by a particular sequence of structures that have been experimented with, a particular sequence of structures that have finally been chosen, and a particular evolutionary path of information. The *inframarginal comparative dynamics* of the Walrasian sequential equilibrium are summarized in table 24.5. For instance, for $s_B > s_B^0$, $s_C > s_C^2$, $L > L_0$, and $k > k_1$, the equilibrium sequence of structures that has been experimented with over periods 0, 1, 2 is ABC, and the equilibrium sequence of structures that has finally been chosen is also ABC. Partial organization information is acquired at the end of period 1 and all organization information is acquired by society at the end of period 2. For $s_B > s_B^0$, $s_C > s_C^1$, $L < L_0$, and $k < k_0$, the equilibrium sequence of structures that has been experimented with over periods 0, 1, 2 is ABC, while the equilibrium sequence of structures that has finally been chosen is AAA. Partial organization information is acquired at the end of period 1 and all organization information is acquired by society at the end of period 2. For $s_B > s_B^0$, $s_C < s_C^2$, and $L > L_0$, the equilibrium sequence of structures that has been experimented with is ABB, and the equilibrium sequence of structures that has finally been chosen is also ABB. Partial organization information is acquired by society. The sequential equilibrium organization information stops evolving at the end of period 2, either because the maximum available amount has already been acquired by society, or because the efficient trade-off between information gains and its cost based on updated information suggests that the information acquisition process should stop. Hence, the chosen structure in period 3 and afterward is always the same as in period 2. But if there are many goods and many structures to try, then the concurrent evolution of division of labor and organization information can occur over many periods.

Since a Walrasian sequential equilibrium is partly determined by a sequence of static corner equilibria, the time paths of individuals' resource allocation decisions, the equilibrium relative prices, and the number of individuals choosing different configurations can be found by putting table 24.1 and figure 24.3 together. For instance, for $s_B > s_B^0$, $s_C > s_C^2$, $L > L_0$, and $k > k_1$, the corner equilibrium in structure B is tried out and chosen in period 1; the corner equilibrium relative prices, numbers of different specialists, and demand and supply in C, given in table 24.1, are tried out and are chosen in period 2. For $s_B > s_B^0$, $s_C > s_C^1$, $L < L_0$, and $k < k_0$, the corner equilibrium in B is tried out in period 1, but the chosen resource allocation in period 1 is the optimum decision in A; the corner equilibrium relative price, number of different specialists, and resource allocation are tried out in period 2, but the chosen resource allocation in period 2 and afterward is the optimum decision in structure A.

As we expected, the Walrasian sequential equilibrium involves some uncertainty about the evolution of the economic organism. In period 0, nobody knows where the evolution of the economy will head. All evolutionary paths in figure 24.3 are possible. This evolutionary uncertainty will gradually be resolved as individuals and society gradually acquire organizational knowledge. But the resulting evolution has a recognizable trend: it involves a progression from a simple organism to a complex one. Although absence of evolution is a possibility, devolution never takes place. The evolution in organization information acquired by society is irreversible too. The intuition for this feature is that since experimental cost is lower for the simple than for the complex organisms, when society is short of organization information it always tries a simple organism before more complex ones. However, this trend does not imply a general relationship between the complexity of organisms and their efficiency.

Interactions between individuals' dynamic decisions and acquired organization information are similar to, though distinct from, the sequential equilibrium in game theory. Individuals' dynamic decisions concerning the sequence of configurations that are experimented with, and the sequence of configurations that are finally chosen, together determine the time path of organization information that they can know, while the evolution of organization information itself determines the adjustment of dynamic decisions. However, each individual does not have perfect sequential rationality. She must use an adaptive decision rule to adjust her dynamic decision as she gradually learns organization information. This is different from Kreps' sequential equilibrium model, where for each subspace of parameters, a player's dynamic decision rule is deterministic and never changes, though the decision itself is contingent upon updated information. Hence, each player has only one dynamic programming problem which is not adjusted over time. But in our model each individual's dynamic programming problem in each period may be different from the one in the next period.

Though there is no information asymmetry in our model, the social learning process may be more sophisticated than in Kreps' sequential equilibrium. In our model, each individual does not know the others' utility and production functions and endowment constraints, and even does not know the distribution functions of states of the physical conditions that others privately know. Hence, this can be considered *absolute information asymmetry*, which is a feature of the Walrasian equilibrium model. The social learning process in our model does not involve the transmission of such private information between individuals and accordingly does not reduce the absolute information asymmetry, though individuals acquire organization information through the price system in this process. All individuals simultaneously acquire organization information at the same rate.

Comparing figure 24.1 and figure 24.3, we can see that if experimental efficiency $s$ is sufficiently high, then the organization information that is acquired by society will spontaneously evolve over time. If transaction efficiency $k$ is sufficiently high too, the evolution of organization information is associated with evolution also in division of labor and in the length of the roundabout production chain, and with the emergence of new machines and related new technology. The essential message from the model is that organization information acquired by society determines the network size and pattern of division of labor, which determine the capacity of society to acquire technical knowledge, which in turn determines productivity and technology progress. Institutional arrangements affect the efficiency of society in using the pricing mechanism to experiment with structures of division of labor and to acquire organization information. Our model shows that free pricing and the market mechanism cannot guarantee that all individuals will obtain all organization information unless all possible structures of division of labor have been experimented with. The free pricing and market system is a vehicle for society to organize and coordinate social experiments with various structures of division of labor in order to acquire organization information.

Our model can be used to show that the application of the notion of a Pareto optimum to economic analysis that involves bounded rationality is much more sophisticated than in neoclassical economics. In our Walrasian sequential equilibrium model, it is a matter of luck to have a Pareto optimum sequential equilibrium. Moreover, the Pareto optimum sequential equilibrium might be meaningless to human society. From table 24.2 and figure 24.3, we can see that structure A is Pareto optimal if $k < k_0$ and $L < L_0$, while the sequential equilibrium achieves the Pareto optimum if $s_B < s_B^0$. This implies that for a sufficiently low transaction efficiency and degree of economies of roundabout production, structure A over all periods is Pareto optimal. If experimental efficiency happens to be low too, then no experiments will take place, so that the Pareto optimum will be achieved. If $s_B > s_B^0$, unnecessary experimental cost will be incurred, despite the fact that organization information is acquired. If $s_B > s_B^0$, $s_C > s_C^2$, $k > k_1$, and $L > L_0$, then the corner equilibrium in structure C is static Pareto optimal and the sequential equilibrium will eventually settle down in the corner equilibrium. However, the sequential equilibrium is not Pareto optimal since society can learn the organization information about the Pareto optimum pattern of division of labor only if it has experimented with all corner equilibria including Pareto inefficient ones. In this sense the nontrivial Pareto optimum Walrasian sequential equilibrium is a utopia. The simple way of pursuing it by restricting experiments with inefficient economic structures is dangerous, since it may discourage experiments that are essential for acquiring information about the Pareto optimum pattern of division of labor.

The model can provide three insights into economic development. First, it explains why those economies with *laissez-faire* policy regimes, such as Hong Kong in recent decades and eighteenth- and nineteenth-century Britain, are more successful in economic development than those with a lot of government intervention, such as seventeenth-century China, which discouraged commerce and had many government industrial policies, and the Soviet Union, which put industrial planning under the complete control of the government. If a government believes that it knows what the efficient industrial structure is, and actively pursues industrial policies to achieve this, then such a naive idea will slow down, and perhaps destroy, the search process for an efficient industrial structure which would otherwise be initiated by spontaneous entrepreneurial activities. The failure during the 1960s and 1970s of many development and industrial policies recommended by neoclassical development economists provides support for our model. China and India used protective tariffs, import substitution, state enterprises, various industrial policies, and central planning to pursue industrialization in the 1950s to 1970s. But their development performance during this period was very disappointing. The Hong Kong government had no interventionist industrial policy, but rather promoted a quite classical *laissez-faire* regime that was duty free (except for cigarette and liquor), had trivial tariffs (just enough to cover custom administration costs), and had a free private enterprise system. But it was the invisible hand in Hong Kong that created the successful labor-intensive export-oriented industrialization pattern which the old industrialized economies had not experienced, and which was later copied by Taiwan, South Korea, Singapore, Thailand, and finally by mainland China and India.

Why is such a successful development pattern always created by the invisible hand rather than by a government with an interventionist policy regime? The answer can be found in our model in this chapter. A *laissez-faire* atmosphere will encourage entrepreneurial activities that lead to spontaneous social experiments with various structures of division of labor, including inefficient ones. This will speed up the process of acquisition of organization information, thereby speeding up economic development. Government planning of industrial development and trade patterns is incompatible with the notion of experiments with various structures of division of labor, including inefficient ones, so that it will slow down the acquisition process of organization information, thereby impeding economic development.

The second insight into economic development that our model can provide relates to the concept of *big-push industrialization*. Big-push industrialization, as described in chapters 6 and 22, implies that the level of division of labor and related size of the input–output network between interdependent specialized sectors discontinuously jumps over many intermediate levels. Many interdependent and highly specialized sectors simultaneously emerge, through comprehensive investment programs, from this process. As we discussed before, a central planning and state enterprise system may slow down the social acquisition process of organization information. However, if developed economies have already acquired a great deal of organization information through a *laissez-faire* regime and through institutional arrangements that protect private property and the residual rights of owners of private enterprises, a latecomer to industrialization may use the free organization information generated by those economies to mimic the efficient structure of division of labor through central planning and a state enterprise system. In this way the latecomer may attempt to jump over many intermediate levels of division of labor and achieve big-push industrialization.

This conjecture is verified by the quite successful big-push industrialization of the Soviet Union in the 1930s and 1950s, and of mainland China and India in the 1950s. This explains why von Mises (1922) and Hayek (1944) failed to predict the survival of the Soviet-style economic system for half of the twentieth century. They did not realize that it is possible to mimic a successful industrialization pattern, despite the fact that they correctly pointed out that the Soviet-style economic system is incapable of searching for an efficient pattern of organization on its own. But the condition for survival of the Soviet-style economic system is imitation of successful organization patterns that have been tried out by the free market system. As the potential for further imitation is exhausted, the fatal flaw of the centrally planned system will destroy it. The Soviet style economic system proceeds by precluding, or destroying, the very institutional infrastructures that create efficient organizational patterns; that is, by killing the golden goose, it ensures that it cannot have its own golden eggs. This is why the new export-oriented big-push industrialization pattern created by Hong Kong cannot be created by a Soviet-style economic system, though the Soviet-style economic system in mainland China has been able to some degree to mimic it in the 1980s and 1990s. This also explains why a transition from a Soviet-style economic system to a free market system is so difficult, since human society has had no experience of such a transition that can be mimicked by Russia and China. When the Chinese communist leaders abandoned the imitation strategy of Stalin and

Lenin and tried to create their own institutions, such as people's communes and public eating halls in 1959, the result was the most devastating man-made economic disaster in history. More than 30 million Chinese people died from the starvation and famine caused by this centralized institutional experiment (Chang and Wen, 1998).

The experience of industrialization in Hong Kong and Taiwan provides evidence that big-push industrialization can be achieved much better through the invisible hand than through a central planning system. Within 50 years, per capita real incomes in those two economies increased from less than US$200 in 1950 to more than US$10,000 in the 1990s. But the early success of China's big-push industrialization based on the Soviet-style economic system in the 1950s could not prevent its failure in the long run. At that time China used the Soviet-style system to successfully implement a comprehensive industrial investment program with 156 large projects, which generated a very impressive jump in the level of division of labor. Many very specialized and interdependent state enterprises simultaneously emerged from the program. In this big push, China systematically mimicked the Taylor scientific management approach of large firms with a high level of division of labor, industrial standardization, mass production and related production lines, a high investment rate, a high growth rate of the producer goods sector compared to the consumption goods sector, and other industrialization patterns created by the capitalist developed economies. The country achieved two-digit growth rates in real GDP and industrial output. However, although it started in 1950 with the same economic conditions and per capita real income as Taiwan, per capita income in China was less than US$1,000 in 1999.

Hence, the third insight that our model can provide is that although state-led big-push industrialization may yield some short-run success, it cannot survive in the long run since it destroys the functioning of the price system in coordinating social experiments with various structures of division of labor, and accordingly restricts the capacity of society to acquire organization information. This insight contrasts sharply with Lange's market socialism (Lange and Taylor, 1964), which many economists still believe in today (see Bardhan and Roemer, 1993), and which is discussed in the following example.

### Example 24.2: market socialism

Lange's *market socialism* works in the following way. A benevolent socialist government owns all firms and production means. Consumers can own consumer goods that they buy. The government delegates management of state firms to managers and asks them to maximize profit, but retains the power of pricing goods and factors. Those prices are determined by a mechanism analogous to the Walrasian auction mechanism. The managers report their profit maximizing quantities of goods supplied and factors demanded to the government, which sets prices according to these reports and the demand for goods by consumers. Then a trial-and-error process is used to work out market clearing prices. If total demand is greater than total supply of a good, the price is increased, and if total demand is short of supply the price is reduced by the government, until the market is cleared. This story is of course consistent with neoclassical general equilibrium models.

Market socialism is criticized by neoclassical economists. First, one may ask why the government would want to clear the market if it is self-interested rather than benevolent? The reality is that the self-interested government would like to prevent the market from clearing, so that its regulatory power dominates the power of the market in allocating resources. Government officials can obtain many tangible and intangible benefits from the imbalance between demand and supply. Second, one may ask what the incentives are for the managers of state firms to maximize profit? In reality, there are no such incentives. The managers are concerned with the security of their positions and the possibilities for promotion. They and their superiors are not accountable for profitability since none of them is a real claimant for the residual rights of any state firm. The managers may collude with workers to overstate demand for factors and understate supply capacity, or pursue welfare benefits for members of a state firm at the cost of long-run investment. They may also be too biased toward the interests of their superiors. Furthermore, the absence of factor markets, including markets for managerial skill and entrepreneurial ideas, will paralyze the functioning of market socialism.

However, the fatal flaw of market socialism relates to the function of the free market in coordinating social experiments with various structures of division of labor. The function of the market is not just to allocate resources, nor is it only to find the efficient network pattern of division of labor. Its more important function is to organize social experiments to acquire organization information. The central planning and state ownership of firms in market socialism are incompatible with the notion of experimentation which involves trial of inefficient patterns of organization. Market socialism gives the government monopoly power in designing institutions and in experimenting with different patterns of economic organization. Hence, the experimental process is not competitive. In particular, entrepreneurs' claims to the residual rights of firms, together with the free price system and the function of the stock market in sharing risk, are crucial for providing entrepreneurs with an incentive to take the risk involved in such social experiments. But market socialism rejects the legitimacy of residual rights to private firms and insists on government monopoly in experimenting with structures of division of labor and residual rights. Hence, the process of acquiring organization information will be much slower under market socialism than in a free market system based on private ownership of property and firms. Our model in this chapter explores functions of the market that are much more sophisticated than in neoclassical general equilibrium models. Hence, Lange's market socialism, based on neoclassical general equilibrium models, can be even more conclusively rejected by our theory in this chapter.

## Key Terms and Review

Walrasian sequential equilibrium and the difference between it and Kreps and Selten's concept of sequential equilibrium.

The difference between lack of information and incomplete information.

Information gains resulting from experiments with various structures of division of labor.

Major determinants of the pattern of concurrent evolution of organization information and division of labor. Bayes updating rule.

Interdependence between organization information and decisions in choosing configuration, and the implications of this for concurrent evolution of organization information and division of labor.

Bounded rationality.

Adaptive behavior.

How can we solve analytically for a dynamic programming problem in choosing the efficient trade-off between information gains and experiment cost, and how can we put the analytical solution of this problem together with the solutions of static corner equilibria of a new classical model to work out Walrasian sequential equilibrium?

What are the implications of the decision horizon in a Walrasian sequential equilibrium model?

## Further Reading

*The sequential equilibrium model in game theory*: Kreps and Wilson (1982), Kreps (1990); *Walrasian sequential equilibrium models*: Yang and Y.-K. Ng (1998), Zhao (1999); *search theory*: Aghion, Bolton, and Jullien (1991), S. Grossman (1989), Morgan and Manning (1985), Reingnum (1982), Stigler (1961), Weitzman (1979), Lippman and McCall (1979); *free riding in the search process*: King (1995), Banerjee (1992*); neoclassical theory and models of big-push industrialization*: Rosenstein-Rodan (1943), Murphy, Shleifer, and Vishny (1989a,b), Nurske (1953), Fleming (1955), Hirschman (1958); *the Soviet Union's big-push industrialization*: Zaleski (1980), Lenin (1939), Sachs and Woo (1994), Sachs, Woo, and Parker (1997); *China's big-push industrialization*: Riskin (1987), World Bank (1984); *Taiwan's big push industrialization*: Rabushka (1987); *evolutionary economics*: Nelson (1995) and references there; *bounded rationality*: Conlisk (1996) and references there; *Market socialism vs. spontaneous order*: Sachs (1993), von Mises (1922), Hayek (1944, 1945), Bardhan and Roemer eds. (1993), Lange and Taylor (1964).

## QUESTIONS

1  Why has the automobile industry developed much more successfully in the US, where the government does not engage in much regulation of this sector, than in China, where the government has very comprehensive industrial policies about the priority order of development of different sectors? The Japanese government had an industrial policy to restrict the development of the automobile industry in the 1950s, since it believed that Japan did not have comparative advantage in this sector. However, private enterprise resisted that industrial policy and developed the most competitive automobile industry in the world. Use the concept of endogenous comparative advantage in chapter 2 and the Walrasian sequential equilibrium in this chapter to analyze why this happened and what the implications are of a private enterprise system for social experiments in acquiring organization information.

2  We have heard many stories about the successful career or business activities of somebody who has advanced through "discovering herself." But from the theory that you have learned in this chapter, you can see that "oneself" is not predetermined. One's professional capacity is determined by one's choice of profession, through which specialized experience can be accumulated. Interdependence between self-confidence in one's professional capacity and accumulation of experience in a professional sector may generate some positive feedback effect (virtual circles). Hence, we may see some cases of a not-so-smart person getting a chance to be involved in a profession and becoming more capable in it than a much smarter guy who did not have the chance to be involved in the profession. Hence, for such success stories "designing oneself" is a better expression than "discovering oneself." In particular, designing oneself is an experiment with possible combinations of one's inherited talent and all kinds of structures of division of labor. Success or failure is, to a certain degree, a matter of luck. Therefore, a positive attitude toward taking reasonable risk may be better than trying something only in the absence of risk. Use the model in this chapter to explain why many successful businessmen, such as Edison, who had no formal education, were once only marginal figures in society.

3  We can use the theory of the firm in chapter 8, the theory about the implications of insurance for the division of labor in chapter 17, and the theory in this chapter to formulate a story about the role of the stock market. The story may be outlined as follows. Suppose there are economies of specialization in acquiring organization information. Hence, a professional entrepreneur may have more organization information than other specialist producers of tangible goods. And hence, there is information asymmetry. The entrepreneur would like to try some structure of division of labor according to her organization information, but others will not follow according to their information. Because of the information

asymmetry, the entrepreneur cannot convince others to participate in the social experiment that she believes to be lucrative. She may use the institution of the firm to buy out others in order to participate in the social experiment that she suggests. However, her organization information may be incomplete despite the fact that she has more information than others. This implies that when she uses the residual rights to a firm to indirectly price her intangible information, she also takes all the risk of the social experiment. If she is risk averse, then she will not choose to specialize in entrepreneurial activities. But if the stock market can be used to disperse the risk of social experimentation, then a higher level of division of labor between professional entrepreneurial activity and the production of tangible goods will occur in equilibrium, so that the sequential equilibrium may be associated with a faster evolution of organization information that is acquired by society. Demonstrate this.

4   Take a case study in which an entrepreneur (or a group of entrepreneurs) uses the stock market to experiment with a large shopping center as a basis for discussing the function of the stock market in sharing the risk of social experimentation, as examined in question 3.

5   Analyze why the success of the McDonalds restaurant network cannot be explained by using marginal analysis, and why inframarginal analysis and social experiment are essential to the explanation.

6   The essence of the model in this chapter is that knowledge of economic organization determines productivity and technical conditions. This point becomes even more evident if many goods are introduced into the model so that the number of patterns of division of labor and the number of experimental patterns are increased. In this case the number of periods necessary for experimenting with all possible patterns of the division of labor will increase more than proportionally. For a completely symmetric model, the number of possible distinct patterns of the division of labor is $m - 1$ if there are $m$ goods. The number becomes $\sum_{n=0}^{m} C^n_m = 2^m$ if $n$ out of $m$ goods are traded and preference and production parameters differ across goods, where $C^n_m$ is $n$ combination of $m$ factors. Suppose there are 100 goods ($m = 100$) and it takes one day for an economy to experiment with one pattern of the division of labor. It will take $2^{100}/365 = 3.34 \times 10^{27}$ years to have experimented with all patterns of the division of labor. Assume that there are 10 final goods and each of them can be produced by a roundabout production chain with 2, 3, ..., or 10 links. Each individual can produce 1, 2, ..., 100 goods. Suppose moreover it takes society one day to experiment with one structure of division of labor. How long will it take society to find the efficient structure of division of labor out of all possible patterns of roundabout production? Use this example to analyze why it took a long time for human society to find the efficient industrial pattern that was realized in the Industrial Revolution.

7   Zhao (1999) specifies a trade-off between the benefit of a long decision horizon, which enables the amortization of fixed investment in organization information over a longer period of time, and the higher computation cost and risk of making more mistakes. Hence, the optimum decision horizon is endogenized. Discuss the implications of the endogenization of the decision horizon.

8   Zhao (1999) shows that if countries are *ex ante* different in some aspects, then their optimum decisions about experiments with various structures of division of labor may be different. If differences in language and culture can isolate the social experiments in different countries, then social experiments with different structures of division of labor can be simultaneously implemented in a short period of time. Use this idea to explain why Europe, with many independent countries, may acquire organization information faster than China, which has had a single government for a long period of time.

9   Discuss the possible free rider problem in the model in this chapter. If all individuals wait for others to experiment with different structures of division of labor in the hope of free riding on the experiments, then the Walrasian sequential equilibrium may involve slower acquisition of organization information. Discuss why in a symmetric model, like the one in this chapter, such free riding would not occur.

# EXERCISES

1. Use the approach in this chapter to dynamize the new classical model with endogenous middlemen in chapter 7. Analyze the implications of the degree of economies of specialization in transacting and production activities, the subjective discount factor, and pricing efficiency for transaction efficiency, emergence of professional middlemen, and trade pattern.

2. Use the approach developed in this chapter to dynamize the new classical model of the institution of the firm in chapter 8. The answer can be found in Zhao (1999).

3. Use the approach in this chapter to dynamize the new classical model of endogenous trade theory in chapter 11. You may assume that each individual considers only the current and the next period when she makes decisions about experiments with different configurations. The answer can be found in Zhao (1999).

4. Use the approach in this chapter to dynamize the trade model with exogenous comparative advantages in chapter 12. Analyze the implications of interdependence between organization information and choice of configuration for the exploitation of exogenous comparative advantage.

5. Use the approach in this chapter to dynamize the new classical model with endogenous cum exogenous comparative advantages in chapter 13. Analyze the implications of interdependence between organization information and choice of configuration for the available number of consumer goods in the market.

6. Use the approach in this chapter to dynamize the new classical model of urbanization in chapter 14. Analyze the implications of institutions that affect pricing cost for development of urbanization.

7. Use the approach in this chapter to dynamize the new classical model of trade-off between leisure and consumption in chapter 15. Analyze the implications of the institutions that affect pricing cost for the efficient trade-off between leisure and consumption.

8. Use the approach in this chapter to dynamize the new classical model of property rights in chapter 16. Discuss the implications of institutions that affect experimental cost for the social search process for efficient institutions.

9. Use the approach in this chapter to dynamize the new classical model of insurance in chapter 17. Analyze the implications of institutions that affect pricing costs for the function of insurance in promoting division of labor.

10. Use the approach in this chapter to dynamize the new classical model of endogenous number of producer goods in chapter 18. Analyze the implications of interdependence between organization information and choice of configuration for the available number of producer goods in the market.

11. Use the approach in this chapter to dynamize the new classical model of an endogenous length of roundabout production chain in chapter 19. Analyze the implications of experimental costs for the evolution of production roundaboutness.

12. Use the approach in this chapter to dynamize the new classical model of the endogenous network hierarchy of wholesale and retail trade in chapter 20. Discuss the implications of the subjective discount factor, transaction cost, degree of economies of specialization, and pricing cost for the evolution of the network hierarchy of wholesale and retail trade.

13    Use the approach in this chapter to dynamize the new classical model of money in chapter 26. Discuss the implications of the subjective discount factor, transaction cost, degree of economies of specialization, and pricing cost for the emergence of money from evolution of division of labor.

14    Follow the approach in chapter 13 to establish an existence theorem of Walrasian sequential equilibrium for a general version of the model in this chapter.

# part X

# MACROECONOMIC PHENOMENA AND THE ENDOGENOUS SIZE OF THE NETWORK OF DIVISION OF LABOR

chapter 25

# INVESTMENT AND SAVING THEORY

## ◆ 25.1 Neoclassical Investment and Saving Theory

Due to the dichotomy assumed between pure consumers and pure producers, it was customary in early neoclassical analysis that the theory of consumption and saving behavior (for instance in Friedman's permanent income model, 1957, and Modigliani's life-cycle model, 1989) was separated from the theory of investment and capital. Many early neoclassical models of saving and investment are macroeconomic models rather than microeconomic general equilibrium models. They do not have a sound microeconomic foundation of saving behavior. In recent microeconomic models of saving and credit the distinction is drawn between self-saving and interpersonal loans. A sound microeconomic foundation of saving and credit is established to explain saving and interpersonal credit as generated by gains from intertemporal trade between individuals. A very good survey of recent neoclassical microeconomic models of saving and credit can be found in Besley (1995).

In this literature there are several types of gain from self-saving. Differences in incomes at different points in time and uncertainty of future income are two common sources of gains. Here, income differences may be caused by differences in endowments or in production capacity. In section 25.2 we consider such a neoclassical model of self-saving. Also, there are several types of gains from intertemporal trade which are based on a general equilibrium mechanism of saving: (a) Differences in subjective discount rates or in tastes for goods at different points in time may generate intertemporal trade. (b) A significant source of gains from intertemporal trade arises from difference in the timing of endowments or production capacities between individuals. (c) Individuals may wish to lend to others who have a better technological advantage for transferring resources over time. (d) There may be a need for purchasing durable goods with a value that is much greater than an individual's income flow at each point in time. In section 25.2, we consider two such neoclassical models of interpersonal loans.

Understanding the productivity implications of saving is essential for explaining the phenomenon observed by Lewis (1955, p. 155): the "central problem in the theory of economic development is to understand the process by which a community which was previously saving . . . 4 or 5 percent of its national income or less, converts itself into an economy where voluntary saving is running at about 12 to 15 percent of national income or more." The most popular theory of the relationship between saving and productivity is called *saving fundamentalism*, which claims an unconditional "if and only if" relationship between current saving and future productivity. Current saving can increase future per capita capital, while labor productivity is a monotonically increasing function of per capita capital. This saving and investment fundamentalism is taken as granted in the growth models of Ramsey (1928), Solow (1956), Lucas (1988), Romer (1986, 1990), and Grossman and Helpman (1989, 1990).

However, we may ask why productivity in the future can be increased by saving today. This positive relationship did not exist 2,000 years ago. For instance, 2,000 years ago, peasants invested corn seeds each year. But that investment could only maintain simple reproduction without much increase in productivity. Also, Chinese peasants invested in houses which were completely self-provided in the 1970s. Productivity based on such investment in durable houses was extremely low (Yang, Wang, and Wills, 1992).

Lucas and Romer point to human capital generated by saving and investment. However, we will again use the Chinese case to argue that investment in human capital and education does not necessarily lead to an increase in productivity. Chinese people have a special preference for saving and for investment in education. However, this did not generate significant productivity increases until the modern school and university systems were introduced into China at the end of the nineteenth century. In traditional Chinese schools, there was no division of labor between teachers. Each teacher taught students a broad range of knowledge, from literature to philosophy. But in a modern university, there is a very high level of division of labor between different specialist teachers and between different specialized colleges. Also, educated individuals are very specialized in their professions after their graduation from universities. It is the high level of division of labor that ensures high productivity in providing education, so that investment in education can contribute significantly to productivity progress. Recent empirical evidence supports our observations. Pritchett (1997) shows that empirical evidence from macro data rejects the unconditional positive relationship between educational capital and the rate of growth of output per worker, despite the positive effects of education on earnings from micro data.

To our question above, Grossman and Helpman might respond by pointing to investment in research and development. However, Marshall attributed the invention of the steam engine by Boulton and Watt to a deep division of labor in the inventing activities (Marshall, 1890, p. 256). Edison's experience is further evidence of the need for division of labor for successful invention. Not only did Edison specialize in inventing electrical machines for most of his life, but he also organized a professional research institution with more than a hundred employees who specialized in different inventing activities (Josephson, 1959).

This implies that investment in physical capital goods, in education, or in research would not automatically increase productivity in the future if the investment were not used to develop the right level and pattern of division of labor. Hence, the essential question around the notion of capital is not so much how much we invest and save, but rather what level and pattern of division of labor are used to invest in machines, education, and research.

The recent empirical evidence that rejects Type IV scale effect (a positive relationship between growth rates in per capita GDP and investment rates) supports our observation (see Jones, 1995a). Hence, most classical economists like Smith, John Stuart Mill, Karl Marx, and Marshall emphasized the connection between the division of labor and capital. Mill's wage fund argument (1848, ch. 2, sec. 2; ch. 5, sec. 3) is somehow inconsistent with the modern dichotomy between investment and consumption. He stated that "capital, although the result of saving, is nevertheless consumed." This proposition implies that a theory of investment should explain why a transfer of consumption goods from their producers to the producers of producer goods can improve productivity. In other words, we should use the concept of general equilibrium to explain gains from interpersonal and intertemporal trade of goods as the engine of investment and economic development rather than following saving fundamentalism.

In section 25.3 we use a new classical model of endogenous specialization to formalize the classical story of investment that is used to increase division of labor in roundabout productive activities. A dynamic general equilibrium model will be used to address the following questions. What is the relationship between saving, which generates investment, and the division of labor, which determines the extent of the market, trade dependence, and productivity? What is the mechanism that simultaneously determines the investment level and the level of division of labor? And what are the determinants of the equilibrium investment (saving) rate, the interest rate, the growth rate, and the equilibrium level of division of labor?

Our new classical story of investment and capital originates with Smith (1776) and Allyn Young (1928), who explicitly spelt out the relationship between the division of labor and capital. According to them, capital and investment is a matter of the development of division of labor in roundabout productive activities.[1] This story runs as follows. There are many *ex ante* identical consumer-producers in an economy where food can be produced out of labor alone or out of labor and tractors. In producing each good, there are economies of specialized learning by doing. A fixed cost is incurred in the period when an individual engages in a job for the first time, or when job shifting takes place. Each individual can choose between specialization and self-sufficiency. The advantage of specialization is to exploit the economies of specialized learning by doing and to avoid job shifting cost. However, it increases productivity in the future at the expense of current consumption because of an increase in transaction cost caused by specialization.

Moreover, in producing a tractor, there is a significant fixed learning cost. The production of a tractor cannot be completed until the learning cost has reached a threshold level. Hence, there are trade-offs among economies of specialized learning by doing, economies of roundaboutness, transaction costs, and fixed learning costs. Each consumer-producer maximizes total discounted utility over the two periods with respect to the level and pattern of specialization and the quantities of goods consumed, produced, and traded in order to efficiently trade-off one against others among the four conflicting forces.

The interaction between these trade-offs determines the nature of the dynamic equilibrium for the economy. If the transaction cost coefficient is sufficiently great, the economy is in autarky in all periods – depending upon the level of fixed learning cost and the degree of economies of roundaboutness, this may entail each individual self-providing food, or self-providing both food and tractor, or it may entail evolution in the number of goods. If the transaction cost coefficient is sufficiently small and economies of specialized learning by doing and of roundaboutness are significant, in the dynamic equilibrium the economy will develop a market structure in which individuals specialize in the production of either tractors or food and trade occurs. For the division of labor there are two patterns of investment and saving. If the fixed learning cost in producing tractors is not large, each individual will sacrifice consumption in period 1 to pay transaction costs in order to increase the level of division of labor, so that productivity in period 2 can be increased. This is a self-saving mechanism which does not involve interpersonal lending. Also, an evolution in the level of specialization and/or in the number of goods may take place in the dynamic equilibrium if the transaction cost coefficient and the degree of economies of specialization and of roundaboutness are neither too large nor too small. If the fixed learning cost in producing tractors is so large that the production of a tractor cannot be completed within one period because of the time required for specialized learning by producing tractors, then an explicit saving arrangement which involves a loan from a specialist producer of food to a specialist producer of tractors in period 1 is necessary for specialization in producing roundabout productive tractors.

Under the assumptions of a high fixed learning cost in producing tractors, a small transaction cost coefficient, and significant economies of specialized learning by doing and roundaboutness, dynamic general equilibrium yields the following picture.

A specialist producer of food produces food using her labor only and makes a loan in terms of food to a specialist producer of tractors in period 1, when the production of a tractor is yet to be completed. In period 2, a specialist producer of tractors sells tractors to a specialist farmer in excess of the value of her purchase of food in period 2. The difference is her repayment of the loan received in period 1. Per capita consumption of food in period 1 is lower than in an alternative autarky pattern of organization. But in period 2, tractors are employed to improve the productivity of food. The discounted gains will more than offset the lower level of per capita consumption in period 1 if the transaction efficiency coefficient and economies of specialized learning by doing and roundaboutness are great. Economic growth takes place not only in the sense of an increase in per capita real income between periods, but also in the sense that total discounted real income is higher than in alternative autarky patterns of organization.

---

### *Questions to Ask Yourself when Reading this Chapter*

♦ What are the gains from intertemporal trade and related saving and credit?

♦ What is the distinction between self-saving and interpersonal lending?

♦ What is the relationship between interpersonal loans and division of labor?

♦ What is the difference between the theory of endogenous gains from saving and the theory of exogenous gains from saving? What are the implications of the difference for the theory of investment?

♦ What is the relationship between transaction efficiency, rate of return to investment, and division of labor in roundabout production activities in the new classical theory of capital?

♦ Under what conditions may the rate of return to investment suddenly jump to 0?

♦ How does the market sort out the efficient levels of saving, interpersonal lending, and investment?

---

## ♦ 25.2 Neoclassical Models of Self-saving and Interpersonal Loans

In this section, we first consider Lenand's model of self-saving (1968), which shows that self-saving level is an increasing function of the degree of uncertainty of future income.

We then consider Diamond and Dybvig's general equilibrium model of interpersonal loans (1983). Finally, we consider Besley, Coate, and Loury's model of rotating savings and informal credit associations (1993).

## Example 25.1: precautionary saving in autarky (Leland, 1968)

An individual's decision problem is

$$\text{Max}_s \; u(y_1 - s) + \delta E[u(y_2 + sr)],$$

where $y_1$ is a certain income level in period 1, $y_2 \sim N(0, \sigma)$ is a random income level in period 2, $s$ is the saving level in period 1, $r$ is a certain return rate of saving, and $sr$ is total return to saving. Utility function $u(.)$ is strictly increasing and strictly concave. According to section 10.4 in chapter 10, the certain equivalent of $E[u(y_2 + sr)]$ is approximately $u(sr - 0.5R\sigma)]$, where $R = -u''(E[y_2 + sr])/u'(E[y_2 + sr]) = -u''(sr)/u'(sr)$ is the degree of risk aversion. A well-known result (Lenand, 1968) says that the optimum saving level $s^*$ increases with the degree of uncertainty $\sigma$, if $u'''(.) > 0$. We use a specific form of $u(x) = \ln x$ to show this. For this specific functional form, the optimum saving $s^*$ is given by the following first-order condition

$$f(\sigma, \delta, r, s, y_1) = r(1 + \delta)s - [(1 - \delta)\sigma/2rs] - (\delta\sigma y_1/2rs^2) - \delta ry_1 = 0.$$

The differentiation of this condition and application of the implicit function theorem yield the comparative statics of the optimum decision:

$$ds/d\sigma = -(\partial f/\partial \sigma)/(\partial f/\partial s) > 0, \qquad ds/d\delta = -(\partial f/\partial \delta)/(\partial f/\partial s) > 0,$$
$$ds/dr = -(\partial f/\partial r)/(\partial f/\partial s) > 0, \qquad ds/dy_1 = -(\partial f/\partial y_1)/(\partial f/\partial s) > 0,$$

where $\partial f/\partial r < 0$ for the positive consumption level in period 2 or for $s^*r > (\sigma/2)^{0.5}$, $\partial f/\partial \sigma < 0$, $\partial f/\partial s > 0$, $\partial f/\partial \delta < 0$, and $\partial f/\partial y_1 < 0$. The comparative statics say that as uncertainty of future income, returns rate of saving, current income, and/or discount factor increase, the optimum saving level increases. Also, the optimum saving level is 0 if $s^*r < (\sigma/2)^{0.5}$ where $s^*$ is given by the first-order conditions as an increasing function of $\delta$, $r$, $y_1$. This implies that if $\delta$, $r$, and $y_1$ are too small and/or $\sigma$ is too large, the individual cannot afford saving, so that the optimum saving level is 0.

In examples 25.2 and 25.3 we consider general equilibrium models that explain saving as generated by gains from interpersonal and intertemporal trade of goods. There are three possible sources of gains from intertemporal trade of goods. In example 25.2, we assume that individuals' subjective discount factors are different, so that those individuals with a lower subjective value of time (those who are more patient) will make loans to those with a higher value of time (those who are more impatient) to allow the latter to consume more at an early point in time in dynamic general equilibrium. Another way to explain gains from intertemporal trade is to assume that individuals' production capacities differ from time to time, so that they will trade goods at different points in time to smooth out fluctuations of consumption flows. In example 25.3, we consider the third general equilibrium mechanism for intertemporal trade of goods. We assume the existence of some durable consumer goods in a general equilibrium model with *ex ante* identical consumers. Since a person's income at each point in time is not enough to afford the durable goods which can be used for many years, consumers can pool their incomes to buy a piece of durable goods for one of them at each point in time. In order to make sure that some of the individuals will voluntarily postpone consumption of durable goods, those who consume the goods earlier must pay an amount of money to compensate those who consume them later. The amount of money can be considered as interest.

### Example 25.2: a neoclassical general equilibrium model with endogenous interest rates, saving, and interpersonal loans (Diamond and Dybvig, 1983)

Consider an economy with two consumer-producers A and B, a consumption good, and two periods of time. Consumer A's subjective discount rate is $\rho \in (0, 1)$, or her subjective discount factor is $\delta = 1/(1 + \rho) \in (0, 1)$. Consumer B's subjective discount factor is $\delta = 1$. Consumer i's consumption of the good at time $t$ is $x_{it}$. Each individual can produce 1 unit of the consumption good in each period. Hence, the two individuals' decision problems are

$$\text{Max: } U_A = \ln x_{A1} + \delta \ln x_{A2} \qquad \text{s.t. } p_1 x_{A1} + p_2 x_{A2} = p_1 + p_2$$

$$\text{Max: } U_B = \ln x_{B1} + \ln x_{B2} \qquad \text{s.t. } p_1 x_{B1} + p_2 x_{A2} = p_1 + p_2$$

where $U_i$ is individual i's total discounted utility over the two periods, $p_t$ is the price of the good at time $t$. The optimum solutions of the two problems yield the two individuals' demand for the consumption good at time $t$:

$$x_{A1} = (p_1 + p_2)/(1 + \delta)p_1, \ x_{A2} = \delta(p_1 + p_2)/(1 + \delta)p_2$$

$$x_{B1} = (p_1 + p_2)/2p_1, \ x_{B2} = (p_1 + p_2)/2p_2$$

Adding the two persons' demand and letting that total demand at time $t$ equal the two persons' total supply at time $t$, which is 2, yields the general equilibrium price of the good at period 2 in terms of that at period 1:

$$p_2/p_1 = (1 + 3\delta)/(3 + \delta)$$

Inserting the equilibrium relative price back into the demand functions, we can see that

$$x_{A1} = 4/(3 + \delta) > 1, \qquad x_{A2} = 4\delta/(1 + 3\delta) < 1$$

$$x_{B1} = 2/(1 + \delta) < 1, \qquad x_{B2} = 2(1 + \delta)/(1 + 3\delta) > 1$$

This implies that person A's demand in period 1 is greater than her supply in period 1 and her demand in period 2 is smaller than her supply in period 2, while person B's position is the opposite. Hence, a loan from person B to person A is made in period 1. Its amount is

$$x_{A1} - 1 = 1 - x_{B1} = (1 - \delta)/(3 + \delta).$$

The repayment of the interpersonal loan in period 2 is

$$1 - x_{A2} = x_{B2} - 1 = (1 - \delta)/(1 + 3\delta).$$

The ratio of the repayment to the loan is

$$(3 + \delta)/(1 + 3\delta) = p_1/p_2.$$

The difference between the ratio and 1 can be considered the *equilibrium real interest rate*, which is

$$r = [(3 + \delta)/(1 + 3\delta)] - 1 = 2(1 - \delta)/(1 + 3\delta) = 2\rho(4 + \rho)$$

where $\delta = 1/(1 + \rho)$ is used. It is not difficult to verify that the equilibrium real interest rate $r$ is an increasing function of person A's subjective discount rate $\rho$. Also, $r$ can be considered an *endogenous* (or *dynamic general equilibrium*) *inflation rate*, since 1 unit of the consumption good in period 1 can exchange for $1 + r$ units of the same good in period 2.

In this general equilibrium model, commercial saving and interpersonal loans are distinguished from self-saving. If we take the same type of good at different points in time as different goods, then the interpersonal loan and its repayment is just the trading of different goods between individuals. The gains to such trade in this model are based on the exogenous difference in the subjective discount factors of the individuals. It is easy to extend the general equilibrium model to explain the gains from such trade by exogenous differences in production conditions or in endowments between individuals and between periods of time, or by the problem caused by differences between the timing of the purchase of durable consumption goods and the timing of consumption of the services that they provide. Compared to other neoclassical models of saving, this general equilibrium model of saving not only endogenizes the interest rate and the inflation rate, but also endogenizes the gains from exchanges of goods at different points in time. The gains from saving are endogenous since we cannot see them until the decisions are made and the equilibrium is worked out. By contrast, in many neoclassical models of saving and capital the gains from saving are exogenously given by an *ad hoc* positive relationship between current saving and future productivity. The productivity gain of saving can be seen from a state equation before the decisions have been made. In the general equilibrium model of saving, the rationale for inflation in the absence of money is gains from trade between goods at different points in time.

However, in the general equilibrium model of saving, saving has no productivity implication. Though its productivity implication can be figured out by introducing intermediate goods or economies of scale in production into the model, the intimate relationship between interpersonal loans and the division of labor cannot be explored by models with no endogenous specialization.

### Example 25.3: rotating savings and informal credit association (Besley, Coate, and Loury, 1993)

There are many informal financial institutions in less-developed countries where exogenous and endogenous transaction costs for founding and developing formal financial markets are very high. Roscas are one of the institutions. They travel under many different names, including *Chit Funds* (India), *Susu* (Ghana, Gambia), *Kye* (Korea), *Dahui* (China), and *Tontines* (Senegal). They operate by having a group of individuals committing to putting a certain sum of money into a pot which each period is allocated to one member of the group by a system of drawing lots (a random rosca) or by bidding. Each period of the process repeats itself, with past winners excluded, until the last member has received the pot.

Imagine a world in which $n$ individuals wish to acquire a durable good that costs $b$. Each has additive preferences over consumption: $v(c)$ without the durable and $v(c) + a$ with it. Ignoring discounting and supposing that each individual has a fixed income flow of $y$ over a life of length $T$, an individual can save up for the durable under autarky and solves the following problem in doing so:

$$\text{Max}_{c, t} \ (T - t)[v(y) + a] + tv(c) \text{ subject to } t(y - c) = b,$$

where $t$ is the acquisition date for the durable and $c$ is consumption during the accumulation phase. The first term in the maximand refers to the period after time $t$ when the durable has been acquired, while the second term is utility during the period of accumulation. The constraint just says that enough saving must have been done before $t$ to buy the durable. By eliminating $t$ in the objective function from the constraint, it is straightforward to see that the value of the autarky program can be written as

$$T[v(y) + a] - b\mu(a),$$

where $\mu(a) \equiv \text{Min}_c \ \{[v(y) + a - v(c)]/(y - c)\}$. The interpretation of this is clear. The first term represents maximal lifetime utility were the durable a free good, i.e., if an individual could own it for her whole life without having to forgo any current consumption. The second represents the utility cost of saving up. A random rosca gives each member of the group of $n$ individuals a $1/n$ chance of winning the pot at each of the rosca's meeting dates. Thus viewed *ex ante*, the rosca gives uniformly distributed acquisition dates on the set $\{1, 2, \ldots, n\}$. Assume that the time for obtaining the durable by self-saving is still $t$. Suppose now that an individual who joins the rosca wins the pot at the $i^{th}$ meeting. Therefore, she gets the durable at time $(i/n)t$. Note the probability for winning at the $i^{th}$ meeting is $1/n$. $E[(i/n)] = \sum_{i=1}^{n}[(i/n)(1/n)] = (n + 1)/2n$. Hence, her lifetime expected utility is

$$(T - t)[v(y) + a] + t[v(c) + (n + 1)a/2n] =$$
$$(T)[v(y) + a] - t\{v(y) - v(c) + [(n - 1)a/2n]\}.$$

Suppose that the rosca aims to maximize the expected utility of its representative member. It maximizes this subject to the budget constraint $t(y - c) = b$, which says that there are enough funds in the pot at each meeting date to buy the durable. Eliminating $t$ in the expected utility function from the budget constraint, the maximized expected lifetime utility in a rosca can be written as:

$$T[v(y) + a] - b\mu[(n - 1)a/2n].$$

where $\mu[(n - 1)a/2n] \equiv \text{Min}_c \ \{\{v(y) + [(n - 1)a/2n] - v(c)\}/(y - c)\}$. It is easy to prove using the envelope theorem that $\mu'(.) > 0$ and hence that, since $(n - 1)/2n < 1$, the random rosca lowers the utility cost of saving up to acquire the durable. The reason is, of course, plain to see. Even if it maintains the same saving pattern as under autarky, the rosca gives each of its members a chance of winning the pot early by drawing lots. In fact, all but the last member of the rosca is better off holding savings fixed. The rosca will, however, choose a lower savings rate than under autarky.

Many neoclassical equilibrium models of saving, credit, and insurance are used to investigate endogenous transaction costs caused by moral hazard, adverse selection, enforcement mechanisms (collateral, reputation including credit history check, social code, culture, peer pressure, and multilateral trading relations or interdependencies). Most of the models are similar to the models of endogenous transaction costs examined in chapters 9 and 10.

## ◆ 25.3 New Classical Theory of Investment and Savings

### Example 25.4: a new classical model of investment (Yang, 1999)

### 25.3.1: The model

We consider a finite horizon (two-period) economy with a continuum of *ex ante* identical consumer-producers of mass $M$. There is a single consumer good (called food) produced by labor alone or by labor and an intermediate good (called a tractor) together. Individuals can self-provide any goods, or alternatively can purchase them on the market. The self-provided amounts of food and of tractors in period $t$ are denoted respectively by $y_t$ and $x_t$. The respective amounts sold and purchased of food in period $t$ are $y^s_t$ and $y^d_t$, and those of tractors are $x^s_t$ and $x^d_t$. The trading efficiency coefficient of x and y is $k$. The total amount of tractors available is therefore $x_t + kx^d_t$. The utility function in period $t$ is

$$u_t = \ln(y_t + ky^d_t), \tag{25.1a}$$

where $u_t$ will be negative infinity if $y_t = y^d_t = 0$.

As in chapter 22 all trade in this economy is mediated through contracts signed in spot and futures markets which operate in period 1. Assume that the futures market horizon and any individual's decision horizon are of two periods. The objective function for an individual's decision problem is therefore total discounted utility, given by:

$$U = u_1 + u_2/(1 + r), \tag{25.1b}$$

where $U$ is total discounted utility, and $r$ is a subjective discount rate.

It is assumed that a fixed learning cost in terms of labor, $A$, is incurred in producing tractors. The fixed learning cost in producing food is $B$. The production functions for an individual are assumed to exhibit economies of specialized learning by doing:

$$y^p_t \equiv y_t + y^s_t = \text{Max} \{(x_t + kx^d_t)^a(L_{yt} - \sigma B), (L_{yt} - \sigma B)\} \tag{25.2a}$$

$$a \in (0.\ 1),\ B \in (0,\ 1)$$

$$x^p_t \equiv x_t + x^s_t = \text{Max} \{(L_{xt} - \sigma A)^b, 0\},\ b > 1,\ A \in (0,\ l) \tag{25.2b}$$

$$l_{yt} + l_{xt} = 1,\ l_{it} \in (0,\ l) \tag{25.2c}$$

$$L_{it} = L_{it-1} + l_{it},\ L_{x0} = L_{y0} = 0 \tag{25.2d}$$

where $y^p_t \equiv y_t + y^s_t$ and $x^p_t \equiv x_t + x^s_t$ are respectively the total output levels of food and tractors in period $t$, $y^s_t$ and $x^s_t$ are respectively the quantities of the two goods sold at time

$t$. $x_t^d$ is the amount of tractors purchased at time $t$. $l_{it}$ is an individual's level of specialization as well as the amount of her labor allocated to the production of good i (i = x, y) in period $t$, and $L_{it}$ is the labor accumulated in producing good $i$ up to period $t$, referred to as human capital. (25.2a) implies that food can be produced either from tractors and labor, or from labor alone. In producing a good in period $t$, $\sigma = 0$ if an individual has engaged in producing the good in period $t-1$ and does not shift between different activities in periods $t$ and $t-1$; $\sigma = 1$ if an individual changes jobs in period $t$ or $t-1$ or engages in producing the good for the first time in period $t$. Each person is assumed to be endowed with $l$ units of labor in each period. The assumption $A \in (0, l)$ implies that it is possible that the production process of tractors cannot be completed in period $t = 1$ if $A = l$, so that a story of investment, saving, and capital may be told. It is assumed that economies of specialized learning by doing and the fixed learning cost are specific to each individual and to each activity. There are economies of specialization in producing each good since a person's labor productivity in producing x increases with her level of specialization in producing x for $b > 1$, and total factor productivity of y increases with her level of specialization in producing y for $a > 0$ when x is used as an intermediate input. If labor alone is used to produce y, then the labor productivity of y increases with the person's level of specialization in producing y, since the utilization rate of the fixed learning cost $B$ increases with her level of specialization. Parameter $b$ represents the degree of economies of specialization in producing tractors. The elasticity of output of food with respect to tractors is $a$. Therefore, the product $ab$ can be interpreted as the degree of Type A economies of roundaboutness. (25.2d) is the state equation and initial condition for human capital $L_{it}$.

We assume that $A + B > l - 1$ to simplify the algebra. It will be clear later on that this assumption implies that self-provision of two goods by each individual in two periods is not an optimal decision. A Walrasian regime prevails because economies of specialized learning by doing are individual-specific and the futures market nullifies the monopoly power which might occur from specialized learning by doing.

## 25.3.2: Configuration sequences and structure sequences

This subsection considers an individual's production and trade decision problem and dynamic equilibrium. The Wen theorem can be applied to the model in this chapter. Hence, each individual sells only one good and does not buy and sell or self-provide a good at the same time. A feasible market structure consists of a set of choices of configurations by individuals. A *sequence of configurations* over 2 periods is a decision variable for each individual. As each individual chooses a certain sequence of configurations, a *sequence of market structures* is determined. For each sequence of market structure, there is a *dynamic corner equilibrium* which satisfies the market clearing conditions and utility equalization conditions, but may not satisfy the condition for maximizing an individual's total discounted utility with respect to choice of sequences of configurations. The remainder of this subsection characterizes the dynamic corner equilibrium for each feasible sequence of market structures and then solves for the *dynamic general equilibrium* where each individual maximizes her total discounted utility. The Wen theorem implies that six configurations – depicted in figure 25.1, where the circles represent configurations and arrow-headed lines represent flows of goods, which constitute four feasible market structures – need to be considered for the optimum decision.

In the first type of market structure, autarky, there is no trade and each individual self-provides any good that is required. Two configurations, E and F, meet the criteria for autarky. For configuration E the quantities traded of all goods are 0, $x_t = 0$, and $y_t > 0$ so that each individual self-provides food without using a tractor. For configuration F, the quantities traded of all goods are 0, but $x_t, y_t > 0$; in this case each individual self-provides both tractors and food. Each of these autarky configurations constitutes a structure. The two configurations are depicted in figure 25.1a.

In the second type of structure there is trade in tractors and/or food. Denote a configuration in which an individual sells tractors and buys food in a period by (x/y), a configuration in which an individual buys food and learns how to produce a tractor but is yet to complete its production by (0/y), a configuration in which an individual sells food and buys tractors by (y/x), and a configuration in which an individual sells food but buys nothing by (y/0).

Given these possible configurations, there are two structures with trade: (i) the structure denoted C consists of a division of the $M$ individuals between configurations (0/y) and (y/0), which are depicted in (b) – that is, professional farmers sell food to professional producers of tractors, retaining an amount for their own consumption; (ii) the structure denoted D consists of a division of the $M$ individuals between configurations (x/y) and (y/x), which is depicted in (c).

There are $2^4 = 16$ sequences of the four structures over two periods: EE, EF, ED, EC, FF, FE, FD, FC, DD, DE, DF, DC, CC, CE, CF, CD, where the first letter denotes the structure in period 1 and the second that in period 2. For instance, CD, as shown in figure 25.2, denotes that structure C is chosen in period 1 and structure D is chosen in period 2. Some of them are obviously infeasible or cannot be equilibrium. For instance, CC involves a specialist producer of tractors choosing configuration (0/y) (buying food but selling nothing) over two periods and a specialist farmer choosing (y/0) (selling food but buying nothing) over two periods. The sequence cannot be equilibrium since it is incompatible with the budget constraint. If the fixed learning cost in producing tractors A = $l$, then sequences Di (i = E, F, D, C), FF, FE, and EF are infeasible and only EE and CD are

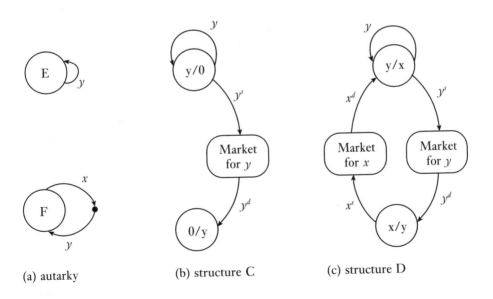

(a) autarky        (b) structure C        (c) structure D

◆ **Figure 25.1:** Configurations and market structures

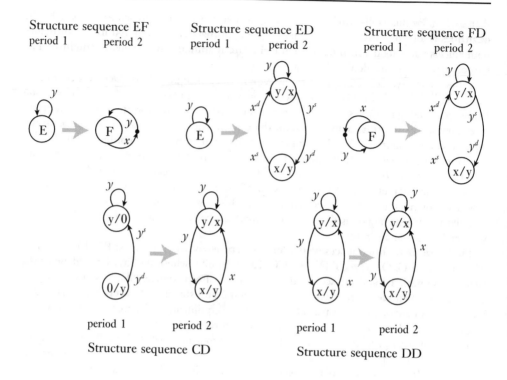

◆ **Figure 25.2:** Investment and evolution of division of labor in roundabout production

feasible. Sequence CD involves explicit saving since a specialist producer of tractors buys food and sells nothing in period 1. This one-way trade can be considered a loan made by a specialist farmer to a specialist producer of tractors.

A dynamic general equilibrium is a fixed point that satisfies the following conditions, which are analogous to the conditions in the fixed point theorem. (i) For a given profile of the sequences of configurations chosen by individuals, a set of numbers of individuals choosing different sequences of configurations and a sequence of relative prices of traded goods at different points in time clear the market for goods and equalize the total discounted utility of all individuals; (ii) for a given set of numbers of individuals choosing different sequences of configurations and for a given set of sequences of relative prices of traded goods, individuals maximize total discounted utility with respect to the sequences of configurations and quantities of goods produced, consumed, and traded.

It is possible to solve for the dynamic general equilibrium in two steps: first, by solving for a dynamic corner equilibrium for each structure sequence; then identifying the Pareto optimum dynamic corner equilibrium that generates the highest total discounted per capita real income. The first step can be divided into two substeps. The first is to solve for an individual's optimum dynamic decision for each sequence of configurations; and the second is to solve for a dynamic corner equilibrium for each structure sequence using the market clearing condition in each period and the condition that total discounted utility must be equalized for all individuals.

In the following subsections, a dynamic corner equilibrium in each of the feasible sequences of market structures is solved for, and an expression is derived for an individual's total discounted real income in each candidate for the dynamic general equilibrium.

### 25.3.3: Dynamic corner equilibria in 16 structure sequences

*1. Sequences EE and FF*: A dynamic corner equilibrium for autarky over two periods is equivalent to the solution to an individual's optimum dynamic labor allocation decision for the sequence of configurations E and/or F over two periods. In configuration E, the quantities traded of all goods are 0, $x_t = 0$ and $y_t > 0$; inserting these values into equations (25.1) and (25.2), and substituting from (25.2) into (25.1a), then into (25.1b), gives the total discounted value of utility for sequence EE as:

$$U(EE) = \ln(l - B) + \ln(2l)/(1 + r) \tag{25.3}$$

where $U(EE)$ is the total discounted utility for sequence EE.

In configuration F, the quantities of all goods traded are 0, and $x_t, y_t > 0$; inserting these values into equations (25.1) and (25.2), and substituting from (25.2) into (25.1a), then into (25.1b), gives the total discounted value of utility for sequence FF. Thus, the decision problem for the sequence is:

$$\underset{l_{xi}}{\text{Max}}\ U = \ln y_1 + \ln y_2/(1 + r) = \ln[x_1{}^a(l_{y1} - B)] + \ln[x_2{}^a(l_{y2} - B)]/(1 + r) \tag{25.4}$$

$$= \ln[(l_{x1} - A)^{ab}(l - l_{x1} - B)] + \ln[(l_{x1} + l_{x2} - A)^{ab}(l - l_{x1} + l - l_{x2} - B)]/(1 + r)$$

subject to  $y_t = x_t{}^a(L_{yt} - B),$    $x_t = (L_{xt} - A)^b$   (production function)
$l_{xt} + l_{yt} = l,$                                   (endowment constraint)
$L_{it} = L_{it-1} + l_{it},$    $L_{i0} = 0$    (state equation and initial condition)

The solution to the decision problem is given by:

$$l_{x1} = [ab(l - B) + A]/(ab + 1), \qquad l_{y1} = (abB + l - A)/(ab + 1), \tag{25.5}$$

$$l_{x2} = abl/(ab + 1), \qquad l_{y2} = l/(ab + 1),$$

$$U(FF) = [(2 + r)/(1 + r)][ab\ln(ab) - (ab + 1)\ln(ab + 1)] + $$
$$[(ab + 1)/(1 + r)][(1 + r)\ln(l - A - B) + \ln(2l - A - B)],$$

where $U(FF)$ is the total discounted per capita real income for sequence FF. As shown above, the autarky configuration F cannot be in equilibrium if $A + B \geq l$, which implies a negative infinite utility in F.

*2. Sequences EF and FE*: Following the above procedure, the corner equilibria in sequences EF and FE and the corresponding total discounted per capita real incomes can be derived. Sequence EF involves an increase in the number of goods and the emergence of tractors in period 2. Sequence FE involves a decrease in the number of goods and the disappearance of tractors in period 2.

*3. Sequence CD*: The structure C consists of configurations (0/y) and (y/0) and structure D consists of configurations (x/y) and (y/x). Hence, this structure sequence consists of the sequence of configurations (0/y) and (x/y) and the sequence of configurations (y/ 0) and (y/x). There are two steps in solving for the dynamic corner equilibrium in the structure sequence: first, for each sequence of configurations the optimum dynamic labor allocation decision and demands and supplies for each good in each period (and hence the indirect total discounted utility of an individual who chooses that configuration sequence) are derived; and second, given the demands, supplies, and indirect utility function of an individual in each configuration sequence, the market clearing conditions and utility equalization conditions are used to solve for the set of corner equilibrium relative prices and the number of individuals choosing different configuration sequences.

3.1. Sequence of Configurations (0/y) and (x/y): In this sequence $x_2^s$, $y_t^d > 0$, $l_{xt} = l$, and $x_1^s = x_t = l_{yt} = y_t = x_t^d = y_t^s = 0$. This sequence will be chosen by an individual only if $A = l$ which means that the production process of a tractor cannot be completed in period 1 due to the large fixed learning cost. If $A < l$, a sequence of (x/y) over two periods will be chosen, since it does not make sense to choose (0/y), which delays the sale of tractors, when a tractor can actually be produced in period 1. Hence, we assume $A = l$ in this configuration sequence, so that the decision problem for sequence of (0/y) and (x/y) is:

$$\text{Max: } U = \ln(ky_1^d) + \ln(ky_2^d)/(1 + r) \tag{25.5a}$$
$$\underset{y_t^d}{}$$

$$\text{s.t.: } x_1^s = 0 \text{ and } x_2^s = (l_{x1} + l_{x2})^b \qquad \text{(production function)}$$
$$l_{x1} = l_{x2} = l \qquad \text{(endowment constraint)}$$
$$p_{x2}x_2^s = y_1^d + p_{y2}y_2^d \qquad \text{(budget constraint)}$$

where $p_{it}$ is the price of good $i$ in period $t$ in terms of food in period 1, which is assumed to be the *numéraire*, and $y_1^d$ is a loan in terms of food made by a specialist farmer to the specialist producer of tractors. The specialist tractor producer's sales in period 2, $p_{x2}x_2^s$, are greater than his purchases in period 2, $p_{y2}y_2^d$. The difference is the repayment of the loan. The solution to (25.5a) is

$$x_2^s = (2l)^b, \qquad y_1^d = (1 + r)(2l)^b p_{x2}/(2 + r), \qquad y_2^d = (2l)^b p_{x2}/(2 + r)p_{y2}, \tag{25.5b}$$

$$U_x = \{(2 + r)[\ln k + b\ln(2l) + \ln p_{x2} - \ln(2 + r)] - \ln p_{y2}\}/(1 + r) + \ln(1 + r),$$

where $x_t^s$ and $y_t^d$ are the supply of tractors and the demand for food in period $t$, respectively, $U_x$ is the indirect total discounted utility function for the sequence.

3.2. Sequence of (y/0) and (y/x): By a similar process, the optimum dynamic decision for this sequence can be found as follows.

$$x_2^d = (2ak^a l p_{y2}/p_{x2})^{1/(1-a)}, \tag{25.6}$$

$$y_1^s = \{l - B - (1 + r)(1 - a)[2p_{y2}l(ak/p_{x2})^a]^{1/(1-a)}\}/(2 + r)$$

$$y_2^s = \{(1 + a + r)[2l(p_{y2}ak/p_{x2})^a]^{1/(1-a)} - (l - B)/p_{y2}\}/(2 + r),$$

$$U_y = (2 + r)\{\ln[l - B + (1 - a)[2p_{y2}l(ak/p_{x2})^a]^{1/(1-a)}] - \ln(2 + r)\}/(1 + r) + \ln(1 + r) - \ln p_{y2}/(1 + r)$$

where $U_y$ is the indirect total discounted utility function for this sequence.

Utility maximization by individuals and the assumption of free entry (when individuals make decisions at $t = 1$) have the implication that the total discounted utility of individuals is equalized across the two sequences of configurations. That is,

$$U_x = U_y. \tag{25.7}$$

Let $M_i$ represent the number of individuals selling good i. The market clearing conditions for the two goods over two periods are:

$$M_x x_2^s = M_y x_2^d, \quad M_x y_t^d = M_y y_t^s, \quad t = 1, 2, \tag{25.8}$$

where $M_x x_2^s$ and $M_y x_2^d$ are market supply and demand, respectively, for tractors in period 2, and $M_x y_t^d$ and $M_y y_t^s$ are market demand and supply, respectively, for food in period $t$. Note that due to Walras's law one of the three market clearing conditions is not independent of the others. There are three independent equations in (25.7) and (25.8), which determine three unknown variables: $M_x/M_y$, $p_{x2}$, $p_{y2}$, where $p_{it}$ is the price of good i in period $t$ in terms of food in period 1 and $M_i$ can be solved using the population size equation $M = M_x + M_y$ as soon as $M_x/M_y$ is determined. The corner equilibrium values of the three variables are thus given by (25.7) and (25.8) as:

$$p_{x2} = (2 - a + r)(l - B)/(1 + r)k(2l)^b,$$
$$p_{y2} = [(2 - a + r)/ak^2(2l)^b]^a(l - B)/(1 + r)(2l)^{1+ab}, \tag{25.9}$$

$$M_x/M_y = ka/(2 - a + r),$$

$$U(\text{CD}) = \ln(l - B) + [(2 - a + r)\ln(2 - a + r) - (2 + r)\ln(2 + r) + (ab + 1)\ln(2l) + a(\ln a + 2\ln k)]/(1 + r)$$

where $U(\text{CD})$ is the total discounted per capita real income for structure sequence CD, which is derived by inserting the corner equilibrium relative prices into the expression for indirect total discounted utility in (25.5) or (25.6).

4. *Sequences ED, FD, DD, DE, DF, DC*: By a two-step procedure analogous to that used to solve for the dynamic corner equilibrium of sequence CD, it is possible to solve for the dynamic corner equilibria in the 8 structure sequences. The other 5 of all 16 sequences, CC, EC, FC, CE, and CF, are obviously infeasible because of their incompatibility with the budget constraint.

## ◆ 25.4 Investment, Capital, and Division of Labor in Roundabout Production

Those corner equilibria that do not generate the highest total discounted utility do not satisfy the condition that each individual maximize her total discounted utility with respect to sequences of configurations. We call the dynamic corner equilibrium that generates the highest total discounted per capita real income the *Pareto optimum dynamic corner equilibrium*. Following the method used to prove the Yao theorem in chapter 6, we can show that only the Pareto optimum dynamic corner equilibrium is the dynamic general equilibrium. Comparisons among the total discounted per capita real incomes for all feasible sequences of structure yield the results in table 25.1.

### 25.4.1 Dynamic general equilibrium

Structure sequence FE is obviously inefficient. Individuals prefer diverse consumption in this model. They do not choose a structure with two goods, such as F, only if the forgone economies of specialized learning by doing are greater than the economies of consumption diversity. If they can afford two goods in structure F in period 1, they will certainly be more able to afford the two goods in F in period 2 because of learning by doing. Hence, FF instead of FE will be chosen. Similarly, it can be shown that DE, which involves devolution in division of labor and in production roundaboutness, is inefficient. If D is better than E in period 1, then the benefit of division of labor must outweigh transaction costs. This will be more so in period 2 because learning by doing is faster in D than in E. A comparison between $U(\text{EF})$ and $U(\text{FF})$ indicates that $U(\text{EF}) > U(\text{FF})$ if $A + B > l - 1$, which is assumed. Hence, we can further rule out structure sequence FF from consideration.

Hence, we can compare total discounted per capita real incomes in 7 structure sequences in table 25.1 to partition the 6-dimension parameter space of $a$, $b$, $A$, $B$, $r$, $k$ into several parameter subspaces. The dividing line between those structure sequences of autarky and those with division of labor is of course determined by some critical value of transaction efficiency $k$, because of the trade-off between economies of specialized learning by doing and transaction costs. The dividing line between CD and DD is determined by the fixed learning cost $A$. For $A < l$, we can show that DD, which has trade in tractors in period 1, is always better than CD, which does not involve trade in tractors in period 1, since it is obviously inefficient not to trade tractors that can be completed in period 1 for $A < l$. Hence, CD will be a candidate for dynamic general equilibrium only if $A = l$, which implies that it takes one period to complete the production of a tractor.

We now consider structure sequences ED, FD, DD, which are candidates for dynamic general equilibrium if $A < l$ and $k$ is sufficiently large. From Table 25.1, we see

**Table 25.1:** Total discounted per capita real incomes in seven structure sequences

| Structure sequence | Total discounted per capita real income |
|---|---|
| EE | $\ln(2l)/(1 + r) + \ln(l - B)$ |
| FF | $[(2 + r)/(1 + r)][ab\ln(ab) - (ab + 1)\ln(ab + 1)] + [(ab + 1)/(1 + r)][(1 + r)\ln(l - A - B) + \ln(2l - A - B)]$ |
| EF | $\{ab\ln(ab) + (ab + 1)[\ln(2l - A) - \ln(ab + 1)]\}/(1 + r) + \ln(l - B)$ |
| ED | $\{a(2\ln k + \ln a) + (1 - a)\ln(1 - a) + ab\ln(l - A) + \ln(2l)\}/(1 + r) + \ln(l - B)$ |
| FD | $\{a(2\ln k + \ln a) + (1 - a)\ln(1 - a) + ab\ln[ab(2l - A - B) + \ln[(ab + 2)l - A - B]\}/(1 + r) + ab\ln(ab) + (ab + 1)[\ln(l - A - B) - (2 + r)\ln(ab + 1)/(1 + r)]$ |
| DD | $(2 + r)\{a(2\ln k + \ln a) + (1 - a)\ln(1 - a)\}/(1 + r) + ab\ln(l - A) + \ln(l - B) + [(1 + ab)\ln(2l)/(1 + r)]$ |
| CD | $\ln(l - B) + [(2 - a + r)\ln(2 - a + r) - (2 + r)\ln(2 + r) + (ab + 1)\ln(2l) + a(\ln a + 2\ln k)]/(1 + r)$ |

$$U(ED) > U(FD) \text{ iff } \gamma > \gamma_0, \tag{25.10a}$$

$$U(DD) > U(ED) \text{ iff } \gamma > \gamma_1, \tag{25.10b}$$

$$U(DD) > U(FD) \text{ iff } \gamma > \gamma_2, \tag{25.10c}$$

where $\gamma = ab\ln(l - A)/(1 + r)$ increases with the degree of economies of specialization in producing tractors, which is $b$, and with the degree of economies of roundaboutness, which is $ab$, and decreases with the discount rate $r$, $\gamma_0 \equiv \{ab\ln[ab(2l - A - B) + l] + \ln[(ab + 2)l - A - B)] - (ab + 1)(2 + r)\ln(ab + 1) - \ln(2l)\}/(1 + r) + [ab\ln(ab) + (ab + 1)\ln(l - A - B) - \ln(l - B)]$, $\gamma_1 \equiv -[\beta + ab\ln(2l)/(1 + r)]/r$, $\beta \equiv a(2\ln k + \ln a) + (1 - a)\ln(1 - a)$, $\gamma_2 \equiv [\gamma_0 - \beta + ab\ln(2l)/(1 + r)](1 + r)^{-1}$. (25.10) imply that

$$U(ED) > U(DD) \text{ and } U(ED) > U(FD) \text{ iff } \gamma \in (\gamma_0, \gamma_1) \text{ which holds only if} \tag{25.11a}$$

$$\gamma_1 > \gamma_0. \tag{25.11b}$$

A comparison between $\gamma_1$ and $\gamma_0$ indicates that $\gamma_1 > \gamma_0$ iff $A + B$ is sufficiently smaller than $l$ but also sufficiently large to be close to $l$. Hence, if $A + B$ is sufficiently smaller than $l$, we can exclude ED from consideration. Then the dividing line between FD and DD is given by (25.10c). Otherwise, (25.11b) holds, so that the set of candidates for dynamic general equilibrium comprises ED, FD, and DD. The dividing lines between them are given in (25.10a,b).

Suppose $k$ is sufficiently close to 0, then all structure sequences with division of labor generate negative infinite total discounted per capita real income. The set of candidates for general equilibrium comprises EE and EF. A comparison between $U(EE)$ and $U(EF)$ generates the dividing line between the two structure sequences, as shown in table 25.2.

Suppose $A = l$. Then, it takes a tractor specialist one period to build up enough human capital to produce a commercially viable tractor. Then, only EE and CD are feasible. ED is infeasible since a tractor is not produced in E in period 1 and it cannot be completed in period 2, even by a tractor specialist (see figure 25.2), a situation that is incompatible with the definition of D, which requires trade in tractors. FD is infeasible, since in F a person self-provides both tractors and food. Even if she allocates all time to the production of tractors in period 1, a tractor can be completed only in period 2, a situation that is incompatible with the definition of F, which requires that a person drives a self-provided tractor to produce food. DD is infeasible, again because D is infeasible in period 1 for $A = l$. A comparison between $U(EE)$ and $U(CD)$ yields the dividing line between EE and CD, as shown in table 25.2.

All of the results of dynamic general equilibrium and its inframarginal comparative dynamics are summarized in table 25.2. EE, as shown in figure 25.2, denotes that all individuals self-provide food in the absence of tractors in both periods. EF, as shown in figure 25.2, denotes that all individuals choose autarky in both periods, but they self-provide only food in period 1 and self-provide both food and tractors in period 2. In other words, tractors emerge in period 2 and there is evolution in the number of goods and in production roundaboutness over time. ED, as shown in figure 25.2, denotes that individuals self-provide food in period 1, while in period 2 some of them specialize in producing food and others specialize in producing tractors. Evolution of division of labor takes place through increases in both individual specialization and the number of goods. FD, as shown in figure 25.2, denotes that individuals self-provide both food and tractors in period 1 and choose specialization and trade the two goods in period 2. In other words, evolution of division of labor takes place through an increase in individual specialization in the absence of changes in production roundaboutness. DD denotes the division of labor and trade in the two goods in the two periods without its evolution, but with an implicit self-saving in period 1. CD, as shown in figure 25.2, denotes the division of labor in the two periods with explicit saving and an interpersonal loan.

In table 25.2, $\rho_0 \equiv [\ln(2l) - \ln(2l - A) + \ln(ab + 1)]/[\ln(2l - A) - \ln(ab + 1) + \ln(ab)]$, $\gamma = ab\ln(l - A)/(1 + r)$ increases with the degree of economies of specialization in producing tractors, which is $b$, and with the degree of economies of roundaboutness, which is $ab$, and decreases with the discount rate $r$, $\gamma_0 \equiv \{ab\ln[ab(2l - A - B) + l] + \ln[(ab + 2)l - A - B)] + (ab + 1)[\ln(l - A - B) - (2 + r)\ln(ab + 1)] - \ln(2l)\}/(1 + r) + [ab\ln(ab) - \ln(l - B)]$, $\gamma_1 \equiv -[\beta + ab\ln(2l)/(1 + r)]/r$, $\beta \equiv a(2\ln k + \ln a) + (1-a)\ln(1 - a)$, $\gamma_2 \equiv [\gamma_0 - b + ab\ln(2l)/(1 + r)](1 + r)^{-1}$, and $\ln k_0 \equiv [(2 + r)\ln(2 + r) - (2 - a + r)\ln(2 - a + r) - a\ln a - ab\ln(2l)]/2a$. Here, $ab > \rho_0$ means that the degree of economies of specialization and roundaboutness is greater than a critical value. $\gamma > \gamma_i$ means that the degree of economies of specialization and roundaboutness is greater and the discount rate is smaller than some critical value. $k > k_0$ means that the transaction efficiency parameter is larger than a critical value. Note that $\gamma_1$ and $\gamma_2$ decrease as $k$ increases, so that DD is more likely to be equilibrium compared to ED or FD if transaction efficiency is higher. Also, $k_0$ decreases with $ab$, so that CD is more likely to be equilibrium compared to EE if the degrees of economies of specialization and roundaboutness are greater. The dynamic general equilibrium and its inframarginal comparative dynamics are also summarized in words in the following proposition.

### Proposition 25.1:

1) The dynamic general equilibrium is an autarky sequence if transaction efficiency, $k$, is low.

   i) Equilibrium is EE where each individual self-provides food over two periods if the degrees of economies of specialization and roundaboutness are not great;

**Table 25.2:** Dynamic general equilibrium and its inframarginal comparative dynamics

| $A < l$ | | | | | | $A = l$ | |
|---|---|---|---|---|---|---|---|
| $k$ is small | | $k$ is large, equilibrium involves division of labor in the absence of explicit saving | | | | $k < k_0$ | $k > k_0$ |
| $ab < \rho_0$ | $ab > \rho_0$ | $A + B$ is close to $l$ | | $A, B$ are small | | EE | CD, |
| EE | EF | $\gamma < \gamma_1$ | $\gamma > \gamma_1$ | $\gamma < \gamma_2$ | $\gamma > \gamma_2$ | autarky with only food produced in 2 periods | division of labor with explicit saving |
| autarky with only food produced in 2 periods | autarky with tractor emerging in $t = 2$ | ED, evolution in specialization, tractor emerges in $t = 2$ | DD, division of labor without evolution | FD, evolution in specialization with 2 goods produced in 2 periods | DD, division of labor without evolution | | |

ii)  Equilibrium is EF, which involves evolution in the number of goods and emergence of tractors in period 2, but without specialization and its evolution if the degrees of economies of specialization and roundaboutness are great.

2) The general equilibrium involves division of labor and/or its evolution but does not involve explicit saving if transaction efficiency is sufficiently high and if $A<l$.

i)  Total fixed learning cost $A + B$ is close to $l$:

a)  Equilibrium is ED if the degree of economies of specialization and roundaboutness is not too great and the discount rate is not too small. The equilibrium sequence involves evolution in specialization as well as in the number of goods;

b)  Equilibrium is DD if the degree of economies of specialization and roundaboutness is great and the discount rate is small. The equilibrium sequence jumps to the highest level of division of labor as soon as possible and stays there;

ii)  Fixed learning costs $A$ and $B$ are small:

a)  Equilibrium is FD if the degree of economies of specialization and roundaboutness is not too great and the discount rate is not too small. The equilibrium sequence involves evolution in division of labor but not in the number of goods;

b)  Equilibrium is DD if the degree of economies of specialization and roundaboutness is great and the discount rate is small. The equilibrium sequence involves no evolution in division of labor nor in the number of goods;

3) If transaction efficiency is high and the fixed learning cost $A = l$, then equilibrium is CD where professional farmers make loans in terms of food to professional producers of tractors in period 1 and this explicit saving is then repaid in period 2 in terms of tractors.

Proposition 25.1 provides a characterization of the conditions under which the various sequences of market structures will occur in dynamic general equilibrium. There are five parameters that determine the inframarginal comparative dynamics of the equilibrium: $A$ (fixed learning cost in producing tractors), $B$ (fixed learning cost in producing food), $k$ (transaction efficiency), $ab$ (degree of economies of specialization and roundaboutness), and $r$ (discount rate). Transaction efficiency determines whether specialization is more likely to take place in the equilibrium compared to autarky. The fixed learning cost $A$ determines whether explicit saving is essential for the division of labor. If $A$ is small, then explicit saving and interpersonal lending are not necessary for the division of labor. When specialization and related trade takes place in DD, there is an implicit investment for increasing specialization, which is in terms of a decrease in consumption of food in period 1 (compared to consumption of food in an alternative autarky structure), caused by a larger transaction cost. However, such investment does not involve interpersonal lending. Hence, investment comes from self-saving rather than from commercial saving. This implicit saving in terms of a lower utility in an early stage of development caused by a faster evolution in division of labor is the same as in the dynamic equilibrium model in chapter 22. The time paths of per capita real income for different structure sequences are shown in figure 25.3, which describes the nontopological features of evolution of division of labor and economic growth.

If $A = l$, then explicit saving and an interpersonal loan are necessary for the division of labor. If $A < l$ but $A + B$ is close to $l$, then FD is infeasible and ED will be equilibrium provided $k$ is large and $ab$ is not great compared to $r$. The degree of economies of specialization and roundaboutness $ab$ determines whether a larger number of goods and/or a higher level of specialization is more likely to take place in the equilibrium. Gradual evolution in individuals' levels of specialization and/or in the number of goods will take place in the equilibrium if $k$ is large but $ab$ is small compared to $r$, or if $k$ is small but $ab$ is large. A larger discount rate $r$ will make a small number of goods and a low level of specialization more likely to take place in the equilibrium.

As in the new classical models in other chapters, increases in the extent of the market, in trade dependence, in the extent of endogenous comparative advantage, in productivity, in the degree of production roundaboutness, in the variety of goods and occupations, in the degree of production concentration, and in the degree of market integration are different aspects of the evolution in division of labor. But in this new model, not only the level of division of labor and the extent of the market are interdependent, but also saving rate, returns to investment, and level of division of labor. Returns to capital are dependent on the level of division of labor, which is determined by saving rate, which is in turn determined by returns to investment. Here, the level of division of labor can be considered *organization capital* that contributes to long-run productivity.

### 25.4.2. Nontopological properties of economic growth and sudden decline of interest rates

So far we have focused our attention on the inframarginal comparative dynamics of general equilibrium and related topological properties of the economic organism. Figure 25.3. shows some nontopological properties of economic growth (increase in per capita real income $u_t$ over time $t$). Panel (a) shows that for $A = l$ and a sufficiently high transaction efficiency, sequence CD generates a lower per capita real income than sequence EE in an early stage of economic development because of transaction costs caused by the division of labor in CD. Later, per capita real income generated by CD is increasingly higher than that in EE because of the effect of specialized learning by doing. Indeed, if the decision horizon involves many periods rather than just two, this feature will be more obvious. Panel (b) shows the similar features of sequences EF, DE, and DD when $A < l$ and transaction efficiency is sufficiently high.

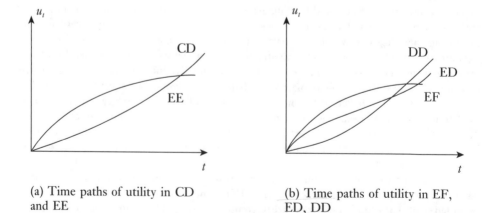

(a) Time paths of utility in CD and EE

(b) Time paths of utility in EF, ED, DD

♦ **Figure 25.3:** Nontopological properties of evolution in divisions of labor and economic growth

If transaction efficiency, $k$, and the fixed learning cost, $A$, are sufficiently large, then dynamic general equilibrium is CD, where a loan in terms of food is made from a professional farmer to a professional producer of tractors in period 1 and repaid in terms of tractors in period 2. A farmer's saving level and saving rate in period 1 are respectively

$$S \equiv y_1^s = a(l - B)/(2 + r), \qquad s \equiv y_1^s/(y_1 + y_1^s) = a/(2 + r).$$

$S$ and $s$ increase with $a$, which positively relates to the degree of economies of roundaboutness, and decrease with the subjective discount rate. But more importantly, transaction efficiency $k$ determines if CD or EE is equilibrium. If transaction efficiency $k$ is very small due to a deficient tax system or a deficient legal system, then EE instead of CD will be equilibrium, which implies a zero saving rate. Also, the magnitude of the fixed learning cost determines whether implicit or explicit saving is essential for a high growth rate of per capita real income. The real saving level in CD can be calculated as the difference in utility between EE and CD in period 1. The real return on saving can be calculated from the difference in total discounted utility between CD and EE in period 2. The real interest rate is the ratio of real return to real saving, which is given as follows.

$$R = [(2 - a + r)\ln(2 - a + r) + 2(1 + r)\ln(1 + r) - (2 + r)\ln(2 + r) + a(b\ln2 + \ln a + 2\ln k)]/(1 + r)[\ln(2 + r) - 2\ln(1 + r) - \ln(2 - a + r)].$$

The inframarginal comparative dynamics of the general equilibrium implies that if values of the parameters of transaction efficiency and economies of specialization and roundaboutness decline to threshold levels, then dynamic equilibrium shifts from CD to EE (autarky), and real returns to saving jump down to 0. The marginal comparative dynamics indicate that as the parameters change within the range defined by the threshold values such that equilibrium stays in CD, then the real interest rate $R$ increases with transaction efficiency and with the degree of economies of specialization ($\partial R/\partial k > 0$, $\partial R/\partial b > 0$). This result can be used to theorize about the successful practice of the Reagan government and the Hong Kong and Taiwan governments in carrying out liberalization and internationalization policies which stimulated investment and trade by reducing tax.

The theory of capital and investment can be used to explain a sudden decline of interest rates. Suppose that the transaction efficiency coefficient and the fixed learning cost are sufficiently large, so that CD is general equilibrium and the saving rate and real interest rate on the saving are positive. However, if the decision horizon is longer than two periods, then the opportunity for investment will suddenly disappear in period $t > 2$ as structure D, which involves the highest level of division of labor in the model, has been reached. If the number of goods is more than 2 in the model, then opportunities for lucrative investment may last longer than two periods. However, there is a limit to the evolution in division of labor, as the highest level of division of labor will eventually be reached, and no more opportunity for investment for increasing division of labor can be pursued if the equilibrium number of professional sectors has reached its upper bound. This is an interesting explanation of a decline in interest rates, which is consistent with the classical theory of capital based on the intimate connection between capital and division of labor, but is substantially different from Keynes' (1936) view of interest rates which focuses on the implication of pure consumers' preference for liquidity, but has nothing to do with the implications of division of labor.[2]

If CD is dynamic general equilibrium, then the growth rate of consumption of food for a specialist producer of tractors is

$$(y_2^d - y_1^d)/y_1^d = [1/(1 + r)p_{y2}] - 1$$

where $p_{y2} = (l - B)[(2 - a + r)/ak^2]^a/(1 + r)(2l)^{1+ab}$ is the price of period 2 food in terms of period 1 food, which can be considered as the price index of consumption goods. This index decreases with the transaction efficiency coefficient, or the discount rate, or labor productivity of food in period 2 compared to that in period 1.[3]

### 25.4.3. The endogenous decision horizon and the effect of liberalization reforms on opportunities for lucrative investment

If the decision horizon is a decision variable, and uncertainty of realizing the gains from investment for increasing division of labor is introduced, there is another interesting trade-off between gains from a longer decision horizon which leads to the amortization of investment cost over a longer period of time and a decreasing probability of realizing the gains. Suppose the fixed learning cost $A = l$ in an extended model which is the same as the original one except that the decision horizon $T$ is each individual's decision variable. The discount rate is assumed to be 0 and $l$ is assumed to be 1 for simplicity. The probability of realizing gains of total discounted utility from a sequence with the division of labor and savings compared to autarky is $f(T) = 1/T$, and the probability that the gain is 0 is $1 - f(T)$, which can be considered the risk of failing to realize the gains from a longer decision horizon. This risk increases as the decision horizon becomes longer. Each individual maximizes expected gains in total discounted utility from choosing the division of labor. Then, it can be shown that the necessary condition for the equilibrium decision horizon is equivalent to the first-order condition for maximizing

$$V = f(T)F(T,k,a,b),$$

$$F(T, k, a, b) = \{[T - a(T - 1)]\ln[T - a(T - 1)] + a(T - 1)(\ln2 + \ln a + 2\ln k) + b[0.5(1 + T)T - 1]\}$$

where $F$ is the difference in total utility over $T$ periods between division of labor and autarky. Application of the envelope theorem to $V = f(T)F(T, k, a, b)$ and of the implicit function theorem to $F$ yields comparative dynamics:

$$dT^*/dk = -(\partial^2 V/\partial k(T)/(\partial^2 V/\partial T^2) > 0, \text{ and } dV(T^*, k)/dk = \partial V(T^*, k)/\partial k > 0$$

where $\partial^2 V/\partial k\partial T > 0$, $\partial^2 V/\partial T^2 < 0$. $T^*$ is the equilibrium decision horizon, which efficiently trades off the gains from a longer horizon against a decreasing probability of realizing them. The policy implication of the result is straightforward. A liberalization and internationalization policy which reduces tariffs, or a better legal system which reduces transaction costs, will increase individuals' efficient decision horizon and increase the opportunities of lucrative investment for increasing division of labor.

Our model shows that investment does not necessarily increase future productivity. Productivity in the future can be increased by an investment that is used to create a higher level of division of labor which can speed up the accumulation of professional experience (human capital) through specialized learning by producing roundabout productive equipment or services. Self-saving is enough for investment for increasing division of labor if the fixed learning cost in roundabout productive activities is not large. A loan from a producer of consumption goods to specialist producers of producer goods is essential for such investment if the fixed learning cost is large. If the transaction cost coefficient is large due to a deficient legal system or to a protectionist tariff, such an opportunity for lucrative investment to increase division of labor does not exist, so that investment may not increase real income. A decrease in the degree of economies of specialization and roundaboutness, an increase in the transaction cost coefficient, and/or exhaustion of the potential for further evolution of division of labor, will reduce real return rates on investment and reduce opportunities for lucrative investment.

This new classical model of investment, capital, and saving endogenizes the gains from investment. There is no "if and only if" relationship between saving and productivity progress. Whether saving and investment can raise productivity is up to the values of several parameters. This mapping is determined by individuals' dynamic self-interested behaviors and interactions between them through the pricing mechanism. This model not only parameterizes the conditions under which investment and saving is lucrative and the conditions under which an interpersonal loan or self-saving are essential for lucrative investment, but also explores the intimate relationship between various patterns of evolution of division of labor and production roundaboutness and various saving mechanisms, such as interpersonal lending and self-savings.

## Key Terms and Review

Capital, investment, saving and the relationship between them and evolution in division of labor.

The difference between interpersonal lending based on differences in the valuation of time between individuals, which generate gains from trade in goods at different points in time, and interpersonal lending based on the development of division of labor in a roundabout production process.

The difference between the function of self-saving in chapter 22 and that of interpersonal lending in this chapter in promoting division of labor.

Endogenous vs. exogenous gains from savings.

The difference between neoclassical saving and investment fundamentalism and new classical productivity implication of savings.

The relationship between returns to investment, transaction efficiency, and division of labor.

The function of the market in determining the efficient levels of saving, interpersonal loans, and investment.

## Further Reading

*Neoclassical macroeconomic theory of saving behavior*: Keynes (1936), Friedman (1957), Modigliani (1989); *neoclassical microeconomic theories of saving, credit*: Besley (1995), Besley, Coate, and Loury (1993), Deaton (1990, 1991), Lenand (1968), Barro (1997); *collateral, information, and credit*: Stiglitz and Weiss (1986); *reputation mechanism of credit*: Diamond (1989), Patten and Rosengard (1991); *neoclassical saving fundamentalism*: Barro and Sala-i-Martin (1995), Romer (1987, 1990), Lucas (1988, 1993), Solow (1956); *empirical evidence to reject saving fundamentalism*: Jones (1995), Olsen (1996), and Liu and Yang (1999); *new classical theory on saving and investment*: Yang and Borland (1991), Borland and Yang (1995), Y.-K. Ng and Yang (1997), Yang (1999); *classical thinking on division of labor and saving*: Mill (1848), Smith (1776), Young (1928), Marshall (1890).

## QUESTIONS

1   Many neoclassical development economists use state equations (such as in Chenery's model of two gaps) or partial equilibrium models to justify worries about the shortage of investment flow into or about capital flight from the less developed economies. But the general equilibrium models of saving and investment in this chapter show that transaction costs, which might be caused by state opportunism and deficient institutions and infrastructure, are responsible for the shortage of foreign investment into and capital flight from less-developed economies. Compare the two analytical methods and discuss their relevance to the real world.

2   According to neoclassical economics, the phenomenon that returns to capital are higher in developing countries than in developed countries is explained by the fact that the developed countries are capital abundant, so that marginal productivity of capital is lower than in developing countries which are short of capital. Use the new classical theory of capital to explain the phenomenon. Analyze the differences between the two explanations and discuss which explanation is more convincing in connection with the following observation. In some less-developed countries, such as pre-reform India, shortage of capital did not imply a high return to capital. Explain why returns to capital in the more open coastal regions of China are higher than in hinterland regions despite the more serious shortage of capital in the latter than in the former. On the basis of your analysis, find empirical evidence for the theory in this chapter against the neoclassical theory of capital.

3   What is the difference between self-saving and interpersonal loans?

4   Outline various possible self-saving mechanisms and discuss the differences between them.

5   Outline the gains from various possible forms of interpersonal lending and discuss the differences between them.

6   What is the relationship between lucrative interpersonal lending and development of division of labor?

7   What is organization capital? Use the following fact to discuss the difference between neoclassical and new classical notions of capital. Many successful entrepreneurs understand that real constraint for the development of their businesses is not availability of investment funds. Instead, potential productivity gains from the division of labor are constrained by transaction conditions. Hence, many entrepreneurs who do not have large investment funds can make a fortune from organization capital.

8   Compare the following two views on saving and investment and discuss their relevance to real economic development. One of them relates to investment fundamentalism which claims an if-and-only-if positive relationship between current saving and future productivity. This view generates worries about shortage of domestic and foreign investment and foreign exchanges as the main obstacle to economic development. The other view focuses on gains from intertemporal trade of goods. According to it, various transaction costs that prevent realization of gains are the main obstacle to economic development.

9   What is the difference between the functions of working capital and fixed capital in facilitating division of labor?

10  Use the examples of the high saving rate of the Soviet Union and of Egypt in 5000 BC to illustrate why a high saving rate may not yield higher productivity progress.

11  What is the difference between saving used to buy durable goods, peasants' saving of corn seeds each year, and the saving that can be used to raise productivity through promoting division of labor?

12  Myrdal (1957, pp. 47–51) argued that despite shortage of capital in less-developed countries, free capital markets never generate much capital movement to underdeveloped countries. Instead, free

markets will generate capital flight from underdeveloped countries. Use statistic data to show that this is a totally wrong claim. Use the Smithian model of capital and investment in this chapter to explain why capital does not flow to some less-developed countries, but does flow to others. Relate your discussion to Hume's (1748, "Of Money," pp. 34–5) classical view on investment: "There seems to be a happy concurrence of causes in human affairs, which checks the growth of trade and riches, and hinders them from being confined entirely to one people; as might naturally at first be dreaded from the advantages of an established commerce. Where one nation has gotten the start of another in trade, it is very difficult for the latter to regain the ground it has lost; because of the superior industry and skill of the former, and the greater stocks of which its merchants are possessed, and which enable them to trade on so much smaller profits. But these advantages are compensated in some measure, by the low price of labor in every nation which has not an extensive commerce, and does not much abound in gold and silver. Manufactures therefore gradually shift their places, leaving those countries and provinces which they have already enriched, and flying to others, whither they are allured and are again banished by the same cause."

# EXERCISES

1  Consider the model in example 25.2. Assume that utility functions are now $u_A = x_{A1}x_{A2}^{\delta}$, $u_B = x_{B1}x_{B2}$. $\delta$ is a positive parameter. Solve for the equilibrium interest rates for $\delta = 1$, $\delta < 1$, and $\delta > 1$, respectively. Identify the condition for person A to borrow money from person B.

2  Assume that in example 25.2 the utility function is the same for the two persons, but person A produces 2 units of a good in period 1, while person B's capacity is always 1 in the two periods. Solve for the equilibrium interest rates.

3  Introduce moral hazard into the models in exercises 1 and 2 to investigate the effects of endogenous transaction cost on the equilibrium saving rate.

4  Assume in example 25.3 that there are only 2 periods and 2 individuals. The person who gets the durable first must pay the other person $R. Solve for the equilibrium value of $R$, which is an interest payment.

5  Rule out the assumption in example 25.4 that $A + B > l - 1$. Show under what conditions structure sequence FF will occur in equilibrium.

6  Assume $B = 0$ in example 25.4. Solve for dynamic equilibrium and its comparative dynamics.

7  Assume that the production function in example 25.4 is $y_i^p = \text{Min}\{x_i + kx_i^d, \alpha(L_{yt} - \sigma B)\}$. Solve for dynamic equilibrium.

# Notes

1  Smith stated (1776, p. 371) that "when the division of labor has once been thoroughly introduced, the produce of a man's own labor can supply but a very small part of his occasional wants. The far greater part of them are supplied by the produce of other men's labor, which he purchases with the produce, . . . of his own. But this purchase cannot be made till such time as the produce of his own labor has not only been completed, but sold. A stock of goods of different kinds, therefore, must be stored up somewhere sufficient to maintain him, and to supply him with the materials

and tools of his work, till such time, at least, as both these events can be brought about."

2 Chapters 16 and 17 show that a trade-off between economies of specialization and coordination reliability may generate a high equilibrium risk of coordination failure, which is efficient as long as economies of division of labor outweigh the welfare loss from the risk. The risk is indeed a risk of mass unemployment. Also, chapter 27 will show that a trade-off between economies of specialized learning by doing in producing durable producer goods and unemployment may generate a dynamic equilibrium which involves efficient business cycles.

3 The relationship between the emergence of money and a high level of division of labor in roundabout productive activities will be investigated in chapter 26.

# chapter 26

# MONEY AND DIVISION OF LABOR

## ◆ 26.1 Neoclassical vs. New Classical Theories of Money

In the previous chapters, we have given no consideration to money. All transactions have been on a barter basis and relative prices have been exchange ratios of goods. In those models, with only final goods and with *ex ante* identical individuals who prefer diverse consumption, all transactions that are essential for division of labor necessarily involve a *double coincidence of demand and supply*. From figures 11.4 and 13.1, we can see that in a model with *ex ante* identical consumer-producers, in the absence of producer goods trade between each pair of trade partners is two-way. This implies that, for each pair of trade partners, if one sells good 1 and buys good 2, then the other must buy good 1 and sell good 2, just like when a boy and a girl simultaneously fall in love with each other: what he wants from her is what she wants to give him, and what she wants from him is what he wants to give her.

However the double coincidence of demand and supply may not hold under at least two circumstances. We will use the Kiyotaki–Wright (KW) model (1989), which involves *ex ante* differences between consumer-producers, to illustrate the first case, and the Borland–Yang (BY) model (1992) to illustrate the second case.

### Example 26.1: the Kiyotaki–Wright (KW) model of money

Consider the KW model, as shown in figure 26.1a, where person A wants good z, but produces only x, person B produces only z, but wants y, and person C wants good x, but produces only y. In this economy with different tastes and production capacities between individuals, trade between each pair of trade partners is one-way only, and a double coincidence of demand and supply does not hold in the absence of money. However, the absence of a double coincidence of demand and supply is necessary but not sufficient for the emergence of money. If all trade partners go to a central clearing house and simultaneously deliver goods to the right buyers according to Walrasian equilibrium prices, money is still not needed. Barter is enough to coordinate all essential transactions.

But if it is impossible to implement all deliveries at the same time in such a central clearing house, money will be essential for this economy. For instance, if the production of y can take place only if person C has received x, then deliveries of x and y cannot be implemented at the same time. If it is impossible to implement all transactions at the same time, then a one-way delivery of x that takes place before deliveries of y and z is a sort of credit arrangement in the expectation of eventual delivery of z. If such a credit system is not available, as is very likely when you buy a good from a stranger on the street who you may never meet again, then person A who delivers x to person C will ask for some commodity as payment for x from C in order to secure property rights. But what A wants is z, which person C does not produce; that is, there is no double coincidence of demand and supply between A and C. Suppose A accepts y, which is produced by C, but is useless for direct consumption by A. Then A can use y to exchange z with B, as shown in figure 26.1b, where all transactions are two-way. Commodity y is here used by person A to facilitate her further transactions. Person A does not use y for her own consumption, or for her production. A commodity that satisfies this condition is called *commodity money*. Hence, in the structure of transactions in figure 26.1b, good y becomes commodity money for person A.

If person A delivers x to person C, and in return C gives A a note which specifies how much C owes to A, then A may give this note to B in exchange for z produced by B. Then B can use this note in exchange for y from C. In this case, the note becomes a *money substitute*. Travelers' checks and money orders are common money substitutes, which themselves have no direct value for consumption and production, but can substitute for commodity money. If the money substitute is enforced by a government legal system and is not backed by any commodity money, we call it *fiat money*. US dollars that we use in daily life are fiat money.

The story described in figure 26.1 predicts that the commodity with the lowest transaction cost will play the role of medium of exchange. This story is not particularly interesting since we can predict this with no formal model. It cannot predict the emergence of

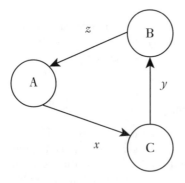

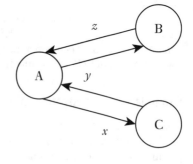

(a) Absence of double coincidence
        of demand and supply

(b) Good y is commodity money

♦ **Figure 26.1:** The absence of double coincidence of demand and supply based on *ex ante* diffenrences between individuals

money, and it cannot explore the intimate relationship between money and division of
labor, since in that story individuals cannot choose their levels of specialization and they
cannot survive in the absence of money or a related credit system. Furthermore, the
productivity implications of money cannot be explored by that story.

Plato (380 BC, pp. 102–6) spelled out the connection between money and division of labor
more than two thousand years ago. Smith (1776, p. 37) and Turgot (1766, pp. 244–6, 64,
70) indicated that specialization is the driving force behind the emergence of money.[1]
Borland and Yang (1992; also see Yang and Ng 1993, ch. 17) develop the first new classical
general equilibrium model to explain emergence of money from evolution of division of
labor in roundabout production. They have shown that even if all consumer-producers are
*ex ante* identical in all aspects, money will emerge from a sufficiently high level of division
of labor in a sufficiently long roundabout production chain. In their model, specialization
and division of labor are necessary but not sufficient for the emergence of money. Also, *ex
ante* differences between individuals are not essential for the emergence of money.

## Example 26.2: Borland and Yang's new classical model of money

The story of the emergence of money from the evolution of division of labor in roundabout production can be illustrated by the graphs in figure 26.2. In that model there

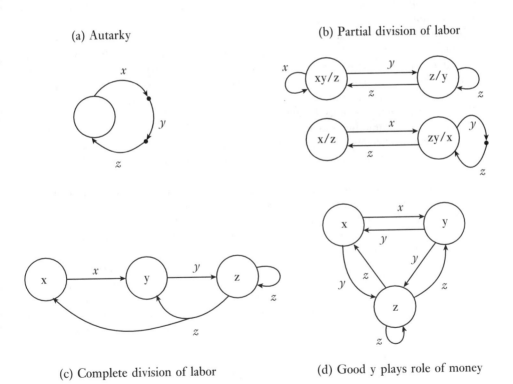

(a) Autarky

(b) Partial division of labor

(c) Complete division of labor

(d) Good y plays role of money

◆ **Figure 26.2**: Emergence of money and evolution of division of labor

are many *ex ante* identical consumer-producers. Each of them can produce steel (x) from labor, then use steel, together with labor, to produce hoes (y), then use hoes, together with labor, to produce food (z) for her own consumption. This is an autarky structure as shown in panel (a), where dots denote the transformation process from intermediate inputs to outputs. For this autarky structure, trade, market, and money are absent. This verifies the statement that division of labor is essential for the emergence of money.

Individuals may choose a structure of partial division of labor: either between configuration (z/y) (complete specialization in producing food) and configuration (xy/z) (producing steel x and hoe y) or between configuration (x/z) (complete specialization in producing steel x) and configuration (zy/x) (producing both hoes y and food z). In this type of structure, shown in panel (b), barter transactions with double coincidence of demand and supply are enough to facilitate partial division of labor. This substantiates the statement that specialization and division of labor are not sufficient for the emergence of money.

The third type of structure with the complete division of labor is shown in panel (c), where each individual completely specializes in producing one good and trade between a specialist in x and a specialist in y or between a specialist in x and a specialist in z is of a one-way nature. A specialist in steel sells steel (x) to a specialist in hoes (y), but she does not need hoes. A specialist in food sells food (z) to a specialist in steel, but she does not need steel. If there is no central clearing house where all traded goods can be simultaneously delivered, then the complete division of labor in the roundabout production chain with three links cannot be realized in the absence of money.

If economies of specialization in producing each good and transaction costs are specified, then the general equilibrium will evolve from autarky to partial division of labor, followed by the complete division of labor as transaction efficiency is improved. In order to facilitate the complete division of labor in the roundabout production chain with three links, either a commodity money, or a money substitute, or a credit system will be used as a medium of exchange. Figure 26.2d shows the structure of transactions with good y as commodity money, where an x specialist exchanges x for y with a y specialist, then exchanges y for z with a z specialist. Commodity y is not used by the x specialist for consumption and production. She uses y as a medium to facilitate further transactions.

It is shown in Borland and Yang (1992) that if a money substitute is not available, or a credit system involves excessive transaction costs due to a war or other social turmoil, then the commodity with the smallest transaction cost coefficient will be used as money. If all commodities have the same transaction cost coefficient, then the commodity in the middle link of the roundabout production chain will be used as money. If a credit system or a money substitute with a much smaller transaction cost coefficient is available, then the credit system or the money substitute will be used as medium of exchange. Money can promote productivity progress through facilitating a high level of division of labor in a long roundabout production chain, which is infeasible in the absence of money. In the model the equilibrium price of commodity money in terms of other goods, the degree of monetization of an economy, and the circulating quantity of money are all endogenized.

In the next two sections, we use a simple new classical general equilibrium model to illustrate the technical substance of this kind of model.

---

### Questions to Ask Yourself when Reading this Chapter

♦ Under what circumstances does the double coincidence of demand and supply not occur? What other condition, in addition to the absence of double coincidence of demand and supply, is needed for the emergence of money?

♦ What is the relationship between the level of division of labor, the length of roundabout production, transaction efficiency, and the emergence of money?

♦ Under what conditions can fiat money or another money substitute play the role of a medium of exchange?

♦ What features of a commodity are important for it to be chosen as money?

♦ What is the relationship between the degrees of commercialization and monetization of an economy, and the level of division of labor?

♦ What are the important determinants of the value of money?

♦ Why can fiat money, money substitutes, and a credit system promote productivity progress?

♦ How does the market sort out an efficient monetary regime and an efficient level of division of labor?

---

## ♦ 26.2 A New Classical Model of an Endogenous Monetary Regime

### Example 26.3: a simplified version of the Cheng model of money (1996)

Consider a new classical model with a continuum of $M$ *ex ante* identical consumer-producers. Each of them has the utility function

$$u = (x + x^r)(y + y^r)$$

where $x$ and $y$ denote the quantity of food and clothing self-provided respectively; and $x^r$ and $y^r$ denote the quantity of food and clothing received for consumption from the market respectively.

An individual incurs a fixed learning cost in terms of labor, 0.2, for each production activity in which she engages. Because of the fixed learning cost, the production system exhibits economies of specialization. Of the two consumption goods, food is produced with single factor labor such that

$$x^p \equiv x + x^s = \text{Max } \{l_x - \tfrac{1}{5}, 0\}$$

where $x$ is the quantity of food produced for self-consumption; $x^s$ is the quantity of food sold to the market; $x^p$ is the total output level of food; and $l_x$ is the proportion of labor devoted to food production.

Clothing is produced with labor and an intermediate good, silk (z), using the Leontief production technology,

$$y^p \equiv y + y^s = \text{Min } \{z + z^r\} \text{ Max } \{l_y - \tfrac{1}{5}, 0\}$$

where $y$ is the quantity of clothing produced for self-consumption; $y^s$ is the quantity of clothing sold to the market; $y^p$ is the total output level of cloth; and $l_y$ is the proportion of labor devoted to clothing production.

Silk is produced with single factor, labor, such that

$$z^p \equiv z + z^s = \text{Max } \{l_z - \tfrac{1}{5}, 0\}$$

where $z$ is the quantity of silk produced for self-production of clothing; $z^s$ is the quantity of silk sold to the market; and $l_z$ is the proportion of labor devoted to silk production. $l_i$ is an individual's level of specialization in producing good i.

Each individual's endowment constraint for time is

$$l_x + l_y + l_z = 1$$

If an individual trades in the market, transaction costs are incurred. The transaction cost coefficient for good i is $(1 - k_i)$. In market transactions, an individual may accept goods in exchange solely for their ability to exchange for some other goods. These accepted goods serve as media of exchange or commodity money, denoted with a superscript $m$. Denoting the total quantity of food, clothing, and silk demanded by an individual for consumption or production and as a medium of exchange as $x^d$, $y^d$, $z^d$, respectively, the quantity that is finally received, net of transaction costs, is therefore $k_x x^d$, $k_y y^d$, $k_z z^d$, respectively. Hence, the material balance equations between what a person receives from a purchase and its use are

$$k_x x^d = x^r + x^m \qquad\qquad (26.1)$$
$$k_y y^d = y^r + y^m$$
$$k_z z^d = z^r + z^m$$

where the left-hand side of each equation is the quantity of a good that a person receives from the purchase and the right-hand side is the allocation of the quantity between consumption or production and medium of exchange. $x^r$, $y^r$, and $z^r$ are the quantities of food, clothing, and silk allocated for consumption or production, respectively; $x^m$, $y^m$, and $z^m$ are the quantities of food, clothing, and silk allocated as a medium of exchange, respectively.

To make the exchange between z and y possible without including inventories in the model, we assume that production is instantaneous once the required factors of production are available. Thus a clothing producer can buy silk from a silk producer, produce clothing, and pay the silk producer with some of the clothing produced. We also assume that trade is strictly bilateral and that an individual cannot trade with two different individuals simultaneously. This rules out the possible existence of a central clearing house and makes sequential exchanges necessary. In addition, we assume a zero discount rate to avoid complications caused by the time dimension; and we make the assumption that no enforceable credit system exists, which we subsequently relax in the discussion of money substitutes.

## ◆ 26.3 Possible Structures and Monetary Regimes

There are 7 market structures we have to consider. The first is structure A where $M$ individuals choose an autarky configuration. Each of them self-provides three goods, as shown in figure 26.3. There are three structures, Ba, Bb, Bc, called partial division of labor. Structure Ba comprises configuration (x/y), which self-provides and sells x and buys y, and configuration (yz/x), which self-provides y and z, sells y, and buys x. Structure Bb comprises configuration (xy/z), which self-provides and sells x, self-provides y, and buys z, and configuration (z/x) which sells z and buys x. Structure Bc comprises configuration (zx/y), which self-provides z and x, sells z, and buys y, and configuration (y/z), which self-provides and sells clothing and buys z. All of the structures are shown in figure 26.3.

There are four structures, $C_y$, $C_z$, $C_x$, and D, referred to as complete division of labor. $C_y$ comprises configurations (x/y), (y/xz), and (zy$^m$/xy). Configuration (x/y) is the same as in structure Ba. Configuration (y/xz) self-provides and sells y and buys x and z. Configuration (zy$^m$/xy) sells z, buys x and y for consumption, and uses part of y as money. Structure $C_z$ comprises configurations (y/xz) selling y and buying x and z, (z/xy) selling z and buying x and y, and (xz$^m$/y), selling x, buying y, and using z as money. Structure $C_x$ comprises configurations (x/y) selling x and buying y, (z/xy) selling z and buying x and y, and (yx$^m$/zx), selling y, buying z and y, and using x as money.

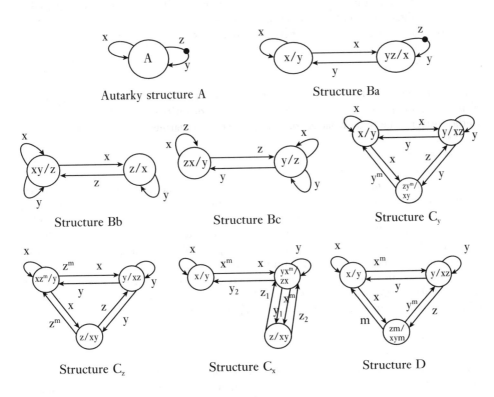

◆ **Figure 26.3:** Market structures and monetary regimes

Finally we consider structure D, where the circulation of commodity money is replaced by fiat money, other money substitutes, or a credit system. If the circulation of commodity money $y^m$ in structure $C_y$ is replaced by the circulation of a money substitute, then a structure with a money substitute that is backed by commodity money y is shown as structure D in figure 26.3. Suppose the circulation of the money substitute involves zero transaction cost, then it makes no difference which commodity money backs the money substitute. Hence, we ignore the distinction between structures with money substitutes that are backed by different commodity monies.

Following the inframarginal analysis that you have been familiar with in the previous chapters, it is not difficult to solve for the corner equilibria in those structures with no money. The procedure to solve for the corner equilibria in those structures with money is slightly more complicated. We show the procedure for structure $C_z$ here and leave solutions to other corner equilibria as exercises.

We first consider a professional farmer choosing configuration $(xz^m/y)$. She sells food x and buys clothing y. Though she does not need silk for consumption and production, she buys silk from the weaver and sells it in exchange for part of the clothing that she consumes from the tailor. Hence, the farmer's total budget constraint is

$$p_y y^d = p_x x^s \tag{26.2a}$$

where trade in z is not explicitly included. The quantity of x that is sold by her is $x^s \equiv x^s_z + x^s_y$, where $x^s_z$ is the quantity sold to the weaver z and $x^s_y$ is the quantity sold to the tailor. The total budget constraint can be decomposed as two bilateral trade balance conditions. When the farmer uses y as money her trade balance with the weaver is

$$p^b_z z^d = p_x x^s_z \tag{26.2b}$$

where $z^d$ is the quantity of silk that the farmer bought from the weaver to use as money, $p^b_z$ is the buying price of silk for the farmer, $x^s_z$ is the quantity of food that the farmer sells to the weaver. The trade balance condition between the farmer and the tailor is

$$p_y y^d = p^s_z z^m + p_x x^s_y \tag{26.2c}$$

where $z^m$ is the quantity of silk, z, resold by the farmer to the tailor, $p^s_z$ is the selling price of silk z, $x^s_y$ is the quantity of food sold by the farmer to the tailor. Silk z is money for the farmer. She cannot have bilateral trade with double coincidence of demand and supply if she does not use silk as money in this particular structure. But if the selling and buying prices of silk are the same for the farmer, or if $p^b_z = p^s_z$, she will not be willing to use money, since the reselling involves extra transaction cost. Hence, the selling price must be higher than the buying price so that the difference can cover the transaction cost. The material balance equation in (26.1) implies $k_z z^d = z^m$ for the farmer since $z^r = 0$ for her. This and trade balance (26.2) can simultaneously hold iff

$$p^b_z = k_z p^s_z$$

where $k_z \in (0, 1)$. The difference between the selling and buying prices can be considered as a price discount that is used by the weaver to attract the farmer to use silk as money. The discount rate is $k_z$. We may still assume that in equilibrium the price of silk is $p_z$, but the farmer can get the discounted buying price $p_z^b = k_z p_z$ from the weaver. Therefore, the decision problem for a farmer choosing configuration $(xz^m/y)$ is

Max: $u = xy^r$  (utility function)

s.t. $x + x_y^s + x_z^s = \frac{4}{5}$  (production function)
$p_x x_z^s = k_z p_z z^d$  (trade balance with weaver)
$p_x x_y^s = p_z z^m = p_y y^d$  (trade balance with tailor)
$k_z z^d = z^m$  (transaction condition for z)

where $x$, $y^r$, $x_y^s$, $x_z^s$, $z^d$, $z^m$, $y^d$ are decision variables and $x_y^s$, $x_z^s$ are respective quantities sold to the tailor and weaver. We leave the solution of this problem to you as an exercise.

The decision problem of a tailor choosing configuration $(y/xz)$ is

Max: $u = x^r y$  (utility function)

s.t. $y + y_x^s + y_z^s = \mathrm{Min}\ \{(z_x^r + z_z^r), \frac{4}{5}\}$  (production function)
$p_y y_z^s = p_z p_z^d$  (trade balance with weaver)
$p_y y_x^s = p_x x^d + p_z z_z^d$  (trade balance with farmer)
$k_x x^d = x^r$  (transaction condition for x)
$k_z (z_z^d + z_x^d) = z_x^r + z_z^r$  (transaction condition for z)

where $y_x^s + y_z^s \equiv y^s$, $y_x^s$ and $y_z^s$ and are the respective amounts of clothing y sold to the farmer and weaver, $z_z^d + z_x^d \equiv z^d$, $z_z^d$ and $z_x^d$, and are the respective amounts of silk bought from the weaver and farmer. $z_x^r + z_z^r \equiv z^r$, $z_z^r$ and $z_x^r$ are the respective amounts of silk that are received from the purchase from the weaver and farmer. Since the tailor uses silk to produce clothing and consumes clothing and food, these commodities are not money to her. The decision variables are $x^r$, $y$, $y_x^s$, $y_z^s$, $z_x^s$, $z_z^r$, $x^d$, $z_x^d$, $z_z^d$. Again we leave the solution of this problem to you as an exercise.

The decision problem of a weaver choosing configuration $(z/xy)$ is

Max: $u = x^r y^r$  (utility function)

s.t. $z_x^s + z_y^s = \frac{4}{5}$  (production function)
$p_z z_y^s = p_y y^d$  (trade balance with tailor)
$k_z p_z z_x^s = p_x x^d$  (trade balance with farmer)
$k_x x^d = x^r$,   $k_y y^d = y^r$  (transaction condition)

where $z_x^s + z_y^s = z^s$, $z_x^s$ and $z_y^s$ are the respective amounts of silk sold to the farmer and tailor. Since the buying price of silk for the farmer is discounted by $k_z$, the weaver's selling price of silk is $k_z p_z$. The decision variables are $x^r$, $y^r$, $z_x^s$, $z_y^s$, $y^d$, $x^d$. From the three decision problems, we can solve for the demand and supply functions of x, y, z and indirect utility functions for the three configurations in structure $C_z$. The utility equalization and market clearing conditions in the structure then yield the corner equilibrium in this structure.

Repeating this calculation for all other structures, we can obtain all information about the corner equilibria in eight structures, which is summarized in table 26.1. You should work out all corner equilibria and compare your answer to the results in the table.

According to the Yao theorem, the general equilibrium is the Pareto optimum corner

**Table 26.1:** Corner equilibria in eight structures

| Structure | Relative number of different specialists | Relative price | Per capita real income |
|---|---|---|---|
| A | | | $\dfrac{(1-2\alpha)(1-4\alpha)\beta}{4(1+\beta)}$ |
| Ba | $\dfrac{M_y}{M_x} = \left(\dfrac{k_x}{k_y}\right)^{\frac{1}{2}}$ | $\dfrac{p_y}{p_x} = \dfrac{(1-\alpha)(1+\beta)}{(1-2\alpha)\beta}\left(\dfrac{k_y}{k_x}\right)^{\frac{1}{2}}$ | $\dfrac{(1-\alpha)(1-2\alpha)\beta}{4(1+\beta)}\dfrac{1}{k_y^{\frac{1}{2}}k_x}$ |
| Bb | $\dfrac{M_x}{M_z} = \dfrac{\beta k_x k_z}{2k_x} + \dfrac{[\beta^2 k_x^2 k_z^2 + 4k_x k_z(1+\beta)]^{\frac{1}{2}}}{2k_x}$ | $\dfrac{p_z}{p_x} = -\dfrac{\beta k_x k_z}{2k_x} + \dfrac{[\beta^2 k_x^2 k_z^2 + 4k_x k_z(1+\beta)]^{\frac{1}{2}}}{2k_x}$ | $\dfrac{(1-2\alpha)^2\beta}{4(1+\beta)}\left\{-\dfrac{\beta k_x k_z}{2} + \dfrac{[\beta^2 k_x^2 k_z^2 + 4k_x k_z(1+\beta)]^{\frac{1}{2}}}{2}\right\}$ |
| Bc | $\dfrac{M_z}{M_y} = \dfrac{1}{\beta k_z}$ | $\dfrac{p_z}{p_y} = \dfrac{\beta k_z}{1+\beta k_z k_y}$ | $\dfrac{(1-2\alpha)^2\beta k_z k_y}{4(1+\beta k_z k_y)}$ |

| Structure | Relative number of different specialists | Relative price | Per capita real income | Circulation of money |
|---|---|---|---|---|
| $C_y$ | $\dfrac{M_y}{M_x} = \dfrac{k_z\beta}{1+k_z\beta}\left(\dfrac{k_x}{k_y}\right)^{\frac{1}{2}}$ <br> $\dfrac{M_y}{M_z} = k_z\beta$ | $\dfrac{p_y}{p_x} = \dfrac{1+k_y k_z\beta}{k_z\beta}(k_y k_x)^{-\frac{1}{2}}$ <br> $\dfrac{p_y}{p_z} = \dfrac{1+k_y k_z\beta}{k_z\beta}$ | $\dfrac{(1-\alpha)^2 k_z\beta}{4}\dfrac{k_z\beta}{1+k_y k_z\beta}$ | $\dfrac{M(1-\alpha)}{2(1+k_z\beta)(1+k_y k_z\beta)} \times \dfrac{k_x^{\frac{1}{2}}k_z\beta}{k_y^{\frac{1}{2}}+k_x^{\frac{1}{2}}}$ |
| $C_z$ | $\dfrac{M_z}{M_x} = \dfrac{2k_x^{\frac{1}{2}}}{2k_x^{\frac{1}{2}}+(1+k_z)k_y^{\frac{1}{2}}k_z\beta}$ <br> $\dfrac{M_y}{M_x} = \dfrac{k_x^{\frac{1}{2}}(1+k_z)k_z\beta}{2k_x^{\frac{1}{2}}+(1+k_z)k_y^{\frac{1}{2}}k_z\beta}$ | $\dfrac{p_z}{p_x} = (k_x k_y)^{-\frac{1}{2}}$ , <br> $\dfrac{p_z}{p_y} = \dfrac{k_z\beta}{1+k_y^{\frac{1}{2}}k_z^{\frac{1}{2}}\beta}$ | $\dfrac{(1-\alpha)^2}{4}\dfrac{k_x^{\frac{1}{2}}k_y k_z^{\frac{1}{2}}\beta}{1+k_y^{\frac{1}{2}}k_z^{\frac{1}{2}}\beta}$ | $M(1-\alpha)k_x^{\frac{1}{2}}\dfrac{4k_x^{\frac{1}{2}}+(1+k_z)k_z\beta(k_y^{\frac{1}{2}}+k_x^{\frac{1}{2}})}{[2k_x^{\frac{1}{2}}+(1+k_z)k_z k_y^{\frac{1}{2}}\beta]^2}$ |

| $C_x$ | $\dfrac{M_z}{M_y} = \dfrac{1}{k_z\beta}$ | $\dfrac{p_{Fx}}{p_{Cy}} = \dfrac{k_x k_z \beta}{1 + k_y^{\frac{1}{2}} k_x^{\frac{1}{2}} k_z \beta}$ | $\dfrac{(1-\alpha)^2}{4}\ \dfrac{k_x k_y k_z \beta}{1 + k_y^{\frac{1}{2}} k_x^{\frac{1}{2}} k_z \beta}$ | $\dfrac{0.5M(1-\alpha)}{1 + k_x + k_z\beta(k_x + k_{y,x}^{\frac{1}{2}\frac{1}{2}z})}$ |
|---|---|---|---|---|
|  | $\dfrac{M_x}{M_y} = \dfrac{1 + k_y^{\frac{1}{2}} k_x^{\frac{1}{2}} k_z \beta}{k_x k_z \beta}$ | $\dfrac{p_x}{p_z} = k_x$ |  |  |
| $D$ | $\dfrac{M_x}{M_y} = \dfrac{1 + k_y^{\frac{1}{2}} k_z \beta}{k_x^{\frac{1}{2}} k_z \beta}$ | $\dfrac{p_y}{p_x} = \dfrac{1 + k_y^{\frac{1}{2}} k_z \beta}{k_x^{\frac{1}{2}} k_z \beta}$ | $\dfrac{(1-\alpha)^2}{4}\ \dfrac{k_x^{\frac{1}{2}} k_y k_z \beta}{1 + k_y^{\frac{1}{2}} k_z \beta}$ | $\dfrac{M(1-\alpha)}{2(1 + k_y^{\frac{1}{2}} k_z \beta)}\ \dfrac{k_x^{\frac{1}{2}} k_z \beta}{1 + k_x^2 + k_z \beta(k_y^{\frac{1}{2}} + k_x^2)}$ |
|  | $\dfrac{M_z}{M_y} = \dfrac{1}{k_z\beta}$ | $\dfrac{p_z}{p_y} = \dfrac{k_z \beta}{1 + k_y^{\frac{1}{2}} k_z \beta}$ |  |  |
|  |  | $\dfrac{p_x}{p_z} = k_x^{\frac{1}{2}}$ |  |  |

equilibrium. The corner equilibrium in structure D is calculated on the basis of the assumption that the transaction efficiency coefficient for the money substitute and fiat money is 1. It is not difficult to show that per capita real income in D is always higher than in other structures with complete division of labor. For simplicity we assume that $k_x = 0.25$. Comparisons between per capita real incomes in three structures with complete division of labor and commodity money indicates that structure $C_x$ is the best if $k_y$, $k_z < 0.25$; $C_y$ is the best if $k_y > k_z$, 0.25; and structure $C_z$ is the best if $k_z > k_y$, 0.25.

Let us now consider the three structures with partial division of labor. A comparison between per capita real incomes in structures Bb and Bc indicates that Bb is better than Bc iff $k_y < k_{y1} \equiv (k^2_z + 30k_z)^{0.5} / k_z [8 - (k^2_z + 30k_z)^{0.5}]$ But $k_{y1}$ is always greater than 1 for any $k_z \in (0, 1)$, while $k_y$ cannot be greater than 1. This implies that Bb is always better than Bc. We can therefore focus on structures Ba and Bb. A comparison between per capita real incomes in Ba and Bb indicates that Ba is better than Bb iff $k_y > k_{y0} \equiv (3/4)^2(k^2_z + 30k_z)$. After this partitioning of the parameter space, we can see that the set of candidates for general equilibrium comprises A, Ba, and $C_y$ if the transaction efficiency of clothing y is higher than that of other goods; A, Bb, and $C_z$ if the transaction efficiency of silk z is higher than that of other goods; and A, Ba or Bb, and $C_x$ if the transaction efficiency of food x is higher than that of other goods.

Based on the partitioning of the parameter space into three subspaces, we can find the critical values of transaction efficiency that further partition each of the parameter subspaces. The resulting general equilibrium and its inframarginal comparative statics are summarized in table 26.2.

In words, the inframarginal comparative statics of the general equilibrium in table 26.2 can be summarized as follows. If transaction efficiency is very low, then the general equilibrium is autarky where the market and money are not needed. As transaction efficiency is improved, the general equilibrium evolves from autarky to partial division of labor, where the market emerges from the partial division of labor, but money is not needed, followed by complete division of labor, where money is essential for the complete division of labor. If social and institutional conditions ensure that the transaction cost coefficient of fiat money, a credit system, or other money substitutes is sufficiently small, then the money substitute will be used as the medium of exchange to facilitate the complete division of labor. But if, for instance, the money substitute can be easily counterfeited, the supply of fiat money increases drastically, so that the value of fiat money declines quickly, or a war impedes the enforcement of the credit system, then the commodity money with the lowest transaction cost coefficient will be used as the medium of exchange to facilitate the complete division of labor.

Cheng (1999) shows that if $k_x$ is a constant between 0 and 1 rather than fixed at 0.25, then structure Bc may be general equilibrium within a parameter subspace. The Borland and Yang model (1992; also see Yang and Ng, 1993, ch. 17) and the Cheng model show that specialization and division of labor are essential but not sufficient for the emergence of money. A sufficiently high level of division of labor that involves roundabout production is essential for the emergence of money. The Borland and Yang model also shows that a sufficiently high level of division of labor in a sufficiently long roundabout production chain is essential for the emergence of money. Because of the trade-off between economies of specialization and transaction costs in the new classical models of money, the emergence of money can promote productivity progress by facilitating a high level of division of labor in a long roundabout production chain. Money promotes productivity progress in an interesting way in the new classical models. Transaction costs may be increased because of

**Table 26.2**: Inframarginal comparative statics of general equilibrium and emergence of money from evolution in division of labor

$k_y < k_{y0}$

| Money substitutes are not available | | | | | | | | | | Money substitutes are available | |
|---|---|---|---|---|---|---|---|---|---|---|---|
| $k_y > k_z$, 1/4 | | | $k_z > k_y$, 1/4 | | $1/4 > k_y$, $k_z$ | | | | | | |
| $k_z < .23$ | $k_z \in (.23, k_{z0})$ | $k_z > k_{z0}$ | $k_z < k_{z1}$ | $k_z > k_{z1}$ | $k_z < 0.23$ | $k_z \in (0.2, k_{z2})$ | $k_z > k_{z2}$ | $k_z < 0.23$ | $k_z \in (0.23, k_{z3})$ | $k_z > k_{z3}$ |
| A | Bb | $C_y$ | Bb | $C_z$ | A | Bb | $C_x$ | A | Bb | D |

$k_y > k_{y0}$

| Money substitutes are not available | | | | | | Money substitutes are available | | |
|---|---|---|---|---|---|---|---|---|
| $k_y > k_z$, 1/4 | | $k_z > k_y$, 1/4 | | | $1/4 > k_y, k_z$ | $k_y < 1/4$ | $k_y \in (0.25, k_{y3})$ | $k_y > k_{y3}$ |
| $k_y < k_{y1}$ | $k_y > k_{y1}$ | $k_y < 1/4$ | $k_y \in (0.25, k_{y2})$ | $k_y > k_{y2}$ | | | | |
| Ba | $C_y$ | A | Ba | $C_z$ | A | A | Ba | D |

*where $k_{y0} \equiv (3/4)^2(k_z^2 + 30k_z)$; $k_{z0}$, is given by $f_0(k_y, k_z) \equiv 2^7 k_y^{3/2} k_z - 9(k_z^2 + 30k_z)^{1/2}(1 + k_y k_z)$ $= 0$; $k_{z1}$, is given by $f_1(k_z, k_y) \equiv 2^7 k_y k_z^{3/2} - 9(k_z^2 + 30k_z)^{1/2}(1 + k_y^{1/2} k_z^{3/2}) = 0$; $k_{z2}$ is given by $f_2(k_z, k_y) \equiv 18(k_z^2 + 30k_z)^{1/2}/[2^7 k_z - 9k_z(k_z^2 + 30k_z)^{1/2}]$; $k_{z3}$ is given by $f_3(k_z, k_y) \equiv 2^7 k_y k_z - 9(k_z^2 + 30k_z)^{0.5}(1 + k_y^{1/2} k_z) = 0$. $k_{y1} \equiv 3/5k_z$, $k_{y2} \equiv 3/5k_z^{3/2}$, $k_{y3}$ is given by $f_3(k_z, k_y) = 0$.*

the emergence of money. For instance, if money and its substitute are not available due to the institutional environment (for instance, use of money is restricted, as in a Soviet-style economic system), and transaction efficiency of goods is sufficiently high, then the equilibrium is a structure with partial division of labor and the complete division of labor is infeasible. As improvements in the institutional environment reduce the transaction cost coefficient for money or its substitute, then money will emerge and the complete division of labor becomes general equilibrium. In the structure with complete division of labor both productivity and transaction costs are increased in comparison to a structure with partial division of labor, provided the productivity progress benefit of a finer division of labor outweighs the increased transaction costs.

Smith conjectured that a more salable commodity is more likely to play the role of medium of exchange. There are two ways to interpret the notion of salability of a commodity. According to some economists, a commodity is more salable if more individuals accept it for their consumption and production. According to our new classical models of money, this interpretation is wrong. A commodity is more likely to be used as money if its transaction cost coefficient is smaller. In the Borland and Yang model of money in which steel is used to produce hoes, which are used to produce food, all individuals accept food for consumption in a structure with complete division of labor, but only specialist producers of hoes need steel. According to the first interpretation of salability, food is more salable than steel and hoes. But according to our interpretation of salability, steel is more salable if its transaction cost coefficient is much smaller than those of hoes and food. Historically, it was some precious metal that very few individuals used for their consumption and production that was used as money. Food, with its low transaction efficiency due to its perishability or the low value of each unit of quantity, is rarely used as money despite the fact that everybody needs it. Commodities that are used as money usually have the following features: a high value of each unit of quantity, so that it costs little to carry the commodity, ease of divisibility, and physical stability (not readily perishable). All of these features imply a low transaction cost coefficient, which includes storage cost and loss of value in transit or in dividing.

Our new classical models of money are general equilibrium models.[2] Hence, the equilibrium quantity of commodity money in circulation is endogenized. Also, the equilibrium price of commodity money in terms of other goods, which includes its value for consumption or production as well as its value as medium of exchange, is endogenized.[3] The circulation volume and value of commodity money not only continuously change within a structure in response to marginal changes in parameters, but also discontinuously jump between structures with various monetary regimes and different network patterns of division of labor as parameter values shift between subspaces.

It can be shown that as transaction efficiency is improved and division of labor evolves in an increasingly longer roundabout production chain, the circulation and value of commodity money increase and the degree of monetization of the economy increases. This is a new classical way to explain the drastic increase of the price of gold during the Industrial Revolution. It can also be shown that use of a money substitute and a credit system can reduce the circulation of commodity money and thereby reduce the price of commodity money in terms of other goods.

## Key Terms and Review

Commodity money, fiat money, money substitutes, credit systems.
Double coincidence of demand and supply and emergence of money.
The relationship between the level of division of labor, the length of the roundabout production chain, transaction efficiency, and the emergence of money.
Conditions for fiat money to substitute for commodity money.
Properties of a commodity that is likely to be used as money.
The relationship between the network size of division of labor, the degree of commercialization, and the degree of monetization of an economy.
Productivity implications of commodity money and fiat money.
The function of the market in searching for the efficient monetary regime and level of division of labor.

## Further Reading

Cheng (1998), Jevons (1893), Borland and Yang (1992), Yang and Y.-K. Ng (1993, ch. 17), Ostroy and Starr (1990), Alchian (1977), Brunner and Meltzer (1971), Clower (1967), Green (1987), Parkin (1986), R. Jones (1976), King and Plosser (1986), Kiyotaki and Wright (1989, 1993), Lucas (1980), Oh (1989), Starrett (1973), Ostroy (1973), Smith (1776, ch. 4), Menger (1871), von Mises (1922).

## QUESTIONS

1   In a Soviet-style economy, the government controls the pricing of most commodities. The official prices under government control are usually far away from the market clearing prices. But those transactions facilitated by barter or commodity money between firms and between individuals can be done without compliance to official prices which are relevant only to transactions in terms of official fiat money. Hence, we can see a lot of "back door" transactions based on barter or commodity money in a Soviet-style economy. Explain why. What is the implication of this feature of a Soviet-style economy for economic development?

2   Since 1990, firms in Russia have preferred barter or transactions in terms of commodity money to transactions in terms of fiat money due to extremely high inflation rates. Use the model in this chapter to explain the phenomenon.

3   Some economists interpret Smith's concept of salability of a commodity as the population share of those who need the commodity for consumption or production. Is this interpretation correct? Why or why not?

4   Use a new classical model of money to illustrate that use of money may increase transaction costs.

5   Discuss the mechanism to endogenize value of money in a new classical model of money. Analyze the implications of monetary policy for productivity progress and evolution of division of labor.

6   How do institutional arrangements determine the degree of monetization, the level of division of labor, and productivity of an economy through affecting transaction efficiency?

7   Test the theory developed in this chapter against empirical observation. For instance, test concurrent evolution of division of labor and the degree of monetization of an economy (income share of economic activities that are facilitated by money).

8   Somebody asks an economist about the quick way to make money. The economist replies: there is no general rule for making money. You have to understand economies of division of labor and the function of money in reducing transaction costs and in facilitating division of labor for a particular business situation, in order to understand the general equilibrium mechanism under which money can be made. Comment on the economist's answer.

## EXERCISES

1   Solve for simplified the Kiyotaki–Wright model where person A's utility function is $u_A = kx$ and her production function is $z = l_A$ where $l_A$ is the fixed labor endowment of person A. Person B's utility function is $u_B = ty$ and her production function is $x = l_B$ where $l_B$ is person B's endowment of labor. Person C's utility is $u_C = sz$ and her production function is $y = l_C$ where $l_C$ is her endowment of labor. $x, y, z$ are respective amounts of three goods and $k, t, s$ are the respective transaction efficiency coefficients of the three goods, which could be interpreted as probabilities for receiving the goods purchased and which relate to probabilities that different types of persons are matched in the original KW model. Trade must be sequential and the discount rate is 0. Identify the condition for a particular good to be money in equilibrium.

2   Solve for the general equilibrium and its inframarginal comparative statics of the Borland–Yang model of money. Each consumer-producer's utility function is $u = z + z^c$, where $z$ is the amount of food self-provided, $z^c$ is the amount of food received for consumption from

purchase in the market. The production function of food is $z + z^s = [(y + y^c)l_z^a]^{0.5}$, where $a > 1$, $z^s$ is the amount of food sold in the market, $y$ is the amount of hoes self-provided, $y^c$ is the amount of hoes that are received from the purchase in the market. $l_z$ is an individual's level of specialization in producing z. The production function for hoes is $y + y^s = [(x + x^c)l_y^a]^{0.5}$, where $y^s$ is the amount of hoes sold, $x$ is the amount of steel self-provided, $x^c$ is the amount of steel that is received from purchase in the market, $l_y$ is an individual's level of specialization in producing hoes. The production function of steel is $x + x^s = l_x - A$, where $x^s$ is the amount of steel sold, and $l_x$ is an individual's level of specialization in producing x. The endowment constraint for working time is $l_x + l_y + l_z = 1$. The material balance between use and production are $tx^d = x^c + x^m$, $ry^d = y^c + y^m$, $kz^d = z^c + z^m$. Superscript $d$ denotes the amount purchased, $c$ denotes the amount used for consumption or production, $m$ denotes the amount used as money. $t$, $r$, $k$ are respective transaction efficiency coefficients for steel, hoes, and food.

3  Suppose that in the Cheng model in example 26.3, $k_x$ is a parameter which might not equal 0.25. Solve for the inframarginal comparative statics of general equilibrium. Calculate the equilibrium value of money in terms of a *numéraire* good. Calculate the equilibrium degree of monetarization. Use your calculation to explain drastic increases and decreases in the price of gold in the nineteenth and twentieth centuries, respectively, and to explain concurrent increases in the degree of monetarization and commercialization as two aspects of economic development. As commodity money is increasingly replaced by fiat money as the medium of exchange at the beginning of this century, what will happen to the price of gold relative to other goods?

4  Assume that the government issues fiat money $Q$ in the model in example 26.3, and uses $Q$ to buy x in period 1, then sells x for fiat money in period 2, then uses fiat money to buy y and z in period 3, and finally sells y and z for fiat money again. What is the effect of change in $Q$ on nominal prices of goods and on the equilibrium level of division of labor and productivity? If $Q$ changes at the end of period 3, will the equilibrium level of division of labor and resource allocation be affected? Use your answer to analyze the implications of monetary policies.

# Notes

1 According to Smith, once the division of labor has been thoroughly established, an individual supplies most of his product to others in exchange for goods he wants. But the exchange "must frequently" be "very much clogged" if one does not have what others want or others do not have what one desires. "In order to avoid the inconveniency of such a situation, every prudent man . . . must have at all times by him, besides the peculiar produce of his own industry, a certain quantity of some one commodity or other, such as he imagined few people would be likely to refuse in exchange for the produce of their industry" (Smith, 1776, p. 37).

2 R. Jones (1976) first developed a model formalizing the idea that money is a natural consequence of the "unconcerted" market behaviour of individuals. His model was later extended by Oh (1989).

3 According to von Mises, "The earliest value of money links up with the commodity-value of the monetary material. But the value of money since then has been influenced not merely by the factors dependent on the 'industrial' uses, which determine the value of the material of which the commodity-money is made, but also by those which result from its use as money" (1922, p. 106).

# chapter 27

# NEW CLASSICAL THEORY OF BUSINESS CYCLES AND UNEMPLOYMENT

## ◆ 27.1 Rethinking Macroeconomics

Macroeconomic phenomena relate to aggregate demand and supply and their relationship with the absolute general level of prices. *Aggregate demand* is the sum of the values of the total market demands for all individual goods. It differs from total market demand for a particular good, which is referred to as a *disaggregate variable*. Aggregate demand, aggregate supply, and the general price level are referred to as *aggregate variables*.

From the new classical static and dynamic general equilibrium models that we have examined in previous chapters, we can see that per capita real income can be considered as the absolute price of labor, which is endogenously determined by the equilibrium level of division of labor. The endogenization of the absolute price level is associated with the endogenization of the network size of division of labor and related aggregate demand in the marketplace. In the new classical framework, a corner equilibrium sorts out resource allocation (relative prices of traded goods and numbers of individuals choosing different occupation configurations), while the general equilibrium sorts out the absolute price level of labor and the network size of division of labor and related aggregate demand. Hence, the marginal comparative statics of a corner equilibrium in the new classical framework has the same explanatory power as the comparative statics of a neoclassical general equilibrium model, while the inframarginal comparative statics of new classical general equilibrium can explain many macroeconomic phenomena that neoclassical models cannot predict. We call the inframarginal comparative statics (or dynamics) analysis of new classical economics *new classical macroeconomic analysis*, and the marginal comparative statics analysis *new classical microeconomic analysis*.

From this discussion, you can see that the focus of new classical economics is on macroeconomic phenomena which relate to the network size of division of labor. In this section, we first consider various ways to explain unemployment and aggregate demand in the new classical framework that relate to the models that we have already studied. Then in the rest of the chapter we develop a new classical dynamic general equilibrium model that can simultaneously endogenize efficient business cycles, efficient unemployment, and long-run economic growth.

## Example 27.1: the new classical model with endogenous risk of mass unemployment

The first new classical general equilibrium models that can endogenize mass unemployment are those discussed in chapter 16 (see also Yang and Wills, 1990) and chapter 17 (see also Lio, 1998). In these models, the efficient trade-offs among economies of division of labor, transaction costs, and coordination reliability of the network of division of labor generate an equilibrium and efficient risk of coordination failure of the network of division of labor. The comparative statics of the general equilibrium indicate that as transaction efficiency is improved, the equilibrium and efficient risk of coordination failure will rise. This risk of coordination failure is indeed a risk of mass unemployment, since when the coordination failure of a very developed network of division of labor takes place, as in the Great Depression, all individuals are forced to choose autarky, which implies that many individuals are excluded from the network of division of labor and the related network of the market, that is, they are unemployed.

This risk of mass unemployment has the following interesting features. First, it is efficient. The market efficiently trades off the positive network effect of division of labor against transaction costs and the risk of coordination failure to determine the efficient risk of mass unemployment, just as we voluntarily choose a higher risk of being killed on the freeway by driving on it more often as transportation conditions are improved. Second, this high risk of coordination failure never exists in an autarchic society. It is associated with a high level of division of labor (or a great degree of commercialization, as we call it in daily language). Unemployment and business cycles are essentially phenomena that are inherent in the nature of the network of division of labor. In autarky each individual produces everything for herself. If her taste or technology changes such that one of the goods is not needed, she will just reduce the resources allocated to the production of that good. If she cannot work in winter or under bad weather conditions, she can just be idle. We would not call this unemployment since she still produces other goods or is busy under better weather conditions. But in a society in which each individual is completely specialized, as consumers' tastes or technical conditions change, a professional sector may be out of the market and all specialists in that sector will be unemployed.

In addition to mass unemployment caused by the efficient risk of coordination failure, there are two more types of unemployment. The first of them is "natural unemployment" and the second is cyclical unemployment. We shall model cyclical unemployment in sections 27.2–27.5. In the rest of this section we consider two ways to explain natural unemployment.

## Example 27.2: natural unemployment caused by the integer problem

The integer problem in new classical models may generate *natural unemployment*. Suppose that in the symmetric new classical model with two goods in chapter 5 there are three individuals ($M = 3$) and the set of individuals is not a continuum. Then, the utility equalization and market clearing conditions yield the numbers of individuals choosing the two occupation configurations $M_x = M_y = 1.5$. This implies that one and a half persons specialize in producing each good. This is not only an unrealistic statement, but it also contradicts the notion of specialization that half a person should specialize in producing $x$ and her other half specialize in producing $y$. Suppose transaction efficiency is so high that person 1 chooses $(x/y)$ and person 2 chooses $(y/x)$, then persons 1 and 2 may establish an "equilibrium" with $M_x = M_y = p = 1$ that generates a higher per capita real income than the real income of person 3 who is forced to choose autarky. Person 3 has an incentive to specialize in producing a good and selling it at a slightly lower relative price than the "equilibrium" one, so that the buyer of the good will turn to her. Thus, the prescribed equilibrium between persons 1 and 2 breaks down and the buyer of the good and person 3 may establish another "equilibrium" that forces the other person to choose autarky. That person will in turn have both the incentive and the capacity to break down the new "equilibrium" again. This process continues, such that an equilibrium can never be reached.

It is not difficult to see that the Walrasian equilibrium does not exist in this two-good economy if the market clearing and utility equalization conditions yield non-integer numbers of different specialists. But if two individuals have much better transaction and production conditions than the other individual, then the two individuals can establish a Nash bargaining equilibrium with the division of labor and the third person is excluded from the market network. Hence, the third person appears to be in involuntary unemployment since she is willing to be involved in the division of labor.

From figure 27.1 we can see that if $M = 3$ in the model in chapters 5 and 6, then the aggregate transformation curve involves three curvilinear figures. Curve $A$ is an individual's transformation curve. If two persons specialize in producing y and the third person

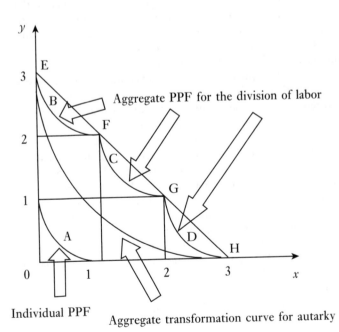

♦ **Figure 27.1**: Aggregate transformation curve for $M = 3$

produces two goods, then we can move curve $A$ up by two units to obtain curve $B$. If two persons specialize in producing x and the third person produces two goods, then we can move curve $A$ to the right by two units to obtain curve $D$. If a person specializes in producing x, the second specializes in producing y, and the third produces two goods, then we can move curve $A$ up by one unit and to the right by one unit to obtain curve $C$. Curves $B$, $C$, and $D$ constitute the aggregate PPF for the production function in chapter 5 if $M = 3$.

Hence the number of curvilinear figures that constitute the aggregate PPF increases with the population size. As the population size tends to infinity, the aggregate transformation curve converges to a straight line and the gap between the aggregate production schedule for autarky and that for the division of labor, which represents the gains from the division of labor, is enlarged.

The equilibrium integer problem disappears as the population size tends to infinity. For instance, in the model with two final goods, the natural unemployment rate is 1/3 if the population size is 3, and is 1/101 if the population size is 101.

If we introduce many consumer and producer goods into the model, then the integer problem will become increasingly serious and complicated. From casual observation, we can see that the natural unemployment rate caused by the integer problem is higher in an economy with a higher level of division of labor than in an autarchic society. But the integer problem in a model with many goods is much more complicated than this intuition suggests. First, unequal incomes may occur in a Nash bargaining equilibrium even between *ex ante* nearly identical individuals. Consider the new classical model with $m$ final goods in chapter 11, where $m = 100$, the number of traded goods is 50 in equilibrium, and the set of individuals is finite and the population size is 101. We assume that those individuals who are marginally less productive than others will be excluded from the network of division of labor if the integer condition does not hold. But the difference in productivity is infinitesimally small, so that the symmetry of the model is retained. The market clearing and utility equalization conditions yield a non-integer number of specialists selling each good, 101/50. Hence, one individual who is marginally less productive than others will be excluded from the network of division of labor and be compelled to choose autarky, or unemployment. The other 100 individuals form two separate networks of division of labor. In each of them, each individual sells one good to and buys one good from each of the other 49 individuals. The equilibrium unemployment rate is 1/101. If transaction efficiency is improved, so that the optimum number of traded goods becomes 80, then 80 individuals will form a symmetric network of division of labor. But there are two possible patterns of organization for the other 21 individuals who are marginally less productive. They may form a symmetric network of division of labor with 21 traded goods if doing so makes them better off than in autarky. In this smaller network of division of labor, economies of division of labor net of transaction costs are not fully exploited, so that per capita real income is lower than in the larger network of division of labor. However, as shown in Yang and Ng (1993, ch. 5), each individual's per capita real income under equilibrium prices might be a nonmonotonic function of the number of traded goods $n$. This case is illustrated in figure 27.2, where the vertical axis represents utility under equilibrium relative prices of traded goods and the horizontal axis represents the number of traded goods.

As shown in Fig. 27.2, an individual's per capita real income is a nonmonotonic function of her number of traded goods. An individual's organization utility is maximized at $n = 80$

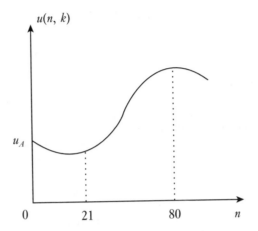

♦ **Figure 27.2:** An individual's organization utility under equilibrium prices

for a given transaction efficiency coefficient $k$. When the number of traded goods is 21, utility is lower than in autarky since transaction costs outweigh economies of specialization for $n = 21$. In this case, 21 individuals will choose autarky in equilibrium and the unemployment rate is $21/101$. This example illustrates that there is no simple monotonic relationship between the level of division of labor and the natural unemployment rate caused by the integer problem. However, it is safe to say that as the equilibrium level of division of labor goes up, the average natural unemployment rate caused by the integer problem is more likely to be higher.

In reality, the natural unemployment caused by the integer problem in a highly commercialized society (with a high level of division of labor) is a very common phenomenon. For instance, suppose that universities in an economy need two more economics professors, but there are three economics Ph.D. graduates of nearly the same quality. Then one of them must be unemployed until new demand emerges. You may ask why the universities cannot hire three part-time professors and require each of them to work for $2/3$ of the full loading time. This cannot be equilibrium because of economies of specialization. Since the part-time professors are only partially specialized they are not as productive as those full-time professors who are completely specialized. From the example of the economy with two goods and three individuals, you can see that if transaction efficiency is sufficiently high, two of the three individuals will have division of labor and complete specialization and will refuse to have division of labor with the other person who is marginally less productive, even if the third person is willing to produce x and y on a part-time basis and to trade with others.

As shown in example 13.1, in a new classical model with *ex ante* different consumer-producers, even if the set of individuals is a continuum, a dual structure may occur in the transitional stage from autarky to the complete division of labor. In this dual structure *ex ante* identical individuals may be divided between an autarky configuration and a specialization configuration. Self-sufficient individuals look underemployed or are unemployed since they cannot find a job to work for the market.

## Example 27.3: natural unemployment caused by changes in the structure of division of labor

The second reason for natural unemployment in a new classical general equilibrium model is changes in the pattern of the network of division of labor caused by exogenous changes in parameters. We use the symmetric new classical model with $m$ consumer goods and $n$ traded goods in chapter 11, where both $m$ and $n$ are endogenous, to illustrate this kind of natural unemployment. Suppose an oil crisis raises the cost of gas and reduces transaction efficiency $k$, so that the equilibrium values of $m$ and $n$ suddenly decline. This implies that, suddenly, the demand for some goods disappears as individuals stop consuming some non-essential goods. The specialist producers of those goods will lose their jobs. But because of fixed learning costs or job shifting costs, these individuals are not as productive as the specialist producers of the other goods which are still demanded, even if the unemployed individuals immediately shift to the professional sectors which are still in the market. Therefore, specialist producers must be unemployed before they get a chance to acquire experience in a profession to which they are new. This kind of unemployment would not take place in an autarchic society where each individual produces all goods for herself. In that case, a change in tastes or production conditions will cause an adjustment of each individual's resource allocation between different goods in the absence of unemployment. It is easy to understand that the higher the equilibrium level of division of labor, the more likely it is that such unemployment will take place in response to exogenous changes in parameters. If the dynamic effect of specialized learning by doing is considered, then any change in the structure of division of labor will force some individuals to change occupations. In the transitional period, old human capital becomes useless, and the acquisition of new professional human capital depends on a new job that creates opportunities for learning by doing. But the unemployed are not competitive with those who have jobs with opportunities for specialized learning by doing, so that unemployment itself prevents the unemployed from finding a new job. Hence, a vicious circle may drive the unemployed out of the market forever.

In exercise 7, the efficiency wage model endogenizes the equilibrium unemployment rate by specifying the trade-off between moral hazard and unemployment. Unemployment can play a role as a device to reduce workers' inefficiency. This model and the three new classical ways, discussed so far, to explain unemployment and the interrelation between network size of division of labor and unemployment are not satisfactory. First, none of these models can predict long-run regular business cycles and related cyclical unemployment. The interdependence between long-run regular business cycles, cyclical unemployment, and long-run endogenous economic growth cannot be explored by these models. In particular, the implications of durable goods, compounded with a sophisticated network of division of labor, for long-run regular and endogenous business cycles and growth cannot be explored by these models. Many experienced businessmen know the intimate relationship between the stock of durable goods and business cycles. In the rest of the chapter, we will use a new classical dynamic general equilibrium model with durable producer goods to endogenize long-run regular efficient business cycles, long-run economic growth, and efficient cyclical unemployment. We will explore the implications of efficient business cycles and efficient unemployment for long-run economic growth and evolution of the network size of division of labor.

The empirical evidence for a positive correlation between business cycles and productivity growth is provided by recent literature of economic growth, although the evidence is still inconclusive. Using cross-sectional data on 47 countries, Kormendi and Meguire (1985) find a significant positive effect of cyclical variability (measured as the standard deviation of real output growth) on the mean annual growth rate. By constructing pooled cross-section/time series data on 113 countries, Grier and Tullock (1989) find a positive and significant effect of the standard deviation of real GDP growth on the average economic growth. Ramey and Ramey (1995) confirm this result for the OECD countries when they use standard deviation of output growth as a proxy for cyclical variability.

There are a number of versions of neoclassical models which concern how cyclical variability may coexist with an increase in economic growth. The first strand of literature explains the positive implication of output fluctuation by assuming that economies face a positive risk–return trade-off in their choice of aggregate technology. Agents collectively would choose riskier technologies only if these were expected to generate a greater return and hence greater economic growth (Black, 1987). The second strand looks at how R&D activities can be boosted when the economy goes through a recession. Typically, firms may find it profitable to reallocate employees to research and reorganization activities in an economic downturn because the opportunity costs in terms of the forgone production are relatively low in a recession (see Aghion and Saint-Paul, 1991). The third line of research emphasizes the precautionary savings motive at recessions. Agents are expected to behave prudently and accumulate physical and human capital as a buffer stock to protect consumption against the bad state of the economy. The precautionary accumulation of human capital is particularly relevant for economic growth. Since low-skilled employment is disproportionately affected by cyclical variability, agents may want to accumulate human capital more rapidly so as to increase job security (see Deaton, 1991, Skinner, 1988, Dellas, 1991). The fourth line in literature is the creative destruction model largely initiated by Aghion and Howitt (1992; see exercise 7 in chapter 21, above). In their endogenous growth model, vertical innovations lead to the replacement of incumbent firms through a Schumpeterian process of creative destruction, and the average economic growth rate and the variance of the growth rate increase with the size of vertical innovations. The fifth line in the literature is the model of implementation cycles constructed by Shleifer (1986). If each innovator must incur a fixed cost in the period prior to innovation, large sales during booms may be necessary to enable the entrepreneur to cover her fixed costs while innovation introduced during the slumps may lose money. Thus a cyclical equilibrium may enhance innovation and productivity growth, while a stabilization policy may be harmful. The sixth line in the literature is the "cleansing effect" model initiated by Caballero and Hammour (1994), where business cycles are good for long-term economic growth because recession may cleanse the production structure by shaking out the least productive firms and allowing the entry of more efficient producers.

All of the neoclassical models cannot explore the intrinsic connection between business cycles and evolution in division of labor. They cannot explore creative destruction based on evolution of division of labor which replaces old occupations of a low level of specialization with highly professional new ones. In particular they cannot simultaneously predict the following concurrent phenomena: increases in each individual's level of specialization and in the degree of commercialization (division of labor) of society as a whole; endogenous, efficient, long-run, and regular business cycles; endogenous, efficient, long-run, regularly cyclical unemployment; endogenous, long-run, and cyclical economic growth; more volatile fluctuations of the output level of durable goods than that of nondurable goods. The new classical dynamic equilibrium model presented in the rest of the chapter can simultaneously predict all of these phenomena.

## Questions to Ask Yourself when Reading this Chapter

◆ What is the relationship between marginal comparative statics and microeconomic phenomena, and between inframarginal comparative statics and macroeconomic phenomena in new classical economics?

◆ What is the relationship between endogenization of the network size of division of labor and endogenization of aggregate demand?

◆ What are the differences between unemployment caused by the integer problem, that caused by risk of coordination failure of the network of division of labor, that caused by changes in the structure of division of labor, and that caused by long-run endogenous regular and efficient business cycles?

◆ What is the difference between exogenous and endogenous business cycles?

◆ What is the relationship between long-run endogenous business cycles and long-run endogenous economic growth?

◆ What is the relationship between the division of labor in producing roundabout productive durable goods and long-run regular endogenous business cycles?

◆ What is the relationship between business cycles, transaction efficiency, economies of specialized learning by doing, job shifting costs, and durability of goods?

◆ What is the trade-off in determining the efficient pattern of business cycles and economic growth in the marketplace?

◆ Why can the equilibrium pattern of business cycles be Pareto efficient?

◆ How does the market sort out the efficient pattern of business cycles, economic growth, and unemployment?

◆ What is the likely consequence of the government's manipulation of the pattern of business cycles and unemployment?

## ◆ 27.2 Long-run Regular Efficient Business Cycles, Cyclical Unemployment, Long-run Economic Growth, and Division of Labor in Producing Durable Goods

In this section, we first tell the story behind the model before you become mired in the algebra and lose your mind for economic thinking. From daily life experience, we can see that many cyclical physical processes can generate much more power than noncyclical processes. The laser is an example: it can generate cyclical light that has much more power than noncyclical light. The human sex life is cyclical; if it were not, we might not be able to have children. Engineers can give you more examples of cyclical physical processes that generate more power than noncyclical processes. The examples remind us that business cycles may have positive productivity implications.

Many economists, from Marx to Keynes and Stiglitz, attribute business cycles to market failure. Many efforts have been made by governments and business communities to rectify this "market failure" by eliminating the cycles. But none of those efforts can change its basic features and regularities. Moreover, the business cycle is not a significant and persistently regular phenomenon in an autarky economy with low productivity, while it is unavoidable in an economy with high levels of specialization, division of labor, and productivity. The concurrence of business cycles, a high level of division of labor, and high productivity remind us that the persistent cycles may have productivity implications and that there is an intricate relationship between the division of labor and the cycle. Economic dynamics with business cycles may be more efficient than noncyclical economic dynamics.

Consider an economy with many *ex ante* identical consumer-producers. Each individual can produce a nondurable consumer good called food and a durable producer good called tractors. A tractor is indivisible and each driver can drive one and only one tractor to produce food at any point in time. There are economies of specialized learning by doing in producing any good, and two types of costs will be incurred if an individual shifts between productive activities. An individual will forget her experience built up in an activity if she shifts from that activity to another. Also there is an entry cost, such as a threshold learning cost, into any activity. Assume, further, that a tractor can be used for two years. Each consumer derives utility from food and maximizes her total discounted utility.

For this simple economy, there are at least three possible organizational structures of production and consumption. The first is autarky structure A, shown in figure 27.4, where each person self-provides each good herself. She spends some time producing a tractor and the rest of the time driving the tractor to produce food in the first year, and produces only food using the tractor in the second year. Therefore, neither business cycle nor unemployment exists for this structure. In the second structure, C (complete division of labor), shown in figure 27.4, the population is divided between the production of tractors and the production of food. Professional farmers drive tractors to produce food in each of the two years. Professional producers of tractors produce them in the first year and are unemployed in the second year. The aggregate output level is higher in the first year than in the second. This is a business cycle of two years with unemployment in the second year. The second cycle occurs over the third and fourth years, and so forth.

The third structure, P (partial division of labor), shown in figure 27.4, is the same as the second except that the producers of tractors shift to the production of food in the second year. In other words, farmers are completely specialized, but producers of tractors, who produce food as well in every other year, are not completely specialized.

Autarky involves job shifting costs but no division of labor and business cycles. Also, structure A involves no transaction costs and cannot exploit productivity gains from specialized learning by doing. Structure C, with complete division of labor, can speed up the accumulation of human capital through specialized learning by doing. It does not incur job shifting costs, but it generates transaction costs as well as cyclical unemployment of physical labor. Structure P, with partial division of labor, involves job shifting costs for producers of tractors but does not generate business cycles. Economies of specialized learning by doing can be more fully exploited by farmers than by producers of tractors. The level of transaction costs in structure P is in-between that in structure A and that in structure C.

Hence, there are many trade-offs among economies of specialized learning by doing, transaction costs, job shifting costs, faster accumulation of human capital, and cyclical unemployment of physical labor. If job shifting costs, transaction efficiency, and economies of specialized learning by doing are sufficiently great, then complete division of labor with business cycles and unemployment is Pareto superior to autarky and partial division of labor without business cycles and unemployment, since the benefit from faster accumulation of human capital through specialized learning by doing and from a lower job shifting cost in structure C outweigh the transaction costs in this structure, compared to structures A and P. Hence, the market mechanism (the invisible hand) will choose the efficient structure with business cycles and unemployment.

In structure C, specialist producers of tractors sell tractors and buy food in years 1, 3, 5, ... The value of tractors that are sold is in excess of the value of food that is purchased. The difference is the saving that the tractor specialists will use to buy food in years 2, 4, 6, ... when they are unemployed, as shown in figure 27.4. Since trade is one-way in years 2, 4, 6, ... and commodity money does not work for this kind of saving of purchase power, fiat money or a credit system is essential for realization of structure C. Because of

(a) Case with high transaction efficiency and job shifting costs and significant economies of specialized learning by doing

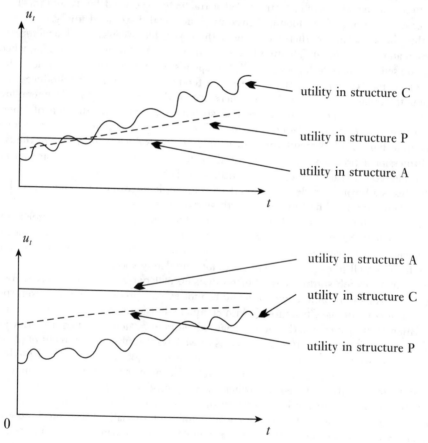

(b) Case with low transaction efficiency and job shifting costs and insignificant economies of specialized learning by doing

◆ **Figure 27.3:** Growth patterns with and without business cycles and unemployment

free choice of profession configurations, total discounted real income must be the same between tractor specialists and professional farmers. In other words, income in the sector producing durable goods must be sufficiently higher than in the sector producing nondurable goods during the boom period, so that the difference is enough to compensate for unemployment in the sector producing durable goods during recession. This implies that the invisible hand (a price mechanism) can coordinate self-interested decisions to sort out the efficient trade-offs among the conflicting forces: economies of specialized learning by doing, transaction costs, and job shifting costs.

The different time paths of per capita real incomes in the three structures within different subspaces of parameter values are shown in figure 27.3. Panel (a) shows the time paths of per capita real incomes in the three structures when transaction efficiency and job shifting cost are high and economies of specialized learning by doing are significant. In the early stage, structure A generates higher per capita real income than structures P and C because of the transaction costs in the two latter structures and the fact that it takes time for economies of specialized learning by doing to speed up accumulation of human capital. As time goes by, per capita real income in structure P first exceeds that in structure A, then per capita real income in structure C overtakes that in structure A and P despite business cycles in structure C.

Panel (b) shows the time paths of per capita real incomes in the three structures when transaction efficiency and job shifting cost are low and economies of specialized learning by doing are insignificant. Structure A always generates a higher per capita real income than structures P and C. Even if the per capita real income in C catches up to that in A and P later on because of a faster accumulation of human capital in C, C may still be Pareto inferior to A and P because of a lower total discounted per capita real income in C than in A and P.

Three features distinguish our new classical theory of business cycles from the existing business cycle models. First, in our model the network size of division of labor and related levels of specialization for each individual are endogenized in a microdynamic equilibrium model. Second, our new classical model generates the following three macroeconomic phenomena simultaneously: persistent, regular, endogenous, and efficient business cycles; endogenous cyclical and efficient unemployment; long-run endogenous economic growth that might be speeded up by business cycles and cyclical unemployment. Our model is characterized by economies of specialized learning by doing, shifting costs between jobs, and indivisibility and durability of producer goods.

These characteristics are necessary for a dynamic equilibrium with the business cycles to be Pareto superior to noncyclical dynamics. Our model explores the implications of business cycles and cyclical unemployment for long-run endogenous economic growth. It predicts that output of durables fluctuates more than output of nondurables, a macroeconomic phenomenon confirmed by a lot of empirical evidence and considered by many economists as one of the important phenomena that need to be explained by macroeconomic theory (see for instance Barro, 1997).

Third, our model can be used to explore the roles of fiat money and saving in enabling the market to use business cycles and cyclical unemployment to speed up accumulation of human capital, thereby speeding up endogenous long-run economic growth. In our model, saving is used to finance purchases by specialist producers of durable goods who are unemployed during recession, such that the market can use business cycles to avoid job shifting costs and speed up human capital accumulation. Hence, the gains from saving are not based on trade between goods at different points in time. Therefore, commodity money cannot be used to facilitate such saving. Money substitutes, fiat money, or a credit system is essential for such saving to facilitate efficient business cycles and efficient cyclical unemployment.

Compared with shock–dependent business cycle models, such as the Samuelson (1939) and the Hicks (1950) models, our model is an endogenous business cycle model which can generate persistent business cycles in the absence of any exogenous shocks. Our model also can generate the productivity implications of business cycles and unemployment which cannot be generated by other endogenous business cycle models, such as those of Vogt (1969) and Goodwin (1951). In contrast to labor shift models (see Lilien, 1982, and Black, 1987), in the model presented in this chapter business cycles and unemployment occur when individuals do not shift between professional sectors, whereas unemployment is caused by such shifts in the labor shift models. Hence, the incompatibility between empirical observations, which indicate much more job shifting during boom periods than during recession, and labor shift models (see Abraham and Katz, 1986, and Murphy and Topel, 1987) may be avoided by our theory. Recently developed real business cycle models (see Kydland and Prescott, 1982, Long, Jr. and Plosser, 1983, and King and Plosser, 1984) need an exogenous stochastic process to generate some "business cycle phenomena" which are not business cycles, according to Prescott (1986). However, our model can generate persistent business cycles in the absence of any exogenous stochastic process. All the forenamed business cycle models are macroeconomic models, whereas our model in this chapter is a microdynamic equilibrium model. Weitzman's microequilibrium model with increasing returns to scale (1982) has endogenized unemployment. However, he considers unemployment as a consequence of coordination failure in the market and his model cannot generate persistent business cycles. The models of monopolistic competition and sticky prices (see for example Mankiw, 1985, Ball, Mankiw, and D. Romer, 1988) and the efficiency wage models (see for example Yellen, 1984, Stiglitz, 1986, and exercise 7) attribute unemployment to a market failure in equilibrating demand and supply. They cannot generate endogenously persistent business cycles. Stiglitz has developed a model (1992) to explain business fluctuations again by the failure of the capital market caused by incomplete information. The business cycles in Ng's (1986, 1992) mesoeconomic model is based also on coordination failure to maintain an efficient equilibrium in an imperfectly competitive economy with a continuum of real equilibria. In contrast, the model in this chapter attributes business cycles *and* unemployment to market success.

## ◆ 27.3 A New Classical Dynamic Equilibrium Model of Business Cycles and Unemployment

### Example 27.4: the Yang–Ng model (1993) of endogenous and efficient business cycles

We consider a model with a continuum of $M$ *ex ante* identical consumer-producers. There is a nondurable consumer good called food and a durable producer good called tractors. At any point in time an individual can drive one and only one tractor to produce food and a tractor can be used for two years. The amount of food which an individual self-provides in year $t$ is denoted by $y_t$. The amount of food sold in year $t$ is $y^s_t$. The amount of food purchased in year $t$ is $y^d_t$. The transaction efficiency coefficient for food is $k$, so that $ky^d_t$ is the amount available for consumption from the purchase of food. The quantity of food consumed in year $t$ is $y_t + ky^d_t$. For the moment we assume that each individual's decision horizon is two years and her subjective discount factor is $\delta \in (0, 1)$. An individual's objective function is her total discounted utility which is a function of the quantity of food consumed:

$$U = \ln(y_1 + ky^d_1) + \delta\ln(y_2 + ky^d_2).$$
(27.1)

In producing food, the output level is determined by tractor input, current labor input, and production experience which depends on the total accumulated labor in producing food. It is assumed that an individual will forget all her experience in producing a good and therefore previous labor has no effect on the current output level of the same good if she shifts between activities. Also, an entry cost into an activity will be incurred in year $t$ if an individual shifts into this activity in year $t$. Hence, the production function of food is specified as follows.

$$y_t + y^s_t = X^\alpha_t(L_{yt} - c_{yt})^a, \qquad a > 1 \text{ and } \alpha > 0$$
(27.2a)

$$X_t = \text{Min } \{\sum_{\tau=1}^t (x_\tau + x^d_\tau), 1\}, \sum_{\tau=1}^t (x_\tau + x^d_\tau) \geq 1$$
(27.2b)

$x_\tau$ and $x^d_\tau$ are non-negative integers
(27.2c)

$L_{yt} = \sum_{\tau=s}^t l_{y\tau}$ where $s$ is the latest time when a person enters into the production of good y; the initial condition is: $L_{y0} = 0$
(27.2d)

$c_{yt} = c$ if a person enters into sector y in year $t$, and
(27.2e)
$c_{yt} = 0$ if a person has stayed in sector y since she previously entered into this sector

where $y_t + y^s_t$ is a person's output level of food. $X_t$ is the effective input level of tractors used to produce food. $x_\tau$ is the self-provided quantity of tractors in year $\tau$, and $x^d_\tau$ is the quantity of tractors bought in year $\tau$. The two variables must be integers because of the indivisibility of a tractor. The output level of food in year 2 depends not only on the input level of tractors in year 2, but also on that in year 1, since the tractor is a durable good that can be used for two years. (27.2b) implies that a person can drive one and only one tractor at any point in time, so that extra tractors have no effect on an individual's output level of food. $L_{yt}$ is a person's level of human capital in producing food in year $t$. This level equals a person's accumulated labor in producing food if no shift between jobs occurs and equals the current labor input level, $l_{yt}$, if any shift between jobs occurs in year $t$ or $t-1$. The entry cost coefficient $c$ is a given positive constant. Expressions (27.2b)–(27.2e) are crucial for the model to generate the productivity implications of business cycles and unemployment.

Letting $x^s_t$ denote the quantity sold of tractors in year $t$, a consumer-producer's production function of tractors is:

$$x_t + x^s_t = (L_{xt} - c_{xt})^b, \qquad b > 1$$
(27.3a)

$L_{xt} = \sum_{\tau=s}^t l_{x\tau}$ where $s$ is the latest time when a person enters into the production of x; the initial condition is: $L_{x0} = 0$
(27.3b)

$c_{xt} = c$ if a person enters into sector x in year $t$
(27.3c)

$c_{xt} = 0$ if a person has stayed in sector x since she previously entered into this sector

where $x_t + x^s_t$ is an individual's output level of tractors, which may not be an integer if we assume that several producers of tractors can produce an integer number of tractors together; $L_{xt}$ is a person's level of human capital in producing tractors; $l_{i\tau}$ is a person's level of labor input into the production of good i as well as her level of specialization in producing good i in year $\tau$.

It is assumed that each consumer-producer is endowed with 2 units of labor and that economies of specialized learning by doing are individual-specific and activity-specific. Hence, there is an endowment constraint in year $t$ for each consumer-producer:

$$l_{xt} + l_{yt} \leq 2 \quad \forall\ t. \tag{27.4}$$

The system of production (27.2)–(27.4) displays economies of specialized learning by doing which imply that a person's labor productivity of any good is higher if she specializes in producing that good over all time than if she shifts between jobs and produces all goods. This system formalizes a trade-off between economies of specialized learning by doing and unemployment which can be avoided by increasing job shifting costs when durable producer goods are indivisible. In order to fully exploit economies of specialized learning by doing, the population should be divided between professional farming and professional tractor manufacturing. But the division of labor will generate unemployment of professional producers of tractors in year 2, since tractors are indivisible durable producer goods. In order to avoid unemployment and associated business cycles, producers of tractors should shift to producing food in year 2. But this will generate shifting costs between jobs and prevent full exploitation of economies of specialized learning by doing. If the decision horizon is much longer than two years, this trade-off will be more obvious.

Also, we have a trade-off between economies of specialization and transaction costs (related to the coefficient $1 - k$). If transaction efficiency $k$ is sufficiently low, then economies of specialization are outweighed by transaction costs. Hence autarky that does not involve any business cycles and unemployment is more efficient than the complete division of labor which may generate business cycles and unemployment. If transaction efficiency is sufficiently high, then the dynamic equilibrium in a decentralized market may be the complete division of labor that generates efficient unemployment in year 2 and business cycles. This story is worked out in the next section.

## ◆ 27.4 Cyclical vs. Noncyclical Corner Equilibria

### 27.4.1 Regime specification, configurations, and market structures

As in chapter 22, all trade is entirely determined in a futures market which operates at $t = 0$ and through two-year contracts. This ensures a Walrasian regime with price taking behavior at $t = 0$. Following the approach to dynamic equilibrium models based on corner solutions, developed in chapters 18 and 25, it can be shown that each consumer-producer's optimal decision in this model is a corner solution and that an individual does not buy and sell the same goods; she sells at most one good at any point in time. Because of the indivisibility and durability of tractors, it is trivial to show that a professional farmer buys one tractor in year 1 and does not buy tractors in year 2. Having taken this into account, there are five possible corner solutions for each consumer-producer. The combinations of the five corner solutions generate three possible market structures.

In the first configuration, autarky, denoted by A and depicted in figure 27.4, there is no trade and each individual self-provides all goods. That is, autarky implies a configuration with $x_t^s = x_t^d = y_t^s = y_t^d = 0$. For configuration A: $y_t$, $x_1 > 0$, so that each individual self-provides a tractor which is an input along with labor in producing food. $M$ individuals choosing configuration A constitute structure A.

The second market structure is referred to as complete division of labor, or simply C. Let $(x/y)$ denote a configuration in which an individual sells tractors in year 1 and buys food in two years, and $(y/x)$ denote a configuration in which an individual sells food in two years and buys a tractor in year 1. Market structure C consists of the division of the $M$ individuals between configurations $(x/y)$ and $(y/x)$, that is, professional farmers exchange food for tractors in year 1 with professional producers of tractors. The latter save some money in year 1 in order to buy food in year 2 when they are unemployed. Market structure C is depicted in figure 27.4.

### 27.4.2 The dynamic corner equilibrium in autarky

The third market structure is referred to as partial division of labor, or simply P. Denote by $(xy/y)$ a configuration in which an individual specializes in producing tractors in year 1, retains a tractor for himself, sells the rest of the tractors in year 1, buys food in both years, and drives the tractor to self-provide part of the food required in year 2. Market structure P consists of the division of the $M$ individuals between configurations $(xy/y)$ and

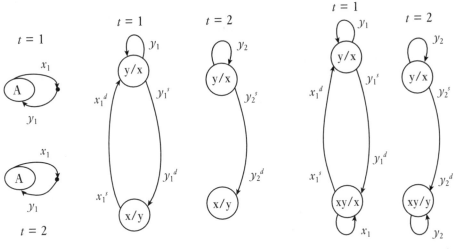

Structure A        Structure C (complete division        Structure P (partial division of
                   of labor with business cycles)        labor without business cycles)

◆ **Figure 27.4:** Structures with and without business cycles

(y/x). In this case, professional farmers are the same as in market structure C, but individuals choosing configuration (xy/y) produce tractors in year 1 and shift to the production of food in year 2. Compared to market structure C, this market structure involves no business cycles and unemployment, but job shifting costs are incurred and economies of specialized learning by doing cannot be fully exploited in configuration (xy/y). Market structure P is depicted in figure 27.4.

A dynamic corner equilibrium in the two years when autarky prevails is defined by the solution to an individual's total discounted utility maximizing labor decision for that configuration. In configuration A, the quantities traded of all goods are 0 and $y_t > 0$, $x_1 = 1$, $x_2 = 0$. Inserting these values into equations (27.1)–(27.4), and substituting from (27.2)–(27.4) into (27.1), gives the decision problem for configuration A as:

$$\text{Max:}_{l_{it}, x_t, y_t} \quad U = \ln y_1 + \delta \ln y_2 \tag{27.5a}$$

$$
\begin{aligned}
\text{s.t.} \quad & y_1 = x_1^\alpha (L_{y1} - c)^a, & \text{(production function of y at } t = 1) \\
& x_1 = (L_{x1} - c)^b = 1, \, x_2 = 0 & \text{(production function of x at } t = 1) \\
& y_2 = x_1^\alpha (L_{y2} - c)^a & \text{(production function of y at } t = 2) \\
& L_{y1} = l_{y1}, \, L_{x1} = l_{x1}, \, L_{y2} = l_{y1} + l_{y2} & \text{(definition of human capital)} \\
& l_{x1} + l_{y1} = 2, \, l_{y2} = 2 & \text{(endowment constraints)}
\end{aligned}
$$

The solution of (27.5a) is $l_{x1} = 1 + c$, $l_{y1} = 1 - c$, $y_1 = (1 - c)^a$, $y_2 = (3 - 2c)^a$, so that:

$$U(A) = \ln(1 - c)^a + \delta \ln(3 - 2c)^a \tag{27.5b}$$

where $U(A)$ is the per capita total discounted real income when an individual chooses configuration A. Note that due to the absence of trade, no transaction costs are incurred in this configuration, but experience cannot be effectively accumulated because of job shifting costs. Hence, $U(A)$ tends to 0 if $c$ is sufficiently large to be close to 1. There is no business cycle and unemployment in this market structure, but accumulation of human capital is very slow since each individual must change jobs in each year. The per capita consumption of food in year 2, $y_2 = (3 - 2c)^a$, is higher than that in year 1, $y_1 = (1 - c)^a$. In particular, as the decision horizon $T$ increases from 2 to a very large number, accumulation of human capital cannot exceed the experience of two years since each individual must change jobs between producing tractors and food every other year. The total discounted per capita real income for $T$ year in autarky is

$$U_T(A) = 2[\ln(1 - c) + \delta \ln(3 - 2c)]S$$

where $S \equiv 1 + \delta^2 + \delta^4 + \ldots + \delta^T = (1 - \delta^{T+2})/(1 - \delta^2)$. The limit of $S$ as $T$ tends to infinity is $1/(1 - \delta^2)$. From the formula, we can see that $U_T(A)$ converges to a constant as $T$ tends to infinity. In other words, there is no long-run continuous accumulation of professional human capital because of frequent shifts between jobs in autarky. Later we will see that structure C can speed up accumulation of human capital through continuous accumulation of professional human capital, so that total discounted per capita real income tends to infinity as $T$ goes to infinity.

### 27.4.3 Market structure C

Structure C consists of configurations $(x/y)$ and $(y/x)$. There are two steps in solving for the dynamic corner equilibrium of a market structure with trade: first, for each type of configuration in the market structure the utility maximizing labor allocation decision and demands and supplies for each good (and hence the total discounted indirect utility of an individual who chooses that configuration) are derived; and second, given the demands and supplies of an individual in each configuration, the market clearing conditions and utility equalization conditions are used to solve for the set of dynamic corner equilibrium relative prices and numbers of individuals choosing each configuration.

*Configuration* $(y/x)$: In this configuration $y_t$, $y_t^s > 0$, $x_1^d = 1$, $l_{yt} = 2$, and $x_t = x_t^s = l_{xt} = x_2^d = 0$. Hence the decision problem for this configuration is:

$$\text{Max: } U_y = \ln y_1 + \delta \ln y_2$$
$$\phantom{xxx}{}_{y_t,\,y_t}$$

s.t.
$y_1 + y^s_1 = (x^d_1)^\alpha (L_{y1} - c)^a,$ (production function of y at $t = 1$)
$x^d_1 = 1$ (integer condition for tractor)
$y_2 + y^s_2 = (x^d_1)^\alpha L_{y2}^a$ (production function of y at $t = 2$)
$L_{y1} = l_{y1} = 2,\ l_{y2} = 2,\ L_{y2} = L_{y1} + l_{y2} = 4$ (endowment constraints)
$p_{y1}y^s_1 + p_{y2}y^s_2 = p_{x1}x^d_1$ (budget constraint)

where $p_{it}$ is the price of good $i$ in year $t$. We assume that food in year 2 is the *numéraire*, that is, $p_{y2} = 1$. The solution to (27.6a) is

$$U_y = (1 + \delta)\ln[p_{y1}(2 - c)^a + 4^a - p_{x1}] - \ln p_{y1} - (1 + \delta)\ln(1 + \delta) + \delta \ln \quad (27.6b)$$

$$y^s_2 = [4^a - \delta p_{y1}(2 - c)^a + \delta p_{x1}]/(1 + \delta), \qquad y_2 = 4^a - y^s_2$$

$$x^d_1 = 1,\ y^s_1 = (p_{x1} - y^s_2)/p_{y1}, \qquad y_1 = (2 - c)^a - y^s_1$$

where $U_y$ is the total discounted indirect utility function, $x^d_1$ and $y^s_t$ are the demand and supply functions for configuration $(y/x)$. Note that a professional farmer's decision involves borrowing money (the income in year 1, $p_{y1}y^s_1$, must be smaller than the expenditure in year 1, $p_{x1}x^d_1$, in order to satisfy the budget constraint).

*Configuration* $(x/y)$: By a similar process, for configuration $(x/y)$

$$U_x = (1 + \delta)[\ln k + \ln(2 - c)^b + \ln p_{x1} - \ln(1 + \delta)] - \ln p_{y1} + \delta \ln \delta \quad (27.7)$$

$$y^d_2 = \delta p_{x1}(2 - c)^b/(1 + \delta),\ x^s_1 = (2 - c)^b,\ y^d_1 = (p_{x1}x^s_1 - y^d_2)/p_{y1}$$

where $U_x$ is the total discounted indirect utility function, $x^s_1$ and $y^d_t$ are the supply and demand functions for configuration $(x/y)$. Note that a tractor specialist's decision involves savings. The income in year 1, $p_{x1}x^s_1$, must be larger than the expenditure in year 1, $p_{y1}y^d_1$, in order to satisfy the budget constraint. It is interesting to see that this market structure cannot operate in the absence of fiat money or a credit system, since professional farmers choosing configuration $(y/x)$ sell and do not buy, and professional producers of tractors buy and do not sell in year 2, while tractors cannot be saved and used to pay for food in year 2 by professional producers of tractors. That is, commodity money cannot facilitate trade across years in this structure.

The utility equalization condition between the two configurations is:

$$U_y = U_x \tag{27.8}$$

where $U_i$ is a function of relative prices of goods in different years. Let $M_i$ represent the number (measure) of individuals selling good $i$, the market clearing condition for food and tractors in two years are

$$M_x x^s_1 = M_y x^d_1, \ M_x y^d_1 = M_y y^s_1, \ M_x y^d_2 = M_y y^s_2 \tag{27.9}$$

where $M_x x^s_1$ is the total market supply of and $M_y x^d_1$ is the total market demand for tractors in year 1, $M_x y^d_t$ is the market demand for and $M_y y^s_t$ is the market supply of food in year $t$. Note that due to Walras's law one of the three market clearing conditions in (27.9) is not independent of the others. The equilibrium relative number of individuals choosing each configuration $M_{xy} \equiv M_x/M_y$ and the equilibrium relative prices $p_{x1}$ and $p_{y1}$ are determined by three independent equations in (27.8) and (27.9). Hence, the dynamic corner equilibrium in market structure C is given by

$$p_{x1} = 4^a (1 + \delta)/\delta[1 + k(2 - c)^b], \ p_{y1} = 4^a/\delta(2 - c)^a, \ M_{xy} = (2 - c)^{-b} \tag{27.10a}$$

$$U(C) = a\delta\ln 4 + [b(1 + \delta) + a]\ln(2 - c) - \ln[1 + k(2 - c)^b] + (1 + \delta)\ln k$$

where $U(C)$ is the total discounted per capita real income for the dynamic corner equilibrium in market structure C.

If the decision horizon is $T > 2$ years, then there are $T/2$ business cycles in market structure C. Each cycle is a duplication of the dynamic corner equilibrium given in (27.10a), except that the initial condition $L_{i0} = 0$ is replaced with a level of human capital accumulated in producing good $i$ at the end of the last cycle. Since no job shift occurs in this market structure, the dynamic corner equilibrium in year $T$ is

$$p_{x1} = (2T)^a(1 + \delta)/\rho[1 + kT^b], \tag{27.10b}$$

$$p_{y1} = (2T)^a/\rho T^a = 2^a/\delta, \ M_{xy} = T^{-b}$$

$$U_T(C) = a\delta\ln(2T) + [b(1 + \delta) + a]\ln(T - c) - \ln[1 + k(T - c)^b] + (1 + \delta)\ln k.$$

It is easy to see that the per capita real income in year $T$ does not involve any job shifting cost $c$ and that $U_T(C)$ increases with $T$. But the per capita total discounted real income in autarky will not increase with $T$ since learning by doing is interrupted by job shifting in each year for autarky.

A comparison between $U(C)$ in (27.10) and $U(A)$ given in (27.5b) indicates that $U(A) > U(C)$ if $k$ is sufficiently close to 0 and if $c$ is sufficiently small, since $U(C)$ tends to negative infinity as $k$ converges to 0 but $U(A)$ is independent of $k$. Also, $U(C) > U(A)$ if $c$ is smaller than 1 but sufficiently close to 1 and $k$ is sufficiently large, since $U(A)$ tends to negative infinity but $U(C)$ is positive as $c$ tends to 1 when $k$ is sufficiently large. This deduction yields

**Lemma 27.1:** The total discounted utility is greater in market structure C than in autarky if $c$ and $k$ are sufficiently close to 1; the total discounted utility is greater in autarky than in market structure C if $k$ and $c$ are sufficiently close to 0; and the total discounted utility increases with the decision horizon $T$ for market structure C and converges to a constant in autarky.

This result is intuitive. Autarky is more efficient if transaction efficiency is too low and if job shifting costs are not too large because autarky does not involve transaction costs but involves job shifting costs, while the division of labor in market structure C involves transaction costs but not job shifting costs.

### 27.4.4 Market structure P

By a two-step procedure analogous to that used to solve for the dynamic corner equilibrium in market structure C, it is possible to solve for the dynamic corner equilibrium in market structure P. Structure P consists of the division of $M$ individuals between configurations $(y/x)$ and $(xy/y)$. The corner solution for configuration $(y/x)$ is the same as in market structure C. The corner solution for configuration $(xy/y)$ is:

$$U_x = (1 + \delta)\ln\{(2 - c)^a - \ln(1 + \delta) + kp_{x1}[(2 - c)^b - 1]\} - \ln p_{y1} + \delta\ln\delta \qquad (27.11)$$

$$x_1 = 1, \quad x^s_1 = (2 - c)^b - 1, \quad y^d_2 = \{\rho k p_{x1}[(2 - c)^b - 1] - (2 - c)^a\}/k(1 + \delta),$$

$$y^d_1 = (p_{x1} x^s_1 - y^d_2)/p_{y1}$$

where $p_{x1}$ and $p_{y1}$ are the respective prices of tractors and food in year 1 in terms of the price of food in year 2. The utility equalization condition $U_x = U_y$ and the two independent market clearing conditions yield the dynamic corner equilibrium relative prices $p_{x1}$ and $p_{y1}$ and the relative number of individuals choosing the two configurations. Although the algebraic form of the dynamic corner equilibrium solution for relative prices, relative number of individuals choosing different configurations, and total discounted utility is very complicated, it is easy to see the effects of the transaction efficiency coefficient $k$, the job shifting cost coefficient $c$, and the number of cycles $T/2$, on per capita real income. Since producers of tractors must shift jobs every other year, they will forget their experience and have to pay entry costs each year. Thus, (27.11) will be the same for each cycle of production and consumption of tractors irrespective of how long the decision horizon is. This implies that the advantage of structure C over structure P is increasingly more significant as the decision horizon increases. The indirect utility function for a professional farmer in structure P is the same as in structure C, given in (27.6b).

The utility equalization condition implies that the total discounted utility must be 0 for all configurations if it is 0 for any one configuration. Hence, the total discounted utility in structure P must become negative as $c$ tends to 2 because $U_x$ in (27.11) tends to negative infinity as $c$ converges to 2 for any positive and finite relative prices of traded goods. The market clearing condition will adjust relative prices such that the utility equalization condition is established. Hence, if $c$ is sufficiently large to be close to 2, the decision horizon is sufficiently long, and the discount factor is sufficiently close to 1, then the total discounted utility in structure C will be higher than in structure P because the former tends to be very large and the latter tends to 0 under these conditions. However, if $c$ is sufficiently smaller than 2 and the decision horizon is not long or the discount factor is sufficiently small, then $U_x$ in (27.11) may be positive but $U(C)$ may be 0 if $k$ is sufficiently close to 0. It is not difficult to see that $U_y$ in (27.6b) is independent of $k$ and $U_x$ in (27.11) may be positive even if $k = 0$, but $U(C)$ in (27.10) tends to negative infinity as $k$ converges to 0. Moreover, $U(A)$ in (27.5b) tends to negative infinity but $U_x$ in (27.11) and $U_y$ in (27.6b) may be positive as $c$ converges to 1 when $c \in (0, 1)$. This deduction leads us to

**Lemma 27.2:** Total discounted utility is greater in structure P than in structures A and C if $c$ is sufficiently close to 1 and $k$ is sufficiently close to 0; total discounted utility is greater in structure C than in structure P if $k$ is sufficiently close to 1, the decision horizon is sufficiently long, the discount rate is sufficiently small, and $c$ is sufficiently close to 2.

Structure P, like structure C, cannot operate in the absence of a money substitute or a credit system because in year 2 professional farmers sell and do not buy and individuals choosing (xy/y) buy and do not sell.

Following the procedure used to prove the Yao theorem in chapter 6, we can establish that theorem for the dynamic general equilibrium model in this chapter. Hence, only the Pareto optimum dynamic corner equilibrium that generates the highest total discounted utility is the dynamic general equilibrium. Therefore, we can identify the dynamic general equilibrium by comparing the total discounted utility levels between different market structures. The comparison, together with lemmas 27.1 and 27.2, yields

**Proposition 27.1:** If transaction efficiency is sufficiently low and job shifting costs are not too high, autarky is the dynamic general equilibrium, and therefore productivity is low, and trade, business cycles, and unemployment do not occur; if transaction efficiency and job shifting costs are sufficiently high, the decision horizon is sufficiently long, and the discount rate is sufficiently small, then the complete division of labor with business cycles and unemployment is the dynamic general equilibrium; if transaction efficiency and job shifting costs are at some intermediate levels, the decision horizon is not long or the discount rate is large, then the dynamic general equilibrium is the partial division of labor without business cycles and unemployment.

Before examining the implications of proposition 27.1, some discussion is required on the question of the existence of equilibrium. From (27.10)–(27.13), we can see that no dynamic corner equilibrium exists for structure C if $k$ is sufficiently close to 0; no dynamic corner equilibrium exists for autarky if $c$ is sufficiently close to 1; and no dynamic corner equilibrium exists for structure P if $c$ is sufficiently close to 2 even if the decision horizon is very long. With these qualifications in mind, the following discussion of the implications of proposition 27.1 is pertinent only if the conditions for the existence of the relevant dynamic corner equilibrium are met.

Suppose the discount rate is sufficiently small, the decision horizon is sufficiently long, and job shifting costs are not too low. Then according to proposition 27.1, as transaction efficiency is improved the dynamic general equilibrium will evolve from autarky, which involves no business cycle or unemployment, to structure C which involves business cycles and unemployment. This implies that our model has endogenized not only the business cycle and unemployment, but also the emergence of the business cycle and unemployment from the evolution of division of labor. This proposition is consistent with the casual observation that business cycles and unemployment occur only in an economy with high levels of division of labor, specialization, productivity, and trade dependence. Contrary to the market failure argument, proposition 27.1 implies that the greater the foresight of individuals, the more likely is the occurrence of efficient business cycles with unemployment in a decentralized market. It seems to us that the productivity benefits of business cycles and unemployment are the reasons for the prevalence of persistent business cycles that involve unemployment.

It is easy to see that autarky and structure P fully employ physical labor but underemploy human capital, while structure C fully exploits human capital but generates cyclical unemployment of physical labor. This difference between the market structure with business cycles and unemployment and those involving no business cycles and unemployment highlights the intuition behind proposition 27.1. Intuitively, if the human capital that is exploited by structure C but not exploited by structures A and P is greater than the physical labor that is employed by structures A and P but not fully employed by structure C, then C is more efficient than other structures and will be the dynamic general equilibrium.

## 27.4.5 Welfare and policy implications of the model

Following the approach used to prove the first welfare theorem in chapter 6, it is not difficult to prove that the dynamic general equilibrium in the Walrasian regime is Pareto optimal. Hence, Pareto improving government policies do not exist. At best, a successful government policy that transfers income from individuals employed to individuals unemployed can play a role equivalent to that of savings in structure C if C is the dynamic general equilibrium in a free market. But such government intervention will certainly generate distortions associated with bureaucracy. Also, such government intervention will paralyze the market mechanism that facilitates the full exploitation of economies of specialized learning by doing through savings. If individuals expect that the government will save for them via income transfers and unemployment welfare, they may have no incentive to save themselves.

However, if individuals are myopic and their decision horizon is one year instead of two, then it is trivial to show that a Pareto improving government income transfer scheme may exist. Indeed, if job shifting costs are sufficiently high, for instance, it is infeasible for a farmer to self-provide a tractor due to prohibitively high shifting costs between farming and tractor manufacturing, then autarky is infeasible. Suppose that individuals' decision horizon is of one year instead of two years, then professional tractor manufacturers will not save any money earned in year 1 for their living in year 2, so that either their total discounted utility over two years tends to negative infinity due to zero consumption in year 2, or they have to change jobs in year 2 and thereby economies of specialized learning by doing cannot be fully exploited. For this case, a Pareto improving income transfer policy exists if the government is less myopic than private businessmen (which is very unlikely). But such an income transfer scheme may institutionalize myopic behavior such that a mature credit market never emerges. Hence, even if short-run benefits may be generated by a government income transfer scheme, its long-run costs are likely to outweigh the benefits.[1]

Casual observation of a capitalist economy indicates the prevalence of structure C, while casual observation of a Soviet-style socialist economy indicates the prevalence of structure P, which does not involve business cycles and unemployment but may be less effective in accumulating human capital than structure C. Hence, one might conjecture that if a socialist government can control the relative number of different specialists and is tempted to rectify the "market failure" that generates business cycles and unemployment, a noncyclical pattern of division of labor without unemployment is more likely to be chosen despite the low productivity of such an organization. In this sense, the prevalence of noncyclical dynamics and associated low productivity in socialist economies is evidence of government failure.

## ◆ 27.5 General Price Level, Business Cycles, and Unemployment Rate

Suppose that transaction efficiency, job shifting costs, the decision horizon, and the discount factor are sufficiently large, then structure C is the general equilibrium. Since the price of tractors in year 2, $p_{x2}$, is irrelevant (tractors are not traded in year 2), the price levels in different years can be compared through the comparison of price levels of food across years. From expression (27.10), it can be seen that the price of food in year $t + 1$ relative to that in year $t$ is

$$p_{yt+1}/p_{yt} = \delta(2T/4T)^a = \delta/2^a < 1 \text{ where } t = 2T - 1 \text{ and } T > 1 \tag{27.14}$$

$$p_{y2}/p_{y1} = \delta[(2 - c)/4]^a < 1$$

where $T/2$ is the number of business cycles. (27.14) implies that the price of the same good is higher in the first year than in the second year of each cycle. The supply of fiat money determines the nominal prices of goods. However, since real variables are determined by the relative prices of goods in different years in this model, nominal prices have no effect on the real variables. Suppose the general equilibrium is structure C and the money supply in year 1 is $m_0$. In order to get around the problem of wealth distribution, we assume that the government, which supplies fiat money, is the middleman who pays fiat money for goods sold by individuals and resells goods to individual buyers. The government first pays $m_0$ for tractors sold by tractor specialists in year 1, so that $m_0 = M_x p_{x1} x^s_1$. Then tractor specialists pay $m_1$ back to the government to buy food where $m_1 = M_x p_{y1} y^d_1 < m_0$ and $m_0 - m_1 = s_1$ is the tractor specialists' savings in the form of fiat money. Then the government pays $m_1$ to farmers for food whose value is $M_y p_{y1} y^s_1 = m_1 = M_y p_{x1} x^d_1$, and this amount of food is delivered from farmers to tractor specialists through the government. Farmers pay $m_1$ back to the government and demand a loan from the government to buy tractors whose value is $M_y x^d_1 = m_0$. The value of the loan is $m_0 - m_1$ and the loan is in the form of tractors. At the end of year 1, tractor specialists hold fiat money $m_0 - m_1$, as savings; farmers hold loan $m_0 - m_1$; and the government holds fiat money $m_1$ as money stock.

In year 2, tractor specialists buy food from and pay $m_0 - m_1 = M_x p_{y2} y_2^d$ to the government and the farmers repay their loan to the government using food whose value is $m_0 - m_1 = M_y p_{y2} y_2^s$. Hence, the value of food in terms of fiat money $m_0 - m_1$ is delivered from the farmers to the tractor specialists through the government. At the end of year 2 all fiat money $m_0$ has been returned to the government, so that the circulation of money has been completed. Suppose that the government increases the money supply by $\Delta m$ at the end of year 2. The increased money supply will determine the nominal prices of all goods in the second business cycle, but will have no effect on any real variables for the following reason. In this model there is no trade across cycles despite the fact that trade may occur across the years in the same business cycle. Also, all real variables are determined by the relative prices within each cycle and nominal prices have no effects on the real quantities of goods. Hence, an increase in the money supply may change the cyclical pattern of the general price level and generate an inflation of nominal prices, but will have no effects on the real business cycle.

This result is consistent with the monetary policy irrelevance argument (Sargent and Wallace, 1975), but the reasons are different. As in Sargent and Wallace's model, our model shows that systematic monetary policy has no effect on real variables, because the money supply affects only nominal prices and has no effect on real variables. However, if the government not only uses money as a medium of exchange in the market, but also allocates money for income transfers via a welfare scheme or money supply is changed in the middle of a cycle, then unexpected monetary policy may matter. Hence an extended model allowing for a function of monetary policy in income redistribution or changes in money supply in the middle of a cycle may be consistent with Lucas's theory (1972, 1973, 1976) that expected monetary policy has no effects but unexpected monetary policy has effects on real variables. Our theory implies that monetary policies may be neutral even if long-term contracts are present. By contrast, long-term contracts may cause unemployment and generate implications of active monetary policy in the theory of labor contract and sticky wages (see Gray, 1976, Fischer, 1977, and Taylor, 1980) and in the theory of monopolistic competition and sticky prices (see for example Mankiw, 1985, and Parkin, 1986).

In exercise 11, it is shown that if unemployment is caused by the integer problem, a Nash bargaining process, which can be done either in a decentralized way or through collective bargaining, may generate a Pareto improving outcome with a lower unemployment than in a Walrasian regime. It can also be shown that if long-run unemployment is caused by the vicious circle based on the effects of learning by doing and changes in structure of division of labor, some government initiatives for the retraining and reeducation of those unemployed may generate Pareto improving outcomes too. However, a better way to analyze the unemployment caused by the vicious circle is to analyze why the market cannot sort this out if there is a Pareto improving possibility. Is this because of some government regulation or entry barriers that prevent private entrepreneurs from using the opportunity, through the institution of the firm and other structures of transactions and ownership, or because the outcome in the market is already an efficient trade-off between conflicting interests?

It is interesting to note that this model can accommodate the Phillips curve (a negative correlation between general price level and unemployment), the monetary policy irrelevance argument, and the inflation–stagnation phenomenon. Suppose that the general equilibrium is structure C, then (27.14) implies that a lower nominal price level is associated with a higher unemployment rate if the money supply does not increase as fast as aggregate real transaction volume. The price of good y is higher in the first year than in the second year, while unemployment is positive in the second year and is 0 in the first year of each cycle. However, if the money supply increases faster than aggregate real transaction volume, then unemployment may be associated with inflation from the second cycle on. But in our model both the Phillips curve phenomenon associated with a moderately increasing money supply and the inflation–stagnation phenomenon associated with a rapidly increasing money supply are compatible with the monetary policy irrelevance argument.

Aggregate output displays a similar cyclical pattern if structure C is the general equilibrium. The aggregate output level in the first year of each cycle in terms of food in the second year of each cycle is

$$Y_1 = M_y p_{y1}(y_1 + y^s_1) + M_x p_{x1} x^s_1 \tag{27.15a}$$

$$= 4^a M[1 + (2 - c)^b(k + 1 + \delta)]/\delta[1 + (2 - c)^b][1 + k(2 - c)^b]$$

$$Y_t = M_y p_{yt}(y_t + y^s_t) + M_x p_{xt} x^s_t$$

$$= (4T)^a M[1 + (2T)^b(k + 1 + \delta)]/\delta[1 + (2T)^b][1 + k(2T)^b]$$

where $t = 2T - 1$ and $T > 1$

where $T/2$ is the numbers of business cycles, $Y_t$ is the aggregate real output level in terms of food in year $t + 1$, $M$ is the population size, $p_{it}$ is given in (27.10), $x^s_1$ given in (27.7), $y_1$ and $y^s_1$ given in (27.6b). $y_t$, $y^s_t$, and $x^s_t$ can be obtained by replacing the initial level of human capital $L_{i0} = 0$ in $y_1$, $y^s_1$, and $x^s_1$ with its level in the end of year $t - 1$.

$$Y_2 = M_y p_{y2}(y_2 + y^s_2) \tag{27.15b}$$

$$= 4^a M(2 - c)^b/[1 + (2 - c)^b]$$

$$Y_{t+1} = M_y p_{yt+1}(y_{t+1} + y^s_{t+1})$$

$$= (4T)^a M(2T)^b[1 + (2T)^b] \text{ where } t = 2T - 1 \text{ and } T > 1$$

where $p_{y2} = p_{yt+1} = 1$ because food in the second year of each cycle is the *numéraire*, $y_2$ and $y^s_2$ are given in (27.6b). $y_{t+1}$ and $y^s_{t+1}$ can be obtained by replacing the initial level of human capital $L_{i0} = 0$ in $y_2$ and $y^s_2$ with its level in the end of year $t - 1$. A comparison between (27.15a) and (27.15b) yields

$$Y_t > Y_{t+1} \ \forall \ t = 2T - 1 \text{ and } T = 1, 2, \ldots \tag{27.16}$$

(27.16) implies that the real aggregate output level is higher in the first year than in the second year of each cycle. It is obvious that there is an upward trend of $Y_t$ despite business cycles because of the positive effects of specialized learning by doing, which is not interrupted in structure C, on productivity and the real output level. The unemployment rate in the second year of each cycle is

$$R = M_x/M = 1/[1 + (2 - c)^b] \text{ for the first business cycle} \tag{27.17}$$

$$R = 1/[1 + (2T)^b] \text{ for other business cycles}$$

Here, the unemployment rate decreases with the degree of economies of specialization in producing tractors, $b$, and with the number of business cycles, $T/2$. However, if there are many producer goods and there is continual evolution of the division of labor in roundabout productive activities as transaction efficiency is improved, then unemployment may increase with the number of business cycles. You are asked in exercise 14 to use a model with food, tractors, and the machine tools which are used to produce tractors, in order to show that the efficient unemployment rate will increase as a longer chain of roundabout productive activities is involved in the division of labor. In that model, capital goods such as machine tools along with physical labor may be unemployed, whereas only physical labor may be unemployed in the model in this chapter. Also, the amplitude and period of the business cycle will increase as a longer chain of roundabout productive activities is involved in the division of labor. Further, it is not difficult to see that an increase in the durability of goods may magnify business cycles and increase the equilibrium unemployment rate during recessions.

## ◆ 27.6 Emergence of Firms and Fiat Money from the Division of Labor

As indicated in the preceding section, structures C and P cannot operate in the absence of fiat money and a credit system. For instance, for structure C, professional farmers sell food but do not buy any goods in year 2, while professional producers of tractors buy food but do not sell any goods in year 2. Professional producers of tractors must save some of their purchasing power generated in year 1 for their living in year 2. The savings cannot be goods since structure C does not involve any savings of goods, so that commodity money does not work. Hence, the savings of purchasing power can only be a money substitute or some kind of credit. This implies that if money substitute and a credit system do not exist, structures C and P cannot be the general equilibrium even if they are Pareto superior to autarky. Hence, the emergence of money substitute or a credit system will improve productivity and individuals' welfare if the conditions for structures C or P to be the general equilibrium are satisfied (i.e., if transaction efficiency, economies of specialized learning by doing, and job shifting costs are sufficiently large).

If the division of labor emerges in a dynamic equilibrium, then there are two institutional mechanisms through which the division of labor could be organized. In the preceding section, one mechanism that organizes the division of labor via the markets for consumer and intermediate goods has been investigated. Suppose that trade in labor is allowed, so that there are three more feasible market structures with the institution of the firm which replaces the market for x with the market for labor. Following the approach developed in chapter 8, it can be shown that if transaction efficiency is lower for an intermediate good than for the labor employed to produce that intermediate good, then the emergence of the division of labor is associated with the emergence of the institution of the firm.

A criticism of the model in this chapter relates to the question: will the result in this chapter change if overlapping generation is allowed? Suppose that a new generation (called the second generation) with the same population size as the first generation emerges in year 2. Then, when the first generation of specialist producers of tractors cannot sell tractors to the first generation of farmers, they can sell tractors to the second generation of farmers, so that unemployment is avoided and business cycles are smoothed out by overlapping generations. It can be shown that this criticism is not right from the point of view of dynamic general equilibrium. The second generation of individuals must be divided between specialized tractor manufacturing and professional farming, since the demand for tractors from the second generation in year 2 will be greater than the quantity supplied by the first generation tractor specialists if the second generation completely specializes in farming. In year 3, the demand for tractors from the first generation of farmers can be met by the supplies of the first generation of tractor specialists, so that the second generation of tractor specialists will be unemployed in year 3 before the tractors that are bought by the second generation of farmers in year 2 have depreciated. Hence, the overlapping generation consideration can to some degree smooth the fluctuations of output, but cannot completely eliminate business cycles and cyclical unemployment.

As shown in exercises 11 and 13 in particular, as the period of depreciation increases from 2 years to 10 years, or as the number of links in a roundabout production chain increases from 2 to 3 or 100, it becomes more difficult to smooth business cycles through overlapping generation considerations. A longer period of depreciation implies that more generations are needed to smooth business cycles to the same degree. But the number of generations that can live at the same time is very limited. If in the model in this chapter, machine tools are needed to produce tractors, then it is much more difficult to smooth business cycles through overlapping generation considerations. The amplitude and period of each business cycle will be changed too. Suppose transaction efficiency, job shifting costs, and economies of specialized learning by doing are all high, so that there is a structure with complete division of labor where population is divided between specialized farming, specialized manufacturing of tractors, and specialized manufacturing of machine tools. Assume that machine tools can be used for two years too. In year 1, machine tool specialists sell these to tractor specialists and buy food from farmers. Tractor specialists buy machine tools, sell tractors, and buy food. In year 2, specialists in tractors and machine tools are unemployed, farmers drive tractors that they bought in year 1 to produce food, while machine tools are unemployed. In year 3 tractors produced in year 1 have been depreciated and new demand for tractors occurs. But machine tools produced in year 1 are still in use since they were not employed in year 2. Hence, in year 3 machine tool specialists are still unemployed, though tractor specialists find jobs and machine tools, which are produced in year 1, are employed in year 3. In year 4, specialists in tractors and machine tools are unemployed, though tractors produced in year 3 are employed. In year 5, specialists in tractors and machine tools find jobs and all labor is fully employed again. We may call years 1, 5, 9, 13 boom years, and years 4, 8, 12 recession years. Output levels and unemployment rates in years 2, 3, 6, 7, 10, 11 are between those in boom years and those in recession years. This example illustrates that as division of labor develops in an increasingly longer roundabout production chain, business cycles and cyclical unemployment will be more difficult to avoid.

Using our new classical models we can show that the following are procyclical factors: the network size of division of labor, the length of roundabout production chain involved in the division of labor, the durability of goods, the income share of durable goods, job shifting costs, transaction efficiency, and the degree of economies of specialized learning by doing. Increases in the magnitudes of these factors will make business cycles and cyclical unemployment more difficult to avoid. The countercyclical factors are: the number of generations that live at the same time, the emergence of new goods that reduce the period of depreciation of the old goods, a decrease in the links in a roundabout production chain, a decrease in the level of division of labor, a decrease in the durability of goods, decreases in transaction efficiency and fixed learning or entry costs in a sector, and a decrease in the effect of learning by doing.

A realistic dynamic general equilibrium model that can be used for practical application must consider all of these factors. We can see that if the procyclical factors dominate countercyclical factors, a regime of business cycles and cyclical unemployment is more efficient than a noncyclical pattern of economic growth. Also, we can see that the green movement's advocacy of abandonment of the use of nondurable paper dishes and other environmentally nonfriendly instant goods entails the cost of more cyclical unemployment and instability of the economy. This kind of analysis can show that a government policy of imposing a high licence fee or other entry costs on a professional sector will promote business cycles and cyclical unemployment.

However, when doing this kind of analysis, we should not forget that under a *laissez-faire* regime, business cycles and cyclical unemployment are the consequence of interactions between self-interested decisions, which efficiently trade off the interests of some individuals against the interests of the others, regardless of whether the business cycles can or cannot be smoothed out, and regardless of individuals' attitudes against or for cyclical unemployment. This is similar to our decision to use a freeway system, which efficiently trades off the benefit of using the freeway against a higher risk of being killed in traffic accidents, despite our feeling against such deaths.

This chapter has developed a dynamic general equilibrium model that has simultaneously endogenized the emergence of the business cycle, unemployment, money substitute, and firms and productivity progress as the different aspects of the evolution of division of labor. The efficient business cycles and unemployment in the dynamic general equilibrium generate productivity implications relating to full exploitation of economies of specialized learning by doing at the cost of unemployment of physical labor. In this sense, business cycles and related unemployment may be the evidence of a market success rather than a market failure.

One more aspect of economic organization has been investigated in this chapter. We have shown that a decentralized market will sort out the efficient pattern of the business cycle and unemployment by trading off economies of specialized learning by doing against unemployment which is necessary for avoiding job shifting costs. Inappropriate government intervention in the market may paralyze the wonderful function of the invisible hand. However, the market cannot function effectively in the absence of a reliable credit system and fiat money, which need to be enforced by the institution of a government.

## Key Terms and Review

Aggregate demand and absolute price level.
Macroeconomic vs. microeconomic phenomena and related inframarginal vs. marginal comparative statics (dynamics) analysis.
Endogenous long-run regular efficient business cycles and cyclical unemployment.
Exogenous unemployment caused by the integer problem of division of labor.
Exogenous unemployment caused by changes in structure of division of labor.
Endogenous and efficient risk of mass unemployment.
Differences between endogenous regular business cycles and output fluctuation caused by exogenous stochastic process or shock.
The relationship between endogenous efficient business cycles and unemployment, evolution of division of labor in roundabout production, and endogenous long-run economic growth.
The trade-off between accumulation of human capital and full employment of physical labor.
The relationship between business cycles, unemployment, transaction efficiency, economies of specialized learning by doing, job shifting costs, and division of labor in producing durable goods.
The function of the invisible hand in searching for the efficient trade-off between accumulation of human capital and full employment of labor.
Possible consequences of government policies to affect the pattern of business cycles and unemployment through manipulating monetary and fiscal policies.

## Further Reading

*Macroeconomics and the relationship between business cycles and durable goods*: Keynes (1936), Samuelson (1947), Stiglitz (1993), Barro (1991, 1997), Akerlof and Yellen (1985), Starrett (1973), Gabisch and Lorenz (1989), Mankiw (1985); *the new classical model of business cycles*: Yang and Y.-K. Ng (1993, ch. 18), Du (2000); *shock-dependent business cycle models*: Schumpeter (1939), Hicks (1950); *the model of endogenous unemployment caused by market failure*: Weitzman (1982), Shapiro and Stiglitz (1984); *models of labor shift*: Lilien (1982), Black (1987), Abraham and Katz (1986), Murphy and Topel (1987); *real business cycle models*: Kydland and Prescott (1982), Long and Plosser (1983), Prescott (1986), King and Plosser (1984, 1986); *monetary policy*: Lucas (1972, 1973, 1976), Sargent and Wallance (1975); *efficiency wage models and endogenous unemployment*: Yellen (1984), Stiglitz (1986), Shapiro and Stiglitz (1984); *macroeconomic models of endogenous business cycles*: Vogt (1969) and Goodwin (1951); *models of monopolistic competition and sticky wages*: Mankiw (1985), Parkin (1986), Ball, Mankiw, and Romer (1988), Rotemberg (1987), Taylor (1980), Fischer (1977), Gray (1976), Wallace (1980); *models of failure of financial markets*: Stiglitz (1992); Segerstrom, Anant, and Dinopoulos (1990); *empirical evidence for positive effects of business cycles on economic growth*: Canton (1997), Kormendi and Meguire (1985), Grier and Tullock (1989), Ramey and Ramey (1995); *neoclassical models to explain the positive correlation between growth and business cycles*: Caballero and Hammour (1994), Deaton (1991), Dellas (1991), Shleifer (1986), Skinner (1988), Basu (1996), Aghion and Saint-Paul (1991), Aghion and Howitt (1998); *empirical evidence for a positive correlation between specialization and company performance*: Berger and Ofek (1995), Bhagat, Shleifer, and Vishny (1990), Comment and Jarrell (1995), Fauver, Houston, and Naranjo (1998), Kaplan and Weisbach (1992), Lang and Stulz (1994), Servaes (1996).

# QUESTIONS

1   Real business cycle models (Kydland and Prescott, 1982, Long and Plosser, 1983) explain fluctuation of output by an exogenously given stochastic process. This mechanism is like the fluctuation of agricultural outputs between good years and bad years before the Industrial Revolution. Analyze the difference between such an irregular fluctuation and regular business cycles.

2   Many macroeconomic models explain unemployment and recessions by exogenous shocks to an economy. Why can this kind of model not generate endogenous and persistent regular business cycles and cyclical unemployment?

3   Most macroeconomic models that explain business cycles and unemployment attribute the cause of the two phenomena to market failure. Why could this view be wrong? Why can persistent business cycles and cyclical unemployment be the consequence of market success?

4   Analyze the difference between reform cycles in previous or current Soviet-style economies and business cycles in a free market economy. Such reform cycles have the feature: "as soon as central planning control is relaxed, chaos follows, as soon as chaos occurs, reforms are reversed and central planning comes back, so that the economic development drive is killed, which causes the next round of reforms."

5   In several newly industrialized economies, such as South Korea and Taiwan, business cycles are blurred out during the take-off stage of economic development. Why could business cycles be smoothed to some degree in the take-off stage of evolution in division of labor?

6   Many economists believe that the market cannot efficiently coordinate self-interested decisions if individuals cannot take account of the macroeconomic consequences of their decisions. They hold that in the presence of network effect, multiple equilibria (similar to multiple corner equilibria in our new classi-

cal models) and coordination failure caused by prisoners' dilemma or externality problems, individuals' self-interested decisions would not take account of the macroeconomic consequences. Marx is an economist who believed that business cycles are evidence of market failure. Use phenomena that are similar to the following example to show that self-interested decisions do account for their macroeconomic consequences through the market price mechanism. In a free market economy, individuals who work in those sectors that are sensitive to business cycles (for instance, the sector producing durable automobiles) have more risk of unemployment in recession than the sectors producing nondurables. Hence, the market wage in the former sectors is higher than in the latter sectors such that the higher pay is enough to compensate for the higher risk of unemployment. Thus, individuals will voluntarily choose a job with a high risk of unemployment.

7   Many textbooks indicate that in the presence of network effect, a person's purchasing decisions will affect the extent of the market for others' produce. If each individual wants to save money and thereby does not buy much, then the entire economy will be in recession because of coordination failure. Use new classical models to show that the very function of the market is to fully utilize the network effect of division of labor. Show that we do not need coordination failure caused by network effect to explain business cycles and cyclical unemployment.

8   In a Soviet-style economy, business cycles and cyclical unemployment were eliminated by central planning. Why do Russians not like that kind of system?

9   Why could an improvement in transaction efficiency promote business cycles and cyclical unemployment?

10   The durability of goods, the number of links in the roundabout production chain involved in the division of labor, and the level of division of labor are procyclical factors, while use of instant goods, the number of generations that live at the same time, and invention of new machines are countercyclical factors. Suppose there is a new classical dynamic general equilibrium with all of these procyclical and countercyclical factors. Discuss the possible dynamics and comparative dynamics and their implications in such a model.

11   Analyze the connection between the tight job market for a professor's position in universities in the 1980s and 1990s, the durability of Ph.D. graduates, and the mass production of Ph.D. graduates after the Second World War.

12   Many aspects of business cycles cannot be investigated using the simple model in example 27.4. For instance, recession may strengthen the discipline of enterprises, weaken monopoly powers, and promote innovation in organization and technology. Discuss the general equilibrium implications of the introduction of this effect into the new classical model of the business cycle.

13   Berger and Ofek (1995), Bhagat, Shleifer, and Vishny (1990), Comment and Jarrell (1995), Fauver, Houston, and Naranjo (1998), Kaplan and Weisbach (1992), Lang and Stulz (1994), and Servaes (1996) provide empirical evidence for negative correlation between diversification of a company and its value and performance. Analyze the trade-off between benefits of specialization and benefit of diversification and the implications of the trade-off for economic development and business cycles.

14   Find empirical evidence for the new classical theory of business cycles in this chapter.

15   Show that the unemployment rate is positive in structure C even if Say's law (demand always equals supply as they are two sides of the division of labor) holds. Explain why it is so.

# EXERCISES

1   An economist uses the graphs below to illustrate the rationale of business cycles and cyclical unemployment. The horizontal axes represent years and the vertical axes represent quantity of a durable good, such as refrigerators. Suppose the period of depreciation is 5 years and total demand is 5 (thousands) at $t = 0$. Panel (a) shows two possible patterns of production capacity. The first is to set up a capacity of 5 units per year as shown by the higher dashed line. Hence, purchase demand equals supply in year 1. But in years 2, 3, 4, 5, there is no purchase demand, though consumption demand is a positive constant. Hence, all production capacity is unemployed until year 6 when all refrigerators produced in year 1 are fully depreciated. The second pattern of production capacity is 1 unit each year as shown by the lower dashed line. Thus, supply is short of demand by 4 units in year 1, by 3 units in year 2, by 2 units in year 3, and by 1 unit in year 4. The market is cleared in year 5. This illustrates the trade-off between unemployment and shortage in producing durables because of nonsynchronous purchase demand and consumption demand of durables. Panel (b) is a pattern of production capacity intermediate between the two extreme cases in panel (a). A capacity of 2 units per year is established in year 0. Hence, supply is short of demand by 3 units in year 1, by 2 units in year 2. Demand is short of supply by 1 unit in year 3 and by 2 units in years 4 and 5. Analyze why this is not a general equilibrium analysis which must endogenize demand as a function of prices. Compare this kind of analysis to the dynamic general equilibrium analysis in this chapter. Then discuss the explanatory power of new classical dynamic general equilibrium models.

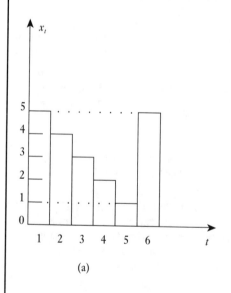

(a)

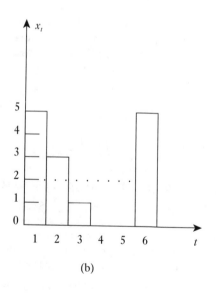

(b)

2   Suppose that the production functions in example 27.4 are the Leontief functions

$$y_t^p = \text{Min} \ \{X_t^d, \ (L_{yt} - c_{yt})\}.$$

Solve for the dynamic general equilibrium and its inframarginal comparative dynamics.

3   Assume that another intermediate good z is needed to produce intermediate good x in the model in example 27.4, so that the production function for x is

$$x_t^p = \text{Min } \{z_t + kz_t^d, (L_{xt} - c_{xt})\}.$$

The production function of z is

$$z_t^p \equiv z_t + z_t^s, \text{Max } \{0, L_{zt} - c_{zt}\}.$$

Solve for the dynamic general equilibrium and inframarginal comparative dynamics. Analyze the implications of the number of links in a roundabout production chain that are involved in the division of labor for business cycles and unemployment.

4   A conventional model to explain the fluctuation of output is the so-called cobweb model. Assume that an *ad hoc* demand function for good x at time $t$ is $x_t^d = a - bp_t$. The quantity supplied at $t$ is determined by the price at $t - 1$, that is $x_t^s = \alpha + \beta p_{t-1}$. The time lag between supply and price is the driving force of fluctuation. Use the market clearing condition at $t$ to solve for the dynamics of the economy. Find the static equilibrium level (steady state) of price and identify the respective parameter interval within which the market price monotonically converges to the static equilibrium, fluctuates around the static equilibrium level as it converges toward it, and fluctuates away from the steady state. (Hint: The static equilibrium level of price is $(\alpha - a)/(b - \beta)$ and the dynamics are given by $p_t = (\beta/b)p_{t-1} + (\alpha - a)/b$ or $\Delta p_t = (\beta/b)\Delta p_{t-1} = (\beta/b)^t\Delta p_0$.)

5   Consider the new classical model in example 5.2. We now introduce the time dimension into the model and assume that time is discrete. There is one period time lag between changes of relative number of professional occupations (x/y) and (y/x) in response to the difference in utility between the two occupations. Hence, $M_x(t) - M_x(t - 1) = \beta[u_x(t - 1) - u_y(t - 1)]$, where $t$ denotes time period and $\beta$ is the sensitivity coefficient of changes in the number of specialist producers of x in response to the difference in utility between two occupation configurations. $M_i(t)$ is the number of specialist producers of good i in period $t$. The indirect utility function $u_i$ for a specialist producer of good i is given in table 5.3. Since $M_x(t) + M_y(t) = M$ where population size $M$ is a given parameter, changes in $M_x(t)$ are proportional to changes in $M_y(t)$ but opposite in direction. For simplicity, we assume that $M = 1$. Further, there is one period time lag between changes of relative price of good y to good x in response to changes in excess demand for good y. Hence, $p(t + 1) - p(t) = \alpha[M_x(t) y^d(t) - M_y(t)y^s(t)]$, where $M_y(t) = 1 - M_x(t)$ and $y^d(t)$ and $y^s(t)$ are given in table 5.3. $\alpha$ is the sensitivity coefficient of changes of relative price in response to excess demand for good y. The initial state of the system is given by $M_x(0) = M_0$, $p(0) = p_0$, and $p(1) = p_1$. Solve for the difference equation for the feedback mechanism. Then simulate it on the computer. Analyze the trade-off between fast convergence to the static equilibrium which can be provided by sensitive feedback and instability of the feedback process caused by very sensitive feedback.

6   Assume that it takes four years to finish a graduate degree and each student's decision in choosing one of two professions is dependent on the relative pay in the two professions. Each graduate can work for 20 years after she finds a job. Develop a new classical dynamic general equilibrium model based on individuals' dynamic optimum decisions with a time lag between price and supply and with rational expectations. If individuals can not only choose between two occupations, but also choose between self-education and a professional university education and between complete self-sufficiency and the division of labor between the two occupations, what are the implications of the endogenization of specialization for fluctuation of excess demand? (Hint: the model is similar to the one in exercise 5.)

7   The efficiency wage model, Shapiro and Stiglitz, 1984: Suppose that a worker's utility
    function is $u = w - e$ where $w$ is wage income and $e$ is the effort level in production. Effort
    level can be high ($e = \alpha$) or low ($e = 0$). The representative firm's production function is $y$
    $= AL^a$ where $a \in (0, 1)$ and $L$ is the amount of labor employed. If a worker is unemployed,
    she receives unemployment benefit $w_0$ from the government. The firm can detect employee
    shirking at probability $q$, but it cannot always observe or verify the effort level of the
    employee. That is, there is moral hazard. The labor supply is $L_0$. Find the firm's demand
    function for labor and the wage rate at which the employee's expected utility for nonshirking
    ($e = \alpha$) is higher than that for shirking ($e = 0$). What is the unemployment level under the
    efficiency wage rate? What are the respective effects of the changes in productivity param-
    eters $A$, $a$, in the high effort level parameter $\alpha$, in detection efficiency parameter $q$, and in
    unemployment benefit parameter $w_0$ on the unemployment rate?

8   Suppose that in preceding exercise the firm can allocate labor to monitoring employees, so
    that detection level $q = \text{Min}\{1, 1/(L_0 - L_m)\}$ where $L_0$ is total labor supply and $L_m$ is the
    amount of labor allocated to monitoring. Solve for the equilibrium level of the unemploy-
    ment rate and analyze if the equilibrium level of the unemployment rate is higher or lower
    than the Pareto optimum level. Discuss the shortcoming of this partial equilibrium analysis
    of endogenous unemployment. Extend this model to describe a general equilibrium mecha-
    nism that simultaneously endogenizes individuals' levels of specialization and unemploy-
    ment rate in society.

9   As in Weitzman's model (1982), investment in physical capital is not specified in example
    27.4, although savings are allocated for investment which is necessary for running the
    efficient pattern of the division of labor and for speeding up accumulation of human capital.
    As shown in chapter 25, if we assume that tractors and machine tools take time to produce
    but each individual must consume final goods at each point in time, then professional
    producers of tractors and machine tools cannot survive in the absence of savings and invest-
    ment. Introduce this investment problem into the model in example 27.4 to investigate how
    the effects of government investment on business cycles and unemployment may be ex-
    plored using an extended model.

10  Consider a new classical dynamic general equilibrium model with the features of the model
    in example 25.1 and of the model in example 27.4. Analyze the interactions between invest-
    ment, business cycles, division of labor in roundabout production, and transaction effi-
    ciency. Use your results to predict the implications for growth and business cycles of
    Kennedy's and Reagan's policies to reduce tax. Can tax reduction simultaneously promote
    investment, long-run growth, and business cycles?

11  Consider the new classical model in example 5.1 and the Nash bargaining model in example 9.1.
    Suppose that the number of finite *ex ante* identical consumer-producers is 3. Show that the
    Nash bargaining equilibrium may avoid unemployment within a certain parameter subspace.
    Use this result to explain why bargaining is an institution to reduce unemployment caused by
    the integer problem. Discuss the trade-off between information cost caused by Nash bargaining
    and unemployment caused by the Walrasian equilibrium. Analyze the welfare loss caused by a
    strike that is used as a threat point in the Nash bargaining in connection with the trade-off
    between economies of division of labor and coordination reliability investigated in part VII.
    What are the equilibrium implications of the trade-offs among economies of division of labor,
    coordination reliability of the network of division of labor, the role of Nash bargaining in
    reducing unemployment, and the welfare loss caused by the threat of strike in Nash bargaining?

12  Du, 2000: Consider one more market structure in example 27.4. In this structure, farmers
    are divided between two groups. The first group produces food and the second is unem-

ployed and receives a loan from the first group in period 1. Hence, the first group demands tractors in periods 1, 3, 5, . . . and the second group demands tractors in period 2, 4, 6, . . . This dis-synchronization of demand for durable goods can avoid business cycles from period 2 on at the cost of unemployment of farmers in period 1. Also, this requires uncollateralized credit to the unemployed. In this structure some individuals choose configuration (y1|x) (an individual remains unemployed in period 1, but starts buying tractors and producing and selling food from period 2 on). Denote (y2|x) as the configuration in which an individual buys tractors and specializes in producing and selling food from period 1 on, and gives a loan of food to feed (y1|x) in period 1. Configuration (x|y) means individuals specialize in producing tractors and buy food from people in (y1|x) and (y2|x). From period 3 on, every two periods constitute a cycle. For simplicity, consider the first two periods as an independent subsystem and solve for its corner equilibrium. Then proceed to the third and fourth periods and solve them as a two-period subsystem, which also leads to a corner equilibrium solution of the cycle to be repeated. Finally, take the discounted sum of intertemporal corner equilibrium total utility for all the subsystems as a proxy for the equilibrium total utility level of the whole intertemporal system. The decision problem of (y1|x) is: Max $U_{y1/x} = \ln(ky_1^d - c') + \delta\ln y_2^d$ s.t. $y_2 + y_2^s = (x_2^d)^\alpha(L_{y2} - c)^a$, $x_2^d = 1$, $p_{y1}y_1^d + p_{x2}x_2^d = p_{y2}y_2^s$, $L_{y2} = 2$, where $c'$ is the transaction cost that is specific to this structure. Assume $p_{y2} = 1$. Here, for simplicity, it is assumed that (y1|x) borrows in period 1 and repays the loan in period 2 as soon as she obtains revenue from selling food. This simplifying assumption confines the effects of uncollateralized credit within the first two periods. (y2|x) extends credit to (y1|x). The decision problem of (y2|x) is given by Max $U_{y2/x} = \ln(y_1^d - c') + \delta\ln y_2^d$ s.t. $y_1 + y_1^s = (x_d^d)^\alpha(L_{y1} - c)^a$, $x_1^d = 1$, $y_2 + y_2^s = (x_1^d)^\alpha(L_{y2})^a$, $p_{y1}y_1^s + p_{x2}x_2^s = p_{x1}x_1^d$, $L_{y1} = 2$, $L_{y2} = 4$. The decision problem of (x|y) remains the same as that in structure C: Max $y_t^d$ $U_x = \ln(ky_1^d) + \delta\ln(ky_2^d)$, s.t. $x_1^s = (L_{x1} - c)^a$, $L_{x2} = 2$, $p_{y1}y_1^d + p_{y2}y_2^d = p_{x1}x_1^s$. Specify the market clearing conditions for tractors and food, and utility equalization conditions for the three configurations and solve for the corner equilibrium for the first two periods of this market structure. From period 3 on, every two periods constitute a cycle that is to be repeated. The decision problem for (y1|x) is given by Max $U_{y1/x} = \delta^2\ln y_3^d + \delta^3\ln y_4^d$ s.t. $y_3 + y_3^s = (x_2^d)^\alpha(L_{y3})^a$, $y_4 + y_4^s = (x_4^d)^\alpha(L_{y4})^a$, $p_{y3}y_3^d + p_{y4}y_4^d = p_{x4}x_4^d$, $L_{y3} = 4$, $L_{y4} = 6$, $x_4^d = 1$. Similarly, the decision problem for (y2|x) is: Max $U_{y2/x} = \delta^2\ln y_3^d + \delta^3\ln y_4^d$ s.t. $y_3 + y_3^s = (x_3^d)^\alpha(L_{y3})^a$, $y_4 + y_4^s = (x_3^d)^\alpha(L_{y4})^a$, $p_{y3}y_3^s + p_{y4}y_4^s = p_{x3}x_3^d$, $L_{y3} = 6$, $L_{y4} = 8$, $x_3^d = 1$. Let $p_{y4} = 1$. Specify the market clearing conditions and utility equalization conditions for this first cycle and solve for the corner equilibrium. To show the following propositions: (1) If the transaction efficiency ($k$) is sufficiently high, the discount factor ($\delta$) is sufficiently large, the transactions cost $c'$ is sufficiently low, then $p_{y1} > p_{y2}$. $p_{y1} - p_{y2}$ is the interest rate that individuals in (y1|x) pay. (2) For the first two periods, if the transaction efficiency $k$ is sufficiently close to 0, the corner equilibrium in this structure is not an equilibrium. The total utility of the first two periods is decreasing in the specific transactions cost $c'$. (3) When $k$ is sufficiently close to 0, the corner equilibrium for the $n$th repeated cycle of this structure would not be a dynamic equilibrium. When $k$ is sufficiently close to 1, but the discount factor is sufficiently close to 0, then it is still not an equilibrium. When $k$ is sufficiently large, the discount factor is not too small, then the total utility of the $n$th cycle of this market structure is higher than that of all structures in example 27.4. (4) If $k$ is sufficiently low and the job shifting cost is not too high, autarky is the equilibrium. If $c'$ is sufficiently large, $k$ and $1/c$ are not too low, the discount factor is sufficiently large, the decision horizon is sufficiently long, then C is equilibrium. If $c'$ is sufficiently small, $k$ and $1/c$ are not too small, the discount factor is sufficiently large, and the decision horizon is sufficiently long, then the structure with unemployment in the first period but full employment and complete division of labor in all subsequent periods is the general equilibrium.

13   Use the results in the preceding exercise to analyze the implications of macroeconomic policies that affect credit market conditions for economic development.

14   Suppose that one more intermediate good is added to the model in example 27.4. Use the extended model to show that as division of labor develops in a longer roundabout production chain, business cycles are more difficult to smooth out by overlapping generation consideration.

15   Calculate the per capita real incomes of two configuration sequences in structure C. Show that per capita real income is not equalized in each period despite equalization of total discounted utilities between occupation configurations. Analyze the effects of eliminating such inequality of income distribution. Recently some empirical work (Deininger and Squire, 1996) shows that inequality of income distribution fluctuates over time. Use the model in example 27.4 to explore growth implications of such a fluctuation.

## Notes

1 It is difficult to draw a distinction between voluntary and involuntary unemployment in our model. In a sense, unemployment in this model can be viewed as voluntary since dynamics with unemployment and business cycles are the outcome of all individuals' optimal decisions. However, such unemployment can also be viewed as involuntary since individuals who are unemployed are willing to work if it is possible. They cannot work during recession time because of a trade-off between full exploitation of human capital and full employment of physical labor. Maybe "involuntary" is the wrong word for this general equilibrium phenomenon. In general equilibrium, each individual is unhappy with the consequence of interactions between self-interested decisions since she always wants more (nonsatiated preferences), but must accept the equilibrium as it is. It is not easy to tell if she accepts the equilibrium voluntarily or involuntarily if the nonsatiated desires are considered.

# REFERENCES

Abdel-Rahman, H. M. (1990), "Agglomeration Economies, Types and Sizes of Cities," *Journal of Urban Economics*, 27, 25–45.

Abraham, K. and Katz, L. (1986), "Cyclical Unemployment: Sectoral Shifts or Aggregate Disturbances?," *Journal of Political Economy*, 94, 507–22.

Aghion, P., Bacchetta, P., and Banerjee, A. (1998), "Capital Markets and the Instability of Open Economies," Working paper, presented at the Harvard University and MIT Growth and Development Seminar.

Aghion, P., Bolton, P., and Jullien, B. (1991), "Optimal Learning by Experimentation," *Review of Economic Studies*, 58, 621–54.

Aghion, P. and Howitt, P. (1992), "A Model of Growth Through Creative Destruction," *Econometrica*, 60, 323–51.

Aghion, P. and Howitt, P. (1998), *Endogenous Growth Theory*, Cambridge, Mass., MIT Press.

Aghion, P. and Saint-Paul, G. (1991), "On the Virtue of Bad Times: An Analysis of the Interaction between Economic Fluctuations and Productivity Growth," CEPR Discussion Paper no. 578.

Aghion, P. and Tirole, J. (1997). "Formal and Real Authority in Organizations," *Journal of Political Economy*, 105, 1–29.

Aiginger, K. and Tichy, G. (1991), "Small Firms and the Merger Mania," *Small Business Economics*, 3, 83–102.

Akerlof, G. (1970), "The Market for Lemons: Quality Uncertainty and the Market Mechanism," *Quarterly Journal of Economics*, 89, 488–500.

Akerlof, G. and Yellen, J. (1985), "A Near-Rational Model of the Business Cycle, with Wage and Price Inertia," *Quarterly Journal of Economics*, Suppl., 100, 823–38.

Alchian, A. (1977), "Why Money?," *Journal of Money, Credit and Banking*, 9, 131–40.

Alchian, A. and Demsetz, H. (1972), "Production, Information Costs, and Economic Organization," *American Economic Review*, 62, 777–95.

Alesina, A. and Rodrik, D. (1994), "Distributive Politics and Economic Growth," *Quarterly Journal of Economics*, 109, 465–90.

Anonymous (1701), *Consideration on the East-India Trade*, in J. R. McCulloch (ed.), *A Select Collection of Early English Tracts on Commerce*, London, 1856, reissued Cambridge, Cambridge University Press, 1954.

Arnott, R. (1979), "Optimal City Size in a Spatial Economy," *Journal of Urban Economics*, 6, 65–89.

Arrow, K. (1962), "The Economic Implications of Learning by Doing," *Review of Economic Studies*, 29, 155–73.

Arrow, K. (1979), "The Division of Labor in the Economy, the Polity, and Society," in G. O'Driscoll, Jr. (ed.), *Adam Smith and Modern Political Economy*, Ames, Iowa, Iowa State University Press.

Arrow, K. (1985), "The Economics of Agency," in J. Pratt and R. Zeckhauser (eds.), *Principals and Agents: The Structure of Business*, pp. 37–51. Boston, Harvard Business School Press.

Arrow, K., Ng, Y.-K., and Yang, X. (eds.) (1998), *Increasing Returns and Economic Analysis*, London, Macmillan.

Azariadis, C. (1975), "Implicit Contracts and Underemployment Equilibrium," *Journal of Political Economy*, 83, 1183–1202.

Babbage, C. (1832), *On the Economy of Machinery and Manufactures*, 4th enlarged edn. of 1835, reissued in 1977, New York, M. Kelly.

Bac, M. (1996), "Corruption and Supervision Costs in Hierarchies," *Journal of Comparative Economics*, 22, 99–118.

Baechler, J. (1976), *The Origins of Capitalism*, trans. Barr Cooper, Oxford, Blackwell.

Baechler, J., Hall, J. A. and Mann, M. (eds.) (1997), *Europe and the Rise of Capitalism*. Cambridge, Mass., Blackwell.

Bag, P. K. (1997), "Controlling Corruption in Hierarchies," *Journal of Comparative Economics*, 25, 322–44.

Baily, M. (1974), "Wages and Employment Under Uncertain Demand," *Review of Economic Studies*, 41, 37–50.

Balassa, B. (1986), "The Employment Effects of Trade in Manufactured Products between Developed and Developing Countries," *Journal of Policy Modeling*, 8, 371–90.

Baldwin, R. E. and Venables, A. J. (1995), "Regional Economic Integration," in G. M. Grossman, and K. Rogoff (eds.), *Handbook of International Economics*, vol. 3. Amsterdam, New York, and Oxford: Elsevier, North-Holland.

Ball, L., Mankiw, N., and Romer, D. (1988), "The New Keynesian Economics and the Output–Inflation Tradeoff," *Brookings Papers of Economic Activities*, 1, 1–65.

Banerjee, A. (1992), "A Simple Model of Herd Behavior," *The Quarterly Journal of Economics*, 107, 797–817.

Banerjee, A. and Newman, A. (1993), "Occupational Choice and the Process of Development," *Journal of Political Economy*, 101, 274–98.

Banerjee, A. and Spagat, M. (1991), "Productivity Paralysis and the Complexity Problem: Why Do Centrally Planned Economies Become Prematurely Gray?," *Journal of Comparative Economics*, 15, 646–60.

Baran, P. (1957), *La economia politica del crecimiento*, Mexico, FCE, 1969.

Bardhan, P. (ed.) (1989), *The Economic Theory of Agrarian Institutions*, Oxford, Clarendon Press.

Bardhan, P. and Roemer, J. (eds.) (1993), *Market Socialism, the Current Debate*, Oxford, Oxford University Press.

Barro, R. (1991), "Economic Growth in a Cross-Section of Countries," *Quarterly Journal of Economics*, 106, 407–44.

Barro, R. (1997), *Determinants of Economic Growth*, Cambridge, Mass., MIT Press.

Barro, R. and Sala-i-Martin, X. (1992), "Convergence," *Journal of Political Economy*, 100, 223–51.

Barro, R. and Sala-i-Martin, X. (1995), *Economic Growth*, New York, McGraw-Hill.

Barzel, Y. (1982), "Measurement Cost and the Organization of Markets," *Journal of Law and Economics*, 25, 27–48.

Barzel, Y. (1985), "Transaction Costs: Are They Just Costs?" *Journal of Institutional & Theoretical Economics*, 141, 4–16.

Barzel, Y. (1989), *Economic Analysis of Property Rights*, Cambridge, Cambridge University Press.

Barzel, Y. (1997), "Property Rights and the Evolution of the State," mimeo, and "Third-party Enforcement and the State," mimeo. Department of Economics, University of Washington, Seattle.

Barzel, Y. and Yu, B. T. (1984), "The Effect of the Utilization Rate on the Division of Labor," *Economic Inquiry*, 22, 18–27.

Basu, S. (1996), "Procyclical Productivity: Increasing Returns or Cyclical Utilization," *Quarterly Journal of Economics*, 111, 719–750.

Baumgardner, J. R. (1988a), "The Division of Labor, Local Markets, and Worker Organization," *Journal of Political Economy*, 96, 509–27.

Baumgardner, J. R. (1988b), "Physicians' Services and the Division of Labor across Local Markets," *Journal of Political Economy*, 96, 948–82.

Baumol, W. J. (1970), *Economic Dynamics*, New York, Macmillan.

Baumol, W. J. (1996), "Productivity Growth, Convergence, and Welfare: What the Long-Run Data Show," *American Economic Review*, 76(5), 1072–85.

Baxer, M. and King, R.G. (1995), "Measuring Business Cycles: Approximate Band-Pass Filters for Economic Time Series," National Bureau of Economic Research working paper no. 5022.

Bazovsky, Igor (1961), *Reliability Theory and Practice*, Englewood Cliffs, NJ, Prentice-Hall.

Becker, G. (1964), *Human Capital: A Theoretical and Empirical Analysis, with Special Reference to Education*, New York, Columbia University Press.

Becker, G. (1965), "A theory of the Allocation of Time," *Economic Journal*, 75, 497–517.

Becker, G. (1981), *A Treatise on the Family*, Cambridge, Mass., Harvard University Press.

Becker, G. and Murphy, K. (1992), "The Division of Labor, Coordination Costs, and Knowledge," *Quarterly Journal of Economics*, 107, 1137–60.

Beckmann, M. (1968), *Dynamic Programming of Economic Decisions*, New York, Springer-Verlag.

Ben-Akiva, M., de Palma, A., and Thisse, J. (1989), "Spatial Competition with Differentiated Products," *Regional Science & Urban Economics*, 19, 5–19.

Benhabib, J. and Joranovic, B. (1991), "Externalities and Growth Accounting," *American Economic Review*, 81, 82–113.

Ben-Ner, A. (1995), "Book Review, Specialization and Economic Organization," *Journal of Institutional and Theoretical Economics*, 151, 571–2.

Berger, Philip and Ofek, E. (1995), "Diversification's Effect on Firm Value," *Journal of Financial Economics*, 37, 39–65.

Berle, A. and Means, G. (1932), *The Modern Corporation and Private Property*, London, Macmillan.

Bernard, A. and Jones, C. I. (1996), "Technology and Convergence," *Economic Journal*, 106, 1037–44.

Besley, Timothy (1995), "Savings, Credit and Insurance," in J. Behrmand and T. N. Srinivasan (eds.), *Handbook of Development Economics*, vol. III, New York, Elsevier Science.

Besley, Timothy, Coate, S., and Loury G. (1993), "The Economics of Rotating Savings and Credit Associations," *American Economic Review*, 83, 792–810.

Bhagat, S., Shleifer, A., and Vishny, R. (1990), "Hostile Takeovers in the 1980s: The Return to Corporate Specialization," *Brookings Papers on Economic Activity: Microeconomics*, Special Issue, 1–72.

Bhagwati, J. and Dehejia, V. (1994), "Freer Trade and Wages of the Unskilled: Is Marx Striking Again?," in J. Bhagwati and M. Kosters (eds.), *Trade and Wages: Leveling Wages Down?*, Washington, DC, American Enterprise Institute.

Bhattacharyya, S. and Lafontaine, F. (1995), "Double Sided Moral Hazard and the Nature of Share Contracts," *RAND Journal of Economics*, 26, 761–81.

Binmore, Kenneth, Osborne, Martin J., and Rubinstein, Ariel (1992). *Noncooperative Models of Bargaining*. New York, Elsevier Science.

Black, F. (1987), *Business Cycles and Equilibrium*, New York: Basil Blackwell.

Black, F. (1995), *Exploring General Equilibrium*, Cambridge, Mass., MIT Press.

Blanchard, O. and Kremer, M. (1997), "Disorganization," *Quarterly Journal of Economics*, 112, 1091–26.

Blitch, C. P. (1983). "Allyn Young on Increasing Returns." *Journal of Post Keynesian Economics*, vol. 5 (Spring), pp. 359–72.

Blitch, C. P. (1995). *Allyn Young: The Peripatetic Economist*. London: Macmillan.

Blomstrom, M. and Wolff, E. (1997), "Growth in a Dual Economy," *World Development*, 25, 1927–37.

Bolton, P. and Dewatripont, M. (1994), "The Firm as a Communication Network," *Quarterly Journal of Economics*, 109, 809–39.

Bolton, P. and Scharfstein, David (1998), "Corporate Finance, the Theory of the Firm, and Organization," *Journal of Economic Perspectives*, 12, 95–114.

Border, K. C. (1985), *Fixed Point Theorems with Applications to Economics and Game Theory*, Cambridge, Cambridge University Press.

Borjas, G., Freeman, R., and Katz, L. (1992), "How Much Do Immigration and Trade Affect Labor Market Outcomes?" *Brookings Papers on Economic Activity*. No. 1, 1–67.

Borland, J. and Eichberger, J. (1998), "Organizational Form outside the Principal–Agent Paradigm," *Bulletin of Economic Research*, 50, 201–27.

Borland, J. and Yang, X. (1992a), "Specialization and Money as a Medium for Exchange," Seminar Paper, Department of Economics, Monash University.

Borland, J. and Yang, X. (1992b), "Specialization and a New Approach to Economic Organization and Growth," *American Economic Review*, 82, 386–91.

Borland, J. and Yang, X. (1995), "Specialization, Product Development, Evolution of the Institution of the Firm, and Economic Growth," *Journal of Evolutionary Economics*, 5, 19–42.

Boserup, Ester (1975), "The Impact of Population Growth on Agricultural Output," *Quarterly Journal of Ecnomics*, 89(2), 257–70.

Bowen, Harry P., Leamer, Edward E., and Sveikauskas, Leo (1987), "Multicountry, Multifactor Tests of the Factor Abundance Theory," *American Economic Review*, 77(5), 791–809.

Braudel, Fernand (1984), *Civilization and Capitalism: 18$^{th}$ Century*, trans. Sian Reynolds, London, Collins.

Brian, Arthur W. (1994), *Increasing Returns and Path Dependence in the Economy*, Ann Arbor, University Michigan Press.

Brown, G. (1978), "Agricultural Pricing Policies in Developing Countries," in T. W. Schultz (ed.), *Distortion of Agricultural Incentives*, Bloomington, Indiana University Press.

Brunner, K. and Meltzer, A. (1971), "The Use of Money: Money in the Theory of an Exchange Economy," *American Economic Review*, 61, 784–805.

Bruton, Henry (1998), "A Reconsideration of Import Substitution," *Journal of Economic Literature*, 36, 903–36.

Buchanan, James M. (1975), *The Limits of Liberty: Between Anarchy and Leviathan*. Chicago, University of Chicago Press.

Buchanan, James M. (1989), *Explorations into Constitutional Economics*. College Station, Texas A&M University Press.

Buchanan, James M. (1991), *Constitutional Economics*. Cambridge, Mass., Blackwell.

Buchanan, James M. (1994), "The Return to Increasing Returns," in Buchanan, J. and Yoon, Y. (eds.), *The Return to Increasing Returns*, Ann Arbor, University of Michigan Press.

Buchanan, James M. and Stubblebine, W. Craig (1962), "Externality," *Economica*, 29, 371–84.

Buchanan, James M. and Tullock, Gordon (1965), *The Calculus of Consent: Logical Foundations of Constitutional Democracy*, Ann Arbor, University of Michigan Press.

Burtless, Gary (1995), "International Trade and the Rise in Earnings Inequality," *Journal of Economic Literature*, 33, 800–16.

Caballero, R. J. and Hammour, M. L. (1994), "The Cleansing Effect of Recessions," *American Economic Review*, 84(5), 350–68.

Calvo, G. and Wellisz, S. (1978), "Supervision, Loss of Control and the Optimal Size of the Firm," *Journal of Political Economy*, 86, 943–52.

Calvo, G. and Wellisz, S. (1979), "Hierarchy, Ability and Income Distribution," *Journal of Political Economy*, 87, 991–1010.

Campbell, R. and Skinner, A. (eds.) (1976), *The Wealth of Nations*, Oxford.

Cannan, E. (ed.) (1937), *The Wealth of Nations*, New York.

Canton, Erik (1997), *Economic Growth and Business Cycles*, Center for Economic Research, Tilburg University, Amsterdam, Thesis Publishers.

Carter, M. (1995), "Information and the Division of Labour: Implications for the Firm's Choice of Organisation," *Economic Journal*, 105, 385–97.

Center for International Comparisons at the University of Pennsylvania (1996–2000), *Penn World*

*Table, http://pwt.econ.upenn.edu.*

Chandler, A., Jr. (1990), *Scale and Scope: the Dynamics of Industrial Capitalism*, Cambridge, Mass., Belknap Press.

Chang, G. and Wen, G. (1998), "Food Availability Versus Consumption Efficiency: Causes of the Chinese Famine," *China Economic Review*, 9, 157–66.

Chen, B.-L., Lin, J., and Yang, X. (1999), "Empirical Evidence for the Endogenous Growth Generated by Evolution in Division of Labor," Development Discussion Paper no. 671, Harvard Institute for International Development.

Chenery, M. (1979), *Structural Change and Development Policy*, Oxford, Oxford University Press.

Cheng, T. (1991), "The Present and Future of China's Residential Registration System," Ph.D. dissertation, Department of Sociology, North-East University, Boston.

Cheng, W. (1999), "Division of Labor, Money, and Economic Progress," *Review of Development Economics*, 3, 354–67.

Cheng, W. (1998), "Specialization and the Emergence and the Value of Money," in K. Arrow, Y.-K. Ng, and X. Yang (eds.), *Increasing Returns and Economic Analysis*, London, Macmillan.

Cheng, W., Liu, M., and Yang, X. (2000), "A Ricardo Model with Endogenous Comparative Advantage and Endogenous Trade Policy Regime," *Economic Record*, 76, 172–82.

Cheng, W., Sachs, J., and Yang, X. (2000), "An Inframarginal Analysis of the Ricardian Model," *Review of International Economics*, 8, 208–20.

Cheng, W., Sachs, J., and Yang, X. (1999), "An Inframarginal Analysis of the Heckscher–Ohlin Model with Transaction Costs and Technological Comparative Advantage," Harvard Center for International Development Working Paper no. 9.

Cheung, S. (1968), "Private Property Rights and Sharecropping," *Journal of Political Economy* Chicago, 76, 1117–22.

Cheung, S. (1969), *The Theory of Share Tenancy*, Chicago, University of Chicago Press.

Cheung, S. (1970), "The Structure of a Contract and the Theory of a Non-exclusive Resource," *Journal of Law and Economics*, 13, 49–70.

Cheung, S. (1974), "A Theory of Price Control," *Journal of Law and Economics*, 17, 53–71.

Cheung, S. (1983), "The Contractual Nature of the Firm," *Journal of Law & Economics*, 26, 1–21.

Chiang, A. (1984), *Fundamental Methods of Mathematical Economics*, London: McGraw-Hill.

Cho, D. and Graham, S. (1996), "The Other Side of Conditional Convergence," *Economics Letters*, 50, 285–90.

Chow, G. (1975), *Analysis and Control of Dynamic Economic Systems*, New York, John Wiley & Son.

Chu, C. (1997), "Productivity, Investment in Infrastructure, and Population Size: Formalizing the Theory of Ester Boserup," *Review of Development Economics*, 1, 294–304.

Chu, C. and Tsai, Y. (1998), "Productivity, Investment in Infrastructure, and Population Size: Formalizing the Theory of Ester Boserup," in K. Arrow, Y.-K. Ng, and X. Yang (eds.), *Increasing Returns and Economic Analysis*, London, Macmillan.

Chu, C. and Wang, C. (1998), "Economy of Specialization and Diseconomy of Externalities." *Journal of Public Economics*, 69, 249–61.

Ciccone, A. and Matsuyama, K. (1996), "Start-up Costs and Pecuniary Externalities as Barriers to Economic Development," *Journal of Development Economics*, 49, 33–59.

Cline, William (1997), *Trade and Income Distribution*, Washington, DC, Institute for International Economics.

Clower, R. (1967), "A Reconsideration of the Microfoundations of Monetary Theory," *Western Economic Journal*, 6, 1–8.

Coase, R. (1937), "The Nature of the Firm," *Economica*, 4, 386–405

Coase, R. (1946), "The Marginal Cost Controversy," *Economica*, 13, 169–82.

Coase, R. (1960), "The Problem of Social Cost," *Journal of Law and Economics*, 3, 1–44.

Coase, R. (1991), "The Nature of the Firm: Origin, Meaning, Influence," in O. Williamson and S. Winter (eds.), *The Nature of the Firm*, New York, Oxford University Press.

Colwell, P. and Munneke, H. (1997), "The Structure of Urban Land Prices," *Journal of Urban Economics*, 41, 321–36.

Comment, Robert, and Jarrell, Gregg (1995), "Corporate Focus and Stock Returns," *Journal of Financial Economics*, 37, 67–87.

Conlisk, John (1996), "Why Bounded Rationality?," *The Journal of Economic Literature*, 34, 669–700.

Conybeare, John A. C. (1987), *Trade Wars: The Theory and Practice of International Commercial Rivalry*, New York, Columbia University Press.

Cooper, R. and Ross, T. W. (1985), "Produce Warranties and Double Moral Hazard," *Rand Journal of Economics*, 16, pp. 103–13.

Cooter, R. (1989), "The Coase Theorem," *The New Palgrave: A Dictionary of Economics*, eds. J. Eatwell, M. Milgate, and P. Newman, London, Macmillan Press, vol. 1, 457–60.

Crafts, N. (1997), "Endogenous Growth: Lessons for and from Economic History," in D. Kreps and K. Wallis (eds.), *Advances in Economics and Econometrics: Theory and Applications*, vol. II, Cambridge, Cambridge University Press.

Cypher, James and Dietz, James (1998), "Static and Dynamic Comparative Advantage: A Multi-period Analysis with Declining Terms of Trade," *Journal of Economic Issues*, 32, 305–14.

Dasgupta, Partha (1995), "The Population Problem: Theory and Evidence," *Journal of Economic Literature*, 33, 1879–1902.

Deardorff, Alan and Stern, Robert (eds.) (1994), *The Stolper–Samuelson Theorem*, Ann Arbor, University of Michigan Press.

Deaton, A. (1990), "Saving in Developing Countries: Theory and Evidence," *World Bank Economic Review (Proceedings of the World Bank Annual Conference on Development Economics, 1989)*, 61–96.

Deaton, A. (1991), "Saving and Liquidity Constraints," *Econometrica*, 59, 1221–48.

Deaton, A. and Muellbauer, J. (1980), *Economics and Consumer Behavior*, Cambridge, Cambridge University Press.

Debreu, G. (1959), *Theory of Value*, New Haven, Yale University Press.

Debreu, G. (1974), "Excess Demand Functions," *Journal of Mathematical Economics*, 1, 15–21.

Debreu, G. (1991), "The Mathematization of Economic Theory," *American Economic Review*, 81, 1–7.

Deininger, K. and Squire, L. (1996), "A New Data Set Measuring Income Inequality," *World Bank Economic Review*, 10, 565–91.

Dellas, H. (1991), "Stabilization Policy and Long Term Growth: Are They Related?," mimeo, University of Maryland.

Delong, B. (1988), "Productivity Growth, Convergence and Welfare: Comments," *American Economic Review*, 78, 1138–54.

Demsetz, H. (1967), "Toward A Theory of Property Rights," *American Economic Review*, 57, 347–59.

Demsetz, H. (1988), *Ownership, Control, and the Firm*, Oxford, Blackwell.

Demsetz, H. and Lehn, K. (1985), "The Structure of Corporate Ownership: Causes and Consequences," *Journal of Political Economy*, 93, 1155–77.

Denardo, E. (1975), *Dynamic Programming: Theory and Application*, Englewood Cliffs, NJ, Prentice-Hall.

Department of Commerce (1972–1999), *Statistical Abstract of the United States*, Washington, DC.

Department of Commerce (1975), *Historical Statistics of the United States*, Washington, DC.

Dewatripont, M. (1988), "Commitment through Renegotiation-proof Contracts with Third Parties," *Review of Economic Studies*, 55, 377–89.

Dewatripont, M. and Maskin, E. (1995a), "Credit and Efficiency in Centralized and Decentralized Economies," *Review of Economic Studies*, 62, 541–56.

Dewatripont, M. and Maskin, E. (1995b), "Contractual Contingencies and Renegotiation," *Rand Journal of Economics*, 26, 704–19.

Dewatripont, M. and Roland, G. (1995), "The Design of Reform Packages under Uncertainty," *American Economic Review*, 85, 1207–23.

Diamond, Charles and Simon, Curtis (1990), "Industrial Specialization and the Returns to Labor," *Journal of Labor Economics*, 8, 175–201.

Diamond, D. W. (1989), "Reputation Acquisition in Debt Markets," *Journal of Political Economy*,

97, 828–62.

Diamond, D. W. and Dybvig, P. (1983), "Bank Runs, Deposit Insurance, and Liquidity," *Journal of Political Economy*, 91, 401–19.

Dicke, T. (1992), *Franchising in America: The Development of a Business Method, 1840–1980*, Chapel Hill & London, University of North Carolina Press.

Diderot, Denis (1713), *Diderot Encyclopedia: the Complete Illustrations*, New York, Abrams, 1978.

Din, M. (1996), "International Capital Mobility and Development Policy in a Dual Economy," *Review of International Economics*, 4, 185–201.

Dixit, A. (1987), "Trade and Insurance with Moral Hazard," *Journal of International Economics*, 23, 201–20.

Dixit, A. (1989), "Trade and Insurance with Imperfectly Observed Outcomes," *Quarterly Journal of Economics*, 104, 195–203.

Dixit, A. (1990), *Optimization in Economic Theory*, Cambridge, MIT Press.

Dixit, A and Nalebuff, B. (1991), *Thinking Strategically*, New York, W. W. Norton & Co.

Dixit, A. and Norman, V. (1980), *Theory of International Trade*, Cambridge: Cambridge University Press.

Dixit, A. and Stiglitz, J. (1977), "Monopolistic Competition and Optimum Product Diversity," *American Economic Review*, 67, 297–308.

Dodzin, Sergei and Vamvakidis, A. (1999), "Trade and Industrialization in Developing Agricultural Economies," International Monetary Fund Working Paper, Washington, DC.

Domar, E. (1947), "Expansion and Employment," *American Economic Review*, 37, 34–55.

Dondran, M. and Minoux, M. (1984), *Graphs and Algorithms*, London, John Willey & Sons.

Dornbusch, Fisher S. and Samuelson, Paul (1977), "Comparative Advantage, Trade, and Payments in a Ricardian Model with a Continuum of Goods," *American Economics Review*, 67(5), 823–39.

Dowrick, S. and Nguyen, D. T. (1989), "OECD Comparative Economic Growth 1950–85: Catch-up and Convergence," *American Economic Review*, 79, 1010–30.

Du, J. (2000), "Endogenous, Efficient Long-run Cyclical Unemployment, Endogenous Long-run Growth, and Division of Labor," *Review of Development Economics*, forthcoming.

Durkheim, E. (1933), *The Division of Labor in Society*, trans. with an intro. by George Simpson, New York, Free Press, 1964.

Dutta, Bhaskar and Mutuswami, S. (1997), "Stable Networks," *Journal of Economic Theory*, 76, 322–44.

Easterlin, R. (1981), "Why Isn't the Whole World Developed?" *Journal of Economic History*, March, 1–17.

Easton, Stephen and Walker, Michael (1997), "Income, Growth, and Economic Freedom," *American Economic Review, Papers and Proceedings*, 87, 328–32.

Eckholm, E. (1975), *The Other Energy Crisis, Firewood*, Washington, DC, Worldwatch Institute; *Economic Literature*, 33, 800–16.

Edwards, Brian K. and Starr, Ross M. (1987), "A Note on Indivisibilities, Specialization and Economies of Scale," *American Economic Review*, 77, 192–4.

Ekelund, Robert, and Tollison, R. (1981), *Merchantilism as an Rent-seeking Society*, College Station, Tex., Texas A & M University Press.

Elvin, Mark (1973), *The Pattern of the Chinese Past*. London, Eyre Methuen.

Emmanuel, A. (1972), *Unequal Exchange: A Study of the Imperialism of Trade*, trans Brian Pearce, New York, Monthly Review Press.

Ethier, W. (1979), "Internationally Decreasing Costs and World Trade," *Journal of International Economics*, 9, 1–24.

Ethier, W. (1982), "National and International Returns to Scale in the Modern Theory of International Trade," *American Economic Review*, 72, 389–405.

Ethier, W. (1988), *Modern International Economics*, 2nd edn., New York, W. W. Norton & Co.

Evans, David (1987), "The Long Run Determinants of North–South Terms of Trade and Some Recent Empirical Evidence," *World Development*, 15(5), 657–71.

Fairbank, John King (1992), *China: A New History*, Cambridge, Mass., Belknap Press.

Fama, E. and Jensen, M. (1983), "Separation of Ownership and Control," *Journal of Law & Economics*, 26, 301–27.

Fang, Xinghai and Zhu, Tian (1999), "Institutional Imperfection and Transition Strategies," *Economic Systems*, 23, 331–48.

Farrell, J. and Maskin, E. (1989), "Renegotiation in Repeated Games," *Games and Economic Behaviour*, 1, 327–60.

Farrell, J. and Saloner, G. (1985), "Standardization, Compatibility, and Innovation," *Rand Journal of Economics*, 16, 70–83.

Fauver, Larry, Houston, J., and Naranjo, A. (1998), "Capital Market Development, Legal Systems and Value of Corporate Diversification: A Cross-Country Analysis," Working Paper, University of Florida.

Fawcett, H. (1863), *Manual of Political Economy*, London, Macmillan.

Feenstra (1998), "Integration of Trade and Disintegration of Production in the Global Economy," *Journal of Economic Perspectives*, 12, 31–50.

Fei, J. and Ranis, G. (1964), *Development of the Labor Surplus Economy*, New York, Richard Irwin Inc.

Fei, J., Ranis, G., and Kuo, S. (1979), *Growth with Equity: the Taiwan Case*, New York, Oxford University Press.

Fischer, S. (1977), "Long-Term Contracts, Rational Expectations, and the Optimal Money Supply Rule," *Journal of Political Economy*, Feb., 85(1), 191–205.

Fleming, Marcus (1955), "External Economies and the Doctrine of Balanced Growth," *Economic Journal*, 65, 241–56.

Friedman, Milton (1957), *A Theory of the Consumption Function*, Princeton, Princeton University Press.

Frye, Timothy and Shleifer, Andrei (1997), "The Invisible Hand and the Grabbing Hand," *American Economic Review, Papers and Proceedings*, 87, 354–58.

Fudenberg, D. and Tirole, J. (1983), "Sequential Bargaining with Incomplete Information," *Review of Economic Studies*, 50, 221–47.

Fudenberg, D. and Tirole, J. (1989), "Noncooperative Game Theory for Industrial Organization: An Introduction and Overview," *Handbook of Industrial Organization*, vol. 1, ch. 5, Oxford, Elsevier Science.

Fudenberg, D. and Tirole, J. (1991), *Game Theory*, Cambridge, Mass., MIT Press.

Fujita, M. (1988), "A Monopolistic Competition Model of Spatial Agglomeration: Differentiated Product Approach," *Regional Science & Urban Economics*, 25, 505–28.

Fujita, M. (1989), *Urban Economic Theory: Land Use and City Size*, New York, Cambridge University Press.

Fujita, M. and Krugman, P. (1994), "On the Evolution of Hierarchical Urban Systems," mimeo, Department of Regional Science, University of Pennsylvania, Philadelphia.

Fujita, M. and Krugman, P. (1995), "When is the Economy Monocentric: von Thünen and Chamberlin Unified," *Regional Science & Urban Economics*, 25, 505–28.

Fujita, M. and Mori, T. (1997), "Structural Stability and Evolution of Urban Systems," *Regional Science and Urban Economics* , 27, 399–442.

Fujita, M. and Thisse, J.-F. (1996), "Economies of Agglomeration," *Journal of Japanese and International Economies*, 10, 339–78.

Fujita, M., Krugman, P., and Venables, A. (1999), *The Spatial Economy: Cities, Regions, and International Trade*, Cambridge, Mass., MIT Press.

Furubotn, E. and Pejovich, S. (eds.) (1974), *The Economics of Property Rights*. Cambridge, Mass., Ballinger Publishing Co.

Gabisch, G. and Lorenz, H. (1989), *Business Cycle Theory: A Survey of Methods and Concepts*, Berlin, Springer-Verlag.

Gale, D. (1986), "Bargaining and Competition. Part I: Characterization and Part II: Existence," *Econometrica*, 54, 807–18.

Gallup, John and Sachs, J. (1998), "Geography and Economic Development," Working Paper,

Harvard Institute for International Development.

Galor, O. (1996), "Convergence? Inferences from Theoretical Models," *Economic Journal*, 106, 1056–69.

Galor, O. and J. Zeira (1993), "Income Distribution and Macroeconomics," *Review of Economic Studies*, 87, 205–10.

Gans, Joshua (1998), "Industrialization Policy and the 'Big Push'," in K. Arrow et al. (eds.), *Increasing Returns and Economic Analysis*, London, Macmillan.

Gibbons, R. (1992a), *A Primer in Game Theory*, New York, Harvester Wheatsheaf.

Gibbons, R. (1992b), *Game Theory for Applied Economist*, Princeton, Princeton University Press.

Gibbons, Robert (1998), "Incentives in Organization," *Journal of Economic Perspectives*, 12, 115–32.

Gilles, Robert (1990), *Core and Equilibria of Socially Structured Economies: The Modelling of Social Constraints in Economic Behaviour*. Krips Repro Meppel.

Gomory, Ralph E. (1994), "A Ricardo Model with Economies of Scale," *Journal of Economic Theory*, 62, 394–419.

Goodwin, R. (1951), "The Non-linear Accelerator and the Persistence to Markets Having Production Lags," *Econometrica*, 19, 1–17

Gordon, B. (1975), *Economic Analysis before Adam Smith*, London, Macmillan.

Gray, J. (1976), "Wage Indexation: A Macroeconomic Approach," *Journal of Monetary Economics*, 2, 221–35.

Green, E. (1987), "Lending and the Smoothing of Uninsurable Income," in E. Prescott and N. Wallace (eds.), *Contractual Arrangements for Intertemporal Trade*, Minneapolis, University of Minnesota Press.

Greenwood, J. and Jovanovic, B. (1990), "Financial Development, Growth, and the Distribution of Income," *Journal of Political Economy*, 98, 1076–1107.

Grier, K. B. and Tullock, G. (1989), "An Empirical Analysis of Cross-National Economic Growth, 1951–80," *Journal of Monetary Economics*, 24, 259–76.

Groenewegen, Peter (1977), *The Economics of A. R. J. Turgot*, The Hague, Martinus Nijhoff.

Groenewegen, Peter (1987), "Division of Labor," in J. Eatwell, M. Milgate, and P. Newman (eds.), *The New Palgrave: A Dictionary of Economics*, London, Macmillan Press, 901–7.

Grossman, G. (1993), "Endogenous Innovation in the Theory of Growth," *Journal of Economic Perspectives*, 8, 23–44.

Grossman, G. (1998), "Imperfect Labor Contracts and International Trade," mimeo, Department of Economics, Princeton University.

Grossman, G. and Helpman, E. (1989), "Product Development and International Trade," *Journal of Political Economy*, 97, 1261–83.

Grossman, G. and Helpman, E. (1990), "Comparative Advantage and Long-Run Growth," *American Economic Review*, 80, 796–815.

Grossman, G. and Helpman, E. (1991), "Quality Ladders and Product Cycles," *Quarterly Journal of Economics*, 106, 557–86.

Grossman G. and Helpman, E. (1994), "Protection For Sale," *American Economic Review*, 84, 833–50.

Grossman G. and Helpman, E. (1995a), "The Politics of Free-Trade Agreements," *American Economic Review*, 85(4), 667–90.

Grossman G. and Helpman, E. (1995b), "Trade Wars and Trade Talks," *Journal of Political Economy*, 103(4), 675–708.

Grossman, G. and Helpman, E. (1995c), "Technology and Trade," in G. Grossman and K. Rogeff (eds.), *Handbook of International Economics, Volume 3*, New York, Elsevier.

Grossman, G. and Levinsohn, J. (1989), "Import Competition and the Stock Market Return to Capital," *American Economic Review*, 79, 1065–87.

Grossman, G. and Richardson, J. D. (1986), "Strategic Trade Policy: A Survey of the Issues and Early Analysis," in Robert E. Baldwin and J. David Richardson (eds.), *International Trade and Finance*, 3rd edn., Boston, Little, Brown, 95–113.

Grossman, G. and Shapiro, C. (1982), "A Theory of Factor Mobility," *Journal of Political Economy*, 90, 1054–69.

Grossman, S. (1989), *The Informational Role of Prices*, Cambridge, Mass., MIT Press.

Grossman, S. and Hart, O. (1986), "The Costs and Benefits of Ownership: A Theory of Vertical and Lateral Integration," *Journal of Political Economy*, 94, 691–719.

Grout, P. (1984), "Investment and Wages in the Absence of Binding Contracts: A Nash Bargaining Approach," *Econometrica*, 52, 449–60.

Hadley, G. (1964), *Nonlinear and Dynamic Programming*, Reading, Mass., Addison-Wesley.

Hahn, F. (1971), "Equilibrium with Transaction Costs," *Econometrica*, 39, 417–39.

Hall, John (1987), "State and Societies: The Miracle in Comparative Perspective," in Baechler, Hall, and Mann (eds.), *Europe and the Rise of Capitalism*, Cambridge, Mass., Blackwell.

Harris, Joseph (1757), *An Essay Upon Money and Coins*, London, G. Hawkins, 1757–8.

Harrod, R. (1939), "An Essay in Dynamic Theory," *Economic Journal*, 49, 14.

Hart, O. (1991), "Incomplete Contract and the Theory of the Firm," in O. Williamson and S. Winter (eds.), *The Nature of the Firm*, New York, Oxford University Press.

Hart, O. (1995), *Firms, Contracts, and Financial Structure*, Oxford, Clarendon Press.

Hart, O. and Holmstrom, B. (1987), "The Theory of Contracts," in: T. Bewley (ed.), *Advances in Economic Theory*, Cambridge, Cambridge University Press.

Hart, O. and Moore, B. (1990), "Property Rights and the Nature of the Firm," *Journal of Political Economy*, 98: 1119–58.

Hart, O. and Moore, B. (1999), "On the Design of Hierarchies: Coordination versus Specialization," *Journal of Political Economy*, 98, 1119–58.

Hartwell, R. (1965), "The Causes of Industrial Revolution: An Essay in Methodology," *Economic History Review*, 18.

Hayek, F. (1944), *The Road to Serfdom*, Chicago, University of Chicago Press.

Hayek, F. (1945), "The Use of Knowledge in Society," *American Economic Review*, 35, 519–30.

Heckscher, E. (1919), "The Effect of Foreign Trade on the Distribution of Income," reprinted in ch. 13 of *AEA Readings in the Theory of International Trade*, Philadelphia, Blackiston, 1949.

Hegel, G. W. F. (1821), *Philosophy of Right*, trans. T. M. Knox, Oxford, Clarendon Press, 1962.

Helpman, E. and Krugman, P. (1985), *Market Structure and Foreign Trade*, Cambridge, Mass., MIT Press.

Helpman, E. and Laffont, Jean-Jacques (1975), "On Moral Hazard in General Equilibrium Theory," *Journal of Economic Theory*, 10, 8–23.

Henderson, J. V. (1974), "The Sizes and Types of Cities," *American Economic Review*, 64, 640–57.

Henderson, J. V. (1996), "Ways to Think about Urban Concentration: Neoclassical Urban Systems versus the New Economic Geography," *International Regional Science Review* 19(1–2), 31–6.

Henderson, J. V. and Quandt, R. (1980), *Microeconomic Theory: A Mathematical Approach*, New York, McGraw-Hill.

Herberg, H., Kemp, M., and Tawada, M. (1982), "Further Implications of Variable Returns to Scale in General Equilibrium Theory," *International Economic Review*, 9, 261–72.

Hicks, J. (1950), *A Contribution to the Theory of the Trade Cycle*, Oxford, Oxford University Press.

Hicks, J. R. (1969). *A Theory of Economic History*, Oxford, Clarendon Press

Hildenbrand, Werner (1974), *Core and Equilibria of a Large Economy*, Princeton, Princeton University Press.

Himmelblan, D. (1972), *Applied Nonlinear Programming*, New York, McGraw-Hill.

Hirschman, Albert (1958), *The Strategy of Economic Development*, New Haven, Yale University Press.

Hobbes, Thomas (1651), *Leviathan, or, The Matter, Forme, & Power of a Common-wealth Ecclesiasticall and Civill*, London, Printed for Andrew Crooke.

Hodrick, R. J. and Prescott, E. (1980), "Post-war US Business Cycles: An Empirical Investigation," working paper, Carnegie-Mellon University.

Holmstrom, B. and Milgrom, P. (1991), "Multitask Principal–Agent Analysis: Incentive Contracts, Asset Ownership, and Job Design," *Journal of Law, Economics, and Organization*, 7, 24–51.

Holmstrom, B. and Milgrom, P. (1995), "The Firm as an Incentive System," *American Economic Review*, 84, 972–91.

Holmstrom, B. and Roberts, J. (1998), "The Boundaries of the Firm Revisited," *Journal of Economic Perspectives*, 12, 73–94.

Houthakker, M. (1956), "Economics and Biology: Specialization and Speciation," *Kyklos*, 9, 181–9.

Hughes, Jonathan (1970), *Industrialization and Economic History*, New York, McGraw-Hill.

Hume, David (1748), *Essays Moreal and Political*, ed. Eugene Rotwein, London, Nelson, 1955.

Hummels, David, and Levinsohn, J. (1995), "Monopolitic Competition and International Trade: Reconsidering the Evidence," *Quarterly Journal of Economics*, 110, 799–836.

Hurwicz, L. (1973), "The Design of Mechanisms for Resource Allocation," *American Economic Review*, 63, 1–30.

Info Press (1999), *The Franchise Annual*, St. Catherines, Ont., Info Press.

International Franchise Association (1997), *Franchise Opportunities Guide*, Washington, DC, International Franchise Association.

Ippolito, Richard (1997), "The Division of Labor in the Firm," *Economic Inquiry*, 15, 469–92.

Jackson, M. and Wolinsky, A. (1996), "A Strategic Model of Social and Economic Networks," *Journal of Economics Theory*, 71, 44–74.

Jacobs, Jane (1969), *The Economy of Cities*, New York, Random House.

Jensen, M. and Meckling, W. (1976), "Theory of the Firm: Managerial Behaviour, Agency Costs, and Ownership Structure," *Journal of Financial Economics*, 3, 305–60.

Jevons, W. (1893), *Money and Mechanism of Exchange*, New York, D. Appleton.

Johnson, Harry G. (1954), "Optimum Tariff and Retaliation," *Review of Economic Studies*, 21(2), 142–53.

Jones, C. I. (1995a), "Time Series Tests of Endogenous Growth Models," *Quarterly Journal of Economics*, 110, 695–725.

Jones, C. I. (1995b), "R & D-Based Models of Economic Growth," *Journal of Political Economy*, 103, 759–84.

Jones, C. I. (1998), *Introduction to Economic Growth*, New York, W. W. Norton & Co.

Jones, Eric L. (1981), *The European Miracle: Environments, Economies and Geopolitics in the History of Europe and Asia*, Cambridge, Cambridge University Press.

Jones, R. (1965), "The Structure of Simple General Equilibrium Models," *Journal of Political Economy*, 73, 557–72.

Jones, R. (1976), "The Origin and Development of Media of Exchange," *Journal of Political Economy*, 84, 757–75.

Josephson, Matthew (1959), *Edison: a Biography*, New York, McGraw-Hill.

Judd, K. (1985), "On the Performance of Patents," *Econometrica*, 53, 579–85.

Kaldor, N. (1957), "A Model of Economic Growth," *Economic Journal*, 67, 591–624.

Kaldor, N. (1967), *Strategic Factors in Economic Development*, Ithaca, Cornell University Press.

Kamien, M. and Schwartz, N. (1981), *Dynamic Optimization: The Calculus of Variations and Optimal Control in Economics and Management*, New York, North Holland.

Kang, Youwei (1980), *Zouxiang Shijie Chuengshu*, Changsha, Hunan People's Press.

Kaplan, Steven, and Weisbach, Michael (1992), "The Success of Acquisitions: Evidence from Divestitures," *Journal of Finance*, 47, 107–38.

Karman, A. (1981), *Competitive Equilibria in Spatial Economics*, Cambridge, Oelgeshloger.

Karoly, L. and Klerman, J. (1994), "Using Regional Data to Reexamine the Contribution of Demographic and Sectoral Changes to Increasing US Wage Inequality," in J. Bergstrand et al. (eds.), *The Changing Distribution of Income in an Open US Economy*, Amsterdam, North-Holland.

Katz, M. and Shapiro, C. (1985), "Network Externalities, Competition, and Compatibility," *American Economic Review*, 75, 424–40.

Katz, M. and Shapiro, C. (1986), "Technology Adoption in the Presence of Network Externalities," *Journal of Political Economy*, 94, 822–41.

Kelley, A. and Williamson, J. (1984), *What Drives Third World City Growth?*, Princeton, Princeton University Press.

Kelly, Morgan (1997), "The Dynamics of Smithian Growth," *Quarterly Journal of Economics*, 112, 939–64.

Kemp, Murray (1991), "Variable Returns to Scale, Non-uniqueness of Equilibrium and the Gains from International Trade," *Review of Economic Studies*, 58, 807–16.

Kemp, Murray and Shimomura, Koji (1995a), "The Apparently Innocuous Representative Agent," *Japanese Economic Review*, 46, 247–56.

Kemp, Murray and Shimomura, Koji (1995b), "On Representative Agents: Reply to Kaneko and Suzumura," *Japanese Economic Review*, 46, 300.

Keren, M. and Levhari, D. (1979), "The Optimum Span of Control in a Pure Hierarchy," *Management Science*, 25, 1162–72.

Keren, M. and Levhari, D. (1982), "The Internal Organization of the Firm and the Shape of Average Costs," *Bell Journal of Economics*, 13, 474–86.

Keren, M. and Levhari, D. (1989), "Decentralization, Aggregation, Control Loss and Costs in a Hierarchical Model of the Firm," *Journal of Economic Behavior and Organization*, 11, 213–36.

Keynes, J. (1936), *The General Theory of Employment, Interest and Money*, London, Macmillan.

Khandker, A. and Rashid, S. (1995), "Wage Subsidy and Full Employment in a Dual Economy with Open Unemployment and Surplus Labor," *Journal of Development Economics*, 48, 205–23.

Kihlstrom, Richard and Laffont, Jean-Jacques (1979), "A General Equilibrium Entrepreneurial Theory of Firm Formation Based on Risk Aversion," *Journal of Political Economy*, 87.

Kim, S. (1989), "Labor Specialization and the Extent of the Market," *Journal of Political Economy*, 97, 692–705.

King, R. and Plosser, C. (1984), "Money, Credit, and Prices in a Real Business Cycle," *American Economic Review*, 74, 363–80.

King, R. and Plosser, C. (1986), "Money as the Mechanism of Exchange," *Journal of Monetary Economics*, 17, 93–115.

King, R. and Levine, R. (1994), "Capital Fundamentalism, Economic Development, and Economic Growth." *Carnegie–Rochester Conference Series on Public Policy*, 40, 259–92.

King, R. and Rebelo, S. T. (1993), "Low Frequency Filtering and Real Business Cycles," *Journal of Economic Dynamics and Control*, 17(1), 207–31.

King, Stephan P. (1995), "Search with Free-riders," *Journal of Economic Behavior & Organization*, 26, 253–71.

Kirzner, Israel (1997), "Entrepreneurial Discovery and the Competitive Market Process: An Austrian Approach," *Journal of Economic Literature*, 35, 60–85.

Kiyotaki, N. and Wright, R. (1989), "On Money as a Medium of Exchange," *Journal of Political Economy*, 97, 927–54.

Kiyotaki, N. and Wright, R. (1993), "A Search-Theoretic Approach to Monetary Economics," *American Economic Review*, 83, 63–77.

Knight, F. (1921). *Risk, Uncertainty and Profit*. Chicago: Hart, Shaffner and Marx.

Knight, F. (1925), "Decreasing Cost and Comparative Cost: A Rejoinder," *Quarterly Journal of Economics*, 39, 332–3.

Kohli, Ulrich and Werner, Augustin (1998), "Accounting for South Korean GDP Growth: Index-number and Econometric Estimates," *Pacific Economic Review*, 3, 133–52.

Kormendi, R. C. and Meguire, P. G. (1985), "Macroeconomic Determinants of Growth: Cross-Country Evidence," *Journal of Monetary Economics*, 16, 141–63.

Kornai, J. (1980), *Economics of Shortage*, Amsterdam, North-Holland.

Kornai, J. (1991), *The Road to a Free Economy*, New York, Norton.

Kornai, J. (1992), *The Socialist System: The Political Economy of Communism*, Princeton, Princeton University Press.

Kravis, I., Heston, A., and Summers, R. (1978), "Real GDP per Capita for More Than One Hundred Countries," *Economic Journal*, 88, 215–92.

Kravis, I. and Lipsey, Robert (1981), "Prices and Terms of Trade for Developed Country Exports of Manufactured Goods," *National Bureau of Economic Research Working Paper* no. 774, Washington, DC.

Kremer, Michael (1993a), "Population Growth and Technological Change: One Million BC to 1990," *Quarterly Journal of Economics*, 108(3), 681–716.

Kremer, Michael (1993b), "The O-ring Theory of Economic Development," *Quarterly Journal of Economics*, 108, 551–75.

Kreps, D. (1990), *A Course in Microeconomic Theory*, Princeton, Princeton University Press.

Kreps, D. and Wilson, R. (1982), "Sequential Equilibria," *Econometrica*, 50, 863–94.

Krueger, A. (1974), "The Political Economy of Rent-seeking Society," *American Economic Review*, 64, 291–303.

Krueger, A. (1997), "Trade Policy and Economic Development: How We Learn," *American Economic Review*, 87, 1–22.

Krugman, P. (1979), "Increasing Returns, Monopolistic Competition, and International Trade," *Journal of International Economics*, 9, 469–79.

Krugman, P. (1980), "Scale Economies, Product Differentiation, and the Pattern of Trade," *American Economic Review*, 70, 950–9.

Krugman, P. (1981), "Intra-industry Specialization and the Gains from Trade," *Journal of Political Economy*, 89, 959–73.

Krugman, P. (1991), "Economics of Geography," *Journal of Political Economy*, 99, 483–502.

Krugman, P. (1992), "Toward a Counter-Counter Revolution in Development Theory," *World Bank Observer*, Supplement, 15.61.

Krugman, P. (1994a), "Europe Jobless, America Penniless?," *Foreign Policy*, 95, 19–34.

Krugman, P. (1994b), "Competitiveness: A Dangerous Obsession," *Foreign Affairs*, 73(2), 28–44.

Krugman, P. (1995), *Development, Geography, and Economic Theory*, Cambridge, Mass., MIT Press.

Krugman,P. and Venables, A. J. (1995), "Globalization and the Inequality of Nations," *Quarterly Journal of Economics*, 110, 857–80.

Krugman, P. and Venables, A. J. (1996), "Integration, Specialization, and Adjustment," *European Economic Review*, 40, 959–67.

Kubo, Y. (1985), "A Cross-country Comparison of Interindustry Linkages and the Role of Imported Intermediate Inputs," *World Development*, 13, 1287–98.

Kurz, M. (1974), "Arrow–Debreu Equilibrium of an Exchange Economy with Transaction Costs," *Econometrica*, 42, 45–54.

Kuznets, S. (1955), "Economic Growth and Income Inequality," *American Economic Review*, March. (Inverted-U hypothesis of inequality.)

Kuznets, S. (1966), *Modern Economic Growth*, New Haven, Yale University Press.

Kydland, F. and Prescott, E. (1982), "Time to Build and Aggregate Fluctuations," *Econometrica*, 50, 1345–70.

Laffont, J.-J. (1990), "Analysis of Hidden Gaming in a Three Level Hierarchy," *Journal of Law and Economic Organization*, 6, 301–24.

Laffont, J.-J. and Tirole, J. (1986), "Using Cost Observation to Regulate Firms," *Journal of Political Economy*, 94, 614–41.

Laffont, J.-J. and Tirole, J. (1993), *A Theory of Incentives in Procurement and Regulation*, Cambridge, Mass., MIT Press.

Lancaster, K. (1980), "Intraindustry Trade under Perfect Monopolistic Competition," *Journal of International Economics*, 10, 151–76.

Landes, David (1998), *The Wealth and Poverty of Nations*, New York, W. W. Norton.

Lang, Larry, and Stulz, Rene (1994), "Tobin's Q, Corporate Diversification and Firm Performance," *Journal of Political Economics*, 102, 1248–80.

Lange, O. (1970), *Introduction to Economic Cybernetics*, Oxford, Pergamon Press.

Lange, O. and Taylor, F. (1964), *On the Economic Theory of Socialism*, New York, McGraw Hill.

Langlois, R. N. (1988). "Economic Change and the Boundaries of the Firm," *Journal of Institutional and Theoretical Economics*, 144, 635–57.

Laslett, Peter (1988), "The European Family and Early Industrialization," in Baechler, Hall, and Mann (eds.), *Europe and the Rise of Capitalism*, Cambridge, Blackwell.

Leamer, Edward E. (1984), *Sources of International Comparative Advantage: Theory and Evidence*, Cambridge, Mass., MIT Press.

Legros, Patrick and Newman, Andrew (1996), "Wealth Effects, Distribution, and the Theory of Organization," *Journal of Economic Theory*, 70, 312–41

Lenand, H. 1968, "Saving and Uncertainty: The Precautionary Demand for Saving," *Quarterly Journal of Economics*, 82, 465–73.

Lenin, V. (1939), *Imperialism, the Highest Stage of Capitalism*, New York, International Publishers.

Leontief, Wassily W. (1956), "Domestic Production and Foreign Trade: The American Capital Position Re-examined," in *Readings in International Economics*, eds. Richard E. Caves and Harry G. Johnson, Homewood, Irwin, 1968.

Lerner, A. P. (1952), "Factor Prices and International Trade," *Economica*, 19(1), 1–15.

Lewis, T. and Sappington, D. (1991), "Technological Change and the Boundaries of the Firm," *American Economic Review*, 81, 887–900.

Lewis, W. (1955), *The Theory of Economic Growth*, London, Allen and Unwin.

Li, Hongyi and Zou, Heng-fu (1998), "Income Inequality is not Harmful for Growth: Theory and Evidence," *Review of Development Economics*, 2, 318–34.

Liebowitz, S. J. and Margolis, Stephen E. (1994), "Network Externality: An Uncommon Tragedy," *Journal of Economic Perspectives*, 8, 133–50.

Lilien, D. (1982), "Sectoral Shifts and Cyclical Unemployment," *Journal of Political Economy*, 90, 777–93.

Lin, J. Y. and Yang, D. (1998), "On the Causes of China's Agricultural Crisis and the Great Leap Famine," *China Economic Review*, 9, 125–40.

Lio, M. (1996), *Three Assays on Increasing Returns and Specialization: A Contribution to the New Classical Microeconomic Approach*, Ph.D. dissertation, Department of Economics, the National Taiwan University.

Lio, M. (1998a), "Uncertainty, Insurance, and Division of Labor," *Review of Development Economics*, 2, 76–86.

Lio, M. (1998b), "The Inframarginal Analysis of Demand and Supply and the Relationship between a Minimum Level of Consumption and the Division of Labor," in K. Arrow, Y.-K. Ng, and Xiaokai Yang (eds.), *Increasing Returns and Economic Analysis*, London, Macmillan.

Lippman, Steven A. and McCall, John J. (1979), "The Economics of Job Search – A Survey," *Economic Inquiry*, 14, 155–89.

Lipton, M. (1977), *Why Poor People Stay Poor*, Cambridge, Mass., Harvard University Press.

Lipton, M. (1984), "Urban Bias Revisited," *Journal of Development Studies*, 20, 139–66.

Liu, Meng-Chun (1999), "Two Approaches to International Trade, Development and Import Protection," Ph.D. dissertation, Department of Economics, Monash University.

Liu, Pak-Wai and Yang, Xiaokai (2000), "The Theory of Irrelevance of the Size of the Firm," *Journal of Economic Behavior and Organization*, 42, 145–65.

Locay, L. (1990), "Economic Development and the Division of Production between Households and Markets," *Journal of Political Economy*, 98, 965–82.

Long, J., Jr. and Plosser, C. (1983), "Real Business Cycles," *Journal of Political Economy*, 91, 39–69.

Loveman, G. and Sengenberger, W. (1991), "The Re-emergence of Small-Scale Production: An International Comparison," *Small Business Economics*, 3, 1–38.

Lucas, R. E., Jr. (1972), "Expectations and the Neutrality of Money," *Journal of Economic Theory*, 4, 103–24.

Lucas, R. E., Jr. (1973), "International Evidence on Output–Inflation Tradeoffs," *American Economic Review*, 63, 326–34.

Lucas, R. E., Jr. (1976), "Econometric Policy Evaluation: A Critique," *Journal of Monetary Economics.*, Suppl. Series, 1, 19–46, 62.

Lucas, R. E., Jr. (1980), "Equilibrium in a Pure Currency Economy," in J. Karenken and N. Wallace (eds.), *Models of Monetary Economics*, Minneapolis, Federal Reserve Bank of Minneapolis.

Lucas, R. E., Jr. (1988), "On the Mechanics of Economic Development," *Journal of Monetary Economics*, 22, 3–42.

Lucas, R. E., Jr. (1993), "Making a Miracle," *Econometrica*, 61, 251–72.

MacFarlane, Alan (1988), "The Cradle of Capitalism: The Case of England," in Baechler, Hall, and Mann (eds.), *Europe and the Rise of Capitalism*, Cambridge, Mass., Blackwell.

MacLeod, W. and Malcomson, J. (1988), "Reputation and Hierarchy in Dynamic Models of Employment," *Journal of Political Economy*, 96, 832–81.

Madison, A. (1991), *Dynamic Forces in Capitalist Development: A Long Run View*, New York, Oxford University Press.

Mailath, George J. (1998), "Do People Play Nash Equilibrium? Lessons from Evolutionary Game Theory," *Journal of Economic Literature*, 36, 1347–74.

Mankiw, N. G. (1985), "Small Menu Costs and Large Business Cycles: A Macroeconomic Model," *Quarterly Journal of Economics*, May, 100(2), 529–38.

Mankiw, N. G., Romer, D., and Weil, D. N. (1992), "A Contribution to the Empirics of Economic Growth," *Quarterly Journal of Economics*, 107, 407–37.

Manne, H. (ed.) (1975), *The Economics of Legal Relationships*, St. Paul, West Publishing Company.

Mantel, R. (1974), "On the Characterization of Aggregate Excess Demand," *Journal of Economic Theory*, 7, 348–53.

Marcouiller, D. and Young, L. (1995), "The Black Hole of Graft: The Predatory State and the Informal Economy," *American Economic Review*, 85, 630–46.

Markusen, J. (1986), "Explaining the Volume of Trade: An Eclectic Approach," *American Economic Review*, 5, 1002–11.

Marshall, Alfred (1890), *Principles of Economics*, 8th edn., New York, Macmillan, 1948.

Marx, Karl (1867), *Capital, a Critique of Political Economy, Vols I–III*, New York, International Publishers, 1967.

Mas-Collell, A., Whinston, M., and Green, J. (1995), *Microeconomic Theory*, New York, Oxford University Press.

Maskin, Eric (forthcoming), "Recent Theoretical Work on the Soft Budget Constraint," *American Economic Review, Papers and Proceedings*.

Maskin, Eric and Tirole, Jean (1997), "Unforeseen Contingencies, Property Rights, and Incomplete Contracts," Harvard Institute of Economic Research Discussion Paper no. 1796, Harvard University.

Maskin, Eric and Xu, Chenggang (1999), "Soft Budget Constraint Theories: From Centralization to the Market," Working Paper, Department of Economics, Harvard University.

Maxwell, Henry (1721), *Reasons Offered for Erecting a Bank in Ireland*, 2nd edn., Dublin.

Mayer, Wolfgang (1981), "Theoretical Considerations on Negotiated Tariff Adjustments," *Oxford Economic Papers*, 33, 135–53

Mayer, Wolfgang (1984), "Endogenous Tariff Formation," *American Economic Review*, 74, 970–85.

McGuirk, A. M. and Mundlak, Y. (1992). "The Transition of Punjab Agriculture: A Choice of Technique Approach," *American Journal of Agricultural Economics*, 74 (Feb.), 132–43.

McKenzie, L. W. (1955), "Equality of Factor Prices in World Trade," *Econometrica*, 23(3), 239–57.

McNeil, W. (1974), *The Shape of European History*, Oxford, Oxford University Press.

Meek, R. and Skinner, A. (1973), "The Development of Adam Smith's Ideas on the Division of Labor," *Economic Journal*, 83, 1094–116.

Meier, G. (1995), *Leading Issues in Economic Development*, New York, Oxford University Press.

Menger, Carl (1871), *Principles of Economics*, trans. James Dingwall and Bert F. Hoselitz, New York, New York University Press.

Milgrom, P. (1987), "Auction Theory," in T. Bewley, (ed.), *Advances in Economic Theory*, Cambridge, Cambridge University Press, 1–31.

Milgrom, P. and Roberts, J. (1982), "Limit Pricing and Entry under Incomplete Information," *Econometrica*, 40, 433–59.

Milgrom, P. and Roberts, J. (1990), "Bargaining, Influence Costs, and the Organization of Economic Activity," in J. Alt and K. Shepsle (eds.), *Perspectives on Positive Political Economy*, Cambridge, Cambridge University Press, 57–89.

Milgrom, P. and Roberts, J. (1992), *Economics, Organization and Management*, Englewood Cliffs, NJ, Prentice-Hall.

Milgrom, P. and Roberts, J. (1994), "The Economics of Modern Manufacturing: Technology, Strategy and Organization," *American Economic Review*, 80, 511–28.

Mill, John Stuart (1848), *Principles of Political Economy*, Harmondsworth, Penguin, 1970.

Mills, E. (1967), "An Aggregative Model of Resource Allocation in a Metropolitan Area," *American Economic Review*, 57, 197–210.

Mills, E. and Hamilton, B. (1984), *Urban Economics*, Glenview, Ill., Scott, Foresman and Co.

Modigliani, Franco (1989), *The Collected Papers of Franco Modigliani*, vol. 5, *Saving, Deficits, Inflation, and Financial Theory*, ed. Simon Johnson, Cambridge, Mass. and London, MIT Press.

Mokyr, Joel (1990), *The Lever of Richs: Technological Creativity and Economic Progress*, New York, Oxford University Press.

Mokyr, Joel (ed.) (1993), *The British Industrial Revolution: An Economic Perspective*, Boulder, Colo., Westview Press.

Mokyr, Joel, (1993), "The New Economic History and the Industrial Revolution," in Mokyr, J. ed. *The British Industrial Revolution: An Economic Perspective*, Boulder, Colo., Westview Press.

Monteverde, K. and Teece, D. J. (1982), "Supplier Switching Costs and Vertical Integration in the Automobile Industry," *Bell Journal of Economics*, 13, 206–13.

Morgan, Peter and Manning, Richard (1985), "Optimal Search," *Econometrica*, 53, 923–44.

Morgan, T. (1970), "Trends in Terms of Trade, and Their Repercussion on Primary Products," in T. Morgan and G. Betz (eds.), *Economic Development Readings in Theory and Practice*, Belmont, Wadsworth.

Morris, C. and Adelman, I. (1988), *Comparative Patterns of Economic Development, 1850–1914*, Johns Hopkins Studies in Development Series, Baltimore and London, Johns Hopkins University Press.

Murakami, N., Liu, D., and Otsuka, K. (1996), "Market Reform, Division of Labor, and Increasing Advantage of Small-scale Enterprises: The Case of the Machine Tool Industry in China," *Journal of Comparative Economics*, 23, 256–77.

Murphy, K., Shleifer, A., and Vishny, R. (1989a), "Industrialization and the Big Push," *Journal of Political Economy*, 97, 1003–26.

Murphy, K., Shleifer, A., and Vishny, R. (1989b), "Income Distribution, Market Size, and Industrialization," *The Quarterly Journal of Economics*, 104, 537–64.

Murphy, K., Shleifer, A., and Vishny, R. (1991), "The Allocation of Talent: Implications for Growth," *Quarterly Journal of Economics*, 106, 503–30.

Murphy, K. and Topel, R. (1987), "The Evolution of Unemployment in the United States, 1968–1985," *NBER Macroeconomics Annual*, 2, 11–58.

Murphy, K. and Welch, F. (1991), "The Role of International Trade in Wage Differentials," in *Workers and Their Wages: Changing Patterns in the United States*, ed. M. Kosters, Washington, American Enterprise Institute.

Myrdal, G. (1957), *Economic Theory and the Underdeveloped Regions*, London, Duckworth.

Naisbitt, John (1990), *Megatrends 2000: The New Directions for the 1990s*, New York, Morrow.

Nash, J. F. (1950), "The Bargaining Problem," *Econometrica*, 18, 115–62.

Nath, S. K. (1962), The Theory of Balanced Growth," *Oxford Economic Papers*, 14(2), 138–53.

National Research Council (1986), *Population Growth and Economic Development: Policy Questions*, Washington, DC, National Academy of Sciences Press.

Nelson, R. (1956), "A Theory of the Low Level of Equilibrium Trap in Under-developed Economies," *American Economic Review*, 46, 894–908.

Nelson, R. (1995), "Recent Evolutionary Theorizing About Economic Change," *Journal of Economics Literature*, 33, 48–90.

Ng, S. (1995), *Economic Openness and Growth*, Ph.D. dissertation, Department of Economics, Monash University.

Ng, Y.-K. (1986), *Mesoeconomics, a Micro–macro Analysis*, New York, Harvester Wheatsheaf.

Ng, Y.-K. (1992), "Business Confidence and Depression Prevention: A Mesoeconomic Perspective," *American Economic Review*, 82, 365–71.

Ng, Y.-K. and Yang, X. (1997), "Specialization, Information, and Growth: A Sequential Equilibrium Analysis," *Review of Development Economics*, 1, 257–74.

Ng, Y.-K. and Yang, X. (2000), "Effects of Externality-corrective Taxation on the Extent of the Market and Network Size of Division of Labor," Seminar Paper, Department of Economics, Monash University.

Nicholson, J. S. (1893), *Principles of Political Economy*, London, A&C Black, 1902.

North, D. (1958), "Ocean Freight Rates and Economic Development," *Journal of Economic History*, 18, 537–55.

North, Douglas (ed.) (1981a), *Structure and Change in Economic History*, New York, Norton.

North, Douglas (1981b), "The Industrial Revolution Reconsidered," in D. North (ed.), *Structure and Change in Economic History*, New York, Norton.

North, Douglas (1986), "Measuring the Transaction Sector in the American Economy," in S. Eugerman and R. Gallman (eds.), *Long Term Trends in the American Economy*, Chicago, University of Chicago Press.

North, Douglas (1987), "Institutions, Transaction Costs and Economic Growth," *Economic Inquiry*, 25, 419–28.

North, Douglas (1990), *Institutions, Institutional Change and Economic Performance*, New York, Cambridge University Press.

North, Douglas (1994), "Economic Performance through Time," *American Economic Review*, 84, 359–68.

North, Douglas and Thomas, R. (1970), "An Economic Theory of the Growth of the West World," *The Economic Review*, 23, 1–17.

North, Douglas and Weingast, Barry (1989), "Constitutions and Commitment: The Evolution of Institutions Governing Public Choice in Seventeenth-Century England," *Journal of Economic History*, 49, 803–32.

Nurkse, R. (1953), *Problems of Capital Formation in Underdeveloped Countries*, New York, Oxford University Press.

Oh, S. (1989), "A Theory of a Generally Acceptable Medium of Exchange and Barter," *Journal of Monetary Economics*, 23, 101–19.

Ohlin, B. (1933), *Interregional and International Trade*, Cambridge, Mass., Harvard University Press.

Olsen, Mancur (1996), "Distinguished Lecture on Economics in Government: Big Bills Left on the Sidewalk: Why Some Nations are Rich and others Poor," *Journal of Economic Perspectives*, 10, 3–24.

Osborne, M. and Rubinstein, A. (1990), *Bargaining and Markets*, San Diego, Academic Press.

Osborne, M. and Rubinstein, A. (1994), *A Course in Game Theory*, Cambridge, Mass., MIT Press.

Ostroy, J. (1973), "The Informational Efficiency of Monetary Exchange," *American Economic Review*, 63, 597–610.

Ostroy, J. and Starr, R. (1990), "The Transactions Role of Money," in B. Friedman and F. Hahn (eds.), *Handbook of Monetary Economics*, vol. 1, Amsterdam, North Holland.

Page, Scott E. (1999), "On the Emergence of Cities," *Journal of Urban Economics*, 45, 184–208.

Palma, Babriel (1978), "Dependency: A Formal Theory of Underdevelopment or a Methodology for the Analysis of Concrete Situations of Underdevelopment?," *World Development*, 6, 899–902.

Patten, R. H. and Rosengard, J. K. (1991), *Progress with Profits: The Development of Rural Banking in Indonesia*, San Francisco, ICS Press.

Parkin, M. (1986), "The Output–Inflation Tradeoff when Prices are Costly to Change," *Journal of Political Economy*, 94, 200–24.

Petty, William (1671), *Political Arithmetics*, in C. H. Hull (ed.), *Economic Writings of Sir William Petty*, New York, Augustus M. Kelly, 1963.

Petty, William (1683), *Another Essay on Political Arithmetics*, in C. H. Hull (ed.), *Economic Writings of Sir William Petty*, New York, Augustus M. Kelly, 1963.

Pigou, A. C. (1940), *War Finance and Inflation*, in Larry Neal (ed.), *Elgar Reference Collection, International Library of Macroeconomic and Financial History* series, vol. 12, Aldershot, UK, Elgar.

Pincus, Jonathan J. (1975), "Pressure Groups and the Pattern of Tariffs," *Journal of Political Economy*, 83, 757–78.

Plato (380 BC) (1955), *The Republic*, trans. H. D. P. Lee, Harmondsworth, Penguin Classics.

Prescott, E. (1986), "Theory Ahead of Business Cycle Measurement," *Federal Reserve Bank of Minneapolis Quarterly Review*, 10, 9–22.

Prestowitz, Clyde V., Jr et al. (1994), "The Fight over Competitiveness," *Foreign Affairs*, 73(4), 186–97.

Pritchett, L. (1997), "Divergence, Big Time," *Journal of Economic Perspectives*, 11(3).

Puga, Diego and Venables, Anthony (1998), "Agglomeration and Economic Development: Import Substitution vs. Trade Liberalisation," Centre for Economic Performance Discussion Paper no. 377, London School of Economics.

Qian, Y. (1994a), "Incentives and Loss of Control in an Optimal Hierarchy," *Review of Economic Studies*, 61(3), 527–44.

Qian, Y. (1994b), "A Theory of Shortage in Socialist Economies based on the 'Soft Budget Constraint,'" *American Economic Review*, 84, 145–56.

Quah, D. (1993), "Galton's Fallacy and Tests of The Convergence Hypothesis," *Scandinavian Journal of Economics*, 95(4), 427–43.

Quah, D. (1996), "Twin Peaks: Growth and Convergence in Models of Distribution Dynamics," *Economic Journal*, 100, 1045–55.

Quigley, John M. (1998), "Urban Diversity and Eonomic Growth," *Journal of Economic Perspectives*, 2(2), 127–38.

Rabushka, A. (1987), *The New China: Comparative Economic Development in Mainland China, Taiwan, and Hong Kong*, Boulder, Colo., Westview Press.

Radelet, Steven and Sachs, J. (1998), "The Onset of the East Asian Financial Crisis," Paper presented in the National Bureau of Economic Research Currency Crisis Conference, Boston.

Radner, R. (1992), "Hierarchy: The Economics of Managing," *Journal of Economic Literature*, 30, 1382–1415.

Radner, R. (1993), "The Organization of Decentralized Information Processing ," *Econometrica*, 61, 1109–46.

Rae, J. (1834), *Statement of Some New Principles on the Subject of Political Economy*, New York, Augustus M. Kelly, 1964.

Ram, Rati (1997), "Level of Economic Development and Income Inequality: Evidence from the Postwar Developed World," *Southern Economic Journal*, 64, 576–83.

Ramey, G. and Ramey, V. (1995), "Cross-Country Evidence on the Link between Volatility and Growth," *American Economic Review*, 85, 1138–51.

Ramsey, F. (1928), "A Mathematical Theory of Saving," *Economic Journal*, 38, 543–59.

Ranis, G. (1988), "Analytics of Development: Dualism," in *Handbook of Development Economics*, eds. H. Chenery and T. Srinivasan, vol. 1, pp. 74–92.

Rashid, Salim (1986), "Adam Smith and the Division of Labor: A Historical View," *Scottish Journal of Political Economy*, 33, 292–7.

Rebelo, S. (1991), "Long Run Policy Analysis and Long Run Growth," *Journal of Political Economy*, 99, 500–21.

Reingnum, Jennifer F. (1982), "Strategic Search Theory," *International Economics Review*, 23, 1–17.

Reynolds, L. (ed.) (1975), *Agriculture in Development Theory*, New Haven, Yale University Press.

Reynolds, L. (1983), "The Spread of Economic Growth to the Third World: 1850–1980," *Journal of Economic Literature*, 21 (Sept.), 956–8.

Reynolds, L. (1985), *Economic Growth in the Third World, 1850–1980*, New Haven, Yale University Press.

Ricardo, D. (1817), *The Principle of Political Economy and Taxation*, London, Gaernsey Press, 1973.

Riezman, Raymond (1982), "Tariff Retaliation from a Strategic Viewpoint," *Southern Economic Journal*, 48, 583–93.

Riskin, Carl (1987), *China's Political Economy: The Quest for Development Since 1949*, Studies of the East Asian Institute of Columbia University, Oxford, Oxford University Press.

Roberts, F. (ed.) (1989), *Applications of Combinatorics and Graph Theory to the Biological and Social Sciences*, New York, Springer-Verlag.

Rodríguez-Clare, A. (1996). "The Division of Labor and Economic Development." *Journal of Development Economics*, 49, 3–32.

Roland, Gerard (2000), *Politics, Markets and Firms: Transition and Economics*, Cambridge, Mass., MIT Press.

Romano, R. E. (1994), "Double Moral Hazard and Resale Price Maintenance," *Rand Journal of Economics*, 25, 455–66.

Romer, P. (1986), "Increasing Returns and Long Run Growth," *Journal of Political Economy*, 94, 1002–37.

Romer, P. (1987), "Growth Based on Inreasing Returns Due to Specialization," *American Economic Review, Papers and Proceedings*, 77, 56–72.

Romer, P. (1990), "Endogenous Technological Change," *Journal of Political Economy*, 98, S71–S102.

Romer, P. (1993), "The Origins of Endogenous Growth," *Journal of Economic Perspectives*, 8, 3–22.

Rosen, S. (1978), "Substitution and the Division of Labor," *Economica*, 45, 235–50.

Rosen, S. (1982), "Authority, Control, and the Distribution of Earnings," *Bell Journal of Economics*, 13, 311–23.

Rosen, S. (1983), "Specialization and Human Capital," *Journal of Labor Economics*, 1, 43–9.

Rosenberg, N. and Birdzell, L. E. (1986), *How the West Grew Rich: Economic Transformation of the Industrial World*, New York, Basic Books.

Rosenstein-Rodan, Paul (1943), "Problem of Industrialization of Eastern and South-Eastern Europe," *Economic Journal*, 53, 202–11

Rostow, W. W. (1960), *The Stages of Economic Growth: A Non-Communist Manifesto*, Cambridge, Cambridge University Press.

Rotemberg, Julio, (1987), "The New Keynesian Micro Foundations," in Stanley Fischer (ed.), *NBER Macroeconomics Annual, 1987*, Cambridge, Mass., MIT Press.

Roumasset, J and Smith, J. (1981), "Population, Technological Change, and the Evolution of Labor Markets," *Population and Development Review*, 7, 401–19.

Rouvray, D., ed. (1990), *Computational Chemical Graph Theory*, New York, Nova Science Publishers.

Rubinstein, A. (1982), "Perfect Equilibrium in a Bargaining Model," *Econometrica*, 50, 97–108.

Rubinstein, A. (1985), "A Bargaining Model with Incomplete Information," *Econometrica* 53, 1151–72.

Rubinstein, A. and Wolinsky, A. (1985), "Equilibrium in a Market with Sequential Bargaining," *Econometrica*, 53, 1133–50.

Ruskin, J. (1851–3), *The Stones of Venice*, in E. T. Cook and A. Wedderburn (eds.), *The Complete Works of John Ruskin*, London, George Allen, 1904.

Rybczynski, T. M. (1955), "Factor Endowments and Relative Commodity Prices," *Economica*, 22, 336–41.

Sachs, J. (1993), *Poland's Jump to the Market Economy*, Cambridge, Mass., MIT Press.

Sachs, J. (1996a), "The Tankers Are Turning – Sachs on Competitiveness," *World Link*, Sept./Oct.

Sachs, J. (1996b), "On the Tigers Trail, – Sachs on Competitiveness," *World Link*, Nov./Dec.

Sachs, J. (1996c), "Notes on the Life Cycle of State-led Industrialization," *Japan and the World Economy*, 8, 153–74.

Sachs, J. and Shartz, H. (1994), "Trade and Jobs in US Manufactures," *Brookings Papers on Activity*, no. 1, 1–84.

Sachs, J. and Warner, A. (1995), "Economic Reform and the Process of Global Integration," *Brookings Papers on Economic Activity*, 1, Washington, DC.

Sachs, J. and Warner, A. (1997), "Fundamental Sources of Long-Run Growth," *American Economic Review, Papers and Proceedings*, 87, 184–8.

Sachs, J. and Warner, A. (1999), "Natural Resource Abundance and Economic Growth," *Harvard Institute for International Development Discussion Paper* 544.

Sachs, J. and Woo, W. T. (1994), "Understanding the Reform Experiences of China, Eastern Europe and Russia," *Journal of Comparative Economics*, 18(3), June.

Sachs, J., Woo, W., and Parker, S. (1997), *Economies in Transition: Comparing Asia and Europe*, Cambridge, Mass., MIT Press.

Sachs, J. and Yang, X. (1999), "Gradual Spread of Market-Led Industrialization," Harvard Center for International Development Working Paper no. 11.

Sachs, J., Yang, X., and Zhang, D. (1999a), "Trade Pattern and Economic Development when Endogenous and Exogenous Comparative Advantages Coexist," Harvard Center for International Development Working Paper no. 3.

Sachs, J., Yang, X., and Zhang, D. (1999b), "Patterns of Trade and Economic Development in the Model of Monopolistic Competition," Harvard Center for International Development Working Paper no. 14

Sah, R. (1991), "Fallibility in Human Organizations and Political Systems," *Journal of Economic Perspectives*, 5, 67–88.

Sah, R. and Stiglitz, J. (1984), "The Economics of Price Scissors," *American Economic Review*, 74, 125–38.

Sah, R. and Stiglitz, J. (1986), "The Architecture of Economic Systems," *American Economic Review*, 76, 716–27.

Sah, R. and Stiglitz, J. (1988), "Committees, Hierarchies and Polyarchies," *The Economic Journal*, 98, 451–70.

Sah, R. and Stiglitz, J. (1991), "The Quality of Managers in Centralized versus Decentralized Organizations," *Quarterly Journal of Economics*, 106, 289–95.

Sala-i-Martin, X. (1996), "The Classical Approach to Convergence Analysis," *Economic Journal*, 106, 1019–36.

Samuelson, P. A. (1939), "Interactions Between the Multiplier Analysis and the Principle of Acceleration," *Review of Economic Statistics*, 21, 75–8.

Samuelson, P. A. (1947), *Foundations of Economic Analysis*, Cambridge, Mass., Harvard University Press.

Samuelson, P.A. (1948), "International Trade and the Equalisation of Factor Prices," *Economic Journal*, 58(230), 163–84.

Samuelson, P. A. (1955), *Economics*, New York, McGraw-Hill.

Sapsford, D. (1985), "The Statistical Debate on the Net Barter Terms of Trade Between Primary Commodities and Manufactures," *Economic Journal*, 95, 781–8.

Sargent, T. and Wallace, N. (1975), "'Rational Expectations,' the Optimal Monetary Instrument, and the Optimal Money Supply Rule," *Journal of Political of Economy*, 83, 241–54.

Say, J. (1803), *A Treatise on Political Economy*, New York, Sentry Press, 1964.

Schiller, F. (1793), *On the Aesthetic Education of Man*, trans. R. Snell, New York, Ungar, 1980.

Schultz, T. (1993), *Origins of Increasing Returns*, Cambridge, Mass., Blackwell.

Schumpeter, J. (1939), *Business Cycles*, New York, McGraw-Hill.

Schumpeter, J. (1942), *Capitalism, Socialism, and Democracy*, New York, Harper & Row.

Schweizer, U. (1986), "General Equilibrium in Space," in J. J. Gabszewicz et. al (eds.), *Location Theory*, London, Harwood.

Scitovsky, T. (1954), "Two Concepts of External Economies," *Journal of Political Economy*, 62, 143–51.

Scott, A.J. (1988), *Metropolis: From the Division of Labor to Urban Form*, Berkeley, University of California Press.

Segerstrom, P. (1998), "Endogenous Growth without Scale Effects," *American Economic Review*, 88, 1290–1310.

Segerstrom, P., Anant, T., and Dinopoulos, E. (1990), "A Schumpeterian Model of the Product Life Cycle," *American Economic Review*, 80, 1077–91.

Seierstad, A. and Sydsater, K. (1987), *Optimal Control Theory with Economic Applications*, Amsterdam, North-Holland.

Selten, R. (1975), "Reexamination of the Perfectness Concept for Equilibrium Points in Extensive Games," *International Journal of Game Theory*, 3–4, 25–55.

Sen, Amartya K. (1977), "Starvation and Exchange Entitlements: A General Approach and Its Application to the Great Bengal Famine," *Cambridge Journal of Economics*, 2, 33–59.

Sen, Partha (1998), "Terms of Trade and Welfare for a Developing Economy with an Imperfectly Competitive Sector," *Review of Development Economics*, 2, 87–93.

Senior, N. (1836), *An Outline of the Science of Political Economy*, rept., London, Allen & Unwin, 1938, 1951.

Servaes, Henri (1996), "The Value of Diversification During the Conglomerate," *Journal of Finance*, 51, 1201–25.

Shapiro, C. and Stiglitz, J. (1984), "Equilibrium Unemployment as a Worker Discipline Device," *American Economic Review*, 74, 433–44.

Shi, H. (1994), "Implications of Imperfect Competition and Specialization on Business Cycles and Economic Structure," Ph.D. dissertation, Department of Economics, Monash University.

Shi, H. and Yang, X. (1995), "A New Theory of Industrialization," *Journal of Comparative Economics*, 20, 171–89.

Shi, H. and Yang, X. (1998), "Centralised Hierarchy within a Firm vs. Decentralised Hierarchy in the Market ," in K. Arrow, Y.-K. Ng, and X. Yang (eds.), *Increasing Returns and Economic Analysis*, London, Macmillan.

Shleifer, A. (1986), "Implementation Cycles," *Journal of Political Economy*, 94, 1163–90.

Shooman, Martin (1968), *Probabilistic Reliability: An Engineering Approach*, New York, McGraw-Hill.

Simon, Curtis and Nardinelli, Clark (1996), "The Talk of the Town: Human Capital, Information, and the Growth of English Cities, 1861–1961," *Explorations of Economic History*, 33, 384–413.

Singh, Nirvikar (1989), "Theories of Sharecropping," in Pranab Bardhan (ed.), *The Economic Theory of Agrarian Institutions*, Oxford, Clarendon Press.

Skaperdas, S. (1992), "Cooperation, Conflict, and Power in the Absence of Property Rights," *American Economic Review*, 82, 720–39.

Skinner, J. (1988), "Risky Income, Life Cycle Consumption, and Precautionary Savings," *Journal of Monetary Economics*, 22, 237–55.

Smith, Adam (1776), *An Inquiry into the Nature and Causes of the Wealth of Nations*, rpt. ed. E. Cannan, Chicago, University of Chicago Press, 1976.

Smythe, D. (1994), "Book Review: Specialization and Economic Organization: A New Classical Microeconomic Framework," *Journal of Economic Literature*, 32, 691–2.

Solow, R. (1956), "A Contribution to the Theory of Economic Growth," *Quarterly Journal of Economics*, 70, 65–94

Sonnenschein, H. (1973), "Do Walras' Identity and Continuity Characterize the Class of Community Excess Demand Functions?," *Journal of Economic Theory*, 6, 345–54.

Spanjers, Willy (1992), *Price Setting Behavior in Hierarchically Structured Economies*, Druk, Wibro Dissertatiedrukkerij, Helmond.

Srinivasan, T. N. (1964), "Optimum Savings in a Two-Sector Model of Growth," *Econometrica*, 32, 358–74.

Srinivasan, T. N. and Whalley, J. (1986), *General Equilibrium Trade Policy Modelling*, Cambridge, MIT Press.

Stahl, I. (1972), *Bargaining Theory*, Economic Research Institute, Stockholm School of Economics.

Starrett, D. (1973), "Inefficiency and the Demand for Money in a Sequence Economy," *Review of Economic Studies*, 40, 289–303.

Stigler, G. (1951), "The Division of Labor is Limited by the Extent of the Market," *Journal of Political Economy*, 59, 185–93.

Stigler, G. (1961), "The Economics of Information," *Journal of Political Economy*, 69, 213–25.

Stigler, G. (1976), "The Successes and Failures of Professor Smith," *Journal of Political Economy*, 84, 1199–1213.

Stigler, G., Stigler, S., and Friedland, C. (1995), "The Journals of Economics," *Journal of Political Economy*, 103, 331–59.

Stiglitz, J. (1974), "Incentives and Risk-sharing in Sharecropping," *Review of Economic Studies*, 41, 219–55.

Stiglitz, J. (1986), "Theories of Wage Rigidity," in J. L. Butkiewicz, K. J. Koford, and J. B. Miller (eds.), *Keynes Economic Legacy: Contemporary Economic Theories*, New York, Praeger Publishers, 153–206.

Stiglitz, J. (1992), "Capital Markets and Economic Fluctuations in Capitalist Economies," *European Economic Review*, 36, 269–306.

Stiglitz, J. (1993), *Economics*, New York, Norton & Co.

Stiglitz, J. (1998), "Sound Finance and Sustainable Development in Asia," Keynote Address to the Asia Development Forum, The World Bank Group.

Stiglitz, J. and Weiss, A. (1986), "Credit Rationing and Collateral," in J. Edwards and C. Mayer (eds.), *Recent Development in Corporate Finance*, Cambridge, Cambridge University Press.

Stokey, Nancy (1991), "Human Capital, Product Quality and Growth," *Quarterly Journal of Economics*, 106, 587–616.

Stolper, Wolfgang and Samuelson, Paul (1941), "Protection and Real Wages," *Review of Economic Studies*, 9, 58–73.

Summer, L. (1992), "The Challenges of Development," *Finance & Development*, March, 6–8.

Sun, Guangzhen (1999), *Increasing Returns, Roundabout Production and Urbanization: A General Equilibrium Analysis of the Division of Labor*. Ph.D. dissertation, Department of Economics, Monash University.

Sun, Guangzhen and Lio, M. (1996), "A General Equilibrium Model Endogenizing the Level of Division of Labor and Variety of Producer Goods," Working Paper, Department of Economics, Monash University.

Sun, Guangzhen and Yang, X. (1998), "Evolution in Division of Labor, Urbanization, and Land Price Differentials between the Urban and Rural Areas," Harvard Institute for International Development Discussion Paper no. 639.

Sun, Guangzhen, Yang, X., and Yao, S. (1999), "Theoretical Foundation of Economic Development Based on Networking Decisions in the Competitive Market," Harvard Center for International Development Working Paper no. 17.

Tabuchi, Takatoshi (1998), "Urban Agglomeration and Dispersion: A Synthesis of Alonso and Krugman," *Journal of Urban Economics*, 44, 333–51.

Tamura, R. (1991), "Income Convergence in an Endogenous Growth Model," *Journal of Political Economy*, 99, 522–40.

Tamura, R. (1992), "Efficient Equilibrium Convergence: Heterogeneity and Growth," *Journal of Economic Theory*, 58, 355–76.

Taylor, J. (1980), "Aggregate Dynamics and Staggered Contracts," *Journal of Political Economy*, 88 (Feb.), 1–23.

Temple, J. (1999), "The New Growth Evidence," *Journal of Economic Literature*, 37, 112–56.

Thompson, Henry (1995), "Free Trade and Income Redistribution in Some Developing and Newly Industrialized Countries," *Open Economies Review*, 6, 265–80.

Tirole, J. (1986), "Hierarchies and Bureaucracies: On the Role of Collusion in Organizations," *Journal of Law and Economic Organization*, 2, 181–214.

Tirole, J. (1989), *The Theory of Industrial Organization*, Cambridge, Mass., MIT Press.

Trefler, Daniel (1993), "International Factor Price Differences: Leontief was Right!," *Journal of Political Economy*, 10(6), 961–87.

Tuck, R. (1954), *An Assay on the Economic Theory of Rank*, Oxford, Blackwell.

Tucker, Josiah (1755), *The Elements of Commerce and Theory of Taxes*, London.

Tucker, Josiah (1774), *Four Tracts on Political and Commercial Subjects*, Gloucester, UK, R. Taikes.

Turgot, A. R. J. (1751), "Lettre a Madame de Graffigny sur les lettres d'une Peruvienne," in G. Schelle (ed.), *Oeuvres de Turgot et Documents le concernant*, vol. I, Paris, F. Alcan, 1913.

Turgot, A. R. J. (1766), *Reflections on the Production and Distribution of Wealth*, in P. D. Groenewegen (ed.), *The Economics of A. R. J. Turgot*, The Hague, Nijhoff, 1977.

Ure, A. (1835), *The Philosophy of Manufactures*, London, C. Knoght; reissued, London, Cass, 1967.

US Department of Labor Employment and Training Administration (1991), *Dictionary of Occupational Titles*, Washington, DC.

Uzawa, H. (1959), "Prices of the Factors of Production in International Trade," *Econometrica*, 27(3), 448–68.

Uzawa, H. (1964), "Optimum Growth in a Two-sector Model of Capital Accumulation," *Review of*

*Economic Studies*, 31, 1–24.

Uzawa, H. (1965), "Optimum Technical Change in an Aggregative Model of Economic Growth," *International Economic Review*, 6, 18–31.

Van Zandt, T. (1995), "Hierarchical Computation of the Resource Allocation Problem," *European Economic Review*, 39, 700–8.

Van Zandt, T. (1996), "Decentralized Information Processing in the Theory of Organisations," in M. Sertel (ed.), *Contemporary Economic Development Reviewed*, vol. 4, *The Enterprise and its Environment*, London, Macmillan Press.

Varian, Hal (1992), *Microeconomic Analysis*, New York, Norton.

Vogt, W. (1969), "Fluktuationen in einer washsenden Wirtschaft under klassischen Bedingungen," in G. Bombach (ed.), *Wachstum, Einkommensverteilung und wirtschaftliches Gleichgewicht*, Berlin, Duncker und Humblot.

von Mises, L. (1922), *Socialism: An Economic and Sociological Analysis*, Indianapolis, Liberty Classics, rpt. 1981.

von Neumann, J. (1945), "A Model of General Equilibrium," *Review of Economic Studies*, 13, 1–9.

Walker, Amasa (1874), *Science of Wealth: A Manual of Political Economy*, Boston, Little Brown: New York, Kraus Reprints, 1969.

Wallace, N. (1980), "The Overlapping Generations Model of Fiat Money," in J. Karenken and N. Wallace (eds.), *Models of Monetary Economics*, Minneapolis, Federal Reserve Bank of Minneapolis.

Walras, Leon (1954), *Elements of Pure Economics, or, The Theory of Social Wealth*, trans. William Jaffe, Homewood, Ill., Richard D. Irwin, 1874.

Wang, J. and Yang, X. (1996), "The Division of Labor and the Pursuit of Relative Economic Standing," *Journal of Comparative Economics*, 23, 20–37.

Wartenberg, C. M. (1966), *Von Thünen's Isolated State*, London, Pergamon.

Weber, Max (1961), *The Protestant Ethic and the Spirit of Capitalism*, Routledge, Chapman & Hall.

Weitzman, M. L. (1979), "Optimal Search for the Best Alternative," *Econometrica*, 47, 641–54.

Weitzman, M. L. (1982), "Increasing Returns and the Foundations of Unemployment Theory," *The Economic Journal*, 92, 787–804.

Weitzman, M. L. (1994), "Monopolistic Competition with Endogenous Specialization," *Review of Economic Studies*, 61, 45–56.

Weitzman, M. L. (1998), "Recombinant Growth," *Quarterly Journal of Economics*, 113, 331–60.

Wen, M. (1997a), "Infrastructure and Evolution in Division of Labor," *Review of Development Economics*, 1, 191–206.

Wen, M. (1997b), *Division of Labor in Economic Development*, Ph.D. dissertation, Department of Economics, Monash University.

Wen, M. (1998), "An Analytical Framework of Consumer-Producers, Economies of Specialisation and Transaction Costs," in K. Arrow, Y.-K. Ng, and X. Yang (eds.), *Increasing Returns and Economic Analysis*, London, Macmillan.

West, E. G. (1964), "Adam Smith's Two Views of the Division of Labor," *Economica*, 3, 23–32.

Williamson, O. (1967), "Hierarchical Control and Optimum Firm Size," *Journal of Political Economics*, 75, 123–38.

Williamson, O. (1975), *Markets and Hierarchies*, New York, The Free Press.

Williamson, O. (1985), *Economic Institutions of Capitalism*, New York, Free Press.

Wong, K.-Y. and Yang, X. (1994), "An Extended Dixit–Stiglitz Model with the Tradeoff Between Economies of Scale and Transaction Costs," Seminar Paper, Department of Economics, Monash University.

Wong, K.-Y. and Yang, X. (1998), "An Extended Ethier Model Model with the Tradeoff Between Economies of Scale and Transaction Costs," in K. Arrow, Y.-K. Ng, and X. Yang (eds.), *Increasing Returns and Economic Analysis*, London, Macmillan.

World Bank (1992), *Development Report 1992. Environment and Resource Problems*, New York, Oxford University Press.

World Bank (1997), *Development Report 1997: The State in a Changing World*, New York, Oxford University Press.

World Bank (1981–99), *World Development Report*, various issues, Washington, DC, World Bank.

Yang, X. (1984), *Jingji Kongzhilun Chubu* (*Introduction to Economic Cybernetics*, in Chinese), Changsha, Hunan People's Press.

Yang, X. (1988), "A Microeconomic Approach to Modeling the Division of Labor Based on Increasing Returns to Specialization," Ph.D. dissertation, Dept. of Economics, Princeton University.

Yang, X. (1991), "Development, Structure Change, and Urbanization," *Journal of Development Economics*, 34, 199–222.

Yang, X. (1994), "Endogenous vs. Exogenous Comparative Advantages and Economies of Specialization vs. Economies of Scale," *Journal of Economics*, 60, 29–54.

Yang, X. (1995), "An Equilibrium Model of Hierarchy," Department of Economics Seminar Paper, Monash University.

Yang, X. (1996), "A New Theory of Demand and the Emergence of International Trade from Domestic Trade," *Pacific Economic Review*, 1, 215–17.

Yang, X. (1997), "Endogenous Transaction and the Theory of the Firm," Working Paper, Department of Economics, Monash University.

Yang, X. (1999), "The Division of Labor, Investment, and Capital," *Metroeconomica*, 20, 301–24.

Yang, X. and Borland, J. (1991a), "A Microeconomic Mechanism for Economic Growth," *Journal of Political Economy*, 99, 460–82.

Yang, X. and Borland, J. (1991b), "The Evolution of Trade and Economic Growth," mimeo, University of Melbourne.

Yang, X. and Borland, J. (1992), "Specialization and Money as a Medium of Exchange," Department of Economics Seminar Paper no. 8/92, Monash University.

Yang, X. and Heijdra, B. (1993), "Monopolistic Competition and Optimum Product Diversity: Comment," *American Economic Review*, 83, 295–301.

Yang, X. and Hogbin, G. (1990), "The Optimum Hierarchy," *China Economic Review*, 2, 125–40.

Yang, X. and Ng, S. (1998), "Specialization and Division of Labor: A Survey," in K. Arrow, Y.-K. Ng, and Xiaokai Yang (eds.), *Increasing Returns and Economic Analysis*, London, Macmillan.

Yang, X. and Ng, Y.-K. (1993), *Specialization and Economic Organization, a New Classical Microeconomic Framework*, Amsterdam, North-Holland.

Yang, X. and Ng, Y.-K. (1995), "Theory of the Firm and Structure of Residual Rights," *Journal of Economic Behavior and Organization*, 26, 107–28.

Yang, X. and Rice, R. (1994), "An Equilibrium Model Endogenizing the Emergence of a Dual Structure between the Urban and Rural Sectors," *Journal of Urban Economics*, 25, 346–68.

Yang, X. and Shi, H. (1992), "Specialization and Product Diversity," *American Economic Review*, 82, 392–8.

Yang, X. and Wills, I. (1990), "A Model Formalizing the Theory of Property Rights," *Journal of Comparative Economics*, 14, 177–98.

Yang, X. and Yeh, Y. (1993), "Economic Organisms and Application of Topology and Graph Theory in Economics," Department of Economics Seminar Paper, Monash University.

Yang, X. and Yeh, Y. (1996), "A General Equilibrium Model with Endogenous Principal–Agent Relationship," Department of Economics Seminar Paper, Monash University.

Yang, X. and Zhang, D. (1999), "International Trade and Income Distribution," Harvard Center for International Development Working Paper no. 18.

Yang, X., Wang, J., and Wills, I. (1992), "Economic Growth, Commercialization, and Institutional Changes in Rural China, 1979–1987," *China Economic Review*, 3, 1–37.

Yellen, J. L. (1984), "Efficiency Wage Models of Unemployment," *American Economic Review*, 74, 200–5.

Young, Allyn (1928), "Increasing Returns and Economic Progress," *The Economic Journal*, 38, 527–42.

Young, Alwyn (1993), "Invention and Bounded Learning by Doing," *Journal of Political Economy*, 101, 443–72.

Young, Alwyn (1998), "Growth without Scale Effects," *Journal of Political Economy*, 106, 41–63.

Young, Leslie (1991), "Heckscher–Ohlin Trade Theory with Variable Returns to Scale," *Journal of*

*International Economics*, 31, 183–90.

Zaleski, E. (1980), *Stalinist Planning for Economic Growth, 1933–1952*, Chapel Hill, University of North Carolina Press.

Zhang, D. (1999), "Inframarginal Analysis of Asymmetric Models with Increasing Returns," Ph.D. dissertation, Wuhan University, Center for Advanced Economic Studies.

Zhang, J. (1997), "Evolution in Division of Labor and Macroeconomic Policies," *Review of Development Economics*, 1, 236–45.

Zhang, J. (1998), "Policy Analysis in a Dynamic Model with Endogenous Specialization," in K. Arrow, Y.-K. Ng, and X. Yang (eds.), *Increasing Returns and Economic Analysis*, London, Macmillan, pp. 205–18.

Zhang, Y. (1999), "Irrelevance of the Size of the Firm: Theory and Empirical Evidence," Ph.D. dissertation, Remin University.

Zhao, Y. (1999), "Concurrent Evolution of Division of Labor and Information of Organization," *Review of Development Economics*, 3, 336–53.

Zhou, L., Sun, G., and Yang, X. (1998), "General Equilibria in Large Economies with Endogenous Structure of Division of Labor," Working Paper, Department of Economics, Monash University.

Zhou, Y. (1997), "A General Equilibrium Model of Hierarchy with Producer Goods," Masters thesis, Department of Economics, Monash University.

# INDEX